# English and American Studies

**Theory and Practice**

Edited by
Martin Middeke, Timo Müller, Christina Wald, Hubert Zapf

Verlag J. B. Metzler Stuttgart · Weimar

Prof. Dr. Martin Middeke is Professor of English Literature at the University of Augsburg and Visiting Professor of English at the University of Johannesburg, South Africa.
Email: martin.middeke@phil.uni-augsburg.de.

Dr. Timo Müller is Assistant Professor of American Studies at the University of Augsburg.
Email: timo.mueller@phil.uni-augsburg.de.

PD Dr. Christina Wald is Assistant Professor of English Literature at the University of Augsburg.
Email: christina.wald@phil.uni-augsburg.de.

Prof. Dr. Hubert Zapf is Professor of American Literature at the University of Augsburg.
Email: hubert.zapf@phil.uni-augsburg.de.


Contact address:
Lehrstühle für Amerikanistik und
Englische Literaturwissenschaft
Philologisch-Historische Fakultät
Universität Augsburg
Universitätsstraße 10
D-86159 Augsburg

Gedruckt auf säure- und chlorfreiem, alterungsbeständigem Papier

Bibliografische Information der Deutschen Nationalbibliothek
Die Deutsche Nationalbibliothek verzeichnet diese Publikation in der Deutschen Nationalbibliografie; detaillierte bibliografische Daten sind im Internet über < http://dnb.d-nb.de > abrufbar.

ISBN 978-3-476-02306-3

© 2012 J.B. Metzler'sche Verlagsbuchhandlung
und Carl Ernst Poeschel Verlag GmbH in Stuttgart
www.metzlerverlag.de
info@metzlerverlag.de

Einbandgestaltung: Ingrid Gnoth
Layout: Ingrid Gnoth | GD 90
Satz: Claudia Wild, Konstanz
Druck und Bindung: Offizin Andersen Nexö Leipzig GmbH

Printed in Germany
Dezember 2012

Verlag J.B. Metzler Stuttgart · Weimar

# Table of Contents

# Preface of the Editors

When we were approached by the publishers of Metzler Verlag to edit an introductory companion to English and American Studies within the new B. A. and M. A. study programs instituted in the Bologna process, we were rather hesitant in our response at first because of the problems of standardization, undue complexity reduction, ready-made information management, and uncritical reproduction of knowledge that an all too utilitarian interpretation and implementation of these new study programs was liable to bring about. And we were certainly not keen on supporting these tendencies by supplying the curricular tools for such a utilitarian instrumentalization of knowledge in our disciplines. Instead, we were—and still are—convinced that university study in the full sense of the word, in particular the study of languages, literatures, and cultures as part of the larger field of the humanities, involves *Bildung* and not just *Ausbildung*, that it requires not merely the ability to reproduce already preexisting knowledge but to be self-reflexively involved in an essentially creative activity. The study of languages, literatures, and cultures in particular involves acquiring and developing various competences such as language proficiency, intercultural translation, textual interpretation, scholarly argumentation, critical reflection, and the creative transformation of such acquired knowledge and competence.

In our subsequent talks with Metzler Verlag, we were pleased to find out that our ideas about the present state and the future of English and American Studies, and consequently of the project of a compendium volume to such Studies, were in principle shared by the publishers. They especially accepted our argument that there was no point in reducing the contents and complexities of knowledge in our disciplines to an imaginary 'basic level' to be provided specifically to B. A. students. They also agreed that we would try to present, however selectively and incompletely, the state of the art of the disciplines and subdisciplines making up the field of English and American Studies in their adequate scope, complexity, and theoretical-methodological reflexivity in a volume which was suitable not only for B. A. students, but also for M. A. and Ph.D. students, and indeed could also serve as a companion for advanced postdoctoral research and teaching. For this purpose, we invited contributions from a great number of colleagues at other universities to realize the project. The result is the present volume, which combines the presentation of fundamental issues, concepts, and developments in the various areas of English and American Studies with theoretical reflection, critical debate, and an awareness of unresolved problems as well as of promising new perspectives.

The editors' thanks go to the contributors for their fruitful cooperation in this project and for submitting highly informed state-of-the-art accounts of their areas of specialization. Our thanks also go to the publishers at Metzler Verlag, especially to Oliver Schütze for his constructive support and his encouraging management of the project from its initial stages through the process of publication. Special thanks go to our Augsburg colleague Wolfram Bublitz for his support in editing the linguistic sections. We further thank our graduate assistants at the University of Augsburg, Anja Haslinger, Georg Hauzenberger, Karla Hirsch, Stephanie Lehner, Selina Udelhofen, Florian Wadas, and especially Aleksandra Cierpinska and Martin Riedelsheimer.

It is our hope that the present volume will be useful both for university study and research and for a more general reading public interested in matters of English and American Studies.

University of Augsburg
Martin Middeke, Timo Müller,
Christina Wald, Hubert Zapf

# Introduction

The present volume offers a systematic survey of the current state of theory and practice in the disciplines commonly subsumed under the umbrella term of English and American Studies. It is intended as a comprehensive study guide and scholarly companion to the contemporary state of knowledge in the major fields of research and teaching related to Anglophone languages, literatures, and cultures. The volume is the collaborative work of leading experts in the field, who have each contributed chapters on their areas of special expertise. In its different parts, the volume reflects the various areas and directions that currently make up the field of English and American Studies as it has been institutionalized in university departments, study programs, scholarly publications, and academic societies. The volume aims to represent core domains of knowledge, which provide exemplary insight into the subject areas, curricular contents, and epistemic frames characterizing the study of Anglophone languages, literatures, and cultures at the Bachelor's and Master's levels, in teacher education, as well as within advanced studies in doctoral programs and postdoctoral work. It is thus a comprehensive reference work for students, researchers, and teachers, but also for a larger public interested in keeping themselves informed about the current state of the art in these disciplines.

In its concept and structure, the volume tries to do justice to the growing **diversification** of the field of English and American Studies in terms of historical-cultural range, areas of specialization, methodologies, theoretical orientations, and disciplinary self-concepts. The **transnational and transcultural dimensions** of Anglophone languages, literatures, and cultures are taken into account, both as a productive extension and a methodological challenge to the traditional scope and boundaries of the various disciplinary fields and subfields. At the same time, the notion of national cultures and literatures remains a pragmatic reference point even with the increasing presence of transnationalism and globalization in all areas of study. The methodological-theoretical approaches, concepts, and tools supplied in the individual chapters are complemented by **exemplary applications** to representative linguistic, textual, and cultural material. While all contributions represent the authors' attempt to cover the most important developments in the field, they also inevitably reflect the theoretical-methodological and personal preferences of the individual contributors—a fact which we do not view as a disadvantage but rather as an indication of the diversity, vibrancy, and open-ended creativity characterizing our areas of study.

As a result of such considerations, the book is organized around the core areas of contemporary English and American Studies, but also contains chapters on recent diversifications and extensions of the field. The first part on **Literary Studies** includes subchapters on British and American Literature, but also on the 'New English Literatures' within a globalized concept of English Studies. Due to its increased importance in international Anglophone studies, the second part is devoted to recent **Literary and Cultural Theory** and some of its most influential approaches. The third part on **Cultural Studies**, again, offers subchapters on British and American Cultural Studies, but also on Transnational and Postcolonial Cultural Studies, as well as on Film and Media Studies as new domains of transtextual and transmedial Cultural Studies. In the fourth part, "**Analyzing Literature and Culture**," the background information provided by the preceding chapters is complemented by exemplary demonstrations of literary and cultural analysis in the genres of poetry, narrative fiction, drama, film, and culture. The next part of the volume, Part V, covers the main domains of current **English Linguistics**, featuring subchapters on the theoretical foundations of the discipline, on historical linguistics, structural linguistics, pragmatics and semantics, and on varieties of English. Part VI on **Didactics** and the teaching of English offers subchapters on the theory and politics of English language teaching, on language learning, and on the teaching of literature. The volume is supplemented by practical sections that are generally useful for students on various levels of their academic development, notably a section on "**Methods and Techniques of Research and Academic Writing**," which offers valuable information and guidelines for one of the major tasks and challenges of academic work, the writing of scholarly papers; a section on "**Study Aids**," with references to recommended book and internet sources. The subject index helps readers to quickly identify and cross-reference key concepts, terms, figures, texts, and historical-cultural phenomena making up the field of contemporary English and American Studies.

Throughout the volume, the main text of the scholarly argument remains the primary medium of representation. For purposes of readability, clarification, and exemplification, the text is complemented by definitions, quotations, sample interpretations, summaries, illustrations, or time tables as additional sources of information, which are either presented on the margins or in inserted boxes within the text. Some key concepts, names, periods, and phenomena are printed in bold type to mark their special structural or thematic signifi-

cance. While new publishing conventions, market considerations, and didactic perspectives should be taken into account in up-to-date surveys of academic knowledge, the volume continues to rely on research-oriented, textually mediated discourse as a main site and source of scholarly study and communication in the field of the humanities. Paying tribute to the broad spectrum covered by this volume, the chapters vary in their use of British and American spelling.

Martin Middeke, Timo Müller,
Christina Wald, Hubert Zapf

# Part I: Literary Studies

# 1 Introducing Literary Studies

Literary studies is a discipline with a long history, during which it has been influenced by fields that we would no longer regard today as central to literary studies, chiefly by biblical exegesis. Hence, the question arises as to what we consider as literature—we instantly would include written imaginative texts such as novels, poems and plays, but what about song lyrics, rap or performance poetry? In the context of increasing interest in psychological and sociological texts, the term could also be extended to, for instance, essays, political speeches, magazines, or newspapers. Scholars have proposed competing notions of literature, and today we can differentiate between **a narrower and a broader understanding of (literary) texts** (the latter would include rap lyrics for instance). The chief quality that helps us distinguish literature from other text sorts is the question of its pragmatic use. In this sense, the definition of literature as a "depragmatized" (Wolfgang Iser) form of text and discourse appears particularly useful. Manuals, for example, have a clear pragmatic use, as have recipes, and we would not consider them literature. By contrast, science fiction novels or absurd plays have little pragmatic use even if readers look out for advice for their everyday lives. In more realistic plays, novels, or poems, such advice may be inferred, but it is not the primary rationale of these texts. Another way of distinguishing literary texts is the question of aesthetics. Does the text under consideration have a special form and language which have implications for its content? Poems usually are the most formalized literary genre, as they are structured in verse, often in rhymes, and have a certain metre, but other genres likewise developed formal characteristics which help us to categorize and interpret.

The question of which texts are considered 'literature' and thus the subject matter of literary studies also depends on the methodological approaches chosen by the reader. Hermeneutic approaches, for instance, seek to investigate an author's intention; formalist approaches such as New Criticism have focussed exclusively on the fictional reality and the structures of the work itself, neglecting many aspects of the history of its production; psychological, sociologist, and Marxist approaches have, by contrast, highlighted the social/historical surroundings or the economical basis of a particular literary text, at the risk of losing sight of its aesthetic structures. While the influential poststructuralist approach led to a resurgence of formal analysis, more recent approaches such as New Historicism or Cultural Materialism have set a much stronger emphasis on historical consciousness while at the same time employing poststructuralist insights. Given this multitude of approaches, we need to keep in mind that whatever method is chosen, some aspects of the literary text will be foregrounded while others will necessarily be overshadowed. If a common denominator can be said to have emerged from this multitude, it is an awareness of the **interdependence of the literary text and the historical conditions** of its production and reception.

Why literary studies? When we acknowledge this interdependence and a dialectical interplay of authors, readers, texts, and the world, it becomes fairly obvious that while literature follows aesthetic rules of its own, its production and reception do not take place in timeless, autonomous realms. Moreover, literature is not a simple copy of reality but a specifically shaped reflection of the world it relates to. Categorizing and interpreting texts, then, can have a twofold function: First, it helps us illuminate the meaning of these texts by laying bare the interrelations that exist between a self (the author, the characters, even the reader) and the world or a particular society. Interrogating the aesthetic rules, laws, and structures of a literary work of art will provide us with some knowledge about that world. Second, the act of interpretation itself is a reflexive process that can provide us with knowledge about ourselves. Studying literature and understanding the different ways in which texts can be interpreted, thus, allows us to shed light on wider questions: for example the psychoanalytic dimension of a text, its stance towards issues of race, class, or gender, but also, more generally, the nature of signification, the functions of the imagination, or the working of artistic creativity in specific aesthetic and historical settings. In a nutshell, analyzing literature heightens our aesthetic competence, offers us a more complex understanding of the world, and can give us a higher level of self-awareness.

Literary studies can hence be described as both formal and cultural-historic analysis, and the requirements for literary analysis are therefore manifold: a knowledge of **(literary) history, of literary** and **cultural theory** as much as the **methods and terminology of literary analysis**. The following sections of this volume therefore aim at introducing all three fields by giving overviews of the periods of literary history (Part I), by introducing various strands of literary theory from structuralism to ecocriticism (Part II), and by providing sample analyses of prose, poetry, drama, and film (Part IV). To illustrate the broad range of cultural studies beyond literature and art (cf. Part III), a short chapter on a phenomenon of popular mass culture is included, namely football.

Problems of Literary History. The chapters on literary history will have to deal, among other things, with the **difficulty of defining historical periods**: The sheer abundance of material and the ensuing specialization of many scholars have made it almost impossible to write a coherent literary history. Moreover, the continual movement of people, ideas, and cultural models in our globalized world is increasingly questioning the usefulness of national boundaries for historiography of any sort. There are no clear-cut delineations between, for example, Romanticism and the literature of the later nineteenth century, or between English and American modernism, but the categories are nonetheless helpful to structure our historical knowledge and to gain insight into literary and cultural developments. While many authors and literary works can be classified rather obviously as typical or indeed formative of their age, others anticipate later developments, still partake in earlier developments, or are rather singular phenomena. Hence, the following chapters do not present mere lists of facts, works, and authors, but instead elaborate on the particular tensions between the works themselves and their cultural/historical surroundings.

A similar problem concerns the issue of **canonization**. Short historical overviews like ours necessarily suggest a canon of centrally important texts, but as our contributors argue throughout, any established canon should be questioned and constantly revised. Indisputably, certain canonical

authors had a strong influence on their contemporaries and later writers, so that their relevance for any literary history should not be downplayed, especially when their texts are characterized less by an affirmative than by a critical attitude toward established notions of the relationship between self and society. The chapters pay tribute to these formative authors and texts, but at the same time, they take into account recent revisions of the canon by discussing authors who were neglected for a long time, e.g. early modern prose authors, female authors of the past, and important voices from English literatures outside Europe and the United States. Given the brevity of the chapters, the authors and texts discussed should be regarded as exemplary choices rather than the only important representatives of their period. The chapters feature boxes of key texts and authors, sometimes because we regard these texts and authors as particularly representative of a certain period or perspective; sometimes because we want to draw attention to significant texts and authors that could not be discussed at length in the chapter or that have previously been omitted from mainstream literary histories. The same selectivity applies to the timelines which accompany most chapters and which unavoidably privilege certain historic events while leaving out others. Again, these timelines are included to provide overviews of developments we deem important for understanding a specific period and to encourage further reading. While the choices of relevant authors and texts as much as the timelines are indebted to insights and conventions of literary studies which cannot be neglected either in teaching or in research, they also reflect the specific views of the experts writing for this volume. Thus, each chapter, on literary history as much as on literary theory, attempts to offer an introduction while at the same time representing the state of academic debate in the respective field.

*Martin Middeke/Timo Müller/*
*Christina Wald/Hubert Zapf*

# 2 British Literary History

The following chapters offer an overview of English literary history, which we have divided in **seven parts**: the **Middle Ages**, the **sixteenth and seventeenth centuries**, the **eighteenth century**, **Romanticism**, the **Victorian Age**, **modernism**, and **postmodernism**. As we have emphasised in the general introduction to Literary Studies, this division has become a standard in literary studies that helps us structure our knowledge of the past and present, but it is by no means absolute. The boundaries between the periods are permeable, and the chapters often comment on authors and works which continue earlier developments or anticipate later strands of literary history. For example, prominent authors of the early modern period like Edmund Spenser drew on medieval literature and deliberately employed an archaic language and a traditional genre to develop a specifically English form of writing. This endeavour also shows that English literature always has to be investigated with a view to its sources and branches outside the British Isles. For instance, in the early modern period, English literature was strongly influenced by Italian, French and Spanish texts; the legacy of ancient Greek and Roman authors persisted into the twentieth century, though it decreased in importance; and ever since the eighteenth century, English literature has been closely associated with American literature and the 'new' English literatures that began to thrive in England's colonies. Accordingly, many of the prestigious Booker Prizes for the best novel of the year have been awarded to Indian, South-African, and Australian authors.

Not only the boundaries, but also the **labels** for each period ('medieval,' 'postmodern') need to be problematised, as they can never cover all literary and cultural developments of their time; in many cases, several labels with differing implications compete, maybe most prominently for the six-teenth and seventeenth centuries which can be called 'Renaissance' just as well as the 'early modern' period, as will be further explained in entry I.2.2. In other cases, several definitions for the same term are in use, as entry I.2.7 points out for 'postmodern,' or a label can only be understood in relation to other periods, as the opening of the following entry explains for the notion of the 'in-between' that underlies our concept of the 'medieval.'

The beginnings of literature written in the English vernacular during the Middle Ages drew on long-standing oral traditions, which continued to exist alongside written texts. Until the establishment of the printing press in the fifteenth century (and often later), texts were circulated in manuscript among a cultural elite and were often read out aloud to an audience; thus, the boundaries between oral and written as much as between performative and literary forms were far from clear-cut. The 'silent,' single reader reading in private became a mass phenomenon in the eighteenth century, which also saw a major shift in the development toward the system of literary genres we know today. Before the eighteenth century, liturgical and secular drama had been the most popular literary genre: performances throughout the country reached people across boundaries of rank and gender. The Renaissance is still regarded as the 'golden age' of English drama, as it produced the most prominent English playwright of all times, William Shakespeare. Poetry was the literary mode of the cultural elite in the sixteenth and seventeenth centuries, and has preserved this status until today; accordingly, the monarch of the United Kingdom still appoints a 'poet laureate' who reflects on courtly and national matters. The last three poets laureate were Ted Hughes, Andrew Motion, and Carol Ann Duffy, the first woman in the long line of prestigious authors that includes Edmund Spenser, Ben Jonson, and William Wordsworth.

The novel, undoubtedly the most popular genre today, only emerged in the eighteenth century, in a period when the essay flourished as well. While poetry was still the chief genre of Romanticism, the novel first superseded poetry and drama in the Victorian Age to become the dominant genre of the nineteenth century. It preserved this status in the modernist period, which is characterised by intense experimentation with narrative forms. Ireland is an exception here, because the Irish Revival was bound up from its beginnings with the establishment of a specifically Irish theatre at the Abbey Theatre in Dublin; hence, drama has had a much more significant political and aesthetic role in Ireland than in the United Kingdom. Since the 1950s, however, drama has gained a greater importance in England, too, with the advent of the 'Angry Young Men,' a group of playwrights, notably John Osborne and Edward Bond, who rejected the traditional 'well-made play' that depicted the lives of the upper classes in conventional structures and instead drew attention to the problems of working-class characters. A second vogue of English drama came with the 'in-yer-face' plays written since the 1990s by Sarah Kane, Mark Ravenhill, Patrick Marber, and others, which have been performed to great acclaim (and controversy) worldwide. Even though English drama is still more conventional than, for example, German drama (which saw the rise of 'post-dramatic theatre'), some authors have experimented with dramatic and theatrical forms in a postmodern fashion, most prominently Caryl Churchill, Sarah Kane, and Martin Crimp.

Considered as a whole, the following chapters address major issues of the development of English literature since the Middle Ages. The chapters reveal that the evolution of major writers, epochs, literary genres and aesthetic styles, trends and traditions is cross-fertilised by gradual developments in **philosophy**, **culture**, **politics**, and **history**. The aesthetics of English literature since the Middle Ages has been flanked by philosophies ranging, to name but a few, from Ancient Greek thinkers, humanism, empiricism, utilitarianism to phenomenology and structuralist/poststructuralist philosophies. The most important cultural and historical phenomena which are reflected in various ways in English literature since the Middle Ages are an ever-growing secularisation and, especially, the scientific revolution and the history of technological progress since the Renaissance and the Enlightenment, which form the basis for the Industrial Revolution and for twentieth-century globalisation. Major changes in the mentalities and personality structures were triggered by Darwinism and the increasing interest in human consciousness which was systematised by psychology and psychoanalysis. These go hand in hand with major political upheavals in the U.K. such as a number of wars and, especially, the rise and subsequent decline of the British Empire. As a consequence, the chapters document the aesthetic shift from biblical, religious, and mythical subject matter to realist negotiations of everyday life and to (post-)modern self-reflexive modes. English literature is indicative of far-reaching changes in literary subjectivity and intersubjectivity (e.g. gender roles) and, thus, of changes in epistemological positions that determine judgements, knowledge, truth and the way of how we attain it. What all the chapters make clear is that literary history is no mere succession and enumeration of facts, but rather a **complex interdependence**: the developments of philosophy, culture, history, politics, etc. influence the development of aesthetics, and at the same time the developments in the field of aesthetics reverberate into the way the world is perceived and understood.

*Martin Middeke/Christina Wald*

The standard German-language history of English literature, ed. Hans Ulrich Seeber, 5th ed. Stuttgart: Metzler, 2012

## 2.1 | The Middle Ages

### 2.1.1 | Terminology

#### Medieval Culture and the Middle Ages

**Definiton**

> → The Middle Ages: "The period in European history between ancient and modern times, now usually taken as extending from the fall of the Roman Empire in the West (ca. 500) to the fall of Constantinople (1453) or the beginning of the Renaissance (14th cent.); the medieval period" (*OED*).

'The Middle Ages,' or 'the medieval period,' is as much a **construct** as the designations of other literary and cultural periods, which tell us more about the time when the period marker came into usage than about the portion of the past they refer to. However, unlike most period names you will encounter in this book, for instance 'the Renaissance,' 'Realism,' or 'Romanticism,' 'the Middle Ages' (*medium aevum*) does not characterize the period in question, other than that it is **a time-span 'in between.'** Since the seventeenth century, the term 'Middle Ages' has been used to label the interval between two eras of greatness: the ancient world of Greece and Rome, and its revival in what was seen as the new golden age ('Renaissance' means rebirth). This "millennium of middleness" (Patterson, "On the Margin" 92) was conceived of as a dark and obscure time by the people who followed and who called themselves humanists. The Italian poet Francesco Petrarca (1304–74) referred to the time following the fall of the Roman Empire as a **period of darkness** (*tenebrae*) and the English poet Sir Philip Sidney (1554–86) called it "a misty time" (Mommsen 226–42; Sidney 133). During the Reformation, religion helped to cement the boundary drawn by the early humanists: Protestantism defined itself against 'outmoded' medieval papism.

The boundary drawn first by the humanists still informs our view of the past. Early modernists in particular have used the Middle Ages as a touchstone against which to define 'their' modern period (Scala and Federico 4). It was the early modern period, they claim, that saw the emergence of modern ideas and characteristics, such as the 'birth' of the individual and a thirst for exploration

(Aers 177–202). As the term 'Renaissance' suggests, this was also a time which saw the 'discovery' of ancient texts and the resurgence of ancient ideas which had allegedly been slumbering in the 'dark' Middle Ages.

The Problem of Terminology. Medievalists have had their share in the perpetuation of the sharp boundary between the modern and the medieval. The school of 'historical' or 'exegetical criticism,' which had a powerful influence particularly in the U.S. between the 1950s and early 1970s, presented the Middle Ages as a homogeneous 'other' (see Patterson, *Negotiating* 3–74). They portrayed a society that was free from class conflicts and other struggles and a literature that was not interested in the psychology of individual characters, but rather in 'types' (Aers 181). It is only in the past three decades that medievalists have started to question the concept of a violent rupture between the Middle Ages and the Renaissance and to reveal what Larry Scanlon has called "one of Medieval Studies' favorite secrets": that "most of what modernity takes to be uniquely its own actually has much older roots" (Scanlon 2). The Renaissance lost its unique status as the term 'Renaissance' was appropriated by medievalists who pointed at a number of earlier 'renaissances,' like the Carolingian Renaissance and the twelfth-century Renaissance (Blockmans and Hoppenbrouwers 3) and by critics who have highlighted the role assigned to the preservation, study and translation of antique texts in the medieval period. The notion of the birth of the individual in the early modern period has similarly been called into question by medievalists like David Aers, who has demonstrated the interest in the individual and in the psychology of character in medieval texts (Aers 181–90). Even the first 500 years after the Fall of the Roman Empire, now referred to as the Early Middle Ages, which had long been defined as a time of ignorance and therefore dismissed as the 'Dark Ages,' are now seen as a "long morning whose creative powers laid down the parameters and future directions of European economic, cultural and political development" (Davis and McCormick 1).

In popular usage, however, 'medieval' is still a pejorative term and is used to mark something as outmoded, tyrannical and cruel (Robinson 752–55), as if violence were unknown to the modern world. The phrase 'to get medieval,' which became a catchphrase with Quentin Tarantino's *Pulp Fic-*

The Middle Ages are still often seen as a period of darkness.

## Timeline: The Medieval Period

| | |
|---|---|
| **410** | Roman occupation of Britain ends |
| **496** | Early Anglo-Saxon kingdoms established |
| **ca. 540** | Christian missionaries arrive |
| **865–877** | Viking invasions |
| **899** | Death of Alfred the Great (King of Wessex) |
| **924–93** | Athelstan of Wessex ends Viking control and becomes first King of England |
| **1066** | Battle of Hastings: Norman invaders under William the Conqueror defeat the Anglo-Saxon King Harold II |
| **1096–99** | First Crusade |
| **1146–48** | Second Crusade |
| **1167** | English students banned from studying at Paris, rapid growth of the University of Oxford |
| **1170** | Archbishop Thomas à Beckett murdered in Canterbury Cathedral |
| **1187–92** | Third Crusade |
| **1214** | King John loses Normandy and other French possessions |
| **1215** | King John signs Magna Carta, limiting the monarch's authority |
| **1337–1453** | Wars between England and France ('Hundred Years' War') |
| **1348–50** | Black Death pandemic in Europe |
| **1377–99** | Richard II King of England, flowering of Middle English Literature |
| **1415** | Battle of Agincourt |
| **1455–85** | 'Wars of the Roses' for kingship between the houses of York and Lancaster |
| **1476** | William Caxton introduces the printing press to England |
| **1485** | Battle of Bosworth: Richard III killed, Tudor dynasty established |

*tion*, suggests a return to unrestricted violence and uncivilized behaviour (Dinshaw 116–63). At the same time, the medieval proliferates in today's popular culture, from films to computer games, fairs and theme parks. Paradoxically then, while 'medieval' is still a term of abuse, the **ubiquity** of medieval themes, images and modes of storytelling in popular culture and the marketability of cultural products that evoke the Middle Ages give credence to Umberto Eco's claim that, after all, "[p]eople seem to like the Middle Ages" (Eco 61).

### The English Middle Ages and Medieval English Literature

The first people to be called 'English' were the **Anglo-Saxon tribes** whose arrival in the British Isles in the mid-fifth century marks the beginning of the English Middle Ages (cf. entry V.3). While the Britons and the Romans referred to the Anglo-Saxons as Saxons, the Anglo-Saxons themselves used the name of the Angles (OE *Engle*) as a collective term. The Anglo-Saxons and the part of Britain they inhabited (the south and east of the island) were known as *Angel-kynn*, their language as *Englisc*. The English and their language thus came to be distinguished from the native inhabitants of the British Isles (the Britons, Picts and Scots), who spoke various Celtic languages. It was not before the early eleventh century that 'England' was used as a place name (*Englaland*: land of the Angles).

The period from the arrival of the Anglo-Saxon tribes to the Norman invasion in 1066 is known as the Anglo-Saxon, Old English, or **Early Medieval period**. This is followed by the **Anglo-Norman period** (1066–ca. 1225), in which Norman French was the language of the rulers and of much literary composition. This led to far-reaching changes in the English language and in English culture in general in the century after the Norman Conquest, on the basis of which philologists fixed the beginnings of Middle English in the first half of the twelfth century. The first half of the fourteenth century saw the resurgence of English as a language for literature.

So when does the 'story' of English literature begin? The earliest extant literary text is the written record of an oral poem: a fragment of a hymn by a 'shepherd-turned-monk' called Caedmon. **Caedmon's Hymn** (657–680) is recorded in Latin and Old English in several manuscripts of Bede's *Historia ecclesiastica gentis Anglorum* (finished 731). Since then, medieval literature was influenced by many places, peoples and cultures. To trace continuity from the first attested Old English poem to literary texts of the late medieval period and beyond is therefore difficult and perhaps not desirable. Rather, its plurality should be celebrated as the hallmark of medieval English literature.

There is not much agreement when it comes to drawing the **boundaries** between the English Middle Ages and the Renaissance. While some scholars acknowledge milestones in book production (e.g. introduction of the printing press to Westminster, 1476); others focus on political events like the accession, or death of, a king (e.g. accession of Henry VII, 1485; death of Henry VIII, 1547); yet others conveniently place it at 1500.

### Medieval Studies and Medievalism

**Medieval Studies** arose in the 1960s as a challenge to the mainly philological conventions of studying the Middle Ages. Combining the disciplines of history, literature, art, architecture, archaeology and historical linguistics, Medieval Studies fosters an **interdisciplinary approach**. Medieval Studies is buoyed by a number of study and research centres, by annual international conferences and various journals. Yet, in January 1990, the Medieval Academy of America's quarterly journal *Speculum* asked whether "medieval studies [have] become irrelevant," whether "medievalists speak a (conservative) language of their own, addressing antiquarian concerns of interest to no one but themselves" (Wenger). While it must be conceded that the engagement of medievalists with theoretical approaches to the study of literature and culture did indeed come late in the day, in the past twenty years links have been forged between contemporary theory and medieval literary and cultural studies (see e.g. Strohm; Solopova and Lee). It has turned out to be quite fruitful to adopt critical terms and concepts from a wide array of theoretical approaches such as New Historicism, postcolonialism, and gender and queer studies. Increasing attention is also given to contemporary (re-)imaginations of the medieval. The question "what does medieval studies matter now" shows the awareness that our view of the past is coloured by the needs and interests of the present, and should therefore only be welcomed.

The place of the medieval in post-medieval times is the concern of scholars working in the field of medievalism. The *OED* defines 'medievalism' as the "[b]eliefs and practices (regarded as) characteristic of the Middle Ages" and as "the adoption of, adherence to, or interest in, medieval ideals, styles, or usages." As a scholarly field, medievalism examines how the medieval period has been remembered, re-imagined, used and abused in subsequent periods, for example in the nineteenth century when the medieval period was celebrated by some for its social and authoritarian order, by others for its primitivism and heroic individuality (cf. section I.2.5).

## Medieval Authors and Medieval Readers

**Authors.** Medievalists have recently traced the incipient emergence of the modern conception of authorship to the late Middle Ages. The meaning usually associated with the term 'author' today is already attested for the late fourteenth century: a "person who originates or gives existence to anything" (*OED*). Yet, medieval ideas of authorship were in many ways different from our own. For instance, authorship in the sense of authority (*auctoritas*) was only ascribed to ancient poets and rhetoricians, not to contemporary and vernacular writers (Minnis 12). However, a number of Middle English writers found ways to bestow authorial status upon their texts, for example by incorporating into their writings academic prologues and other commentaries of the kind academia commonly produced for classical texts (e.g. Osbern Bokenham's Prologue to his *Legendys of Hooly Wummen*, 1443–47).

Only a few works by **female authors** survive. This has been explained by their lack of access to institutions of learning, their lack of skill in writing and by the fact that authorship was regarded to be incompatible with femininity (Summit 91–109; Barratt 5; Kern-Stähler 29–31). Since many medieval writings are anonymous or circulated under a false name, it may well be that some of the texts we consider as male-authored were, in fact, written by women. Among the best known works composed by women are *A Revelation of Divine Love*, in which the mystic Julian of Norwich records a series of vision she experienced in 1373, and the early fifteenth-century *Book of Margery Kempe*, which provides an insight into the semi-religious life of a laywoman. While Julian of Norwich wielded the pen herself, Margery Kempe dictated her experiences to an amanuensis, which suggests that women who were not skilled in writing may still be regarded as the composers of texts.

**Readers.** Similarly, it has been suggested that the term 'reader' should be redefined for the medieval context. While the majority of women were not literate in the medieval sense of being able to read and write and having at least a minimal com-

Frontispiece to *Troilus and Criseyde*, Corpus Christi College, Cambridge, MS 61

---

**Focus on Medieval Women**

**Women as authors and readers** are the concern of *The Cambridge Companion to Medieval Women's Writing* (Dinshaw and Wallace) and of a number of articles in *Women and Literature in Britain, 1150–1500* (Meale). A selection of **medieval women's writing** is anthologized in *Women's Writing in Middle English* (Barratt). *The Book of Margery Kempe* is available in a Modern English translation by Barry Windeatt.

petence in Latin, many women were in fact able to read in English and French, some also in Latin. And, what is more, reading was also a communal activity in that texts were read to others (*lectio*), often during mealtimes. Thus, women who were unable to read still had access to book culture by listening to texts.

### 2.1.2 | Anglo-Saxon Literature

*The emergence of an English literary culture*

From the ninth to the eleventh centuries, an English literary culture was established. Monastic scholars and scribes developed a literary language and recorded some of the poetry of the Germanic tribes in England. Although the original texts were composed at different times and in different dialects, the Old English manuscripts show hardly any traces of these differences. These scholars also introduced a Christian ethos into the pagan spirit of their source texts and thus worked as co-generators of Old English literature as we know it. Old English poetry, then, constitutes a social text of the ninth and tenth centuries, rather than reflecting any original authors' words.

The pattern of Anglo-Saxon verse craft relied on **alliteration**: it established coherence of lines, line-breaks were nearly immaterial and stanza divisions unknown. This poetry offers some insight into the ideals of a warrior society. Courage and loyalty are praised, and so is the generosity of the warlord to his men. Success in battle and a happy life within the warriors' community, though, cannot be taken for granted: fate may always interfere and bring death. Then courage has to manifest itself as brave endurance unto the brink of destruction.

### *Beowulf* and the Christian Epic

In their praise of courage and wisdom, the 3,182 lines of the heroic poem ***Beowulf*** still reflect the spirit of Germanic warrior society; indeed, it alludes to events and characters of fifth and sixth-century Scandinavia. But the late version of the story—our only manuscript witness was produced around the year 1000—is a Christianizing reworking of a preliterate version.

The **story** can be reduced to a series of three battles fought by Beowulf: first, as a young man, against the monster Grendel, and then against its mother, and finally, as an aged king caring for his people, against a fire-breathing dragon. In this last

battle he is mortally wounded, and the poem ends with his funeral. The celebration of strength in the young warrior and of self-sacrifice in the ruler should remind the settlers in England of the traditional virtues of their forefathers. When, despite Beowulf's final victory, the poem predicts the downfall of his people, the opposition between **cultural order and chaos** adds a typically Germanic thought to the conflict: strength, courage and good rule make for an honourable life—yet personal triumph can only defer the final victory of the forces of evil. Against this background of a hostile universe, Beowulf's heroic behaviour and his spirit of magnanimity gain their values as Germanic as well as Christian virtues. The enemies Beowulf fights are also creatures hateful to God—Grendel, for instance, lives as an outlaw "siþðan him scyppend forscrifen hæfde" (since the Creator had condemned him; line 106)—and Beowulf's short triumphant moods are balanced by an awareness of man's restricted strength to resist evil. Defeat is always near, as is the judgment at Doomsday. The poem draws attention to this dark lesson when it frames the hero's life story by two funerals, thus interweaving a nostalgic view of pagan life "in geardagum" (in a bygone era; line 1) with an essentially Christian set of values.

> **Focus on Reading *Beowulf***
>
> A good place to start reading *Beowulf* is the translation by the Nobel prize-winning poet Seamus Heaney. *Klaeber's Beowulf* provides a magisterial survey of research.

*The Battle of Maldon* also praises the ideal of heroism in a hostile world; at the same time, it undermines its praise by pointing out that the military strategy adopted in that battle was based on arrogance. Obviously, the heroic defiance of the enemy by the military leader Byrhtwold is meant to cover up a military blunder:

Hige sceal þe heardra, heorte þe cenre,
mod sceal þe mare, þe ure mægen lytlað. (lines 312–13)
(Minds will be the tougher, hearts the keener, courage the greater, while our strength lessens.)

Old English Saints' lives can be read as examples of **pagan poetry** transformed as part of the missionary effort: they use the conventions of heroic poetry for their appeal to Germanic audiences admiring warriors of a proud disposition. Therefore, the Christian ideal of humility had to be played down, and evil was presented in the shape of Satanic enemies who could only be defeated in battles fought in the spirit of traditional heroism. Among those works, *Andreas* is remarkable for its Christian redefinitions of the meaning of some of the old heroic terms. Humility is demonstrated in *The Dream of the Rood*. Here, the Cross speaks as a retainer who suffers wounds and insults together with Christ to fulfil God's will most loyally. Although it uses heroic language, courage has now been replaced by reluctant obedience: "þær ic þa ne dorste ofer dryhtnes word / bugan oððe berstan" (35–36) (Then I dared not bend or break against the Lord's word).

## The Elegies

The so-called elegies (an unhelpful term) are **meditative monologues** contrasting loss and consolation. Their speakers suffer from exclusion from the society of their kinsmen or fellow warriors and voice their loneliness. Yet their distance from the old society leads to spiritual growth and they accept the rival view of the world, the teaching of the Gospel. When, in their minds, God has replaced their warlord, they feel consoled. Exile and loneliness, then, characterize the human condition in this world:

forþon ne mæg weorþan wis wer, ær he age
wintra dæl in woruldrice (*The Wanderer*, lines 65–66)
(no man acquires wisdom before he has spent his share of winters in the kingdom of this world.)

As both the pagan world and the future afterlife share the quality of happiness, there is a certain ambiguity in the evaluation of pagan society: was it as good as Paradise, or is it a stage of which one has to divest oneself?

## Old English Prose

The literary culture of the Anglo-Saxons also developed prose, both as a medium subtle enough to be used in theological arguments, and as a rhetorically powerful tool for sermons. The moving spirit behind many of the translations of the late ninth century was **King Alfred** (849–899) who entrusted a group of scholars with the task of providing vernacular texts for the training of priests. In this context, the translation of Pope Gregory's *Cura Pasto-*

*ralis* served a double purpose: it provided the Church with a manual for future bishops, and it served as a reminder of the man who had organized the evangelization of the English South in 597. Alfred's translators also made available histories of the English Church—translating **Bede**'s *Historia ecclesiastica gentis Anglorum*—and of the Church generally—by producing an Old English version of **Orosius**' *Historia adversum Paganos*. Alfred also inspired secular writings in Old English, most notably a chronicle of Anglo-Saxon history since the early settlements. When this annalistic survey had finally been compiled in 899, manuscript copies were sent to various monastic centres, some of which took up the implied challenge: seven continuations, in varying degrees of narrativization of the annalistic skeleton, have been preserved.

About a century later, a renewed cultivation of prose writing was meant to spread the principles of the Benedictine reform in England. The great writers, **abbot Ælfric** (955–1020) and **Archbishop Wulfstan of York** (d. 1023), developed rhetorically heightened styles. In his homilies, Ælfric lays down theologically accepted exegetical readings of the Bible, thus providing models for priests of how to preach to the laity. Wulfstan's sermons urge his listeners to reform their lives, using, in rhythmical, alliterative prose, the continued threat of Viking invasions as a means to remind the morally lax English of God's anger.

*Anglo-Saxon literature between pagan and religious traditions*

## 2.1.3 | Middle English Court Cultures

In 1066, the Normans conquered England. As they spoke Anglo-Norman—a North French idiom—the production of Old English literature ceased to enjoy official backing. The invaders began to cultivate a type of English literature which used imported French literary matter and forms (end rhyme and regular metres, for instance). This interest in the native language resulted in a flowering of Middle English literature at the court of **Richard II** (d. 1400) and also at some provincial courts. At Richard's court, John Gower wrote an English work, the *Confessio Amantis*, which illustrates 133 sins against love by narratives which, taken together, draw a depressing picture of mankind. There is no moralising, but obviously England is presented as morally corrupt because of a prevailing spirit of individualism.

The Bayeux tapestry shows the Norman invasion of England in 1066.

## Geoffrey Chaucer

*Troilus and Criseyde.* Courtly literature made England familiar with Italian and Latin writers. A free reworking of Boccaccio's *Il Filostrato* (ca. 1338), a story from the Trojan War, was Geoffrey Chaucer's most important contribution to this project. His *Troilus and Criseyde* follows the stages of a tragic love affair: first, proud Troilus falls in love despite all his intentions, then he needs his uncle's help to set up his love affair with Criseyde, next he is found in 'heaven' only to become jealous when Criseyde is sent to the Greek camp and there strikes up a new relationship, and finally, deserted Troilus seeks death in battle. Throughout this sequence of events, love is presented in ambiguous terms: it is seen as an ennobling experience, yet at the same time Boethius' warning against trusting in the stability of anything in this world offers a sobering commentary on Troilus' elated feelings. The love story can be read in two ways, and as an amusing emphasis on the practicalities of a love affair undermines any tendency towards a moralist reading. Obviously, one cannot find ideals without physical experience—yet the clash between ideals and reality cannot be resolved:

I [have] seyd fully in my song
Th'effect and joie of Troilus servise,
Al be that ther was som disese among. (3.1814–16)

*Canterbury Tales.* In his *Canterbury Tales* (unfinished, late 1380–1400) Chaucer uses a variety of literary strategies to offer, again, competing moral perspectives without any evaluation. Firstly, he links the pilgrims' tales by a frame which is spoken by a narrator who restricts himself to the business of 'reporting' accurately what the other pilgrims' stories were like. This disengagement from any responsibility for the moral content of narratives is new in medieval literature and, indeed, *The Canterbury Tales* contain their share of questionable stories and rude language.

Secondly, the religious character of the pilgrimage is suspended by the Host's suggestion to turn the journey into an **entertainment**: each pilgrim is asked to contribute tales to shorten the time of the journey, and the best story-teller is promised a prize at the end. The pilgrims' progress becomes a challenge to win a worldly contest which in turn deprives the single tales of a morally binding frame. Finally, the tales, freed now of any expected mode of reception, form groups which discuss the same problem with different, purely personal answers.

The series of 24 tales starts with two stories of a **love triangle**. Whereas the rhetorically impressive *Knight's Tale* employs philosophical concepts to convince readers that the rival lovers have to subordinate themselves to the rule of *providentia*, the highest order, the following *Miller's Tale* presents the pilgrims with a crude story of lust in a plain style. But if *The Knight's Tale* was really meant by the author to be presented by the Knight (the teller-tale relationships are debated among Chaucerians), then this narrator cannot claim a greater authority than the Miller: *The Canterbury Tales* are prefaced by a series of pilgrims' portraits from which it emerges that the Knight is but a mercenary who might well have fought against the English on one occasion. Another set of tales is concerned with the role of wives (the 'Marriage Group') and the range of perspectives on this issue extends from praise of absolute subjection to a husband's wishes (*The Clerk's Tale*), via an example of privately practised marital equality (*The Franklin's Tale*), to a voice proudly claiming to have survived five husbands (*The Wife of Bath's Prologue*). All the reader can take away from *The Canterbury Tales* by way of a moral is the reminder that the religiously sanctioned order is incompatible with the messiness of actual life. Chaucer's *Canterbury Tales* refrain—in an amused way, at that—from judging human society.

## John Lydgate

Though living away from London in an East Anglian monastery, John Lydgate obtained patronage for some of his literary work at the royal court. His *Troy Book* (ca. 1420), a detailed history of Troy in verse, was based on a Latin prose source, yet is transformed to bear some relevance to court politics: Lydgate employs legendary history to discuss the House of Lancaster's right to the throne. *The Fall of Princes* (ca. 1431–1438), based on a French translation of Boccaccio's *De casibus virorum illustrium*, shows, by means of countless examples, the influence of Fortune on the makers of history, providing again a comment on Lancastrian politics. Lydgate's admiration for Chaucer engaged him in the literary game of continuing *The Canterbury Tales*: *The Siege of Thebes* (ca. 1421) was devised to serve as a companion piece to *The Knight's Tale*. Whereas Chaucer's version is about accepting the force of Providence, Lydgate's more 'modern' view airs the possibility of strategically managing Fortune, Providence's agent, by avoiding situations where Fortune is allowed to act as a decisive force:

But as fortune and fate, both yffere,
List to dispose with her double chere
[...]; wherfor ech man be war
Vnavysed a were to bygynne.
For no man woot who shal lese or wynne.
(*Siege of Thebes* lines 4647–52)

## Literature at Provincial Courts

Literary texts of formal intricacy, and ambiguity of meaning, also found an audience at provincial courts in the North of England. The **Gawain poet** (North-West Midlands) combined native long alliterative lines with the imported convention of end rhymes to good effect in all his works. *The Pearl* (before 1390) follows the stages of mourning, culminating in a vision of the heavenly Jerusalem which works as a powerful consolation, and yet marks the distance between God and imperfect man. Problems of accepting one's imperfection also form the subject of *Sir Gawain and the Green Knight* (before 1400). When Gawain has accepted a seemingly impossible challenge, he leaves King Arthur's court, travels through a wintry England and spends the last days before his appointment with the Green Knight in a castle, alone and preoccupied with thoughts of his imminent death. But with one minor exception, he is unflinchingly

brave. Against all odds, he succeeds in his mission, but when he returns to Arthur's court he cannot join in the general merriment due to shame at his lack of absolute perfection, and remains mentally separated from his fellow knights. Gawain is resigned to his fate, brave to the outside world and yet full of self-doubt:

Þe knyȝt mad ay god chere,
And sayde, "Quat schuld I wonde? [...]
What may mon do bot fonde?" (lines 562-65)
(The knight made a brave face and said: "Why should I shy away?
What can man do but try?")

## 2.1.4 | Romances and Malory

Middle English romances, 116 texts of narrative literature in verse such as *Guy of Warwick*, *Sir Isumbras*, *The Squire of Low Degree* entertained a less sophisticated audience with fictional tales. The basic plot, a chain of adventures and fights, varies the pattern of the socially or geographically displaced knight who slowly regains his high position in society. By this reintegration, romance plots present the nobility as worthy of admiration: their courage and strength can protect the people from foreign rule. This message is often linked with the imaginary construction of a glorious national past when British virtues were embodied in King Arthur and his noble knights (cf. Putter and Gilbert). The great popularity of romances is also attested by the large number of printed editions of reworkings of these stories in Early Modern England.

*Romances were a highly popular form at the time.*

Malory's *Le Morte Darthur* (ca.1468–1470), a compilation of many **Arthurian stories** in prose, uses the conservative vision of the superior quality of noble blood as a foil against which the selfishness and corruption of fifteenth-century nobility is revealed. Malory makes the success of Arthur's knights dependent on their chivalric value: only idealistically motivated acts will bring honour. But in the course of Arthurian 'history,' chivalric ideals lose their power, and rivalries begin to develop among the knights until, at the end, a desolate picture of Arthur's kingdom emerges. The decline begins when some knights no longer ignore queen Guinever's adultery with Launcelot. As a consequence, the Arthurian knights are forced to take sides—with Arthur, or with Mordred, Arthur's illegitimate son who embodies the new non-chivalric spirit. Unfortunately, loyalty no longer rules: "The most part of all England held with Sir Mordred, the people were so new-fangle" (bk. 21). Their armies clash, and the dying Arthur is forced to realize how the 'newfangled' world of material values takes possession of the field where what was once the flower of chivalry lie dead or wounded:

He saw and hearkened by the moonlight, how that pillers and robbers were come into the field, to pill and to rob many a full noble knight of brooches, and beads, of many a good ring, and of many a rich jewel; and who that were not dead all out, there they slew them for their harness and their riches. (Bk. 21)

Malory's elegy for the chivalry of the past is to be read as a lesson of good rule for the contemporary nobility of England, unprofitably involved in the Wars of the Roses.

### 2.1.5 | Late Medieval Religious Literature

Much of late medieval religious writing expresses and promotes **affective piety**. Meditations, lyrics, sermons and religious drama call upon the reader or listener to meditate on the humanity of Christ and the Virgin Mary and to identify emotionally with their human experiences. One of the most widely circulated texts, Nicholas Love's *Mirror of the Blessed Life of Jesus Christ*, a fifteenth-century translation of the thirteenth-century *Meditationes Vitae Christi*, urges the reader to feel compassion with Jesus and his mother. Religious lyrics also encourage an emotive response to the passion, sometimes providing the reader with a role model to imitate: "Whan I thenke on Cristes blod / That he

schad upon the rode, / I lete teris smerte" (qtd. in Gray 34).

*Medieval religious drama*, too, was meant not only to teach and to entertain but also to stir the affection of the audience. The origin of medieval drama lies in the enactment of the *Visitatio Sepulchri*, the three Maries' visit to Christ's tomb, where the angel addresses them with the question "Quem quaeritis" (Whom do you seek?). Stage directions survive for the Benedictine monks at Winchester from as early as the tenth century. Other scenes re-enacted in the church were the deposition and the elevation, in which a crucifix or a wooden puppet of Christ was laid into, and then taken out of, the Easter sepulchre. Liturgical drama which was linked to a specific day of the church calendar and performed in the church is only one type of medieval drama. From the thirteenth century onwards, religious plays in the vernacular were performed on church squares, market places and in the streets.

The best known plays are the **Cycle Plays** (also known as **Mystery Plays**), which presented the history of the creation, fall and salvation of humankind. The cycle plays were originally written for the Corpus Christi procession; the earliest document dates from 1376. The titles of some Cycle Plays point at the cities in which they were performed, e.g. the York Plays or the Chester Plays. The Cycle Plays were performed on a series of pageants (wooden wagons), each of which was set up by a craft or religious guild. The pageants were

A pageant from the Coventry Plays
(nineteenth century illustration)

drawn through the city along a prearranged route. The first pageant (showing, for example, the Creation) would perform at the first station as early as 4.30 a.m. and then proceed to the next station, the second pageant following close behind. In York there were as many as 12–16 stations and over fifty pageants, so the performance of a Cycle Play would have taken all day.

Unlike these cycles of biblical drama, **Saints' or Miracle Plays** dramatize the lives and miracles of saints. The origin of these plays lie in the saints' legends, many of which were assembled in collections, such as the thirteenth-century *South English Legendary*. Among the surviving Saints' or Miracle Plays are the Digby *Conversion of St Paul* and *Mary Magdalen* (ca. 1500) and the fifteenth-century Croxton *Play of the Sacrament*. Under Queen Elizabeth I, all performances of plays on religious subjects were banned. After a long period of neglect, medieval religious drama has seen a revival since the 1950s.

---

**Focus on Medieval Religious Drama**

- Selections from all genres of **medieval drama** are brought together in Walker.
- As **introductory reading**, we recommend Beadle and Fletcher; Dillon; and Normington.
- The following website provides easily accessible **play texts** of several cycle plays: www.umm. maine.edu/faculty/necastro/drama/

---

## 2.1.6 | Oppositions and Subversions

### Langland and the Literature of Social Discontent

Middle English Literature also exploited the **polemical potential** of writing. Well before the Reformation, the alliterative dream vision *Piers Plowman* (various revisions 1362–1394, probably written by William Langland) raises doubts about the contemporary church's precepts and examples of right living. Nearly all principles of "being kynde"—of living as a human being created by God—melt away for Will, the dreamer, when he reflects on the permanent obligation to choose between good and evil. Will presents his thought process by resorting to satire of social life and ecclesiastical abuse, and personification allegory al-

lowing for the introduction of teachers and examples of ways of life. In the barrage of competing voices and modes of life, Piers, the simple man, stands for a way of life characterized by carrying out all the duties laid upon him by God and man, but Will—also a figure with allegorical significance—knows that this life of 'Dowel,' of obedience, is lacking in essential qualities. Via the stage of 'Dobet,' a turning away from this world, 'Dobest' is reached, a compromise between conscious efforts devoted to save one's soul and humble submission to God's laws of Grace. Having reached this mode of existence, the establishment of a reformed Church is meant to replace the existing one and do away with ecclesiastical corruption. No other Middle English text is so critical of the institutionalized church, and *Piers Plowman* was influential in shaping the literature of religious and political dissent in the late Middle Ages.

### Robert Henryson

When, in the fifteenth century, the **Great Vowel Shift** began to change the quality of all long vowels (cf. section V.3.4.1), affecting individual words at different times, writing end-rhyme poetry became a near impossible task in England. However, these vowel changes did not affect Scotland at the time, and, consequently, the centre of literary production shifted to the North. Among the Scottish *makars* of the later fifteenth century, Robert Henryson is remarkable for taking the first steps towards alternative, post-medieval interpretations of traditional narratives. In his **Testament of Cresseid** (ca. 1490) he invents a sequel to Chaucer's *Troilus and Criseyde* and exempts the heroine from moral stricture. As this amounts to justifying physical love, Henryson's narrative breaks fairly radically with the medieval convention of applying religious standards when evaluating the behaviour of literary figures. Henryson seems to take literature's moral autonomy for granted, and as this must have come as a surprise, *The Testament* again and again foregrounds its readers' assumed responses.

This spirit of independence is also manifest in his collection of 13 **Morall Fabilis** (ca. 1484). Here, he contrasts the allegorical meaning given in the Middle Ages to animals and their typical characters with the moral conclusions the beasts, as representatives of common man, draw for themselves after their adventures. When, for instance, the cock scraping for food in a dunghill fails to see the value of the jasper he has found, he displays a matter-of-fact sensibility: jewels, after all, do not have any nutritional value. Would the story really make sense if the cock stood for those ignorant people who despise "prudence" (line 128) as the story is understood by the narrator? With Henryson, it is up to the reader to decide whether the narrator's—quite often unrelated—moral conclusions to the fables usurp interpretive authority or whether the animals' sensible reasoning should be taken as the meaning of the story. In view of this

discrepancy, readers are empowered to apply the literary text to their own frames of thinking, and by offering such scope, Henryson radicalizes *The Canterbury Tales'* **moral ambivalence**: he introduces narrators who, when they resort to moralizing, also (and incongruously) claim independence from authority: "Quha wait gif all that Chauceir wrait was trew?" (*Testament of Cresseid* line 64) (Who knows if Chaucer's writings contain the truth?).

## Recommended Primary Texts

### Old English

*Beowulf*. **Trans.** Seamus Heaney. New York: Norton, 2002.
Fulk, R. D., Robert E. Bjork, and John D. Niles, eds. *Klaeber's Beowulf*. 4th ed. Toronto: University of Toronto Press, 2008.
*The Wanderer* and *The Dream of the Rood*. Both in: E. Treharne, ed. and trans. *Old and Middle English. An Anthology*. Oxford: Blackwell, 2000. 42–47 and 108–15.

### Middle English

**Chaucer, Geoffrey.** *The Canterbury Tales*. Ed. Jill Mann. London: Penguin, 2005.
**Chaucer, Geoffrey.** *Troilus and Criseyde*. Ed. Barry Windeatt. London: Penguin, 2003.
**Henryson, Robert.** *Robert Henryson: The Poems*. Ed. Denton Fox. Oxford: Oxford University Press, 1987.
**Julian of Norwich.** *Revelations of Divine Love and The Motherhood of God*. Ed. and trans. Frances Beer. Cambridge: D. S. Brewer, 1999.

**Langland, William.** *The Vision of Piers Plowman*. Ed. A. V. C. Schmidt. London: Dent, 1995.
**Love, Nicholas.** *The Mirror of the Blessed Life of Jesus Christ: A Reading Text*. Ed. Michael G. Sargent. Exeter: Exeter University Press, 2004.
**Malory, Thomas.** *Le Morte Darthur*. Ed. Stephen H. A. Shepherd. New York: Norton, 2004.
*Sir Gawain and the Green Knight*. Trans. Simon Armitage. London: Faber, 2007.
**Tolkien, J. R. R., E. V. Gordon, and Norman Davis, eds.** *Sir Gawain and the Green Knight*. 2nd ed. Oxford: Clarendon, 1967.
**Walker, Greg, ed.** *Medieval Drama. An Anthology*. Oxford: Blackwell, 2000. In particular, we recommend the York "Adam and Eve" and "Joseph's Trouble about Mary," and the Croxton "Play of the Sacrament." 25–37, 213–34.
**Windeatt, Barry, trans.** *The Book of Margery Kempe*. Harmondsworth: Penguin, 1985.
**Windeatt, Barry.** *The Oxford Guides to Chaucer: Troilus and Criseyde*. Oxford: Oxford University Press, 1995.

## Select Bibliography

**Aers, David.** "A Whisper in the Ear of Early Modernists; or, Reflections on Literary Critics Writing the 'History of the Subject.'" *Culture and History: 1350–1600: Essays on English Communities, Identities and Writing*. Ed. David Aers. Detroit: Wayne State University Press, 1992. 177–202.
**Archibald, Elizabeth, and Ad Putter, eds.** *The Cambridge Companion to Arthurian Legend*. Cambridge: Cambridge University Press, 2009.
**Barratt, Alexandra.** *Women's Writing in Middle English*. London: Longman, 1992.
**Beadle, Richard, and Alan J. Fletcher.** *The Cambridge Companion to Medieval English Theatre*. Cambridge: Cambridge University Press, 2008.
**Blockmans, Wim, and Peter Hoppenbrouwers.** *Introduction to Medieval Europe*. Trans. Isola van den Hoven. New York: Routledge, 2009.
**Brown, Peter, ed.** *A Companion to Medieval English Literature and Culture: ca.1350-ca.1500*. Chichester: Wiley-Blackwell, 2007.
**Cooper, Helen.** *The Oxford Guides to Chaucer: The Canterbury Tales*. 2nd ed. Oxford: Oxford University Press, 1996.
**Davis, Jennifer R.,** and Michael McCormick. "The Early Middle Ages: Europe's Long Morning." Introduction. *The*

*Long Morning of Medieval Europe. New Directions in Early Medieval Studies*. Eds. Jennifer R. Davis and Michael McCormick. Aldershot: Ashgate, 2008. 1–10.
**Dillon, Janette.** *The Cambridge Introduction to Early English Theatre*. Cambridge: Cambridge University Press, 2006.
**Dinshaw, Carolyn.** "Getting Medieval: Pulp Fiction, Gawain, Foucault." *The Book and the Body*. Ed. Dolores Warwick Frese and Katherine O'Brien O'Keeffe. Notre Dame: University of Notre Dame Press, 1997). 116–63.
**Dinshaw, Carolyn, and David Wallace, eds.** *The Cambridge Companion to Medieval Women's Writing*. Cambridge: Cambridge University Press, 2003.
**Eco, Umberto.** *Travels in Hyperreality*. Trans. William Weaver. San Diego: Harcourt Brace, 1986.
**Fulk, R. D., and Christopher M. Cain.** *A History of Old English Literature*. Malden: Blackwell, 2003.
**Galloway, Andrew.** *Medieval Literature and Culture*. London: Continuum, 2006.
**Gray, Douglas.** *Themes and Images in the Medieval English Religious Lyric*. London: Routledge, 1972.
**Kern-Stähler, Annette.** "Gender, Creation and Authorship in the Late Middle Ages." *Gender and Creation: Surveying Gendered Myths of Creativity, Authority, and Au-*

*thorship*. Ed. Anne-Julia Zwierlein. Heidelberg: Winter, 2010. 25–42.

**Klaeber's Beowulf.** 1950. Eds. Robert D. Fulk et al. 4th ed. Toronto: University of Toronto Press, 2008.

**Meale, Carol, ed.** *Women and Literature in Britain: 1150–1500*. 2nd ed. Cambridge: Cambridge University Press, 1996.

**Mehl, Dieter.** *English Literature in the Age of Chaucer*. Harlow: Longman, 2001.

**Minnis, Alastair.** *Medieval Theory of Authorship: Scholastic Literary Attitudes in the Later Middle Ages*. 1984. 2nd ed. Philadelphia: University of Philadelphia Press, 2009.

**Mommsen, Theodor E.** "Petrarch's Conception of the 'Dark Ages.'" *Speculum* 17 (1942): 226–42.

**Normington, Katie.** *Medieval English Drama*. Cambridge: Polity Press, 2009.

**Patterson, Lee.** *Negotiating the Past. The Historical Understanding of Medieval Literature*. Madison: University of Wisconsin Press, 1987.

**Patterson, Lee.** "On the Margin: Postmodernism, Ironic History, and Medieval Studies." *Speculum* 65 (1990): 87–108.

**Pulsiano, Phillip, and Elaine Treharne, eds.** *A Companion to Anglo-Saxon Literature*. Oxford: Blackwell, 2001.

**Putter, Ad, and Jane Gilbert, eds.** *The Spirit of Medieval English Popular Romance*. Harlow: Longman, 2000.

**Robinson, Fred C.** "Medieval, the Middle Ages." *Speculum* 59 (1984): 745–56.

**Scala, Elizabeth, and Sylvia Federico.** "Getting Post-Historical." Introduction. *The Post-Historical Middle Ages*. Eds. Elizabeth Scala and Sylvia Federico. New York: Palgrave Macmillan, 2009. 1–11.

**Scanlon, Larry. Introduction.** *The Cambridge Companion to Medieval English Literature: 1100–1500*. Ed. Larry Scanlon. Cambridge: Cambridge University Press, 2009. 1–8.

**Sidney, Sir Philip.** *An Apology for Poetry*. Ed. Geoffrey Shepherd. London: Nelson, 1965.

**Solopova, Elizabeth, and Stuart Lee.** *Key Concepts in Medieval Literature*. Houndsmill: Palgrave Macmillan, 2007.

**Strohm, Paul, ed.** *Oxford Twenty-First Century Approaches to Literature: Middle English*. New York: Oxford University Press, 2007.

**Summit, Jane.** "Women and Authorship." *The Cambridge Companion to Medieval Women's Writing*. Ed. Carolyn Dinshaw and David Wallace. Cambridge: Cambridge University Press, 2003. 91–108.

**Treharne, Elaine, and Greg Walker, eds.** *The Oxford Handbook of Medieval Literature in English*. Oxford: Oxford University Press, 2010.

**Wallace, David, ed.** *The Cambridge History of Medieval English Literature*. Cambridge: Cambridge University Press, 1999.

**Wenger, Luke.** "Editor's Note." *Speculum* 65.1 (1990): n. pag.

*Annette Kern-Stähler/Stephan Kohl*

# 2.2 | The Sixteenth and Seventeenth Centuries

## 2.2.1 | Overview

At first glance, the field of early modern studies may appear so heterogeneous as to hardly justify the use of a common term. There is no consensus as to how such labels as '**Renaissance**,' '**Humanism**,' '**early modern**,' or '**Restoration**' are to be understood or precisely which periods of time they cover in their respective European contexts. All of them carry reductive and sometimes misleading connotations—whether they harness our attention to the assumption of a wholesale cultural revival of classical antiquity, structured according to earlier processes on the continent (e.g. the Florentine Renaissance or the Spanish *Siglo de Oro*); privilege certain areas of learning, scholarship, and education together with a concept of 'the human'; transport a hidden bias about degrees, stages, and values of modernity and its ultimate arrival; or concentrate on political developments, postulating caesuras at the expense of continuities in other areas of reality, or modelling them according to patterns of disruption and return. While this state of terminological affairs appears unsatisfactory, it also seems hardly possible to mend it. Still, one way out of the difficulties that arise if we rely on traditional period divisions may be to stress kinds of continuity capable of bracketing together the two centuries of cultural and political history between the reigns of Henry VIII (1509–1547) and William of Orange (1689–1702): transformations of antiquity, the emergence of new science and new philosophy, the long process of the Reformation, systems of literary patronage and beginning professionalisation, and the project of nation-building.

The major structures of **Tudor as well as Stuart aesthetics** bridge the extremes between urbane accomplishment and technical brilliance on the one side, built on an increasing awareness of the multiplication of perspectives and realms of knowledge, and on the other, a generalised sense of anxiety, discord and disintegration with a loss of certainties deepening even to despair. This consciousness of a growing and irreducible plurality of world views—i.e. "the cultural principles of pluralism and plenitude" (Kinney, Introduction 6) implying the proximity and relatedness of human dignity and misery articulated by continental Humanists at the beginning of the period as well as a vague sense of a multiplicity of 'worlds'—continues to inform artistic production in England right into the eighteenth century.

In the period which saw the emergence of Humanistic education, emphatic notions of literary authorship and its first professionalizations, men (and some women) were educated to be "**rhetorical men**" (cf. Lanham), human beings whose central competence was eloquence—a verbal and semantic versatility which as "self-fashioning" and performance in a multitude of ways informed the whole of life (cf. Greenblatt, *Renaissance Self-Fashioning*). Far from the moral dubiousness of hypocrisy, authorial dissimulation is part and parcel of this all-embracing theatricality, a generalisation of the courtly model, which was to become a signature of the period as a whole. Antiquity, to Rhetorical Man, is a central part of his lexicon and the major treasury of his invention. The "Invention of the Human" claimed by Harold Bloom for Shakespeare's theatre may, after all, amount to just this: a mentality whose mainstay is the idea of performative humanity (beyond a Humanism which provided the scholarship and the ancient materials) and poetic subjectivities relying on imaginative transformations of a selectively perceived and re-shaped antiquity.

| Timeline: Tudor and Stuart Dynasties | |
|---|---|
| 1485–1509 | Henry VII: Inauguration of Tudor dynasty |
| 1509–1547 | Henry VIII |
| 1526 | William Tyndale's English translation of the New Testament |
| 1534 | Separation from Roman Catholicism: Henry VIII head of the Church of England |
| 1547–1553 | Edward VI |
| 1553–1558 | Mary I (return to Catholicism) |
| 1558–1603 | Elizabeth I (return to Protestantism) |
| 1599 | Opening of the Globe Theatre |
| 1603–1625 | James I: Inauguration of Stuart dynasty |
| 1607 | Establishment of the first English colony in the New World |
| 1625–1649 | Charles I |
| 1642–1649 | Civil War; Closing of theatres; Charles I executed in 1649 |
| 1649–1660 | Interregnum |
| 1660 | Restoration of Charles II; Foundation of Royal Society; Reopening of theatres |
| 1685–1688 | James II |
| 1688–1689 | Glorious Revolution; Accession of William of Orange (1689–1702) |

## 2.2.2 | Transformations of Antiquity

The philosophical and literary transformations of antiquity constitute one form of continuity in the sixteenth and seventeenth centuries, as the intensely verbal and textual culture of English early modernity depends, and indeed thrives on, the textual cultures of classical antiquity. True, transformations of antiquity neither begin nor end with the period of time under consideration. But in their characteristically sixteenth- and seventeenth-century profile they contain the promise to accommodate both the salient changes and the perduring cultural sameness which give the period a recognisable consistency. In England, the early modern period is not a time in which philosophical systems are originated or, like Cartesian thought in France, systematically developed from first principles. Neither are systematic positions elaborated by Greek and Latin thinkers handed down unchanged through the centuries, to be 're-born' in the belated English Renaissance. Rather, these are selected, recomposed and changed—transformed, as elements from heterogeneous schools of thought are reorganised in versions, mode and media aimed at cultural situations very different from their origins. Thus, the 'transformative' approach tries to avoid connotations of an unmodified 'return' or 'reception' of the paradigms of Graeco-Roman Antiquity. It also attempts to accommodate an interest that guides much recent research in explaining the mentalities that shaped the period and made possible its extraordinary cultural achievements.

### Spenser and Browne

In a poem from his sonnet sequence *Amoretti* (1594), Edmund **Spenser**, or his poetic *persona*, appears to be enjoying something we might expect him to reject rather than celebrate, namely the beauty of created beings, intensely and sensually experienced. Thus, in sonnet 72 the poet imagines his soul as a bird of prey in a moment of perfect relaxation:

Oft when my spirit doth spred her bolder winges,
   In mind to mount up to the purest sky:
   it down is weighd with thoght of earthly things
   and clogd with burden of mortality,
Where when that soverayne beauty it doth spy,    5
   resembling heavens glory in her light:
   drawne with sweet pleasures bayt, it back doth fly,
   and unto heaven forgets her former flight.
There my fraile fancy fed with full delight,
   doth bath in blisse and mantleth most at ease:   10
   ne thinks of other heaven, but how it might
   her harts desire with most contentment please.
Hart need not wish none other happinesse,
   but here on earth to have such hevens blisse.

Instead of soaring to the highest spiritual heights, the speaker's "spirit" appears, in the second half of the poem, to be content with the contemplation of earthly beauty. But what is it that motivates him to this ambitious ascent in the first place, and why does he break it off in order to opt for the second-best? And is it really the inferior option? Why should he imagine his soul as a bird of prey? Why does this kind of subject call for precisely this form of a fourteen-line poem in iambic pentameter and a complicated rhyme scheme? What is it that leads a late sixteenth-century poet to cast love in terms of a "flight unto heaven" supposed to help him shed all "thoght of earthly things"? Is the soul's, and in particular: the imagination's ("my fraile fancy"), return to the "sweet pleasures" below a kind of failure or really another kind of success? What exactly do these pleasures consist in, seeing that they promise both sensual and spiritual delight? And why is it that this soul-bird feels so blissfully self-satisfied, although it has just missed its aim?

In order to answer questions of this kind we need to know something not only about **Neoplatonic philosophy** in late antiquity but also about the shapes the Neoplatonic doctrine of the soul had assumed in Spenser's time. These were in many respects a far cry from the original—as witnessed, for instance, by this poem and its bold remodelling of typical Neoplatonic structures of cyclical 'conversion' in favour of a pattern of artistic self-affirmation. The point is that, while we might argue that early modern writers to some extent invented their own antiquity, the implication is not so much that they thereby distorted it, but that, by making the transformations serve new and unforethought ends, they productively **re-functionalised** the former ideas, thoughts, and systematic configurations.

Interpretation

Interpretation

Our second example is separated by more than half a century from Spenser's text. Sir Thomas **Browne** opens a treatise he calls *Hydriotaphia, Urne-Buriall, or, A Discourse of the Sepulchrall Urnes lately found in Norfolk* (1658) as follows:

In the deep discovery of the Subterranean world, a shallow part would satisfie some enquirers; who, if two or three yards were open about the surface, would not care to rake the bowels of *Potosi* and regions towards the Centre. Nature hath furnished one part of the Earth, and man another. The treasures of time lie high, in Urnes, Coynes, and Monuments, scarce below the roots of some vegetables. Time hath endlesse rarities, and shows of all varieties; which reveals old things in heaven, makes new discoveries in earth, and even earth it self a discovery. That great Antiquity *America* lay buried for thousands of years; and a large part of the earth is still in the Urne to us.

Obviously, here the emphasis appears to be less on the spiritual than on the material and natural. But what exactly does the speaker refer to when he mentions that "Nature" has "furnished one part of the Earth"? Are we therefore entitled to excavate and exploit earth's treasures like the legendary silver mines of Potosi? And are there indeed other, subterranean worlds to discover? Can there be other worlds besides the one we occupy? Is it permitted to imagine them? If we do, as the text whimsically seems to suggest, by dying and being buried, in a quite literal sense "furnish" the earth, turning it into a kind of necropolis that only waits to be discovered by later generations, very much like the New World "*America*" (here wittily referred to as a "great Antiquity"— just as desirable, of course, to an antiquarian, as any brand-new world): if the new is really the old, and vice versa, are we then justified in treating both as mere material for our research? Are the things that are "still in the Urne to us" connected to the living individuals they once were—and if so, how? Finally, if what we find and explore are indisputably objects to be experienced by means of our senses, how do we then reconcile our findings with metaphysical doctrines of the immortality of the soul and indeed, the resurrection of the body?

Again, these questions are underpinned by a sense that, in this rather dizzying opening paragraph to a far-ranging treatise on burial customs, we are dealing with transformations of antiquity, blended with the special antiquarian sense the term acquired in the seventeenth century and playfully spiced with a grain of the discoverer's enthusiasm. Here, we may be faced with Browne's own version of **Epicurean materialism** as well as a Naturalism that seems to have been processed by thinkers as unorthodox as himself and interested in the possibility of 'other worlds' (such as Giordano Bruno). Still, we should be fatally wrong if we tried to identify Browne with just one of these ways of thinking. At one point in his extended autobiographical essay *Religio Medici*, he warns us not to pin him down to any one of the available schools of thought: "I have runne through all sects, yet finde no rest in any, though our first studies & *junior* endeavors may stile us Peripateticks, Stoicks, or Academicks, yet I perceive the wisest Heads prove at last, almost all Scepticks, and stand like *Janus* in the field of knowledge" (pt. 2, sect. 8). As could be shown, however, what looks like a confessed allegiance to the **Scepticism** fashionable in seventeenth-century England, is itself to be taken with a pinch of salt. Like the other philosophies mentioned—Aristotelianism, Stoicism, Platonism—Pyrrhonism is just part of a large quarry from which Browne and his contemporaries break the chunks they need in order to fashion their own, syncretistic and often very special literary identities.

## Ancient Philosophy in Early Modern Mentalities

Much like the other topics discussed in this chapter, the complex transformations of antiquity which structure our period could be unfolded along overlapping parameters of performance, narrative, discursive reflection, and, not least, the formation of poetic subjectivities—quite literally self-created, public images of 'makers' (cf. Greek *poiein*) who were proud of their achievements and confidently fashioned themselves as artists capable of making a difference in the world for which they wrote. Prior to considerations of this kind, however, a fundamental question arises: **Which antiquity do we refer to?** If literature grows from, and is capable of changing, historical mentalities, we should turn to them first and enquire in particular into those parts of their profile which owe so much to older formations. True, the presence of Graeco-Roman thinking has always been recognised as a hallmark of the period, invented to mark the difference between one's own enlightened and the preceding 'dark' age. Nonetheless, as indicated by the above examples, the English Renaissance is clearly neither a unified nor a comprehensive re-birth of classical antiquity. Especially with respect to its natural philosophy, the period is arguably still to a very large extent **Aristotelian**. For university syllabi as well as individual scholars, the Latin Aristotle and his scholastic commentators remained the major authorities, to be challenged only with the beginnings of the New Science (see our next section). However, with respect to ethics, the cultures of the self and of everyday life, it should be stressed that it is above all Hellenistic, that is to say, late antiquity with its Stoic, Sceptic, Neoplatonic, and increasingly also Epicurean thinkers which provided the models and the formative texts. As these were gradually becoming available in Latin or even in English, they attracted an interest that went beyond the scholarly and its specialist disciplines. By way of multiple mediations through texts, artefacts, social practices, and especially literary culture, their ideas and precepts percolated into the everyday. In this process of selective adoption and recombination, philosophical positions derived from antiquity were blended into sometimes contradictory and often idiosyncratic wholes with other elements, above all with Christian thought.

Still, Hellenistic profiles often remain visible in their outlines. Thus, the **Stoicisms** of Epictetus, Marcus Aurelius, and especially Cicero furnished not only humanist scholars from John Colet to Thomas More with some of the mainstays and many ingredients of their writings and respective arts of life. Fusing with other elements of ancient (and medieval) faculty theory and the affective regimes associated with these, they contributed to shaping a mentality and *habitus* in which the management of the passions together with a technique and economy of the self, including its public service and contribution to the commonwealth, played a major role and which retained its validity throughout the seventeenth century. With Cicero's *De officiis* serving as one of the central texts in grammar school education, Stoic *romanitas* comes to inspire Elizabethan notions of 'virtue'—including its masculinist implications.

That the cultural transfer of Stoicism need not be channelled institutionally and did not depend on a university education is borne out by the scholarly

---

**Definition**

→ **Stoicism:** a strongly rationalist school of thought founded by Zenon of Kition, Chrysippus, and Cleanthes and popularised by Roman thinkers such as Cicero, Seneca, and Marcus Aurelius. While ancient Greek Stoicism developed a system of logic, metaphysics and physics that explained the world as well-ordered *cosmos* held together by sympathetic relationships, Roman Stoics tended to stress the ethical dimension of their philosophy, presenting it above all as an art of life. Since the world, for the Stoic, is well-ordered, it is reasonable to accept the inevitable, and most important to remain unmoved (in a state of *apathia*) in the face of obstacles, catastrophes, and blows of fate. The main thing is to 'live according to nature,' that is, to follow the flow of life, keep a mental distance from external events as well as inner turmoil. Stoicism goes well with ideologies of military heroism and political virtue. Elizabethans loved it, and since the writings of Cicero and Seneca were read at grammar school, the notion of Stoical virtue, selfless public service, and generalised 'Roman-ness' was deeply ingrained at all levels of culture.

---

qualities of Ben Jonson's writings as well as William Shakespeare's—witness the intense topicality of passages such as Polonius' admonition of Laertes in *Hamlet* ("to thine own self be true," Act 1); the Duke's exhortation in *Measure for Measure* ("Be absolute for death," Act 3) addressed to the imprisoned and ultimately unreceptive Claudio; or Ulysses' famous 'degree' speech in *Troilus and Cressida* (Act 1), with the various characters' unsuccessful attempts to come to terms with their passions. In all of these, pieces of Stoic wisdom have already been transformed into, and can be evoked as, commonplaces. It is in this topical and essentially a-systematic shape that they now form part of new, and complex, literary configurations; not only, but prominently, in Shakespeare's Roman Plays or in Jonson's 'classicism.'

Side by side with the Stoic, we find Sceptic modes of thought infiltrating English literature after 1562, the publication date of Henri Etienne's Latin edition of the *Outlines of Pyrrhonism*, the manifesto of Late Antique **Scepticism** by Sextus Empiricus. Mediated, most prominently, through Montaigne's *Essays* (especially the "Apology for Raimond Sebonde") congenially translated by John Florio (1601) and later through Thomas Stanley's *History of Philosophy*, 'structural' scepticisms abound in sixteenth- and seventeenth-century English literature and inform its imaginative energy.

Again, Shakespeare's *Hamlet* is a case in point, but this also holds for *The Tempest*, with its almost verbatim allusions to Montaigne in combination

→ **Scepticism** (or **Pyrrhonism**): Hellenistic way of thinking, finding its origins in the eponymous Pyrrhon of Elis, a radical philosopher who, however, left nothing in writing. The most important Sceptical author in late antiquity was Sextus Empiricus (2nd half of the 2nd century) with his *Outlines of Pyrrhonism*. In the face of controversy, Sceptics abstain from making up their minds and committing themselves. They remain undecided, preferring to put the warring positions in brackets (*epoché*) and to suspend judgment in order to preserve their mental equilibrium (*ataraxia*).

with literary strategies which actively create and stage aporetic situations in which readers and spectators cannot but respond with the sceptical *epoché* later to be ambiguously recommended by Thomas Browne: We are asked to suspend judgment and direct our thoughtful attention to problems that admit of no ready solution. Cleopatra's death at her own hands in *Antony and Cleopatra*—"Let's do't after the high Roman fashion" (Act 4)—presents another, complex example. It combines the Stoic element of constancy with hedonistic, 'Epicurean' voluptuousness and the "Immortal longings" (Act 5) reminiscent of yet another kind of Hellenism in a manner which makes it impossible to reduce the aesthetic experience offered on stage to any of these ideological certainties—a structurally Sceptical effect.

Elements of **Epicureanism** also gain a foothold in English mentalities, increasing through the sixteenth century and gaining prominence, indeed notoriety, in the second half of the seventeenth. While Elizabethans still tended to reduce the teaching of Epicurus to its hedonistic stereotypes (and to repudiate them accordingly), a growing number of translations of Lucretius' long didactic

→ **Epicureanism:** a school of thought going back to the teachings of Epicurus, a materialist thinker who explained everything as the result of atoms and their movements and who taught that the aim of life is to attain happiness (*hedonè*, or pleasure), which in turn consists in freedom from fear and follows from an ascetic lifestyle. Only a few fragments of Epicurus' writings have survived, and we owe most of our knowledge about his doctrine to Lucretius and his great didactic poem *De rerum natura*. In the 17th century, many natural scientists found in atomist thought explanations of natural phenomena closer to experience and common sense than those provided by speculative thought in the tradition of medieval Aristotelianism ('scholasticism') and its commentators.

poem *De rerum natura*, its major literary compendium, contributed to a much more varied reception, ranging from the ethical to the scientific.

From the 1770s, "Lucretius English't"—in parts or in its totality—by John Evelyn (1656–1657), Thomas Creech (1682), John Dryden (1685) and, first but never published, by the Puritan Lucy Hutchinson (ca. 1650) was greeted with enthusiasm. At one end, it furthered downright Libertinist stances such as the Earl of Rochester's, and, in unlikely hybridisations with modified Neoplatonic and Sceptic structures, Aphra Behn's; at the other, Lucretian naturalism and atomism afforded confirmation as well as arguments to natural philosophers, virtuosos, and empirical scientists interested in the corpuscular make-up of the universe. Again in surprising combinations, these surface in the writings of Thomas Browne. The capacities of the atomistic model to account for material as well as psychological and spiritual phenomena rendered it particularly attractive to avid (if less discriminating) readers and writers such as Margaret Cavendish, whose prolific fictions, poetry, and expository writings cover the whole range of explanatory possibilities available to contemporary theory, fusing them to experimental and often adventurous configurations.

Finally, let us turn to the philosophy which inspired the Italian Renaissance like no other: **Platonism**, especially the **Neoplatonism** of Plotinus and his followers. It was epitomised in thinkers, translators, and cultural mediators like Marsilio Ficino and Giovanni Pico della Mirandola, remained virulent in the syncretistic naturalism of Giordano Bruno, and continued to resonate in various transformations through the sixteenth and seventeenth centuries in England. We have already seen it at work in Spenser's *Amoretti* 72, in its speaker's fascination with the possibilities of a spiritual ascent to the highest as well as his awareness of the challenges to sensuality and the appreciation of beauty this poses. Ancient Neoplatonism not only persists subculturally in Hermeticist and Occultist writings; it has also strongly informed English Petrarchism since its inception in *Tottels Miscellany* and the poetry of Wyatt and Surrey, to be continued and modified in sonnet sequences by Sidney, Spenser, and Shakespeare as well as in Sidney's romance novel sui generis, the *Arcadia*. It is thus part of the freight of philosophical implications carried by the sonnet form. But it also drives and structures Spenser's allegory in *The Faerie Queene*. In its transformations, it inspires English courtli-

## Definition

> → **Neoplatonism:** a school of thought, a metaphysical philosophy and a way of life pursued by followers of Plato and founded by Plotinus. Neoplatonists tend to be concerned, above all, with truth, beauty, and goodness—which, in their view, are ultimately identical—, and also with the way everything flows from a single source of being ("the One") and returns to it in one unbroken chain of simultaneous descent and ascent. Its disciples strive to participate with mind, soul, and body in this self-reflexive movement towards union with the transcendent One. Neoplatonism plays an important role on several levels of early modern culture—in love poetry, religion, courtliness as well as the self-presentation of monarchy.

ness through the medium of Castiglione's and Hoby's *Book of the Courtier*. And it provides the ideological context in which 'Seraphic' friendships flourish in the seventeenth century, prefiguring the new epistolary and literary culture of sensibility which, prepared by Aphra Behn's *Love-Letters Between a Nobleman and His Sister*, was to give distinctive profile to the eighteenth-century novel from Richardson to Jane Austen.

## Literary Transformations

It cannot be stressed enough that, in the literary texts of the period (and often in the non-fictional as well), the above-mentioned mindsets freely, and often surprisingly, intermingle. Hardly ever do we find unalloyed reproductions of ancient ways of thinking—not even in the works of the Libertine John Wilmot, Earl of Rochester, or the enthusiastic Christian Neoplatonist Thomas Traherne. What we do find are **selective perceptions and inventive recombinations of Hellenisms**, which amount to sometimes astonishing interventions in ancient reference texts and their systematic structures. Ancient texts, ideas and modes of thinking are thus profoundly altered through succeeding stages of interpretation, translation, and edition. Antiquity is re-functionalised in keeping with new and fairly specific historical and cultural requirements. That the latter span a wide spectrum, sometimes covering polar opposites, becomes obvious even if we

consider only the field of affective regimes—these extend from the restrictive and ascetic disciplines to be derived from Stoic, Sceptic, and Epicurean techniques and arguments aimed at achieving tranquillity of the soul (*apathia* and *ataraxia* respectively) to the enthusiastic recommendations articulated by Neoplatonic models in order to achieve spiritual union with the highest.

In these processes of productive transformation, the principle of plenitude—not to be confused with arbitrariness or indifference—appears to rule supreme. This may be indicated by reference to one of the earliest examples, **Thomas More's** *Utopia* (1516). Originally published in Latin, the text was translated into English in 1551. Preceded by a 'Dialogue of Counsel,' it depicts the social and religious customs of an imaginary island called Utopia. More's highly influential *jeu d'esprit* has given the genre of utopia its name. In addition to numerous other facets of knowledge and ideology, More's text abounds with Stoical wisdom, proverbs and precepts drawing in many cases on the copious collection of *Adagia* compiled by his friend Erasmus. It seems to propagate Epicurean naturalism in the areas of marital ethics and certain social practices, combining the description of hedonistic elements in Utopian society with ascetic ones. Yet in matters of theology and religion as well as in some aspects of politics, the Utopians appear to advocate monistic, Platonising models, while their church government approximates that of an enlightened Catholicism. None of these, however, can safely be ascribed to Thomas More himself. This is due to the structural Scepticism of a highly ironical narrative constituted by the multiple embedding and inconclusive dialogues of pseudo-authorial voices (the narrator, the traveller Hythloday, the 'More'-figure in the text).

It is precisely this kind of **irreducible pluralism** with its possibilities of juridical and philosophical argument as well as serious play which is a major source of the aesthetic delight provided by More's text. While similar descriptions could be given of the Hellenistic elements and strategies employed and interlaced in works written around the middle of the period and especially during the enormously productive decades towards the end of the sixteenth century, such

Frontispiece of More's *Utopia* (1516), showing a woodcut of the island

as the great epics of Sidney's *Arcadia* or Spenser's *Faerie Queene*, it should be pointed out that this holds even for late seventeenth-century texts which at first glance follow a wholly different poetic ratio. Thus, **Andrew Marvell's poetry**, composed by an author with known Protestant and Republican affiliations, engineers, through the way his verses marshal mutually exclusive ways of thinking, ironical effects which amount to an almost total elusiveness of the stance they might be seen to advocate. Resonating with Classical scholarship in unexpected places, Marvell's "Poetry of Criticism" (to echo Rosalie Colie), for instance in "The Garden," "On a Drop of Dew," but also in his long and perplexing topographical masterpiece "Upon Appleton House," evokes and scrutinises both central and recondite ideas of ancient Neoplatonism, experimentally and provocatively combining them with Naturalisms of a sometimes extreme, materialistic kind. Ultimately, his verse provides matrices of poetic reception and effect, in turn spanning the poles that the period as a whole tries to encompass—immanence and transcendence, enthusiasm and melancholic despair, harmony and disintegration, plurality and oneness.

### 2.2.3 | New Science and New Philosophy

It is in the transformative context described above that changes of mind-set are to be seen which took their beginnings in the sixteenth century but became more pronounced and gained institutional stability in the seventeenth. Although some of the developments responsible for these changes appear to be primarily of a contextual kind, these, too, affect and are in turn affected by, the literature of the period. The phenomena we need to consider here are related to the emergence of new methods, concepts, theories, and institutions in what were to become the natural sciences; a process often referred to as **Scientific Revolution**. Recent intellectual historians schooled by Quentin Skinner have explored this complex in a way immediately relevant for literary studies (cf. e.g. Mulsow and Mahler). For if literature is also a way of thinking, it will not remain unaffected by

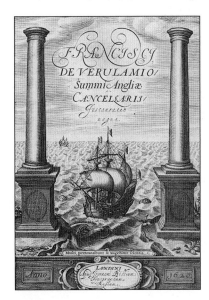

Title Page of Bacon's *Instauratio Magna* (1650)

fundamental changes in other ways of thinking about the world and, concomitantly, the self. The history of Science, its origins as well as the processes leading to its disciplinary emancipation, consolidation, and institutional establishment in the Royal Society, including the important role played in this by the writings of **Francis Bacon**, are at present still hotly debated. The answers to some of the questions raised in the course of this discussion are not without relevance to the study of the literature of the period. Besides, they also involve transformations of antiquity. Hence, it matters whether the origins of scientific culture are assumed to be somehow autochthonous and its beginnings abrupt and dateable or whether, as has recently been suggested (among others by Dieter Groh and Stephen Gaukroger), they are to be sought in the Middle Ages, possibly as early as the 'Renaissance' of the twelfth century, and here not only in natural philosophy, but also in theology (cf. entry I.2.1). Therefore, we can no longer understand New Science exclusively (and perhaps not even predominantly) as a product of greater processes of secularisation, for example as a result of the internal dynamics of physical research and mechanical experimentation. On the contrary, it will be seen to emerge at least equally from the attempt to harmonise scientific observations systematically with religious faith, to discern traces of God's creative action in a universe which was still considered as divine economy and perceived to be structured by relations of analogy and correspondence, sympathy and antipathy in accordance with ancient models.

What seems to be fairly undisputed, notwithstanding the outcome of this debate, is the crucial role, culminating in the English seventeenth century, of **experimentalism** and the **Royal Society** which was founded in 1660 to promote scientific, experimental research. Still, here too, interactions with developments on the continent (some of these mediated through English Royalist exiles) have been noted which relativise notions of insularity: both Cartesian rationalism and diverse attempts, most vigorously pursued by Gassendi and his followers, to reconcile Epicurean atomism with Christian theology form parts of the horizon of both English and continental thinkers interested in the New Science. One of the most familiar examples (with earlier precursors such as the aristocratic Northumberland Circle) is the **Cavendish Circle** around the exiled Duke and Duchess of Newcastle, which included, if only temporarily, René Descartes and Thomas Hobbes, and more continuously, Walter Charleton. Charleton's attempt to reconcile the various possible approaches to knowledge of the natural world resulted in his *Physiologia Epicuro-Gassendo-Charltoniana* (1654)—a treatise typically mirroring in its monstrous title both the heterogeneity of its subject matter and the ambition to weld it into a new whole. But even within the more traditional and institutionally secure scholarly networks, such as the Cambridge Platonists, we find the strong impulse to integrate different types of knowledge and styles of thinking; most impressively perhaps in the person and writings of Henry More, correspondent of Descartes and inventor of the term 'Cartesianism,' himself a scientific dilettante of sorts, interested in Cabbala and Hermeticism and believer in witchcraft, but simultaneously an eminent Christian theologian, aspiring poet, and Platonist. Among his numerous works, the *Democritus Platonissans* (1646) possibly bears most eloquent witness to the length to which he and his contemporaries were prepared to go in order to bring together what threatened to fall apart.

For some, of course, this had already happened. Their **sense of disorientation and disintegration** was aptly summarised by John Donne's much-quoted and easily generalised lament in *The First Anniversarie* that "new Philosophy cals all in doubt" (line 205) and "'Tis all in pieces, all cohearence gone" (213). What is shared, however, by the protagonists in this scenario of scientifically acerbated simultaneity of the non-simultaneous is not only remarkably consistent in its central aspects, but also, again, prominently displays literary features. For what the anti-Aristotelism, or rather: anti-scholasticism, typical of the proponents of the New Science amounted to was above all a strong resentment of a certain style of thinking, speaking, and writing—in other words, the kind of rhetoric epitomized by the 'schoolmen' and characterised by abstraction, speculation, endless ramifications of commentary, and the dogmatism of competing 'schools.' Spokesmen of the Royal Society such as Robert Hooke and Thomas Sprat sought to counter scholastic culture by propagating a new type of scientific communication that had the additional advantage of conforming with the ideals of Protestant preaching: **plain style.**

## The Literary Productivity of the Scientific Revolution

Scientific ferment and philosophical disorder thus turn into a source of **epistemological as well as literary productivity**. The seventeenth century develops into a laboratory situation of an unprecedented kind, with a sense of experimentalism and the excitement of exploring the reaches of the new knowledge and methodology side by side with intensified emphasis on the need for stability, rock-bottom truth, and the (re-)discovery of first and unshakeable principles. Thanks to Humanist philology, the textual materials were available and ready to be searched and re-employed with an 'experiential' curiosity which, in the essayistic boldness of some of its results, paralleled the experiments performed and recorded by virtuosos and natural scientists. Thus, for all its flaunting of anti-scholasticism, the rise of the experimental sciences is intimately connected with changes in the system of literary 'kinds,' or genres and modes of writing (Colie, *Resources of Kind*). Not only does the period appear obsessed with ways of finding and ascertaining truth, inspired by religious and confessional fervour on the one hand and scientific zeal on the other, but also with the desire to articulate and present it adequately. It is the media and modes in which knowledge is communicated and insight made possible which matter. But while the rhetorical norm of *delectare et docere*, requiring literary texts both to delight and teach, still held sway in poetics, it did make a difference whether the truth to be taught was felt to be spiritual, hidden and divine, perhaps ultimately inaccessible, or physical and material, sensually apprehensible and, because immanent, ultimately accessible by mechanical means. Accordingly, we find considerable inventiveness with respect to poetic forms, especially in the **poets** later called '**Metaphysical**' (Donne, Herbert, Marvell, and, in a different manner, Crashaw and Vaughan), but also—resuming

*Plurality of genres*

| Definition |
| --- |

The name → 'metaphysical poets' was belatedly given to a group of English poets who wrote religious poems in the seventeenth century. The poems have become famous for their 'conceits,' that is, for their innovative use of witty metaphors, as well as for their frequent blending of the erotic and the religious. Important poets are John **Donne**, George **Herbert**, Richard **Crashaw**, Andrew **Marvell** and Henry **Vaughan**.

some of the innovatory momentum of Elizabethan non-dramatic writing—in prose.

Here, one of the most fertile and imaginative inventors is certainly **Margaret Cavendish,** the Duchess of Newcastle. Her copious writings cover the whole range from the poetic to the expository, including the dramatic. Although she has, over the last decade, grown into one of the icons of historical feminism, her admittedly eccentric but certainly symptomatic contribution to the contemporary scientific and philosophical debates (albeit nowhere near as learned or systematic as *The Principles of the Most Modern and Ancient Philosophy* by Anne Conway) as well as to the genres of utopia and science fiction in her *Blazing World* (1666) and other texts still deserves closer attention. Another writer, already canonical in some respects, who is coming to be recognised as the author of texts that can be considered as paradigmatic for the period by virtue of their very contradictoriness and 'experimental' openness that never cease to surprise is Sir **Thomas Browne.** He has long been admired, particularly in his *Religio Medici*, his *Hydriotaphia, or Urne-Buriall*, and his *Garden of Cyrus*, as one of the early masters of English prose (and severely criticised for his seeming illogicality). Now he is beginning to be appreciated also for the analytical as well as integrative qualities that render his texts so typical of his century's untiring, fascinated, and radical search for truth—a truth capable of accommodating the metaphysical with the natural without compromising either. Undaunted by the dangers of religious heterodoxy, yet mindful of the respect merited by all kinds of belief, aware of uncertainties and incoherence, yet unwilling to content himself with them, Browne seeks to present this truth in literary strategies which throw into relief his own poetic subjectivity and a curiosity which extends to the microscopic structures of immanence as well as to a transcendence not to be apprehended by the telescope.

## 2.2.4 | Religious Literature: A Long Reformation

*Politics of religion and privacy of confession*

No outline of Renaissance and early modern literary mentalities can be complete without taking into account their religious dimension. Despite Bacon's attempts to divide science and theology, in this period neither scholarly nor scientific world views are easily separable from matters of belief.

Conversely, religion was anything but a private or institutionally contained matter: attended by troubling and highly contested questions with respect to the shape Christianity was to take in England under the auspices of the Reformation, it is intimately connected with public affairs of all kinds. However, the **inseparability of religion and politics** on the one hand corresponds, on the other, to a remarkable individual secretiveness about personal beliefs, indeed, their widespread dissimulation. Heterodoxy could have terrifying consequences in an age that witnessed several radical switches between old and new faiths, between Roman Catholicism and various brands of Protestantism, following the volte-faces in church politics instigated by the respective monarchs from Henry VIII through Edward VI, 'Bloody' Mary Tudor, and Elizabeth in the sixteenth century, from Stuart rule to Puritan Interregnum and back again in the seventeenth. Hence, early modern subjects, like their rulers, tended to keep their own counsel with respect to their innermost convictions (cf. King). The consequences, for the literature of the period, go far beyond biographical questions concerning the tacit beliefs of individual authors—despite the present debate as to whether Shakespeare was a crypto-Catholic and to which extent this affects his writings and their reception (Wilson).

The difficulties of charting the course of the **Protestant Reformation** in England, in its inextricable mixture of political and theological factors, its spectrum of theological positions between Calvinist radicalism and Anglo-Catholic moderation, and its wide range of hotly contested issues from matters of liturgy, vestments, ritual and music to questions of ecclesiastic law or the constitution of individual congregations are further compounded by the asynchronies of social and regional developments, with parts of the English aristocracy in the North retaining their older religious allegiances, many Scots developing a strong attachment to Geneva, and Ireland (with the exception of 'colonial' settlements in the northern counties) adhering to Rome. While generalisations appear hardly possible, it seems worthwhile to recall that the Reformation in the British Isles did not originate as a theological, let alone univocal, movement. Accordingly, despite the ordainment of its initial steps 'from above' in consequence of Henry VIII's marriage politics, it neither took a linear course, following a teleology that inexorably led to the triumph of Protestantism, nor did it happen abruptly, with people's minds switching from the old to a new religion in one historical instant. Instead, we are faced with **overlapping and intermittent processes**, with "the vagaries of dynastic politics and the survival of Catholic resistance to changes in religion" (King 106) over roughly two centuries.

In this field of highly charged symbolic moves, often revolving around the Lutheran twin demands focussed on the Word—*sola scriptura*—and the individual believer's soul—*sola fides*—**religious writing**, too, acquires important, but multiple and shifting, not to say duplicitous, functions. Formal, ideological, public and personal agendas do not always coincide. Hence, as Heather Dubrow has pointed out with respect to the Renaissance lyric, "we need to approach it from many critical perspectives, alert to both technical virtuosity and ideological imperatives and thus to the complex interplay between formal potentialities and cultural history" (197). With a view to this sharpened tension between the textual and the contextual in a situation of intense interplay between literary and extra-literary traditions and agents, it is indeed due to its formal and thematic potentialities that the religious literature of the period systematically runs a twofold risk that nonetheless ultimately accounts for its productivity. As a Renaissance literary 'kind,' it is expected to be, above all, oriented towards God and the divine. Both the presentation of authorial interiority and the ostentation of poetic art for their own sakes fall under generic restraints the more severe as they are theologically motivated. Neither the poet's self nor the aesthetic perfection of the piece ought to attract more interest than absolutely necessary for the achievement of its rhetorical purpose. If the end of poetry is to teach and move, the end of religious poetry is to lead the soul towards God. Even more than in other genres, textual delight here is not to be caused (or experienced) without ulterior purpose, but serves as a vehicle for the recognition and praise of the Highest. Within this normative frame, to place the means before the end would imply theological as well as poetic failure, a falling short of the aim and a settling for the merely human, i.e., at the utmost, the second best.

## Between Subjectivity and Didacticism

While this raises systematic obstacles, it nonetheless does not exclude religious literature from the two signature achievements of the period—**the development and consolidation of poetic subjectivity** as well as the emancipation of aesthetic functions from ideological precepts and didactic or edifying purposes. On the contrary: against the changing background of new emphases on the text concerning its accessibility, readability, the modes of its interpretation as well as the literate believer's states of mind, this prescriptive poetics may be observed to enable what it seemed out to prevent—in the works of Protestant as well as Catholic writers. Under scrutiny, many pieces of religious writing will reveal strategies which effectively circumvent generic restrictions. In fact, some of them, especially (though not exclusively) examples of seventeenth-century Metaphysical Poetry, might even be seen as particularly congenial media for the unfolding of poetic inwardness together with unprecedented aesthetic brilliance. In these cases, the palpable poetic sign, through functioning as a perfect means of sacred communication, does indeed paradoxically achieve seemingly irreconcilable ends—literary perfection together with theological insight, textual beauty coinciding with heavenly. While Spenser's *Faerie Queene* or Bunyan's *Pilgrim's Progress* employ and transform the resources of allegory in different ways and with the didactic still often overruling the aesthetic, Spenser's *Fowre Hymnes* may be considered a case in point, aided by an explicitly Neoplatonic poetics; equally, Southwell's "The Burning Babe" and many of George Herbert's poems; certainly also Andrew Marvell's extraordinary "On a Drop of Dew," or Traherne's rapturous *Centuries*. But then, as these successful stagings of transcendence take place as it were under the cover of a presumptively innocuous literary kind, they may themselves—even in confessional or laudatory modes (as, for example, in Marvell's ambivalent celebrations of Cromwell)—be taken as evidence of the dissimulation so characteristic of the period as a whole. Thus, and perhaps surprisingly, it is in the systematic ambiguities attending the modes of religious literature and literary culture that many of the innovative aspects of early modern writing—including issues of personal authorship, poetic subjectivity, inwardness and sensibility, and aesthetic reflexivity—prepare themselves, leading, in some of their eminent protagonists, from Wyatt and Surrey, through Spenser to Donne, Herbert, Milton, and Marvell, to productive perplexities and resonant duplicities that point far beyond the cultural conflicts from which they emerge.

Having said this, it must immediately be conceded that a huge amount of texts remain well

How can poetic
and spiritual perfection
be reconciled?

within the pale of **traditional religious rhetoric** and **conventional didactic**—especially those composed for everyday use and with polemic purposes. Foremost among these is a proliferation of controversialist, polemical, and satiric writings engaging in the conflicts of the day—with texts ranging from contributions to the vestments and Admonition controversies to Milton's treatise *On Church Government* or Marvell's *Rehearsal Transpros'd* and other polemics of the second half the seventeenth century; from the Marprelate tracts through resistant propagandist writing by Marian continental exiles on the one hand, on the other, Catholic underground writing and recusant literature from the 1570s onwards, in the wake of the Jesuit mission to England; from anti-papist broadsheets to large and immensely popular works like John Foxe's *Acts and Monuments of the English Martyrs* (1563), or the weighty foundational text of Anglican ecclesiology, Richard Hooker's *Of the Laws of Ecclesiastical Polity* (1559). Thus, we find a great diversity of writings, especially of prose texts whose aspirations are not in the first place literary—from sermons to fables, anecdotes, or adventure narratives, but also of popular verse genres, including ballads, songs, and epigrams. An impressive variety of these is contained in Foxe's *Book of Martyrs* alone. Foxe effectively models his Protestant martyrology on Roman Catholic hagiography and legend, adding, as 'historical' evidence, numerous illustrations in the shape of lurid woodcuts that illustrate how the Protestant 'saints' suffered in bearing witness to their faith, how they showed their exemplary constancy, and how, more often than not, providence would intervene in favour of the persecuted. If these can be said to constitute new, iconic media, which lend stark profile to some

Protestant mentalities, contemporary spirituality was also shaped by symbolic practices of a different provenance: As Louis Martz observed in his landmark study of 1954, there was a considerable influx, increasing during the seventeenth century, of devotional literature from the continent, appreciated not only by Catholic believers. Thus, patterns of classical Ignatian meditation and affective discipline can be seen to structure the English religious imagination across the denominational divide, for instance in the poetry and sermons of John Donne.

## Translations and Millenarian Writing

Another highly influential area of religious writing is that of translation (cf. Cummings for theological controversies surrounding, for example, a term like 'justification'). Stimulated by humanist educational reform stressing the return to the Greek (and Hebrew) source texts, and furthered by attempts to raise the English vernacular to a standard comparable in dignity to Latin and in versatility with that of continental dialects such as the Italian of Petrarch, the striving after a codification of ritual in the national language found expression in Cranmer's *Book of Homilies* (1547) and the *Book of Common Prayer* (1549). Possibly even more important, Protestant respect for, and philological attention to, the Word of God gives rise to a succession of **Bible translations** in the period, beginning with Tyndale's highly influential New Testament (Worms 1526), followed in 1535 by the first complete English Bible, the Coverdale Bible, and the Great Bible (1539) under Henry VIII. Protestant exiles under Mary produced the Geneva Bible (1560), with annotations, concordance, illustrations, and further aids to a close evangelical understanding, also with a clear Calvinistic bias; to be followed by the less controversial Bishops' Bible (1568) and the Rheims-Douai Bible (1582; 1609–1610), produced by Catholic exiles and close to the Vulgate; finally by the King James Bible or Authorised Version in 1611. While these translations are literary achievements in their own right, the influence Biblical diction (especially in the Tyndale and King James versions) exerted—and to the present day exerts—on everyday language as well as the literature of the period can hardly be overestimated.

If we find the—occasional or frequent—Biblical turn of phrase in Spenser and Shakespeare, other Renaissance authors also tried their hand at a more specialized Biblical genre: that of **psalm**

**translation**. Again, this literary kind can be seen to fulfil a number of functions, not all of them purely religious. Thus, in the explosive atmosphere of the 1530s at the court of Henry VIII, the renderings of the Penitential Psalms by Henry Howard, the Earl of Surrey, and Sir Thomas Wyatt were much more than a pious exercise. Mediated through the psalmist's voice, David the kingly poet and singer par excellence, these texts served the purposes of authorial self-expression, bitter lamentation and protest, as well as barely veiled criticism of the translator's treatment at the monarch's hands. If there arose the need for individual courtly dissimulation under Henry, on a different level and far from courtly concerns, we find open communal proclamation of faith under his son Edward VI, albeit in the same medium: the so-called Sternhold-Hopkins psalter, *The Whole Book of Psalms* in a versified translation by Thomas Sternhold and John Hopkins, gained immense popularity among Protestants and ran to numerous editions in both centuries. While 'English'd' psalms thus lent voice not only to the suffering individual but also assisted the building of nonconformist Protestant congregations, in Mary and Philip Sidney's important metrical translation of the complete psalter they became, under Elizabeth I, a medium for poetic experiment on an unprecedented scale. And, once again, they help to dissemble individual faith while displaying literary virtuosity, for, as in the *Arcadia*, the Sidney siblings' collaboration yields no indication or evidence of their 'true' confessional allegiances.

While concern with Last Things is a hallmark of religious writing, the sixteenth and seventeenth centuries also saw a marked increase in **apocalyptic and millenarian writing**. Some of it displays interesting affiliations with the growing scientific fervour of the day, Bacon's *Valerius Terminus* affording instructive insights into the period's eschatological vein. Yet growing concern with the (possibly imminent) end of the world found its counterpart not least in **Milton**'s monumental effort to interpret its beginnings in *Paradise Lost*. The grandiose display of learning in Milton's epic and the self-consciously artistic accomplishment to be found also in his minor poetry once again describe the figure that characterises much of early modern religious literature: that of a subjectivity ostensibly effacing itself, but at the same time asserting its validity and dynamic versatility through its poetic skill. We have become used to discerning it in **John Donne's** poetry, whose speakers pretend so eloquently to minimise themselves, often histrionically, in their struggles for *metanoia* or conversion (sometimes to annihilation, as for instance in the "Nocturnal upon St. Lucy's Day, Being the Shortest Day," but also in many of the Holy Sonnets). Repeatedly, even abjectly, they protest utter heteronomy in poems like "Good Friday, 1613. Riding Westward," but at the same time they transparently manage to aggrandise themselves in their poetic artistry. While this sense of an assertive ego, present and vigorous even in devotion and self-humiliation, appears less pronounced in the verse of **George Herbert**, here too, if less obtrusively, we can observe the poetic subject finding itself under scrutiny. Herbert's speakers, however, recognise themselves in the eyes of an Other, and, while speaking not only of their own afflictions but of divine redemptive action, repeatedly and sometimes surprisingly succeed in spreading "Easter Wings."

If this type of paradoxical 'heterology' is one of the signatures of early modern religious writing, it finally becomes possible to also perceive a major way in which it points towards later developments—for instance to the literature and culture of sensibility of the succeeding centuries (cf. entry I.2.3). From this perspective, too, we might expect some of the familiar emphases in the Early Modern canon to shift towards lesser known writers. Thus, it is perhaps time to rediscover the seraphic vision of **Thomas Traherne** with its all-encompassing theme of felicity and enjoyment of the visible world. While the second half of the seventeenth century, especially in dissenting and Puritan milieus, sees a flourishing of the literary modes of soul-searching, in diaries, letters, and confessional outpourings, which for many critics have long been among the discursive forerunners of the eighteenth-century novel, the theologically much more orthodox Traherne, in his exuberant, second-person prose meditations as well as his reflexive poetry, produces strikingly unorthodox writings. Here is a poetic voice only seemingly eccentric. Considered in the context of a newly emerging cult of 'seraphic' friendships in unlikely (courtly as well as scholarly) circles, his insistence on universal relatedness and the immanence of paradise affords an alternative view of English religious literature. Perhaps Traherne's undogmatic enthusiasm for the delights of the visible as amiable lineaments of the transcendent marks a kind of ending to the age of Reformation.

Literature as serious play
leading to happiness

## 2.2.5 | The Literary Culture of the Court and Popular Literature

### Print, Patronage, and Professionalisation

In early modern England, the royal court was the centre not only of power, but also of the arts and learning. Many of the most famous early modern writers were courtiers, for instance Sir Thomas Wyatt, Henry Howard, Earl of Surrey, Sir Philip Sidney and Sir Walter Raleigh. Some writers of lower social status, such as John Lyly, Samuel Daniel and Michael Drayton, sought careers as civil servants and advertised their skills and their reverence to the crown or to aristocratic patrons via their literary works. Many literary texts originated from courtly entertainments or from the stylised rituals of courtship, and they were initially only exchanged among the courtly coterie in manuscript form. Print established itself only gradually; especially at the court, literature kept circulating in **manuscript form** throughout the sixteenth and seventeenth centuries. Aristocrats who wrote poetry, plays or narratives did not openly consider their works as a serious occupation, but as a pastime that displayed their wit, rhetorical sophistication and education. In fact, aristocrats avoided the publication of their works, since writing for money and for the public was considered vulgar.

This 'stigma of print' applied particularly to **female authors**, since the gender ideals of the day opposed female speaking (or writing) in public. As a consequence, the few existing women authors mainly translated devotional literature. However, during the seventeenth century, prolific female authors evolved: the poetry by Elizabeth Tyrwhitt, Anne Dowriche, Isabelle Whitney, Mary Sidney, and Aemilia Lanyer has been explored by early modern scholars in recent years; the *Tragedy of Mariam* (1613), the first play by an English female author, Elizabeth Cary, was published (albeit not performed) before women acted on English stages, and important female authors of long prose narratives emerged, including Margaret Cavendish, Mary Wroth, and Aphra Behn.

**From aristocratic to professional authorship**

The attitude towards print of aristocrats and those aspiring to a career at court began to change in the seventeenth century, when, for example, Ben Jonson collected his own works in an impressive folio edition (1616). Working as a professional author was difficult in the early modern period, and those who attempted such a career, like Robert Greene and Thomas Nashe, often suffered poverty. Neither copyrights nor royalties were paid, and the writers only received a small fee when they delivered their books to the printers. Therefore, authors sought patronage from wealthy aristocrats, whose support sometimes involved inclusion in intellectual and artistic circles. For instance, Lucy Russell, a close confidante of Queen Anne, supported John Donne, Ben Jonson, Michael Drayton, and Samuel Daniel. When Charles I was executed in 1642, the **patronage system** that centred on the court life collapsed, too, and many leading authors lost their positions, were imprisoned or fled the country. As a result of the disintegration of aristocratic circles in which manuscripts were exchanged, more authors began to publish their work from the 1640s onwards.

### Early Modern Drama

Dramatists, especially when they were shareholders of theatres as William Shakespeare was, had better chances to make a living from writing, since the theatre was a commercialised form of entertainment in late sixteenth-century and seventeenth-century England, with the exception of the Civil War and the Interregnum years (1642–1660), when public theatres were shut down by official decree. Public theatres had been built since the 1560s (Shakespeare's famous **Globe Theatre** opened in 1599), and each accommodated roughly two thousand spectators. Theatre companies also sought patronage by aristocrats, but for legal rather than financial reasons, since unsponsored groups were prone to punishments as vagrants. For instance, Shakespeare's troupe was first called 'The Lord Chamberlain's Men,' and after 1603, when James I took over their patronage, 'The King's Men.'

**Shakespeare's plays** are the most famous literary works of the early modern period. Nonetheless, we should keep in mind that the Elizabethan and the Jacobean period had a rich theatre culture which staged plays by a variety of authors including Christopher Marlowe and Ben Jonson. The roughly forty plays by Shakespeare cover the whole dramatic range from tragedies (*Hamlet*, *King Lear*, *Macbeth*) and comedies (*A Midsummer Night's Dream*, *Twelfth Night*), to the so-called 'romances' which blend comic and tragic elements with a sense of the marvellous (*The Winter's Tale*, *The Tempest*), and 'history plays' (*Richard II*, *King John*). Drawing on a wide array of sources, from historiographies and travel reports to prose narratives and the dramatic tradition, the plays addressed particularly early modern concerns; for example, the legitimisation of royal sovereignty, the rise of commerce, and the role of colonisation. At the same time, they raise such fundamental topics (and are written in such rich and engaging style and constructed with such an artful dramaturgy) that they have remained attractive for theatre audiences today and are an integral part of the curricula at schools and universities worldwide. For example, the humorous exploration of **gender roles** in Shakespeare's comedies is still engaging today. Shakespeare frequently has his characters disguise themselves across the boundaries of gender and thus tests out to which degree gender is essential and to which degree it is a result of performance (see entry II.6 for a theoretical exploration of this issue). In *As You Like It*, this question is heightened, because the protagonist undergoes a multiple gender transformation: Rosalind dresses up as Ganymede and then play-acts Rosalind for Orlando, who fell in love with the young gentlewoman but does not recognise her in her male attire. Because female roles were embodied by boy actors on the Renaissance stage, early modern audiences saw a fourfold gender performance that also complicated the erotic attraction between the figures. Besides gender and sexuality, also Shakespeare's exploration of **ethnicity** remains a topical issue today. His tragedy *Othello* depicts the mechanisms of racism as well as the exoticist fascination of the foreign in such a complex manner that theatre productions and films keep performing and adapting Shakespeare's text.

Shakespeare's plays partake in the important early modern developments outlined in this chapter: They transform the **heritage of antiquity**, for example by staging political events of the Roman Empire as in *Antony and Cleopatra* and *Julius Caesar*, by adapting classical sources such as Ovid's *Metamorphoses* (e.g. in *Titus Andronicus* and *A Midsummer Night's Dream*) and by engaging with philosophic discourses of antiquity as discussed above. The plays also register the advent of new science, for example in their astrological metaphors. Recently, scholars have investigated the impact of the Reformation on Elizabethan drama and have explored how abandoned Catholic rituals were creatively modified on Shakespeare's stage. One example of such a concern with abandoned Catholic rites is discussed in the exemplary analysis of *Hamlet* in entry IV.3. When the ghost of Hamlet's father returns and demands that his son

Shakespeare's Globe Theatre has been reconstructed on London's Southbank.

take revenge for his murder, the play invokes the notion of purgatory, which was denounced by the Reformed state religion. Further examples of the relevance of **religion** for Shakespeare's plays are encounters with the other, for example with Jewishness in *The Merchant of Venice*. *The Merchant* is also interesting with regard to genre. The fact that it is called a "comical history" in its title shows us that Shakespeare's contemporaries would have perceived the play as a comedy. However, one of its central concerns, anti-Semitism, and the fact that the disadvantaged Jewish character, Shylock, in the end falls victim to a biased pseudo-legal trial makes the play hardly a comedy for audiences today. *The Merchant* is therefore a good example for how notions of genre change over the centuries, and that they change not only because of literary renewal, but also because of political and cultural developments.

The importance of Shakespeare's history plays for the project of **nation-building** has long been acknowledged in early modern studies; looking back at England's past, they investigate the legitimisation of the Tudor rule (see interpretation on p. 32).

When theatres were reopened in the **Restoration period** after 1660, comedies of manners became the most widespread form of entertainment. These witty comedies by authors like George Etherege, William Wycherley, Aphra Behn and William Congreve mock the follies and power struggles of the English upper society and depict

### William Shakespeare, *Richard III*

*Richard III* revisits the beginning of the Tudor dynasty by chronicling events of the 1480s, when the Wars of the Roses came to an end. In order to legitimise the Tudor rule as the onset of a more civilised and peaceful era, Richard III, who was defeated by the first Tudor king, Henry VII, is depicted as a cruel tyrant who is deformed physically as much as morally. This characterisation follows the biased historiographies written during the reign of Elizabeth I, but at the same time, Shakespeare gives the villain alluring wit and he lets him engage intimately with audiences from his soliloquy at the beginning of the play.

Therefore, while *Richard III* on the one hand conforms to the Tudor myth (it ends with a speech by Henry VII who prays that his offspring will "Enrich the time to come with smooth-faced peace / With smiling plenty, and fair prosperous days"), on the other hand it makes a straightforward condemnation of Richard difficult for the audience. Apart from *Richard III*'s historical significance, its exploration of totalitarianism and of the fascination of evil as much as the witty rhetorics and spectacular political role-play of Richard have made the play attractive for audiences (and actors) until today.

the immoral erotic schemes of libertines. Simultaneously, heroic plays, chiefly by John Dryden, staged the conflict between honour and love on a more serious note. The Restoration stage saw an important innovation in performance practice, as female actors entered the stage.

The location of the public theatres outside of the city of London, on the South bank of the Thames, signals the **low cultural status of the theatre** in the early modern period: the buildings were neighboured by taverns, brothels and arenas for bear-baiting and cock fights. Accordingly, the performances were frequently criticised by religious hardliners for their amoral impact on audiences. Later, indoor theatres were erected within the limits of the city, which, by contrast to the open-air buildings on the South bank, were artificially lit and were visited by more wealthy spectators. For example, John Webster's *The Duchess of Malfi* (1612–1613) was written for the Blackfriars, an indoor theatre, and its staging accordingly requires a number of special lighting effects. The fact that *The Duchess* was later also performed at the Globe is representative of the broad social appeal of Elizabethan and Jacobean plays: They addressed both the cultural elite, well-educated aristocrats who would, for example, appreciate rhetorical finesse or intertextual allusions to classical sources (as would many of the non-aristocratic spectators who profited from the Humanist school education), and the less privileged inhabitants of London, who presumably paid for a thrilling plot and engaging characters. The theatre was hence a **'popular' form** in the sense established by Peter Burke, since it stands for a common culture shared by early moderns across the ranks, ages and genders. This phenomenon of an intermingling of the elite and the popular also holds true for other literary kinds; for example, jest-books, which are usually considered a socially and aesthetically low text sort, were also read by Edmund Spenser, and they were almost exclusively devised by aristocrats.

Besides the popular South bank stages and the more restricted indoor theatres, an elite form of theatrical entertainment was staged at the court: **the masque**. Masques were performances for special occasions, such as weddings or visits by important foreign guests, which mostly depicted mythological subjects. Courtiers, sometimes even the queen herself, took part as actors in these masques, and at the end, other courtiers joined the masquers in a dance. By contrast to the reduced scenery of the popular theatre, masques, in particular in Stuart times, afforded lavish costumes and expensive scenery; but they shared with the South bank performances an inclusion of music and dance (Ravelhofer). Ben Jonson, the most famous author of courtly masques, collaborated with the stage designer Inigo Jones on many masques. Jonson is said to have established the proscenium stage by 1620. Together with the elaborate scenery, the proscenium stage allowed for a more realistic illusion than the word scenery ('Wortkulisse') of the popular open-air stage surrounded on three sides by the audiences. Shakespeare's *The Tempest* includes a wedding masque to celebrate the betrothal of Miranda and Ferdinand, and Prospero here comments on the illusionary power of the masque (and, at the same time, the 'magic' of theatre in general), "the baseless fabric of this vision," "such stuff as dreams are made on" (Act 4).

### Thomas Nashe, *The Unfortunate Traveller*

Thomas Nashe's narrative *The Unfortunate Traveller* (1594) is indicative of a turn to **'popular' forms of literature**, such as the jest-book and the cony-catching pamphlet (stories of tricksters), which are deliberately opposed to 'elite' kinds in order to appeal to readers of middle ranks rather than aristocratic patrons.

Nashe's protagonist is not a young prince or princess, as typical of the chivalric and erotic romances written by Philip Sidney, Robert Greene, and Thomas Lodge and adapted in Shakespeare's plays, but a servant called Wilton—whom Nashe specifies as a 'page,' thus setting up a metafictional meaning of his tale. The protagonist accompanies Surrey, the pre-eminent Henrician courtly poet, during his travels on the European continent, and ultimately comes to compete with his aristocratic superior in a scenario that blends sexual and literary rivalry. Here, the narrating protagonist mocks the outworn, sterile Neoplatonic Petrarchan poetry of his master, which makes Surrey "leap into verse" and "with [...] rhymes assault" his beloved. Rather than being interested in winning her, however, Surrey appears to be "more in love with his own curious forming fancy than her face; and truth it is, many become passionate lovers only to win praise to their wits." The narrator Wilton himself is more pragmatic than "to woo women with riddles." Instead, he seduces the woman whom both men adore: "My master beat the bush and kept a coil and a prattling, but I

caught the bird; simplicity and plainness shall carry it away in another world." Boasting with his sexual success, Wilton contrasts the aristocratic, elitist poetry of his master with his own "dunstable [i.e., plain] tale" with "some cunning plot" which "made up my market." The 'simplicity' and 'plainness' of the 'page' hence have an important metafictional meaning (even though Nashe's own style does not always follow this demand of 'plainness'; the claim is an emancipatory strategy rather than an apt characterisation of Nashe's prose): the plain, cunningly plotted narrative outdoes the master's elaborate rhymed poetry as a means of courtship, but also on the print market frequented by non-aristocratic consumers. Accordingly, the narrator of *The Unfortunate Traveller* repeatedly addresses his implied readers of middle ranks with whom he allies against the aristocratic other—a strategy which is unusual and daring in 1594, but became more common in the seventeenth century.

Thus, the narrative sets up a contrast between literary **modes** (poetry versus narrative), **styles** (elaborate rhetorics versus plainness), **distribution forms** (manuscript versus print), classes (aristocratic versus middle rank), **generations** (father-figure versus son), but also between **nations** (Italianate versus English). The latter distinction became increasingly important in early modern England, which found itself caught in a paradox of continuous cultural exchange and a new interest in nation-building.

## Plain Style and the Emergence of Popular Prose Fiction

During the Restoration, a new predominant style of elegant simplicity was established, which was often seen in opposition to the highly rhetorical style of Elizabethan and Jacobean literature, maybe most succinctly represented in the work of John Lyly, whose extravagant style in his two *Euphues* tales established a literary fashion full of antitheses and alliterations that was called 'Euphuism.' However, the 'new' simplicity, which was represented, for example, by Marvell and Dryden and which was partly influenced by the above-discussed turn to science, the Protestant appreciation of plain style, and an indebtedness to classical ideals of rhetorical clarity, had been prepared much

earlier. When we take a closer look at Elizabethan narratives, a new predilection for simple, straightforward writing can be observed, and this form of literature was often presented by its authors as an anti-courtly gesture (by contrast to Dryden's work, most prominently his heroic plays, which still referred to aristocratic ideals of honour).

## 2.2.6 | European Englishness? Cultural Exchange versus Nation-Building

In the early modern period, we can trace a **gradual emancipation of England** in linguistic and literary terms, a development which went hand in hand with a growing sense of being a distinct nation and with a beginning sense of patriotism on the national scale (by contrast to the more regional allegiances typical of the Middle Ages). The break with Roman Catholicism and the establishment of the Anglican Church isolated the country from a transnational network of religious and political allegiance and endorsed a view of England as a self-contained national unit. The concomitant Protestant turn to the English vernacular (most notably in the *Book of Common Prayer* and the English Bible as discussed above) together with the increase in literacy during the last quarter of the sixteenth century (if, however, chiefly among the male population) contributed to the creation of language and reader communities, which arguably formed the basis for envisioning a national community. As Benedict Anderson has argued in a seminal study, nations have to be understood as imagined communities, and critics have shown that many of Anderson's arguments, which he developed mainly for the eighteenth century, also apply to sixteenth-century England in crucial respects (cf. Helgerson; Shrank). Sometimes, a sense of the nation included the Irish, Welsh, and Scottish, but most often, the English defined themselves against the other peoples on the Isles. Be it the imagined communities of readers of printed narratives, or the experienced communities during vernacular church services, in early modern theatres or during aristocratic gatherings when poetry was read out aloud, literature and language played a decisive role in the shaping of Englishness. Additionally, many texts and performances also engaged on the level of content with the growing sense of nationhood, most straightforwardly those which represented English history: for example, Shakespeare's history plays and the popular genre of (sometimes fictionalised) chronicles, which Helgerson calls "the Ur-genre of national self-representation" (11), most famously Raphael Holinshed's *The Chronicles of England, Scotlande, and Irelande* (1577).

Therefore, the establishment of a **sense of Englishness** in the sixteenth century was a process of imagination, of construction, of writing and reading. Textual cultures of the word and the world were closely intertwined, as, for example, the catchy title of John Florio's *A World of Words* highlights (see Pfister, "Die englische Renaissance"). Beforehand, the English had often been thought of as being characterised by a *lack* of specific traits and by their changeability and easy infatuation with things foreign. In a number of pamphlets, an inability to resist the attraction of novelty and change, then called

*Early modern literature fostered a sense of nationhood.*

'newfangledness,' was presented as an inherently English quality. At times, it was explained by geographic specificities; living on an island, the English were thought to be so liable to the influence of the moon and the tides that they were changeable in their political, cultural, and religious allegiances. William Rankins's *Seven Satires* in the late sixteenth century still chastised the changeable English who "with the Moone participate their minde," and thus with "[t]he vainest Planet, and most transitory." Hence, Rankins mocked, they "*Proteus*-like [...] change their peeuish shape" ("Satyr Primus: Contra Lunatistam").

## Establishing an English Literary Culture

The earlier sixteenth century was characterised by a **fascination with foreign lands, languages, and literatures**. Travel, in particular the educative 'grand tour' of Europe, was regarded highly in Henrician times, and classical or contemporary foreign tales, poems and plays were read widely in England, either in the original or in translations, which sometimes offered rather free adaptations of the sources and hence were one of the starting points of English vernacular literature. However, in the course of the century, the English increasingly began to define themselves against Continental countries, and with the discovery of the New World and beginning colonialism, also against more distant people. This development went hand in hand with an **increasing rejection** of foreign phrases and literary models. In particular, the English tried to outgrow the long-standing notion of British barbarism, which had originated with the contempt of early Italian humanists for the *barbari Britanni*, the Oxford Scholastics and logicians who had frequented Italian universities since the fourteenth century. Ever since a letter of Petrarch likened the Oxford writers to the Cyclopes of Sicily, the stereotype of barbarism haunted the English. Accordingly, Thomas More's *Utopia* (1516) was written in the more prestigious language of Latin rather than in English, and it aimed at an international community of highly educated readers. This attitude changed throughout the century, as a result of which *Utopia* was translated into English in the 1550s. Thomas Hoby declared his 1561 translation of Castiglione's *Courtier* to be part of an emancipatory project: "that we alone of the worlde maye not bee styll counted barbarous in oure tunge, as in time out of minde we haue bene in our maners." The "brightness and full perfection" of the English tongue can compete with the Italian original, Hoby maintained ("The Epistle of the Translator"). Perhaps most famously, Spenser called for a validated literary English in a letter to Gabriel Harvey in 1580: "Why a God's name, may not we, as else the Greeks, have the kingdom of our own language?" (qtd. in Smith 99)—a desire reflected in E.K.'s epistolary to Spenser's *Shepheardes Calender*, too.

And yet, even if authors agreed that English had to be legitimised as a **literary language**, the question remained: Which English? The English language was only slowly homogenised by print, and authors felt that they had to actively shape the 'new' English language. In this context, vocabulary-building became a crucial aspect of nation-building (Blank; Müller). However, linguistic policies differed radically. Some adhered to a descriptive poetology and accepted the large amount of loan words in English, while others developed a normative poetology and called for a purer English literary language. In a similar manner, while some accepted the transcultural nature of English literature, others began to reject European literary models. For some authors, genuine 'Englishness' became a new, important yardstick to measure their oeuvre. Roger Ascham, a leading humanist and tutor of Elizabeth I, criticised the harmful impact of Italian literature on English readers: "those books" will "corrupt honest living" and "subvert true religion. More papists be made by your merry books of Italy than by your earnest books of Louvain" (*The Schoolmaster* bk. 1). According to Ascham, fictional literature has a greater impact on readers than theological treatises of the counter-Reformation printed in Louvain. Although Ascham criticises medieval erotic romances written in the English vernacular, too (cf. entry I.2.1), he sees Italianate books as more dangerous for "the simple head of an Englishman": "And yet ten *Morte Darthurs* do not the tenth part so much harm as one of these books made in Italy and translated in England. They open [...] such subtle, cunning, new, and diverse shifts to carry young wills to vanity and young wits to mischief" (*The Schoolmaster* bk. 1).

Despite the publication of Ascham's highly influential *Schoolmaster* in 1570, most authors kept using foreign sources for their own works. Nonetheless, a number of authors attempted to construct **a genuinely English mode of writing**. They employed various strategies to mark their works as English. In addition to the use of a plain style, as discussed above, they turned to medieval modes and sometimes used archaic language, too; most famously in Edmund Spenser's *The Faerie Queene*, which creates an artificially archaic English. In a typical move of the Renaissance humanist, Philip Sidney, in his influential *Apology for Poetry*, despises the medieval period as "that uncivil age," but he nonetheless incidentally confesses his inclination towards medieval literature: "Certainly, I must confess my own barbarousness, I never heard the old song of Percy and Douglas that I found not my heart moved." In his preface to Greene's *Menaphon*, Nashe goes a step further, as he criticises the slavish imitation of foreign sources, in particular the "English Italians" who are infatuated with "Petrarch, Tasso, Celiano, with an infinite number of others" and disregard the English tradition of "Chaucer, Lydgate, Gower."

In addition to creating a distinct English style and to recovering traditional English forms, authors mocked an infatuation with things foreign on the level of content. We saw an example of how the Italianate Englishman was parodied in Elizabethan literature in Nashe's *The Unfortunate Traveller*. In the seventeenth century, the Frenchified Englishman became a stock character of ridicule. For example, Jonson in "On English Monsieur," published in 1616, asks mockingly,

Would you believe, when you this Monsieur see,
That his whole body should speak French, not he?
That so much scarf of France, and hat, and feather,
And shoe, and tie, and garter should come hither
And land on one whose face durst never be
Toward the sea, farther than half-way tree?
That he, untravelled, should be French so much,
As Frenchmen in his company should seem Dutch? (lines 1–8)

Despite these attempts at establishing a truly English form of writing and ridiculing Italianate and Frenchified Englishmen, English authors kept translating foreign texts, working with European literary models and integrating foreign sources into their own texts. There was a shift from a ma-

### Focus on Reading Early English Books

Almost all the key texts of the early modern period have been digitised and are available on **Early English Books Online** (http://eebo.chadwyck.com), which should be accessible via your university's campus network. All the primary literature that is quoted in this entry can be found there as well.

jority of Italian translations in the sixteenth century to French texts in the seventeenth century, a change which partly had to do with Charles II's predilection for French modes when he returned from his exile in France together with his French wife Henrietta Maria. Thus, in political as much as literary respects, a fascination for foreign modes coincided with xenophobia and with an increasing national pride—and this holds true for cultures of the word as much as of the world.

## Select Bibliography

**Anderson, Benedict.** *Imagined Communities: Reflections on the Origin and Spread of Nationalism.* London: Verso, 2006.

**Blank, Paula.** *Broken English: Dialects and the Politics of Language in Renaissance Writings.* London: Routledge, 1996.

**Bloom, Harold.** *Shakespeare: The Invention of the Human.* New York: Riverhead, 1998.

**Burke Peter.** *Popular Culture in Early Modern Europe.* London: Temple Smith, 1978.

**Colie, Rosalie L.** *"My Ecchoing Song": Andrew Marvell's Poetry of Criticism.* Princeton: Princeton University Press, 1970.

**Colie, Rosalie L.** *The Resources of Kind: Genre-Theory in the Renaissance.* Ed. Barbara K. Lewalski. Berkeley: University of California Press, 1973.

**Cummings, Brian.** *The Literary Culture of the Reformation: Grammar and Grace.* Oxford: Oxford University Press, 2002.

**Dubrow, Heather.** "Lyric Forms." Kinney, *Cambridge Companion* 178–99.

**Fish, Stanley.** *Self-Consuming Artifacts: The Experience of Seventeenth-Century Literature.* Berkeley: University of California Press, 1974.

**Gaukroger, Stephen.** *The Emergence of a Scientific Culture: Science and the Shaping of Modernity: 1210–1685.* Oxford: Clarendon Press, 2006.

**Groh, Dieter.** *Göttliche Weltökonomie: Perspektiven der Wissenschaftlichen Revolution vom 15. bis zum 17. Jahrhundert.* Frankfurt/M.: Suhrkamp, 2010.

**Greenblatt, Stephen.** *Renaissance Self-Fashioning: From More to Shakespeare.* Chicago: University of Chicago Press, 1980.

**Greenblatt, Stephen.** *Shakespeare's Freedom.* Chicago: University of Chicago Press, 2010.

**Hadfield, Andrew.** *Literature, Travel, and Colonial Writing in the English Renaissance: 1545–1625.* Oxford: Oxford University Press, 1998.

**Hadfield, Andrew.** *Shakespeare, Spenser, and the Matter of Britain.* Houndmills: Palgrave Macmillan, 2004.

**Harris, Frances.** *Transformations of Love: The Friendship of John Evelyn and Margaret Godolphin.* Oxford: Oxford University Press, 2002.

**Helgerson, Richard.** *Forms of Nationhood: The Elizabethan Writing of England.* Chicago: University of Chicago Press, 1992.

**King, John N.** "Religious Writing." Kinney, *Cambridge Companion* 104–31.

**Kinney, Arthur F., ed.** *The Cambridge Companion to English Literature: 1500–1600.* Cambridge: Cambridge University Press, 2000.

**Kinney, Arthur.** *Humanist Poetics: Thought, Rhetoric, and Fiction in Sixteenth-Century England.* Amherst: University of Massachusetts Press, 1986.

**Kinney, Arthur.** Introduction. Kinney, *Cambridge Companion* 1–10.

**Lanham, Richard A.** *The Motives of Eloquence. Literary Rhetoric in the Renaissance.* New Haven: Yale University Press, 1976.

**Lobsien, Verena Olejniczak.** *Skeptische Phantasie: Eine andere Geschichte der frühneuzeitlichen Literatur.* Munich: Fink, 1999.

**Lobsien, Verena Olejniczak.** *Transparency and Dissimulation: Configurations of Neoplatonism in Early Modern English Literature.* Berlin: de Gruyter, 2010.

**Long, A. A.** *From Epicurus to Epictetus: Studies in Hellenistic and Roman Philosophy.* Oxford: Clarendon Press, 2006.

**MacCulloch, Diarmaid.** *A History of Christianity: The First Three Thousand Years.* London: Penguin, 2010.

**MacCulloch, Diarmaid.** *Reformation: Europe's House Divided: 1490–1700.* London: Allen Lane, 2003.

**Martz, Louis L.** *The Poetry of Meditation: A Study in English Religious Literature of the Seventeenth Century.* 1954. New Haven: Yale University Press, 1978.

**Müller, Wolfgang G.** "Directions for English: Thomas Wilson's Art of Rhetoric, George Puttenham's Art of English Poesy, and the Search for Vernacular Eloquence." *The Oxford Handbook of Tudor Literature: 1485–1603.* Eds. Michael Pincombe and Cathy Shrank. Oxford: Oxford University Press, 2009. 307–22.

**Mulsow, Martin, and Andreas Mahler, eds.** *Die Cambridge School der politischen Ideengeschichte.* Frankfurt/M.: Suhrkamp, 2010.

**Pfister, Manfred.** "Die englische Renaissance und der Dialog mit Europa." *Renaissance – Episteme und Agon: Für Klaus W. Hempfer anläßlich seines 60. Geburtstages.* Eds. Andreas Kablitz and Gerhard Regn. Heidelberg: Winter, 2006. 351–64.

**Pfister, Manfred.** "Die Frühe Neuzeit: Von Morus bis Milton." *Englische Literaturgeschichte.* Ed. Hans Ulrich Seeber. 5th ed. Stuttgart: Metzler, 2012. 51–159.

**Ravelhofer, Barbara.** The *Early Stuart Masque: Dance, Costume, and Music.* Oxford: Oxford University Press, 2006.

**Schmitt-Kilb, Christian.** *"Never Was the Albion Nation Without Poetrie": Poetik, Rhetorik und Nation im England der Frühen Neuzeit.* Frankfurt/M.: Klostermann, 2004.

**Shrank, Cathy.** *Writing the Nation in Reformation England: 1530–1580.* Oxford: Oxford University Press, 2004.

**Skinner, Quentin.** "Meaning and Understanding in the History of Ideas." *History and Theory* 8.1 (1969): 3–53.

**Skinner, Quentin.** *Reason and Rhetoric in the Philosophy of Thomas Hobbes.* Cambridge: Cambridge University Press, 1996.

**Smith, G. G.** *Elizabethan Critical Essays.* Oxford: Clarendon Press, 1904.

**Wilson, Richard.** *Secret Shakespeare: Studies in Theatre, Religion and Resistance.* Manchester: Manchester University Press, 2004.

*Verena Olejniczak Lobsien (2.2.1–4)/*
*Christina Wald (2.2.5–6)*

## 2.3 | The Eighteenth Century

### 2.3.1 | Terminology and Overview

In English literary history writing, the eighteenth century has been redefined and reinvented again and again. Even the exact time period one refers to as 'the eighteenth century' has been subject to negotiation: many scholars have worked within the demarcations of a '**long eighteenth century**' spanning from 1660, the year of the monarch's restoration to the throne, to 1832, the year of the First Reform Bill and Sir Walter Scott's death. Alternatively, the Victorian critic (and father of Virginia Woolf) Sir Leslie Stephen saw the eighteenth century as beginning in 1688. Others have set a narrower scale from 1688 to 1789, in which a shortened eighteenth century begins and ends with a revolution. This chapter refrains from marking such definite periodical boundaries. Instead it outlines the key paradigms of the eighteenth century: Enlightenment, Neoclassicism, and Sensibility.

**Political Changes.** Britain underwent major changes between ca. 1700 and 1800. The Glorious Revolution of 1689 and the Revolutionary Settlement had produced a new **balance of power** between king and parliament, landed and moneyed interests etc., setting the stage for the further rise of the middle class; the political union with Scotland came about in 1707, necessitating a rethinking of what it was to be English or British; by 1714, the first Hanoverian King (who spoke little English and spent much of his time in Hanover), George I, was on the British throne. The American colonies gained independence in 1776 (whereas Ireland remained a colony until 1800); elsewhere, Britain had asserted and continued to assert itself as the prime imperial and naval power. At home, the country's topography, demography, and social structures saw significant changes. Enclosures (i.e. the conversion of common land into private property, which had affected most of the country before 1700) modified the landscape in many areas. By 1700, the majority of the population already worked outside agriculture, and the number increased slowly throughout the century. Urbanization proceeded swiftly, and London's population almost doubled in the period. (Yet even in 1800, most of the population lived in the countryside). After mid century, the country's population grew rapidly to levels never previously achieved without a drop in living standards. At the same time, the mechanization of industry got under way. Despite the continued dominance of the aristocracy and gentry in politics, trade ("moneyed interest") generated a new culture of commerce and consumerism as well as a flourishing print culture.

**Cultural Changes.** Located in a new middle-class "public sphere," and effectively aiming to assert itself and, at the same time, to embrace the upper class, it is this new culture based on class-consolidation that has traditionally laid claim to marking the distinct quality of eighteenth-century culture, more specifically its first forty years or so. Politically and culturally, its hallmark is optimism, thus the traditional view. The **Augustan Age** is marked by the hope for a new 'golden age' similar to the first Golden Age of Latin literature (the reign of Augustus, 27 BC-14); its aesthetic correlative is **Neoclassicism** with its belief in the superiority and ideal exemplarity of ancient art and literature. Alexander Pope paradigmatically represents this Augustan interweaving of political and cultural optimism, poignantly articulated in his much cited line "One truth is clear, whatever is, is right" (*Essay on Man*, Epistle I, line 294).

**The concept of the New Eighteenth Century**, proclaimed by Felicity Nussbaum and Laura Brown in 1987, challenged the traditional, somewhat one-sided view of the Augustan Age (and of the entire century). Of course, earlier literary histories had also acknowledged the disappointed hopes of the Augustans, articulated in the many **satires** addressing contemporary life and politics. Works like John Gay's *The Beggar's Opera* (1728), Jonathan Swift's

### Timeline: The Long Eighteenth Century

| | |
|---|---|
| **1660** | Restoration of Charles II to the throne |
| **1667** | Milton's *Paradise Lost* published |
| **1688** | Glorious Revolution |
| **1707** | Act of Union: the Kingdoms of England and Scotland are united to form the Kingdom of Great Britain |
| **1714** | George I becomes the first British King from the House of Hanover |
| **from ca. 1750** | Technological innovations lead to the industrialization of production, improvements in infrastructure, and widespread urbanization |
| **1755** | Johnson's *Dictionary of the English Language* published |
| **1775–1783** | American War of Independence: Britain defeated |
| **1789** | French Revolution: an important inspiration for British Romanticism |
| **1803–1815** | Napoleonic Wars fought across Europe; Britain is Napoleon's staunchest enemy |

Satire is an artistic form that seeks to ridicule its objects, their transgressions, vices, or folly. There are two common modes of English neoclassicist satire that go back to formal verse satire in Roman antiquity: the scathingly harsh **Juvenalian satire** (e.g. Swift's "A Modest Proposal" and Pope's *The Dunciad*) and the mockingly playful **Horatian satire** (e.g. Pope's *The Rape of the Lock*). The long eighteenth century, and particularly the "Augustan Age," produced a plethora of satirical writing—not least because Augustan writers discovered satire as an effective medium for political (e.g. John Dryden's *Absalom and Achitophel*) or private invective (e.g. *The Dunciad*).

"A Modest Proposal" (1729), or the art of William Hogarth castigated hunger and poverty, injustice, greed, moral depravity and the corruption of Sir Robert Walpole's administration. Yet satire was a literary genre and practice firmly steeped in Augustan neoclassical principles. Authors like Pope and Samuel Johnson established their authority by translating and rewriting classical texts (e.g., Pope's *The Rape of the Lock*, 1712; Johnson's "London: A Poem in Imitation of the Third Satire of Juvenal," 1738). Satire operated to address contemporary issues within a classical frame of reference. Its double edge displays the political, social, and cultural tensions within the Augustan world.

The proponents of the New Eighteenth Century, however, significantly redefined and broadened the picture, advocating "a revision or problematization of period, canon, tradition, and genre in eighteenth-century literary studies" (Nussbaum and Brown 14). Its scholars turned towards race, class, and gender as constitutive facets of individual and collective cultural identities. The origins of the novel were revised, discarding a simple history of generic evolution. Hitherto marginalized fields, issues, writers, and genres—nationalism and imperialism/empire, cultural identities, domesticity, women writers, the diary, scandalous memoirs etc.—received critical attention from "Marxist, Foucauldian, new historical, or feminist" perspectives (Nussbaum and Brown 2). The **extension and revision of the canon**, along with the turn to theory, performed a self-conscious critical departure from the traditional 'resistance to theory' (Paul de Man) that had obstinately governed eighteenth-century English studies. The effect was "the discipline's move from formalism to historicisms, and a resistance of the top-down, rarefied voice of Augustan literary history" (Backscheider and Ingrassia 5–6). Even if it had never appeared homogeneously bright and coherent, the eighteenth century was definitely no longer seen as the Augustan age of order, coherence, wit, and common sense.

It is now more than twenty years ago that the New Eighteenth Century was first announced. In the meantime, it has itself turned into a "cliché" (Backscheider and Ingrassia 5), leaving us, perhaps, within a Post-New Eighteenth Century paradigm. There has been a movement towards a more extensive investigation of contexts and a fresh concern with material culture. Neglected authors are being re-evaluated and new fields and issues explored: the literature of the labouring classes (Goodridge); previously unconsidered genres like tales of spying or women's friendship poems (Backscheider); the intricate ideology of the discourse on slavery and transnationalism (Boulukos; Hulme); book culture (Runge and Rogers); literacy and the politics of reading; popular culture; the role of science; poverty, prostitution, economic and literary practices (Backscheider and Ingrassia; Wall; Rosenthal; and others). Recent scholarship, especially on the (re-)writing of London (e.g. Bond), has performed a **spatial** or **topographical turn** in eighteenth-century English studies, while, at the same time, branching out into the material reality of culture, focussing on the Streets of London with its waste and filth, prostitution, begging, and thieving (e.g., Gee; Rosenthal; Wall). There is also new research addressing the fascination of the age with fakes, frauds, forgeries and deception (what Jack Lynch has called "fake studies"). Indeed, the eighteenth century abounded with forgeries and frauds such as Macpherson's famous *Ossian* (the ostensible ancient Gaelic author of a cycle of poems which Macpherson claimed to have translated). The case of Ossian especially divided the literary scene into believers and non-believers, defendants and hostile critics. What was at stake was authenticity, but also the juridical and commercial concern with authorship.

## 2.3.2 | The Enlightenment and the Public Sphere

Perhaps like no other subject in English eighteenth century studies, the nature of the **public sphere** has been the key point of contention. To a large extent, the controversy has focussed on Jürgen Habermas' seminal concept of the bourgeois "public sphere," which, according to Habermas, evolved in the eighteenth century as a (virtual) community

## Key Authors: Augustan Age

John Dryden (1631–1700)
Alexander Pope (1688–1744)
Jonathan Swift (1667–1745)
Joseph Addison (1672–1719)
Sir Richard Steele (1672–1729)
John Gay (1685–1732)

of private individuals, a realm of public social life formed in the face of and in opposition to the lack of institutionalized political power of the middle class at the time. As such, it operated to mediate between society and state authority. Its discursive form was public rational-critical debate; its forums were continental *salons*, *Tischgesellschaften*, coffee-houses, clubs, and periodicals.

Coffee-houses indeed played a key role in the formation of public opinion, as they were intimately connected to the **periodical press**, which could be read, discussed, circulated, and at times even written on the premises. *The Tatler* by Richard Steele and its successor *The Spectator*, the enormously popular series of periodical essays co-produced by Steele and Addison and published daily (except Sundays) in 1711–12 and 1714, are prime examples. Each signed by "Mr Spectator," the *Spectator* essays feature a variety of fictional characters representing different social types and points of view, and they cover diverse topics ranging from social customs, women's education, fashion, and manners to literary taste and the imagination. Not only does the *Spectator* offer models of social and moral behaviour to the middle classes, it also seeks to generate its own reader qualified by the gentlemanly culture of reason, politeness, and taste. Its stylistic ideal is the "free and easy" discourse of the coffee-house.

Although they varied in size, composition and choice of topics, Habermas claims that the forums of the public sphere shared a disregard for social status within the realm of rational social intercourse, replacing "the celebration of rank with a tact befitting equals" (Habermas 36). More recent scholarship, however, has dismissed this claim as idealism or "myth" (Downie), attacking Habermas' version of the public sphere on the grounds of insufficient historical evidence, neglect of material factors such as the systems of distribution of print material, overgeneralization, and blindness to gender and processes of exclusion and social distinction (e.g. Eagleton; Eger et al.; Downie).

Notwithstanding its necessary revisions, Habermas' concept helps us to understand the function of literature (and criticism) in the early to mid-eighteenth century (cf. Eagleton). Its place was neither an autonomous sphere, nor the court; rather, literature operated at the heart of the public sphere, intersecting and engaging with a plurality of discourses, negotiating political, social, and moral issues according to trans-literary standards. Its political prerequisites were the Act of Toleration (1689), which provided a certain degree of religious tolerance, and the lapse of the Licensing Act in 1695, effectively terminating pre-publication censorship. The subsequent copyright legislations of 1709 and 1774 provided the legal framework for the ensuing conceptual and functional changes of literature and its authors. While prior to the eighteenth century, the author would have depended on support by the court or an aristocratic patron, the new copyright legislation eventually enabled the professional author to produce for a **literary market**, independent of the restraints of patronage. Women writers like Anne Finch, Charlotte Lennox, or Frances Burney tended to publish anonymously in order to avoid publicity. In any case, throughout at least the first half of the century, so-called "hack" writing for payment was generally considered a disrespectable way of making one's living associated with London's Grub Street. Samuel Johnson defined it in his *Dictionary of the English Language* (1755): "Grubstreet: Originally the name of a street in Moor-fields in London, much inhabited by writers of small histories, dictionaries, and temporary poems; whence any mean production is called *grubstreet*."

Johnson himself, the "great cham of literature" (Tobias Smollett) in the latter half of the eighteenth century, famously came to dismiss patronage: "Is not a patron, my lord, one who looks with unconcern on a man struggling for life in the water, and, when he has reached ground, encumbers him with help?" he wrote in his "Letter to the Earl of Chesterfield" (1755). As many of his contemporaries, Johnson depended on

Coffee-House at the beginning of the eighteenth century

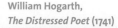

William Hogarth,
*The Distressed Poet* (1741)

subscription publishing, a mode of publication that entailed the financial risk by guaranteeing purchasers prior to printing in return for the bookseller's agreement to publish a book at an agreed price. In spite of his own rise to enormous reputation as versatile author, lexicographer, and critic (leading to a pension from the king in 1762), Johnson never condemned hack writers as a species, unlike Pope, who one generation earlier had castigated Grub Street authors in his verse satire of *The Dunciad* (1728–1743).

### 2.3.3 | Pope and Neoclassicism

Alexander Pope's own career was one of impressively successful self-promotion. His subscription project for his translation of Homer's *Iliad* (1714) freed him from the need of patrons for good, and his commercial success enabled him to gloss over his modest and precarious family background. (His father was a catholic linen merchant, subjected to anti-catholic legal discrimination). By 1715, Pope had established himself among the cultural and social elite. According to his aristocratic taste, he fashioned his famous villa in the Palladian style in Twickenham, imitating—on a much smaller scale—the landed aristocrat's estate. He had his riverside garden connected to the basement of his villa by an underground passage, which he turned, by way of ornament, into a grotto. Although Pope's garden design retained some formality, it helped to shape the aesthetic ideal of the **English landscape garden** with its preference for natural appearance, changing "prospects," alternating light and shade, and variety in opposition to the formal rigidity and symmetry of French and Italian gardens.

Some of Pope's literary and aesthetic ideals are articulated in his early, pre-Twickenham poem "Windsor-Forest." Written in two parts in 1704 and 1712 and published in February 1713 to celebrate the Treaty of Utrecht (signed in April 1713), this topographical poem perfectly encapsulates Pope's Enlightenment neo-classical aesthetics, Augustan cultural optimism, political Toryism or Jacobitism, and English patriotism. (Jacobites were dedicated to the restoration of the Stuarts to the British throne).

Completing the poem towards the end of a long war, Pope articulates a deeply optimistic vision of historical progress in his poem. It begins with an evocation of a paradisal, pastoral Windsor (the location of his family home):

> Thy forests, *Windsor*! and thy green Retreats,
> At once the Monarchs and the Muse's seates,
> Invite my Lays. Be present, Sylvan Maids!
> Unlock your Springs, and open all your Shades.
> *Granville* commands: Your Aid O Muses bring!
> The Groves of *Eden*, vanish'd now so long,
> Live in Description, and look green in Song:
> *These*, were my Breast inspir'd with equal Flame,
> Like them in Beauty, should be like in Fame.
> Here Hills and Vales, the Woodland and the Plain,
> Here Earth and Water seem to strive again,
> Not *Chaos-like* together crush'd and bruis'd,
> But, as the World, harmoniously confus'd:
> Where Order in Variety we see,
> And where, tho' all things differ, all agree.
> Here waving Groves a chequer'd Scene display,
> And part admit, and part exclude the Day (lines 1–18).

Pope envisages a perfectly harmonious place; its keyword is **Order in Variety**. The harmony clearly extends beyond formal aesthetic concerns, as politics, (imperial) economics, and history are interwoven into the poetic topography. Not only does "Windsor-Forest," modelled on Virgil's agricultural poem *Georgics*, stress Britain's economic productivity, but this happy state is given a specific historical context:

> Rich Industry sits smiling on the Plains,
> And Peace and Plenty tell, a Stuart reigns (41–42).

William Turner, *Pope's Villa, at Twickenham* (1808)

In the subsequent lines, the poem indeed tells a history of progress from a savage past, the tyrannies of William the Conqueror, to the present state of harmony and plenty. In contrast to the destruction and exploitation of the land by the Norman kings (conveyed through extensive images of hunting), Queen Anne is celebrated as "Fair *Liberty*, *Britannia's* Goddess," who "leads the golden Years" (91–92) of the present Stuart reign. The poem's historical narrative thus culminates in the present Queen,

Whose Care, like hers, protects the Sylvan Reign,
The Earth's fair Light, and Empress of the Main (163-64).

The semantics of these lines suggests a larger map than the Forest of Windsor, and indeed the poem's final part progresses along the river Luddon and "Old Father *Thames*" (330) into the wider world. Interweaving classical mythology (specifically Ovid's metamorphoses) and topography, it evokes an imperial image of world peace and liberty:

At length great ANNA said—'Let Discord cease!'
She said, the World obey'd, and all was *Peace*! (327-28)

The hope for peace, patriotism, and imperial vision go hand in hand:

There Kings shall sue, and suppliant States be seen
Once more to bend before a *British* QUEEN. [...]
Oh stretch thy Reign, fair *Peace!* from Shore to Shore,
Till Conquest cease, and Slav'ry be no more (383-408).

The poem thus celebrates the Popeian unity of Tory or Jacobite politics, imperial patriotism, and neoclassical poetics. At the same time, with its topographical ideal of "order in variety," it anticipates the English landscape garden that Pope would create in Twickenham.

Next to Pope, among the principle advocators of the English garden were William Kent (who brought the Palladian style to England and was influenced by Pope), William Shenstone, Lancelot "Capability" Brown, and Horace Walpole, the Gothic novelist and influential theorist of gardening. Among the typical features of the English garden such as undulating grass, groups of trees, winding paths, a lake of irregular shape, a temple, ruin and a grotto, Walpole propagated the installation of a "ha-ha," a sunken fence allowing extensive views and showing "that all nature was a garden" (qtd. in Hunt and Willis 313). With its topographical preferences and its paradoxical agenda to create a seemingly natural landscape, the English garden in turn paved the way for and helped to shape what was to become the fashion of the **picturesque**, which sought to discover in nature the qualities of seventeenth-century French and Italian landscape paintings. A naturally pictorial quality of scenery was its ideal; its "materials," according to the chief theorist of the picturesque William Gilpin, "*mountains—lakes—broken grounds—wood—rocks—cascades—vallies—and rivers*" (Gilpin, *Observations on the Mountains and Lakes of Cumberland and Westmoreland*, 1793) were assembled into a whole picture that combined features of the beautiful and the sublime. Increasingly, travellers or travel writers like Thomas Gray pursued and celebrated the qualities of the picturesque not only in the traditional locations of the **grand tour** to France and Italy, but also in the wild landscapes of the Lake District, Scotland, and Wales—topographies that eventually came to be considered essentially Romantic.

## 2.3.4 | The Public Sphere, Private Lives: The Novel 1719–1742

The eighteenth century is, above all, the **age of the novel**. In the context of Enlightenment discourses on moral values, what made a good life, manners and ways of relating to one another, gender roles, etc., the novel evolved as a key genre to negotiate such issues of general concern. In some ways, it operated next to, sometimes fed on, and fictionalized the popular literary 'species' of **biography**

### Focus on the Rise of the Novel

Both the contributory factors and the historical timeline of the **eighteenth-century novel** have been subject to scholarly controversy. In his seminal study *The Rise of the Novel* of 1957, Ian Watt proposed a causal chain from the rise of the middle class and the rise of literacy to the rise of the novel. Subsequent studies have emphasized the important role played by non-fictional genres (religious tracts and pamphlets, biography, conduct books, journalism), both as popular middle-class reading matter and as antecedent textual modes contributing to the formation of the novel in the seventeenth and early eighteenth centuries (e.g., Hunter). And whereas Ian Watt defined the new exclusive quality of the novel as its "**formal realism**" (influenced by the philosophies of Descartes and John Locke), scholars have since drawn a more complex picture. Rather than simply give a "full and authentic report of human experience" (Watt 32), the novel responds to and negotiates new, pressing social and epistemological "problems that are central to early modern experience" (McKeon 20), relating to questions of **truth** and questions of **virtue**. McKeon's own project has been to dialectically retrace the novel's movement from "romance idealism" and "aristocratic ideology" to "naive empiricism" and "progressive ideology" and subsequently to "extreme skepticism" and "conservative ideology" (21).

(climaxing in James Boswell's canonical *Life of Johnson* of 1794).

*Robinson Crusoe*

**The novels of Daniel Defoe** align with formal realism, empiricism, and progressive ideology alike. In his enormously successful *The Life and Strange Surprizing Adventures of Robinson Crusoe* (1719), Defoe combines and transforms the forms of travel and adventure narratives, diary, and spiritual autobiography into the fictional autodiegetic narrative of a 'homo oeconomicus.' As the hero leaves his home and family to venture out into the imperial world and eventually finds himself shipwrecked, he primarily strives to look after himself, be it to engage in adventurous trading for profit or to survive on the lonely island frequented by cannibals. Again and again, the protagonist protests his Puritan recognition of God's "Providence," but his narrative foregrounds his own mastery of the environment. Robinson's self-account is largely devoted to the particulars of his secular concerns, rather than to spiritual introspection.

**Samuel Richardson.** If Defoe created a realist "circumstantial view of life" (Watt 32), Samuel Richardson gave psychological depth and a distinct dimension of gender to the novel. In 1740, Richardson, who ran a printing business, was invited to publish a collection of *Familiar Letters on Important Occasions* (publ. in 1741), i.e. a series of model letters offering advice on appropriate responses to a variety of situations, which he then

*Pamela*

transformed into his first epistolary novel, *Pamela, or Virtue Rewarded. In a Series of Familiar Letters from a Beautiful Young Damsel to her Parents* (1740). Consisting almost entirely of the heroine's letters to her parents, the novel tells the story of "virtue in distress." Pamela, a young, innocent, yet articulate and literate maid, is pursued, sexually harassed and even kidnapped by her young gentleman employer. Yet not only are his intimidating attempts to make her his mistress successfully allayed by her resilience, but her female, middle-class claim to virtue (defined as virginity) defeats his male aristocratic notions of superiority, honour and reputation. In spite of her frequent weeping and fainting, Pamela is neither inferior to her importunate "master" in intellectual or rhetorical strength, nor is she unaware of his financial and personal attractions. In the face of her unrelenting resistance, Mr B. eventually proposes to his maid, turning the story of a "damsel in distress" into one of female social elevation by means of virtue/chastity, middle-class self-assertion and sociability. By the end of the narrative, Pamela has

converted her surroundings to a (effeminized) culture of social bonding through the power of "sentiment."

Pamela's sentimental story was much praised and copied by her contemporaries, yet it also provoked malicious or satirical responses. Henry Fielding famously attacked the heroine and her author for hypocrisy in his *Shamela* (1741). He used his second anti-Richardsonian novel *Joseph Andrews* (1742) to formulate in the "Preface" what amounts to a classical counter-agenda for the novel, which he termed a "'comic epic poem in prose'" aiming to expose, by ridicule, "vanity, or hypocrisy."

## 2.3.5 | Scepticism, Sentimentalism, Sociability: The Novel After 1748

Sentiment and sensibility form the new paradigm of mid eighteenth-century literature and culture, hence the term "**Age of Sensibility**." Among its writers and theorists are the philosophers David Hume, Francis Hutcheson and Adam Smith (and partially Anthony Ashley Cooper, Third Earl of Shaftesbury), the sentimental novelists Richardson, Laurence Sterne (*A Sentimental Journey Through France and Italy*, 1768), Oliver Goldsmith (*The Vicar of Wakefield*, 1766), Henry Mackenzie (*The Man of Feeling*, 1771), Frances Burney (*Evelina or the History of a Young Lady's Entrance into the World*, 1778), and to some degree sentimental playwrights like Steele, Richard Sheridan, Goldsmith, and Elizabeth Inchbald. These writers are all "committed to the resources of a language of feeling for the purpose of representing necessary social bonds; all discover in their writings a sociability which is dependent upon the communication of passions and sentiments" (Mullan 2; my emphasis). The basis of such sociability is the "sensitive and socialized body—the site where the communicative power of feeling is displayed, but also where sensibility can become excessive or uncontrollable" (Mullan 16). Sentimental novels celebrate a natural, seemingly inadvertent bonding between individuals, allowing—often through shared physical symptoms like weeping—human beings to feel deeply connected and committed to the thoughts and feelings of others. The keyword is **sympathy**, which signifies the human faculty of sharing another's sentiments by spontaneous transmission

(David Hume) or by an act of imagining oneself in the place of the other (Adam Smith). Sympathy thus constitutes the basis of social and moral consciousness both in moral philosophy and literature. Furthermore, it operates as the key principle in a variety of disciplines and discourses from medicine to theories of acting/theatre (David Garrick) and notions of aesthetic response in various literary/aesthetic theories (see box). Even Samuel Johnson, although not a sentimental philosopher, resorted to the psychological mechanism of sympathy when explaining the impact of reading biographies or novels (*The Rambler* 4 and 60, 1750).

**Richardson's *Clarissa*.** While the mid-century novel and its readers played a crucial role in the formation of a culture of sentiment and sociability, it also came to be the forum for its critique, or for the negotiation of its limits. In *Pamela*'s immediate successor and possibly the longest novel in English literature, *Clarissa, or, the History of a Young Lady* (1748), Richardson already draws a far more ambivalent picture of the power of sympathy. While on the one hand, the angelic heroine comes to inhabit a space of perfect moral autonomy and self-command gained through sympathy turned inward, there is ultimately no world for such a perfect being as Richardson's ideal woman. On the other hand, the price for the heroine (and the reader) to pay is high indeed. The excessive "trials" of her physical and personal integrity culminate in Clarissa's rape by Lovelace, her demonic antagonist of almost Miltonic proportions, and they lead to radical isolation from her friends and unsympathetic family, and to her eventual death. The bonds of sympathy and sentiment thus prove precarious, or even impossible to sustain in a hostile world.

**Fielding's *Tom Jones*.** There is, then, a sceptical dimension to Richardson's tragic novel, albeit glossed over by the final sentimental deathbed scenes staging mourning admirers of Clarissa's angelic virtue. The scepticism of his rival, Henry Fielding, goes further, and is of a different nature. In his comic novel *The History of Tom Jones, a Foundling* (1749), Fielding employs a self-consciously omniscient, authorial narrator to spin a plot that Coleridge was to call one of "the three most perfect plots ever planned" (*Table Talk*, 1834). As the rash young hero, a foundling, moves through various social spheres to prove his innate good nature against false accusations, to be finally rewarded with the subject of his ad-

| Key Texts: Literature and Sympathy |
| --- |

**Edmund Burke**, *A Philosophical Enquiry into the Origin of our Ideas of the Sublime and Beautiful* (1757)
**Alexander Gerard**, *An Essay on Taste* (1759)
**Lord Kames (Henry Home)**, *Elements of Criticism* (1762)
**James Beattie**, *Essays, on the nature and immutability of truth in opposition to sophistry and scepticism. On poetry and music as they affect the mind. On laughter and ludicrous composition. On the utility of classical learning* (1776)
**Hugh Blair**, *Lectures on Rhetoric and Belles Lettres* (1783)

oration, the reader is taught a lesson in the fallibility of judgement. While he/she has never been left in any doubt as to Tom's good nature (despite his lack of prudence), the reader is initially tempted to draw false conclusions as to the hero's origins. It is only in retrospect that the reader—along with Tom's adoptive father, a worthy gentleman and justice of peace—is forced to recognize that he/she has jumped to conclusions all too easily. Similar to the **epistemological scepticism** in David Hume's *Treatise of Human Nature* (1739–1740), Fielding's narrator thus demonstrates how our judgements often depend on unreliable inferences. At the same time, he propagates an ethics of benevolence (inspired by Shaftesbury) in a mild and humorous way that allows for human error and weaknesses while ridiculing hypocrisy.

**Sterne's *Tristram Shandy*.** Benevolence, compassion, and a deeply sceptical viewpoint also permeate Laurence Sterne's nine-volume sentimental novel *The Life and Opinions of Tristram Shandy, Gentleman* (1759–1767). *Tristram Shandy* radically explores the unknowability and instability of the self and its inability to communicate with others. The novel playfully converts the notion of "association of ideas," formulated by the empiricist philosopher John Locke (*An Essay Concerning Human Understanding*, 1690) as the fundamental operation of the human mind, into a parody of the mechanisms of autobiographical self-consciousness. As the hero undertakes to tell the story of his life, he is forever tempted and forced to pursue pre-histories and side-lines. The result is a novel that, on one level, abounds with communicative blunders and misunderstandings, leaving human beings ridden by their "hobby-horses" and ultimately unknowable to themselves and others. On another level, it stages a narrative marked by seemingly infinite digression and excess.

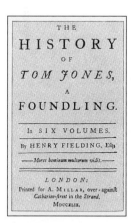

Title page of the first printing of Henry Fielding's *Tom Jones* (1749)

## 2.3.6 | Literature of the Sublime: The Cult of Medievalism, Solitude and Excess

Despite its significance, popular success, and critical acclaim, *Tristram Shandy* remains a singular, radical phenomenon in the history of the eighteenth-century novel. Far more influential was a trend that also destabilized key Enlightenment beliefs and played on notions of excess. The **Gothic fictions** of Horace Walpole (*The Castle of Otranto*, 1764), Ann Radcliffe (*Mysteries of Udolpho*, 1794), M. G. Lewis (*The Monk*, 1796), and others transport their readers into the Middle Ages or to remote foreign (catholic) scenes to create a genre committed to the evocation of astonishment and horror in the face of excess, violent events, and the overpowering force of the supernatural. Inspired by the contemporary cult of medievalism, they rely on the effect of the "**sublime**," an ancient concept revised by Edmund Burke in his *Philosophical Enquiry*. The effect of the sublime, pertaining to the vast, the powerful, with darkness and infinitude, but also with the radical solitude of the self, was, according to Burke, a "delightful horror" (pt. II, section VIII)—a feeling much stronger than pleasure, which was associated with the beautiful. The

The first Gothic novels date from the eighteenth century.

Burkean notion of sublimity was to permeate Romantic poetry and art—from the sublime landscapes of the Lake District and Scotland to figures of the political sublime in the writings of the radical political theorist, novelist, and biographer William Godwin, particularly in his political Gothic novel *Things as They Are; or, The Adventures of Caleb Williams* (1794).

In a way, then, the figures of the sublime in the Gothic novel are linked to another phenomenon of Pre-Romanticism in the eighteenth century, **Graveyard Poetry**, named after its preferred locations. William Collins, Edward Young, Thomas Gray, and others conflated traditional topoi such as melancholy, *memento mori*, sympathy, etc. with new notions of genius and originality (as formulated in Young's *Conjectures on Original Composition*, 1759), and with new configurations of a highly self-conscious, self-reflective gloomy solitary self as poet. Along with the poems of William Cowper, Thomas Gray's "Elegy Written in a Country Churchyard" (1751) proved one of the most widely read texts of the eighteenth century. With its figure of the poet in sympathetic bonding with the rural community and yet radically set apart, it was to inspire and anticipate the concerns of the Romantic poets.

## Select Bibliography

**Backscheider, Paula.** *Eighteenth-Century Women Poets and their Poetry. Inventing Agency, Inventing Genre*. Baltimore. Johns Hopkins University Press, 2005.

**Backscheider, Paula, and Catherine Ingrassia, eds.** *A Companion to the Eighteenth-Century English Novel and Culture*. Malden: Wiley-Blackwell, 2009.

**Bender, John.** *Imagining the Penitentiary: Fiction and the Architecture of Mind in Eighteenth-Century England*. Chicago: University of Chicago Press, 1987.

**Bond, Eric.** *Reading London: Urban Speculation and Imaginative Government in Eighteenth-Century Literature*. Columbus: Ohio State University Press, 2007.

**Boulukos, George.** *The Grateful Slave: The Emergence of Race in Eighteenth-Century British and American Culture*. Cambridge: Cambridge University Press, 2008.

**Brown, Marshall.** *Preromanticism*. Stanford: Stanford University Press, 1991.

**Damrosch, Leo, ed.** *The Profession of Eighteenth-Century Literature: Reflections on an Institution*. Madison: University of Wisconsin Press, 1992.

**Downie, J. A.** "Public and Private. The Myth of the Bourgeois Public Sphere." *A Concise Companion to the Restoration and Eighteenth Century*. Ed. Cynthia Wall. Malden: Blackwell Publishing, 2005. 58–79.

**Eagleton, Terry.** *The Function of Criticism: From 'The Spectator' to Post-Structuralism*. London: Verso, 1984.

**Eger, Elizabeth, et al., eds.** *Women, Writing and the Public Sphere, 1700–1830*. Cambridge: Cambridge University Press, 2000.

**Gee, Sophie.** *Making Waste: Leftovers and the Eighteenth-Century Imagination*. Princeton: Princeton University Press, 2010.

**Goodridge, John, ed.** *Eighteenth-Century English Labouring-Class Poets*. London: Pickering & Chatto, 2003.

**Habermas, Jürgen.** *The Structural Transformation of the Public Sphere: An Inquiry into a Category of Bourgeois Society*. Trans. Thomas Burger and Frederick Lawrence. Cambridge: Polity Press, 1989.

**Hammond, Brean S.** *Pope*. Brighton: Harvester Press, 1986.

**Hammond, Brean S.** *Professional Imaginative Writing in England, 1670–1740: 'Hackney for Bread.'* Oxford: Clarendon Press, 1997.

**Hulme, Peter.** *Colonial Encounters: Europe and the Native Caribbean: 1492–1797*. London: Routledge, 1986.

**Hunt, John Dixon, and Peter Willis.** *The Genius of the Place: The English Landscape Garden, 1620–1820*. Cambridge: MIT Press, 1988.

**Hunter, J. Paul.** *Before Novels: The Cultural Contexts of Eighteenth-Century English Fiction*. New York: Norton, 1990.

**Lynch, Jack.** *Deception and Detection in Eighteenth-Century Britain*. Aldershot: Ashgate, 2008.

**McKeon, Michael.** *The Origins of the English Novel: 1600–1740*. Baltimore: Johns Hopkins University Press, 1987.

**Mullan, John.** *Sentiment and Sociability: The Languages of Feeling in the Eighteenth Century*. Oxford: Clarendon Press, 1990.

**Nisbet, H. B., and Claude Rawson, eds.** *The Eighteenth Century*. Cambridge: Cambridge University Press, 1997.

Vol. 4 of *The Cambridge History of Literary Criticism*. H. B. Nisbet and Claude Rawson, gen. eds. 9 vols. to date. 1989-.

**Nussbaum, Felicity, and Laura Brown, eds.** *The New Eighteenth Century: Theory, Politics, English Literature*. New York: Methuen, 1987.

**Rawson, Claude Julien.** *Order from Confusion Sprung: Studies in Eighteenth-Century Literature from Swift to Cowper*. London: Allen & Unwin, 1985.

**Rosenthal, Laura J.** *Infamous Commerce: Prostitution in Eighteenth-Century British Literature and Culture*. Ithaca: Cornell University Press, 2006.

**Runge, Laura L., and Pat Rogers, eds.** *Producing the Eighteenth-Century Book: Writers and Publishers in England, 1650–1800*. Newark: University of Delaware Press, 2009.

**Todd, Janet M.** *The Sign of Angellica*: *Women, Writing, and Fiction 1660–1800*. New York: Columbia University Press, 1989.

**Wahrman, Dror.** *The Making of the Modern Self: Identity and Culture in Eighteenth-Century England*. New Haven: Yale University Press, 2004.

**Wall, Cynthia, ed.** *A Concise Companion to the Restoration and Eighteenth Century*. Malden: Blackwell Publishing, 2005.

**Watt, Ian.** *The Rise of the Novel: Studies in Defoe, Richardson, and Fielding*. London: Pimlico, 1957.

*Helga Schwalm*

## 2.4 | Romanticism

Periodization

There is an awareness in recent studies of Romanticism that the Romantic period "is typically granted representation out of all proportion to its duration" in literary and cultural histories (Chandler 9). To be sure, in the wake of the strictly historicised (and historicizing) focus of Jerome McGann's critical investigation of *The Romantic Ideology* (1983), the 1980s and '90s inaugurated an unprecedented **turn in Romantic studies** which—very much in line with the debates about the New Eighteenth Century—took into account the broader contexts of *British Culture, 1776–1832* (thus the subtitle of the seminal *Oxford Companion to the Romantic Age* edited by Iain McCalman in 1999). That an era which had to come to terms with the accumulated effects of the American, French and industrial revolutions, population increase and social unrest as well as the shifting cultural parameters of an increasingly print-based and professionalized public sphere and an emerging consumer society—that such an era should be accessible through the works of a handful of poets, the so-called **Big Six** (see box), seemed increasingly doubtful. Consequently, revision and expansion of the canon was the order of the day and led to the recovery and re-establishment of a number of female writers, while the unified understanding of Romanticism as influentially expounded by René Wellek and M. H. Abrams was questioned in a resurgence of A. O. Lovejoy's early insistence that "we should learn to use the word 'Romanticism' in the plural" (235; see also Ferguson).

More recently, however, the undeniable persistence of the **aesthetic** coordinates established in the Romantic period (as opposed to the many other modernizing impulses of the eighteenth century at large) has motivated a shift back to acknowledging the historical centrality of the aesthetic principles around which Wellek and Abrams built their conceptualisation of Romanticism, focussing on "the workings […] of poetic **imagination**, […] **nature** and its relation to man, and […] a use of **imagery, symbolism, and myth** which is clearly distinct from that of eighteenth-century neoclassicism" (Wellek 160–61). In an attempt at resuscitating *and* historicizing these ideas, the early twenty-first century has seen the emergence of a consensus that one "need[s] to think of Romantic literature not as escapist in the way the term 'Romantic' seems sometimes to suggest, but as literature that tries passionately to come to terms with the modern world as it emerges through a series of wrenching changes" (O'Flinn 3). It has become increasingly clear that in the decades at the close of the long eighteenth century "the categories of 'aesthetics' and 'poetics' both underwent serious transformation in ways that still matter in the early twenty-first century" because the period saw "the emergence of what might be called a cultural idiom, a whole way of being in the world"; what is more, this cultural idiom was framed by the introduction of a new mode of writing which we "still call 'imaginative literature'" (Chandler 1–2, 5).

### 2.4.1 | Romanticism as a Cultural Idiom

What exactly is this specifically Romantic way of being in the world? William Wordsworth's poem "Nutting," written in the last months of 1798 and first published in the second edition of the *Lyrical Ballads* in 1800, may serve as a point of entry here (cf. Mason 296–98). The poem opens with the following sentence:

> It seems a day,
> (I speak of one from many singled out)
> One of those heavenly days which cannot die,
> When forth I sallied from our cottage-door,

---

**Key Authors: Romanticism**

| The 'Big Six': | (Re-)Established Woman Writers: |
|---|---|
| William Blake (1757–1827) | Mary Shelley (1797–1851) |
| William Wordsworth (1770–1850) | Charlotte Smith (1749–1806) |
| Samuel Taylor Coleridge (1772–1827) | Mary Robinson (1757–1800) |
| Percy Bysshe Shelley (1792–1822) | Anna Letitia Barbauld (1743–1825) |
| John Keats (1795–1821) | Joanna Baillie (1762–1852) |
| George Gordon Lord Byron (1788–1824) | |

---

And with a wallet o'er my shoulder slung,                   5
A nutting crook in hand, I turned my steps
Towards the distant woods, a figure quaint,
Tricked out in proud disguise of beggar's weeds
Put on for the occasion, by advice
And exhortation of my frugal Dame.                          10

Typically of Wordsworth, the appositional syntax roams freely across the line breaks of the chosen blank verse (i.e. unrhymed iambic pentameter) lines, challenging the reader to follow the poem's argument, which slowly moves from the striking conjectural present-tense of the opening half-line (line 1) through an insistence on 'singling out' one day from many (2) to a claim of that particular day's immortality (3) before finally establishing the past-tense frame for the narrated episode from the speaker's younger days (4, 6). With this opening, the poem hovers somewhat uneasily between imaginative construction (as emphasised in lines 1–3) and detailed (and presumably faithful) remembrance of an episode from the speaker's past. The latter reading is supported by the 1843 note written by Wordsworth for Isabella Fenwick in which he stresses the autobiographical character of "Nutting":

Written in Germany: intended as part of a poem on my own life, but struck out as not being wanted there. Like most of my school-fellows I was an impassioned nutter. For this pleasure, the vale of Esthwaite, abounding in coppice wood, furnished a very wide range. These verses arose out of the remembrance of feelings I had often had when a boy [...]. (qtd. in Mason 377)

The poem, we learn here, was originally part of, but not included in, Wordsworth's life-long autobiographical poetic project which was only post-humously published as *The Prelude* in 1850, and the oblique and unexplained allusion to 'my frugal Dame' at the end of the first sentence, identified by later editors as "Ann Tyson, Wordsworth's beloved landlady in his schooldays" (Mason 297n), hints at just such a private, autobiographical frame of reference. But then, the opening lines insist that there is more to it, and when Wordsworth introduced classifications of types of poems for his post-*Lyrical Ballads* collections of poetry, "Nutting" did not turn up among the 'Poems Relating to the Period of Childhood' but rather among the 'Poems of the Imagination,' a decision vindicated in the poem's climactic scene in which the conjectural mode established in the opening lines resurfaces (marked in italics in the following):

Wordsworth's "Nutting" is set in the Vale of Esthwaite. Steel engraving ca. 1840

                              Among the woods,
And o'er the pathless rocks, I forced my way
Until, at length, I came to one dear nook         15
Unvisited, where not a broken bough
Drooped with its withered leaves, ungracious sign
Of devastation, but the hazels rose
Tall and erect, with milk-white clusters hung,
A virgin scene!—A little while I stood,           20
Breathing with such suppression of the heart
As joy delights in; and with wise restraint
Voluptuous, fearless of a rival, eyed
The banquet, *or beneath the tree I sate*
*Among the flowers, and with the flowers I played;*   25
*A temper known to those, who, after long*
*And weary expectation, have been blessed*
*With sudden happiness beyond all hope.*
*Perhaps it was a bower beneath whose leaves*
*The violets of five seasons re-appear*           30
*And fade, unseen by any human eye;*
*Where fairy water-breaks do murmur on*
*For ever*, and I saw the sparkling foam,
And with my cheek on one of those green stones
That, fleeced with moss, beneath the shady trees,  35
Lay round me, scattered like a flock of sheep,
I heard the murmur and the murmuring sound,
In that sweet mood when pleasure loves to pay
Tribute to ease; and, of its joy secure,
The heart luxuriates with indifferent things,     40
Wasting its kindliness on stocks and stones,
And on the vacant air.

Here, the initial mode of "**hypothetical recon-struction**" (Mason 296n) or even imaginative construction breaks through the mode of straightforward recollection characteristic of the intervening passages, and it is striking that the poem's one approximation of rhyme occurs in the context of this backshift into the initial conjectural mode ('eyed'—'sate'—'played,' lines 23–25). This paves the way for a fully-fledged imaginary abode beyond even the natural run of the four seasons (30; see also 'For ever,' 33) which is characterised as "unseen by any human eye" (31). This transcendent vision of oneness with nature is grounded in breathing (21–22), seeing (22–23, 33), touching (34–36), and finally listening (37), when, back in the past-tense mode of recollection from line 33 onwards, the speaker distinguishes between the 'murmuring sound' (which can be perceived, 37) and the deeper 'murmur' (32, 37) of which the sound is a mere echo. This deeper murmur, the poem suggests, can only be experienced in the unfocused state of being described in the closing lines of the passage (38–42) in the wake of the mystic communion with nature *imagined* earlier (29–33).

After this, it is all the more surprising that the poem does not end on this happy note. Without any transition or explanation, the poem continues:

Then up I rose
And dragged to earth both branch and bough, with crash
And merciless ravage; and the shady nook
Of hazels, and the green and mossy bower,          45
Deformed and sullied, patiently gave up
Their quiet being;

Continuing after a mere semicolon, the speaker suggests that, even in retrospect, he cannot make sense of his act of vandalism and that ever since, he has had mixed feelings about it, oscillating between exultation and pain:

and, *unless I now*
*Confound my present feelings with the past,*
*Even then, when from the bower I turned away*
*Exulting, rich beyond the wealth of kings,*          50
*I felt a sense of pain when I beheld*
*The silent trees and the intruding sky.—*

Here, the spirit of hypothetical reconstruction reasserts itself once again (marked by italics in the quotation), and we have finally reached the **cultural idiom** of Romanticism, the specifically Romantic and thus modern way of being in the

world: the speaker perceives, in spite of his longing for unity, that there is an insurmountable **difference between himself and nature**, a difference which can only be overcome in the imagination, as the seemingly unconnected closing lines of the poem indicate in a faint attempt at re-confirming the earlier vision. The lines are addressed to an as yet unmentioned maiden who is identified in associated manuscripts as the enigmatic and idealized Lucy (Mason 298n), figuring more prominently in Wordsworth's Lucy poems as the epitome of innocence saved from experience by dying young:

Then, dearest maiden! move along these shades
In gentleness of heart; with gentle hand
Touch—for there is a Spirit in the woods.          55

Quite clearly, this afterthought does not really affect the core of the poem, which has been identified by the critic and writer Gabriel Josipovici as a primal scene of cultural modernity:

The poem is so shocking because we sense that it is not so much the act of violence which is seen as a rape of nature as the very presence of the child; the act merely dramatises what had been latent all along [...]. The paradox for Wordsworth is that only in the midst of nature does he feel fully himself [...], and yet his very presence in nature robs it of precisely that which made it such a source of healing and joy. (54)

Romanticism, then, marks the emergence of a specifically **modern way of perceiving the world** and making sense of the experience, uneasily hovering between experience and expression, between being and representation, between subjectivism and a longing for integration and continuity, between emphatically embracing the world as nature and a retreat into art. Romantic practices have been concerned ever since with the "self and experience in a mediated world" and with the "reinvention of publicness" under these conditions (Thompson 207, 235).

## 2.4.2 | Theorising Romanticism

The most influential theoretical statement about many of these concerns can be found in the preface William Wordsworth wrote for the second edition of his and Samuel Taylor Coleridge's **Lyrical Ballads** which had first come out in 1798, and was then revised and expanded largely by Wordsworth alone for republication in 1800 (among the added poems was "Nutting"). Here, Wordsworth famously, and in direct contrast to neoclassical decorum, twice defined poetry as "the spontaneous overflow of powerful feelings" and has thus been traditionally hailed as the spearhead of the 'Romantic revolution.' However, closer inspection has revealed in the meantime that the revolutionary turn towards subjectivity had actually taken place much earlier in the context of a poetics of sensibility (cf. McGann, *Poetics of Sensibility*); Wordsworth and others were, in fact, concerned with the consequences of this revolution: they were trying to find out how the fleeting realm of subjective experience in its highly individualized actual existence could claim any kind of cultural authority. The answer to this question can actually be found in what follows the much-quoted slogan (see box). In Wordsworth's *complete* definition, poetry is *not* the spontaneous overflow of powerful feelings, but rather a *re-enactment* or *re-presentation* of emotion after recollecting and contemplating it at a later point in time, preferably in tranquillity. In the process of thinking long and deeply, an emotion *similar* to the one originally experienced is gradually produced in the mind, and *this* emotion can then be expressed or embodied in a poem (see, for example, Wordsworth's "I Wandered Lonely as a Cloud," also known as "The Daffodils," of 1804, which provides a very straightforward poetic illustration of the basic assumptions).

What is added here, in spite of Wordsworth's insistence on the near-identity of the emotions, is the dimension of **reflection**, and it is through this dimension that the raw material of subjective experience is transposed into the realm of culture. Taking into account Wordsworth's full argument in his preface to the *Lyrical Ballads*, one can see that he is deeply worried about anything that cannot be rationally controlled. He does not want to re-enact and communicate excessive overflows of powerful feelings in his poetry, but to impart only "that quantity of pleasure […] which a poet may *rationally* endeavour to impart" (my emphasis). To make sure that this is the case, the "language really used by men" which is so central to Wordsworth's innovative poetic stance has to be "purified […] from what appear to be its real defects," and this purification is effected both by selection and through the transposition into metrical composition:

[A] selection of the language really spoken by men [will] wherever it is made with true taste and feeling […] of itself form a distinc-

In the preface to *Lyrical Ballads*, → Wordsworth's definition of poetry reads as follows:
"[A]ll good Poetry is the spontaneous overflow of powerful feelings; but though this be true, Poems to which any value can be attached were never produced […] but by a man who, being possessed of more than usual organic sensibility, had also thought long and deeply. […] I have said that Poetry is the spontaneous overflow of powerful feelings; it takes its origins from emotion recollected in tranquillity; the emotion is then contemplated till by a species of reaction the tranquillity gradually disappears, and an emotion, kindred to that which was before the subject of contemplation, is gradually produced, and does itself actually exist in the mind."

tion […] and entirely separate the composition from the vulgarity and meanness of ordinary life; and, if metre is superadded thereto, […] a dissimilitude will be produced altogether sufficient for the gratification of the rational mind.

Whenever there is the danger of "excitement […] carried beyond its proper bounds," Wordsworth insists that "the co-presence of something regular […] cannot but have great efficacy in tempering and restraining the passion." All this is far from the traditional idea that the Romantic revolution opened up modern culture for an unmediated influx of subjectivity and emotion, and Wordsworth's frequent invocations of rationality indicate that it is too simplistic to describe Romanticism as being in direct and unequivocal opposition to Enlightenment concerns. Instead, it can be described as the Enlightenment's twin or shadow, trying to come to terms with those aspects of modernity which are elided in the project(s) of Enlightenment but nevertheless intransigent, such as the unavoidable cultural dimensions of subjectivity on the one hand and language and media opacity on the other.

What Romanticism is concerned with, then, is the **transposition of subjective experience into cultural relevance and authority**, and the latter can only be gained through expressing and communicating experience. Throughout the preface, Wordsworth is searching for a genuine mode of existence and experience which has apparently been overwhelmed by recent cultural developments, as a highly prescient passage of cultural criticism suggests:

For a multitude of causes, unknown to former times, are now acting with a combined force to blunt the discriminating powers of the mind and [...] to reduce it to a state of almost savage torpor. The most effective of these causes are the great national events which are daily taking place, and the increasing accumulation of men in cities, where the uniformity of their occupations produces a craving for extraordinary incident, which the rapid communication of intelligence hourly gratifies.

Poetry, Wordsworth insists, is one possible medium for recovering the discriminating powers of the mind and a less alienated existence and experience, but the problem is that poetry is already at a remove from experience, separated from it, as we have seen, by retrospective reflection and, what is more, the inscription of the recollected experience into the media of writing, print and poetic form. There is no way back from the realm of representation to the realm of existence, or from experience to innocence, as **William Blake** showed in his programmatic introductory poem to his *Songs of Innocence* (1789) even before he supplemented the collection with his *Songs of Experience* (1793) (see box).

Wordsworth, we have seen, is similarly aware of this, as the bout of frustration barely contained by the poem "Nutting" illustrates. In this sense, "Nutting" provides an interesting example of what

John Keats called, in an influential formulation which intriguingly covers the potential of art and poetry *and* the predicament of the modern condition, "***Negative Capability***, that is when man is capable of being in uncertainties, Mysteries, doubts, without any irritable reaching after fact & reason" (Letter to George and Thomas Keats, Dec 21, 1817). However, "Nutting" is not very typical of Wordsworth, who tends to focus on the successful poetic re-enactment of harmonious experiences in nature and to sublimate his awareness of difference into poetic meditations rather than ecological vandalism. Samuel Taylor Coleridge, on the other hand, in an equally influential formulation, was aware of the fact that what he called the "primary **IMAGINATION**," i.e. "the living power and prime agent of all human perception [...] as a repetition in the finite mind of the eternal act of creation in the infinite I AM" is only accessible to human beings as an "echo [...] coexisting with the conscious will" which he called "secondary [imagination]," but which still "dissolves, diffuses, dissipates in order to recreate [and] struggles to idealize and to unify"; mere "**FANCY**, on the contrary, has no other counters to play with but fixities and

---

Interpretation

### William Blake, *Songs of Innocence*

In his "Introduction" to his *Songs of Innocence* (1789), the poet, painter and engraver William Blake reflects upon the gap between being and representation by introducing the figure of a piper whose art moves from the realm of innocent involvement to the realm of representation. Interestingly, this fall from grace is inaugurated by a child who urges the piper to broaden the functional potential of his art by enriching first its affective and then, in a move from pure music to singing and writing, its semantic and representational potential:

Piping down the valleys wild
Piping songs of pleasant glee
On a cloud I saw a child,
And he laughing said to me;

"Pipe a song about a lamb";          5
So I piped with merry chear.
"Piper, pipe that song again—"
So I piped, he wept to hear.

"Drop thy pipe, thy happy pipe,
Sing thy songs of happy chear."          10
So I sung the same again
While he wept with joy to hear.

"Piper sit thee down and write
In a book that all may read—"
So he vanished from my sight.          15
And I plucked a hollow reed,

And I made a rural pen,
And I stain'd the water clear,
And I wrote my happy songs
Every child may joy to hear.          20

In the course of the poem, the fall from grace is clearly depicted as a **fall into language** which has the capacity to add joy to the world (lines 12, 20) but lets the world vanish from sight (15). Writing about the world is necessarily at a distance from the world, it "stain[s]" (18) its original being. In Blake's frontispiece for the collection, the piper/writer is depicted in the act of stepping out of the world of original being into experience.

definites" (*Biographia Literaria*, ch. 13). Thus, human creativity is grounded in imagination as the highest good, but it will always remain at a remove from the world in its totality because anyone who says 'I' will of necessity impose a difference on the world.

## 2.4.3 | Modes of Romantic Poetry

Against this background, **two basic orientations** of Romantic poetry can be identified:

*Processes of Naturalization: Voice.* On the one hand, Romantic poetry pursues the project of validating the cultural relevance and authority of subjective experience by integrating it into a larger framework which transposes Romantic notions of nature into the cultural realm and establishes a new understanding of culture as 'folk culture,' 'the people's culture', and 'national culture' in the process, an understanding which marks a clear contrast to the cosmopolitan culture of the educated elites on which neoclassicism was built. This strand of poetry avoids all artistic ostentation and retains just a bare minimum of poetic form in order to culturally domesticate and validate its staged (or represented) voices along the lines suggested in Wordsworth's preface to the *Lyrical Ballads.* As the title of this influential collection indicates, these poems try to combine the folk culture credibility of formerly oral ballad and song traditions with the subjective imaginative potential of the lyric. Characteristically, this new type of poem adapts the forms which can be found in these traditions:

- the **ballad stanza**: quatrains in alternate four- and three-stressed iambic lines with at times irregular unstressed syllables added, rhyming abcb;
- the **common metre** (or common measure) drawn from hymns, which is basically similar to the ballad stanza but more regular and rhymes abab;
- the **long metre**: iambic tetrameter, abab, as in Blake's "Introduction" (see box on p. 50).

In addition to narrative poems (i.e. ballads such as Coleridge's "The Rime of the Ancient Mariner" or Wordsworth's "Goody Blake, and Harry Gill," both in the 1798 *Lyrical Ballads*) and lyric song-like poems (such as Blake's *Songs of Innocence and of Experience* 1793 or Wordsworth's Lucy poems (1798–1801), there is also a more individualized and

situational mode of poetry in blank verse such as, for example, Wordsworth's "Nutting" as analyzed above. In extended form, such poems trace an individual speaker's reflections in what Coleridge has termed '**conversation poems**' (when there is an addressee for the speaker's ruminations as in his "The Eolian Harp," 1796, and "Frost at Midnight," 1798) or in highly subjective free-form variants of the ode (such as, for example, Wordsworth's "Lines Written A Few Miles Above Tintern Abbey," 1798, and "Ode: Intimations of Immortality," 1804). Between them, these latter modes of poetry have influentially been identified as the specifically Romantic genre of the 'Greater Romantic Lyric' (cf. Abrams, "Structure and Style"). The 'Greater Romantic Lyric' shares with ballads and songs its prioritization of voice as opposed to poetic form. But as opposed to the more collective framing of ballad and song forms, the Greater Romantic Lyric provides an opening for an individualization of voice which, when taken to its logical conclusions, could also entail an individualization of poetic form. And this is, in fact, the second basic orientation of Romantic poetry.

*Processes of Individualization: Poetic Form.* As opposed to the processes of naturalization outlined above, Romantic poetry also pursues the project of validating the cultural relevance and authority of subjective experience by emphatically embracing individuality and transforming it into an emphatic understanding of (modern) art and literature as an autonomous realm which provides an opening for the highest form of individuality, **genius**. Genius, one could say, transcends individuality into universality by taking it to extremes *without* losing relevance. As the hallmark of genius is originality which had to be detectable in the works themselves, this turn towards heightened individuality instigated a dynamics of formal innovation which in the long run resulted in the modernist alienation of poetry from the common reader. In the Romantic period itself, however, this was held at bay by the very processes of naturalization described above, and Wordsworth's ideal of "man speaking to man" (preface to the *Lyrical Ballads*) is part of this project.

Nevertheless, a turn towards formal innovation can be observed in the Romantic **sonnet revival**, which was inaugurated by Charlotte Smith with her *Elegiac Sonnets* (first edition 1784, nine further, continuously growing editions until 1811). Smith picked up an early modern tradition of poetic self-examination and self-stylization that ran

The Greater Romantic Lyric

John Keats in an 1828 oil painting by T. Sampson, based on the 1816 mask of the poet made by Keats's friend, Benjamin Robert Haydon

from the Petrarchism of Wyatt, Surrey, Spenser and Sidney through Shakespeare's individualization of the form in his *Sonnets* (publ. 1609) to the metaphysical poets and Milton, but was then interrupted by the neo-classicists' aversion to poetic subjectivity in the earlier eighteenth century, and she used the sonnet form as a medium for hypothetically reconstructing and imaginatively constructing autobiographical material in order to project a public persona of herself. In Smith's wake, Romantic poets like Wordsworth and Coleridge were creatively engaging the double tradition of established formal conventions (fourteen lines, iambic pentameter, rhyme scheme abba abba [turn] cde cde [or cdc dcd] in the Italian tradition or abab cdcd efef [turn] gg in the English tradition), but it took some time until fully individualized sonnets emerged, such as, for example, Percy Bysshe Shelley's "Ozymandias" (1818) or John Keats's poetological sonnet "If by dull rhymes our English must be chain'd" (1819).

If by dull rhymes our English must be chain'd,
    And, like Andromeda, the Sonnet sweet
        Fetter'd, in spite of pained loveliness;
Let us find out, if we must be constrain'd,
    Sandals more interwoven and complete     5
To fit the naked foot of Poesy;
        Let us inspect the Lyre, and weigh the stress
Of every chord, and see what may be gain'd
    By ear industrious, and attention meet;
        Misers of sound and syllable, no less     10
Than Midas of his coinage, let us be
    Jealous of dead leaves in the bay wreath crown,
So, if we may not let the Muse be free,
    She will be bound with garlands of her own.

The sonnet establishes its very own formal principle of semantically charged, not fully regularly correlated rhyme chains (a: lines 1, 4, 8 "chain'd/constrain'd/gain'd"; b: 2, 5, 9 "sweet/complete/meet"; c: 3, 7, 10 "loveliness/weigh the stress/no less"). It is certainly no accident that the central message of the poem emanates from the deviation from emerging regularity in line 6, and pronounces "Poesy/be/free" in chain d (6, 11, 13), while the final chain e (12, 14) remains incomplete and impure ("crown/own").

A sonnet like this amounts to a declaration of formal independence, and many highly innovative and individualized forms begin to emerge, among them highly elaborate bound-form variants of the **ode** (such as, for example, Keats's famous "Ode on a Grecian Urn," 1819) and the dazzling combination of *terza rima* lines in four sonnets (aba bcb cdc ded ee) in Shelley's "Ode to the West Wind" (1819). The latter is actually a good example of what Stuart Curran, following Wordsworth, has called "composite orders" (cf. Curran, *Poetic Form* 180–203), i.e. highly experimental forms trying to bring together, for example, the lyric and the epic as in Wordsworth's autobiographical *The Prelude*, written in blank verse and posthumously published in 1850, or the satirical and the epic as in Byron's never-ending *Don Juan* (1819–1824), written, in a dazzling display of formal craftsmanship and wit, in highly irreverent *ottava rima* stanzas (iambic pentameter, abababcc). The high degree of formal innovation and reflexivity indicated by these texts actually reaches its climax in the elaborate meta-commentary on all available discursive forms of the period formulated in Charlotte Smith's long blank verse meditation *Beachy Head* (1807), which has, after a long period of neglect, re-emerged as one of the most important texts of the revised and expanded canon of Romantic writing in recent years, shedding interesting light on the time-honoured classics in the field and standing next to Coleridge's "Kubla Khan"

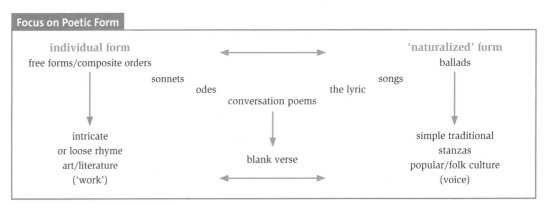

**Focus on Poetic Form**

individual form — 'naturalized' form

free forms/composite orders        ballads

sonnets        songs

odes    the lyric

conversation poems

intricate        simple traditional

or loose rhyme        stanzas

art/literature    blank verse    popular/folk culture

('work')        (voice)

(1797/98, pub. 1816) as another possible candidate for the highly productive genre of the "Romantic Fragment Poem" (cf. Levinson) which indicates how great the newly-won formal freedom was, even making incompleteness and open-endedness acceptable (cf. Schmitt).

## 2.4.4 | Other Genres

While the genre of poetry was busy establishing the new paradigm of imaginative literature with a pronounced **emphasis on aesthetic autonomy**, it took some time for the genres of fiction and drama with their stronger social and institutional embedding and their less pronounced personal and subjective dimensions to find their place in the new regime. Accordingly, they occupy a seemingly less central place in the field of English Romantic Literature, and the following remarks will indicate why this is the case and how fiction and drama can be related to the conceptualisation of Romanticism outlined in this chapter.

Fiction. In contrast to Germany, where the moniker 'the Romantic novel' designates a clearly identifiable set of texts and where the centrality of the novel as a genre for the new Romantic understanding of what (modern) literature should be about has been theoretically expounded at a very early stage by Friedrich Schlegel, there is no such thing as 'the Romantic novel' in England. Traditionally, the history of English fiction has been written as a history of **realist fiction**. When held against this norm, the second half of the eighteenth century has been perceived as an interruption in the emergence of the classic realism of the nineteenth century from its early eighteenth-century predecessors. While fictional genres and types of novels proliferated—among the most prominent period designations were sentimental fiction, Gothic novel, oriental tale, moral tale, Jacobin novel, society novel—there was little sense of a coherent synthesis which could be retrospectively integrated into smooth accounts of the history of the English novel. Against the background of the understanding of Romanticism put forward here, however, the two most prominent genres of fiction in the second half of the eighteenth century, the **Gothic novel** and **sentimental fiction**, can be clearly identified as being part of the subjective revolution of sensibility (cf. McGann, *Poetics of Sensibility*) which preceded Romanticism. Both were very much concerned with the subjective dimensions of feeling even to the point of irrationality, and it is interesting to note that both genres were to a certain extent relegated to the sphere of popular culture when realism re-asserted itself as a means of domesticating subjective experience very much along Wordsworthian lines in the novels of Jane Austen and Sir Walter Scott.

The Gothic novel was inaugurated by Horace Walpole with the publication of *The Castle of Otranto* in 1764. Ever since the Renaissance, the term 'Gothic' had been associated with a medieval and thus distinctly non-classical 'Northern' past, and in the eighteenth century this meaning was extended to cover anti-Enlightenment connotations. Walpole drew on these connotations in suggesting (in his preface to the second edition 1765) that he was trying to resuscitate the imaginative potential of the old type of romance which had been replaced by the realist novel in order to be able to get at the undomesticated, irrational aspects of human experience and desire. In this design, the supernatural serves as a pretext for an engagement with the unspoken and sometimes extreme thoughts and feelings of individuals; it is, in a sense, an artificial and imaginative replacement for nature in Edmund Burke's aesthetic programme of the awe-inspiring and potentially cathartic Sublime, and it is meant to work accordingly. And it did—*The Castle of Otranto* was a spectacular success which inspired numerous successors such as Clara Reeve's *The Old English Baron* (1777), Anne Radcliffe's *The Mysteries of Udolpho* (1794), and Matthew Lewis's *The Monk* (1796). By the end of the century, the genre had become so formulaic that a reviewer in *The Spirit of the Public Journals for 1797* offered a satirical recipe:

*Take*—An old castle, half of it ruinous.
A long gallery, with a great many doors, some secret ones.
Three murdered bodies, quite fresh.
[...]
Mix them together, in the form of three volumes, to be taken
at any of the watering places, before going to bed.

(qtd. in Greenblatt 602)

With Mary Shelley's *Frankenstein* (1818) marking a prominent exception, the Gothic novel had become a medium of entertainment rather than literature by the end of the eighteenth century, and the same applies to the varieties of **sentimental fiction**. The emerging larger reading public for fiction was by no means acknowledged as an adequate

Gothic novels were highly popular at the time.

audience for the new literature. As Coleridge witheringly comments retrospectively in his *Biographia Literaria* (1817): "For as to the devotees of the circulating libraries, I dare not compliment their *pass-time*, or rather *kill-time* with the name of *reading*" (ch. 3; emphasis in original). With this, Coleridge picks up where Wordsworth left off 17 years earlier, when he complained in his preface to the *Lyrical Ballads* that the "invaluable works of our elder Writers […] are driven into neglect by frantic novels, sickly and stupid German tragedies, and deluges of idle and extravagant stories in verse." It is against these developments that the 'invaluable works' of newer writers like Wordsworth and Coleridge are trying to carve out their cultural niche through claims of universal relevance—and while poetry is the medium of choice, fiction and drama seem to be part of the problem rather than answers to it.

**Drama.** While fiction was at least in its principal coordinates of communication comparable to poetry—both are based on texts written by individuals and then distributed in print and read privately by individuals again—, drama was suspicious to many Romantic writers because of its public institutional framing. This fault-line can be nicely illustrated with the help of the German word '**Vorstellung**,' which covers both '**performance**' and '**imagination**': Quite clearly, drama did not easily fit the emergent paradigm of modern literature with its ideological preferences as indicated in the chart below, and the rich theatre scene of the eighteenth century with its emphasis on spectacle did not easily accommodate the interiority-oriented priorities of Romantic writers. The perceived gap between dramatists and literary writers in the new sense was never fully bridged, and while some Romantic writers wrote successfully for the stage—most notably Elizabeth Inchbald with the farces *Appearance Is Against Them* (1785) and *A Mogul Tale* (1788) and the comedies *I'll Tell You What* (1786), *Such*

*Things Are* (1788) and *Everyone Has His Fault* (1793), as well as Joanna Baillie with her huge cycle of *Plays on the Passions* (1798–1812)—their works did not really make it into the canon of literature while the dramatic works of posthumously famous Romantic poets such as Wordsworth's *The Borderers* (1796–1799) or Coleridge's *Remorse* (1813) were not successful on the stage and remain marginal to their oeuvre. Nevertheless, Romantic writers were fascinated or even obsessed with the theatre, but many of their dramatically oriented or inspired works remained safely in the imaginative realm of either **dramatic poetry** or **closet drama** (i.e. drama for reading rather than performance) such as, famously, Byron's *Manfred: A Dramatic Poem* (1816/17) or Shelley's *Prometheus Unbound* (1820).

## 2.4.5 | Historicising Romanticism

It remains the challenging task of Romantic studies to integrate this varied field of literary practice with related fields of artistic practice (such as painting and music) and other cultural realms (such as science, politics, and popular culture) in a way which no longer imposes the ideological predispositions of Romanticism itself on the historical complexity of the period in question. In this respect, the study of Romanticism is clearly part of, as well as a continuation of, the larger project of establishing a **New Eighteenth Century**. At the same time, and in clear contrast to the aesthetic self-descriptions of the Augustan Age which have clearly become obsolete, it is crucial to acknowledge the formative effect that the cultural idiom of Romanticism has had on aesthetic and cultural practices ever since, so that all attempts at historicising Romanticism and the aesthetic are inevitably caught up in a certain degree of cultural complicity with their object of study.

'Vorstellung'

| theatre | literature |
| --- | --- |
| performance, spectacle | imagination |
| proliferation of genres | synthesis as ideal |
| the actor as star | the author as genius |
| institutional dependence | autonomy |
| public and social constraints | private individuality, freedom |

Drama between Theatre and Literature

## Select Bibliography

**Abrams, M. H.** *The Mirror and the Lamp: Romantic Theory and the Critical Tradition.* New York: Norton, 1953.

**Abrams, M. H.** *Natural Supernaturalism: Tradition and Revolution in Romantic Literature.* New York: Norton, 1971.

**Abrams, M. H.** "Structure and Style in the Greater Romantic Lyric." *The Correspondent Breeze: Essays on English Romanticism.* By Meyer H. Abrams. New York: Norton, 1984. 76–108.

**Bode, Christoph.** *Selbst-Begründungen: Diskursive Konstruktion von Identität in der britischen Romantik I: Subjektive Identität.* Trier: WVT, 2008.

**Breuer, Rolf.** *Englische Romantik: Literatur und Kultur 1760–1830.* Munich: Fink, 2012.

**Chandler, James, ed.** *The Cambridge History of English Romantic Literature.* Cambridge: Cambridge University Press, 2009.

**Curran, Stuart.** *Poetic Form and British Romanticism.* New York: Oxford University Press, 1986.

**Curran, Stuart, ed.** *The Cambridge Companion to British Romanticism.* 2nd ed. Cambridge: Cambridge University Press, 2010.

**Fay, Elisabeth A.** *A Feminist Introduction to Romanticism.* Malden: Blackwell, 1998.

**Ferber, Michael.** *Romanticism: A Very Short Introduction.* Oxford: Oxford University Press, 2010.

**Ferguson, Frances.** "On the Numbers of Romanticisms." *English Literary History* 58 (1991): 471–98.

**Greenblatt, Stephen, et al., eds.** *The Norton Anthology of English Literature.* 8th ed. 2 vols. New York: Norton, 2006.

**Josipovici, Gabriel.** "I Heard the Murmur and the Murmuring Sound." *What Ever Happened to Modernism.* By Gabriel Josipovici. New Haven: Yale University Press, 2010. 48–62.

**Levinson, Marjorie.** *The Romantic Fragment Poem: A Critique of Form.* Chapel Hill: University of North Carolina Press, 1986.

**Lovejoy, A. O.** "On the Discrimination of Romanticisms." *PMLA* 39 (1924): 229–53.

**Mason, Michael, ed.** *Lyrical Ballads.* By William Wordsworth and Samuel Taylor Coleridge. 2nd ed. Harlow: Pearson Longman, 2007.

**McCalman, Iain, ed.** *An Oxford Companion to the Romantic Age: British Culture: 1776–1832.* Oxford: Oxford University Press, 1999.

**McGann, Jerome.** *The Poetics of Sensibility: A Revolution in Literary Style.* Oxford: Clarendon, 1996.

**McGann, Jerome.** *The Romantic Ideology: A Critical Investigation.* Chicago: University of Chicago Press, 1983.

**O'Flinn, Paul.** *How to Study Romantic Poetry.* 2nd ed. Basingstoke: Palgrave, 2001.

**Reinfandt, Christoph.** *Englische Romantik: Eine Einführung.* Berlin: Schmidt, 2008.

**Roe, Nicholas, ed.** *Romanticism: An Oxford Guide.* Oxford: Oxford University Press, 2005.

**Ruston, Sharon.** *Romanticism.* London: Continuum, 2007.

**Schmitt, Franziska.** *Method in the Fragments: Fragmentarische Strategien in der englischen und deutschen Romantik.* Trier: WVT, 2005.

**Thompson, John B.** *The Media and Modernity: A Social History of the Media.* Cambridge: Polity, 1995.

**Wellek, René.** "The Concept of Romanticism in Literary Scholarship." 1949. *Concepts of Criticism.* By René Wellek. New Haven: Yale University Press, 1963. 128–98.

*Christoph Reinfandt*

## 2.5 | The Victorian Age

### 2.5.1 | Overview

The Victorian Age (1832–1901) carries central characteristic features of Romanticism forward, although Victorian subjectivity presents itself as far less excessive than the striving for the infinite inherent in the Romantic cult of subjectivity. The Victorian self is constituted intersubjectively in a relation of self and society, but for the most part this interaction turns out to be a precarious one. Despite the progress in technology, social reform, individual freedom, and independence in the Victorian era, by the end of the nineteenth century, the formation of an individual self was accompanied by all the psychological drawbacks of modern humanity: estrangement from the world, **alienation**, **disorientation**, **loss of meaning**. This impression is further enhanced by the intensification of **historicism** in all disciplines in the nineteenth century, which since the cornerstone of the French Revolution has conceived of human beings, culture, and society as transient and ever-changing phenomena. While Romanticism, in a famous definition by Henry H. H. Remak, has been looked upon as "the attempt to heal the break in the universe" via imagination and "the painful awareness of dualism coupled with the urge to resolve it in organic monism" (35), by the end of the Victorian Age, such synthesising has to a large extent become impossible; in fact, by that time, the wound of the 'break in the universe' is gaping wider than ever before.

Social and political developments. The historical period of 'Victorianism' owes its name to the extraordinarily long life and reign of **Queen Victoria**, who succeeded William IV on the throne in 1837. While the time span marked by Victoria's enthronement and her death in 1901 is thus rather a coincidence, it would also be well justified to make the Victorian Age start five years earlier with the political landmark of the First Reform Bill in 1832. In a more generic denotation of the term 'Victorian Age' or 'Victorianism,' the Reform Bill meant the beginning of a new age predominated by the power of middle-class economic interests, as it vitalised the British political landscape in the period of the **Industrial Revolution**, which started in the mid-eighteenth century and reached its climax in nineteenth-century England and then spread all over Europe, the United States, and Japan. The bill made the number of citizens entitled to vote rise from 400,000 to 650,000; many, though not all, of the so-called 'rotten boroughs' (small boroughs with so few inhabitants that they were felt to be overrepresented in parliament) were disenfranchised, while the new big industrial cities of the north (i.e. Manchester, Birmingham, Sheffield, Leeds) were granted boroughs and the right to vote for representatives in parliament. With the benefit of hindsight, the bill constitutes the beginning of a modern democracy in Britain, although it falls far short of solving all the problems inherent in the Industrial Revolution and the change from an agricultural to an industrial society. Even though a first attempt at universal suffrage was made, 95 % of the population (all women amongst them) still did not have the vote. Huge social inequalities could not be alleviated because the right to vote was bound to the holding of property worth the still respectable sum of £10. Whereas the bill implied that aristocratic voices feared that the Reform Act gave too much strength to the House of Commons, it also enhanced a split between the working classes and the middle class, which gave rise to the **Chartist Movement**, the first working class mass movement that aimed at political reform between 1838 and 1848. Named after The People's Charter in 1838, its beginnings were among such skilled labourers as shoemakers, printers, and tailors. For achieving their objectives of universal male suffrage and secret ballots, for instance, the Chartists endorsed strikes and did not shy away from using violence.

Queen Victoria of Great Britain and Ireland, Empress of India (1819–1901)

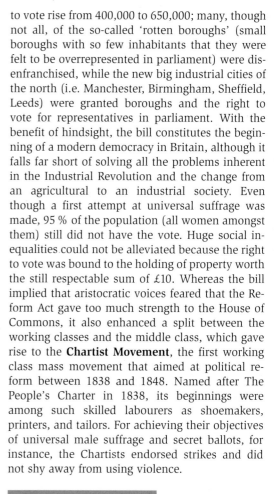

**Timeline: The Victorian Age**

| | |
|---|---|
| **1832** | First Reform Bill |
| **1838** | 'People's Charter' by the Chartist Movement |
| **1851** | Great Exhibition of Science and Industry at the Crystal Palace, London |
| **1859** | Charles Darwin publishes *Origin of Species* |
| **1867** | Karl Marx publishes *Das Kapital*; Second Reform Bill |
| **1870** | Married Women's Property Act |
| **1877** | Queen Victoria made Empress of India |
| **1891** | Free elementary education |
| **1899** | Anglo-Boer War |
| **1901** | Death of Queen Victoria |

**Periodisation.** Historians have subdivided the Victorian Age into three major phases: **Early-Victorian** (1830–1848), **Mid- or High-Victorian** (1848–1870), and **Late-Victorian** (1870/80–1901). Surveying the entire nineteenth century worldwide, the German historian Jürgen Osterhammel has argued that the period of 1830 until 1880 constitutes a time-span which, at least for Europe, concentrates all the features generally held as distinguishing the nineteenth century worldwide. By contrast, for Osterhammel, the 1880s mean the turning point of the Fin de Siècle, which arguably lasts until the First World War. In a pan-European context then, 'Victorianism' denotes the economical and military predominance Britain held in the world. It is also justified to speak of epoch-making characteristics of the Victorian age, as Britain was the first country to bring the rational use of resources to perfection (Osterhammel 102–16). Since the 1830s, the age of fossil fuels had begun, and man- as well as animal-power were successively replaced by organic energy (coal). Looms, spindles, pumps, ships, and railways were powered by steam-engines, which allowed for mass production and turned Victorian times into an age of speed, acceleration, interconnectedness, national integration and imperial control (Queen Victoria became Empress of India in 1876).

The early phase of the Victorian age was characterised by severe economical crises, which brought Britain to the brink of revolution. Social grievances and inequality were blatant, the industrial labourers had to face dramatically increasing pauperisation, which lead to Chartist uprisings in 1839 and 1849, the introduction of the 10-hour workday in 1847, and—after more than ten Factory Acts—the restriction of child labour to the minimum age of twelve in 1901. Since the first reform bill, a continuous process of further political reform had involved the Second and Third Reform Bills (1867 and 1884), the latter of which at least bestowed voting rights to all adult males. It seems remarkable that, in the seven decades of the Victorian age, the will to democratic reform pervaded all political parties, conservatives ('Tories') as well as liberals ('Whigs,' later 'Liberals'). The mid- or high-Victorian years can be seen as years of consolidation, prosperity, and flourishing agriculture, trade and industry. If Victorian times ever had the connotation of an optimistic look towards the future, such optimism would be grounded in this middle period. London saw the Great Exhibition in 1851, compulsory education was introduced in 1870, standard literacy was almost universal by 1900, voting rights were given to the (male) working classes, Britain was the world's most powerful banker, had the biggest merchant fleet in the world, and, by the end of the century, the British Empire had also taken hold of much of Africa reaching out from the Cape to Cairo (see map).

**The way of progress and the sense of crisis.** Thus, the Victorian Age marks a **period of change** unprecedented in history. The seven decades until Queen Victoria's death witnessed an enormous expansion of trade, commerce, manufacturing and economic growth. London replaced Paris as the centre of European civilisation, and its population grew from two to six and a half million inhabitants within Victoria's reign. The society changed from largely rural landownership to an urban economy based on trade and manufacturing (see Abrams and Greenblatt 2:1043–65). On the one hand, these developments entailed such 'wonders' of science, technology, and urbanisation as the interconnection of the globe with telegraph and rail-

Child labour in the Industrial Revolution

The British Empire 1812/1914

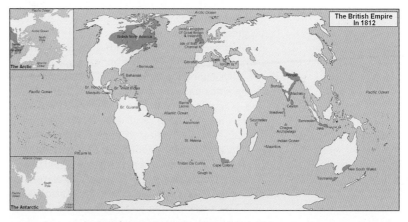

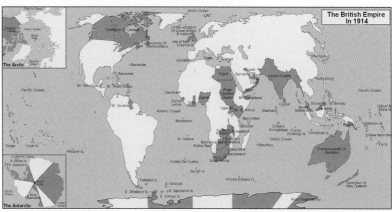

## Timeline: Important Inventions

| 1814 | steam locomotive | George Stephenson | British |
|------|------------------|-------------------|---------|
| 1825 | electromagnet | William Sturgeon | British |
| 1831 | electric dynamo | Michael Faraday | British |
| 1835 | mechanical calculator | Charles Babbage | British |
| 1837 | telegraph | Samuel Morse | American |
| 1839 | hydrogen fuel cell | William Robert Grove | British |
| 1855 | sewing machine motor | Isaac Singer | American |
| 1866 | dynamite | Alfred Nobel | Swedish |
| 1876 | telephone | Alexander Graham Bell | British |
| 1877 | cylinder phonograph | Thomas Edison | American |
| 1877 | first moving pictures | Eadward Muybridge | British |
| 1878 | electric light bulb | Joseph Wilson Swan | British |
| 1880 | seismograph | John Milne | British |
| 1882 | machine gun | Hiram Stevens Maxim | American |
| 1885/86 | automobile | C. Benz/G. Daimler | German |
| 1887 | radio waves | Heinrich Hertz | German |
| 1895 | x-ray diagnosis | Wilhelm C. Roentgen | German |
| 1895 | cinematograph | Lumière Brothers | French |

way, and were further fuelled by ground-breaking discoveries and inventions which changed the path of economical and historical civilisation and progress (see timeline). By the end of the century, steam power had been put to full exploit, electricity had been introduced, the railways had changed the physiognomy of the British landscape, and steam-ships had conquered the ocean, and a **second phase industrial revolution** based on innovation in chemistry and electrical-engineering started. All this meant a triumph of progress and doubtlessly changed human life for the better. On the other hand, however, the severe social and economical problems due to the unregulated nature of the development became obvious to everyone. The late Victorian phase from 1880 onwards changed the prevailing optimism into a more sceptical, pessimistic and often almost despaired world-view which permeated the economy, politics, and especially the arts and literature. The Victorians could no longer hide the fact that the social, technological, and economic progress, firstly, could not do away with the widening gap between rich and poor and that, secondly, the human psyche was not able to bear up against this rapid change of society and experience. As early as 1850, in his "Stanzas From the Grande Chartreuse," **Matthew Arnold** describes a feeling of

Wandering between two worlds, one dead,
The other powerless to be born,

With nowhere yet to rest my head,
Like these, on earth I wait forlorn.
Their faith, my tears, the world deride—
I come to shed them at their side. (lines 85–90)

When he further on in the poem speaks of a "gloom profound," a "holy pain," an "exploded dream" and "melancholy," he gives expression to a thorough sense of spiritual crisis which permeated Victorian sensibilities and which bled out profusely in late Victorian times—a feeling of utter displacement, alienation, and indeed melancholy, an uneasy sense that something was irretrievably lost on the way of progress. This sense of crisis concerned Victorian psychology, economy, and foreign affairs where Britain had to face major drawbacks. Germany, for instance, began to threaten Britain's predominant position in trade and industry. After the Civil War, the United States of America developed and spread railways from the east to the west coast, unlocking new ways of transportation of products from there, and hence put pressure on industrial markets; likewise, the United States and Canada were able to participate in the grain market worldwide, which meant lower grain prices and a totally new scale of productivity in agriculture, which Britain could not even dream to match. Severe economical depressions followed in Britain in the 1870s, which led many people to emigrate. Britain also had to pay the high price of rebellions and ill-fated wars for being the world's most powerful imperial power: The

'**Irish Question**,' for instance, remained unresolved. England had shamefully neglected its imperial duties during the Great Famine (1845–1848) and hence further instigated the Irish desire for Home Rule, which lead to the Easter Rising in 1916, the Anglo-Irish War (1919–1921) and the Anglo-Irish Treaty and the partition of Ireland in 1922. Furthermore, the disasters of the Indian Mutiny, the Jamaica Rebellion, the massacre of Karthoum in the Sudan, and the Boer Wars, bitter guerrilla wars in which the British sought to annex two colonies in the south of Africa, were very much unlikely to generate much confidence in the omnipotence of the 'age of the first capitalist globalisation' and the 'prime time of the capital' (see Osterhammel 44).

## 2.5.2 | The Spirit of the Age: Doubts, Unresolved Tensions, and the Triumph of Time

The spirit of the Victorian age can therefore best be characterised as a **period of transition**, of unresolved tensions, frictions, anxieties, irreconcilable differences, and contradictions. These can be accounted for in every area of public and private life, and these are also reflected in Victorian literature and culture: Pessimism stands besides optimism, the harking back to the past alongside positive and negative views of the future, fatalism next to activism and social criticism, utter conservatism next to innovation and experiment, enthusiasm towards the imperial mission adjacent to criticism of it. Even with regard to ethics, the Victorian insistence on middle-class values such as the sacrosanct family, rigid gender relations, moral earnestness and duty, involving a severe denial of treating sexuality openly, found their (hypocritical) counterparts and flipsides in a discrimination and even pathologisation of a self-conscious female identity that would deviate from the gender norm. By the end of the century, the allegedly domesticated subconscious had fully struck back when a new, modernist late-Victorian attitude towards life and sex had paved its way into the twentieth century while it was at the same time stigmatised as '**decadence**' or, in the words of the notorious Austrian critic Max Nordau, even as "degeneration." The reasons for this contradictory attitude toward life indicative of Victorian life are manifold and can be traced further by looking at the major intellectual trends of the time.

### Utilitarianism

The ethical concept of utilitarianism is widespread in nineteenth-century ethics, social philosophy, law and economics. Though traces of utilitarian thought can be found in eighteenth-century philosophy (de Mandeville, Hobbes, Adam Smith, and others), its systematic conceptualisation hearkens back to the English philosophers Jeremy Bentham and James Mill. It is further developed by the latter's son, John Stuart Mill. In his *Introduction to the Principles of Morals and Legislation* Bentham claims that the penultimate aim of utility is a purely instrumental one—the best possible maximising of benefit and pleasure for both individual and communal interests. In utilitarian ethics, actions are not measured by inner motives, but exclusively by their consequences. What is more, the outcome of such actions must be rationally calculable and empirically verifiable. This is to guarantee the **maximum of happiness** for all humanity. Legislation is deemed necessary in order to remind the individual of his communal responsibility. In order to be able to influence individual behaviour accordingly, this includes 'sanctions' such as affection or thankfulness on the one hand, but also, if necessary, punishment on the other. Bentham even transferred his instrumental ethics and their empirical verifiability onto the architecture of prisons when he designed the panopticon-prison in an entirely utilitarian spirit, a circular structure with an inspection house at its centre which enables the prison staff to observe the inmates at all times, who could never be sure whether they were being watched or not (for an illustration see entry II.4). From a utilitarian, instrumental point of view, all this makes perfect sense, as it leads to a reduction of costs for staff and produced constant fear among the inmates— yet at the same time entails unbearable psychological strain and dreadful psychological consequences (see Foucault). Thus, while this concept may be in accordance with utilitarian rules, it is obviously counteracting modern ideas of justice and even a vague idea of a prison reforming (rather than breaking) its delinquents. In *Utilitarianism* John Stuart Mill defended the utilitarian idea that any right was based on the idea of a general utility, yet he also saw the clash of utilitarian rules with justice and that individual rights must be considered regardless of the consequences for the common good. Hence, he somewhat mitigated rule utilitarianism into a weaker form when he ac-

Jeremy Bentham and John Stuart Mill: Proponents of utilitarianism

knowledged that certain circumstances allowed for an exception to the rule: saving a life, for instance, might possibly necessitate lying or stealing in order to satisfy the rule of striving for greatest happiness of all.

It cannot come as a surprise that the utilitarian principle of utility, that any arbitrary action is approved of or dismissed ('sanctioned') by its tendency to increase the happiness of the party whose interests are at issue, would seem cold-hearted and materialistic and that it could easily be considered a 'carte blanche' justifying ethical egotism. The entrepreneurs and factory-owners of the Industrial Revolution could readily use utilitarian principles to legitimate a **laissez-faire capitalism** relying on the power of unregulated markets for the 'common' good of secure economic growth and international competitiveness while utterly neglecting the individual conditions of work and health of their labourers. One of the most influential and groundbreaking publications of the Victorian age was **Karl Marx's** *Capital: Critique of Political Economy*. Marx argued that capitalism was ultimately tantamount to the exploitation of labour: the less you paid your worker the higher your profit and potential surplus value would turn out. In the capitalist process of growing mass-production, Marx saw work turn to abstract work, alienating worker and work from each other and reducing individual work force to the commodity of human capital. Marx severely attacked both Bentham and Mill quite consistently for their utilitarian ethics and ridiculed the former as a "genius of middle-class stupidity" (492, my trans.). Characteristically too, there is no single renowned Victorian literary work of art that would opt for utilitarian ethics. Certainly the most acrimonious reckoning of utilitarianism is **Charles Dickens's** novel **Hard Times**, which portrayed the industrial workers as mere 'hands' in the eyes of their employers and which satirically castigated the utilitarian understanding of education of schoolmaster Thomas Gradgrind and teacher Mr M'Choakumchild and their absurd insistence on the instrumental measurability of educational success as the mindless rehashing of positivist facts and, indeed, the utilitarian 'cho(a)king' of all creative fancy and imagination.

*Critique of capitalism*

'Now, what I want is, Facts. Teach these boys and girls nothing but Facts. Facts alone are wanted in life. Plant nothing else, and root out everything else. You can only form the minds of reasoning animals upon Facts: nothing else will ever be of any service to them. This is the principle on which I bring up my own children, and this is the principle on which I bring up these children. Stick to Facts, sir!' (*Hard Times* ch. 1)

The tension between liberal and conservative utilitarian thinking and its manifold critique represents an unstable equilibrium pervading the Victorian age. It explains the coexistence of modernisation, technological progress, capitalist interest, successful efforts for reform (i.e. Reform Bills, New Poor Law, Custody of Infant Act, trade-unions), and also (late-)Victorian, post-Industrial Revolution pessimism. It should not be concealed, however, that this conflict lasts and that utilitarian ethics have influenced philosophical, political and economical thinking until today (i.e. Thatcherism).

## Darwinism, Theory of Evolution, Religion

**Charles Darwin.** In the entire human cultural history there are only very few scientists and scholars who have changed the self-understanding of humankind as profoundly and irreversibly as Charles Darwin has done. Building on earlier research done by Carl von Linné, who had also doubted the constancy of species, Immanuel Kant, Jean Baptiste de Lamarck, and Charles Lyell's *Principles of Geology*, Darwin's **On the Origin of Species** constitutes a culmination point of historicism, a world view which had begun in the eighteenth century, was celebrated by the French Revolution and Romanticism and then truly spread with the systematic rise of the humanities and sciences in the nineteenth century. When Darwin returned from his five-year journey on the HMS Beagle (1831–1836) and started analysing the observations he had made of flora, fauna, and geology, he realised how far his findings had taken him away from biblical genesis. He felt that his theories came close to "confessing a murder" (of God), and conscience had taken him away from publishing his findings for more than twenty years. Darwin's central thesis is a twofold one: all species have a common origin and, in a process of transmutation, no species in nature is ever constant.

On the contrary, all species have emerged and reside in an evolutionary process over tremendous periods of time. This insight discards all Christian belief in divine creation. Darwin defines the principle of natural selection as the preserving of survivable variants and, at the same time, as the extinction of less survivable, disadvantageous, or even harmful variants of a species. Both processes—survival and extinction—follow a mechanism in which organisms better adjusted ('fitter') to their surroundings have a greater chance for survival and for the reproduction of the species than less adjusted ones who, in the course of evolution, are superseded and eventually die out. The process of natural selection, therefore, is subject to a fight for survival, a 'struggle for existence.' Darwin knew that '**natural selection**' and 'struggle for existence' were complex metaphors only, which denoted abstract processes completely cut off from human influence and teleological action. Darwin's work unsettled the Victorian society to its core, as the Victorians all of a sudden peered into the abyss of a **godless universe**, in which human beings are only minor characters, barely more than a complex accident in an evolutionary process beyond their control. Darwin himself always believed that, by using their intelligence, human beings were able to face the conditions of their biotope and thus reach for ultimate perfection. The biologist Thomas Henry Huxley, by contrast, in a much more pessimist fashion, also took a retrograde evolution of mankind into consideration, and the late-Victorian winged words of 'degeneration,' 'decadence,' and 'depression' among other things reflected this regressive, uncertain awareness of life generated by the theory of evolution.

Social Darwinism. In a much different and, from today's perspective, altogether pejorative way, the term 'Social Darwinism' has transferred Darwin's ideas of natural selection of species to the realms of sociology, economics, and politics. Indeed it was the eminent sociologist Herbert Spencer, who coined the phrase of the '**survival of the fittest**.' Thomas Robert Malthus had argued earlier in his *Essay on the Principle of Population* that distress in a society (and especially in the working classes) was due to overpopulation and that the benefit of a whole society was dependent upon holding the increase of a population within resource limits. Social Darwinism, then, takes Darwin's metaphor of the 'struggle for existence' literally as a justification for social inequalities: Some individuals (groups, nations, races) are able to support themselves, others are not, and this is merely considered a matter of being 'fitter' (i.e. better adapting to the circumstances) and finding the right survival tactics. It goes without saying that laissez-faire capitalism, imperialism, or racism would unhesitatingly luxuriate in Social Darwinist settings.

Secularisation. Not only have Darwinism and Evolution Theory (generally in unison with the proceeding secularisation brought about by the Industrial Revolution and capitalism) cast most severe doubt on the existence of God in that they literally contradicted the belief in a biblical genesis of the world and of human beings, they also made God "disappear" (Miller) in a figurative sense. Darwinist thought, just like historicism in general, has assumed "the relativity of any particular life and culture" (Miller 9), stable world views are all of a sudden replaced by a multitude of perspectives, belief systems, gradually corroding a social and moral consensus and threatening to plunge individuals into an abyss of psychological nothingness and existential isolation. The historicist understanding of the world ultimately amounts to the doubting of the validity of any world view or philosophy, the interrogation of institutions, beliefs, laws, morals, and customs, and the awareness that the articles of faith could no longer be brought to satisfactory proof (see, for example, Miller 12–13; Houghton 95–180; Gilmour 63–110). Phenomena of secularisation and modernisation such as a growing indifference towards religious matters and agnosticism were evidentially hollowing out the Anglican Church.

Religious renewal. At the same time, however, the Victorian Age witnessed powerful attempts at religious renewal. The Church of England in the mid-nineteenth century consisted of three major branches: Low Church, Broad Church, and High Church. Religious life also saw protestant groups outside the Church of England, known as Nonconformists or Dissenters, such as Methodists, Baptists, or Congregationalists. The Low Church movement of the Evangelicals, for instance, was responsible for the abolition of slavery in the British Empire in 1833, and very influentially advocated for a strict Christian life following severe Puritan standards demonising all wordliness. Dogmatism, rigidity, duty, and earnestness (Houghton) were the moral keywords of the age intentionally set against the alienating forces of religious and social crisis, rigidly tabooing human sexuality and, consequently, accounting for what is today almost proverbially called '**Victorian prudery**.'

Though human passion is hardly to be controlled by either concealment or censorship, the Evangelical movement was the primary source of the revival of the ethic of purity. Furthermore, since the mid-1830s, religious life in the Victorian age had also witnessed High Church reform, which accentuated the Catholic principles within the Anglican Church and opted for a rehabilitation of tra-

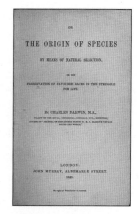

Title page of the first printing of *On the Origin of Species* by Charles Darwin (1859)

In the Victorian home swarming with children sex was a secret. It was the skeleton in the parental chamber. No one mentioned it. Any untoward questions were answered with a white lie (it was the great age of the stork) or a shocked rebuke. From none of his elders—parent, teacher, or minister—did the Victorian child hear 'so much as one word in explanation of the true nature and functions of the reproductive organs.' This conspiracy of silence was partly a mistaken effort to protect the child, especially the boy, from temptation (initially from masturbation, which was condemned on grounds of health as well as morals), but at bottom it sprang from a personal feeling of revulsion. For the sexual act was associated by many wives only with a duty and by most husbands with a necessary if pleasurable yielding to one's baser nature: by few, therefore, with an innocent and joyful experience. The silence, which first aroused in the child a vague sense of shame, was in fact a reflection of parental shame, and one suspects that some women, at any rate, would have been happy if the stork had been a reality. (Houghton 353)

dition and authority. The most important movement in the context is known as the **Oxford Movement** or **Tractarianism**. Following the tenets of their major representatives John Keble, Edward Bouverie Pusey, and John Henry Cardinal Newman, who all taught at Oxford University, the tractarians argued against liberal tendencies and attempted to renew the Church by, for instance, strengthening medieval elements of religious and Church ritual. Both Evangelicalism and the Oxford Movement embodied a counterculture to the prevailing sense of doubt in the Victorian age—sheet anchors, as it were, in the stormy "Sea of Faith" Matthew Arnold described in his poem "Dover Beach" (1867; see interpretation below).

**Uncertainty without scepticism.** In order not to confuse these anxieties with the relativism of a postmodernist bend, for instance, it must be noted that the alleged sense of doubt which characterised the Victorian age only gradually changed to downright scepticism. The feeling of arbitrariness, relativity, and historical contingency grew from the 1830s to the Fin de Siècle. The early- and mid-Victorian sentiment of doubt was felt by people who were uneasy and truly baffled about what to believe in, or how to cope with a world which was—with breath-taking speed—bringing about a vast increase of scientific and historical knowledge. Some lost their belief in God, others did not; some lamented the loss of faith, others, like Tennyson, quietly acquiesced: "So be it. It is God's will. I still believe, though I cannot see. And I have faith that God will be waiting for me when I have crossed the bar" (qtd. in Miller 13). Until 1870,

doubts never reached that epistemological vantage point when the mind was no longer regarded as a valid instrument of finding the truth.

The loss of faith and manifold attempts at its renewal constituted a characteristically unstable equilibrium. Victorians were uncertain about their position in their society, they were uncertain about the new theories they were confronted with, but, then, their principal capacity to arrive at truth rationally was not fundamentally questioned—in fact, the consensus that truth is attainable somehow is the one Victorian certainty left, politically, sociologically, economically, and, as we shall see later, aesthetically. John Ruskin argued against the utilitarian spirit of the age by turning to art history, and Matthew Arnold, otherwise thoroughly pessimistic about the signs of the times, adhered to the redeeming value of culture and still points out in 1869, at a time when high-Victorianism was well on the wane:

Now, then, is the moment for culture to be of service, culture which believes in making reason and the will of God prevail, believes in perfection, is the study and pursuit of perfection, and is no longer debarred, by a rigid invincible exclusion of whatever is new, from getting acceptance for its ideas, simply because they are new.
The moment this view of culture is seized, the moment it is regarded not solely as the endeavour to see *things as they are*, to draw towards a knowledge of *the universal order* which seems to be intended and aimed at in the world, and which it is a man's happiness to go along with or his misery to go counter to,—to learn, in short, *the will of God*,—the moment, I say, culture is considered not merely as the endeavour to see and learn this, but as the endeavour, also, to make it prevail, the moral, social, and beneficent character of culture becomes manifest. (Arnold 32; my emphasis)

It was not until about 1870 when this belief in "things as they are" and in the existence of a "universal order of things" was more and more shattered, quite in proportion to how the **relativity of knowledge** and the **subjective character of thought** were likewise enhanced. It no longer seemed a question of what unmistakably and immutably *is*, but in what particular light a situation, a character, a culture, or the world appear. More and more gradually, the **autonomy of consciousness** was established, which decidedly contradicted the causal connection of what people saw happening around them and which produced broken images of countless perspectives in which ultimate truths were dissolving by degrees. Graphic examples of this process are Vincent van Gogh's famous impressionist sunflower paintings produced between 1888 and 1889. The meticulous differences making each painting a singular object reveal that there is potentially a myriad of perspectives of looking at a sunflower, reflecting upon multiple attitudes towards life.

## Victorian Gender Relations

This transformation of attitude gradually yet fundamentally affects the construction of gender roles as well, especially the view of women in the Victorian Age. The relation of men and women was traditionally characterised by **separate spheres**, which, most of all, can be regarded as an implication of the Industrial Revolution. While formerly family members worked side by side in and around their home, the shift from such home-based activities to factory production made men leave the house to earn their wages and women stay at home to perform (unpaid) domestic work. In Victorian society, marriage, domesticity, and motherhood were largely considered well sufficient emotional fulfilment for women. The role model of this attitude was Queen Victoria herself, whose marriage to her beloved husband Albert was mostly centred around the private sphere of Balmoral Castle, surrounded by their many children, suggesting to the people an image of marital bliss and a haven of homely comfort. Following the evangelical ideal of constancy in marriage and woman's innate purity and goodness, an idealisation of woman occurred that envisaged women as dutiful, subordinate, virtuous, comforting, passive yet thoroughly busy, upright and morally superior, albeit hardly human, creatures. Another eponymous role model was what Coventry Patmore in the (otherwise minor) poem of the same title called the "The Angel in the House":

*Man must be pleased*; but *him to please*
*Is woman's pleasure*; down the gulf
Of his condoled necessities
*She casts her best, she flings herself.*
How often flings for nought, and yokes          5
Her heart to an icicle or whim,
Whose each impatient word provokes
Another, not from her, but him;
While she, too *gentle* even to force
His penitence by *kind* replies,          10
*Waits* by, expecting his remorse,
With *pardon* in her pitying eyes;
And if he once, by shame oppress'd,
A comfortable word confers,

*She leans and weeps against his breast,*          15
*And seems to think the sin was hers;*
Or any eye to see her charms,
At any time, she's still his wife,
Dearly devoted to his arms;
She loves with love that cannot tire;          20
And when, ah woe, she loves alone,
Through passionate duty love springs higher,
As grass grows taller round a stone.
(bk 1, Canto 9, Prelude 1; my emphasis)

Home, here, is obviously a refuge from the chaos of politics, business, public services or factory life the man is involved in, and the woman, or rather the wife, is the man's pleasurable, condoling, emotional, patient, gentle, kind, pardoning, self-sacrificing redeemer (see illustration on p. 64). The social function of woman as wife, mother, and domestic manager precluded women from work outside of the home, although since by far not all middle-class families used to have servants, household work often involved physical labour such as carrying water, washing, ironing, hemming of bed-linen, which turned out to be difficult enough in women's dresses, when corsets made work or any other physical activity an at least cumbersome undertaking and often left little time for Victorian female pastimes such as embroidery and playing the piano. The redeeming function of women was seen even on the grander scale of social life when many associations—the Sunday Schools, for instance—and institutions for the care of the sick or for orphans were put on women's shoulders.

The normative understanding of what a successful female 'career' was supposed to look like, the ideal of woman's purity, the domestication and tabooing of all levity, sexual impulses, and personal freedom in favour of chastity, duty, and earnestness yielded a terrible, though self-evident, downside. With the hindsight of all our present Post-Freudian psychoanalytical knowledge, those taboos can appear as hardly more than (hypocritical) flights from open secrets. Obviously, the virtual deification of the '**Angel in the House**' and its ensuing cult of virtue and earnestness could not do away with adultery, seduction, and countless illegitimate children born by unmarried women. Once 'fallen' (from the path of virtue), these women led the lives of outcasts with little else to turn to for support than prostitution. 50,000 prostitutes were recorded in England and Scotland in 1850, in London there were 8,000 prostitutes alone. The French historian Hippolyte Taine indi-

"The Angel in the House"

Victorian Family
Scene (left)

"The New Woman—
Wash Day" (right)

cated that in the Haymarket and the Strand "every hundred step one jostles twenty harlots" (qtd. in Houghton 366).

Though it is conventional in its conclusion, Alfred Lord Tennyson's narrative poem "The Princess" centres on a princess, who founds a university for women where men are not allowed to enter and articulates many of the injustices suffered by women. While the Prince's father unequivocally swears by the separate spheres men and women are meant to inhabit—"Man with the head and woman with the heart: / Man to command and woman to obey; / All else confusion"—Princess Ida, by contrast, embodies the "New Woman" who rebels against legal and social bondage, boredom in being locked up at home, and who is passionate about equality in education and professional careers:

Everywhere
Two heads in council, two beside the hearth,
Two in the tangled business of the world,
Two in the liberal offices of life,
Two plummets dropt for one to sound the abyss
Of science and the secret of the mind;
Musician, painter, sculptor, critic, more.
(Tennyson, "The Princess" lines 155–161)

Types of Victorian femininity

It cannot be concealed that it took feminism a long time, until the last quarter of the nineteenth century, to gain true momentum in the Victorian age. Carrying forward Mary Wollstonecraft's argument in favour of the equality of the sexes in *A Vindication of the Rights of Woman*, John Stuart Mill, in his essays *On Liberty* and *The Subjection of Women*, opposed the rigid exclusion of women from public activities and legal rights from his consistent utilitarian perspective. Thoroughly influenced by the advent of such plays by Henrik Ibsen as *A Doll's House* or *Hedda Gabler*, the type of '**New Woman**' provocatively revolted against the limits imposed on women in the 1890s. They wore comfortable clothes, rode on bicycles, smoked cigarettes in public with ostentation (see illustration). Female suffrage was a political topic from 1832 onwards, the national movement of women's suffrage in the United Kingdom began in 1872, and from the first decades of the twentieth century (1903–1928) the **suffragette movement** and their figureheads Emmeline and Christabel Pankhurst fought for women's right to vote—which only became law in 1918—with more and more radical means. Instead of subordinating to the norm of female self-sacrifice, the New Woman of the late-nineteenth century self-consciously and self-confidently believes in political as well as sexual equality, independence and individual fulfilment. New Women are activists, reformers, and also artists and writers. Characteristically, this new female self-consciousness has often been associated by those (men) anxious of or scandalised by such behaviour with decadence, degeneration, perversion or even crime (see Shires; Robotham; Dowling; Greenslade; Dijkstra; Ledger; Bronfen), visible, for instance, in the deluded position of positivist criminology brought forward by Cesare Lombroso in notorious studies like *The Female Offender*. Such pathologisation made the fight for women's equal rights all the harder.

These various types of Victorian femininity (and such topical masculine counterparts as the

'Gentleman' or the ('seducer') pervade Victorian literature, as only a quick glance at George Eliot's work makes clear. Here, the reader encounters living female saints such as the Methodist preacher Dinah Morris in *Adam Bede* or, in the same novel, the tragic fate of fallen women such as Hetty Sorrel, who is seduced, made pregnant, jilted, and then abandons her child and is tried for child murder. Dorothea Brooke in Eliot's *Middlemarch* and Gwendolen Harleth in *Daniel Deronda*, by contrast, are early prototypes of the New Woman. The New Woman became a phenomenon many writers—male and female—have turned to with utter fascination since 1870. George Gissing's novels spring to mind, focussing on the fate of emancipated women in a male-dominated society, or unforgettable characters like Thomas Hardy's Eustacia Vye in *The Return of the Native*, Sue Bridehead in *Jude the Obscure*, indeed Henry James's Isabel Archer in *The Portrait of a Lady* and the extraordinary relationship between the two feminists Olive Chancellor and Verena Tarrant in *The Bostonians* respectively, Grant Allen's Herminia Barton in *The Woman Who Did*, Mona Caird's Hadria Fullerton in *The Daughters of Danaus*, and the character of Elizabeth Caldwell Maclure ('Beth') in Sarah Grand's autobiographical novel *The Beth Book*.

## The Triumph of Time

**Triumph of man over time.** In 1866, the British poet Charles Algernon Swinburne publishes the poem "The Triumph of Time," which must be considered one of the most important catchphrases summarising the unresolved tensions and the gradual change of the Victorian spirit, oscillating between optimism, enthusiasm and anxious pessimism. On the one hand, in the Victorian era, the 'triumph of time' is tantamount to a veritable triumph of man *over* time because, in a socio-cultural and -historical sense, no other epoch in human history has seen a similar standardisation of time. The beginning of the nineteenth century still featured a vast array of different local *times* and time cultures. Every place or at least every region set their clocks commensurate with their estimation of the culmination point of the sun. A hundred years later, this plethora of times had taken the level, order, but also the pace of a coordinated World Time. The standardisation of clock-time posed a challenge, absorbing governments, rulers, and engineers alike,

and was detachable only after the invention and introduction of transmitting electric impulses over vast distances via telegraph. Since the eighteenth century, nautical standards amongst seaman had already come to an agreement as regards a 'normal time' based on the longitude of the prime meridian at the Royal Observatory in Greenwich. By 1855, 98% of public clocks in Britain were set according to Greenwich Mean Time (GMT), which became official in 1880. Finally, in 1884, an international conference in Washington agreed upon a **Standard Time** by subdividing the globe in twenty-four consistent time zones comprising of fifteen degrees of longitude each, made necessary by the temporal coordination needed for reliable and efficient railway travel. The idea of standard time was proposed by the Scottish-born Canadian engineer Sandford Fleming, who may well be called "one of the most influential globalisers of the nineteenth century" (Osterhammel 90). These developments were possible only in those societies used to measuring time by the clock. Victorian times witnessed a pervasive 'chronometerisation,' that is, in effect, the democratisation of time as the industrial mass production of clocks and watches set in. The city of Geneva, for example, exported 54,000 pocket watches in 1790; by 1818, the number of clocks produced in the whole canton of Neuchâtel amounted to almost a million. Close to another hundred years later, by 1908, the German watch and clock manufacturer Junghans was the biggest of its kind in the world producing 3,000,000 clocks and watches in a year (Wendorff 387–429). The fact that in the 1890s the American manufacturer Ingersoll lowered the price of a pocket watch to one dollar was almost symbolic of the fact that the social difference between people with or without watches was outweighed once and for all.

**Triumph of time over man.** On the other hand, however, the 'triumph of time' and the distribution and omnipresence of clocks and watches did not only have positive implications. Surely, it accounted for the **quantification and perpetuation of working processes**, which back in pre-industrial circumstances had proceeded in irregular and erratic rhythms. However, as the division of labour and the organisation of production were increasing and the general rhythm of everyday life was accelerated and had to be more coordinated (in adjusting to railway time-tables, for instance), workers had to face a much stricter time regiment forced

*The democratisation of time*

upon them both by their employers and by the requirements of the market itself. Longer and more efficient working hours represented useful effects, but at the same time the subordination under a concept of abstract time entailed time pressure and, thus, a psychologically precarious drifting apart of private ('subjective time'), social and public rhythms ('social time'), the clash of which turned out to be a matter of social discipline as well as of cultural and psychic alienation (see Middeke 60–78 and also Foucault 171–293 for the aspect of temporal disciplining). Seen from this angle, the 'triumph of time' shapes up as a triumph of time *over man*, and this impression of time felt as oppressive and overwhelming is borne out in an even more general way by the relation between Victorian consciousness, individual man and the cosmic long-term perspective of life and nature embodied, for instance, by Darwin's theory. Losing an ultimate meaning and a metaphysical stability in reality and social life quite congruously entailed for the individual that the temporal dimension of life came to the fore. In Swinburne's poem, "the loves and hours of the life of a man" are "swift and sad, being born of the sea." We "rejoice" and "regret" only "for a span," we are "born with a man's breath," and we are unable to "save" anything "on the sands of life, in the straits of time" ("The Triumph of Time," lines 72–82). Swinburne's poem, though originally depicting the lyrical I's mourning for a lost love, is indicative of time felt as being the opponent of mankind in a situation where the Victorian consciousness has lost bearing upon the hitherto safe metaphysical laws of existence. Revealing a heartfelt grieving for the loss of such metaphysical security and fixed moral and ethical standards of conduct, the conflict with time was both the symptom and the cause of a widespread feeling of insignificance and transitoriness amongst the Victorians. The deep **melancholy** inherent in the loss of time is a central motif in Victorian life and literature. Such a mid- and late-Victorian view that looks upon time as a force disrupting individual self and social consensus is clearly opposed to the much more optimistic stance of Thomas Babington Macaulay, who was, besides Thomas Carlyle, the most eminent Victorian historian. Macaulay's *The History of England* can be considered one of the intellectual mouthpieces of a middle-class, common sense point of view that is derived from a confident belief in progress and the continuity of past traditions, personalities, and democracy into an open and rather sanguine future.

### 2.5.3 | The Novel

**Increasing literary market.** The process of a broadening reading public, which was begun in the eighteenth century, was continued and intensified in the Victorian Age. Readership numbers increased rapidly, both among the lower middle-class as well as among industrial workers, and were brought forward by social reform and various ensuing socio-cultural developments (see Abrams and Greenblatt 2:1043–65). While the history of public libraries went back into the fifteenth century, **circulating libraries** first appeared in the eighteenth century and further flourished in Victorian times, the most commercially successful one being founded by Charles Edward Mudie in 1840 in London, which developed into a chain and quickly acquired branches in other British cities. In 1848, W. H. Smith opened the first railway station bookshop where inexpensive books could be bought or borrowed. As newspapers were still quite expensive until 1855 when the tax on newspapers ('Stamp Duty') was abolished, members of the lower classes could turn to broadsides (tabloid types of street literature) and chapbooks for information and entertainment. Hundreds of **magazines** covering all the fields of contemporary life ranging from politics, science, and medicine, to culture, art, and literature sprang up like mushrooms. These developments certainly made for one central thing besides an increased accessibility of literary products: Whereas the Romantic era clearly had its aesthetic highlights in the form of poetry, Victorian literature witnessed the **triumphal procession of the novel**, which—though still disdained at the beginning of the century—became the most representative and productive literary genre in the nineteenth century.

The economic demands of commercial circulating libraries like Mudie's made it a typically nineteenth-century publishing practice that novels originally appeared as so-called '**three-decker-novels**' (see illustration), the first volume virtually whetting the readership's appetite for the next two.

The price of each volume was half a guinea (10s 6d), which equals about £20 today, and made buying the volumes unattainable even for many mid-

'Three-decker-novel,' here: Charles Dickens's *Oliver Twist* (1838)

dle-class readers. Cheaper one-volume editions of successful novels for 6s were indeed published, but with much delay (see Seeber 273–75). Hence, the power and influence of people the likes of Mudie were considerable, as they were not only able to buy large quantities of a first edition of a novel, but were also able to promote and channel the career of a writer (Nünning 21–22). Writers from Dickens to Hardy also chose to have their novels published in the form of instalments in magazines such as *Household Words*, *The Saturday Review*, or *The Cornhill Magazine*. For writers, the three-decker-novel or publishing in magazines meant financial success but also accommodating to literary conventions, most prominently the happy ending or poetic justice as well as the strict avoidance of reference to all matters sexual. What is striking to observe across the entire Victorian era is the change that takes place with regard to which parts of the readership were (meant to be) reached by the novel. Novels by Dickens and poems by Tennyson were read by almost all ages and all social classes. However, since the last decades of the Victorian age, a much more liberal treatment of moral issues and literary conventions in connection with much more complex aesthetic structures in novels by Walter Pater, Henry James, or Joseph Conrad, for instance, have procured an enduring **split in the readership**, disconnecting the aesthetics of the novel from the taste and understanding of the masses, which is prevalent until today.

**Continuing traditions.** The Victorian novel continued the traditions started in the eighteenth-century novel and in Romanticism (cf. entries I.2.3 and I.2.4). The models of the ***Bildungsroman*** and the **sentimental novel** (in the wake of Fielding's *Tom Jones* or Richardson's *Pamela*) or, more generally, novels focussing their plotlines on the development or education of their (female) protagonists were as constructive as the continuation of the **historical novel** after Walter Scott and the **Gothic novel** strand of Romanticism. Likewise, in epoch-making and until today widely read novels such as *Sense and Sensibility*, *Pride and Prejudice*, or *Emma* Jane Austen combined aspects of moral education with a meticulous portrayal of family issues, class, manners, love, marriage, and courtship. Such topics were as productive as Austen's early **stream-of-consciousness technique**, which combines direct discourse with narratorial comment focussing on individual, subjective perspectives in the narrative. Not only did both Austen's

| Key Texts: The Victorian Novel |
|---|
| **Elizabeth Cleghorn Gaskell,** *Mary Barton* (1848) |
| **Emily Brontë,** *Wuthering Heights* (1847) |
| **Charlotte Brontë,** *Jane Eyre* (1847) |
| **William Makepeace Thackeray,** *Vanity Fair* (1847–1848) |
| **Charles Dickens,** *Bleak House* (1852–1853) |
| **George Eliot,** *Middlemarch* (1874) |
| **Henry James,** *The Portrait of a Lady* (1881) |
| **Walter Pater,** *Marius the Epicurean* (1885) |
| **Thomas Hardy,** *Jude the Obscure* (1895) |
| **Joseph Conrad,** *Lord Jim* (1900) |

subject matter and form betray, her keen concern with individuality, subjectivity and human emotion, the plotlines of her novels also present a character's future as emphatically open. Today, especially Austen's use of free indirect speech seems much ahead of her time as the rigorous use of this technique leads way towards the late-nineteenth century novel and, indeed, literary modernism.

**Diversification.** Beyond that, the Victorian novel witnessed an immense diversification of these traditions, evolving sub-genres like 'silver-fork' novels or novels of fashion (based on upper-class lifestyles), political novels, social novels, religious novels, regional novels, novels depicting female developments and education, panoramic views of society, sensational novels (the predecessor of crime fiction), fantasy fiction, or utopian and dystopian novels (for concise overviews see, for instance, David; Wheeler, *English Fiction*; Nünning; Pordzik) generating an unprecedented plurality of texts, bringing forward a sheer abundance of new writers, and creating whole scores of different intentions for different readers ranging in quality from highest aesthetic claims to broadest mass entertainment.

**Two modes: realism and romance.** The aesthetics of the Victorian novel and all its sub-genres follow two fundamental ideal types: The modes or varieties of realism and of romance. Obviously, all ideal types are hypothetical constructions in the abstract. Hence, considering these two modes and their characteristics must firstly acknowledge that individual variants und understandings of 'realism,' for example, may be quite different by comparison of individual texts and writers, and secondly, that the opposition suggested here in fact denotes another tension, an oscillation movement between the two poles. Both the modes of realism and romance entail a particular way of looking at

**Definition**

Realism and Romance
- → Realism is characterised by **verisimilitude**, the likeliness of a representation to reality, and the very probability of an action (for an extended definition see section I.3.3.1). Things, persons, actions, places, events, and situations must be recognisable and identifiable to a wide majority of readers beyond a particular author's perspective and consciousness; what happens must be credible to be likely to have happened the way it is described. Realism implies linear chronology and continuity, causal interconnectedness of the events described in chronological order; and, after all, everyday subject matter and a heterodiegetic, heteroreferential, omniscient narrator and point of view (cf. entry II.9). In the words of the postmodernist British novelist John Fowles, the (Victorian) realist "novelist stands next to God. He may not know all, yet he tries to pretend that he does," pulling "the right strings and his puppets will behave in a lifelike manner" (*The French Lieutenant's Woman*, ch. 13).
- The → romance, by contrast—originating in medieval heroic verse and prose narratives—is centred on adventures, quests, and love. Other than the realist novel, the romance contains the generic elements of the **supernatural**, the marvellous, and the *un*common that shine through its incidents, which render the romance a much more heightened and idealised genre.

the world, and analysing both modes in the Victorian novel makes clear that their shares in the aesthetics of a particular novel may be weighed differently, often they even overlap in a co-existence of various elements taken from each mode and produce complex genre-hybrids.

Realism, then, must most of all be looked upon as a mode of fictional writing that intends and allows for generalisations to be made. Realism is based upon and at the same sets out to produce **consensus**, that is, a common horizon, an equality of viewpoints grounded in the shared conviction of the existence and achievability of identity and truth: "the *oneness* or the invariant structure by which we recognize a thing, by which we judge it under varying circumstances to be the same" (Ermarth 5). Realist narratives are characterised by **past-tense narrators** whose overall intention is to generate a collective experience, "a recollection of all points of view and of all private times under the aegis of a single point of view and in a common time" (Ermarth 54). In such a view, the mode of fictional representation suggests, to repeat Matthew Arnold's words, that things can indeed be perceived "as they are" (for a vast number of people sharing that view) and, hence, these 'things as they are' would not change even if the perspective

on them varied. Beyond such epistemological prerequisites of realism, the common sense realist world-view is strengthened by structural conventions such as, for instance, the **causal coherence** of the plotline and the **happy ending**, that is, closure in the sense of poetic justice.

## The Development of the Victorian Novel

Surveying the development of the Victorian novel from the 1830s to the end of the nineteenth century, it can be ascertained that, quite proportional to the loss of social and political consensus outlined above, the epistemological, cultural, and philosophical preconditions for realism subside more and more and, thus, the aesthetics of the novel change. Famous examples of the Victorian *Bildungsroman* like Dickens's *Oliver Twist* (1838) and *David Copperfield* (1849–50) present their young protagonists at odds with, yet desperately searching for, their identity, their place in society, and in the universe. Oliver, quite symbolically, is a foundling and a waif; David suffers from his cruel stepfather, who almost beats him to death; both are afflicted by circumstances entirely indifferent to their fates. In both cases, though, Dickens in the end devises a place, a career, and a future for them in an at least potentially ordered society where all the characters get what they deserve. Even though the Victorian novel did not break through to the radical formal and narratological experiments carried out later by Modernist writers like James Joyce and Virginia Woolf, by the end of the century, the world nevertheless no longer seemed an 'objective' entity or fact, but rather a subjective projection, a form of consciousness. In a moral or ethical sense even, hitherto unquestioned Victorian key values like duty, honour, valour, or earnestness in late Victorian novels like Joseph Conrad's *Lord Jim* or Henry James's *What Maisie Knew* and *The Ambassadors* only exist anymore because (some) characters believe in them. As these novels by James and Conrad prove, recognising the world has become a matter of individual interpretation, which, in turn, calls for new forms of narrative beyond the realist consensus that has gone stale by this time.

The social problem novel. Before innovation in literature has an impact on aesthetic structure and form, it affects new subject matter. In the early-Victorian period, the most innovative sub-genre was the social problem novel that made new subject areas accessible as it portrayed industrial life in hitherto unprecedented ways. Authors like Benjamin Disraeli, Elizabeth Cleghorn Gaskell or Charles Kingsley commented on developments and movements (in particular, Chartism or strikes as one proletarian antidote to exploitation) and set out to confront especially their middle-class readership with the wrong side of the transformation process inherent in the Industrial Revolution. In a realist and poignant fashion, they pointed out to these privileged classes the hardships of working class living conditions in the big cities: unemployment, bitter poverty, hunger, or unacceptable standards of hygiene. Disraeli's *Sybil, or the Two Nations* tackled the issue of an impending split between the misery of the working class and the luxury of the upper class. Gaskell turned this difference geographical in that she juxtaposed the rural south and the industrialised north of England in *North and South*. Gaskell's *Mary Barton* is a realistic depiction of the proletarian squalor in the slums of Manchester. Kingsley's *Yeast* provides insight into agricultural labour, while in *Alton Locke* Kingsley makes his tailor/poet-protagonist movingly narrate his own fate and, unconventionally, denies a happy ending to him. In most other cases of the social problem novel, the happy ending seems all too artificially precipitated, as it often derives from an exerted ensnarement of social realism on the one hand and a romance love-plot on the other. While this incongruent mix deflected the actual solution to the social problem into the realm of emotional compassion, Disraeli's *Coningsby, or the New Generation* devised a marriage between the aristocracy and the middle-class industrial magnates and, much more politically, called for eminent and responsible leaders to get on top of the social maladies.

**Thomas Carlyle: hero-worship.** This demand for leaders echoes the philosophy of one of the greatest Victorian thinkers: Thomas Carlyle. In 1841, Carlyle's historiographical study *On Heroes, Hero Worship, and the Heroic* sees the salvation of society in emulating 'super'-leaders ("Capitains") such as Dante, Shakespeare, Luther or Napoleon. Carlyle's earlier biographies on Friedrich Schiller, Frederick II of Prussia, essays such as "Biography," "Boswell's *Life of Johnson*" and the autobiographical novel *Sartor Resartus* testify to Carlyle's belief that the life of an excellent personality and the **hero-worship** involved in its recounting can be foundation stones of inspiration in an otherwise completely unheroic world. In the tradition of Goethe's *Wilhelm Meister*, the protagonist of *Sartor Resartus*, the German professor Diogenes Teufelsdrökh, transforms the nihilistic impression of an "everlasting No" into an "everlasting Yea" when he comes to the conclusion that the central act of knowledge is accepting a will of God beyond the world's fate. The world is perceived as a gigantic steam engine, relief from which can again only be procured by quasi-feudal leaders. In an earlier, yet programmatic essay on the "Signs of the Times" Carlyle points out that "were we required to characterise this age of ours by a simple epithet, we should be tempted to call it, not an Heroical, Devotional, Philosophical, or Moral Age, but, above all others, the Mechanical Age." Carlyle ironically lays bare that the optimism derived from progress and industrialisation is an illusion, the price for which is a likewise mechanical utilitarian thinking producing callous, de-individualised monster-human beings.

**Charles Dickens.** No other Victorian writer has given that much life to the big industrial city, its dirt, its bad smells, its labyrinthine streets as Charles Dickens. Dickens's novels, short stories, and tales (i.e. *Sketches by Boz*, *The Pickwick Papers*) are unique hybrids including elements from the **social problem novel** and the **sensational novel**, and also incorporate picaresque and farcical elements of **humour**. In no other Victorian writer is the pure energy and bustle of industrial city life captured that well and reflected in such a rich kaleidoscope of unforgettable and eccentric characters and such haunting images as, for instance, the fog that is indicative of a nebulous legal system in *Bleak House*. At times, Dickens's tone may perhaps be hard to digest, as it often all too suddenly and superficially blends the social criticism with sentimental melodrama. However, what Dickens most of all sets against the alienating forces of the times is a veritable triumph of the imagination, the choice of names for his characters alone, though these are often openly moralising and telling names, displays Dickens's playful relish in language: Wopsle (the parish clerk in *Great Expectations*), Luke Honeythunder (*The Mystery of Edwin Drood*), Paul Sweedlepipe (the barber in *Martin Chuzzlewit*), Mr Fezziwig (*A Christmas Carol*), Anne Chickenstalker (*The Chimes*), Serjeant Buzfuz (*The Pickwick Papers*) or Polly Toodle (the nurse in *Dombey and Son*), beyond all satire, betray Dickens's insight into the pure materiality of signifiers, which has rendered his work open even to deconstructive readings (cf. entry II.4). The ultimately benign optimism that

*The triumph of the imagination*

Interpretation

## "Coketown" in Charles Dickens's *Hard Times*

It was a town of red brick, or of brick that would have been red if the smoke and ashes had allowed it; but, as matters stood it was a town of *unnatural red and black like the painted face of a savage*. It was a town of machinery and tall chimneys, out of which interminable serpents of smoke trailed themselves for ever and ever, and never got uncoiled. There was a canal in it, and *a river that ran purple with ill-smelling die*, and vast piles of building full of windows where there was rattling and a trembling all day long, and *where the piston of the steam-engine worked monotonously up and down like the head of an elephant in a state of melancholy madness*. It contained several large streets all very *like one another*, and many small streets still more *like one another*, inhabited by people equally *like one another*, who all went in and out at the *same* hours, with the *same* sound upon the *same* pavements, to do the *same* work, and to whom every day was the *same* as yesterday and tomorrow, and every year the counterpart of the last and the next. (Dickens, *Hard Times* ch. 5, my emphases)

The unimaginable fatigue of the monotonous routine of the mechanical workflow in the industrial cities, its mindless repetition, and its terrifying, hostile impact on man is portrayed in this nightmarish sketch of Coketown, which Dickens dedicated to Carlyle.

shines through Dickens's early work later makes way for a resounding pessimism. Rewriting the negative first ending, which Dickens had originally designed for Pip in *Great Expectations*, meant nothing but a major concession to Victorian literary conventions, while mature novels like *Bleak House* or *Our Mutual Friend* are indicative of the fact that Dickens must have felt the consensus between social role and private self lastingly disrupted, so that determining the balance of what society expects and what individuals must do to remain true to themselves became increasingly impossible. Striking leitmotifs like the river (of time and eventual renewal), money, and the waste heap in *Our Mutual Friend*, thus, advance as fictional models of the world.

**The historical novel.** The role-model Sir Walter Scott set for the historical novel—a fictitious hero is placed in historical surroundings and his adventures confront him (and the reader) with historical figures and incidents—is only rather fitfully continued. Many popular writers trivialise the historical setting and make use of it for purely entertaining reasons. Even for writers like Dickens (e.g. *Barnaby Rudge*) or George Eliot (*Romola*) the historical framework is really not much more than a decorum illustrating contemporary ideas. The most convincing example of the Victorian historical novel after Scott is **William Makepeace Thackeray**'s *Henry Esmond*, which constitutes a development of Scott's model because not only does it involve a psychological transformation process of the protagonist, it also turns out disenchanted about Scott's view of history as heroic events. Thackeray's masterpiece *Vanity Fair* and Anthony Trollope's novels constitute meticulously crafted, panoramic profiles of Victorian society. *Vanity Fair*, as its subtitle makes clear, is "a novel without a hero" and, thus, satirically and often parodistically debunks Victorian stereotypes and narrative conventions. Both writers share the contempt of romance-like coincidences and black-and-white moralising, as the portrayal of Amelia Sedley and Rebecca Sharp in *Vanity Fair* makes irrevocably clear: Amelia is virtuous and passive, yet cowardly and naïve; Becky is ruthless and sly, but active and determined at the same time. Thackeray's altogether pessimist vision is obviously fascinated by this ambivalence, his characters are, thus, beyond good and evil and entirely entangled in that fair of the vanities which surrounds them. Likewise, but less satirically so, the characters of Trollope's novels inhabit a God-less, entirely human world of inter-subjective relations. Both writers testify to a weakening of the omniscient, authorial narrator. Thackeray's last sentence in *Vanity Fair* still invites the reader to "shut up the box and the puppets, for our play is played out" (ch. 67), but it has been a 'play' devoid of a clear moral judgment hinting at the beginning breakdown of an authoritative system of ethical norms. Still, what looks like a discontinuous array of specific cases and multiple viewpoints is given a (realist) form through the distance of a narrator-consciousness.

**Female novelists.** Out of a vast number of novels written by female novelists in the Victorian Age, which deal with social issues, manners, (female) education and development, religious matters or explicitly with the 'woman question' (for overview see, for instance, Thompson; Mergenthal, *Autorinnen*), the novels of **Charlotte, Emily, and Anne Brontë** and Mary Ann Evans—best known under her pen-name **George Eliot**—clearly stand out in the way they challenge traditional gender-stereotypes and have unusual aesthetic structures evolved from a decidedly psychological interest in their characters. Attesting to the difficulties for women to publish and pursue an intellectual career, the Brontës also used pseudonyms (Currer, Ellis, Acton Bell) in order to make sure that their works were taken seriously in an era when female authors were usually associated with romantic novels. The Brontës grew up in the seclusion of their remote Yorkshire home and, hence, had little choice but to concentrate on depicting the inner life of their protagonists. Charlotte Brontë's *Jane Eyre* follows the structure of the educational novel and the *Bildungsroman*, but also borrows from Gothic fiction. When Jane and Rochester finally unite, Brontë seems to envision them as having become true equals.

The uncanny character of Bertha Mason, however, the angry 'madwoman in the attic' whom Rochester married in the Caribbean and who in rage, yet quite symbolically, sets the estate on fire, can be seen as the repressed colonial 'other,' but also appears as the uncanny double of the ireful and passionate 'other' side of Jane's psyche herself (see Gilbert and Gubar), which leaves the psychological problem of conscious and unconscious human behaviour in the open. More radically even, Emily Brontë's *Wuthering Heights* incorporates elements from the sensational novel such as passion, insanity, hallucinations, and dreams into her novel. She portrays the central, destructive, and unhappy relationship between Heathcliff and Catherine, who love each other but cannot be together other than in death, as an uncontrollable force of nature. This psychological point of departure is further enhanced by the narrative structure of the novel: Refusing ultimate authorial control to her narrative, Brontë masterfully chooses two unreliable narrators (cf. entry II.9) to present the events, leaving the reader behind with "unquiet slumbers for the sleepers in that quiet earth" (*Wuthering Heights* ch. 34). George Eliot's *Middlemarch* provides a panoramic, multi-perspective overview of a provincial town. Her **psychological realism** combines Eliot's interest in the inner motivations of actions (conscience or psychic dispositions) with an almost scientific analysis of social structure. As a formal reflection of a complex world, the authorial narrative skilfully weaves the threads of the plotline, albeit no longer claiming absolute validity for its judgements but indicating an insight in the fact that "signs are small measurable things, but interpretations are illimitable" (*Middlemarch* ch. 3). Accordingly, her earlier

novel *The Mill on the Floss* is one of the first Victorian novels to end tragically.

**The negative Bildungsroman.** The decisive acknowledgment of incommensurable forces and drives working the human consciousness and psyche coupled with the sense of epistemological and ontological crisis permeating the Victorian society since the 1880s made the plotlines of the late Victorian novel change substantially (see illustration). Traditionally, the happy ending brought objectives to a successful conclusion, both in the sense of private and public happiness. For the characters, these objectives not only ended in failure now, sometimes it also seemed hard to take the necessary steps of actualisation or even to define the objectives in the first place, and the *Bildungsroman* therefore transformed into a negative *Bildungsroman* (Broich). Formerly causally structured plotlines developed into what Gillian Beer called "**Darwin's plots**" accentuating temporal contingency, unpredictability, fatality, and the transitoriness of human action and existence.

Influenced by evolution theory and the German philosopher Arthur Schopenhauer, who saw the human psyche and our coping with reality governed by "will/*Wille*" (i.e. desire, striving, nature) and "ideas/*Vorstellung*" (i.e. the subjective images of how we perceive and frame the external world), especially **Thomas Hardy**'s later novels (i.e. *The Return of the Native*; *Tess of the d'Urbervilles*) portray individuals struggling with a meaningless, absurd world. *Jude the Obscure* is the epitome of a negative *Bildungsroman*. Jude's failure is a fourfold one: society, his genes, his individual psychic disposition, and nature itself, which is entirely indifferent to his personal fate, lead to his tragic end-

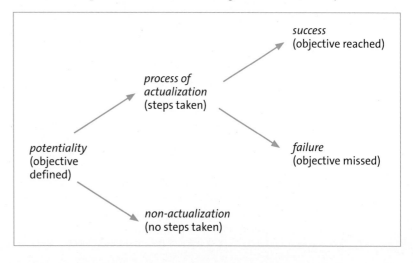

ing. A similar plot development is visible in **Samuel Butler**'s masterpiece *The Way of all Flesh*, in which Butler portrays his (anti-)hero Ernest Pontifex inconclusively struggling against his biological and historical/cultural heritage.

**Major strands in nineteenth-century European aesthetics**

Three major strands in the history of European nineteenth-century aesthetics have enhanced such pessimistic yet innovative views:

- Firstly, **naturalism** as a pan-European movement meant a radicalisation of realist poetics (cf. section I.3.3.4). Naturalist representations of reality (in the novels of Hardy, Gissing and George Moore, for instance) went beyond any realist idealising or didactic intentions in favour of an accurate portrayal of social milieu and all negative and harsh aspects of human life which were often described in shockingly grotesque imagery.

- Secondly, **aestheticism** was the flight to the realm of the beautiful and, thus, represented a counter-discourse to the alienating side effects of the Industrial Revolution and its positivist scientific ideals. Taking their cue from French symbolism, aestheticists such as Walter Pater were striving for a concept of the novel that focused on the refuge of the fleeting moment in what otherwise seemed a remorseless flow of time. Pater's *Marius the Epicurean* is clearly opposed to the idea of an omnipotent rationality of man, hence it makes the attaining of knowledge and insight no longer a matter of reasoning but of isolated moments of vision which clearly prefigure the aesthetics of 'epiphanic' visions in James Joyce and Virginia Woolf (cf. entry I.2.6). Oscar Wilde's *The Picture of Dorian Gray* is a much more transitional novel: its aestheticist preface claims that "there is no such thing as a moral or an immoral book" and that "all art is quite useless," yet the practice which Dorian's life puts this theory into turns out to be both asocial and highly immoral.

- Thirdly, **impressionism** heavily influenced the late Victorian novel focussing on movement, time, multiple perspectives, and individual experience and consciousness. The elusive 'reality' in Henry James's novels is entirely filtered through individual streams of consciousness, making extensive use of free indirect discourse. The protagonist in Joseph Conrad's *Lord Jim* does not even have a say in the novel, and Jim's character and the moral dilemma which his fate implies are a-chronologically depicted in umpteen contradictory versions. The "sovereign power enthroned in a fixed standard of conduct" (ch. 5) seems dead and buried. In the preface to *The Nigger of the Narcissus* Conrad emphasises that

the aim of art, which, like life itself, is inspiring, difficult—obscured by mists; it is not in the clear logic of a triumphant conclusion; it is not in the unveiling of one of those heartless secrets which are called the Laws of Nature. It is not less great, but only more difficult.

In the preface to the New York edition to *The Tragic Muse*, Henry James famously asks in almost the same way, "what do such large, loose, baggy monsters, with their queer elements of the accidental and the arbitrary, artistically *mean*?" The question expresses his disdain with the aesthetics of the Russian realists or writers like Trollope, against the authorial narrative of which James set a single "center of consciousness" in novels like *The Golden Bowl* or *The Ambassadors*. Obviously, by the turn of the century in writers such as James and Conrad, the novel is formally drawing near to modernist aesthetics.

*Sensational novel and scientific romance.* The trends in children's literature, fantasy fiction, and, especially, the late-nineteenth-century **sensational novel** corroborate this diagnosis in terms of subject-matter and form: The episodic structure of Charles Lutwidge Dodgson's (a.k.a. Lewis Carroll) famous *Alice's Adventures in Wonderland* and its sequel *Through the Looking Glass, and What Alice Found There* reveals his interest in dreams, fairy tales, and playful nonsense, which heavily influenced writers and movements such as James Joyce and surrealism. Drawing on earlier novels such as Wilkie Collins's *The Woman in White* or Sheridan LeFanu's *Carmilla*, Bram Stoker's *Dracula* or Robert Louis Stevenson's *Dr Jekyll and Mr Hyde* allowed new glimpses into the unknown of the subconscious. The **scientific romance** at the turn of the century designed dystopian visions of the future (e.g. H. G. Wells's *The Time Machine*, *The Island of Dr Moreau*) which are clearly set apart from earlier utopian outlooks on society such as Edward Bulwer-Lytton's *The Coming Race* or Edward Bellamy's *Looking Backward* and rather prefigured the modern dystopia in George Orwell and Aldous Huxley. Even Britain's imperial mission had gone stale by the turn of the century. While writers like Rudyard Kipling believed in the 'noble' enterprise of British imperialism ("The White Man's Burden"), the character of Kurtz in Conrad's *Heart of Darkness*, by contrast, starts out his business in the Congo in the best tradition of that 'white man's burden,' becomes corrupted though, and finally ends "hollow at the core."

## 2.5.4 | Poetry

Victorian poetry continued on the path of the **Romantic tradition**. Poets like Wordsworth, Shelley, and Keats were still seen as exemplary, even though the radical expression of the self, which distinguished Romantic subjectivity and set it apart from the Neoclassicism, was largely avoided. Victorian poetry was characterised by a rich **variety of forms**, the most productive of which were dramatic monologues, monodramas, ballads, sonnets, pastoral poetry, and, especially, elegies. Furthermore, all major writers still attempted to write epic or longer narrative poetry. Very different from the novel, Victorian poetry eschews addressing contemporary subject matter or problems overtly. Both the contemporary world and the self of the poet are turned to only indirectly in encoded or embellished form as most of the poetry by the major writers is deflected into the realms of the historical and the mythical. Nevertheless, similar to the novel, melancholy was one significant mental state emanating from the poetry, both in the sense of private loss and death as well as in a more general understanding of losing stability, orientation, and meaning. The elegiac tone of many poems and the retreat into mythical times and dreams can be regarded as one appropriate way of facing and, at the same time, transcending the pains generated by separation and uncertainty. Far fewer others, like Tennyson's "Ulysses," sought to face the strife of life with affirmative heroism (see Seeber 311). If we acknowledge a little irony on Tennyson's part, however, Ulysses's concluding affirmative purpose "Made weak by time and fate, but strong in will / To strive, to seek, to find, and not to yield" may be taken with a pinch of salt.

**Alfred Lord Tennyson** is a contradictory figure, whose personality aptly reflects the tensions prevalent in Victorian times. He was Poet Laureate for more than forty years, ennobled by Queen Victoria and both embodied and pronounced Victorian values thoroughly. But then he also cultivated private spheres of exotic sentiment that appeared sceptical about the modern comforts of progress and sought for a retreat from the alienating forces within society. However, these private spaces of his imagination no longer had the power to challenge the utilitarian spirit of the times politically. The view of reality remains an indirect one, as the example of Tennyson's famous ballad "The Lady of Shalott" (1833/42), who cannot view reality other than in a mirror and through a window pane, but dies when she beholds the world directly, makes clear. The immensely associative poem comments on Tennyson's own outsider status estranged from society, it also makes a poetological reference to the position of a poet faced with the (impossible) task of representing reality, and, of course, hints at the marginalised position of women in Victorian times. Tennysons's dramatic monologues such as "Lotos-Eaters" (1832) and "Ulysses" (1842), longer poems like *In Memoriam* (1850) or his monodrama *Maud* (1855) present his intense examination of death as their essential subject matter. Tennyson's epic poem *The Idylls of the King* (1859–85) takes up the myth of King Arthur.

By comparison, **Robert Browning**'s work exhibits a more optimistic fascination with vitality and heroic potential in the face of all difficulties and troublesomeness. His shorter poems, dramatic monologues, and narrative poetry centre on the experience of love, on loneliness, on the incommensurable relationship between life and art ("My Last Duchess," 1842; "Fra Lippo Lippi," 1855), on the conflict between guilt and innocence (*The Ring and the Book*, 1868/69), and they often contemplate the secular in conflict with the religious ("Fra Lippo Lippi") which makes a divine truth discernible among otherwise fragmented perspectives. His wife **Elizabeth Barrett Browning** was an ardent admirer of Mary Wollstonecraft's ideas, and her blank verse epic poem *Aurora Leigh* (1856), though stylistically flawed, is of political interest in the context of women's rights as are other political poems dealing with, for instance, her argument against slavery. Her sonnet cycle *Sonnets from the Portuguese* (1850) juxtaposes a consciousness of transitoriness and decay with an eventual regeneration found in love.

The poetry of **Matthew Arnold** is governed by the impression of the transitoriness of human existence and the diagnosis of a time devoid of beliefs and of a meaningless universe. This is coupled with melancholy memories of a better past. Thus, weariness of life and ennui dominate poems like "The Scholar Gypsy."

Victorian poetry was given fresh and innovative impulses by the work of **Charles Algernon Swinburne** and **Gerald Manley Hopkins**. As argued above, Swinburne was obsessively concerned with time and temporality and, more strongly than in Arnold or Tennyson, his work is characterised by an almost morbid fascination with death. Death is seen as ultimate loss, but also as the moment when human life at last finds rest from the burden of life:

Tennyson and Browning were the major poets of the Victorian Age.

Then star nor sun shall waken,
Nor any change of light;
Nor sound of waters shaken,
Nor any sound or sight;
Nor wintry leaves nor vernal,
Nor days nor things diurnal;
Only the sleep eternal
In an eternal night.
(Swinburne, "The Garden of Proserpine" lines 89–96)

Swinburne challenged Victorian (religious) morals as he ostensibly turned to provocative topics such as homoerotic love, sadomasochism, and liberal sexual attitudes. Moreover, he radicalised the 'tamer' poetic language of the older generations of Victorian poets by incorporating international influence (Baudelaire and Richard Wagner) and introducing new elements of prosody and metre. Gerald Manley Hopkins also brought linguistic innovation to Victorian poetry; poems like "The Wreck of the Deutschland" and "The Loss of the Eurydice" both centred on historical shipwrecks and featured a veritable fireworks of alliterations, sprung rhythms, assonances, regular/run-over

## Interpretation

### Matthew Arnold, "Dover Beach"

Matthew Arnold's "Dover Beach" (1867) is one of the key-texts documenting the **alienation** felt by the Victorian age in the face of an industrial, urban world when former certainties melt down.

The sea is calm to-night.
The tide is full, the moon lies fair
Upon the straits; on the French coast the light
Gleams and is gone; the cliffs of England stand;
Glimmering and vast, out in the tranquil bay.      5
Come to the window, sweet is the night-air!
Only, from the long line of spray
Where the sea meets the moon-blanched land,
Listen! you hear the grating roar
Of pebbles which the waves draw back, and fling,   10
At their return, up the high strand,
Begin, and cease, and then again begin,
With tremulous cadence slow, and bring
The eternal note of sadness in.

Sophocles long ago                                 15
Heard it on the Ægaean, and it brought
Into his mind the turbid ebb and flow
Of human misery; we
Find also in the sound a thought,
Hearing it by this distant northern sea.           20

The Sea of Faith
Was once, too, at the full, and round earth's shore
Lay like the folds of a bright girdle furled.
But now I only hear
Its melancholy, long, withdrawing roar,            25
Retreating, to the breath
Of the night-wind, down the vast edges drear
And naked shingles of the world.

Ah, love, let us be true
To one another! for the world, which seems         30
To lie before us like a land of dreams,
So various, so beautiful, so new,
Hath really neither joy, nor love, nor light,
Nor certitude, nor peace, nor help for pain;
And we are here as on a darkling plain             35
Swept with confused alarms of struggle and flight,
Where ignorant armies clash by night.

Unlike the Romantics, the speaker can no longer find imaginative refuge in nature. What at first sight seems an idyllic night scene at sea in Arnold's poem—"The sea is calm tonight," "The tide is full," "the tranquil bay" (lines 1–4)—is apparently threatened by "the grating roar" (9) of cobble stones moved by the sea in a repetitive rhythm which produces an "eternal note of sadness" (14). The speaker likens himself to the Greek tragedian Sophocles, and transfers the nature image onto the realm of philosophy. Like the sea in the present moment of contemplation, "The Sea of Faith" (21) was once "at the full" (22), but has now withdrawn and has only left a "melancholy, long […] roar" carried away by the wind (25). In the face of this loss the speaker resorts to love and clings to his partner, "Ah, love, let us be true / To one another" (29–30), although the lovers find themselves exposed to "naked shingles of the world" (28) and surrounded by chaos, disorientation, and utter helplessness on a strange, amorphous battle field "where ignorant armies clash by night" (37). This bleak vision of a world in which there is "neither joy, nor love, nor light/ Nor certitude, nor peace, nor help for pain" (33–34) is structurally echoed by the three truncated stanzas that barely recall the first one which is loosely reminiscent of the sonnet structure.

rhymes, and, especially, puns, wordplay and neologisms which bespeak Hopkins's playful use of language.

A beetling baldbright cloud thorough England
Riding: there did stores not mingle? And
Hailropes hustle and grind their
Heavengravel? wolfsnow, worlds of it, wind there?
("The Loss of the Eurydice" lines 25–28)

During his studies at Oxford, Swinburne came into contact with the **Pre-Raphaelites** (or: Pre-Raphaelite Brotherhood), a group of English painters, poets, and critics which was founded in 1848 by William Holman Hunt, John Everett Millais, and Dante Gabriel Rossetti. Rossetti's paintings as well as his poetry are characterised by a meticulous study of detail focussing on a dream-like cult of beauty, medieval culture and myth, which entailed a strange and exotic historical dislodgement. The Pre-Raphaelites considered themselves aesthetic reformers, and the exquisiteness of their imagery can certainly be regarded as a counter-discourse to and a subtle flight from the oppressive everyday experience of the Victorian age. The poetry of Rossetti's sister, Christina Georgiana Rossetti, is characterised by a rich and complex psychology, which combines the melancholic consciousness of anxiety and unhappy love with eroticism and a deeply felt need for female self-assertion, spirituality and religiousness.

The cult of exquisite and beautiful experience was continued and intensified in the poetry of the Fin de Siècle in writers such as Oscar Wilde, Ernest Christopher Dowson, Arthur William Symons and Lionel Johnson. This group, who were associated during their lifetime with "**decadence**," took their cue from Walter Pater. In *Studies in the History of the Renaissance* (1873), Pater has famously and controversially argued in favour of the aesthetic moment and the triumph of form over content, which he thought could only perfectly coalesce in music. Pater looked upon life as an inexorable and irresistible flux—each moment was separated from another by inevitable temporal difference. Thus, what was left for the artist or the poet, or any other man, amidst this process of constant change was to never tire in capturing as many of these unique flickering impressions as possible. "While all melts under our feet," Pater wrote in the "Conclusion" to *The Renaissance*, "we may well catch at any exquisite passion, or any contribution to knowledge that seems by a lifted horizon to set the spirit free for a moment, or any stirring of the senses, strange dyes, strange colours, and curious odours, or work of the artist's hands, or the face of one's friend." This was misunderstood by many contemporaries as equalling a licentious hedonism and amorality. Further influenced by the **French symbolists** (Charles Baudelaire, Stéphane Mallarmé, Paul Verlaine), the poets of the Nineties turned to the exquisite beauty of the moment as a means of a definitive protest against the utilitarian spirit of the age. Named after the notorious "yellow book" (apparently Joris-Karl Huysmans's *À rebours*, 1884), which Dorian is given and misled by in Wilde's *The Picture of Dorian Gray* (1891), the leading illustrated magazine of the 1890s in England was *The Yellow Book*.

In France and in England, 'yellow' was the colour associated with the often erotic and lascivious subject matter of the texts and, augmented by Aubrey Beardsley's famous illustrations (see illustration), the whole decade is often called '**yellow Nineties**.' Notable contributors to the journal besides Dowson and Symons were Henry James, H. G. Wells, and the young William Butler Yeats, who was later to become the most important Anglophone poet in the first half of the twentieth century (cf. section I.2.6.4). He was one of the founding fathers of the **Irish Revival**, fought for Irish freedom and independence, which he thought should be based upon the self-conscious recourse to the Irish tradition of legends and folk tales. His early poetry, *The Wanderings of Oisin* (1889), *Crossways* (1889), *The Rose* (1893), *The Wind among the Reeds* (1899), reveals various influences ranging from Irish mythology, occultism, the mysticism of William Blake and French symbolism. These sources became means to a radical, often hermetic and dream-like articulation of a personal experience in a search for a hidden, subjective truth in the world of phenomena.

Aubrey Beardsley, "The Toilet of Salome, for Salome," first version (1894)

## 2.5.5 | Drama

Innovation in drama only took place within the last two decades of the Victorian era. In early Victorian times, only three theatres—Covent Garden, Drury Lane, and the Haymarket—were licensed to stage plays, while others saw the performance of musical

The rise of popular drama

pieces such as brief comical opera ('burlettas'). By 1851, these restrictions fell away, and by the end of the century more than sixty theatres were putting on stage plays in London. The result was a spectacular increase of popular theatre dedicated merely to people's entertainment, which very appropriately could be compared to the cultural importance of the cinema nowadays, which saw its beginnings in late Victorian times as well. Directed at a mass audience, these plays had to be hits at the box-office, the domineering genres, therefore, were **farce** and **melodrama**. Melodrama was an essentially middle-class genre focussing on moral struggles and hazarding the consequences of a black and white moralising in which there was a clear-cut distinction made between good and evil, or love and hate. Its dramaturgy was determined by flat characters or types (i.e. 'the villain'), the main intention of its aesthetics was to create thrilling suspense by incorporating violence, crime, pathos or even horror elements. The significant representative of the popular drama of the time was Dion Boucicault, whose provocative farce *London Assurance*, much in the fashion of seventeenth-century Restoration Comedy (cf. section I.2.2.5), held a mirror up to society's hypocrisy and also had an important impact on Oscar Wilde's later drawing-room comedies, though it was at the same time fairly grounded in Victorian values. Obviously, this popular drama was the perfect opposite to the 'elitarian' **verse drama** or **closet drama** by authors like Tennyson, Browning, Arnold, or Swinburne.

Melodrama's inherent struggle against moral corruption and injustice and its didactic function to make the audience realise this through pathos helped to pave the way for the **social problem play** by writers like Arthur Wing Pinero or Henry Arthur Jones, who attempted realist portrayals of the social issues of the time. In the 1890s, this development was further instigated by the advent of Henrik Ibsen's plays in London. George Bernard Shaw wrote *The Quintessence of Ibsenism* in 1891, which, for Shaw, meant the basis of his rigorous attack on Victorian values in social problem plays such as *Widowers' Houses* and *Mrs Warren's Profession* (published as *Plays Unpleasant* in 1898) and many more plays that made Shaw one of the leading playwrights of the twentieth century. Farce and melodrama were both structural elements in the dramatic work of Oscar Wilde, the aesthetic highlights of his entire writing career were farcical comedies like *Lady Windermere's Fan*, *A Woman of No Importance*, *An Ideal Husband*, and, particularly, *The Importance of Being Earnest*. Elegant, witty, provocative, relishing in linguistic paradox and puns, Wilde challenged and exposed the moral (i.e. 'earnestness') as well as the theatrical conventions of the time. In fact, Wilde's comedies constituted elaborate parodies of these conventions. The playful and artificial lightness which characterised their tone and the entire absence of any didactic purpose pointed towards a modern, self-reflexive use of language.

## Select Bibliography

**Abrams, M. H., and Stephen Greenblatt, eds.** *The Norton Anthology of English Literature.* 7th ed. 2 vols. New York: Norton, 2000.

**Arnold, Matthew.** *Culture and Anarchy.* Ed. Samuel Lipman. New Haven: Yale University Press, 1994.

**Beer, Gillian.** *Darwin's Plots: Evolutionary Narrative in Darwin, George Eliot and Nineteenth-Century Fiction.* London: Routledge and Kegan Paul, 1983.

**Bremond, Claude.** "La logique des possibles narratifs." *Communications* 8 (1966): 60–76.

**Broich, Ulrich.** "Der 'negative Bildungsroman' der Neunziger Jahre." Pfister and Schulte-Middelich 197–226.

**Bronfen, Elisabeth.** *Over Her Dead Body: Death, Femininity, and the Aesthetic.* Manchester: Manchester University Press, 1993.

**Buckley, Jerome Hamilton.** *The Triumph of Time: A Study of the Victorian Concepts of Time, History, Progress and Decadence.* Cambridge: The Belknap Press of Harvard University Press, 1966.

**Dalziel, Nigel.** *The Penguin Atlas of the British Empire.* London: Penguin, 2006.

**David, Deirdre, ed.** *The Cambridge Companion to the Victorian Novel.* Cambridge: Cambridge University Press, 2001.

**Dijkstra, Bram.** *Idols of Perversity: Fantasies of Feminine Evil in Fin de Siecle Culture.* Oxford: Oxford University Press, 1986.

**Dowling, Linda.** *Language and Decadence in the Victorian Fin de Siecle.* Princeton: Princeton University Press, 1986.

**Ermarth, Elizabeth Deeds.** *Realism and Consensus in the English Novel: Time, Space and Narrative.* Princeton: Princeton University Press, 1998.

**Foucault, Michel.** *Überwachen und Strafen: Die Geburt des Gefängnisses.* Frankfurt/M.: Suhrkamp, 1994.

**Gilbert, Sandra M., and Susan Gubar.** *The Madwoman in the Attic: The Woman Writer and the Nineteenth-Century Literary Imagination.* New Haven: Yale University Press, 1979.

**Gilmour, Robin.** *The Victorian Period: The Intellectual and Cultural Context of English Literature, 1830–1890.* London: Longman, 1993.

Goetsch, Paul. *Die Romankonzeption in England 1880–1910*. Heidelberg: Winter, 1967.

Greenslade, William. *Regeneration, Culture and the Novel: 1880–1940*. Cambridge: Cambridge University Press, 1994.

Houghton, Walter E. *The Victorian Frame of Mind: 1830–1870*. New Haven: Yale University Press, 1957.

Kern, Stephen. *The Culture of Time and Space, 1880–1918*. Cambridge: Harvard University Press, 1983.

Ledger, Sally. *The New Woman: Fiction and Feminism at the Fin de Siècle*. Manchester: Manchester University Press, 1997.

Marshall, Gail, ed. *The Cambridge Companion to the Fin de Siècle*. Cambridge: Cambridge University Press, 2007.

Marx, Karl. "Das Kapital. Kritik der politischen Ökonomie." *Karl Marx und Friedrich Engels Gesamtausgabe*. Vol. II/5. Berlin: Dietz Verlag, 1983.

Mergenthal, Silvia. *Autorinnen der viktorianischen Epoche: Eine Einführung*. Berlin: Schmidt, 2003.

Mergenthal, Silvia. *Erziehung zur Tugend. Frauenrollen und der englische Roman um 1800*. Tübingen: Niemeyer, 1997.

Middeke, Martin. *Die Kunst der Gelebten Zeit: Zur Phänomenologie literarischer Subjektivität im englischen Roman des ausgehenden 19. Jahrhunderts*. Würzburg: Königshausen & Neumann, 2004.

Miller, J. Hillis. *The Disappearance of God: Five Nineteenth-Century Writers*. Cambridge: Harvard University Press, 1963.

Nowak, Helge. *Literature in Britain and Ireland: A History*. Tübingen: UTB-Francke, 2010.

Nünning, Vera. *Der englische Roman des 19. Jahrhunderts*. Stuttgart: Klett, 2000.

Osterhammel, Jürgen. *Die Verwandlung der Welt: Eine Geschichte des 19. Jahrhunderts*. Munich: Beck, 2009.

Pfister, Manfred, and Bernd Schulte-Middelich, eds. *Die 'Nineties: Das englische Fin de siècle zwischen Dekadenz und Sozialkritik*. Munich: Francke, 1983.

Pittock, Murray, ed. *Spectrum of Decadence: The Literature of the 1890s*. London: Routledge, 1993.

Pordzik, Ralph. *Der englische Roman im 19. Jahrhundert*. Berlin: Schmidt, 2001.

Remak, Henry H. H. "A Key to West European Romanticism." *Colloquiua Germanica* 2 (1968): 37–46.

Robotham, Sheila. *Women in Movement: Feminism and Social Action*. London: Routledge, 1993.

Schalk, Fritz. "Fin de Siècle." *Fin de Siècle: Zu Literatur und Kunst der Jahrhundertwende*. Ed. Roger Bauer. Frankfurt/M.: Klostermann, 1977. 3–15.

Schnackertz, Hermann Josef. *Darwinismus und literarischer Diskurs. Der Dialog mit der Evolutionsbiologie in der englischen und amerikanischen Literatur*. Munich: Fink, 1992.

Schopenhauer, Arthur. *The World As Will and Idea*. Trans. R. B. Haldane and J. Kemp. 3 vols. London: Routledge & Kegan Paul, 1883–1886.

Seeber, Hans Ulrich, ed. *Englische Literaturgeschichte*. 5th ed. Stuttgart: Metzler, 2012.

Shires, Linda M. *Rewriting the Victorians: Theory, History, and the Politics of Gender*. London: Routledge, 1992.

Thompson, Nicola Diane. *Victorian Women Writers and the Woman Question*. Cambridge: Cambridge University Press, 1999.

Thornton, R. K. R. "'Decadence' in Later Nineteenth-Century England." *Decadence and the 1890s*. Ed. Jan Fletcher. London: Arnold, 1979. 15–30.

Wendorff, Rudolf. *Zeit und Kultur. Geschichte des Zeitbewußtseins in Europa*. Opladen: Westdeutscher Verlag, 1980.

Wheeler, Michael. *Death and the Future Life in Victorian Literature and Theology*. Cambridge: Cambridge University Press, 1990.

Wheeler, Michael. *English Fiction of the Victorian Period 1830–1890*. London: Longman, 1985.

Zwierlein, Anne-Julia. *Der physiologische Bildungsroman im 19. Jahrhundert: Selbstformung, Leistungsethik und organischer Wandel in Naturwissenschaft und Literatur*. Heidelberg: Winter, 2009.

*Martin Middeke*

## 2.6 | Modernism

### 2.6.1 | Terminology

The term '**modernism**' is used to describe a set of cultural and aesthetic practices developed in the early part of the twentieth century and marked by a revolt against the dominant values and poetics of the nineteenth century. It sparked a sceptical attitude towards Christian religion, the Empire and nationalism, the idealization of the family and women's role within society and privileged subjective viewpoints and psychological interests. Ezra Pound's injunction to "Make it New" (the title of his 1934 essay collection) served as a common denominator to a cultural movement which was by no means restricted to literature, but rather encompassed painting, sculpture, music, architecture, dance and other artistic fields. Insofar as it is an **international phenomenon** (cf. entry I.3.4) and covers such diverse tendencies as naturalism, symbolism, imagism, futurism, cubism, vorticism, expressionism, and surrealism, it seems more appropriate to speak of '**modernisms**' in the plural form instead of one overarching 'modernism.' Generally speaking, modernist aesthetics relies on modes of abstraction and introspection and with reference to literature in particular, modernism denotes a style which is often termed avantgardist because of its focus on formal experiment. In Britain, modernism had far less impact on drama than on prose fiction and poetry, even though some European playwrights such as Antonin Artaud, August Strindberg and Henrik Ibsen influenced modernism across the genres (Childs 102).

---

**Key Texts: Modernism**

**James Joyce,** *A Portrait of the Artist as a Young Man* (1916)
**D. H. Lawrence,** *Women in Love* (1920)
**William Butler Yeats,** "The Second Coming" (1920)
**T. S. Eliot,** *The Waste Land* (1922)
**James Joyce,** *Ulysses* (1922)
**Katherine Mansfield,** *The Garden Party* (1922)
**Virginia Woolf,** *Mrs Dalloway* (1925)
**Virginia Woolf,** *To the Lighthouse* (1927)
**Dylan Thomas,** "Fern Hill" (1945)

---

### 2.6.2 | Scope and Periodization

**What Was Modernism?** All modernist writers share a marked concern with the nature of selfhood, consciousness, and experience, and they try to reach beyond conventional notions of time, reality and language. In Brian McHale's words, the dominant aspect of modernist fiction is therefore **epistemological**—it asks questions such as "How can I interpret the world of which I am a part? And what am I in it?" (9). These issues arise from a growing uncertainty about human experience as it is aptly expressed in **Virginia Woolf**'s statement on the challenges the modern novelist has to face:

Examine for a moment an ordinary mind on an ordinary day. The mind receives a myriad impressions—trivial, fantastic, evanescent, or engraved with the sharpness of steel. From all sides they come, an incessant shower of innumerable atoms; and as they fall, as they shape themselves into the life of Monday or Tuesday, the accent falls differently from of old [...]. Life is not a series of giglamps symmetrically arranged; life is a luminous halo, a semi-transparent envelope surrounding us from the beginning of consciousness to the end. Is it not the task of the novelist to convey this varying, this unknown and uncircumscribed spirit, whatever aberration or complexity it may display, with as little mixture of the alien and external as possible? ("Modern Fiction")

The preoccupation with new ways of thinking and feeling about the world was shaped significantly by developments in psychology and psychoanalysis, but also triggered by a changing **political consciousness**. Some of the aims of modernist authors were to render the new zeitgeist and changing human relations, which were seen to be conditioned by the technological inventions and increasing speed of the machine age, by an awareness of the growing gap between the wealthy and the poor as well as by the effects of urbanization and transformations in the sex/gender system.

Modernism's diversity stems not only from its broad range of concerns and approaches; it is also due to the fact that it was an international affair. The European metropolis, especially **London, Paris, and Berlin**, was the centre of attraction and meeting place for numerous artists and writers, many from the English-speaking world. Thus Paris was chosen by the Irish novelist James Joyce and by American poet Gertrude Stein as a new long-term abode and place of artistic production, while the American Thomas Stearns Eliot spent most of his creative life in London and even became a British citizen in 1927. This experience of exile, which served as a stimulus to a lot of modernist writing, was not limited, perhaps not even primarily related, to the authors' status as foreigners, but more often than not arose from a subjective sense of alienation from 'home' and their culture of origin.

**When Was Modernism?** The term 'modernism' itself was never used by any specific group of artists or writers of the period. Although the first reference in the sense of a modern(ist) aesthetic style—here applied to architecture—can be found as early as 1929 (Hitchcock 205), the term only came into widespread use retrospectively, namely by Anglo-American critics from the 1960s onward. The exact beginning and end of modernism has always been and continues to be a matter of debate. One extreme position was held by German philosopher Theodor W. Adorno, who argued that modernism is a qualitative and not a chronological category (218). In determining the beginning, some critics follow Virginia Woolf, who claimed in her 1924 essay "Character in Fiction" that "on or about December 1910 human character changed." That month saw the death of the British king, Edward VII, which meant the end of the Edwardian age. It was also the opening month of the influential Post-Impressionist Exhibition in London, organized by art critic and **Bloomsbury Group** member Roger Fry. This latter event seems to constitute a more decisive turn, since the show allowed the British public a first encompassing and, for many, disturbing encounter with the works of 'modern' European **painters** like Vincent van Gogh, Paul Cézanne, Georges Seurat or Paul Gauguin. Their radically new styles, their experiment with perspective, their use of vivid colours, texture and unusual brushwork provoked shocked reactions in the viewers (the exhibition was retrospectively labelled 'the Art Quake of 1910') but were a source of inspiration for many modernist writers who subsequently attempted in their own literary medium a decentering of perspective and tried out new forms of literary composition such as montage or cinematic techniques.

1910 to 1930 are usually considered the puritanical boundaries of modernism, and there is a general critical consensus that the rise and climax of literary modernism occurred in the 1920s. **1922** is often regarded as a particularly important year because it saw the first publication of two milestones of modernism—James Joyce's novel **Ulysses** and T. S. Eliot's poem **The Waste Land**. However, from

**Focus on the Bloomsbury Group**

The ➔ Bloomsbury Group was a loose association of leading English intellectuals who frequently met in Bloomsbury, London between 1905/06 and World War II. It included such prominent members as **Virginia Woolf**, **E. M. Forster**, **Roger Fry**, **Vanessa Bell**, and the economist **John Maynard Keynes**. These key figures of modernism exerted a strong influence on contemporary artistic and social discourse.

a gender-critical point of view, it seems counterproductive to focus exclusively on the 1920s, because even though some 1930s literary texts tended to be more politically charged than formally experimental, a great number of modernist women writers only started their careers during that decade. One of the most frequent temporal framings of modernism therefore is 1910 to 1939, 1940 or even 1941 (depending on whether the outbreak of World War II is viewed as a 'natural' point of termination or whether the suicide of one the main representatives of literary modernism, Virginia Woolf, is taken to be constitutive). Most critics agree nowadays that modernism only became possible after a long transitory period of detachment from and subversion of Victorian norms of literary writing (cf. entry I.2.5), which started in the 1890s at the latest.

**Who Was Modernism?** The term 'modernism' was and is controversially discussed within literary and art criticism. As early as 1934, British architect Reginald Blomfield published an anti-modernist polemic against what he considered 'Modernismus' of German origin, and debased it as an epidemic that had invaded Britain since the

Paul Gauguin,
*Three Tahitians* (1899)

war. In recent years, several critics have expressed their scepticism of modernism's alleged elitism and narrow scope, which arise from the sole focus on aesthetic or formal innovation, disregarding less conspicuously experimental texts and a great number of thematically innovative works. A certain irony is involved in the fact that the authors and artists now considered as outstanding representatives of high modernism only reached small audiences and were rather unsuccessful commercially in their own time, the early twentieth century. Avantgardist writing constituted only a small part of the literary field which was mainly directed at a mass readership.

**Modernism Studies.** For the last decades, modernist works have served as principal objects of analysis and modernist style has been an inspiration to Anglo-American literary studies. Modernism seems to have advanced to the status of an academic critical category in the 1960s, partly out of resistance against a contemporary culture that was dominated by the postmodern turn away from depth and concern with the past and that was instead directed towards surface structures and the present (Wilson 135). However, from the 1970s, poststructuralist theorists increasingly turned to modernist studies which they regarded as a rich resource for linguistic experiment and subversion. **Poststructuralism** shares with modernism a marked concern with language as an arbitrary and instable system of signification and as a shaping force of human experience and epistemology. This is probably one reason why poststructuralist critics such as Roland Barthes, Julia Kristeva or Jacques Derrida tend to concentrate on modernist writing rather than on postmodern texts and why even much of their own critical output seems to be based on modernist aesthetics (cf. entry II.4).

In the 1980s and 1990s, feminist literary critics initiated a more gender-adequate scope of the exploration of modernism. Not only did they challenge the alleged centre of Anglo-American literary modernism, i.e. the exclusive status of Wyndham Lewis's "Men of 1914" (Ezra Pound, T.S. Eliot, James Joyce, Wyndham Lewis) but they also questioned their implicit reliance on very specific notions of gender, class and ethnicity. Their call for an inclusion of women writers in the canon of modernist writing and a widening definition of modernism to account for writers and works that were successful in the literary market of the 1920s and 1930s has resulted in a range of studies that

*Extensions of the modernist canon*

take both formal and thematic innovation as a point of departure (Linett). Thus, they typically investigate both 'aesthetic modernism' and 'historical modernity' (Felski), which has led to an **extension of the modernist spectrum** that now often encompasses female authors like Dorothy Richardson, Jean Rhys, May Sinclair and in some cases, Vita Sackville-West, Rebecca West, Rosamond Lehmann, Elizabeth Bowen, and Radclyffe Hall.

In recent years, postcolonial literary studies have increasingly focussed on modernism's relationship to the categories of place, nation and colonialism (e.g. Booth and Rigby). The postcolonial approach prefers to focus on modernist texts which engage closely with issues of imperialism and are subtly subversive of its ideologies. This critical interest leads to the analysis of the role of the 'primitive' and of 'othering' in modernist writing, and it includes investigations into the relationship between modernism, imperialism and the degeneration paradigm (Edmond).

## 2.6.3 | Modernist Aesthetics

**Intermedial Relations.** The period of modernism is characterised by an intense dialogue between the arts (Zwernemann 229–30). These intermedial relations meant, on the one hand, that literary modernism was influenced by painting, film, etc., and on the other, that individual artists frequently worked in more than one medium (this is true e.g. for D. H. Lawrence, Wyndham Lewis and Mina Loy). **Artistic circles** such as the Bloomsbury Group or Vorticism (see box), which included writers, painters, sculptors and art critics, transgressed medial boundaries. Many literary authors saw painting as their sister art, and strove to develop similar techniques, especially because innovations in painting seemed to be highly advanced in comparison to literary experiment. One famous example is Gertrude Stein, an artist who saw a particularly close relationship between her own texts and Pablo Picasso's cubist paintings. At times, this close interdependence between different fields of creativity would also prove problematic for individual artists as D. H. Lawrence's example shows. Because of their emphasis on sexuality, his paintings as well as two of his novels (*The Rainbow*, 1915, and *Lady Chatterley's Lover*, 1928) called the British censor into action, and they were banned as pornographic under the Obscene Publications Act.

In their attempt to break with traditional aesthetic conventions, artists and literary authors used different innovative techniques, all of which emphasized the difficulties of representation (Lewis 3). These innovations included non-objective or 'abstract' painting, which renounced traditional subject-matter for the sake of mere patterns of lines and colours, and cubism, which abandoned the central perspective that had been normative since the Renaissance. A questioning of the central perspective also occurred within narrative fiction, where new techniques of representing the **consciousness** of characters (usually subsumed under the heading of 'stream of consciousness') and of **narrative transmission** ('figural narration') aimed at disempowering the omniscient narrator. In the realm of poetry (e.g. by Ezra Pound or T.S. Eliot), **free verse** with its rather loose syntax began to substitute well-formed stanza structures and intricate rhyme schemes and meter. Individual rhythm, both visual and textual, became an important aesthetic principle, as imagist poetry as well as futurist and vorticist paintings show. The **crisis of representation** also made itself felt in the theatre, where the 'invisible fourth wall' separating the audience from the actors was broken down and actors thematized their status as characters. Aesthetic language, whether verbal or visual, was no longer trusted to render reality in a one-to-one relationship, but was instead regarded as a system of signification which constitutes rather than mirrors the 'real.' This sense of a crisis of representation provides the crucial link between modernism and postmodernism. Its aesthetic products triggered a lot of hostility because critics and the public often found modernist paintings or writings difficult to access.

Changes in the Literary Market: The 'Little Magazines.' One of the questions raised by modernist literature is how it was possible for highly experimental and avantgardist literary texts, which were unlikely to reach large readerships, to enter the book market at all (McDonald). In the first three decades of the twentieth century, the publication of modernist texts on both sides of the Atlantic was largely enabled by numerous so-called 'little magazines,' which increasingly replaced late Victorian commercial magazines and periodicals that had catered to mainstream tastes. The editors of little magazines—some of them wealthy patrons of the arts with no need for large profits—instead aimed at adopting the new aesthetic and intellectual ideas from Europe, especially France, and em-

## Focus on Imagism and Vorticism

The early twentieth century was the heyday of **artistic movements** such as imagism, vorticism, and Italian futurism—associations of artists that had their own aesthetic and sometimes political agendas which they self-confidently expressed and reflected.

→ Imagism was a movement around Ezra Pound that distanced itself from the poetics of Romanticism (cf. entry I.2.4) and sought to reduce poetic expression to a single image "which presents an intellectual and emotional complex in an instant of time." In his essay "A Retrospect," Pound identified three principles of Imagism:

- Direct treatment of the 'thing' whether subjective or objective.
- To use absolutely no word that does not contribute to the presentation.
- As regarding rhythm: to compose in sequence of the musical phrase, not in sequence of the metronome. (Pound, "A Retrospect")

→ Vorticism was founded by Pound, Wyndham Lewis, and others in an effort to make imagism more dynamic and to incorporate cubist and futurist elements. Its short-lived literary magazine, *BLAST*, contained both theoretical aesthetic discussions and original literary works by writers such as Pound, Lewis, T.S. Eliot, and Ford Madox Ford.

phasized the arts at the cost of political and social issues. This also meant that they foregrounded an intermedial interest, linking contemporary literature and the visual arts especially. Thus, the American little magazine *The Dial* (1880–1929) published photographs of works by Henri Matisse, Amedeo Modigliani and Pablo Picasso alongside new literary works by T.S. Eliot, Ezra Pound and William Carlos Williams (Wilson 120; cf. also entry I.3.4). The little magazines were especially appropriate for the publication of short stories, which advanced to a prominent status within modernist literature (Buchholz). From the point of view of gender, it is interesting to note that the modernist profile of little magazines such as *The Little Review* or *The Egoist* was significantly shaped by their female owners and editors. However, most little magazines had to face serious financial problems and censorship struggles, since they often sold by subscription only, and by the end of the 1920s, *The Dial, The Little Review* and *The Egoist* had all ceased publication.

The Debate on Highbrow, Middlebrow, and Lowbrow Literature. Highbrow modernist authors who are canonized today, such as Woolf, Lawrence or Eliot, were neither very popular nor highly regarded in their own time. The more traditional,

Richard Boix's "Walking Architecture" is one of the many drawings published in *The Dial*.

conventional novelists such as Arnold Bennett (1867–1931) and John Galsworthy (1867–1933; Nobel Prize for Literature 1932) were much more successful financially and reached larger readerships. Their more popular style of writing—often classified as '**middlebrow**'—was predominantly realist, often with a slant of social criticism, and alongside romance fiction and crime novels (categorized as 'lowbrow literature') they attended to mainstream tastes. As critics like Andreas Huyssen have pointed out, high modernist writers tended to emphasize the seemingly unbridgeable gap between an **elite culture and the masses**, which he calls 'the great divide': "Modernists such as T. S. Eliot and Ortega y Gasset emphasized time and again that it was their mission to salvage the purity of high art from the encroachments of urbanization, massification, technological modernization, in short, of modern mass culture" (163). According to Rainey (33), by the end of the first decade of the twentieth century, this modernist polarization between 'high' and 'low' literature was already firmly established. One symbolically charged scene which shows the modernist contempt for mass-produced literature can be found in James Joyce's novel *Ulysses* (1922) where the protagonist Leopold Bloom uses pages torn from the popular Victorian weekly *Tit-Bits* to wipe his bottom.

With the spread of cultural and gender studies within literary academia, middlebrow and even lowbrow texts from the period of modernism have received new critical attention—as cultural artefacts to be read against contemporary cultural discourses, as works that have influenced highbrow modernist writing in many ways, and in conjunction with other medial forms such as radio and film (Habermann). Narrative fiction thus turns out to have been an important contribution to the leisure industry of the modernist period, with novels becoming more affordable because of technological improvements in printing that facilitated the transition from the expensive three-decker novel of the nineteenth century to cheap one-volume editions.

### 2.6.4 | Central Concerns of Modernist Literature

The First World War. Even today, World War I continues to be called the 'Great War' in Britain, and is considered the central political event of the early twentieth century. In the cultural consciousness of many Britons, World War I was perceived as a definite caesura, and this "sense of a gap in history that the war engendered became a commonplace in imaginative literature of the post-war years" (Hynes xiii). To modernist artists and writers, coming to terms with an experience of hitherto unknown wartime losses, of the values of Western 'civilization' renounced and of the outbreak of violence and destruction with the help of new, cruel methods of warfare served as a major creative trigger. Modernism's literary responses reflected the **social disruption** that the war represented to those affected by it and emphasized "alienation, plight, chaos, unreason, depression and disenchantment with culture" (Childs 163).

However, the war itself was seldom depicted in modernist works, even though its consequences were visible everywhere in the 1920s: millions of people were left wounded, disabled, displaced, traumatized and grieving, and the idea of 'a lost generation' dominated cultural memory. Instead of centering on the war itself, modernist works written during or in the decade after the war frequently took a **nostalgic look at the past** and tried to recreate it imaginatively (Stevenson 138–40; Erll). This is true for James Joyce's modernist novel *Ulysses* (1922), which reconstructs life in Dublin in 1904, as it is true for Virginia Woolf's *To the Lighthouse* (1927), which depicts the untroubled and idyllic summer holidays of the Ramsay family in the first part, mourns their loss in the middle part "Time Passes" by portraying the summerhouse in decay and devoid of human life, and portrays the bleak post-war world in its third and last part.

While the so-called **soldier poets** such as Siegfried Sassoon, Richard Aldington, Robert Graves, Edward Thomas, and Wilfred Owen resist classification as modernists in an aesthetic sense, their response to the war can partly be aligned with narrative writings, e.g. the pessimistic portrayal of shell-shocked war veteran Septimus Smith in Woolf's *Mrs Dalloway* (1925). If the first two years of the war saw the production of war poetry that celebrated patriotic enthusiasm and displayed it in an elevated, idealized diction with the central terms of 'honour,' 'glory,' and 'England,' after the disastrous Battle of the Somme in 1916, war poems were characterized by a thinly veiled criticism and sense of disillusionment with the war (Erll 238–41). Anti-war poetry focussed very concretely on the everyday reality of trench warfare, on the horrors and suffering of war and its fatal aesthetization; yet in its radical questioning of the progress of history, its turning inward and foregrounding of paradoxes and incoherences, it is not so far removed from the concerns of high modernism (Hynes 457–58).

A similar shift from initial enthusiasm to disillusionment with the war took place in the field of narrative fiction: **Pro-war narratives** such as Gilbert Frankau's *Peter Jackson* (1920) and Ernest Raymond's *Tell England* (1922) continued the literary tradition of the imperialist boy's adventure story of the nineteenth century, trivialized the war as a game of sports and staged myths of male heroism. By contrast, an even earlier wartime novel, Rose Macaulay's *Non-Combatants and Others* (1916), centres on a young woman's experience of life at the British homefront, which she—as a social outsider with a physical disability—perceives as useless, and inscribes the pointlessness of war into its narrative structure through fragmentation and stasis.

Psychology and Psychoanalysis. Modernism was strongly influenced by developments within psychology and especially psychoanalysis (Frosh). Thus, Sigmund Freud's discovery of the **unconscious** was highly influential for many modernist artists and writers since it challenged faith in rationality and allowed for a new concept of human behaviour as contingent. The idea that conscious and unconscious parts of the mind interact with each other and that unconscious and unknowable desires derive their energy from bodily instincts challenged the validity of Victorian moral concepts such as self-control, discipline and restraint. Another way in which Freud's theory appealed to modernist writers was that he considered unconscious meanings to be at work in language. The Freudian notion of the unconscious as a dynamic and disruptive force undermined the traditional concept of the autonomous subject of liberal humanism and foregrounded the importance of dreams and dream-like states—aspects which found diverse reverberations in modernist literature (for further information on psychoanalysis and its impact on literary studies, cf. entry II.7).

The modernist interest in character psychology led to the development of new, specifically narrative techniques of representing consciousness. These are usually subsumed under the heading of '**stream of consciousness**'—a term initially introduced into psychological discourse by American psychologist William James in his *Principles of Psychology* (1890):

Christopher Nevinson's Vorticist painting *A Bursting Shell* (1915) expresses the 'shell shock' many soldiers experienced in World War I.

Consciousness [...] does not appear to itself chopped up in bits. Such words as 'chain' or 'train' do not describe it fitly as it presents itself in the first instance. It is nothing jointed; it flows. A 'river' or a 'stream' are the metaphors by which it is most naturally described. In talking of it hereafter, let us call it the stream of thought, of consciousness, or of subjective life (vol. 1, ch. 9).

### Eliot and Yeats

In the field of poetry, T. S. Eliot's **The Waste Land** is generally regarded as a key work of modernism because of its concentration of typical high modernist elements such as an imagist condensation of meaning, a fragmentation of myths and other cultural elements and evocation of a sterile and broken civilization. At the same time, although *The Waste Land* may not be a direct representation of the war, it abounds with images of decay and destruction, of death and loss. Its very first lines,

April is the cruellest month, breeding
Lilacs out of the dead land

not only refer intertextually to Geoffrey Chaucer's *Canterbury Tales* (cf. section I.2.1.3), but can also be read as an implicit cultural reference, since the major military offensives on the Western Front took place in springtime (Erll 244). Eliot's *The Waste Land* stages a deeply felt sense of cultural crisis and disorientation with its sudden shifts of location and language—a poetic structure clearly shaped by the experience of the war. (For an interpretation of the poem in the context of American modernism see section I.3.4.3.)

William Butler Yeats's poem **"The Second Coming"** (1920) is more explicitly rooted in the realities of the war. The poem can be regarded as a pessimistic reflection on the uncertainties and anxieties created by the aftermath of World War I. The apocalyptic overtones and nightmarish visions of the poem are corroborated by the use of violent, terrifying imagery and an archaic, ritualistic language.

Interpretation

### James Joyce, *Ulysses*

James Joyce's novel *Ulysses* is considered a classic of experimental modernism despite its rather banal subject-matter. The novel chronicles one day in the life of three Dublin-based characters—the middle-aged Jewish advertising salesman, Leopold Bloom, his wife Molly, and the young intellectual poet Stephen Dedalus, who was the protagonist in Joyce's earlier novel *A Portrait of the Artist as a Young Man* (1916). The exceptional literary status of *Ulysses* is due to Joyce's use of a varied and sophisticated stream-of-consciousness technique, in which free indirect thought and interior monologue complement authorial control. These narrative choices allow Joyce to achieve almost cubist character portrayals by creating constantly alternating perspectives and effortless switches between a character's inner consciousness and a seemingly objective narratorial distance. The novel, whose characters and incidents are intertextually related to Homer's verse epic *The Odyssey*, thus works against any narrow, "one-eyed" vision of reality (Stevenson 52).

Interestingly, the first person to apply the notion of 'stream of consciousness' to the field of literary production was a novelist and critic herself. **May Sinclair**, who was familiar with the works of Sigmund Freud and C. G. Jung, employed it in a 1918 review of the first volumes of Dorothy Richardson's novel-sequence *Pilgrimage* (1915–1967) to describe a narrative technique which renders a character's consciousness as a flux. She praises Richardson's narrative achievement, which consists in an exclusive centering on the consciousness of the protagonist Miriam Henderson, i.e. by restricting herself to one reflector figure for more than 2,000 pages of text. Sinclair herself also adopted numerous concepts from contemporary psychology and psychoanalysis in her literary works. This alliance with psychoanalysis against Victorian values emerges clearly from her novel *Life and Death of Harriett Frean* (1922) in which she thematizes the harmful effects of repression to her female protagonist, who remains fatefully entangled in an oedipal triangulation all her life and never manages to break with her parents' injunction to "behave beautifully," that is to keep to the Victorian feminine ideals of self-denial and renunciation. Unlike Sinclair's earlier eponymous heroine in *Mary Olivier* (1919), Harriett Frean is unable to achieve sublimation, to channel her desires into some socially acceptable new dimension such as art or literature or music. By remaining trapped in her role as her parents' daughter socially, emotionally and even somatically, Harriett Frean illustrates one of the basic tenets of psychoanalysis—that our childhood and our parents shape our lives.

**Time and Space.** At the beginning of the twentieth century, there was a widespread sense that the pace of life was quickening. Innovations in the transport sector (automobiles, airplanes, an improved railroad system) as well as in communication technology (telegraph, telephone) transformed the experience of time significantly. Since the late nineteenth century, there had been attempts in Britain and the U.S. to standardize time, which resulted in the consensus of 25 countries in 1884 to make Greenwich the zero meridian and thus to establish **World Standard Time**. The late nineteenth and early twentieth centuries have thus come to be called "the clock's final triumph in ordering life" (Stevenson 119; cf. Kern).

The increasing importance attributed to the subject-dependency of perception received scientific support through Albert Einstein's **theory of relativity** introduced first in 1905 and then, in a more general framework, in 1916. With Einstein, the traditional Newtonian distinction between the categories of time and space was radically questioned. His theory of relativity required a rethinking of the seemingly objective-because-measurable notion of clock time and fuelled reflections on subjective mind time. Even though Einstein did not exert any direct influence on modernist writing, his insight that a sequence of events might seem to take place in a different temporal order if it is observed from two separate viewpoints moving in different directions or at a different speed probably served as an inspiration to plot experiments in narrative fiction (Lewis 24).

The ideas of Anglo-French philosopher Henri Bergson (1859–1941) found even more immediate reverberations with modernist writers and intellectuals, especially the Bloomsbury Group (Gillies). Bergson distinguished between time as 'duration'—as the indivisible, continuous flow experienced only by the individual through intuition—and time as divisible, quantitative and studied by science, the 'public' time of the external world. If public time or 'clock time' spatializes time, i.e. divides, names and regularizes it in order to analyse and explain, duration indicates most truthfully the nature of existence because it is a qualitative and not quantitative category. It mingles past and present and accounts for the subjective perception of time speeding up or slowing down:

Pure duration [*durée*] is the form which the succession of our conscious states assumes when our ego lets itself *live*, when it refrains from separating its present state from its former state [...] [I]n recalling these states, it does not set them alongside each another, but forms both the past and the present states into an organic whole, as happens when we recall the notes of a tune, melting, so to speak, into one another. (Bergson 100)

For Bergson, memory was a way of suggesting the relation between the material and the 'spiritual' worlds, a relationship which he thought public, spatialized time denied. This notion of memory and a newly subjectivized concept of time strongly influenced modernist literature, particularly Marcel Proust's *A la recherche du temps perdu* (1913–1927) and Virginia Woolf's novel *Mrs Dalloway* (see box).

During the first few decades of the twentieth century, space underwent a process of subjectivization similar to that of temporal experience.

The **visual arts**, cubism and futurism in particular, experimented with space on the canvas by splitting it into several—often contradictory—perspectives. In cubist paintings such a fragmentation of the represented object(s) suggested the simultaneity of diverse subjective angles depending on the observer's position; in the case of futurist paintings, it was used to suggest dynamic movement in a static medium and thus to find a visual equivalent to the interdependency of time and space. Just as in painting, space in literary writing is no longer represented as a mere setting, but is often presented through the subjective lens of one or more characters, in a fragmented fashion and grasped synesthetically, through the simultaneous use of several senses. The cultural space of the metropolis, with its specific range of mentalities, its atmospheric attraction and more liberal moral attitudes, advances to a privileged status within many modernist novels, and the individual dynamization of space is reflected in the figure of the **urban flaneur** or flaneuse as well as in the—male and female—traveller (Würzbach).

Cyril Edward Power's futurist linocut *Whence and Whither?* (1930) expresses the dynamics of the modernist city.

---

**Time in the Modernist Novel: *Mrs Dalloway* and *Stephen Hero***

In *Mrs Dalloway* (1925) **Virginia Woolf** introduces an enormous number of perspectives with numerous shifts from one character to another. The system that nevertheless produces cohesion consists in the bells of Big Ben and of other London churches, which signal to the reader that a certain amount of time has passed on the June day of 1923 to which the story time in *Mrs Dalloway* is restricted. The novel presents the reader with characters who each show very different proportions of duration and measurable time in their lives. Both clock and mind time are used as techniques of implicit characterization. One example would be Lucrezia Warren Smith, the wife of traumatized war veteran Septimus Smith, who feels that the London church bells assume the authoritarian attitude of psychiatrist Dr. Bradshaw when they turn into unrelenting and threatening 'Bradshaw time' after a visit paid to the doctor: "Shredding and slicing, dividing and subdividing, the clocks of Harley Street nibbled at the June day, counselled submission, upheld authority, and pointed out in chorus the supreme advantages of a sense of proportion" (133). Some of Woolf's characters also experience time in a specifically intense and emotionally charged manner. These highly subjective and overwhelming experiences of a particular moment in time resemble what **James Joyce**, in his unfinished manuscript of the novel *Stephen Hero* (1944), termed 'epiphanies'—a sudden moment of vision, revelation or awakening which affects the character deeply on a spiritual level but does not necessarily result in a palpable new insight or knowledge: "By an epiphany he meant a sudden spiritual manifestation, whether in the vulgarity of speech or of gesture or in a memorable phase of the mind itself. He believed that it was for the man of letters to record these epiphanies with extreme care, seeing that they themselves are the most delicate and evanescent of moments" (ch. 25).

Interpretation

**Sex/Gender, Sexuality, and the Body.** In Britain, the topic of human sexuality had entered public consciousness in the last two decades of the nineteenth century thanks to the writings of Havelock Ellis, John Addington Symonds and Edward Carpenter. Sexologists like Ellis and Symonds started to fuel research into sexual identities, sexual behaviour and sexual relationships much earlier than Freud's theories did, although sexological research only reached its peak in the 1920s and 1930s. This new discipline took two different directions: On the one hand, it acknowledged sexuality as a human (not only a male) necessity and took a sceptical attitude towards traditional family structures; on the other hand, it drew attention to so-called 'deviant' sexualities, i.e. homosexuality, or sexual inversion, as Ellis preferred to call it, prostitution and asexuality (Gutenberg 69–75). Sexologists thus pleaded for a depathologising recognition of hetero-, homo- and bisexual orientations at the same time as they were establishing **new sexual norms** themselves (such as the eroticization of female subordination in heterosexual relationships and the requirement of actively practising sexuality—to 'perform' adequately in order to maintain one's health).

*Discussions of sexuality in modernist novels*

Some literary authors of the period such as Radclyffe Hall (1880–1943) or E. M. Forster (1879–1970) adopted these sexological explanations to motivate the behaviour of their fictive characters. Hall's novel *The Well of Loneliness* (1928), which can almost be read as a textbook example of Havelock Ellis's theory of sexual inversion, was clearly meant to be a serious political intervention and was understood as one by the British censorship authorities who banished it directly after the first publication (while they ignored similar narrative representations in the comic mode, such as Compton Mackenzie's *Extraordinary Women*, 1926). Hall's text is anti-modernist in a formal and aesthetic sense, but is highly modern in the way it reflects contemporary debates on the 'third sex.' With her didactic appeal for compassion and tolerance towards her invert protagonist Stephen Hall, she inscribes herself into the discourse of sexological classification.

Such a watering down of the Victorian doctrine of separate spheres and the concurrent dichotomous sex/gender system was not limited to the spiritual or psychological realm, though. Especially narrative texts of the 1920s and 1930s—not necessarily modernist ones in a formally experimental sense—tend to stage gender transgressions concretely, even physically at times, in the form of parasite and vampire figures or of metamorphoses from human into animal form (Gutenberg). Such **borderline characters** are either functionalised as threats to the dominant system of heterosexuality (e.g. in novels written as a polemic against sexual inversion such as Clemence Dane's *Regiment of Women*, 1916) or they are presented as embodiments of a revolutionary potential and hope for the future (as the witch-like eponymous heroine in Sylvia Townsend Warner's novel *Lolly Willowes*, 1926). If non-canonized and long neglected texts like these are read against the works of some modernist writers, they can shed new light on their rather conservative sexual politics. This is true for most of D. H. Lawrence's novels, which can be viewed as progressive in their sexual explicitness but reactionary in the way they base human well-being, that is psychological and physical health, on very conventional, hierarchically organized heterosexual relationships.

## Select Bibliography

**Adorno, Theodor W.** *Minima Moralia: Reflections on a Damaged Life*. Trans. E. F. N. Jephcott. New York: Verso, 2005.

**Baldick, Chris.** *The Modern Movement: 1910–1940*. Oxford: Oxford University Press, 2004. Vol. 10 of *The Oxford English Literary History*. Ed. Jonathan Bate. 13 vols. 2001–2006.

**Batchelor, John.** *The Edwardian Novel*. London: Duckworth, 1986.

**Bell, Michael.** *Literature, Modernism and Myth: Belief and Responsibility in the Twentieth Century*. Cambridge: Cambridge University Press, 1997.

**Bergson, Henri.** *Time and Free Will*. Trans. F. L. Pogson. New York: Harper and Row, 1913.

**Blomfield, Reginald Theodore.** *Modernismus*. London: Macmillan, 1934.

**Booth, Howard J., and Nigel Rigby, eds.** *Modernism and Empire*. Manchester: Manchester University Press, 2000.

**Bradshaw, David, ed.** *A Concise Companion to Modernism*. **Malden:** Blackwell, 2003.

**Buchholz, Sabine.** *Narrative Innovationen in der modernistischen britischen Short Story*. Trier: WVT, 2003.

**Calinescu, Matei.** *Five Faces of Modernity: Modernism, Avant-Garde, Decadence, Kitsch, Postmodernism*. Durham: Duke University Press, 1987.

**Childs, Peter.** *Modernism*. London: Routledge, 2000.

**Edmond, Rod.** "Home and Away: Degeneration in Imperialist and Modernist Discourse." Booth and Rigby 39–63.

**Erll, Astrid.** "Der Erste Weltkrieg in Literatur und Erinnerungskultur der 1920er Jahre." *Kulturgeschichte der* englischen Literatur: Von der Renaissance bis zur Gegenwart. Ed. Vera Nünning. Tübingen: Francke, 2005. 237–50.

Felski, Rita. "The Gender of Modernity." *Political Gender: Texts and Contexts.* Eds. Sally Ledger, Josephine Mc-Donagh, and Jane Spencer. Hemel Hempstead: Harvester Wheatsheaf, 1994. 144–55.

Frosh, Stephen. "Psychoanalysis in Britain: 'The rituals of destruction.'" Bradshaw 116–37.

Fussell, Paul. *The Great War and Modern Memory.* London: Oxford University Press, 1975.

Gillies, Mary Ann. "Bergsonism: 'Time out of mind.'" Bradshaw 95–115.

Gutenberg, Andrea. *Körper, Sexualität und Moral: Die Auseinandersetzung mit Degenerationsvorstellungen in englischer Literatur und Kultur: 1910–1940.* Trier: WVT, 2009.

Habermann, Ina. "Modifikationen des Modernismus: Medialität, Identität, Populärkultur." *Kulturgeschichte der englischen Literatur: Von der Renaissance bis zur Gegenwart.* Ed. Vera Nünning. Tübingen: Francke, 2005. 251–63.

Henke, Suzette A. "Modernism and Trauma." *The Cambridge Companion to Modernist Women Writers.* Ed. Maren Tova Linett. Cambridge: Cambridge University Press, 2010. 160–71.

Hewitt, Douglas. *English Fiction of the Early Modern Period: 1890–1940.* London: Longman, 1988.

Hitchcock, Henry Russell. *Modern Architecture: Romanticism and Reintegration.* New York: Payson & Clarke, 1929.

Huyssen, Andreas. *After the Great Divide: Modernism, Mass Culture, Postmodernism.* London: Macmillan, 1986.

Hynes, Samuel. *A War Imagined: The First World War and British Culture.* New York: Macmillan, 1990.

Kern, Stephen. *The Culture of Time and Space: 1880–1918.* Cambridge: Harvard University Press, 2003.

Lewis, Pericles. *The Cambridge Introduction to Modernism.* **Cambridge:** Cambridge University Press, 2007.

Linett, Maren Tova, ed. *The Cambridge Companion to Modernist Women Writers.* Cambridge: Cambridge University Press, 2010.

McDonald, Peter D. "Modernist Publishing: 'Nomads and Mapmakers.'" Bradshaw 221–42.

McHale, Brian. *Postmodernist Fiction.* **London:** Routledge, 1987.

Nünning, Vera, ed. *Kulturgeschichte der englischen Literatur: Von der Renaissance bis zur Gegenwart.* Tübingen: Francke, 2005

Rainey, Lawrence. "The Cultural Economy of Modernism." *The Cambridge Companion to Modernism.* Ed. Michael H. Levenson. Cambridge: Cambridge University Press, 1999. 33–69.

Stevenson, Randall. *Modernist Fiction: An Introduction.* Hemel Hempstead: Harvester Wheatsheaf, 1992.

Williams, Keith, and Steven Matthews, eds. *Rewriting the Thirties: Modernism and After.* London: Longman, 1997.

Williams, Raymond. *The Politics of Modernism: Against the New Conformists.* Ed. Tony Pinkney. London: Verso, 1989.

Wilson, Leigh. *Modernism.* London: Continuum, 2007.

Woolf, Virginia. *Mrs Dalloway.* 1925. Oxford: Oxford University Press, 1992.

Würzbach, Natascha. *Raumerfahrung in der klassischen Moderne: Großstadt, Reisen, Wahrnehmungssinnlichkeit und Geschlecht in englischen Erzähltexten.* Trier: WVT, 2006.

Zwernemann, Jens. "Das Bild des Menschen in modernistischer Literatur und Malerei." *Kulturgeschichte der englischen Literatur: Von der Renaissance bis zur Gegenwart.* Ed. Vera Nünning. Tübingen: Francke, 2005. 225–36.

*Andrea Gutenberg*

## 2.7 | Postmodernism

Postmodernism can be seen as both a **continuation of and a reaction against modernity**. It has become an important concept under which a variety of concerns in late twentieth and contemporary Western literature and culture have been subsumed and negotiated. Its proponents see it heralding a new era and finally terminating the project of modernity, whose continuities since the Renaissance and the Enlightenment postmodernism is said to have irrevocably and radically severed.

### 2.7.1 | Terminology

**Postmodernism: An American Phenomenon?** Pointing to globalization as both one of its conditions and hallmarks, the American critic **Fredric Jameson** presents postmodernism as a product of "the brief 'American century' (1945–73) […] while the development of the cultural forms of postmodernism may be said to be the first specifically North American global style" (*Postmodernism* xx; cf. also entry I.3.5). This view seems to be supported by attitudes in Britain, Ireland and other parts of Europe where postmodernism has been at least as much criticised as it has been celebrated (e.g. Norris; Eagleton), and where the importance of postmodernism as a cultural influence or explanatory concept has regularly been played down. This general assessment has its merits, but it also occludes outstanding European contributions without which neither the origins nor the later developments of postmodernism as it appears today can be adequately conceptualized. Finally, the specific forms of postmodernism which can be found in various nations, cultures or ethnicities as well as in various historical phases, disciplines, or art forms can vary immensely and need specific and carefully individualized exploration. This is what will be done in the following for literature and culture in Britain and Ireland, even if the wider context cannot always be excluded.

**Terminology and Definitions.** In general usage but also in academic discourse, '**postmodernity**' and '**postmodernism**' are often used synonymously. Nevertheless, differentiating between them makes sense. Glenn Ward has the following proposal:

[Postmodernism] refers to cultural and artistic developments (i.e. in music, literature, art, film, architecture, and so on), while [postmodernity] has to do with social conditions and the 'mood' that these conditions give rise to. (12)

Thus, postmodernity has the wider reach. Bran Nicol, following Jameson's assessment, suggests that 'postmodernity' should be used in the political and socio-economic context where it formed a stage of 'postindustrial' or 'late capitalist' development: "It means that areas of society which were previously unaffected by the logic of the market, such as the media, the arts, or education became subject to the laws of capitalism […] and the advance of what we now call the 'globalization' of consumerism" (3). The two respective adjectives 'postmodern' and 'postmodernist' are used accordingly, but here 'postmodernist' clearly seems to occur less frequently. Whereas Ward argues that 'postmodernism' has come to cover the semantic field of 'postmodernity' (12), the reverse tendency can be observed on the adjectival level, thus making 'postmodern' as the adjective and 'postmodernism' as the noun the safest bets in everyday usage.

### 2.7.2 | Period, Genre, or Mode?

These formal semantic delimitations do not yet say much about the meaning of the terms as such. Two related questions arise next. First, the prefix 'post-' begs the question of postmodernism's relation to modernism and modernity and, second, the status and range of the concept itself have to be explored.

First, the prefix suggests the **chronological sequence** of postmodernism following after modernism. This may sound reasonable enough, but has its complications and will be further explained below.

Second, and more importantly, the prefix points to a **radical break with modernity** which modernism, for all its claims to novelty, is not usually credited to have effected with the same vehemence as postmodernism. Brian McHale points out: "I want to emphasize the element of logical and historical *consequence* rather than sheer temporal *posteriority*. Postmodernism follows *from* modernism, in some sense, more than it follows *after* modernism" (*Postmodernist Fiction* 5; his italics). Drawing on both the first and second implications, the prefix 'post-' seems to suggest that modernism, with its ways of making sense of the world and its specific forms of writing, has come to an end. This conclusion has, however, met with increasing scepticism. Thus, Peter Gay calls the last chapter of his magisterial survey of modernism "Life after Death?" and Marjorie Perloff argues that, "from the vantage point of the new century, the rejection of modernism no longer makes much sense" (571). This suggested continuance of modernist writing and culture into and beyond postmodern times has its reverse movement in the contention that postmodernist modes of writing could be identified within and before modernism. Here, a differentiation between the prehistory of the term on the one hand and the concept on the other seems helpful.

The prehistory of the term 'postmodern' has been variously described (e.g. Cahoone 2–3; Hassan, "Postmodernism" 6–7; Ward 6–8); it reaches back at least as far as the British painter John Watkins Chapman who used the term in the early 1870s (Higgins 7; there erroneously dated to the 1880s) to refer to a style of post-Impressionist painting. The German writer and philosopher Rudolf Pannwitz used it in 1917 to describe an amoral, nihilistic attitude which he observed among his contemporaries (64). In 1934, the Spanish literary critic Federico de Onis (xviii-xix) used *postmodernismo* to describe a reaction to the difficulty and experimentalism in modernist writing. For the theologian Bernard Iddings Bell, 'postmodernism' expressed the failure of secular modernism and the return to religion, while in the same year of 1939 the British historian Arnold Toynbee introduced a period after 1875 which he called the "post-Modern age" (Toynbee 5:43 and 8:338). None of the occurrences of the term 'postmodernism' listed so far tallies with its current usage, even if overlaps or similarities emerge. And, as Ihab Hassan ("Postmodernism" 7) notes, albeit somewhat underplaying Onis's position above, "only in the late sixties and early seventies [...] does postmodernism begin to signify [...] a critical modification, if not actual end, of modernism."

Postmodern Writing. As distinct from the prehistory of the term, incidents of postmodernist writing can be discovered in works published long before the term was available or the time had arrived when it became a wide-spread artistic and cultural phenomenon. These could be called instances of 'proto-postmodernism.' Bran Nicol lists the following as the most important features of postmodern texts (xvi):

1. A self-reflexive acknowledgement of a text's own status as constructed, aesthetic artefact.
2. An implicit (or sometimes explicit) critique of realist approaches both to narrative and to representing a fictional 'world.'
3. A tendency to draw the reader's attention to his or her own process of interpretation as s/he reads the text.

Looking at novels such as, famously, Lawrence Sterne's *Tristram Shandy* (1759–1767) or Denis Diderot's *Jacques le fataliste* (1771) and, more recently, possibly aspects of Samuel Beckett's novels and James Joyce's *Finnegans Wake* (1939), these texts could arguably be classed as postmodern by means of Nicol's criteria. Moreover, Nicol himself realizes that "none of these features are exclusive to postmodern fiction," and he emphasizes that "the question is really one of degree" (xvi). In Nicol's account, then, the characteristics of postmodern writing are not restricted to a certain time, but their intensity and frequency in the late twentieth century as well as their embeddedness in corresponding cultural and social developments nevertheless allow us to speak of a **postmodern period**. This is also a view Brian McHale accepts when he concedes that "postmodernist literary expression, and maybe postmodernism in general, behaves like earlier cultural periods and phenomena behaved." However, he also harks back to the French poststructuralist Jean-François Lyotard and the notion of a "perpetual postmodernism" (McHale and Neagu n. pag.) with postmodern features discernible throughout history.

**In conclusion,** the postmodern can be accepted as summarizing predominant features of writing in the period which started in the 1960s; it has an as yet unclear ending, and chronologically follows modernism, even if modernist writing may not have died out under its sway. At the same time, the postmodern has acquired a modal value in John Frow's sense (65–66) which could be used to highlight features of texts from all (literary) historical periods, even if, in practice, this modal application of an "adjectival" use (cf. Fowler 106) of the postmodern is not very common.

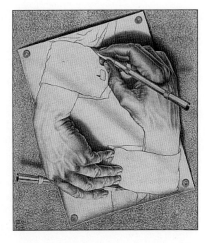

Representation and reality in M. C. Escher's *Drawing Hands* (1948)

### 2.7.3 | Conceptual Focus: Representation and Reality

Postmodernism can be conceptualized from many perspectives and within a variety of frameworks. Choosing a focus on referentiality and representation in the following is therefore undoubtedly eclectic, even if the choice will be shown to have some foundational validity, as postmodernism may be seen as the logical consequence of a '**crisis of representation**.' Modernists had reacted against the realist mode of writing of the preceding century mainly in two ways. First, they had become more sceptical towards the representational powers of language and, not unconnected to that, their interest shifted to other aspects of reality, mainly the 'inner' life, thought and consciousness of their characters much in line with the rise of Sigmund Freud's research in the human psyche. Still, it is important to realize that, ultimately, the modernists did not abandon the realist project of representing some form of 'reality out there' in writing. It is only that the objects of representation and the strategies of representation shifted; the referentiality of language had become complicated for them, but that was all the more reason to understand its nature to try to explore and possibly regulate it. This is clearly visible in developments in the philosophy of that time, epitomized in **Ludwig Wittgenstein**'s *Tractatus Logico-Philosophicus* (1921) where the Austrian philosopher had laid down rules for meaningful statements and denied all meaning to statements such as those to do with ethics, meaning or the self which did not follow these rules, famously ending the *Tractatus* with the aphorism: "Whereof one cannot speak, thereof one must be silent" (108). These scientific precepts for the precise calibration of referential language were clearly a modernist project and can be seen refracted in such diverse literary phenomena as T. S. Eliot's concept of an "objective correlative" in poetry (58) where Eliot attempted to extend the precision of language to the poetic representation of emotions, or in Ernest Hemingway's insistence on truth in fiction, as his alter ego in *A Moveable Feast* encourages himself: "All you have to do is write one true sentence. Write the truest sentence that you know" (ch. 2).

**Linguistic Turn.** Later, however, Wittgenstein drastically revised his positions put forward in the *Tractatus*. His new outlook, posthumously published in 1953 as *Philosophical Investigations*, epitomizes what has come to be called the '**linguistic turn**,' a phrase used already in the 1950s but popularized by Richard Rorty in 1968 and symptomatically visible in Wittgenstein's turnaround. Instead of optimizing the referentiality of language, Wittgenstein now radically continued the thought started in Ferdinand de Saussure's *Cours de linguistique générale* of 1916 (cf. section II.1.4). This dissociation of the signifier from the signified led Wittgenstein to seek the constitution of meaning in the relationship of signifiers among each other, and not in the referential function of a signifier (cf. *Philosophical Investigations* 2). He famously described this relationship between signifiers in analogy to the regulatory framework of a game. The most important consequences of this understanding of **language as a game** are

- first, that **meaning is contingent**, i.e. words, like chess pieces, have their specific signifying functions only within the regulatory framework of this particular 'game'; outside of these they are meaningless.
- Second, **meaning is produced within language**, through the process of contrasting and differentiating between individual words; meaning is not outside language where it might be mirrored or represented.

**Emergence of Postmodernism.** Adopting this view itself has far-reaching consequences. The linguistic turn is the 'Ur'-turn behind numerous further reconceptualizations in various disciplines and fields of knowledge (cf. Bachmann-Medick 33–36). Ultimately, the linguistic turn recalibrates the view on reality and radically reverses the perspective. Language no longer mirrors or refers to reality, but reality is a product and function of language and is not to be found outside of language. Fredric Jameson harks back to Friedrich Nietzsche

---

**Key Texts: Postmodern Theory**

**Michel Foucault**, *The Order of Things* (1966)
**Jacques Derrida**, *Of Grammatology* (1967)
**Roland Barthes**, "The Death of the Author" (1967)
**Paul de Man**, *Blindness and Insight* (1971)
**Gilles Deleuze** and **Félix Guattari**, *Anti-Oedipus* (1972), *A Thousand Plateaus* (1980)
**Jean-François Lyotard**, *The Postmodern Condition* (1979)
**Richard Rorty**, *Philosophy and the Mirror of Nature* (1979)
**Jean Baudrillard**, *Simulacra and Simulation* (1981)
**Fredric Jameson**, *Postmodernism, or the Cultural Logic of Late Capitalism* (1991)

when he speaks of the "prison house of language" in his book of that title, and Jacques Derrida famously coined the phrase that "**there is nothing outside of the text**" ("il n'y a pas de hors-texte"; 158). Roland Barthes, in his essay "The Reality Effect," shows how realist writers used certain narrative strategies to produce a literary effect which created the impression in the reader that the things presented in the text were 'real' (cf. section I.3.3.1). For Jean Baudrillard, this mechanism is not innocent, however, but could take the form of occluding people's perception in simulation. He writes:

> Representation stems from the principle of the equivalence of the sign and of the real (even if this equivalence is utopian, it is a fundamental axiom). Simulation, on the contrary, stems [...] *from the radical negation of the sign as value*, from the sign as the reversion and death sentence of every reference. [...]
> The transition from signs that dissimulate something to signs that dissimulate that there is nothing marks a decisive turning point. (6; italics in the original)

Baudrillard calls the latter kind of sign a 'simulacrum.' His famous example is Disneyland, which has the function of an empty signifier (see section II.4.3). Its overt fantasy points to a reality outside, which in Baudrillard's view does not exist anymore, thus producing a reality of the second order, or 'hyperreality.' The tables are turned and the 'real' world now needs Disneyworld to exist and is, ultimately, its product.

**Objections to Postmodernism.** This textual or linguistic fundamentalism, so to speak, has led, on the one hand, to scepticism, if not outright rejection of the postmodernist agenda. If 'reality' is a product of language or 'texts,' there is no way to get behind these and find meanings or points of reference outside of them. It horrified Marxist and neo-Marxist thinkers, such as Jameson (*Postmodernism*) or Terry Eagleton, who saw the traditional Marxist priority of the material base over the superstructure reversed and who feared that the subversion of referentiality to an outside, material world could imply a subversion of any political and social impact they expected from literature and the arts (cf. section II.2.2). Similar problems would arise for anyone who wanted to see literature and the arts as committed to a cause and as endowed with the mission to make a difference in culture and society, such as feminist or postcolonial writers. Again, if the order of the world was to be seen as a linguistic or textual one which had no

space for an Archimedean point outside itself, the foundations of most traditional conceptions of ethics were seen to crumble: 'Anything goes' is the catchphrase usually employed to criticize postmodernity's radical relativism. When there are no 'grand,' 'master' or 'meta-' narratives which provide legitimation, order and orientation in this 'postmodern condition' in Jean-François Lyotard's analysis (37 and *passim*), there is no outside reality to vouchsafe for referentiality and to anchor representation, and there is no profound or ultimate meaning deep down in the signifying structures of texts, 'below' their surface or 'behind' their first semantic appearance; there is only contingency, context, contiguity.

'Anything goes'

But this surface without depth or transcendent meaning, this metonymical reading at the expense of the metaphoric, produces its own order. That is often understood in Gilles Deleuze and Félix Guattari's concept of the '**rhizome**,' a network structure without centre or limits where everything can link up to everything else on the same level, such as, notably, pop and folk culture with 'serious' art, the trivial with the elitist, 'high' and 'low' culture, but also the historical in irreverent pastiche and insouciant intermixture with the contemporary, the exotic with the homegrown.

**Conclusion.** Postmodernism's essentially linguistic or textualist outlook need not, however, lead to chaos, but may simply imply that reality, referentiality and ethics are themselves to be understood textually, which some might say they have been all along; postmodernism would then have taught to give up the illusion of a hard and fast reality beyond **human 'ways of world-making' through language**, an illusion which is a specifically modern institution; which appeared with the rise of modernity; and which is on the wane as modernity is abandoned or revitalised in postmodernism. Values need not be less real or important for their textuality. The fact that Wittgenstein introduced the concept of 'game' in our understanding of language need not entail the conclusion that postmodernism is not to be taken seriously. Indeed, the ludic side of it is perhaps the most serious aspect of postmodernism, since games can only be played on the basis of a community with generally accepted rules and regulations; and these regulations are the result of negotiation and voluntary agreement; a potentially liberating move, after all.

## 2.7.4 | Genre and Postmodern Literary History

The lines of postmodernist thought sketched out so far, from the late modernist crisis of representation to the celebration of narrative or textuality and beyond, can also serve as a trajectory for recent literary history in Britain and Ireland, notably in the field of prose writing. Here, the novel in particular must be seen as the main arena for postmodernist developments, and will hence be the focus of the following considerations. Still, drama and poetry have their postmodern developments, albeit in different ways and partly in different time frames.

**Status of Poetry.** Brain McHale points out with reference to poetry: "what I think makes a pretty sound argument in the context of fiction, doesn't look nearly as sound in the case of poetry. Poetry from certain points of view had been postmodern before the postmodern, or had always already been postmodern" (McHale and Neagu, n. pag.). For Redell Olsen, poetry is the one genre that he describes as "relatively uninvested in the capital of a culture industry, which is currently terming itself in its latest guise as 'postmodern'" which is why, "[p]aradoxically, [...] poetry has the potential to be the most 'postmodern' and the most 'anti-postmodern' of the arts" (42). Thus, the poem "To Whom It May Concern" by Andrew Motion, poet laureate from 1999 to 2009, begins "This poem about ice cream / has nothing to do with government, / with riot, with any political scheme." Despite the first line's announcement, the poem never really gets round to its professed, trivial subject of ice cream, but is spent on continual asseverations that nothing 'serious' or 'political' which could upset the reader will be addressed. It therefore constitutes a highly self-reflexive way of criticising a line of poetry as well as a specific type of poetry readers' expectation that contemporary poetry is a pleasant play on words involving only harmless, quotidian scenarios without virulence or political substance, and the poem ironically carries this message by being precisely this, a playful consolation of an implied reader frightened of politics, recent history, and social commitment. In search of form (**New Formalism** is a watchword here) and of accessibility at the same time, poetry sits perhaps most precariously on the fence, looking in on the postmodern developments to be described now for the genre of the novel and, to some extent, paralleled in certain developments of British drama.

## 2.7.5 | Postmodern Developments in Britain and Ireland

The development of postmodernism is variously described and subdivided. Thus, Steven Connor lists "accumulation; synthesis; autonomy; and dissipation" (1) as subsequent stages in its development while Hans Bertens describes a move from "Anti-Modernism" to a phase in the 1970s to "Theorizing the Postmodern Condition" in the 1980s to the establishment of "The Postmodern as a New Social Formation." A description of the literary developments in Britain and Ireland will, however, be better served by phases reflecting on the styles of writing and on the narrative strategies employed.

**'Literature of Silence.'** Following this precept, Ihab Hassan's book title and phrase to describe the work of Henry Miller and Samuel Beckett, "the literature of silence," seems helpful to grasp the transition from Modernism to Postmodernism. Indeed, **Beckett** epitomizes this transition to a large degree, and his work has proved a major influence and inspiration on early postmodernist writers. Beckett's six major novels—and much of his drama can be included here—all explore and ultimately subvert questions of realist representation. As Bran Nicol sums it up: "Each of his fictions is a prolonged and increasingly more bleak and alienating exercise in questioning the status of the represented world of fiction and its relationship to the real world" (54). Beckett's novels display increasing physical immobility of their characters. While *Molloy* still has a quest motif with outward movement and action, all movement in Beckett's subsequent novel, *Malone Dies*, has come to a standstill. The protagonist Malone is in bed, waiting for

> ### Key Writers: Postmodern Poetry
>
> John Betjeman (1906–1984)
> Philipp Larkin (1922–1985)
> Ted Hughes (1930–1998)
> Sylvia Plath (1932–1963)
> Seamus Heaney (b. 1939)
> Andrew Motion (b. 1952)
> Carol Ann Duffy (b. 1955)
> John Burnside (b. 1955)
> Simon Armitage (b. 1963)

death. Hardly able to move, he tells stories. Although there is a parallel to Scheherazade in the *Arabian Nights*, the fictionality of the stories told is never out of sight. But not only the outward movement has come to a complete stop for the narrator; narration as such seems to fold back on itself, becoming ever more narrowly focalized, albeit often with an ironic twist:

I fear I must have fallen asleep again. In vain I grope, I cannot find my exercise-book. But I still have the pencil in my hand. I shall have to wait for day to break. God knows what I am going to do till then.
I have just written, I fear I must have fallen, etc. I hope this is not too great a distortion of the truth. (236–37)

Malone has just described the loss of his exercise-book: but where could he write that down if his exercise book is where readers are meant to assume the whole story is being written? This is, of course, a little joke on Beckett's part. However, its serious contention is that the narration can never catch up with what is to be narrated; narrating time takes much longer than the narrated time. The author exists only in so far as he is author and narrates; there is no existence in excess of narration and the author constitutes himself in the process of narration, thus becoming an example of Baudrillard's simulacrum: the function of narrator implies a reference to something else, an implication which is not realized, however, as it is turned back on itself by referring only to itself. That, too, is only a fiction, of course, as it all happens within the text.

By the time he wrote his last novel, Beckett had begun his career as a dramatist, notably with the success of **Waiting for Godot** (1952). From then on, both his drama and his prose seem to shrink into increasingly reduced forms, often just the length of a few pages down to the one page of *Breath* (1969), together with a growing emphasis on the breakdown of communication. In one sense, Beckett seemed bent on the paradoxical quest of expressing or approaching silence with words, silence appearing as the point where misunderstanding and the uncertainties of referentiality ended, but also where communication would finally collapse.

**Experimental Postmodernism.** Where Beckett and other dramatists of the theatre of the absurd had tackled the break-down of communication by writing plays about the break-down of communication and, in Beckett's case, by getting as far as possible to actually writing and acting this col-

lapse and crisis, other writers began to experiment in different directions. Thus, **James Joyce**, in his last, enigmatic novel, **Finnegans Wake** (1939), explores the limits of language in different ways. With the fall of man evoked as a motif right at the beginning of the novel, the postlapsarian nature of language appears as an important theme. Before the fall, there was direct communication between humans and between humans and God. But the book does not have a tragic structure, as the Fall into language is no reason to despair; it has its humorous side, as the immediate reference to Humpty Dumpty right at the beginning also seems to suggest:

The great fall of the offwall entailed at such short notice the pftjschute of Finnegan, erse solid man, that the humptyhillhead of humself promptly sends an unquiring one well to the west in quest of his tumptytumtoes: and their upturnpikepointandplace is at the knock out in the park were oranges have been laid to rust upon the green since devlinsfirst loved livvy. (ch. 1)

*Finnegans Wake* and
the fall into language

Other experiments in narrative style and technique followed from the 1960s onwards. Thus, Christine Brooke-Rose's (born 1923) monosyllabic titles—*Out* (1964), *Such* (1966), *Between* (1968), *Thru* (1975)—already point to **innovative technique**, which comes in bilingual neologisms, the exposal of the novel's textuality and focus on language, and stylistic experiment, *Thru* being written in the present tense throughout. Bryan Stanley William Johnson (1933–1973) depicts the London of his time, but all his seven novels are highly experimental. *Alberto Angelo* (1964) has holes cut in pages to allow a view into the future (which, textually, is the next page), and *The Unfortunates* (1969) contains unbound sections in a box which readers have to assemble for themselves. Gabriel Josipovici (born 1940) has similar metafictional techniques when he provides the inventory of a dead man's belongings in *The Inventory* (1968), uses the present tense throughout in the aptly entitled *The Present* (1975), or writes almost exclusively in dialogue in *Now* (1998).

The most frequently quoted departure from the realist mode is **John Fowles**'s *The French Lieutenant's Woman* (1969). Fowles presents a Victorian setting in the realist mode until the narrator steps out of the illusory mode in chapter 13:

If I have pretended until now to know my characters' minds and innermost thoughts, it is because I am writing in (just as I have assumed some of the vocabulary and "voice" of) a convention universally accepted at the time of my story: that the novelist stands next to God. He may not know all, yet he tries to pretend that he does. But I live in the age of Alain Robbe-Grillet and Roland Barthes; if this is a novel, it cannot be a novel in the modern sense of the word.

Further anti-realist devices follow. Starting from chapter 45 when the story has come to a happy ending, the reader is again addressed by the narrator and subsequently offered alternative endings, with the author figure repeatedly appearing in metaleptic fashion. The metafictional aspects which Fowles introduces in his novel and the irreverent use he makes of history by unmasking it as a narrative convention is certainly one of the early high points of postmodernist writing in Britain.

In the **theatre**, experimentation is possible on at least three levels, in the dramatic text, in directors' interpretations and in the ways of theorizing drama and theatre, but combinations are frequent. Postmodern ideas have been translated into **experimental forms of drama, theatre, performance or theory** by such famous figures as the American directors Robert Wilson or Richard Schechner, the German playwright Heiner Müller, the Polish director Jerzy Grotowski and his Laboratory Theatre, or theorized by the American director Herbert Blau, but impact of these radical new departures has been much more moderate in Britain. Although British theatre had its own contributions to make, such as the pioneering site-specific performances of the Welsh drama group Brith Gof realizing the 'spatial turn' in theatrical practice, the overall experimental impetus has remained guardedly moderate.

A scene from Martin Crimp's *Attempts on Her Life* (National Theatre, London, 2007, dir. Katie Mitchell)

**'Cornucopian' Postmodernism.** Experimentation in Fowles's generation never reached the radical extreme which Joyce had presented in *Finnegans Wake*. Traditional narrative retained its importance, even if its realist vein was continually subverted in metafictional reflexivity. By the 1980s, with Margaret Thatcher's premiership (1979–1990) often seen as the onset of the negative, late capitalist aspects of postmodernity in Britain, novelists seemed to have internalised the narrative techniques and strategies of the earlier experiments as a set of useful tools for new narrative coherence. Apart from their consciously postmodern self-referentiality, these novels deal with serious cultural, political and social issues. Thus, **Martin Amis**'s *Money: A Suicide Note* (1984) is the most well-known engagement with the political and cultural agenda Thatcher epitomized. His *Time's Arrow* (1991) reverses narrated time, starting with the death and ending with the birth of its protagonist, to approach the horrors of the Holocaust.

At the same time, narrative itself—one might speak of a narrative turn here—was proposed as a major epistemological tool, prefiguring human knowledge and culture. Thus, **Graham Swift** self-reflexively uses specifically local narrative as constitutive of history and human social interaction in general, notably in *Waterland* (1983) and *Last Orders* (1996). The narrative overlap between memory and fiction has not only developed into an important critical paradigm (cf. entry II.11), but has been a source of important inspiration in novels which explore the insight that human access to the past is mainly shaped by memory and that memory itself can be seen as following narrative conventions, so that narrative itself is a prime means of constituting and negotiating the past. This is shown in an exemplary way in the novels of **Kazuo Ishiguro**, such as *A Pale View of Hills* (1982) and the Booker Prize-winning *The Remains of the Day* (1989).

While the intermingling of experimental approaches, self-reflexive writing and more traditional realist conventions, often with a humorous note, has led to a situation in British writing where 'anything goes,' the result is far from banal. Many of the issues and points of contention which the modernists had criticized have remained, but they are now no longer seen as tragic and causes of despair. The lack of realist referentiality has brought about a **promethean unbound(ed)ness** which, far from being bogged down by scepticism about the precision and reliability of language has accepted contingency and the relativity of truth. But precisely because truth and values are seen as language-based and bound in narrative, the production of such narrative fiction has proliferated in postmodernism. The sheer multitude of narrative possibilities, experimental and avant-garde, but equally traditional and well-known, which come together in the contemporary novel in Britain could be called the 'cornucopian' version of postmodernism as the potential of the innovative moves through and beyond modernism as well as realism now appears to have opened in its full range and richness.

**Multiculturalism.** Such richness has been significantly increased thematically, but also formally, by the emergence of authors from Britain's fast-growing multicultural and multi-ethnic context. Although many of these texts have postcolonial themes and traits, they can by no means be reduced to reactions to Britain's colonial past and its consequences; rather, they must be seen as genuine contributions at the centre of what makes British society and culture today. **Salman Rushdie** looms large here as a pioneering figure. He catapulted himself to fame with *Midnight's Children* (1981), and later to more fame but also to Islamist hatred with *The Satanic Verses* (1988). He is certainly one of the most distinguished living writers in English. Although his *Satanic Verses* approaches the life of Indian expatriates in Britain in tantalizingly innovative ways, Rushdie himself, born in India, long a resident in Britain, now living mainly in the United States and writing about many cultures and themes world-wide, may resist appropriation to any national literature. He is, however, certainly a good example for a postmodern novelist, not only because of his itinerant, diasporic biography, but because he uses a wide range of narrative techniques and traditions in his work, such as history, myth, and magical realism, and fuses them into a style of his own which seems particularly apt to deal with the postmodern concerns of uprootedness, migration, globalization and the intermingling of cultures he so frequently writes about. In *The Ground Beneath Her Feet* (1999) his portrayal of the rock star Vina Apsara can be seen to combine many issues of postmodernity and to present a trenchant analysis and, possibly, critique of the 'postmodern condition' as such.

Many British writers from multi-ethnic backgrounds have followed in Rushdie's footsteps. **Hanif Kureishi** has colourfully illuminated the life

### Key Texts: Postmodern Drama

**Samuel Beckett,** *Waiting for Godot* (1952), *Endgame* (1957)
**Harold Pinter,** *The Birthday Party* (1958), *The Caretaker* (1960)
**Tom Stoppard,** *Rosencrantz and Guildenstern Are Dead* (1966)
**Caryl Churchill,** *Top Girls* (1982), *The Skriker* (1994)
**Sarah Kane,** *Blasted* (1995), *Cleansed* (1998)
**Mark Ravenhill,** *Shopping and Fucking* (1996)
**Martin Crimp,** *Attempts on Her Life* (1997), *Fewer Emergencies* (2005)
**Martin McDonagh,** *The Pillowman* (2003)

of Pakistani immigrants in London, starting with his acclaimed novel *The Buddha of Suburbia* (1990). He swiftly moved on to other themes in his more recent work such as *Intimacy*, *Gabriel's Gift*, or *Something to Tell You*, human relations and gender roles among them, meeting up with other traditions of writing, such as Jeanette Winterson's acclaimed explorations of the narrative constructions of gender as in *Sexing the Cherry* (1989) or *Written on the Body* (1992). Zadie Smith and Monica Ali come next to Kureishi in their recent rise to fame and in the similarity and the roll call of novelists writing from similar backgrounds on similar social and cultural situations is long, especially when the many writers from the English-speaking world are taken into account who are not writing in or about Britain, but whose books have found a wide market and many interested readers there.

The 'cornucopian' phase of postmodernism also fits the character of recent **theatrical productions** in Britain. While innovative and experimental staging techniques have been acknowledged and are being employed by British playwrights today, much of contemporary drama remains within the wider conventional setting, notably from the pen of such outstanding playwrights as Alan Ayckbourn, Howard Brenton, David Edgar, Brian Friel, or Tom Stoppard. It is at least possible to see this restraint in experimentation connected to a persistently radical streak informing this tradition from the **Angry Young Men** of the 1950s and 1960s onwards, where new topics (gender, ethics, religion, politics, history) are addressed in ever varying ways with traditional as much as with innovative dramatic techniques. Indeed, this 'radical' side can be understood as endemic to the genre, as it were, since, according to Tim Woods (80), drama "goes against the grain of our dominant technological and cultural practices" which are centred on film and the electronic media. In social and cultural comment, much innovative work has been done, notably in the field of gender and multi-ethnic contexts (see Griffin).

### 2.7.6 | After Postmodernism?

With this image of vibrancy and vitality in the British scene of writing, the question of an end to postmodernism seems futile, even if new departures keep being noticed (e.g. Stierstorfer; McHale, "What Was Postmodernism?"; Kirby). When, for example, Malcolm Bradbury renegotiates enlightenment values in *To the Hermitage* (2000) and em-

phasizes the materiality of texts as other writers recently re-emphasize the paradoxical combination of spirituality and materiality in the human body, as Michael Symmons Roberts has done in *Breath* (2008), there still does not seem to arise the need to announce a new period or paradigm. While the most radically experimental postmodernism may be passé and modernist concerns may admittedly remain, postmodernism as a project and development in the arts and in literature seems far from spent. As far as period divisions go, it is therefore fully justifiable to look at contemporary British literature from the perspective of a specifically British version of the postmodern in its mature and highly productive phase.

### Select Bibliography

**Bachmann-Medick, Doris.** *Cultural Turns: Neuorientierungen in den Kulturwissenschaften.* 3rd ed. Reinbek: Rowohlt, 2009.

**Barthes, Roland.** "The Reality Effect." *The Rustle of Language.* Trans. Richard Howard. Oxford: Blackwell, 1986. 141–48.

**Baudrillard, Jean.** *Simulacra and Simulation.* Trans. Sheila Faria Glaser. Ann Arbor: University of Michigan Press, 1994.

**Beckett, Samuel.** *Molloy, Malone Dies, The Unnamable.* 1958. New York: Alfred Knopf, 1997.

**Bell, Bernard Iddings.** *Religion for Living: A Book for Postmodernists.* London: The Religious Book Club, 1939.

**Bertens, Hans.** *The Idea of the Postmodern: A History.* London: Routledge, 1995.

**Cahoone, Lawrence.** Introduction. *From Modernism to Postmodernism: An Anthology.* Ed. Lawrence Cahoone. 2nd ed. Oxford: Blackwell, 2009. 1–13.

**Connor, Steven.** Introduction. *The Cambridge Companion to Postmodernism.* Ed. Steven Connor. Cambridge: Cambridge University Press, 2004. 1–19.

**Deleuze, Gilles, and Félix Guattari.** *A Thousand Plateaus, Capitalism and Schizophrenia.* Trans. Brian Massumi. Minneapolis: University of Minnesota Press, 1987.

**Derrida, Jacques.** *Of Grammatology.* Trans. Gayatri Chakravorty Spivak. Baltimore: Johns Hopkins University Press, 1974.

**Eagleton, Terry.** *The Illusions of Postmodernism.* Oxford: Blackwell, 1996.

**Eliot, T. S.** "Hamlet and His Problems." 1920. *The Sacred Wood and Major Early Essays.* By T. S. Eliot. Mineola: Dover Publications, 1998. 55–59.

**Fowler, Alastair.** *Kinds of Literature: An Introduction to the Theory of Genres and Modes.* Oxford: Clarendon Press, 1982.

**Frow, John.** *Genre: The New Critical Idiom.* London: Routledge, 2006.

**Gay, Peter.** *Modernism: The Lure of Heresy from Baudelaire to Beckett and Beyond.* London: Vintage, 2009.

**Griffin, Gabriele.** *Contemporary Black and Asian Women Playwrights in Britain.* Cambridge: Cambridge University Press, 2003.

**Hassan, Ihab.** "From Postmodernism to Postmodernity: The Local/Global Context." *Philosophy and Literature* 25.1 (2001): 1–13.

**Hassan, Ihab.** *The Literature of Silence.* New York: Random House, 1967.

**Higgins, Dick.** *A Dialectic of Centuries: Notes Towards a Theory of the New Arts.* New York: Printed Editions, 1978.

**Jameson, Fredric.** *Postmodernism, or the Cultural Logic of Late Capitalism.* London: Verso, 1991.

**Jameson, Fredric.** *The Prison-House of Language: A Critical Account of Structuralism and Russian Formalism.* Princeton: Princeton University Press, 1972.

**Kirby, Allan.** "Successor States to an Empire in Free Fall." *Times Higher Education.* 27 May 2010. 3 Sept. 2010 <http://www.timeshighereducation.co.uk/story.asp?storycode=411731>.

**Lyotard, Jean-François.** *The Postmodern Condition: A Report on Knowledge.* 1979. Trans. Geoff Bennington and Brian Massumi. Minneapolis: University of Minnesota Press, 1984.

**McHale, Brian.** *Postmodernist Fiction.* London: Routledge, 1987.

**McHale, Brian.** "What Was Postmodernism?" *Electronic Book Review.* 20 Dec. 2007. 3 Sept. 2010 <http://www.electronicbookreview.com/thread/fictionspresent/tense>.

**McHale, Brian, and Adriana Neagu.** "Literature and the Postmodern: A Conversation with Brian McHale." *Kritikos* 3 (2006). 12 Aug 2010 <http://intertheory.org/neagu.htm>.

**Nicol, Bran.** *The Cambridge Introduction to Postmodern Fiction.* Cambridge: Cambridge University Press, 2009.

**Norris, Christopher.** *The Truth About Postmodernism.* **Oxford:** Blackwell, 1993.

**Olsen, Redell.** "Postmodern Poetry in Britain." *The Cambridge Companion to Twentieth-Century English Poetry.* Ed. Neil Corcoran. Cambridge: Cambridge University Press, 2007. 42–55.

**Onis, Federico de.** *Antología de la poesia española e hispanoamericana: 1882–1932.* Madrid: Junta para Ampliación de Estudios e Investigaciones Científicas, 1934.

**Pannwitz, Rudolf.** *Die Krisis der Europäischen Kultur.* Nürnberg: Hans Carl, 1917.

**Perloff, Marjorie.** "Epilogue: Modernism Now." *A Companion to Modernist Literature and Culture.* Eds. David Bradshaw and Kevin J. H. Dettmar. Malden: Blackwell, 2006. 571–78.

**Rorty, Richard, ed.** *The Linguistic Turn: Essays in Philosophical Method: With Two Retrospective Essays.* Chicago: Chicago University Press, 1968.

**Rose, Margaret.** *The Post-Modern and the Post-Industrial: A Critical Analysis.* Cambridge: Cambridge University Press, 2001.

**Stierstorfer, Klaus, ed.** *Beyond Postmodernism: Reassessments in Literature, Theory, and Culture.* Berlin: de Gruyter, 2003.

**Toynbee, Arnold.** *A Study of History.* 12 vols. Oxford: Oxford University Press, 1934–1961.

**Ward, Glenn.** *Teach Yourself Postmodernism.* London: Hodder Headline, 1997.

**Wittgenstein, Ludwig.** *Philosophical Investigations.* 1953. Trans. G. E. M. Anscombe. 3rd ed. Oxford: Blackwell, 2001.

**Wittgenstein, Ludwig.** *Tractatus Logico-Philosophicus.* 1921. Trans. G. K. Ogden. Mineola: Dover Publications, 1999.

**Woods, Tim.** *Beginning Postmodernism.* Manchester: Manchester University Press, 1999.

*Klaus Stierstorfer*

# 3 American Literary History

The chapters of this section cover the five periods into which American literary history is usually divided: early American literature; the American Renaissance; realism/naturalism; modernism; and postmodern and contemporary American literature. Traditional literary historiography has situated the **beginnings of American literature** in the early seventeenth century, when the first English settlers arrived in Virginia and Massachusetts and wrote travel accounts, histories, and religious texts. As entry I.3.1 points out, however, the English were latecomers to American colonization, and if we look beyond national and language boundaries the beginnings of American literature can be dated back to 1492, when Columbus wrote his first letters about the new continent. More important still, there was a wide range of native cultures to whom the continent was not new at all. While our chapters focus on written literature, it must be kept in mind that Native American myths, legends, and chants were usually transmitted orally from generation to generation; they form a literary history of their own that dates back centuries before the Europeans arrived. The twentieth-century revival of Native American literature is covered in entry I.3.5.

These reflections raise the related question of what we mean by **'America'** when we speak about American literary history. In English and American Studies, 'America' traditionally refers to the United States, while Canada and the Caribbean are usually covered under the heading of 'postcolonial' or 'New English' literatures (cf. entry I.4). In recent years, however, these demarcations have become less clear-cut, since authors, texts, and ideas are crossing national boundaries with increasing frequency. The tendency in scholarship is to acknowledge the traditional categories but to draw attention to the fuzzy boundaries of these categories and the interactions across them.

While the beginnings of American literature are hard to pin down, the succession of styles and movements from the nineteenth century on is somewhat easier to define. The early nineteenth century saw the gradual emergence of a 'literary field' in the northeast, a substantial number of authors, critics, and publishers who were aware of each other and could define their literary creed in mutual discussion. It was from these circumstances that the relatively unified movement of transcendentalism emerged, and the authors associated with it in various degrees came to shape the period now known as 'American Romanticism' or the **'American Renaissance'** (entry I.3.2). The latter term suggests the epochal significance of writers like Emerson, Hawthorne, Melville, Thoreau, and Whitman, as well as of other equally important writers little recognized at the time, such as Emily Dickinson and Edgar Allan Poe. The American Renaissance is said to have ended with the Civil War (1861–1865), and indeed the shocking experience of that war and the social injustice of the Industrial Revolution in the following decades introduced a new style of writing that can be broadly defined as **realist and naturalist**. Entry I.3.3 defines these styles of writing, the second of which was much more prominent in the United States than in England, and shows how the alienating experience of unrestrained industrial capitalism motivated some writers to address these problems outright while others explored alternatives to the existing order. The popularity of 'local color' literature at the time indicates the literary mapping of the regional diversification of the United States, often accompanied by nostalgia for the simpler values and closeness to nature associated with rural America.

In the course of the nineteenth century, American literature had thus already achieved a considerable degree of cultural and literary independence, even if much of the mainstream literary production still followed European trends. In the twentieth century the currents of literary influence began to turn, and many pioneers of international literary **modernism** came from the United States.

The standard German-language history of American literature, ed. Hubert Zapf, 3rd ed. Stuttgart: Metzler, 2010

The poets Ezra Pound and T.S. Eliot in particular became enormously influential after they had moved to Europe in the wake of the First World War, where they joined Henry James and Gertrude Stein in establishing a new aesthetic and a literary field in which this aesthetic could thrive (entry I.3.4). While the 1910s are today regarded as the first modernist decade, however, the bestseller lists were dominated by the established naturalist writers long into the 1920s; the neat definitions of literary historians often conceal such overlaps. The same can be said for the transition from modernism to postmodernism after the Second World War. Entry I.3.5 begins with chapters on the continuities between these periods, especially in poetry and in drama, where the defining figures of the mid-twentieth century (Tennessee Williams, Arthur Miller) elude classification as either modernist or postmodernist. While **postmodernist** fiction reaches its high point in the 1960s and 70s, the aesthetic and epistemological assumptions of postmodernism remain a powerful influence into the later twentieth and the early twenty-first centuries. At the same time, the ethnic differentiation of American literature leaves its irreversible mark. Within the context of an ever-accelerating process of globalization, American literature is now undergoing another transformation in which realist and postmodernist, experimental and traditional styles of writing seem to converge in multiple new ways. Topics like trauma, ethics, ecology, the family, migration, and transcultural encounters are forming the narrative matrix of intensely personal and yet cosmopolitan narratives, in which American lives are examined as part of a globally shared life on the planet.

*Timo Müller/Hubert Zapf*

# 3.1 | Early American Literature

## 3.1.1 | Overview

John Smith's *A Map of Virginia* (1612), one of the earliest eyewitness accounts of America in the English language, begins:

VIRGINIA is a Country in America that lyeth betweene the degrees of 34 and 44 of the north latitude. The bounds thereof on the East side are the great Ocean. On the South lyeth Florida: on the North nova Francia. As for the West thereof, the limits are unknowne. (sect. 1)

This brief opening is characteristic of the **colonial worldview** in a number of ways. First, there is the foundational act of naming the country in print, a mental appropriation fittingly complemented by the physical measurement of space, a drawing of boundaries and borders. Next, there is the striking contrast between enclosure (to the East, South, and North) and the limitless expanse to the West: a space of copious opportunities that will determine American self-descriptions for centuries to come. Finally, and perhaps most importantly at the time, there is the inevitable framework of European power struggles: boxed in between French and Spanish holdings, Virginia beckons in Smith's tract as a promise yet to be fulfilled, an English dreamscape of pressing necessity but uncertain reality.

Competition over territories and resources fostered competing visions of America. Early European descriptions of the new continent were shaped as much by the wonder of the unexpected as by the need to legitimize their own existence. **Writing and settlement** were so closely interwoven that 'American literature' in its original form often looks like a double conjuring act: making itself appear self-evident while giving reality to a cultural realm improbably close to and yet marvelously removed from Europe. In important ways, it has remained so ever since: to read American literature means to read a literature which is different from others, not because of some unmistakable national character or exceptional heritage and destiny, but because of its inescapable investment in the **problematical term** *American*. Recursive to a degree so obvious it is easy to overlook, American literature has always been concerned with the conditions of its own possibility: with the power of words and narratives to create what they describe. How unlikely is it that the expansive name *America* came to denote, in the ordinary speech of most people in the world today, the United States? American Studies is about this unlikelihood; the discipline's defining concern is with the culture-making force of American self-descriptions.

It is sometimes said that America already existed in the European imagination before it was discovered. And true, literature has always fantasized about new worlds. The Western story repertoire abounds with model places of spiritual regeneration and perfect government. Christopher Columbus, too, went on his sea voyage with interpretive preconceptions in tow that were derived from his **readings**, although not of utopian philosophy or tales of earthly paradise but of the Bible and Marco Polo. It bears repeating that the latter's accounts of China shaped Columbus's project in more than rhetorical terms. Asia, physically so much more concrete than the myth of Atlantis or Plato's ideal Republic, provided a rationale and a destination for Europe's first American voyages. The goal was to find a Western passage to India; the aim, by going west, was to arrive in the Far East. In order to comprehend the astonishment produced by Columbus's inadvertent discovery in 1492, it is useful to remember that the Western hemisphere entered the European mind as an unexpected space. It may have already been filled with images and narratives of territorial self-transcendence, but once its dimensions became clear, they were staggering: a **New World** indeed. This surprise still reverberates 115 years later in

| **Timeline: The Making of 'America'** | |
|---|---|
| 1492 | Columbus lands in America |
| 1607 | Jamestown, the first permanent English settlement, is founded |
| 1620 | The Pilgrim Fathers found Plymouth Plantation in New England |
| 1630 | Massachusetts Bay Colony |
| 1692 | Salem witch trials |
| 1773 | Boston Tea Party |
| 1775–1783 | American War of Independence |
| 1776 | Declaration of Independence |
| 1791 | Bill of Rights ratified (the first ten amendments to the U.S. constitution) |
| 1803 | Louisiana Purchase: the U.S. acquires most of the American Midwest |
| 1812 | War of 1812 between the U.S. and Great Britain |
| 1823 | The Monroe Doctrine asserts U.S. influence over the Americas |

Smith's statement about the American West: "the limits thereof are unknown." After the empirical precision of the preceding sentences, this terse remark opens up bright vistas of possibility. No longer a realm of geographical transition, the West has become a massive challenge to the European imagination.

### 3.1.2 | Labor and Faith: English Writing, English Settlement (1584–1730)

England was a latecomer to the colonial race. Largely a Reformed nation—although Reformation theology took some idiosyncratic turns off the continent—it followed a course of colonization markedly different from Spain, Portugal, and France. In hindsight, it is hard to argue with the success of the English model, if success can be measured by the longevity of settlements, the sustained cultivation of resources, and long-term economic wealth. In intellectual terms, England brought two conflicting traditions to the New World: radical **Protestantism** and **Baconian empiricism**. In conjunction with the latter, early English authors tended to imagine the Western hemisphere not only as a natural paradise for exploitation or seclusion but as an explicitly political testing ground: a place to remake society. Appropriately, the early modern genre of *utopia* was launched by an English author, with Thomas More's Renaissance classic from 1516 (in Latin, translated into English in 1551; cf. section I.2.2.2). Francis Bacon followed suit in 1627 with *The New Atlantis*.

**Colonization.** But actual colonization started out differently. The first attempt at English settlement was initiated and overseen by **Sir Walter Raleigh**. It failed miserably. In 1584, Raleigh founded a colony on Roanoke Island, off the coast of today's North Carolina. Six years later, in Raleigh's absence, the settlement had mysteriously disappeared. All of the colonists were gone; only a signpost with the word "CROATOAN" remained. Unperturbed by the tragedy of the 'lost colony,' Raleigh turned his attention to South America, publishing *The Discovery of Guiana* in 1595, a tract promoting large-scale, Spanish-style settlements on the Orinoco river. Raleigh's book stands as one of the strongest expressions of the road not taken by English colonialism. It described Guiana as a land where riches could be acquired easily: "every stone that we stouped to take up, promised either

*Roanoke, the 'lost colony'*

golde or silver by his complexion" (pt. 4). *The Discovery of Guiana* urged Queen Elizabeth I to get a foothold in South America, because if she did not, Spain would enlarge its transatlantic holdings and become a colonial superpower. Not mincing his words, Raleigh recommended that a virgin land be raped:

> Guiana is a countrey that hath yet her maydenhead, never sackt, turned, nor wrought, [...] the graves have not bene opened for golde, the mines not broken with sledges, nor their Images puld downe out of their temples. It hath never bene entered by any armie of strength, and never conquered or possessed by any Christian Prince. (pt. 5)

A list of negatives, but its reasoning was unmistakably **imperialistic**: a rhetoric of national competition for resources and glory. In the end, England chose a different path to empire. Partly because of the costly failure of Roanoke, parliament and the crown decided to sidestep established models of settlement that relied either on private initiative or large-scale government commitment (as in the Spanish case). In contrast to these policies, England would concentrate on small bases which were to be financed by joint-stock companies and granted royal charters. Two companies were founded in this way: the Virginia Company of Plymouth (no relation to the later Puritan settlement in Plymouth, Massachusetts) and the Virginia Company of London, which in 1607 established the first permanent English settlement in Jamestown.

**Writing in the Jamestown Settlement.** In terms of its literary representation, Jamestown is inseparably linked with Captain **John Smith**, British America's first great prose stylist. Smith's description of the Powhatan Indians in *A True Relation of Virginia* (1608), though inflected by promotional purposes and Christian prejudices, counts among the earliest proto-ethnographic texts in American literature, evincing an empiricist ethos of observation and experiential knowledge. Even though Smith stayed in Jamestown for only two years, he shaped English colonial discourse in profound and lasting ways. Apart from being the author of some of the earliest English-language descriptions of the New World, Smith also became one of America's first self-made literary characters, mainly through his relationship with Powhatan's daughter Pocahontas, which he increasingly dramatized in later writings.

Like Raleigh, Smith believed that England required colonies to keep up with other European powers. Moreover, he feared that English society, with its economic imbalances between the lower and the upper classes, was heading toward a crisis. He was particularly troubled by the dependency of farmers on their landlords, but also by the growing number of young people who lived off their inheritances. The New World provided a solution to these problems; it made unprofitable labor profitable and counteracted rising unemployment, offering a purpose to aimless youngsters in the bargain. The underlying idea was as simple as it was convincing: **send England's surplus people overseas** to make them become productive elsewhere. For centuries, this formula, so different from the Spanish model, encapsulated the socio-economic rationale behind English (and later British) settlement efforts. In bettering their own condition, colonists were supposed to open up new resources for the home-country. And vice versa: by benefiting the market at home, they would improve themselves. Thus, the relationship between England and its colonies was considered to be a mutually beneficial and contractual one (during the American Revolution, this model would become the source of many a dramatic misunderstanding between parliament and the Anglo-American colonists).

Little wonder that Smith rejected "the shimmering mirage of gold [...] through which the sixteenth century saw the New World" (Gunn 65). Instead of Raleigh's emphasis on easy wealth, Smith stressed the importance of **diligent employment**. *A True Relation of Virginia* and *A Map of Virginia* reinforced this point, constantly repeating the need for *industry* in a fertile but demanding environment. Prototypically, these writings envisioned America as a place where hard-working young men and poor people could become self-sufficient and act in their own interests. Long before the liberal theoreticians of the Enlightenment, Smith maintained that land-ownership and private property were able to stabilize society. Believing that common wealth leads to commonwealth, Smith managed to do without the double-edged topos of America as a virgin to be raped or to be protected from modern corruption. Nor was Smith's America a paradise regained (in paradise there is no toil). Rather, the America of John Smith made a reasonable promise to those willing to exert themselves for their own and their community's welfare. Describing sustainable subsistence rather than sudden prosperity as the New World's boon, Smith's was an ideology of labor fulfilled,

---

**Focus on Pocahontas**

**Pocahontas** (ca. 1596–1617) was the daughter of Powhatan, a Native American chief in Virginia. She has become famous through Smith's account of how, as a small girl, she saved his life from execution at the hands of her father by shielding him with her own body. The historical accuracy of this account is dubious, however.

A nineteenth-century drawing of Pocahontas saving John Smith's life

---

extolling self-interested work and the satisfaction and safety that come with it.

Needless to say, there was a gap between these lofty ideals and the facts on the ground. Smith nearly despaired of the fortune-seekers in Jamestown, "ten times more fit to spoyle a Commonwealth, then either begin one, or but helpe to maintaine one" (*The Genrall Historie of Virginia* bk. 3, ch. 12). After he left in 1609, social and economic discipline in Jamestown deteriorated dramatically, as did relations with the natives. Virginia was saved from failure only when John Rolfe, the later husband of Pocahontas, developed a successful system of planting and exporting tobacco in 1612. However, to the extent that discourses create realities, it was important for the future course of North America that Virginia first described itself in terms of John Smith's socio-economic philosophy.

**Writing in Puritan New England.** A similar philosophy, with an additional ingredient, ruled Puritan New England. Calvinist theology crossed the Atlantic with those who founded **Plymouth Plantation** (1620) and the nearby Massachusetts Bay colony in Boston (1630). While holding fast to radical Protestant doctrines of divine sovereignty and predestination, these settlements developed flexible religious systems that balanced theological principles with the political and economic realities of an overseas colony. Rather than establishing strict theocracies, Plymouth and Massachusetts Bay separated religious and political authority at the level of local institutions, but committed both to a unified social ideology based on Christian notions of justice and morality, most famously expressed in **John Winthrop**'s lay-sermon *A Model of Christian Charity* (1630). Later revolutionaries, such as John Adams, regarded this Congregationalism as a forerunner of the enlightened separation of church and state.

The tension between Puritan theology and colonial *realpolitik*, faith and facts, dominates early literature from Massachusetts. **William Bradford,** the first governor of Plymouth, chronicled his settlement's history in *Of Plymouth Plantation,* written in two parts in 1630 and 1646–1648, and first published in 1856. Composed in the Puritan *plain style* which avoided ornamental rhetoric in favor of unadorned speech close to the vernacular, Bradford's book illustrates the mutual dependency of religious typology (i.e. the figural interpretation of worldly events as biblical symbols) and secular necessities. Everyday desires needed to be brought into accordance with a religious language that, in turn, gave meaning to the colonial experiences of displacement, exposure, and loss. Thomas Shepard's *Autobiography* (1646, published 1832) and the poems of **Anne Bradstreet** (written 1632–1672) bear witness to this sensual dimension of early American life. In fact, Bradstreet's records of her religious doubts and sexual longings for her

husband, sometimes described by modern scholars as covertly rebellious, were fully compatible with Puritan conceptions of faith and marriage. Later, American writers from Nathaniel Hawthorne to H. L. Mencken and Arthur Miller found it convenient to turn the Puritans into exemplars of sexual repression and American exceptionalism, but the texts speak a different language.

The more the colony thrived, the harder it became for Bradford to negotiate between the settlement's worldly success and its religious purity. Thus, the second part of his chronicle laments the decline of faith among the colonists, turning *Of Plymouth Plantation* into a jeremiad, the admonitory tale of a better past, which according to Sacvan Bercovitch is one of the central genres of North American writing. However, what Bradford saw as impending failure was the outline of an unequaled success story: Massachusetts' slow rise to become a mercantile force in the British empire. Bradford writes:

[T]he people of the plantation began to grow in their outward estates, by reason of the flowing of many people into the country, especially into the Bay of Massachusetts. By which means corn and cattle rose to a great price, by which many were much enriched and commodities grew plentiful. And yet in other regards this benefit turned to their hurt, and this accession of strength to their weakness. [...] And this I fear will be the ruin of New England, at least of the churches of God there, and will provoke the Lord's displeasure against them. (ch. 23, "Anno Dom: 1632")

A similar fear informed one of the most famous Puritan self-descriptions, John Winthrop's "**city upon a hill**" passage from *A Model of Christian Charity* (1630). Frequently quoted as an example of America's self-confident sense of mission, on closer inspection Winthrop's sermon reveals more anxiety than triumphalism. Its historical and intellectual contexts would have nothing to do with the imperial aspirations for which it was so often appropriated:

Now if the Lord shall please to hear us, and bring us in peace to the place we desire, then hath He ratified this covenant and sealed our commission, [and] will expect a strict performance of the articles contained in it; but if we shall neglect the observation of these articles [...] and prosecute our carnal intentions, seeking great things for ourselves and our posterity, the Lord will surely break out in wrath against us; be revenged of such a perjured people and make us know the price of the breach of such a covenant. [...] For we must consider that we shall be as a city upon a hill. The eyes

John Winthrop, Puritan writer and second governour of the Massachusetts Bay colony

### William Bradford, *Of Plymouth Plantation*

The conflicting claims of faith and facts structure *Of Plymouth Plantation* and the colonial imagination at various levels. Among other things, they frame Bradford's depictions of intercultural encounters. At one point, his chronicle relates how the English newcomers stumbled upon a store of Indian corn and freely helped themselves. Predictably, Bradford offers a typological interpretation of the event: "And here is to be noted a special providence of God, and a great mercy to his poor people, that here they got seed to plant them corn the next year, or else they might have starved, for they had none nor any likelihood to get any" (ch. 10). The question of who owns the corn seems to be conveniently avoided, because if it was placed by God, the taking of it cannot be theft. However, Bradford is thoroughly aware of the pragmatic vicissitudes of the situation, i.e. the fact that the Indians—potential trade partners and military allies—have stored the corn for purposes other than feeding the Christians. Therefore, he complements his religious interpretation with the following remark: "Also there was found more of their corn and of their beans of various colours; the corn and beans [we] brought away, purposing to give them full satisfaction when [we] should meet with any of them as, about some six months afterwards [we] did, to their good content" (ch. 10).

Bradford's insistence that the corn was properly exchanged in a trade-off would be unnecessary if his view of the natives were guided by typological conviction alone. But an exclusive reliance on theological discourse is prevented in this case by Bradford's knowledge that his struggling community will be dependent on Native assistance and instruction—not least in order to learn how to properly plant and grow the seeds they have just borrowed, with the help of God, from their future neighbors. Even later military conflicts, such as the Pequot War of 1636, did not divide neatly among ethnic or religious lines, but combined tribal and colonial groups in coalitions of interest, often dictated by internecine power struggles in European and Native communities.

of all people are upon us, so that if we shall deal falsely with our God in this work we have undertaken, and so cause Him to withdraw His present help from us, we shall be made a story and a by-word through the world. We shall open the mouths of enemies to speak evil of the ways of God, and all professors for God's sake. We shall shame the faces of many of God's worthy servants, and cause their prayers to be turned into curses upon us till we be consumed out of the good land whither we are going. (pt. 2)

In fact, the eyes of all people were not on Massachusetts. The world—addressed also by Thomas Jefferson 146 years later in the *Declaration of Independence*—could not have cared less what a small group of sectarians was doing in some wild, faraway province. New England's pervading sense of provincialism explains a lot about the colonists' need for self-assertion. Nothing short of divine providence would legitimize their presence in this godforsaken place. Thus, in American writing, the declaration of communal cohesion has all too frequently been a sign of the natural lack thereof, from settler cultures clinging to their biblical self-images to citizens pledging allegiance to the flag of a country without a royal family, state religion, or long inherited symbols expressive of a common heritage. American nationalism is a strange phenomenon, for it has a strange history, still different in important ways from those of other nations, entangled histories and worldwide webs of communication notwithstanding.

## 3.1.3 | A Revolutionary Literature (1730–1830)

Emphasizing faith over works, seventeenth-century Protestantism constantly needed to balance its appraisal of individual experience with the mediating agency of religious institutions, embodied by pastors and ministers. From the beginning, the Congregational establishment of New England worked hard to contain its faith's inherent tendency towards **antinomianism**, i.e. the privileging of subjective spiritual justification over the communal letter of the law. But Puritanism's propensity for self-radicalization broke through again and again, for the first time in 1636 with Anne Hutchinson's ultra-Puritan rebellion against the ministers and magistrates of Boston. Hutchinson was banned and became an implausible martyr in later American narratives (among other things, she served as inspiration for Nathaniel Hawthorne's *The Scarlet Letter*, 1850, and was

→ **Puritanism**, which originated as a reform movement within the Church of England, greatly influenced American life and politics in the sixteenth and seventeenth centuries. Its adherents hoped to purify church and society through an emphasis on God's sovereignty, the individual experience of grace, and a generally skeptical attitude toward institutional hierarchies. The Bible was seen as the only necessary dogmatic authority. Faith, rather than good works, served as the most important way to salvation.

featured in the 1964/65 TV series *Profiles in Courage*, based on John F. Kennedy's 1955 book of the same title).

**The Great Awakening.** In the eighteenth century, antinomianism could no longer be so easily controlled. Following the travels of British Methodist minister George Whitefield (pronounced *Whitfield*), a wave of evangelical revivals collectively known as the **Great Awakening** swept the thirteen British colonies in the 1730s and 1740s. The Great Awakening changed America's religious landscape forever, challenging the dominance of Congregational (in New England), Quaker (in Pennsylvania) and Anglican (in the Southern colonies) establishments with a welter of new evangelical denominations that preached immediate grace and sensuous rebirth. Revivalists such as Gilbert Tennent and—to a lesser degree—Jonathan Edwards held that God's grace touches the believer suddenly and without mediators, in one supremely intimate yet eminently consequential moment of spiritual conversion. The evangelical vocabulary, with its insistence on *revival*, *regeneration*, *rebirth*, etc. put a high premium on sensual immediacy— an anti-institutional philosophy that resonated with the enlightened epistemologies of the day. Combined with spatially transgressive forms of communication (itinerant preachers such as Whitefield proved to be extremely adept in their use of the press), evangelicalism turned socially explosive. Belief in the spiritual benefit of transformative experience became increasingly widespread—and such a mentality was reinforced by the rise of modern practices of **publicity**, themselves inherently transformative and wide-spreading. Thus, the commercial marketing of charismatic preachers, the newspaper coverage of sensational mass awakenings, and the public competition of religious goods benefited the evangelical movement as much as it fostered a steadily growing, largely secular consumer culture.

Even though the Great Awakening was not an overtly political movement, it did more than diversify American religion: through its influence on colonial media, it paved the way for the revolt of 1776. As the first truly common experience of all thirteen colonies, it inaugurated a trans-colonial **public sphere**, which the secular elites of the American Revolution would put to political use in the 1760s and 1770s. Moreover, the Great Awakening drew many people from the lower classes and marginalized groups into Protestant churches and sects, staking out a place of public speech for women, African Americans, and Native Americans. The sentimental reform movements of the nineteenth century, most notably abolitionism, owe a good deal to the doctrines and practices of the Great Awakening, as does the literary rhetoric of Harriet Beecher Stowe's *Uncle Tom's Cabin* (1852).

In ideological terms, the Revolution would dissipate religious concerns in favor of issues of taxation, representation, and government. The revolutionary pathos of **Thomas Paine**'s call for independence, *Common Sense* (1776), was still indebted to the rhetoric of evangelical enthusiasm, but after a decade of struggling statehood, there was a new language: the authors of the American Constitution (1789) founded a political entity that was resolutely secular. It was also resolutely innovative, even as it masked its originality with a vocabulary of classical republicanism. Most of all, it was *self-made*, not in the congratulatory sense of having freed itself from outside influences but in the sense of conjuring up its own presence. As Mitchell Meltzer observes, no nation and no national literature had ever "before been the product of conscious invention" in quite the same way. Hence the Constitution created a fictional voice called "**We the People**" whose authorship and authority "would somehow override the sheer arbitrariness of simply setting out" (110). According to Meltzer, the Constitution is "a made-up thing, and yet such knowledge has never inhibited the nation from believing in it. It has been the burden, and the originality, of at least one central strain of American literary tradition to suffer this ever-new ambition of finding poetic forms that will participate in the nation's founding paradox" (112).

**Political Writing After the Revolution.** One such paradox was the young nation's simultaneously expansive and post-colonial self-understanding. A brilliant solution to this dilemma was offered by the Constitutional definition of statehood, prepared in the **Northwest Ordinance** (1783). The Northwest Ordinance held that the United States of America would not be a colonial nation on the model of European power politics. The existing thirteen states would not expand into Western territories, competing over borders and spheres of influence. Instead, the West would supply new states—*more* states, whose sheer existence and number would diminish the influence of the original polities and strengthen the power of the union.

The Federalist Papers. The question remained of how such an unlikely union could be made more probable. This question is at the core of American literature between the 1780s and the 1830s and beyond. The most sustained answer was formulated by **James Madison**, Alexander Hamilton and John Jay, writing collectively under the pen-name Publius in *The Federalist Papers* (1787/88), their defense and explication of the new Constitution. Arguably America's biggest contribution to political thought, *The Federalist Papers* overhauled the philosophical inventory of the European Enlightenment to make it fit the conditions of a provincial power-to-be, a paradoxical nation that was hoping for continental proportions but committed itself to republican government. Neither the civic virtues of classical republicanism nor the market values of economic liberalism foresaw this possibility (while the catchphrases of both were cunningly reinterpreted by Publius). Thus, *The Federalist Papers* proposed an **oxymoronic policy of pluralizing consolidation** that defied received wisdom. If you want to curb the power of interests, Madison perplexingly argued, multiply their number. This doctrine was to be installed at all levels of social interaction: the more states, the lower the influence of individual states. The more religious denominations, the lower the risk of a state religion. The more social groups, the lower the chance that one will usurp public opinion. This was Madison's iconoclastic idea of an "**extended republic**": a sphere of political organization that would provide cohesion by encompassing dissimilar multitudes.

The punch line of this idea rested on the word *republic*, so ripe with associations of civic solidarity and face-to-face communication. Madison held that such republicanism could be achieved even in a geographically extensive and socially diversified society—*if* the involved players were integrated within the same system of communicative rules and procedures. It was a breathtakingly modern conjecture: rather than calling on people's morality, and rather than counting on virtuous rulers or

voters, Madison acted on the assumption that politicians are naturally power-driven and voters beholden to their local interests. Common welfare was nonetheless possible, if competition was enlarged and rendered dynamic to such a degree that no monopoly seemed probable, and if rival practices were restricted through procedural entanglements. At the level of national government, this translated into the Constitution's famous principle of **checks and balances**, i.e. the competitive overlap of administrative responsibilities and competencies, which was inconceivable under European conceptions of a mere 'separation' of powers.

At its heart, then, the extended republic was a procedural republic. From today's perspective, we can easily identify it as the first *nation-state* in the modern understanding of the term. In the context of literary studies, it is significant that Publius conceived of it as a dynamic construction—or to use Benedict Anderson's felicitous phrase, as an **imagined community**. What is meant by this is a space of virtual communication in which people do not have to personally know each other to recognize and respect one another as members of the same community. In other words, Madison's concept of the extended republic already imagined the United States as a **media nation**. It looked beyond the polite networks of correspondence that had characterized enlightened discourse in Europe and the colonies, welcoming instead the era of national newspapers and envisioning an intensely networked public sphere that could span an entire

Title page of the first printing of *The Federalist Papers*

A call to solidarity in the colonies (woodcarving in the *Pennsylvania Gazette*)

continent. It is no coincidence that the United States, built on this model of procedural governance, would in time become the world's major purveyor of stories and images. "What is an American," Hector St. John de Crèvecoeur (who was no friend of the new Constitution) had asked before the Revolution. He had answered his question with a virtue-bound hope for European self-realization. *The Federalist Papers* cleared the ground for more modern conceptions that saw Americans recognizing themselves as Americans through technology-savvy acts of imagination, i.e. through the stories they tell and consume, and even more so through their shared participation in the same media public, which constantly reinforces itself, even when the media content is not about the nation.

### 3.1.4 | Fictional Writing in the Early Republic

*Patriotic poems*

However, the earliest examples of United States fiction, poetry, and drama frequently did choose the nation as subject matter. Many poems of the early republic were patriotic to the point of parody—and probably had to be, given the lack of collective heritage in a multi-state society. Only with writers such as Philip Freneau ("The Wild Honey-Suckle," 1786, "The Indian Burying Ground," 1788) and William Cullen Bryant ("Thanatopsis," 1821, "The Prairies," 1834) did American poetry gradually turn away from the over-wrought pathos of national epics such as Joel Barlow's *The Vision of Columbus* (1787) and embraced more self-reflective forms of literary expression. Meanwhile, American playwrights such as Royall Tyler dutifully reproduced the stage conventions of British Restoration drama and infused them with patriotic messages in plays such as *The Contrast* (1787).

In 1789, William Hill Brown published the **first American novel**, *The Power of Sympathy*, a conventional sentimental story modeled on the works of Samuel Richardson (cf. section I.2.3.4). At the time, no one could have foreseen that the novel would become America's defining art form (together with the twentieth-century motion picture). No other literary genre has shaped American self-conceptions more thoroughly, and no other genre has been shaped as profoundly by American contributions. The first highlights, paving the way for the masterpieces of the nineteenth century, were written in the **sentimental** and **Gothic** mode. Su-

*Rip van Winkle as imagined by the contemporary American painter George F. Bensell*

sanna Rowson's *Charlotte Temple* (1791), a bestseller of the time, told a cautionary tale of female waywardness and the dangers of masculine seduction, arguing for the ideal of well-educated, sexually vigilant women who contributed to the nation's welfare by fulfilling their civic responsibility as 'republican mothers.' Somewhat more irritatingly, Hannah Webster Foster's *The Coquette* (1797) employed epistolary multiperspectivity to great effect, granting a forceful voice to subjective desires that were quite at odds with the republican moral of the tale. Even more disconcerting were the Gothic novels of **Charles Brockden Brown** (no relation to William Hill Brown): *Wieland, or the Transformation* (1798), *Ormond, or the Secret Witness* (1799), *Arthur Mervyn, or Memoirs of the Year 1793* (1799), and *Edgar Huntly, or Memoirs of a Sleep-Walker* (1799). These writings painted an unsettling underground image of America at the turn of the century. In Brown's universe, subjective misjudgments and the dark urges of the soul always threaten to dispel the enlightened confidence of empirical reason on which the nation was supposedly built. *Wieland*, in particular, probed deep into the invisible undercurrents of American republicanism, setting its heroine and narrator Clara awash in a sea of uncontrollable intentions and unreliable voices (the tale centers on ventriloquism). Fully aware of the political dimension of the term, Brown's novel dealt with the ambiguities of *representation*; it bespoke deep-seated anxieties about the possibility of a rational social order based on *vox populi*. Brown sent a copy of his book to fellow writer Thomas Jefferson, but apparently never received an answer.

Brown was one of the first American authors who tried to live on his writing. However, professional authorship required a national literary sphere. Brown worked hard to create one, with *The Monthly Magazine and American Review* (1799–1800) and other magazine projects, but the time was not ripe. The first Americans who managed to make a living as professional authors (not counting Benjamin Franklin, who became rich with the annual publication of *Poor Richard's Almanac*, 1732–1758) were **James Fenimore Cooper** and **Washington Irving**, but this was largely because of their success in the English market (both moved to Europe and spent large parts of their careers there). At the time, the search for a national literature mainly meant to demonstrate that the New World contained proficient material for established (read: British) artistic forms. Hence, Barlow, Freneau, Rowson, Foster, Brown, and after them

Cooper and Irving adapted traditional literary genres to American subject matter. Irving transposed European fairy tales to the countryside of New York in "Rip van Winkle" (1819) and "The Legend of Sleepy Hollow" (1820). Cooper, in turn, successfully Americanized the historical novel in his five *Leatherstocking* books (1823–1841), with Indian characters parlaying like highlanders from Walter Scott's works (cf. section I.2.5.3). What marked these tales and novels as American were their settings. Thematically, however, they revealed an undertone of discontent in the so-called Era of Good Feelings after the War of 1812. Cooper's *The Pioneers* (1823) and *The Last of the Mohicans* (1826) certainly perpetuated the crypto-imperialist romanticism of the 'vanishing Indian' motif, but they also voiced doubts about the ecological consequences of America's Westward expansion. Irving even introduced a **new type of American hero** with Rip van Winkle, the anti-Franklin who sleeps through the Revolution and shrinks from domestic responsibility as much as he dreads political agitation, preferring to spend his time alone and unprofitably in the woods.

## 3.1.5 | Voices From the Margins

Less idyllic expressions of dissent animated the life-writing and post-revolutionary pamphleteering of authors from marginalized groups, especially women, African Americans, and Native Americans. Their strongest strategy was to remind the nation of its commitments, entangling its self-image in discursive contradictions. Early slave narratives such as *The Interesting Narrative of Olaudah Equiano, the African, Written by Himself* (1789) espoused capitalist values and evangelical spirituality in order to demonstrate the economic imperfection and moral depravity of the slave trade. Equiano was an important inspiration for the more openly oppositional and more explicitly African American writings of Frederick Douglass after 1845. Similarly,

### Focus on Native Americans in Literature

Literary representations of Native Americans often relied on a few stereotypes. The motif of the **noble savage** combined the notion of the Indians' social and cultural backwardness on the one hand and their primitive natural virtue and innocence on the other. The opposite of the noble savage is the intrinsically evil and treacherous **ignoble savage**. The motif of the **vanishing Indian** emerged from the assumption that the gradual displacement of the native population was inevitable, due to the impact of civilization and its superiority to native "savagery." In eighteenth- and nineteenth-century literature it was often connected with nostalgia or a sense of tragedy. In recent years, studies have emphasized the degree to which these motifs were projections on the settlers' part that served either to justify or to gloss over their political and military domination of native populations.

William Apess's native autobiography *A Son of the Forest* (1829) used the rhetoric of the Protestant conversion narrative to object to Andrew Jackson's Indian Removal policy. Finally, the *Seneca Falls Declaration of Sentiments* (1848), mostly authored by Elizabeth Cady Stanton, turned away from the republican feminism of the young republic and demanded female suffrage—but it did so invoking the *Declaration of Independence*.

Ever since, American protest voices have repeatedly insisted on taking the nation's founding documents at their word. This strategy, in turn, has produced powerful new descriptions of America, from tales of self-despair in the face of national hypocrisy to the conceptualization of **America as an unfulfilled promise**—a view of American history later called progressivism. From a less involved perspective, one can observe the generative dynamism at work in these American self-descriptions. There is perhaps no other literature so self-referential and at the same time so able to accommodate, even generate, oppositional perspectives by recourse to its own foundational fictions. In order to gauge the cultural force of this improbable semantics, it is necessary to read American self-descriptions *as* self-descriptions, not simply as Anglophone writings that happen to have been written in a non-European place.

## Select Bibliography

Anderson, Benedict. *Imagined Communities: Reflections on the Origin and Spread of Nationalism*. London: Verso, 1983.

Armstrong, Nancy, and Leonard Tennenhouse. *The Imaginary Puritan: Literature, Intellectual Labor, and the Origins of Personal Life*. Berkeley: University of California Press, 1992.

Bercovitch, Sacvan. *The American Jeremiad*. Madison: University of Wisconsin Press, 1978.

Davidson, Cathy N. *Revolution and the Word: The Rise of the Novel in America*. Oxford: Oxford University Press, 2004.

Elliott, Emory. *Revolutionary Writers: Literature and Authority in the New Republic*. New York: Oxford University Press, 1982.

Fluck, Winfried. *Das kulturelle Imaginäre: Eine Funktionsgeschichte des amerikanischen Romans 1790–1900*. Frankfurt/M.: Suhrkamp, 1997.

Gray, Richard. *Writing the South: Ideas of American Region*. Cambridge: Cambridge University Press, 1986.

Greenblatt, Stephen. *Marvelous Possessions: The Wonder of the New World*. Chicago: University of Chicago Press, 1992.

Gunn, Giles, ed. *Early American Writing*. Harmondsworth: Penguin, 1994.

Hoffman, Ronald, and Peter J. Albert, eds. *Women in the Age of the American Revolution*. Charlottesville: University of Virginia Press, 1989.

Jehlen, Myra, and Michael Warner, eds. *The English Literatures of America: 1500–1800*. New York: Routledge, 1997.

Jones, Howard Mumford. *O Strange New World: American Culture: The Formative Years*. New York: Viking, 1964.

Kelleter, Frank. "1776: John Adams Disclaims Authorship of *Common Sense* But Helps Declare Independence." *A New Literary History of America*. Eds. Marcus Greil and Werner Sollors. Cambridge: Harvard University Press, 2009. 98–103.

Kelleter, Frank. *Amerikanische Aufklärung: Sprachen der Rationalität im Zeitalter der Revolution*. Paderborn: Schöningh, 2002.

McDougall, Walter A. *Freedom Just Around the Corner: A New American History: 1585–1828*. New York: Harper Collins, 2004.

Meltzer, Mitchell. "1787: A Literature of Secular Revelations." *A New Literary History of America*. Eds. Marcus Greil and Werner Sollors. Cambridge: Harvard University Press, 2009. 108–12.

Meserole, Harrison T. *American Poetry of the 17th Century*. New York: University Press, 1993.

Spengemann, William C. *A New World of Words: Redefining Early American Literature*. New Haven: Yale University Press, 1994.

*Frank Kelleter*

## 3.2 | American Renaissance

### 3.2.1 | Terminology

In 1941, the eminent critic F.O. Matthiessen published a magisterial work on Romantic writing in America which he titled *American Renaissance: Art and Expression in the Age of Emerson and Whitman*. In his pioneering study, Matthiessen discussed at length the works of Ralph Waldo Emerson, Henry David Thoreau, Nathaniel Hawthorne, Herman Melville, and Walt Whitman. These five authors he judged the true representatives of this formative period of American literature, although—with the possible exception of the later Whitman—none of these writers was known to more than a relatively small fraction of American audiences (a fraction which, furthermore, was concentrated mainly in New England). To **Edgar Allan Poe**, a prominent if controversial figure of antebellum literature, Matthiessen would not dedicate a chapter of his own, because he shared Emerson's distrust of "the jingle man" (Matthiessen 136), a derogatory reference to Poe's alleged lack of moral dimension and his affinity with the realm of popular literature and culture. The latter, he tells his readers in the introduction, "still offers a fertile field for the sociologist and for the historian of our taste. But I agree with Thoreau: 'Read the best books first, or you may not have a chance to read them at all'" (xi). Nor would he discuss **Emily Dickinson**, the reclusive Amherst poet, later to become one of the most widely known American women poets ever. For Matthiessen, only the above male writers were trying to continue the great tradition of European classical high art against the onrush of cheap mass literature. Matthiessen called the period between, roughly, 1830 and 1865 the "American Renaissance," because he clearly saw the debts of these writers to John Milton and the seventeenth-century metaphysical poets (cf. sections I.2.2.3–4). What did not register with him, however, was to how great a degree all of them were struggling to come to grips with the rapidly changing conditions of American society and, particularly, the uncertainty of their own position as professional literary authors vis-à-vis a new socio-economic framework and the rampant materialism of Jacksonian society.

Later scholars, though generally following Matthiessen's attempt to establish the "American Renaissance" as a crucial stage in the formation of an American national literature, increasingly emphasized the often conflicted involvement of these au-

→ **American Renaissance** is today the most widespread term for the period from, roughly, 1830–1865. The period before the Civil War is also called the **antebellum era**, and critics often refer to texts written in that era as antebellum literature. The term **American Romanticism**, which is sometimes used synonymously, implies a more transcultural perspective on the period by stressing the response to European Romanticism and German Idealism in American literature of the time.

thors with their socio-cultural environment. Especially critics writing in the wake of what came to be known as 'Cultural Studies' (cf. Part III) claimed "that all forms of cultural production need to be studied in relation to other cultural practices and to social and historical structures" (Grossberg 4). Because culture was now defined as the whole of the symbolic modes by which we encode our daily lives, the production of literary texts could be seen as responding—in a critical or affirmative manner—to the political, economic, and technological processes in which it is embedded. While Matthiessen still conceived of literature as a privileged mode of discourse which is self-reliant and independent of the larger society, more recent critics underlined that authors of the American Renaissance struggled with such issues as the devastating effects of **industrialization**, a growing **distrust of Puritanism**, the role of **African Americans** and **women** in a democratic society, or the atrocities of **modern warfare** as it unfolded from the fierce battles of the Civil War. If some felt repelled by the onslaught of cheap mass culture and the widespread utilitarianism of nineteenth-century American society, by and large, Romantic writers of the period Matthiessen calls the "American Renaissance" were in no way conservative rebels who tried to resist the negative influences of modern society by harkening back to the great tradition of European art. Rather, the symbolic complexity and often ambiguous, mixed meaning that marks American writing of the American Renaissance seems informed by an effort to explore the paradoxes and socio-political implications of **modern authorship**. Put another way, Romantic authors in America, their

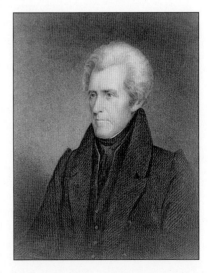

Andrew Jackson, seventh president of the United States (1829–1837), profoundly reformed the state's democratic system by strengthening the common (white) man's political influence and economic rights.

| Key Texts: American Renaissance |
| --- |

**Ralph Waldo Emerson,** "The American Scholar" (1837), "The Poet" (1844)
**Edgar Allan Poe,** short stories
**Frederick Douglass,** *Narrative of the Life of Frederick Douglass* (1845)
**Nathaniel Hawthorne,** *The Scarlet Letter* (1850)
**Herman Melville,** *Moby-Dick* (1851)
**Harriet Beecher Stowe,** *Uncle Tom's Cabin* (1852)
**Henry David Thoreau,** *Walden* (1854)
**Walt Whitman,** "Song of Myself" (1855)
**Emily Dickinson,** poems (mostly published posthumously)

sometimes opaque, allegorical styles notwithstanding, clearly registered the far-reaching social, economic, and technological changes during the middle decades of the nineteenth century. In both their fictional texts and in their essays, journal entries, and personal letters (as in the oft-quoted Melville-Hawthorne correspondence), American Renaissance writers addressed the tensions arising from the rapid technological progress, the populism of Jacksonian democracy, the ongoing debate over the geo-political destiny of the New Nation, the emerging women's movement, or the dividing issue of slavery and the looming prospects of Civil War.

### 3.2.2 | Wider Historical Context

According to the French historian of science and philosopher Michel Foucault, the end of the eighteenth century marks an important shift in the way many humanist sciences—Foucault mentions natural history, geography, economics, and linguistics—study the topics and phenomena of their respective fields. During the period from, roughly, 1775 through 1825 the positivism and rationalism of the Enlightenment, Foucault argues, is being transformed into a new, essentially **historical understanding of scientific knowledge**. Classification and ordering, the founding principles of all scientific activity, are no longer based exclusively on similarity and ontological sameness, but on relations that unfold, and therefore become visible, only over the course of historical development. In other words, modern science has shifted from explaining natural and/or cultural phenomena on their own terms to historicizing them, to showing them as related over time, even though they have frequently become subject to historical change. Thus, what Adam Smith's analysis of economic prosperity, Hegel's philosophy of (univer-

sal) history, and Darwin's theory of evolution have in common is their distinct sense of historicity, their proposition of a larger, organizing time frame. If Romanticism (both in Europe and the U.S.), as Hans Eichner claimed, "is, perhaps predominantly, a desperate rearguard action against the spirit and the implications of modern science" (8), it is probably equally true that Romantic writing mirrored and also reinforced the paradigm shift that Foucault saw at work in the sphere of the sciences. By probing the underlying connections between nature and culture, body and mind, appearance and essence, or collective history and the fate and place of the individual, Romantic authors not only criticized the processes of **modernization** from the outside, from a "world elsewhere," as Richard Poirier famously put it; they became part and parcel of a widespread attempt within modern society to come to terms with the rapid transformation from an agrarian to a capitalist mode of production. The tensions and paradoxes that often accompany Romantic writing, which in turn reflects the paradoxes of modern society at large, are particularly visible in the writings of the American Renaissance. Because of its consistently utilitarian orientation, capitalist America, as historian Daniel Boorstin aptly put it, has become at once "the laboratory and nemesis of romanticism" (173).

| Timeline: Mid-Nineteenth Century America | |
| --- | --- |
| 1829 | Andrew Jackson inaugurated as President |
| 1830 | Removal Act exiles Indian tribes to the West |
| 1845 | John O'Sullivan coins the term "manifest destiny" to legitimize westward expansion |
| 1846–48 | Mexican-American War |
| 1849 | Gold Rush in California |
| 1850–51 | Peak of the American Renaissance: *The Scarlet Letter* and *Moby-Dick* published |
| 1850 | Fugitive Slave Law leads to intensified debates about race, abolitionism, and the unity of the nation |
| 1852 | *Uncle Tom's Cabin* published |
| 1860 | Abraham Lincoln elected President, Southern states secede |
| 1861–65 | Civil War |
| 1863 | Emancipation Proclamation slavery outlawed in the U.S. |

## 3.2.3 | The Formation of an American Cultural Identity

**American Exceptionalism.** America was literally born out of a conflict of identity or, in psychological terms, an identity crisis. As the previous chapter has shown, early settlers and emigrants, who had fled Europe for religious reasons, increasingly invested the "New World" with the time-worn myth of a paradise to-be-regained (usually located in the still unexplored Western Hemisphere) and the religious promise of a **New Canaan**, a New Jerusalem upon the Hill (cf. section I.3.1.2). America, to be sure, had never been a 'new,' pristine land at all (just think of the history and cultural achievements of Native Americans), but the idea persisted that the colonies provided plenty of "elbow room," as the Puritans had it, for God's chosen people. Yet the notion of an as yet unknown paradise in the West was not altogether a religious idea; it could also be found in the writings of Thomas More (*Utopia*, 1516), Francis Bacon (*Novum Organum*, 1620), and, especially, the Irish philosopher and Bishop George Berkeley who believed that in history Western empires had always succeeded the ones in the East and that therefore "**Westward the course of empire takes its way**"—Greece had given way to that of Rome, Rome had yielded to Northern Europe and France, Spain had waned once Britain increased its power, and now America was about to replace Britain as the leading power in the world (Smith 8). America, as a matter of fact, was considered to represent 'newness' to such a degree that it prompted the English philosopher John Locke to use it metaphorically for the idea of origins and new beginnings in general: "In the beginning," Locke writes in "The Second Treatise of Civil Government" (1689), "all the world was America" (sect. 49).

Although the notion of **American exceptionalism**, of America as "virgin land" (Smith) and pristine utopian space was widespread, historically there had never been a complete break with the cultural and political traditions of the Old World. Even after the Revolutionary Wars had finally led to American independence, it would take at least another half-century for a genuine American culture to evolve. Since the Declaration of Independence did not lead to a sudden hiatus in social and cultural development, historians now agree that the first half of the nineteenth century was actually the most important period in American cultural history. It is thus crucial to keep in mind that the heyday of Romantic writing in America coincided with the formative decades of a cultural, social, and economic national future which had been, for the first time, widely independent from external pressure and influence.

**The Myth of the Common Man.** It is equally worth noting that the new nation, though struggling to discharge the idea of caste, of social hierarchy according to birth, was nevertheless marked by a relatively rigid class structure. Thus, only the frontier and the new states west of the Mississippi Valley clung to the **Jeffersonian ideal of the "common man,"** the land-holding farmer who tills his own soil and constitutes the political backbone of the Republic. While the American South slowly metamorphosed into an elitist planter's society based on brutally enforced racial division, by the 1850s, the Northeast had already developed into an industrialized area, with a considerable working class and more complex social stratification in general. Contrary to the widespread notion of America as a land of social and economic opportunity, there was only little upward mobility during the first half of the nineteenth century. Through the 1850s, the editor and politician Horace Greeley popularized the slogan "Vote Yourself a Farm," a slogan based on the older Jeffersonian ideal of the land-owning yeoman, though there was no evidence that industrial workers became farmers on the Western frontier in great numbers (cf. Bailyn 334).

The shifting social and political reality notwithstanding, the notion of the 'common man' still remained a potent **national myth** of far-reaching consequences. To many mid-nineteenth-century Americans, the new nation was distinct from all other nations in that it gave expression to and was informed by the physical prowess and willpower of the common laborer (farmers, settlers, craftsmen, etc.). So powerful was this ideal of the 'common man' that in 1827 the Philadelphia gentleman Pat Lyon, who had made a fortune as a locksmith and builder of fire engines, had himself represented in a famous portrait by John Neagle not in his jacket and formal attire, as was customary, but as a laborer at work at his anvil, in a leather apron with his sleeves rolled up. Walt Whitman, who had included a paean to the common American worker, titled "A Song for

John Neagle, *Pat Lyon at the Forge* (1829)

Occupations," as one of the twelve poems of the original 1855 edition of *Leaves of Grass*, echoes Lyon's posture in the frontispiece, which shows him in laborer's clothes as an American Everyman. In a similar vein, Ishmael, the principle narrator of Melville's classic novel *Moby-Dick; or, The Whale* (1851), who embarks on a whaling voyage to cope with his impending "hypochondria" (an ailment particularly reminiscent of the Old World), does not want "ever to go to sea as a passenger." Nor does he intend to embark on a career "as a Commodore, or a Captain, or a Cook." A true American, Ishmael deliberately abandons the "distinction of such offices" for the community and solidarity of the common sailor:

*The communal vision of Melville's Moby-Dick*

> No, when I go to sea, I go as a simple sailor, right before the mast, plumb down into the forecastle, aloft there to the royal mast-head [...] I always go to sea as a sailor because of the wholesome exercise and pure air of the forecastle deck. For as in this world, head winds are far more prevalent than winds from astern [...] so for the most part the Commodore on the quarter-deck gets his atmosphere at second hand from the sailors on the forecastle. He thinks he breathes it first; but not so. In much the same way do the commonality lead their leaders in many other things, at the same time that the leaders little suspect it. (ch. 1)

Because of their historical role in the exploration and settling of the American continent and as representations of an important, burgeoning sector of American economy, **ships** figured prominently in the cultural imagination of nineteenth-century Americans. This is especially true of New Englanders, who lived near the Eastern shore and participated in one of the first truly global businesses, the bloody harvesting of the sperm whale. In the early nineteenth century, according to maritime historian Nathaniel Philbrick, "people didn't invest in bonds or the stock market, but rather in whale ships" (20). As novels such as James Fenimore Cooper's *The Pilot* (1824), Poe's *The Narrative of Arthur Gordon Pym From Nantucket* (1838), Richard Dana's *Two Years Before the Mast* (1840), or Melville's *Moby-Dick* (to name just the most widely known of his numerous seafaring narratives) attest, in antebellum American literature, ships repeatedly served to articulate and also to question the democratic orientation of the new nation. Transforming the actual seagoing experience into a kind of **spiritual journey**, American Renaissance writers frequently depicted the world-as-ship or, as in *Moby-Dick*, the ship-as-world. Melville's Pequod is actually a human microcosm, a floating world replete with sailors from all walks of life. The economic nature and physical hardships of the whaling business notwithstanding, theirs is a community of equals that cuts across the boundaries of both class and race. As the doomed journey of the vessel reveals, the communitarian ideal of the simple sailor is eventually threatened. Though ultimately a critique of the shallowness of the democratic myth, Melville's idealized treatment of maritime life nevertheless helped to establish the sea as a utopian counter-space to the increasing rigidity and social divisiveness of modern American society.

## 3.2.4 | Literary Marketplace

During the first half of the nineteenth century, America also saw the formation of a new kind of culture: formerly local networks of oral communication were gradually displaced by the increasing presence of **printed matter** (newspapers, magazines, books). What first began to take shape during the decades immediately following the Revolution, that is, the creation of a literary marketplace (cf. Davidson), ushered in dramatic changes and a tremendous increase in the sheer numbers of books available for circulation in the decades preceding the Civil War. Not only had the literary market changed and expanded so that it reached into almost every American household; it was during this crucial period in American history that it became an important economic and cultural force (cf. Teichgraeber).

**Technological innovations** such as the cylinder rotary press, stereotyping, electrotyping and, somewhat later, the introduction of cheap, mass-produced spectacles were as instrumental in bringing about these changes as were the marketing of new varieties of books and the creation of new formats to popularize the latest literary products or scientific inventions. There were designed books to add prestige to the mere possession of the volume, lavishly ornamented literary annuals, gift books, and compendiums of articles and poetry. Publishers also experimented with the series format that included biographies, histories, natural science, and travel literature. As one prominent American publisher estimated, 52 books had been published on average annually between 1832 and 1842. In 1853, when Henry David Thoreau's *Walden* appeared, 733 works had been printed, an increase of more than 800 percent in less than twenty years. Given that contemporary first editions usually comprised nearly 10,000, with some editions peaking as high as 100,000 copies, it is fair to say that mid-nineteenth century was seeing a veritable landslide regarding the numbers of books written and produced for an ever-growing readership.

**Media.** As regards the publication of **newspapers and magazines**, similarly dramatic changes had occurred. If, in 1825, fewer than 125 American magazines had been in business, by 1870 the number of periodicals had increased to more than 1,200! Though religious periodicals still outnumbered the newly introduced genre of the popular literary magazine, none of them ever managed to become as influential and widely circulated as their secular counterparts. Leading monthlies included *Godey's Lady's Book* (1830–98), *Peterson's Ladies National Magazine* (1842–98), *Harper's New Monthly Magazine* (1850–), all of which claimed to have more than 100,000 paid subscribers. In addition, there were less long-lived publications such as *Graham's Magazine* (1841–58), *Putnam's Monthly Magazine* (1853–57), *The United States Magazine and Democratic Review* (1837–59), or *Sartain's Union Magazine* (1847–52). Authors and contributors to these monthlies were usually paid between $4 to $12 a page for prose and $10 to $50 for a poem, with sometimes higher rates for more famous contributors. Of perhaps even greater consequence was the simultaneous emergence of daily and weekly newspapers. As the nation's "second breakfast" (Ralph Waldo Emerson), their numbers almost tripled from 1,200 to 3,000 during the 1840s through 1850s, with a much greater variety and total numbers than in Europe at the time. Even though their reliability as a source of information varied, they represented perhaps the most palpable change, according to Richard Teichgraeber, "in the reading matter of ordinary Americans as the nation moved gradually from an era of scarcity to that of abundance" (674).

It would be foolish, however, to frame the enormous growth of reading in early nineteenth-century America as simply a replacement of oral by literary culture. As critic Donald Scott has shown, the important **national lecture system** and the spreading of newspapers and dailies reinforced rather than excluded each other. And while the numbers of novels and fiction writers skyrocketed during the decades preceding the Civil War, the authors responsible for the increased output of books often also appeared as public speakers in town halls and lyceums, where similar topics were

discussed as those found in books, magazines and newspapers. To get a sense of the dynamic forces triggered by this new American literary market, just note that in 1826, Cooper's best-selling novel *The Last of the Mohicans* sold a mere 5,750 copies; by contrast, in 1852, Harriett Beecher Stowe's *Uncle Tom's Cabin* reached total purchases as high as five million copies. In other words, print had indeed changed antebellum culture, but it cannot be understood as a force isolated from other factors and cultural activities. America had gone from being a society where public information had been scarce (and largely under the control of the learned and wealthy) to one in which a new abundance of public information became available to a diverse variety of consumers by way of both specialized printing and public speech. **New patterns of public information diffusion** were thus at the roots of new forms of cultural fragmentation and diversity. What is more, writers of poetry and prose were now compelled to come to terms with an altogether new culture in which literature had been reduced to the status of a commodity, and where success for writers now meant appealing to an anonymous, distant, and unknown audience. Paradoxically, then, the decades that became known as the American Renaissance were decisive in widening the gap between mass and high culture while, at the same time, they mark a more serious involvement of professional writers with popular cultural forms.

### 3.2.5 | The Role of Women Writers

Among the many women writers of the nineteenth century, **Margaret Fuller**'s career as professional author, teacher, editor, newspaper correspondent, and ardent defender of women's rights stands out as a glaring example of the tenacity and intellectual

*Godey's Lady's Book,*
Cover, June 1867

**Definition**

→ **American Transcendentalism** was a literary-philosophical and social movement that developed during the 1830s and 1840s as a reaction against the rampant materialism in American culture and society and against the concomitant waning of spiritual values. Major representatives were: **Amos Bronson Alcott, Orestes Brownson, Ralph Waldo Emerson, Margaret Fuller, Theodore Parker, George Ripley,** and **Henry David Thoreau.**

rigor of female authors vis-à-vis the sexist, patriarchal stereotypes women like Fuller had to face. Although she never had a formal college education, Fuller befriended various young Harvard scholars with whom she formed lasting intellectual friendships, among them James Freeman Clarke and W.H. Channing, the later coeditors of her *Memoirs* (1852). She also became a close friend of Emerson and edited *The Dial*, the famous Transcendentalist magazine, from 1840 to 1842. Her controversial essay **"The Great Lawsuit"** originally appeared in *The Dial* of July 1843. (A revised and extended edition was later published by Horace Greeley as *Woman in the Nineteenth Century*, 1844.)

Sentimental Novels. "The Great Lawsuit" was written at the high-water mark of female fiction in America during the nineteenth century. Between the publication of Catharine Sedgwick's *New-England Tale* in 1822 and Susan Warner's *Wide, Wide World* in 1850, literally hundreds of so-called 'sentimental' novels had been published, many of which were economically successful and were thereby steadily increasing the demand of publishers for manuscripts that might appeal to the staggering numbers of female readers. America's first best-selling novel, Susanna Rowson's *Charlotte Temple: A Tale of Truth* (1791), had paved the way for this kind of sentimental fiction, which was based on the ideal of the 'home' as an educational cultural space where the tribulations and hazards of the public sphere should be kept at bay. If sentimental novels were primarily concerned with sensational topics such as love, marriage, and the loss or betrayal of the husband, they also mark a genuine achievement of female authorship. What is more, as critic Nina Baym has put it, "they are written by women, are addressed to women, and tell one particular story about women" (22). Since many of these novels are set in the home as the central space where much of the action takes place, they were also called "domestic" fictions and they were accused, particularly by modern

---

**Interpretation**

**Frances Harper, "The Two Offers"**

The conjunction of social reform, domesticity, and the complicated symbolism of sensibility also informs Frances Ellen Watkins Harper's short story "The Two Offers." The story was written in 1860 and, together with "The Triumph of Freedom—A Dream," it marked the beginning of Harper's published fiction. Harper was one of the leading **African-American** poets of her time and she had gained a national reputation for her participation in political movements such as abolition, suffrage, temperance, and education. As one of her earliest biographers put it, "she only ceased from her literary and Anti-slavery labors when compelled to do so by other duties" (William Still, qtd. in Foster 18). "The Two Offers" takes up as its central motif an argument already developed in Margaret Fuller's essay "The Great Lawsuit." Fuller had repeatedly linked her struggle against the discrimination of women to the struggle for abolition and the freedom of enslaved African Americans. In "The Great Lawsuit" the character who represents the male view in the dialogue on the "woman question" makes this connection explicit:

"Is it not enough," cries the sorrowful trader, "that you have done all you could to break up the national Union, and thus destroy the prosperity of our country, but now you must be trying to break up family union, to take my wife away from the cradle, and the kitchen hearth, to vote at polls, and preach from a pulpit? Of course, if she does such things, she cannot attend to those of her on sphere. She is happy enough as she is. She has more leisure than I have, every mean of improvement, every indulgence."

In "The Two Offers" Harper turns the tables on such chauvinist arguments by criticizing at once the popular male idealization of women and their enforced confinement in a supposedly romantic relationship with men. The two protagonists of the story, Laura Lagrange and her cousin Janette Alston, are engaged in a discussion of two offers for marriage that Laura has recently received. Since the latter cannot decide which one she should accept, Janette proposes to decline both and instead to turn towards philanthropy, public service, and the pressing cause of abolition.

critics, of promulgating a "cult of domesticity" that was largely affirmative of the ascription of women to the house. This, however, may ultimately not do justice to the controversial valorization of the home by female authors. As Nina Baym and other critics have argued, women were not supposed to stay out of the public sphere because of their obligations and educational duties at home; rather, they were seen as reformers who would bring their principles and ideals of human relations to also improve the conditions of public and social relations at large.

The emphasis on **feminist and racial issues** in writers such as Frances Harper (see box on p. 116) betrays an acute awareness among mid-nineteenth-century women writers, both white and black, of the importance of literature in addressing and negotiating social conflict. Its occasional innocent posture to the contrary, female writing during the antebellum era often reflects, in the words of Judith Fetterley, an astonishing "degree of self-consciousness towards the act of writing" (5). Unwilling to neglect the social embeddedness of their writing, Fetterley argues, "American women writers early concentrated on describing the social context that shapes the individual self, and thus they created a literature concerned with the connection between manners, morals, social class, and social value" (9). Hawthorne's oft-quoted diatribe against the "d—d mob of scribbling women" (304), which he considered an obstacle to the development of a serious American literary tradition, may thus have been triggered not by the lack of professional commitment on the part of women authors, but by their self-conscious presence, visibility, and striking commercial success in the literary marketplace.

## 3.2.6 | Industrialization, Technology, Science

"The splendors of this age outshine all other recorded ages," Emerson wrote in his journal in 1871, adding a list of recent innovations that had struck him as important driving forces of modern history: "In my lifetime, have been wrought five miracles, namely, 1. the Steamboat; 2. the railroad; 3. the Electric telegraph; 4. the application of the Spectroscope to astronomy; 5. the photograph; five miracles which have altered the relations of nations to each other" (*Journals*, June

1871). Though one may argue about the actual role of these inventions in changing the course of modern history, there is no doubt that to the eminent New England philosopher technological progress represented not just a list of "improved means to an unimproved end," as his disciple Henry David Thoreau sarcastically put it (*Walden*, ch. 1), but the ambivalent legacy and future of modern society at large. Given the increasing presence of the machine in early-nineteenth-century America, the extent to which technical inventions influenced the form and content of American Renaissance writing can hardly be overrated.

When Harvard professor Jacob Bigelow, in a study titled *Elements of Technology* (1829), defined technology as the application of the sciences to the so-called useful arts, he seemed convinced that once technology was instituted as a common practice there would be no return to an earlier, pre-technological state of being. "The augmented means of public comfort and of individual luxury, the expense abridged and the labor superseded, have been such," he writes in view of the uneasiness of many of his fellow Americans about technology's rapid progress, "that we could not return to the state of knowledge which existed even fifty or sixty years ago, without suffering both intellectual and physical degradation" (6). Though fervently brandishing the age's mechanical orientation, Emerson's friend, the English critic Thomas Carlyle, seems to have shared Bigelow's insight into the irreversibility of technological progress. In the conclusion to his influential essay "Signs of the Times" (published the same year as Bigelow's *Elements*), Carlyle outlines his hopes for the future by explicitly approving of the progress made in learning and the arts:

Doubtless this age also is advancing [...] Knowledge, education are opening the eyes of the humblest; are increasing the number of thinking minds without limit. This is as it should be; for not in turning back, not in resisting, but only in resolutely struggling forward, does our life consist [...] Indications we do see [...] that Mechanism is not always to be our hard taskmaster, but one day to be our pliant, all-ministering servant.

Given the staggering number of mechanical inventions during the first half of the nineteenth century, all three, Bigelow, Carlyle, and Emerson, agreed that all men are being continuously shaped by modern technology, and that this process can hardly be reversed.

Technological progress was widely debated.

## Timeline: Technological Innovations

| | |
|---|---|
| **1802** | First steamboat line in the U.S. (between New York and Albany) |
| **1809** | Electric light invented |
| **1810** | Improved printing press invented |
| **1814** | First photograph taken by a 'camera obscura'; the process takes eight hours |
| **1829** | Typographer, a predecessor to the typewriter, invented |
| **1831** | First commercially successful reaper. Electric dynamo invented |
| **1835** | Mechanical calculator invented |
| **1836** | Samuel Colt invents the first revolver |
| **1837** | Samuel Morse invents the telegraph |
| **1839** | Daguerreotype photography |
| **1843** | Lithographic rotary printing press introduced, a much faster device than traditional presses |

While technological progress soon became synonymous with the pioneering efforts to build the nation, it also spelled out an unflinching belief in the essential **power of knowledge**. In line with fundamental ideas of the Enlightenment and the emphasis it placed on the human capacity to better social conditions and to envision a future perfected state of society, the Founding Fathers had actively endorsed the invention of labor-saving machinery and other useful contrivances. Though apprehensive of the negative impact of the machine on communal life, technological expertise was essential not only as a means to serve the needs of the individual citizen but also to promote the republic's higher humanitarian goals. Even Thomas Jefferson, who in his *Notes on the State of Virginia* (1785) promulgated a pastoral America immune to the social and moral corruption of industrial production, eventually conceded that technology could well be a major ingredient of historical progress. To Robert Fulton, the successful inventor of a new steamboat, he wrote in 1810: "I am not afraid of new inventions or improvements, nor bigoted to the practices of our forefathers. It is that bigotry which keeps the Indians in a state of barbarism in the midst of the arts" (qtd. in Meier 21). For Jefferson and his fellow Americans, the importance of technology was thus actually twofold. First, technological advancement figured, in a very literal sense, as a means to conquer and eventually possess the whole of the continent. Second, it was taken to vindicate synecdochically the historical destiny of America and the accompanying exploitation of natural resources that almost led to the extinction of its native population.

**Criticizing Historical Progress.** Of the most famous American Renaissance writers, **Poe and Hawthorne** in particular took issue with this widespread metaphorical conflation of technology and historical progress. In his political satire "**The Man That Was Used Up**" (1839), Poe turned the tables on Americans' naive readiness to assume an intrinsic connection between progress and technology. By relating the creation of the republic and the violence associated with its geographical expansion to an authentic historical figure, Poe launches a scathing critique of historical progress as the fulfillment of America's special destiny. In the story, technological progress defines the main character to such a degree that his very name calls forth commendations on the age's inventiveness and mechanical expertise. Whenever the narrator mentions General John A. B. C. Smith, supposedly a veteran Indian fighter of the late Bugaboo and Kickapoo campaign and alias of former Vice President Richard M. Johnson, the general's friends and acquaintances invariably reiterate a paean to the "wonderful age" of invention. While the General seems to be well recognized among his contemporaries as a living emblem of the marvelous prospects of modern times, the enthusiastic responses to the narrator's query about his actual identity remain strikingly evasive and tautological. With each interlocutor, the fabulous soldier becomes increasingly entangled in a skein of elliptic discourses that are bound to mystify rather than uncover the history of his mysterious personality. In the end, General Smith remains but a narrative construct, a hollow (and horrible) signifier of both technological ingenuity and historical myth.

If "The Man That Was Used Up" questioned antebellum Americans' love affair with machinery by exposing its inherent (self-)destructive powers, Hawthorne took a different, yet in no way less critical, approach. In his short story "**The Celestial Railroad**" (1843) he satirizes the historical role that many ascribed to the onrush of technical inventions by making technology the center of a burlesque rewriting of John Bunyan's *The Pilgrim's Progress* (1678). Machines abound in this allegorical tale. Not only does Hawthorne's modern Christian alleviate the burden of his pilgrimage to the Celestial City by riding on the newly established railroad, he also encounters such engineering achievements as, for example, a daring bridge whose foundations have been secured by "some scientific process," a tunnel lit by a plethora of communicating gas lamps, and a steam-driven ferryboat.

Significantly, Hawthorne's adoption of **techno-logical metaphors** in the story blurs with his critical stance on specific cultural practices and religious trends. When the narrator finally arrives at the present-day Vanity Fair, where "almost every street has its church and […] the reverend clergy are nowhere held in higher respect," he ridicules the traveling lecturers of these burgeoning sects as "a sort of machinery" designed to distribute knowledge without the encumbrance of true learning. On the surface a critique of facile latitudinarianism, a prominent, pseudo-rational strain of thought within the Anglican church, and the contemporary fad of providing instruction through oral rather than literary discourse, the passage also betrays Hawthorne's anxiety about the ongoing mechanization of American society in general. Moreover, the "etherealizing" of literature, which appears to be his core complaint, epitomizes the difficult position of literary authors within an increasingly technological, differentiated sphere of cultural production. Much as Hawthorne tries to defend the superior quality of the literary text (versus the sheer "machinery" of trivial lectures), his rhetorical strategy also lays bare the degree to which he himself has become a part of the new machine environment. If he dismisses the shallow libertarian sects as a movement inevitably leading to moral and intellectual destruction, his very use of machinery as an emblem of such inevitability attests to the symbolic power of modern technology, a power that held enthralled even the most conservative of antebellum writers.

### 3.2.7 | Materialism vs. Idealism

Similar ambiguities vis-à-vis an increasingly technological environment can be traced throughout the major works of the period. The establishment of the literary profession within the socioeconomic network of nineteenth-century American society required its differentiation from other specialized professions such as engineering or manufacturing, and it rested on a rationalization of the creative process as exempted from the materialist exigencies of industrial production. The notion of modern authorship, in other words, developed along the lines of strong **anti-materialist** biases that emphasized the spiritual over the physical implications of writing. Romantics often conceived of

Thomas Cole's *River in the Catskills* (1843): The train in the background heralds the industrialization of an idyllic landscape.

their work as a disembodied process that turned on an effort to transcend both the bodily confines of the writer and the material constraints of the text to be produced. That the Romantic poetics of disembodiment were closely tied to contemporary discussions of technology can be seen, among others, in Hawthorne's metafictional short story "The Artist of the Beautiful" (see box on p. 120).

**Complex Self-Representations.** Boorstin's aforementioned observation that capitalist America has turned out to be both "the laboratory and the nemesis of romanticism" underscores the complex self-representations of American Renaissance writers and their contradictory relations with antebellum society. His critical satires notwithstanding, Poe responded positively to the wave of new technology on the whole. Despite his emphasis on the exceptional cognitive status of creative work, his definition of authorship was utterly technological. Given the fervor with which Poe embraced, for example, 'anastatic printing' (also known as 'relief etching' that reproduced a facsimile impression of the original) as a way of experimenting with and ultimately increasing the representational value of written texts, he foreshadows the constructivist tradition within modern art, mainly identified with early-twentieth-century avant-garde movements. Rather than figuring as the downfall of the writer's profession, science and technology provided for Poe a "laboratory" of new ideas from which he concocted the symbols and metaphors that are now closely associated with his literary oeuvre.

**Search for Professional Identity.** Nor would Hawthorne or Melville conceive of the contemporary technological environment as the "nemesis"

### N. Hawthorne, "The Artist of the Beautiful"

Hawthorne's 1844 story effectively juxtaposes the materialist foundations of modern technological society and the ethereal, disembodied work of the Romantic writer. Resonating with references to early industrial manufacturing and the emphasis that Jacksonian America placed on punctuality and the utilitarian ideal of the 'useful arts,' "The Artist of the Beautiful" reflects the **cultural changes** concurrent with rapid technological advancement and the burgeoning of antebellum American economy. Not only does Hawthorne apprize the conflict between the practical and the beautiful by creating a character who is both watchmaker and artist; he also has his protagonist, Owen Warland, embark on a highly symbolic project. Searching for a material form that will communicate his aesthetic ideals, the watchmaker builds a synthetic creature, a mechanical butterfly, which combines his artistic ambitions and the difficulties arising from his ambivalent professional status.

Hawthorne's text cogently portrays the human body as the antithesis to everything that is beautiful and aesthetically important. Having set his heart upon the realization of an abstract concept, biological life matters only insofar as it is conditional to the accomplishment of Warland's task. Whereas the technological—and the body as its physical-material counterpart—operates in direct opposition to the artist's ethereal strivings, the story as a whole might well be taken as an attempt to amalgamate the divergent forces of creativity and materiality. The ironic and ambiguous ending, which has left many readers puzzled as to the true relation of art, nature, and material culture in the story, could also be read as a plea for the inclusion—rather than exclusion—of technology into the realm of artistic production. In keeping with the organic principle of Romantic writing, Hawthorne provides his watchmaker with the power to animate, to spiritualize, machinery. Warland's ambition, we are told, is not "to be honored with the paternity of a new kind of cotton machine," but to produce a "new species of life and motion." It is thus not by imitating nature but by competing with her, by putting forth "the ideal which nature has proposed to herself in all her creatures, but has never taken pains to realize" that the watchmaker becomes an artist. However frail and transient his imaginative child may be, as carrier of an original idea it takes on a quality more real than reality itself. "When the artist rose high enough to achieve the beautiful," as we learn in the concluding paragraph of the story, "the symbol by which he made it perceptible to mortal senses became of little value in his eyes while his spirit possessed itself in the enjoyment of the reality."

of literary creativity. Aware of the ubiquitous presence of the machine in antebellum America, these writers examined the changing conditions under which they labored in sometimes excruciating detail. The numerous representations of literary work in both their shorter fiction and in many of their full-fledged romances and adventure novels need therefore be assessed in light of an imaginative search for professional identity. Far from advocating the writer's withdrawal from society, American Renaissance writers addressed the processes of modernization in a pragmatic manner. To find a place of their own amidst an American society dramatically shifting from an agrarian virgin land to a Tartarus of industrial labor, Hawthorne and Melville had recourse to highly symbolic modes of self-representation that helped to deflate the rising tensions between the materiality of the printed text, on the one hand, and the original ideas it conveyed, on the other. Since the conflict between modern authors and the economic and technological environment often turned on the rival ideologies of idealism and materialism, to weave technical, corporeal, and spiritual imagery into a complex cyborgean skein, as Hawthorne did in "The Artist of the Beautiful," became a formal option preferred by many writers of the American Renaissance (cf. Benesch, *Romantic Cyborgs*).

### 3.2.8 | Art and Society

However widespread the urge to compete on the marketplace of specialized labor, American Renaissance writing is also marked by the somber prospects of the author's inevitable alienation from society. In Melville's "**Bartleby, the Scrivener**," isolation and estrangement of the literary worker set in after a period of extreme productivity. Since

Melville's literary reputation was already flagging when the story first appeared in 1853, the text encapsulates, on one level, its author's doomed struggle for public recognition. On another level, however, it is the first in a row of mid-nineteenth-century American texts in which authorship appears to be entirely overwhelmed by either industrialization or the economic strategies of American capitalism. There is no escape for Bartleby from the prison house of Wall Street and the mass production of written texts; mired in physical deterioration and increasing muteness, the scrivener's initial resistance to the growing mechanization of his office environment eventually turns into a hollow gesture of all-encompassing passivity.

Melville's symbolic depiction of Bartleby's fragmented, immobilized body ties in with concerns equally traceable in the work of two other American Renaissance writers, **Rebecca Harding Davis** and **Walt Whitman**. To bring into conjunction writers as different as Melville, Davis, and Whitman is by no means an easy task. If Davis's social realism already differs considerably in both its form and its setting from Melville's Romantic self-representation, Whitman's democratic, all-embracing pose seems to be even farther apart from the deeply pessimistic stance which dominates Melville's later texts. However, in both Davis's *Life in the Iron Mills* (1861) and in Whitman's *Drum-Taps*, a cluster of poems about the Civil War first published in 1865, the besieged artist is as muted and paralyzed as the starving scrivener. It is this struggle to negotiate the staggering gap between the realm of art and the world outside that allows us to discuss these writers in the same context. This does not mean to deemphasize the many differences among representatives of the American Renaissance. Rather, it means that where the relationship between literature and society is concerned, individual writers should not be discussed in isolation. When brought into dialogue, the diverse writings of the American Renaissance conjoin to make this a more complicated and, in fact, contentious period than Matthiessen originally envisioned in his famous study. If American capitalism, as Boorstin suspected, turned out to be both the laboratory and the nemesis of Romantic writing in the U.S., it also spawned a self-conscious

reaction among the writers of the American Renaissance. Their joint response, though differing in form and content, was to poise the negative consequences of modern society with a new style and a new perspective on core issues such as race, gender, class, and the widening gap between culture and nature. Judging from the continuing appeal of Melville and Thoreau for critics in both literary and cultural studies, the American Renaissance now appears to be not merely a formative period of classic American literature, but of our modern understanding of authorship and the contested relations of art and society in general. While Melville has been repeatedly acknowledged as one of the most far-reaching modern voices on slavery, race, and class, Thoreau remained a constant reference point for generations of American writers to come as well as an important source of inspiration for the burgeoning new field of ecocriticism (cf. entry II.14) and environmentally conscious literary studies.

A similarly powerful and anticipatory role of art in society at the interface of ecological, ethical, and aesthetic concerns is exemplified in the poetry of **Emily Dickinson**, a singular figure in American Renaissance literature, who both represents and transcends the historical-cultural conditions of her time in her highly complex and experimental writings. Her style is often fragmented and syntactically broken, intensely symbolic and reflexive, and full of tensions and paradoxes. Dickinson's poems open up new imaginative spaces and explore the interstices between body and soul, mind and matter. Her preferred topics range from subjectivity to society, from gender issues to religion, from death to love, from natural to artistic creativity.

Dickinson is considered today one of the most important voices of American poetry. In 2011, one of her poems was adapted to music by contemporary French composer Philippe Manoury in his piece for soprano, choir, electronics and big orchestra, *Noon*. Like Thoreau's, Dickinson's life and work has remained a model and a point of reference for many modern readers and authors alike. The continuing modern interest in her poetry and poetics goes to show that the American Renaissance is indeed a crucial and vital period in American literature and culture at large.

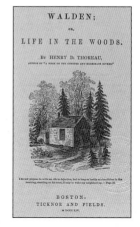

Thoreau's hut at Walden Pond—the illustration is from the original cover of *Walden*—became a mythic place for later generations.

Interpretation

### Emily Dickinson, "Poem 986"

A narrow Fellow in the Grass
Occasionally rides—
You may have met Him—did you not
His notice sudden is—

The Grass divides as with a Comb—          5
A spotted shaft is seen—
And then it closes at your feet
And opens further on—

He likes a Boggy Acre
A floor too cool for Corn—                  10
Yet when a Boy, and Barefoot—
I more than once at Noon
Have passed, I thought, a Whip lash
Unbraiding in the Sun
When stopping to secure it                   15
It wrinkled, and was gone—

Several of Nature's People
I know, and they know me—
I feel for them a transport
Of cordiality—                               20

But never met this Fellow
Attended, or alone
Without a tighter breathing
And Zero at the Bone—

This poem demonstrates particularly well the **interaction of ecological, ethical, and aesthetic concerns** in Dickinson's writings. The referential content of the poem seems obvious enough—it is the presence of a snake as a special creature in a certain natural environment. The grass, a boggy acre, cool and unfit for human cultivation, are mentioned as the snake's habitat, along with the personal encounter of the child with this creature, which continues to exert its shock-like, at once fascinating and paralyzing effect on the adult speaker. Yet the text only begins to unfold its rich semantic potential when we look at the ways in which this primary experience is conveyed. The poem lives from the strangeness of the familiar—a 'fellow' is someone with whom one shares a familiar code and life-world, and yet this particular fellow is also characterized by strangeness, by the unexpected and unpredictable, by breaking out of habitual patterns of feeling, behavior, and per-

ception. What is conveyed here, therefore, is the vital interconnection of the human subject with a symbolic life force that is nevertheless unavailable, with an other that is radically alien yet also affects the innermost core of the self. What the poem thus unfolds in its formal composition and its interfusion of metaphor and narrative is an uncanny **dialectic of familiarity and strangeness**, of the visible and the invisible (second stanza), of presence and absence (third stanza), of communication and isolation, of life and death (third and fourth stanzas) as basic forms of being in the world. The snake is one of the most frequently recurring archetypes of the human imagination, occurring in Western and non-Western literature alike throughout the ages as a powerful image of danger inspiring both fear and fascination. Beyond this archetypal, transhistorical level, however, the snake has also special significance within the context of American culture. On this level, it represents a counterforce to the pastoral interpretation of America as a new garden of Eden, a colonial project in which, as American literature again and again illustrates, the presence of the alien and unavailable is already implicated in its very conception of order, mastery, and control over the human and nonhuman world. The image in which the boy at first perceives the snake, the "whip lash," is a sign of this cultural illusion of mastery and control over a brightly visible, passive and literally "graspable" nature, which however at the attempt of "securing it" turns into something ungraspable, active, shape-changing, and absent—"It wrinkled and was gone." The whip as an icon of master-slave relations, of dominance and domestication, which in the context of mid-nineteenth-century America has additional overtones, is transformed here into a subversive counterforce. In the third stanza, we have a further alienating effect in that the identity of the human subject, too, breaks out of conventional patterns such as gender roles when Dickinson's poetic self surprises the reader by turning herself into a "boy," thereby imaginatively changing her place and perspective on life, in fact participating in the shape-changing process and resistance to any fixed notion of knowledge and identity that the poem enacts. The biophilic mutuality between human and nonhuman nature in stanza four, finds its counterpoint in the fifth stanza in the biophobic, paralyzing experience of potential threat and annihilation. The z or s sound, which irregularly occurs throughout and appears once more in the "Zero at the bone" at the poem's end, signifies the negative climax of a series of unexpected changes which run as if in irregular serpentine waves through the text, making the snake not only the theme but a shaping image of the text's semiotic movement (Zapf).

## Select Bibliography

Bailyn, Bernard et al. *The Great Republic: A History of the American People*. Lexington, MA: Heath, 1977.

Baym, Nina. *Woman's Fiction: A Guide to Novels by and about Women in America: 1820–1870*. Ithaca: Cornell University Press, 1978.

Benesch, Klaus. "Where I Lived, and What I Lived For? Thoreau's Platial Iconicity." *American Cultural Icons: The Production of Representative Lives*. Eds. Bernd Engler and Günter Leypoldt. Würzburg: Königshausen & Neumann, 2010. 107–21.

Benesch, Klaus. *Romantic Cyborgs: Authorship and Technology in the American Renaissance*. Amherst: University of Massachusetts Press, 2002.

Bigelow, Jacob. *Elements of Technology*. Boston: Boston Press, 1829.

Boorstin, Daniel. *The Genius of American Politics*. Chicago: University of Chicago Press, 1953.

Bromell, Nicholas K. *By the Sweat of the Brow: Literature and Labor in Antebellum America*. Chicago: University of Chicago Press, 1993.

Buell, Lawrence. *The Environmental Imagination: Thoreau, Nature Writing, and the Formation of American Culture*. Cambridge: Harvard University Press, 1995.

Davidson, Cathy. *Revolution and the Word: The Rise of the Novel in America*. New York: Oxford University Press, 1986.

Eichner, Hans. "The Rise of Modern Science and the Genesis of Romanticism." *PMLA* 97 (1982): 8–30.

Fetterley, Judith, ed. *Provisions: A Reader from 19th-Century American Women*. Bloomington: Indiana University Press, 1985.

Foster, Frances Smith, ed. *A Brighter Coming Day: A Frances Ellen Watkins Harper Reader*. New York: The Feminist Press at CUNY, 1993.

Foucault, Michel. *The Order of Things*. New York: Vintage, 1973.

Gilbert, Sandra M., and Susan Gubar. *The Madwoman in the Attic: The Woman Writer and the Nineteenth-Century Literary Imagination*. New Haven: Yale University Press, 1984.

Gilmore, Michael T. *American Romanticism and the Marketplace*. Chicago: University of Chicago Press, 1985.

Grossberg, Lawrence, Cary Nelson, and Paula Treichler. *Cultural Studies*. New York: Routledge, 1992.

Hawthorne, Nathaniel. *The Letters, 1853–1856*. Eds. Thomas Woodson et al. Columbus: Ohio University Press, 1987.

James, C. L. R. *Mariners, Renegades, and Castaways: The Story of Herman Melville and the World We Live In*. 1953. London: Allison & Busby, 1985.

Karcher, Carolyn L. *Shadow over the Promised Land: Slavery, Race, and Violence in Melville's America*. Baton Rouge: Louisiana State University Press, 1980.

Levy, Andrew. *The Culture and Commerce of the American Short Story*. Cambridge: Cambridge University Press, 1993.

Marx, Leo. *The Machine in the Garden: Technology and the Pastoral Ideal in America*. New York: Oxford University Press, 1964.

Matthiessen, F. O. *American Renaissance: Art and Expression in the Age of Emerson and Whitman*. London: Oxford University Press, 1941.

McMurry, Andrew. *Environmental Renaissance: Emerson, Thoreau, and the Systems of Nature*. Athens: University of Georgia Press, 2003.

Meier, Hugo A. "Thomas Jefferson and a Democratic Technology." *Technology in America: A History of Individuals and Ideas*. Ed. Carrol W. Pursell, Jr. Cambridge: MIT Press, 1990. 17–44.

Pease, Donald E. *Visionary Compacts: American Renaissance Writings in Cultural Context*. Madison: University of Wisconsin Press, 1987.

Philbrick, Nathaniel. *In the Heart of the Sea: The Tragedy of the Whaleship Essex*. New York: Viking, 2000.

Poirier, Richard. *A World Elsewhere: The Place of Style in American Fiction*. New York: Oxford University Press, 1966.

Pratt, Lloyd. *Archives of American Time: Literature and Modernity in the Nineteenth Century*. Philadelphia: University of Pennsylvania Press, 2009.

Scott, Donald. "Print and the Public Lecture System." *Printing and Society in Early America*. Eds. William Joyce, David D. Hall, Richard D. Brown, and John B. Hench. Worcester: American Antiquarian Society, 1983.

Smith, Henry Nash. *Virgin Land: The American West as Symbol and Myth*. Cambridge: Harvard University Press, 1950.

Teichgraeber, Richard F., III. "Literary Marketplace." *American History Through Literature: 1820–1870*. Eds. Janet Gabler-Hover and Robert D. Sattelmeyer. Detroit: Scribner, 2006. 673–79.

Williams, Susan S. *Reclaiming Authorship: Literary Women in America: 1850–1900*. Philadelphia: University of Pennsylvania Press, 2006.

Zapf, Hubert. "Literary Ecology and the Ethics of Texts." *New Literary History* 39.4 (2008): 847–68.

*Klaus Benesch*

## 3.3 | Realism and Naturalism

### 3.3.1 | Terminology

Realism can be discussed from a vast array of perspectives: as an artistic, literary and intellectual movement emerging in Europe in the 1850s; as an era in American literary history from roughly 1880 to 1900; as a perennially popular representational convention still present on the contemporary literary scene; and finally as a philosophical dispute, beginning in antiquity and still unresolved, concerned with the question of truthful representation of reality, or mimesis.

In this dispute, one of the most essential concerns of Western epistemological discourse is at stake. This problem concerns artistic accounts of reality and leads to crucial questions surrounding the concept of **mimesis**: can literature relate directly to reality, can it depict reality truthfully, and what artistic techniques are particularly appropriate here? These questions have been debated hotly and answered very differently over the centuries. In ancient philosophy, where the debate began, Plato and Aristotle demarcated the central positions. Plato, in his dialogue *Sophist,* raises the essential question: do artists create mere duplications of reality or is mimesis rather a creation allowing for artistic freedom in the construction of reality? Plato's dialogues argue that the latter is the case, yet the question remains open of how to evaluate the element of poetic license. In this debate, Aristotle took a more positive stance and elaborated on the potential of artistic freedom, whereas Plato strictly condemned it and saw works of art as twice removed from a truthful rendering of reality, and thus as precarious.

While the discussion of the dangers and possibilities of mimesis has persisted over centuries, it gained particular intensity—and radicalism—in the poststructuralist debates of the twentieth century. Here the truthful rendering of reality in an artwork was repudiated altogether. That literature does not—*cannot*—represent reality in any immediate way is one of the bedrock assumptions of poststructuralism (cf. entry II.4). Yet as careful readings of literary texts reveal, literature paradoxically *does* seem to be in close interaction with its historical context. The various twentieth century schools of literary theory have gone to great lengths to account for this **contradiction**, and most theoretical approaches concentrate on explanations of how fiction exploits the fluid realm between creation and re-creation that Plato's deliberations posited, a space where *a* fictional reality is created that both depends on that which is, *the* reality, and at the same time supersedes and supplements it.

**Realism as a Convention of Representation.** If this space between the actual and the created is characteristic of fiction in general, realist fiction in particular exploits it with a view to achieving a particular effect. It aims to create what the French thinker Roland Barthes, in 1968, famously called a "**reality effect**" (141). He argues that a realist text does not—cannot—represent reality truthfully, but *pretends* to do so, or rather poses as reality by confronting the reader with an abundance of superfluous details in the description of characters, objects or places. The technique of rendering a multitude of details and thereby evoking a feeling of recognition in the reader, also called **verisimilitude**, is one of the most prominent qualities of realist writing.

The many **narrative characteristics** of realist texts are all geared to creating the illusion of a text's truthful rendering of reality. Among these features, as Philippe Hamon has shown, are certain rhetorical procedures. For instance, they establish narrative coherence through the measured integration of summaries or plausible predictions; they exhibit the psychological motivation of the characters; and they seek to provide verifiable information and circulation of knowledge through the integration of reliable narrative authorities in the text. These various stylistic and rhetorical procedures that characterize the realist convention of representation can be found in one form or another in virtually all literary epochs. They have never lost their appeal, as various resurgences over the course of the twentieth century in the form of neo-realism, magic realism, dirty realism, minimalism, and many others have shown, yet they were most coherently pursued in the classic realist literature of the nineteenth century.

---

**Definition**

→ **Realism** may refer to
- a philosophical dispute concerned with the question of mimesis;
- a convention of representation that aims to render reality in its objective truth;
- an artistic movement emerging in Europe in the 1850s (cf. entry I.2.5.3);
- a period in American literary history from roughly 1880 to 1900.

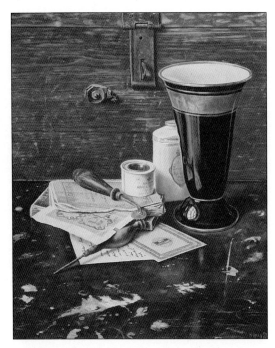

Verisimilitude in the visual arts: Manfred Hönig, *Zeitfragmente* (2008)

**Realism as an International Literary Movement.** Realism as an international literary movement started to gain momentum in the 1850s in Europe with the works of such eminent writers as Gustave Flaubert and Edmond de Goncourt in France, Leo Tolstoy and Fyodor Dostoyevsky in Russia, Charles Dickens, William Makepeace Thackeray, and George Eliot in Britain, and Theodor Fontane and Theodor Storm in Germany. The many differences notwithstanding, the works of these writers are connected through the dominance of the realist aesthetic as discussed above, but also through the way the authors understood their own role as well as the function of literature in general. To them, literature was to explore the **social realities** of their times, and they, as authors, were to truthfully record these realities like sociologists. In marked contrast to the approach of the preceding Romantic period, now the social conditions in the industrializing societies became the unveiled focus of literature's concern. More precisely, it was the living conditions and conventions of the middle class that these authors tried to chronicle with as much accuracy as possible.

## 3.3.2 | The Poetics of American Realism

As with most artistic developments that emerged in Europe in the eighteenth or nineteenth century, it took a while for realism to be fully absorbed into the American literary context (and to be deeply transformed in the process of adaptation). Thus, when the era of European literary realism was coming to an end in the 1880s, it was at its height on the American scene. It is difficult to fix the precise beginning of the realist period in the United States. Standard literary histories have often dated it at 1865, after the **end of the Civil War**, with the most prolific period coming in the 1880s. Yet there is reason to push this time frame backwards, as some recent scholarship has argued that texts by women writers, such as Rebecca Harding Davis's *Life in the Iron-Mills* (1861), should count as pioneering works of realist fiction (cf. section I.2.2.8). Undoubtedly, some of the earliest works of American realist fiction are John W. De Forest's postwar novel *Miss Ravenel's Conversion from Secession to Loyalty* (1867) and Mark Twain's satirical travelogue *The Innocents Abroad* (1869).

William Dean Howells was one the most important and influential proponents of realism in the U.S. He was a novelist, critic, and editor of the literary magazine *Harper's New Monthly* (founded in 1850) and was the friend and in some cases the patron of leading American realist writers such as Henry James, Mark Twain, Mary Eleanor Wilkins Freeman, Sarah Orne Jewett, Charles Chesnutt, Charlotte Perkins Gilman, and Paul Laurence Dunbar. Howells was also one of the main targets in the so-called **Realism War** which was waged in the literary magazines in the 1880s and 1890s. In this war, realism was attacked aggressively as being artless, cheap, and devoted to "worship of the vulgar, the commonplace and the insignificant […] which is the last stage of decadence," as one

---

**Key Texts: American Realism/Naturalism**

**Henry James,** *The Portrait of a Lady* (1881)
**Stephen Crane,** *The Red Badge of Courage* (1895)
**William Dean Howells,** *The Rise of Silas Lapham* (1885)
**Mark Twain,** *The Adventures of Huckleberry Finn* (1885)
**Kate Chopin,** *The Awakening* (1899)
**Frank Norris,** *McTeague* (1899)
**Theodore Dreiser,** *Sister Carrie* (1900)
**Jack London,** *The Sea Wolf* (1904)

of Howells's main adversaries, the writer Maurice Thompson, held (20). The squad of realist writers on the opposite side, although connected by a certain trust in the civilizing power of the realist novel (which will be discussed shortly), were a much less homogeneous and firmly organized group than their opponents took them to be. The following quotation from a letter that **Stephen Crane**, author of the remarkable Civil War novel *The Red Badge of Courage* (1895), wrote in 1894, illustrates this point:

> So I developed all alone a little creed of art which I thought was a good one. Later I discovered that my creed was identical with the one of Howells and Garland and in this way I became involved in the beautiful war between those who say that [...] we are the most successful in art when we approach the nearest to nature and truth, and those who [...] keep Garland and I out of the big magazines. Howells, of course, is too powerful for them. (*Letters* 31–32)

In one of his many theoretical deliberations on the subject of realism, published in *Harper's*, Howells pondered in 1887 a letter from one of his readers: "Whatever in my mental make-up is wild and visionary, whatever is untrue, whatever is injurious, I can trace to the perusal of some work of fiction" (43). To Howells, this was a most welcome criticism, as he could use it to explain that this charge against fiction writing is just only when directed against dated forms of the novel, not against realist fiction. The outdated novel, he holds, only wants to entertain; it unfolds melodramatic plots in unlikely settings where for the "gaudy hero and heroine" love and passion always win over reason. Novels like these mislead the reader into total immersion in these phantas-

mal fictional realities; reading them is comparable to "opium eating" (44).

These, Howells argues, are the novels of the past, whereas the realist novel is the novel of the future. The realist novel addresses its readers as adult human beings and aims to establish a **rational dialogue** with them. What is more, it wants to **educate** them in forms of responsible behavior and the correct assessment of social realities. In order to distinguish one form from the other, Howells proposes a test. He puts forward a question that to his mind critics should ask of any fictional text: "Is it true?—true to the motives, the impulses, the principles that shape the life of actual men and women?" (45–46). A positive answer would prove the author's commitment to realism and thus to the novel's truthful representation of reality. As an example of one of the novels that have passed this test, Howells refers to **Henry James**'s *Princess Casamassima*, in his opinion "incomparably the greatest novel of the year [1886]" (47). This test and question tie in with the European realist tradition, yet in another of Howell's assessments, the particularly American angle of literary realism becomes clearly visible. In praising **Mark Twain**'s successful *The Innocents Abroad* (1869) and *Roughing It* (1872), Howells claims: "Let fiction cease to lie about life; let it portray men and women as they are, actuated by the motives and the passions *in the measure we all know*" (49; my emphasis). His formulation "in the measure we all know" bases his demand for truthful fiction on the reliability of common knowledge and common experience, thereby expressing his belief that realism is a profoundly democratic—and thus American—project.

The notion that realism is a **democratic and civilizing project** was introduced by the German Americanist Winfried Fluck, who in his groundbreaking work *Inszenierte Wirklichkeit* turned against the traditional view that understood American realism simply as a more or less successful attempt to adopt European strategies and objectives. In elaborating on his perspective on American realism as a cultural strategy based on the civilizing potential of experience, Fluck sums up its concerns as follows: "If there is one common denominator that dominates the various forms of American realism, ranging from the historical and political novel, travel literature and local color fiction to the novel of manners and the utopian novel, [...] it is [...] the attempt to provide instances of an exemplary learning process in which the main characters finally learn to trust their own instinct and experience as the only reliable source of knowledge" ("Declarations of Dependence" 26). The prime example of such a learning process is provided by Henry James's ***The Portrait of a Lady*** (1881). In this paradigmatic American realist novel, the protagonist Isabel Archer, a young and innocent American girl, undergoes a maturation process in Europe. After Isabel in her naïveté has fallen for the wrong man, she painfully begins to trust her perceptions, to interpret them correctly, and to learn from her experiences, until she is finally able to decipher the scheming of her untrustworthy husband and his accomplice. After the revelation of the conspiracy, in an exemplary instance of mature behavior, she decides to accept her responsibilities and remain in her unhappy marriage.

### 3.3.3 | William Dean Howells and the Historical Context of the Gilded Age

Howells himself published fine examples of American realist literature, and a close reading of his novel *A Hazard of New Fortunes* (1889) may illuminate further the conventions of realist writing. The novel is set amid the dramatic social changes and upheavals accompanying the massive industrialization of the U.S. during the 1880s and 1890s, the "**Gilded Age**." This period saw the accumulation of great fortunes in the emerging class of the super rich, the so-called robber barons, on one side, and on the other the growing slums in the big cities that absorbed and accommodated the constant inflow of immigrant labor. Jacob Riis's *How the Other Half Lives: Studies Among the Tenements of New York* (1890), a masterful work of photojournalism, documents the abysmal living conditions in the slums. Howells picks up the turmoil of these social transformations and firmly establishes the perspective of the middle class as his narrative center.

The opening paragraph of *A Hazard of New Fortunes* (see box on p. 128) confronts the reader with the core of American realism's objective: this new form of the novel was to communicate the **power of rational dialogue**, because it put its trust in the rational, democratic development of American society as a whole. It puts forward visions of commonality and individual liberation through the power of mutual exchange. Winfried Fluck holds that the realist novel addresses readers "as demo-

cratic equals who are invited to an ongoing dialogue on the nature and current state of American civilization, and yet are left alone to form their own conclusions because of a basic trust in their common sense and innate morality" ("Declarations of Dependence" 29).

This civilizing project can be traced very clearly in the canonized masterpieces of American realist literature published in the 1880s, be they James's *The Portrait of a Lady* (1881), Mark Twain's *The Adventures of Huckleberry Finn* (1885), or Howells's *The Rise of Silas Lapham* (1885). In all of these novels, the protagonists have to learn to rely on their own experiences and to draw the right conclusions from them.

**Variety of Realist Writing.** There were, however, more forms of realism to be noted in the American context. The most prominent realist sub-group was **local color or regionalist writing**. Local color writers shared the general interest of late nineteenth century American society in exploring and mapping out their reunified nation after the war. Thus, local color writers—many of them female—were interested in the local customs, mores and dialects of a certain U.S. region, and like local historians, depicted those truthfully and in great detail, very often in the form of short stories or anecdotes. Local color writers recording rural life on the East coast were, to name but a few, Mary Eleanor Wilkins Freeman (*A New England Nun and Other Stories*, 1891), Sarah Orne Jewett (*The Coun-*

Illustration from Jacob Riis's *How the Other Half Lives*

Interpretation

### William Dean Howells, *A Hazard of New Fortunes*

Howells' protagonist is the writer Basil March who, supported by his wife Isabel, is the rational and moral voice of the novel. He is persuaded by his friend Fulkerson to give up his job in the insurance business, move to New York City and become the editor of the new literary magazine *Every Other Week*, a magazine financially backed by Jacob Dryfoos, a nouveau riche gas magnate and self-made millionaire. The moral crisis and climax of the novel arises when Dryfoos tries to force the editors to no longer print articles by the socialist Lindau, who has criticized him for his brutal leadership style, reminiscent of Manchester capitalism. Fulkerson and March have to take sides and to weigh their own financial wellbeing against the defense of their independence as editors and the democratic right of freedom of expression. The novel depicts the process of the editors' coming to terms with the situation and making the courageous decision to defy Dryfoos through the extensive presentation of rational dialogue—thereby giving the reader a model of ideal behavior.

A closer look at the opening of the novel will illustrate its realist character:

"Now you think this thing over, March, and let me know the last of next week," said Fulkerson. He got up from the chair which he had been sitting astride, with his face to its back, and tilting toward March on its hind legs, and came and rapped upon his table with his thin bamboo stick. "What you want to do is to get out of the insurance business, anyway. You acknowledge that yourself. You never liked it, and now it makes you sick; in other words, it's killing you. You ain't an insurance man by nature. You're a natural-born literary man; and you've been going against the grain. Now I offer you a chance to go *with* the grain. I don't say you're going to make your everlasting fortune, but I'll give you a living salary, and if the thing succeeds, you'll share in its success. We'll all share in its success. That's the beauty of it. [...]."

He put his leg up over the corner of March's table and gave himself a sharp cut on the thigh, and leaned forward to get the full effect of his words upon his listener.

March had his hands clasped together behind his head, and he took one of them down long enough to put his inkstand and mucilage bottle out of Fulkerson's way. (Howells, *A Hazard of New Fortunes* pt. 1, ch. 1)

As far as the **conventions of realist representation** are concerned, this passage exhibits many of the traditional features: there is no aesthetic experiment that would defamiliarize the textual surface or cloud the text's intentions. Very much to the contrary, the text tries to evoke the effect of intense reality through the description of the office interior, down to the mentioning of such mundane objects as an inkstand and a mucilage bottle. It tries to evoke the friendship between the two men by describing their relaxed, informal postures in detail: Fulkerson sitting astride a chair, tilting on its hind legs, then putting his leg up over the corner of March's table, March having his hands clasped together behind his head. Howells attempts to convey a real-life, familiar atmosphere through employing the non-standard grammar of spoken language ("You ain't an insurance man by nature").

Yet this opening passage is also a prime example of the particular nature of the American realist tradition. The reader enters this fictional reality *in medias res*, i.e., does not get any introduction into the characters, setting or story line and is not guided by a controlling narrative voice. The novel thus loses no time in subtly establishing how it intends to address its readers: as responsible, mature persons who are expected to be able to adequately interpret an unfamiliar scene upon which they enter. The text also immediately presents its dominant mode of communication: that of rational dialogue. We take in the arguments that Fulkerson uses to persuade his friend to leave the insurance business and follow his true nature and talents. We are convinced easily by their commonsensical force and have no doubt that March will be also. Furthermore, the middle-class milieu and perspective are established from the start. The office setting leaves no doubt about the bourgeois ambience, while the whole enterprise which Fulkerson proposes is not about making millions or heading off on a wild adventure, but about finding and living one's true vocation with the anticipated payoff of a moderate income and solid peace of mind. Finally, the whole endeavor is a collaborative effort in whose success all will share.

*try of the Pointed Firs*, 1896), and Harriet Beecher Stowe (*Old Town Folks*, 1869). Among regionalist writers from the South were Kate Chopin (*Bayou Folk*, 1893) and George Washington Cable (*Old Creole Days*, 1883), famous for their portrayals of Creole life in Louisiana. Notable Midwestern writers include Hamlin Garland (*Prairie Folks*, 1893), Edward Eggleston (*The Hoosier Schoolmaster*, 1871), and Bret Harte, who in *The Outcasts of Poker Flat* (1869) gives a memorable depiction of life during the California gold rush.

---

### 3.3.4 | American Naturalism

Some realist novels took up pressing topics of the time such as political corruption (Henry Adams, *Democracy*, 1880), divorce (Howells, *A Modern Instance*, 1882), or alcoholism (Howells, *The Landlord at Lion's Head*, 1897). The concern with urban squalor turned more radical towards the end of the century when a more extreme version of realist writing, naturalism, gained influence. What connects both forms, realism and naturalism, is their reliance on scientific theory, in particular the belief in objectivity and the method of close observation. What differentiates them is naturalism's alliance with the philosophical theories of **determinism** and **Social Darwinism** (for a definition see entry I.2.5.2) Realist authors perceived themselves not only as authors, but also as sociologists taking precise notes on the social reality around them. Naturalist writers, however, took their note pads into areas that had been unacceptable or downright tabooed for realist writers: they wanted to deal with the underbelly of the urban landscape, with poverty, abnormality, violence, sexuality and the pure struggle for survival, and to depict these unadorned in their novels. As with realism, the impulse for this kind of literature came from Europe, from the French novelist **Émile Zola**.

In his influential essay *Le Roman expérimental* (1880), which is seen as **naturalism's manifesto**, Zola explains that the naturalist novel can serve as a stage for conducting a scientific experiment to demonstrate that human agency is determined socially and biologically and thus is not free. The author, functioning like a scientist, can set characters in motion in his fictional universe and show that what happens to them is determined by abstract forces, by heredity and the environment, not by any notion of free will. Clearly this world view

> #### Definition
>
> The → Gilded Age is the name given by Mark Twain and Charles Dudley Warner to the period in U.S. history between the end of the Civil War and the end of the nineteenth century. The rebuilding of the nation after the Civil War was accompanied by massive industrialization and drastic socio-economical changes to the structure of society, fuelled by capitalistic materialism. The term "gilded" ironically hints at the difference between the shining lifestyle of the wealthy few and the drab poverty of the masses.

is in strong opposition to the realists' trust in the power of rational discourse, mutual exchange and malleable social development, and in comparison to the naturalists' stark approach to the truthful representation of reality, realist literature now seemed effete. Thus it comes as no surprise that towards the end of the century, naturalism came to be the new and exciting literary development, realism was losing influence, and formerly prominent men of letters like William Dean Howells fell into oblivion. Sinclair Lewis went so far as to openly dismiss him in his Nobel Prize address of 1930: "Mr. Howells was one of the gentlest, sweetest, and most honest of men, but he had the code of a pious old maid whose greatest delight was to have tea at the vicarage. He abhorred not only profanity and obscenity but all of what H. G. Wells has called 'the jolly coarsenesses of life.'" The coarseness of life was certainly the material in which the naturalist writers indulged.

If it is an act of fate (the lottery win) and revenge that ruins the protagonists' lives in Frank Norris's *McTeague* (see box on p. 130), Carrie Meeber, in **Theodore Dreiser**'s *Sister Carrie* (1900), described as merely passive and given over to the forces of fate, leaves a trail of crushed masculine lives behind her on her way from country bumpkin to fame as a New York City actress. In **Jack London**'s work, one of the major examples of American naturalist writing, it is usually the pattern of man versus nature that serves as a testing ground for the battle between civilization and the power of natural instincts. Around the turn of the century, the old Victorian traditions and values were beginning to be seen as oversocialized and demure, and the topic of the wilderness gained recognition as a possible antidote to this tendency of effeminization. London, who had spent years as a hobo traveling through the American landscape and had gone to Alaska during the Klondike gold rush in the late 1890s, used the experiences he had

Interpretation

## Frank Norris, *McTeague*

In one of the finest examples of American naturalist writing, Frank Norris's *McTeague* (1899), the protagonist is shown in his descent from man to beast, the process being determined by heredity and environment, as the product of his temperament. McTeague, a man of immense physical strength but moderate intelligence, practices as a dentist in his San Francisco shop without having had any formal education in his profession. He marries a woman, Trina, who shortly after their engagement wins a large sum in a lottery. The couple is happy at first, although Trina soon shows distinct stinginess as one of her major character traits and won't allow the lottery money to be spent for their daily necessities. The catastrophe begins when McTeague is denounced by his rival and debarred by the authorities from further work as a dentist. He has to give up his shop and the couple has to move to increasingly cheaper apartments. McTeague succumbs to drinking—he has inherited the disposition for alcoholism and a certain inclination to violent behavior, or so the narrator informs the reader. When Trina comes to him for the first time to get some dental work done, he is tempted to rape her when she is lying before him unconscious in the surgical chair:

Suddenly the animal in the man stirred and woke; the evil instincts that in him were so close to the surface leaped to life, shouting and clamoring. [...] Below the fine fabric of all that was good in him ran the foul stream of hereditary evil, like a sewer. The vices and sins of his father and of his father's father, to the third and fourth and five hundredth generation, tainted him. The evil of an entire race flowed in his veins. Why should it be? He did not desire it. Was he to blame? (ch. 2).

Film still from *Greed* (1924), Erich von Strohheim's adaptation of *McTeague*

Of course not, would be the answer in the context of a naturalist experiment, and the tragedy proceeds. McTeague becomes more and more violent towards his wife. As Trina still refuses to spend the lottery money, McTeague, in scenes of domestic violence, is consumed by cannibalistic tendencies and repeatedly bites her. He eventually murders her and flees with the lottery money, chased by his rival. The two opponents meet in the middle of Death Valley and McTeague murders his rival, only to find out that the latter has managed to handcuff himself to his murderer before his death. In the final scene, McTeague is shown with his last water gone in Death Valley, chained to his victim and holding in his fist his only possession, his beloved caged canary bird, both doomed to die.

The story of McTeague clearly displays the main ingredients of a **naturalist experimental scenario**. Essential to this is always some stark catastrophic event in the form of a natural disaster, extreme social circumstances or pure coincidence that sets the drama in motion. Contrary to the realists' trust in the power of rational behavior, naturalist writers wanted to show just how thin the layer of civilized behavior really is and how easily it can be stripped from any member of society. Then the human being is easily ruled by animalistic instincts and libidinal desires, just as McTeague's loss of his profession is enough to spur his alcoholic predisposition and awaken his violent, cannibalistic and murderous instincts. Thus, the inevitable catastrophic plot construction of a naturalist novel, a phenomenon that led Frank Norris to declare in an 1896 essay that "[t]errible things must happen to the characters of the naturalistic tale. They must be twisted from the ordinary, wrenched out from the quiet, uneventful round of every-day life, and flung into the throes of a vast and terrible drama that works itself out in unleashed passions, in blood, and in sudden death. The world of M. Zola is a world of big things; the enormous, the formidable, the terrible, is what counts; no teacup tragedies here" (72).

there to write naturalist fiction that told time and again the story of overcivilized men regaining their true nature in the wilderness—or losing the fight there, as does the protagonist in London's most famous short story "To Build a Fire" (1902).

One of London's most famous novels, **The Sea Wolf**, published in 1904, is inspired by the theories of Darwin, Spencer, and Marx. *The Sea Wolf* follows the tradition of the *Bildungsroman* and tells the story of the overcivilized and sickly writer Humphrey Van Weyden, the narrator of the story, who relates how he accidentally got aboard the ship of Captain Wolf Larsen, a highly intelligent yet brutish and supernaturally strong human being. Larsen and Van Weyden mirror and provoke one another, and a dramatic life-or-death battle between the antagonists unfolds aboard the ship.

The war is waged on many levels: a confrontation of ideologies in which Larsen represents the dog-eat-dog position, or a fight against the elements of nature or among the crew members, whose community can be read as an allegorical microcosm of the brutal living conditions of the lower classes in the Gilded Age in general. Along with this battle, Van Weyden undergoes a process of remasculinization. He becomes healthy and strong and learns to listen again to his reawakened instincts. Because he also possesses the advantage of high civilization, in contrast to his opponent, he eventually wins the battle. In this novel, London defines a new middle position in naturalist writing: in the battle of **survival of the fittest**, it is not instincts and strength alone that win, but a combination of nature and civilization that proves superior.

## Select Bibliography

Barthes, Roland. "The Reality Effect." 1968. *The Rustle of Language*. Trans. Richard Howard. Berkeley: University of California Press, 1989. 141–48.

Beaumont, Matthew, ed. *A Concise Companion to Realism*. Chichester: Wiley-Blackwell, 2010.

Bell, Michael Davitt. *The Problem of American Realism: Studies in the Cultural History of a Literary Idea*. Chicago: University of Chicago Press, 1993.

Crane, Stephen. *Letters*. Ed. R. W. Stallman et al. New York: New York University Press, 1960.

Fluck, Winfried. "Declarations of Dependence: Revising Our View of American Realism." *Victorianism in the United States: Its Era and Its Legacy*. Eds. Steve Ickingrill et al. Amsterdam: VU University Press, 1992. 19–34.

Fluck, Winfried. *Inszenierte Wirklichkeit: Der amerikanische Realismus: 1865–1900*. Munich: Fink, 1992.

Glazener, Nancy. *Reading for Realism: The History of a U.S. Literary Institution, 1850–1910*. Durham: Duke University Press, 1997.

Hamon, Philippe. "Philippe Hamon on the Major Features of Realist Discourse." Trans. Lilian R. Furst and Seán Hand. *Realism*. Ed. Lilian R. Furst. New York: Longman, 1992. 166–85.

Howard, June. *Form and History in American Literary Naturalism*. Chapel Hill: University of North Carolina Press, 1985.

Howells, William Dean. *Selected Literary Criticism*. Ed. Donald Pizer. Vol. 2. Bloomington: Indiana University Press, 1993.

Kaplan, Amy. *The Social Construction of American Realism*. Chicago: University of Chicago Press, 1988.

Kearns, Catherine. *Nineteenth Century Literary Realism: Through the Looking-glass*. Cambridge: Cambridge University Press, 1996.

Lamb, Robert Paul, et al., eds. *A Companion to American Fiction, 1865–1914*. Malden: Blackwell, 2005.

Lewis, Sinclair. "The American Fear of Literature." Nobel Lecture. 12 Dec. 1930. *Nobelprize.org*. 13 Oct 2010 <http://nobelprize.org/nobel_prizes/literature/laureates/1930/lewis-lecture.html>.

Martin, Jay. *Harvests of Change: American Literature, 1865–1914*. Englewood Cliffs: Prentice Hall, 1967.

Newlin, Keith, ed. *The Oxford Handbook of American Literary Naturalism*. New York: Oxford University Press, 2011.

Norris, Frank. "Zola as a Romantic Writer." *The Literary Criticism of Frank Norris*. Ed. Donald Pizer. Austin: University of Texas Press, 1964. 71–72.

Papke, Mary E., ed. *Twisted from the Ordinary: Essays on American Literary Naturalism*. Knoxville: University of Tennessee Press, 2003.

Pizer, Donald, ed. *The Cambridge Companion to American Realism and Naturalism: Howells to London*. Cambridge: Cambridge University Press, 1995.

Pizer, Donald. *The Theory and Practice of American Literary Naturalism: Selected Essays and Reviews*. Carbondale: Southern Illinois University Press, 1993.

Smith, Christopher, ed. *American Realism*. San Diego: Greenhaven Press, 2000.

Thompson, Maurice. "The Analysts Analyzed." *The Critic: A Weekly Review of Literature and the Arts* ns 6 (1886): 19–22.

Trachtenberg, Alan. *The Incorporation of America: Culture and Society in the Gilded Age*. New York: Hill and Wang, 1982.

*Susanne Rohr*

## 3.4 | Modernism

### 3.4.1 | Terminology

Like other epochal terms in literary history, that of 'modernism' suggests a unity of concept and practice that the texts we call 'modern' do not always confirm. The term not only ignores the considerable differences that mark the theories and national practices of modernism, but also its distinctly different phases of development. In its most inclusive sense, modernism is an **international phenomenon** that took place between, roughly, **1890 and 1930**, the result of a cultural conflict between generations: the radical break of sons, obsessed by a desire for innovation, with the culture of their Victorian fathers. It originated in the modernizing societies of Western Europe (including Western Russia) and the United States, and it prospered in its metropolitan centers: Paris, London, Berlin, New York (on British modernism see entry I.2.6).

At the beginning of the twentieth century, there were a number of artistic movements or individual practices in the U.S. claiming to be committed to the New. But in comparison to Europe, the U.S. was an aesthetic diaspora in a culture dominated by principles either of moral austerity or commercial usefulness. Those who could not stand it went to Europe—first Gertrude Stein, then Ezra Pound and T. S. Eliot. Those who stayed (Robert Frost, Wallace Stevens, William Carlos Williams, Marianne Moore) developed their own, '**home-made**,' modernist idiom.

The experimental writer Gertrude Stein believed that modernism was the logical translation of the social process of modernization into art and literature. Since America had begun that process earlier than any other nation, it was in essence modern—even if its art was not (yet) modernist. The philosopher George Santayana argued in a similar vein: "Americanism," he wrote in 1903, "apart from the genteel tradition, is simply modernism—purer in America than elsewhere because less impeded and qualified by survivals of the past" (135).

Gertrude Stein, portrait by Pablo Picasso, 1906

### 3.4.2 | The Two Discourses of Modernism

In American literature, the 'modern' became manifest in two discourses which are different from each other but also, in a complex manner, interconnected.

- One, congruent with a tradition of rationality as well as strategies of artistic and literary realism, makes the **experience of modernity** (and of the process of modernization) the very topic of its representations—the contradictions and ambivalences of that experience, the tensions felt between a desire for cultural order and for the flow of experience slowly eroding it. To this discourse we owe a number of realist and naturalist novels such as Kate Chopin's *The Awakening* (1899), Frank Norris's *McTeague* (1899), Theodore Dreiser's *Sister Carrie* (1900), Edith Wharton's *The House of Mirth* (1905), or James Weldon Johnson's *The Autobiography of an Ex-Colored Man* (1912). These are novels, placed in zones of mixing (between classes, races, ethnic cultures or concepts of gender, between high culture and popular culture), whose protagonists test new concepts of self and social role by abandoning themselves to the experience of the moment. This literature of transition between Victorianism and Modernism is fascinated with areas hitherto tabooed by the dominant order: the despised and yet secretly desired life below the threshold of the rational order (cf. entry I.3.3). In the literature and social writings of the time, Africa becomes a metaphor of unknown regions of society as well as of the psyche. Although this first discourse of modernity pushes beyond the borders of the existing cultural order, it nevertheless remains defined by it. It also stays within the realm of traditional narrative conventions, its search confined to exploring new areas of experience.

- The second discourse is that of **modernism proper**: It turns the cultural into a textual category, represents new experiences via new forms of expression. Thus, the poet William Carlos Williams, aware of the incessant flow of perception, wants to develop a language that can register "instantaneously" the movement and ongoing transformation of the perceived object as well as of the perceiving self (*Imaginations* 89). In a similar vein, Gertrude Stein develops, in a fast changing sequence of linguistic experiments, open or de-centered systems of composition. In "Melanctha" (the second story of *Three Lives*, 1906) and in her "portraits" of Cézanne and Picasso, she tests compositional designs that represent the nature of their object, via repetition and variation of linguistic patterns, as dynamic form-in-motion. Her texts thus project spaces of language and reflection "filled with moving" that, analogous to a filmic sequence of almost identical frames, render movement in and as a "continuous present" (198).

Both discourses display their modernity differently. The first, by its representation of **new contents** and ways of experience; the second, via the transformation of new modes of perception into **new forms** and techniques of artistic representation. Although the second discourse follows the first in temporal sequence and dominates it in the twenties, both continue existing next to each other, the first becoming dominant again during the thirties in a period of economic distress. Modern literature in the U.S. unfolds from the tension between them; one cannot be understood without the foil of the other: the first ('progressive' or 'realistic') discourse is driven toward formal innovation by the increasingly problematic status of the real; the second (that of modernism proper), although breaking with the conventions of realism, remains mimetically tied to a world outside the text (as the examples of Williams, Dos Passos or Hemingway demonstrate).

## 3.4.3 | Early Modernism: Stein, Pound, Eliot

**Gertrude Stein.** No author of American modernism, however, was as consequently avant-garde in her aesthetic convictions and compositional practice as Gertrude Stein. Since she did not belong to any clique, she was an avant-garde all to herself from whose experiments several generations of modernists profited. By 1912, long before Pound, Joyce or Eliot had found their modernist stylistic signature, Stein had run a whole gamut of linguistic and compositional experiments. Yet she was not counted among the 'masters' of modernism, nor were her works considered 'masterpieces' the way Joyce's *Ulysses* or Eliot's *The Waste Land* were immediately considered 'masterpieces' of modernist literature. For a long time she was merely an ex-centric figure, a 'writer's writer.' Stein pursued persistently what Williams called "the principal move in imaginative writing today": the tendency "away from word as symbol to word as a reality in itself" ("Excerpts" 107). And yet, the center of the movement was formed by others: first by Pound, then by Eliot.

**Focus on International Modernism**

The **internationalization** of the literary scene in the twentieth century is indicated, among other things, by the fact that many modernist writers are included in histories of both English and American literature (cf. entry I.2.6). Pound was born in the United States but lived in London during the formative period of modernism and exerted a strong influence there. Eliot even settled permanently in England and became a British citizen in 1927. Conversely, Auden moved to the United States in 1939 and eventually adopted American citizenship.

**Ezra Pound** had come to Europe only a few years after Stein (in 1908). He first went to London, then, at the beginning of the twenties, to Paris until he settled in Rapallo in 1924. Stein took her cues from modern painters—Cézanne, Matisse, and especially Picasso. She did not seek for models in literature (with the possible exception of Henry James), certainly not in the literature of earlier centuries. Pound, in contrast—although familiar with futurism and other avant-garde movements—pursued the linguistic purification of contemporary poetry by going back to a multitude of literary traditions: "to get back to something *prior* in time even as one is MAKING IT NEW" (Perloff, *Dance* 22). *The Cantos*—the central poetic endeavor of his life—were begun in 1917; he worked on them for the next fifty years, and then fell silent. The 109 cantos published are—among other things—a critical reflection on the corruption of the modern world by "usury," against which Pound projects the values of a universal classicism, especially the value of right "measure" in which the individual and social are conjoined in the poet's right "application of word to thing" (*How to Read* 21). At the same time, they circle around quasi-mystical moments of illumination when the "gods" reveal themselves sensuously in the perceived object.

The identification of the aesthetic with the social and political was the basis of Pound's creative work, but also the cause of his political blunders. Like Williams and Hart Crane, Pound saw the poet's voice legitimized by its **public function**. However, this quasi-utopian concept of an organic community which gave the poet purpose and to which he gave expression, ran counter to the actual reduction of the poet's status in contemporary society. Pound's hope for a possible union of the aesthetic with the social and political order (a hope he had originally connected with a modern American Renaissance) was so desperate that he

Interpretation

### T. S. Eliot, *The Waste Land*

Eliot's *The Waste Land* is by far the most famous modernist poem and in its immediate impact only comparable to Joyce's *Ulysses*, also published in 1922. Pound called it "the justification of the 'movement,' of our modern experiment since 1900" and "enough … to make the rest of us shut up shop" (*Selected Letters* 9 July). For others—most of all for William Carlos Williams—Eliot's poem, its linguistic and formal virtuosity notwithstanding, constituted treason to the project of creating the poetic language of a genuinely American modernism. (Williams rejected especially Eliot's acceptance of traditional blank verse as a metric basis, no matter how subtly it was varied.) We now know how much Eliot owed to his "miglior fabbro" Ezra Pound (as he called him in the dedication to *The Waste Land*) for trimming the poem to its published form. Pound cut it by half and, by dividing it into five parts, created at least a semblance of structural coherence.

The impact of the poem is, most likely, the result of its dissonant, yet extremely suggestive linguistic surface. There is no consistent lyrical self or speaker but a **multiplicity of changing voices**, sociolects, and languages. The language of Elizabethan drama is set next to the jargon of London streets. In addition, Eliot quotes from close to forty texts of English, French, Italian and German literature as well as from the Baghavad Gita. Images and motifs of diverse provenance are strung together in loose association: images from the experiential context of modern metropolitan life—of hastening city crowds, of its human and industrial "waste"—but also from Wagner operas, Greek, Egyptian and Christian mythology together with cards of the Tarot (the Wheel of Fortune, the Hanged Man). They function as **leitmotifs** connecting the different parts of the poem; yet whether they build a coherent structure or only display the fragments of a culture in ruins remains open. (For an interpretation of the poem in the context of English modernism see section I.2.6.2.)

came to believe it had found fulfillment in Mussolini's fascism.

As dubious as Pound's role was in politics, his importance as "midwife" of modernist American poetry during the twenties is beyond any doubt. Marianne Moore, H. D., Mina Loy, William Carlos Williams, E. E. Cummings and, especially, T. S. Eliot profited from his critique and support. His critical writings established standards of discussion and thus a basis for the reception of modern literature in subsequent years. In this function, they were surpassed only by Eliot's essays.

**T. S. Eliot** had come to Europe in 1915, after he had given up his study of philosophy at Harvard. "The Love Song of J. Alfred Prufrock"—written in 1911 but only published in 1915—gave him instant reputation as a new and original voice in contemporary poetry. The famous first lines of this poem—"Let us go then, you and I, / When the evening is spread out against the sky / Like a patient etherized upon a table"—were unmistakably influenced by the French symbolist Jules Laforgue, but their ironic deconstruction of Romantic nature imagery seemed revolutionary. In the figure of Prufrock, Eliot staged a sensibility in whose melancholic and self-deprecatory narcissism a whole generation recognized itself; and the ironic-satirical tone of the poem, the dissonant juxtaposition

of its images were perceived as a lyrical language never heard before—at least not in the realm of English poetry.

Partly in response to Pound, Eliot made himself the theoretical spokesman of Anglo-American modernism via a number of **influential essays**. His critical positions were similar to Pound's but where Pound argued polemically, Eliot assumed an aloof intellectual stance as "man of letters," thus laying the foundation for the later academic absorption of modernism into the theoretical discourse of the New Critics (cf. entry II.1). His most famous essay, "Tradition and the Individual Talent" (1919), conceives of tradition as an organic ensemble of works that changes with every individual work newly added to it. In this process, tradition has priority since it encompasses individual expression. Accordingly, the creative process is not an act of self-affirmation but of self-abnegation for the sake of something higher. Eliot's anti-Romantic rhetoric culminates in a sentence that influenced American poetry and its criticism until the 1960s: "The progress of an artist is a continual self-sacrifice, a continual extinction of personality."

Eliot's later development as poet had little impact on American poetry—although as editor of the influential journal *Criterion* and as the author of a number of essays in literary and cultural theory he increasingly became the literary 'Pope' of Anglo-American modernism. But his conversion to the Anglican Church in 1927 and his assumption of British citizenship (together with his professed Royalism) seemed to confirm Williams's judgment of him—even though the influence of his earlier poems and critical pronouncements remained undiminished.

### 3.4.4 | Home-Made Modernism

Only few poets before and after World War I had resisted the temptation to follow the example of Stein, Pound and Eliot. Hilda Doolittle (H.D.), in Pound's tracks, had gone to London in 1911 and never returned to the U.S. The English poet Mina Loy who, during her short literary career, was first associated with the Futurist Marinetti, then with the New York avant-garde, moved between two worlds, as did many American modernists. To be sure, during and after World War I, some European avant-garde artists also went to New York (Duchamp, Picabia, and Varèse, for instance), but the pull of Europe, especially of Paris, increased during the twenties, partly for economic reasons. The legendary 'expatriates' (Hemingway, Fitzgerald, Djuna Barnes, and others) formed an American avant-garde in voluntary exile with its own magazines and publishing outlets.

Those who stayed—like Moore, Stevens and Williams—did so on the basis of professional or personal commitments, so that finding their own poetic voice was unavoidably connected to their **rootedness** in local conditions. Especially for Williams, the project of developing a specifically American form of modernism could not be separated from a commitment to the local.

Marianne Moore. For a long time all three stood in Eliot's shadow; least, perhaps, Marianne Moore whose status as a 'major minor poet' was guaranteed by Eliot's preface to her *Selected Poems* (1935). As editor of the journal *The Dial*, she published the poems of both groups. Yet although she held contact with Pound and Eliot, she was closer to Williams. They shared a dedication to the precise image and to a democratic aesthetic of the common (which included common speech). Thus she begins her famous poem "Poetry" with a laconic: "I, too, dislike it" and then lists the hard facts and materials—from baseball to a market report—that can be of use to the imagination. Accordingly, she says, her poems are "imaginary gardens with real toads in them." This poetological tension between ordinary facts and the imagination's power to transform them is characteristic of modernist American poetry in general. But Moore's poetry is singular in its combination of dry wit with clear and yet highly dense images. She developed her own stern form of syllabic verse, a verse structure, modeled on the French classical tradition, consisting of lines that contain an equal amount of syllables. Animals of all sizes are the preferred objects of her poems. In precise contour and concrete detail, they appear as linguistically rendered facets of the imagination.

Wallace Stevens and William Carlos Williams—although never completely forgotten—were discovered as central figures of American modernism only in the 1950s and 1960s. When Stevens published his first volume of poetry, *Harmonium*, in 1923, he was already forty-four years old and had been employed in an insurance company for seven years. (He later became its vice-president.) *Harmonium,* already an accomplished work even as his first, proved Stevens to be a singular voice in American poetry: meditatively abstract, yet also sensuous and ironic, extravagant in its wordplay, virtuoso in its mastery of poetic conventions. Like Eliot, Stevens was influenced by the French Symbolists, like Eliot he loved the sound and flair of the exotic word and linked poetry to music more than to the clear outline of the image (in that respect, *Harmonium* is a programmatic title). But the religious nostalgia of Eliot's early poetry was foreign to him. Especially "Sunday Morning" rejects "the holy hush of ancient sacrifice" in favor of a life-affirming sensuousness based on the awareness of death's inevitability. Stevens, like Williams, places the imagination at the center of his poetological thought. Their theoretical positions touch indeed; their poetical practices, however, do not. While Williams, by empathetic perception, translates the materiality of the perceived into the imaged materiality of the linguistic object (e.g in "Young Sycamore"), for Stevens the "thing" (nature) is forever the ungraspable Other, the world becoming real only through the mind's creation, a *mundo* (as he called it) made by the poet's words. In "The Idea of Order at Key West" it is the creative power of the imagination which gives voice to an elusive world, creates and orders it in the process of reflective naming:

Cover of the first printing of Wallace Stevens's *Harmonium*

[...] Then we,
As we beheld her striding there alone,
Knew that there never was a world for her
Except the one she sang and, singing, made.

It is this self-reflexive action of shaping a world in the very process of thinking and writing it that made Stevens interesting for a later generation of postmodern poets (such as John Ashbery, cf. section I.3.5.4).

William Carlos Williams was the one who suffered most from Eliot's prominence, and felt almost personally slighted by it. When the hierarchy of modernism was challenged and overturned in the sixties, Williams became the father figure of a younger generation of poets (Allen Ginsberg, Frank O'Hara, Robert Creeley) who deeply questioned the concept of modernism that had become identified with Eliot's critical position as much as his poetic practice. Williams was a pediatrician and general practitioner for more than forty years. Like Stevens, he found his own style comparatively late. His breakthrough came with the publication of two experimental texts, *Kora in Hell* (1920) and *Spring and All* (1923). Their linguistic experiments served the purification of the senses (especially of the visual sense), blurred by conventional names and significations. The poem was to create things anew by turning them into sensuously and imaginatively perceived word objects. For Williams, "the work of the imagination" stands not in metaphorical but in metonymical relation to reality, as "co-extensive," "transfused with the same forces which transfuse the earth," and therefore as part of reality, not as its mirror image: "Reality is not opposed to art but apposed to it" (*Imaginations* 121). In his late long poem *Paterson*, published in five sections between 1946 and 1958, Williams tries to bring together the aesthetic and public aspirations of his work, both rooted in the local, in a last poetic counter-statement to Eliot's cosmopolitanism. It juxtaposes different kinds of texts, fragments of private and collective history, and aims at revealing buried continuities, forgotten origins, via a "descent" into the social and mythological past of the now industrial city of Paterson. This motif of "descent"—an opening "downward" toward regenerative origins—is enacted in his poetry time

Modernist 'primitive' painting: Pablo Picasso, *Bust of a Man* (1908)

and again for reasons that are surely a matter of personal vision but also part of a counter-cultural desire that had characterized modernism from early on.

## 3.4.5 | African American Modernism

Modernism's rebellion against the established cultural order and its literary conventions can be easily linked to what Freud diagnosed as Western civilization's inherent discontent. In a similar vein, the anthropologist Stanley Diamond argued that modernization and the **desire for the 'primitive'** were two sides of the same coin. Together with the social and cultural pressures of the modernizing process—which became increasingly identified with the idea of civilization itself—grew the desire for the repressed other of the civilized (white) soul. In Europe, this became apparent primarily as an aesthetic appropriation of 'primitive' art forms (or, on the level of popular culture, in the huge success of Josephine Baker). In the U.S., the real presence of African Americans and the virulent racism of the dominant culture (the twenties were also a good time for the Ku Klux Klan) made appropriation much more problematic. Harlem was a social reality, yet also a place where white fantasies of 'blackness' and the realities of black life intermingled and clashed. The border zones of interaction were therefore areas of intense stereotyping: of racist clichés on the one hand and of idealizing counter-images of the 'primitive' on the other.

The Harlem Renaissance. The (re)discovery of the 'primitive' is enacted in the (white) literature of the twenties in many different, often grotesque ways (e.g. in Vachel Lindsay's poem "The Congo"). Even Carl Van Vechten, a friend of Gertrude Stein and Langston Hughes (see below) and certainly one of the most important mediators between white and black avant-gardes during the twenties, demonstrated in his novel *Nigger Heaven* (1927) that any attempt, however well intended, at passing for black and entering "Ethiopean psychology" was at least structurally analogous to the blackening up of white actors in the minstrel show. For African Americans who were neither metaphors nor incarnations of white fantasies yet forced to live with them, the 'primitivism' of modernism was a trap as much as it opened possibilities. The writers of the Harlem Renaissance, the flowering of African American literature in the 1920s, saw themselves caught between the oppositional clichés of the 'old' and the 'new negro.' What for Van Vechten may have been empathetic (if condescending) mind-expansion, was for the poet Claude McKay painful stereotyping: the African American writer moved through a minefield of Janus-faced racism. McKay had grown up in Jamaica as the child of a black middle class proud of its ability to speak "pure" English. His white patron, however, loved the primitive speech of the lower classes and wanted McKay to write poems of dialect (thus making him indeed discover the richness of black Jamaican speech). When McKay went to the U.S., however, he was confronted with another poetry tradition of black dialect in which dialect confirmed black cultural inferiority. (Dialect and 'local color' were, for a long time, the only forms of publication open to black writers.) Therefore McKay's turning to the conventions of white poetry (to the sonnet, specifically) was surely a rejection of white stereotypes of "primitive blackness" but, at the same time, an acceptance of white poetic forms (which, as in his sonnet "If We Must Die," he made convey a "black" message of resistance; cf. North 100-23).

McKay's dilemma was symptomatic of the precarious cultural status of the Harlem Renaissance in general. Just as black Harlem was a product of modernization (of the 'great migration' of African Americans from the rural South to the industrial cities of the North), the Harlem Renaissance was a product of the modernist movement. It was created in a borderland of **overlapping white and black dreams**. The desire for revitalizing white culture by opening it "downward" toward the "primitive" met the hopes of a new black urban elite of artists and intellectuals to inscribe themselves into a shared American culture by developing a written culture of African American expression that would "beat barbaric beauty out of a white frame," as Claude McKay phrased it in *Home to Harlem* (1928).

In the introductory essay to his anthology *The New Negro* (1925), the writer and philosopher Alain Locke called Harlem "**a race capital**" (7), the capital and intellectual center of all those whose origin was Africa. It was thus a new fact also in the consciousness of black America and the basis for a distinctly new African American culture in the sign of the modern. The times were favorable since a white modernist movement in search of its national origins converged with the project of a new generation of African Americans to create a culture of their own. If white modernists looked to Africa for aesthetic inspiration, then, inversely, African American artists could—via the art of modernism—connect their own art to that of Africa.

Locke's '**new Negro**' and his vision of a new African American culture thus issued from a transgressive exchange between "white" and "black" on all levels—an exchange made possible by a modern experimental consciousness thriving especially in the metropolitan context of New York. Obviously, this exchange was socially lopsided and culturally precarious. White fantasies and black realities overlapped only marginally, and with the beginning of the Great Depression they fell apart. The Harlem race riots of 1934 made the "deferred" dreams of the Harlem Renaissance indeed "explode," as Langston Hughes wrote in his famous poem, "Harlem." Hughes—poet, dramatist, story writer and novelist—was the most visible and certainly the most prolific author of the Harlem Renaissance. Like Zora Neale Hurston, he played ironically with the white fantasies of black people—without being able to escape from them completely. He tried to combine the democratic gestures of Whitman's language with the themes and rhythms of the Blues. His poems deal, satirically and plaintively, with black experience. They were folksy and deceptively artless—and thus not what Alain Locke possibly envisioned as an African American contribution to the art of modernism.

Jean Toomer's *Cane* (see box on p. 138) is a key text of African American literature since it does not establish the ethnic voice as (subordinate) counterdiscourse, but attempts to anchor the transformation of orality into written text within the very center of American modernism. It is this literary consciousness in Toomer's treatment of the oral that may also have encouraged Zora Neale Hurston to discover and preserve the folk spirit of the South's black oral culture for an urban audience. But whereas Toomer translates the poetic power of the oral into the 'white frame' of the modernist text, Hurston tried to create a written oral text—a text that preserves its oral quality—through subtle innovations of narrative technique. Her novel *Their Eyes Were Watching God* (1937) is thus a written representation of black oral performance. From formal achievements such as these issued a tradition of black modernism that includes the work of Ralph Ellison and culminates in that of Toni Morrison (cf. section I.3.5.4).

Claude McKay and Langston Hughes expressed the conflicts of African American life in their poetry.

Interpretation

**Jean Toomer, *Cane***

The author who came perhaps closest to Locke's ideal (see above) was Jean Toomer. In *Cane* (1923)—a book that comprised poems, lyrical prose and dramatic text—he transformed the material of **black oral culture** (the "stuff" the blues was made of) into a highly stylized written text influenced by the linguistic experimentalism of the modernist avant-garde. *Cane* was the result of a trip into the American South where Toomer hoped to discover the roots of a genuine black cultural tradition as well as of his own identity. His seeming identification with black culture exposed him to massive stereotyping by his white avant-garde friends—which he rejected, just as he tried to escape the embrace of Alain Locke and other writers of the Harlem Renaissance: "there are seven race bloods within this body of mine. French, Dutch, Welsh, Negro, German, Jewish, and Indian. […] One half of my family is definitely colored. For my own part, I have lived equally among the two groups. And, I alone, as far as I know, have striven for spiritual fusion analogous to the fact of racial intermingling" (Hutchinson, "Jean Toomer" 231).

"**Fusion**" is indeed the thematic and symbolic center of the book. In its cryptic epigraph: "Oracular, redolent of fermenting syrup, purple of the dusk, deep-rooted cane," (sugar) cane is the emblem of African-American culture in the South, connected with it through the economy of slavery. This culture is oral ("oracular") and sensuous, part of the soil as much as of a history of victimization, but also a culture of the past, alive only in narration and in song. *Cane* is thus also a record of cultural memory: of sung and narrated stories of love and suffering transformed into the beauty of the written word and preserved for an urban and industrial present which has lost the vital cultural nurture of the 'folk spirit.'

For Toomer, oppositions between rural and urban, soil and city, rootedness and fragmentation, black oral tradition and urban non-communication are not primarily racial but cultural. They constitute an inner space of cultural consciousness divided and turned against itself, and they signal the absence of a life-giving tradition, a hunger for synthesis that could be stilled by the spiritual nourishment of 'cane' (the book as much as the culture it preserves)—if the reader, black or white, would only take it. Toomer's search for "a spiritual fusion analogous to the fact of racial intermingling" was directed toward a new American identity that would leave race consciousness behind and "differ as much from white and black as white and black differ from each other" (Hutchinson, "Jean Toomer" 228; 231).

## 3.4.6 | Modernism and the Urban Sphere

Modernism is an aesthetic movement created by the metropolis. It thrived on the city's energy and sensuous stimuli even where its imagery betrayed its unease with the city or even fed on (and into) anti-urban discourse (as is most obvious in Eliot's *The Waste Land*). The breathtaking expansion of the cities at the end of the nineteenth and the beginning of the twentieth century ran more or less parallel to early modernism's artistic revolt. The big cities were not only the sites of fundamental change (of new technologies, of new media), they also made these changes immediately and sensuously apparent: The famous skyline of Manhattan—that most impressive icon of New York's modernity—was constructed during the first three decades of the new century; and with it grew a new urban society of cultural, ethnic, even of racial mixing: 'mongrel Manhattan.'

Although not all modern authors felt themselves tied to the city, most of them, succumbing to its lure, had come from the Midwest, or the South—first to Chicago, then to New York and from there, in some cases, to London or Paris. These cities were **centers of literary and cultural innovation**: new forms of expression went hand in hand there with an experimental style of living that thrived on the freedom of the city's anonymity.

But from the very beginning, the experience as well as the representation of the metropolis was deeply ambivalent: its anonymity liberates and isolates; its energies, its stimulation of the senses exhilarate and distract, overwhelm and threaten. Just as ambivalent as the artistic treatment of the city was the perception of technology and **the machine**: They were central agents of the modernization process and therefore, like the city, metaphorically linked with it. In literature and art, the machine was treated in diverse ways: It was seen as instrument and symbol of an accelerating process of mechanization representing a new reality of technology and rationality that was marked by the loss of an original unity with nature. Accordingly, the function of a truly contemporary art was not to deny the machine (as some did) but to transform it into a fact of consciousness. By thus revealing the machine's inherent creative power, art might help restore a lost sense of "wholeness." (A vision Hart Crane saw realized in the beauty of that technological wonder: the Brooklyn Bridge.)

Others tried to escape the pull of this Romantic tradition by perceiving city and machine from a more matter-of-fact or constructivist position. The painter and photographer Charles Sheeler, for example, conceived of the new industrial and urban landscape quite literally as a second, a man-made, nature equivalent to that of art. Therefore the machine marked neither a fall from nature, nor a break with American values; rather it embodied continuity: of an ethics of workmanship, of a tradition of carefully crafted objects. From this perspective, the machine was like an aesthetic object and the artist brother to the craftsman or engineer.

**Hart Crane.** In 1923, at a point when American modernism was coming into its own, the poet Hart Crane began writing the first drafts of his cyclical poem *The Bridge*, which he finished seven years later at the beginning of the Great Depression. Like Williams, Crane saw Eliot's *The Waste Land* as betraying the project of creating a modern art expressive of America's material and spiritual resources. In contrast to Williams, however, he was deeply influenced by Eliot's metaphoric brilliance, which he turned into a densely and dynamically expressive medium of his own. Only if the poet would open himself to the sensuous stimulation of the city and translate the energies of its environment into a consciousness-assaulting dynamics of metaphor could his poetry fulfill its true "contemporary function," as he put it. Crane's poetic apotheosis of the Brooklyn Bridge tries to symbolically reconcile the contradictory experience of modernity by making the Bridge the very incarnation of a spiritual "wholeness" whose presence lies unbroken underneath the painful fragmentariness of urban life.

**John Dos Passos.** Crane's totalizing mystic vision of the city is completely alien to John Dos

*The Bridge*

A contemporary engraving of Brooklyn Bridge (1915)

Passos's comprehensive representation of metropolis in *Manhattan Transfer* (1925), where fragmentariness becomes a principle of composition. It is the very immensity of the object, New York City, that forces Dos Passos to break with realistic conventions of city representation and to emphasize compositional over mimetic principles. Not unlike Crane, Dos Passos seeks the analogy of music when he describes the structure of his work. He calls *Manhattan Transfer* "symphonic"—probably because it connects a great variety of themes, motifs and images into a polyphonic sequence. Another metaphor he takes from **film**: its cuts and montages, the techniques the Russian filmmaker Eisenstein used to create jarringly condensed sequences of images, or from **Cubist collage** that places materials of diverse provenance next to each other (cf. section III.5.2.2). Although Dos Passos maintains a basic linear structure in his narrative, he nevertheless breaks up its surface. The novel narrates thirty years of New York history (from about 1890 till 1920) as a **'simultaneous chronicle'** (Dos Passos's term) composed from the cut-up histories of a multiplicity of figures. Although their intersecting life stories form a loose network of coherence, the city is nevertheless a fragmented world that robs its creatures of reflection, depth, and distance: it functions as a system that deforms consciousness and individual character. All figures are constantly in hectic motion, all their senses continuously exposed to the onrush of sensuous impressions. With the exception of Jimmy Herf, who finally leaves the city to save himself, the protagonists are reduced to 'puppets' and 'mechanical toys'—mere caricatures of self.

Although the new city culture is dynamic, it is also spiritually and morally empty. Its loss of semantic depth becomes topical in Dos Passos's novel. It is, however, compensated for by a general increase in aesthetic value: the exhilarating yet devouring Moloch of the city is aesthetically transformed and controlled by formal innovation and artistic design.

**Definition**

The term → objective correlative was introduced by **T. S. Eliot** in his seminal essay "Hamlet and His Problems" (1919) and quickly became a central concept of modernist literary aesthetics. Eliot wrote: "The only way of expressing emotion in the form of art is by finding an 'objective correlative'; in other words, a set of objects, a situation, a chain of events which shall be the formula of that *particular* emotion; such that when the external facts, which must terminate in sensory experience, are given, the emotion is immediately evoked."

### 3.4.7 | Modernist Fiction

Especially in its early phase, the medium of modernist expression was poetry more than fiction. In comparison to the novel, poetry was a private medium addressing a small audience (an audience more or less confined to the readers of the small and short-lived journals that also published Stein's and Joyce's prose). In contrast, the novel—mediated through the literary market—depended on a larger reading public. It was usually the result of a negotiation between the author's aesthetic commitment to his medium and his (and his publisher's) desire to be commercially successful. Thus Ernest Hemingway tried to convince his publisher Horace Liveright that *In Our Time* would be a book "that will be praised by highbrows and can be read by lowbrows. There is no writing in it that anybody with a high-school education cannot read" (31 March 1925). Yet Hemingway as much as Scott Fitzgerald was plagued by the fear that the very success he so ardently desired might eventually ruin his creative talent.

**Fitzgerald and Hemingway.** In 1924, their paths crossed for the first time. Hemingway was busy with his first book, *In Our Time*; Fitzgerald with writing *The Great Gatsby*, the novel he hoped would guarantee him a place in American literary history. Both books appeared in 1925. Fitzgerald was already famous then—although not as a representative of the literary avant-garde. At least in his early phase, he had taken writing to be an easy way to fame and fortune. Hemingway, on the other hand, was still at the beginning of his career. Like Fitzgerald, he came from the Midwest, but left for the East coast and went directly to Europe as a journalist. His stylistic effort at laconic precision can be partially explained by the journalist's need to express himself concisely via transatlantic cable but even more by his aversion against all idealizing rhetoric. The experience of war (he took part in World War I as the driver of an ambulance) made the words and values of a patriarchal 'genteel culture' seem absurd to a new generation. Therefore, what was needed most of all was a **purification of language**. In this, Hemingway's aesthetic interests coincided with those of Pound, Stein, and Williams. For the early Hemingway, the duty to be linguistically precise was an aspect of an ethics of craftsmanship and authenticity—which gave special pathos to *his* version of Pound's concept of the clear-cut image and of Eliot's 'objective correlative.' Subjective emotion was to be mediated authentically through the precise linguistic enactment of the "real event, the sequence of motion and fact" that evoked it; so that years later the reality of the emotion could still be felt by the reader (qtd. in Levin 94). In a famous analogy, he compared his linguistic strategy with the movement of an iceberg that revealed only a tenth of its real size (*Death in the Afternoon*, ch. 16). Hemingway's simplicity of language is thus a deceptive surface. Through its gaps and condensations, the reader has to discover the text hidden underneath its surface. While Hemingway seems to be indebted to Pound and to the visual precision Pound demanded of the image, Fitzgerald appears closer to Eliot's fascination with symbolic cipher and metaphor.

**William Faulkner** neither belonged to these cosmopolitan 'expatriates,' nor could he compete with the literary reputation they gained during the twenties and thirties, even though, after the moderate success of his first novels, he was not entirely unknown. Yet with his fourth book, *The Sound and the Fury* (1929), the cornerstone for his later fame as 'master' of the modern novel, he seemed to take himself out of the literary business altogether, forgetting about publishers, writing only

### F. Scott Fitzgerald, *The Great Gatsby*

In *The Great Gatsby*, Scott Fitzgerald combined the strategies of the romance with those of the realist novel of manners: he projected a social and geographical space peopled with types more than characters, filled with excessively symbolic landscapes, with glossy surface images of magazines, posters, advertisements (the city seen from Queensboro Bridge "as if for the first time," the valley of ashes, the empty eyes of Dr. Eckleburg, the green light marking the object of Gatsby's desire, etc.). Filmic gestures, richly textured clothes, expensive things as means of self-expression—these are parts of a coded language of allusion and suggestion.

**Social ambition** takes the form of a quasi-religious yearning for a beauty that, when grasped, reveals its meretriciousness. Consequently, the romance of money, beauty and desire barely hides a submerged reality of fact and corruption; as becomes evident in a series of contrapuntal images and figurations: the beautiful Daisy, "gleaming like silver, safe and proud above the hot struggle of the poor" (ch. 8), willingly relies on the brute strength of her husband to defend the interest and privilege of class. Gatsby's "extraordinary gift for hope" is financed and supported by the New York underworld. The dynamic beauty of the city, seen and remembered in its first wild promise of all the "mystery and beauty of the world" (ch. 6), creates literally (out of its wastes and ashes) and metaphorically (out of the emotional waste of its original promise) the shadow image of the lost pastoral life, the "valley of ashes."

Very early in the novel, the familiar conviction "that life was beginning over and again within the summer" (ch. 1) is connected with the **movies**, where time can be reversed and each moment endlessly repeated. The strength of Gatsby's hope is based on the belief that the past can indeed be repeated—whereas really each moment is lost in the current of time. In Fitzgerald's entropic world, dream-wastage increases constantly. Since Gatsby's dream is real only at the very moment of its inception, myths accumulate at both ends of time: in Gatsby's projection of his hopes into an "orgiastic future" as well as in Nick's nostalgic transfiguration of the past when man, discovering the virgin continent, was "face to face for the last time in history with something commensurate to his capacity for wonder" (ch. 9).

On one hand, the novel aims—in the manner of the realistic novel—at **unmasking illusions** and at re-anchoring a chimeric world of lies, legends and mere surface in the firm ground of the real; on the other, it elevates the fate of the fallen Gatsby into an **idealizing countermovement**. It is the creative power of his hope that makes him, the up-start figure on the social margins, admirable even in Nick's class-restricted eyes. If all material fulfillments are indeed inauthentic, the only authenticity remaining is the pure and passionate intensity of Gatsby's "I want." The spiritual emptiness of the period is mercilessly revealed in this novel, but at the same time transcended in its conflation of excessive desire with creative energy. The novel unmasks the "meretricious" culture of the city at the same times that it absorbs it in its language and aesthetic design. Like Dos Passos's *Manhattan Transfer*, it thrives aesthetically on what it ethically condemns.

Interpretation

for himself. Like many of his later works, *The Sound and the Fury* is situated in an imaginary South, the Yoknapatawpha County of his own invention whose capital is Jefferson. It tells a story of decay—the decay of a family, the Compsons, as well as of the South. (He deals with the history of both again in his great historical novel of 1936, *Absalom, Absalom!*) In a later interview, Faulkner remembered how the novel grew out of two scenes he vividly saw in his mind's eye: of children playing by a brook and dirtying themselves; and of children watching their grandmother dying through a window. Out of these, the constellation of the figures and their complex interrelation unfolded. There is Caddy, courageous and loving, who loses her innocence early, falls out of the order of bourgeois life (but is still actively present in her siblings' consciousness); there is her mentally disabled brother Benjy, who constantly mourns Caddy's absence; there is Quentin, the older brother, who is haunted with incestuous desire for his sister Caddy and commits suicide while at Harvard; there is Jason, his calculating younger brother; then a father who slowly drinks himself to death; an egocentric mother for whom sickness is escape; and Dilsey, the black housekeeper and real mother to the children who stands, as Faulkner says in the second version of his introduction to the novel, "above the fallen ruins of the family."

Faulkner tells this story in four episodes, on four days, and by four different narrative voices. The first, Benjy's story, occurs on April 7, 1928 (his thirty-third birthday); the second, Quentin's, eighteen years earlier, on June 2, 1910 (the day he commits suicide); the third, Jason's, a day earlier than Benjy's, on April 6, 1928 (when Caddy's daughter, also called Quentin, steals money from him); the fourth, Dilsey's (the chronologically last and the only one told by an omniscient narrator) on April 8, 1928, Easter Sunday. The first two parts in particular challenge the reader to an extraordinary degree. Benjy's episode is told in the voice of a mentally disabled narrator who can neither speak nor think coherently. Accordingly, Benjy's associations are not ordered in any logical, causal or chronological sequence: he associates simultaneously (and via all his senses) events, memories, sensations of his past quasi-conscious life. The second part (the fictive narrative of a person already dead) is Quentin's highly conscious, yet unstructured stream of reflections, associations, memories culminating in his suicide. With the last two episodes—the narrative of the rational, prag-

matic Jason and the authorial narrator of Dilsey's part—Faulkner apparently returns to a conventional order of narration. Except that, by now, *that* order (as much as the concept of order itself) has been fundamentally undermined. When at the end, Luster—Dilsey's son and Benjy's nurse—drives the coach left instead of right around the square, as is his wont, Benjy howls until habitual order has been restored: "The broken flower drooped over Benjy's fist and his eyes were empty and blue and serene again as cornice and facade flowed smoothly once more from left to right; post and tree, window and doorway, and signboard, each in its ordered place" (ch. 4).

The **fragility** of this reality, ordered by habit and everyday ritual, is enacted by Faulkner on the thematic as well as on the formal level. Thematically, the decay of order is dramatized in the social and biological decline of the Compsons. Against their sense of pain and mourning (most evident in Benjy's howling), Faulkner, however tentatively, places an image of surviving order at the novel's end: the communication still possible "there" in the Easter service of the black community. This has its echo on the formal level in the seeming return to realist narrative in the final section, where it nevertheless marks not a recovery but a weakened sense of the Real, a loss of ontological faith that can only be found elsewhere, if at all.

**Djuna Barnes.** Among the authors of American modernist fiction, Djuna Barnes holds a special place. She was unknown to a larger audience, but a legendary and elegantly eccentric marginal figure, first in New York's Bohème, later among the Paris expatriates. In 1931, she began work on a novel that was published five years later, after several rejections by American publishers, by Faber & Faber as *Nightwood*. It is an image-intense and atmospherically dense book dealing with the "nightwood" of the corrupt or decadent societies of Old Europe. Vienna, Berlin, Paris are fused in one symbolic space: the night side of social life as well as of the human psyche, peopled by the lost, the losers and the desperate—figures on the margins who suffer from themselves or from love to others, clutching them in self-destructive passion. In the changing constellation of protagonists, emphasis shifts from Felix Volkbein, the Viennese Jew, to Robin Vote, a young French woman he meets and marries in Paris; and from her to the American Nora Flood, who falls in love with Robin. Their short harmonious relation is broken up by Jenny Petherbridge, who abducts Robin—always pas-

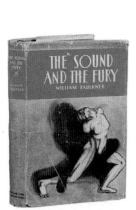

Cover of the first printing of Faulkner's novel (1929)

sionately in search of something—to America. Nora remains, inconsolable ("bloodthirsty with love") together with the drinker, fake physician, and verbose provider of consolation, Matthew O'Connor. He is the connecting link between the novel's chapters as well as its characters, the powerful/powerless "watchman" whom Nora asks to tell her "everything about the night" (ch. 5). But the only truth he knows is that of suffering, and the only consolation he is able to provide is the consolatory gesture of language itself, its meaning hidden underneath a protective cloak of rhetoric: the consoler as charlatan.

British critics praised *Nightwood* euphorically, perhaps on the basis of the preface Eliot had written for it. The reaction to the American publication a year later was more reserved. Indeed, Barnes's novel evoked the symbolic landscape of Eliot's *Waste Land* more than it referred to any relevant context of the thirties, when Americans, confronted with economic depression, turned to fundamental beliefs and social commitments.

## 3.4.8 | Late Modernism

"In 1930," Malcolm Bradbury wrote, "all book titles changed, and it was clear that a great literary corner had [been] turned" ("American Literature" 9). This cultural turn of the thirties was not an American phenomenon alone. It also marked European developments in art and culture during the late twenties and early thirties: a general "return to order," be it social or narrative, in music or in visual representation (cf. Nochlin). In the U.S., it was characterized by a return to agrarian values, to the experience of "common people," to the shared values of democracy and "honest work"—in short, by a rejection of everything the previous decade had embraced. In literature, it was also marked by a return to realist or naturalist forms of representation. Implied in Bradbury's phrase is the **politicization** of intellectuals, artists, writers and critics—their shift to the Left. It coincided with a widening of the institutional basis of literature: a new generation of intellectuals of ethnic and "proletarian" descent (during the thirties these were largely synonyms) began to participate in the process of literary production and its critical reception. For many of these new critics (mostly from the Left), this meant a fundamental rejection of modernist aesthetics and its elitist appeal.

Perhaps this was more a matter of ideological controversy among critics than a matter of artistic practice. The artistic production of the period was neither marked by a radical rejection of modernism nor by a whole-hearted return to the realist mode. Rather, it signaled another turn in the ongoing mediation between the two discourses of modernity mentioned in the first part of this chapter: the one emphasizing contemporary content and experience, the other, modern forms of representation. Underneath a dominant rhetoric of anti-modernism, modernism continued and changed in the dialogue between positions that mutually reflect and question each other—modernism becoming more "realistic" (as visible in the development of Hemingway or Dos Passos), and "realism" absorbing modernist probings into the status of the real. This is true of Henry Roth's *Call It Sleep* (1934), which begins as an ethnic/working-class novel and ends in a Joycean stream-of consciousness; and even of James T. Farrell's trilogy *Studs Lonigan*, which tries to control its mass of factual material via modernist techniques.

*The two discourses of modernity*

**James Agee and Walker Evans.** However, I conclude this chapter with the discussion of a text that embodies and thematizes the inner tensions of the period with agonizing self-awareness. By radically renouncing the fictional and the aesthetic, James Agee and Walker Evans attempted in *Let Us Now Praise Famous Men* (1941) to grasp the essence of the real, but were forced, by this very renunciation, to reflectively explore the limits of the real *and* the aesthetic, of the imaged, the imagined, and the unimaginable.

The book owes its existence to the documentary impulse of the period. *Fortune Magazine* had asked Agee and Evans to document in writing and photography the living and working conditions of tenant farmers in the South. What it expected was a reportage, illustrated with images of a famous American photographer. What it got was something else entirely—so different indeed that *Fortune* refused to publish it. The book (published several years afterwards) cannot be defined in terms of genre. It is an uninterrupted reflection on the status of the perceived object, on the unavoidable subjectivity of all perception as well as on problems of representation and the representational.

While he and Evans lived with three tenant families in Alabama as intense observers of the everyday life they shared with them, Agee was always conscious that the act of observation, inevitably, also was an act of manipulation. To write on

*Portrait of a Southern woman in Let Us Now Praise Famous Men (1935/36)*

and to document the life of the poor meant interfering with their lives. To that extent, the act of writing only duplicated their social and economic exploitation. Writing about them could never simply be reportage. It had to counter the element of dominance in their skewed relationship by intense self-awareness of the perceiving consciousness. But doing so meant to question documentary realism's trust in fact and evidence. Agee was so impressed by the "dignity" and "beauty" inherent in the lives of these families that he doubly distrusted his representation: first, because he was afraid he would betray their lives by aestheticizing them, and, second, because he feared their existence might elude the grasp of linguistic representation altogether.

Agee was so fully convinced of the **"sacredness" of the Real** (the democratic dignity of the common and everyday) that he carefully and painstakingly described the material culture of these families: the materiality of their houses, their objects of daily use, the texture of their clothes, the simple things they used to enhance their living space, etc. And so conscious was he of the inability of "mere words" to represent these lives and objects, to grasp their innate value, that his vain yet stubborn attempt to do justice to what lay in front of his eyes became the very topic of his representation. It was, paradoxically, his faith in "pure existence" (i.e. in a reality anteceding consciousness) that threw the possibility of realism into doubt; as much as it made him doubt (and despise) any effort of transforming it into "Art." It is this almost desperate attempt to not betray the Real by making it aesthetic ("Above all else: in God's name, don't think of it as Art"; ch. 1) that makes Agee's book a central aesthetic document not only of the period but also of the tensions and contradictions of American modernism.

## Select Bibliography

Baker, Houston. *Modernism and the Harlem Renaissance*. Chicago: University of Chicago Press, 1987.

Berman, Marshall. *All That is Solid Melts Into Air: The Experience of Modernity*. New York: Simon and Schuster, 1982.

Bradbury, Malcolm. "American Literature and the Coming of World War II." *Looking Inward – Looking Outward*. Ed. Steve Ickringill. Amsterdam: VU University Press, 1990. 8–21.

Bradbury, Malcolm. *The Modern American Novel*. New York: Oxford University Press, 1986.

Bradbury, Malcolm, and James McFarlane, eds. *Modernism*. Hardmondsworth: Penguin Books, 1976.

Capetti, Carla. *Writing Chicago: Modernism, Ethnography, and the Novel*. New York: Columbia University Press, 1993.

DeKoven, Marianne. *A Different Language: Gertrude Stein's Experiental Writing*. Madison: University of Wisconsin Press, 1893.

DeKoven, Marianne. *Rich and Strange: Gender, History, Modernism*. Princeton: Princeton University Press, 1991.

Diamond, Stanley. *In Search of the Primitive: A Critique of Civilization*. New Brunswick: Dutton, 1974.

Dijkstra, Bram. *The Hieroglyphics of a New Speech*. Princeton: Princeton University Press, 1969.

Douglas, Anne. *Terrible Honesty: Mongrel Manhattan in the 1920s*. New York: Farrar, Strauss & Giroux, 1995.

Eysteinsson, Astradur. *The Concept of Modernism*. Ithaca: Cornell University Press, 1990.

Gelpi, Albert. *A Coherent Splendor: The American Poetic Renaissance: 1910–1950*. Cambridge: Cambridge University Press, 1987.

Gubar, Susan. *Racechanges: White Skin, Black Face in American Culture*. New York: Oxford University Press, 1997.

Hemingway, Ernest. *Selected Letters: 1917–1961*. London: Granada, 1981.

Hutchinson, Charles. *The Harlem Renaissance in Black and White*. Cambridge: Harvard University Press, 1995.

Hutchinson, George. "Jean Toomer and American Racial Discourse." *Texas Studies in Literature and Language* 35.2 (1993): 226–50.

Jameson, Fredric. *The Modernist Papers*. London: Verso, 2007.

Kenner, Hugh. *A Homemade World*. New York: William Morrow, 1975.

Kenner, Hugh. *The Pound Era*. Berkeley: University of California Press, 1971.

Klein, Marcus. *Foreigners: The Making of American Literature: 1900–1940*. Chicago: University of Chicago Press, 1981.

Klepper, Martin, and Joseph Schöpp, eds. *Transatlantic Modernism*. Heidelberg: Winter, 2001.

Lemke, Sieglinde. *Primitivist Modernism: Black Culture and the Origins of Transatlantic Modernism*. Oxford: Oxford University Press, 1998.

Lentricchia, Frank. *Modernist Quartet*. Cambridge: Cambridge University Press, 1994.

Levin, Harry. *Memories of the Moderns*. London: Faber & Faber, 1980.

Locke, Alain, ed. *The New Negro: Voices of the Harlem Renaissance*. 1925. New York: Atheneum, 1975.

McAlmon, Robert, and Kay Boyle. *Being Geniuses Together: 1920–1930*. San Francisco: North Point Press, 1984.

Miller, J. Hillis. *The Linguistic Moment*. Princeton: Princeton University Press, 1985.

Nicholls, Peter. *Modernisms: A Literary Guide*. London: Macmillan, 1995.

Nochlin, Linda. "Return to Order." *Art in America* (1981): 74–83.

North, Michael. *The Dialect of Modernism*. New York: Oxford University Press, 1994.

Perloff, Marjorie. *The Dance of the Intellect*. Cambridge: Cambridge University Press, 1985.

Perloff, Marjorie. *The Futurist Moment*. Chicago: University of Chicago Press, 1986.

Perloff, Marjorie. *The Poetics of Indeterminacy*. Evanston: Northwestern University Press, 1999.

Pound, Ezra. *How to Read*. London: Faber & Faber, 1954.

Pound, Ezra. *Selected Letters*. New York: New Directions, 1971.

Riddel, Joseph. *The Turning Word: American Literary Modernism and Continental Thought*. Philadelphia: University of Pennsylvania Press, 1996.

Santayana, George. *The Genteel Tradition*. Cambridge: Harvard University Press, 1967.

Scott, Bonnie Kime, ed. *The Gender of Modernism*. Bloomington: Indiana University Press, 1990.

Singal, Daniel Joseph, ed. *Modernist Culture in America*. Spec. issue of *American Quarterly* 39.1 (1987): 5–174.

Stein, Gertrude. *Lectures in America*. 1935. Boston: Beacon Press, 1957.

Tashjian, Dickran. *Skyscraper Primitives: Dada and the American Avantgarde: 1910–1925*. Middleton: Wesleyan University Press, 1975.

Tichi, Cecelia. *Shifting Gears: Technology, Literature, Culture in Modernist America*. Chapel Hill: University of North Carolina Press, 1987.

Torgovnick, Marianne. *Gone Primitive: Savage Intellects, Modern Lives*. Chicago: University of Chicago Press, 1990.

Trask, Michael. *Cruising Modernism: Class and Sexuality in American Literature and Social Thought*. Ithaca: Cornell University Press, 2003.

Williams, William Carlos. *Imaginations*. New York: New Directions, 1970.

Williams, William Carlos. "Excerpts from a Critical Sketch: A Draft of XXX Cantos by Ezra Pound." *Selected Essays*. New York: New Directions, 1969. 105–12.

*Heinz Ickstadt*

# 3.5 | Postmodern and Contemporary Literature

## 3.5.1 | Overview

The discontinuous developments

As the preceding entry on modernism has demonstrated, American literature of the twentieth century defies any easy categorization or linear-teleological narrative. Instead, it is characterized by various national and transnational currents and countercurrents, by heterogeneous developments, and by constant discontinuous revisions and transformations of the themes, styles and aesthetic conceptions through which writers shaped what emerged as modern American literature. Like other historical periods, American literary modernism is not a monolithic phenomenon but is made up of various tendencies and continuities. Avantgarde poetry, for instance, refers back to previous poetic models like Whitman (cf. entry I.3.2) and at the same time points forward to postmodern models like the Beat poets; the Harlem Renaissance rediscovers creative potentials of African American culture while preparing the way for the rich production of African American literature in the later twentieth century. Generalizing labels like 'modernism' and 'postmodernism' are therefore to be treated with caution. Accordingly, the subsequent chapter is not organized on the basis of a schematic opposition between these and other styles of writing but in the sense of continuous interactions, tensions, conflicts, overlappings, and mutual transformations between them.

## 3.5.2 | American Drama From Modernism to the Present

Drama as a genre has had a much more difficult and culturally contested fate in American than in other national literatures. Between the deep-rooted suspicion towards drama and theater in colonial Puritanism and the commercialization of the theater in the nineteenth century, not much creative space, cultural prestige, and practical stage opportunities were available to potential playwrights. In the early twentieth century, however, in a climate shaped by the experimental styles of the international avant-garde, American drama finally came into its own through the efforts of individual artists, university circles, and "**little theaters**," which saw themselves as a noncommercial, artistic alternative to the star system of Broadway. Apart from the Washington Square Players, the most famous of these alternative theater groups were the **Provincetown Players**. Their director, George Cram Cook, was influenced by modern European playwrights such as August Strindberg and Henrik Ibsen and above all by Friedrich Nietzsche, whose Dionysian concept of drama and art provided both a critical and revitalizing energy for the new American plays that the group produced, mostly as one-act plays, since the year 1915. Their success was mainly due to two of their members, who would become leading figures in the emergence of an artistically significant drama and theater in the U.S.: Susan Glaspell and Eugene O'Neill.

### The Experimental Phase of Modernist Drama

Susan Glaspell, like Cook and O'Neill, was strongly influenced by Nietzsche's radical cultural critique, which she specifically related to the question of female self-empowering in a highly conventionalized and gender-determined society. Her well-known early play, *Trifles* (1916), is the parodistic inversion of a conventional detective play, tracing in small, apparently insignificant details the story of the murder of a New England farmer. After *The Verge* (1921) about a female Frankenstein and mad scientist ruthlessly trying to create new life, and *Alison's House* (1930), about a passionate, unconventional poet modeled on Emily Dickinson, Glaspell stopped writing plays in the 1930s, when she supported the Federal Theater Project, which was launched in the FDR Roosevelt era during the Great Depression to enable the impoverished working classes to stage, perform and experience drama and theater.

Eugene O'Neill. The main impetus for the success of this first wave of experimental drama in the U.S., however, came from an author who dominated the development of American drama until the mid-twentieth century: Eugene O'Neill. O'Neill, who went through a deep personal crisis before he turned to playwriting, used the therapeutic potential of drama not only as a strategy of personal survival but for a psycho-cultural analysis of the desires, anxieties and pathologies of life in American society. With his experimental dramatic style influenced by European Naturalism and Expressionism, he challenged conventional American theater, of which his father, the famous actor James O'Neill, was a major protagonist.

*Eugene O'Neill, The Emperor Jones*

Brutus Jones, whose vernacular version of Black English dominates the stage language, has escaped from an American prison after killing a brutal overseer, and after his flight to an island in the West Indies, he has made himself "emperor" of the natives there. When the natives start a rebellion against his autocratic rule, Jones has prepared everything for his escape, but gets lost in the nightly forest. There, he is confronted with hallucinations from scenes of his personal memory, but also of the collective memory of African Americans from slavery, on the Middle Passage, and from African mythology. As Jones' encounter with his repressed deeper self intensifies, the dominance of words gives way to **expressionis-** tic nonverbal effects as highlighted in the constantly intensifying rhythm of the rebels' drums, which simultaneously expresses the accelerating heartbeat of the hunted emperor.

Interpretation

The famous African American actor Paul Robeson as Emperor Jones in a contemporary production

One of his early experiments is ***The Emperor Jones*** (1920), in which an African American for the first time becomes the protagonist of a tragic drama (see box). The mixing of mask and face, role and person in modern society is of special interest to O'Neill, as in the surrealist play ***The Great God Brown*** (1926), where he explicitly uses masks to illuminate the paralysis of personal relations within the modern success myth, but also to revitalize theater with the help of pre-modern forms of mythological drama.

**Other attempts** at renewing American drama followed, using different modes and styles of drama: satirical expressionism in Elmer Rice's *The Adding Machine* (1923); folk drama such as *Porgy*, produced by the Theater Guild in 1927 and turned into an opera, *Porgy and Bess* (1935), by George Gershwin; or the drama of the Harlem Renaissance (cf. section I.3.4.5), which combined elements of minstrel show, dance, song, and the experience of African Americans. Apart from such innovations on the margins of American drama and theater, realist and well-made plays continued to dominate the cultural mainstream in the 1920s with playwrights such as Maxwell Anderson, Sidney Howard, or Philip Barry. Meanwhile, the musical emerged as a significant new form combining drama, show, dance, and popular music. At the same time, film theaters began to replace traditional theater as the site of modern mass entertainment. The new film industry incorporated the popular preference for melodrama and the star system of conventional theater in its commercial success strategy.

### Drama in the 1930s between Politics and Anthropological Universalism

As in other genres, the '**Red Decade**' of the 1930s saw a politicization of drama and theater as well. Especially the Group Theater, with its collective style of production inspired by East European figures such as Stanislavski, was an influential proponent of political drama. Their most important author was **Clifford Odets**, whose play *Waiting for Lefty* (1935) was probably the best-known production of a leftist proletarian theater that was performed across the country in the newly established worker's theaters. The play shows the characteristic structure of the agitprop play in its stereotyping of characters, its melodramatic confrontation between workers and capitalists in an historical struggle between good and evil (in which the union representative has been corrupted by capitalism as well), and in the transgression of the boundary between stage and audience in the final collective call to strike. Another, less explicitly political playwright of this decade is **Lillian Hellman**, whose *The Children's Hour* (1934) deals with rumors of lesbianism between teachers as a challenge to the social system. With her husband Dashiell Hammett, Hellman also wrote screenplays for Hollywood, but was more or less forgotten in her later life after she became one of the victims of McCarthyism in the post-war years.

A central role in this politicization of theater in the 1930s was played by the state-supported **Federal Theater Project**, which helped to produce more than 300 new plays from 1935 to 1939. Some of the productions followed the model of the Living Newspaper, presenting current news in the form of montage-like episodic scenes with the help of loudspeakers, posters, and screen projections such as in Arthur Arent's *Ethiopia* (1936), about Mussolini's invasion of Ethiopia, or his famous *One Third of a Nation* (1938), about slum life in American cities.

Leftist political theater
in the 1930s

In other developments of drama and theater at the time, politics retreated into the background in favor of tragedy, poetic drama, and formal experiments. While Maxwell Anderson's verse drama *Winterset* (1935) about the Sacco and Vanzetti case was still overtly political, William Saroyan's successful verse plays were affirmative versions of the American Dream. Still less political, and instead focused on universal human topics, are the plays of **Thornton Wilder**. Wilder was the first American playwright who systematically used the techniques of 'epic theater' as Bertolt Brecht had developed it. Unlike Brecht, who wanted to achieve a change of social awareness in his audience with his alienation-effect (*V-Effekt*), Wilder's answer to the turbulences of the Great Depression was his retreat to the ever-returning archetypal conditions of human existence. His plays employ epic effects such as stage managers, meta-dramatic comments and direct audience involvement, but also make use of Chinese, Japanese, classical and medieval models, as well as of marionette and popular revue theater, thus gaining a cosmopolitan dimension. This way, the dramatic form of his plays is universalized as well as their content—such as in *Our Town* (1938), in which the three acts are organized around the birth, marriage, and death of a young woman in the context of everyday life in small-town America, or in his synopsis of human evolution in *The Skin of Our Teeth* (1942), in which the three catastrophic scenarios of the Ice Age, the Great Flood and a World War form the background for the ever-recurring human struggle for survival.

## American Tragedy as a Cultural-Critical Project

O'Neill represented a continuing presence in American drama from the 1920s to the mid-twentieth century, earning him the Nobel Prize in 1936. In *Mourning Becomes Electra* (1931), O'Neill attempted to transfer the spirit of Greek tragedy into America within the historical context of the Civil War, basing character relations on the oedipal model of Freudian psychoanalysis. In the battle between *eros* and *thanatos*, which constitutes the play's conflict, the char-

acters are victimized by a fate that is both within them and beyond their control, and the play ends in a gesture of defiant negation of the world by the single surviving protagonist, Lavinia (Electra). Even more disillusioned, and yet of a feverishly intense dream quality, are O'Neill's late plays, in which he returns from mythical models to autobiographical experiences. In **Long Day's Journey into Night** (1956), which is still probably the most frequently performed play by O'Neill, he deals with the story of his own family in the exemplary situation of a crisis on one day in 1912, bringing together the drug addiction of his mother, the alcoholism of the male family members, and the diagnosis of his own tuberculosis. In this metaphorical journey from day to night, from light into darkness, which is symbolically underlined by the increasing fog, the mutual world of lies and illusions between the characters is destroyed, while glimpses of truth and momentary communication form a dramaturgical counterpoint to the overall sense of isolation and melancholia that pervades the play. With O'Neill, American drama for the first time became a force in world theater which gained influence on European theater programs as well.

Tennessee Williams. In post-war American drama, Tennessee Williams was the first important Southern playwright. Indeed, the crisis of the South between a declining tradition and an aggressive-materialist culture of modernity very much defines the background and thematic focus of his plays. In his intimate psycho-dramas, roles and masks are shattered in radical acts of disillusionment, and the forces of sexual desire and of repressed vitality play themselves out in both destructive and liberating ways. *The Glass Menagerie* (1944), which brought his breakthrough, fictionalizes the problematic relationship to his fragile sister in the form of a lyrical memory play, in which a collection of glass animals becomes the symbolic center of a personal dream world that is shattered in its collision with the real world. The conflict between poetic imagination and naturalistic disillusionment is staged much more brutally in *A Streetcar Named Desire* (1947), where the decadent hypersensitive Southern aristocrat Blanche DuBois is contrasted with the physically powerful immigrant worker Stanley Kowalski, who in the end destroys her personality by raping her and having her sent into a mental institution. In eleven scenes, different aspects of the relation between imagination and reality are played out in a multifaceted theatrical performance accompanied by music and light effects, underlining Williams's conception of what he calls "plastic theater," a kind of *Gesamtkunstwerk* idea.

Arthur Miller was the other dominant figure in mid-twentieth-century drama. Different than Williams's symbolist-psychological drama, Miller specialized in what has been called **social domestic drama**, in which the interdependence between psychology and society, private and public sphere, domestic and economic-political domains becomes the focus of an intensely ethical form of playwriting. The American Dream as the dream of personal happiness through material success forms the context of his modern tragedies, as above all in ***Death of a Salesman*** (1949), which has become a classic on the stage and in the classroom. Willy Loman (the modern *low man* as tragic hero) is an aging and unsuccessful salesman who, however, tries to maintain the charisma of his profession and the dignity of his person at all costs. When he sees no other way out, he commits suicide to provide his family, especially his beloved son Biff, with his life insurance money. In a combination of realism and stream-of-consciousness technique, interior and exterior world are contrasted with and blended into each other. The leitmotiv of the flute, "telling of grass and trees and the horizon" (Act One), indicates the absence of nature in the walled-in space of urban capitalism in which the characters live. ***The Crucible*** (1953) deals with the paranoia of witch-hunting in America, explicitly in the historical case of the witchcraft trials in Salem in 1692, implicitly in the contemporary climate of the anti-communist witch-hunt of the **McCarthy era**, during which Miller himself was cited before the House Un-American Activities Committee.

I never thought of making a play out of it. It just was a fascinating thing to me that a town of this kind could suddenly erupt in explosive hysteria. I just couldn't understand how it could happen.[...] Well, the whole attitude of the fifties started to develop. People were persecuted, and they were jumping out of the windows. Friendships were being destroyed. There were disasters all around. The repetitiousness of it brought up the idea of the Salem witchcraft trials, where on a different level with different folkways essentially the same phenomenon was occurring. [...] I wanted to tell people what had happened before and where to find the early underlying forces of such a phenomenon. (Evans 71 f.)

Miller continued to write plays until the late twentieth century, among them the screenplay for a film with his wife Marilyn Monroe, *The Misfits* (1961), and two full-length plays *The Price* (1968) and *Broken Glass* (1994).

## Postmodern Drama

While the modernist aesthetic of Williams and Miller still assumed the possibility of mimetically representing world and self on the stage, postmodern drama was characterized by a more skeptical and self-reflexive attitude. The boundary between fact and fiction became radically blurred, coherent forms of identity were dissolved, and theatrical signifiers lost their referential certainties (see below for an explanation of 'postmodernism').

Edward Albee was influenced both by the theater of the absurd and by Artaud's theater of cruelty, but adjusted both to American themes and to his own idiosyncratic dramatic style. His first play, ***The Zoo Story*** (1959), deals with the encounter between two strangers, Peter and Jerry, at a park bench in New York, in which the failing attempt at a mutual understanding escalates into the climax of an assisted suicide. After a gradual transition from verbal to nonverbal communication, the piece develops as a narrative performance in which a bizarre "dog story" becomes the nuclear fantasy of the multilayered "zoo story" that unfolds as an allegory of the imprisonment of humans in anonymous urban environments. Albee wrote a companion piece in 2001, *Homelife*, which portrays the loneliness of Peter's domestic life before his meeting with Jerry. Albee's most successful play was ***Who's Afraid of Virginia Woolf?*** (1962), in which the marriage of the history professor George to the college president's wife Martha becomes the site of intense gender and culture wars, which are disguised as games but reveal hidden family secrets in an highly ambivalent process of mutual confrontation and humiliation. The psycho-dramatic interactions between the characters and their double-bind situations have been taken as a model of problems of human communication in general (cf. Watzlawick, Beavin, and Jackon). In numerous experimental plays, Albee used different techniques such as the ***mise en abyme*** in *Tiny Alice* (1964), the splitting up of characters into different selves interacting with each other at different ages in *Three Tall Women* (1991), or the unmasking of family conventions in the transition from farce to tragedy in *The Goat or Who is Sylvia?* (2000)—always discovering new possibilities of the theater through the exploration of its own performative potential.

Other important postmodern playwrights are **Arthur Kopit**, whose *Indians* (1968) is an anarchic farce between history and fiction, which de-

Albee's plays became postmodern classics.

constructs the Wild West myth and its medial representations; **David Mamet**, who is influenced by Harold Pinter and combines naturalism and postmodern language games in a satirical analysis of modern capitalism as in *American Buffalo* (1975) or *Glengary Glenn Ross* (1983); and **Sam Shepard**, who is not only a playwright but a film-maker, actor, and rock musician. His plays are shaped by these intermedial influences, as well as by the work of Beckett and Pinter, the Western and cowboy myth, but also the postmodern hyper-world of cultural signifiers that have become independent of their signifieds. His characteristic themes like rock music (*The Tooth of Crime*, 1972), family structures (*Buried Child*, 1978), media and reality (*True West*, 1981), or gender and violence (*A Lie of the Mind*, 1986), are acted out in the tension between simulacrum and authenticity, between anonymous and personal realities. The postmodern loss of values is staged in a more cynical, provocative way in **Neil LaBute**'s plays, in which the white middle class is exposed in its brutal selfish normality, such as in *The Shape of Things* (2001) or in the sequence of short plays *autobahn* (2004), in which all scenes are set inside of an automobile on a highway, exploring the dramatic possibilities of a limited space for a diagnosis of postmodern society.

Beyond individual authors, American drama since the 1960s has also profited from the activities of various groups and **theater collectives**. The

Living Theater has been one of them, with off-off-Broadway productions such as *Paradise Now!* (1969), an improvisational play including the audience in its erotic utopia. Also, the **musical** celebrated worldwide successes with *My Fair Lady* (1956), *West Side Story* (1957), *Hair* (1967), and *A Chorus Line* (1975). Postmodern **performance theater** continued to thrive in the later twentieth century in Richard Schechner's Group/Environmental Theater, Lee Breuer's multimedial 'total theater', in Richard Foreman's experiments and Robert Wilson's 'theater of vision', which uses painting, music, and dance in a mixture of images, sound collages, and slow motion techniques for a mythographic sign language of the theater, as in the monumental spectacle *The CIVIL warS* (1983–84), which was performed in different parts in Rotterdam, Tokyo, Cologne and Rome.

### Drama, Gender, and Sexuality

Since the 1960s, **feminist theater groups** had participated in the experimental, political and postmodern renewal of American drama and theater (such as the New Feminist Repertory, Women's Experimental Theatre, or Womanspace Theater). Also, women playwrights emerged as individual authors. **Beth Henley** began her career at the Actors Theatre in Louisville, and moved on to write her own plays in the grotesque mode, in which fears and neuroses of everyday life become the subject of psycho-dramatic crisis scenarios. Her first and best-known play, *Crimes of the Heart* (1978), deals with the traumas of three sisters in their relation to their grandfather, from whose overpowering influence they liberate themselves in the course of the play. **Marsha Norman** also started out at the Actors Theatre Louisville, and her major play, *'night, Mother* (1982), deals with a traumatic crisis as well. It is about the announcement of the suicide of the 40-year-old daughter Jessica, which she carries out in the end in spite of her mother's attempts to prevent it. This existential borderline situation creates the tension of a psycho-thriller, while it also enables for the first time an open, authentic communication between mother and daughter. More than Henley and Norman, **Wendy Wasserstein** is oriented on the comic genre. Sociopolitical problems, especially of women in intellectual milieus, are staged in an ironically playful and humorous tone. Conflicts between different female role models in *Uncommon Women and Others* (1977) and the quest for independent individual self-determination within the unfolding women's movement in *The Heidi Chronicles* (1988) are some of her characteristic themes.

**Gay and lesbian plays** have been part of this experimental-political differentiation of American drama. Tony Kushner's *Angels in America* (1991/92) has been celebrated for counteracting the conservatism of the Reagan/Bush years by presenting AIDS not as God's punishment for homosexuality but as a symbol of cultural alternatives related to the liberating force of sexuality. Sexual abuse is the theme of **Paula Vogel**'s *How I Learned to Drive* (1997), in which scenes from the past are interspersed with the present in a similar, though more realist manner than in **Richard Greenberg**'s tragicomedy *Take Me Out* (2002), about the disastrous consequences of the coming out of a baseball star. In the course of this increased focus on body and culture, sickness and death have become a topic in various contemporary plays. Among them is **Margaret Edson**'s *Wit* (1995), which deals with the final stages of terminal cancer of an English literature professor, who encounters in the clinic a scientific attitude of efficiency but personal indifference that she tries to cope with through reference to the spiritual comforts of literature, especially to John Donne's sonnet "Death Be Not Proud."

### Drama and Ethnic Diversity

As in all branches of literature, ethnic minorities contributed to drama as well, even though perhaps less visibly so than in other genres. **American Indians** had, of course, their own traditional rituals, dances, chants, ceremonies, and communal forms of drama, such as the *Navajo Night Chant*. Among the relatively few contemporary playwrights are Hanay Geiogamah (Kiowa), who confronts the problem of alcoholism in Indian reservations in *Body Indian* (1972) and the role of cultural stereotypes in *Foghorn* (1973), which contains historical references to the Wounded Knee Massacre of 1890. **African American plays** were already produced since the Harlem Renaissance by Langston Hughes for example, but became more important in the course of the Civil Rights Movement with plays like Lorraine Hansberry's *A Raisin in the Sun* (1959) about ghetto life, James Baldwin's *Blues for Mr. Charley* (1964) about the Emmet Till lynching case of 1955, or Amiri Baraka's political dramas *Dutchman* (1964) about the dangers of naive racial integrationism, or *The Slave* (1964) about the contradictions of a revolutionary between racist cli-

chés. Ed Bullins' militant drama lives from the resuscitation of African myths, music, dance, jazz, and bebop, while Ntozake Shange combines dance and poetry in her remarkable *for colored girls who have considered suicide/ when the rainbow is enuf* (1975), a "choreopoem" between ritual and theater. More recently, August Wilson has emerged as a leading figure by contributing "a cycle of ten plays about African American life, each chronicling a different decade of the twentieth century" (Saddik 90). Of these, *Fences* (1985) and *The Piano Lesson* (1987) have been especially successful. The focus of Suzan-Lori Parks' *The American Play* (1990–93) and *Topdog/Underdog* (2001) is the cultural invisibility of African Americans, which the first play tries to convey in a non-realist, the second in a realist mode (Grabes and Schwank 10).

In **Hispanic drama**, problems of Mexican immigrants since the 60s led to political forms of drama by Chicano/a writers, as in Luis Valdez' Teatro Campesino with its sketch-like agitprop-plays ("Actos"). More recently, Milcha Sanchez-Scott in *Roosters* (1987) presents elements of Mexican traditions in a mixture of magical and realist modes. Among Asian American playwrights are Frank Chin with *The Chickencoop Chinaman* (1971) or *The Year of the Dragon* (1975), and David Henry Hwang with *The Dance and the Railroad* (1982) about the Chinese workforce in the railroad industry, or with *M. Butterfly* (1988), where the Puccini opera is used to dissolve stereotypes between East and West and between genders. From a Japanese American perspective, Philip Kan Gotanda in *Sisters Matsumoto* (1998) dramatizes questions of identity and cultural recognition by mainstream society.

The Teatro Campesino fostered political consciousness among Hispanic Americans.

### 3.5.3 | Transitions to Postmodernism in Poetry and Prose

By the middle of the twentieth century, modernism had its high point not only in drama but in poetry, fiction and criticism. The so-called New Criticism (cf. section II.1.2) became the dominant school of poetics and of literary studies with figures such as T.S. Eliot, Allen Tate, or Cleanth Brooks, who advocated the formal unity of the artwork as an autonomous sphere of the aesthetic that had to be seen independently from politics, history, biography, and life. It was against this creed, as well as against the post-war mentality of an increasingly ideological middle class America, that a group of young intellectuals emerged in the late 1940s as a loose movement of countercultural writing later called the **Beat Generation**. Unlike the more international, existentialist Lost Generation of post-World War I, the Beat Generation primarily originated from a reaction to an inner-American situation. The students that first met at Columbia University in 1944—**Allen Ginsberg**, **Jack Kerouac**, and **William Burroughs**—formed the core figures of the group, which however became more numerous when it moved to the West Coast and gathered for a famous poetry reading in 1955 at the City Lights Book Store in San Francisco. In their life and writing, the Beats looked for radical alternatives to mainstream America, using drugs, sex, mobility, jazz, and transcendental meditation as escape routes from the depressing circumstances of society, and searching for states of intensified experience and inspired ecstasy that would open up a direct path to higher life and creativity. Literature and art were no longer separate from life but an enhancement and anarchic celebration of life that was stifled in a conformist society. In this mixture between rebellion and hedonism, satire and *eros*, individualism and communitarianism, the Beats prepared the way for the more collective spirit of revolt, social change, and alternative life styles which would become the hallmark of the counterculture of the 1960s and 70s.

In their writing, the Beats were influenced by imaginative models of European Romanticism, especially William Blake, by the anarchic individualism of American transcendentalists such as Ralph Waldo Emerson and Henry David Thoreau, by the Dionysian free verse and pan-erotic celebratory tone of Walt Whitman, but also by the poetry of W. C. Williams. On the other hand, they also strongly related to non-Western traditions of thought and writing such as Hinduism or Zen-Buddhism, but also, in the case of Gary Snyder, Native American mythologies.

A cult text of the movement is Kerouac's **On the Road** (1951/58), which he supposedly typed in a three-week manic writing period on one continuous roll of paper in a technique he called "spontaneous prose." The novel combines elements of the

### Interpretation

#### Allen Ginsberg, *Howl*

In his best-known poem *Howl* (1955), Allen Ginsberg practiced his theory of In-Spiration, which holds that the breath length is the measure of poetic rhythm, resulting in a spontaneous visionary poem of free verse with the famous beginning lines

I saw the best minds of my generation destroyed by madness, starving hysterical naked [...]

The text is organized in four sections—(1) rebellion against the normal life, (2) vision of the God Moloch as epitome of modern alienation, (3) incantation of the mad poet Carl Salomon, and (4) footnote to *Howl* in a sanctification of the Moloch's victims and the supersedure of fragmentation by "holistic" thinking (both in the sense of *holi*ness and of *whole*ness).

picaresque with the frontier and road novel to celebrate personal mobility in the journey of Sal Paradise with Dean Moriarty through the U.S. to Mexico, a trip of nonconformist nomadic outsiders through worlds of drugs, visions, and sexuality for the purpose of self-expansion and enhanced vitality. The nightmarish side of such experiments is described in Burroughs' surreal-apocalyptic novel *The Naked Lunch* (1959), which is a discontinuous series of drug hallucinations within a totalitarian system of power in aleatory textual assemblages.

The Beats have been criticized for their excessive individualism and their patriarchal gender attitudes. On the other hand, an important contribution of the Beat Generation can be seen in their openness to non-Western forms of thought, in their highly personal poetics, in their creative intermedial dialogue with other art forms such as Bebop or Action Painting, and in their ecological awareness of nature, which became one of the lasting features of the poetry of Gary Snyder, to date certainly one of the most prominent American eco-poets. The Beats also influenced central figures of the popular counterculture such as the poetry and rock music of **Bob Dylan**, whose songs "Like a Rolling Stone," "Blowing in the Wind," or "The Times They are A-changing," were like a wake-up call to a new mass movement of protest, rebellion and the search for alternative life forms that had been anticipated, on a smaller scale, by the Beat Generation.

### Definition

The various aspects of the → Beat movement are illustrated by the three meanings of "beat": "beaten" in the sense of depressed, "beat" in the sense of rhythm and musical sound, and "beatific" in the sense of the search for ecstatic transcendental happiness.

## 3.5.4 | American Poetry in the Later Twentieth and Early Twenty-First Centuries

In other developments, American poetry since the mid-twentieth century opened up to new themes and forms as well.

**The Black Mountain School** of poetry was associated with a reform college where various important artists were cooperating from architecture, design, composition, dance, choreography, and literature. Among them, Charles Olson and Robert Creeley, who edited the journal *Black Mountain Review*, became especially influential, along with Robert Duncan, Denise Levertov, and John Wieners. In his "Projective Verse" (1959), Olson postulated an **open form of poetry** liberated from fixed generic and metrical patterns and based on bodily individual experience as manifested in the personal rhythms of speech and breathing. From the group emerged the **San Francisco School**, experimenting with forms of avant-garde music, while on the East coast the New York Poets Frank O'Hara and John Ashbery explored the connections between poetry and painting, especially action painting and aleatory soundscapes.

**Confessional Poets.** At about the same time, the so-called Confessional Poets wrote from the experience of personal crisis in a psycho-cultural tension between depression and self-therapy. **John Berryman**, who admired Whitman but didn't share his affirmative attitude to life, examined in his *Dream Songs* (1964/69) the failure of his quest for the self in various poetic roles. While **Robert Lowell** critically confronted the patriarchal New England tradition from a male perspective, **Anne Sexton** and **Sylvia Plath** tried to overcome the traumas of restrictive social gender roles from the perspective of female self-assertion. Sexton's *Live or Die* (1966) is a high point of this confessional poetry, in which she reflects in free verse about life and death, love and loneliness from a basically positive attitude to existence. Plath, like Sexton, struggled with depression and suicidal impulses, but also produced powerful poetry from the extreme tensions and contradictions of her personality. In *The Bell Jar* (1963), she describes in prose the development of her fictional self, Esther, between hope and disillusion, tracing her recovery from a nervous breakdown until her return to college. Plath's increasing bitterness about society, especially after her failed marriage to the British poet Ted Hughes, led to a more radical and violent tone in her collection *Ariel* (1965), in which the figure of her father in the poem "Daddy" merges with threatening images from the holocaust, and in which "Lady Lazarus" becomes the symbolic medium of a self-staged poetic resurrection.

Another major woman poet, who was active from the 1950s through the 1990s, both reflecting and actively shaping characteristic transformations of poetry in these decades, is **Adrienne Rich**. Starting out with formally well-made poems in the high modernist style, she turned to feminist and autobiographical forms of writing in the 60s and 70s, and then moved on to include nature and ecological themes in her later poetry.

**Experimental Poetry.** In a more visibly experimental and language-conscious way, the school of L = A = N = G = U = A = G = E poetry since the 1970s foregrounded the medium of poetry, language and words as a material sign system which could be explored in new dimensions by focusing on its concrete visual and acoustic implications.

**Native American poets** themselves have found inspiration both from this contemporary scene and from their own oral traditions of poetry and story-telling, and this hybrid combination has proved to be highly productive. A prominent voice is Simon Ortiz, whose "The Creation, According to Coyote" is an example of this transcultural hybridity, in which the biblical account of creation is overwritten by a Native American version related by the trickster figure of coyote. In the poems of Ray Young Bear, Linda Hogan, Joy Harjo, or Rita Dove as well, traditional forms and rituals are resuscitated and productively integrated into postmodern American literature and society in manifold ways.

In these poetic stagings of cultural memory, the ecological dimension is very prominent, since nature is an integral part of Native American thinking and poetics. Yet in mainstream poetry as well, ecological issues have become increasingly important in the course of the twentieth and in the early twenty-first century. The living interrelatedness between culture and nature is not only a thematic focus but a creative matrix of numerous texts—notably in poems by A. R. Ammons, Robert Hass, Mary Oliver, Ed Roberson, or Ruth Stone.

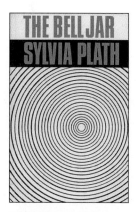

Sylvia Plath, *The Bell Jar* (1963), dust jacket of the 1966 printing

### 3.5.5 | Postmodern and Contemporary Fiction

#### Between Modernism and Postmodernism

While the Beats experimented with poetic and psychedelic forms of counter-writing, American novelists of the post-war period continued with broadly **realist forms** of fiction that focused, more than before, on the place of the individual within an anonymous mass society and between different cultural identities. Ethnic issues were foregrounded and at the same time related to universal models of a cosmopolitan human identity. The **social outsider** became a cultural representative.

The best-known novel of adolescence in this line is probably *The Catcher in the Rye* (1951; see box); another is **Saul Bellow**'s *The Adventures of Augie March* (1953), in which a young picaresque hero tries to find his identity in a bewildering plurality of social roles that other people attempt to impose on him. Bellow, winner of the Nobel Prize in 1976, sees the Jewish intellectual as an existentialist outsider who simultaneously represents general human qualities, acquiring, as in *Seize the Day* (1956), a new form of wisdom through his failures and suffering. Bellow's major novel *Herzog* (1964) deals with the crisis of a modern intellectual, who tries to come to terms with the broken relationship to his wife and to society in general by obsessively writing letters he never sends off. Like Bellow, **Bernard Malamud** is a Jewish American writer of Russian descent, who uses mythical and biblical motifs in a mixture of realist and symbolic styles in novels that depict the suffering Jew as a social outsider, who can nevertheless become the redemptive figure of a higher humanity. An exemplary case is *The Assistant* (1957), in which the Italian criminal Frank Alpine is humanized by his encounter with the poor, saint-like Jewish grocer Morris Bober. In the course of the novel, Frank is transformed into a second Bober, symbolically uniting the religions of Christianity and Judaism in a higher form of universal humanity.

**Philip Roth.** Whereas writers like Malamud and, even more so, Isaac Bashevis Singer, who reactivates Yiddish story-telling traditions in an American context, try to integrate Jewish tradition and modern America, Philip Roth sharply and often provocatively distances himself and his protagonists from that tradition and particularly from the repressive side of orthodox forms of Judaism. His early fiction such as the story collection *Goodbye, Columbus* (1959), which contains the much-anthologized "The Conversion of the Jews," is characterized by an ironic-satirical tone and a comic reversal of all conventional pieties, including the sexual norms of American middle class life. His later novels are more explicitly political and ethical, focusing on fundamental topics of modern society such as the Holocaust, the Vietnam war, terrorism, sickness, trauma, and the independence of writers and intellectuals in an age of collective ideologies. In his sequence of Zuckerman novels, Roth follows the biography of his fictional alter ego, the writer Nathan Zuckerman, through his overcoming of writer's block in *My Life as a Man* (1974), his fantasy of reversing history by saving Anne Frank from the Nazis in *The Ghost Writer* (1979), the ambivalences of literary success in *Zuckerman Unbound* (1982), and his conflict with the cultural establishment in *The Anatomy Lesson* (1983). *The Human Stain* (2000) is a masterful novel about the deformations of personal life in a world of racism, ideology, and social conformism. The protagonist Coleman Silk is a professor of classical philology, who has denied his African American roots and assumed a Jewish identity to circumvent racist obstacles to his success in the

---

**Interpretation**

#### J. D. Salinger, *The Catcher in the Rye*

A **cult novel** of the 1950s and beyond was J. D. Salinger's *The Catcher in the Rye* (1951), in which the adolescent hero Holden Caulfield is an outsider in a "phony" society of adults, who experiences a series of disillusions that in the end lead to his psychic breakdown and his being committed into a mental institution, telling his story both as an act of social satire and of personal self-therapy. The coolness of his narrative tone, with which he sets himself off from the traditional *Bildungsroman*, "that David Copperfield kind of crap," contrasts with his inner fragility and his sentimental idealization of childhood, which he wants to preserve against the corruptions of the adult world. With its youthful narrator and its oral story-telling, the novel belongs to a tradition of American novels of adolescence and initiation, of which Mark Twain's *Huckleberry Finn* (1885) is the prototype.

academic world. In the novel, Silk's repressed past returns with tragic irony when he is charged with racism against two black students and loses his job at the college. His fight for his rehabilitation, in which he is helped by the narrator Zuckerman, is only one side of the unfolding story, however. The other side is his passionate affair with the cleaning woman Faunia Farley, who brings Silk into new contact with life outside conventions and prejudices, even though she is herself severely traumatized by the loss of her two children and by her violent Vietnam War veteran husband.

John Updike's work, like that of Roth, spans the second half of the twentieth century and fundamentally continues the mimetic-realist tradition of modern fiction as a symbolic representation of its age and culture. His Rabbit Angstrom tetralogy (1960–90) is based on a humanist poetics, aiming to portray the everyday life of an average human individual against the background of major political, social and cultural events in America in successive decades—the 1950s in *Rabbit, Run*, the 60s in *Rabbit Redux*, the 70s in *Rabbit is Rich* and the 80s in *Rabbit at Rest*. The protagonist's name marks his character as an un-heroic everyman figure, dominated by fear and failure rather than courage and success, and repeatedly frustrated in his attempts to break out of the normative prison-house of middle class existence.

Joyce Carol Oates has also been one of the the most prolific American fiction writers of recent decades. In her mixture of 'high' and 'popular' literary forms, she appeals both to a university audience and a wide reading public. Characteristic features of her writings are their focus on violence, their exploration of deeply traumatized states of mind, their often shocking use of grotesque and Gothic modes inspired by Poe, and their enormous narrative and linguistic flexibility, creating dream-like textures that seem to be floating over abysses. Often, adolescent characters are focalizers of narratives of female initiation into an extremely alienating and surreally incomprehensible world. A major later work is *The Falls* (2004), in which the Niagara Falls become an ecocultural energy center and textual vortex around which the characters and events in the novel revolve.

John Irving is another highly successful novelist, whose work is likewise positioned between, or rather outside, usual labels of literary style and genre. More so than Oates, Irving writes in a consciously popular, audience-friendly mode, and where Oates explores the internal terrors of the modern psyche, Irving externalizes the hidden fears, dreams and nightmares of modern individuals into bizarre scenarios of action, in which the grotesque deformations of life under the conditions of a chaotic modern world are exposed in drastic concreteness. Violence, sex, rape, and terrorism are recurring ingredients of his plots, in which the fantastic collides with the real in often unexpected and shock-like turns of events, as in his cult novel *The World According to Garp* (1978). Transitory, metamorphous states of the self, androgynous and transsexual characters, dismemberment and mutilation of bodies, carnivalesque subversion of categories are the hallmarks of Irving's tragicomic narratives, which are at the same time novelistic parables about the relationship between his fictional artist figures and their imaginary material. Irving's works are bestsellers which have gained him a worldwide reading public. Their narrative fascination for the reader is nevertheless connected with considerable artistic craft and intellectual sophistication.

## Postmodernism

Against these remarkable continuities of fiction writing in America since late modernity, the period of postmodernism in a more narrow sense, as a phenomenon largely from the 1960s to the 1980s, stands out as a phase of **radical innovation and experiment**. General features of postmodernism have been discussed above in the context of English literature (see entry I.2.7), even though the major impulse towards postmodern experimentation came from American literature. In the volume *Postmodernism: The Key Figures* (Bertens and Natoli), a handbook referring to international postmodernism in literature, theater, photography, and art, the vast majority of representatives is Ameri-

---

**Focus on Postmodernist Literature**

Postmodernist texts often take a skeptical stance toward realism, the 'grand narratives' of historiography, and the notion of a stable identity. They subvert such constructs by using techniques like
- parody and pastiche
- metafictionality
- intertextual and intermedial references
- multiperspectival narration
- non-linear time structures
- open or alternative endings

can. Under the influence of theories of poststructuralism and deconstructionism, writers broke away from the normative poetics of the New Criticism and practiced a radically open, innovative, and language-conscious form of writing. In one sense, they continued the impulse of the modernist avant-garde and shared its epistemological skepticism and its sense of a fundamental crisis of values and civilization. On the other hand, they rejected the elitist concept of modern art and sought to combine it with popular art forms. The dissolution of the closed work of art, the experimental exploration of its own mediality, and the dialogue with other media became hallmarks of postmodern fiction, which thereby moved from fiction to meta-fiction, from mimetic representation to semiotic performance, from text to intertext. Fiction becomes indistinguishable from reality, and history becomes accessible only in imaginative form. The **recycling of previous genres, styles, and texts** is the paradoxical form of postmodern creativity. Favorite textual metaphors are the maze, the mirror-hall, the *mise en abyme*, the imaginary library, the intertextual echo-chamber, the web or network of signifiers.

**Vladimir Nabokov**, the cosmopolitan writer of Russian descent, was a central figure in the emergence of American postmodernism. His scandal-provoking novel *Lolita* (1955) about the pedophilic relationship of the 37 year-old European Humbert Humbert to the twelve-year old American Lolita, is a proto-postmodernist novel in which the unreliability of narration, the multiple forms of textual self-reflexivity, the parodistic language games, and the wealth of literary allusions provided an infinitely complex, even though formally unspectacular model of postmodern fiction. *Pale Fire* (1962) clearly demonstrates as well the postmodern mode in its self-reflexive staging of the relations between text and life, art and reality, consisting of a four part poem of 999 lines by a fictitious poet John Shade that is edited and supplied with a preface and 200 pages of notes by his friend Charles Kinbote.

**Thomas Pynchon**, also called the James Joyce of postmodernism, is one of Nabokov's most famous disciples. Like Salinger he gained cult status by living in hiding for most of his life. His novel *V.* is about the search for a woman named Victoria Wren in the chaotic labyrinths of history, which turn out to be worlds of proliferating signifiers without any clearly identifiable signified. In *The Crying of Lot 49* (1966) civilizational power is con-

trasted to, but also strangely interconnected with, a mysterious underground organization Tristero, whose code word W. A.S. T.E is a programmatic motto for the ways in which the multiple wastelands of human history become the subject and creative force of the text, while the muted posthorn signifies both the mobilizing energy and the inevitable failure of the search for truth and communication that the protagonist Oedipa Mass sets out for. *Gravity's Rainbow* (1973) was a bestseller widely read in the countercultural scene, framing a chaotic-apocalyptic series of episodes with the launching and impact of a V-2 rocket, and involving countless characters in a nonlinear narration in heterogeneous worlds. In *Against the Day* (2006), Pynchon published his most massive novel so far of over 1000 pages, an example of the postmodern genre of historiographic metafiction, in which the historical past is explored as a discursive intertextual field in which facts and fantasy are indistinguishably mixed. The novel covers the period from the 1893 Chicago World Fair to the aftermath of World War I in various parts of the world in multiple, not always conclusive plots, and in a variety of different registers and stylistic modes.

**John Barth** is both a postmodern fiction writer and a university professor, exemplifying in his person the interplay between theory and text which characterizes his writings. In his story collection *Lost in the Funhouse* (1968), subtitled "Fiction for Print, Tape, Live Voice," the written medium is foregrounded through the use of italics, ellipses, explicit comments on stylistic conventions, and convolutions of syntax. The reader is confronted with surfaces of signs and collage-like permutations of signifiers, which refer to each other in endlessly recursive feedback loops. Other formal experimenters in the mode of what has been called "surfiction" are Donald Barthelme, Raymond Federman, Richard Brautigan, Robert Coover, and Ronald Sukenick.

**The Topic of History.** Postmodern fiction, however, also engages in serious, if unorthodox ways, with history. Examples are John Hawkes's *The Cannibal*, in which World Wars I and II are conveyed in apocalyptic scenes of violence and chaos that present historical events as the mad visions of psychiatric patients; Joseph Heller's *Catch-22* (1961), in which the absurdities of the war are exposed in the inescapable ethical paradoxes in which the protagonist, who wants to escape the madness of events, nevertheless remains trapped; Kurt Vonnegut's *Slaughter-House Five* (1969), in

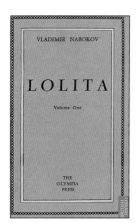

VLADIMIR NABOKOV

LOLITA

Volume One

THE OLYMPIA PRESS

Initially banned in the United States, *Lolita* was first published in Paris by the Olympia Press.

which the firebombing of Dresden in World War II becomes the subject of a nonlinear, time-transcending science fiction narrative; or E.L. Doctorow's **Ragtime** (1975), in which the turn of the nineteenth to the twentieth century provides the material for a work of historiographic metafiction, which is composed around different strands of plot and combines fact and fiction to illuminate the connections between racism, Jewish immigrants, and the life of African Americans, whose improvisational ragtime music shapes the narrative style of the novel.

While these postmodern experiments dominated the literary evolution of the later twentieth century, they were accompanied from the beginning not only by the continuities of mainstream novel writing, but also by deliberate attempts to radicalize the potential of literary realism. Truman Capote had taken a real murder case as the basis for his factographic novel *In Cold Blood* (1966), Norman Mailer in the *Armies of the Night* (1968) described with documentary evidence and from his own observations the largest anti-Vietnam-war demonstration in 1967. Tom Wolfe wrote in this mode of a "new journalism" as well, practicing a neorealist style of urban fiction writing in his New York novel *The Bonfire of the Vanities* (1987). Other representatives of different kinds of neorealism are Gore Vidal, Tobias Wolff, T.C. Boyle, and the minimalists Ann Beattie and Raymond Carver.

## The Multicultural Differentiation of American Literature

The United States had been a multiethnic and multicultural project from its beginnings, but while this fact was covered over for a long time by enforced concepts of national unity and homogeneity, it became an increasingly visible aspect of American culture and literature in the twentieth century.

African American writing had already emerged in the early republic and had produced new genres like the slave narrative and musical forms such as the jazz, but it only began to articulate itself on a broader scale since the Harlem Renaissance of the 1920s and 30s (cf. section I.3.4.5). From this period of creative explosion across different art forms, it became a distinct branch of American literature that developed its own sociocultural and literary dynamic while also interacting with the development of American society and literature at large. After Richard Wright's naturalist study *Na-*

*tive Son* (1940), the African American novel manifested itself powerfully in the 1950s in **Ralph Ellison**'s *Invisible Man* (1952), in which the modern condition of the alienated individual in a conformist mass society is presented in the form of a picaresque trickster novel that uses African American forms of folklore, blues, and jazz in combination with modern narrative traditions (Melville, Twain, Dostoyevsky, Joyce, Eliot). While **James Baldwin** also practices such a culturally hybrid form of writing, he deals with racism in American society from a more explicitly political and religious perspective, such as in *Go Tell it on the Mountain* (1953). In the context of the 1960s Civil Rights and Black Power movements, people like Amiri Baraka postulate a more polemical and separatist Black Aesthetic, while at the same time writers like **Ishmael Reed** consciously adapt postmodern techniques as in his *Mumbo Jumbo* (1972), an experimental novel based on a collage-like mixture of texts, pictures, songs, newspaper clippings, voodoo elements, and an improvisational jazz poetics which shapes the texture of the novel.

In another development especially since the 1980s, women novelists moved from the margins to the center of African American literature. Following the model of Zora Neale Hurston's *Their Eyes Were Watching God* (1937), writers like **Alice Walker** focus on the creative potential of African American folklore, culture, and community life, and particularly on the role and identity of women in the racist tensions between black and white America. In her epistolary novel *The Color Purple* (1982), Walker mixes vernacular and standard English to trace the liberation of the protagonist Celie from male suppression and her discovery of female solidarity and self-empowerment. The novels of **Toni Morrison** gain their enormous linguistic and narrative power from their combination of African American traditions of story-telling, folk mythology and jazz poetics, with formal techniques of modern and postmodern narration. Her prize-winning *Beloved* (1987) is significantly located on "Blues[-]tone road," setting the tone for the blues rhythm of the narrative, which uses a broad range of historical material for an imaginative reconstruction of nineteenth century slavery as a deep-rooted trauma of American history. The plot centers around the killing of the two-year old daughter Beloved by her mother, the fugitive slave Sethe, in a desperate attempt to prevent her child from being taken back into slavery. After 18 years, a stranger, who acts like the ghost of Beloved, con-

Toni Morrison was
the first African American
to win the Nobel prize
for literature.

Interpretation

### Toni Morrison, *Beloved* (1987)

A fully dressed woman walked out of the water. She barely gained the dry bank of the stream before she sat down and leaned against a mulberry tree. All day and all night she sat there, her head resting on the trunk in a position abandoned enough to crack the brim in her straw hat. Everything hurt but her lungs most of all. Sopping wet and breathing shallow she spent those hours trying to negotiate the weight of her eyelids. The day breeze blew her dress dry; the night wind wrinkled it. Nobody saw her emerge or came accidentally by. If they had, chances are they would have hesitated before approaching her. Not because she was wet, or dozing or had what sounded like asthma, but because amid all that she was smiling.

The emergence of Beloved evokes a moment of birth, but also a return from death. She appears like a drowned person, who uneasily gropes her way back to life, but also like a hybrid being in a state of metamorphosis, about to assume a new, unknown and yet instinctively anticipated state of existence. She is soaking wet, but fully dressed, and is thus a natural creature placed in a cultural context. The traces of the past are recognizable in her thin, scarred neck, which she can barely keep upright, and the two scratches on her head. Beloved thus has from the beginning something fascinating, pitiful and monstrous, as if the parts of her personality do not fit into a coherent whole. Even though she looks like a human shape externally, she seems internally "dismembered," like Sethe's real daughter, striving to gain back her lost wholeness through the "rememory" of the other characters' story-telling, which her reappearance sets off (pt. I, ch. 5).

fronts Sethe with her repressed past and thus makes possible the symbolic exorcism of the demon of slavery through story-telling and ritual regeneration. Polyphonic narration and associative stream-of-consciousness technique work together in this collective trauma therapy and cultural 'rememory' (a term Morrison introduces in *Beloved*).

Apart from slavery, Morrison also deals with other periods and issues of African American history from a perspective not only of victimization and deprivation but of survival, regeneration, and creative self-empowerment as in *Song of Solomon*, *Jazz*, *Paradise*, or *A Mercy* (2008). Other novelists as well, like Gloria Naylor, Octavia Butler, Saidiya Hartman or Edward P. Jones, continue to explore and differentiate both the traumas and the fascinating complexities of African American history into the twenty-first century in different styles and thematic contexts.

American Indian literature, even though dating back to pre-colonial times in its oral traditions, only fully established itself as a written culture of literature with the Native American Renaissance of the 1960s and 70s. With **Scott Momaday**'s *House Made of Dawn* (1968), a new form of novel emerged that combined modern forms of multiperspectival narration with the reactivation of oral traditions and rituals, such as the *Navajo Night Chant*, from which the novel's title is taken. The plot relates the return of Abel, a traumatized World War II veteran, and his attempts to find a way back into the Indian community, which repeatedly fails but in the end succeeds with the help of resusci-

tated memories and healing ceremonies. **Leslie Marmon Silko**'s *Ceremony* (1977) is like a follow-up novel to Momaday's, also aiming at cultural and personal regeneration through the revitalization of Indian traditions. Somewhat different from Momaday, however, these traditions must be changed and newly invented in the process of their historical actualization in order to be effective. The novel is framed by the poetic imagination of the mythical story-teller Spider Woman:

Thought-Woman, the spider,
Named things and
As she named them
They appeared.

She is sitting in her room
Thinking of a story now

I'm telling you the story
She is thinking. (Prologue)

Her poems and stories intersect with the experiences of the war veteran Tayo and his attempts at a reintegration of his identity under the conditions of a destructive modern civilization, which is epitomized both in his traumatic war experiences in Japan and in the atomic bomb that was built from uranium mined on reservation land in New Mexico. The quest for identity between white and Indian society also shapes the grotesque novels of James Welch, while a more postmodern approach to the question of Native American identity char-

Leslie Marmon Silko's
*Ceremony* (1977), cover

acterizes the novels of Gerald Vizenor, Louise Erdrich, and Sherman Alexie. Both in fiction and poetry, Native American writing remains an important and productive branch of contemporary American literature, even though, as in African American or indeed in Chicano or Asian American literatures, transculturally hybrid rather than separatist forms and styles seem to be characteristic of current developments.

Hispanic or Chicano/a literature as well, as the literature of mainly Mexican immigrants, has become an important branch of American literature since the 1960s with the novels of, among others, Rudolfo Anaya, such as *Bless Me, Ultima* (1972) or *Heart of Aztlan* (1976) about the mythical homeland of the Chicanos that is superseded by the urban industrialism of capitalist America. The barrios of immigrant communities and the borderlands between the U.S. and Mexico are favorite sites of identity conflicts and intercultural clashes of values in various novels by Rolando Hinojosa, Alejandro Morales, Arturo Islas or Miguel Mendez M. Gender issues are articulated in the narratives by Sandra Cisneros in her much-anthologized *The House on Mango Street* (1983) or by Ana Castillo in her magical-realist *So Far From God* (1993). Both of these prominent Chicana writers continue to be productive in the twenty-first century, Cisneros with her generational novel *Caramelo* (2002), Castillo with her *Watercolor Women / Opaque Men: A Novel in Verse* (2005). The special emphasis on the border as metaphor and reality initiated by Gloria Anzaldúa's influential *Borderlands/La Frontera: The New Mestiza* (1987), combining cultural hybridity, marginality and feminine sensibility, has produced new important work by numerous authors, among them Pat Mora, Luis Alberto Urrea or Cecile Pineda.

Asian Americans as well have articulated their diverse ethnic-intercultural identities, with major writers like Maxine Hong Kingston, Amy Tan (Chinese), Chang-Rai Lee (Korean), Lois-Ann Yamanaka (Japanese), Bharati Mukherjee, Kiran Desai (Indian), Diana Abu-Jaber (Iraq), and many more. Multiethnicity in a transnational and globalized context remains one of the most productive factors in contemporary American literature.

## American Literature in a Globalized World

Postmodernism has remained an important cultural and aesthetic reference frame for American literature, even while neorealist and multicultural forms of writing demonstrated a renewed interest in apparently discarded categories such as reality, identity, ethics, and the power of art and the word. Rather than binary oppositions, the hybrid **mixture of styles** and aesthetic concepts has characterized the literary evolution at the turn of the twentieth to the twenty-first century. The shock of the **terrorist attacks of 9/11** was seen by many as a turning point in postmodernism as well, since it marked a return of the "real" to a cultural studies debate primarily concerned with self-referential signifiers. Important literary responses to 9/11 were, most notably, Art Spiegelman's graphic novel *In the Shadow of No Towers* (2004), Jonathan Safran Foer's *Extremely Loud & Incredibly Close* (2005), John Updike's *Terrorist* (2006), and Don DeLillo's *Falling Man* (2007), all of which emphasized, unlike the official 9/11 Commission Report by the American Government, the personal and collective traumatization of characters beyond national, cultural, and ideological binaries. Yet 9/11 has only been one factor in a more general shift within the literary culture towards a more realist and representational attitude to language and narrative. Other factors are a new emphasis on ethical questions, the critique of an omnipresent media culture, an increased ecological awareness, and the return to questions of individual identity and the social networks in which it is defined.

Don DeLillo is one of the key figures illustrating this transformation of postmodern literature into the medium of a critical reflection of contemporary society, engaging with ecological issues such as toxic waste in *White Noise* (1984), with political issues in the Kennedy assassination novel *Libra* (1988), with the role of the writer in a mass media world in *Mao II* (1991) with the Cold War and the threat of nuclear power in *Underworld* (1997), and with the trauma of 9/11 in *Falling Man*. DeLillo places American events and topics in multinational contexts, combines narrative montage and collage with complex webs of relationships, and breaks through the surface of a simulated media world by emphasizing the concrete descriptive and communicative power of language.

Paul Auster also continues with postmodern experiments, however not in the sense of pure linguistic self-reflexivity, but always as attempts to examine, from different narrative angles and perspectives, the life of individual characters under the pressures of collectivism in contemporary society. His brilliant **New York Trilogy** (1988) is the parody of a detective novel, in which the differ-

Cover of Art Spiegelman's
graphic novel *In the
Shadow of No Towers*
(2004)

ence between fiction and reality is blurred, and in which the characters observe each other as in a mirror hall of second selves. At the same time, the novel is a critique of dogmatic language theories, demonstrating how the ideal of a pure original prelapsarian language destroys human life, while the footsteps of a character walking through Manhattan are interpreted as forming the letters "TOWER OF BABEL." Auster's concept of the self and the novel is polyphonic in a Bakhtinian sense. A high degree of intertextuality and self-referentiality is fused in his works with realist, historiographic, and (auto-)biographical narration from various perspectives but also with fantastic elements. In recent novels such as *The Brooklyn Follies* (2006) or *Invisible* (2009), Auster continues to write about traumatization and the comedy of human survival in multiple narrative frames and contexts, in which the relationship between text and world, life and writing is explored in ever new variants and configurations.

**Family relations** have gained new relevance in the novels of Jonathan Franzen, Jeffrey Eugenides, Jonathan Safran Foer, Nicole Krauss, Cormac McCarthy, Richard Powers, and Siri Hustvedt. Franzen's *The Corrections* (2001) examines life in contemporary society in the microcosm of a mid-western family gathering for Christmas. The demented father, who considers taking the Alzheimer medicine Correctall, forms the symbolic center around which the futile attempts of the family members towards a "correction" of their various failures in life are narrated in a style that harks back to the realist traditions of nineteenth century novels. In *Freedom* (2010) as well, Franzen tells a family saga in an American middle class milieu, in which the farcical flaws and confusions of the characters are nevertheless gradually transformed into an attitude of deeper understanding. Eugenides' *Middlesex* (2002) is a large-scale narration in the tradition of ancient Greek epic, spanning almost the whole twentieth century, whereby the hero/ine Cal/Calliope is a modern hermaphrodite version of the Greek muse of epic poetry, illuminating multiethnic and transgender aspects of modern life from the experience of multiple marginalization, but also from an exuberant energy of multi-voiced storytelling. Jonathan Safran Foer traces the history of his family in his fictional search for his ancestors in the Ukraine in *Everything is Illuminated* (2002) in which he reconstructs the colorful history of the imaginary town of Trachimbrod up to its destruction by the Nazis in a highly unsettling story of both victimization and complicity, a story that also gains comic overtones, however, through the intercultural dialogue between the narrators. Nicole Krauss' *The History of Love* (2005) relates the history of two young lovers separated in Poland in World War II and finding each other again through a manuscript about their relationship entitled *The History of Love*, without however being able to return to their former intimacy. **Cormac McCarthy** recycles the genre of the Western in his intensely self-reflexive novels of violence, in which narrative is put to extreme tests in borderline-situations of

---

**Interpretation**

### Siri Hustvedt, *What I Loved* (2003)

Siri Hustvedt has emerged as a new voice in American fiction in the early twenty-first century. She transforms autobiographical material into intensely personal narratives in which the intrinsic plurality and dialogicity of the self becomes the source of both fascinating and unsettling experiences. Like her other novels, *What I Loved* deals with existential experiences of love and death, with trauma, suffering, loss, and sickness, but also with vitality, *eros*, and creative energy, which unfold beyond the individuality of the aging male narrator in a multi-voiced interaction of various characters that are mutually dependent on and define each other.

The dialogic conception of human identity in *What I Loved* is formulated by the main female protagonist Violet:

I've decided that *mixing* is a key term. It's better than suggestion, which is one-sided. It explains what people rarely talk about, because we define ourselves as isolated, closed bodies who bump up against each other but stay shut. Descartes was wrong. It isn't: I think, therefore I am. It's: I am because you are. That's Hegel—well, the short version. (ch. 1)

The ideology of individualism, which has defined American culture through such concepts as the 'self-made man,' is rejected here in favor of a communicational ethics which postulates people's dependence on each other as a fundamental axiom of human existence.

characters who have lost all ethical or existential certainties or even, as in *The Road* (2006), the world itself, leaving only the father-son relationship as a last source of hope in a global posthuman wasteland.

**Richard Powers** writes highly intellectual novels which illuminate the conditions of individual life in the context of family and social history. Hallmarks of his writings are their transnational and transcultural orientation and their complex mediations between different forms of cultural creativity, especially between the sciences and the arts. In *The Goldbug Variations* (1991), he explores

analogies between the compositional techniques of J. S. Bach, the narrative plot of Poe's short story, and the double helix of the DNA structure; in *Galatea 2.0* (2002), the relationship between literary art and artificial intelligence research; in *The Time of Our Singing* (2003), the connections between musical time and the relativity theory of time in modern physics in a transatlantic context of racism in the twentieth century; and in *The Echo Maker* (2006), the role and limits of neuroscience for trauma therapy and the understanding of human identity in the case of a brain-damaged accident victim.

## Select Bibliography

Allen, Donald, and Warren Tallmann, eds. *The Poetics of the New American Poetry.* New York: Grove Press, 1973.

Aranda, José F. *When We Arrive: A New Literary History of Mexican America.* Tucson: University of Arizona Press, 2003.

Bertens, Johannes W., and Joseph Natoli, eds. *Postmodernism: The Key Figures.* Malden: Blackwell, 2002.

Breinig, Helmbrecht, ed. *Imaginary (Re-)locations: Tradition, Modernity, and the Market in Contemporary Native American Literature and Culture.* Tübingen: Stauffenburg, 2003.

Connor, Steven, ed. *The Cambridge Companion to Postmodernism.* Cambridge: Cambridge University Press, 2004.

Evans, Richard. *Psychology and Arthur Miller.* New York: Dutton, 1969.

Franco, Dean J. *Ethnic American Literature. Comparing Chicano, Jewish, and African American Writing.* Charlottesville: University of Virginia Press, 2006.

Gates, Henry Louis, Jr. *The Signifying Monkey: A Theory of Afro-American Literary Criticism.* New York: Oxford University Press, 1988.

Grabes, Herbert, and Klaus Schwank, eds. *Das neue amerikanische Drama: Autoren – Entwicklungen – Interpretationen.* Trier: WVT, 2009.

Greil, Marcus, and Werner Sollors. *A New Literary History of America.* Cambridge: Harvard University Press, 2010.

Hoffmann, Gerhard. *From Modernism to Postmodernism: Concepts and Strategies of Postmodern American Fiction.* Amsterdam: Rodopi, 2005.

Hornung, Alfred. "Postmoderne bis zur Gegenwart." Zapf 305–92.

Hutcheon, Linda. *The Poetics of Postmodernism. History, Theory, Fiction.* New York: Routledge, 1989.

Kramer, Michael P., and Hanna Wirth-Nesher, eds. *The Cambridge Companion to Jewish American Literature.* Cambridge: Cambridge University Press, 2003.

Lyotard, Jean-François. *The Postmodern Condition. A Report on Knowledge.* Trans. Brian Massumi. Manchester: Manchester University Press, 1984.

Saddik, Annette J. *Contemporary American Drama.* Edinburgh: Edinburgh University Press, 2007.

Seed, David, ed. *A Companion to Twentieth-Century United States Fiction.* Chichester, West Sussex: Wiley-Blackwell, 2010.

Taylor, Victor E., and Charles E. Winquist. *Encyclopedia of Postmodernism.* London: Routledge, 2001.

Versluys, Kristiaan. *Out of the Blue: September 11 and the Novel.* New York: Columbia University Press, 2009.

Watzlawick, Paul, Janet H. Beavin, and Don D. Jackson. *Pragmatics of Human Communication: A Study of Interactional Patterns, Pathologies, and Paradoxes.* New York: Norton, 1967.

Wu, Jean, Yu-wen Shen, and Min Song, eds. *Asian American Studies: A Reader.* New Brunswick: Rutgers University Press, 2000.

Zapf, Hubert, ed. *Amerikanische Literaturgeschichte.* 3rd ed. Stuttgart: Metzler, 2010.

*Hubert Zapf*

# 4 The New Literatures in English

## 4.1 | The History of the New Literatures in English

The New Literatures in English are not that new altogether. They have emerged from **processes of colonization** that transformed large tracts of the world from the late fifteenth century onwards, and some of them can trace their beginnings to the nineteenth or even late eighteenth century, when English, Irish or Scottish settlers in the Caribbean, Canada or South Africa first began to create an 'overseas literature,' and enslaved or colonized people first began to reflect on their current situation and future perspectives utilizing the medium of what was then 'the colonizer's tongue.' Other literatures in English are indeed new, sometimes startlingly so: as distinct literary fields, West African literature in English emerged in the 1950s, East African literature in English in the 1960s, indigenous writing in Canada, Australia and New Zealand in the 1970s, and Black and Asian British Literature in the 1980s. All of these new literatures in English have—in remarkably diverse ways—been shaped by experiences of colonization and their legacies, and all of them have—to varying degrees—moved beyond the original colonial matrix to remake the forms and functions of English as a global language and to engage with a wide variety of political, cultural and literary contexts in various parts of the world. If colonialism and its aftermath mark the nexus from which the new literatures have emerged, their current trajectories are defined by complex **transcultural networks** and the negotiation of sociocultural diversity in an increasingly globalized world.

While the scope and significance of the new literatures in English thus clearly extend far beyond their colonial, anticolonial and postcolonial dimensions, there are nevertheless sound reasons to begin a survey of these literatures with an overview of the historically widely divergent experiences of colonialism. Not only are the histories of

these literatures inextricably entangled with these colonial experiences, but different types of colonial regimes have also given rise to different post-independence societies, which in turn have shaped the divergent paths which the new literatures have followed. Even the English language that at first sight seems to provide a pragmatic common denominator has been moulded by these colonial experiences and their legacies into a globally interlinked network of Englishes: today it is no longer only Britain and the USA, but some 70 countries throughout the world that are "divided by a common language" (George Bernard Shaw).

The new literatures in English have been decisively shaped by three main types of colonial experience: **plantation slavery** (as in Britain's 'New World' colonies in the Caribbean, and in Indian Ocean locations such as Mauritius), **European settlement** (as in Canada, Australia and New Zealand, but also in African countries such as Kenya, Zimbabwe or South Africa), and **colonial conquest** (as in South Asia and most of the territories acquired by Britain during the late nineteenth century 'Scramble for Africa'; see the map in section I.2.5.1). Although these colonial experiences often

Countries in which English is an official language. In most of these countries, anglophone literatures have emerged, even where English is not the first language for the majority of the population.

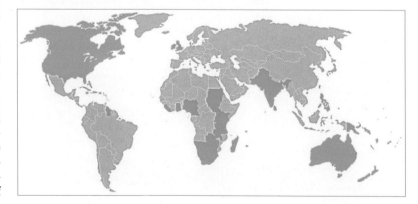

## Timeline: The British Empire

| | |
|---|---|
| **1600** | East India Company founded (for trade rather than colonization) |
| **1607** | Jamestown settlement starts British colonization of America; Britain participates in transatlantic slave trade |
| **1757** | Battle of Plassey makes East India Company the dominant political force on the subcontinent |
| **1763** | Peace of Amiens eliminates France as colonial rival |
| **1788** | Colonization of Australia, mainly with convicts |
| **1877** | Queen Victoria crowned Empress of India; Britain participates in 'Scramble for Africa' in late nineteenth century |
| **1914** | British Empire at its zenith, comprises 20 % of world's population |
| **1931** | Statute of Westminster: Virtual independence of 'White Dominions' |
| **1947** | India becomes independent; Partition |
| **1949** | 'Commonwealth of Nations' replaces 'British Commonwealth' |
| **1960s** | Most British colonies in Africa and the Caribbean become independent |

blended into each other within the larger history of "overlapping territories and intertwined histories" (Said 3) brought into being by the British Empire, they nevertheless gave rise to distinct social, cultural and linguistic patterns that transformed large parts of the world and generated powerful legacies, some of which have remained in place long after the global demise of colonialism.

**Plantation slavery.** Historically speaking, these patterns can all be traced back several centuries to the very beginning of the colonial enterprise. From the late fifteenth century onwards, Europe's colonial interests were directed not only to the 'New World,' but also to Africa and Asia; in terms of their repercussions in global history, Bartholomew Diaz' journey around the Cape of Good Hope in 1487 and Vasco da Gama's sea voyage to India in 1498 were no less consequential than Christopher Columbus's 'discovery' of the Bermudas in 1492. When Britain entered the global struggle for colonial power in the late sixteenth and early seventeenth century, first to contest and later to supplant the hegemony of Portugal and Spain, the first two colonial global play-

ers, it embarked both on conquest (e.g. by wresting Jamaica from the Spanish in 1655) and on settlement (e.g. of Barbados in 1624). Yet, from the mid-seventeenth century onwards, plantation slavery began to replace earlier patterns of European settlement in Britain's New World colonies; by the eighteenth century, the **Triangular Trade** between Britain (manufacturing cheap industrial goods and weapons), Africa (providing slaves) and the New World colonies (producing plantation goods such as tobacco, cotton and sugar) was well established, and millions of enslaved Africans had been transported to the New World in what became known as the **Middle Passage**. Modern plantation slavery gave rise to social regimes based on brutal oppression on the one hand and covert resistance on the other. It also engendered a world-wide struggle for its abolition (resulting first in the abolition of the slave trade in 1807 and later in the abolition of slavery within the British Empire in 1834). Its most significant legacy today consists in long-standing processes of **creolization** that gave the lie to colonial visions of order as well as racist fantasies of purity, and produced a new mixed breed of people, cultures, religions and languages that has remained a constitutive feature of areas such as the Caribbean to the present day.

**European settlement** emerged as the dominant form of colonization in other parts of the world. When Britain emerged victoriously from its global contest with France for colonial hegemony in South Asia, the Americas and the Pacific after a protracted series of wars in the eighteenth century, the stage was set for an unprecedented influx of settlers from England, Scotland and Ireland to Canada (which had originally been explored and settled by the French), Australia and New Zealand during the nineteenth century. European settlers claiming 'pioneer' status soon outnumbered and displaced the original indigenous populations in these colonies, most blatantly in Australia, where the notorious *'terra nullius'* **doctrine** negated some 50,000 years of aboriginal settlement and became the cornerstone of a vicious racism that plagued Australian society far into the twentieth century and beyond. From the mid-nineteenth century onwards, these colonies (later designated as '**White Dominions**') edged their way towards national integration and independence from a colonial power that had learned its lesson from the American Revolution and avoided snubbing its remaining settler colonies; by the early twentieth century they had developed nationalisms of their own and finally became

Loading plan of a ship transporting slaves from Africa to America

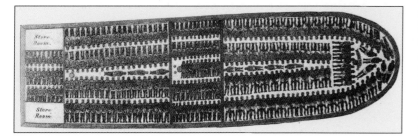

sovereign nation states (as laid down in the Statute of Westminster in 1931), albeit with the British Crown as nominal head of state. Despite earlier legislation to maintain the British or at least the European character of the settler colonies by curbing non-European immigration (particularly from Asia), Canada, Australia and New Zealand became **multicultural societies**. During the last decades of the twentieth century, they all acknowledged this status (e.g. through Canada's Multiculturalism Act that made Canada the first country to officially declare itself a multicultural nation in 1988) and began a process of reconciliation with the indigenous populations that had proven far more resilient in social, political and cultural terms than earlier fantasies of 'vanishing peoples unfit for modernity' had thought possible. In linguistic terms, the former settler colonies developed the largest communities of mother tongue speakers of English outside Britain and the USA, whose distinct varieties of English were supplemented by further varieties of indigenous and immigrant Englishes.

The European settler colonies in **Africa** followed a rather different pattern of development. Although South Africa was somewhat implausibly counted among the 'White Dominions,' nowhere in Africa did white settlers outnumber the African population, and they remained a small minority in most British colonies. The political influence of that minority grew beyond all proportions, however, when white settlers blocked decolonization and the transition towards independence initiated after World War II and thus sparked off bloody conflicts such as the Mau-Mau movement in Kenya in the 1950s or the liberation war in Rhodesia (today's Zimbabwe) in the 1970s. When even South Africa's infamous **Apartheid system**, the most resilient of these settler regimes, was forced to hand over power to the country's black majority in the early 1990s, the era of European settler domination in Africa finally came to an end. While this era has left few cultural or linguistic legacies in most parts of Africa, post-Apartheid South Africa

today is home to a large number of mother tongue speakers of South African English that have become part of the 'rainbow nation's' cultural and linguistic mosaic.

Colonial conquest. It was neither plantation slavery nor white settlement, however, that became the dominant experience for the vast majority of Britain's globally dispersed colonial subjects. The conquest of India from the mid-eighteenth century onwards and the '**Scramble for Africa**' during the 1880s and 90s brought hundreds of millions of people under British colonial control, many of whom continued to be governed by Maharajas and Nizams, Emirs and Paramount Chiefs. Under the widespread system of '**Indirect Rule**' practiced throughout the British Empire, these traditional rulers acknowledged British suzerainty and organized the fiscal and economic incorporation of their subjects into British-run systems of domination. Approximately half of British India and large territories in Africa were governed in this manner, but even where direct rather than indirect rule prevailed (as in the other half of India), Britain's colonies of conquest were controlled by relatively few Europeans: at the height of the British Raj in India, some 300 million Indians were ruled by no more than 125,000 British administrators, soldiers and traders. An iron-fisted '**Pax Britannica**' made sure that British interests prevailed throughout the British Empire, but in contrast to France and its centralized system of colonial rule that regarded 'départements d'outre mer' located thousands of kilometres away from the French mother country as integral parts of the French nation, Britain never dreamt of 'overseas counties' and did not attempt to systematically transform its colonies of conquest into replicas of itself. Instead, Britain sought to create a small "class who may be interpreters between us and the millions whom we govern," as Thomas Babington Macaulay recommended in his notorious "Minute on Education" in 1835: "a class of persons Indian in blood and colour, but English in taste, in opinions, in morals, and in intellect" (94).

*The 'Scramble for Africa' marked a peak of European colonialism.*

## 4.2 | Global Englishes: Colonial Legacies, Multiculturalism, and New Diversity

Although the majority of people throughout South Asia and what is somewhat misleadingly often referred to as 'Anglophone Africa' did not, in fact, speak English during colonial times (and do not do

so today), the English language nevertheless became a vitally important means of communication—not only as the language of colonial administration, but also as a medium of education, commerce and politics. English became the '**second language**' in the modern nation states of South Asia that emerged from the partition of British India in 1947 (India, Pakistan and Bangladesh) as well as Burma (renamed Myanmar by its military rulers) and Sri Lanka (known during colonial times as Ceylon), as well as in independent Nigeria, Ghana, Kenya, Sambia and numerous other sub-Saharan African countries. In all these locations, English today is not only the language of globalization, but also a locally adapted *lingua franca* (cf. section VI.1.1) that has diversified into countless second language varieties of English and has become part of multilingual societies where it interacts with a plethora of other languages—some huge, like Hindi, Bengali, Haussa or Kiswahili, some extremely small, like various 'tribal languages' in India or languages of small ethnic groups in Africa. The relationship of second-language speakers—and writers—to their "stepmother tongue" (Skinner) may be complicated or even strained for a wide variety of historical, political and cultural reasons, but second-language literatures today constitute one of the fastest-growing and most productive sites of world literature written in English.

In close conjunction with colonial structures and policies at first, but increasingly with dynamics of their own, the cultural processes within which the new English literatures emerged have moved towards a high level of transnational and transcultural interrelatedness and enmeshment. While the spread of English as a globalized—also literary—language through the process of colonization and its aftermath is a central factor for the emergence of the so-called new literatures in English, the forced and voluntary mobility of populations during and after the colonial period presents another important axis along which to conceptualize this development, both historically and contemporarily. Forced migration, such as the institution first of slavery and then of indenture that brought workers from India to Fiji, East and South Africa, and to the Caribbean after the abolition of slavery in 1834, have created African and Indian (as well as a wide variety of other) communities across the British Empire. Decolonization, the dissolution of the British Empire, and increasing migration from the former colonies after the Second World War brought about new manifestations of a process that had begun much earlier.

## 4.3 | The Concept of Diaspora

Estimates vary for the Atlantic slave trade, but it is assumed that between the 1500s and the nineteenth century, 11 million Africans were shipped as slaves to South America, the Caribbean, and North America; between 1837 and 1920, over a million Indians were brought to the Caribbean, the Pacific Islands as well as to South and East Africa. Both forms of involuntary migration as well as later movements onwards to other countries formed the basis of communities of Africans, or respectively Indians, all over the British Empire.

The populations that were thus displaced were—at least in their primary displacement—highly heterogeneous: African slaves came from different peoples, spoke different languages, and brought with them different cultural practices. These forced new community formations, however, came to be perceived over time as sharing certain cultural traits as well as a 'homeland.' It was in part these perceived commonalities that have led to the appropriation of the concept of 'diaspora' for displaced communities—as well as for literatures growing out of these communities—in the context of the British Empire and later global constellations after World War II.

The term '**diaspora**' has been defined in a number of different, occasionally even contradictory ways (see box). A relatively restrictive use would highlight not only the migration 'away from home' and the memory kept of that home over generations, a memory often critically or affirmatively addressed in literary texts; it would also not lose sight of the forced character of the

**Definition**

Very generally, drawing historically on the Jewish displacement from Palestine under Roman occupation in the first and second centuries AD, → diaspora used to refer to populations that have been displaced from a homeland, settled in two or more places away from this homeland, and that have retained over generations a memory (and often idealization) of 'home' constitutive of group identity (see e.g. Clifford). In contemporary usage, the concept has become somewhat inflationary, as it increasingly tends to designate any migrant community.

original displacement—Jewish, Armenian, African, or Indian. But even within these populations, scholars increasingly distinguish between **'old' diasporas**, that is, those established by forced displacement such as slavery, indenture, or genocide; and **'new' diasporas** of populations that may claim such forced migrations as part of collective history but that contemporarily tend to be based on voluntary migration, such as for educational purposes or economic opportunities (Clifford). The understanding of both, old and new diasporas, is complicated by migration movements that have been termed 'double' or even "**triple diasporization**": for instance, the primary dislocation of Indians to the Caribbean or East Africa, where they made a home, and then onwards for instance to the U.S., Canada, or Great Britain (Fludernik; Hall).

'Diaspora' differs from related terms such as 'exile' in that it does not primarily focus on the individual, but on the community. Linking diaspora to concepts of hybridity and multiculturalism, Monika Fludernik suggests that the concept of diaspora functions—through its focus on the collective—to resolve "problems inherent in the individualistic design of the hybridity concept, and that both scenarios [diaspora and hybridity] are answers to the tensions and contradictions present in the politics of multiculturalism" (xxiv). Diaspora is thus understood not only historically, as referring to the spatial and cultural displacements experienced by specific populations as a result of colonial policies, but also with regard to contemporary constellations in countries such as Great Britain or Canada which, since the second half of the twentieth century, have struggled for appropriate ways to accommodate ethnic difference, politically and culturally.

This analysis of the function—not only the content—of the term 'diaspora' highlights yet another central point: diasporas, as the importance of memory attests to and as Vijay Mishra has illustrated with regard to the Indian diaspora, are never simply social realities of collective displacement. Diaspora has a strongly imaginary aspect appropriately termed—in reference to Benedict Anderson's concept of the '**imagined community**' of the nation—the diasporic imaginary (Fludernik). In this context, notions such as 'nation,' 'community' or 'diaspora' are understood not primarily as social facts, but as 'imagined' in the sense that social constellations need to be imagined as providing a common ground of identification for individuals in order to be socially and politically effective. This is accomplished, for instance, by educational institutions, but also through literature (Anderson). Hence, the concept of diaspora has a significant impact on the new literatures in English: as a framework in which authors write and to which they refer; as a topic about which they write; and as a central part of community construction. At the same time, diasporic communities and their cultural manifestations challenge the very understanding of culture—and, by extension, literature—as firmly rooted in a particular place of origin: for while there is the often idealized notion of or at least the implicit reference to a 'homeland,' historical as well as contemporary processes of cultural transformation and **hybridization** call into question the ongoing 'rootedness' of culture and literature in the face of large-scale migrations.

Diaspora writing points to the constructedness of notions of home and origin.

## 4.4 | Globalization

This opens up a related, but discursively distinct context, the context of globalization, in which the emergence and development of the new literatures in English has to be understood. Very generally, globalization means a high level of **interrelatedness** in terms of diversified economic, cultural, social, or ecological structures, etc.; so in contrast to much of the everyday understanding of globalization, it is neither purely economic nor simply culturally homogenizing. If British colonialism presented a globalizing phenomenon, the economic, political, cultural, and technological developments that have shaped the second half of the twentieth century significantly sped up and intensified earlier connections.

As a consequence, local events are affected significantly by what happens in distant locations; thus, spatial constellations, as theorists of modernity such as Anthony Giddens have argued, have become abstract; more concrete places now have to be understood in relation to the abstraction of space in the context of globalization, which fundamentally changes the ways in which place offers a sense of identity.

## 4.5 | Anglophone Literatures

This obviously has a significance for literature and culture that is hard to underestimate. Not only is culture not inextricably bound up with place anymore (if it ever was), but the mobility of culture also suggests processes of **hybridization** and **transculturation**. For the study of literatures in English, this implies not only a necessary and growing scepticism with regard to national or regional concepts of literature, as the varying national pigeon-holes—Indian, British, Caribbean, African, Canadian, American—for authors such as Sam Selvon, Salman Rushdie, M. G. Vassanji, or Bharati Mukherjee attest to. Also, literary texts more often than not deliberately draw on a broad variety of themes and models, cultural codes and frameworks, aesthetics and forms that connect literary production, even those texts that refer to a very specific regional or ethnic context, to globalized networks of culture.

Representative surveys In the following, this process of cultural transformation within and across national frameworks will be illustrated by focusing on distinct examples, that is, the development of Anglophone literatures in Trinidad/Tobago, India, Canada, and Nigeria. Each example takes as its starting point a specific form of colonial organization and experience, as sketched in the historical overview. However, none of these literatures can be reduced to their colonial history; rather, each example with its specificities highlights the historical and contemporary dynamics of the development of Anglophone literature and eventually problematizes the category of 'national literature.'

### 4.5.1 | Trinidad/Tobago

**Caribbean Literature.** The literatures of Trinidad/Tobago are usually considered in the context of 'Caribbean literature.' The 'Caribbean' is a term that subsumes a number of comparable, but nevertheless in their historical and contemporary constellations highly specific countries. As a cultural region, the Caribbean is shaped by shared historical experiences of European (Spanish, French, British, and Dutch) colonialism, and since the late nineteenth century also by frequent political and military interventions by the United States; the contemporary situation is characterized largely by external economic (and, by extension, political)

dependencies—that run counter to regional integration—on the one hand, and by the development of culturally independent, hybridized forms of artistic expression (Gewecke) on the other. In terms of political independence, there are important differences between the countries that make up the Caribbean: from Haiti as the first independent nation in the Caribbean (1804) to still-dependent overseas territories such as Montserrat (UK) or Martinique (France), there is a broad spectrum of political constellations and developments as well as languages, from standard English and other European languages to different Creole languages as a result of cultural and linguistic processes of hybridization.

These legacies of colonization and enforced dislocation as well as of contemporary diaspora have resulted in uniquely diverse Caribbean cultures of creolization and transculturation; literary negotiations between the effects of transnational movements and aesthetics, on the one hand, and the insistence on the specificity of locale on the other have shaped cultural production in the Caribbean. Hence, in contrast to other postcolonial national literatures, for instance those of Canada, Caribbean literatures tend to be less concerned with (critical or affirmative) investigations of 'the nation,' but rather with the exploration of often highly conflictual cultural dynamics in specific locations as well as across and beyond the Caribbean.

**Historical Background.** Trinidad/Tobago in particular illustrates painfully well the historical and contemporary contradictions of the Caribbean, as well as the development of independent literatures in Anglophone parts of the region. Trinidad/Tobago has been shaped historically by slavery and the plantation economy; demographically, the people of Indian and African descent form the two largest groups (over 80%), less than 20% of the population is of Chinese or European heritage. Like other Caribbean countries, Trinidad/Tobago's

---

**Key Texts: Trinidad**

**C. L. R. James,** *Minty Alley* (1936)
**Sam Selvon,** *The Lonely Londoners* (1956)
**V. S. Naipaul,** *A House for Mr. Biswas* (1961)
**Earl Lovelance,** *The Dragon Can't Dance* (1979)
**Derek Walcott,** *Omeros* (1990)
**Shani Mootoo,** *Cereus Blooms at Night* (1997)

development, politically and culturally, is grounded in its economic transition from a plantation society and its impact on the relationship between the different ethnic groups; in the process of decolonization (it became independent in 1962); in the emergence of Creole/hybridized identities and cultural forms; and, since after World War II, large-scale migration to Great Britain, the United States, and Canada (see Gewecke).

Given the historical background of colonialism and a plantation economy built on strict racial hierarchies, it is not surprising that early Caribbean literature was produced by the white elite, and primarily so in Jamaica and British Guinea (Gohrisch). It was only in the 1920s and 1930s that a more vital literary scene emerged that encompassed Trinidadians of African and Indian descent; critics have called this period the '**Trinidad Renaissance**' (Saunders). This analogy to the Harlem Renaissance emerging at the same time in New York points to a boom of literary activity that was anti-colonial while aesthetically adhering to European models. For instance, the novel *Minty Alley* (1936) by C. L. R. James—political historian and co-founder of the first anti-colonial literary journal in the Caribbean, the *Beacon*—related in a naturalistic style the life of ordinary people in an urban backyard in Trinidad and set the tone for prose writing in Trinidad, as it was also taken up by writers like the Nobel prize winning V. S. Naipaul in novels such as *Miguel Street* (1959; see Döring, *Postcolonial Literatures*).

**The question of language** was crucial from the beginning. As postcolonial critics have frequently pointed out, colonial power manifests itself significantly in the power of naming (Ashcroft, Griffiths, and Tiffin), and Anglophone postcolonial writers in all parts of the former British Empire (as in other formerly colonized countries) have struggled with the question of how to productively use and transform a colonial language in postcolonial contexts (Ashcroft, Griffiths, and Tiffin; Talib; for the Caribbean in particular, with different foci, see for instance Döring, *Passages*; James). Early on, some writers shifted away from standard English to an emphasis on spoken language, the use of **vernaculars** and **Creoles**. For instance, while the above-named and many other texts use standard English for the narrative and Creole at most for individual characters' direct speech, Sam Selvon's novel *The Lonely Londoners* (1956), the story of Caribbean immigrants in London, is told by a third-person narrator in Creole. While this is a novel of social

critique, this choice of narrative voice has also to be regarded as a strong cultural statement: this seeming adjustment to 'how people speak' is also to be read as part of the ongoing attempt to find a genuine 'West Indian' voice, a form of cultural decolonization. It generally raises the question of language, the diversification of English, and of the assumptions underlying linguistic and literary standards. Just as creoles are fully developed languages, not the 'incorrect' versions of standard English (or French or Dutch) as which they have been too often seen, texts that use creoles or specific cultural references to Caribbean cultures and traditions (such as Earl Lovelace's *The Dragon Can't Dance*, 1979) were and are no more or less 'particular' than those—usually European—works that had previously been regarded as 'universal.'

The question of language is thus to be placed in the context of a more broadly understood engagement of Caribbean writers with issues such as colonial cultural legacies, cultural autonomy, and processes of transculturation and globalization. In Trinidad and Tobago, writers like Derek Walcott (the first Caribbean author to win the Nobel prize in 1992, who was born in Saint Lucia, but spent formative years in Trinidad from the late 1950s to the 1970s) engaged directly with the European canon by critically re-writing canonical texts in a postcolonial Caribbean context both in his poetry and his plays (e.g. in *Pantomime*, 1978, the epic poem *Omeros*, 1990, or *Odyssey: A Stage Version*, 1993). This engagement, however, is not to be understood as limited to an investment in countering 'European' cultures; rather, writers like Walcott explored the specificities of Caribbean (or as Walcott rather had it, New World) modernities, a critical and creative move that challenged the very notion of modernity as 'Western' and 'European.'

The 1980s and particularly the 1990s saw an increasing **diversification of themes and styles** in works by Trinidadian authors. Namely, with the increasing prominence of women writers, gender relations and gender constructions came into focus; more recently, writers like Shani Mootoo in *Cereus Blooms at Night* (1997) and *Valmiki's Daughter* (2008) or Lawrence Scott in *Aelred's Sin* (1998) also took up issues of homosexuality and transgender.

**Transcultural Perspectives.** The previous examples, despite their differences in approach, language, genre, and style point to an inherent tension within Trinidadian literary development: the oscillation between local/national Trinidadian/

*Derek Walcott's Nobel prize fostered interest in Caribbean literature.*

The difficulties
of regional and national
categorization

Caribbean frameworks and transnational contexts, both with regard to the texts' settings and to the authors' lives. At present, most prominent Trinidadian writers live outside of the Caribbean. This more generally raises questions about categories such as 'national literature' or 'regional literatures' that have dominated postcolonial literary studies until recently; consequently, it also prompts us to question assumptions about 'national culture,' since all of these writers deliberately draw on a variety of cultural resources and deploy strategies that are increasingly discussed from a transcultural perspective.

In fact, despite all differences, this links the Caribbean and 'Caribbean literature' to the other regions and countries discussed here: the contemporary literary scene is shaped by migration, diaspora, and transcultural dynamics that fundamentally unsettle taken-for-granted cultural, ethnic, and national ascriptions. Would Austin Clarke be considered Canadian or Caribbean? Is Caryl Phillips a Caribbean or a British writer? These questions, that implicitly or explicitly are so common in the classroom and the media as well as in literary scholarship, obviously make less and less sense. In the picture that emerges here, post-colonial countries like India, Nigeria, or Trinidad/Tobago are marked by significant literary out-migration as well as **transmigration**; the literary landscape of largely 'receiving' countries such as Canada or the UK at the same time is also fundamentally changed—primarily by the categorical questions that these movements pose for literary analysis and institutionalization.

## 4.5.2 | India

**Historical Background.** Like the Caribbean, but in contrast to most of Africa (with the significant exception of South Africa where colonial rule lasted for less than a century), significant parts of the Indian subcontinent were dominated by Britain for more than two centuries. The **British East India Company** was founded as early as 1599, and in the seventeenth century set up 'factories' in Surat, Madras, Bombay and Calcutta to organize and safeguard its trading activities with India; from the mid-eighteenth century onwards, 'John Company' (as the East India Company was called in India) began a systematic conquest first of Bengal, later of other regions, that secured its control over India's

economy and forced Indian rulers to acquiesce to its hegemony on the subcontinent. After the defeat of the so-called '**Indian Mutiny**' of 1857, which had severely threatened that hegemony, India became a Crown Colony, partly administered directly by Britain and partly under the nominal sovereignty of 'princely states' that remained formally independent, but acknowledged Britain's suzerainty with regard to economic, fiscal, military and diplomatic matters. When Queen Victoria was crowned 'Empress of India' in 1877, the British Raj (as Britain's Indian empire was known on the subcontinent) seemed impregnable, but less than a decade later the Indian National Congress was founded and (at first fairly moderate) nationalist agitation began. After World War I, the nationalist movement led by the charismatic Mahatma Gandhi became a serious challenge to British colonial rule. When the British Raj finally came to an end in 1947, the subcontinent was partitioned into the new nation states of India and Pakistan, with up to a million people losing their lives and some 15 million people losing their homes.

**The Question of Language.** This long-standing conflictual relationship between Britain and India decisively shaped not only the linguistic set-up of the Indian subcontinent, but also the emergence of English-language literature in India. After British India (still under 'John Company' rule at the time) had decided to adopt an 'Anglicist' policy (focusing on English as a medium of communication) rather than an 'Orientalist' approach (utilizing Persian and Sanskrit) in its efforts to educate a small native elite that should act as 'middlemen' in its dealings with India, English was—quite rightly—seen as an instrument of colonial hegemony by many; during the later stages of the nineteenth century, it also became the medium of expression of the Anglo-Indians, people of English or 'mixed' descent who were born or lived permanently in India. At the same time, English became an important medium of communication, education and political agitation among English-educated Indians who began to use their education to further social reform and political change. The debate over the legitimacy and utility of English in India thus reaches far back into the nineteenth century: while Hindu reformers such as Ram Mohan Roy and Gopal Krishna Gokhale advocated the use of English as a medium of education and social change, radical nationalists such as Bal Gangadhar Tilak denounced English as a foreign imposition that should eventually disappear from Indian public life—although for reasons of political expediency the latter also founded the English-language newspaper *The Mahratta*.

**English-language Literature.** During the nineteenth century, English-language literature in India thus followed two quite distinct trajectories: on the one hand, Anglo-Indian authors such as Nobel laureate Rudyard Kipling projected their vision of Indian life, culture and (colonial) society, a vision that rarely challenged the rationale of colonial rule, but at times—as in Kipling's *Kim* (1901)—moved decisively beyond the orientalist fantasies and stereotypes that often characterized British writing on India. On the other hand, members of the newly emerging English-educated Indian middle class began to use English (often alongside other Indian languages) to promote their ideas of social reform in journalistic and essayistic writing—as in Ram Mohan Roy's *Conference between an Advocate for, and an Opponent of the Practice of Burning Widows Alive* (1818, published in both English and Bengali), or in Romesh Chunder Dutt's *Three Years in Europe* (1872). While some of the protagonists of the '**Bengali Renaissance**' also wrote English-language poetry and fiction (the first Indian novel written in English was Bankim Chandra Chatterjee's *Rajmohan's Wife*, serialized in 1864), many nineteenth-century Indian creative writers preferred to write in Indian languages.

Given the vitality and popularity of Indian-language print media and book publishing, English-language literature has remained a relatively small segment within India's overall multilingual media landscape until today, but both its scope and its impact changed dramatically during the twentieth century. From the 1930s onwards, three major writers placed Indo-English writing firmly onto India's literary map and contributed significantly to making Indian literature known to a wider world: Mulk Raj Anand exposed the social injustice not only of colonial rule, but also of tradi-

tional Indian caste oppression and the exploitation of cheap labour in novels such as *Untouchable* (1935), *Coolie* (1936), and *Two Leaves and a Bud* (1937), and proposed a socialist humanism to overcome the social rifts characterizing Indian society; Raja Rao wrote a classic of anticolonial literature (*Kanthapura*, 1938) that not only exposed the arrogance of British colonial rule in an archetypal Indian village, but also highlighted the transformation of 'traditional' India through the revolutionary thought of Gandhiism, and in later works such as *The Serpent and The Rope* (1960) explored the potential of India's philosophical heritage for an understanding of Indian modernity; R. K. Narayan surveyed the multiple ironies engendered by the clash between 'traditional' village life worlds and rapid modernization processes as well as by India's cultural, linguistic and social diversity in a humorous mode that became the hallmark of works like *The Guide* (1958), an ironic portrayal of India's fascination with charismatic spiritual leaders, and a whole series of novels set in the fictitious small South Indian town Malgudi.

The three 'grand old men of Indian letters' were only part of a much wider literary dynamic, however, to which many other writers contributed, including well-known women authors such as Ruth Prawer Jhabvala, Kamala Das, Kamala Markandaya, or Anita Desai, whose work not only presented a critical view on patriarchal ideologies and gender relations in modern India, but—as in Desai's *In Custody* (1984)—also dealt with the sociocultural rift between Hindi and Urdu culture on the subcontinent. The publication of Salman Rushdie's *Midnight's Children* (1981) marked a new phase of Indian-English literature: combining long-standing traditions of drawing on India's ancient epic literature and its rich oral tradition in modern literature with a postmodern narrative stance, **magical realist** fabulation and a thorough critique of the political mythologies of post-independence India, Rushdie's novel paved the way for a new generation of Indian writers such as Vikram Chandra (*Red Earth and Pouring Rain*, 1995), Kiran Nagarkar (*Cuckold*, 1997), or Arundhati Roy (*The God of Small Things*, 1997), who used a wide array of postmodernist techniques to critically explore the intricacies and contradictions of the subcontinent's turbulent history as well as the predicaments of contemporary India faced with the manifold challenges of an increasingly globalized world.

**Transnational Dimensions.** While English-language writing on the Indian subcontinent has al-

*Indian literature through the twentieth century*

---

**Key Texts: India**

**Mulk Raj Anand,** *Untouchable* (1935)
**Raja Rao,** *Kanthapura* (1938)
**R. K. Narayan,** *A Tiger for Malgudi* (1983)
**Anita Desai,** *Clear Light of Day* (1980)
**Salman Rushdie,** *Midnight's Children* (1981)
**Arundhati Roy,** *The God of Small Things* (1997)
**Amitav Ghosh,** *Sea of Poppies* (2008)
**Aravind Adiga,** *The White Tiger* (2008)

ways had **transcultural** features, the **transnational** dimensions of Indian English literature and the interaction between Indian diasporic writing and literature on the subcontinent have become more pronounced in recent decades. Writers like Salman Rushdie, Amitav Ghosh, Kiran Desai and Aravind Adiga, who have lived outside India for much of their lives, not only continue to contribute to Indian literature in English by addressing Indian themes and concerns, but also thematize time and again the diasporic or transnational connections that tie India not only to its neighbouring countries on the Indian subcontinent, but also to Africa, Europe, the Americas and the Pacific region. Thus, Ghosh's *The Circle of Reason* (1986) not only scrutinizes the impact of refugees created by the Indo-Pakistani conflict on a Bengali village, but also sends a cast of characters on an intricate flight following traditional Indian migration routes to the Gulf states, North Africa and Europe; Kiran Desai's *The Inheritance of Loss* (2006) stages an intricate narrative relationship between an illegal Indian migrant in the USA and a young woman in India who are both struggling for a viable sense of identity beyond the conventional confines of nationalism; Aravind Adiga's epistolary novel *The White Tiger* (2008) takes a critical look at 'traditional' forms of social oppression and exploitation that underlie India's globally booming IT industry through a series of letters written by an Indian entrepreneur in Bangalore to the Chinese premier Wen Jiabao; and Salman Rushdie's *The Enchantress of Florence* (2008) explores long-standing historical parallels between the sixteenth-century India of Akbar the Great and the Renaissance Florence of Niccolò Machiavelli. Indian writing in English has been situated from its early beginnings at the intersection of various national, regional and transnational cultural and literary dynamics; in the twenty-first century, it can be confined less than ever before to a narrowly territorialized understanding of national literature.

Global perspectives in
recent Indian writing

## 4.5.3 | Canada

**Two Colonial Traditions.** Canada and its literature can be seen on the one hand as exemplary for the development in those colonies in which European settlers formed a demographic majority. On the other hand, there are a number of specificities that have to be noted. A central feature is the **bifur-cated literary history** growing out of two colonial traditions, French and English; while France was replaced as a colonial power in North America after the Seven Years' War (or the Indian Wars, as they were called in North America) in 1763, the tension-ridden relationship of the French and English settlers in what became 'Canada' has helped shape contemporary constellations. While French-language literature underwent a very distinct development (for a literary history that covers both English- and French-language literatures in Canada see for instance Nischik), the coexistence of these two strong European-based traditions and literatures continues to be a central factor for the understanding of Canada and its literatures, as does Canada's highly regionalized political and cultural development.

Among the so-called settler colonies, Canada was the first one to achieve the status of a Dominion in 1867 through the British North America Act (BNA). This did not mean full sovereignty or independence from Great Britain, but entailed a certain degree of autonomy that helped foster the development of a national consciousness over the decades following the BNA.

**The Confederation Poets.** While this was not immediately reflected aesthetically in the prose of the time, the poetic development was innovative and has to be seen as part of this growing self-confidence of Canada as a nation. In this context, the so-called **Confederation Poets** Charles G. D. Roberts, Bliss Carman, Archibald Lampman, and Duncan Campbell Scott played an important role. The Confederation Poets were not a poetic school in the sense that they shared an artistic agenda; rather, their commonalities can be found in their shared decade of birth (the 1860s, that is, the decade of confederation), their social and educational background, their literary shaping by the English Romantics and by American models such as Emerson or Whitman, their constant direct reference to one another, and their agenda of establishing 'Canada'—for instance the Canadian landscape—as a legitimate theme of poetry (see New; Nischik).

The Confederation Poets are interesting in yet another sense, for they illustrate the 'double-bind' of Anglophone Canadian literary development since the second half of the nineteenth century: by their orientation towards international models, first British, then American, and later in a more comprehensive sense '**internationalist**'; and by the attempt to define and develop specifically na-

## Key Texts: Canada

**Susanna Moodie,** *Roughing it in the Bush* (1852)
**Margaret Laurence,** *The Stone Angel* (1964)
**Mordecai Richler,** *St. Urbain's Horseman* (1971)
**Joy Kogawa,** *Obasan* (1981)
**Tomson Highway,** *The Rez Sisters* (1986)
**Michael Ondaatje,** *The English Patient* (1992)
**Margaret Atwood,** *The Blind Assassin* (2000)
**Dionne Brand,** *What We All Long For* (2005)

tional themes and modes of expression. While the orientation towards Britain and the United States was not exclusively due to the artistic models they provided, but also to the publishing infrastructure which Canada lacked, later internationalist tendencies—such as the development of modernist poetry and to some extent short stories (and also art) in the 1920s and, belated in the 1950s with Sheila Watson's *The Double Hook*, long prose—have to be read rather in terms of a self-understanding of Canadian writers as part of international developments and as a refusal to be instrumentalized for cultural-nationalist purposes.

**Modernism.** While the First World War led to a boost of national self-confidence in Canada, it also gave rise to an increasing openness and the attempt by Canadian artists to connect themselves to international movements such as modernism. In the 1920s for instance, poets such as F. R. Scott, A. M. Klein and A. J. M. Smith criticized both the derivative artistic form chosen by the Confederation Poets and their successors and the focus on 'Canadian' themes. In his often-cited 1927 poem "The Canadian Authors Meet," Scott bitingly takes up what he sees as superficial nationalism and self-congratulatory artistic posing.

The cultural nationalist perspective by no means dominated only the literary and historical periods that could be seen as constitutive for Canada as a political and cultural nation. In 1972, **Margaret Atwood** published the study (and programmatic pamphlet) *Survival: A Thematic Guide to Canadian Literature*, in which she identifies—in direct line with literary scholar Northrop Frye's concept of the **garrison mentality**—survival as the central theme in Canadian literature. This hypothesis is both descriptive and prescriptive for what Atwood sees as Canadian victim positions and the transformation to a culturally and politically self-affirmative 'Canadian' stand. Since its

publication, the concept of 'survival' has received severe criticism, but it nevertheless remains important for understanding the attempt to come to terms with 'outside' cultural influences and the search for 'genuinely Canadian' modes of artistic expression.

**Regional Differentiation.** At the same time, this search for a self-confident grounding of a 'Canadian experience' found expression—somewhat paradoxically—in a strong regional differentiation. Margaret Laurence, for instance, in her so-called 'Manawaka Cycle' consisting of four novels and a collection of short stories written between 1964 and 1974, sketches individual, closely intertwined lives in the fictional Manitoba town of Manawaka; and, with a focus on the Scottish population in the Maritimes, Alistair MacLeod's short stories explore the importance of specific places and their history for individuals and communities. However, while these and other writers—Robert Kroetsch, Rudy Wiebe, Aritha van Herk among them—are often grouped as **'regional writers,'** their work investigates 'region' in the larger framework of the nation as well as transnational processes: Margaret Laurence grounds her protagonists' lives in historical migrations and investigations of contemporary social structures that exceed the confines of the specific region, and MacLeod's short stories investigate the characters' conflicts against the background of specific localities as affected by national and transnational economic processes.

This careful, at times even anxious, self-reflexivity with regard to place, community, and identities can be seen, with reservations, as characteristic

Lawren Harris, "Lake and Mountains" (1928). In art, the Canadian landscape became an expression of national identity with the so-called Group of Seven.

Interpretation

### F. R. Scott, "The Canadian Authors Meet" (1927)

Expansive puppets percolate self-unction
Beneath a portrait of the Prince of Wales.
Miss Crotchet's muse has somehow failed to function,
Yet she's a poetess. Beaming, she sails

From group to chattering group, with such a dear     5
Victorian saintliness, as is her fashion,
Greeting the other unknowns with a cheer—
Virgins of sixty who still write of passion.

The air is heavy with Canadian topics,
And Carman, Lampman, Roberts, Campbell, Scott,     10
Are measured for their faith and philanthropics,
Their zeal for God and King, their earnest thought.

The cakes are sweet, but sweeter is the feeling
That one is mixing with the *literati*;
It warms the old, and melts the most congealing.     15
Really, it is a most delightful party.

Shall we go round the mulberry bush, or shall
We gather at the river, or shall we
Appoint a Poet Laureate this fall,
Or shall we have another cup of tea?     20

O Canada, O Canada, O can
A day go by without new authors springing
To paint the native maple, and to plan
More ways to set the selfsame welkin ringing?

In this 1927 poem, F. R. Scott satirizes what he believed to be a stale, self-congratulatory, and uninspired literary atmosphere in early twentieth century Canada. Written in a seemingly simple alternate rhyme scheme, the poem is both a critique of the formal adherence to Victorian poetry (and thus to British models already outdated in Britain at the time) and of a superficial 'Canadianism' manifest in the obsessive use of natural images. The lines "The air is heavy with Canadian topics / And Carman, Lampman, Roberts, Campbell, Scott," refer to the 'Confederation Poets' mentioned in this chapter. Since the late nineteenth century, this bitingly suggests, little has happened in the Canadian literary scene, and those who understand themselves as poets have become complacent: it is not art that matters but a false artistic atmosphere ("The cakes are sweet, but sweeter is the feeling / That one is mixing with the *literati*"), and the sentiments expressed in poetry lack any connection to creativity and life ("Virgins of sixty who still write of passion"). The last stanza plays with "O Canada," the first line of the song that—first performed in 1880 and later played for instance at the Diamond Jubilee of the Confederation in 1927—was to become the national anthem in 1980. By the use of an enjambment—the first two lines have to be read without break after "O can"—it ironically shifts from national celebration to lament and disgust with the repetition of 'Canadian' imagery such as the maple.

for Canadian literature. This concerns both the cultural nationalist perspective as well as its criticism from a more internationalist standpoint.

**Internationalist Orientation.** The 1980s in particular can be regarded as the beginning of a more consciously internationalist decade. This is largely an effect of fundamental societal transformations: Canada's immigration laws were changed in the mid-1960s, and these changes for the first time eliminated 'race' as a category for immigration; and in 1971, Prime Minister Pierre Trudeau declared **multiculturalism** an official policy (followed 17 years later by the Multiculturalism Act). This led to a significant shift with regard to Canadian self-understanding as a multicultural society. The presence of 'ethnic' or even 'visible' minorities in Canada is not a new phenomenon: Asian immigration began in the mid-1800s (and was

banned beginning in the late nineteenth/early twentieth centuries until the 1960s), Blacks have lived in eastern Canada since the late eighteenth century, and the presence of First Nations precedes that of Europeans; however, the demographic shifts following the new immigration laws and the importance attributed (at least officially) to cultural diversity as a *value* had a significant impact also on the development of Canadian literature. In contrast to earlier attempts to link Canadian developments with those abroad, as in modernism, the 1980s hence brought about a different shift: so-called minority writers began to play an increasing role in and for Canadian literature. Michael Ondaatje's focus on immigrant communities and their role in 1930s Toronto in his novel *In the Skin of a Lion* (1987), Joy Kogawa's groundbreaking *Obasan* (1981) on the effects of Japanese Canadian internment during the Second World War, Dionne Brand's poetry and prose that exposed racism, sexism, and homophobia in Canadian society, Thomas King's postmodernist blend of Native oral traditions with a comic re-writing of canonical texts and Canadian historiography in *Green Grass, Running Water* (1993) are all examples of an increasing critical investigation of Canadian society from the perspective of ethnic minorities, but also a clear indication for a changing understanding of Canada as a multicultural nation.

Many have regarded this development critically as a process of fragmentation and hence an obstacle to a truly 'national' literature. At the same time, at least more recently, the diversity of Canadian literature—**CanLit** as it is both ironically and affectionately called—has become a source of national pride or even characteristic of Canadian literature per se; a development not only seen critically by those who fear for Canadian 'unity' but also for those who see these writers potentially instrumentalized for a national agenda (Mathur). Authors who have previously been leaning more towards a cultural nationalist position such as Margaret Atwood have become not only internationally known, but internationalist writers. Diversity and international orientation have come to be seen as central to the understanding of Canadian literature. At the same time, and highly ironically so, it is this diversity and the multiple transnational connections referred to and deployed by authors—in their lives and their literature—that calls into question the very model of a national literature.

## 4.5.4 | Nigeria

Like many modern African nation states, Nigeria was 'invented' both by colonialism (that merged various ethnicities and political units into a colonial territory encompassing a large variety of cultures and languages) and by nationalist anticolonialism (that organized an independence movement in the colonial territory which in turn sought to give meaning to the new sovereign nation-to-be through an act of conscious 'nation-building'). Thus from its very beginnings, Anglophone literature in Nigeria formed part of a culturally and linguistically diverse social reality, and participated in a complex process of sociocultural reawakening, self-invention and transformation. Neither the widespread notion that English-language liter-

ature constitutes a 'foreign' imposition on Africa nor the equally widespread idea that African literature in English is essentially a reflection of 'African culture' are thus sufficient to grasp the manifold origins and affiliations of Anglophone writing in Nigeria.

**Beginnings of English-Language Literature.** The earliest stages of English-language literature in West Africa reach back far beyond the creation of modern Nigeria. In the late eighteenth century, Olaudah Equiano published his famous autobiographical slave narrative *The Interesting Narrative of the Life of Olaudah Equiano, or Gustavus Vassa, the African* (1789), a major contribution to the abolitionist cause in the contemporary debates on the abolition of the slave trade in Britain that included a lengthy account of his childhood in the Ibo region of today's Nigeria (the authenticity of which has been contested in recent scholarship, however). In the second half of the nineteenth century, black intellectuals associated with Christian missions and the first institutions of higher education in West Africa such as Edward W. Blyden (Liberia) and J. E. Casely Hayford (Gold Coast, today Ghana) began to publish mainly political and educational texts concerned with the current state and future perspectives of a yet to be colonized Africa; Casely Hayford's *Ethiopia Unbound* (1911), a blend of biographical narrative and political essay focussing on the life of a British-educated West African and his intellectual, religious and political aspirations, has often been considered the first West African novel written in English.

**Anticolonial Literature.** While colonialism in most parts of Nigeria (as in much of West and East Africa) lasted only some 70 years (Britain's systematic colonization of West Africa began in the late 1880s during the '**Scramble for Africa**,' led to the establishment of the 'Colony and Protectorate of Nigeria' in 1914, and ended with Nigeria's independence in 1960), it nevertheless played an im-

---

**Key Texts: Nigeria**

**Chinua Achebe,** *Things Fall Apart* (1958)
**Wole Soyinka,** *The Interpreters* (1965)
**Buchi Emecheta,** *The Joys of Motherhood* (1979)
**Ken Saro-Wiwa,** *Basi and Company: Four Television Plays* (1988)
**Ben Okri,** *The Famished Road* (1991)
**Chimamanda Ngozi Adichie,** *Purple Hibiscus* (2004)
**Chris Abani,** *Graceland* (2004)
**Helon Habila,** *Oil on Water* (2010)

Engaging with European
depictions of Africa

portant role in the emergence and early stages of Nigerian literature in English. Writing in Nigeria began to flourish during the last stages of colonial rule, when a new generation of writers challenged colonialism and its ideological underpinnings (such as European myths of the 'barbarism' of African cultures and societies) and sought to project a new self-confidence based on the aspirations of the independence movement. Chinua Achebe's novel *Things Fall Apart* (1958), a classic of modern African literature and one of the first works by a West African author to gain world-wide recognition, explored the social, cultural and religious life of Umuofia, an Ibo village in Eastern Nigeria, before and during the first encounter with colonialism, and engaged in a conscious act of '**writing back**' (Ashcroft, Griffiths, and Tiffin) to European accounts of 'primitive' Africa in novels such as Joseph Conrad's *Heart of Darkness* (1899/1902) and Joyce Cary's *Mister Johnson* (1939). Achebe's highly innovative literary style that entangled an English-language narrative in a network of allusions to Ibo forms of oral art such as riddles and proverbs (and thus demonstrated the extraordinary creative potential of orality for modern African literature) became an inspiration for a whole generation of African writers exploring the literary uses of 'Africanized' English. At the same time, his seeming acceptance of patriarchal oppression as a 'normal' feature of 'traditional' African culture was challenged by Nigerian women writers such as Flora Nwapa and Buchi Emecheta in the 1960s and 70s, e.g. in Emecheta's novel *The Bride Price* (1976) that presented a critical perspective on gender relations in an Ibo village.

**Postindependence Writing.** As in many other new literatures in English, 'writing back' to colonial discourses and their legacies did not remain a major preoccupation of Nigerian literature for long. Only a few years after independence, a '**literature of disillusionment**' began to grapple with the contemporary social and political realities of Africa's newly independent nations and developed an increasingly critical stance towards ruling elites who seemed to have abandoned the aspirations and ideals of the anticolonial movements. Corruption, abuse of power and the manipulation of ethnic differences for political ends became a major theme in novels such as *The Beautyful Ones Are Not Yet Born* (1968) by the Ghanaian writer Ayi Kwei Armah, or in *The Interpreters* (1965), the first novel by Nige-

ria's Nobel laureate Wole Soyinka. Chinua Achebe's fourth novel, *A Man of the People* (1966), signaled a decisive break with his earlier preoccupation with pre-colonial history and the critique of colonialism and offered a somber diagnosis of the populism and graft of Nigeria's post-independence civilian rulers. The military takeover prognosticated at the end of Achebe's novel became reality as the book was being published: Nigeria plunged into civil war and entered a long-drawn phase of military dictatorship that continued into the 1990s.

From the 1970s onwards, the traumatic legacies of the **Biafra War** (1967–1970), the oppressive impact of military rule on society and the new democratic movements that emerged in the 1980s became important themes in Nigerian literature in English. Once more, English-language writing became a prime means of addressing national issues, e.g. in Wole Soyinka's satirical plays on the deadly power-lust and corruption of Nigeria's military regimes (*From Zia, with Love*, 1992, and *King Baabu*, 2001), in Chinua Achebe's fifth novel highlighting civil society resistance to military rule and the (re)invention of a democratic counter-culture (*Anthills of the Savannah*, 1987), in Ken Saro-Wiwa's popular plays and TV soap operas on the corruption of everyday life in Lagos (*Basi and Company: Four Television Plays*, 1988), and in Helon Habila's magical realist account of student opposition to military oppression (*Waiting for an Angel*, 2002).

**Transnational Dimensions.** Like most of the new literatures in English, Anglophone African writing emerged in a contact zone encompassing a wide variety of transcultural and transnational connections, and contemporary Nigerian writing in English is no exception to this rule. Many of Nigeria's best-known writers have studied, lived or taught abroad, and the experiences and perspectives of Africa's new diasporas have long since become inextricably intertwined with the history of Nigerian literature. Writers such as Ben Okri (*The Famished Road*, 1991), Diran Adebayo (*Some Kind of Black*, 1996), Chimamanda Ngozi Adichie (*Purple Hibiscus*, 2004), Chris Abani (*Graceland*, 2004) and Helon Habila (*Measuring Time*, 2007) testify to the importance of this new **Nigerian diaspora** in African letters and demonstrate that Nigerian literature in English has long outgrown any attempt to restrict it to a nationalistically or territorially circumscribed idea of 'national culture.'

## 4.6 | Conclusion

As the four exemplary 'new literatures in English' presented in this chapter testify to, Anglophone writing in the formerly colonized parts of the world has been shaped by a wide variety of colonial experiences as well as highly diverging patterns of post-independence modernity. On the one hand, the emergence of these literatures is historically rooted in British colonialism and its political, cultural, and linguistic policies; on the other hand, they have responded to new social, political and cultural constellations that have emerged after the end of colonialism. Long-drawn processes of migration (forced and voluntary, transcontinental as well as within newly-independent nation states) have resulted in new patterns of ethnic, cultural and linguistic diversification that belie any attempt to 'place' these literatures into homogenous contexts of 'national' or 'regional' cultures. The new literatures in English are thus **no longer simply 'postcolonial'**: just like the English language they have come to employ as first or second language, they are not only shaped by local circumstances and experiences, but also by globalization processes and intricate networks of transcultural connections. Writing from formerly colonized parts of the world is no longer the voice of a putative 'other,' but part of the constantly transforming and diversifying system of contemporary world literature.

### Select Bibliography

Anderson, Benedict. *Imagined Communities: Reflections on the Origin and Spread of Nationalism.* London: Verso, 1991.

Ashcroft, Bill, Gareth Griffiths, and Helen Tiffin. *The Empire Writes Back: Theory and Practice in Post-Colonial Literatures.* London: Routledge, 1989.

Atwood, Margaret. *Survival: A Thematic Guide to Canadian Literature.* Toronto: Anansi, 1972.

Braziel, Jana Evans, and Anita Mannur, eds. *Theorizing Diaspora: A Reader.* Malden: Blackwell, 2003.

Clifford, James. *Routes: Travel and Translation in the Late Twentieth Century.* Cambridge: Harvard University Press, 1997.

Döring, Tobias. *Caribbean-English Passages: Intertextuality in a Post-Colonial Tradition.* London: Routledge, 2002.

Döring, Tobias. *Postcolonial Literatures in English.* Stuttgart: Klett, 2008.

Fludernik, Monika, ed. *Diaspora and Multiculturalism: Common Traditions and New Developments.* Amsterdam: Rodopi, 2003.

Frye, Northrop. "Conclusion to a Literary History of Canada." *Literary History of Canada.* Ed. Carl F. Klinck. Toronto: University of Toronto Press, 1965. 213–50.

Gewecke, Frauke. *Die Karibik: Zur Geschichte, Politik und Kultur einer Region.* Frankfurt/M.: Vervuert, 2007.

Giddens, Anthony. *The Consequences of Modernity.* Stanford: Stanford University Press, 1991.

Gohrisch, Jana. "Caribbean Literature II: Themes and Narratives." *Reading the Caribbean: Approaches to Anglophone Caribbean Literature and Culture.* Ed. Klaus Stierstorfer. Heidelberg: Universitätsverlag Winter, 2007. 51–72.

Groß, Konrad, Klooß, Wolfgang, and Nischik, Reingard, eds. *Kanadische Literaturgeschichte.* Stuttgart: Metzler, 2005.

Hall, Stuart. "Cultural Identity and Diaspora." *Contemporary Postcolonial Theory: A Reader.* Ed. Padmini Mongia. London: Arnold, 1996. 110–21.

Held, David, and Anthony McGrew, eds. *The Global Transformation Reader: An Introduction to the Globalization Debate.* Cambridge: Polity Press, 2004.

James, Louis. *Caribbean Literature in English.* London: Longman, 1999.

Macaulay, Thomas Babington. "Minute on Education (1835)." *South Asian Literatures.* Eds. Gerhard Stilz and Ellen Dengel-Janic. Trier: WVT, 2010. 92–94.

Mathur, Ashok. "Transubracination: How Writers of Colour Became CanLit." *Trans.Can.Lit.: Resituating the Study of Canadian Literature.* Eds. Smaro Kamboureli and Roy Miki. Waterloo: Wilfrid Laurier University Press, 2007. 141–52.

Mishra, Vijay. *Literature of the Indian Diaspora: Theorizing the Diasporic Imaginary.* London: Routledge, 2008.

New, William Herbert. *A History of Canadian Literature.* London: Macmillan, 1989.

Nischik, Reingard, ed. *History of Literature in Canada: English-Canadian and French-Canadian.* Rochester: Camden House, 2008.

Said, Edward W. *Culture and Imperialism.* New York: Vintage, 1993.

Saunders, Patricia Joan. *Alien-Nation and Repatriation: Translating Identity in Anglophone Caribbean Literature.* Lanham: Lexington Books, 2007.

Skinner, John. *The Stepmother Tongue: An Introduction to New Anglophone Fiction.* Basingstoke: Macmillan, 1998.

Talib, Ismail. *The Language of Postcolonial Literatures: An Introduction.* London: Routledge, 2002.

*Katja Sarkowsky/Frank Schulze-Engler*

# Part II: Literary and Cultural Theory

# 1 Formalism and Structuralism

## 1.1 | Origins

The origins of reflection on the nature, the task, and the formal aspects of literature can be found in ancient Greece. Plato and Aristotle offered comments on, for instance, the nature of poetry, the role of the poet in society, and the attempt to represent reality in literature. However, in spite of this long tradition of theoretical thinking about literature, our modern understanding of literature and literary criticism was shaped in the nineteenth century. Of utmost importance in this context were the English and German Romantics who insisted on the poet's self-creation by means of his idiosyncratic work of art—the poet's will to form could not but break with the tradition. The letters of the nineteenth-century French writer Gustave Flaubert, who was one of the first genuinely modern novelists, are full of passages where he expresses the difficulty of finding the adequate form for his works. In a famous letter to his friend Louise Colet, Flaubert underscores his desire to write "un livre sur rien," a book about nothing which is all form and style, free of the burden of content. In literature, as well as in painting (for instance, French impressionism), the idea of aesthetic form became increasingly important in the nineteenth century. Yet it is crucial to note that literary criticism did not adequately react to this **idea of form**. At the end of the nineteenth century, the work of literary critics in Europe and America was mostly governed by biographical, historical, and psychological approaches. Furthermore, literary criticism was often impressionistic and humanistic. Many American critics, developing theories of realism and naturalism, were preoccupied with the task of shaping a specifically American literary tradition, and in so doing, contributing to the establishment of a national identity.

Focus on form rather than content

## 1.2 | Russian Formalism

The question of literary or aesthetic form was not, of course, completely ignored by these nineteenth-century critics, but it often played only a minor role in their texts. This utterly changed in the twentieth century. Twentieth-century literary criticism and theory cannot be understood without appreciating the role and function of form. As the German philosopher Theodor W. Adorno put it in his *Aesthetic Theory*: "Art has precisely the same chance of survival as does form, no better" (141). Concerning this question of form, the role of Russian Formalism can hardly be overestimated. Russian Formalism had a profound impact on twentieth-century literary studies. The Russian Formalists were a very diverse group. Most of them were born in the 1890s, came to prominence in Russian letters during World War I, flourished throughout the 1920s, and became marginalized with the rise of Stalinism in the late 1920s.

From its inception, Russian Formalism was split geographically into two centers. In 1915, the **Moscow Linguistic Circle** was established whose members were Roman Jakobson, Osip Brik, Grigory Vinokur, and Petr Bogatyrev. The Petersburg **OPOJAZ** (Society for the Study of Poetic Language) was founded in 1916. Among its members were Viktor Shklovsky, Boris Eichenbaum, and Yuri Tynyanov. Another important critic associated with this movement was the folklorist Vladimir Propp. The Russian Formalists intended to make literary criticism more scientific, primarily by applying the insights of formal linguistics to the field of literary studies. Their critique was directed against biographical or historical criticism, against

**Focus on Mikhail Bakhtin**

Bakhtin's work was influenced by both formalism and structuralism. He wrote most of his books and essays in relative obscurity during the 1920s and 1930s but became highly influential among Western critics from the 1970s onward. His key concepts include:

**Polyphony** ('multi-voicedness'), or the plurality and anti-hierarchical coexistence of voices in an utterance or text. In literary works polyphony can occur on two levels: a single voice can be 'populated' by various speech patterns or worldviews, and the author can admit polyphony among his characters by granting each a perspective entirely independent from his own.

**Dialogism** refers to the interplay and interdependence of utterances or voices. Every utterance, Bakhtin argues, must be seen in the context of other utterances, by which its form and meaning are influenced. This concept has inspired the notion of 'intertextuality,' which stresses that texts are not the isolated product of a single author but participate in a dialogic network of other texts. For the coexistence of different speech codes in a text, Bakhtin coined the term 'heteroglossia.'

**Chronotope** is a term Bakhtin introduced to describe the specific time-space configuration of a literary text. He suggested that chronotopes can help define genres and tell us something about the time in which they were current. He also identified chronotopic motifs such as the road, meeting, and the salon.

**The Carnivalesque** is a powerful but temporary suspension of the social order. Its characteristics, Bakhtin argues, have occasionally been transferred into literature and inspired a poetics of 'carnivalization' marked by such principles as eccentricity, *mésalliance*, and profanation.

the view of literature which connects it with a philosophical system and which regards it as containing a transcendent truth, and against the idea of symbolism. According to the Formalists, any mimetic theory of art and literature had to be criticized, and the autonomy of literature had to be defended against attempts to demonstrate that it was impossible to discuss literary texts without considering political, religious, sociological, psychological, or historical questions. Eichenbaum characterizes the Formalists' attitude thus:

[O]ur Formalist movement was characterized by a new passion for scientific positivism—a rejection of philosophical assumptions, of psychological and aesthetic interpretations, etc. Art, considered apart from philosophical aesthetics and ideological theories, dictated its own position on things. We had to turn to facts and, abandoning general systems and problems, to begin "in the middle," with the facts which art forced upon us. Art demanded that we approach it closely; science, that we deal with the specific. (1065)

Seeking to find out how literary texts actually worked, the Russian Formalists regarded the text as a material fact, that is, as a particular and idiosyncratic organization of language. Hence, it was the task of the critic to analyze the specific laws, structures, and devices (like imagery, rhetorical figures, narrative technique, syntax, and meter) of the literary work. The scientific study of literature, according to the Formalists, would concentrate on the text's **literariness** and on the way literary language **defamiliarizes** ordinary language. Literary language, especially poetic language, makes the ordinary world strange, changes the reader's habitual responses and perceptions of objects, and at the same time calls attention to its own complexity and self-referentiality.

## 1.3 | New Criticism

Many of the characteristics of Russian Formalism can also be found in the American New Criticism. As a literary theory, the New Criticism was the most influential critical movement in American academia from the 1930s to the late 1950s. However, its influence lasted well into the 1970s. It is crucial to see that some of the important features of the New Criticism originated in England during the 1920s. The poet T.S. Eliot, who was born in the U.S., has to be named in this context, as well as the literary scholar I.A. Richards and his student William Empson. Richards's *Principles of Literary Criticism* and *Practical Criticism* and Empson's *Seven Types of Ambiguity* prepared the ground for the New Critical method.

The American New Critics were also known as the Fugitives and the Southern Agrarians. They sought to defend the values of the Old South against the economically advanced North. To the New Critics, the industrial North stood for science, technology, and rationalism, and the alienation and reification of industrial capitalism was seen as a serious threat to the rather aesthetic life of the Old South. New Critics such as John Crowe Ransom, Allen Tate, Cleanth Brooks, Robert Penn Warren, W.K. Wimsatt, and R.P. Blackmur held that only poetry could offer a solution to this problem. Only the radically autonomous work of art, the poem as an autonomous verbal structure, could function as a refuge from the vulgarity, disorientation, materialism, and sterility of modern life.

**Main Characteristics of the New Critical School.** First, the New Criticism strives to purify literary criticism from extrinsic concerns such as the study of sources, social and historical backgrounds, the history of ideas, and politics. In its intrinsic approach, it concentrates exclusively on the literary text itself. Second, the New Criticism focuses on the structure of a work and not on the mind of the respective author or the reaction of the readers. W. K. Wimsatt and Monroe Beardsley call the attempt to find out what was going on in the author's head at the time of composition of the literary text an **intentional fallacy**. Moreover, they use the term **affective fallacy** to refer to the confusion of the emotional responses of particular readers with the poem's meaning. Wimsatt and Beardsley elaborate on these two types of fallacy as follows:

The Intentional Fallacy is a confusion between the poem and its origins, a special case of what is known to philosophers as the Genetic Fallacy. It begins by trying to derive the standard of criticism from the psychological *causes* of the poem and ends in biography and relativism. The Affective Fallacy is a confusion between the poem and its *results* (what it *is* and what it *does*), a special case of epistemological skepticism, though usually advanced as if it had far stronger claims than the overall forms of skepticism. It begins by trying to derive the standard of criticism from the psychological effects of the poem and ends in impressionism and relativism. The outcome of either Fallacy, the Intentional or the Affective, is that the poem itself, as an object of specifically critical judgments, tends to disappear. (1388)

As a third characteristic, one has to mention that the New Criticism champions an **organic theory of literature** which refuses a dualistic conception of form and content and which pays special attention to the coherence and unity of a literary work of art. This organic unity, as the New Critics contend, often depends on ambiguity, paradox, or irony. Fourth, the New Criticism practices a method called **close reading**. This is a way of reading individual texts which avoids paraphrase and thematic statements and which instead attends scrupulously to nuances of words, rhetorical figures and tropes, and shades of meaning. By reading closely, the critic can hope to find out how each of the text's parts is connected with the others, and how those parts, in spite of or because of their tensions, eventually form an organic unity.

The similarities between Russian Formalism and the American New Criticism are important if one seeks to understand the history of formalism in the twentieth century. Both theoretical schools offered a clearly language-oriented criticism which regarded the literary text, primarily the poem, as an autonomous verbal construct. Both concentrated on an analysis of form, structure, and the multilayered complexity of poetic language. Furthermore, both sought to elucidate the insufficiencies and shortcomings of traditional academic literary criticism. Raising literary standards, both schools also tried to redefine the canon of great works. Within the framework of a strictly intrinsic approach which analyzed aspects of form, structure, and narrative technique, many former great works appeared in a different light. (For an example of New Criticism in practice see section IV.2.2)

New Criticism:
The American variant
of formalism

## 1.4 | French Structuralism

A brief discussion of the main difference between the Russian Formalists and the New Critics will lead to the next stage of the development of formalism, namely, French structuralism. In comparison with the New Critics, the analyses of the Formalists were much more theoretical and abstract in nature. The latter sought to grasp the general nature of literature and the various literary devices. They developed large-scale projects in **theoretical poetics**, often avoiding interpretation altogether. By contrast, the proponents of the New Criticism engaged in practical criticism of individual works, that is, they were mainly concerned with the practice rather than the theory of close reading. In spite of its formalist gesture, at least to a certain degree, the New Criticism continued the Western tradition of (aesthetic) humanism, whereas the Russian Formalists' attempt to make literary studies and criticism more scientific ought to be seen as preparing the ground for structuralism.

**Saussure.** Most of structuralism's key concepts and main ideas go back to Ferdinand de Saussure's *Course in General Linguistics*. Saussure, who was born in Switzerland, was the founder of modern structural linguistics (cf. section V.2.2.2). Saussurean linguistics radically broke with nineteenth-century historical linguistics and philology. Language, to Saussure, is a system of signs which must not be studied diachronically, that is, in its historical development, but **synchronically**, that

Saussure's understanding
of the linguistic sign

is, one should analyze the system and its elements at a given point in time as a functional whole. Saussure not only gave the idea of synchrony priority over diachrony, but he also profoundly changed people's understanding of **the linguistic sign**. He saw the sign as consisting of two inseparable elements: a **signifier** (French "*signifiant*," German "Signifikant") which is the sound-image or its graphic equivalent, and the **signified** (French "*signifié*," German "Signifikat") which is the concept or meaning. According to Saussure, the relation between the signifier and the signified is arbitrary and conventional. Cultural and historical convention also governs the relation between the whole sign and what it refers to (what Saussure terms the **referent**, for instance, the actual tree in the garden, the actual car in the driveway). It is crucial to appreciate that for Saussure the relationships between signifier and signified as well as sign and referent cannot be explained by using phrases like natural resemblance or causal connection, but they ought to be seen as being defined by convention or law.

Saussure's contention is that language is a system of **differences**. A sign is not a positive entity, it does not have an essence, but each sign in the system has meaning only because it differs from all the other signs in the system or structure. In other words, meaning is not immanent in a sign (which could be analyzed in isolation), but meaning is the result of a system of relations and oppositions whose elements must be defined in formal, differential terms. The last point that should be mentioned with regard to Saussure's structural linguistics is that he thinks that one must not try to analyze people's actual speech acts or utterances (what he calls *la parole*), but that one should rather focus on the underlying system or structure which makes those speech acts possible in the first place. Saussure maintains that this system of a language, which he calls *la langue*, is the proper object of linguistics. The Saussurean kind of analysis can be summarized as follows: "He fostered inquiry into rules rather than expressions, grammar rather than usage, models rather than data, competence rather than performance, systems rather than realizations, langue (*language*) rather than parole (*speech*)" (Leitch 239).

**Modern structuralism**, as it developed in France in the 1960s and in the U.S. in the 1970s, attempted to apply this Saussurean linguistic theory to a variety of other fields such as literary studies, anthropology, psychoanalysis, political theory, historiography, film studies, art history, and others. Instead of structuralism, scholars and intellectuals started using the term **semiotics** or semiology (meaning a general science of signs) to denote this broadened application (cf. entry II.8). The French anthropologist **Claude Lévi-Strauss**, for instance, analyzed tribal kinships by structuralist means, while the French literary theorist and critic **Roland Barthes** used a structuralist or semiotic approach in order to illuminate how people wrote about fashion (*Système de la mode*). The works of Lévi-Strauss, Barthes, and others made clear that structuralism not only bracketed off the referent or real object, but that it was also responsible for what would later be called "the disappearance of the subject." According to the structuralists, the individual does not speak, he or she is spoken by the system. He or she neither originates nor controls the codes and conventions, and the author of a literary text is proclaimed to be dead (it was Barthes who in 1968 announced "la mort de l'auteur"—the **death of the author**). Structuralism is clearly antihumanistic, since it regards the self as a construct, the result of systems of conventions. The functions of the self are taken up by the combination of interpersonal systems that operate through it.

According to **Jonathan Culler**, one of the leading proponents of structuralism in the U.S., there is no such thing as a structuralist method. However, in his opinion, "there is a kind of attention which one might call structuralist." He defines this structuralist attention thus: "a desire to isolate codes, to name the various languages with and among which the text plays, to go beyond manifest content to a series of forms and then to make these forms, or oppositions or modes of signification, the burden of the text" (302).

Structuralism or semiotics arrived in the U.S. together with that which would eventually lead to its demise, namely, poststructuralism. It was especially the work of the French philosopher **Jacques Derrida** which undermined the foundations of structuralism and semiotics and which at the same time radicalized many of its insights (cf. section II.4.1). This Franco-American dialogue which governed literary and cultural theory in the last three decades of the twentieth century cannot be adequately understood, as it has been shown, without considering the development of formalism.

## Select Bibliography

Adorno, Theodor W. *Aesthetic Theory*. 1970. Trans. Robert Hullot-Kentor. Minneapolis: University of Minnesota Press, 1997.

Barthes, Roland. "The Death of the Author." *The Rustle of Language*. Trans. Richard Howard. New York: Hill and Wang, 1986. 49–55.

Barthes, Roland. "Introduction to the Structural Analysis of Narratives." *A Roland Barthes Reader*. Ed. Susan Sontag. New York: Vintage, 1993. 251–95.

Blumensath, Heinz, ed. *Strukturalismus in der Literaturwissenschaft*. Cologne: Kiepenheuer & Witsch, 1972.

Culler, Jonathan. *Structuralist Poetics: Structuralism, Linguistics, and the Study of Literature*. 1975. New York: Routledge, 2002.

Eichenbaum, Boris. *The Theory of the 'Formal Method.'* 1927. *The Norton Anthology of Theory and Criticism*. Eds. Vincent B. Leitch et al. New York: Norton, 2001. 1062–87.

Fietz, Lothar. *Strukturalismus: Eine Einführung*. Tübingen: Narr, 1992.

Habib, M. A. R. *A History of Literary Criticism and Theory*. Oxford: Blackwell, 2005.

Jameson, Fredric. *The Prison-House of Language: A Critical Account of Structuralism and Russian Formalism*. Princeton: Princeton University Press, 1972.

Leitch, Vincent B. *American Literary Criticism from the Thirties to the Eighties*. New York: Columbia University Press, 1988.

Macksey, Richard, and Eugenio Donato, eds. *The Languages of Criticism and the Sciences of Man: The Structuralist Controversy*. Baltimore: Johns Hopkins University Press, 1970.

Ransom, John Crowe. *The New Criticism*. Norfolk: New Directions, 1941.

Scholes, Robert. *Structuralism in Literature: An Introduction*. Rev. ed. New Haven: Yale University Press, 2009.

Selden, Raman, ed. *From Formalism to Poststructuralism*. Cambridge: Cambridge University Press, 1995. Vol. 8 of *The Cambridge History of Literary Criticism*. 9 vols. 1989–2005.

Sturrock, John, ed. *Structuralism and Since: From Lévi-Strauss to Derrida*. Oxford: Oxford University Press, 1979.

Wimsatt, Jr., William K., and Monroe Beardsley. "The Affective Fallacy." 1949. *The Norton Anthology of Theory and Criticism*. Eds. Vincent B. Leitch et al. New York: Norton, 2001. 1387–1403.

*Ulf Schulenberg*

# 2 Hermeneutics and Critical Theory

## 2.1 | The Philosophy of Universal Interpretation: Hermeneutics

Interpretation is a central human activity. Every day human beings have to interpret texts, situations, feelings, and people. Hermeneutics, the art of interpretation (see box), was developed in fields which were concerned with the interpretation of holy or canonical texts. Theologians developed a 'hermeneutica sacra,' while jurisprudence came to be governed by a 'hermeneutica iuris.' In philology, a 'hermeneutica profana' became increasingly important. This long tradition of biblical exegesis, legal hermeneutics, and philological hermeneutics culminated in the work of **Friedrich Schleiermacher** and **Wilhelm Dilthey**. In contrast to his precursors, Schleiermacher no longer focused exclusively on the interpretation of classical texts, but rather conceived of hermeneutics as a general activity. Moreover, he, in a Kantian manner, sought to illuminate the conditions for the possibility of understanding.

For the development of hermeneutics in the twentieth century, Dilthey's work is even more important. He called attention to the fact that understanding always involves a historical dimension. Furthermore, Dilthey established a distinction between the human sciences (*Geisteswissenschaften*) and the natural sciences. If the human sciences really desired to present themselves as a science, they had to develop their own method, which had to be grounded on firm foundations and therefore comparable to the methodology of the natural sciences. With Dilthey, hermeneutics turned into a methodological reflection on the scientific status of the human sciences and their claim to truth.

**Heidegger and Gadamer.** Twentieth-century hermeneutics is closely connected with the work of two German philosophers: Martin Heidegger and his student Hans-Georg Gadamer. It is crucial to appreciate that with twentieth-century hermeneutics we leave the field of epistemology and move into the area of what Heidegger called 'fundamental ontology.' Instead of being concerned with understanding something, and instead of claiming that we are capable of rationally analyzing the world as an object 'out there,' he argued, we should learn to regard understanding as our way of being-in-the-world. Understanding is man's fundamental way of existing, which is prior to cognition, rational analysis, or intellectual activity in general. Heideggerian ontological hermeneutics "replaces the question of understanding as knowledge about the world with the question of being-in-the-world" (Holub 262). One can speak of an **existentialist turn** in hermeneutics in this context. To Heidegger, there is no such thing as a neutral or objective understanding. Understanding, as a primordial state or power of being, confirms man's embeddedness in practical situations, his or her constant dialogue with the world which is shaped by his or her concrete concerns. Understanding, therefore, should rather be seen as a 'pre-understanding.' It is man's prejudices and presuppositions which make understanding possible in the first place.

In *Sein und Zeit* (*Being and Time*), **Heidegger** not only makes clear that understanding is radically historical, but he also places a special emphasis on the significance of language. It is language which opens the world for us, without language there is no world for us. Language is not simply a means of communication, but it is rather the realm in which man unfolds. It pre-exists the individual subject and has an existence of its own. Heidegger's view of language had a profound impact on many twentieth-century theoretical approaches (for instance, structuralism, poststructuralism, and deconstruction; cf. entries II.1 and II.4). Concern-

| Definition |
| --- |

→ **Hermeneutics** (from Greek *hermeneia*, 'explanation' or 'interpretation') is the art of interpretation or the art of understanding and interpreting texts correctly. Originally, hermeneutics was confined to the interpretation of written texts, but its scope has widened to include all forms of communication.

ing the task of interpretation, Heidegger maintains that to understand a text does not mean to discover a meaning produced by the author, but that understanding refers to a contemplation of the unfolding or 'un-concealing' of Being indicated by the text.

In many respects, **Gadamer** continued Heidegger's hermeneutic project. While Dilthey offered a methodological understanding of hermeneutics, Heidegger and Gadamer sought to turn hermeneutics into a **universal philosophy of interpretation**. They claimed for hermeneutics a universal status and regarded understanding as the essence of man's being-in-the-world. Gadamer's magnum opus *Wahrheit und Methode* (*Truth and Method*) offers a critique of the methodology of the natural sciences. While the experimental method of the natural sciences is usually associated with truth, Gadamer intends to problematize the conjunction 'and' which connects the two nouns in the title of his book. Directing attention to Dilthey's attempt to illustrate the human sciences' claim to truth, Gadamer does not advance the idea that hermeneutics provides a new and more efficient method, but rather uses hermeneutics to question the seemingly natural connection between methodology

and truth. He wants to show that the work of art not only produces aesthetic bliss, but that it also offers a special experience of truth. Gadamer seeks to redefine the concept of truth by demonstrating that the sphere of art allows man to enter into a **dialogue** with the respective work of art, and that it is by means of this dialogue that he or she is offered the possibility of redefining his or her understanding of truth and knowledge. However, this non-methodological mediation of truth typical of the work of art also offers man the possibility of gaining a new understanding of himself.

Following Gadamer, all interpretation is historical and situational, and all understanding is productive, creative, and a confrontation with otherness. In this context it is crucial to note that, according to Gadamer, all understanding is dominated by the '**hermeneutic circle**,' that is, the detail is understood within the whole, and the whole from the detail. To describe the event of understanding, he speaks of a "Horizontverschmelzung" (289), which means a fusion of one's own horizon of historical meanings, assumptions, and prejudices with the historical horizon of the text or work of art.

Gadamer continued
Heidegger's hermeneutical
project.

## 2.2 | The Frankfurt School and Critical Theory

Gadamer's work has provoked numerous reactions. E. D. Hirsch, Gadamer's main critic in the U.S., introduced his own conservative version of hermeneutics in *Validity in Interpretation*. The French philosopher **Paul Ricoeur** also used Gadamer's texts in order to develop his brand of hermeneutics (which famously distinguishes between a hermeneutics of the sacred and a 'hermeneutics of suspicion' which he identifies with Marx, Nietzsche, and Freud). One of the most creative and provocative readings of Gadamer was offered by the American pragmatist philosopher **Richard Rorty** in his *Philosophy and the Mirror of Nature*. Rorty's book is a severe critique of metaphysics and epistemological foundationalism. The Gadamerian notion of 'Gespräch' (conversation) is of particular value for Rorty in this context. In his opinion, Gadamer's hermeneutics is not a method for attaining truth, but rather "a redescription of man" which calls attention to the significance of "the romantic notion of man as self-creative" (358). Rorty underscores that his **pragmatist** version of hermeneutics must not be seen as a succes-

sor subject to epistemology, and that one should try to grasp the possibilities offered by a new view of culture as conversation rather than as a structure erected upon immutable and firm foundations.

Gadamer teaches us, according to Rorty, that instead of striving to represent things accurately, we should concentrate our energies on "finding new, better, more interesting, more fruitful ways of speaking" (360). Rorty uses the term '**edification**' for this hermeneutic project, and he clearly differentiates between systematic philosophy and edifying philosophy. His reading of Gadamer's *Truth and Method* is important for literary scholars, since it suggests that the "'poetic' activity of thinking up [...] new aims, new words, or new disciplines" (Rorty 360) ought to play a central role in a contemporary critique of metaphysics, foundationalism, and representationalism. Rorty characterizes edifying philosophers thus:

Edifying philosophers want to keep space open for the sense of wonder which poets can sometimes cause—wonder that there is something new under the sun, something which is *not* an accurate representation of what was already there, something which (at least for the moment) cannot be explained and can barely be described. (370)

Critical Theory. While Rorty productively uses Gadamer in order to make the idea of a genuinely postmetaphysical culture look attractive, other theorists have criticized various aspects of Gadamer's work. Of primary concern in this context is Gadamer's conservatism. Members of the 'Frankfurt School,' within their leftist framework of Critical Theory, developed a version of ideology critique whose basic ideas made it incompatible with hermeneutics. Although there are also some crucial parallels, and reciprocal influences, between hermeneutics and Marxist Critical Theory, the differences between these two approaches have turned out to be more important for twentieth-century theoretical discussions. Jürgen Habermas, for instance, as the foremost representative of the second generation of the Frankfurt School, avers that while Gadamerian hermeneutics correctly underlines the importance of historicity, the dialogical nature of language, and the situatedness of the interpreter, and thus is directed against positivism, objectivism, and empiricism, it is of no great help as regards the development of an emancipatory politics. What Habermas misses in Gadamer, in other words, is a critical dimension which does not praise the value of tradition, but which on the contrary contributes to the development of conceptual tools which might be used in the attempt to radically question and critique the hegemony of tradition. The English Marxist theorist and literary critic Terry Eagleton characterizes Gadamer's notion of tradition as follows: "Tradition holds an authority to which we must submit: there is little possibility of critically challenging that authority, and no speculation that its influence may be anything but benevolent" (63).

The theorists of the Frankfurt School offered a multilayered analysis of the vicissitudes of the Enlightenment and of Enlightenment reason, as well as a sophisticated critique of capitalist modernity and its ideological apologists. Theodor W. Adorno, Max Horkheimer, Walter Benjamin, Herbert Marcuse, Erich Fromm, and other members of the Institute for Social Research, which was founded in 1924, used the Hegelian-Marxist method of dialectical analysis in order to discuss phenomena as various as fascism, monopoly and late capitalism, the authoritarian personality, reification, commodification, fetishism, the culture industry, and the fate and function of art in late capitalism. Concerning the development of a Marxist literary and aesthetic theory, Adorno's writings have proven to be of crucial importance. Contrary to his fellow Marxist aesthetician Georg Lukács, Adorno contends that the form-content dialectics of the work of art is clearly dominated by the category of form. Adorno abhors the notion of realism and the idea that the work of art or literary text realistically and objectively mirrors the outside world. In his opinion, this idea of a materialist reflection theory has always been problematic, but it has turned out to be singularly inadequate as far as the attempt to artistically represent the complexity and totality of late capitalism is concerned. In his late *Ästhetische Theorie* (*Aesthetic Theory*), but also in many of the essays collected in *Noten zur Literatur* (*Notes to Literature*), Adorno repeatedly insists on the importance of aesthetic form for the radically autonomous work of art. It is aesthetic form, in its radical nature and newness, that separates the authentic and hermetic work of art from the standardized products of the culture industry. In Adorno's opinion, originality has withdrawn "into the artworks themselves, into the relentlessness of their internal organization" (172).

In order to confront the permanent threat of heteronomy, the artist has to realize the importance of form, since it is form which offers the possibility of a separation from the empirical sphere and thus of aesthetic autonomy. It is crucial to see that Adorno's aesthetic thought not only warned against vulgarizations of materialist aesthetic theory, but that it showed above all that a discussion of aesthetic form had political implications and that it did not necessarily lead to a confirmation of an anemic and otherworldly formalism. Regarding twentieth-century literary and aesthetic theory, the importance of the following two sentences can hardly be overestimated: "The concept of form marks out art's sharp antithesis to an empirical world in which art's right to exist is uncertain. Art has precisely the same chance of survival as does form, no better" (Adorno 141).

## 2.3 | Postmodern Marxism

The work of the Frankfurt School had a profound impact on theoretical discussions in the latter half of the twentieth century. It is important to note that the influence of the Critical Theorists has not been limited to Germany. In Great Britain, contemporary theorists like Raymond Williams, Terry Eagleton, and Stuart Hall, to varying degrees, have been influenced by the Frankfurt School. However, it is the American literary and cultural theorist **Fredric Jameson**, whose reading and mapping of the dialectical tradition has produced the most interesting and stimulating results. Jameson, it can be said, has developed a postmodern Marxism which is capable of conceptually confronting a globalized or multinational capitalism and its cultural logic. Since the publication of his study *Marxism and Form* in 1971, he has tried to mediate between his own Hegelian Marxism and various other theoretical discourses such as formalism (New Criticism), Lacanian psychoanalysis (cf. entry II.7), Gilles Deleuze and Félix Guattari's micropolitics of desire, structuralism, Louis Althusser's structuralist Marxism, poststructuralism, American deconstruction (cf. entry II.4), and New Historicism (cf. entry II.5). The emergence of an open and mostly undogmatic Marxist discourse is the result of his understanding of **dialectical criticism**. Jameson has constantly tried to work through other philosophical and theoretical positions in order to prove the efficacy of the Hegelian Marxist model. It has been his intention to translate the insights developed within those other theoretical discourses into the Hegelian Marxist discourse. He explicitly speaks of his own discourse as a "translation mechanism" (Zhang 365) which is capable of translating and subsuming other theoretical perspectives within an overarching Marxian framework. With books like *Postmodernism, or the Cultural Logic of Late Capitalism*, *The Seeds of Time*, *The Cultural Turn*, and *Archaeologies of the Future* Jameson has established himself as one of the foremost theorists of postmodernism and postmodernity.

Since its inception as a theoretical discourse, Marxism has been attacked from numerous sides. This critique has also led to a new understanding of the heritage of Critical Theory and its function at the beginning of the twenty-first century. Proponents of postcolonial studies, multiculturalists, and cultural studies scholars, for instance, have argued that the notion of art and aesthetics which can be found in texts by authors associated with the Frankfurt School is too eurocentric and elitist, as well as too dominated by an orthodox version of Marxism. Undoubtedly, this critique is important, but it partly ignores that, in contrast to many other theoretical approaches, Marxism has often been governed by a self-critique of its proponents. Faithful to the dialectical heritage, Marxist theoreticians, and those strongly influenced by the Hegelian-Marxist tradition, have advanced a critique of the obsolescence of certain Marxist axioms and premises and have thus sought to adapt leftist thought to a radically changed (late-) capitalist society. Since the 1980s, those theoretical endeavors directed against classical and orthodox Marxism have been subsumed under the somewhat unfortunate term '**post-Marxism**.' Important post-Marxist texts are, for instance, Ernesto Laclau and Chantal Mouffe's *Hegemony and Socialist Strategy*, Slavoj Žižek's *The Sublime Object of Ideology*, Jacques Derrida's *Specters of Marx*, and Michael Hardt and Antonio Negri's *Empire* and *Multitude*. Important precursors in this context are Antonio Gramsci (*Selections from Prison Notebooks*) and Louis Althusser (*For Marx*). Although the influence of Critical Theorists such as Adorno and Benjamin on those post-Marxist texts often is not directly discernible, the complexity of the latter cannot be fully appreciated without considering the heritage of the Frankfurt School.

In a renewed form, both theoretical approaches discussed in this chapter, Hermeneutics and Critical Theory, play an important role in contemporary debates and will continue to do so in the future.

---

**Focus on Hegelian Dialectics**

According to the German philosopher Georg Wilhelm Friedrich **Hegel**, the development of thought is a dialectical process, i.e., it results as a synthesis from the conflict between a thesis and an antithesis. It is an infinite process in which the synthesis is never final but becomes the thesis for a new dialectical cycle. In this, Hegel's dialectic is very similar to the hermeneutic circle. Karl **Marx** criticized Hegel's abstract idealism and applied the dialectic principle to the concrete social scenario of class struggle (*Klassenkampf*).

Interpretation

**William Faulkner, *The Sound and the Fury***

*The Sound and the Fury*, William Faulkner's fourth novel, was published in 1929. It depicts the decay of a Southern family, the Compsons, who once belonged to the plantation aristocracy. The narrative present is Easter weekend 1928. The novel consists of four parts. Each of the first three sections covers a day narrated by one of the Compson brothers, and in all three sections, Faulkner uses the stream-of-consciousness technique. It is only in the final section, which centers on the black servant Dilsey, that the author tells the story from the perspective of an omniscient narrator. *The Sound and the Fury* is a genuinely modernist text which is utterly fragmented, seemingly incoherent, and which employs an avant-garde narrative technique, comparable to the complexity of James Joyce's *Ulysses*, in order to tell the story of the decline of the Compsons. A sophisticated Marxist interpretation first pays attention to the fragmentation, the lack of chronology, and the discontinuities which are present on the surface of the text. Following the model introduced by Fredric Jameson in *The Political Unconscious*, the next step in the analysis is the attempt to conceptually grasp the totality of the unconscious of the text which is necessarily connected with the social and economic realities out of which the novel was created. In the case of Faulkner's novel, this textual unconscious is directly related to the shift in socio-economic realities from the system of the nineteenth-century Southern plantation aristocracy to a modern industrial or monopoly capitalism. What this boils down to is that a sophisticated Marxist interpretation no longer has use for a simplistic notion of mimesis or reflection theory, and hence no longer underlines the significance of traditional forms of realism, but that it strives to elucidate the meaning of aesthetic form and the complex mediating function of narrative between individual experience and social totality. In this context, Jameson speaks of "the ideology of form" (*Political Unconscious* 76). The final step in the interpretation would bring one to view the decay of this formerly "aristocratic" family not merely in connection with the Southern past but to read it as a parable of the alienation, reification, and disintegration of modern man. As their sections make clear, all three Compson brothers are no longer sustained by familial and cultural unity, and hence are utterly isolated and lost in their private worlds and words.

## Select Bibliography

**Adorno, Theodor W.** *Aesthetic Theory*. 1970. Trans. Robert Hullot-Kentor. Minneapolis: University of Minnesota Press, 1997.

**Callari, Antonio, Stephen Cullenberg, and Carole Biewener, eds.** *Marxism in the Postmodern Age: Confronting the New World Order*. New York: Guilford Press, 1995.

**Derrida, Jacques.** *Specters of Marx: The State of the Debt, the Work of Mourning, & the New International*. Trans. Peggy Kamuf. New York: Routledge, 1994.

**Eagleton, Terry.** *Literary Theory: An Introduction*. 1983. 2nd ed. Oxford: Blackwell, 1996.

**Gadamer, Hans-Georg.** *Wahrheit und Methode*. 1960. 6th ed. Tübingen: Mohr Siebeck, 1990.

**Grondin, Jean.** *L'Herméneutique*. Paris: Presses Universitaires de France, 2006. (German translation published as *Hermeneutik*. Göttingen: UTB, 2009).

**Hardt, Michael, and Antonio Negri.** *Empire*. Cambridge: Harvard University Press, 2000.

**Holub, Robert.** "Hermeneutics." *The Cambridge History of Literary Criticism*. Ed. Raman Selden. Vol. 8. Cambridge: Cambridge University Press, 1995. 255–88.

**Horkheimer, Max.** *Traditionelle und Kritische Theorie: Fünf Aufsätze*. Frankfurt/M.: Fischer, 1992.

**Iser, Wolfgang.** "Hermeneutical Theory: *Gadamer*." *How to Do Theory*. Malden: Blackwell, 2006. 28–42.

**Jameson, Fredric.** *Marxism and Form: Twentieth-Century Dialectical Theories of Literature*. Princeton: Princeton University Press, 1971.

**Jameson, Fredric.** *The Political Unconscious: Narrative as a Socially Symbolic Act*. London: Methuen, 1981.

**Jameson, Fredric.** *Postmodernism, or the Cultural Logic of Late Capitalism*. New York: Verso, 1991.

**Jay, Martin.** *Marxism and Totality: The Adventures of a Concept from Lukács to Habermas*. Cambridge: Polity Press, 1984.

**Palmer, Richard E.** *Hermeneutics: Interpretation Theory in Schleiermacher, Dilthey, Heidegger, and Gadamer*. Evanston: Northwestern University Press, 1969.

**Ricoeur, Paul.** *The Conflict of Interpretations: Essays in Hermeneutics*. Trans. Don Ihde. Evanston: Northwestern University Press, 1974.

**Rorty, Richard.** *Philosophy and the Mirror of Nature*. Princeton: Princeton University Press, 1979.

**Zhang, Xudong.** "Marxism and the Historicity of Theory: An Interview with Fredric Jameson." *New Literary History* 29 (1998): 353–83.

*Ulf Schulenberg*

# 3  Reception Theory

We have stated in our "Introduction to Literary Studies" (entry I.1) that what is considered literature, what the subject matter of literary studies is and how we analyse and interpret literature depends upon the methodological approaches we—as interpreters and readers—choose to apply. We have highlighted the interdependence, the dialectical interplay, and the semantic/semiotic oscillation which exists between authors, readers, texts and the world and in which meaning is generated. This communicative interplay has been foregrounded since the 1960s and 1970s in what was from various viewpoints and methodological angles called *Rezeptionsästhetik* and, in its special American variant, **reader-response criticism** and **reader-response theory**. To put the matter more simply, these approaches are here subsumed under the generic heading 'reception theory.'

What they have in common is the conviction that texts do not produce meanings by themselves. We can easily see that even scholars, as readers, disagree about interpretations and that reading a text is neither an unambiguous nor an altogether inactive process. In fact, the reader takes a vital part in the construction of meaning. Martin Heidegger points out in *Being and Time* that whenever readers interpret a text or a situation, they project their own potentials onto their objects of contemplation. Moreover, Heidegger argues, readers must always have somehow understood beforehand what they strive to understand (195). Drawing on this insight, Hans-Georg Gadamer asserts that the reader "projects a meaning for the text as a whole as soon as some initial meaning emerges in the text" (267). He famously phrased this projection process of meaning as "the fore-conception of completeness" (294). As this is a clearly formal condition of all understanding, the active part of readers in interpretation and, in fact, in any form or method of criticism becomes palpable.

In a very broad understanding of the term, then, any theory or any criticism is a kind of reception theory. At a closer view, however, the term 'reception theory' refers to those theories which shift their attention away from the author, the production processes of literature, and the text itself to the reader. This focus obviously bears resemblance to Heidegger's and Gadamer's phenomenological hermeneutics (cf. section II.2.1), but has also broadly found its way since then into contemporary literary theory, which no longer sees literature as an entirely text-based, fixed, rigid, and almost timeless matter, but rather as a complex and ever-changing interaction and dialogue. In this context, an important predecessor to reception theory was Mikhail Bakhtin and his concepts of **dialogicity** and intertextuality (cf. section II.1.2). Indeed the almost ostentatious predilection of twentieth and twenty-first century literature for intertextual writing in all genres has proven this shift to open, dialogic forms which overtly address the activity of the 'reader-detective' who is engaged in the (re-)construction of meaning.

*Terminology*

## 3.1 | Reader-Response Criticism in the United States

Since the 1960s, many scholars in the United States have investigated the phenomenon of reader-response with a clear emphasis on the individual experience of the reader. Two major representatives of this branch of reception theory are Norman N. Holland and Stanley Fish.

**Norman N. Holland.** In *The Dynamics of Literary Response*, Holland largely draws on a mostly American direction of psychoanalysis called ego-psychology. Different from more deconstructive psychoanalysis (cf. entry II.7), ego-psychology is fairly optimistic about its ability to define a sense of a stable identity, self, and subject. Accordingly,

Holland starts his analysis of reader activity on the premise that each reader evolves a specific ego based upon childhood experience and further projects this distinctive ego onto his readings of texts. Holland's assumption of a **transaction between reader and text**, therefore, can be delineated as a relationship which is regulated by a feedback structure in which the reading of a text enables the readers to re-create their prominent identities. Holland suggests a model mechanism inherent in this transaction process of reading in which the reader passes through various successive stages: defence → expectation → fantasy → transformation (DEFT). In the brain of each individual, Holland argues, there is a specific **identity theme**, a unique core that facilitates a behavioural cohesion. Such cohesion, for instance, becomes visible in individual readings. Holland proves this by probations of readings of individual texts by different readers. Reading a (literary) text is seen by Holland as a controversial yet fruitful means of self-assertion. Though this is, of course, a fascinating idea in itself, it should be pointed out here that Holland does little to link these insights to the actual structures of the texts at issue. He simply presumes these structures to correlate with the individual psychic parameters, interests, and predilections of readers because for him there is no difference between interpreting the world or a literary text. In the end, then, Holland's cognitive objective is a primarily psychological one.

Stanley Fish calls his contribution to reader-response criticism **affective stylistics** and also overtly sets this concept against the text-based New Criticism (cf. section II.1.3). For Fish, the text itself is important only as it arouses certain expectations in the reader. What he has in mind when he speaks of 'the reader' is an **ideal reader**, who is well-informed and who can relish in the mysteries and indeterminacies the text offers. What an 'ideal reader' is can perhaps best be described using the example of such a highly complex postmodernist novel as Umberto Eco's *The Name of the Rose*. This bestselling novel can be and indeed has been read by many readers focussing exclusively on the murder mystery as an intriguing and entertaining variant of detective fiction. The novel, however, contains much more than that, and an 'ideal reader' would both be able and willing to unravel the discourses of theological dispute the novel touches upon, the historical framework of the Middle Ages, the dense network of intertextual references and associations, and the novel's metafictional semiotic

interest in how meaning is generated. For Fish, therefore, the meaning of a text is never determined outside a reader's understanding of that text.

Furthermore, Fish argues that our everyday life is governed by interpretations of indefinite objects, and these interpretations are influenced by the structures of our knowledge and control mechanisms, such as cultural norms. For Fish, each mental model of perceived, and hence also interpreted, objects is a product of these socio-cultural norms. The influential term Fish coins to denominate these normative factors in the processes of generating meaning is **interpretive communities**:

[I]t is interpretive communities, rather than either the text or the reader, that produce meanings and are responsible for the emergence of formal features. Interpretive communities are made up of those who share interpretive strategies not for reading but for writing texts, for constituting their properties. In other words these strategies exist prior to the act of reading and therefore determine the shape of what is read rather than, as is usually assumed, the other way around. (14)

It follows that members of the same interpretive community are very much likely to arrive at the same meanings and interpretations of texts simply because their interpretations adhere to the very standards of values, purposes, goals, and intentions characteristic of their respective community. In other words, interpreters/readers also judge the quality of their interpretations as they are able to understand and reflect upon the mechanisms of their interpretive communities. It needs to be emphasised at this point, though, that even though Fish's approach can explain why and how we favour one interpretation over another (because one protocol of a respective community is preferred to another), he still largely ignores the individual psychic dispositions of individual members of an interpretive community. There is certainly much truth in the notion that a text gains its meaning in the context of a set of cultural assumptions made about, for instance, authorial intentions. The manifold and diverging interpretations of Joseph Conrad's *Heart of Darkness* are a significant example of how these processes can be put to work. Many readers have juxtaposed the narrator Marlow's common-sense perspective with the abject, free-floating subjectivity of Kurtz. Other readers have focussed on the undertakings of human civilisation and enlightenment and have placed these against the perversion of such civilisation by the horrors procured by colonialism. Famously arguing from the perspective of the interpretive community of post-colonialism, the Nigerian scholar Chinua Achebe (cf. section I.4.5.4) has read Conrad's portrayal of Africa and of African culture as reductionist, dehumanising, and, after all, forthrightly racist. And again, other scholars arguing from a psychoanalytical point of view have entirely reassessed the postcolonial difficulty and have interpreted Marlow's voyage into the heart of darkness as a voyage into the human subconscious. No doubt these approaches to Conrad's novel often complement or even contradict each other and thus reveal how competing cultural assumptions and constructions determine our ways of reading literary texts. Nevertheless, Fish's emphasis on interpretive communities very likely risks lumping readers together all too crudely.

## 3.2 | The Constance School

Another pertinent strand of reception theory was developed in Germany in the late 1960s and early 1970s at the University of Constance. The concepts of reception history (*Rezeptionsgeschichte*) and reception aesthetics (*Rezeptionsästhetik*) are inextricably linked to the work of Hans Robert Jauß and Wolfgang Iser.

**Hans Robert Jauß.** In a more historicist way than Iser, Jauß's *Rezeptionsgeschichte* originated an entirely new branch of literary historiography. Jauß inquires into the analysis and interpretation of the history of the manifold ways of how people read a particular literary work. In order to explain this, Jauß introduces the term **horizon of expectations** ('Erwartungshorizont'), which encompasses the historical and aesthetic expectations that surround a particular text. The history of a text's reception may change considerably over years and centuries, quite in proportion to the evolution of tastes and interests, moral judgements, ethical standards, world views, cultures, and societies. Jauß's own example for such changes in the horizons of expectations is Gustave Flaubert's novel *Madame Bovary*, but one might with equal ease point to writers like D. H. Lawrence or texts such as James Joyce's *Ulysses*, who and which have seen extremely changeable histories of reception (cf. section I.2.6.4). *Ulysses*, for instance, was banned for obscenity and pornography in England and the United States well into the 1930s, and even though it was not banned in Ireland it was still unavailable there. While the expectations of readers and the authorities may be satisfied or challenged, in the latter case they were seriously frustrated with regard to both the complex narrative structure of the novel and its, at times, unreserved sexual undertones and encounters. Needless to say that today Joyce's novel is broadly recognised as the most ground-breaking piece of fiction of the twentieth century, and while its narrative is still a challenge to Joyce scholars and students alike, its sexual notoriety has worn off. Jauß explains such a change in reception as the result of a complex interaction between the text and its readers. In the course of time, the aesthetics of particular texts are able to change the aesthetic taste of their readers who, likewise, change their expectations in a literary work. Hence, Jauß understands the history of reception as a gradual process of a merging of the horizons of text and its interpreter. For Jauß, a literary work contains a **semantic potential** which can only realise itself fully in the course of various historical stages of its reception. Although this has proved to be a convincing and influential argument in itself, the concept of the merging horizons of text and reader remains speculative, after all, and some problems arise: Firstly, the further you go backwards into the past for the reconstruction of horizons of expectations, the more difficult it will become to retrieve truly reliable data. Secondly, Jauß's concept is firmly grounded in the belief that it is possible to decipher a relatively dominant mindset in the reception of a work of literature. While this might be easier to accomplish in former centuries, the present (post-)modern intellectual climate of Western culture, for instance, which is characterised by plurality, multiculturalism, individuality, and fragmented and hybrid, often collage-like aesthetic forms, renders the assumption of such a 'dominant' mindset increasingly difficult to maintain.

**Wolfgang Iser.** Where Jauß is focussing on historical issues, Iser's concept explicitly concentrates on the aesthetic and intra-fictional dimension and structures of literature. In two seminal publications—*The Implied Reader* and *The Act of Reading*—he sets out to systematise not only how the reader actively partakes in the communication process with the text, but also how this reader communication is inscribed into the fictional structure of the texts. But the question also re-

*From historical to aesthetical and structural considerations*

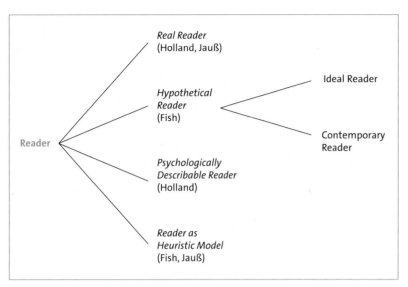

Four categories of the reader according to W. Iser

In the act of reading, the reader is not confronted with the text as a complete whole. On the contrary, what readers have to face while they are reading are incomplete fragments which will have to be pieced together in the reader's imaginary. The appeal structure of the implied reader, therefore, is shaped by what Iser calls **gaps** or **blanks** in the text which prompt the reader to fill these in the process of reading. As deconstructive criticism has amply proved, any signifier in language owns an incommensurable semantic substratum to which it is impossible to ascribe a univocal meaning; thus, semantic as well as semiotic gaps are produced (cf. entry II.4). In a more direct way, such gaps and blanks can be verified, for instance, in techniques of montage and fragmentation of narrative structures, in the commentary of a narrator which accompanies and often relativises the surrounding plotlines and character developments, in irony or other rhetorical characteristics of speech. In short, gaps which make the implied reader visible are instances which—directly or indirectly, overtly or covertly—generate indeterminacy in a literary text which the reader then has to substantiate. It should be noted, however, that such indeterminacy does not advocate an encompassing relativity and arbitrariness of interpretation, but rather re-anchors the interpretive movements of the reader in textual signals that readers face and react to in their encounter with the text. A notoriously indeterminate, floating signifier such as 'Godot' in Samuel Beckett's play *Waiting for Godot* (1952) shows the implied reader at work, as Beckett's neologism self-consciously reflects upon the insufficient validity of all systems of the production of meaning by a radically open formal structure in which readers of all backgrounds find their respective interpretive consciousness activated yet at the same time frustrated. 'Godot' illuminates the response-inviting structure of literature, while at the same time it functions as a response-projection mechanism in the reader himself. Indeed, an answer to what or who 'Godot' ultimately is could be that 'Godot' is anything that gives meaning to a particular reading of it.

mains for Iser as to who the readers are. Drawing on research done by other scholars, he identifies four categories of the reader (*Act of Reading* 27–34): the "real reader" as envisaged by Jauß when the history of responses is being studied; the "hypothetical reader" who is assumed when a potential effect of the text is the object of investigation (this category can be further divided into the "ideal reader" (as in Fish) and the contemporary reader); the "psychologically describable reader" (as in Holland); and finally, a group of readers under the category of "the reader as heuristic model" (as in both Fish and Jauß) (see box).

Though acknowledging their merits and possibilities, Iser points to the limitations of each of these concepts and proposes a concept of his own: the **implied reader**. The implied reader is not a historical reader but rather a reader-response pattern which is composed into the **appeal structure** ("Appellstruktur") of the text. Iser understands this appeal structure as a structure of indeterminacies on the level of textual composition which concerns both textual repertoire and textual strategies. Hence, the implied reader is best conceived of as a phenomenological construct with a double role: the implied reader is at the same time a textual structure and also triggers structured acts of reading in the actual reader.

# 3.3 | Applying Reception Theory

Thus, reception theory highlights the **interaction** that exists between the world, the text, and the reader in order to actualise the meaning potential inherent in that interaction. In this respect, but with specific differences both with regard to their interests and methods, the four approaches outlined above feature similarities. If we apply their findings to the interpretation of a particular text, however, thoroughly different 'meanings,' emphases, perspectives, and accentuations come to light.

Interpretation

### Thomas Hardy, *Tess of the d'Urbervilles*

Thomas Hardy's *Tess of the d'Urbervilles: A Pure Woman Faithfully Presented* (1891) centres on the feigned idyll of the village of Marlott and on the family of John Durbeyfield, who believes that he is a descendant of one of the oldest families of the country, the d'Urbervilles. Dreaming of social ascent and in order to make her contribute to their living, John and his wife send their beautiful daughter Tess to Tantridge, the ancestral home of the d'Urbervilles. An important irony of the novel consists in the fact that those d'Urbervilles whom Tess meets are nothing but pretentious upstarts who have only bought the old family name. Tess is courted by the reckless Alec d'Urberville, whom she finds hard to keep at bay. The pivotal scene of the novel, which prefigures Tess's tragic ending, takes place when Alec rides with Tess into a forest in darkness after saving her from an awkward situation in the village. Characteristically, Hardy's description leaves it entirely open for the reader if the sexual encounter, in which Tess becomes pregnant, is a seduction or a rape.

The obscurity was now so great that he could see absolutely nothing but a pale nebulousness at his feet, which represented the white muslin figure he had left upon the dead leaves. Everything else was blackness alike. D'Urberville stooped; and heard a gentle regular breathing. He knelt and bent lower, till her breath warmed his face, and in a moment his cheek was in contact with hers. She was sleeping soundly, and upon her eyelashes there lingered tears.

Darkness and silence ruled everywhere around. Above them rose the primeval yews and oaks of The Chase, in which were poised gentle roosting birds in their last nap; and about them stole the hopping rabbits and hares. But, might some say, where was Tess's guardian angel? Where was the providence of her simple faith? Perhaps, like that other god of whom the ironical Tishbite spoke, he was talking, or he was pursuing, or he was in a journey, or he was sleeping and not to be awaked.

Why it was that upon this beautiful feminine tissue, sensitive as gossamer, and practically blank as snow as yet, there should have been traced such a coarse pattern as it was doomed to receive; why so often the coarse appropriates the finer thus, the wrong man the woman, the wrong woman the man, many thousand years of analytical philosophy have failed to explain to our sense of order. (ch. 11)

Studying Hardy's novel or this passage in particular, ideal readers—in the light of Stanley Fish's theory—would have to be informed about major developments of the nineteenth century. They would, for instance, have to be in the know about technological progress and would see this exemplified in the major changes in agricultural labour which the novel discusses. While agriculture as portrayed in *Tess* witnesses the increasing use of machinery, Tess herself is an image of a "pure woman" representing untouched nature, as is indicated in the subtitle of the novel.

■ Fish would link the question of whether readers assume that Tess is raped or seduced by Alec to their affiliation with interpretive communities. A decidedly feminist point of view, for example, accentuating how women have been wronged and marginalised by patriarchy over centuries, could easily plead (and has indeed pleaded) that what Alec does to her in the wood is against her will.

■ Elaborating on the reception history of *Tess*, Jauß's approach would find excellent evidence for the thesis of shifting horizons of expectation by looking at the question of why Hardy's novel used to cause such a great scandal at the time and could only be published in an extenuated version. Hardy's attack on the sexual politics of the times and especially on the moral double standards is severe, and no matter if Hardy's criticism drew on well-known socio-political reforms in the nineteenth century, the overt depiction of the tragic fate of a visibly (and sexually) self-conscious 'fallen woman' was as innovative as the unhappy ending of the novel was in a formal sense. Both concepts, however, were obviously overstraining the expectations of the reading public, as both were deviating from established aesthetic norms. This challenged existing horizons of expectation and, what is more, was ultimately also conducive to the change of these horizons, as many of Tess's problems seem to have disappeared more than a century later.

- Looking at the passage above from the theoretical stance of Iser's implied reader is also extremely fruitful. In fact, the density of gaps/blanks and of narrative indeterminacy is blatant: The scenery is set in utter "obscurity," and a "pale nebulousness" is pervading. As the narrator, who of course knows about Victorian moral conventions and norms, tells us, Tess was missing a "guardian angel," and Alec's pursuit of her is likened to a characteristic "coarse pattern" which besmirches Tess's alleged purity. The hardly shrouded sexual charging of the "beautiful feminine tissue, sensitive as gossamer" is no-

ticeable, which emphasises that Tess was bitterly wronged. Characteristically, though, in the next chapter of the novel time has moved on several weeks, and Tess—pregnant by now—decides to leave Tantridge and tells Alec that she loathes and hates herself for her "weakness" (ch. 12). Thus, while some of the imagery may indeed point to the violence of Alec's action, Tess's speaking of her own weakness might refer to her regret that she may have given in to Alec's seduction. In the end, the incident and the ensuing question if she was raped or seduced remain opaque and open to readers' conjecture. The implied reader, thus, functions in terms of the text's indeterminate appeal structure, which likewise confronts and involves the reader in the process of generating meaning.

### Focus on the Legacy of Reception Theory

There have been various approaches to reception theory alongside the four representative theories outlined above. As early as in the 1960s, **David Bleich** collected statements of students about the feelings and associations they had when reading a text. Bleich used this material and integrated the results into a theory of classroom teaching of literature. The concepts of the 'ideal reader' and the 'implied reader' were also taken up, discussed, and modified in scholarly work by **Jonathan Culler** and **Michel Riffaterre**, who introduced the category of a "superreader" of a text composed of its author, the critics, the translators, and even the footnotes made by the critics. The lasting legacy of reception theory rests in the strong emphasis on the communication process in which the production of meaning in any literary work of art is always embedded. The interrelation between the production and reception of (literary) texts has also been examined in **narratology** (Nünning) and in areas such as **cognitive poetics** (see the overview in Strasen).

### Select Bibliography

**Achebe, Chinua.** "An Image of Africa: Racism in Conrad's *Heart of Darkness*." *Massachusetts Review* 18.4 (1977): 782–94.

**Bleich, David.** *Subjective Criticism*. Baltimore: Johns Hopkins University Press, 1978.

**Culler, Jonathan.** *Structuralist Poetics: Structuralism, Linguistics, and the Study of Literature*. Ithaca: Cornell University Press, 1975.

**Fish, Stanley.** *Is There a Text in this Class? The Authority of Interpretive Communities*. Cambridge: Harvard University Press, 1980.

**Gadamer, Hans-Georg.** *Truth and Method*. 1960. London: Continuum, 1989.

**Heidegger, Martin.** *Being and Time*. 1927. Trans. John Macquarrie and Edward Robinson. New York: Harper & Row, 1962.

**Holland, Norman N.** *The Dynamics of Literary Response*. New York: Norton, 1975.

**Holland, Norman N.** *5 Readers Reading*. New Haven: Yale University Press, 1975.

**Iser, Wolfgang.** *The Act of Reading: A Theory of Aesthetic Response*. 1976. Baltimore: Johns Hopkins University Press, 1980.

**Iser, Wolfgang.** *The Implied Reader: Patterns of Communication in Prose Fiction from Bunyan to Beckett*. 1972. Baltimore: Johns Hopkins University Press, 1974.

**Jauß, Hans Robert.** *Literaturgeschichte als Provokation*. Frankfurt/M.: Suhrkamp, 1970.

**Nünning, Ansgar.** "*Unreliable Narration* zur Einführung: Grundzüge einer kognitiv-narratologischen Theorie und Analyse unglaubwürdigen Erzählens." *Unreliable Narration: Studien zur Theorie und Praxis unglaubwürdigen Erzählens in der englischsprachigen Erzählliteratur*. Ed. Ansgar Nünning. Trier: WVT, 1998. 3–39.

**Riffaterre, Michel.** "Describing Poetic Structures: Two Approaches to Baudelaire's 'Les Chats.'" Tompkins 26–40.

**Strasen, Sven.** *Rezeptionstheorien: Literatur-, sprach- und kulturwissenschaftliche Ansätze und kulturelle Modelle*. Trier: WVT, 2008.

**Tompkins, Jane, ed.** *Reader-Response Criticism: From Formalism to Poststructuralism*. Baltimore: Johns Hopkins University Press, 1980.

**Warning, Rainer, ed.** *Rezeptionsästhetik: Theorie und Praxis*. Munich: Fink, 1975.

*Martin Middeke*

# 4 Poststructuralism/Deconstruction

Much like postmodernism in its relation to modernism, poststructuralism was both a critical revision and a radicalization of structuralist thought (cf. section II.1.4). Its most influential proponent, **Jacques Derrida**, argued that the crucial contribution of structuralism was not its claim that all human thought and activity follows structural patterns. What Derrida found much more important was the insight that no structure has ever succeeded in explaining its central organizing principle, its 'center,' in its own terms. No religion can explain its god, for example, and no Enlightenment philosopher arrived at a satisfactory definition of reason. After structuralism, Derrida suggested, one can no longer suppress the thought that such centers are mere constructs whose role is to fend off thoughts that threaten to subvert the structure—thoughts such as "God is dead," or "unreasonable statements can be true." There are two ways of dealing with this situation, Derrida argued: "to question systematically and rigorously ... the founding concepts of the entire history of philosophy," or to make these concepts "criticize themselves" by using them playfully, "here and there denouncing their limits, treating them as tools which can still be used" (*Writing* 358–59). Derrida adopted the second strategy, which he called **deconstruction**; the first was pursued most successfully by Michel Foucault, another pioneer of poststructuralism.

## 4.1 | Derrida: Deconstruction

Derrida's early philosophy, which he brought forward in such seminal studies as *Of Grammatology*, *Writing and Difference*, and *Speech and Phenomena* (all originally published in 1967), takes its cue from structuralism, psychoanalysis, phenomenology, and existentialism, but it goes beyond these approaches in that it is based entirely on language. It starts from de Saussure's assumption that the

**John Fowles, *The French Lieutenant's Woman***
It cannot come as a surprise that deconstructive thought has been extremely productive with postmodern, experimental literature, which highlights ambiguity, fragmentation and challenges traditional notions of originality, authenticity, causality, and narrative control and consensus in such open modes of writing as **parody, pastiche, travesty,** or **metafiction**. In John Fowles's 1969 metafictional novel *The French Lieutenant's Woman*, which is set in Victorian England, a third-person, omniscient narrator spends twelve chapters with setting up the illusion of a Victorian love story. Chapter 12 ends on a question about the female protagonist of the novel—"Who is Sarah?"—which any nineteenth-century omniscient narrator would clearly and necessarily have answered readily. Fowles's narrator, however, who turns out to be a shockingly self-conscious one, frustrates all traditional expectations by stating: "I do not know. This story I am telling is all imagination. These characters I create never existed outside my own mind" (Chapter 13). The metafictional strategy of the novel, thus, produces its own double reading that subverts a seemingly realist consensus and its conventions into its very parody laying bare the created illusion as mere *fiction*. What becomes deconstructed here is that, as the narrator goes on to explain, "in the age of Alain Robbe-Grillet and Roland Barthes" former centers no longer hold, which is corroborated by the fact that Fowles provides multiple endings for his novel that deny any idea of structural as well as epistemological closure.

*Interpretation*

relationship between a *signifier* and the *signified* to which it relates is arbitrary (cf. section II.1.4). Derrida radicalizes Saussure's concept, however, by suggesting that, on closer inspection, the relationship does not even exist, since the very link of signifier and signified is highly unstable. There is no guarantee that a signifier will evoke the intended signified. In other words, language resists the attribution of a unified or fixed 'meaning.' Rather, meaning is continually constructed and destructed in the act of communication (hence the term 'deconstruction'). In deconstructive thinking, then, signifiers are conceived as **free-floating** and engaged in **free play**. A deconstructive approach to language highlights this very quality inherent in language and in all other signification processes and thus reveals that such processes are always already deconstructing themselves.

**Key Concepts.** Consequently, Derrida directs deconstruction against the Western philosophical tradition, which he thinks is engaged in a **metaphysics of presence**. Metaphysics, for Derrida, means "the enterprise of returning 'strategically,' 'ideally' to an origin or to a priority thought to be simple, intact, normal, pure" (*Limited Inc* 236). Similar to Martin Heidegger, for instance, he rejects the privileging of presence in Edmund Husserl's phenomenology, because anything that *is* and, accordingly, any hypostatized concept of an absolute 'now' are always already exhausted in the experience of time. There is no absolute moment in time. In other words, before we are able to speak of something that *is*, we would first have to inquire into the very conditions that render such a presence possible. Derrida points out that traditional philosophy has to adopt transcendental or ontological positions, and thereby construct **oppositions and dualisms**, in order to be able to conceive of such an absolute presence in the first place. One of the central dualisms Derrida identifies is the dualism between oral and written language. In the history of Western philosophy (especially Plato, Rousseau, Saussure, Lévi-Strauss) there has been a clear preference for oral language as natural, original, and primordial, while written language has at the same time been seen as secondary and subordinated. While traditional theories look upon *logos* (speech, spoken words) as direct reflections of mental images, they regard written language as a symbol of already existing symbols and, thus, as second-hand and artificial. Derrida rejects this privileging as an undue **logocentrism** based on false oppositions such as primary/secondary or natural/artificial. The same is true, for him, of what he calls 'phallogocentrism': the entire set of patriarchal privileges based on the oppositions of male/female and dominant/subordinated. Derrida argues that speech is itself preceded by **writing/*écriture***, which he understands not simply as written signs on a page, but rather as an 'arche-writing,' a possibility of representation that emphasizes the gap that exists between what one wants to communicate and what actually is or may be communicated.

For this gap between the signifier and the signified, between the intention of an utterance and its pragmatic outcome, between the oral and the written, Derrida coins the neologism **differance**. What makes *differance* and *difference* different is inaudible in spoken speech: this emphasizes the importance of writing for any inquiry into language. Moreover, the change of the second 'e' into an 'a' marks the ineluctable gap that exists between the sign and its alleged univocal meaning, as the signifier denotes both "to differ" and "to defer." Thus, any stable meaning of the signifier 'difference' is itself deferred. Accordingly, Derrida replaces the idea of a clearly definable origin, which would have to precede the attribution of a pure signified, by a blank which he calls **trace** because it already leads to what is absent in meaning, to the breach inherent in all signification. Aside from this absence, but equally unavoidable, a signifier always carries a surplus of meaning and rhetoric—it can mean more than is said or intended—which he calls **supplement**.

**Against Speech Act Theory** as proposed by J.L. Austin and John Searle (cf. section V.5.1.6), Derrida famously argued that in order to function in communication, a sign needs to be iterable, that is, repeatable and hence intelligible beyond the presence of addressee and writer/speaker. In fact, the **iterability of the sign** constitutes the backbone of all communication. Writing as an iterative structure, however, has an inherent lack of ultimate authority. As each sign can be isolated from the sequence or chain of written speech it appears in and be "grafted" (*Limited Inc* 9) onto other sequences, the iterability of a sign documents its belonging to a process of **dissemination** and **decentering**, in which multiple perspectives and meanings can be generated because no speaker/writer, therefore, can be in total control of his utterances or speech acts. The deconstructive quality of language, hence, is the complex interplay of signs and chains of signs, to which there is neither a stable meaning nor a clearly defined origin and end. This corrects one of the most persevering misconceptions about deconstruction. Deconstruction does not say that there is *no* meaning or *no* intention. On the contrary, it insists that there is a multitude of meanings and a plethora of possible interpretations of an utterance, so that binary oppositions, dualisms, and essentialisms such as right/wrong, good/evil, man/woman, human/animal, etc. that require unequivocal attributions of meaning come to appear as unattainable, invalid logocentric ideas. Deconstruction replaces univocal truth, substance, and essence with free play, undecidability, decentering, and aporia. While traditional approaches highlight origins, authorities, authenticity, and (inter-)subjectivity, deconstruction focuses on instability, rhetoric, and (inter-)textuality. Derrida makes deconstruction interrogate, expose, and ultimately obliterate these oppositions.

**Applying Deconstruction.** Derrida himself always pointed out that he never conceived of deconstruction as a clearly defined method of interpretation. Nevertheless, the following passage from *Of Grammatology* shows how a reading may expose the deconstructive quality inherent in language:

The movements of deconstruction do not destroy structures from the outside. They are not possible and effective, nor can they take accurate aim, except by inhabiting those structures. Inhabiting them *in a certain way*, because one always inhabits, and all the more when one does not suspect it. Operating necessarily from the inside, borrowing all the strategic and economic resources of subversion from the old structure, borrowing them structurally, that is to say without being able to isolate their elements and atoms, the enterprise of deconstruction always in a certain way falls prey to its own work. (24)

Derrida is candid enough to admit that to say what deconstruction *is* remains caught up in the same ambiguous process of deferring that any other signifier is enmeshed in. At the same time, he points out that deconstruction is characterized by a **double movement**, which, on the one hand, remains true to the 'old structure' and then, on the other hand, subversively goes beyond it to prove its instability. Deconstructive interpretations, therefore, are characterized by a careful, close reading of texts, which discloses an oscillation between fidelity to and transgression of the 'old structure' in the second reading of the text at issue and which, thus, displaces any 'definite' or 'ultimate' meanings.

Any given text can be subjected to a deconstructive reading in this fashion when the reader selects parts of a text and investigates intensely

---

**James Joyce, *A Portrait of the Artist as a Young Man***

James Joyce's autobiographical narrative portrays the development of Joyce's alter ego Stephen Dedalus from childhood, school time, university to the point when Stephen realizes that his destiny in life is to become an artist and that in order to follow his vocation he has to leave his country, the Church, and his family. Stephen self-confidently writes in his diary: "Welcome, O life! I go to encounter for the millionth time the reality of experience and to forge in the smithy of my soul the uncreated consciousness of my race" (Part V). A straightforward reading following the aesthetic paradigms of the *Künstler-* or *Entwicklungsroman* would see this resolution as the authentic culmination of self-realization and the fulfillment of the personal development which the novel describes. A deconstructive approach, then, would acknowledge this but in a second reading could, for instance, point to the ambivalence of the verb "to forge" which denotes "to create" but also "to

fake." This second, subversive reading clearly challenges the authority given to Stephen's resolution and self-assertion, as it produces a breach between the perspectives of Stephen, who does not even seem to be aware of the ambiguity in his choice of words, and the (implicit) author, who appears to be much more reserved about Stephen's resolution. As the narrative in this final section turns from a third-person figural point of view into a first-person narrative in diary form, one may argue that, on the one hand, Stephen has at last found a true, pure and authentic voice ("I") and self. The deconstructive second reading, however, would decenter such certainties and the alleged coherence of Stephen's account and, thereby, render him an increasingly unreliable narrator. The binary oppositions of truth/fiction, authenticity/inauthenticity, reliability/unreliability are also broken down by the very title of the novel, in which Joyce characteristically chooses to speak of *a* portrait (out of many possible ones) rather than *the* (one and only valid) portrait.

*Interpretation*

into its language and its rhetoric in order to accentuate how this text untangles its own assumptions and, thus, generates a surplus of meaning that can no longer be unified and that contradicts the idea of a stable truth and essence. While it is true that deconstruction may appear as a relatively isolated analysis of language games immanent to language, and while it is also true that deconstruction shifts the analytical perspective from semantics to semiotics, this does not mean that deconstruction entails a semiotic nihilism or an epistemological as well as methodological 'anything goes.' As Jonathan Culler rightly points out, there are **strong** and **weak readings**. A strong reading is one that reveals through close analysis of the text's rhetoric the shifting, non-transparent relationship between the network of signifiers and their referents in the world outside.

The high wave of deconstructive criticism has ebbed away, as much criticism since the 1970s has turned to the question of how the language games and the multiplicity of meanings highlighted by deconstruction function in social, political, and historical settings (see box). These developments show the lasting importance of deconstruction, which rests upon crucial insights that seem incontestable today. We are aware of the central importance of language and rhetoric for our lives, and we recognize that discourses of any provenance (cultural, political, historical) share in fictionality. Deconstruction can be a sensitizing force in unfolding the power structures inherent in discourse—an ethical perspective that Derrida himself developed in his later work and that Foucault pursued in many of his writings (see the following section and entry II.12)—and it reminds us that expecting essential truth and harmonious, 'ultimate' meaning may amount to self-deception.

---

**Focus on Poststructuralist Legacies**

Poststructuralist thought and deconstructive approaches have influenced a number of disciplines. Beside Derrida and Foucault, the foremost poststructuralist of the first generation was the psychologist **Jacques Lacan**, who developed his ideas in deconstructive interaction with Freud (cf. entry II.7). Later, poststructuralism was a major influence on postcolonial theorists **Edward Said** and **Homi K. Bhabha** (cf. entry III.4) and on the pioneer of contemporary gender studies, **Judith Butler** (cf. entry II.6).

---

## 4.2 | Foucault: Discourse, Knowledge, Power

**The Concept of Discourse.** The French term *discours* has several meanings, most of which are shared by its English counterpart. In general usage, as well as in rhetoric, it refers to a public speech. In linguistics it broadly refers to a stretch of actual spoken or written language, based both on linguistic rules and on the social rules underlying the communicative situation. In narratology it is distinguished from 'story,' or series of events, and means the way in which the story is told. **Foucault**'s concept of discourse, which has been highly influential in the social sciences and the humanities, partakes of all of these meanings. It refers to a set of actual spoken or written statements by people who are accorded authority on the subject of these statements. (A priest, for example, can be part of religious discourse; the weatherman on TV can be part of meteorological discourse, and so on.) Like a public speaker, these people are listened to because they are supposed to be authorities on the subject, but in another way of looking at it, they have a say on what constitutes an authority on their subject *because* people are listening to them in the first place (Dreyfus and Rabinow 44–52). In a way, they are the narrators who determine how the story gets told, since their version is the one in which people believe. This problem led Foucault to two central conclusions: we need to examine the linguistic and social rules underlying such discourses, and we need to rethink our notions of knowledge and power.

**Analyzing Discourse.** Foucault developed his concept of discourse in a series of historical studies devoted to specific discourses or discursive phenomena (a project he summed up as *The Archeology of Knowledge* in his 1969 publication of that title). To name one example, the first of his historical studies, *Madness and Civilization*, traced the process by which **madness** became abnormal as "mad" people were first separated from society, then locked away like criminals, then studied as medical cases. Foucault shows that definitions of madness changed quite drastically over time and that they depended on the discourses that regulated the debate on madness. In the Renaissance there was no categorical distinction between the normal world and the world of madness. Mad people moved around rather freely and were taken seriously on a number of subjects. During the political and economic turmoil of the seventeenth century, madmen were criminalized because they were regarded as depriving the community of much-needed manpower. In the nineteenth century madness came under the authority of the emerging discipline of psychiatry, which distinguished mad people from criminals and brought them under the subtler but more effective regime of the mental clinic. More fundamentally, however, madness became a **means of defining normalcy**. The more thoroughly madness was defined as abnormal, the more powerful became complementary notions such as reason and sanity—to the extent that nowadays reason is synonymous with being right (*avoir raison* in French) and that the medical apparatus takes up an ever-increasing portion of our resources.

As this example and others show, Foucault assumes that discourses follow certain rules that change over time and that can be studied and systematized. These rules determine how one can speak about a phenomenon: in what words, from what theoretical standpoints, in what social context, from what subject position, and so on. In his lecture "**The Order of Discourse**" Foucault pointed out that the main function of a discourse is to limit what can be said about a phenomenon: many possible statements are ruled out as being unreasonable, incorrect, taboo; others fall outside of disciplinary boundaries or are ruled out by previous scholarship ("authoritative definitions"); and many discourses require long, rigid courses of study that impress their spoken and unspoken rules upon potential speakers. More or less directly, all of Foucault's historical studies suggested that the human sciences—and by implication, all attempts to order knowledge—are not a linear progress toward truth. On the contrary, the fundamental shifts Foucault found in the history of science indicate that different periods and cultures have their own notions of truth, so that **truth is the outcome of discourse** rather than the yardstick by which discourse can be measured. Like Derrida, though in a different way, Foucault subverted the logocentric view that history, and the history of knowledge in particular, follows universal principles such as truth, reason,

or linear progress. In his view, the history of our culture is the history of a continual but ultimately arbitrary reordering of knowledge, and it is the historian's job to trace these orders that delimit what and how we think.

**Knowledge and Power.** While Foucault's early work was mainly concerned with the systematic study of discourse, from the early 1970s on it increasingly focused on the connections between discourse and power. The example of the public speaker's authority shows that power and knowledge depend on each other: without knowledge the speaker would not be regarded as an authority, but as an authority he can influence the discursive rules that define what kind of knowledge is authoritative—and, indeed, 'true.' For Foucault, then, power is not something that certain people, groups of people, or institutions 'have' while others do not. Power comes not from above but from below: every social relation is also a power relation since it involves questions of authority (of narrating a story one's own way) and since all communication takes place in a network of discursive patterns and practices that limits our choice of words, perspectives, and subject positions. Oppressive structures are not only found in dictatorships but in many everyday situations where discursive and non-discursive factors subject the individual to certain modes of behavior. As a historian, Foucault identifies this **microphysics of power** as typical of modern Western society. He locates its origins in the Enlightenment project of forming each individual into an ideal member of society. The basics of this project are laid out in his study *Discipline and Punish: The Birth of the Prison*. Instead of punishing criminals in spectacular symbolic rituals such as public floggings or beheadings, Foucault argues, the Enlightenment philosophers and their followers meant to 'discipline' criminals. They confined them to an enclosed space, regulated their activities, constantly monitored their behavior, and subjected them to all kinds of study and treatment. This is a much more efficient (and microstructural) way of exerting power than the traditional punishments because it eventually makes individuals monitor *themselves* to ensure that they behave normally. Foucault suggests that it can be found not only in prisons but also in schools, hospitals,

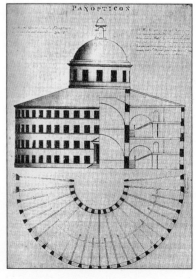

The 'panopticon' was designed by eighteenth-century thinker Jeremy Bentham. The drawing is contemporary.

factories, the military, and all other disciplinary institutions. The prototypical disciplinary structure, for him, is the 'panopticon,' where all inmates constantly feel that they are under observation from a central tower (see illustration and also section I.5.2). Foucault's work on the power/knowledge nexus further eroded the belief in ideals such as neutrality, objectivity, and reason. It was taken up by political theory, cultural criticism, and literary studies. Political approaches to literature such as the New Historicism (cf. entry II.5)

and postcolonial theory (cf. section III.4.1) began to examine the way in which literary texts both shape and are shaped by the power relations underlying our transmission of knowledge. Jürgen Link drew on Foucault's discourse theory to argue that literature functions as an **interdiscourse**: through various devices, it brings together knowledge from various specialized discourses and makes it accessible to a larger public. This notion can also be found in some ecocritical approaches to literature (cf. section II.14.5).

## 4.3 | Other Poststructuralist Thinkers

**Roland Barthes.** One of the best-known theorists of his time, Barthes drew attention to the arbitrariness and manipulability of signs in his popular magazine columns, where he analyzed the semiotic strategies behind the media presentation of everyday phenomena such as red wine, magazine covers, and jet pilots. In literary studies his most influential contribution was his essay "**The Death of the Author**" (1967), which refuted the traditional notion that every text has a single meaning intended by the author that must be deciphered by the reader. A more modern view, Barthes suggested, would acknowledge that every reader in fact rewrites each text he reads because he inscribes his own ideas and interpretations into the text: "every text is eternally written in the *here and now*." Barthes praised contemporary experimental literature for supporting this process by leaving more work for the reader to do. He called such literature 'writerly texts' (*textes scriptibles*), as opposed to traditional 'readerly texts' (*textes lisibles*) that expect a passive reader.

**Jean Baudrillard.** Like Barthes, Baudrillard was concerned that representation was coming to overlay or even replace reality in Western society (cf. section I.2.7.3). He approaches this problem from a historical perspective and argues that modern culture lost faith in the connection between its symbols and the real. It counterbalanced the loss of this 'symbolic order' by producing signs that did not refer directly to reality anymore ('simulacra'), a process that Baudrillard calls **simulation**. Contemporary Western society, he suggests, has reached the highest level of simulation, in which the distinction between copy and original, reality and illusion, has been annihilated and these poles have merged. Reality is no longer "that of which it is possible to provide an equivalent reproduction" but "that which is always already reproduced" (73). In other words, the signifiers in our culture have set themselves free from their signifieds and have assumed a self-referential status, replacing reality in such a way that they constitute a new reality of altogether self-referential signs: **hyperreality**. Baudrillard takes a more skeptical stance than Derrida on this "freeplay of signifiers" as it helps mass media and capitalist institutions to manipulate our perception.

**Jean-François Lyotard.** Drawing on many of Derrida's and Foucault's ideas, Lyotard took poststructuralism in a more openly political and ethical direction. Foucault's influence can be detected in Lyotard's argument that societies and individuals think of themselves in narratives, and that the power structures implied in these narratives need to be studied. His best-known book, *The Postmodern Condition*, draws on this argument to define postmodernism as the end of **grand narratives** that subsume all aspects of a society under

Disneyland is one of Baudrillard's examples for the condition of hyperreality.

a universal concept such as progress or freedom. Lyotard advocated an ethics of 'little narratives' that have their own rules and can better accommodate individual backgrounds and opinions. His second major study, *The Differend*, is devoted to the question of what to do when two such little narratives come into conflict because they cannot describe a problem in the same terms—a situation he calls a "differend," or irreconcilable clash of languages. He suggests that literature can "bear witness to differends by finding idioms for them" (13).

**The Yale School.** Literary critics Harold Bloom, Geoffrey Hartman, J. Hillis Miller, and Paul de Man, all of whom taught at Yale in the 1970s, played an important role in spreading deconstruction in the United States. In their own work they took poststructuralist thought in various directions and developed individual methodological perspectives. While Bloom is best known for his model of 'anxiety of influence,' which mainly draws on other theoretical sources, Miller defended deconstruction against the criticism of established American scholars and offered practical applications in his studies of nineteenth-century literature. De Man closely cooperated with Derrida and deconstructed what he saw as the traditional privileging of metaphor over metonymy and symbol over allegory.

**Another generation of poststructuralism** can be said to have emerged following the work of Gilles Deleuze and Félix Guattari, which is strongly influenced by psychoanalysis, ranges across a variety of discourses, and critiques the dominance of capitalism in modern society. Important representatives of this new generation include Fredric Jameson, Alain Badiou, and Slavoj Žižek.

## Select Bibliography

**Baudrillard, Jean.** *Symbolic Exchange and Death.* Trans. Iain Hamilton Grant. London: Sage, 1993.

**Culler, Jonathan.** *On Deconstruction: Theory and Criticism after Structuralism.* Ithaca: Cornell University Press, 1982.

**Derrida, Jacques.** *Limited Inc.* Evanston: Northwestern University Press, 1988.

**Derrida, Jacques.** *Of Grammatology.* Trans. Gayatri Spivak. Baltimore: Johns Hopkins University Press, 1976.

**Derrida, Jacques.** *Writing and Difference.* Trans. Alan Bass. Chicago: University of Chicago Press, 1978.

**Dreyfus, Hubert L., and Paul Rabinow.** *Michel Foucault: Beyond Structuralism and Hermeneutics.* Chicago: University of Chicago Press, 1982.

**Flynn, Bernard.** "Derrida and Foucault: Madness and Writing." *Derrida and Deconstruction.* Ed. Hugh J. Silverman. New York: Routledge, 1989. 201–18.

**Foucault, Michel.** "The Order of Discourse." *Untying the Text: A Post-Structuralist Reader.* Ed. Robert Young. Boston: Routledge, 1981. 48–76.

**Kammler, Clemens.** "Historische Diskursanalyse." *Neue Literaturtheorien. Eine Einführung.* Ed. Klaus-Michael Bogdal. Opladen: Westdeutscher Verlag, 1990. 31–55.

**Link, Jürgen.** "Literaturanalyse als Interdiskursanalyse: Am Beispiel des Ursprungs literarischer Symbolik in der Kollektivsymbolik." *Diskurstheorien und Literaturwissenschaft.* Eds. Jürgen Fohrmann and Harro Müller. Frankfurt: Suhrkamp, 1988. 284–307.

**Lyotard, Jean-François.** *The Differend: Phrases in Dispute.* Trans. Georges Van Den Abbeele. Manchester: Manchester University Press, 1988.

**Lyotard, Jean-François.** *The Postmodern Condition: A Report on Knowledge.* 1979. Trans. Geoff Bennington and Brian Massumi. Minneapolis: University of Minnesota Press, 1984.

**Norris, Christopher.** *Deconstruction.* London: Routledge, 1991.

**Stocker, Barry.** *Derrida on Deconstruction.* London: Routledge, 2006.

**Zima, Peter V.** *Die Dekonstruktion: Einführung und Kritik.* Stuttgart: UTB, 1994.

*Martin Middeke / Timo Müller*

# 5  New Historicism and Discourse Analysis

## 5.1 | General Aspects

New historicism and discourse analysis are cross-disciplinary practices of critical inquiry that study literary texts and their socio-cultural functions. Both explain the **circulation and production of meaning** in specific historical moments, and share a micro-analytic mode of interpretation. They distrust holistic and monological explanations applied by historicism and intellectual history. New historicism and discourse analysis stress the reciprocity and the mutual constitution of the linguistic and the social: "On the one hand, the social is understood to be discursively constructed; and on the other, language-use is understood to be always and necessarily dialogical, to be socially and materially determined and constrained" (Montrose 15). New historicism and discourse analysis oppose the transparency of linguistic signs (cf. entry II.4) and deny the assumption of an underlying truth in texts of the past. Their interpretative procedures start from a position within history, society, institutions,

politics, class, and gender conditions. They reinforce text analysis that investigates "both the social presence to the world of the literary text and the social presence of the world in the literary text" (Greenblatt, *Renaissance* 5).

New historicism and discourse analysis are **contextualizing methods of interpretation**. New historicism emphasizes cultural intertextuality: Literary texts relate to one another in contexts that are inseparable from the cultural and historical moment. New historicism dissolves the distinction between literature and social life, and, in doing so, heralds the notion of culture as text. Discourse analysis studies the syntactic and semantic structures of texts (i.e., literary, political, religious, scientific) within socio-cultural moments. Moving from Marxist theory and its critique of ideology to discourse analysis, new historicists examine texts as particular discursive practices (popular or elitist). They expound the ways in which literary discourses interact with and are determined by other discourses, institutions, and practices of society in a specific historical situation. Literary discourse contains the "dynamic, unstable, and reciprocal relationship between the discursive and material domains" (Montrose 23). Similarly, new historicists regard literary texts as "collective social constructions" (Greenblatt, Introduction 6).

> **Definition**
>
> While → discourse analysis examines the social production of knowledge, → New Historicism discusses the social production of literature.

## 5.2 | Emergence and Characteristics

New historicism and discourse analysis differ from each other in their chronology of emergence and the theoretical schools from which they derive their critical impulse.

Discourse analysis theory takes its beginnings in structural linguistics (cf. section V.5.2). It has developed into a critical practice that explores the social production of knowledge in many areas, i.e.

sociology, history, or anthropology. In general terms, discourse analysis studies the structures of texts and considers both their linguistic and socio-cultural dimensions in order to determine how meaning is constructed. While earlier studies of discourse analysis concentrate on verbal exchanges or linguistic segments of discourse (utterances, sentences, words) to determine the relations of meaning, more recent studies examine "social discourse" as literary and non-literary material related to broader cultural, institutional, and political contexts. Marc Angenot defines discourse as "all that is said or written in a given state of society." Discourse analysis focuses upon "generic systems, the repertories of topics, the enunciative rules which, in a given society, organize the *sayable*—the narratable and the arguable" (13; emphasis in original, my trans.). For instance, a study of nineteenth-century realism would explain narrative realism as a way of making sense of the world in various discourses: medical, sociological, and economic. In discourse analysis, the study of literature as a singular and autonomous text loses its privileged place in favor of a study of discursively shared strategies which contribute to the general production of knowledge and power. **Michel Foucault** explores the articulation of knowledge and power in medical, disciplinary, and historical discourse. His notion that power is a "productive network which runs through the whole social body" (119) has greatly influenced the new historicist notion of an interplay between social and aesthetic discourse (cf. section II.4.2). In his study *Renaissance Self-Fashioning: From More to Shakespeare*, Stephen Greenblatt, for instance, demonstrates the ways in which literature goes beyond mirroring society and plays a central part in the production of power and the self in early modern England.

New Historicism. Two developments characterize the rise of New Historicism in the 1980s: In Great Britain, New Historicism emerges within Renaissance Studies opposing the history-of-ideas approach of works such as E. M. W. Tillyard's *The Elizabethan World Picture,* that attempts to extract the age's thought and attitudes from literary texts (cf. entry I.2.2). In the United States, it evolves from the so-called "French turn" in the North American academy and the challenges against formalist thinking by poststructuralism and deconstruction (cf. entry II.4). American New Historicism mainly draws upon Michel Foucault's analysis of power and discourse. Other important sources of influence are Louis Althusser's concept of ideology as a system of meaning that positions everybody in imaginary relations to the real relations in which one lives, Raymond Williams' analyses of the institutions of culture (forms of drama and fiction, the press, language, education, and literacy), Michel de Certeau's idea of heterology (i.e. history writing as a science of the "other"), and Clifford Geertz's conceptualization of culture as an accumulated body of symbolic forms and systems that are socially constituted and historically transmitted.

*Foucault's influence on both discourse analysis and New Historicism*

## 5.3 | Critical Practice and Key Concepts

Critics are divided on whether historicism can be seen as the intellectual predecessor of New Historicism. Whereas historicism favors a synecdochic and organic interpretation of history that adds up to an empirical whole, New Historicism follows a poststructuralist view of history that is best characterized as chiastic. At the center of New Historicism is a "reciprocal concern with the **historicity of texts** and the **textuality of history**" (Montrose 20). Montrose's famous chiasmus refers to both the fact that all writing is embedded in a specific social and historical situation and the poststructuralist premise that we do not have unmediated and authentic access to the past. To the new historicist, history disintegrates into ever widening relations of discourses, and he thus questions any trans-historical theory of textual meaning like hermeneutics (cf. entry II.2). Claire Colebrook sees New Historicism as a "form of texual inductivism" (24) that does not worship pre-given totalities such as 'world-picture' or 'civilization.'

New historicist investigations focus on the interaction between text and the world. Stephen Greenblatt, for instance, calls for a critical practice that no longer considers literary works as "a fixed set of texts that are set apart from all other forms of expression" (Introduction 6), but rather interprets their interplay with textual forms and symbolic structures perceivable in the larger social world. Texts function as **mediators** between diverse discourses in society such as religion, philosophy, the sciences, and the arts.

In order to trace textual connections, practitioners of New Historicism (foremost among them Stephen Greenblatt, Catherine Gallagher, Louis Montrose, Aram Veeser) consider literary texts as focal points of "social energy" (cf. Greenblatt, *Negotiations*). They seek to reveal the **cultural transactions** contained within literary texts which they

*The historicity of texts and the textuality of history*

define as a "site of institutional and ideological contestation" (Greenblatt, *Negotiations* 3). Since history is seen as a global text, both literary and non-literary texts transform into a dynamic field of force in which many voices of culture converge and interact. For Greenblatt, therefore, the study of genre (such as Renaissance drama) is "an exploration of the **poetics of culture**." The poetics of culture gives emphasis to the productive power of representation and its links "to the complex network of institutions, practices, and beliefs that constitute the culture as a whole" (Introduction 6).

New historicists rely on a vocabulary of interpretation that demystifies traditional assumptions of a mimetic conceptualization of art, and they debunk any notions of stable meanings, as in humanist thought. Literature connects to history through all the texts that circulate in a specific moment in time and by showing the interrelatedness of human activities. The key terms, **circulation,**

Interpretation

### Phillis Wheatley, "On Being Brought"

New historicism can be understood as a critical practice that treats the literary text as a space where power relations become visible. The following reading of Phillis Wheatley's "On Being Brought from Africa to America" (1773) exemplifies what New Historicism calls the poetics of culture.

'Twas mercy brought me from my Pagan land,
Taught my benighted soul to understand
That there's a God, that there's a Saviour too:
Once I redemption neither sought nor knew,
Some view our sable race with scornful eye,
"Their colour is a diabolic die."
Remember, Christians, Negroes, black as Cain,
May be refin'd, and join th' angelic train.

Wheatley's poem seeks to reverse misconceptions about the black race that are motivated by Christian religion. The speaker of the poem conveys her subtle critique by using puns or wordplays which carry implications that go beyond the surface of the poem's meaning. Words like "sable race" (line 5), "die" (6), and "Cain" (7) connect the poem to the larger context of the Black Atlantic and counter negative racial connotations. Sable, for instance, derives from the language of heraldry and denotes the color black in a coat of arms. A sable is also a mammal that is valued highly for its dark and soft fur. The poem's wordplays evoke images of racial pride to question some of the widely held racial stereotypes of Wheatley's white Christian brethren. In line six, the speaker of the poem quotes them verbatim: "Their colour is a diabolic die." This statement aligns Black people with the Biblical source of evil, but, at the same time, the end-rhymes "eye" and "die" redirect the reader's perception and open up a different layer of meaning

and contextual reading. In the context of slavery, "die," alludes to the blue indigo dye which was produced by black slaves in the West Indies and gained significant wealth for many white Christians in the colonies and England. The statement thus opens the reader's "eye" for the questionable moral double standards which underlie the "scornful eye" of white Christians who profit from forced labor. Hinting also at its superficial nature, the use of "die" challenges any moral judgments based on the color of skin alone. Similarly, the biblical reference to "Cain" in the concluding couplet contains further intertextual references. Cain is a homonym (similar in sound, but different in meaning) for cane or sugar cane, another commodity of the West Indies, produced by black slaves and central to the triangular trade between Africa, America, and Europe. Ironically, although black people belong to the "cursed race," their forced work sustains the wealth and progress of white Christian societies. Thus, if white Christians "remembered" all of this, they would have to recall their Christian obligation toward their black brethren.

The example demonstrates New Historicism's practice of interpretation. New historicists link the literary to historical circumstances and the text to social effect. Literature turns into an "agonistic field of verbal and social practices" (Montrose 30). The relation between the text and its historical context is one of exchange and negotiation. Wheatley's poem can be interpreted either as a repetition of the white power which occurs in the real world and is embodied by religion, or as a subtle reflection upon power's dependence on linguistic performance, as in the case of the "diabolical die," in which reality is renegotiated through the poem's cultural intertextuality. (For additional examples of the use of New Historicism in literary analysis see sections IV.2.3 and IV.3.2).

exchange, negotiation, and struggle, are derived from the nascent capitalism of the early modern period. Similar to the circulation of material commodities, new historicists investigate the proliferation and circulation of representations which resonate within a given text and let it "reach out beyond its formal boundaries to a larger world" (Greenblatt, "Resonance" 79). Stories become meaningful through circulation, reproduction, and exchange.

Rather than looking for unity in a literary work, new historicists elicit its messy vitality. Their readings aspire to find distortions, voices of the excluded, and subversive patterns. Regarding anecdotes as the raw material of history, they frequently use them to develop **alternative histories** or microhistories that retrieve the voices of the once-forgotten and seek for the return of the oppressed. According to Samuel Johnson's *Dictionary*, an anecdote is a secret history. For new historicists, anecdotes function as history's 'other,' a digression that highlights contingency and deviates from the master narratives of totalizing and progressive history.

## 5.4 | New Historicism and Contemporary Criticism

Since its emergence in the 1980s, New Historicism has been fervently disputed by literary critics and historians alike. While many critics object to New Historicism's methodology, especially its fallacy of finding significance everywhere, others, like feminist critics, challenge its limited scope, as most studies focus on canonical texts and demonstrate blindness to gender questions. Many scholars take issue with new historicists' hunt for analogies, balkanization of literature, and retrospective liberalism. Paul Cantor puts it tersely: "One good anecdote, one semi-plausible homology, and you are in business" (23). Other critics contest New Historicism's relativism and its poststructuralist textualization of history, which downplays the importance of an extra-textual social and historical background. In light of de-centering any master narrative, Terry Eagleton refers to the **absence of a macro-historical perspective** characterizing New Historicism. Focusing on anecdotes evokes the arbitrariness of history, but leaves aside the socio-economic condition of history and the subject's role in it. Given the fact that its most prominent exponents have come out of the English department at the University of California, Berkeley, he concludes: "Perhaps it is easier in California to feel that history is random, unsystematic, directionless, than in some less privileged places in the world" (198). The British answer to American New Historicism and its emphasis on poststructuralism and discourse analysis has been **cultural materialism**. In contrast to American New Historicism, it explicitly analyzes literature and the self as always being socially, materially, and historically conditioned.

Despite its controversial nature and its lack of a systematic theory, New Historicism has irrevocably dissolved the distinction between historical and formal methods in literary criticism. Given the vast expansion of work on culture in the 1980s and 1990s, the return to history has brought about contextual interpretations where literary and non-literary texts interact, and has thus contributed to a widening cultural perspective in literary criticism. If, as Jacques Derrida asserts, nothing is extratextual, literary critics have directed their theory-driven lenses upon 'texts' (semiotic products) of all kinds—from soccer matches to soap operas, from *Hamlet* to talk shows. Particularly, under the influence of journals such as *Representations* and monograph series such as "The New Historicism: Studies in Cultural Poetics," the American branch of New Historicism has transformed into a unified field of criticism with productive relations between literary critics and historians (Hayden White, Dominick LaCapra), postcolonial critics (Edward Said, Tzvetan Todorov), and ethnologists like Clifford Geertz. Another field of critical interest for American New Historicism is Romanticism. Unlike Renaissance historicism, literary critics like Jerome McGann, Jon Klancher, or Alan Liu show a stronger affiliation to Foucault and claim their own oppositional historicism while reading Romanticism as an 'ideology.' New historicism's material relativism and its anti-hermeneutic impulse currently find entrance into theories of social practice that oppose textualism and examine the routines and enactments of social life by interpreting culture through objects, discourse, knowledge, and agency.

The return to history
in literary criticism

## Select Bibliography

**Angenot, Marc.** *1889: Un état du discours social*. Québec: Le Préambule, 1989.

**Cantor, Paul A.** "Stephen Greenblatt's New Historicist Vision." *Academic Questions* 4 (1993): 21–36.

**Colebrook, Claire.** *New Literary Histories: New Historicism and Contemporary Criticism*. Manchester: St. Martin's Press, 1997.

**Eagleton, Terry.** *Literary Theory: An Introduction*. Oxford: Blackwell, 2008.

**Foucault, Michel.** *Power / Knowledge: Selected Interviews and Other Writings, 1972–1977*. Ed. Colin Gordon. New York: Pantheon Books, 1980.

**Gallagher, Catherine, and Stephen J. Greenblatt.** *Practicing New Historicism*. Chicago: University of Chicago Press, 2000.

**Greenblatt, Stephen J.** Introduction. *Genre* 15.1–2 (1982): 3–6.

**Greenblatt, Stephen J.** *Renaissance Self-Fashioning: From More to Shakespeare*. Chicago: University of Chicago Press, 1980.

**Greenblatt, Stephen J.** "Resonance and Wonder." *Literary Theory Today*. Eds. Peter Collier and Helga Geyer-Ryan. Cambridge: Polity, 1990. 74–90.

**Greenblatt, Stephen J.** *Shakespearean Negotiations: The Circulation of Social Energy in Renaissance England*. Oxford: Clarendon Press, 1988.

**Montrose, Louis A.** "Professing the Renaissance: The Poetics and Politics of Culture." *The New Historicism*. Ed. H. Aram Veeser. New York: Routledge, 1989. 15–36.

**Scheiding, Oliver.** "Intertextualität." *Gedächtniskonzepte der Literaturwissenschaft: Theoretische Grundlegung und Anwendungsperspektiven*. Eds. Astrid Erll and Ansgar Nünning. Berlin: de Gruyter, 2005. 53–72.

**Spiegel, Gabrielle M., ed.** *Practicing History: New Directions in Historical Writing After the Linguistic Turn*. New York: Routledge, 2005.

**Veeser, H. Aram.** *The New Historicism*. New York: Routledge, 1989.

*Oliver Scheiding*

# 6 Gender Studies, Transgender Studies, Queer Studies

## 6.1 | Changing Concepts of Gender

What is known today as Gender Studies emerged in the late 1960s and 1970s in the wake of the second wave of the Women's Movement. At its core were an analysis of hierarchical gender structures that oppressed women and a critique of androcentrism, of a male-dominated world-view masquerading as a universal standpoint. At first, the focus was on the study of the most obviously excluded group, i.e. on women, which was reflected in the term **Women's Studies**. Women's Studies was gradually renamed **Gender Studies**, a shift that indicated a greater emphasis on gender relations, gender regimes, and the structural function of gender in society.

This and further developments are closely related to changing concepts of gender resulting from various theoretical interventions. The first to mention is the conceptual differentiation between **sex**, which denotes the biological difference between male and female, and **gender**, which refers to the social and cultural differentiation of masculinity and femininity, in the 1960s. The social and cultural **construction of gender**—rather than its 'natural' derivation from sex—can be further specified. In psychological terms, gender is used in the sense of gender identity. From a sociological perspective, gender is constructed in social interaction in the sense that we perform our own gender through specific gender markers like voice, hairstyle, clothes, ways of behaving etc. and that we read other people's gender on the basis of these signs. Thirdly, gender must be considered as a social institution that "establishes patterns of expectations for individuals, orders the social processes of everyday life, is built into the major social organizations of society, such as economy, ideology, the family, and politics" (Lorber 1). These various definitions were instrumental in analysing the power relationships governing the cultural gender order. In this context, Michel Foucault's work on discourse formation and the interplay of power and resistance in the shaping of discourse as well

as the productive force of discourse itself has been invaluable (cf. section II.4.2).

All these theoretical moves concentrate on the category of gender while leaving sex untouched, because they are based on the assumption that sex is biologically determined and hence 'natural.' Judith Butler in her seminal study **Gender Trouble** of 1990 questions this essentialist view of sex and instead argues for a constructivist perspective of both sex and gender as entities that are culturally produced. Butler claims that the notion of sex as a 'natural' category that exists beyond any discourse is nothing but the effect of a specific discourse: "gender is also the discursive/cultural means by which 'sexed nature' or 'a natural sex' is produced and established as 'prediscursive,' prior to culture, a politically neutral surface on which culture acts" (7). Butler does not deny the materiality of the body as such, but claims that it emerges within the confines of a regulatory norm which produces a gendered body based on a binary system (male or female) that circumscribes the parameters of its intelligibility as a human body (see *Bodies That Matter*). The constant repetition of that norm through 'doing gender,' what Butler calls **performativity**, results in its sedimentation and contributes to its naturalisation, while an unsettling of that norm can be achieved through introducing differences into the process of repetition.

The dissociation of both gender and sex from a 'natural' order paved the way to a historical analysis of the changes these categories underwent in the course of time and in different geographical and cultural contexts, as well as the cultural interventions that contributed to these modifications. Joan W. Scott's argument for the productivity of gender as a category of historical analysis provided a useful theoretical basis for a great number of historical studies, e.g. the massive five-volume *A History of Women in the West* under the general editorship of Georges Duby and Michelle Perrot, to name but the most ambitious project. The most influential book to deal with different constructions of the sexed body and sexual difference was Thomas Laqueur's *Making Sex: Body and Gender from the Greeks to Freud*, which traces the gradual change from a one-sex model (the two genders aligned hierarchically on a single axis according to the degree of their metaphysical perfection, with the man on top of the scale) to a two-sex model (two incommensurable sexes grounded in a radical biological dimorphism) in the course of the eighteenth century. Laqueur's analysis, which was mainly derived from medical sources, corroborated previous socio-historical research that had located the cementing of gender difference through the construction of biologically determined sexual characteristics at around the same time.

To capture the power structures governing gender relations in a patriarchal system, Antonio Gramsci's notion of hegemony has gained a certain currency, especially in masculinity studies since the 1980s. R. W. Connell uses the term **hegemonic masculinity** to denote the historically varying forms of masculinity that occupy the hegemonic position in a given social order. Hegemonic masculinity is normative and refers both to a pattern of practices and a set of ideals, fantasies and desires that serve as a model to be aspired to. According to Connell, the field of multiple and shifting masculinities is divided into hegemonic masculinity and subordinated masculinities (e.g. gay men), which are defined in a hierarchical relation to this norm. Although hegemonic masculinity is enacted by a relatively small number of men, the majority of men benefit from its systemic value—Connell calls this the patriarchal dividend—and therefore entertain a relationship of complicity with it (Connell; Connell and Messerschmidt).

## 6.2 | Transgender Studies and Queer Theory

Important theorists
of gender

**Michel Foucault**, whose work inspired both Laqueur's and Butler's theories of the construction of sex, also makes a strong case for the discursive production of sexuality in his seminal *History of Sexuality*. He delineates a discursive explosion around sex since the eighteenth century and the emergence of sexuality as a field of knowledge in the nineteenth century. Most crucially, rather than hailing sexuality as a liberating and transgressive force of resistance against societal regulations, he places it squarely within the realm of power and identifies it as an apparatus of power in its own right, for example in the area of biopolitics and the regulation of reproduction through specific mechanisms of control. With respect to (male) homosexuality he establishes a shift from same-sex relations as discrete acts of sodomy treated as temporary aberrations to the homosexual as a species, whose whole being is defined by his sexuality in the second half of the nineteenth century, a process Foucault calls the **incorporation of perversions**.

**Judith Butler**'s theoretical interventions foreground and dismantle two key categories of the cultural gender norm: heterosexuality and the binary structure of gender. The cultural construction of sex challenges the duality of sex and gender. This opens up an area beyond or between male and female that can be conceptualized as a 'third space' or pluralisation of genders and sexualities and that is encompassed by the term **transgender**. Transgender functions as an umbrella term for all kinds of gender diversity that, explicitly or implicitly, question the binary gender order (including transsexuality, intersexuality, cross-dressing, and other formations) and has initiated a separate area of research: transgender studies (cf. Stryker and Whittle).

The interdependence of sex, gender and sexuality has been variously described in terms of a coherent system that significantly underpins social structures. Gayle Rubin calls the cultural logic that turns anatomical sex into social gender within the framework of a heterosexual matrix the sex/gender system. Similarly, authors like Monique Wittig or Adrienne Rich conceptualize heterosexuality as a cultural institution rather than a personal desire. Butler builds on these functional analyses in her characterization of the heterosexual matrix as "that grid of cultural intelligibility through which bodies, genders, and desires are naturalized" (*Gender Trouble* 151). This structural connection between the duality of gender and heterosexuality that is inscribed not only in individual bodies, subjectivities and personal relationships but also in the political, economic, legal and symbolic systems of a society is now known as **heteronormativity** (Engel 21) and has been most thoroughly theorized in the context of Queer Theory and Queer Studies (cf. Degele).

Queer Theory is closely connected to Lesbian and Gay Studies on account of its primary focus on sexuality. However, queer is decidedly anti-identitarian and emerged in opposition to identity categories like lesbian and gay. Instead, queer functions as a kind of catalyst that strategically decentres identity positions without becoming a site of identity itself. Queer politics does not support any kind of minority, group or issue but derives its political force from undermining any constellation that congeals into a stable structure. It is a cultural practice that dismantles heteronormativity and other norms and processes of normalisation and categorisation and directs our attention to the blank spaces and exclusions, that which is not culturally intelligible in any given order. The permanently decentring dynamic of queer makes it very productive for a rigorous questioning of normative structures and identities, but it proves nevertheless problematic as an instrument of intervention on behalf of the marginalised subject, whose very survival might depend on some degree of stability and anchoring. Butler addresses this dilemma in *Undoing Gender* when she states that "[t]he critique of gender norms must be situated within the context of lives as they are lived and must be guided by the question of what maximizes the possibility for a livable life" (8). Consequently, she suggests a shift from queer as a rejection of identity to queer as a rejection of the *policing* of identity, thus focusing on the deprivileging of hegemonic identities in favour of pluralisation and an open field of subjectivities.

The concept of heteronormativity highlights the mutual dependence of gender and sexuality, which in extension raises the problem of analysing gender as an isolated category. This had already become evident in the early stages of Gender Studies when lesbians criticised the heterosexual bias of feminist criticism and women of colour its white middle-class focus. The last two decades have seen a more systematic investigation into different axes of social differentiation and their intersections, a term introduced by the legal scholar Kimberle Crenshaw to describe multiple forms of discrimination, sexism and racism in particular. This has resulted in the conceptualization of **gender as an interdependent category**, and the development of models for the analysis of context-specific processes of categorization along different social vectors (e.g. Walgenbach et al.).

Gender as a productive
category for literary
analysis

## 6.3 | Gender and Sexuality in English and American Studies

Gender, as a central organising principle of our culture and society, has become relevant for historical and cultural analyses across the disciplinary spectrum (cf. Bußmann and Hof; Braun and Stephan, *Genus*), which in turn have served as important reference points for literary studies. A number of context-specific investigations focus on the interaction of literature with extra-literary discourses and theoretical models to explore the productivity of literature in handling and reshaping concepts of gender and sexuality (e.g. the Enlightenment discourse on 'natural' gender differences and the domestic fiction of the time, or the late nineteenth/early twentieth-century medical discourse on homosexuality and the literary production of Aestheticism and Modernism).

Probably the most prominent area of investigation has proved to be the impact of gender norms on the individual in different historical formations and the role of gender for subject formation in general (cf. also entry II.7). This resulted in a thorough reworking of various (auto)biographical genres from a gender perspective, most notably the *Bildungsroman* and the novel of development from the eighteenth century to the present, but also (fictional) (auto)biographies or the picaresque novel. Queer theory approaches emphasize the potential of **dissident genders** (transgender, genderqueer) to transgress and reconfigure the binary gender system (e.g. Halberstam, *Female Masculinity*; Kilian) as well as heteronormative biographical patterns and their generational time structure (Halberstam, *Queer Time*).

Explicitly or implicitly, these studies owe much to the Foucauldian model of power and resistance in the shaping of discourse, concepts that also apply to the production of academic knowledge, for example to the structuring of the literary field and its parameters. Research on the gender-bias of historical concepts of authorship contributed to a rethinking of the scope and defining features of specific literary movements (e.g. Romanticism or Modernism) and the texts and authors they are represented by. By extension, an ongoing debate about the mechanisms of canon formation and the reorganisation of existing literary canons has led to an **opening of traditional canons** to hitherto excluded texts and to the production of alternative canons. Ina Schabert presented one of the most sustained and successful attempts to rewrite English literary history from a gender perspective, which differs both in focus and aim from traditional literary histories. Her two-volume work covers the period from the Early Modern Age to the end of the twentieth century. It reads the history of English literature in terms of a history of gender relations and gender difference, its primary emphasis lying on the historically changing gender norms and their production and negotiation in literary and extra-literary discourses as well as their impact on the ordering of the literary field. Her choice of material does not reflect the 'great works,' but the variety of writing available at a given time and the intertextual connections between the writings of female and male authors. These particular ordering principles make visible the presence of women in literary life and turn this alternative literary history into an important piece of feminist historiography.

Last but not least, the impact of Gender Studies on narrative theory has been an issue since the emergence of **feminist narratology** in the 1980s, and later **queer narratology**. It has provoked a systematic enquiry into the cultural embeddedness of narrative structures, notably their function in the (de)construction or performativity of gender and sexuality (e.g. Mezei; Nünning and Nünning). Queer Studies has inspired a number of queer readings of literary texts. These are close readings both of works that explicitly deal with queer issues and ostensibly 'straight' texts. They exploit textual structures of excess and indeterminacy to demonstrate the inherent instability of the binary gender system and of the heterosexual/homosexual dichotomy and to reveal traces of dissidence and resistance to dominant structures (Dollimore; Hall 113–71). Eve Kosofsky Sedgwick's readings (see box) are based on two central hypotheses: First, the sex/gender system is not only upheld by heterosexuality but, more importantly for her purpose, by **homophobia** or '**homosexual panic**.' Consequently, homosocial relations between men can only be sustained by homophobia to mark the clear boundary between the social and the sexual. Homosexual desire has to be routed through the heterosexual paradigm, a process that is often mirrored in triangular constellations in literature (two men and one woman). Secondly, literary texts employ strategies of revelation and concealment as part of an 'epistemology of the closet,' i.e. a regime of knowing that consists of a complex interplay of (sometimes strategic) ignorance and knowledge, (open) secrets and silences, the speakable and the unspeakable.

---

*Interpretation*

**Henry James, "The Beast in the Jungle"**
Sedgwick puts her own framework to use in her compelling and unorthodox interpretation of Henry James's story "The Beast in the Jungle" (1903), in which the protagonist John Marcher has a long-standing friendship with May Bartram without ever entering into a love relationship with her. Marcher has a secret that is vaguely referred to as his foreboding that something crucial will happen to him and overwhelm him like a beast in the jungle. While most critics have read Marcher's moment of recognition after Bartram's death as his final knowledge that he forfeited life and happiness with her while waiting for the unexpected, Sedgwick establishes through a close scrutiny of individual passages that Marcher's unnamed secret has a homosexual content. On this basis, she claims that Marcher's final recognition that he should have loved May Bartram is not a flash of lucid, though tragically late, self-knowledge, but an instant of irredeemable self-ignorance, which is reflected in his compulsion to turn his desire for a male mourner he sees in the graveyard into an identification with that man's loss of a beloved woman.

# Select Bibliography

Braun, Christina von, and Inge Stephan, eds. *Gender@Wissen: Ein Handbuch der Gender-Theorien*. Cologne: Böhlau, 2005.

Braun, Christina von, and Inge Stephan, eds. *Gender-Studien: Eine Einführung*. 2nd ed. Stuttgart: Metzler 2006.

Bußmann, Hadumod, and Renate Hof, eds. *Genus: Geschlechterforschung/Gender Studies in den Kultur- und Sozialwissenschaften*. Stuttgart: Kröner, 2005.

Butler, Judith. *Bodies That Matter: On the Discursive Limits of 'Sex.'* New York: Routledge, 1993.

Butler, Judith. *Gender Trouble: Feminism and the Subversion of Identity*. New York: Routledge, 1990.

Butler, Judith. *Undoing Gender*. New York: Routledge, 2004.

Connell, R. W. *Masculinities*. Cambridge: Polity Press, 1995.

Connell, R. W., and James W. Messerschmidt. "Hegemonic Masculinity: Rethinking the Concept." *Gender and Society* 19 (2005): 829–59.

Crenshaw, Kimberlé. "Demarginalizing the Intersection of Race and Sex: A Black Feminist Critique of Antidiscrimination Doctrine, Feminist Theory and Antiracist Politics." *The University of Chicago Legal Forum* 139 (1989): 139–67.

Degele, Nina. *Gender/Queer Studies: Eine Einführung*. Paderborn: Fink, 2008.

Dollimore, Jonathan. *Sexual Dissidence: Augustine to Wilde, Freud to Foucault*. Oxford: Clarendon Press, 1991.

Engel, Antke. *Bilder von Sexualität und Ökonomie: Queere kulturelle Politiken im Neoliberalismus*. Bielefeld: transcript, 2009.

Foucault, Michel. *The Will to Knowledge*. 1976. Trans. Robert Hurley. London: Penguin, 1998. Vol. 1 of *The History of Sexuality*. 3 vols.

Halberstam, Judith. *Female Masculinity*. Durham: Duke University Press, 1998.

Halberstam, Judith. *In a Queer Time and Place: Transgender Bodies, Subcultural Lives*. New York: New York University Press, 2005.

Hall, Donald. *Queer Theories*. Basingstoke: Palgrave Macmillan, 2003.

Kilian, Eveline. *GeschlechtSverkehrt: Theoretische und literarische Perspektiven des gender-bending*. Königstein: Helmer, 2004.

Kroll, Renate, ed. *Metzler Lexikon Gender Studies/Geschlechterforschung*. Stuttgart: Metzler 2002.

Laqueur, Thomas. *Making Sex: Body and Gender from the Greeks to Freud*. 1990. Cambridge: Harvard University Press, 1992.

Lorber, Judith. *Paradoxes of Gender*. New Haven: Yale University Press, 1994.

Mezei, Kathy, ed. *Ambiguous Discourse: Feminist Narratology and British Women Writers*. Chapel Hill: University of North Carolina Press, 1996.

Nünning, Vera, and Ansgar Nünning, eds. *Erzähltextanalyse und Gender Studies*. Stuttgart: Metzler, 2004.

Rich, Adrienne. "Compulsory Heterosexuality and Lesbian Existence." 1980. *Blood, Bread and Poetry: Selected Prose: 1979–1985*. London: Virago, 1987. 23–68.

Rubin, Gayle. "The Traffic in Women: Notes on the 'Political Economy' of Sex." *Toward an Anthropology of Women*. Ed. Rayna R. Reiter. New York: Monthly Review Press, 1975. 157–210.

Schabert, Ina. *Englische Literaturgeschichte aus der Sicht der Geschlechterforschung*. Stuttgart: Kröner, 1997.

Schabert, Ina. *Englische Literaturgeschichte des 20. Jahrhunderts: Eine neue Darstellung aus der Sicht der Geschlechterforschung*. Stuttgart: Kröner, 2006.

Scott, Joan W. "Gender: A Useful Category of Historical Analysis." 1986. *Coming to Terms: Feminism, Theory, Politics*. Ed. Elizabeth Weed. New York: Routledge, 1989. 81–100.

Sedgwick, Eve Kosofsky. *Between Men: English Literature and Male Homosocial Desire*. New York: Columbia University Press, 1985.

Sedgwick, Eve Kosofsky. *Epistemology of the Closet*. 1990. London: Penguin, 1994.

Stryker, Susan, and Stephen Whittle, eds. *The Transgender Studies Reader*. New York: Routledge, 2006.

Walgenbach, Katharina, et al. *Gender als interdependente Kategorie: Neue Perspektiven auf Intersektionalität, Diversität und Heterogenität*. Opladen: Barbara Budrich, 2007.

Wittig, Monique. *The Straight Mind and Other Essays*. Boston: Beacon Press, 1992.

*Eveline Kilian*

# 7 Psychoanalysis

## 7.1 | Freud's Psychoanalysis

When **Sigmund Freud** characterized writers as valuable allies of psychoanalysts (cf. "Der Dichter"), he alluded to the fact that many psychoanalytic concepts were formulated in literary texts, long before Freud developed his own theory of the interplay between **the body, subjectivity and culture** on the basis of both his work with neurotic patients and his readings of literature. Freud's work evolved by constant revision and does not constitute a unified theory; over time psychoanalysis has developed into a vast array of many different and sometimes even warring schools.

Due to his invention of the "talking cure" of verbalized free association, Freud learned to read the patient's speech and symptoms as expressions of unconscious wishes, feelings of guilt and anxieties connected to the patient's family history. He came to regard childhood and adolescence as processes of internalizing cultural restraints of sexual desire and of modelling one's affects and identifications after the parents and other figures of authority. Modern subjectivity is thus conceived of as the result of a culturally determined process of human self-domestication whose socio-historical parameters have been studied extensively since Freud.

The structural parallels Freud construed between dreaming, phantasizing and writing on the one hand, and between reading and psychoanalyzing on the other, are complex. In the first decades of the twentieth century, these parallels were developed by Freud himself and others into textual analyses which (1) treated literary characters as if they were patients, and read their actions and utterances as neurotic symptoms, or (2) concentrated on the relation between the author's personal life and the symptomatic character of his or her work, or (3) developed a psychoanalytic theory of readers' responses to literary texts (cf. Wright). **Jacques Lacan**'s poststructuralist return to Freud has crucially contributed to new conceptions of textuality and reading since the 1970s. Lacanian psychoanalysis also provides a conceptual framework for contemporary cultural studies, particularly for scholars focusing on gender and race.

## 7.2 | The Model of the Dream

In Freud's writings, *Die Traumdeutung* (1899) has a special status: he analyzed the dream as a universal non-pathological psychic phenomenon to demonstrate the systematic character of his **theory of the unconscious**. Comparing the manifest dream to a hieroglyphic script or a picture puzzle, Freud split it into its components and used the dreamer's free associations in order to fathom the semantic richness of all details and their interconnectedness. Out of these findings he constructed the latent meaning of the dream, which he identified as the hallucinatory fulfillment of an unconscious wish deemed inappropriate and embarrassing to the dreamer's internalized social norms. Building on a large sample of interpreted dreams, Freud subsequently formalized the laws of dreamwork by which an unconscious agency of censorship prevents an unconscious wish from becoming conscious, but allows it access to the dreamer's perceptual apparatus in distorted form. The manifest dream is composed from verbal material linked to the most recent experiences of the subject; this material is then subjected to processes of condensation (which repress certain words and replace them by other words linked to the repressed words by semantic or acoustic similarity or spatial proximity), and to processes of displacement (which shift the emphasis to unimportant words). To these two factors of dream-work two more must be added: considerations of representability (since some words are transformed into visual images) and processes of secondary revision which connect the words and images of the dream by inventing a narrative logic for them. The aim of dream-work is to relieve psychic tensions by fulfilling the illicit wish in hallucinatory form: the dream is unintelligible for the conscious subject who tries to make sense of it according to normative conventions of representation, but not for the subject of the unconscious (Freud, *Traumdeutung*).

The **dream** constitutes Freud's basic psychoanalytic model for the literary text, with some qualifications. The writing of literature starts as day-dreaming, i.e. a combination of unconscious and conscious phantasies, which are then stripped by the author of personal contents in order to give them socially acceptable form. In conscious phantasies, the narcissistic wishes of the ego are imaginarily fulfilled; these phantasies may also serve as a trajectory for unconscious phantasies, provided that the latter are submitted to distortion and displacement. The artistic necessity to give phantasies a literary form—to turn them, say, into a narrative or a play by inventing characters and a plot—serves as another layer of distortion and is the source of conscious aesthetic pleasure. The readers will consciously share this pleasure of form, while they will unconsciously indulge in the various phantasies encoded in the text ("Der Dichter").

Addressing himself or herself to the public at large in an act of communication marked by culture as phantasy and art, the writer is awarded a greater freedom of expression than others. This freedom benefits the reader: to read a literary text means to engage with somebody else's phantasy, which reduces the grip of unconscious self-censorship. It means to identify with characters and phantasmatically partake in their actions; not only morality, but also social transgressions can thus be given their due. For this reason, literary texts are an important medium in the cultural production, circulation and change of cultural forms of identity, of types and modes of object-relations, and of ethical norms and social values. Depending on the individual text, the individual reader, and the general social climate, reading literature may lead to 'sympathies with the devil,' or amount to an escapist compensation for libidinal sacrifices demanded by society.

The dream as the psychoanalytic model for the literary text

## 7.3 | Poststructuralist Psychoanalysis

**Lacan**'s notion of the **imaginary** and the **symbolic** integrates Freud's concepts of the subject into a new framework. His notion of the imaginary is focussed on identification, as a term that encompasses processes of projection, imitation, and internalization. They constitute the basis of the infant's integrated body image and later, of a subject's conscious identity. The primordial libidinal object (the maternal breast) is not recognized by the baby as ontologically distinct, but experienced as a part of its being; the presence of the object causes not only physical satisfaction, but narcissistic completeness and bliss, and its absence a crisis of narcissistic lack and anxiety. When the infant later recognizes its **mirror-image**, it identifies with it as a narcissistic ideal ego with defined bodily boundaries: the infant thus claims an ontological autonomy for itself, while at the same time developing a notion of the other as equally autonomous and distinct. This formation of the ideal ego is bound up with the disavowal of a lack of being, and to that extent builds on the earlier experience of narcissistic bliss. But the experiences of lack insist and threaten to shatter the ideal ego, because the object (the breast) is now recognized as external to the infant's body. As a result, the primordial object becomes an **object of desire** which is withheld, so the infant believes, by 'the Other'; Lacan uses this term, sometimes also called 'the big Other' to describe a radical form of otherness which cannot be assimilated through identification. To ward off an anxiety now predicated both on the lack of the desired object and the threat of bodily disintegration, the ego is formed by fashioning itself according to the perceptual, affective and cognitive image it perceives the Other wanting it to be, in order to attain the desired object (Lacan 75–81). This process is bound up with the infant's learning to use words. The imaginary relation between the ego and the other underlies all verbal

The Oedipus complex

communication. Growing up, the child learns to give up the desired object and replace it with other objects, and the appeal to the other loses its existential urgency.

This moment of having to give up the desired object and replace it by other objects prefigures the Oedipus complex, a Freudian notion elaborated by Lacan on the grounds of findings of structuralist anthropology. According to Lacan, the complex refers to the process by which the body of a subject becomes a cultural sign inscribed in the symbolic, i.e. in the codes of gender and sexuality which ensure exogamy and sexual reproduction by structuring and limiting sexuality. Infantile sexuality is bisexual and polymorphous. In the Oedipal complex, sexuality is genitally reorganized; it is linked to the subject's sex; and it is bound to a culturally prohibited incestuous object. The Oedipal law is based on anatomical differences and their symbolic meaning, but internalized by way of the imaginary: sexual difference is interpreted as the physical possession of the phallus or its lack, and gender identity constructed on the basis of this (erroneous) interpretation. When the pre-Oedipal desire for the maternal object is reconfigured as sexual desire for the mother, the father is experienced as a preferred rival. For the boy, sexual desire for the mother is accompanied by castration anxiety, that is, a feared punishment by the father which is overcome by an identification with the father as aggressor. This identification with the father leads to the psychic construction of a self-censoring ego ideal, effects the repression of incestuous desire, encourages **sublimation** (i.e. a displacement to non-sexual cultural objects), and brings about a displacement of sexual desire to other women as permitted substitute sexual objects. For the girl, the maternal object constitutes the pre-oedipal object of desire as well. However, the imaginary interpretation of sexual difference produces feelings of resentment against the mother, as mother and daughter and indeed all women share the imaginary injury of castration, and feelings of envy against males. In the Oedipus complex, the girl has, therefore, already displaced her earlier desire for the maternal object to the father as a sexual object to obtain the missing phallus, but as this desire is prohibited as incestuous,

it must be repressed, sublimated and displaced to other men as substitute sexual objects.

Both Freud and Lacan argued that the Oedipus complex is conceptual shorthand for a much more complex process, since the subject's pre-Oedipal identifications are not aligned with gender, and both parents can be sexual objects for both sexes. At any event, the subject's submission to the Oedipal law is never complete: the split within the subject created by ego-formation widens due to repressed identifications with persons of the opposite sex, and the internalization of the Law by way of the ego ideal goes together with creating the psychic space of **unconscious repressed desire**. The imaginary brings about a basic conformity of all subjects as far as gender identity is concerned, and facilitates or wards off certain substitute objects of incestuous desire, but cannot determine heterosexual object-choice.

The conscious subject that submits itself to self-scrutiny and self-control, and the subject of repressed unconscious desire are thus both produced by the **interplay of the symbolic and the imaginary**, but as they never coincide, they cannot be cognitively syncretized. Freud's analysis of the mechanisms of dream-work, which he also discovered in neurotic symptoms, phantasies, *lapsus linguae*, jokes, and literature, and identified as articulations of unconscious desire, were elucidated by Lacan by referring to Saussure's and Jakobson's work in structural linguistics (cf. section II.1.4). The differential structure of verbal signs as well as the rhetorical operations within sentences are general conditions of language. Linguistic meaning is never stable and definite: there is a continuous "gliding of the signifier" in any use of language which is made invisible by conventions of communication and by context. Freud's dream-work is but a variant of this general linguistic structure. When in **free association**, the analysand's speech is liberated from the restrictions of ordinary language use, the unconscious desire of the subject becomes legible: the analysand appeals to the analyst as a representative of the Law and articulates his or her unconscious desire in a transferential relation that repeats earlier processes of imaginary ego-formation and brings out the phantasmatic dimension of speech.

## 7.4 | Poststructuralist Psychoanalytic Literary Theory

**Shoshana Felman** argued in her Lacanian reading of Henry James's story "The Turn of the Screw" (1898) that psychoanalysis and literature must be regarded as two distinct yet overlapping practices of reading and writing which both acknowledge the fact that words may say something entirely different than what they mean. Defining sexuality as the conflict between the forces of desire and repression, Felman conceives of "The Turn of the Screw" not just as representing but as performing that conflict as an irresolvable and unreadable division of meaning in all its textual layers. Reading the story, then, either means to unconsciously support one or the other side of the conflict and "receive [one's] own message back [...] in an inverted form" (Lacan 246)—or to reconstruct the textual economy of ambiguity (see box).

All reading, thus, is transferential, since it invariably takes the text as a communication by a subject for a subject, i.e. as an appeal to the reader's understanding (in her work on holocaust testimony, Felman elaborates the ethical implications of this point, cf. Felman, *Testimony*). All readings construct meaning for a subject, and find their limit in the *unreadability* of the text founded on its irreducibly ambiguous play with the literal and figurative meanings of language.

### Henry James, "The Turn of the Screw"

Felman's analysis of James's text differs from Freud's by treating literary form—the construction of the embedded narratives, the unreliable narrators, the ambivalent relations between the characters, the repetition of key words, the function of metaphor, the performance of irony—not as a "veil" or an extra-layer of aesthetic pleasure, but as the textual site where the conflict of desire and repression plays itself out. At the core of James's text is a story told by a governess who believes to have seen the ghost of a dead servant and suspects that the children she is looking after might have been seduced by this servant. By observing the interplay of literal and figurative meanings of key terms of the text such as "to see," "to grasp" and "to know," Felman shows that the governess is presented in the text as a reader of ambiguous signs whose capability of "seeing" is driven by a desire to determine their true meaning (which she suspects to be a sexual secret). However, the governess's interrogations of the children only produce ambiguous answers and lead to the death of a child. The governess writes the story down and sends it as a letter to a friend, who in turn reads it to a circle of friends, one of whom is the narrator of the text as a whole. The governess's tale is thus an intimate communication turned public, and the reader is positioned as either the governess's confidant or an outside observer in a circle of friends.

This structure allows Felman to elucidate the process of reading **literature as transference**. The habitual transferential structure of reading is one of intimacy: addressing the narrative to himself/herself, projecting himself/herself into the main characters, and sharing their point of view, the reader unconsciously absorbs the phantasmatic content of the text. In "The Turn of the Screw" this intimacy is disrupted when the governess turns out to be an unreliable narrator (she sees a ghost). The reader will then rely on the realist frame of the story, take up the position of the outside observer, diagnose the governess as neurotic—and resume transference. For in "The Turn of the Screw," this outside observer's position is contained in the text, which helps Felman to make a general point: no reader can attain an outsider's position vis-à-vis any text.

Interpretation

## 7.5 | Psychoanalysis and Gender Studies

For Lacan, masculinity and femininity are social constructions of identity by which a symbolic difference is naturalized. From a feminist perspective, **Judith Butler** has taken up this construction, but focuses on the heteronormative dimension of the Oedipus complex (cf. section II.6.2). Defining the Law not as repressive vis-à-vis a given sexual desire, but, following Foucault, stressing the

Law's productivity as a discursive practice that carves out a psychic space for sexual desire in the first place, she argues that both sanctioned heterosexuality and prohibited homosexuality are productions of the Law in order to coerce subjects into conformity with hegemonic configurations of power. As psychoanalysis has demonstrated, desire does not follow from gender; nor is gender bound up with an ontological category of sex, as Butler shows using the example of drag. Butler conceives of gender identity as an inscription on the body performatively brought about by a "stylized repetition of acts" through time (*Gender Trouble* 140); these acts cite/repeat/reconstitute the set of discursive practices which make up a cultural style of **doing gender**. Gender is a historically contingent, fluid, and internally dissonant discursive construction, and malleable in principle by political intervention and discursive prac-

tices of resignification. Referring to Freud and Lacan, Butler argues that desire is not categorically opposed to identification, but is rather produced and sustained or repudiated by identification as the mode to relate to a desired object in a way that enables identity. If homosexual desire is no longer culturally repudiated, the set of discursive practices of doing gender and producing identification proliferates, and the normative terms of gender identity can be dismantled in the long run (cf. *Bodies That Matter* 99). Butler's concept is widely used in literary criticism to show how literature as a practice of representation partakes in the inscription of normative gender identity, but also performs subversive resignifications. To conceive literary textuality with Felman as a use of tropes that exposes the illusionary character of what is otherwise regarded as reality is crucial in the latter regard.

## 7.6 | Critical Race Studies, Postcolonial Studies

Studying the
psychoanalysis of race

Critical race studies have used the Lacanian concepts of the symbolic and the imaginary to explain the psychic functions of social hierarchies in which **racialized subjects** figure as a threatening Other against which racially unmarked whiteness is defined as the representation of cultural norms of civility, rationality and self-control (cf. entry III.4). This construction is created by an interpretation of skin color in the imaginary which naturalizes a symbolic hierarchy of race vs. whiteness in hegemonic culture and society by fashioning distinct and coherent social identities for racialized subjects and whites. In competitions for social objects such as access to economic resources or political power, whites identify with other whites on the basis of their common difference from the racialized Other and institute social practices of exclusion. For the racialized subject in turn, socialization not only means to identify with the social Other and thus internalize racist stereotypes, but may also amount to an identification with whites as the embodiments of social norms, as **Frantz Fanon** puts it. The symbolic hierarchy between racialized subjects and whites can only be sustained over time, however, if sexual intercourse between the two groups is prohibited. To justify such a law, black men are typically ascribed a natural inclination to sexual violence which allegedly requires particular vigilance by

whites, while the history of slavery provides ample evidence for sexual violence of white men against black women—which attests to the eroticization of racist power-relations, and demonstrates the paranoid inversions of the logic of social practices in the racist imaginary.

The consequences for literary analysis are manifold. Apart from close readings of texts that observe the intersections of race, power, sexuality and gender in narrative representations of characters and their actions, there is also a critical emphasis on textual disruptions of representation as an irritation or refutation of racial stereotyping. **Homi Bhabha**'s readings of colonial texts highlight the colonialists' desire to disavow the differences within the colonized population in order to sustain social hegemony over a stereotypical Other. He shows how these differences return within the hegemonic discourse itself, where they are figured as a menace of the Other who cannot be contained by the colonizer's conceptual apparatus. Such paranoid transferential constructions are sustained, but also challenged by textual performances of ambivalence: the tropological figurations of literary meaning testify to the latent instability of social semantics, and allow for a critical re-articulation of identifications of self and Other that challenges the totalizing binarisms of the social imaginary. Referring to Lacan, Bhabha reads all cultural acts of identification in the colonial imaginary as the production of a split in the subjects of discourse: disavowed by dominant culture (and often by minoritarian culture as well), there is an unconscious **third space** in all performative acts of identification as they align a specific subject in the present with the historically sedimented discursive repertoire of identity. The objective for postcolonial criticism, then, is to work against ossified juxtapositions of self and Other, and elaborate the contingent and the liminal in historical and actual representations of subjects (cf. Bhabha 179).

## Select Bibliography

Bhabha, Homi K. *The Location of Culture*. London: Routledge, 1994.

Butler, Judith. *Bodies That Matter: On the Discursive Limits of "Sex."* New York: Routledge, 1993.

Butler, Judith. *Gender Trouble: Feminism and the Subversion of Identity*. New York: Routledge, 1990.

Fanon, Frantz. *Black Skin, White Masks*. New York: Grove Press, 2008.

Felman, Shoshana. *Testimony: Crises of Witnessing in Literature, Psychoanalysis, and History*. New York: Routledge, 1992.

Felman, Shoshana. "Turning the Screw of Interpretation." *Literature and Psychoanalysis: The Question of Reading: Otherwise*. Ed. Shoshana Felman. Baltimore: Johns Hopkins University Press, 1980. 94–207.

Freud, Sigmund. "Der Dichter und das Phantasieren." *Studienausgabe*. Vol. 10. 1969. 69–179.

Freud, Sigmund. *Die Traumdeutung*. *Studienausgabe*. Vol. 2. 1969.

Freud, Sigmund. "Der Witz und seine Beziehung zum Unbewussten." *Studienausgabe*. Vol. 4. 1969. 9–220.

Freud, Sigmund. *Studienausgabe*. Eds. Alexander Mitscherlich, Angela Richards, and James Strachey. 10 Vols. Frankfurt/M.: Fischer, 1969.

Freud, Sigmund. *Vorlesungen zur Einführung in die Psychoanalyse und Neue Folge. Studienausgabe*. Vol. 1. 1969.

Lacan, Jacques. *Ecrits: The First Complete Edition in English*. Trans. Bruce Fink. New York: Norton, 2007.

Laplanche, Jean, and Jean-Bertrand Pontalis. *The Language of Psychoanalysis*. Trans. Donald Nicholson-Smith. London: Karnac, 2006.

Wright, Elizabeth. *Psychoanalytic Criticism: Theory in Practice*. New York: Methuen, 1984.

*Ulla Haselstein*

# 8 Pragmatism and Semiotics

## 8.1 | Classical Pragmatism

Pragmatism is a philosophical tradition that originated in the United States in the latter half of the nineteenth century. It has many strains and variants, but all share a key tenet found in the 'pragmatic maxim,' which states that the meaning of a concept is determined by the practical consequences that its adoption might have, not by antecedent data. Thus meaning in pragmatism is always connected to a **real-world context** and to human action within it. Furthermore, pragmatism emphasizes the social character of human experience as well as the inherent creativity in human action.

The **reception** of pragmatism in European philosophy was mixed. Although some voices recognized pragmatism's new way of thinking and some major European intellectuals such as Wittgenstein and Heidegger dealt with similar topics, pragmatism as a whole was considered rather parochial and crude in Europe, mainly due to the dissemination of out-of-context quotations such as William James's infamous statement on the 'cash value' of truth (cf. entry V.5.1).

The key thinkers who developed pragmatism *Key thinkers* were Charles S. Peirce, William James, John *of pragmatism* Dewey, and George Herbert Mead. To characterize their work briefly,

- **Peirce**, the founder of pragmatism, was generally interested in developing a theory of scientific knowledge, whereas
- **James**, who worked mainly in the field of psychology, significantly expanded Peirce's work to encompass moral and religious questions as well as questions of personal belief and commitment.
- **Dewey**, who can be called an instrumentalist, brought Peirce's epistemological and James's psychological work into a dialogue and concentrated on the issue of how theories and concepts might function as instruments for problem-solving.
- **Mead** developed a theory of the particular features of human communication in which the self is seen as defined entirely by social structures.

After World War II, pragmatism lost much of its impact and was displaced by the so-called **linguistic turn** in analytical philosophy, yet in the late twentieth century there was a renewed interest in it. Thinkers such as Richard J. Bernstein hold that the pragmatists had really been ahead of their time and had initiated a sea change that analytical philosophy, struggling with similar themes, was slow to fully realize and acknowledge. Thus in retrospect, American pragmatist thinking, at first ignored or condemned as petty and unsophisticated, proved very influential in the end, even on a global scale (Bernstein ix-xi). Today, pragmatism is seen by many as the "single most important, most inventive, most vigorous, most distinctly American philosophical movement between the end of the Civil War and the end of World War II" (Margolis 1). Names connected to the renewed interest in pragmatism include, to name only a few, Richard Rorty, Jürgen Habermas, Hilary Putnam, and Cornel West.

The term '**pragmatism**' began to circulate after William James used it in a lecture, "Philosophical Conceptions and Practical Results," in 1898. Although he explicitly referred to his close friend Peirce as the originator of pragmatism and credited him with having developed its theoretical framework decades before, pragmatism remained connected to James's work as it gained international prominence. This is presumably due to William James's influential position as an important public intellectual and Harvard professor, while Peirce suffered unfortunate personal circumstances and a failed professional career. Nonetheless, Peirce's work was certainly the more original and systematic, and his writings on logic and the philosophy of science are still hailed as major contributions to those fields. His two articles, "The Fixation of Belief" and "How To Make Our Ideas Clear," undisputedly count as the founding documents of pragmatism.

## 8.2 | The Pragmatic Maxim

In these texts, Peirce develops the **pragmatic maxim**, which in his notoriously difficult style of writing reads like this: "Consider what effects, that might conceivably have practical bearings, we conceive the object of our conception to have. Then, our conception of these effects is the whole of our conception of the object" (Peirce 5:402). Another way of putting it would be to say that theories and models must be judged **by their consequences, not by their origins**. Sometimes Peirce used biblical imagery to explain the basic proposition of the maxim: "Ye may know them by their fruits" (Peirce 5:402n2). The ground-breaking strategy that Peirce used here is from theory to practice, a move away from *a priori* reasoning towards the analysis of the systematic implications of a concept, including the action to which it ultimately would give rise. Understanding all of these implications, according to the maxim, leads to understanding the concept in question. That is, meaning in pragmatism cannot be perceived outside of human action and lived experience and is thus always context-bound.

## 8.3 | A Key Tenet of Pragmatist Thinking: Anti-Cartesianism

Pragmatism really begins with a radical critique of Cartesianism, that is, with a critique of Descartes's methodological principle of universal doubt that is bound to the subjective contemplation of the individual. Pragmatism transforms this notion of a doubting individual into a social process. We cannot begin with complete doubt, so the pragmatists think. Substantial doubt does not arise in solitary, systematic contemplation, but in concrete contexts when our habitual beliefs and actions are challenged by some incident. A cyclical, social and intersubjective process evolves, in which the individual overcomes doubt, developing new beliefs and habits until these are challenged anew by doubt. In the cycle, new knowledge, new interpretations of reality emerge which are better adapted to understanding the context in which doubt arose, until a new incident elicits doubt and the process begins anew.

The pragmatist move of exchanging the central position of the doubting subject for an **intersub-jective process** has profound implications, not least for the definitions of truth and reality. For the endless dynamic of doubt and belief is above all a cooperative search for truth. Contrary to common misunderstandings, truth in pragmatism is neither relative nor an abandonment of the ideal of true knowledge but a ceaseless approximation of the final opinion on which those involved in the search will ultimately agree, a view that cannot be improved. Truth here is not eternal, but it is not subjective, either; it can be determined by the success of action based on it. Clearly, the state of affairs in the succession of doubt and belief cannot but be somewhat provisional, hence the proviso of fallibilism that for pragmatism strictly characterizes the status quo of every proposition: "our knowledge is never absolute but always swims [...] in a continuum of uncertainty and of indeterminacy" (Peirce 1:171).

Pragmatism questions
the central role of the
doubting subject.

## 8.4 | Reality—A Somewhat Precarious Affair

If knowledge is never absolute but in a constant process of revision, a process fueled by the doubt-belief dynamic, then clearly what we perceive as real can never be absolute or unchanging. In a decidedly anti-Kantian turn, pragmatism defines the real not as incognizable, but as **endlessly**

**cognizable**. What is more, the real is not seen as the *origin* of processes of cognition but as their *product*, that which "sooner or later, information and reasoning would finally result in" (Peirce 5:311). Thus concepts of the real, like those of truth, fall under the proviso of **fallibilism** and make for an understanding of the real as something volatile and open to endless interpretation and re-interpretation. And it is at this point precisely that pragmatism and semiotics converge, for the process of interpreting the real is seen as a sign process. To be precise, it is a process of interpreting signs that at the same time is carried out through signs.

It was again Peirce who had systematically integrated semiotics into his elaborate classification of sciences and ascribed to it a central position. For Peirce held that the decisive micro-moment in pragmatist thinking is the moment of **abductive inference**. This is the instant when we literally make guesses about the real, the moment of making sense of our own perceptions, of interpreting and explaining to ourselves what it is that we perceive. It is the moment when we transform our perceptions into perceptual judgments (and these may give rise to action or to doubt), the moment of a move from image to text. This whole operation is understood as a process of interpretation carried out through signs. With this concept, we can place Peirce in the epistemological tradition of semiotics, as opposed to the linguistic one.

## 8.5 | A Very Brief History of Semiotics

Semiotics, or the general science of signs, began its systematic development in antiquity with the writings of Aristotle, Plato, and Augustine. Before these thinkers, the dominant concept of representation followed the 'aliquid stat pro aliquo' (something stands for something else) rule in the straightforward understanding that, for instance, smoke stands for a fire, a red dot on the skin stands for a particular illness, or the word /tʃeə(ɹ)/ stands for a chair. Aristotle in *De Interpretatione* and Plato in *Cratylus* then developed the landmark concept that a sign does not refer to its object in any direct way but only via a concept that is located in the sign user's mind. Aristotle called this concept broadly 'the content of consciousness' (see illustration). That is, when one is confronted with the word /tʃeə(ɹ)/ it first refers to the **con-cept** of a chair one has in one's mind. Only by way of the concept can the sign refer to any concrete chair, and only in this indirect way can a sign fully *represent* its object to the mind. Augustine, in *De Doctrina Christiana*, was the first to systematically explore the idea that signs are the indispensable means of any communication whatsoever

After these groundbreaking contributions, the semiotic discussion continued over the centuries with a clear epistemological focus, and as such was firmly located in the discipline of philosophy. The debate centered mainly on the question of how to define the status of the concept or '**content of consciousness.**' Whence its origin? Is it given by God? Is it fixed like Plato's ideas and thus eternal? If this were the case, the concept would be the same for everyone, but if differences are acknowledged, how to account for them? Or is it the other way around and the concepts are fully individual and different for everyone? In that case, how would communication and understanding be possible at all? Clearly, these are fundamental questions that have persisted since ancient times. Many different names have been given to the 'content of consciousness' over the centuries and in the context of the various philosophical approaches, such as Locke's 'ideas' or Hegel's *Vorstellung* (conception). Contributing significantly to this epistemological tradition was Charles Sanders Peirce, who called the 'content of consciousness' the 'interpretant.' With his work, the triadic sign model was firmly integrated into the pragmatist theory of human action.

The Aristotelian model of the sign

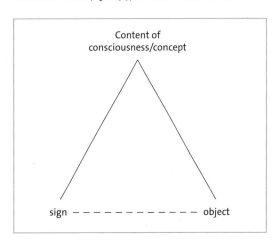

Content of consciousness/concept

sign – – – – – – – – – – object

In literary analysis, a pragmatist perspective can produce very **different readings**. If for instance this perspective is applied to realist fiction—literature that was produced in the late nineteenth century, a time of extreme social unrest—the many passages of elaborate dialogue typical of the realist novel can be reframed under pragmatist parameters. In these extended dialogues the characters in endless acts of communication try to come to terms with a confusing reality, thereby demonstrating the intersubjective, cooperative search for truth that defines pragmatism at its core. Novels by Henry James or William Dean Howells would beautifully serve as material for analysis (cf. entry I.3.3).

In modernist literature, where the focus shifts decidedly from intersubjectivity to subjectivity, other questions may be asked from a pragmatist perspective. The demanding modernist literature of the early twentieth century shares pragmatism's deep interest in the subjective dimensions of reality construction. Both philosophy and literature examine how what is perceived as real is the product of cognition. That is, in their respective discursive fields they both investigate how individuals make sense of their perceptions, interpret and explain them, thereby creating reality in the first place. The reader, in trying to make sense of enigmatic modernist texts, has to perform the very same procedure and thus can reflect on it from within. Gertrude Stein's and William Faulkner's aesthetically challenging writing would be suitable material for this kind of interpretation (cf. entry I.3.4).

## 8.6 | The Linguistic Turn

A sea change in the whole debate occurred at the beginning of the twentieth century with the work of the Swiss linguist **Ferdinand de Saussure**. Saussure shifted the whole semiotic debate out of the philosophical/epistemological realm into a purely linguistic context (hence the term 'linguistic turn,' denoting the paradigm change that the humanities in general underwent in the twentieth century when, following Saussure, they came to rest on a language-oriented or semiotic basis). Saussure's most radical move consisted of transforming the triadic sign model into a dyadic one, bringing together just two elements, thought and sound. In other words, he connected the concept, which he called the **signified**, and a sound image, the **signifier**. The third element in the old triadic model, the object, is abandoned altogether. The reasoning is that the linguistic sign *cannot* refer directly to objects, an insight established by Aristotle, yet Saussure radicalized it by abandoning the reference to the object entirely. Saussure's model would thus look like this:

Saussure then further particularized this definition of the sign by a number of important specifications: he explained that the connection between signifier and signified is arbitrary (i.e. there are no inherent reasons why a chair should be called /tʃeə(ɹ)/), but that it is nonetheless immutable once it is in use by a linguistic community (cf. section V.2.2.2). How then does meaning enter into this arbitrary combination of signifier and signified? According to Saussure, via the dynamic of **difference**: "In language there are only differences. Even more important: a difference generally implies positive terms between which the difference is set up; but in language there are only differences without positive terms" (Saussure 120). A sign gets its meaning through its difference from other signs, which also implies that every sign is tacitly connected to all other signs. That is, something is something because it is not something else, or even because it is not *everything* else, as one sign seems to bear the traces of all other signs through their endless interconnectedness. The meaning of one sign thus seems impossible to pin down, and by analogy, the meaning of complex sign conglomerates such as literary or cultural texts seems to be evasive and forever out of one's grasp (cf. section II.1.4).

A whole new field of research opened up for the humanities after these decisive insights were formulated by Saussure and a language/semiotic-based foundation had been established. Due to the radical move of severing the sign's connections to the world of objects and the emphasis put on the play of differences in the generation of meaning, literary and cultural studies in particular were busy tracing and exploiting all the systematic implications of the paradigm change. Questions of the construction of meaning or identity now became of utmost importance. The theoretical elaborations grew ever more sophisticated over the course of the twentieth century, from structuralism to post-structuralism and deconstruc-tion (cf. entry II.4). Although the language-based semiotic debate was without doubt overwhelmingly dominant in the twentieth century, the epistemological strand was never given up entirely. In this context, attempts have been made to apply the insights of what was primarily Charles Sanders Peirce's semiotic-pragmatist theory to literary and cultural analysis.

## Select Bibliography

Bernstein, Richard J. *The Pragmatic Turn*. Malden: Polity Press, 2010.

Cobley, Paul, ed. *The Routledge Companion to Semiotics*. New York: Routledge, 2010.

De Waal, Cornelis. *On Pragmatism*. Belmont: Thomson-Wadsworth, 2005.

Margolis, Joseph. "Pragmatism, Retrospective, and Prospective." Introduction. *A Companion to Pragmatism*. Eds. John R. Shook and Joseph Margolis. Malden: Blackwell, 2006. 1–10.

Peirce, Charles Sanders. *Collected Papers of Charles S. Peirce*. Eds. Charles Hartshorne, Paul Weiss, and Arthur W. Burks. 8 vols. Cambridge: Harvard University Press, 1931–58.

Rohr, Susanne. *Die Wahrheit der Täuschung: Wirklichkeitskonstitution im amerikanischen Roman: 1889–1989*. Munic: Fink, 2004.

Rohr, Susanne. "Pragmaticism: A New Approach to Literary and Cultural Analysis." *REAL* 19 (2003): 293–306.

Saussure, Ferdinand de. *Course in General Linguistics*. Trans. Wade Baskin. Eds. Charles Bally and Albert Séchehaye. New York: McGraw-Hill, 1966.

Sebeok, Thomas A. *Signs: An Introduction to Semiotics*. 2nd ed. Toronto: University of Toronto Press, 2001.

Talisse, Robert B., and Scott F. Aikin. *Pragmatism: A Guide for the Perplexed*. London: Continuum, 2008.

Trabant, Jürgen. *Zeichen des Menschen: Elemente der Semiotik*. Frankfurt/M.: Fischer, 1989.

*Susanne Rohr*

# 9 Narratology

## 9.1 | Definition

Narratology refers to the study of narrative qua narrative. Narratology attempts to analyse what is typical of narrative as a (macro)genre or text type in contrast to description, instruction, argumentation, etc., or in contrast to drama or the lyric (in literary studies). Narratology is typically concerned with the question of what is narrative, with answers ranging from essentialist proposals (e.g. minimal definitions in Prince's *Dictionary of Narratology*, see box) to fuzzy concept solutions (Ryan) and constructivist frameworks (Fludernik, *Towards*). Besides the **what of narratives**, narratologists have additionally been interested in the **how**: in the delineation and functions of narrative elements or aspects, and in their systematic analysis. Several typologies of narrative texts have been devised (see box). These typologies distinguish between different *kinds* of narrative, for instance according to the identity of the narrator persona, the point of view from which the story is told, or the temporal relationship between telling and told; in some cases they propose prototypical combinations of these features as in Stanzel's narrative situations. Narratologists moreover study the 'making' of narratives by considering the effects of the devices and elements in their functional interrelation. The most important categories of narratology will be explained in section 9.3 below.

Development. Whereas originally, narratology—since it was part of linguistic and literary studies—focussed exclusively on literary narratives, especially on novels and short stories and other fiction (the fairytale), more recently it has been turning into a master discipline concerned with any kind of storytelling. As a result, narratologists now deal with historical writing, with conversational narratives in dinner-table exchanges, with narratives in psychotherapy, with storytelling in cartoons, films, and the electronic media, and much more (see section 9.2 below). Narratology has been extending its object realm into narratives in different media but also into factual storytelling (narrative in law, in economics, in psychotherapy, etc.). At the same time, it increasingly considers narratives written before the invention of the novel and tries to accommodate storytelling traditions from outside Europe, thus broadening its range in diachronic and intercultural analysis.

Status. The status of narratology among the sciences cannot be determined with any conclusiveness. Narratology is no 'theory,' though often taught as part of theory classes. It was originally closely linked to Structuralism (e.g. in the work of Barthes, Greimas, Bremond) and to structuralism's formalist antecedents (Shklovsky, Jakobson, Mukařovský, Propp, Lotman; cf. section II.1.2) and was heavily influenced by the structuralist linguistics of Saussure and Benveniste. One can therefore describe narratology as an applicational type of structuralism, or "**low structuralism**" (Stanzel, "Low-Structuralist"). One argument for such a view of narratology could be that narratology does not provide readings of (narrative) texts in the same manner as psychoanalytic, feminist, or postcolonial literary criticism. Narratological analysis has no ideological impetus, and as a methodological tool, it lends itself to various quite different approaches. It operates more like rhetoric or stylistics: narratological analysis can be equally fruitful for an analysis of a colonial tract and an anti-colonial or postcolonial manifesto; the narrative devices used in either text (like the rhetorical or stylistic features) would tend to be the same, though

---

**Key Texts: Narratology**

**Franz Karl Stanzel,** *Die typischen Erzählsituationen im Roman* (1955); *A Theory of Narrative* [*Theorie des Erzählens*] (1979)
**Gérard Genette,** *Narrative Discourse: An Essay in Method* (1972)
**Seymour Chatman,** *Story and Discourse* (1978); *Coming to Terms* (1990)
**Mieke Bal,** *Narratology: Introduction to the Theory of Narrative* (1980)
**Susan Lanser,** *The Narrative Act* (1981)
**Gerald Prince,** *Narratology* (1982); *A Dictionary of Narratology* (1987)

employed for entirely contrary purposes. In this respect, narratology is more of a methodology or toolbox (Nünning, "Cultural"). Finally, as Jan Christoph Meister has recently argued, narratology can also be conceptualized as a *discipline*, especially on account of its institutional anchoring (regular conferences, associations, journals) and its cross-disciplinary position (attracting members from English studies, German studies, historians, anthropologists, film theorists, linguists, conversation analysts, etc.).

**Focus on Terminology**

Coined by Tzvetan Todorov in his *Grammaire du Décameron* (1969) and first used as the title of a scholarly study in Mieke Bal's *Narratologie* (1977), the term **narratology** has now superseded alternatives such as *narrative studies*, *stylistics*, and *rhetoric* (Booth). In German, by contrast, *Erzähltheorie*, *Erzählforschung* (Lämmert) and the neologism *Narrativik* (Ihwe) are still in use.

## 9.2 | Narrativity

One of the most controversial questions of the discipline of narratology concerns its very object of study—narrative. The problem touches both on the definition of what is a narrative and on the range of objects that such a definition allows one to include. Thus, can some kinds of music, painting, sculpture or lyric poetry be treated as (partially) "narrative"? Traditionally, on account of the institutional anchoring of narratology within literary studies, definitions of narratology have focused on (1) a sequence of events (plot) together with (2) the presence of a narrator or narratorial medium (this is true of definitions by Prince, Genette, and Lanser). This approach also highlights the **double temporality** of narrative: the dynamics between the retrospective act of narration and the structuring of events. Chatman formalizes this double temporality by stipulating that narrative must have a **story** and a **discourse** level (see section 9.3 below). More recent definitions tend to include what Monika Fludernik calls experientiality. This feature relates to the evocation of the human experience of being in the world, and to the dynamics of what makes a narrative exciting (tellability) and significant (point). Experientiality is now often posited as either the exclusive defining feature of narrativity (Fludernik, *Towards*), subsuming plot under its umbrella, or as a comple-

*Narrating events vs. events narrated*

mentary constituent of narrativity within a prototype or family resemblance concept of narrativity. A typical example of the second type is Marie-Laure Ryan's definition:

Narrative must be about a *world* populated by individuated existents. This world must be situated in time and space and undergo *significant transformations*. The transformations must be caused by nonhabitual physical events. Some of the participants in the events must be intelligent agents who have a *mental life* and *react emotionally* to the states of the world. Some of the events must be purposeful actions by these agents, motivated by identifiable goals and plans. The sequence of events must form a unified causal chain and lead to closure. The occurrence of at least some of the events must be asserted as fact for the story world. The story must *communicate something meaningful* to the recipient. (Ryan 8; our emphases)

On the whole, narrativity, originally conceptualized in essentialist fashion, has increasingly become a scalar concept, allowing for more or less, better or less pronounced narrativity. Fludernik (*Towards*) additionally proposes a constructivist model in which texts that do not meet essentialist definitions of narrativity can be *treated as* or *read as* narratives. Thus, Joyce's question-and-answer chapter of *Ulysses* ("Ithaca") is non-narrative if one applies a restrictive definition of narrativity, but easily becomes a narrative if one chooses to read it as one.

# 9.3 | Major Categories of Narratology

Owing to restrictions of space, only a few major terminological distinctions current in narratology can be presented here. We will illustrate them on the example of James Hogg's *Private Memoirs and Confessions of a Justified Sinner* (1824).

**Story vs. Discourse.** This distinction contrasts the level of mediation or representation (cf. Stanzel's *mediacy* or *Mittelbarkeit*) with the level of the narrated events or storyworld; in verbal/written narratives, it refers to the text (discourse) vs. the events (story). In Hogg's novel, what actually happened in the story may remain mysterious, but the book provides three accounts, i.e. discourses trying to establish what occurred in the story: by an omniscient narrator, by a first-person narrator, and by the editor of the first-person narrative. (Although the first part is titled "The Editor's Narrative," it represents the events in omniscient narration.) Discourse, if an oral or written verbal narrative, can itself be subdivided into two aspects: that of the narrative as *énoncé*, i.e. the utterance or text, and that of the *énonciation*, the act of speech or writing, which Genette calls "narration" (27).

**Narrator.** Owing to its focus on the novel, and its reliance on traditional storytelling, narratology has focused extensively on the figure of the narrator. The narrator is traditionally distinguished from the author, who—in fictional stories—remains outside the textual framework (see Cohn). The narrator figure in fictional texts can be foregrounded ("overt") by means of several narrational functions. These include, for example, (1) the use of the first-person pronoun in addresses to the reader figure (narratee; e.g.: "Sure, you will say, it must be an allegory"); (2) the voicing of opinions and evaluations, the uttering of so-called gnomic truths ("But the better all the works of nature are understood, the more they will be ever admired"); and (3) meta-narrative statements (e.g.: "in recording the hideous events which follow, I am only relating […] matters of which [Scots] were before perfectly well informed"). The narrator's discourse, whose product is the text we are reading, has a number of functions, among them most prominently the reportative function (see Nünning, "Erzählinstanzen").

Narrators can be **homo- or heterodiegetic** (Genette's terminology), depending on whether the storyteller is also a character in his story or merely a teller outside the world of the story. Thus, in the first part of the memoir, the editor-narrator is an omniscient narrator who is not a character in the fiction (heterodiegetic) and his story concerns George and Robert and Mrs. Logan and Mrs. Calvert in the seventeenth century. In the second part of the novel, Robert writes his memoir; he is a first-person narrator and writes his own story (homodiegetic, more specifically **autodiegetic**—the narrator is the major protagonist). In the third part of the novel, the editor becomes part of the story since he is one of a team unearthing the skeleton of Robert and the memoir buried with him. Here, the editor is also a homodiegetic narrator, but not the central character, hence not autodiegetic; Stanzel would call him a peripheral first-person narrator. The traditional distinction between first- and third-person narrative (Booth; Stanzel) has become problematic since writers have begun to use second-person narrative, in which the protagonist is referred to not as *I* (homodiegesis) or *he/she* (heterodiegesis), but as *you*.

Narrators can also be either **extra- or intradiegetic**. This distinction refers to narrative levels. According to Genette, any narrative requires a narrative act that takes place outside of that narrative; this 'outside' narrative he calls extradiegetic. If another narrative act occurs within the narrative, for example when a character tells a story, this 'inside' narrative can then be called intradiegetic or simply diegetic. If this story contains yet another narrative, i.e. when a character tells a story in which a character tells a story, Genette speaks of the **metadiegetic** or, better, **hypodiegetic** level. Thus, in Hogg's novel, the omniscient narrator's narrative constitutes the first or extradiegetic level; the conversation between Mrs. Calvert and Mrs. Logan therefore occurs on the diegetic level (level

Homodiegetic narrators are characters in their story, heterodiegetic narrators are not.

> **Definition**
>
> The term → unreliable narrator is used when a text suggests that the narrator—intentionally or not—is providing wrong, insufficient, or one-sided information. There are various textual indicators for unreliable narration, including contradictions in the narrator's account, contradictions between different accounts (in multiperspectival narration), discrepancies between the narrator's self-characterization and the way other characters perceive him, and explicit admissions to insufficient knowledge on the narrator's part.

2) of the story told by the omniscient narrator; the events of Mrs. Calvert's story constitute level 3 (meta/hypodiegetic level); and when Mrs. Calvert tells of telling the story of her miseries to her customer, these events of her former life are situated on level 4 (metametadiegetic/hypohypodiegetic).

**Narratee.** Besides the narrator, narratologists have also analysed the figure of the addressee, variously called the narratee or reader figure (Prince, "Introduction"; Goetsch). The real reader, like the real author, plays a role only in factual narratives; in fiction, narratees can be extra- or intradiegetic. Thus, Hogg's "Surely, you will say, ..." is directed at an extradiegetic narratee, whereas Mrs. Logan as the addressee of Mrs. Calvert's story would be an intradiegetic narratee, i.e. a person located in the world of the fiction. (On the question of address in fiction see also Rabinowitz, who distinguishes a narrative and an authorial audience.)

**Time.** A second area of investigation in narratology has been the handling of the relationship between the **time of narration and narrated time** (the distinction goes back to Günther Müller). Genette distinguishes retrospective (the most common type) from simultaneous, prospective and intercalated modes of narration. He points out, moreover, that the narrational act can be shorter than the events described (summary), or even elide elements of the story (gap), but it can also attempt to be synchronic (scene), e.g. when rendering a dialogue. It can even stretch the duration of events (as in filmic slow-motion) or create a pause (while the narrator delineates the beauties of the heroine or engages in philosophical musings, time stands still on the plot level). Finally, Genette's theory has become most famous for its discussion of **anachronies**, i.e. the reordering of events on the discourse level. Thus, rather than narrating events in sequence from beginning to end, the narrative discourse may actually start at the end and then go back to the beginning and relate the story chronologically after that; or it can alternate between earlier and later situations (using **flashbacks**, which Genette calls **analepses**). Anticipations of future events (**prolepses**) or gaps which are filled later may also be employed. Hogg's novel is particularly interesting in this respect since it starts with a quasi-omniscient narrative that fails to uncover the mystery of the real circumstances of George Colwan's murder. In the memoir of Robert Wringhim, it then supplies a counter-narrative that presents many of the same events from Robert's perspective (on this term, see below), but also mentions events

*Most narratives are retrospective: They narrate past events.*

not noted in the earlier account, for instance that of Robert's alleged rape of a young lady or the murder of his mother (presumably committed by Satan, who takes Robert's shape). The final part of the novel supplies further details of Robert's suicide and discovers the memoir's whereabouts, but does so as a recovery of the past inside an early nineteenth-century frame.

**Point of View, Perspective, Focalization.** A third area of narratological analysis examines what is variously known as point of view, perspective, or focalization (Genette). The questions asked here concern the following issues, among others: What is the distribution of knowledge about characters' minds (can/does the narrator present their thoughts and feelings)? From which standpoint does the narrative present the hero or events (from an external or an internal perspective)? Where is the centre of focalization? How is the story told in terms of ideology or style? Is it presented in a slanted or an objective manner? Is the language used by the narrator indicative of a particular class and register? Whereas Stanzel, who distinguishes between external and internal perspective, is more interested in access to the characters' psyche, Uspensky examines psychological along with ideological, phraseological, and spatio-temporal perspective. Vision is the central metaphor for all of these terms (point of view, perspective, focalization), but not all narratologists agree that the (heterodiegetic) narrator actually "sees" (Chatman, *Coming to Terms*, and Fludernik, *Towards* insist that such narrators only report but do not "see"). Genette's model, as Bal has pointed out (171), confuses different types of vision. Thus, in his category of **external** focalization, the narrative presents the characters from outside and has no access to their minds; in his **internal** focalization we witness the fictional world through the "eyes" of a character, whose mind is presented in detail; and his category of non-focalized narration (corresponding to omniscient narrative) allows for a variety of focuses, combining external and inside views of characters. Bal more logically distinguishes between the **focalizer** (from whose viewpoint something is seen) and the **focalized** (that which is seen). The focalized can be either visible or invisible; if the focalizer is a character, as in Genette's internal focalization (equivalent to Stanzel's figural narrative situation), this focalizer cannot see into other people's minds; feelings or thoughts of other people are an invisible focalized. If there is a narrator-focalizer, on the other hand, the consciousness of characters can be either a visible or an invisible focalized, depending on whether the narrator is omniscient or not in traditional parlance.

Focalization is put to extensive use in narrative texts. Creative use can be made of this technique in the interest of **multiperspectivism**, i.e. the contrasting or combining of different perspectives (see Nünning and Nünning). Thus, in Hogg's novel, the juxtaposition of what is generally known or what is seen from George Colwan's perspective with what we learn from Robert's memoir (especially regarding the mysterious stranger, who seems to be the devil) enriches the account of the uncanny events related in the book without, ingeniously, ruining the suspense about the stranger's identity.

**Stanzel's Narrative Situations.** Whereas Genette keeps his various categories of analysis distinct and sees them as unrestrictedly combinable, Stanzel (*Theory*) has proposed three prototypical combinations of what he calls **person** (identity or non-identity of narrator and protagonist, i.e. homo-/heterodiegesis), **perspective** (external vs. internal perspective, roughly equivalent to non-focalization vs. internal focalization in Genette) and **mode** (explicit narration by a narrator persona vs. presentation through the consciousness of a protagonist). These three prototypical scenarios are called narrative situations. Stanzel's *Typenkreis* (see illustration) visualizes the interrelations between the three narrative situations and shows that they form a continuum rather than a set of neatly separable categories.

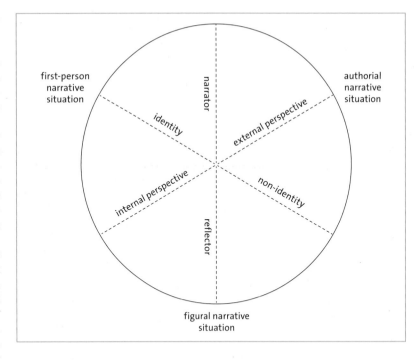

One could enumerate a number of other aspects of narrative treated at length by narratologists (plot structure, the representation of thought and speech, narrative levels and their crossing in metalepsis, the representation of space in narrative, *mise en abyme*), but for lack of space, interested readers are referred to the large number of introductions to narratology, some of which are listed in the bibliography.

Stanzel's Typenkreis
(following Stanzel 1984, 56)

## Select Bibliography

Bal, Mieke. *Narratology: Introduction to the Theory of Narrative*. 1985. Toronto: University of Toronto Press, 1997.

Booth, Wayne C. *The Rhetoric of Fiction*. 1961. Chicago: Chicago University Press, 1983.

Chatman, Seymour. *Coming to Terms: The Rhetoric of Narrative in Fiction and Film*. Ithaca: Cornell University Press, 1990.

Chatman, Seymour. *Story and Discourse: Narrative Structure in Fiction and Film*. Ithaca: Cornell University Press, 1978.

Cohn, Dorrit. "Signposts of Fictionality: A Narratological Perspective." *Poetics Today* 11.4 (1990): 775–804.

Cornils, Anja, and Wilhelm Schernus. "On the Relationship Between the Theory of the Novel, Narrative Theory, and Narratology." *What is Narratology? Questions and Answers Regarding the Status of a Theory*. Eds. Tom Kindt and Hans-Harald Müller. Berlin: de Gruyter, 2003. 137–74.

Fludernik, Monika. "Narratology in the Twenty-First Century: The Cognitive Approach to Narrative." *PMLA* 125.4 (2010): 924–30.

Fludernik, Monika. *Towards a 'Natural' Narratology*. London: Routledge, 1996.

Genette, Gérard. *Narrative Discourse: An Essay in Method*. 1972. Trans. Jane E. Lewin. Ithaca: Cornell University Press, 1980.

Goetsch, Paul. "Reader Figures in Narrative." *Style* 38.2 (2004): 188–202.

Hamburger, Käte. *The Logic of Literature*. 1957. Trans. Marilynn J. Rose. Bloomington: Indiana University Press, 1993.

Hogg, James. *The Private Memoirs and Confessions of a Justified Sinner*. 1824. Ed. John Carey. Oxford: Oxford University Press, 1981.

Ihwe, Jens. "On the Foundation of a General Theory of Narrative Structure." *Poetics* 1.3 (1972): 5–14.

Lämmert, Eberhard. *Bauformen des Erzählens*. 1955. Stuttgart: Metzler, 1993.

Martínez, Matías, and Michael Scheffel. *Einführung in die Erzähltheorie*. Munich: Beck, 1999.

Meister, Jan Christoph. "Narratology." *Handbook of Narratology*. Eds. Peter Hühn et al. Berlin: de Gruyter, 2009. 329–50.

Müller, Günther. "Erzählzeit und erzählte Zeit." 1948. *Morphologische Poetik*. Ed. Elena Müller. Darmstadt: WBG, 1968. 269–86.

Nünning, Ansgar. "Die Funktion von Erzählinstanzen: Analysekategorien und Modelle zur Beschreibung des Erzählverhaltens." *Literatur in Wissenschaft und Unterricht* 30 (1997): 323–49.

Nünning, Ansgar. "Towards a Cultural and Historical Narratology: A Survey of Diachronic Approaches, Concept, and Research Projects." *Anglistentag 1999 Mainz: Proceedings*. Eds. Bernhard Reitz and Sigrid Rieuwerts. Trier: WVT, 2000. 345–73.

Nünning, Vera, and Ansgar Nünning, eds. *Multiperspektivisches Erzählen: Zur Theorie und Geschichte der Perspektivenstruktur im englischen Roman des 18. bis 20. Jahrhunderts*. Trier: WVT, 2000.

Prince, Gerald. "Introduction to the Study of the Narratee." *Essentials of the Theory of Fiction*. Eds. Michael J. Hoffman and Patrick D. Murphy. Durham: Duke University Press, 1988. 313–35.

Prince, Gerald. *Narratology: The Form and Functioning of Narrative*. Berlin: Mouton de Gruyter, 1982.

Rabinowitz, Peter J. "Truth in Fiction: A Reexamination of Audiences." *Critical Inquiry* 4 (1977): 121–41.

Ryan, Marie-Laure. *Avatars of Story*. Minneapolis: University of Minnesota Press, 2006.

Stanzel, Franz Karl. "A Low-Structuralist at Bay? Further Thoughts on a Theory of Narrative." *Poetics Today* 11.4 (1990): 805–16.

Stanzel, Franz Karl. *A Theory of Narrative*. Trans. Charlotte Goedsche. Cambridge: Cambridge University Press, 1984.

Todorov, Tzvetan. *Grammaire du Décameron*. The Hague: Mouton, 1969.

Todorov, Tzvetan. *The Poetics of Prose*. 1971. Trans. Richard Howard. Oxford: Blackwell, 1977.

Uspensky, Boris. *A Poetics of Composition*. Trans. Valentina Zavarin and Susan Wittig. Berkeley: University of California Press, 1973.

*Monika Fludernik / Caroline Pirlet*

# 10 Systems Theory

Not very far into William Blake's huge multi-media epic *Jerusalem* (1804–1820), the mythical but very modern character Los cries out indignantly: "I must Create a System, or be enslaved by another Man's. / I will not Reason & Compare: my business is to Create" (Plate 10). To this day, every attempt at introducing systems-theoretical thinking to the fields of literary and cultural studies faces frequent resistance along similar lines: Why would one resort to another man's—or another discipline's—system, when the very word 'system' itself seems to be alien to the flexibility and personal relevance of many of the aesthetic practices examined in literary and cultural studies? The following observations will try to counter these charges. While a variety of systems-theoretical approaches have found their way into literary studies (cf. Reinfandt, "How German" 276–78), **Niklas Luhmann**'s sociological systems theory of modernity seems to offer the most compelling framework for an inclusive but highly differentiated re-conceptualisation of many of the central concerns of recent literary and cultural theory. Luhmann participates in the late-twentieth-century shift from

the regulative idea(l) of 'identity' to a full acknowledgement of the constitutive function of 'difference' for all notions of truth and knowledge. But he replaces the focus on language and text(uality), which twentieth-century (literary) theory insisted on after the 'linguistic turn' (cf. entries II.1 and II.4), with a very different **focus on observation and communication**. These key terms provide an alternative to the fixation on matters of representation which characterises the mainstream of (literary) theory. In reconnecting representation to sophisticated notions of practice, process, and mediality, a systems-theoretical approach introduces a culturally and socially embedded as well as strictly historicised understanding of textual and media-based phenomena. While the terminology of systems theory seems to be highly abstract at first glance, it nevertheless opens up new perspectives on text-context relations and texts' social functions. It is thus highly conducive to inquiries under the banner of the 'cultural turn,' as the following sketch of the systems-theoretical potential for work in English and American Studies will demonstrate.

## 10.1 | Consciousness and Communication

Modern society, according to Niklas Luhmann, consists of communications which, in referring exclusively to themselves and to other communications, create their own dynamics of systemic formation and closure. Thus, modern society at large differentiates itself into autonomous, autopoietic (i.e. self-generating) subsystems ('**social systems**') catering to different functions, such as economy, law, politics, religion, art, education, science and literature. All these social systems operate according to their own norms and horizons of meaning (*Sinn*). On the other hand, Luhmann considers human beings as a combination of 'organic systems' and '**psychic systems**' and locates them in the environment of social systems and

hence outside society, which is one of the most controversial aspects of his theory. He also claims that social systems and psychic systems operate differently: In contrast to social systems, which consist of an ongoing series of interconnected communications, psychic systems operate on the basis of interconnected thoughts. Meaningful human thoughts, Luhmann argues, cannot readily be transferred into the realm of communication because this transferral imposes the distinction of information and message with their respective dimensions of selectivity. This leads, as will be explained in the section 'Layers of Mediality (1)' below, to a completely different horizon of meaning from the one surrounding the original thought.

For Luhmann, social systems consist of communications, psychic systems of thoughts.

This is the first theoretical challenge, which, however, provides an interesting explanation for typically modern phenomena like alienation, fragmentation and loss or lack of meaning.

The second theoretical challenge is the following: We have seen that both human consciousness and social communication exist only as a series of events which are, as such, fleeting, evanescent, continually passing out of existence and thus discontinuous. How is it, then, that both persons and

societies generate a fairly stable understanding of their respective existence? How can this fundamental discontinuity be overcome so that the system can construct its continuous identity in self-description and, in parallel, its very own 'view' of the world on the basis of its specific constitutive difference from its environment? Luhmann provides the answer to these challenges with the help of a radical rethinking of the concept of '**medium**.'

## 10.2 | Medium vs. Form

Systems-theoretical terms are never formulated as free-standing notions but rather as **observer-dependent distinctions**. The term 'observer' does not refer to human action but rather to the systemic operation of drawing a distinction by marking something off from the unmarked space surrounding it. This operation is also constitutive for the systems themselves: every system can only exist—and be adequately theorized—in its specific difference from its environment. For example, the subsystem of (modern) literature 'observes' the world (i.e. constructs its own environment) with a strong emphasis on the subjective experience of psychic systems. The subsystem of (modern) science, on the other hand, tries to relegate subjectivity to the sidelines in order to 'observe' the world (construct its environment) objectively in an attempt to maintain ontological notions of truth under modern conditions. Both literature and science thus provide text-based *Observations of Modernity* (Luhmann 1998; note that modernity has to be understood as both the subject and the object of observation). Their descriptions (constructions) of the world, however, will only partially overlap, thus contributing to modern culture's overwhelming sense of plurality and fragmentation.

*Medium as a relative category*

A crucial position in systems theory's repertoire of distinctions (so far, system/environment, operation/observation, consciousness/communication) can be assigned to the distinction of '**medium**' and '**form**.' Theoretically, Luhmann draws upon the psychologist Fritz Heider, who suggested that media provide loosely coupled elements which can be rigidly coupled in forms. David Wellbery has described this persuasively, with reference to Daniel Defoe's *Robinson Crusoe*, as "the Friday theory of media":

Consider a stretch of sand on an apparently uninhabited island. As such, it is just what it is: sand. However, if I, like Crusoe, happen to encounter a footprint in it, it becomes a medium for bearing form. The grains of sand—'loosely coupled' in the sense of having no fixed arrangement and being susceptible to rearrangement—are brought into a particular array that exhibits the form 'human footprint.' Friday has left his trace and this trace is a datum that is itself distinguished from, but related to other data ('animal spoor', 'wind swirl'). The footprint is a 'rigid coupling' of the loosely coupled elements (the grains of sand) in the sense that not just any indentation of the beach will do. The sand thus becomes a medium when it is imprinted with, receives, or comes to bear the form; and the footprint becomes a form when the loosely coupled elements of the medium are brought into an alignment that makes a difference ('That's Friday's footprint, not the footprint of a turtle!'). (301–2)

Starting from this general distinction of medium/form, Luhmann develops a multi-layered expansion of the media concept which goes beyond received notions in literary, cultural and media studies because "[f]rom the perspective of systems theory [...] the terms *form* and *medium* are relative; what counts as a medium will depend entirely on the plane of analyses selected" (Wellbery 302). What potential does this concept hold for literary and cultural theory?

### 10.2.1 | Layers of Mediality (1): Meaning

Most strikingly, Luhmann uses his reconceptualisation of the term 'medium' in order to establish that social systems and psychic systems constitute themselves within the medium of **meaning** (*Sinn*). The constitutive operations of social and psychic systems, i.e. communications and thoughts respectively, generate a temporal horizon which establishes the system's very own past, present and future. On this basis, meaning(fulness) can be produced and assessed on a strictly functional (and relative) basis: Everything which facilitates the continuation of a system's specific operations is meaningful, but only for that particular system. Thus, many of the more hermetic texts of high modernism do not seem to make any sense at all for 'normal readers' (and sometimes not even for academics), but they make perfect sense within the confines of the system of modern literature at that particular stage of its evolution. The medium of meaning, then, provides a solution to the challenge posed by the fundamental discontinuity of the system's operations. Both psychic and social systems rely on it, albeit in fundamentally different modes: While perception and imagination enable consciousness to transform information into meaningful **units of experience**, communication remains insurmountably grounded in difference, and this is why the identity of experience is inevitably compromised by its expression. According to Luhmann, communication comprises a three-fold process of selection in which the difference between what is being communicated ('information') and how it is being communicated ('message') has to be successfully processed ('understanding'; again: not alluding to human action) before **connectivity** (*Anschlussfähigkeit*) can be reached in the form of either acceptance or rejection (which would, either way, maintain the system's continuing existence as it necessitates another communication). In contrast to traditional sender-receiver models of communication, there is a strong sense of simultaneity in which the message actually creates information and not the other way round, very much like the emergence of form actually brings about the medium-status of the mere sand in the Friday theory of media. On a more general note, these ideas sit comfortably with recent developments in epistemology (constructivism) and narratology, where discourse is assumed to bring a story into existence instead of merely recounting it.

## 10.2.2 | Layers of Mediality (2): Language

The co-evolution of psychic and social systems has brought forth an additional layer of mediality which allows for a 'structural coupling' between autonomous systems, even if one system's meaning can never be another system's meaning: No information can ever cross from one system into another be-

cause all a system gets from its environment (including other systems) is stimuli which will have to be transformed into information according to the system's very own rules – information can only be constructed (and thus generated) internally. This additional layer of mediality is **language**, which Luhmann, in contrast to assumptions from modern linguistics and (post-)structuralism (cf. entries II.4 and V.2), conceives not as a system but rather as the medium which makes structural coupling between consciousness and communication possible. Thus, language facilitates a history of **mutual stimulation** between systems, which results in their coordination despite the systems' insurmountable autonomy and closure. (Modern) literature, for example, has long been the privileged arena for playing out the dimension of subjective experience as it unfolded in modern culture. In spite of this affinity, however, it has always processed the stimuli from psychic systems according to its own rules, which has led, with high modernism marking a crucial turning point, to an increasing sense of alienation and overwhelming difficulty on the part of the psychic systems (cf. entries I.2.6 and I.3.4). At the same time, (modern) literature has maintained fruitful relationships with the systems of politics and religion, but these were also punctuated by acts of censorship, restrictive regulations and even death sentences against authors like, most recently, Salman Rushdie, which clearly indicates the limits of mutual understanding.

Language in this sense works on two levels simultaneously: on the one hand, it provides a medium for the **symbolic generalization** of meaning *within* the systems (i.e. a semantic detachment of signs from their potential reference at the cost of particularity, see 'Layers of Mediality (4)' below), raising the potential for connectivity to unprecedented heights; on the other hand, it serves as a medium of communication by means of **material signs**, and it is on this materially graspable and observable level that structural coupling is facilitated even to the point where Romantic poems are written and read by psychic systems as authentic and immediate outpourings of feelings in spite of the fact that the marks on a page are completely disconnected from their author once they are 'out there' and can only be processed and made sense of in the new systemic context (communication/'literature'). The interconnectedness of both levels adds two new qualitative dimensions to the functional understanding of meaning introduced above: First, language holds the potential of nega-

Language mediates between different systems.

tion, thus doubling the potential for meaningful selections at one stroke. Secondly, language provides a semantic dimension which creates a second dimension of differentiation at a distance from reality, potentially reflecting—but also alleviating and thus countering and sometimes even negating—the effects generated on the operational level of the systems involved. Notions of identity, for example, tend to be, if at all, wrested from difference in such a compensatory fashion. They are, as such, largely a semantic phenomenon, while the operations of systems keep on processing difference in order to maintain their operational identity. Thus, modern literature as a social system has provided many opportunities for the self-fashioning of psychic systems as modern subjects, and the genres of poetry and fiction have provided suitable blueprints for this exercise with their additional shaping of the mediality of language. However, the dynamics of the system have also undermined these very same constructions in the course of the system's evolution: The emphatic speaking subjects of Romantic poetry vanished into the mere voices of modernist poetry which in turn increasingly acknowledged their own textual/written/printed status in a move from modernist universality to postmodernist particularity, returning psychic systems to their own devices, and with increased ontological insecurity at that. Similarly, the realistically grounded and embedded subject positions of realist fiction became increasingly detached from the world with the modernist turn into interiority and experientiality, which again could only be re-connected to the world with a postmodernist acknowledgement of their textual/written/printed status. As opposed to the cognitive orientation of some constructivist approaches, systems-theoretical thinking manages to combine cognitive and social orientations by grounding the mediality of language in the mediality of meaning and acknowledging the importance of both dimensions for the interplay between psychic and social systems.

## 10.2.3 | Layers of Mediality (3): Writing, Print, Electronic Media

While language facilitates the emergence of face-to-face interaction (oral communication) with heightened semantic potential, social systems in Luhmann's sense would have to rely on additional layers of mediality. Here, writing is of seminal importance because it liberates communication from the limitations of interaction. While the **storage and distribution** functions of writing introduce the possibility of covering spatial and temporal distances with the concomitant effects of building an archive and facilitating specialization of vocabulary and genre, it is the technologizing of writing in print which brings forth modern culture and society as we know it. Only on the basis of print can various textuality-based historical semantics such as, for example, (modern) love with its grounding in individuality and subjectivity (cf. Luhmann, *Love as Passion*), form a virtual reality of sorts. This virtual reality of modernity becomes all-permeating with the advent of electronic media and their ultimate convergence into what Luhmann calls, in the title of a monograph, *The Reality of the Mass Media*, insisting in its notorious opening sentence that "[w]hatever we know about our society, or indeed about the world in which we live, we know through the mass media" (1).

## 10.2.4 | Layers of Mediality (4): Symbolically Generalized Media of Communication

While the layers of mediality identified so far are all part and parcel of media studies and cultural studies as currently practiced, there is one additional layer which has as yet not been addressed in terms of its mediality. This layer starts from a surprising observation: In spite of the innumerable occasions for communication induced by the contemporary mediascape and by the increasing functional differentiation of modern society into specialized autonomous sub-systems, successful communication in any given system does not become more likely—in fact, paradoxically, it becomes even less likely. So each functionally differentiated social system has to cope with this increasing improbability of successful communication, which is generated by the print-induced severance of production and reception (cf. Luhmann, "Improbability"): every potential reader of a text may at all times opt for reading a different text or even doing something completely different, and the writer has no way of making sure that a particular text is going to be read at all—and even if the text is read, the writer has no way of making sure that it is understood in any particular way, be it according to the writer's intentions or, on the functional level, according to the specific horizon of meaning of a particular social system. To counter these developments, social systems establish their own functionally determined horizons of meaning by imposing a **secondary medium of communication** on writing, print, and the electronic media. These secondary 'success media,' as Luhmann calls them in his as yet untranslated *magnum opus, Die Gesellschaft der Gesellschaft,* make the continuation of systems-specific communication more likely by establishing a distinct symbolically generalized horizon of meaning and a specific binary code for each social system. For example, the medium of money facilitates the ongoing communicative negotiation of +/– ownership in the economic system, publications facilitate the ongoing communicative negotiation of +/– truth in the science system, and works of art and literature facilitate the ongoing communicative negotiation of +/– beauty, interestingness, aptness or whatever symbolic preference value one would like to propose for modern art and literature.

As one can see here, systems theory provides a plausible explanation for the increasing specialization, fragmentation and destabilization of traditional notions of meaning under modern conditions. At the same time, it provides a consistent set of terms for addressing the various layers of meaning which are 'inscribed,' as it were, in any text. Meanwhile, systems-specific communication is always surrounded by an environment of other social systems as well as what Luhmann terms 'general social communication.' General social communication precedes and prepares (but also picks up impulses from) the communication in functionally differentiated subsystems of modern society, which is in turn based on the relationship between psychic and social systems that can be described in terms of 'socialisation' and 'inclusion/exclusion.' The functionality of social systems themselves can be described with regard to the three basic systemic references of function, performance, and reflexivity. The level of **function** refers to the system's relationship with modern society as a whole, in which the emergence of a specific subsystem is motivated by a specific function no other system caters to. On this level, textual analysis would have to address the dominant systemic reference of a given text, along with the specific discursive rules applicable at a given moment

in that system's evolution. In the case of literature, for example, these rules would also have to be differentiated with regard to their applicability to processes of production (by authors who are actively socialised in the literary system) as opposed to processes of reception (by readers who are only passively socialised in the literary system). In the system of science, on the other hand, all readers are, as scientists, also writers, so that the systems-specific communication rests exclusively on active socialisation, which explains why modern scientific communication has evolved into a much more specialized discourse than modern literary communication: Scientists may write for scientists exclusively, while literary authors may never completely forget the common reader, even if modern literature as a social system reached unprecedented levels of specialisation with modernism. The level of **performance** regulates the system's relationship with other systems in its environment in terms of structural coupling, and the manifold relations among social systems can be balanced against relations between social and psychic systems with their variable modes of inclusion/exclusion. Here, a systems-theory approach to literature would look at the complex interactions of the literary system with the systems of law (e.g. copyright), economy (the literary market), education (schools), science (literary studies), etc. This inbuilt polycontextuality of literature can then serve as a starting point to explain its frequently compensatory but at times also reflexive and expansive performance for individual readers or groups of readers: Literature can confirm its readers' prejudices and preconceptions and thus give them a sense of security, but it can also motivate readers to re-think their assumptions and to learn something new about the phenomena it describes. Finally, the level of **reflexivity** determines a system's identity by means of self-observation and self-description as well as the specific workings of a system's symbolically generalized medium of communication with its binary code of preference value vs. reflection value. On this level, the transformation from 'text' to 'work' can be described in terms of textual features against the background of the evolution of the modern literary system. The level of reflexivity thus establishes the inner-systemic dimension of the exterior dimensions addressed under the rubrics of function and performance.

The function of literature

The literary system and its relations to other systems

## 10.3 | Systems Theory and Reading/Analysing Texts

Luhmann's innovative concepts of meaning and mediality position modern literature in its specific horizon of meaning which combines objective, subjective and reflexive dimensions. Accordingly, every text can be analyzed in terms of its (fictional) referentiality, in terms of its relation to subjective experience, and in terms of its mediality. While the first two dimensions have been traditional concerns of literary studies, it is actually the third dimension which regulates the terms and conditions of how a text works at a given historical moment. Thus, systems theory provides an integrated framework for analyzing individual texts in terms of their mediality which in turn links the individual text to its particular genre and its specific functionality at a given moment in the evolution of modern literary communication (for a glimpse of the implications for poetry, fiction and drama at a crucial historical turning point, see for example entry I.2.4). Broadly

---

### Focus on Literature as a Social System

The **emergence of the novel** as the central genre of modern literature provides a suitable example for the emergence of literature as a social system, which had to demarcate its distinctive function as opposed to other emerging social systems, unfold its performative potential for these other social systems as well as for psychic systems, and finally establish its operative identity through continuous self-reference and thus reflexivity.

In terms of function, early novels like Daniel Defoe's *Robinson Crusoe* had to legitimize their new project of presenting fictional but realist narratives about the contemporary world by insisting on its status as a true story that is "told with modesty, with seriousness, and with a religious application" (Preface). One would assume, however, that contemporary audiences were much more interested in the "wonders of this man's life [which] exceed all that [...] is to be found extant," and it is certainly no coincidence that the preface praises these attractions which point forward to a new understanding of literature in terms of imagination and entertainment *before* it insists on the morally exemplary qualities of the tale. Similarly, it can be safely assumed that audiences' interest in the *Harry Potter* of the eighteenth century, Samuel Richardson's *Pamela* with all its spin-offs, was more directed at the interior of young women's bedrooms and minds than the moral point of *Virtue Rewarded*. In terms of the novels' literary status, however, readers' enthusiasm for spectacle and piquancy brought the dangers of coarseness and genuine popularity, which in turn undermined the new genre's cultural authority. No wonder, then, that Henry Fielding, who truly emancipated modern fiction by establishing the authorial narrator and thus liberated fiction from the constraints of first-person narration, tried to fend off the uneducated by using the uncommon adjective 'eleemosynary' in the very first sentence of *Tom Jones* after he had legitimized the new genre with recourse to neoclassical poetics as a 'comic epic poem in prose' in the preface to his earlier novel *Joseph Andrews* (1742).

Whatever the strategies of insisting on novels' status as literature in the emerging new sense, however, the **performative potential** of the new genre remained to a certain extent unchecked by these. To this day, nothing can keep readers of fiction from reading novels for mere entertainment without any regard for literary ambition as manifested in, for example, formal complexity, and nothing can keep readers from identifying with characters or looking for a message or moral which could be applied to their own lives. Accordingly, novels (and modern literature at large) perform all kinds of services for psychic systems and, depending on which registers of meaning are foregrounded in the reading process, establish more or less close performative ties with other social systems. While this can result in exclusively religious, political, economic or whatever readings, the fact that the text at hand provides an **integrative vehicle** for this multiplicity emerges as one of the strong points of modern literature.

As this sketch shows, function and performance are only loosely coupled. The relationship between the two will have to be continuously negotiated and calibrated in the processes of self-observation and self-description characteristic of modern literary communication. **Reflexivity** thus becomes the **hallmark of modern literature**, and a history of modern fiction could be written with a focus on the variety of metaliterary, metanarrative or metafictional strategies displayed in novels since the eighteenth century. Such strategies are one of the decisive markers of 'literary fiction' even today, while some subgenres of the novel, such as the Gothic novel, lost their status as literature on these grounds (cf. entry I.2.4).

speaking, the evolution of modern literature has been marked by the emergence of subjectivity as the basis of modern culture in a movement from negotiating its relation to the world (reference) through emphatic validations of subjective experience to an increasing acknowledgement of its conditioning through textuality and mediality (cf. Reinfandt, "Reading"), but one of the distinctive features of modern literature is the persistent compensatory co-presence of all three dimensions with varying dominants. Depending on the contexts of their reception, modern literary texts carry the potential for manifold readings. Systems-theoretical approaches in literary and cultural studies provide a dynamic framework for acknowledging the polycontextuality and the historical dynamics shaping the underlying processes of production and reception.

The four-dimensional topography of layers of modern mediality outlined above suggests that Niklas Luhmann's sociological theory of moder-nity provides a repertoire of distinctions that on the whole allow for a more precise and differentiated analysis than comparable approaches in cultural theory, such as, for example, Stephen Greenblatt's metaphorical notion of 'the circulation of social energy' or Michel Foucault's concept of 'discourse' (cf. entries II.4 and II.5). What is more, the theory is self-reflexive in that it acknowledges its own positioning in the very cultural continuum of modernity that it describes: sociological systems theory is only one more example for the creativity of systems, which forms the basis for everything there is. The dangers of enslavement as envisioned by Blake in the opening quotation of this entry can perhaps best be countered with the help of an approach which charts the multidimensional layers of systemic creativity as well as the dangers of their mutual encroachment upon each other on a sophisticated theoretical footing which acknowledges the systems' fundamental operative closure and autonomy.

## Select Bibliography

**Luhmann, Niklas.** *Art as a Social System*. Stanford: Stanford University Press, 2000.

**Luhmann, Niklas.** *Die Gesellschaft der Gesellschaft*. Frankfurt/M.: Suhrkamp, 1997.

**Luhmann, Niklas.** "How Can the Mind Participate in Communication?" *Materialities of Communication*. Eds. Hans Ulrich Gumbrecht and K. Ludwig Pfeiffer. Stanford: Stanford University Press, 2004. 370–87.

**Luhmann, Niklas.** "The Improbability of Communication." *Essays on Self-Reference*. New York: Columbia University Press, 1990. 86–98.

**Luhmann, Niklas.** *Introduction to Systems Theory*. Cambridge: Polity, 2011.

**Luhmann, Niklas.** *Love as Passion: The Codification of Intimacy*. Cambridge: Polity, 1986.

**Luhmann, Niklas.** *Observations on Modernity*. Stanford: Stanford University Press, 1998.

**Luhmann, Niklas.** *The Reality of the Mass Media*. Stanford: Stanford University Press, 2000.

**Luhmann, Niklas.** *Social Systems*. Stanford: Stanford University Press, 1995.

**Luhmann, Niklas.** "What is Communication?" *Communication Theory* 2 (1992): 251–59.

**Moeller, Hans-Georg.** *Luhmann Explained: From Souls to Systems*. Chicago: Open Court, 2006.

**Müller, Harro.** "Luhmann's Systems Theory as a Theory of Modernity." *Niklas Luhmann*. Spec. issue of *New German Critique* 61 (1994): 39–54.

**Reinfandt, Christoph.** "How German Is It? The Place of Systems-Theoretical Approaches in Literary Studies." *Systems Theory and Literature*. Spec. issue of *EJES: European Journal of English Studies* 5.3 (2001): 275–88.

**Reinfandt, Christoph.** "Reading the Waste Land: Textuality, Mediality, Modernity." *Addressing Modernity: Social Systems Theory and U.S. Cultures*. Eds. Hannes Bergthaller and Carsten Schinko. Amsterdam/New York: Rodopi, 2011. 63–84.

**Wellbery, David.** "System." *Critical Terms for Media Studies*. Eds. W. J. T. Mitchell and Mark B. N. Hansen. Chicago: University of Chicago Press, 2010. 297–309.

**Werber, Niels, ed.** *Systemtheoretische Literaturwissenschaft: Begriffe – Methoden – Anwendungen*. Berlin: de Gruyter, 2011.

*Christoph Reinfandt*

# 11 Cultural Memory

## 11.1 | Definition

Cultural memory is a theoretical perspective which links English and American Studies closely to interdisciplinary research in the humanities and social sciences. Memory studies is a broad convergence field, with contributions from cultural history, social psychology, media studies, political philosophy, and comparative literature. With the term '**cultural memory**,' scholars describe all those processes of a biological, medial, or social nature which relate past and present (and future) in socio-cultural contexts. Cultural memory entails remembering *and* forgetting. It has an individual and a collective side, which are, however, closely interrelated (see Erll, *Memory in Culture*).

**Ways of studying memory in literature**

There are many different ways of engaging in memory studies from the vantage point of English and American Studies. Some scholars are, for example, interested in the significance of ancient mnemotechnics (*ars memoriae*) for English philosophy of the early modern period, others study intertextuality as 'literature's memory,' canon formation as a way of defining cultural heritage, the relation of narrative, memory and identity, or British and American sites of memory. From this wealth of possible approaches, this chapter will—very selectively—present three topics which are currently much-discussed in interdisciplinary memory studies and at the same time pertain to key areas of English and American Studies:

**1. The representation of 'traumatic pasts' in media such as literature and film.** This topic links memory research to Holocaust studies and the cultural history of war and violence. English and American Studies contributes to an understanding of mediated memories by analyzing Holocaust writing, war movies, '9/11' novels, the poetry of World War I, and the ways in which historical injustices and the violation of human rights are represented in the Anglophone world (e.g. British colonial wars, slavery in the U.S., South African Apartheid, or the Australian 'stolen generation'). The logic of individual and cultural trauma, narrative and other aesthetic forms used to represent memory, and the social functions of literature and film are some of the central questions memory studies has to deal with in this area of research.

**2. The 'afterlife' of literature.** The study of literary afterlives (which is reminiscent of Aby Warburg's research on art's afterlife) opens up a diachronic perspective. Stories appear, disappear, and reappear. Literary works are read, reread, and rewritten across decades and centuries. In the process, they are constantly transformed and put to ever-new uses. **Intertextuality**, **rewriting**, **intermediality** and **remediation** are key concepts which describe the 'social life' of texts and other media in a mnemohistorical perspective.

**3. Transnational and transcultural memory.** Most recently, memory studies has begun to turn away from its prevailing methodological nationalism and become interested in forms of remembering *across* nations and cultures. A similar development can be observed in English and American Studies, namely an increased interest in transcultural English literatures, in world literature, and in the effects of colonialism and decolonization, migration, cultural globalization, and cosmopolitanism within the Anglophone world (cf. entry I.4).

## 11.2 | The Representation of Memory in Literature and Film: 'Traumatic Pasts'

Literature and film can vividly portray individual and collective memory—its contents, its workings, its fragility and its distortions—by coding it into aesthetic forms, such as narrative structures, symbols, and metaphors. Fictional versions of memory are characterized by their dynamic relationship to memory concepts of other symbol systems, such as psychology, religion, history, and sociology: they are shaped by them, and shape them in turn; they may perpetuate old or anticipate new images of remembering and forgetting.

It is at least since the modernist writings of Marcel Proust and Virginia Woolf that this close relationship of literature to social discourses of memory has become obvious. In 'memory novels' such as *Mrs Dalloway* (1925; cf. section I.2.6.4), ideas about the **individual memory** which had been circulating at the beginning of the twentieth century (e.g. Sigmund Freud's concept of the unconscious and Henri Bergson's *mémoire involontaire*) are staged with specifically literary forms, such as free indirect discourse and a complex time structure.

**English and American Studies** have shown how memory is represented in poetry, drama, and fiction (e.g. Assmann; Nünning, Gymnich, and Sommer). Metaphors of memory, the narrative representation of consciousness, the literary production of mnemonic space and of subjective time are some of the key issues in literary studies' engagement with memory. From a narratological viewpoint (cf. entry II.9), it is interesting to note that the distinction between an 'experiencing I' and a 'narrating I' already rests on a (largely implicit) concept of memory, namely on the idea that there is a difference between pre-narrative experience on the one hand, and, on the other, narrative memory which creates meaning retrospectively. The preoccupation with first-person narrators is thus always a preoccupation with the literary representation of individual remembering. Referring to these and other literary forms, and using Charles Dickens's *David Copperfield* as an example, Martin Löschnigg subsumes under the term 'rhetoric of memory' those narrative means with which the illusion of authentic autobiographical remembering is created.

The possibilities and limits of literary representation are gauged when it comes to the **memories of violent history**, such as war, terror, and genocide.

Recent studies, often comparative in their approach, have looked at the literary memory of the world wars, the experience of colonialism and decolonisation, of authoritarian regimes, genocide, and of global terror. In British media culture, for example, the 'Great War' is still one of the major traumatic memory sites (Korte, Paletschek, and Hochbruck). 9/11 can be conceived of as a global traumatic event. It has brought forth a large body of writing which tries to give literary shape to its impact on cultural memory (e.g. the novels of Don DeLillo, Jonathan Safran Foer, Mohsin Hamid, and Ian McEwan). It is, however, clearly the Holocaust which takes centre stage in the project of conveying traumatic pasts through literature and other art forms. As in the mnemohistory of other events, we can distinguish between different generations and perspectives of writing about the Holocaust—for example, survivors' testimonies (Primo Levi), writers of the second generation (Art Spiegelman), and various other forms of imaginative reconstruction (from Anita Desai to Anne Michaels)—and ask how the memories of those who experienced the events first-hand are transmitted to their children and grandchildren (transgenerational memory) and to people not immediately involved in the events (prosthetic memory, see below).

It is especially within American discussions that the notion of trauma as a 'crisis of representation' has gained great prominence. This idea was introduced to literary studies in the framework of poststructuralist thinking, notably by Cathy Caruth's *Unclaimed Experience*. In a clearsighted, critical survey of the expanding field of trauma studies, Ruth Leys (267–68) identifies at its heart the concern with the "constitutive failure of linguistic representation in the post-Holocaust, post-Hiroshima, post-Vietnam era." In poststructuralist trauma discourse, "the Holocaust is held to have precipitated, perhaps caused, an epistemological-ontological crisis of witnessing, a crisis manifested at the level of language itself." Such equations between the individual and the cultural, the biological and the linguistic levels, can of course be highly misleading and the ethical consequences of trauma studies' tendency to personify texts, to conflate literary works with real people, must be critically assessed.

**Media studies** approaches to memory are perhaps better suited to get to grips with the question

**Literary representations of traumatic memory**

of how literature and film represent traumatic pasts—and to what degree these 'pasts' are always already mediated memories. Marita Sturken, for example, in *Tangled Memories*, investigates how the Vietnam War and the AIDS epidemic were turned into elements of cultural memory by means of television, movies and other popular media. Sturken brings out the complex entanglements of memory and media in the social arena. She emphasizes the active and memory-productive role of media: "Cultural memory is produced through objects, images, and representations. These are technologies of memory, not vessels of memory in which memory passively resides" (9). Addressing the experiential dimension of mediated memory, Alison Landsberg introduced the notion of 'prosthetic memory.' Landsberg studies the age of mass culture, with a particular focus on the effects that representations of slavery and the Holocaust in literature, cinema and museum exhibits have on memory. She argues that what makes mass media so powerful in memory culture is that they allow us to "take on" other people's and groups' experiences and memories "like an artificial limb" (20). For Landsberg, prosthetic memory has deeply ethical implications: it is characterized by its "ability [...] to produce empathy and social responsibility as well as political alliances that transcend race, class, and gender" (21).

## 11.3 | The 'Afterlife' of Literature

Literary texts as actualizations of memory

Approaches to the 'life' and ongoing impact of literary stories and patterns address the **basic process of memory in culture**: that of continuation and actualization. In reconstructing the 'social life' of a literary text, we may ask how it was—across long periods of time—received, discussed, used, canonized, forgotten, censored, and re-used. What is it that confers upon some literary works, again and again, a new lease on life in changing social contexts, whereas others are forgotten and relegated to the archive? These questions can be addressed from social, medial, and textual viewpoints—and the phenomenon of literary afterlives will arguably be tackled best by a balanced combination of all three.

- The social perspective emphasizes the active appropriations of a literary text by social actors. How do changing social formations—with their specific views of history and present challenges, their interests and expectations, discourses and reading practices—receive and re-actualize literature? How do different generations respond in changing ways to the same literary work? The worldwide reception of Shakespeare, Bunyan or Milton across the centuries gives ample evidence of how different audiences de- and resemiotize literary works, and how different readings may be related to transformations in society.

- Looking at literary afterlives from a media culture perspective means directing attention to the intermedial networks which maintain and sustain the continuing impact of certain stories: intertextual and intermedial references, rewriting and adaptation, forms of commentary and cross-reference. Using the concepts of premediation and remediation I have shown elsewhere (Erll, *Prämediation*) how the narratives and iconic images of the 'Revolt of 1857' (a colonial war in Northern India against British rule) were pre-formed by stories and images of similar earlier events (such as the 'Black Hole of Calcutta' of 1756), then remediated in colonial and postcolonial contexts across the spectrum of available media technologies (from newspaper articles to novels, photography, film, and the Internet), in order to turn, finally, into premediators of other stories and events (such as the Amritsar massacre of 1919, nostalgic post-imperial novels of the 1950s, or current debates about terrorism).

- In a more text-centred perspective, we may ask if there are certain properties of literary works which make them more 'actualizable' than others, properties which cause the works to lend themselves to rereading, rewriting, remediating, and continued discussion. For example, studying the long and rich afterlife of Walter Scott's *Ivanhoe*, Ann Rigney (215–16) has shown that the novel's continuing appeal can be attributed to a combination of two (seemingly contradictory) characteristics of its plot: More than any other novel by Walter Scott, *Ivanhoe* is both "highly schematic" *and* highly "ambivalent." On the one hand, it offers a basic narrative paradigm that can be used as a model "for dealing with *other* events"; on the other hand, it keeps readers puzzled and engaged by its "de-stabilizing tension between the outcome of the story and its emotional economy."

The 'afterlives approach' asks, in a diachronic perspective, about the **continuing impact of literature**, how it manages to 'live on' and remain in use and meaningful to readers. It addresses the complex social, textual and intermedial processes involved in this dynamic, and therefore requires a sophisticated combination of various approaches, some of which can boast a long tradition in English and American Studies: close textual and media analysis, the study of intermediality and intertextuality, the history of literary functions, and the social history of literature and art.

## 11.4 | Transnational and Transcultural Memory

Memory studies was long characterized by its '**methodological nationalism**.' This is best exemplified by Pierre Nora's influential *Lieux de mémoire* (1984–1992), a collection of essays about French sites of memory. Many critics drew attention to the nation-centeredness of Nora's approach and to the fact that the *Lieux* project in fact 'forgets' the history of cultural exchange within Europe, cultural transactions with the French colonies, and the significance of migrants' memories. Such entangled histories also impinge on memories in the Anglophone world: British trade and colonialism, the multi-ethnic foundations of, say, Canada and the United States, and the complex migration patterns of the twentieth century have all led to a wealth of shared, transnational and transcultural sites of memory (cf. Hebel).

For those interested in **transcultural memory**, postcolonial studies, with its focus on the persistence, or working-through, of the colonial past, can offer valuable insights. Key concepts, such as 'writing back,' the Middle Passage as 'traumatic event,' or 'colonial nostalgia,' clearly display a memory dimension (cf. entry III.4). One characteristic feature of the New English Literatures (cf. entry I.4) is that they often represent and construct transcultural memory: Caribbean literature 'remembers' the Black Atlantic (Eckstein); Black British Literature plays with genre memories (Rupp), migrant and diasporic writing creates 'figures of displacement' (Baronian, Besser, and Jansen). With a view to South African fiction, Sarah Nuttall has developed concepts such as 'negotiation' and 'entanglement,' which help address literary responses to the divergent and contested memories arising from different racialized identity groups.

What current discourses of globalization and '**memory in the global age**' (Levy and Sznaider) sometimes tend to overlook—and what a decidedly historical perspective on memory will quickly bring to light—is that transcultural remembering has a long genealogy. It is actually since ancient times that contents, forms and technologies of memory have crossed the boundaries of time, space, and social groups, and been filled in different local contexts with new life and new meaning. The 'transcultural' is therefore not only a category for studying memory in our current globalizing age, but a perspective on memory that can, in principle, be chosen with respect to all historical periods. English and American Studies can contribute to an understanding of such 'traveling memory' by reconstructing the routes of powerful stories (like that of Odysseus or the 'Pilgrim's Progress'), mnemonic rituals (e.g. the 'Two Minutes Silence'), or media-technologies and -formats (such as docufiction) in their local, translocal, and global dimensions.

### Select Bibliography

**Assmann, Aleida.** *Erinnerungsräume: Formen und Wandlungen des kulturellen Gedächtnisses.* Munich: Beck, 1999.

**Baronian, Marie-Aude, Stephan Besser, and Yolande Jansen, eds.** *Diaspora and Memory: Figures of Displacement in Contemporary Literature, Arts and Politics.* Amsterdam: Rodopi, 2007.

**Caruth, Cathy.** *Unclaimed Experience: Trauma, Narrative, and History.* Baltimore: Johns Hopkins University Press, 1996.

**Eckstein, Lars.** *Re-membering the Black Atlantic: On the Poetics and Politics of Literary Memory.* Amsterdam: Rodopi, 2006.

**Erll, Astrid.** *Memory in Culture.* Basingstoke: Palgrave Macmillan, 2011.

**Erll, Astrid.** *Prämediation – Remediation: Repräsentationen des indischen Aufstands in imperialen und post-kolonialen Medienkulturen (von 1857 bis zur Gegenwart).* Trier: WVT, 2007.

**Hebel, Udo, ed.** *Sites of Memory in American Literatures and Cultures.* Heidelberg: Winter, 2003.

Korte, Barbara, Sylvia Paletschek, and Wolfgang Hochbruck, eds. *Der Erste Weltkrieg in der Populären Erinnerungskultur*. Essen: Klartext, 2008.

Landsberg, Alison. *Prosthetic Memory: The Transformation
of American Remembrance in the Age of Mass Culture*.
New York: Columbia University Press, 2004.

Levy, Daniel, and Natan Sznaider. *The Holocaust and Memory in the Global Age*. Trans. Assenka Oksiloff. Philadelphia: Temple University Press, 2006.

Leys, Ruth. *Trauma: A Genealogy*. Chicago: University of
Chicago Press, 2000.

Löschnigg, Martin. "'The Prismatic Hues of Memory ...':
Autobiographische Modellierung und die Rhetorik
der Erinnerung in Dickens' *David Copperfield*."
*Poetica* 31.1–2 (1999): 175–200.

Nora, Pierre, ed. *Les lieux de mémoire*. 3 vols. Paris:
Gallimard, 1984–92.

Nünning, Ansgar, Marion Gymnich, and Roy Sommer, eds.
*Literature and Memory: Theoretical Paradigms—
Genres—Functions*. Tübingen: Narr, 2006.

Nuttall, Sarah. *Entanglement: Literary and Cultural Reflections on Post Apartheid*. Johannesburg: Wits University
Press, 2009.

Rigney, Ann. "The Many Afterlives of Ivanhoe." *Performing
the Past: Memory, History, and Identity in Modern Europe*. Eds. Karin Tilmans, Frank van Vree, and J. M. Winter. Amsterdam: Amsterdam University Press, 2010.
207–34.

Rupp, Jan. *Genre and Cultural Memory in Black British
Literature*. Trier: WVT, 2010.

Sturken, Marita. *Tangled Memories: The Vietnam War, the
AIDS Epidemic, and the Politics of Remembering*. Berkeley: University of California Press, 1997.

Warburg, Aby. *Der Bilderatlas MNEMOSYNE*. Ed. Martin
Warnke. 3rd ed. Berlin: Akademie Verlag, 2008.

*Astrid Erll*

# 12 Literary Ethics

Literary ethics is a concept referring to the interconnectedness of **literature, literary criticism, and ethics**. When talking about literary ethics nowadays we usually think of the field of ethical criticism which has been flourishing ever since the so-called "ethical turn in literary studies" in the late 1980s and 1990s (cf. Gras). However, the history of critical analysis of the connections between notions of the good, values, morals, and the resulting norms on the one hand, and literature on the other, reaches back much further than that, in fact right to the beginnings of literary criticism.

## 12.1 | Early Conceptualizations of the Connection Between Literature and Ethics

**Antiquity.** In ancient Greece, for example, **Plato**, in his *Republic*, claims that "there is an old quarrel between philosophy and poetry" (*Republic* 607b5–6), and in Book X, he has Socrates exile the poets from the ideal city, accusing them of producing lies because poetry is based on imitation, producing mere images of the phenomenal world, i.e. images of images, and thus not providing knowledge of intelligible forms, although they pretend to describe reality. Consequently, the poets are to be seen as enemies of truth and unfit as educators of the philosopher-guardians who should rule the *polis*. Furthermore, Plato's Socrates points out that the poets privilege desire over reasoning, and thus foster both ignorance and desire, which can lead to the corruption of readers or of the audience and produce negative ethical effects.

**Renaissance.** The Renaissance writer Ben Jonson translated Horace's *Ars Poetica* into his mother tongue, and when this translation was published posthumously in 1640 as *The Art of Poetry*, it provided an argument in English which attributed an ethical function to literature, namely to **teach and delight**. Sir Philip Sidney, in *An Apology for Poetry*, had already reinterpreted Plato as an apologist of poetry trying to preserve literature from being abused. Sidney, in Horatian manner, defined "poesy" as "an art of imitation [...] with this end, to teach and delight" (9), and he specified that the kind of imitation "whereof Poetry is, hath the most conveniency to Nature of all other" (21). This furthers the ethical function of literature which, according to Sidney, consists in the fact that it "doth intend the winning of the mind from wickedness to virtue" (21).

**Eighteenth Century.** Literature was defined again as an art closely related to ethics when Johann Christoph Gottsched, in his *Versuch einer critischen Dichtkunst vor die Deutschen*, attributed to literature the task of **moral education** through the mimetic representation of nature/reality and the provision of examples illustrating general moral rules. In his famous *Briefwechsel über das Trauerspiel* with Moses Mendelssohn and Friedrich Nicolai, Gotthold Ephraim Lessing reacts to the position of the latter two, according to which tragedy is to be placed beyond the moral realm. Lessing, however, looks back to Aristotle and holds that it is the task of tragedy to sharpen the audience's sensibility by creating fear and compassion, the cathartic effect of which can form an ethical basis for the moral state of the newly rising middle class.

**Nineteenth Century.** Literary and cultural value were linked to ethics by Matthew Arnold, who, in *Culture and Anarchy*, discussed a situation of accelerated cultural change and complexity in an age which increasingly saw old cultural patterns questioned by new developments in the natural and social sciences as well in the humanities. He turned culture in general and literature in partic-

Literary criticism
was concerned with
ethical questions from
the beginning.

ular into the instrument of a civilizing mission that could bind together the various elements of the English nation beyond the faultlines of class hierarchy, social, religious, and philosophical fragmentation and "make the best that has been thought and known in the world current every-where; [...] make all men live in an atmosphere of sweetness and light" (70). Literature and culture were thus given the humanist ethical mission of providing a **new sense of orientation** in a world that was increasingly perceived to be falling apart.

## 12.2 | Twentieth-Century Literary Ethics Before 1970

In the twentieth century, the connection between ethics and literature attracted a lot of interest largely due to the epistemic crisis of a period in which many felt that "[t]hings fall apart; the centre cannot hold," as W. B. Yeats famously put it in his poem "The Second Coming." The **New Critics**, for example, tried to attribute to literature a role in creating a better world in which a more moral existence was possible. This was not to be achieved by using extra-textual moral norms in reading and evaluating literature, however. On the contrary, the New Critics pursued an ideal of reading based on a formalist text-immanent analysis of literature vying with the natural sciences for disinterestedness and objectivity (cf. section II.1.3). For I. A. Richards, in his *Practical Criticism*, "[t]he critical reading of poetry is an arduous discipline: few exercises reveal to us more clearly [...] the immense extension of our resources" (350–51). To Richards, it is through this widening of our awareness of the potency of humanity that the ethical project of improving the world can be fostered. For Richards, as for T. S. Eliot in "Tradition and the Individual Talent" and for Matthew Arnold, ethics and culture are closely linked, and writing and reading literature become the practical manifestations of a concern with ethics. English literature, to them, became a **civilizing tool** and part of a humanist ethics, which was unashamedly Western, patriarchal, and, ultimately, colonialist.

F. R. Leavis, taking up Eliot's lead, sees the humanist ethics of this project embodied in a specific canon of English literature comprised of the novels of what he refers to as the **great tradition** which, according to him, provides a moral criticism of life. Leavis developed this position in the pages of his periodical *Scrutiny* as well as in *The Great Tradition*, and he thus linked aesthetic and ethical issues. Leavis read the novels of Jane Austen, George Eliot, Henry James, and Joseph Conrad, the main representatives of his great tradition, as moral fables with a special ethical significance for life.

## 12.3 | Hard Times for Literary Ethics

The impact of poststructuralism

With the rise of literary and cultural theory in the 1970s and 1980s, this kind of literary ethics fell on hard times. It was accused of an untenable foundationalist humanism characterized by a patriarchal Western essentialism that disregarded deconstruction's and poststructuralism's insights into the linguistic constructedness of reality and values (cf. entry II.4) and tried to install an ethics that pretended to be universal and disinterested, but was in fact shamelessly predicated on a specific positionality, and therefore relative. For a while, it seemed as if literary ethics was a dying approach, and it became rather unpopular to analyze literary texts with reference to ethics, morals, or values in a postmodern climate characterized by skepticism towards grand narratives.

However, the polycentric and **plurivocal playfulness of postmodernism** (cf. entry I.2.7) with its self-awareness and its emphasis on the relativity of any positionality and thus, by implication, of any cultural pattern, any value, any norm, did not only produce a liberating effect by taking away old barriers of thought and opening up a new space of freedom characterized by the principle of "anything goes," in the terms of Paul Feyerabend's epistemological anarchism (23). After an initial phase of celebration, transgression and experimentation, there followed a more sobering period of a renewed search for frameworks of orientation in a world which was seen as ever more plural, complex, heterogeneous, fragmented, multicultural and global, and consequently also as confusing and challenging any self-positioning whatsoever. How was it possible to touch moral ground in the age "after virtue," as Alasdair MacIntyre called it? This question led to the ethical turn of the 1990s.

## 12.4 | The Ethical Turn of the 1990s and After

To begin with, however, theory now found itself in a dilemma, in as far as the insights of poststructuralism, deconstruction and postmodernism had made untenable the approach represented by the literary ethics of the liberal humanist tradition outlined above while there was felt to be an urgent need, on an anthropological as well as a psychological and a cultural level, for reconstructing the possibility of a valid self-positioning in the sense of an identity-constitution that could provide orientational markers again. Critical theory was thus caught in between the Scylla of absolute relativism or valuelessness and the Charybdis of essentialism. What was needed was an ethics that was able to cater to the needs of humans as pattern-building animals (Antor, "Ethical Plurivocity" 40; "Ethics of Criticism" 67–69) and that at the same time avoided the old liberal humanist errors. Essentialist moral systems masking their own constructedness and relativism behind a façade of supposed ethical truths with an ontology of their own were no longer a feasible option. This was not only an issue of ethics, however, but also one that was intimately linked to **discourses of identity**, which have been very prominent in critical theory in recent years. Wayne C. Booth has pointed out that the Greek term *ethos* also means "character" or "collection of habitual characteristics" (*Company* 8), i.e. custom or habit, and thus points to the identity-constituting element of the self-positioning that creates both an *ethos*, a character, and the habits and customs that make up a culture. Similarly, the philosopher Charles Taylor describes the connection between ethics and identity when he points out that

doing without frameworks is utterly impossible for us; [...] the claim is that living within [...] strongly qualified horizons is constitutive of human agency, that stepping outside these limits would be tantamount to stepping outside what we would recognize as integral, that is, undamaged human personhood. [...] To know who I am is a species of knowing where I stand. (27)

Ethics, identity and culture are thus inevitably linked, but the insights of poststructuralism and postmodernism have created a **crisis of legitimacy** for the cultural patterns or frameworks used earlier. If cultural values can only be constructed through language, which in turn is characterized by the infinite deferral of meaning effected by the endless sliding of the signified under the signifier (in Derridean deconstructive terms) this inevitably means that ethical concepts are susceptible to a similar process of constant postponement. Nevertheless, as Richard Rorty points out, humans need at least an imagined teleology in order to have a sense of orientation and to be able to feel at home and exist in the world.

All this became relevant to the discussion of literary ethics because literature came to be seen as one of the prime tools humans use in order to position themselves in their environment, i.e. to create an *ethos* in the etymological sense of the word. The pattern-building activity of human beings often takes on the form of story-telling, and thus, as Graham Swift has it in his novel *Waterland*, man is "the story-telling animal" (ch. 8). The ethical problem of self-positioning in the (post-) postmodern world is thus also one of how the world and the self are narrativized and read, how humans can use literature/ stories as tools of constructing the world and creating an orientation in it, making it meaningful and manageable. Culture is thus to be understood as a **system of narrativizations**, and literary ethics deals with how these narrativizations are used and negotiated.

The dilemma mentioned above has been approached in different ways by different critics. J. Hillis Miller is still very much indebted to deconstructive practices and stresses the fact that language can never be transparent in the sense of being an unproblematic medium providing reliable access to a reality or truth beyond the text. Consequently, he places himself, on the one hand, in a Kantian tradition and presupposes the existence of a universalist "moral law as such" (*Ethics of Reading* 22), but on the other hand declares that law to be unattainable because it could only be represented through text which invariably places

Bringing together
poststructuralism
and ethics

**New ethical perspectives: Literature as dialogue**

us "within the space of a perpetual deferral or direct confrontation of the law" (*Ethics of Reading* 25). The only tenable ethics of reading, then, according to Miller, is one that acknowledges the ultimate **unreadability** of any text, thus doing away with notions of literature as a means of providing a meaning that can furnish us with a *telos* in our yearning for orientation.

Other critics and philosophers have taken up a less extreme position in as far as they do not contradict Miller's diagnosis but supplement the latter's deconstructive contribution by reconstructively salvaging the notion of the useful functions of the fiction of teleology. Richard Rorty, Martha Nussbaum and Wayne C. Booth take seriously humans' need for a sense of direction and draw our attention to the value of literature, stories, **texts as a catalytic tool** that makes different readers of the world (as text) and of (literary) texts use narrative to understand and evaluate the world, to invest it with meaning, but also to dialogically compare and negotiate their various attempts at thus positioning themselves. These critics are aware of the infinite openness of processes of creating meaning, of constructing values and identities, but this does not invalidate efforts to do so in their eyes. They are aware of and accept the linguistic constructedness, subjectivity and relativity of any ethical positionality and value the conversation about alternative possibilities of creating an *ethos* above any attempt at reaching an ultimate consensus. They accept the "contingencies of value" (Smith) without reverting to the absolute relativism of "anything goes." The model of literary ethics propounded by these critics is an eminently **dialogic** one, in which the hermeneutic and democratic open conversation between self and other, between a reader and a text or between different readers, is an end in itself rather than a means to an ultimately unattainable *telos*. Such an ethics can live with the co-existence of incommensurable positionalities

without refusing the "conversational gambit" (Booth, *Company* 135) of the other.

Such an approach draws attention to the role of **alterity** in literary ethics. Respect for otherness in a process of understanding that is dialogic and must remain open or unfinished is thus seen as an ethical effect of the process of reading. The literary text constitutes a singular instance of otherness and, as such, appeals to the reader to deal responsibly with it. This entails engaging seriously with the text and entering into a hermeneutic conversation with it that negotiates both the text's and the reader's horizons or positionalities without one being imposed on the other and including the risk for the reader of ending up elsewhere, with a changed *ethos*. The idea of an ethical commitment to the other fostered by literature is partly still indebted to the hermeneutics of Hans-Georg Gadamer (cf. section II.2.1), but much more so to the philosophy of alterity suggested by Emmanuel Levinas who, in *Totality and Infinity*, criticizes the totalizing gestures of earlier philosophical approaches and replaces them by an ethics that situates us within infinity. This de-essentializing gesture is combined in *Otherwise than Being or Beyond Essence* with an appeal for being-for-the other. Levinas's contribution thus combines some of the radical insights of recent philosophy with an emphasis on the anteriority of responsibility, and it links attention to the linguistic constructedness of texts with a commitment to the world beyond text.

The ethical turn of the 1990s has reinvigorated literary ethics in as far as it has moved beyond the foundationalist assumptions of an older liberal humanism and taken seriously the critical interventions of deconstruction, poststructuralism and postmodernism while pushing even beyond the limitations of these latter approaches towards a "post-postmodern critical neo-humanism" (Antor, "Ian McEwan's") that takes seriously humans' need for orientation and frameworks without having recourse to old essentialisms.

## Select Bibliography

**Adamson, Jane, Richard Freadman, and David Parker, eds.** *Renegotiating Ethics in Literature, Philosophy, and Theory*. Cambridge: Cambridge University Press, 1998.

**Antor, Heinz.** "Ethical Plurivocity, or: The Pleasures and Rewards of Reading." *Text – Culture – Reception: Cross-Cultural Aspects of English Studies*. Eds. Rüdiger Ahrens and Heinz Antor. Heidelberg: Winter, 1992. 27–46.

**Antor, Heinz.** "The Ethics of Criticism in the Age After Value." *Why Literature Matters: Theories and Functions of Literature*. Eds. Rüdiger Ahrens and Laurenz Volkmann. Heidelberg: Winter, 1996. 65–85.

**Antor, Heinz.** "Ian McEwan's Black Dogs (1992) and the Ethics of a Post-Postmodern Critical Neo-Humanism." Arizti and Martínez Falquina 42–50.

**Arizti, Bárbara, and Silvia Martínez Falquina, eds.** *On the Turn. The Ethics of Fiction in Contemporary Narrative in English*. Newcastle: Cambridge Scholars Press, 2007.

**Arnold, Matthew.** *Culture and Anarchy*. Cambridge: Cambridge University Press, 1970.

**Booth, Wayne C.** *The Company We Keep: An Ethics of Fiction*. Berkeley: University of California Press, 1988.

**Booth, Wayne C.** "Are Narrative Choices Subject to Ethical Criticism?" *Reading Narrative: Form, Ethics, Ideology*. Ed. James Phelan. Columbus: Ohio State University Press, 1989. 57–78.

**Connor, Stephen.** *Theory and Cultural Value*. Oxford: Blackwell, 1992.

**Eaglestone, Robert.** *Ethical Criticism: Reading After Levinas*. Edinburgh: Edinburgh University Press, 1997.

**Feyerabend, Paul.** *Against Method: Outline of an Anarchistic Theory of Knowledge*. London: New Left Books, 1975.

**Gibson, Andrew.** *Postmodernity, Ethics and the Novel*. London: Routledge, 1999.

**Gras, Vernon W.** "The Recent Ethical Turn in Literary Studies." *Mitteilungen des Verbandes Deutscher Anglisten* 4.2 (1993): 30–41.

**Handwerk, Gary J.** *Irony and Ethics in Narrative: From Schlegel to Lacan*. New Haven: Yale University Press, 1985.

**Hoffmann, Gerhard, and Alfred Hornung, eds.** *Ethics and Aesthetics: The Moral Turn of Postmodernism*. Heidelberg: Winter, 1996.

**Larson, Jil.** *Ethics and Narrative in the English Novel: 1880–1914*. Cambridge: Cambridge University Press, 2001.

**Levinas, Emmanuel.** *Otherwise than Being or Beyond Essence*. Pittsburgh: Duquesne University Press, 1998.

**Levinas, Emmanuel.** *Totality and Infinity*. Pittsburgh: Duquesne University Press, 1969.

**MacIntyre, Alisdair.** *After Virtue*. London: Duckworth, 1981.

**Miller, J. Hillis.** *The Ethics of Reading*. New York: Columbia University Press, 1987.

**Miller, J.** Hillis. "Is There an Ethics of Reading?" *Reading Narrative. Form, Ethics, Ideology*. Ed. James Phelan. Columbus: Ohio State University Press, 1989. 79–101.

**Norris, Christopher.** *Truth and the Ethics of Criticism*. Manchester: Manchester University Press, 1994.

**Nussbaum, Martha.** *Love's Knowledge: Essays on Philosophy and Literature*. New York: Oxford University Press, 1990.

**Onega, Susana, and Jean-Michel Ganteau, eds.** *The Ethical Component in Experimental British Fiction since the 1960's*. Newcastle: Cambridge Scholars Press, 2007.

**Richards, I. A.** *Practical Criticism*. 1929. London: Routledge, 1964.

**Rorty, Richard.** *Contingency, Irony, and Solidarity*. Cambridge: Cambridge University Press, 1989.

**Sidney, Philip.** "An Apology for Poetry." *English Critical Texts*. Eds. D. J. Enright and Ernst de Chickera. Delhi: Oxford University Press, 1962. 3–49.

**Smith, Barbara Herrnstein.** *Contingencies of Value: Alternative Perspectives for Critical Theory*. Cambridge: Harvard University Press, 1988.

**Taylor, Charles.** *Sources of the Self: The Making of the Modern Identity*. Cambridge: Cambridge University Press, 1989.

*Heinz Antor*

# 13 Cognitive Poetics

## 13.1 | Definition

Cognitive poetics is a relatively new and still emerging discipline in the field of literary studies and involves the critical practice of understanding and analyzing literary texts in terms of cognitive linguistics and psychology. The phrase itself was introduced by Reuven Tsur to denote a cognition-based approach to poetry and its perception, but recently it has been used in a much wider sense, referring to "any approaches to literary craft that take models from cognitive science as their descriptive frameworks" (Stockwell 8). According to Peter Stockwell, practitioners of cognitive poetics do not merely use literary texts as data to illustrate insights made in cognitive linguistics and psychology (6). Rather, they take the **cognitive turn** seriously and aim to answer some of the central questions of literary studies by engaging in "a thorough re-evaluation of all of the categories with which we understand literary reading and analysis" (7). Hence, instead of discarding terms and concepts drawn from literary criticism and linguistic analysis, they re-conceptualize them along the line of cognitive poetics and thus establish a new mode of understanding literature. Stockwell even goes so far as to claim that "cognitive poetics is essentially a *way of thinking* about literature rather than a framework in itself" (7; emphasis in original).

## 13.2 | Beginnings

*Introducing Conceptual Metaphor Theory*

**George Lakoff** and **Mark Johnson** laid the groundwork for the cognitive poetic approach to literature in their now classic study *Metaphors We Live By* (1980). In contrast to the prevalent conception of 'metaphor' as a mere rhetorical device primarily used in poetry, they regarded it as an omnipresent cognitive mechanism. As Lakoff puts it in his article "The Contemporary Theory of Metaphor," "the locus of metaphor is not in language at all, but in the way we conceptualize one mental domain in terms of another" (267). If we say, for instance, "I am at a crossroads in my life" or "He is without direction in his life," our statements display the metaphoric conceptualization of the mental domain 'life' in terms of the other domain 'journey.' In short: we view 'life' as a 'journey.' Lakoff and Johnson refer to such statements as "metaphorical linguistic expressions" and argue that they make manifest underlying 'conceptual metaphors' in which a 'target domain' ('life') is understood in terms of a 'source domain' ('journey'). Usually entities of the target domain are abstract concepts such as life, ideas, and argument while entities of the source domain are more concrete (and structured) ones such as journey, money, and war (e.g., we often understand 'life' as a 'journey,' 'ideas' as 'money,' and 'argument' as 'war'). Far from being singular cognitive phenomena, conceptual metaphors are highly conventionalized or 'well-entrenched,' that is, deeply ingrained in our mind, and therefore happen mostly unconsciously and almost automatically. As such, they not only shape the way we think and act in our everyday lives, but also permeate our cultural creations such as literary texts (for a more detailed discussion of Conceptual Metaphor Theory see section V.2.5.2).

## 13.3 | Conceptual Metaphor Theory and Blending Theory

Opening the door to numerous cognitive poetic investigations of metaphoricity in literature, George Lakoff and Mark Turner demonstrate the ubiquity of conceptual metaphors underlying literary texts in their study *More Than Cool Reason: A Field Guide to Poetic Metaphor*. They argue that complex conceptual metaphors in literature are combinations of basic everyday metaphors. "Poets," they state, "may compose or elaborate or express them [basic metaphors] in new ways, but they still use the same basic conceptual resources available to us all. If they did not, we would not understand them" (26). Lakoff and Turner illustrate their argument with several analyses of poems (see box). Their cognitive approach to literary texts, especially poetry, has paved the way for a plethora of interpretations that highlight the pervasiveness of everyday conceptual metaphors in literature.

Interpretation

**Emily Dickinson, "Because I Could Not Stop for Death"**
Here is Lakoff and Turner's interpretation of the nineteenth-century poet Emily Dickinson's "Because I Could Not Stop for Death" (ca. 1863).

The three stanzas of the poem are on the left; the right-hand column details the conceptual metaphors used according to Lakoff and Turner. Conceptual metaphors are conventionally presented in small capitals.

| | |
|---|---|
| Because I could not stop for Death— | LIFE IS A JOURNEY |
| He kindly stopped for me— | DEATH IS DEPARTURE |
| The Carriage held but just Ourselves— | DEATH IS GOING TO A FINAL DESTINATION |
| And Immortality. | |
| | |
| We slowly drove—He knew no haste | |
| And I had put away | |
| My labor and my leisure too, | |
| For His Civility— | |
| | |
| We passed the School, where Children strove | |
| At Recess—in the Ring— | |
| We passed the fields of Gazing Grain— | PEOPLE ARE PLANTS |
| We passed the Setting Sun— | A LIFETIME IS A DAY AND DEATH IS NIGHT |

According to the two cognitive scientists, Dickinson's poem manifests a combination of several basic metaphors: e.g., LIFE IS A JOURNEY (the first person narrator perceives her life as a journey and presents us with a sequence of life-stages such as childhood in the third stanza), PEOPLE ARE PLANTS (the speaker views her life cycle as the yearly cycle of plants; thus, the phrase "Fields of Gazing Grain"—the grain is mature—refers to her maturity), A LIFETIME IS A DAY (this metaphor permits us to understand birth as dawn and Dickinson's phrase "Setting Sun" as a reference to death; DEATH IS NIGHT is a related metaphor), and DEATH IS GOING TO A FINAL DESTINATION (the speaker regards her death as the final stopping point of her journey).

## 13.4 | Cognitive Poetics and Jazz Literature

A different path can be taken by reconceptualizing the idea of **intermediality** in literature with the help of Conceptual Metaphor Theory (and Blending Theory). Instead of perceiving the relationship between two media such as speech and writing or music and writing as an imitational one (Gr. *mimesis*), it can be viewed as a metaphoric relation between two distinct conceptual domains: a writer does not 'imitate,' 'mimic,' or 'represent' the original source (speech, music) in his or her

Interpretation

Langston Hughes, "The Cat and the Saxophone (2 a.m.)"

The capitalized lyrics in Langston Hughes's jazz poem "The Cat and the Saxophone (2 a.m.)" (1926) invite readers to identify the literal meaning of the words and, at the same time, metaphorically 'translate' the lines into the melody indicated by the lyrics. Here is an excerpt from the poem:

EVERYBODY
Half-pint,—
Gin?
No, make it
LOVES MY BABY
corn. You like
liquor,
don't you, honey?
BUT MY BABY
Sure. Kiss me,
DON'T LOVE NOBODY
daddy.
BUT ME.

LYRICS ARE A MELODY

THE LYRICS OF "EVERYBODY LOVES MY BABY (BUT MY BABY DON'T LOVE NOBODY BUT ME)" ARE THE MELODY OF "EVERYBODY LOVES MY BABY (BUT MY BABY DON'T LOVE NOBODY BUT ME)"

While the regular lines of the initial part of the poem describe a brief exchange between a hip black man, the "cat" from the title of the poem, and the bartender as well as a conversation between the "cat" and his girlfriend ("honey") in a cabaret, the upper case lines ask the readers to imagine that both dialogues take place while a saxophonist plays the melody of the standard jazz tune "Everybody Loves My Baby (But My Baby Don't Love Nobody But Me)" composed in 1924. The metaphoric understanding of intermediality enables readers to discover the metaphoric dimension of intermedial literary texts such as jazz poems.

writings, but rather 'translates' the source domain into the target domain. The product of such conceptual metaphors are metaphorical linguistic expressions that allow for literal and figurative readings (see box above).

In order to explain cognitive phenomena that are not covered by the target-source model of Conceptual Metaphor Theory, Gilles Fauconnier and Mark Turner introduced a conceptual integration network of multiple spaces. Accepting some of the basic tenets of Lakoff's and Johnson's theory of conceptual metaphor (e.g., conceptual 'mapping') and Fauconnier's early work on so-called '**mental spaces**,' they contend that "blending" is a pervasive cognitive process of mapping and integration that happens in a network of mental spaces. They define a mental space as "small conceptual packets constructed as we think and talk, for purposes of local understanding and action" (Fauconnier and Turner 40) and claim that a mental space network always includes one or more "blended mental spaces," or simply "blends" into which "struc-

ture from two mental spaces is projected" (47). A "conceptual blend" makes use of several mental spaces (a generic space, two input spaces, and a blend) and gives rise to an emergent structure that is "not copied there directly from any input" (48). Many literary critics have utilized Fauconnier and Turner's theory of **conceptual blending** (or mental space theory) to account for metaphoric blends as well as non-metaphorical phenomena in literature. Elena Semino, for instance, applies the model to Ernest Hemingway's narrative "A Very Short Story" in order to provide an account of the 'online' text processing performed by readers of the story (Semino 83–98). The mental space network can also be used to explain non-metaphoric cognitive processes performed by readers while 'translating' a jazz poem into a rich, conceptually integrated aesthetic experience (e.g., blending the literal meaning of words and phrases with the remembered music of jazz recordings, recollections of a jazz concert, images of jazz musicians, and the smell of cigarette smoke).

## 13.5 | Other Approaches

Stockwell and other critics have developed further cognitive poetic approaches to literature and, for example, suggest the use of the linguistic concept of 'prototypicality' and cognitive grammar to shed some light on generic deviations from the 'norm' as well as on styles used in literary works.

Prototypicality. Cognitive linguists consider 'prototypicality' as the basis of our conceptual system for categorization and argue that the latter "is not like an 'in or out' filing cabinet, but an arrangement of elements in a *radial* structure or network with *central* good examples, *secondary* poorer examples, and *peripheral* examples. The boundaries of the category are fuzzy rather than fixed" (Stockwell 29; emphasis in original). For instance, we consider apples and oranges as good examples of the category 'fruit' and exclude potatoes from the category 'fruit.' Yet we could find shared attributes between apples and potatoes (e.g. both are 'round') and classify 'potatoes' as an element at the fuzzy boundary between 'fruit' and 'vegetables' (29). According to Stockwell, critics can use the concept of prototypicality to revise genre categories by giving more weight to some generic attributes than to others and explore linguistic deviations from 'prototypical' styles and literary texts, such as parodies and satires.

Grammar. An additional cognitive poetic approach to literature draws on cognitive grammar models mainly developed by Ronald Langacker to highlight the connection between our conceptual system and grammatical constructions featured in literary texts. His grammatical concept of "action chains," for instance, allows for the investigation of verbal patterns in literature. Langacker claims that the roles played by "participants" of a clause are based on role archetypes which make up the basic relationships expressed by a clause: that is, agent, patient, instrument, experiencer, and mover (Stockwell 64). This semantic approach to grammatical categories enables readers to recognize that a writer has neglected the category of 'agent' in saying "the window broke" instead of "Tom broke the window" and has foregrounded the 'mover' in "the earthquake made many people homeless" instead of "people were made homeless because of the earthquake." Readers aware of such semantic foregrounding find it easier to see the writer's focal point. The perceived relationship between the two grammatical entities and semantic categories such as 'agent' and 'patient' is called cognitive profiling. Literary critics have used the notion of cognitive profiling and the concept of "action chains" to track action chains (e.g., a series of verb profiles) and participant roles in literary texts. Craig Hamilton, for instance, analyzes the sequence of verb profiles in Wilfred Owen's sonnet "Hospital Barge" (1917) to determine the experience of reading the poem (Hamilton 55–66).

## 13.6 | The Impact of Cognitive Poetics

The use of the above mentioned cognitive linguistic concepts and theories in literary studies has gained a broader acceptance in recent years because it directs attention to the cognitive processes documented and triggered by literary texts. Critics of cognitive poetic approaches to literature have argued that the latter tend to revisit already-existing literary insights. However, such criticism overlooks a number of new perspectives made possible by cognitive poetics: if we treat the use of cognitive linguistic theories in literary studies, for instance, as a conceptual metaphor, whose target domain is 'literature' and whose source domain is 'cognitive theories' (LITERATURE IS COGNITIVE THEORIES), then we can create correspondences between the two distinct domains and disciplines and highlight features of literary texts which we could not have focused on if we had simply relied on our 'normal' reading skills (see, for instance, the ubiquity of everyday conceptual resources in literature). The focus on how our conceptual system works also enables readers to pay more attention to the **cognitive processes used to create a literary text**—as an author *and* as a reader—and thus highlights factors that influence interpretation. What is truly underestimated by traditional literary studies is the way cognitive poetic rethinking of literary terms and issues raises questions that only seem to have been answered (see the discussion of *mimesis* above). Therefore, cognitive poetics is needed as a new discipline that brings together the insights and techniques of

Metaphors reveal correspondences between different domains.

cognitive science and other disciplines to study the premises and processes within the realm of literature. It allows us to challenge given assumptions through empirical textual research and thereby create new perspectives. As Stockwell puts it: "It [cognitive poetics] offers a grounding of critical theory in a philosophical position that is scientific in the modern sense: aiming for an account of natural phenomena (like reading) that represents our current best understanding while always being open to falsifiability and a better explanation" (59).

## Select Bibliography

Brône, Geert, and Jeroen Vandaele. *Cognitive Poetics: Goals, Gains and Gaps*. Berlin: De Gruyter, 2009.

Fauconnier, Gilles, and Mark Turner. *The Way We Think: Conceptual Blending and the Mind's Hidden Complexities*. New York: Basic, 2003.

Gavins, Joanna, and Gerard Steen, eds. *Cognitive Poetics in Practice*. London: Routledge, 2003.

Hamilton, Craig. "A Cognitive Grammar of 'Hospital Barge' by Wilfred Owen." Gavins and Steen 55–66.

Lakoff, George. "The Contemporary Theory of Metaphor." *The Cognitive Linguistics Reader*. Eds. Vyvyan Evans, Benjamin K. Bergen, and Jörg Zinken. London: Equinox, 2007. 267–315.

Lakoff, George, and Mark Johnson. *Metaphors We Live By*. 1980. Chicago: University of Chicago Press, 2003.

Lakoff, George, and Mark Turner. *More Than Cool Reason: A Field Guide to Poetic Metaphor*. Chicago: University of Chicago Press, 1989.

Langacker, Ronald W. *Cognitive Grammar: A Basic Introduction*. New York: Oxford University Press, 2008.

Redling, Erik. *From Mimesis to Metaphor: Intermedial Translations in Jazz Poetry*. Forthcoming.

Semino, Elena. "Possible Worlds and Mental Spaces in Hemingway's 'A Very Short Story.'" Gavins and Steen 83–98.

Stockwell, Peter. *Cognitive Poetics: An Introduction*. London: Routledge, 2002.

Tsur, Reuven. *Toward a Theory of Cognitive Poetics*. Brighton: Sussex Academic Press, 2008.

*Erik Redling*

# 14 Ecocriticism and Cultural Ecology

## 14.1 | Emergence and Definitions of Ecocriticism

One of the most significant developments in the late twentieth and early twenty-first century has been the emergence of ecocriticism as a new trans-disciplinary paradigm in literary and cultural studies. In a most general sense, ecocriticism represents a response of the humanities to the environmental crisis which modern civilization has brought about in its uncontrolled economic and technological expansionism. In addition to categories like class, race, gender, ethnicity, or sexuality, **nature** (together with related terms such as environment, place, earth, planet) has become a central category of cultural studies—albeit a strangely **hybrid category** located somewhere between world and text, realist concept and discursive construct. Urgent environmental issues such as climate change, loss of species diversity, oil spills, deforestation, soil erosion, desertification, diminishing water supplies, limited fossile energies, the uneven distribution of industrially caused environmental risks, or the unmanageable hypertrophies of human waste have become topics of academic investigation as well as of fictional treatments in texts, films, and other media. In the light of increased political and public attention to environmental issues, ecocriticism and ecological art and literature are positioned in an interdisciplinary field of information circuits, in which the sciences represent both a necessary source of knowledge and yet also a subject of critical reflection, since they were instrumental in the technological-economic expansion of modern civilization that has led to the current environmental problems.

'Ecology' was first defined by nineteenth-century scientist Ernst Haeckel as "the whole science of the relationships between the organism and its environment" (qtd. in Nennen 73). Ecocriticism as it emerged in the 1990s was analogously defined in the first major ecocritical volume, *The Ecocriticism Reader*, as the "study of the relationship between literature and the physical environment," advocating an "earth-centered approach to literary studies" (Glotfelty xviii). The **first phase of ecocriticism** in the early 1990s therefore involved a preference for nonfictional genres of nature writing, romantic nature poetry, and wilderness narratives. The ecocritical movement was significantly shaped and theoretically underpinned by such landmark studies as Lawrence Buell's *The Environmental Imagination*, which rehabilitated the referential and representational dimension of textuality that, in Buell's view, had been unduly neglected in poststructuralist theories. Buell's prime examples were classics of nonfictional American nature writing in the tradition of Henry David Thoreau, but also contemporary novels with a clearly recognizable environmental agenda such as Leslie Marmon Silko's *Ceremony* (1977). For an exemplary ecocritical reading in this vein see section IV.1.1.

**In the twenty-first century**, the realist epistemology and ecodidactic orientation of earlier ecocriticism has been extended and transformed through its dialogue with cultural studies, with theory, postmodernism, and the postclassical natural sciences.

From ecology
to ecocriticism

## 14.2 | Directions of Ecocriticism

Rather than positing distinct stages or "waves" of ecocriticism (Buell, "Ecocriticism"), it seems preferable to speak of palimpsestic layers or coexisting directions within a field of interacting ecocritical approaches and orientations. While some ecocritics focus on the local, personal and experiential dimensions of ecocritical writing, and, on this basis, advocate what Scott Slovic has called "narrative scholarship" (Slovic xiv), others explore the global and systemic aspects of ecology, integrating experiential with scientific aspects of ecological knowledge and focusing on the unforeseeable consequences of a contemporary "risk society" characterized by information technologies and worldwide economic interdependencies in an "environmental imagination of the global" (Heise), which translates these new experiences into postmodern aesthetic practices.

Within the broad range of contemporary ecocriticism, **environmentalism** as a political-pragmatic position can be distinguished from **deep ecology** as a philosophical-spiritual position, from **social ecology** respectively **eco-marxism** as community- and class-oriented positions, and from **ecofeminism** as a gender-oriented position (Garrard 16–32). In the case of ecofeminism, the tension that is observable in ecocriticism in general between celebratory, 'nature-endorsing' and culturalist, 'nature-sceptical' views, is especially virulent (cf. Soper), but in its complex negotiations between these positions, ecofeminism has become a productive branch of ecocriticism, both in terms of theory and of textual interpretation.

In **postcolonial** versions of ecocriticism, the issue of environmental justice has become especially relevant, and the unequal distribution of environmental risk and disaster caused by the industrialized world in different cultures and social classes is critically examined on both a regional and global scale. At the same time, postcolonial

ecocriticism also attempts to bring together modern concepts of ecology with non-Western modes of protoecological thought—as, for example, in Native American, Latin American, African or Asian traditions. Global interconnectedness and local knowledge go together in these versions of ecocriticism in forms of creative symbiosis—such as between Taoism and modern ecology in Chinese ecocriticism.

Ecocriticism is thus not a fixed or monosystemic approach but a "transformative discourse" related to "wider social context" (Garrard 7). From a linguistic-epistemological aspect, this links up with Gregory Bateson's observation that ecological thinking is closer to metaphoric than to logocentric speech (*Sacred Unity* 237–42). Garrard distinguishes some of the characteristic metaphorical concepts or "tropes" which govern "the production, reproduction and transformation of large-scale metaphors" within the discourse of ecocriticism: Pollution, Wilderness, Apocalypse, Dwelling, Animals, Earth, Health (Garrard). In various ways, these conceptual tropes form characteristic foci of attention that pervade both the thematic concerns of ecocriticism and the fictional scenarios of ecoliterature. In the course of this differentiation and diversification of the field of ecocriticism, attention has been expanded towards new branches of ecology such as 'urban ecology,' in which the binary opposition between city and country is destabilized and positive values such as "sociability, walkability, cosmopolitanism, spontaneity, and diversity" are associated with cities, and new forms of culture-nature symbiosis in urban life are envisioned (Goodbody 211). A complementary development is the emergence of 'ecopsychology,' in which the deep-rooted dependency and interconnection of the human psyche with experiences of nature is explored in terms of sickness and health, trauma and therapy.

A recent overview of directions of ecocriticism (Goodbody and Rigby)

## 14.3 | Critical Theory and Ecocriticism

Contrary to polemical arguments in the 1990s, an ecological perspective on culture and literature is neither entirely new in the history of Critical Theory (cf. entry II.2.2), nor is it necessarily opposed to positions of modern and postmodern aesthetics and theory. Apart from the highly influential role

of Romantic theories about the complex-dynamical rather than the normative-systemic character of art, certain modern versions of Critical Theory anticipated an ecological perspective in a broad sense—e.g., Nietzsche's dionysian concept of art as life-enhancing form of productive cultural energy, Heidegger's concept of poetic dwelling, or Adorno and Horkheimer's *Dialectic of Enlightenment*, in which art represents a resistance of nature, however oblique, against the totalizing claims of instrumental reason. In his own way, a postmodern thinker such as Lyotard links up his critique of totalizing master narratives to a form of 'ecology' that aims at discursively empowering the concrete, manifold forms of human life, which are overshadowed or silenced by those dominant grand narratives. Deleuze and Guattari's concept of a rhizomatic rather than a structuralist-systemic discourse likewise has affinities to an ecological paradigm. In the later Derrida as well, the deconstruction of binary oppositions such as between mind and body, or culture and nature, entails an opening of poststructuralism towards an ecological perspective. To think and speak in a non-anthropocentric way requires a literary rather than a philosophical mode, because the latter offers the possibility of opening the text to nonhuman nature, while at the same time remaining aware of its irreducible alterity (Derrida 372).

This turn towards ecology in later postmodernism represents a significant move beyond its earlier positions, supplementing concepts of difference and heterogeneity with concepts of connectivity, feedback loops, networks and webs of relationships, which underlie the complex phenomena of life and which are fundamental to any ecology of knowledge. In this context, the project of a "**material ecocriticism**" (Iovino) has developed from the attempt to bridge the gap between ecology and postmodernism, as well as between scientific and cultural forms of ecology. Aiming to overcome the dichotomy between mind and matter, culture and nature in an ecocritical dialogue with science studies, this project clearly intersects with and indeed has substantial affinities to the paradigm of cultural ecology.

## 14.4 | From Natural Ecology to Cultural Ecology

Cultural Ecology is a new direction of ecocriticism, which is both connected to and different from natural ecology. Cultural ecology was initiated by Gregory Bateson in the 1970s, but has gained considerable visibility in recent years. In his project of an *Ecology of Mind*, Bateson considers culture and the human mind not as closed entities but as open, dynamic systems based on living interrelationships between the mind and the world, and within the mind itself. Culture is seen as an **evolutionary transformation** and metamorphosis rather than a binary opposite of nature. Cultural and natural evolution are interconnected in the sense that culture remains dependent on natural energy cycles, while at the same time it has gained relative independence and follows its own semi-autonomous dynamics in the course of cultural evolution. While causal deterministic laws are therefore not applicable in the sphere of culture, there are nevertheless productive analogies which can be drawn between ecological and cultural processes.

Evolutionary Cultural Ecology, an approach developed primarily by Peter Finke, fuses Bateson's ideas with concepts from systems theory and linguistics. The various sections and subsystems of society are described as cultural ecosystems with their own processes of production, consumption, and reduction of energy—involving physical as well as psychic energy. This also applies to the cultural ecosystems of art and of literature, which follow their own internal forces of selection and self-renewal, but also fulfil an important function within the cultural system as a whole. From the perspective of this kind of cultural ecology, the internal landscapes produced by modern culture and consciousness are as important for human beings as their external environments. Human beings are, by their very nature, not only instinctual but also cultural beings, as it were; their habitats are not only external physical environments but the cultural ecosystems of the societies in which they live. Literature and other forms of cultural imagination and cultural creativity are necessary in this view to continually restore the richness, diversity, and complexity of those inner landscapes of the mind, the imagination, the emotions, and interpersonal communication, which make up the cultural ecosystems of modern humans, but are threatened by impoverishment from an increasingly overeconomized, standardized, and depersonalized contemporary world.

This basic premise of a vital interrelatedness and yet evolutionary difference between culture and nature has significant consequences for ecocriticism. While it helps to overcome the deeply entrenched **culture-nature dualism** and its anthropocentric ideology of supremacy and exploitative dominance over nonhuman nature, it also resists opposite attempts to simply dissolve culture into nature and replace an anthropocentric ideology by a physiocentric or ecocentric naturalism (as e.g. in Abram). The ethical challenge that lies in this double, paradoxical condition of cultural ecology has perhaps best been formulated by Serenella Iovino in her plea for a "nonanthropocentric humanism" (Iovino).

## 14.5 | Literature as Cultural Ecology

Within such a transdisciplinary context, literature can itself be described as the symbolic medium of a particularly powerful form of "**cultural ecology**" (Zapf, *Literatur*). This theory is based, on the one hand, on assumptions of general cultural ecology, and on the other hand on the insights of literary theory and, indeed, of the literary texts themselves, which in this view must be taken seriously as sources of cultural knowledge in their own right. Literary texts have staged and explored the complex interactions of culture and nature in ever new scenarios, and have derived their specific power of innovation and cultural self-renewal from the creative exploration of this boundary. The aesthetic mode of textuality involves an overcoming of the mind-body-dualism by bringing together conceptual and perceptual dimensions, ideas and sensory experiences, reflective consciousness and the performative staging of complex dynamical life processes. Literature as a medium of cultural ecology thus specifically focuses on 'life' as a complex phenomenon on the boundary between culture and nature, and on the relational dynamics between self and other, mind and body, anthropocentric and biocentric dimensions of existence.

Literature as an ecological force within cultural discourses breaks up ossified forms of language, communication, and ideology, symbolically empowers the marginalized, and reconnects what is culturally separated. With a view to narrative texts, this transformative function of literature as cultural ecology can be described in a triadic functional model (Zapf, *Kulturökologie* and "Literary Ecology"), in which imaginative literature fulfills a threefold function within the larger system of historical-cultural discourses (see box on the left).

Literature in this sense is, on the one hand, a sensorium for what goes wrong in a society, for the biophobic, life-paralyzing implications of one-sided forms of consciousness and civilizational uniformity, and it is, on the other hand, a medium of constant cultural self-renewal, in which neglected biophilic energies can find a symbolic space of expression and of (re-)integration into the larger ecology of cultural discourses. Literary texts are a mode of sustainable textuality, since they are sources of ever-renewable creative energy (Rueckert). They are self-reflexive models of cultural creativity, which constantly renew ossified forms of language, thought and cultural practice by reconnecting an anthropocentric civilization to the deep-rooted memory of the biocentric coevolution between culture and nature, of human and nonhuman life. In such a perspective, literature and art represent an ecological force within cultural discourses, which is translated into ever new aesthetic practices, and which is systematically articulated in the theories and interpretative procedures of ecocriticism.

---

**Focus: The Triadic Model of Literature as Cultural Ecology**

1. As a **cultural-critical metadiscourse**, which identifies and exposes petrifications, coercive structures, and traumatizing implications of dominant civilizational reality systems—e.g., the system of puritanism in Hawthorne's *The Scarlet Letter*, the system of global economic expansionism in Melville's *Moby-Dick*, the Victorian gender system in Chopin's *The Awakening*, or the system of slavery in Morrison's *Beloved*.

2. As an **imaginative counter-discourse**, which foregrounds and symbolically empowers the culturally excluded and marginalized—as in the counter-discursive force of the scarlet letter A in Hawthorne, of the white whale in Melville, of the sea in Chopin, or of the reincarnated ghost of the dead daughter in Morrison.

3. As a **reintegrative interdiscourse**, which brings together the civilizational system and its exclusions in new and transformative ways, and thereby contributes to the constant renewal of the cultural center from its margins—as in all of the above mentioned texts, in which the reconnection of the culturally separated constitutes a tentative ground for systemic self-corrections and for potential new beginnings.

**A. R. Ammons, "Reflective"**
The following reading of the poem "Reflective"
by the contemporary American writer A. R. Ammons illustrates the cultural-ecological approach
to literature.

> I found a
> weed
> that had a
> mirror in it
> and that
> mirror
> looked in at
> a mirror
> in
> me that
> had a
> weed in it.

The poem establishes a **mutual relationship** between the speaker and a phenomenon of nature,
a weed, which is neither beautiful nor sublime,
but rather insignificant, useless, and irrelevant,
an inconspicuous organism that does not fit into
the utilitarian forms of order and significance
that human civilization has imposed on domesticated nature. The weed is an image of 'wild' nature outside the anthropocentric dominance of
civilization, which, however, is shown to be intrinsically interconnected with the human subject. The speaker and the weed are connected by
the image of a mirror, which has been a central
cultural metaphor of human knowledge and
self-knowledge in the classical and enlightenment periods, but is employed here in such a way
that the subject-object-position is reversed and
the phenomenon of nature is turned from an observed object into an observer of its own reflection in the human subject. In a playful defamiliarization of conventional perceptions, the text
reconnects the minimalist symbol of wild nature
with the cultural symbol of civilizational self-reflection in a fractal ecology of weed in which the
interconnection of what is culturally separated
becomes the focus of the poem's process.

Interpretation

## Select Bibliography

**Abram, David.** *Becoming Animal: An Earthly Cosmology.*
New York: Pantheon, 2010.

**Bate, Jonathan.** *The Song of the Earth.* London: Picador,
2000.

**Bateson, Gregory.** *A Sacred Unity: Further Steps to an
Ecology of Mind.* London: Paladin, 1991.

**Bateson, Gregory.** *Steps to an Ecology of Mind.* London:
Paladin, 1973.

**Buell, Lawrence.** "Ecocriticism: Some Emergent Trends."
*Qui Parle* 19.2 (2011): 87–115.

**Buell, Lawrence.** *The Environmental Imagination: Thoreau,
Nature Writing, and the Formation of American Culture.*
Cambridge: Harvard University Press, 1995.

**Clark, Timothy.** *The Cambridge Introduction to Literature
and the Environment.* Cambridge: Cambridge University Press, 2011.

**Derrida, Jacques.** "The Animal That Therefore I Am (More
to Follow)." *Critical Inquiry* 28 (2002): 371–418.

**Finke, Peter.** "Die Evolutionäre Kulturökologie: Hinter-
gründe, Prinzipien und Perspektiven einer neuen Theorie der Kultur." *Literature and Ecology.* Spec. issue of
*Anglia* 124.1 (2006): 175–217.

**Garrard, Greg.** *Ecocriticism.* London: Routledge, 2004.

**Gersdorf, Catrin, and Sylvia Mayer, eds.** *Nature in Literary
and Cultural Studies: Transatlantic Conversations on
Ecocriticism.* Amsterdam: Rodopi, 2006.

**Glotfelty, Cherryl.** "Literary Studies in an Age of Environmental Crisis." Introduction. Glotfelty and Fromm
xv–xxxvii.

**Glotfelty, Cherryl, and Harold Fromm, eds.** *The Ecocriticism
Reader: Landmarks in Literary Ecology.* Athens: University of Georgia Press, 1996.

**Goodbody, Axel.** *Nature, Technology and Cultural Change
in Twentieth-Century German Literature: The Challenge
of Ecocriticism.* Basingstoke: Palgrave Macmillan, 2007.

**Goodbody, Axel, and Kate Rigby, eds.** *Ecocritical Theory:
New European Approaches.* Charlottesville: University
of Virginia Press, 2011.

**Gras, Vernon W.** "Why the Humanities Need a New Paradigm which Ecology Can Provide." *Anglistik* 14.2 (2003):
45–61.

**Guattari, Félix.** *Die Drei Ökologien.* Ed. Peter Engelmann.
Vienna: Passagen, 1994.

**Heise, Ursula.** *Sense of Place and Sense of Planet: The Environmental Imagination of the Global.* Oxford: Oxford
University Press, 2008.

**Hornung, Alfred, and Zhao Baisheng, eds.** *Ecology and Life
Writing.* Heidelberg: Winter, 2012.

**Iovino, Serenella.** "Ecocriticism and a Non-Anthropocentric
Humanism." *Local Natures, Global Responsibilities: Ecocritical Perspectives on the New English Literatures.* Eds.
Laurenz Volkmann et al. Amsterdam: Rodopi, 2010.
29–53.

**Müller, Timo.** "Between Poststructuralism and the Natural
Sciences: Models and Strategies of Recent Cultural
Ecology." *Anglistik* 21.1 (2010): 175–91.

**Müller, Timo, and Michael Sauter, eds.** *Literature, Ecology,
Ethics: Recent Trends in Ecocriticism.* Heidelberg: Winter,
2012.

**Nennen, Heinz-Ulrich.** *Ökologie im Diskurs: Zu Grundfra-gen der Anthropologie und Ökologie und zur Ethik der Wissenschaften.* Opladen: Westdeutscher Verlag, 1991.

**Rueckert, William.** "Literature and Ecology: An Experiment in Ecocriticism." 1978. Glotfelty and Fromm 105–23.

**Slovic, Scott.** *Going Away to Think: Engagement, Retreat, and Ecocritical Responsibility.* Reno: University of Nevada Press, 2008.

**Soper, Kate.** *What Is Nature?* Oxford: Blackwell, 1998.

**Zapf, Hubert, ed.** *Kulturökologie und Literatur: Beiträge zu einem transdisziplinären Paradigma der Literaturwis-senschaft.* Heidelberg: Winter, 2008.

**Zapf, Hubert.** "Literary Ecology and the Ethics of Texts." *New Literary History* 39.4 (2008): 847–68.

**Zapf.** Hubert. *Literatur als kulturelle Ökologie: Zur kulturel-len Funktion literarischer Texte an Beispielen des ameri-kanischen Romans.* Tübingen: Niemeyer, 2002.

*Hubert Zapf*

# Part III: Cultural Studies

# 1 Transnational Approaches to the Study of Culture

## 1.1 | Cultural and National Specificity of Approaches

Although the development of English and American Studies, just like other disciplines in the humanities, has been characterized by an on-going trend towards internationalization and globalization, there are still marked **differences** between various national research cultures and traditions. These differences can hardly be overlooked when comparing, for instance, the ways in which literary criticism as practised in British universities differs from the German tradition of *Literaturwissenschaften* (see Zima). Similar differences can be observed when pitting British Cultural Studies against German *Kulturwissenschaften*, both of which are also characterized by cultural and national specificity (cf. sections 1.2 below, III.2.3, and III.2.4).

Such differences between national approaches testify to the fact that the study of culture, and of literature, one might add, is itself very much a cultural practice and that it is characterized by cultural and national specificity. Different approaches to the study of culture are themselves culturally and historically conditioned and thus subject to change and cultural variation. The latter nonetheless pose serious obstacles to both the transfer of approaches and concepts from one national research culture to the other, and the development of genuinely transnational approaches to the study of culture.

There are several reasons why approaches to the study of culture as developed and practised in different countries still display considerable differences, even in an age of globalization and world-wide mobility, especially among academics. Among the most important reasons that can explain such cultural and national differences are language, intellectual styles, the cultural contexts and historical developments of disciplines and approaches, and institutional differences between research cultures and their traditions.

As the comparison between German *Kulturwissenschaften* and British Cultural Studies in section 1.2 below will serve to show, the differences between these national traditions of studying culture are still so big that it would be unwarranted to speak of transnational approaches as though they actually existed. While there is a broad range of different national traditions of studying culture, including various kinds of British Cultural Studies and American Cultural Studies, but more recently also of 'Latino/a Cultural Studies' (see Allatson), the development of genuinely transnational, or even trans-European, approaches to the study of culture is still a desideratum for future research. Since separate entries in this volume are devoted to the delineation of British Cultural Studies and American Cultural Studies (cf. entries III.2 and III.3), this entry will focus on approaches not primarily associated with either Britain or the U.S., but developed independently in other contexts.

The present outline of transnational approaches to the study of culture refers to a project that does not yet exist as a fully-fledged theoretical or analytical framework. Therefore, this entry can speak of it only in a largely programmatic manner, outlining how it could be fostered and what it could be. In addition to exploring some of the differences between national research traditions to the study of culture, it will provide an overview of recent contributions to research that have fostered, or are fostering, the development of transnational approaches to the study of culture. These include approaches that either cut across national traditions or that have successfully travelled from one research culture to others, a number of influential '**cultural turns**' (Bachmann-Medick, *Cultural Turns*) in the humanities, or 'cultural sciences' (*Kulturwissenschaften*), and the notions of '**travel-**

ling concepts' (Bal) and '**translation**' as promising ways of overcoming boundaries between different research cultures and national traditions. Thus, this entry outlines possible trajectories for how Anglo-American varieties of cultural studies, German *Kulturwissenschaften* and other approaches associated with particular national research cultures and traditions could be transformed into a truly Transnational Study of Culture (cf. Sommer, "From Cultural Studies").

## 1.2 | The Study of Culture in an International Context

*Defining Kultur-*
*wissenschaften*

Although British and American varieties of cultural studies and their rough equivalent of German *Kulturwissenschaften* are all concerned with the study of culture in the widest possible sense, they nonetheless display considerable differences. For students doing English and/or American Studies at a German, Austrian, or Swiss university, it is important to be aware of such differences and to be able to assess and deploy different approaches. Just as there is arguably a 'national style' of English literary criticism, historiography, and cultural studies (cf. Nünning, "Englishness"), German *Kulturwissenschaften* likewise share a number of epistemological claims, discursive strategies, and institutional practices that set them off from their American and British counterparts.

German *Kulturwissenschaften*. To begin with, the German term *Kulturwissenschaften*, just like *Literaturwissenschaften*, is lost in translation. It serves to emphasize the scientific nature of the discipline that it designates, implicitly claiming that the study of culture can be as scientific as any discipline in the hard sciences. As Peter Zima has shown in a pioneering article, the term *Literaturwissenschaften* in the German sense is very much "a language-and culture-bound phenomenon" that "becomes questionable as soon as it is projected into an intercultural context" (26). The same holds true for the term ***Kulturwissenschaften***, which should not be confused with the English term 'cultural studies.' What is at stake here is much more than just a question of terminology, in that there is a semantic rupture between the German and English sociolinguistic contexts that concerns the constitution and traditions of the respective disciplines and research cultures as a whole, including the ways in which they construct their objects, define their objectives, and practise the study of culture.

Despite many attempts, the term *Kulturwissenschaft(en)*, just like the term 'cultural studies,' is used as a catch phrase for a wide range of different approaches and concepts (see Nünning and Nünning). Many scholars have acknowl-

edged that it is notoriously hard to define and that it does not exist as an independent and clearly circumscribed discipline (cf. Bollenbeck and Kaiser 617). The main difficulty of any attempt at definition has to do with the fact that the term is used to cover a **multiplicity of different fields** of research and trends in the humanities; that it functions as an umbrella term for open and interdisciplinary discussions, and that the scope of its application and extension is subject to debate. Like the term 'cultural studies,' the terms *Kulturwissenschaft* and *Kulturwissenschaften* have become a catch-all, which is used in at least four different senses:

**1.** in a very broad usage *Kulturwissenschaft(en)* stands for an **interdisciplinary frame of reference**, which is supposed to integrate the whole spectrum of the traditional disciplines in the humanities;

**2.** the term *Kulturwissenschaft* is also used as a **key concept** for the call for change and for an opening of the traditional philologies, especially, literary studies, but also of the humanities at large;

**3.** in a more narrow and specialized sense, *Kulturwissenschaft* denotes a **special subdiscipline** within the individual philologies. A closer look reveals that this often amounts to little more than a new label for a traditional approach that is often denounced as old-fashioned: the study of the geographical, social, economical and cultural characteristics of individual countries, known as *Landeskunde* at German universities.

**4.** The discipline that used to be called '**Volkskunde**' (i.e. folklore studies) or '**Europäische Ethnologie**' (which could be translated as 'European ethnic studies') is now also sometimes referred to as *Kulturwissenschaft*.

Main Differences between *Kulturwissenschaften* and Cultural Studies. In spite of some similarities with regard to subject matter and methods, the German version of *Kulturwissenschaften* should be distinguished from the special brand of cultural studies developed in Britain. At the risk of oversimplification, the main differences between British (and American) Cultural Studies and German *Kulturwissenschaften* can be located on at least four levels (cf. Sommer, *Grundkurs*; Assmann 16–26).

**1.** British Cultural Studies were developed as a response to concrete social and political challenges of the British class system and as a politically motivated project aimed at producing changes in society and strategies of resistance; in this research tradition, culture and politics have been inextricably intertwined. By contrast, the German tradition of *Kulturwissenschaften*, which can be traced back to the late nineteenth and early twentieth century (see Böhme, Matussek, and Müller), has quite a different genealogy and non-political agenda, being largely an academic enterprise which explores cultural phenomena as objects of academic research, not with an eye to engendering political change.

**2.** While British Cultural Studies is characterized by an ideological position and marked by a Marxist approach, German *Kulturwissenschaften* display a more pluralistic, multiperspectival theoretical orientation, exploring symbolic forms and ways of worldmaking (Goodman).

**3.** As the very name of its most renowned and important institution, the "Birmingham Centre for Contemporary Cultural Studies" already indicates, British Cultural Studies has tended to expand the concept of culture from high-brow culture to popular culture, paving the way for a new approach to contemporary popular culture, on which the Birmingham school largely focussed. By way of contrast, German *Kulturwissenschaften* has favoured a broader anthropological and semiotic concept of culture (see section 1.4 below), taking a wider range of cultural objects and a broader diachronic perspective into consideration.

**4.** Being an integral part of the respective national, institutional and academic cultures from which they have emerged, British Cultural Studies and German *Kulturwissenschaften* have developed different research questions, topics, and methods (cf. Assmann 16).

These differences between British Cultural Studies and German *Kulturwissenschaften* show that national traditions in the study of literature and culture are shaped by the '**intellectual style**' (to use Johan Galtung's felicitous term) predominant in a culture, which colours the research process. According to Galtung, the intellectual style is located on a "level between the individual and the universal": "Broadly speaking, it is the civilizational or sub-civilizational—in other words macro-level" (808). It is no coincidence that most of what Galtung writes about the Saxon style is also true for English literary criticism, historiography, and forms of doing cultural studies, just as his observations on the 'Teutonic' intellectual style pertains to the German traditions of *Literaturwissenschaften* and *Kulturwissenschaften*.

**Theorizing vs. Facts.** Such differences in intellectual style manifest themselves in a number of concrete and tangible ways, shaping both prevalent research agendas and practices. While German *Kulturwissenschaften* display a predilection for **theorizing**, what constitutes the lowest common denominator of most of the features specific to British Cultural Studies is a clear preference for **particulars** and concrete 'facts,' and a concomitant distrust of generalities and abstractions. The national style of English literary history and cultural studies is not only marked by a number of prominent stylistic traits (e.g. a strong dislike of theory, focus on individual writers and their works as well as on facts and figures, preference for the tradition of empiricist discourse) and by ideas of Englishness (see Easthope) but it simultaneously serves to reinforce such collectively held concepts (cf. Nünning, "Englishness").

**Problematic Transfer.** One of the problems and impediments for the development of transnational approaches to the study of culture results from the prevailing tendency to 'import' British (or American) Cultural Studies into other (e.g. German) academic and institutional contexts and merely emulate or imitate the imported model. The main problem with such a transfer, however, is that while British Cultural Studies must be seen against the background of Britain's class system, the American debates about race, class, and gender, or the revision of the Western canon, only make sense in the context of the U.S. multicultural society. The strength of English and American Studies as they are practised in Germany, or France, the Netherlands, or Spain, for that matter, resides precisely in the fact that they view literatures and cultures of the English-speaking world from the outside. Moreover, they can apply the differences between their own and the foreign culture(s) in a fruitful manner. Both the canon debates (and revisions) with their focus on race, class, and gender and the British and American forms of Cultural Studies can thus themselves be seen as (highly interesting!) objects of inquiry,

Defining British
Cultural Studies

both from the point of view of English and American Studies as practised and taught at German universities and in a broader transnational framework for the study of culture(s). It is also important not to forget or ignore the indigenous research tradition developed for the study of culture in Germany, which is called *Kulturwissenschaft* or *Kulturwissenschaften*.

## 1.3 | Trans/national Concepts of Culture

*Different ways
of studying culture*

The term 'study of culture' does not refer to any narrow definition or the understanding of the object of study, or to a particular theoretical approach or school of thought, as is the case with, for example, "cultural studies," "cultural analysis" (Bal 6–8), "cultural materialism," or "cultural criticism" (Belsey). Instead, the goal is to enhance the **dialogue** among the disciplines and among different cultures of research, thus fostering self-reflexive, interdisciplinary, international, and potentially even transnational approaches to the study of culture. As both the interest that various disciplines in the humanities and social sciences have paid to culture, and the co-existence of various kinds of British Cultural Studies, American Cultural Studies, German *Kulturwissenschaften*, and other national traditions already serve to demonstrate, the study of culture is essentially an interdisciplinary and an international field of research. With regard to both the range of disciplines that are concerned with culture and its international dimension, the study of culture is characterized by theoretical and methodological pluralism as well as multiperspectivism (cf. Nünning and Nünning). During the last three decades, the study of culture has been one of the most rapidly developing research fields in European and American, but increasingly also in Asian and Australian scholarship. As a newly emerging interdisciplinary field, the study of culture forges new relations between literary studies, film studies, media studies, theatre and performance studies, and musicology, for example, but it also engages in dialogue with neighbouring disciplines such as anthropology, architecture, art history, cultural geography, cultural psychology, political science, and sociology.

In addition to interdisciplinary cooperation, research into the broad range of domains that fall under the purview of the study of culture also presupposes **theoretical and methodological pluralism**. The development of transnational approaches to the study of culture does not privilege any one approach to the study of culture, but must display a commitment to diversity, including empirical approaches, quantitative analysis, and thick description (sensu Clifford Geertz). Approaches that have cut across disciplinary and national research traditions include cultural semiotics (*Kultursemiotik*, see Posner), cultural anthropology, historical anthropology, literary anthropology, the new cultural history, cultural ecology and area studies, among others (for an overview, see Nünning and Nünning).

**Typology of Concepts of Culture.** Already in 1952, Kroeber and Kluckholm provided a systematic overview of no fewer than 175 different definitions of the word 'culture.' Since then, the number of competing concepts of culture has increased significantly, because many disciplines have developed a plethora of new concepts of culture (see Ort). Reckwitz offers a useful typology of concepts of culture, according to which one can distinguish between four basic kinds or types of concepts of culture (64):

**1.** **The normative concept of culture** ("der normative Kulturbegriff") is based on an evaluative definition of those aesthetic phenomena and objects that are considered to belong to 'high' culture and regarded as worth including in the canon of great works of art that are preserved by institutions and cultural memory. Since such a normative definition is relatively narrow and restrictive, it has been challenged by proponents of cultural studies, which are more interested in the products of popular culture which such a narrow view tends to exclude.

**2.** **The totalizing concept of culture** ("der totalitätsorientierte Kulturbegriff"), in contrast to such a normative definition, refrains from any aesthetic value judgements, taking into consideration instead "the whole way of life" (Williams). According to such a non-normative understanding, which has dominated in anthropology and ethnology, for example, the concept of culture is used as an umbrella term that subsumes all the collectively shared ways of thinking, feeling, and believing, the structures of attitudes, and the hierarchies of norms and values that are characteristic of a given community, group or nation and that set them off from other collectives. Accepting the basic equality of different cultures and cultural manifestations, such a broad, holistic, and totalizing concept of culture draws attention to the full range of cultural expressions, objects, and practices, including institutions, rituals, and other social practices.

**3.** The difference-theoretical concept of culture ("der differenztheoretische Kulturbegriff") is much more restrictive again, focussing solely on the "narrow field of art, education, science, and other intellectual activities" (Reckwitz 6). Originating from sociology and systems theory, this concept of culture is based on the notion that culture is a particular sub-system of modern society, viz. the system that is specialized in intellectual and aesthetic ways of worldmaking.

**4.** The semiotic and constructivist understanding of culture ("der bedeutungs- und wissensorientierte Kulturbegriff"), adopted by many scholars today, understands culture as the entire complex of discursive formations, ideas, values, and meanings created by humans and materialized in symbolic systems. In this definition of culture, not only are material forms of expression (for example, artistic artefacts) part of culture, but social institutions and mentalities are as well, and without them the creation of such artefacts would not even be possible. Cultures possess not only a material aspect—the cultural assets/goods/treasures of a nation—but also social, emotional, and cognitive dimensions (see box).

The three dimensions of culture are not isolated phenomena, but interdependent and complementary elements within the study of culture. Research in these fields revolves around the synchronic and diachronic plurality of cultural formations through a broad spectrum of areas of study, which range historically from antiquity through the Middle Ages to the postmodern era, and geographically from the Anglo-American to the Latin American, Asian, African, and Eastern European contexts.

Proceeding from an anthropological, semiotic, and constructivist understanding of culture, the

---

**Focus on Dimensions of Culture**

Culture needs to be studied in its various dimensions:

- The **material dimension** is evident primarily in the wide variety of media studied (from language and literary texts to historical sources, texts of any kind, interviews, photography, film and the new media). Yet elements of material culture or performative acts of a transitory nature (such as theatre, rituals, and festivals) are also regarded as material objects of study.
- The **social dimension** is studied in the form of institutions, political organizations, and social hierarchies and roles, as well as in the social components of media systems.
- The **cognitive dimension**—mentalities, systems of values and norms, taboos, and concepts of identity—characterizing a culture is at the centre of almost all research projects, although it is only indirectly observable via its material and social dimensions.

---

project of developing transnational approaches to the study of culture attempts to merge different traditions and conceptualizations of culture. Moving beyond a narrow and normative concept of culture, solely understood as the field of artistic and intellectual creation, the study of culture is concerned with cultural expressions, discourses, cultural heritage, and artistic objects, and a wider anthropological notion of culture, understood as the broad realm of whole ways of life, or human life forms, including material manifestations, collective habits and mentalities, social institutions, practices, and rituals, as well as shared values and social norms. Instead of privileging a particular domain, an interdisciplinary and transnational approach conceives of culture as the totality of discourses, texts, images, performances, and other products of media culture, but it also takes into consideration political culture, institutions, rituals, mentalities, as well as norms and values (see Nünning, "Literatur, Mentalitäten"). It explores how artistic and literary creation is embedded in, and shaped by, social conditions, and prefigured by cultural heritage, and how it can in turn be considered as having performative power, as an active force in its own right, and as an intervention in its respective context.

## 1.4 | Cultural Turns in the Humanities

As Doris Bachmann-Medick has shown in *Cultural Turns*, in addition to the approaches mentioned above, there have also been a number of 'cultural turns' in the humanities that cut across disciplinary and national boundaries and that have significantly changed the ways in which research agendas have developed. All of the turns covered in Bachmann-Medick's book have helped to move beyond the boundaries of disciplines and national borders, fostering the processes of *Internationalizing Cultural Studies* (Abbas and Erni) and of developing new approaches for *The Contemporary Study of Culture* (Bundesministerium and IFK). Devoting a chapter to each turn, she systematically explores in detail the research questions, epistemic ruptures, theoretical frameworks, and possibilities of application offered by the following cultural turns, all of which not only provide important concepts for the study of culture, but have also been, and continue to be, instrumental in internationalizing and transnationalizing it:

- the interpretive turn, i.e. the redirection of attention towards cultural meanings, negotiations and interpretations that was ushered in by cultural anthropology and that initiated both an understanding of culture as a huge repertoire of texts and an anthropological turn in literary studies (Bachmann-Medick, *Kultur als Text*);
- the performative turn, i.e. the complementary as well as corrective move to an understanding of 'culture as performance,' a view that takes into consideration all the factors, institutions, social processes and practices that are involved in the practical production of cultural meanings;
- the reflexive/literary/rhetorical turn, i.e. an enhanced critical and self-conscious exploration of the complex issues involved in the representation and writing of culture as well as of the forms and structures of texts and other cultural ways of worldmaking;
- the postcolonial turn (for details, cf. entry III.4);
- the translational turn, i.e. an explicit focus on translation processes across the humanities and a sustained analysis of the mediation processes and problems of transfer involved in cultural exchanges conceived of as translations (cf. section 1.6 below);
- the spatial turn, i.e. a cross-disciplinary focus on, and analysis of, the categories of space, place, borders, and border-crossings based on a new understanding of space as a relational cat-

egory and as a result of social relations, practices, and orders of knowledge;
- the iconic turn, i.e. the immense importance of, and the widespread cross-disciplinary interest in, the functions of images and visualization in today's media culture.

While all of the cultural turns discussed by Bachmann-Medick have greatly increased interest in what Jerome Bruner called "The Narrative Construction of Reality" and in what the philosopher Nelson Goodman felicitously christened "Ways of Worldmaking," the transnational study of culture is, of course, interested in **cultural ways of worldmaking** like media and narratives (cf. Nünning, Nünning, and Neumann). All of these turns have been conducive to transcending the limitations of national research traditions, in fostering transnational as well as transcultural approaches to the study of culture, and to foregrounding both global and transnational cultural issues and the concept of transnationalism itself. The latter has mainly been explored by global historians, but cultural theory has also developed a keen interest in the concepts of transnationalism and transculturality (cf. Welsch), as the recent development of postcolonial studies (cf. entry III.4), for instance, demonstrates.

Itself a major mode of the diffusion, transfer and problematization of key concepts, the transnational perspective epitomizes the emergent character of concepts and the necessity of greater self-reflexivity. The concept of **transnationalism** draws attention not only to transnational cultural phenomena (e.g. Hollywood and Bollywood movies, popular music and MTV, a new understanding of world literature) that have proliferated in the age of globalization, but also to the far-reaching effects transnationalization has had on the historical and heuristic reconfiguration of the interdependence of culture, society, and the polity. Both such transnational cultural phenomena and various transnationalization processes underline the fact that the development of transnational approaches to the study of culture is a great desideratum, especially in the present age of globalization and world-wide migration.

# 1.5 | Travelling Concepts and Translation

**Several key concepts**, or meta-concepts, present themselves as possible models for framing and fostering the development of transnational approaches to the study of culture. They include the notions of

- travelling concepts (Bal),
- translation (cf. Bachmann-Medick, *Cultural Turns* 238–83),
- cultural exchange or cultural transfer,
- emergence.

Though the focus in this section will be on the potential of 'travelling concepts' as a metatheoretical framework for developing a transnational perspective for the study of culture, recent insights of the other fields and approaches, i.e. translation studies, cultural exchange, and cultural transfer, converge in a number of ways that impinge on any attempt to develop transnational approaches to the study of culture.

What the notions of travelling concepts, translation, cultural exchange, and cultural transfer have in common is that they share at least two central epistemological assumptions: first, the assumption that concepts are 'operative terms' (Welsch), i.e. that they are never merely descriptive but "also programmatic and normative" (Bal 28) and that they construct and change the very objects they analyse (cf. Welsch 20), "entailing new emphases and a new ordering of the phenomena within the complex objects constituting the cultural field" (Bal 33); second, the assumption that there are no universal concepts for the study of culture, society or politics, and that no approach or theory can ever claim any universal validity.

**Differences.** Though all of these approaches are concerned with the dynamic processes involved in the traffic between cultures and disciplines, and are thus intertwined in a number of ways, they focus on different aspects. Bal's cross-disciplinary project of 'travelling concepts' is mainly concerned with the development of a "concept-based methodology" (Bal 5) and with fostering interdisciplinary research projects in the humanities. The other approaches look much more closely at the historical and social contexts, the actual people and institutions who adapt concepts, goods or practices from another country, the multilayered processes involved in the acts of translation, or appropriation, and the transformations that theories, concepts or other cultural phenomena undergo as they are transferred from one (for instance, academic) context into another.

**Problems.** Approaches and concepts in the humanities are not only heavily imbued with, and shaped by, very particular historical, intellectual, and national traditions, they also come with ideological freight and unconscious biases, as the insights of postcolonial theory and globalization studies have demonstrated. As Dipesh Chakrabarty has shown in his influential book *Provincializing Europe*, every case of transferring a cultural, economic or political model or theory from one context to another is always "a problem of translation" (17) as well—a translation of existing worlds, their "conceptual horizons" and their thought-categories into the context, concepts and horizons of another life-world (cf. 71). He draws attention to the fact that any seemingly "abstract and universal idea" can "look utterly different in different historical contexts," that no country is "a model to another country," that "historical differences actually make a difference," and that "no human society is a *tabula rasa*" (xii). What Chakrabarty observes about the "universal concepts of political modernity," is also true of every approach and concept for the study of culture that is transferred from one academic context to another: such travelling concepts "encounter pre-existing concepts, categories, institutions, and practices through which they get translated and configured differently" (xii). All of this should be borne in mind when trying to gauge the challenges and possibilities offered by the notion of travelling concepts, as well as of translation, cultural exchange, and cultural transfer, for the development of transnational approaches to the study of culture.

**Intersubjectivity.** One of the most promising ways of fostering the development of transnational approaches to the study of culture was suggested by the Dutch narratologist and cultural theorist Mieke Bal in her book *Travelling Concepts in the Humanities: A Rough Guide* (2002). Her project proceeds from the assumption that concepts are indispensable for the study of culture because they are "the **tools of intersubjectivity**" in that "they facilitate discussion on the basis of a common language" and that they "offer miniature theories" (22). More often than not, however, the "meaning, reach, and operational value" (24) of concepts differ between diverse disciplines, different academic cultures, and historical periods. Though various

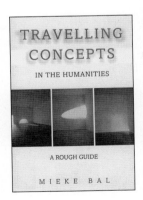

The transnational study
of culture foregrounds
interaction.

key concepts are at the core of many disciplines in the social sciences and humanities concerned with the study of culture, they are usually not univocal and firmly established terms. Rather, they are dynamic and flexible, undergoing semantic changes as they travel back and forth "between disciplines, between individual scholars, between historical periods, and between geographically dispersed academic communities" (24), which are often shaped by different national research cultures. Some concepts and theories tend to travel better than others: while some concepts are roughly translatable, others may contain cultural connotations or implications that defy translation. The travelling of concepts thus serves to show that the very assumption of translatability in general and the 'translatability of cultures' (cf. Budick and Iser) in particular may not quite hold (cf. Chakrabarty 74).

**Interdisciplinarity.** With the move towards greater interdisciplinarity, the dynamic exchange of concepts, as well as of metaphors and narratives, between different disciplines has considerably intensified (cf. Neumann and Tygstrup). Concepts and metaphors are not only shaped by cultures and theories, but also in turn shape the latter (cf. Grabes, Nünning and Baumbach). Through constant appropriation, translation, and reassessment across various fields, approaches to and concepts of cultural phenomena have acquired new meanings, triggering a reorganisation of prevalent orders of knowledge and opening up new horizons of research in the social sciences as well as the humanities. To the extent that the meaning of such travelling concepts must, therefore, be constantly renegotiated, a sustained enquiry into the dynamics of such travelling, into the "'translational' processes" (Chakrabarty 19) and into politics involved, and in the genealogies of the concepts in question is a prerequisite for both the development of transnational approaches to the study of culture and a higher degree of self-reflexivity of any approach to this blossoming and increasingly diverse field.

**Travelling.** In order to provide theoretical, conceptual, and methodological backbones to any project concerned with either the travelling, and translation, of concepts, or the development of transnational approaches to the study of culture, four axes along which approaches, theories, concepts, metaphors, and narratives can travel can be distinguished:

1. travelling between academic disciplines: crossing disciplinary boundaries;
2. travelling between academic and national cultures and cultures of research: crossing national borders;
3. travelling diachronically across time: crossing the boundaries between historical periods;
4. travelling synchronically between functionally defined subsystems: travelling between academia and society.

**Cotexts and contexts.** The complexity of such theoretical and conceptual transfers resides in the fact that concepts are always embedded in their respective cotexts and in various contexts. The latter include the theories, frameworks, or paradigms in which a given concept was developed, the discipline from which it originates as well as the respective disciplinary discourses associated with it, and the academic research culture with its concomitant institutional practices, national traditions, and intellectual styles. Therefore, concepts always have a number of disciplinary, formal, and functional features that can be derived either from their position and role in a particular theory, conceptual system or discipline, or from the traditions from which it originates and the respective intellectual styles. Whenever a concept is transferred from its original context(s), it is never innocent or travels alone, but always comes with theoretical baggage and possibly even ideological freight, both of which may, however, be lost in transit or translation. The incorporation of concepts adapted from other disciplines or research cultures therefore always entails acts of recontextualization, i.e. relating the adapted concepts to established frameworks and theories in the new disciplinary and institutional context.

**Challenges and risks.** Although such conceptual transfers across any of the axes identified above constitute a promising way for the development of interdisciplinary and transnational approaches to the study of culture, they are also inevitably fraught with some challenges and risks. Important challenges are arguably the tasks of paying critical attention to the processes of translation and of successfully mediating between different cultural traditions, as well as between academic and theoretical differences. In doing so, one has to avoid the danger that the travelling of concepts can result in bringing together two non-commensurable cultural or theoretical frameworks. The most obvious risks include the danger of **oversimplification** and of loss of terminological precision, theoretical consistency, analytical insight, and epistemological and heuristic power. When concepts travel they may also become mere commonplaces or metaphors, which can result in the dissolution of a concept as a whole. On the other hand, the importation of concepts from other fields can be an important heuristic move and tremendously productive, yielding new combinations of insights and leading to the revision of established disciplinary theories or the discovery of unknown phenomena. Moreover, it can "trigger and facilitate reflection and debate on all levels of methodology" (Bal 29), enhance disciplinary innovation, and even redefine a discipline and its boundaries, generating new theoretical frameworks, disciplinary research domains or even new fields of interdisciplinary research.

The most important gain that can result from concepts travelling across disciplinary and national boundaries is thus arguably the emergence of new areas or fields of research for the transnational study of culture, or even of new and truly interdisciplinary academic fields that cut across traditional disciplines. The emerging fields of cultural memory studies (cf. entry II.11) and cross-disciplinary narrative research (cf. Heinen and Sommer) provide typical cases in point of such emergent transnational approaches to the study of culture and transdisciplinary fields of research, though there are a number of equally pertinent examples, including, among others, postcolonial studies, ritual studies (see Dücker), visual studies, as well as performance studies and cultures of performativity.

New fields of research

## 1.6 | From Cultural Studies to the Transnational Study of Culture

What is needed for the development of transnational approaches to the study of a culture is an enhanced degree of **self-reflection** about, and a much more detailed and comprehensive investigation of, the different national traditions and styles of 'doing' cultural studies, or the study of culture, the promotion of greater "transnational literacy" (Bal 291), and a willingness to endorse interdisciplinarity, to question one's own academic routines, and to negotiate between different national research traditions and intellectual styles. In this day and age, in which "there is increased awareness that a particular national literature can look quite different from a different national perspective" (Thomas 10), there is also an increased need to compare not just the literatures and cultures of different countries but also the various national traditions of studying literature and culture, and to move beyond the epistemological limitations of national boundaries, of institutionally driven conceptual frameworks, and of particular intellectual styles (cf. Galtung).

In order to be able to gauge the complex problems of developing transnational and transcultural approaches to the study of culture, English and American Studies need to get to grips with, and transcend, the different national traditions that have emerged and that have become institutionalized. Worldwide migration and the global interfacing of cultures require **different approaches** from those championed by British or American Cultural Studies, approaches that are no longer limited to a national research tradition and concept of culture, but it is much harder to actually devise new models for a transnational study of culture freed from the shackles of the hitherto dominant British or American approaches. In order to move beyond such nationally based boundaries and academic styles, English and American Studies needs to investigate in detail the presuppositions, discursive practices, and structural features of its own research traditions, which have so far been largely unacknowledged and have tended to become naturalized. Therefore, transnational and transcultural approaches to the study of culture require the development of a new set of guiding principles, travelling concepts and other ways of academic worldmaking that expand the limited horizons of British Cultural Studies, American Cultural Studies, German *Kulturwissenschaften*, and other nationally specific research traditions.

## Select Bibliography

Abbas, Ackbar, and John Nguyet Erni, eds. *Internationalizing Cultural Studies: An Anthology*. Malden: Blackwell, 2005.

Allatson, Paul. *Key Terms in Latino/a Cultural and Literary Studies*. Malden: Blackwell, 2007.

Assmann, Aleida. *Einführung in die Kulturwissenschaft: Grundbegriffe, Themen, Fragestellungen*. Berlin: Erich Schmidt, 2006.

Bachmann-Medick, Doris, ed. *Kultur als Text: Die anthropologische Wende in der Literaturwissenschaft*. Frankfurt/M.: Fischer, 1996.

Bachmann-Medick, Doris. *Cultural Turns: Neuorientierungen in den Kulturwissenschaften*. Reinbek: Rowohlt, 2006.

Bal, Mieke. *Travelling Concepts in the Humanities: A Rough Guide*. Toronto: University of Toronto Press, 2002.

Belsey, Catherine. "Beyond Literature and Cultural Studies: The Case for Cultural Criticism." *Belgian Journal of English Language and Literatures* ns 1 (2003): 91–100.

Böhme, Hartmut, Peter Matussek, and Lothar Müller. *Orientierung Kulturwissenschaft: Was sie kann, was sie will*. Reinbek: Rowohlt, 2000.

Bollenbeck, Georg, and Gerhard Kaiser. "Kulturwissenschaftliche Ansätze in den Literaturwissenschaften." Jaeger and Straub 615–37.

Bruner, Jerome. "The Narrative Construction of Reality." *Critical Inquiry* 18 (1991): 1–21.

Budick, Sanford, and Wolfgang Iser, eds. *The Translatability of Cultures: Figurations of the Space Between*. Stanford: Stanford University Press, 1996.

Bundesministerium für Wissenschaft und Verkehr, and Internationales Forschungszentrum Kulturwissenschaften, eds. *The Contemporary Study of Culture*. Vienna: Turia + Kant, 1999.

Chakrabarty, Dipesh. *Provincializing Europe: Postcolonial Thought and Historical Difference*. 2000. Princeton: Princeton University Press, 2008.

Dücker, Burckhard. *Rituale: Formen – Funktionen – Geschichte: Eine Einführung in die Ritualwissenschaft*. Stuttgart: Metzler, 2007.

Easthope, Antony. *Englishness and National Culture*. London: Routledge, 1999.

Erll, Astrid, and Nünning, Ansgar, eds. *Cultural Memory Studies: An International and Interdisciplinary Handbook*. Berlin: de Gruyter, 2008.

Galtung, Johan. "Structure, Culture, and Intellectual Style: An Essay Comparing Saxonic, Teutonic, Gallic and Nipponic Approaches." *Social Science Information* 20.6 (1981): 817–56.

Goodman, Nelson. *Ways of Worldmaking*. 1978. Indianapolis: Hackett, 1992.

Grabes, Herbert, Ansgar Nünning, and Sibylle Baumbach, eds. *Metaphors Shaping Culture and Theory*. Tübingen: Narr, 2009.

Heinen, Sandra, and Roy Sommer, eds. *Narratology in the Age of Cross-Disciplinary Narrative Research*. Berlin: de Gruyter, 2009.

Jaeger, Friedrich, and Burkard Liebsch, eds. *Grundlagen und Schlüsselbegriffe*. Stuttgart: Metzler, 2004. Vol. 1 of *Handbuch der Kulturwissenschaften*. 3 Vols.

Jaeger, Friedrich, and Jürgen Straub, eds. *Paradigmen und Disziplinen*. Stuttgart: Metzler, 2004. Vol. 2 of *Handbuch der Kulturwissenschaften*. 3 Vols.

Kroeber, Alfred L., and Clyde Kluckholm. *Culture: A Critical Review of Concepts and Definitions*. Cambridge: Peabody Museums, 1952.

Neumann, Birgit, and Frederik Tygstrup. "Travelling Concepts in English Studies." *Travelling Concepts in English Studies*. Eds. Birgit Neumann and Frederik Tygstrup. Spec. issue of *EJES: European Journal of English Studies* 13.1 (2009): 1–12.

Nünning, Ansgar. "Literatur, Mentalitäten und kulturelles Gedächtnis: Grundriß, Leitbegriffe und Perspektiven einer anglistischen Kulturwissenschaft." *Literaturwissenschaftliche Theorien, Modelle und Methoden: Eine Einführung*. 1995. Ed. Ansgar Nünning. Trier: WVT, 2004. 173–97

Nünning, Ansgar. "On the Englishness of English Literary Histories: Where Literature, Philosophy and Nationalism Meet Cultural History." *Critical Interfaces: Contributions on Philosophy, Literary Theory and Culture in Honour of Herbert Grabes*. Eds. Gordon Collier, Klaus Schwank, and Franz Wieselhuber. Trier: WVT, 2001. 55–83.

Nünning, Ansgar, ed. *Metzler Lexikon Literatur- und Kulturtheorie*. 1998. 4th ed. Stuttgart: Metzler, 2008.

Nünning, Ansgar, and Vera Nünning, eds. *Einführung in die Kulturwissenschaften: Theoretische Grundlagen – Ansätze – Perspektiven*. Stuttgart: Metzler, 2008.

Nünning, Vera, Ansgar Nünning, and Birgit Neumann, eds. *Cultural Ways of Worldmaking: Media and Narratives*. New York: de Gruyter, 2010.

Ort, Claus-Michael. "Kulturbegriffe und Kulturtheorien." Nünning and Nünning 19–38.

Posner, Roland. "Kultursemiotik." Nünning and Nünning 39–72.

Reckwitz, Andreas. *Die Transformation der Kulturtheorien: Zur Entwicklung eines Theorieprogramms*. Weilerswist: Velbrück, 2000.

Sommer, Roy. *Grundkurs Cultural Studies/Kulturwissenschaft Großbritannien*. Stuttgart: Klett, 2003.

Sommer, Roy. "From Cultural Studies to the Study of Culture: Key Concepts and Methods." *English Studies Today: Recent Developments and New Directions*. Eds. Ansgar Nünning and Jürgen Schlaeger. Trier: WVT, 2007. 165–91.

Thomas, Brook. "Placing Literature in Written English." *Literature and the Nation*. Ed. Brook Thomas. Tübingen: Narr, 1998: 1–31.

Welsch, Wolfgang. "Transkulturalität." *Universitas* 52.607 (1997): 16–24.

Williams, Raymond. *Culture and Society 1780–1950*. 1958. Harmondsworth: Penguin, 1963.

Zima, Peter V. "Die Stellung der Literaturwissenschaft zwischen den Kulturen: Eine textsoziologische Betrachtung." *Literaturwissenschaft: intermedial – interdisziplinär*. Eds. Herbert Foltinek and Christoph Leitgeb. Vienna: Verlag der Österreichischen Akademie der Wissenschaften, 2002. 25–38.

*Ansgar Nünning*

# 2 British Cultural Studies

*Cultural Studies is dead!* Its spiritual home, the Centre for Contemporary Cultural Studies (CCCS) in Birmingham, had to close its doors in 2002, not quite forty years after its inauguration in 1964. In the USA, where British Cultural Studies found a new home (cf. entry III.3), loud demands for "Stopping Cultural Studies" can be heard (Warner and Siskin), and plans for a life at "The University After Cultural Studies" are already being made. (Such was the title of a plenary panel at the seventh annual meeting of the *Cultural Studies Association* in Kansas City in 2009.) What would it mean, however, to stop doing cultural studies? Would it mean that we stop analysing the texts, films, plays, images, and songs that contribute to our cultures? Does it mean that we no longer examine the artefacts and symbols that form (British) ways of living? It does not.

*Long live cultural studies!* To stop doing (British) Cultural Studies means only to stop studying culture one particular way. The aim of this text is to first trace the paths that led to the ends, but also to the beginnings of British Cultural Studies. Following this account will be an outline of what the study of culture could look like after the demise of British Cultural Studies. My perspective on the history and place of cultural studies is one originating within the field of **English Studies in Germany** (*Anglistik*)—one of the many disciplines that gave a fruitful home to British Cultural Studies. The following remarks, therefore, will switch between a description of cultural studies as it was first formed in Great Britain on the one hand, and an outline of English Studies (in Germany) as a mode of cultural studies on the other. British Cultural Studies, consequently, means two things to me: cultural studies as it has been practiced in Britain, and the study of the cultures of Britain.

## 2.1 | The Rise and Fall of Cultural Studies

In order to understand what British Cultural Studies *is*, one has to understand its *use*. Cultural studies, just as every other discipline or research paradigm, is bound up in the history of social and scientific structures: it is not just an artefact of intellectual, theoretical achievement ('learning'), but also rooted in social practices and mentalities ('a whole way of life'). Therefore, I will begin by examining one of the stories which try to make sense of the relationship between *Anglistik* and cultural studies. The analysis of such stories (i.e. narratology) and their intended effects (i.e. rhetoric) are central tools for the study of culture, a culture of which cultural studies is a part.

**Current Condition.** When two of the leading figures of English Studies in Germany were asked to define the status quo of '**English Studies Today**' they strongly expressed their disappointment in the current condition of the discipline. It appears helpful to take a closer look at the somewhat provocative, but nonetheless very representative story these authors have to tell about the causes for this demise. The two professors are clear about what they do not like about the present state of English Studies: they criticise the "disorders of our academic minds" (Nünning and Schlaeger 14) and the "centrifugal forces" (14) that have led to the "unfocussed and fragmentary nature" (13) of the field, which reveals a lack of even "a modicum of unity and coherence" (15); not even some sort of "common purpose and standards or shared preferences" (12) are discernible. If disorderly behaviour

A history of
cultural studies

is the offence, the prosecution is, however, less straightforward in naming the accused. The first time that one is allowed a glimpse of the culprit is in the form of a (rhetorical) question: "If you don't like Byron, Dickens, Eliot or Marlowe why not occupy yourself with Batman, Diana, Eminem or Madonna, or Manchester United, for that matter?" (11). All that is rotten in the state of English Studies, it transpires, seems to be fruits from the fields of non-literary **popular culture**—a classical topic of cultural studies, that is (cf. section III.3.3).

**Rise.** After enumerating various examples of misled research, the authors become somewhat more precise. First, they claim that the rise of 'Theory,' and poststructuralism in particular (cf. entry II.4), led to a "loss of prestige of our disciplines" (Nünning and Schlaeger 18). At this moment of crisis, when English Studies was at its weakest, enfeebled by the infection from (frenchified) "intellectual coteries" (17), cultural studies apparently took over a defenceless English Studies: "The vacuum was filled by the next candidate in line: cultural studies" (18). At the beginning, the authors admit, the newcomer was not without merits as it "not only allowed literary scholars and, to a certain extent, also linguists to focus their attention on cultural utterances that had been deemed not worth the effort until then" (18). It also strengthened English Studies' "claims for social relevancy through the inclusion of political agendas which seemed to move the field right back into the centre of contemporary intellectual, political and ethical concerns" (18). With the traditional canon of 'good literature' apparently destroyed by postcolonial, feminist, Marxist, and poststructuralist theories (cf. entries III.4, II.6, II.2.3, and II.4 respectively), cultural studies and its emancipatory project seems to have promised to revive a dwindling discipline: with cultural studies, one was able to explain *why* (ordinary) people read/watched what they actually read/watched, not what they *should* read (and *should not* watch).

**Fall.** Such rise in relevance was not to last, however. Even though cultural studies might have had its time providing giddy "excitement" and "interesting perspectives" (Nünning and Schlaeger 18), its unorganised descriptions of the ordinary should be shown the door now in order to make room once again for more serious matters. The argument is more suggestive than logical, resting on little backed premises, but obvious nonetheless: a) cultural studies invaded what "was once a more or less unified philological discipline" about "three

decades ago" (8), b) since then, cultural studies lost its "relevancy and prestige" (18) outside English Studies; ergo: English Studies spiralled into "uncontrolled diversification and fragmentation" (18). Although the authors are quick to add that "there is probably no direct causal link" (18) between the rise (and fall) of cultural studies and the demise of English Studies, the chronological correlation, and especially the fact that no other possible causes are considered, suggest otherwise. Finally, the question of (British) Cultural Studies becomes the question of the future of English Studies (in Germany): "Quo vadis, *Anglistik*?" (7)

**Outlook.** The authors are cautious when it comes to suggesting how to restore unity, order, and coherence once cultural studies has been dismissed. The final lines of the 'argument' against cultural studies, however, offer us at least an inkling of what they consider to be the centre of English Studies when they speak of "English Studies and other modern philologies" (Nünning and Schlaeger 18). English Studies, it appears, is essentially a study of words (and reason), i.e. texts, and as neither Diana nor Madonna nor ManU are especially famous for primarily textual outputs, they should not be studied by philologists. And indeed, they should not. If we keep defining English Studies as 'philology,' there are good reasons to exclude Madonna, Diana, and the rest of the ladies from the playing field—and return, hardened through the experience of crisis, to the more serious and reasonable utterances of Byron, Dickens and Eliot. The more interesting question, however, is whether English Studies should really (still) be considered a **philological enterprise**. The term might, although even that is doubtful, give a home to both Literary Studies and Linguistics, but it surely excludes cultural studies in any meaningful sense—that is, in a sense that goes beyond understanding 'culture as text' (Huck and Schinko).

Instead of suggesting a restorative solution to the problem of English Studies by bringing philology in line against cultural studies, I would like to suggest a model for the study of culture(s) that might not threaten, but instead stimulate English Studies. Such a model would not aim at providing (idealist and normative) orientation in an ever more complex society (Frühwald et al.); nor would it content itself with mere (empiricist and arbitrary) descriptionism. Rather, a methodological examination of **contingency** as modern society's defining attribute (Luhmann, *Observations*) could disclose the interdependency of **meaning** and **materiality** for every world-observing **actor**, reveal latent potentialities, and create new possibilities. In order to develop such a future model

of English Studies as cultural (media) studies, I want to go back to the beginnings of cultural studies in Britain.

## 2.2 | A Cultural History of Cultural Studies

Cultural studies began with an attack against the traditional canon of English Studies as it was represented in the work of New Critics (cf. section II.1.3). Two texts are commonly identified as the **starting point** of cultural studies: *The Uses of Literacy* by Richard Hoggart, from 1957, and *Culture and Society* by Raymond Williams, published only a year later. Both texts propagate the notion that there is no such thing as an elite culture, but only an elitist view of culture (Lindner, *Stunde* 20); both texts emphasise that (high) *culture* ('arts and learning') and *society* ('a whole way of life') are always interdependent, that *literacy* is a question of *use*, that art is always related to life.

In his introduction to *Culture and Society*, Williams traces back the meaning of the word 'culture' to conclude that whereas "*culture* meant a state or habit of the mind, or the body of intellectual and moral activities, it means now, also, a whole way of life" (xviii). Culture, Williams stresses, is not just Byron, Dickens, Eliot, but everything that gives meaning to people's lives in specific social circumstances—and that could also be Diana, Madonna, or ManU. It does not mean, however, that Byron's poems are *not* culture—they are just not all there is, and they do not mean the same for everyone. And neither does it mean that all cultural products are the same, or that they all have the same function.

From an exclusive **idea of culture** as the "best that has been thought and said in the world" (Arnold 52) Williams moves to an anthropological, inclusive notion. Williams calls this new understanding "the 'social' definition of culture, in which culture is a description of a particular way of life, which expresses certain meanings and values not only in art and learning but also in institutions and ordinary behaviour" (*Long Revolution* 41). Consequently, society can no longer be divided into a cultivated bourgeoisie and an unrefined lower class—and 'high' cultural products could no longer hold to represent all of British culture.

It is this objection against a narrow definition of culture as a collection of great works and the demand for the recognition of working class life as

being 'cultural' that gave rise to the project of cultural studies. While such an enlarged notion of culture might appear to us today as a sound *theoretical* construct, it nonetheless emerged from a vital personal *experience* of difference and a subsequent demand for a *practice* of recognition. And it is this experience of cultural difference (and unity) that, above all, gave momentum to the emergence of cultural studies. Cultural studies, from the beginning, was more than just an academic project.

Hoggart formulates the particular social and psychological conditions of '**scholarship boys**' in a chapter of *The Uses of Literacy*. Although, as Hoggart points out, there are 'scholarship boys' who feel comfortable in their new environment, a great number of 'boys' depart from their original (working class) milieu without ever fully arriving—and subsequently feeling at home—anywhere else. Instead, they are stuck "at the friction-point of two cultures" (225). Aspiring to social advancement and being dissociated from his family to a certain degree, the 'scholarship boy' can no longer fully identify with working class val-

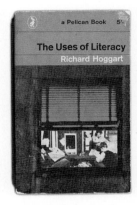

Hoggart's study was one of the starting points of Cultural Studies.

---

**Focus on Early Cultural Studies**

In order to understand the relation between theory, experience, and practice it is helpful to look at Williams and Hoggart's **life-narratives**, which reveal similar social experiences. **Hoggart**, born in Leeds in 1918, grew up in a working class district with his grandmother, who supported his educational efforts that would lead to a scholarship for the University of Leeds (Lindner, "Hoggart" 165–6). **Williams** was born into a Welsh family in an agrarian environment in 1921; his father was a railway worker, but the rest of his family had been working on farms for generations ("Culture is Ordinary" 3–4). Like Hoggart, Williams was the first person in his family to come into contact with higher education, earning himself a **scholarship** to Cambridge. They both represented a new generation of British intellectuals of the 1950s who came from a working class environment and attended secondary schools and then (elite) universities on a scholarship. Various political, social, and economic changes in post-WWII Britain made these careers possible (e.g. Education Act 1944), as well as international developments (e.g. Stalinism, Cold War) (Winter). What I want to look at here are the intellectual consequences of such careers (Bromley, Lindner, *Stunde*, and Sommer, "From Cultural Studies").

ues (integrity, solidarity), but neither wholeheartedly adopt middle-class values (betterment, individuality).

Williams seems to overcome this inability to relate acquired knowledge to working class experience and, apparently, combines the two parts of his identity. Nevertheless, since he has moved away from his social origins but still identifies with the working class, he feels located in a "border country" ("Culture is Ordinary" 7). The double affiliation to these two cultures, without fully belonging to either, makes Williams a 'cultural hybrid' who is able to analyse working class culture from within but with the attitude of an outsider (Lindner, *Stunde* 25). This outside perspective on the familiar seems to be the essence of Williams' and Hoggart's intellectual productivity (Williams, "Future" 152, 156).

Rolf Lindner, an ethnologist of Western culture, argues that **working class culture** could be lived without reflecting that it actually is a form of *culture* because it has traditionally been thought of as a *natural* state of being (*Stunde* 46)—in contrast to the cultivated, or rather: civilised middle and upper class. It is the comparison of one's own habits with another's, however, that enables self-reflexivity, and only the 'scholarship boys' had the required cognitive competence to bring their individual experience to bear on theory. The autobiographic parallels in Hoggart's and Williams' career form a generational theme that made itself felt not only in the academic world, but in the fields of political and artistic activities, too (Lindner, *Stunde* 27, 36). Their position in-between two cultures provided this generation with the potential to see the community they left with different eyes (92–93). Artists and academics alike were able to express the specificity of working class culture in the academic and artistic vocabulary of the traditional cultural elite—and demand recognition for a culture that hitherto had been neglected at best, and denigrated at worst.

### 2.2.1 | Marginalised Expressions of Culture

As a consequence of such experiences, the **objects of research** in cultural studies pre-eminently used to be cultural groups that were socially underrepresented, as well as cultural products that had formerly been excluded from the canon of English Studies (Hall, "Emergence" 21). The aim of cultural studies was to bring recognition to marginalised expressions of culture, and to recognise these expressions as cultural in the first place. Here was a generation of scholars who had to find out that huge parts of their lived experience were not represented in the academic world—and that those works that were present were analysed by New Critics without reference to "those social, cultural, ideological, regional, and generational" (Weimann 261) forces that shaped their form and content. Williams and Hoggart had experienced first-hand that one reads texts differently according to one's social background, and that one chooses different cultural products according to one's social environment, one's habits, rather than one's intellectual capacity. As a consequence, both bringing new texts into the classroom and explaining old texts differently, but also understanding the formation of different cultural groupings that determine one's taste in and appreciation of cultural products, became the central objectives of cultural studies.

**Cultural contact** as experienced by Williams and Hoggart is the prerequisite for a culture to be recognised as a 'culture' at all (Baecker 16): neither the bourgeoisie nor the working class were considered (contingent) cultures before they met on equal terms—however cultivated they might have been; rather, they were considered as more or less civilised. Varying forms of behaviour, however

---

**Definition**

While → culture is often used synonymously with the term 'arts,' another, anthropological tradition understands culture to refer to a structured collective of humans. **E. B. Tylor**, for example, defined culture as "that complex whole which includes knowledge, belief, art, morals, law, custom, and any other capabilities and habits acquired by man as a member of society" (1:1). However, as **Gregory Bateson** has shown, culture is not a given set of characteristics defining social groups, but a means of comparing, distinguishing and thereby first of all creating these groups. Cultures, thus, are contingent constructions. **Raymond Williams**, finally, emphasises that "we use the word culture in [...] two senses: to mean a whole way of life—the common meanings; to mean the arts and learning—the special processes of discovery and creative effort. Some writers reserve the word for one or the other of these senses; I insist on both, and on the significance of their conjunction" ("Culture is Ordinary" 4). To be more precise, Williams actually distinguishes three aspects of culture: (a) material artefacts, (b) observable social behaviour (e.g. institutions, habits), and (c) the unobservable and not yet fully figured 'mentality' behind this behaviour. To analyse the conjunction of these aspects is a central tenet of cultural studies.

unrealised, are at the same time a prerequisite for recognizing difference. Cultures, consequently, become relative terms: their existence and their identity rely on the chosen reference group: this could be a class, a nation, a gender, a religion, a region, an ethnicity, etc. Cultural studies, consequently, came into being when culture, as a level of comparability between compared groups, was discovered in cultural contact.

The insistence on culture in the anthropological sense opened English Studies (in Great Britain) to new concerns: **cultural difference** and the **power relations** that govern the relations between different cultures on the one hand, and the relation between **cultural texts** and **lived experience** on the other. The anthropological sense of culture made the study of cultural products (books, films, etc.) by no means obsolete: Williams, for example, develops an interest in the complex relations between what he calls "structures of feeling"—defined "as social experiences *in solution*, as distinct from other social semantic formations which have been *precipitated* and are more evidently and more immediately available" (*Marxism and Literature* 133–34)—and cultural products, that is, between "meanings and values as they are actively lived and felt" (132) on the one hand, and concrete cultural products such as texts and films on the other. While for Williams culture encompasses not only material artefacts, but also the observable social behaviour and the underlying unobservable 'mentality' (see box), it is the relation between all of these aspects that is central to his vision of cultural studies.

## 2.2.2 | The Centre for Contemporary Cultural Studies

The position on the margins of culture, or rather: in the contact zone of cultures, applies to many who worked for the Centre for Contemporary Cultural Studies in (the marginalised city of) Birmingham, which was founded in 1964 by Richard Hoggart (Hall, "Emergence" 12). **Stuart Hall**, Hoggart's assistant and successor as director of the CCCS, shifted the focus of cultural studies away from cultural products in the sense of 'arts and learning' towards more sociological questions, where cultural products play a vital, but nonetheless secondary role. Hall was born in Jamaica of African descent and moved to Britain in the early 1950s as

**Focus on the CCCS**

The **Centre for Contemporary Cultural Studies (CCCS)** at the University of Birmingham was founded in 1964 by Richard Hoggart. Its establishment helped to broaden the scope of English Studies beyond the arts to include sociological questions. A number of key figures in British Cultural Studies, such as Hoggart, Stuart Hall, Dick Hebdige, Angela McRobbie, and Paul Gilroy were associated with the CCCS and strongly influenced the discipline through their work. The CCCS was closed in 2002.

part of the Windrush generation; again, a scholarship paved his way to study in Oxford, and once again, the experience of cultural difference led to a theoretical interest in culture (Interview 13). Hall, after studying English Literature in Oxford, went on to become professor of sociology at the Open University and president of the British Sociological Association; with him the CCCS moved from the English Department to that of Sociology. Rather than looking for a (lost) working class culture, Hall's research concentrated on the role of the mass media in organising society and the (active) role of the audience in consuming popular culture. Central to Hall's concern became the question of how cultural products contributed to the constitution of a **hegemonic culture**—a culture, that is, which convinces people to act according to an ideology that is not necessarily beneficial to their own life without coercing these people (by force).

Several graduates from the CCCS expanded the field of cultural studies in important directions. **Paul Willis** introduced ethnographic methods to study the resistance of subcultures to hegemonic culture; these new research methods (participant observation, interviewing) made it possible to highlight the appropriations of cultural products in actual use. **Dick Hebdige** concentrated on those material expressions of youth and subcultures that subverted the official, hegemonic use; such recognition of subcultures opened the way for understanding the heterogeneity of any culture/society. **Paul Gilroy** focused on ethnic representations of national identity and the marginalisation of migrant identities, criticizing especially the (outdated) idea of the Empire. **Angela McRobbie** emphasised the relevance of (hierarchical) gender relations for youth and other cultures. Consequently, when the CCCS was finally closed in 2002, fields of research included the role of popular culture and mass media in the (hegemonic) formation of society; the ways in which gender, ethnic, and class habits, but also experiences of

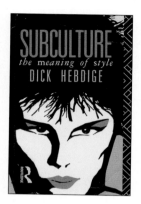

Dick Hebdige put the focus on subcultures.

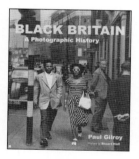

Paul Gilroy pioneered the study of black life in Britain.

sexual orientation, age, and ability structure power relations within society; possibilities of resistance to hegemonic culture. While cultural studies began with an agenda of recognition, it soon had to put questions of identity and difference at the centre of research. From now on, (representational) identity politics rule: if culture is a **construct**, it can be made and re-made.

Arrival in Germany. It is in this later form that (British) Cultural Studies arrived in Germany. When Jürgen Kramer and Bernd Lenz welcomed cultural studies in their inaugurating editorial to the newly founded *Journal for the Study of British Cultures*, they characterised it as follows: "It has been predominantly, but by no means exclusively, concerned with analytical categories (such as class, 'race'/ethnicity, gender, nation/nationality, language, generation) and with signifying processes, above all the mass media and their wide-spread cultural products. Thus, its main objective has been to analyse social and signifying processes on the one hand and processes of identity formation on the other" (5). As a consequence, the authors recommend that "Departments of English and American Studies" incorporate cultural studies of the following form "in their research and teaching" (5): "The objects of Cultural Studies in research and teaching can be grouped under three headings:—social processes (historical developments, political institutions, the economy etc.);—signifying processes (the arts, the media, life styles etc.);—processes of identity formation (mentalities, social roles, norms and values etc.)" (4). It is this wide definition of cultural studies that came to be viewed as

a cause of disorder and fragmentation only a decade later by Nünning and Schlaeger.

Criticisms. There are a number of criticisms that have been brought forward against this (later) version of cultural studies: too much emphasis on popular culture without regard to aesthetic concerns (of literature); as a consequence, too much emphasis on contemporary culture, which is, unfortunately, dominated by popular culture, and a subsequent lack of historiography; a "politically (and ideologically) correct type of moralism" (Weimann 264) instead of a scientific methodology and a sound theoretical framework. Even the most prominent figure within British Cultural Studies, Stuart Hall, seems to be weary of the direction in which cultural studies is heading: "I really cannot read another cultural studies analysis of Madonna or *The Sopranos*" (Interview 29). Why? Because it is too political (i.e. 'left'), too populist, too contemporary, too un-scientific, too disorderly? No. Hall's disappointment in the state of the discipline stems from quite different expectations. Hall is concerned by the fact that "cultural studies ceased to be troubled by the grubby worldliness [...], the worldliness in which culture has always to exist" (Interview 28). Cultural studies, it seems, had come full circle: where the New Critics had ignored culture as a 'whole way of life' because they believed literary texts to exist independently of such life, the '**New Culturalists**' seem to think they can ignore culture as a 'whole way of life' because everything is a text anyway; in the end, these practitioners of cultural studies turn out to think as a-historically (and a-materially) as their predecessors.

## 2.3 | Cultural Studies in Germany as Discipline and/or as Perspective

If the objects of cultural studies in Germany are to be all those things that Kramer and Lenz (5) enlist, many have to practice cultural studies: historians, political scientists, economists, art historians, musicologists, sociologists, anthropologists, ethnologists, etc. Since the so-called **cultural turn**, everything that used to be humanities (*Geisteswissenschaften*) has been remodeled as some sort of cultural studies (*Kulturwissenschaften*): everything that humans create (artefacts), or even think (mentalities) or do (actions), is culture. In this rather unspecific sense, 'cultural studies' does not so much denominate a discipline, but a perspec-

tive—a perspective that can shed more or less light on (nearly) everything. However, if *Kulturwissenschaft* wants to be anything more than *Geisteswissenschaft*'s new clothes, it has to provide a third space rather than an alternative (Eagleton 4–5, Stierstorfer 11): instead of looking for empirically observable laws (*Naturwissenschaft*) or philosophical ideas and subjective intentions (*Geisteswissenschaft*), the cultural turn suggests that one look for **contingent patterns of meaning** that structure economic, political, and social relations and which are *articulated* (Hall, "On Postmodernism and Articulation") in books, films, paintings,

III. 2.3

Cultural Studies

Cultural Studies
in Germany as Discipline
and/or as Perspective

songs, buildings, billboards, etc. 'Contingency' as a new research paradigm might be able to mediate between the strict opposition of a two-cultures paradigm that sets mind in opposition to matter, subject against object, history against nature, *tekhnè* against *physis*, autonomy against heteronomy, freedom against determination. Under this new perspective, a reformed English Studies would be a sub-discipline of *Kulturwissenschaften*—that sub-discipline that concentrates on the English-speaking world.

On the other hand, however, cultural studies is a **sub-discipline** of English Studies (*Anglistik*). English Studies, then, consists of Literary Studies, Linguistics, and cultural studies, complemented by Language Training and Didactics for those training to become teachers (Sommer, *Grundkurs* 13). Under this paradigm, the manifold tasks that Kramer and Lenz (5) enumerate have, obviously, to be cut down to size, as to attempt all of them from within English Studies would indeed seem a somewhat hubristic enterprise bound to end in dilettantism. The obvious way to scale down cultural studies seems to be to enclose it within the field of philology: "English (cultural) studies in Germany remain [sic] a textual or interpretive science [...]. This emphasis on textual(ised) culture marks the disciplinary boundary between hermeneutic, and historical studies of cultural representation on the one hand and sociological research on the other" (Sommer, "From Cultural Studies" 172). While Williams and Hall worked towards a combination of hermeneutic/historical and sociological research, although with different emphases, many within English Studies re-emphasise this disciplinary boundary.

Using Williams' terminology, one could say that English Studies has tried to open the category of 'arts and learning' to even those objects that are part of a 'whole way of life'—without however trying to approach this 'whole way of life,' i.e. social behaviour, habits and institutions, which are considered to be the object of sociology or anthropology; this way, English Studies was superficially, i.e. in terms of its objects of research, able to renew itself, without, however, having to question its practice of research, i.e. *reading* texts. While, on the surface, English Studies gained relevance through opening itself to cultural studies, it stretched its traditional framework without being willing to renew its own foundation.

**Solutions.** Practically, the conundrum that English Studies is as much a sub-discipline of a general *Kulturwissenschaften* as cultural studies is a sub-discipline of English Studies has led to a number of solutions. One attempt can be found in accumulating the various disciplines that study the culture of Britain (or the USA) in an interdisciplinary centre. The *Großbritannienzentrum* in Berlin—similar to the *John F. Kennedy Institut für Nordamerikastudien*—brings together historical, political, economic, juridical, literary, and linguistic studies concentrating on British culture. To think of cultural studies as a discipline is not necessary according to this conception, as it becomes the perspective under which diverse disciplines collaborate.

However, those forms of Literary Studies that contribute to such collaborations are often understood as a mode of a general cultural studies. Such ***Kulturwissenschaftliche Literaturwissenschaft*** ('cultural studies literary studies') analyses literary works as "media expressions through which a culture becomes observable" (Nünning and Sommer 19; my trans.) and concentrates on a text's relations to its con*text*, the 'mentalities' in which it is embedded, and the political, economic, and social circumstances that determine its form. Less often, *Kulturwissenschaftliche Literaturwissen-*

## Focus on Textuality and Representation

Cultural studies within English Studies is bound to analyse "**culture as text**," that is, textual manifestations of British cultures, whereby films and even "the internet" and architecture are also considered "texts" (Sommer, *Grundkurs* 5, 65, 85). It is such limited understanding of both **texts as (cultural)** *representations*, waiting to be hermeneutically/semiotically interpreted, and sociological research, which is apparently coming to its conclusions without interpreting culture, that makes a new conceptualisation of the discipline difficult. If anything, it is the inability to adopt "non-representational theories" (Thrift) that might lead to a "loss of prestige of our discipline." "Representation," however, made it possible for Literary Studies to allow cultural studies perspectives into its field without fundamentally changing its approach. The common defence against cultural studies by Literary Studies proponents can be summarised as follows: "critics of sociological approaches to popular culture point to methodology as the main problem: English Studies are [sic] not an empirical discipline and thus never concerned with cultural processes *as such*, but a textual science concerned with the analysis and interpretation of *representations*, of those processes" (Sommer, "From Cultural Studies" 179–80). 'Representations,' in this approach, seem to be easily separated from 'cultural processes as such'—as if representations were not part of cultural processes, as if 'representations,' could exist without being cultural artefacts, not only re-presenting 'cultural processes' after the fact, but forming and prefiguring them by laying out models, schemata, scripts, distinctions, values, etc.—as if representations, even more importantly, were not *present* in cultural processes.

*schaft* examines the effects of literature, of its canonization and tradition, on culture and society. What it does not consider is the presence of literature in cultural processes. Cultural studies (as opposed to 'cultural studies literary studies'), under this paradigm, is to deal with everything that is not literature: TV, cinema, video games, pop music, etc.—within the methodological and theoretical framework of literary studies, however. In this way, apparently, English Studies could regain relevancy without getting its hands dirty at the 'grubby worldliness' of culture.

## 2.4 | Cultural Studies, *Kulturwissenschaft*, and *Medienwissenschaft*

In German-speaking countries, the study of culture had a tradition of its own long before the advent of British Cultural Studies in the 1980s. Philosophers and sociologists discussed and analysed the role of culture in society since at least the late eighteenth century (Kittler; Böhme et al.). While there is no space here to recapitulate this story, I want to highlight one specific moment in this history that shares some significant features with the British developments in the late 1950s. In the 1920s, building on the groundbreaking work by sociologists of culture like Georg Simmel and Max Weber, a group of (secular) Jewish intellectuals brought together various ideas then circulating and, although not a 'school' in the narrow sense, created a research perspective that might be able to add to the study of culture what cultural studies might lack: **history** and **materiality**. Like their British working class counterparts, these researchers also argued from the margins of cultures and disciplines.

Ernst Cassirer, a professor of philosophy in Hamburg before the Nazis forced him to emigrate to New York, shifted attention away from the study of mind (*Geisteswissenschaften*) to that of cultural expressions. In his central three-volume work *Die Philosophie der symbolischen Formen* (1923–1929), Cassirer emphasises the active role of **symbolic forms** (art, language, myths, law, etc.) in the construction of the (meaningful) world humans inhabit. Cultural products were no longer thought of as either representations of universal ideas or subjective expressions of the human mind, but as an emergent level in the organisation of cultural patterns; culture, here, is not only something produced, but also something productive.

Walter Benjamin, like his successors at the CCCS, was a bold trespasser of disciplinary boundaries, writing on literature, film, art, shopping arcades, and street lighting alike. Following Cassirer, Benjamin highlights the **constructive role of media**: "The way in which human perception is organised—the medium in which it occurs—is conditioned not only by nature but by history" (23). In his studies of literature and film, Benjamin emphasises especially the role of technological media (the printing press, the cinematic apparatus) in the production and reception of cultural products: the same story told by an oral narrator or read in a novel is no longer the same story, the mechanically reproduced image no longer the same as the original painting. Media change what we see in cultural products, and, consequently, how we see the world. It is not only the materiality of media and its influence on signifying processes that Benjamin highlighted, but the importance of the material world in general (street lamps, shopping malls) in the creation of cultural meaning. As a consequence, the study of culture becomes reciprocal: the very concepts that we use to interpret the semantics of cultural products are formed by the media that bring these into existence. A safe vantage point from which to observe such contingent developments becomes as hard to find as a place outside history—or culture. Media, in the basic sense developed by Benjamin, are the very places where meaning and materiality are forever intricately interwoven.

---

**Key Texts: German *Kulturwissenschaft***

**Ernst Cassirer,** *Die Philosophie der symbolischen Formen* (3 vols., 1923–1929)
**Walter Benjamin,** "Das Kunstwerk im Zeitalter seiner technischen Reproduzierbarkeit" (1936)
**Walter Benjamin,** *Das Passagenwerk* (1927–1940, unfinished)
**Siegfried Kracauer,** *Die Angestellten* (1930)
**Aby Warburg,** *Der Bilderatlas MNEMOSYNE* (posthumous, 1929)
**Theodor W. Adorno** and **Max Horkheimer,** *Dialektik der Aufklärung* (1944/1947)

**Siegfried Kracauer**, too, began to analyse the everyday worlds of urban entertainment. Like Benjamin, with whom he collaborated at the *Frankfurter Zeitung* throughout the 1920s, Kracauer was a keen observer of everyday culture, writing about film, design, advertising, tourism, cabaret, architecture, dime novels, and related topics; like Benjamin, and like Williams and Hall, too, Kracauer was looking for ways of renewing Marxist thought, adding cultural forces, values, and ideologies, to those of history and economy. It was of central importance to Kracauer, therefore, to find a method of analysis that made possible the combination of empirical observations and theoretical approaches that guide such observations. For him, the **study of everyday culture** is more political than any explicitly political critique dedicated to "extreme cases—war, crude miscarriages of justice, the May riots, etc." (Kracauer 101). Only in the study of everyday culture can the reflexivity of meaning and materiality, each forming the other, be observed. The tube-stations, shopping malls, and amusement parks Kracauer studies could be read as 'symptoms' of an age; more importantly, however, the media and materialities observed condition the very possibilities of interpreting them. The objects that Kracauer examines are not only (performative) signs, but media in the formative sense that Benjamin emphasised.

Such reciprocal determinations within an emergent and contingent culture can neither be studied solely by pure empirical observation nor without it. Kracauer's description of a **methodology** particular to the study of culture seems to me as fresh and important today as it must have been in 1930, and therefore worth quoting at length:

> For a number of years now, reportage has enjoyed in Germany the highest favour among all types of representation, since it alone is said to be able to capture life unposed. Writers scarcely know any higher ambition than to report; the reproduction of observed reality is the order of the day. A hunger for directness that is undoubtedly a consequence of the malnutrition caused by German idealism [read today: French theory, C. H.]. Reportage [read today: philology, C. H.], as the self-declaration of concrete existence, is counterposed to the abstractness of idealist thought, incapable of approaching reality through any mediation. But existence is not captured by being at best duplicated in reportage. The latter has been a legitimate counterblow against idealism, nothing more. For it merely loses its way in the life that idealism cannot find, which is equally unapproachable for both of them. [...] Certainly life must be observed for it to appear. Yet it is by no means contained in the more or less random observational results of reportage; rather, it is to be found solely in the mosaic that is assembled from single observations on the basis of comprehension of their meaning. (32)

'Observations' and 'comprehension,' 'sociological research' and 'hermeneutic studies,' here, are no longer oppositions, but different aspects that have to be fruitfully combined if the contingency of culture, based on the possibilities of materiality and the potentialities of meaning alike, is to be studied.

**Aby Warburg**, in whose *Kulturwissenschaftliche Bibliothek* Ernst Cassirer was a regular visitor, worked as an art historian who integrated his analyses of paintings in a context of a wider visual culture that includes press photography, advertising, and stamps. His examinations were crossing cultural boundaries between high and low, and also between regional cultures. Equally important, however, was his diachronic view of culture, revealing the forgetting and remembering (cf. entry II.11), the repression and canonisation of figures and motives through the ages. This attention to the work of memory has become central to the study of culture in Germany. (After Warburg's death in 1929, his library was transported to London in order to save it from the Nazis.)

**Theodor W. Adorno and Max Horkheimer**, who collaborated with Walter Benjamin at the *Institut für Sozialforschung*, continued the analysis of popular culture after the war, albeit with a different impetus, in their famous *Dialektik der Aufklärung* (1944/1947). Horkheimer and Adorno, equally under the influence of the Nazi-propaganda that drove them to emigrate to the USA and the Hollywood schmaltz that welcomed them, identify the mass media and the 'culture industry' as purely conservative forces that promote the values of a capitalistic society and dupe consumers into passive acceptance of such a state. It is this negative opposition of mass culture to folk culture that became one of the stepping stones for (British) Cultural Studies.

**'German Media Theory', Old and New.** All in all, the *Kulturwissenschaftler* of the 1920s and 1930s had discovered many of the same topics that British Cultural Studies highlighted in the 1950s and 1960s: (popular) culture, mass media, visual forms, power, practice, marginalisation. More than their British counterparts, they focused on the materiality and the **formative powers of media**, but also on the historicity of cultural forms. Following this lead, German Studies developed its own branch of *Medienkulturwissenschaft* (e.g. Siegfried J. Schmidt, Friedrich Kittler, Hartmut Böhme), emphasising the role of mediality in all forms of culture; mediality, therefore, goes beyond the study of contemporary mass media (cf. entry

III.5). But it is not only in Germany that the role of media is granted a more prominent place in the study of culture. Warner and Siskin, after their pleading for "Stopping Cultural Studies," suggest an engagement with (historical) media in a section of their essay entitled 'Starting.' Also, *New Cultural Studies*, a collection of a self-proclaimed 'new generation' of (British) Cultural Studies proponents (Hall and Birchall), suggests, amongst other things, 'German Media Theory' as an important contributor to a new form of cultural studies.

## 2.5 | Theory and Methodology of Cultural (Media) Studies

**Remodeling British/English Studies.** That "[c]ultural studies has not paid much attention to the classical questions of research methods and methodology" (Barker 31) is a claim so often repeated that some scholars have started to celebrate it as an achievement of freedom. Today, however, the study of culture can no longer claim a marginal position that would justify a consequent preference for exploratory, eclectic, and politically engaged studies. Thus, if the study of culture is to have a future within English Studies, its central concerns and methodologies should be clarified. The aim of this section, then, is to remodel British/English Studies (*Anglistik*) as a form of cultural studies in which the study of **language**, **literature**, and **media** are three integrated and supplementary sub-disciplines of a discipline that revolves around historical manifestations of a specific cultural area and era. On the basis of those stories of origin narrated above, I will try to sketch the outlines of a possible path into the future of the study of British/English cultures.

The aim of the following section, then, is neither to provide a complete theory of culture nor to provide a comprehensive set of research techniques. Rather, I want to suggest a model of English Studies in general, and **cultural (media) studies within English Studies** especially, that identifies objects of research and provides a frame for possible approaches to these objects; such a theoretical model and methodology is derived from the practice of English Studies rather than a philosophical, sociological, psychological or other (grand) theory that was never devised to deal with culture, let alone cultural products. This is not to say that such theories are not valuable as background knowledge and inspiration for English Studies, or that they cannot enable valuable approaches—they are just not useful as a theoretical framework for English Studies, I think. Theory, here, is not a master-narrative (Marxism, psychoanalysis, deconstruction; cf. entries II.2.3, II.7, and II.4) which the study of literature and other cultural products can only confirm, or not; rather, this theoretical model is to provide nothing more, and nothing less, than a framework for open-ended research questions. That such a theoretical model is not without its own premises, that it is not neutral, goes without saying; what these premises are shall be elaborated in the following.

My definition of English Studies (*Anglistik*) begins with an acknowledgement that it is part of cultural studies in the general sense of *Kulturwissenschaften*. Its aim is to provide observations of everyday (signifying) practices giving meaning to social life, in so far as these practices are condensed and manifested in linguistic and non-linguistic media. If culture is made up of the various social processes whereby humans make sense of their worlds, one way to access these meanings is their (iterative, symbolic) communications. Hence, culture goes beyond art and includes all social practices through which individuals interpret and define their worlds and find their place in it. English Studies' objects of analysis and interpretation are contingent and condensed manifestations of historically and culturally specific processes of creating, disseminating, transferring, and regulating meaning; particular attention is given to the material and media conditions of these communicative manifestations.

These objects of research are termed "**cultural condensations**" (Beck 48) here, rather than continuing the hypostatization that comes with the term 'cultural product.' Cultural condensations are not solely 'works' produced by individual artists, but visually, audibly, and haptically perceptible formations of and within culture; nonetheless, English Studies concentrates on lasting condensations rather than transitory formations, such as dances or similar rituals (Posner 51). 'Cultural condensations' are related to those *precipitations* that Williams distinguishes from culture *in solution*; in the terms of systems theory, condensations are tight couplings of those elements of culture that remain unobservable in their usual state of loose coupling (Luhmann, *Gesellschaft* 198–201). Only in the form of tight couplings, i.e. *condensations*, can culture be disseminated, transferred, and negotiated.

The focus of research in English Studies lies on revealing the **constructedness** of traditions and knowledge regimes (cf. section II.4.2) as well as of personal and collective identities, that is, to disclose the processual character of the condensation of meaning in its historical and cultural variability as well as their functions and effects. The tight couplings of cultural elements, *articulations* in Stuart Hall's sense, feed back on the culture from which they emerge. (When trying to understand such processes, however, it is obligatory to consider one's own historically and culturally specific observer position.)

The purpose of these (second-order) observations and reconstructions is to help society understand itself by teaching individuals how to interpret those cultural condensations that form their identities, and which create the very horizons that shape these interpretations. At best, such studies can enable students to gain sovereignty over their culture, to realise the contingency of its state and to envision alternatives. Central to English Studies, therefore, is the education of students who can transfer the results of such reflections back into society, as teachers or cultural workers in general. (Complex didactic, instructive, and communicational skills and proficiencies are, of course, prerequisites for such transfer.)

English Studies concentrates on processes of creating, disseminating, and regulating meaning in English-speaking cultural areas (for an example see entry IV.5), but also considers the effects of the acculturation of cultural condensations from Great Britain in other cultural areas, especially Germany. It draws on several disciplinary approaches (cf. the respective entries in this volume):

**Linguistics** concentrates on the development, structure, and use of the English language, its historical and cultural variability as well as the regulating processes that determine these variations and the cultural identities these engender. As language is key to communication and consequently constitutive to the formation of culture, linguistics is key to the study of culture—a culture of which one is, qua language, always already a part.

**Literary Studies** focuses on textual communications and their relations to other media. Special attention is given to fictional texts that enable the exploration of alternative or hitherto unrealised interpretations of reality; such traditions, knowledge regimes, and identities are to be analysed in relation to their specific historical, political, institutional, and social contexts. In order to understand these relations to heteronomous forces, literary studies concentrates on the autonomous structures of texts, the specific forms, techniques, and traditions of texts that enable the recognition of alien perspectives and the revelation of new ones. As literature reflects everyday uses of language, and as few other cultural condensations know a similar history of autonomous structures, the study of literature has an important position within English Studies, both historically and methodologically.

**Cultural Media Studies**, as the third component of English Studies, concentrates on multimedia cultural condensations, building on the semantic and textual work of Linguistics and Literary Studies, including visual, auditory, and material formations as well. Emphasizing the media-material condition and the pragmatic dimension of cultural condensations, cultural media studies is concerned with the technological, economic, institutional, political, ecological, and receptive determinants of cultural condensations as well as the reciprocal determinants of materiality, semantics, and pragmatics. Rather than concentrate on aesthetic objects only, as literary studies does, cultural media studies also

---

**Focus on Questions of English Studies**

English Studies as *Kulturwissenschaft* analyses the functions of cultural condensations, that is, the creation, negotiation, dissemination, affirmation, regulation, and negation of cultural norms and values through cultural artefacts. Artefacts, thus, can be analysed as **cultural condensations**, if they can be related to the creation, negotiation, affirmation, and negation of cultural norms and values. While culture is its *raison d'être*, English studies, according to this model, takes cultural condensations as its methodological vantage point. Such cultural condensations are then questioned

- for their embeddedness within social practices,
- for their relations to (imaginary) horizons of norms and values, and
- for their material determinants.

These aspects of cultural condensations are examined in order to determine their function for the meaning-producing recipient-consumer:

- Why does an individual turn to a specific artefact?
- What can it tell him/her?
- How can it influence him/her?

To understand this, one also has to understand the socio-cultural environment and the material basis of cultural condensations—but only in so far as they are relevant for the study of the relation between cultural meaning, materiality, and (human) actors.

examines the *aisthetic* dimension of our everyday environment (Böhme 17).

There are, of course, other forms of cultural studies possible (Johnson)—but this is the one I see most promising for evolving the traditions and qualifications of English Studies. Cultural practices less condensed, less mediated, less linguistic, and less permanent are the objects of ethnology, anthropology, sociology, and others.

Studying cultural condensations

Cultural condensations, under this definition, are analysed because they promise access to the **social self-interpretation** of specific groups at particular times. In this sense, they could be described as second-order mirrors (Stichweh 87). Here, individuals are not directly looking at themselves, i.e. they cannot read books or see films and simply identify what their culture is like; instead, they have to look at others looking at others and deduce (speculatively) the average value of other people's observations to form a 'compact impression' (Luhmann, *Gesellschaft* 597) of the world they live in. While sense-making is an individual process, it cannot be practised alone; through **cultural sense-making** the individual is connected to society; the meaning of signs is always already shared. Cultural condensations do not deliver representations of the world, but, at best, a shared interpretation of the world; this way, contingent condensation can provide orientation within contingent cultures. Why certain cultural condensations gain a representative status, and why others are marginalised, is a central research question rather than a starting point.

What is more, cultural condensations are more than mere representations of 'grubby worldliness,' they are **part of this world**. Contrary to a purely (poststructuralist) semiotic point of view, cultural media studies does not hold that "the object is *nothing*," that "it matters little what object is involved" (Baudrillard 63, 64) in the meaning creating processes of a culture. But neither do material objects determine their own meanings autonomously. Instead, such 'things'

participate in social practices just as human beings do. To be sure, these things are 'interpreted' by the human agents in certain ways, but at the same time they are applied, used, and must be handled within their own materiality. [...] 'Things' thus have the status of 'hybrids': On the one hand, they are definitively not a physical world as such, within practices they are socially and culturally interpreted and handled. On the other hand, these quasi-objects are definitively more than the content of cultural 'representations,': they are used and have effects in their materiality. (Reckwitz 208–9)

**Cultural condensations are hybrids of potentiality and actuality, meaning and materiality.** Examples for cultural condensations relevant to English Studies are films, plays, books, but also games, packaging, and buildings, in short: everything that is at the same time part of our world and forms a distinctively structured realm of itself. Cultural condensations neither imitate a forgone world, nor figure the invisible structures of such a world, but participate in it; they are articulations, tight couplings of an unobservable culture. They can, of course, present themselves as mere (fictional) representations, and they can also be received as doing so—in doing so, however, they participate in constituting the very world they claim to re-present. Cultural condensations are products of a culture, but they also produce culture. Whereas culture, however, remains a speculative entity, cultural condensations exist (Konersmann 8). Concentrating on cultural condensations, it becomes necessary to relate meaning and materiality in non-reductive ways, and it is in this sense that Williams' cultural materialism proposes "the analysis of all forms of signification, including [...] writing, within the actual means and conditions of their production" (*Writing in Society* 210); the relation between meaning and materiality, here, is a matter of (historical) contingency, neither necessary nor arbitrary.

New research paradigms, finally, ask for new methodological approaches. Traditional hermeneutic and semiotic procedures form a sturdy basis for analysing the semantics of cultural condensations. However, if one is interested in materialities and practices also, new, empirical methods must be tried that can answer questions about production, circulation, reception, and consumption. The hybrid status of cultural condensations as meaning and materiality (in practice) demands a combination of methods of understanding and explaining. While meaning has to be understood, materiality is open to empirical research, even if only through the archive; the perspective of the actor, finally, can be examined by phenomenological and ethnographic methods as well as reception studies. If we agree that the media-materiality of the cultural condensation informs the very way in which actors interpret it, we will have to employ hermeneutic procedures on the basis of empirical reconstructions of materiality (Koschorke 11). **Contingency** means that every specific cultural formation is neither the way it is by necessity nor arbitrarily so. As a new paradigm for research, contingency demands that we analyse both how something became what it is (*Genesis*) and why it is valued over other possible states (*Geltung*); we have to explain what is and understand which options have remained latent. As there is no causality in the development of cultures, we have to interpret the interpretations that led to its existence; as the development of cultural formations is no pure coincidence, we can trace their path empirically.

Cultural condensations, finally, can be examined according to **three dimensions**. This model (see box), although simplifying matters, should provide orientation to the following explications.

Meaning. First of all, there is the dimension of *meaning*, in the sense of a semiotic figuration that consists of any combination of textual, visual or auditory signs: a detective novel, a Shakespeare drama, a rock album, a video game, a Wordsworth poem, a thriller movie, a dress or a guildhall. Such semiotic figurations, of course, cannot be understood without reference to other diachronic and synchronic 'texts' and contexts. In order to understand a given semiotic figuration it is necessary to know its history, the genre rules it follows and the language regimes it partakes in, and the difference it makes compared to other 'texts' within a given discourse. As semiotic figurations, cultural condensations refer to (possible) worlds, although never directly: every signifier refers to a signified that mediates between sign and world.

Materiality. However, no image, no song, and no book merely refers to something other than itself (*reference*)—they also present themselves in their own existence, they reveal their own *materiality*, although in varying degrees, a dress maybe more so than a poem. Semiotic figurations stand in a double relation to the (material) world. On the one hand, they refer to it. On the other hand, every signified needs a material signifier to be perceivable through the senses. The material mediality that meaning employs to become, however, shapes this very meaning in an act of *mediation*—the words we use to communicate, for example, contribute to what we say as much as to what we think. Only as materiality can texts be stored and disseminated, can they be presented and passed on. Because semiotic figurations need materiality, they become part of economic and technological processes. However, a signifier can only be related to a signified because somebody does this relating; a sign is a sign only for someone: an individual, an *actor*. Consequently, cultural condensations exist

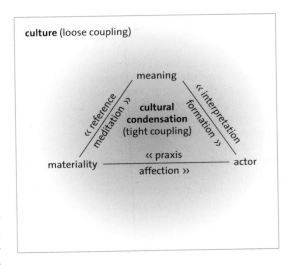

culture (loose coupling)

meaning

« reference
meditation »

**cultural
condensation**
(tight coupling)

« interpretation
formation »

materiality ——— « praxis ——— actor
affection »

Cultural condensations
are the central objects of
a reformed English Studies,
with meaning, materiality,
and actors as their most
relevant aspects.

within the triangular force field of *meaning*, *materiality*, and *actor*.

The actor, of course, does not exist independently of the semantic figuration s/he observes; s/he simultaneously observes ( = follows) the rules of the semantic figuration s/he observes ( = reads), s/he forms what s/he observes and is being formed by it. The actor's very subject position, the scripts, schemata, and distinctions s/he employs in order to *interpret*, are shaped and formed by the semantic figuration s/he consumes (*formation*); 'subjects' interpret cultural condensations and are in turn formed by the culture from which these condensations emerge and to which they contribute. Through the use of such cultural condensations, every actor becomes part of a larger formation, i.e. a particular culture. The actor's individual stance, finally, is a function of culture—which is always social.

What is more, the process of observing is not only a cognitive-intellectual procedure. The **actor as a hermeneutic being** is bound to a specific place and space, to a specific (material) history by the actor's corporeal existence that determines the individuality of his/her interpretations; the stance of the actor is thus both a prerequisite and a consequence of his/her encounter with cultural condensations. The corporeal stance of the actor also ensures that this encounter goes beyond volitional interpretation. As a material artefact, the cultural condensation exists in the same world as the actor, who is *affected* by both the materiality of the signifier and the material world the signified refers to; at the same time, the actor is subject to the visual and aural regimes that cultural condensations pro-

The example of tourist
guidebooks to the
Lake District

duce and partake in. Actors, finally, do not only exist corporeally and consequently re-act affectively to the materiality of the wor(l)d. They also act on and interact with this materiality, handling artefacts according to their specific materiality within specific spatial arrangements and a specific social *praxis*—they scratch with records and use the 'walkman' to find privacy in public places. It is such a triangulation of *meaning, materiality*, and *actor* that can be employed in order to examine *cultural condensations* as articulations of *culture*.

**Exemplarity and Embeddedness.** Such a complex triangulation of cultural condensations can only be performed exemplarily for historically and culturally specific occurrences. To understand *the* British culture, or even *the* English-speaking culture and *the* impact of its cultural condensations on other cultures is a task without end. Rather, the work of cultural condensations and their contribution to the contingency of cultures is to be revealed exemplarily—not at least in order to teach the method of second-order observation. Nonetheless, particular studies are meaningless as long as they are not embedded in a more global perspective that reveals repeating patterns as well as discontinuities over time and across cultures; identity and

difference, as I tried to explain, are matters of comparison. Even something as specific as, for example, tourist guidebooks to the Lake District in the mid-nineteenth century are connected to large-scale social transformations (the emergence of a leisure class), material revolutions (the introduction of the railway system), new mentalities (romanticizing nature), and new social practices (colonial travel). A particular phenomenon cannot be understood without reference to wider developments which in turn can only be revealed through particular analyses. Detailed descriptions have to lead to abstract terminology and theories, as much as such terminology has to be employed to interrogate specific phenomena; at the same time, this terminology has to be refined in this process of interrogation. Central to such hermeneutic procedure, also, is the acknowledgement of the researcher's particular stance: his/her theoretical paradigm, institutional practices, and individual preferences bond the researcher to his/her context in the same way as the actor is bound to his/hers. English Studies in Germany, for example, practices cultural hermeneutics (cf. entry II.2) from a different starting point as do similar endeavours in the U.S. or Great Britain.

## 2.6 | Future Cultural (Media) Studies

The establishment of cultural media studies in the way outlined above within a reformed discipline of English Studies would make it necessary to devise a new curriculum focussing on questions of culture. Linguistics, then, would ask about the role language plays within culture, and how the English language itself has been formed by Anglo-American cultures. Literary studies would ask about the role literature plays within Anglo-American cultures, and how literature itself has been formed by these cultures. Cultural media studies would ask how other cultural condensations (films, video games, music videos, etc.) contribute to Anglo-American cultures, and how they themselves are in turn formed by these cultures. Finally, a **transcultural perspective** would be necessary to understand the formation of differences and identities through comparison. The aim of research and teaching would be to reveal contingencies and enable reflective and refined self-observation. Pragmatic concerns like media literacy or direct political action cannot be central; rather, research

should produce a surplus of meaningful possibilities from which society (politics, protest movements, art, economy) is then to select. That cultural patterns are contingent forms means that they *can* be changed, but not just so—if they have become what they are through history, new cultural patterns have to create their own histories to gain stability.

English Studies after cultural studies—in the sense of: having gone through cultural studies (and poststructuralism) and coming out the better—would neither be a 'study of everything,' nor a return to philology, but the **study of cultural condensations**, both formed by their specific historical circumstances and producing these in turn. In order to be able to do so, English Studies has to employ historical, political, economic, and sociological studies in the way that we use, for example, computers; that is, it has to be able to handle the results of such studies critically, but it does not necessarily have to be able to produce these results itself. Instead of doing the work of historians, economists, sociologists, and others, English Studies has to be able to build on the results of these disciplines. When it comes to cultural condensations, however, English Studies should be able to examine empirically the history, economy, and praxis of such manifestations. Rewarding new research, therefore, will not be possible without a broad knowledge of the findings of relevant related disciplines, a thorough familiarity with the history of one's own discipline, methodological rigour, and theoretical validation.

To establish this will probably take a few (academic) generations—if it ever happens. The task at hand differs greatly from what has been done so far: it is neither another turn asking to look at the same old phenomena (texts) from yet another angle; neither is it about looking at new phenomena (comics, music videos, etc.) from a well-known angle (psychoanalysis, semiotics, etc.). A truly reformed English Studies asks for a completely new form of knowledge that allows those that have acquired it to analyse cultural condensations both as productions and producers of (social) realities. One has to become, as the CCCS required from the beginning, both an expert in culture and society, literary studies and sociology—and, if possible, also in film and art studies, history, ethnology, anthropology, etc. To achieve this daunting task, we not only need a theoretical foundation for the study of culture (which we are getting close to) and a fitting set of methodologies (which are still slow in coming), but also an adequate curriculum and disciplinary setting (which is nowhere yet to be seen).

If you think this is an impossible task, think again, and consider the various fields a medical scientist has to be an expert in: chemistry, biology, physics, psychology, surgical crafts, etc. The medical profession, consequently, asks for a curriculum that seems to be amongst the most demanding: to study humans is considered to be one of the most complex tasks in the world, and students are eager to invest heavily to learn the trade. But if humans are such complex systems, how complex is that which all humans who ever lived have created together, that is, culture? Why should it be less demanding to study cultures than to study humans? And why should it be less rewarding (at least intellectually)?

Just as medicine does not make physics, chemistry, and so on obsolete, the study of (British) cultural condensations does not make obsolete media studies, literary studies, art history, sociology, ethnology, anthropology, economics, etc. Rather, like medicine, using other knowledge systems selectively for the study of humans, the study of cultural condensations uses the aforementioned knowledge systems to understand such cultural condensations and the cultures that create them—or at least to open a space between being made and making, between actuality and potentiality.

*Toward a new form of knowledge*

## Select Bibliography

**Arnold, Matthew.** *Literature and Dogma: An Essay Towards a Better Apprehension of the Bible.* London: Smith, Elder & Co., 1891.

**Baecker, Dirk.** "Globalisierung und kulturelle Kompetenz." *Wozu Kultur?* Ed. Dirk Baecker. Berlin: Kulturverlag Kadmos, 2003. 11–32.

**Barker, Chris.** *Cultural Studies: Theory and Practice.* 3rd ed. Los Angeles: Sage, 2008.

**Bateson, Gregory.** "Culture Contact and Schismogenesis." 1935. *Steps to an Ecology of Mind.* New York: Ballantine 1972. 61–72.

**Baudrillard, Jean.** *For a Critique of the Political Economy of the Sign.* St. Louis: Telos, 1981.

**Beck, Ulrich.** *Ecological Politics in an Age of Risk.* 1988. Trans. Amos Weisz. Cambridge: Polity Press, 1995.

**Benjamin, Walter.** *The Work of Art in the Age of its Technological Reproducibility, and other Writings on Media.* 1936. Ed. Michael William Jennings. Harvard: Harvard University Press, 2008.

**Böhme, Gernot.** *Aisthetik: Vorlesungen über Ästhetik als allgemeine Wahrnehmungslehre.* Munich: Fink, 2001.

**Böhme, Hartmut, et al.** *Orientierung Kulturwissenschaft: Was sie kann, was sie will.* 3rd ed. Reinbek: Rowohlt, 2007.

**Bromley, Roger.** "Cultural Studies gestern und heute." *Cultural Studies: Grundlagentexte zur Einführung.* Eds. Roger Bromley, Udo Göttlich, and Carsten Winter. Lüneburg: zu Klampen, 1999. 9–24.

**Cassirer, Ernst.** *Die Philosophie der symbolischen Formen.* 1923–1929, 3 vols. Hamburg: Meiner, 2010.

**Eagleton, Terry.** *The Idea of Culture.* Oxford: Blackwell, 2000.

**Frühwald, Wolfgang, et al.** *Geisteswissenschaften heute: Eine Denkschrift.* Frankfurt/M.: Suhrkamp, 1991.

**Gilroy, Paul.** *There Ain't no Black in the Union Jack: The Cultural Politics of Race and Nation.* London: Hutchinson, 1987.

**Hall, Gary, and Clare Birchall, eds.** *New Cultural Studies: Adventures in Theory.* Edinburgh: Edinburgh University Press, 2006.

**Hall, Stuart.** "The Emergence of Cultural Studies and the Crisis of the Humanities." *The Humanities as Social Technology* 53 (1990): 11–23.

Hall, Stuart. Interview by Colin MacCabe. *Critical Quarterly* 50 (2008): 12–42.

Hall, Stuart. "On Postmodernism and Articulation: An Interview with Stuart Hall, by Lawrence Grossberg." *Journal of Communication Inquiry* 10.2 (1986): 45–60.

Hebdige, Dick. *Subculture: The Meaning of Style*. London: Methuen, 1979.

Hoggart, Richard. *The Uses of Literacy: Aspects of Working-Class Life with Special Reference to Publications and Entertainments*. 1957. New Brunswick: Transaction Publishers, 1992.

Huck, Christian, and Carsten Schinko. "The Medial Limits of Culture: Culture as Text vs. Text as Culture." *GrenzGänge—BorderCrossings: Kulturtheoretische Perspektiven*. Eds. Gerd Sebald, Michael Popp, and Jan Weyand. Münster: LIT, 2006. 57–71.

Johnson, Richard. "What is Cultural Studies Anyway?" *What is Cultural Studies? A Reader*. Ed. John Storey. London: Arnold, 1998. 75–114.

Kittler, Friedrich. *Eine Kulturgeschichte der Kulturwissenschaft*. Munich: Fink, 2000.

Konersmann, Ralf. *Kulturphilosophie zur Einführung*. Hamburg: Junius, 2003.

Koschorke, Albrecht. *Köperströme und Schriftverkehr: Mediologie des 18. Jahrhunderts*. Munich: Fink, 1999.

Kracauer, Siegfried. *The Salaried Masses: Duty and Distraction in Weimar Germany*. 1930. Trans. Quintin Hoare. London: Verso, 1998.

Kramer, Jürgen, and Bernd Lenz. "Editorial." *Journal for the Study of British Cultures* 1.1 (1994): 3–7.

Lindner, Rolf. "Richard Hoggart (*1918): 'A shabby cat from the council house': *The Uses of Literacy* und das *Centre for Contemporary Cultural Studies*, Birmingham." *Culture Club II: Klassiker der Kulturtheorie*. Eds. Martin Ludwig Hofmann, Tobias F. Kortas, and Sibylle Niekisch. Frankfurt/M.: Suhrkamp, 2006. 164–83.

Lindner, Rolf. *Die Stunde der Cultural Studies*. Vienna: WUV, 2000.

Luhmann, Niklas. *Die Gesellschaft der Gesellschaft*. Frankfurt/M.: Suhrkamp, 1998.

Luhmann, Niklas. *Observations on Modernity*. 1992. Trans. William Whobrey. Stanford: Stanford University Press, 1998.

McRobbie, Angela. *Feminism and Youth Culture*. London: Routledge, 1990.

Nünning, Ansgar, and Jürgen Schlaeger. "Quo vadis, *Anglistik*? Recent Trends in and Challenges for English Studies." *English Studies Today: Recent Developments and New Directions*. Eds. Ansgar Nünning and Jürgen Schlaeger. Trier: WVT, 2007. 7–22.

Nünning, Ansgar, and Roy Sommer. "Kulturwissenschaftliche Literaturwissenschaft: Disziplinäre Ansätze, theoretische Positionen und transdisziplinäre Perspektiven." *Kulturwissenschaftliche Literaturwissenschaft: disziplinäre Ansätze—theoretische Positionen—transdisziplinäre Perspektiven*. Eds. Ansgar Nünning and Roy Sommer. Tübingen: Narr, 2004. 9–31.

Posner, Roland. "Kultursemiotik." *Einführung in die Kulturwissenschaft: Theoretische Grundlagen—Ansätze—Perspektiven*. Eds. Ansgar Nünning and Vera Nünning. Stuttgart: Metzler, 2008. 39–72.

Reckwitz, Andreas. "The Status of the 'Material' in Theories of Culture: From 'Social Structure' to 'Artefacts.'"

*Journal for the Theory of Social Behaviour* 32.2 (2002): 195–217.

Sommer, Roy. "From Cultural Studies to the Study of Culture: Key Concepts and Methods." *English Studies Today: Recent Developments and New Directions*. Eds. Ansgar Nünning and Jürgen Schlaeger. Trier: WVT, 2007. 165–91.

Sommer, Roy. *Grundkurs Cultural Studies / Kulturwissenschaft Großbritannien*. Stuttgart: Klett, 2003.

Stichweh, Rudolf. *Inklusion und Exklusion: Studien zur Gesellschaftstheorie*. Bielefeld: transcript, 2005.

Stierstorfer, Klaus. "Einleitung: Anmerkungen zur Interdisziplinarität der Kulturwissenschaft." *Kulturwissenschaft Interdisziplinär*. Eds. Klaus Stierstorfer and Laurenz Volkmann. Tübingen: Narr, 2005. 9–18.

Thrift, Nigel. *Non-Representational Theory: Space—Politics—Affect*. London: Routledge, 2007.

Tylor, Edward Burnett. *Primitive Culture: Researches Into the Development of Mythology, Philosophy, Religion, Language, Art and Custom*. Vol 1. 1871. Whitefish: Kessinger, 2007.

Warner, William B., and Clifford Siskin. "Stopping Cultural Studies." *Profession* (2008): 94–107.

Weimann, Robert. "Towards a History of Twentieth-Century *Anglistik*: Cultural Studies and the Question of Aims and Methods." *Anglistik: Research Paradigms and Institutional Policies:1930–2000*. Ed. Stephan Kohl. Trier: WVT, 2005. 253–70.

Wiesing, Lambert. "Was sind Medien?" *Was ist ein Medium?* Eds. Stefan Münker and Alexander Roesler. Frankfurt/M.: Suhrkamp, 2008. 235–48.

Williams, Raymond. *Culture and Society: 1780–1950*. London: Chatto & Windus, 1958.

Williams, Raymond. "Culture is Ordinary." 1958. *Resources of Hope: Culture, Democracy, Socialism*. Ed. Robin Gable. London: Verso, 1989. 3–18.

Williams, Raymond. "The Future of Cultural Studies." *The Politics of Modernism: Against the New Conformists*. Ed. Tony Pinkney. London: Verso, 1989. 151–62.

Williams, Raymond. *The Long Revolution*. London: Chatto & Windus, 1961.

Williams, Raymond. *Marxism and Literature*. Oxford: Oxford University Press, 1977.

Williams, Raymond. *Writing in Society*. London: Verso, 1983.

Willis, Paul. *Learning to Labour: How Working-Class Kids Get Working-Class Jobs*. Aldershot: Gower, 1977.

Winter, Rainer. *Kunst des Eigensinns: Cultural Studies als Kritik der Macht*. Weilerswist: Velbrück, 2001.

*Christian Huck*

(Much of section 2 was written with the help of Geneviève Nario-Rivera. An earlier version of the definition of *Anglistik* in section 5, although not the theoretical model, has been devised together with colleagues from both literary studies and linguistics in English and American studies, namely: Lieselotte Anderwald, Ute Berns, Roger Lüdeke, Birgit Neumann, and Erik Redling; they cannot be made responsible, however, for any misgivings in the current revised version. Moreover, I would like to thank Alexander Joachimsmeier, Stefan Bauernschmidt, and Doris Feldmann for valuable comments on earlier drafts of this text.)

# 3 American Cultural Studies

## 3.1 | Beginnings

The recent cultural turn in the humanities provides a belated support for the direction the newly established field of American Studies took after its formation in the 1930s. **American Studies** emerged as a synthesis of intellectual history and literary studies, and from the very beginning, culture was a key concept of the new field—so much so, in fact, that one of its pioneers, Henry Nash Smith, could define American Studies as "the study of American culture" in a programmatic essay entitled "Can American Studies Develop a Method? " Against a then dominant approach in literary studies, the formalism of the New Criticism, scholars in American Studies insisted that literary texts can only be adequately understood and appreciated if they are seen as part of their culture (whereas the New Criticism focused exclusively on the literary text itself; cf. section II.1.3). Intellectual historians had traditionally inquired what traditions and ideas were crucial in forming society. Now they argued that societies gain their identity and cohesion not primarily through ideas but through myths and symbols, that is, **cultural forms**.

Methods of Studying American Culture. Thus, in order to understand American society, one had to focus on its culture. Cultures provide a common horizon for national self-definitions, but they are also realms of individual expression, so that, in studying them, we can gain access to a subjective dimension of social life. However, what is the best way of studying culture? What methods should **American Cultural Studies** (from here on **ACS**) use? In focusing exclusively on the aesthetic autonomy of the literary work of art, literary studies could not provide any viable model. Neither could Marxist or other sociological approaches, because these methods were based on a mirror reflection model (*Widerspiegelungstheorie*) in which culture merely reflects economic and social conditions. Such a concept of culture cannot account for the possibilities of reinterpretation, reconfiguration, and resignification of social phenomena that culture opens up, nor is it able to deal with the expressive dimension of culture. A "**third way**" between the formalism of literary studies and the literalism of sociological content analyses was needed, in which the aesthetic and the social dimension could be meaningfully linked. This analysis should keep in view the social embeddedness of cultural phenomena, while not ignoring their distinct modes of communication and expression. It was one of the major challenges for the newly established ACS to develop a theory and method for such a type of cultural analysis.

Until World War II, an independent study of American culture had not yet been institutionalized at universities, neither in the U.S. nor outside, because American culture was considered **epigonal** and **provincial**. There was a common perception that American society had perverted the idea of culture by an unfettered commercialism, resulting in a standardized mass culture in which culture's potential to serve as a counter-realm of non-instrumental values was betrayed. This verdict was particularly damning in the post-War years in which the U.S. had become the leading power in the West. As long as the U.S. was considered a materialistic society that had no place for culture, it seemed to lack the moral and intellectual authority to act as leader of the "Free World." Thus, American cultural diplomacy actively promoted studies of American culture. But the main inspiration came from left-leaning liberals who wanted to influence American self-perceptions and self-definitions. Their aim was to define an American cultural tradition outside of mass culture, not only to demonstrate that American soci-

**Key Texts**

> Pioneers of American Cultural Studies:
> **Perry Miller,** *The New England Mind* (1939, 1953)
> **F. O. Matthiessen,** *American Renaissance* (1941)
> **Lionel Trilling,** *The Liberal Imagination* (1950)
> Myth and Symbol School:
> **Henry Nash Smith,** *Virgin Land* (1950)
> **R. W. B. Lewis,** *The American Adam* (1955)
> **Leo Marx,** *The Machine in the Garden* (1964)
> **Richard Slotkin,** *Regeneration Through Violence* (1973)

judgments implied decisions about what texts should be introduced into liberal arts curricula in schools and at the university.

The pioneer studies of ACS (see box) can be seen as attempts to identify distinct and representative texts of American culture and to read them as significant expressions of American society. How this can best be done emerged as one of the major challenges for ACS and has become the main issue in a series of debates on the theory and method of the field. A historical reconstruction of the directions these debates have taken and, linked with it, of their competing claims about how a cultural analysis should proceed, appears to be the best way of presenting the different models of cultural analysis that the field has developed. Tracing these developments may also offer the best chance for comparing their respective strengths and weaknesses.

ety had developed a notable culture of its own, but also to strengthen its influence on American society. If culture provided the key to national identity, critical judgments about what should be considered the best and most valuable American culture were of crucial importance, especially since such

## 3.2 | Myth and Symbol School

The first generation of ACS focused on the concepts of myth and symbol as key concepts for understanding American culture. The term still used today for describing their approach is therefore that of the Myth and Symbol School. **Myth** here refers to a foundational narrative that has crucially shaped American national identity. As a synthesis of thought and emotion, such "non-rational" narratives can be more powerful than other forms of national self-definition, because they link descriptive concepts with emotional and imaginary elements. **Symbols** are inherently ambiguous images that can invite intense imaginary engagements due to their semantic openness and indeterminacy. These qualities explain the centrality of myths and symbols in the national imaginary and their amazing resilience even in the face of ideological criticism; although often refuted by fact, myths seem to be immune to criticism and deconstruction (cf. entry II.4), because they articulate beliefs, fantasies, and desires of a culture. For cultural analysis, a focus on myth and symbol can thus be especially rewarding for gaining a deeper understanding of American society and culture.

**American Myths.** The most influential studies of the Myth and Symbol School already evoke central American myths in their titles (see box above). However, contrary to later perceptions, the Myth and Symbol School is not celebrating these myths

uncritically. On the contrary, it focuses on them, because it wants to draw attention to some of the harmful consequences these myths have had for American society—and, in some cases, continue to have: "A people unaware of its myths is likely to continue living by them" (Slotkin 4). For Smith and Leo Marx, a **pastoral agrarianism**, that is, the myth of an unspoilt land that gave Americans the chance for a new beginning, is one of the major reasons why industrialization had not played a central role in American self-descriptions and why Americans rarely took a closer look at the social consequences of the industrial revolution. Richard Slotkin argues that the myth of individual and collective regeneration through violence explains not only the expansion to the American West but also imperial steps beyond national borders to countries like Vietnam. And, as Annette Kolodny claims in her study *The Lay of the Land* (1975), cultural conventions of describing the land as female paved the way for its exploitation and "rape."

**Myths and Society.** In all of these cases, it is the goal of ACS to make Americans aware of the role their own **mythic self-perceptions** have played in shaping American politics and society. However, the Myth and Symbol School does not want to restrict its cultural analysis to such a critique. In studying American culture, it also wants to focus on the work of those writers (like Emerson, Thoreau, Hawthorne, Melville, and Whitman, all authors of the so-called 'American Renaissance'; cf. entry I.3.2) that have problematized the claims of American myths and have thereby established the seeds of an oppositional counter-tradition. These writers do not suppress conflicts and contradictions of a culture but articulate them, often by means of image or symbol, and thereby complicate the perception of myths. For example, when a steamboat destroys the raft on which Huck and Jim lead an idyllic, pastoral existence in Mark Twain's novel *Adventures of Huckleberry Finn*, the novel draws attention to the conflict between **pastoralism and industrialization** in American culture, and creates a tension between the two that undermines any naive belief in progress.

Revealing Hidden Conflicts. In their essay "Literature and Covert Culture," the most ambitious methodological self-description of the Myth and Symbol School, Leo Marx and his co-authors describe an interpretive procedure designed to bring such "hidden" conflicts to light. In official representations, and in popular culture, national myths are usually uncritically affirmed. But on a second, covert level, doubts, fears, and anxieties contradict and undermine the seemingly unambiguous surface. It is therefore not enough to study myths, because they only represent the common belief, not the critical response to it. For the study of **critical responses**, literature can be especially useful in revealing covert patterns of a culture, because it uses images and metaphors, that is, forms that do not simply denote something but carry additional cultural connotations. By doing so, they function as voices of opposition and negation that challenge official American ideology with an emphatic "No! In Thunder" (an expression coined by Melville and often used by the Myth and Symbol School).

The hopes the Myth and Symbol School puts in the negating potential of certain works explains the central role that high literature still plays in their cultural analysis. This would later become one of the major points of criticism, in part because of the reasons offered in defense of this central role: literary texts that had originally been selected for their aesthetic value were now said to also provide "deeper" insights into American culture precisely because of this value. The **aesthetic value** of a work thus becomes its major source of cultural insight; where a text is described as aesthetically valuable, we can assume that it is also especially rewarding for a cultural analysis. Or, as Leo Marx puts it: "I would submit that the argument for the usefulness of *Moby-Dick* in the kind of inquiry I have described is identical with the argument for the intrinsic merit of *Moby-Dick* as a work of literature" (Marx, "American Studies" 89). However, how can Marx be so sure about the "intrinsic merit" of a literary text? Ironically, the criteria are taken from the very formalism ACS wanted to replace, the then dominant New Criticism. Formal elements emphasized by New Critics in order to emphasize the aesthetic autonomy of the literary text—such as irony, paradox, ambiguity, but also patterns of repetition—determine the text's usefulness for a cultural analysis, because they promise to provide access to underlying conflicts and tensions of a culture (Fluck, "Das ästhetische Vorverständnis").

National Identity. Even more important for later assessments of the Myth and Symbol School has been another critical objection that is not so much a methodological but a political one: in trying to describe the American mind or the American character, American society is defined as a homogeneous entity without any inner difference. Myth and symbol are ideally suited for this type of cultural analysis because of their promise to capture the meaning of this entity in one narrative or image. Those texts in which they play a central role are therefore privileged sources for providing "deeper" knowledge about U.S.-America. On the other hand, minority and diaspora cultures are of little interest, because their goal is not to define "America" in terms of a unified national character or identity. Thus, the assumption of a **unified national identity** does not only ignore the multicultural diversity of American society, it also establishes the idea of a national identity as a tacit norm that excludes those subcultural, ethnic, and oppositional groups that, for whatever reason, do not want to accept an exceptionalist definition of the U.S.: "The notion of an all-encompassing American identity, in literature as in society, now appeared not only incomplete but, in its denial of nonhegemonic difference, actually repressive" (Jehlen 4).

Leo Marx and the Myth and Symbol School

# 3.3 | Popular Culture Studies

**From Mass Culture to Popular Culture.** If one wants to understand a culture, what kinds of cultural phenomena should one analyze? What texts and objects are representative? At a time when one of the most prominent scholars of the Myth and Symbol School, Leo Marx, still defended the priority of special artistic and intellectual achievements for cultural analysis in his essay "American Studies—A Defense of an Unscientific Method" and argued that a novel like Herman Melville's *Moby-Dick* would be more useful for an understanding of American culture than any popular text, other scholars in ACS were beginning to take different views. These changing attitudes find expression in a terminological shift: the term **mass culture** commonly used to that point is replaced by the term **popular culture**—which also means that cultural objects like Hollywood movies that had so far been dismissed as "mere entertainment" or the worst kind of escapism should now be reevaluated as expressions of popular beliefs and wide-spread cultural attitudes. Claiming that popularity must be seen as culturally significant, scholars like John Cawelti, Will Wright, and Janice Radway argue that the best way to understand American culture is not to focus on central myths but to look at popular culture. Their arguments usher in a serious study of popular culture and, soon to follow, of youth and ethnic subcultures.

How can the claim be supported that such popular genres as the **Western**, the **detective novel**, the **melodrama**, or the **romance** provide important insights into American culture? For the Myth and Symbol School, significant cultural insights are dependent on the aesthetic value of a cultural object. Popular culture, on the other hand, was considered aesthetically inferior. Under these circumstances, there were only two possibilities to

make a case for the usefulness of popular culture for cultural analysis: one was a defense of popular culture as by no means aesthetically inferior, the other consisted in the claim that special insights into American culture could be gained precisely from those features that had been considered aesthetically inferior until now.

**Narrative Formulas.** Critics who dismissed popular culture as aesthetically inferior usually pointed to its formulaic character that seemed to stand in the way of individual creativity and any "authentic" cultural expression. If ACS wanted to change this perception, it had to address the issue. The answer it came up with was that formula fiction is by no means "meaningless," because in cultural production, narrative formulas are not mindlessly repeated but constantly revised and reconfigured. As Cawelti argues in his study *Adventure, Mystery, and Romance*, it is not the narrative formula in itself that carries the meaning but its different use in changing narrative contexts. Narrative formulas, not myths, should therefore be the primary object of analysis in ACS. Whereas Slotkin regards violence as the central myth of American culture and sees his task in clarifying its meaning and tracing its impact, Cawelti demonstrates in his essay "Myths of Violence in American Culture" how the meaning and cultural significance of violence will vary and change, depending on the narrative context. Myths, symbols, and formulas thus have to be seen in their changing narrative contexts to become culturally meaningful. Cawelti's argument provides the theoretical basis for another look at standardized genre conventions such as adventure and love stories, soap operas, and, above all, the classical Hollywood film. In the Myth and Symbol School, the word Hollywood served as a short-hand for cheap mass culture; now classical Hollywood movies become one of the major objects of analysis in ACS.

**Extending the Cultural Field.** The acceptance of popular culture as a significant object of analysis has far-reaching consequences for the field. As long as culture is defined as a counter-realm of "higher," non-materialistic values, not everything can count as a legitimate object of cultural analysis. Consequently, it is one of the major tasks for the ACS scholar to separate the wheat from the chaff and to select those objects that are seen as the best manifestations of the intellectual and artistic potential of American culture. If, on the other

---

**Key Texts: Popular Culture Studies**

**John Cawelti,** *Adventure, Mystery, and Romance: Formula Stories as Popular Art and Popular Culture* (1976)
**Janice Radway,** *Reading the Romance: Women, Patriarchy, and Popular Literature* (1984)
**Lawrence Levine,** *Highbrow/Lowbrow: The Emergence of Cultural Hierarchy in America* (1988)
**Christoph Decker, ed.,** *Visuelle Kulturen der USA: Zur Geschichte von Malerei, Fotografie, Film, Fernsehen und Neuen Medien in Amerika* (2010)

hand, the aesthetically less valuable object can be regarded as **equally relevant** for an understanding of American culture, then the field can be extended to potentially everything American culture has to offer. Film and television, comics and advertisement, jazz and popular music, fashion and theme parks become legitimate areas of analysis and the same applies to cultural phenomena that had so far been considered the epitome of banality or queerness, such as Fast Food, Drag Car Racing, or Drag Queens. In view of this extension of the cultural field, it is not surprising to see that the terms 'Popular Culture Studies' and 'Cultural Studies' are increasingly used interchangeably.

Aesthetic Reevaluation. There is also a second line of argument in ACS, however, to justify popular culture as a field of study, and that is the rejection of a view of popular culture as aesthetically inferior. Instead, popular forms are praised as examples of a new aesthetic, characterized aptly in the title of Robert Warshow's essay collection *The Immediate Experience*, a pioneer work of Popular Culture Studies. Warshow's title draws attention to those elements of representation that are characterized by a direct, sensuously intense appeal. Media like popular music or film, and film genres like the musical and other "body genres" that have a strong sensuous impact and often provide an experience of immersion, are cultural phenomena that have received new and increased attention as a result of this aesthetic reevaluation. One of the reasons why the Western played an important role in the initial attempts to justify the study of popular culture was that it had a thematic focus that could still be connected to the founding myths of American culture. In contrast, even those popular forms can now gain attention that, at first sight, seem to be meaningless and seem to stand for "nothing but" entertainment.

Highbrow/Lowbrow. Popular culture has become an important area of study for ACS, then, not only because of its popularity and wide cultural resonance, but also because, as a sensuously strong and immediate experience, it seems to be a more authentic cultural expression than many high cultural forms. Many popular culture scholars therefore have a different view of America than the Myth and Symbol School: they see a vibrant common culture with an original aesthetic of its own. In his cultural history of the nineteenth century, Lawrence Levine describes the gradual differentiation of American culture into the taste levels highbrow and lowbrow as betrayal of a common

American culture by elites that introduced the concept of high culture in order to cement social hierarchies. Several studies have provided sympathetic interpretations of this anti-elitist common culture and its strong elements of performance—among them studies of the stage melodrama of the nineteenth century, the minstrel show, the Vaudeville theater, amusement parks, new dance forms, and the silent movies. To highlight the new type of aesthetic experience provided by the latter, Tom Gunning has coined the term "cinema of attractions," which, in its emphasis on spectacle and sensuous immersion, could also be used as description for many of the other popular forms.

Reinterpretation. In both lines of argument— that of a reconsideration of popular formulas and that of an aesthetic reevaluation—an equation of aesthetic value with certain formal features is challenged and replaced by a concept of aesthetic experience taken from reception aesthetics. Janice Radway's study *Reading the Romance* provides an example. As her ethnographic study of the reception of romances by female readers shows, a literary text cannot fully determine the meaning readers take from it (cf. entry II.3); rather, the text must be seen as a script that takes on its final meaning only in the imagination of the reader. Cultural objects can thus change meanings, including the possibility of **subversive reinterpretations**. Even an unmistakably conservative film like the movie *Rambo* can contain elements that may be used for an at least partially subversive or oppositional reading. This has opened up new possibilities for interpreting Hollywood films, television series, and other forms of popular culture, as a by now seemingly endless stream of subversive readings demonstrates. Whereas for the Myth and Symbol School, only the best high cultural works held the prospect of a counter-perspective, popular culture, too, can now serve as a reservoir of oppositional gestures.

This leads to a central problem of ACS. Clearly, the love romances analyzed by Radway are based on an unwavering affirmation of patriarchal structures. If this is the case, however, why do female readers expose themselves to these texts again and again? Traditional explanations point to the power of ideology that prevents female readers from realizing their own situation. However, if the act of reception activates the reader's imagination and provides her with some freedom of her own to reinterpret the text, then reading can also open up spaces for resignification and wayward readings, and the text's effect and social function cannot simply be equated with its ideology of submission. Instead, the text can also be seen as an articulation of utopian wishes. Traditionally, popular culture had been criticized as an illusory solution of real conflicts. Now the focus of interpretation is shifted not to the solution but to the utopian wishes that have created the conflict. Even though these may be contained or punished at the end of the text, they have nevertheless been articulated and, thus, introduced into the culture. The very feature that seemed to devalue popular culture for cultural analysis, its often criticized '**escapism**,' now becomes a culturally significant phenomenon and may even become a cultural source of subversion.

**Americanization.** The realization that meaning and effect are not inherent properties of cultural objects but can change, depending on different contexts of use, is of special importance for a debate that has been central for ACS outside the U.S. The issue is whether the world-wide influence of American popular culture after World War II has led to an 'Americanization' of other national cultures as a way to secure and consolidate for the U.S. an international cultural hegemony. As long as American culture was seen as primarily a com-

*The background of U.S. international cultural hegemony*

mercialized mass culture, the growing market share of this mass culture could indeed be a matter of concern, and counter measures like national quotas or tax breaks for national productions could make sense. However, in this case, too, an increasing number of reception studies provided growing evidence that text and effect are not identical. Recipients make selective use of media content and interpret it within frameworks of explanation derived from their own cultural horizons. Accordingly, the meaning of culture changes, once one regards reception as an important constituent of meaning and cultural significance: whereas the impact of myths is still attributed to their unifying power, culture now becomes a reservoir of signs, forms, styles, and performances from which recipients take different elements for their own aesthetic experiences. Unexpectedly, 'Americanization' may even have a certain subversive potential in this context and may lead to value changes that are not necessarily negative—for example, when the Prussian ideal of the military man is displaced, as it was in the 1950s in Germany, by images of masculinity taken from rock'n'roll and other expressive forms of American popular culture (Maase; Fluck, *Romance* 239–67).

## 3.4 | Ideological Criticism, New Historicism, New Americanists

Every cultural analysis rests on a basic network of assumptions that are logically linked. If, as is the case with the Myth and Symbol School, the idea of America is, in principle, still the major value, but certain "materialistic" developments are deplored, then those aspects of American culture will be especially important for ACS that highlight culture's potential for negation and resistance. As a rule, these texts will be intellectually and aesthetically ambitious and will therefore require a fairly sophisticated method of interpretation, such as, for example, the covert culture-approach by Leo Marx and his collaborators. All of these assumptions are radically revised in the 1970s when new social movements begin to have a growing influence on debates and research agendas in ACS. The idea of America is no longer associated with the promise of a new historical beginning, but with a system that is hiding its true nature behind a liberal facade. Myth is redefined as **ideology**, and aesthetic value is no longer a potential source of negation and resistance but an especially cunning source of

seduction and misrecognition. Reflecting a growing radicalization of ACS, new approaches are introduced into the field that completely change the research agendas and interpretive procedures of cultural analysis.

**Ideological Criticism.** One of these new revisionist approaches is a turn towards ideological criticism, most influentially in the work of Sacvan Bercovitch, who began his scholarly career as a specialist on American Puritanism. Initially, his studies focused on the jeremiad, a ritual of complaint about the decline of Puritanism that had the paradoxical effect of reaffirming and strengthening Puritan ideals as something that should be protected and saved. For Bercovitch, the jeremiad became a model of the fate of dissent in American society, and led to a reconceptualization of the concept of ideology. In contrast to Marxist approaches (cf. section II.2), ideology is no longer defined as false consciousness (which might still be overcome by enlightened critique from another position), but as the only available consciousness—and therefore as a seemingly self-evident truth for which no alternative exists. At the center of his redefinition of the idea of America as an ideological system stands the liberal idea of America as the land of freedom; even in criticizing America, the idea of America is reaffirmed because this criticism illustrates the freedom provided by the system. There is no need for change because there is freedom of dissent. Even oppositional criticism of a fundamental nature has the effect of providing renewed support for the idea and ideals of America. Bercovitch's approach—a critique of an American liberalism that sees itself "beyond ideology," because it freely admits dissent— is obviously influenced by Herbert Marcuse's idea of repressive tolerance and marks the arrival of European Critical Theory (cf. section II.2.2) in ACS.

If dissent can only give renewed legitimation to that which it criticizes, then culture takes on a new function. Where Myth and Symbol School-scholars still see a potential for negation, Bercovitch and other ideological critics only see an especially cunning form of ideological containment. In the left liberal world of the Myth and Symbol School, a literary text can be only one of two things, "aesthetically valuable" or "ideological." If literature succeeds as art, it transcends ideology. In contrast, Bercovitch claims that "a work of art [...] can no more transcend ideology than an artist's mind can transcend psychology; and it is worth remarking as a possibility that our great writers [...] may be just as implicated in the dominant culture as other, contextual writers, and in the long run perhaps more useful in perpetrating it" ("America" 99–100). What used to be the major source of negation in the Myth and Symbol School, the aesthetic value of a text, is now redescribed as a form of ideological obfuscation. Ambiguity, for example, had been seen as a characteristic of the symbol that seemed resistant to ideological appropriation, because it cannot be pinned down to one unequivocal meaning. In New Critical formalism, ambiguity is thus seen as one of literature's key devices to distance itself from ideology. However, if there is no longer any categorical difference between art and ideology, then even ambiguity may have an ideological function in providing a fiction of choice. Instead of transcending ideology, the literature of the American Renaissance turns out to be an especially effective medium of this ideology, because it gives support to a liberal illusion of resistance by art. This ideological critique paves the way for reading literary works

or cultural objects as directly infused with social and political issues, such as, most importantly, slavery (Sundquist).

Starting with Sacvan Bercovitch's and Myra Jehlen's essay collection *Ideology and Classic American Literature* and its redefinition of myth as ideology, a variety of politically oriented revisionist approaches emerged in response to the Myth and Symbol School—from **Marketplace Criticism** to **New Historicism** (cf. entry II.5), the **New Americanists**, and their subsequent emphasis on the idea of empire. However, despite many disagreements, these different manifestations of a new kind of political criticism all had one starting premise in common: they all postulated, although to varying degrees of emphasis, that hopes for political subversion or resistance by literature were illusionary. The different approaches that emerged as part of this political revisionism illustrate subsequent stages in the radicalization of this argument.

In Marketplace Criticism, the market, until then *the* commercial antithesis to art, has already begun to invade even the work of the best artists—that is, the form of literature on which the hopes of the Myth and Symbol School had rested (Gilmore). However, even though writers like Hawthorne or Henry James may not always have been as aloof from commercial considerations as they claimed, it is in principle still possible to resist market forces. In contrast, in New Historicism the question is no longer whether artists were able to resist the market. Since art is part and parcel of culture, its aesthetic dimension can no longer constitute a separate sphere (Michaels). On the contrary, the aesthetic may have the function of representing power in a way that makes its disciplinary effects even desirable (Brodhead). The aesthetic now becomes part of the system's disciplinary power. In a book on Henry James, Mark Seltzer accordingly redefines the power of art as the art of power.

The New Americanists further radicalize this critique in that they add a political dimension to a basically neohistoricist method to overcome the separation of cultural and political life. 'America' is therefore politically redefined as a nation-state and hence as an exemplary space of governmental rule, most obviously in a by now almost permanent state of exception. Such a state is in need of legitimation, and the idea of America functions as imaginary core of an American national identity that interpellates Americans into a fantasy of exceptionalism and allows them to disavow the racism, sexism, homophobia, and imperialism per-

Sacvan Bercovitch
and Myra Jehlen were
pioneers of the new
political approaches.

vading American society (Kaplan and Pease). Phenomena like racism or imperialism are therefore not leftovers from other, less enlightened periods. They have been key elements in the formation of U.S.-American culture from the beginning. The traditional definition of empire—rule over colonies—is replaced by a new definition, that of an **internal cultural power regime**. New Americanists "aim to argue more radically that the state and the political economy of the United States are themselves entirely dependent on the internal, imperial racialization of the population" (Radway, "What's in a Name" 54).

And if American society is shaped by phenomena like racism and imperialism, this must also be true for American culture which has been instrumental in 'naturalizing' racial and imperial politics. Since the starting premise of this type of cul-

tural radicalism is that ideology and power pervade all aspects of American society and no position outside exists, one can conclude that racism, sexism, and homophobia are also all-pervasive in American culture, even where the textual surface does not explicitly exhibit them (Kaplan, *Anarchy of Empire*). The characteristic mode of analysis of the New Americanists is therefore **metonymical**: wherever a textual element can be interpreted as, for example, racist or imperialist, this part can stand for the whole. There is no longer any need here to establish a canon or to make selections. Texts are no longer 'exemplary' because they criticize or affirm, but simply because they exemplify the culture of which they are a part. One text is therefore as good as another for analyzing the constituent dimensions of American culture, since they are all shaped by the same forces.

## 3.5 | Race and Gender Studies

**Multiculturalism/Diversity.** In its early stages, ACS saw culture as a source of national identity that provides American society with cohesion and a distinct national character. Even though it redefines myth as ideology, ideological criticism retains the idea of a single, unified national culture. However, with the emergence of the new social movements in the wake of the **Civil Rights Movement**, the idea of a unified American identity was increasingly criticized as suppression of the heterogeneity and diversity of American society. There is, it was argued, no common American culture; by claiming otherwise, a norm of 'Americanness' is established that excludes those groups which do not fit the idea of a 'specifically' American culture.

In the heyday of the Myth and Symbol School, these groups were considered irrelevant for understanding the true nature of American society and culture. The new social movements ushered in by the 1960s, among them the women's movement, African Americans, Native Americans, Mexican Americans, Asian Americans, and gays and lesbians changed all that by challenging ACS to fully recognize their different cultures and thereby to compensate for a long history of misrecognition.

The starting premise of this **politics of recognition** is the claim that degrading images of groups that do not fit the official cultural norm of "Americanness" will have a crippling impact on the self-image of the group and its members who will internalize feelings of inferiority and unworthiness. Two strategies have been developed to counter such negative effects: one is the critique of degrading stereotypical representations, the other the search for alternatives that could help to overcome these stereotypes. This is the starting point for a challenge to dominant cultural canons and curricula that has led to sweeping revisions, most impressively exemplified by ever expanding anthologies of American literature that aim at extensions of the traditional canon and have led to the rediscovery of many long-forgotten, ignored, or rejected works (see box). **Multiculturalism**, the concept most often used to describe this approach, expresses the hope that a cultural politics of mutual

---

**Key Texts**

Many of the texts recovered by the multicultural approach in American Cultural Studies can be found in these anthologies:

**Paul Lauter, ed.,** *The Heath Anthology of American Literature*

**Nina Baym, ed.,** *The Norton Anthology of American Literature*

**Sandra M. Gilbert and Susan Gubar, eds.,** *The Norton Anthology of Literature by Women*

**Henry Lous Gates, ed.,** *The Norton Anthology of African American Literature*

**Nicolas Kanellos, ed.,** *Herencia: The Anthology of Hispanic Literature of the United States*

**Marc Shell and Werner Sollors, eds.,** *The Multilingual Anthology of American Literature*

recognition will lead to a peaceful coexistence of different ethnic groups in American society (Takaki), especially since ethnicity has often become symbolic ethnicity by now (Hollinger). The challenge for ACS, then, is to recover this diversity fully within the explanatory framework of a politics of recognition in which difference is accepted in its own right and for its own sake and curricula serve the needs of a multicultural democracy. American culture is redefined as multicultural.

Whiteness Studies. This model of cultural pluralism has been criticized, however, because it tacitly assumes that the history of discrimination has been similar for all minorities. In consequence, one may overlook the profound differences that exist between immigration and slavery, European ethnic groups and people of color (Wald). Although the history of European immigration to the U.S. may not always have been a happy one, and may have been shaped by many social and cultural conflicts, there is nevertheless an unmistakable trajectory of gradual integration into American society. In contrast, blackness constituted an unbridgeable difference and barrier. In fact, as the critical approach of *Whiteness Studies* argues, the integration of ethnic groups such as the Irish or the Jews, who had initially been subject to far-reaching discrimination, became possible because these groups could define themselves as white (and thus as "American") in sharp differentiation from blacks. One place to do so were the widely popular **minstrel shows**, a genre that had been seen as an embarrassment in ACS before, but now takes on a center-stage role in explanations of the formation of American culture. *The Wages of Whiteness* by David Roediger, *Whiteness of a Different Color* by Matthew Jacobson, *Playing in the Dark* by Toni Morrison, and *Love and Theft* by Eric Lott have described these processes from different perspectives and, in doing so, have responded to the methodological challenge of identifying the opposition black/non-black as central for even those aspects of (white) American culture where they do not seem to play any role. For Toni Morrison, the opposition between black and white pervades all of American culture, because racial prejudice was constitutive of American identity from the very beginning. The black presence is thus central to understanding American culture.

Race and Gender Studies. A cultural construction of inferiority that is based on corporeal characteristics such as black skin cannot be fully grasped from the perspective of ethnic studies or multiculturalism. Thus it made sense to introduce the concept of race, class, and gender studies to draw attention to the consequences unbridgeable difference can have for the constitution of identity (cf. also entries II.6 and III.4). Class, however, never really became the basis for a consistent research agenda in ACS, so that the more fitting term is that of race and gender studies. Gender and race are terms designed to increase our understanding of how identities are shaped through cultural constructions of sexual and racial difference. Gender refers to the cultural construction of differences between the sexes, race to the cultural construction of any racial identity, including whiteness. Although the term has no biological basis, ACS nevertheless continue to use it in order to be able to analyze the cultural consequences of racial fictions.

It continues to be an important goal for race and gender studies to criticize and reject especially demeaning stereotypes as, for example, the figures of Sambo, Mammy, or Uncle Tom that dominated the representation of African Americans in the nineteenth and large parts of the twentieth century. Such stereotypes deny the depicted characters the status of a subject. To regain this subject status is the goal of a second project of race and gender studies in which degrading images are to be replaced by models of positive and alternative identities. The identity politics of the **Black Power Movement** and its redefinition of "authentic" blackness (for example in clothing, hair-, and musical styles), or the description of specific characteristics and achievements of black culture (Levine, *Black Culture*) provide exemplary cases. An important part of this project is the attempt to describe distinctively "black" forms of expression, including vernacular traditions, "the elaborate modes of signification implicit in black mythic and religious traditions, in ritual rhetorical structures such as 'signifying' and 'the dozens'" (Gates, *Black Literature* 6–7). For Gates, blacks have always been masters of figurative language, because they had to say one thing in order to mean something else.

In the search for other examples of cultural empowerment, those **studies of slavery** that describe uses of culture by slaves to carve out a certain, although limited sphere of agency have been of special interest. A number of studies in the 1970s focus on 'ordinary,' **everyday culture** such as family structures, religious practices, musical and dancing performances, harvest festivities, or elements of African traditions, and identify them as key re-

*Criticizing stereotypes*

| Definition |

→ "Black Power" is the slogan used by a controversial strand of the Civil Rights Movement in the late 1960s and 1970s. The term reflects the African American pursuit of increased socio-economical, cultural, and political influence and the intention to establish a genuinely black identity. The **Black Power Movement** was a heterogeneous group containing peaceful members and black nationalists as well as separatist militants.

sources in the struggle against discrimination and oppression (Blassingame). The meaning of culture is thus revised again, from a mythic national identity to culture's potential as a resource for resisting the racism of white hegemonial culture and for preserving a certain degree of self-respect. For this type of cultural analysis, creativity is key and not the dehumanizing consequences of slavery.

This 'culturalist' social history draws on new archives. Since no significant written records exist, other sources such as census data, city directories, or the archives of plantations must be analyzed to give slaves a voice and liberate African American history from the invisibility which had been its fate in American historiography until 1960 (Gutman). This methodological reorientation introduces a **new empiricism** into ACS. Statistical methods like census data seem to indicate objectivity. But these data have to be interpreted and have to be inserted into a narrative in which they gain larger cultural significance. Reflecting the origin of the social history approach in the social activism of the 1960s, these narratives show a recurring pattern: they want to prove that African Americans (or white workers) had "cultural resources of their own to resist oppression and maintain a sense of their dignity and worthiness as human beings" (Fredrickson 115). Although empirically grounded, they do not seem to be aware of the impact that discursive frameworks of explanation have on the interpretation of their sources.

**Women's Studies/Gender Studies.** A politics of identity also has another problem. If it is the purpose of cultural analysis to replace cultural misrecognition by a positive description of group identity that could provide the basis for equal recognition, then the question arises of who defines this identity. The problem is illustrated by the development of women's studies to gender studies. In women's studies, which emerged in the 1960s in the wake of the women's movement, the initial project was the criticism of those images that had

been instrumental in justifying a gender hierarchy. The so-called 'images of women'-approach focused on traditional stereotypes of the 'weaker sex,' because of their crucial role in the formation of female identity and because of their social consequences: "Feminist critics reinforced the importance of their enterprise by emphasizing the connections between the literary and the social mistreatment of women, in pornography, say, rape" (Showalter 5). In her essay "Melodramas of Beset Manhood," Nina Baym provides an eye-opening analysis of how such images have even shaped theories of American literature and culture. But if the association of inferiority, linked with these images, is to be effectively refuted, then a necessary next step must consist in the recovery of a female literary tradition with its own essential characteristics and an aesthetic of its own (which French feminists called *l'écriture feminine*).

In ACS, one of the examples of this search for a specific women's culture with its own aesthetic is Jane Tompkins' study *Sensational Designs,* which takes its point of departure from the historicist claim that aesthetic value is always relative and culture-and-institution-specific. In order to determine the value of a text, one therefore has to look at its cultural and institutional contexts. For a particular type of sentimental literature, called **domestic novels**, which had long been perceived as conventional, conformist, and aesthetically inferior, this context was women's culture of the nineteenth century. From this perspective, domestic novels can be reevaluated as an effort to reinterpret society from the woman's point of view. Where critics see aesthetic flaws, Tompkins tries to reverse these negative judgments by describing the functionality of these features for a female culture of the nineteenth century which has "a theory of power that stipulates that all true action is not material, but spiritual" (151). This explains the ethics of submission by which domestic novels are dominated and redefines it as an effective form of female self-empowerment.

No matter how convincing or unconvincing such an attempt to identify a female culture of the nineteenth century may be, its implication is that it is possible to define an identity and aesthetic that is specifically female. However, can such an identity also include African American women who were often exposed to triple discrimination (race, class and gender)? Apart from obvious differences in living conditions, Hazel Carby has pointed to the open racism of the American Temperance and Suffragette movements. A more general, but nevertheless valid, objection criticizes the reductions that are connected with all attempts to define an essentially female identity (Opfermann). Finally, an interpretation of the culture of sentimentality as a culture of female self-empowerment has been subjected to a radical critique by feminists who have insisted on the complicity of this culture with institutionalized forms of racial oppression (Samuels).

Protests against the essentialism of identity politics have not been restricted to feminism, however. An obvious example is the group of Asian Americans that is so heterogeneous that the group name cannot provide a cultural identity and is only acceptable in the form of a "strategic essentialism" (Lowe). A politics of recognition must thus be extended to include a recognition of difference within minority groups. Hence, a politics of identity has been replaced by a **new politics of difference**." In his essay "New Ethnicities," Stuart Hall has given this perspective a programmatic profile by claiming that "the end of the innocent notion of the essential black subject" has been reached:

> What is at issue here is the recognition of the extraordinary diversity of subjective positions, social experiences and cultural identities which compose the category 'black'; that is, the recognition that 'black' is essentially a politically and culturally *constructed* category, which cannot be grounded in a set of fixed trans-cultural or transcendental racial categories. (443)

This critique of the essentialism of identity politics has also provided a point of departure for approaches that have further developed the research agenda of gender studies, such as masculinity studies and queer studies. They cannot be discussed here but, generally speaking, they have also followed a theoretical trajectory from a critique of representation to analyses of the (verbal and visual) discourses and cultural performances through which engendered identities have been constructed in American culture. Exposing misrecognitions of otherness is the common project that links all of these approaches in race and gender studies.

## 3.6 | Border Crossings, Multiple Identities, and Transnationalisms

With the arrival of a new **politics of difference**, an important point of theoretical reorientation has been reached in ACS. Various versions of the idea of mobility promise to liberate the field from a dead-end into which a certain type of power analysis has led it. In the approaches we have traced so far, the relation between individual agency and cultural ascription has steadily moved to the side of cultural ascription. Myths, as they have been described by the Myth and Symbol School, may be powerful cultural frameworks of explanation, but there are nonconformists who successfully resist. Even the all-pervasive American ideology described by Bercovitch still leaves the option of several positions within that ideology. But in race and gender studies and the New Americanism, it is now the cultural system that constitutes the subject and ascribes an engendered and racialized identity to him or her (Voelz). If the system's power is most effectively at work in the formation of identity, however, then it must become a central project of ACS to understand the role culture plays in the **formation of identity**. From a sociological perspective, identity is the result of a long-drawn process of socialization. In ACS, this model of identity formation is radically revised by drawing on the concept of interpellation as a term for discursive subject positioning. One example for the formation of a gender identity by interpellation (or "hailing") is the often heard exclamation "What a sweet little girl!" Before the girl is able to develop an identity of her own in the process of socialization, she is already positioned in a gendered identity.

This shift to the side of cultural ascription can best be understood as a transition from political to cultural radicalism. In political radicalism, dominant until the late 1960s, there are still institutions like progressive political parties, or the labor unions, or the student movement, or simply the institution of art, that hold a promise for resistance or negation. In cultural radicalism, such hopes are rejected as liberal self-delusions, because for this type of radicalism the actual source of power does not lie in particular institutions, but in culture and its processes of subject formation (Fluck, "Humanities"). The stability of social systems is no longer secured by repression, but by cultural structures of whose power effects individuals cannot be aware, because these structures provide the very concepts and explanatory

*The transition from political to cultural radicalism*

frameworks through which they make sense of the world. Before an individual can hope to reach any degree of agency, she has already been interpellated into a subject position that has become second nature to her. Methodologically, in following the influence of the French cultural historian Michel Foucault (cf. section II.4.2), the concept of discourse is now used as a description of the ensemble of linguistic structures, media and significatory practices through which culture exerts its power.

How are individual agency and resistance still possible then? Since ACS can no longer define culture as a utopian counter sphere, the only way out lies in the project of deconstructing cultural forms of identity formation, for example, by "dis-identification" or "dis-interpellation." New Americanists like Don Pease see such a possibility in moments of crisis that undermine the identificatory lure of identity ascriptions (Pease, *New American Exceptionalism*).

But more influential in this search for a way out of the cultural power effects of interpellation has been the concept of **multiple or flexible identities**. The concept can be seen as the logical extension of hopes once ascribed to minority positions outside of the imaginary hold of a unified national identity. Because definitions of national identity exclude certain minorities, the argument goes, these minorities have not identified with the American nation-state and can therefore provide an outside perspective. In fact, this is the theoretical reason why the study of minorities has moved to the center of ACS. They became crucial, not only to do justice to the diversity of U.S.-America, but because minorities, in their position outside of the interpellative powers of a national identity, have become central for outlining the possibility of oppositional perspectives. However, after the critique of the essentialism of identity politics had problematized an automatic equation of resistance with an outsider position, the only remaining option was no longer a position on the margins of the system, but a movement between different positions. Concepts of **hybridization** or '**in-between-**

ness' have therefore become central in ACS. One example is provided by border studies, in which the border area of Mexico and the U.S. is defined as a space in-between different national, ethnic, and gendered identities (Anzaldúa). Similarly, the concept of diaspora has found renewed attention, no longer in its original meaning, but as another space in-between with the potential of creating multiple and flexible identities (Mayer).

But the logic of border crossings has opened up still another option that erases national borders altogether and redefines ACS as transnational studies. Already in 1916, Randolph Bourne had argued that U.S.-America does not have a specific national identity but is characterized by a diversity that he calls "transnational America." The exceptionalism that dominated ACS in the post-World War II period had ignored this transnational dimension and had obscured the role cultural exchanges have played in the formation of American culture. But while Bourne still thought in terms of separate ethnic cultures, **transnationalism** now emphasizes the dimension of constant interaction, exchange, and hybridization. Cultures cannot be neatly demarcated by national borders, they are always spaces of interaction between different cultures and international influences. The influence of African culture on American musical developments that later gained world-wide popularity provides a case in point. Such processes of cultural exchange are not restricted to Transatlantic Studies. The transnational paradigm has been expanded to Hemispheric Studies, Pacific Rim Studies, and Border Studies to identify and analyze other transnational spaces (Porter). At present, the question is how far this transnational redefinition of ACS should go. Should we continue to focus on US-America as our primary object of analysis and expertise and draw on transnational perspectives where they can help to better understand this object, or should ACS transform itself into a field of cosmopolitan studies? Transnationalism is still a relatively new development in ACS, but it is already clear that it can be used for different goals and agendas (Fluck, "A New Beginning?").

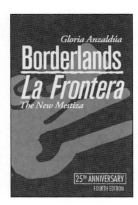

Gloria Anzaldúas
*Borderlands/La Frontera*
(1987)

# Select Bibliography

Anzaldúa, Gloria. *Borderlands/La Frontera: The New Mestiza*. San Francisco: Aunt Lute Books, 1987.

Arac, Jonathan. "The Politics of The Scarlet Letter." Bercovitch and Jehlen 247–66.

Baym, Nina. "Melodramas of Beset Manhood: How Theories of American Fiction Exclude Women Authors." *American Quarterly* 33 (1981): 123–39.

Bercovitch, Sacvan. "America as Canon and Context: Literary History in a Time of Dissensus." *American Literature* 58 (1986): 99–108.

Bercovitch, Sacvan. "The Problem of Ideology in American Literary History." *Critical Inquiry* 12.4 (1986): 631–53.

Bercovitch, Sacvan. *The Rites of Assent*. London: Routledge, 1993.

Bercovitch, Sacvan, and Myra Jehlen, eds. *Ideology and Classic American Literature*. Cambridge: Cambridge University Press, 1988.

Blassingame, John W. *The Slave Community: Plantation Life in the Antebellum South*. Oxford: Oxford University Press, 1972.

Bourne, Randolph. "Trans-National America." *The American Intellectual Tradition*. Eds. David A Hollinger and Charles Capper. Vol. 2. New York: Oxford University Press, 1989. 2 vols. 153–63.

Brodhead, Richard H. *Cultures of Letters: Scenes of Reading and Writing in Nineteenth-Century America*. Chicago: University of Chicago Press, 1993.

Burgett, Bruce, and Glenn Hendler, eds. *Keywords for American Cultural Studies*. New York: New York University Press, 2007.

Carby, Hazel V. *Reconstructing Womanhood*. Oxford: Oxford University Press, 1987.

Cawelti, John. "Myths of Violence in American Popular Culture." *Critical Inquiry* 1 (1975): 521–41.

Cawelti, John. *Adventure, Mystery, and Romance: Formula Stories as Popular Art and Popular Culture*. Chicago: University of Chicago Press, 1976.

Engler, Bernd, and Oliver Scheiding, eds. *Key Concepts in American Cultural History from the Colonial Period to the End of the 19th Century*. Trier: WVT, 2007.

Fisher, Philip, ed. *The New American Studies: Essays from "Representations."* Berkeley: University of California Press, 1991.

Fluck, Winfried. "American Literary History and the Romance with America." *American Literary History* 21.1 (2009): 1–18.

Fluck, Winfried. "Das ästhetische Vorverständnis der American Studies." *Jahrbuch für Amerikastudien* 18 (1973): 110–29.

Fluck, Winfried. "California Blue: Americanization as Self-Americanization." *Americanization and Anti-Americanism: The German Encounter with American Culture after 1945*. Ed. Alexander Stephan. New York: Berghahn Books, 2005. 221–37.

Fluck, Winfried. "The Humanities in the Age of Expressive Individualism and Cultural Radicalism." Pease and Wiegman 211–30.

Fluck, Winfried. "A New Beginning? Transnationalisms." *New Literary History* 42.3 (2011): 365–84.

Fluck, Winfried. *Romance with America? Essays on Culture, Literature, and American Studies*. Heidelberg: Winter, 2009.

Fluck, Winfried, and Werner Sollors, eds. *German? American? Literature? New Directions in German-American Studies*. New York: Peter Lang, 2002.

Fluck, Winfried, Donald Pease, and John Carlos Rowe, eds. *Re-framing the Transnational Turn in American Studies*. Hanover: Dartmouth College Press, 2011.

Fredrickson, George M. *The Arrogance of Race*. Hanover: Wesleyan University Press, 1988.

Gates, Henry Louis, ed. *Black Literature and Literary Theory*. New York: Methuen, 1984.

Gates, Henry Louis. *The Signifying Monkey: A Theory of African American Literary Criticism*. Oxford: Oxford University Press, 1988.

Gates, Henry Louis. "The Trope of a New Negro and the Reconstruction of the Image of the Black." Fisher 319–45.

Gilmore, Michael T. *American Romanticism and the Marketplace*. Chicago: University of Chicago Press, 1985.

Gilroy, Paul. *The Black Atlantic: Modernity and Double Consciousness*. Cambridge: Harvard University Press, 1993.

Gunning, Tom. "The Cinema of Attractions." *Early Cinema*. Ed. Thomas Elsaesser. London: British Film Institute, 1990. 56–62.

Gutman, Herbert G. *The Black Family in Slavery and Freedom: 1750–1925*. New York: Pantheon, 1976.

Hall, Stuart. "New Ethnicities." *Critical Dialogues in Cultural Studies*. Eds. David Morley and Kuan-Hsing Chen. New York: Routledge, 1996. 441–49.

Hollinger, David A. *Postethnic America*. New York: Basic Books, 1995.

Jacobson, Matthew F. *Whiteness of a Different Color*. Cambridge: Harvard Unversity Press, 1998.

Jehlen, Myra. "Beyond Transcendence." Bercovitch and Jehlen 1–18.

Kaplan, Amy. *The Anarchy of Empire in the Making of U.S. Culture*. Cambridge: Harvard University Press, 2002.

Kaplan, Amy, and Donald Pease, eds. *Cultures of United States Imperialism*. Durham: Duke University Press, 1993.

Kerber, Linda. "Diversity and the Transformation of American Studies." *American Quarterly* 41 (1989): 415–31.

Kimmel, Michael. *Manhood in America: A Cultural History*. New York: Oxford UP, 2011.

Kolodny, Annette. *The Lay of the Land: Metaphor as Experience and History in American Life and Letters*. Chapel Hill: University of North Carolina Press, 1975.

Levine, Lawrence W. *Black Culture and Black Consciousness: Afro-American Folk Thought from Slavery to Freedom*. Oxford: Oxford University Press, 1977.

Levine, Lawrence W. *Highbrow/Lowbrow: The Emergence of Cultural Hierarchy in America*. Cambridge: Cambridge University Press, 1988.

Lott, Eric. *Love and Theft: Blackface Minstrelsy and the American Working Class*. Oxford: Oxford University Press, 1993.

Lowe, Lisa. *Immigrant Acts*. Durham: Duke University Press, 1996.

Maase, Kaspar. *BRAVO Amerika: Erkundungen zur Jugendkultur der Bundesrepublik in den fünfziger Jahren*. Hamburg: Junius, 1992.

Martschukat, Jürgen, and Olaf Stieglitz, eds. *Väter, Soldaten, Liebhaber: Männer und Männlichkeiten in der Geschichte Nordamerikas*. Bielefeld: transcript, 2007.

**Marx, Leo.** "American Studies: A Defense of an Unscientific Method." *New Literary History* 1 (1969): 75–90.

**Marx, Leo.** *The Machine in the Garden: Technology and the Pastoral Idea in America*. Oxford: Oxford University Press, 1964.

**Marx, Leo, Bernard Bowron, and Arnold Rose.** "Literature and Covert Culture." *Studies in American Culture*. Ed. Joseph Kwiat. Minneapolis: University of Minnesota Press, 1960. 84–95.

**Matthiessen, F. O.** *American Renaissance: Art and Expression in the Age of Emerson and Whitman*. Oxford: Oxford University Press, 1941.

**Mayer, Ruth.** *Diaspora: Eine kritische Begriffsbestimmung*. Bielefeld: transcript, 2005.

**Michaels, Walter Benn.** *The Trouble with Diversity: How We Learned to Love Identity and Ignore Inequality*. New York: Henry Holt, 2006.

**Morrison, Toni.** *Playing in the Dark: Whiteness and the Literary Imagination*. Cambridge: Harvard University Press, 1992.

**Opfermann, Susanne.** *Diskurs, Geschlecht und Literatur: Amerikanische Autorinnen des 19. Jahrhunderts*. Stuttgart: Metzler, 1996.

**Pease, Donald.** *The New American Exceptionalism*. Minneapolis: University of Minnesota Press, 2009.

**Pease, Donald, and Robyn Wiegman, eds.** *The Futures of American Studies*. Durham: Duke University Press, 2002.

**Porter, Carolyn.** "What We Know That We Don't Know: Remapping American Literary Studies." *American Literary History* 6 (1994): 467–526.

**Radway, Janice A.** *Reading the Romance: Women, Patriarchy, and Popular Literature*. Chapel Hill: University of North Carolina Press, 1984.

**Radway, Janice A.** "What's in a Name?" Pease and Wiegman 45–75.

**Roediger, David R.** *The Wages of Whiteness: Race and the Making of the American Working Class*. London: Verso, 1991.

**Rotundo, E. Anthony.** *American Manhood: Transformations in Masculinity from the Revolution to the Modern Era*. New York: Basic Books, 1993.

**Samuels, Shirley, ed.** *The Culture of Sentiment: Race, Gender, and Sentimentality in Nineteenth Century America*. Oxford: Oxford University Press, 1992.

**Seltzer, Mark.** *Henry James and the Art of Power*. Ithaca: Cornell University Press, 1984.

**Showalter, Elaine.** "The Feminist Critical Revolution." Introduction. *The New Feminist Criticism*. Ed. Elaine Showalter. New York: Pantheon, 1985. 3–17.

**Slotkin, Richard.** *Regeneration Through Violence: The Mythology of the American Frontier: 1600–1860*. Middletown: Wesleyan University Press, 1973.

**Smith, Henry Nash.** "Can American Studies Develop a Method?" *American Quarterly* 9 (1957): 97–208.

**Smith, Henry Nash.** *Virgin Land: The American West as Symbol and Myth*. Cambridge: Harvard University Press, 1950.

**Smith-Rosenberg, Carroll.** *Disorderly Conduct: Visions of Gender in Victorian America*. New York: Oxford University Press, 1985.

**Sundquist, Eric J.** *To Wake the Nations: Race in the Making of American Literature*. Cambridge: Belknap Press of Harvard University Press, 1993.

**Takaki, Ronald.** *A Different Mirror: A History of Multicultural America*. Boston: Little, Brown & Co., 1993.

**Tompkins, Jane.** *Sensational Designs: The Cultural Work of American Fiction 1790–1860*. Oxford: Oxford University Press, 1985.

**Voelz, Johannes.** *Transcendental Resistance: The New Americanists & Emerson's Challenge*. Hanover: Dartmouth College Press, 2010.

**Wald, Alan.** "Theorizing Cultural Difference." *Melus* 14.2 (1987): 21–33.

*Winfried Fluck*

# 4 Postcolonial Studies

## 4.1 | Postcolonial Theory: A Contested Field

In the last two decades, postcolonial studies has emerged as one of the fastest-growing and most influential fields in international academia, particularly by way of postcolonial theory as a framework of analysis for a broad range of cultural forms and political and historical constellations. Like other such frameworks, postcolonial theory is characterized by a pronounced and often puzzling internal diversity; as far back as 1995, one of its prominent protagonists noted wryly that "the attributes of postcolonialism have become so widely contested in contemporary usage, its strategies and sites so structurally dispersed, as to render the term next to useless as a precise marker of intellectual content, social constituency, or political commitment" (Slemon 7). Despite (or possibly because of) this perplexing fuzziness, postcolonial theory has been productively applied (and controversially debated) in a wide array of disciplines, and has long since proliferated beyond the field of literary and cultural studies where it made its first appearance: today, it not only plays a major role in new fields such as globalization and diaspora studies, but also in long-established disciplines such as sociology, medieval studies, or ancient history.

This entry will explore major currents and usages of postcolonial theory in cultural and literary studies. It is based on a perception of postcolonial theory as a loosely knit network of approaches rather than as a unified field, and seeks to identify important new perspectives opened up by different currents within postcolonial theory as well as major areas of controversy they have given rise to. While many of the great expectations generated by postcolonialism, particularly with regard to the social and political relevance of cultural and literary theory, have clearly not been fulfilled, the diverse, often controversially interlocked strands of postcolonial theory have initiated a transformation process in many fields of the humanities that is far from finished today.

Postcolonial theory as a network of approaches

## 4.2 | Colonial Discourse Analysis

Colonial discourse analysis is undeniably one of the central and most influential strands within postcolonial studies. Drawing on Michel Foucault's understanding of discourse (cf. section II.4.2), it was initiated by **Edward Said**, a renowned Palestinian cultural and literary theorist, with his groundbreaking study *Orientalism*, published in 1978. Said's study analysed European representations of 'the Orient' (mainly the Middle East and North Africa), particularly in ethnography and in literature, and was based on the seminal idea that 'Orientalism' is a discourse that had come into existence under specific circumstances and func-tioned according to specific rules; colonial discourse analysis was thus faced with the challenge of examining the genesis of these rules and of analysing how precisely they work.

*Orientalism* identifies five major modes in which this discourse can be analysed.
**1.** It can be examined as a **construct**—a fantasy about places and people allegedly located in the real world that discursively sets up an imaginary "parallel universe" into which these places and people are incorporated. The central task of colonial discourse analysis is thus to scrutinize the tropes, images, and figurations that make up this

'parallel universe.' One of the characteristics of these tropes, images, and figurations that Said identifies in his study is that they come in binary arrangements.

**2.** A more specific task of colonial discourse analysis thus lies in **identifying** (and thus opening up to critical scrutiny) these pairs that set up **an essentialized difference** between 'Europe' and 'the Orient': 'progress' versus 'timelessness', the 'civilized' European versus the 'violent' Arab, the 'lazy' Indian or the 'inscrutable' Chinaman, the strong 'male' European whose culture is at its peak versus the 'effeminate,' decadent Oriental whose culture is in decline.

**3.** Another mode of analysis is concerned with the institutionalization of Orientalism as a **scientific practice**, e.g. in ethnography, Oriental Studies, and a wide range of further disciplines, and examines the mechanisms through which the 'parallel world' of orientalist discourse became transformed into allegedly 'objective' knowledge about Europe's colonized 'Others.' Since orientalist discourse also pervaded European literature, culture, and art, the Orient became a general cultural construct reflected in many aspects of 'Western' life.

**4.** A mode of discourse analysis thus explores both the **'latent' presence** of Orientalism as a deep undercurrent of European literature, culture, and art, and its 'manifest' appearance, i.e. in stereotypical cultural representations of 'orientals' as Europe's essential 'Others.'

**5.** Finally, orientalist discourse also served (and, according to Said, continues to serve) as **legitimation** of first European and later more generally 'Western' claims to rule over other parts of the world. A fifth mode of analysis is thus concerned with the mobilization of orientalist tropes in political discourse.

Critiques of *Orientalism.* Said's analysis of orientalism combined Foucault's discourse theory with a salient interest in the workings and legacies of colonialism in the world at large and thus established a nexus between poststructuralist theory and postcolonial politics that has remained a hallmark of postcolonial studies ever since—and has given rise to intense controversies. Thus, critics have questioned the feasibility of combining the theoretical rigour of Foucauldian discourse analysis with the political concerns of anticolonial resistance, since poststructuralist theory inevitably deconstructs the very ideas of agency and (collective) subjectivity that are vitally important for anticolonial politics. Others have criticized the ahistorical

timeframe of Said's 'Orientalism' concept, which not only covers the whole era of European colonialism together with postcolonial phenomena such as late twentieth century American foreign policy, but also postulates a continuity of Orientalism reaching all the way into antiquity. Finally, the question has been raised whether the very notion of 'Western discourse' does not simply replicate the deep structure of 'Orientalism' itself and homogenize and simplify what is in fact an internally riven, contradictory, and far from linear history: "Talking of 'Western capitalist modernity since 1492' can easily become [...] an evocation of a past flattened into a blunt tool useful for showing the ugly flip side of European progress, but not for building up other ways of narrating and explaining a complex history" (Cooper 416–17).

Edward Said himself was well aware of this danger and warned against turning colonial discourse analysis into a form of reverse '**Occidentalism**.' His *Culture and Imperialism* provides an impressive example of a historically specific investigation into the colonial entanglements of Europe's canonical literature and culture ranging from the novels of Jane Austen to the operas of Giuseppe Verdi that carefully avoids reproducing binary oppositions between 'East' and 'West' and highlights the "overlapping territories" and "intertwined histories" that emerged during long centuries of European colonial rule (3–61). Colonial discourse analysis was further refined by **Homi Bhabha** (cf. section 4.5 below), whose nuanced readings of colonial 'mimicry' focused on the mode of colonized subjects to "almost, but not quite" adapt to the norms and lifestyles of their colonial masters (89) and highlighted the inherent instability and anxiety of a colonial discourse caught in the paradox of aiming at the 'enlightenment' and social transformation of 'the colonized races,' on the one hand, and needing to maintain a gap of absolute alterity in order to justify the colonial project in the first place on the other.

A look at nineteenth century European art as 'orientalist' in the many facets of Said's model reveals both the productive potential and the limitations of colonial discourse analysis. With the decline of the Ottoman Empire and with Napoleon's campaigns in Egypt in the early 1800s, the number of travellers and artists to 'the Orient' had increased significantly (see e.g. Depelchin). With them, visual depictions of the Orient multiplied; however, while these depictions can be called 'orientalist' in the numerous ways elaborated above, they cannot be subsumed under a single agenda (see box).

## Orientalism and Women

The depiction of women is a particularly good example for the complexities of Orientalism. On the one hand, and with regard to the portrayal of 'oriental' women, it illustrates the ways in which the 'western' imagination of both the Other and the self was **projected** onto the Orient—presentations of the 'Harem,' as in Théodore Chassériau's *Le Harem* (1851/52) for instance, or Thomas Rowlandson's erotic engraving *The Harem* (after 1812) were purely fictional as European men usually had no access to this space; thus, these renderings revealed more about the desire of the artist and his cultural images of the Orient than about the Orient itself (Depelchin 30). On the other hand, in these artistic depictions, the **fear of the Oriental** became manifest: the abduction of 'white' (that is, 'western') women was a popular theme, e.g. in Henri Félix Philippoteaux's *The Kidnapping* (1844) or Jean-Baptiste Huysman's *The Captive* (1862). Catering to the fear and titillation that 'other' masculinities evoked, it also found an expression in the allegorization of the Occident as a woman, threatened by an Orient imagined as masculine savage, as in Eugène Delacroix's *Greece on the Ruins of Missolonghi* (1826), a painting illustrating the—in the mid-1820s seemingly hopeless—Greek war of independence against the Ottoman Empire and the sympathy with which "painters participated fully in the philhellenic embrace" (Peltre, *Orientalism* 40). While these images have in common that they project European expectations, desires, or fears onto a cultural 'Other,' the agenda of these depictions is far from homogenous: As Peltre argues, women are associated with eroticism as well as spirituality, for example in Léon Joseph Bonnat's *Woman with Child* (1870) (Peltre, "Und die Frauen" 158–64); and while they serve for European male projections as the Oriental woman, women as Occidental figures also embody Europe, usually as threatened—so the Orient may be feminine as well as masculine, threatening and threatened. What this example highlights is thus the need for strict contextualization—the link between power and knowledge, as formulated by Foucault and taken up by Said as well as Bhabha, is not as clear-cut and unidirectional as Said in particular suggests in his earlier work. Also, and this is a debate that concerns other fields of postcolonial studies as well, the exclusive focus on one category of representation and 'othering' tends to ignore overlapping categories of identification—in this example, gender plays a central role for understanding the process of Orientalist depiction and identification.

Théodore Chassériau, *Le Harem* (1851/52)

Interpretation

While the theories and methods of colonial discourse analysis have made a major contribution to the critical study of colonialism and its manifold legacies, and have become an integral part not only of postcolonial studies, but also of Cultural Studies in general, the **predominance of colonial discourse analysis** in the field has also caused considerable concern, particularly among critics working on contemporary literatures and cultures in formerly colonized parts of the world who are apprehensive of the fact that a primary focus on (European) colonial discourse may once more privilege the former colonial centres and relegate the alleged peripheries to a critical back seat. Thus, Diana Brydon warned more than two decades ago that "the new directions of the last few years have led us in a circle, revitalizing readings of the Raj and silencing the new literatures" (29). On a more general level, Amartya Sen has highlighted the dangers inherent in an overabundance of cultural memory focussing on the colonial past in the formerly colonized regions of the world:

> It cannot make sense to see oneself primarily as someone who (or whose ancestors) have been misrepresented, or treated badly, by colonialists, no matter how true that identification may be. [...] [T]o lead a life in which resentment against an imposed inferiority from past history comes to dominate one's priorities today cannot but be unfair to oneself. It can also vastly deflect attention from other objectives that those emerging from past colonies have reason to value and pursue in the contemporary world (88–89).

In assessing the potential and impact of postcolonial studies for contemporary Cultural and Literary Studies, it is thus important not to reduce its scope to colonial discourse analysis alone, despite the fact that this particular mode of postcolonial studies has acquired particularly high prestige in international academia. The 'recentring' dynamics inherent in studying Europe's representations of its "Others" thus arguably has to be balanced by the 'decentring' logic embodied in other modes of postcolonialism that focus on the diversity of cultural representations, in an increasingly transculturally interlinked world of globalized modernity.

## 4.3 | Cultural Nationalism

A particularly influential mode of representing this diversity within postcolonial theory takes its cue from a strong national framework serving as the major point of reference for cultural and literary studies. This mode has its origins in the close connections between anti-colonial movements for national independence and cultural struggles to "**decolonize the mind**" (Ngũgĩ) in colonial and postcolonial settings. In this context, a form of 'cultural nationalism' developed next to political nationalism, insisting on both the importance and the specific character of 'national cultures.'

While this connection between the struggle for national independence and the insistence on a 'national culture' to some extent also characterized the 'first wave' of decolonization in the nineteenth century (i.e. the so-called settler colonies Canada, Australia and New Zealand that gained far-reaching autonomy from Great Britain), it became arguably even more important for the independence movements in Asia, Africa, and the Caribbean in the mid-twentieth century.

**The Paradox of Nationalism.** A post-Renaissance development with its roots in Europe, nationalism, including cultural nationalism, is something of a paradox in postcolonial contexts. As critics have frequently pointed out, the concept and even more so the myths of the nation in the nineteenth century are intimately linked to the expansion of national control through imperialism (Ashcroft, Griffiths, and Tiffin, *Post-Colonial Studies*). At the same time, the narrative of the nation, with its focus on cohesion and common origin, has been adopted in postcolonial contexts for the purpose of resistance against colonization and as a

*Nationalism fueled both colonization and the resistance against colonization.*

basis for the creation of postcolonial nation states in Africa, Asia, and the Americas. This usually entailed a reference to a pre-colonial cultural and political past as the basis for a post-colonial national future. As Ashcroft et al. have put it, "anti-colonial movements employed the idea of a pre-colonial past to rally their opposition through a sense of difference, but they employed this past not to reconstruct the pre-colonial social state but to generate support for the construction of post-colonial nation-states based upon the European nationalist model" (*Post-Colonial Studies* 139).

There is nothing 'natural' about the nation; it is a relatively new discursive construction that nevertheless provides the basis for powerful mobilization and identification. 'Culture' and a strong sense of difference from other (national) cultures are central for the sense of exclusiveness and belonging that nationalism creates (Anderson). Therefore, in the context of independence movements and later also in their academic conceptualizations, national culture may be recognized as constructed; nevertheless, strategically (and all too often also in essence), it provides an unquestioned basis for anti-colonial resistance and for the construction of the post-colonial nation state. Gayatri Spivak has called this position "**strategic essentialism**" (11). This applies to the ways in which literature, for instance, was understood in its relationship to the nation in the context of decolonization, that is, as a tool in nation building, on the one hand. On the other hand, it is also relevant for understanding literary criticism and its theorization of this relationship. To once again quote Ashcroft and his colleagues: "The develop-

Cultural nationalism:
The examples of African
and Canadian literature

ment of national literatures and criticism is fundamental to the whole enterprise of post-colonial studies" (*Empire* 17).

Cultural nationalism played a major role, for example, in the emergence of modern **African literature**. A writer like Chinua Achebe (cf. section I.4.5.4), author of the classical anticolonial novel *Things Fall Apart*, saw it as his duty to educate his African readers about their own traditional culture that had been vilified by colonialism and "to help my society regain belief in itself and put away the complexes of the years of denigration and self-abasement" (Achebe 44). Achebe's portrayal of pre-colonial culture and society in *Things Fall Apart* was strongly geared towards dismantling colonial prejudices about 'savage Africa' and sought to portray the cosmology, religious norms and social order of an Ibo village in late nineteenth century Eastern Nigeria. This cultural nationalist orientation did not result in an Edenic vision of pre-colonial Africa, however, since Achebe's novel also addressed some of the weaknesses of traditional Ibo society. That Achebe's cultural nationalism went beyond an uncritical cultural essentialism can also be inferred from his espousal of an "anti-racist racism" that would help to dismantle the obnoxious binaries between 'civilized' Europe and an allegedly inferior and primitive Africa in order to pave the way for African self-understanding and future dialogue with the rest of the world—an understanding of the political role of cultural self-definitions that strongly echoes (or rather, prefigures) Spivak's "strategic essentialism."

**More Recent Cultural Nationalist Positions.** Despite its important role for independence movements, cultural nationalism has met with serious criticism in postcolonial studies: it is regarded as implicitly or explicitly essentialist, that is, it is seen as assuming some kind of cultural essence of a nation that can be clearly delineated and that sets this nation apart from all others. Thus, despite its originally emancipatory agenda in the postcolonial context, it is charged with the production of new mechanisms of exclusion. In short, cultural nationalism presents itself as a highly contradictory stand. Nevertheless, and in spite of significant shifts within the field of postcolonial theory that tend to highlight cultural hybridity and hence the crossing of cultural boundaries, the model of post-colonial national literatures and national cultures has had and continues to have a significant impact on postcolonial literatures and their studies—as a political concept, but also as an analytical position. And this influence is clearly not restricted to the time of decolonization.

In **Canada**, for instance, strong positions of cultural nationalism can be identified in the 1970s. Based on the work of literary critic Northrop Frye and his concept of the "garrison mentality" as a marker for Canadian literature, Margaret Atwood identified *survival*—physical, spiritual, psychological—as the defining theme in Canadian literature, both Anglophone and Francophone. While Frye's notion of the garrison mentality is not explicitly political, Atwood's understanding of 'survival' clearly is; it is both an analytical and a normative concept, a typical feature of cultural nationalism. Atwood identifies four 'victim positions'—from the victim who cannot or does not want to recognize her- or himself as such, through various stages to the former victim who has managed to gain agency and to overcome the status of a victim. On the one hand, these positions are the result of an interpretation of literature; this is the analytical aspect of the concept. On the other hand, Atwood interprets these positions as stages of literary and cultural development in Canada; this is clearly a normative project, for Atwood defines Canada as a colony and thus contextualizes her reading in a process of decolonization. She writes:

Let us suppose, for the sake of argument, that Canada as a whole is a victim, or an 'oppressed minority,' or 'exploited.' Let us suppose in short that Canada is a colony. A partial definition of a colony is that it is a place from which a profit is made, but *not by the people who live there:* the major profit from a colony is made in the centre of empire. [...] Of course there are cultural side-effects which are often identified as 'the colonial mentality,' and it is these which are examined here; but the root cause for them is economic. (36)

Here, the implied colonizer is not the former colonial mother country Great Britain; rather, Atwood writes against a background of increasing cultural antagonism between Canada and the United States and Canadian fears of being dominated by an overwhelmingly powerful U.S.-American cultural industry (as well as by a politically and economically much more potent neighbor to the south). Hence, the political context has clearly shifted, but the mobilizing force remains a close and empowering link between nation, culture, and literature. Atwood's cultural nationalism relies on the basic assumption of the distinctiveness of national cultures and literatures as well as on their political, anti-colonial function for the production of collective (and individual) identities. Atwood herself has exemplified the concept of survival in the novel *Surfacing*, published in 1972, the same year as *Survival*.

Tribal Nationalism. The two previous examples highlight the historical importance of cultural nationalism in different geographical and political contexts. However, the concept has also found more recent application, as the final example will illustrate. In the context of identity politics and the revival of ethnic consciousness during the 1990s, cultural nationalism has found expression in the writings of many indigenous theorists as **tribal nationalism**, a form of nationalism that shares an analytic and normative thrust with the previous examples. The position of native populations in Canada, the United States, Australia, and New Zealand is one of 'internal colonization,' often interpreted by indigenous activists as ongoing colonization. In Canada, the very term 'First Nations' that is now used to designate the indigenous population signals a political claim based on a—strategic or essentialist—connection between nation, population, territory, language, and culture. Lakota critic and writer Elizabeth Cook-Lynn has formulated tribal cultural nationalism as a clear obligation for indigenous authors; an obligation that many writers no longer fulfill—as Cook-Lynn sees it—for reasons of commercial success. She calls this situation a "postcolonial incoherence" (83) that leads to a dangerous misconception about the status of indigenous groups in North America (and probably, by extension of the argument, in other parts of the world, too)—in the eyes of the majority population, but also for indigenous peoples themselves. This misconception, she warns, has a negative impact on the project of political and cultural decolonization, for it leads to the assumption

that tribes are not nations, that they are not part of the Third World perspective vis-à-vis colonialism, and that, finally, they are simply 'colonized' enclaves in the United States, some kind of nebulous sociological phenomena. It is crucial to understand that such an assessment is in direct opposition not only to the historical reality of Indian nations in America, but also to the contemporary work being done by tribal governmental officials and activists, politicians, and grassroots intellectuals to defend sovereign definition in the new world. (82)

The concept of the nation that Cook-Lynn refers to is closely linked with the understanding of tribal cultures as distinctive and closed. With the French Orientalist Ernest Renan, she defines 'nation' as a "spiritual principle" (87), and stronger than in Atwood's concept, cultural nationalism for Cook-Lynn is a normative project in the context of cultural and political decolonization.

Such cultural nationalist definitions of indigeneity have not gone unchallenged, however. In a very different vein, the Maori writer Witi Ihimaera has used the image of "the rope of man" linking present-day Maori people to their ancestral generations. For Ihimaera, this rope embodies both the continuity of cultural specificity and the inevitability of transformation and change:

Some Maori believe that with the coming of the Pakeha [the white New Zealanders] it became frayed [...] It renewed itself, thickened, matted with strong twisting fibres and was as strong as it had been originally. But it was a *different* rope. It was different because the Pakeha became added to the rope, the strands of Pakeha culture entwining with ours, the blood of the Pakeha joining ours and going into the rope with our blood. Some people might think that diminished our strength. I like to think the opposite. The Pakeha has become included with us in singing not our songs but *our* songs. ("The Return," ch. 3)

In all the examples presented above, culture and literature are central elements of decolonization processes and struggles for cultural and political independence, as different as their contexts may be. Against this background, national culture is often conceptualized as clearly distinguishable and identifiable, and in reference to understandings of culture and nation as formulated in the eighteenth and nineteenth centuries. At the same time, these cultural nationalist conceptions interact—and clash—with theories and experiences of transnational culture, the mixing and transformation of cultural traditions, and cultural globalization, which will be addressed in more detail further below.

A key work of
Postcolonial Studies

## 4.4 | Writing Back

One of the most popular strands of contemporary postcolonial theory has evolved around the 'writing back' paradigm that was first systematically set out in 1989 in *The Empire Writes Back* by Bill Ashcroft, Gareth Griffiths, and Helen Tiffin, and has since had a major impact in literary and cultural studies. Drawing heavily on postmodern and poststructuralist theories of language, this paradigm postulates that postcolonial literatures are engaged in an **imaginative rewriting of European 'master**

**narratives'** that have shaped the ways in which the West has perceived the colonized parts of the world and often enough also the ways in which the colonized saw themselves. The writing back paradigm combines an endorsement of anticolonial politics with a strict critique of essentialist notions of cultural authenticity. Instead, it sees literature in terms of poststructuralist accounts of language and literature, for example by stressing the necessary indeterminacy of language produced by the ambiguous relationship between the signifier and the signified. Postcolonial literatures are thus seen as essentially deconstructive and subversive:

Hence it has been the project of post-colonial writing to interrogate European discourse and discursive strategies from its position within and between two worlds […]. Thus the rereading and rewriting of the European historical and fictional record is a vital and inescapable task at the heart of the post-colonial enterprise. These subversive manoeuvres, rather than the construction of essentially national or regional alternatives, are the characteristic features of the post-colonial text. Post-colonial literatures/cultures are constituted in counter-discursive rather than homologous practices. (Ashcroft, Griffiths and, *Empire* 196)

The **counter-discursive dimensions** of 'postcolonial' literature, art, film and new media practices, music, and performance have become a major field of postcolonial analysis in the last two decades. Such analysis has sought to explore the complex intertextual and intermedial relationships between (fictional and non-fictional) European 'master texts' and their postcolonial 'rewritings' and has often focused on the ironical or satirical modes by which 'postcolonial texts' seek to dismantle hierarchies of knowledge based on the legacies of empire. While this approach has become particularly fruitful with regard to work produced in the context of anticolonial movements or in the immediate aftermath of political decolonization, the more general idea that "the characteristic features of the postcolonial text" are grounded in "subversive manoeuvres" directed against the cog-

nitive, intellectual, and cultural legacy of colonialism has increasingly met with criticism. On the one hand, more than half a century after the end of European colonialism in most parts of the world, the idea that 'experiences of colonialism' and resistance to colonial imposition still constitute the mainspring of 'postcolonial' cultures and literatures is rapidly losing plausibility. On the other hand, writers and artists from Africa, India and other parts of the formerly colonized world have pointed out that the 'writing back' paradigm severely restricts the scope of cultural production and effectively sidelines a wide variety of other concerns that inform contemporary cultural practices—and have thus often rejected the label 'postcolonial' altogether (see, for example, Osundare; Trivedi and Mukherjee).

As for instance Thomas King's work illustrates, 'writing back' provides a tool to analyze specific aspects of indigenous literatures, for example, but the texts always very self-confidently do more than 'resist' or 'write back'; besides their own agenda, they pose questions to the categories of 'writing-back' and 'resistance' as concepts that implicitly subscribe about the very power structures they seek to debunk and that do not take into account processes of transculturation. Texts like King's draw on numerous cultural strategies and sources and thus present a 'cultural mixture' that cannot simply be reduced to categories such as 'resistance' or 'writing back.'

Thomas King, *Green Grass, Running Water*

A recent example for the writing back-paradigm, its complexities and ambivalences, is the novel *Green Grass, Running Water* (1993) by Cherokee author Thomas King. The novel self-confidently draws on a variety of aesthetic strategies: it incor-

porates and imitates oral storytelling, its narrative is in many ways postmodern in its fragmentation, it strongly deploys intertextuality and citation practice, it is highly self-reflexive—and it 're-writes' a number of canonical texts, such as the biblical Book of Genesis, Daniel Defoe's

Interpretation

*Robinson Crusoe*, James Fenimore Cooper's *Leatherstocking Tales*, and Herman Melville's *Moby-Dick*, as well as the stories of pop-culture heroes like the Lone Ranger or Hollywood Western movies. The very title of the novel is a citation, referring to the (usually broken) treaties between Europeans and Native Americans in which the set aside land was supposedly guaranteed to the indigenous population "as long as the grass is green and the water runs."

*Green Grass, Running Water* is a good example for the interpretative opportunities offered by the writing back-paradigm, but also (maybe even more so) its limits. Set in present-day Alberta, Canada, it tells the interwoven stories of a number of Blackfoot individuals.

Four trickster figures, named Lone Ranger, Ishmael, Robinson Crusoe, and Hawkeye structure the main parts of the novel, each one an attempt 'to tell it right,' and in each, one canonical or popular narrative is taken up. One that comes closest to the classic writing back-paradigm is the story of Changing Woman, a Native mythological figure, who finds herself on Captain Ahab's ship. Through her exchange with Ishmael (whose name she eventually takes) and Captain Ahab, King draws attention to the assumptions and power structures which underlie the culture that produced and canonized *Moby-Dick*, including its will to dominate and its destructive tendencies:

And. When they catch the whales. They kill them. This is crazy, says Changing Woman. Why are you killing all these whales? Oil. Perfume, too. There is a big market in dog food, says Ahab. This is a Christian world, you know. We only kill things that are useful or things we don't like. (ch. 1)

It is Changing Woman's no-nonsense questions (and the re-interpretation of the great white—male—whale as a great black—female—whale) that strip *Moby-Dick* of both its metaphorical layers and its claim to cultural authority.

But despite some of the characteristics of 'writing-back'—that is, the retelling of a canonical story from a subaltern point of view and hence a subversion of the claim to cultural authority carried by the 'original'—the novel does not pursue an agenda focused exclusively on debunking the power of the text; it is not solely an act of resistance or subversion. Instead, *Green Grass* refuses to subscribe to the center-periphery model on which the writing-back paradigm is built. Indigenous stories as well as the mode of oral storytelling as such are imbued with claims to cultural authority in their own right: the adaptation of canonical stories becomes a (trans)cultural incorporation and indigenization that goes far beyond the deadlock of resistance. Thomas King himself has repudiated the application of postcolonial paradigms to indigenous literatures; Native writing, he argues, is not limited to resistance to European or Euro-American/-Canadian models but undergoes developments that may engage with these models, but on terms of their own and with effects of their own.

## 4.5 | Hybridity

The ongoing processes of cultural transformation and adaptation that postcolonial literatures and cultures attest to have been theoretically captured in a multiplicity of terms. Syncretism, creolization, transculturation, Mestisaje and hybridity are the most prominent examples, each with a specific focus:

- **syncretism** originally mainly referred to cultural 'mixture' in the field of religion and has more recently been employed in cultural theory and theater studies;

- **creolization** is originally a linguistic concept that has become an influential concept in Cultural Studies;

- **transculturation** and **Mestisaje** were developed in specific geographical contexts (the Caribbean and Mexico/the U.S.-American Southwest, respectively).

While each of these concepts has widened its meaning and has come to encompass cultural phenomena beyond the context of its emergence, it is the concept of **hybridity** that has emerged as probably one of the most influential concepts in postcolonial theory.

**Terminology.** The term itself goes back to biology, and particularly in the nineteenth century was closely linked to the debate around the question of polygenesis or monogenesis (that is, the question whether human beings, regardless of race, are of common origin) and hence to highly problematic conceptions of 'race.' Notions of race, in turn, cannot be understood independent of attempts to justify racial hierarchizations within the human species as well as the prohibition of racial mingling (see for instance Young). The negative connotation one might thus expect to be connected to 'hybridity' has been critically remarked upon (Young), but contemporary understandings of the term are usually dissociated from these earlier biological connotations. Drawing rather on a number of theoretizations of cultural 'mixture'—such as the notion of transculturation formulated by the Cuban theorist Fernando Ortiz in the 1940s—hybridity nowadays has become associated most notably with Homi Bhabha and his seminal *The Location of Culture* (1994); further explorations of the concept will focus on this dominant—but not uncontroversial—understanding.

**Bhabha's theory of hybridity** is closely connected to the specific situation in colonial India and marked by a sense of ambivalence. While colonialism is clearly shaped by power differentials, Bhabha nevertheless sees colonized and colonizers engaged in a process of mutual cultural constitution, a process that is fed not only by cultural contact per se, but also by the 'civilizing' agenda and the pedagogical claims put forward by the British in India. In this context of 'civilizing India,' Bhabha argues, cultural purity becomes an obsession of the colonizers. Since this notion of purity insists on an ontologically founded boundary between 'English' culture and Indian culture(s), cultural influence is supposed to be only unidirectional, for instance through the implementation of the British school system, Christian missions, and the spread of the English language. This view of cultural processes, Bhabha holds, is an illusion born out of fear, since the process of colonization changes not only the culture of the colonized, but also that of the colonizers: "A contingent, borderline experience opens up *in-between* colonizer and colonized. This is a space of cultural and interpretive undecidability produced in the 'present' of the colonial moment" (206). This openness of a cultural in-between results in an uncontrollability of cultural processes

generally; thus, it produces unexpected effects that fundamentally question the possibility of fixed boundaries between cultures. Even culture itself becomes such an effect when Bhabha writes: "To see the cultural not as the *source* of conflict—*different* cultures—but as the *effect* of discriminatory practices—the production of cultural *differentiation* as signs of authority—changes its value and the rules of recognition" (114).

Therefore, the concept of hybridity as such undermines the credibility of juxtaposing ethnic and cultural groups as supposedly homogenous units. With Bhabha, hybridity is to be understood as a process of cultural formation, in which the criteria to **identify 'difference'** are not fixed from the start, but have to be constantly re-negotiated in a discursive space that Bhabha calls the "third space of enunciation" (37).

Bill Ashcroft, Gareth Griffiths, and Helen Tiffin directly relate this space to the development of individual and collective cultural identities when they write: "Cultural identity always emerges in this contradictory and ambivalent space [the third space of enunciation], which for Bhabha makes the claim to a hierarchical 'purity' of cultures untenable" (*Post-Colonial Studies* 118). This **'third space'** is therefore also the prerequisite for the articulation of a non-static, that is, in its criteria not-predefined form of cultural difference; for Bhabha, this distinguishes cultural hybridity from interculturality or multiculturality, since "the theoretical recognition of the split-space of enunciation may open the way to conceptualizing an *inter*national culture, based not on the exoticism of multiculturalism or the diversity of cultures, but on the inscription and articulation of culture's *hybridity*" (38). Bhabha's understanding of hybridity thus emphasizes the inherent **heterogeneity of cultures**; cultures are understood as porous, constantly transforming constellations rather than as identifiable units. At the same time, hybridity is conceptualized as the phenomenon of a specific colonial formation, that is, British colonialism on the Indian subcontinent. This background is central for the understanding and application of the term, an instance that is often ignored.

**Shift to Transculturality.** This is one of the reasons why, roughly since the early 2000s, there has been a shift from 'hybridity' to 'transculturality' (Huggan, "Postcolonialism"; Schulze-Engler and Helff). This shift is paradigmatic in so far as it differs from both hybridity and the early

Key theorist of the postcolonial condition: Homi Bhabha

term 'transculturation' (see above) in its focus on ongoing cultural transformation processes in globalized contexts. While these processes more often than not are embedded in power asymmetries (a constellation stressed by transculturation and hybridity against their specific contexts, the Caribbean and India), the development does not only question notions of cultural purity (as 'hybridity' does), but also moves beyond the binaries of specific colonial power hierarchies to investigate the manifold transcultural and transnational connections that shape cultures in virtually all locations in a rapidly globalizing world (Hannerz) and the "constitutive transculturality" (Ashcroft) of texts produced and read in complex cultural settings.

## 4.6 | Future Perspectives: Postcolonial Studies in the United States and Europe

While postcolonial studies developed primarily with regard to those former colonies of the British Empire that became independent during the nineteenth and twentieth centuries, major debates have also emerged about the potential application of postcolonial concepts to the United States and, more recently, Europe. The implications of these discussions are far-reaching, since they suggest an impact of colonialism not only on the former settler colonies and on former colonies in Africa, the Caribbean, the Pacific, and Asia, but also on former colonizing countries such as Britain, France, or Germany, and on a United States that is often perceived as a (neo)imperial successor to European colonialism.

**United States.** With regard to the United States, this discussion revolved around three main issues: the theoretical question of whether the U.S. should be included in the field of postcolonial studies, and if so, what its exact positioning should or could be vis-à-vis countries like India or Nigeria; the actual application of postcolonial theory in fields such as ethnic studies; and the effects of academic institutionalization on the theory and methodology of postcolonial studies.

The position of the United States within postcolonialism has been a problematic one from the beginning. Bill Ashcroft, Gareth Griffiths, and Helen Tiffin in *The Empire Writes Back* saw the United States and its "relationship with the metropolitan centre as it evolved over the last two centuries [as] paradigmatic for post-colonial literatures everywhere" (2). This acknowledgement of U.S.-American 'postcoloniality' notwithstanding, the authors leave the literatures of the United States largely aside in their subsequent analyses of postcolonial writing.

Against this background, Peter Hulme has diagnosed a large-scale **exclusion** of the U.S. in postcolonial theory when he noted that "America—in a

continental sense—barely features on the [postcolonial] map at all" ("Including" 118). While Hulme focuses on a neglect of 'America' rather than just the U.S. in postcolonial theory, the United States nevertheless remain a special case: given its early independence and even more so its geo-political position as a superpower and central player in contemporary exploitative global structures, the label 'postcolonial'—positioning the U.S. in one category with Ghana or Bangladesh—seems to be absurd at first glance. However, as Hulme points out, "because 'postcolonial' should not be used as a merit badge, the adjective implies nothing about a country's behavior […] a country can be postcolonial and colonizing at the same time" ("Including" 122).

By contrast, Anne McClintock, referring to Ashcroft et al.'s inclusive definition of 'postcolonial' as covering "all the culture affected by the imperial process from the moment of colonization to the present day" (Ashcroft, Griffiths, and Tiffin, *Empire* 2) has sharply rejected the inclusion of the U.S. in the 'postcolonial world': "by what fiat of historical amnesia can the United States of America, in particular, qualify as 'post-colonial'—a term which can only be a monumental affront to the Native American peoples" (McClintock 256).

**American Studies and Postcolonial Studies.** Despite the initial heatedness of these debates about the applicability of postcolonial theory to the U.S.-American context, postcolonial theory *was* de facto applied in the context of American Studies from the 1990s onwards, and has become a crucial and by now indispensable theoretical framework, particularly in the field of ethnic studies. While this has remained controversial with regard to Native American—and across the border First Nations—Studies (see for instance King; Emberley), postcolonial theory has offered important theoreti-

Is the United States a postcolonial country?

cal tools for the analysis of power relations between ethnic groups: the close attention postcolonial theory pays to the linkage between power and knowledge, for instance, or to the effect of historical colonial relationships on contemporary societal constellations ties in with long-standing concerns, particularly of African American and Chicano/Chicana Studies. Also, postcolonial theory has become crucial to the discussion about transnational migration movements and the analysis of diasporic communities within the United States, most prominently the South East Asian diaspora.

By now, postcolonial studies are firmly institutionalized in the United States—as part of American Studies, but even more so in English departments. As in other contexts, these academic institutionalizations have had direct effects on the field: the increasing dominance of U.S. institutions and the presence of important theorists at American universities such as Harvard (Bhabha) or Columbia (Spivak, the late Said) has 'Americanized' postcolonial studies both in focus and perception. An important aspect of postcolonial studies has been a focus on the global dominance of the U.S. as a new 'Empire,' and this shift has, in part, led to a problematic reduction of postcolonial studies to a U.S. framework and to debates that assess the significance of postcolonial theory only with regard to this specific field—without always making this narrowed focus explicit (see for instance Agnani et al.).

Europe. Recent debates on bringing Europe into postcolonial studies have followed a somewhat different trajectory, because 'Europe' is, paradoxically, both everywhere and nowhere in postcolonial discourse. On the one hand, it is everywhere, because long traditions of "Provincializing Europe" (Chakrabarty)—of combating Europe's Orientalism, of dismantling Europe's intellectual, political, and economic legacies of Empire, and of analysing how postcolonial literatures 'write back' to the former European centres of colonial and imperial power—have been central to the academic and political concerns of postcolonial studies worldwide. On the other hand, Europe is nowhere, because it has effectively been written out of the idea of a 'postcolonial world' (which in many varieties of postcolonialism continues to function as a half-defiant, half-nostalgic latter-day synonym of 'Third World') and because postcolonial discourse has largely abstained from addressing the consequences of the complex and contradictory dynamism of contemporary European unification for its own intellectual and institutional practice.

In recent years, "Postcolonial Europe" (see Huggan, "Perspectives"; Ponzanesi and Blaagard) has become an important issue in postcolonial studies for at least three interrelated reasons.

**1. The legacy of colonialism** for the political, social and cultural make-up of contemporary Europe has become a pressing issue against the background of a wave of xenophobia and racism that has accompanied the process of European integration. The loss of Europe's overseas empires was never properly reflected in a European integration process geared towards overcoming the legacies of fascism and war, but not of colonialism: the process of European integration began when Britain, France, Belgium, and the Netherlands were still largely in possession of their colonial empires, and there were no international law courts to deal with Europe's colonial crimes, nor was there a Truth and Reconciliation Commission to make the voices of Europe's colonial victims heard. Europe is thus arguably in dire need to face up to its own colonial past and its current "postcolonial condition" (Hulme, "Beyond" 54) in order to overcome its "Postcolonial Melancholia" (Gilroy).

**2. New patterns of migration** that emerged from the mid-twentieth century onwards have transformed Europe from a continent that had traditionally exported its population across the globe to a major destination of world-wide immigration flows, many of which were and continue to be connected to Europe's colonial past. The realities of Europe's "inner cosmopolitanization" (Beck 166) and multicultural transformation have thus generated conflicts and opportunities that in many respects resemble sociocultural constellations (i.e. in Canada, Australia or New Zealand) that have already become a focus of postcolonial studies and to which postcolonial approaches can be fruitfully applied. In addition, a uniquely European mode of postcolonial analysis has emerged through the application of postcolonial paradigms to post-Communist societies and cultures in East and Central Europe (see, for example, Kelertas; Korek).

**3. The "feral beauty of postcolonial culture, literature, and arts** of all kinds [that] is already contributing to the making of new European cultures" (Gilroy 142) has increasingly become addressed in European postcolonial studies. Thus "postcolonial Britain" (Dawson), "postcolonial France" (Barclay), "postcolonial Italy" (De Donno), "postcolonial Spain" (Hanley) and even "postcolonial Germany" (Ha, al-Samarai, and Mysorekar) have long since become established categories in postcolonial literary and cultural studies. Beyond the national frameworks that paradoxically still inform many of these studies (particularly with regard to Black and Asian British Literature in Britain), European postcolonial studies has also begun to explore the wider European dimensions of postcolonial cultures and literatures, e.g. with regard to migrant literatures (Ponzanesi and Merolla) and to Afro-European literature (Brancato; Bekers, Helff, and Merolla).

The factual extension of postcolonial studies to both Europe and the U.S. presents a further challenge to an academic field of analysis that is currently engaged in a thoroughgoing process of introspection and self-transformation. Major publications in recent years have called for "Revisioning Post-Colonial Studies" (Mayer), "Reframing Postcolonial Studies" (Gopal and Lazarus) and "Re-routing the Postcolonial" (Wilson, Şandru, and Lawson Welsh) or have explored new perspectives relating to "Postcolonial Studies and Beyond" (Loomba et al.). Although the diverse perspectives suggested in these and similar publications are often hard to reconcile, they nevertheless seem to concur in identifying globalization as a major challenge that postcolonial studies will have to contend with in order to safeguard its own credibility and institutional future. In such a scenario, the transition in postcolonial studies from an earlier anticolonial politics and emphasis on literatures and cultures of a 'postcolonial world' (that could be set against a 'non-postcolonial' part of the world) towards more general models of cultural complexity, interaction, and conflict in a world of decentered, globalized modernity is likely to gather pace.

## Select Bibliography

**Achebe, Chinua.** "The Novelist as Teacher." *Morning Yet on Creation Day*. London: Heinemann, 1977. 42–45.

**Agnani, Sunil, et al.** "Editors' Column: The End of Postcolonial Theory?" *PMLA* 122.3 (2007): 633–50.

**Anderson, Benedict.** *Imagined Communities: Reflections on the Origin and Spread of Nationalism*. London: Verso, 1991.

**Ashcroft, Bill.** "Reading the Other: Constitutive Transculturality in a Hong Kong Classroom." *Beyond 'Other Cultures': Transcultural Perspectives on Teaching the New Literatures in English*. Eds. Sabine Doff and Frank Schulze-Engler. Trier: WVT, 2011. 17–30.

**Ashcroft, Bill, Gareth Griffiths, and Helen Tiffin.** *The Empire Writes Back: Theory and Practice in Post-Colonial Literatures*. London: Routledge, 1989.

**Ashcroft, Bill, Gareth Griffiths, and Helen Tiffin.** *Post-Colonial Studies: The Key Concepts*. London: Routledge, 2007.

**Atwood, Margaret.** *Survival: A Thematic Guide to Canadian Literature*. Toronto: Anansi, 1972.

**Barclay, Fiona.** *Writing Postcolonial France: Haunting, Literature, and the Maghreb*. Lanham: Lexington, 2011.

**Beck, Ulrich.** *The Cosmopolitan Vision*. Cambridge: Polity, 2006.

**Bekers, Elisabeth, Sissy Helff, and Daniela Merolla, eds.** *Transcultural Modernities: Narrating Africa in Europe*. Spec. issue of *Matatu* 36 (2009): 1–442.

**Bhabha, Homi.** *The Location of Culture*. London: Routledge, 1994.

**Brancato, Sabrina.** *Afro-Europe: Texts and Contexts*. Berlin: Trafo, 2009.

**Brydon, Diana.** "New Approaches to the New Literatures in English." *Westerly* 3 (1989): 23–30.

**Centre for Contemporary Cultural Studies.** *The Empire Strikes Back: Race and Racism in 70s Britain*. London: Routledge, 1982.

**Chakrabarty, Dipesh.** *Provincializing Europe: Postcolonial Thought and Historical Difference*. Princeton: Princeton University Press, 2000.

**Cook-Lynn, Elizabeth.** *Why I Can't Read Wallace Stegner and Other Essays: A Tribal Voice*. Madison: University of Wisconsin Press, 1996.

**Cooper, Frederick.** "Postcolonial Studies and the Study of History." Loomba et al. 401–22.

**Dawson, Ashley.** *Mongrel Nation: Diasporic Culture and the Making of Postcolonial Britain*. Ann Arbor: University of Michigan Press, 2007.

**De Donno, Fabricio.** "Colonial and Postcolonial Italy." *Interventions: International Journal of Postcolonial Studies* 8.3 (2006): 371–539.

**Depelchin, Davy.** "Im Banne des Orients: Motive und Erscheinungsformen einer künstlerischen Strömung." *Orientalismus in Europa: Von Delacroix bis Kandinsky*. Eds. Roger Diederen and Davy Depelchin. Munich: Hirmer, 2011. 15–32.

**Emberley, Julia.** *Thresholds of Difference: Feminist Critique, Native Women's Writing, Postcolonial Theory*. Toronto: University of Toronto Press, 1993.

**Frye, Northrop.** "Conclusion to a Literary History of Canada." *Literary History of Canada*. Ed. Carl F. Klinck. Toronto: University of Toronto Press, 1965. 213–50.

**Gilroy, Paul.** *Postcolonial Melancholia*. New York: Columbia University Press, 2005.

**Gopal, Priyamvada, and Neil Lazarus, eds.** *After Iraq: Reframing Postcolonial Studies*. Spec. issue of *New Formations* 59 (2006): 1–171.

**Ha, Kien Nghi, Nicola al-Samarai, and Sheila Mysorekar.** Introduction. *Re/visionen: Postkoloniale Perspektiven von People of Colour auf Rassismus, Kulturpolitik und Widerstand in Deutschland*. Eds. Kien Nghi Ha, Nicola al-Samarai, and Sheila Mysorekar. Münster: Unrast, 2007. 1–21.

**Hanley, Jane.** "Vanishing Empires: Francisco Solano and Spain's Postcolonial Present." *Conflict, Memory Transfers and the Reshaping of Europe*. Eds. Helena Gonçalves da Silva et al. Newcastle: Cambridge Scholars, 2010. 231–37.

**Hannerz, Ulf.** *Transnational Connections: Culture, People, Places*. London: Routledge, 1996.

Huggan, Graham. "Perspectives on Postcolonial Europe." *Journal of Postcolonial Writing* 44.3 (2008): 241–49.

Huggan, Graham. "Postcolonialism, Globalization, and the Rise of (Trans)Cultural Studies." *Towards a Transcultural Future: Literature and Society in a 'Post'-Colonial World.* Eds. Geoffrey V. Davis et al. Amsterdam: Rodopi, 2004. 27–35.

Hulme, Peter. "Beyond the Straits: Postcolonial Allegories of the Globe." Loomba et al. 41–61.

Hulme, Peter. "Including America." *ARIEL* 26.1 (1995): 117–23.

Ihimaera, Witi. "The Return." In: Ihimaera, *The Rope of Man.* Auckland: Reed, 2005. 169–322.

Kelertas, Violeta, ed. *Baltic Postcolonialism.* Amsterdam: Rodopi, 2006.

King, Thomas. "Godzilla vs. Postcolonial." *World Literature Written in English* 30.2 (1990): 10–16.

Korek, Janusz, ed. *From Sovietology to Postcoloniality: Poland and Ukraine from a Postcolonial Perspective.* Huddinge: Södertörns Högskola, 2007.

Loomba, Ania, et al., eds. *Postcolonial Studies and Beyond.* Durham: Duke University Press, 2005.

Mayer, Igor, ed. *Critics and Writers Speak: Revisioning Post-Colonial Studies.* Lanham: Lexington, 2006.

McClintock, Anne. "The Angel of Progress: Pitfalls of the Term 'Postcolonialism.'" *Colonial Discourse/Postcolonial Theory.* Eds. Francis Barker, Peter Hulme, and Margaret Iversen. Manchester: Manchester University Press, 1994. 253–66.

Ngũgĩ wa Thiong'o. *Decolonising the Mind: The Politics of Language in African Literature.* London: Currey, 1986.

Ortiz, Fernando. "El fenómeno social de la transculturación y su importancia en Cuba." *Revista Bimestre Cubana* 46 (1940): 273–78.

Osundare, Niyi. "How Post-Colonial is African Literature?" *Caribbean Writers Between Orality and Writing / Les Auteurs Caribéens entre l'oralité et l'écriture.* Eds. Marlies Glaser and Marion Pausch. Spec. issue of *Matatu* 12 (1994): 203–16.

Peltre, Christine. *Orientalism in Art.* New York: Abbeville, 1998.

Peltre, Christine. "Und die Frauen?" *Orientalismus in Europa. Von Delacroix bis Kandinsky.* Eds. Roger Diederen, Davy Depelchin. Munich: Hirmer, 2011. 156–65.

Ponzanesi, Sandra, and Bollette B. Blaagaard. "Introduction: In the Name of Europe." *Social Identities* 17.1 (2011): 1–10.

Ponzanesi, Sandra, and Daniela Merolla, eds. *Migrant Cartographies: New Cultural and Literary Spaces in Post-Colonial Europe.* Lanham: Lexington, 2005.

Pratt, Mary Louise. *Imperial Eyes: Travel Writing and Transculturation.* 1992. London: Routledge: 2008.

Rushdie, Salman. "The Empire Writes Back with a Vengeance." *The Times,* 3 July 1982 : 8.

Said, Edward W. *Culture and Imperialism.* New York: Vintage, 1993.

Said, Edward W. *Orientalism.* 1978. London: Penguin, 2003.

Schulze-Engler, Frank, and Sissy Helff, eds. *Transcultural English Studies: Theories, Fictions, Realities.* Amsterdam: Rodopi, 2009.

Sen, Amartya. *Identity and Violence: The Illusion of Destiny.* 2006. New York: Norton, 2007.

Slemon, Stephen. "Introductory Notes: Postcolonialism and its Discontents." *ARIEL* 26.1 (1995): 7–11.

Spivak, Gayatri Chakravorty. "Criticism, Feminism, and the Institution." *The Post-Colonial Critic: Interviews, Strategies, Dialogues.* Ed. Sarah Harasym. New York: Routledge, 1990. 1–16.

Trivedi, Harish, and Meenakshi Mukherjee. *Interrogating Post-Colonialism: Theory, Text, and Context.* Shimla: Indian Institute of Advanced Study, 1996.

Wilson, Janet, Cristina Şandru, and Sarah Lawson Welsh, eds. *Rerouting the Postcolonial: New Directions for the New Millennium.* London: Routledge, 2010.

Young, Robert. *Colonial Desire: Hybridity in Theory, Culture and Race.* London: Routledge, 1995.

*Katja Sarkowsky / Frank Schulze-Engler*

# 5 Film and Media Studies

## 5.1 | Introduction: Media Culture in the Electronic Age

When Marshall McLuhan, the celebrated Canadian media and communication theorist and 'high guru' of media culture, first coined the phrase "global village" in 1964, no one could have predicted the level of information-dependency of our planet today. The mechanical age has been left behind and has given way to a postmodern electronic age. We spend an incredible amount of time every day using media, which in itself is a sign of their ubiquity. They represent a huge industry, and are all-powerful for the very reason that they have such a profound effect on us. They shape our ideas, behaviour and what we experience as reality and, due to the computerization of even remote geographic regions of the world, they guarantee that individuals are linked across languages and cultural borders. The **increased importance of media** in society and the intensified scholarly discussion of media and their interplay that came with it are a result of the differentiation and expansion of communication technologies in the latter part of the twentieth century:

The dissemination of audiovisual media at the beginning of the 20th century has led to changes in the relationship between text and image as well as to shifts in the relational structure between speaking and writing, between orality and literacy. Since the middle of the 20th century, television was the medium that took root, making audiovisuality into a constitutive factor of culture, challenging the boundaries of established differentiations—for example, between globality and locality or between the public and the private realms. With the pervasive expansion of computer technology and the development of networked communication towards the end of the 20th century, renewed shifts in cultural structures could be experienced leading to transformations in the various communicative cultures. (Jäger, Linz, and Schneider 9)

The Iconic Turn. One of the most characteristic features of the electronic age is the increase of mediated images and visual messages circulated by the media. While visuality has been an important paradigm within Western culture ever since classical antiquity, the invention and development of new visual media, such as panoramas, dioramas and, in particular, photography in the nineteenth century and television, video and digital technologies in the twentieth, have produced a deluge of pictures and further intensified the visual aspects of everyday life to such a degree that W.J.T. Mitchell (*Picture Theory*) speaks of an "**iconic turn**" within our culture. Other cultural critics today also detect an ongoing **marginalization of writing and printing** which they interpret as a symptom of the approaching demise of our book culture and the "Gutenberg galaxy" (McLuhan, *The Gutenberg Galaxy*). Nicholas Mirzoeff claims that "visualizing makes the modern period radically different from the ancient and medieval world in which the world was understood as a book" (6) and when works of art still had an aura, i.e. a singular cult value (Benjamin, "Work of Art"). Computer enthusiast Jay David Bolter maintains that today's U.S. newspapers and television show a general tendency to "replace words with images" and that on the worldwide web "the verbal text must now struggle to assert its legitimacy in a space increasingly dominated by visual modes of representation" (261 and 271). Obviously not all cultural critics today subscribe to an iconic turn; in fact, with

### Focus on Marshall McLuhan

**Marshall McLuhan** (1911–1980) was a Canadian communication theorist whose work strongly influenced modern media theory. He coined the term **global village** to describe the effect that progress in information and communication technology has on human societies. The global village is to be understood as the era that follows the **Gutenberg Galaxy** the period during which print media were the prime influence on human thought. Whilst the Gutenberg Galaxy saw the rapid growth of literacy and the rise of scientific methodology together with a strong focus on individual authorship, the development of electronic media has led to the bridging of communication gaps and the rapid global exchange of ideas and information in the global village.

regard to the new media such as the Internet, many emphatically believe in a new oral culture, which helps to restore what has allegedly been lost in the "Gutenberg age," namely face-to-face interaction. It was Walter Ong who predicted that TV, radio and the telephone as transmitters of talk would produce a "secondary orality" in the electric age; however, it has transpired that the development of computer networks has also led to a "secondary literacy": e-mail and Internet chat rooms contend with media such as TV, radio and the telephone. Georg Franck has highlighted another important aspect of our media culture, namely its new **economy of attention**. The leading concept of the new media such as TV and the Internet is the attracting of attention, which is hailed as the most important resource of the 'information society.' In a situation where the production of information is as all-pervading as it is in our contemporary Western societies, attention is the most precious commodity, and what indeed would be a better tool for attracting the attention of 'users' of the new media than eye-catching and appealing pictures with their enhanced memorability and high emotional impact? Certainly the success of the visual has disrupted and challenged any attempt to define our Western world in purely linguistic terms. But the variety and abundance of mixed media today suggest that it is premature to think of a complete transition from the verbal to the visual. The **increasing proliferation of visual images** in our digital culture brings about more and more diverse forms of conjunction and co-operation between the media, which warrant analysis. After all, media collaborate to enable human communication and the storage of knowledge.

## 5.2 | Media Studies: Medium—Mediality—Materiality

### 5.2.1 | Anglo-American vs. German Traditions

Theoreticians of culture have claimed that the twentieth century saw at least three turns in the humanities: the linguistic turn in the first half, the iconic turn in the second half and the media turn at its close. The media explosion that followed in the wake of the so-called digital revolution gave a tremendous boost to media studies.

In Anglo-American universities the academic disciplines of Film and Media Studies have become increasingly important since the 1960s. While the term 'film studies' is self-explanatory, the term 'media studies' is more complicated, because the terms 'medium' and 'media' have been defined in different ways in English- and German-speaking academia (for an overview of the expansion of media studies in the U.S., England and Germany cf. Voigts-Virchow 6–16). **Media Studies** in the English-speaking academic world deal with mechanical, electronic and digital media such as photography, film, TV, video, the internet etc., i.e. with new media technologies, with the way mass media communicate and with popular culture (for a critique of standardized mass culture and culture industry cf. Horkheimer and Adorno; cf. section II.2.2). They investigate the specific characteristics of mass media as well as their role in society. The task of studying various forms of communication, including mediated communication, has been shared with scholars in sociology, political science, psychology, rhetoric, journalism, other social sciences and the humanities.

In German universities the investigation into medium, mediality and media is a more encompassing field. Clearly, the Anglo-American tradition of Media Studies had its influence on German universities in the 1970s and 1980s, when Film and Media Studies were in their infancy and literary studies departments reshaped in order to deal with questions concerning the role of literature in an increasingly mass-mediated world. During the 1980s and 1990s, English/American literature de-

---

**A Very Short Timeline of the Media**

Some notable pivotal events in the history of the media and civilization are the invention of

- **writing** in ancient time (4000–3000 BC)
- **print** (Gutenberg's printing press, mid-fifteenth century)
- **photography** (first half of the nineteenth century) and **film/cinema** (ca. 1895)
- **electronic communications** (in 1896, Marconi introduced improvements to the telegraph in Britain which helped to establish radio in the decades to follow; the 1930s brought the first TV services, but national television emerged only after WW II)
- **electronic writing and computer networks** (since the 1980s, computers have been used on a broad scale).

partments at German universities focused on film and literature, on TV and screenplays. Now the field has diversified and includes more general areas of investigation such as general media theory, media anthropology, intermediality and media hybridity. *Medienwissenschaft* in German-speaking academia today investigates the materiality and specific nature of different media, the relationships between them, and analyzes the functions of literary texts in our post-modern electronic age. From the 1980s, research was extended towards the exploration of mediality, leading to discussions concerning problems such as the 'materiality of the sign' and the interrelationship between materiality and meaning in literary texts (Gumbrecht and Pfeiffer). While hermeneutics, in the tradition of Wilhelm Dilthey and Hans-Georg Gadamer had *Sinn* ("meaning") and *Geist* as their central concepts—they asked the question "what's the meaning of a literary text?"—, since the 1980s, **medium** and **mediality** have become the new core terms of literary debates, terms which demonstrate the heightened awareness of the material side of the production of meaning. According to the Swiss linguist Ferdinand de Saussure (cf. section V.2.2.2), a sign has two sides, the signifier (the physical object, e.g. sound) and the signified (mental concept). However, semioticians, especially structural and cognitive ones such as Louis Hjelmslev, concentrated in their research almost exclusively on the content, the *signifié-* or cognitive side while neglecting the material *signifiant*-side of the sign. The linguist Ludwig Jäger has therefore spoken recently of a displacement or repression of the problem of mediality, i.e. the sensuous side of a sign (Jäger 13). Whereas semiotics and a post-Saussurean logocentrism see language as the master discourse of all media, scholars working with concepts like mediality and materiality use interdisciplinary approaches and are interested in media differentiations, but also, and increasingly so, in the relationships between media, the historical interplay between the media, culture and communication, specific media-cultural configurations as well as the role media played in Western societies, which defined themselves as information-, knowledge- and media-societies. This has triggered many **comparative and historical media analyses** and acknowledges the fact that 'mediality' (also 'mediumhood') is a relational property, which has to be discussed through comparison of media. The discipline of comparative media studies helps to overcome the shortcomings of

*Theorizing mediality*

*Einzelmedienwissenschaft* and individual case studies. It takes into account today's convergence of media in the form of digital code and computer processing: different media converge in the social production of meaning, hence they can no longer be studied in isolation. *Medienwissenschaft* has become an important field of research in German universities and has subsequently led to repercussions in the English-speaking academic world.

## 5.2.2 | Terminology and Classification

Media allow for the production, distribution and reception of signs, hence they enable communication. They function as intermediaries, i.e. they are a means of increasing mediacy and overcoming distance. Without media there is no message, hence no meaning. But while these general functions of media are easily identified, it is far more difficult to define and classify them. Etymologically, the term *medius* in Latin means 'middle' and 'intermediate,' *Vermittler* (in German). It entered the English language around 1930 to designate channels of communication. However, since then, it has become a highly ambiguous term. In the plural form, 'media,' it is often equated with mass and popular culture:

> Ask a sociologist or cultural critic to enumerate media, and he will answer: TV, radio, cinema, the Internet. An art critic may list: music, painting, sculpture, literature, drama, the opera, photography, architecture. A philosopher of the phenomenological school would divide media into visual, auditory, verbal, and perhaps gustatory and olfactory (are cuisine and perfume media?). An artist's list would begin with clay, bronze, oil, watercolor, fabrics, and it may end with exotic items used in so-called mixed-media works, such as grasses, feathers, and beer can tabs. An information theorist or historian of writing will think of sound waves, papyrus scrolls, codex books, and silicon chips. 'New media' theorists will argue that computerization has created new media out of old ones: film-based versus digital photography; celluloid cinema versus movies made with video cameras; or films created through classical image-capture techniques versus movies produced through computer manipulations. The computer may also be responsible for the entirely new medium of virtual reality. (Ryan, Introduction 15–16)

The pioneering work of two Canadians, Harold Adams Innis and **Marshall McLuhan**, has inspired the work of scholars in media studies and media theory on both sides of the Atlantic for many decades. In his book-length study *Understanding Media*, published in 1964, McLuhan defines media in a very general way as a sort of prosthesis, as "any extension […] of man" (3) be it of the body or the consciousness. He differentiates between

- "hot" media such as the radio, movies and photography (characterized by high definition and filled with data), and
- "cool" media such as the telephone, television, cartoons (which have relatively little data and require interaction from the listener or viewer. (22–23)

**Friedrich A. Kittler**, a literary scholar who has worked on the history of material media and developed an archaeology and a hermeneutics of media technologies, uses the term "medium" exclusively when talking about technical channels and acoustic and optic media for transmitting and storing information such as the typewriter, film, television etc. In contrast, Aleida Assmann and Horst Wenzel understand "medium" in a much more general way; for them the term also includes non-technical media such as spoken language, writing, painting, the human body etc. This short overview of terminology has demonstrated that the meaning of the term "medium" is notoriously shifting and ambiguous; what constitutes a medium depends very much on the purpose of the investigator.

**Siegfried J. Schmidt** has argued that media systems consist of four components:

1. a semiotic instrument of communication, the prototype being natural oral language
2. a media technology; since the development of writing, examples of media technologies have included print, film, both kinds of "notebooks"
3. a social system, that is, institutions on which technologies are based, such as schools or TV stations
4. media products or offerings such as literature or music that provide the opportunity to study aspects like production, distribution, reception, and processing.

In addition, the entry for 'medium' in *Webster's Ninth Collegiate Dictionary* is enlightening. It includes two definitions of 'medium' which are essential:

1. a channel or system of communication, information, or entertainment.
2. material or technical means of artistic expression.

The first definition is a transmissive one and presents a medium as a particular technology or cultural institution for the transmission of information. **Transmissive media** include television, radio, the internet, the gramophone, the telephone,

but also cultural channels such as books and newspapers. As Marie-Laure Ryan points out, in this conception of medium, "ready-made messages are encoded in a particular way, sent over the channel, and decoded on the other end. TV can, for instance, transmit films as well as live broadcasts, news as well as recordings of theatrical performances. Before they are encoded in the mode specific to the medium in sense 1, some of these messages are realized through a medium in sense 2. A painting must be done in oil before it can be digitized and sent over the Internet" (Introduction 16). Communicative media are not simply conduits and hollow pipes, but also carry out configuring action. Obviously, each medium has certain constraints and possibilities, i.e. built-in properties, which shape the message they encode. As Stuart Hall, towering figure of the renowned communication and cultural-studies department at the University of Birmingham (closed since 2002; cf. section III.2.2.2) has demonstrated in a famous article entitled "**Encoding/Decoding**" (1973) on TV audience research, the transmission line and the decoding are far from being simple and unambiguous processes either. He posits three reading strategies, a "dominant" one (overlapping with the dominant ideology), a "negotiated" one (the viewer's real-life situation provokes some with critical inflections) and a "resistant" one (in opposition to the dominant ideology).

Of the two definitions of the term 'medium' given by *Webster's Dictionary* listed above, the first one, medium as channel of communication, has been far more influential in Anglo-American media studies, where media studies commonly concern themselves with technologies of mass communication and cultural institutions developed in

Stuart Hall's encoding/
decoding model

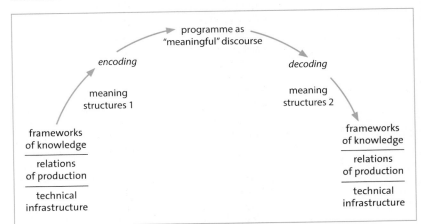

the twentieth century. The second definition of the term *medium*, material means of expression, has become more relevant for German *Medienwissenschaften* from the 1980s onwards. Defined in such a broad way, the phenomenon of media is as old as humankind, which is why Hans H. Hiebel in his article "Media: Tabelle zur Geschichte der Medien-Technik" (1991) starts his encompassing media chronicle in 4000 BC.

To summarize: The narrow use of the term **medium** which focuses solely on technological and sociological aspects and highlights media differences and specificities is now passé. It has been replaced by a broad understanding of the term which triggers an investigation of how meaning is generated by cross-medial references and allows for a systematic analysis of inter- and multimedial constellations. Media scholars for a long time investigated individual media, but they now agree that the specific characteristics of media can only be reconstructed through a comparative analysis of media. The history of individual media is too limited and cannot explain how intricately the history of one medium is linked to the history and development of other media. Faulstich and others plead for a more holistic *Medienkulturgeschichte* which takes into account the history and collabora-

tions of all media, their network of connections. As a consequence, the majority of literary scholars today also concurs that literature can no longer be understood in splendid isolation, but has to be questioned as to its role in a cultural field characterized by the competition and collaboration of different media. Questions concerning literature's "mediality," i.e. its status as verbal or written text, as printed (Eisenstein; Giesecke) or digitally encoded (Landow) document are crucial to the understanding of how meaning is produced. The new bibliography scholarship (Kastan), for instance, has achieved new insights into Shakespeare's texts by reading them against the backdrop of the history of manuscript culture, publishing and printing, i.e. within their material contexts. Bibliographers believe that the meaning of a text is intrinsically embedded in the medium in which the text is transmitted to its readers. Roger Chartier has recently brought the necessity of connecting the issue of meaning with that of materiality into relief:

In contrast to the representation of the ideal, abstract text—which is stable because it is detached from all materiality [...]—it is essential to remember that no text exists outside of the support that enables it to be read; any comprehension of a writing, no matter what kind it is, depends on the forms in which it reaches the reader. (161)

## 5.3 | Intermediality and Remediation

### 5.3.1 | Terminology I: Intra-, Trans-, and Intermediality

Like mediality, **intermediality** is a semantically shifting term, but this shifting quality might be the very reason why it has become so strikingly successful in German academic debates in literary studies since the 1980s and, subsequently, gained growing international recognition over the last decade (Todorow). Although Dick Higgins published a pioneer article called "Intermedia" in 1966, it was Aage Hansen-Löve, a scholar of Russian literature, who introduced the German term "Intermedialität" in a 1983 article. Whereas he applied it to text-picture relations such as modern Russian pattern poems, where both media, i.e. writing and pictures, are co-present, today intermediality is considered as an umbrella term which also includes ekphrastic phenomena (cf. section III.5.3.2 below), where only one medium, writing, is pres-

ent. Since the 1980s, the term intermediality has also played a major role in film studies (Paech, "Intermedialität") and communication theory (Luhmann, whose work inspired intermediality researchers like Paech).

Although intermediality as a research field requires interdisciplinary approaches and the collaboration between literary scholars, art historians, musicologists, film and media scholars, etc., literary scholars initially tended to understand intermediality as a neglected extension of **intertextuality**, i.e. of text-text relations as theorised by Gérard Genette, Renate Lachmann, and others. Since a definition of intermediality as a sub-branch of intertextuality superimposes textual criteria on other media, it produces problems. Hence it is more helpful to define intermediality in a more general and comprehensive way as the name for a field of studies dealing with interrelations between different media—in the case of the philologies, such relations can exist between texts and paintings, texts and sculptures, texts and architecture, texts and films, and texts and various forms of music.

Major theoreticians of intermediality like Werner Wolf and Irina O. Rajewsky have presented typologies which help to differentiate a wide range of intermedial phenomena. As Rajewsky points out, "researchers have begun to formally specify their particular conception of intermediality through such epithets as transformational [Spielmann], discursive, synthetic, formal, transmedial, ontological [Schröter], or genealogical intermediality [Gaudreault and Marion], primary and secondary intermediality [Leschke], or so-called intermedial figuration [Paech, 'Intermediale Figuration']" (Rajewsky 44). For Rajewsky, intermediality is an umbrella-term and hyperonym for all kinds of phenomena, which take place between media:

- 'intermedial' designates those configurations which have to do with a crossing of borders between media
- 'intramedial' phenomena do not involve a transgression of medial boundaries
- 'transmedial' phenomena are, for instance, the appearance of a certain motif or style across a variety of different media.

Intermedial phenomena can be studied from a synchronic research perspective, which allows scholars to develop typologies of specific forms of intermediality; and a diachronic perspective, which investigates the history of the media and their intersections and collaborations. According to Rajewsky, the current debate reveals two basic understandings of intermediality, "a broader and a narrower one, which are not in themselves homogeneous. The first concentrates on *intermediality as a fundamental condition or category* while the second approaches *intermediality as a critical category for the concrete analysis of specific individual media products or configurations*" (47, emphasis in original). Rajewsky's literary conception of intermediality in the latter and more narrow sense encompasses three subcategories, but it goes without saying that single medial configurations will match more than just one of the three subcategories:

**1.** Media combination (also called multi-media, pluri-media as well as mixed media); the examples she gives are opera, film, theatre, performances, illuminated manuscripts, comics, computer installations, etc. In this subcategory intermediality is "a communicative-semiotic concept, based on the combination of at least two medial forms of articulation" (52).

**2.** Medial transposition as, for example, film adaptations, novelizations, etc. This category is production-oriented, the intermedial quality "has to do with the way in which a media product comes into being, i.e., with the transformation of a given media product (a text, a film, etc.) or of its substratum into another medium" (51).

**3.** Intermedial references, for instance references in a literary text to a piece of music (the so-called 'musicalization of fiction'), the imitation and evocation of filmic techniques such as dissolves, zoom shots, montage editing, etc.; descriptive modes in literature which evoke visual effects or refer to specific visual works of art ('ekphrasis'). Intermedial references contribute to the overall signification; like the first category, they are of a communicative-semiotic nature, but they involve by definition only one medium. It is important to note that a mere mentioning of another medium or medium-product does not justify the label intermedial but only such media-products which evoke or imitate formal and structural features of another medium through the use of their own media-specific means ('as if' character and illusion-forming quality of intermedial references); they create the illusion of another medium's specific practices.

Apart from Rajewsky, narratologist Werner Wolf is the literary scholar who has published most widely on 'intermediality.' Wolf points out that intermediality studies had a forerunner in 'interart studies,' a sub-branch of the so-called 'Comparative Arts' or 'Comparative Literature' which dealt throughout the twentieth century with a range of contacts between literature and the 'high' arts such as music and painting. Wolf, however, argues in favour of a literature-centred investigation of contacts between verbal art and works of other media regardless of their status as high art, i.e. he includes artefacts, performances, and new media whose status as art is not obvious. Intermediality applies in its broadest sense to any transgression of boundaries between media, and thus is concerned with "'**heteromedial' relations** between different semiotic complexes" (Wolf, "Intermediality" 252). According to Wolf, intermediality deals with media as conventionally distinct means of communicating cultural content. Media in this sense are specified principally by the nature of their underlying semiotic systems (involving verbal language, pictorial signs, music, etc. or in cases of 'composite media' such as film, a combination of several semiotic systems); their technical or institutional channels are merely secondary. There are three main phenomena (253–55):

- 'intramediality,' which involves only one medium
- 'transmediality,' which describes such transmedial phenomena that are non-specific to individual media (motifs, thematic variation, narrativity)
- 'intermediality,' a category subdivided into two variants of intermedial relations/references. The involvement with another medium may take place explicitly ("whenever two or more media are overtly present in a given semiotic entity" 254) or covertly, i.e. indirectly (e.g. musicalization of fiction or ekphrasis, i.e. visualization of fiction/poetry). For many critics, the mere thematization of another medium is not enough, they reserve the term 'intermediality' for an evocation of certain formal features of another medium); change of the medium (i.e. film adaptation of a novel), combination of media ("multi-" or "plurimediality": ballet, opera, film, comic strips, technopagnia).

The typologies developed by Rajewsky and Wolf are attempts at charting the vast field of intermedial relations. As in all classifications there are many borderline cases, and multiple labellings of one and the same phenomenon are sometimes necessary.

## 5.3.2 | Text-Picture Relationships: History and Literary Examples

Emblem "Scripta manent" ("writinges laste"), 1586

According to W. J. T. Mitchell, there is no such thing as a "pure" medium: "all arts are 'composite' arts (both text and image); all media are mixed media" (*Picture Theory* 94–95). This implies that intermedial qualities inhere in cultural phenomena in general and works of art in particular. Not only questions concerning the specific material qualities of words, images and music/sound, but also investigations into the ways different media of one culture interact with one another and the role they have in the communication processes of post-modern societies have transformed literary studies into a more interdisciplinary field. The intermedial relationships between words and images in particular have become a central field of investigation. For centuries, poetry and painting were considered as "sister arts," closely following Horace's doctrine **ut pictura poesis** and thus believed to function according to the same rules. Aristotle outlined the earliest agenda for cross-me-

dial studies in his *Poetics*; the eighteenth-century German poet and playwright G. E. Lessing developed a detailed comparative study of the artistic media painting and poetry, their strengths and limitations. In his 1766 essay *Laocoön: An Essay on the Limits of Painting and Poetry* he attempted to differentiate decisively between words and pictures on a semiotic and medial basis. He separated the two sign systems as two radically different and independent modes of representation. Whereas language follows the rules of arbitrariness, successivity and time, images adhere to the laws of simultaneity and space. Although Lessing's essay was widely read and accepted at the time, the succeeding generation of Romantics began to blur Lessing's neat line of demarcation between the two arts. The late Romantic writer Walter Pater, for instance, stated in his essay on "The School of Giorgione" (1877) that

although each art has thus its own specific order of impressions, and an untranslatable charm, while a just apprehension of the ultimate differences of the arts is the beginning of aesthetic criticism; yet it is noticeable that, in its special mode of handling its given material, each art may be observed to pass into the condition of some other art, by what German critics term as *Anders-streben*—a partial alienation from its own limitations, through which the arts are able, not indeed to supply the place to each other, but reciprocally to lend each other new forces.

In his *New Laokoon* (1910) Irving Babbitt subsequently accused Romantic writers of "eleutheromania," i.e. of not respecting medial borderlines between the arts, and thereby distorting and perverting them. Babbitt asked for a new art, a modern art, which would develop a new generic and medial pu-

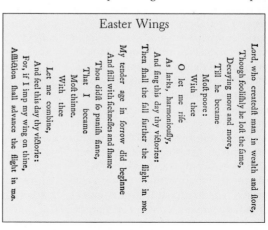

George Herbert, "Easter-Wings" (1633)

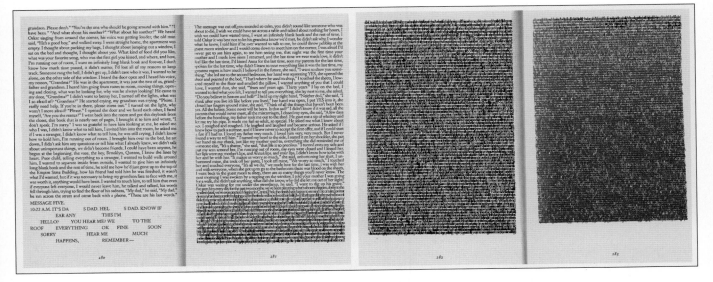

rity and accept the uniqueness of the different arts. The approaches of Lessing, Pater and Babbitt are examples of the different ways of defining the relationship between words and images. But no matter how such a relationship is conceived of, pictures have always been measured against their medial other, that is texts, and vice versa.

Literary texts have always had close ties with images: They are surrounded by cover pictures or frontispieces; they sometimes include miniature paintings, as is the case with many medieval texts; other texts are illustrated or arranged in an iconic form, or they allude verbally to pictures by describing them. **Intermedial text-picture relationships** in Anglo-American literature can be subdivided into three main categories:

**1.** Typographical experiments, where text and image are simultaneously present and actually form a unit, as is the case in so-called pattern/figure poems or technopaignia, a genre which dates back to antiquity but which has been successful throughout literary history.

George Herbert's "Easter-Wings" combines language's discursive character with iconic simultaneity. The meaning of the poem is intensified by the iconic arrangement of the words (see illustration on p. 320). Another example of typographical experiments in contemporary American fiction can be found in Jonathan Safran Foer's novel *Extremely Loud & Incredibly Close* (2005), which also contains reproductions of photographs and other visual material. In this typographical experiment (see above), Foer turns writing into a black canvas.

Jonathan Safran Foer, *Extremely Loud & Incredibly Close* (2005)

Graphic novel-adaptation of Paul Auster's *City of Glass* (2004)

**Ekphrasis** is a Greek term which etymologically means simply "to speak out" or "to show clearly and completely" and which the *OED* records as first used in English in 1715. According to James A. W. Heffernan's widely accepted definition, ekphrasis is "the verbal representation of visual representation" (*Museum* 2). There are a surprising number of contemporary novels and poetry collections, such as A. S. Byatt's *Still Life* (1985), and Charles Simic's *Dime-Store Alchemy* (1992), which are replete with ekphrastic passages, indicating that many contemporary writers have dealt with the

"iconic turn" and the new plethora of images. Their literary texts demonstrate convincingly that instead of simply proclaiming the death of the verbal and the victory of the pictorial or visual, the verbal today needs to be carefully dissected with regard to its collaboration, interaction and competition with the visual and vice versa. Here is an excerpt from Simic's poem "Cléo de Mérode," which consists partly of an ekphrastic description of a work of art, the box "L'Égypte de Mlle Cléo de Mérode cours élémentaire d'histoire naturelle" of the American Surrealist artist Joseph Cornell, constructed in 1940 (see illustration):

Doll's forearm, loose red sand, wood ball, German coin, several glass and mirror fragments, 12 corkstopped bottles, cutout sphinx head, yellow filaments, 2 intertwined paper spirals, cut-out of Cléo de Mérode's head, cutout of camels and men, loose yellow sand, 6 pearl beads, glass tube with residue of dried green liquid, crumpled tulle, rhinestones, pearl beads, sequins, metal chain, metal and glass fragments, threaded needle, red wood disc, bone and frosted glass fragments, blue celluloid, clear glass crystals, rock specimen, 7 balls, plastic rose petals, three miniature tin spoons for a doll house.

Simic's ekphrasis reduces language to nouns and adjectives with the effect that narrative time and movement come to a standstill. With this abstinence from verbs, Simic overcomes the mediality of language itself, its "sequentiality"— to use a term introduced by Lessing in his 1766 essay *Laocoön*—and thus to approximate poetic language to the graphic/plastic arts.

**2.** Text and picture are simultaneously present in a work, but as separate parts. Emblems are examples of this type of text-picture interaction (e.g. "Scripta Manent," see p. 320), as are graphic novels, for instance Paul Karasik and David Mazzucchelli's graphic novel-adaptation of Paul Auster's *City of Glass* (2004, see p. 321).

Another important example are illustrated literary texts, as for instance Virginia Woolf's short story "Kew Gardens" (1919) which includes not only woodcuts of Woolf's sister, the visual artist Vanessa Bell, but also testifies to the visual, often cinematic qualities of modernist literary texts.

**3.** Descriptions in literary texts can also count as a type of text-picture relationship. Here only one medium, text, is present, and the second medium, the image, is only evoked via verbal description (and is not present as a material form). If descriptive strategies are used to evoke general visual qualities, critics usually speak of "description," sometimes of "pictorialism" (Rippl). If, however, specific pictures or sculptures (which may or may not exist) are described, this is categorized as **ekphrasis**—a genre or mode of writing which has recently been the subject of many vibrant debates within literary and art history departments (see box).

## 5.3.3 | Terminology II: Remediation, Digitality and Hyper-Mediality

**Digitality** plays a crucial role when it comes to defining intermediality, and media scholars have asked whether the concept should be restricted to the analogue arts and media, because only there the materiality of a medium is actually present (Paech and Schröter). Henry Jenkins has introduced the term "convergence" to describe the series of intersections between different media systems in our digitalized world, and when Jay David Bolter and Richard Grusin discuss intermedial relationships in connection with digital media, they use a different term, namely **remediation**, a metaphor of media ecology which has replaced McLuhan's vision of media as network. Bolter and Grusin claim that in current (digital) media "*all* mediation is remediation" (55), understanding the concept of "remediation" as a particular kind of intermedial relationship through processes of medial refashioning. They define remediation as "the formal logic by which new media refashion prior media forms" (273); remediation is thus "*the mediation of mediation*: Each act of mediation depends on other acts of mediation. Media are continually commenting on, reproducing, and replacing each other, and this process is integral to media. Media need each other to function as media at all" (55); a medium "is that which remediates. It is that which appropriates the techniques, forms, and social significance of other media and attempts to rival or refashion them in the name of the real" (65):

[New] visual technologies, such as computer graphics and the World Wide Web […] are doing exactly what their predecessors have done: presenting themselves as refashioned and improved versions of other media. Digital media can best be understood through the ways in which they honor, rival, and revise linear-perspective painting, photography, film, television, and print. No medium today, and certainly no single media event, seems to do its cultural work in isolation from other media, any more than it works in isolation from other social and economic forces. What is new about new media comes from the particular ways in which they refashion older media and the ways in which older media refashion themselves to answer the challenges of new media. (14–15)

In the face of the recent technological developments, the question of how literature conceives of its relationship not only to the ubiquitous and powerful picture but also to the computer as a new hyper-medium is of pivotal importance. Obviously, the term 'literature' itself has undergone a considerable change in meaning. In the age of electronic media, the term 'literature' can actually be used for two distinct cultural phenomena:

**1.** It defines literary texts which exist **in printed form**, i.e. in black letters on white paper. Literary texts that appear in this medial form are usually associated with the concept of the 'strong author' whose work belongs to the Western canon and is therefore carefully edited, commented on, and activated by school and university curricula. In this tradition, a text is commonly defined as a fixed and linear set of verbal signs, the arrangement of which does not necessarily have to be recorded in a written mode, but can also be reproduced orally from memory. However, what is important is the identical reproduction of signs and words.

**2.** In the age of the computer and other electronic media, "literature" can also refer to another, new sort of literary texts, namely hypertextually encoded fictions such as Michael Joyce, *Afternoon: A Story* (1990), Stuart Moulthrop, *Victory Garden* (1991), Simon Biggs's *The Great Wall of China* (1996), and Caitlin Fisher's hypermedia novella *These Waves of Girls* (2001, http://www.yorku. ca/caitlin/waves) which exist only in an elec-

| **Focus on Remediation** |

Bolter and Grusin describe the **representation of one medium within another** as remediation and argue that "remediation is a defining characteristic of the new digital media" (45) and a basic trait of all medial practices. But as Rajewsky has rightly pointed out, while Bolter and Grusin's concept of remediation is a subcategory of intermediality in the broad sense, it is nevertheless "hardly reconcilable with conceptions of intermedial subcategories like medial transformation, media combination, or medial references" for the very reason that remediation "necessarily implies a tendency to level out significant differences both between the individual phenomena in question and between different media with their respective materiality; differences that come to the fore as soon as detailed analyses of specific medial configurations, their respective meaning-constitutional strategies, and their overall signification are at stake" (Rajewsky 64).

tronic medial form. **Hyperfiction** is characterized by its (quasi-)interactive features which persistently question and challenge traditional notions of "text," "author" and "reader." As hyperfictions request their readers to co-create the text, they do not have the same stability and linear form as traditional texts; and as they challenge the positions conventionally ascribed to reader and author respectively, they require us to revise our concept of the "strong author." On top of that, their interactive and multimedial form invites us to rethink the concept of a purely verbal art. Landow defines a hypertext as a "text composed of blocks of words (or images) linked electronically by multiple paths, chains, or trails in an open-ended, perpetually unfinished textuality described by the terms link, node, network, web, and path" (3). As a huge number of hypertextually structured fictions are created day by day, they ask for critical attention and invite literary scholars to further specify and apply the existing theoretical approaches to these new phenomena. Computer philology has become a new field of investigation in literary studies, which focuses on the issues sketched above (Jannidis).

# 5.4 | Literature and the (Audio-)Visual Media: Photography—Film—TV

What has been said so far demonstrates the desirability of a *Medienkulturwissenschaft* which aims at analyzing the relationship between meaning and medium and asks how literature at specific times related to other medial configurations. For some time, literary scholars have shown a certain resistance to the topics of materiality, mediality

and intermediality. In 1999, Jörg Schönert published an article called "Germanistik als Medienwissenschaft oder als radikale Philologie?"—a title that summarizes the situation of literary studies in Germany today. Whereas in the 1970s the philologies and humanities were geared towards the social sciences, they are now requested to metamorphose into media and cultural studies. The central terms *Sprache—Geist—Bildung* have been replaced by "culture" or "collective and cultural memory" and the new holy trinity *Medien—Kultur—Kompetenz*, that is, "media," "culture" and "knowledge society." This new trinity requires philologists to teach their students not only the traditional methods and canonical literary texts, but also bring about a **media and computer literacy**, a consciousness of the critical uses of the different media, as well as some basic knowledge of the history, theory and aesthetics of the media and their interplay. The new programme has provoked counter-reactions and emphatic calls for a "radical philology." This radical philology would once again exclusively rely on text competence and verbal material. These calls for a restricted, narrow approach might well be explained by philology's deep-rooted fear of losing its independence. While this fear is understandable, it is still a fact that a huge number of modern and postmodern Anglo-American writers have discussed the role of literature against the backdrop of the increasing prevalence of media such as photography, film and TV. A return to the text as a context-independent entity, which ignores the text's interaction with other media, is therefore no real option. Hence this chapter ends with a discussion of three central media and an investigation into how literary texts have replied to the ubiquitous technical and electronic images they produce.

## 5.4.1 | Photography

**History.** The Anglo-American novelist Henry James commenced writing in an era that witnessed the image becoming a mass produced article due to the invention of photographic techniques which permitted the large-scale technical reproduction of images for the first time in human history. Since James viewed text-picture relationships as inherently competitive ones, his novels and narratives were almost entirely devoid of illustrative pictures. James, who thought of himself metaphorically as a "painter of life" (James 198), did not consider the new medium photography an art form, although it had become a powerful metaphor for literary realism. In his short story "The Real Thing" (1893), he spells out why this is the case: photography represents merely the surface of things; real art, however, investigates what is underlying the surface, it

*Henry James: A novelist on photography*

interprets life. Only later in his career did James commission pictures by the young American photographer Alvin Langdon Coburn which came to serve as frontispieces for the complete edition of his works. Coburn's photographs, in whose production James was significantly involved, in that he gave the young photographer accurate instructions for the choice of motifs and their composition, correspond to James's conception of restrained illustrations, which do not compete with the text and its "verbal images."

In spite of resistance by major cultural protagonists such as James, photography (= light writing) rapidly became successful due to its 'democratic' character, i.e. the fact that the medium allows for the inexpensive reproduction of images. There is hardly an area of modern life untouched by photography; celebrity culture, advertisement, pornography and topographic views are some of the areas which would not thrive without photography. In the 1920s and 1930s, the German philosopher and critic Walter Benjamin argued that photography should be understood as a technology of the **"optical unconscious"** ("Small History"), bringing into view what escaped standard vision—an insight which certainly still applies to some of the subject areas of photography mentioned above. A central division has generated our understanding of photographic categories: the distinction of 'documentary' and 'art' photography.

**Documentary photography** (war photographs, etc.) is perceived to be "a neutral, styleless, and objective record of information. The document is usually thought to be devoid of subjective intention, even of human will—it is frequently claimed that the camera produces images automatically, as if unaided by an operator. [...] Photographic art, in contrast, lays claim to intention, subjective expression, spiritual uplift, and aesthetic effect" (Edwards 12). Documentary photographs allegedly "entail an objective, unmediated record of facts. Documentary is said to provide its viewers with direct access to truth" (Edwards 27). Allegedly, there is no retouching, no posing, no staging, no additional lighting or dramatic light effects. Whereas during the early decades following its invention, photography was considered a documentary medium rather than an art form, during the latter decades of the nineteenth century, many photographers insisted that photography is an art just like painting.

**Art Photography.** One of the English pioneers of photography, Julia Margaret Cameron (1815–79), who is famous for her portraits of her artfully posed contemporaries such as Thomas Carlyle, John Herschel, and Alfred Lord Tennyson, turned photography into an art form by making her portraits and *tableaux vivants* intentionally out of focus. In a letter to Herschel (December 31, 1864) she commented on her technique as follows:

[I] believe in other than mere conventional topographic photography—map-making and skeleton rendering of feature and form without that roundness and fulness of force and feature, that modelling of flesh and limb, which the focus I use only can give, tho' called and condemned as 'out of focus'. What is focus—and who has a right to say what focus is the legitimate focus? My aspirations are to ennoble photography and to secure for it the character and uses of High Art by combining the real and the ideal and sacrificing nothing of Truth by all possible devotion to Poetry and beauty. (qtd. in Gernsheim 14)

Cameron's art of photography can certainly be defined as "**pictorial photography**," a tradition pursued by Gertrude Käsebier at the beginning of the twentieth century. Likewise, Alfred Stieglitz and Edward Steichen were early twentieth-century promoters of art photography. Stieglitz, who ran '291' gallery on fifth Avenue, New York, and additionally published the magazine *Camera Work* from 1903 to 1917, became the chief promoter of art photography in North America.

A decade or two later, Walker Evans, Dorothea Lange and others rediscovered **photographic realism**. In the USA the 1930s and 1940s brought about several documentary reportages of the social, economic and agricultural crisis, which were the product of a collaboration between photographers and writers. The most famous of these joint ventures of pen and camera were Erskine Caldwell and Margaret Bourke-White's *You Have Seen Their Faces* (1937), Dorothea Lange and Paul S. Taylor's *An American Exodus* (1939), Richard Wright and Edwin Rosskam's *12 Million Black Voices* (1941) as well as James Agee and Evans's study of cotton tenantry in Alabama, *Let Us Now Praise Famous Men* (1941). Walker Evans (1903–75) is an American photographer known for his documentary style and photographic realism. He rebelled against the "aestheticism" of the leading photographers of his day, Stieglitz and Steichen, who had fought for the acceptance of photography as fine art. Indeed, Evans propagated a straight documentary style, i.e. sharp, hard-focus pictures, not photographic abstractions or impressions. Between 1935 and 1938, Evans worked as a photographer for the government (Farm Security Administration) in Alabama and across the whole of the Deep South. While many critics have praised Evans's straight style, sobering clarity, sharp focus, and choice of commonplace subject matter, it is now a well-known fact that during his photographic sessions in the sharecroppers' homes in Alabama he occasionally moved their belongings and rearranged things or even had them removed. This demonstrates that documentary photography is indeed an aesthetic mode or style; it is neither simply devoid of style nor an objective recording technology of truth/reality.

Julia Margaret Cameron, *Lancelot and Guinevere* (1874)

### Digital vs. Analogue Photography.

While in the world of the news media, people might still believe in the proof and authenticity value of photography, the invention of digital photography in the 1980s has superseded the idea that photography is a faithful and lasting re-presentation. A digital image may look just like a photograph when published in a newspaper, but "it actually differs profoundly from a traditional [analogue] photograph" (Mitchell, *The Reconfigured Eye* 4), for the very reason that a digital photograph is differently produced, circulated and stored. The fact that in "analogue" forms of photography there still exists a chemical bond between light and silver salt has an impact on our under-

Walker Evans, photograph from *Let Us Now Praise Famous Men* (1941)

standing of photography. As Roland Barthes, one of the most influential theoreticians of analogue photography has rightly pointed out, in photographs there exists a trace of the objects which were before the lens at a specific place and time. The American Pragmatist philosopher Charles Sanders Peirce (cf. entry II.8), a pioneer semiotician, developed a typology of three components of signs (iconic, indexical and symbolic components), thus working out how signs, which are always embodied in a material vehicle (a medium), construct meaning and enable communication. Since photographs can visually resemble the object they depict and since they bear a causal connection to those objects (which at a point in time were in front of the lens and have left their trace on the photographic picture), photographs are signs with iconic and indexical features.

New Approaches. Since the 1970s, photographers have increasingly interrogated the role of the photographic medium in society. One prominent example is Cindy Sherman's picture series *Untitled Film Stills*, begun in 1977, which remediates the conventions of cinema (and melodrama in particular) "to unmask some powerful ideologies of femininity as appearance" (Edwards 65). Sherman's photographs are a contemporary art form which explores post/modern culture and its values and exposes the fact that pictures are not "natural," but always dependent on conventions. For Susan Sontag photography functions as a *memento mori* and Barthes also understands photographs as reminders of the passing of things and as discernment of an impending misfortune. One of the main functions of photography is as a vehicle for acts of **remembrance**: private ones (the photos in a family album) as well as public and popular ones (Sherman's pictures of the *Untitled Film Stills* series refer to a collective cultural memory). Most recently, Ulrich Baer has explored the striking parallels between the workings of the photographic camera and the structure of traumatic memory, i.e. the common structural features of photography and the illusion of the medium to have caught a "slice of time" or a "frozen moment" and the phenomenon of trauma—experiences that have "remained unremembered yet cannot be forgotten" (7).

*Photography and memory*

## 5.4.2 | Film

### Film History, Style and Genre

Around 1895, the new medium film—also called cinema, motion picture and movie—started its victorious career, which led to the labelling of the twentieth century as 'the century of the cinema'; sound was introduced in the mid-1920s to mid-1930s, *The Jazz Singer* (Alan Crosland, 1927) being one of the early "talkies" in the USA. Although film became the new medium only around 1900, the critic Leon Edel sees Henry James's visual fiction with its characteristic point-of-view technique as already displaying many early parallels to the work of a film camera. For Edel, the invention of the novel is an anticipation of the film camera: "Novelists have sought almost from the first to become a camera. And not a static instrument but one possessing the movement through space and time which the motion-picture camera has achieved in our century" (177). The manifold **intermedial relationships between modernist literature and film** with its montage technique are conspicuous and have become an important research topic, but they are not the only connection between film and literature. Like the latter, film is often considered a narrative medium; and like drama, it is a multimedial art form combining pictures, language and sound (but unlike drama it is shown in a cinema and is thus not a live event). Not only is watching a film in the cinema a collective public experience, its production is also a collaborative process, involving writers, producers, directors, actors, cinematographers, editors, etc. The style of a film depends on the use of significant techniques, which involves the

- **mise-en-scène:** setting, lighting, costume and the behaviour of the figures,
- **editing:** coordinating one shot with the next via such devices as the fade-out, the fade-in, the dissolve and the wipe
- **sound:** the audio code of a film encompasses three kind of sounds: noise, speech, and music. However, sound can be either diegetic, emanating from a source in the current scene, or nondiegetic, i.e. when the source of noise, speech and music is not located in the current scene
- **cinematography** (i.e. "writing in movement"; Thompson and Bordwell 156–350) which refers to *how* a shot is filmed and involves three factors: the photographic aspects of the shot, the framing of the shot and its duration. The vocabulary used to

describe the visual code of moving pictures (Jahn) includes terms such as "frame" or "cell" (which show a single picture; it needs a sequence of 24 frames per second on a screen for the human eye to be deceived into seeing a moving image), "shot" (a sequence of frames filmed in a continuous "take" of a camera); a sequence of shots makes up a "scene" (a sequence of action segments which take place, continuously, at the same time and in the same place). Shot types which indicate the camera's distance from the object as well as the size of the object, have been subdivided into extreme close-up, close-up, medium shot, American shot, full shot, long shot and extreme long shot.

Film studies have inherited some of their major fields of investigation from literary studies: apart from questions regarding narration and medium specificity, genre theory and its problems have received a lot of attention (cf. entry IV.4).

In addition to the grouping of films based upon ideas of how they were made (three major **types** of filmmaking are documentary, experimental and animation), **genre** is a popular way of grouping fiction film (Grant; Thompson and Bordwell 93–109). All filmmakers and viewers are familiar with genres such as Westerns, musicals, war films, science fiction, horror movies and action films, screwball comedies, romances, detective dramas, *films noirs*, etc., however, the boundaries between these genres are not clear-cut. Hence, genre as a category should always be used in a descriptive rather than a prescriptive and evaluative way. Moreover, genres change over time, filmmakers tend to play with the old formulas, they deviate from the conventional pattern and iconography (i.e. recurring symbolic images that carry meaning from film to film), thus allowing for innovation.

## Film Theory

When we turn to film theory, it is interesting to note that while W. J. T. Mitchell proclaimed a "pictorial turn" (*The Reconfigured Eye*) for the later twentieth century, America's first poet-critic and film theoretician Nicholas Vachel Lindsay already claimed a shift from a literate to a visual culture in his own time. Lindsay characterized North American culture at the beginning of the twentieth century by using the term "hieroglyphics," which came to play a major role in his impressionistic rather than systematic film theory, *The Art of the Moving Picture* in 1915:

American civilization grows more hieroglyphic every day. The cartoons of Darling, the advertisements in the back of the magazines and on the bill-boards and in the street-cars, the acres of photographs in the Sunday newspapers, make us into a hieroglyphic civilization far nearer to Egypt than to England. [...] Hieroglyphics are so much nearer to the American mood than the rest of the Egyptian legacy that Americans seldom get as far as the Hieroglyphics to discover how congenial they are. Seeing the mummies, good Americans flee. But there is not a man in America writing advertisements or making cartoons or films but would find delightful the standard books of Hieroglyphics sent out by the British Museum, once he gave them a chance. They represent that very aspect of visual life which Europe understands so little in America, and which has been expanding so enormously even the last year. (11–12)

According to Lindsay's theses, modern American life resembles life in ancient Egypt, in that life in both cultures has a strong visual quality and is characterized by a deluge of pictures. The ubiquity of advertisements, cartoons and films, which disseminate the new "hieroglyphics" and picture-words in the USA, cannot be found in its mother country England. The visual mode of thinking in hieroglyphics is for Lindsay a specific mental feature of America, and that is the reason why Lindsay suggests abolishing alphabetic writing and substituting it by the introduction of a new Esperanto, the hieroglyphic system best represented by the pictorial language of film.

Lindsay's *The Art of the Moving Picture* demonstrates that film theory began shortly after the invention of film. Film theory is in fact an **international and multicultural enterprise**, "yet too often it remains monolingual, provincial, and chauvinistic" (Stam, *Film Theory* 4). French theorists have not referred to work in English for a long time, and Anglo-American film theory tends to cite from French, German, Italian, Portuguese, Russian, Spanish, Hungarian and Asian theorists only if their works have been translated into English. "First World film theory" (Stam, *Film Theory* 158) can be subdivided into four complementary (rather than contradictory) categories, which "do not supersede one another in a linear progression" (9):

> **Key Texts: Film Theory**
>
> **Nicholas Vachel Lindsay,** *The Art of the Moving Picture* (1915)
> **Hugo Münsterberg,** *The Photoplay: A Psychological Study* (1916)
> **Laura Mulvey,** "Visual Pleasures and Narrative Cinema" (1975)
> **Gilles Deleuze,** *Cinéma I, l'image-mouvement* (1983) and *Cinéma II, l'image-temps* (1985)

the early theory of silent film, classical film theory, contemporary film theory, and, most recently, cognitive film theory. Common interests concern aesthetics, medium specificity (which assumes that each art form has uniquely particular norms and capabilities of expression), realism, and genre—categories which are also central in literary studies and have, due to their contested and complex nature, triggered many debates.

Early silent film theory considered whether film, rooted in scientific experiments and based on mechanical means of visual recording is an art form or not—a question answered in the affirmative by classical film theorist Rudolf Arnheim in the 1950s. The first systematic film theory is Hugo Münsterberg's *The Photoplay: A Psychological Study* (1916), which puts emphasis on the active spectator and thus anticipates the reception theory of the 1980s, Gilles Deleuze's philosophical film theory and cognitive film theory of the 1990s. Early silent film theory gave way in the 1920s to the more in-depth reflections of the Soviet montage theorists and filmmakers such as Sergei Eisenstein, whose silent film *The Battleship Potemkin*, made in 1925, brought him international fame. He was influenced by another important source for film theory, namely the Russian Formalists Shklovsky and Eikhenbaum (cf. section II.1.2). Their ideas of defamiliarization, making strange and making difficult suited Eisenstein's own ideas of montage (according to Eisenstein, montage is not the mere linkage of shots, but their collision, which helps to trigger an emotional response from which arises a concept or idea) and cinema as a social practice and thought-provoking constructivist medium to interrogate and transform ideology.

Due to its photographic basis, some critics have considered film a realist medium which serves the truthful representation of everyday life. André Bazin and Siegfried Kracauer, for instance, investigated the democratic realist aesthetic of the medium of film in the 1960s. Another concern was **auteurism**, a movement which dominated film theory and criticism in the late 1950s and early 1960s: If film is considered an art form, then it must be possible to assume the existence of an artist responsible for a filmic work of art.

Contemporary film theory started in the mid-1960s, when structuralist and Bakhtinian ideas (cf. section II.1.2) were absorbed and film theory was called "screen theory." Its central claim was that film is a kind of language, an idea promoted partic-

ularly through the works of Christian Metz, but already developed in the writings of Hungarian film theorist Béla Balázs from the 1920s through the late 1940s. Film theory of the 1970s and 1980s gave way to a second wave of semiology by invoking poststructuralist thinkers. Psychoanalysis, in particular the writings of Jacques Lacan (cf. entry II.7), became central to the understanding of the medium film. Spectatorial desire, i.e. the viewers's psychic and emotional responses to film, was now the focus. The influence of feminism (Laura Mulvey, Teresa de Lauretis, Kaja Silverman; cf. entry II.6) has led to analyses of the gendered nature of vision and the ideological substratum in film, which constructs a masculinist view of women. Laura Mulvey's seminal 1975 essay "Visual Pleasures and Narrative Cinema" analyses the gaze in classical Hollywood cinema and how it reinscribes patriarchal conventions and asymmetrical power relations. While feminist film theory was mainly interested in recognizing that spectatorship was gendered, theoreticians in the decade to come noted that spectatorship is also "sexualized, classed, raced, nationed, regioned, and so forth" (Stam, *Film Theory* 232).

From the 1980s, film theory was influenced by two books by Gilles Deleuze, *Cinéma I, l'image-mouvement* (1983) and *Cinéma II, l'image-temps* (1985). Using Peirce's theory of signs, Deleuze argues against Metzian film linguistics and Lacanian psychoanalytical ideas of cinematic desire. Following the French philosopher of becoming, Henri Bergson, he foregrounds what has been neglected by linguistic approaches to cinema, namely **film as "movement" and event**. Since the mid-1980s, cognitive film theory has gained ground, dismantling the speculative tenets of 1970s screen theory. Amongst its main proponents are the members of the 'Wisconsin School' of neo-formalist film analysis, David Bordwell, Kristin Thompson, Noël Carroll and Janet Staiger, who try to blend their interest in formalist aesthetics and historical poetics (film style studied in historical context) with findings from cognitive psychology which help to explain the viewer's emotional responses to film (Smith; Tan). Recently, the intermediality of film (Paech, *Film*) has been an innovative theoretical approach, as have been investigations into film sound, which helped to undermine the view that film is a predominantly visual medium (when in fact three of this audiovisual medium's five tracks, image, phonetic sound/dialogue, noises, written materials, and music, are aural).

## Adaptation

Another thriving field of film theory and criticism is adaptation. Since 2005, several book publications on literature on screen have appeared (Cartmell and Whelehan; Hutcheon; Leitch; Stam and Raengo) as a reaction to the fact that adaptations are so widespread today, whether on the movie screen, television, DVD, the internet, or in comic books and graphic novels. While filmic adaptations of novels (i.e. David Fincher's film adaptation of Chuck Palahniuk's novel *Fight Club*; cf. entry IV.4) and short stories have for a long time been considered as aesthetically derivative, hence inferior secondary versions of popular culture, in our "postmodern age of cultural recycling" (Hutcheon 3), "fidelity," i.e. faithfulness to the source, as a criterion for judging adaptation has to be reconsidered due to its basis in essentialist arguments (Stam, "Theory and Practice" 14–15). As a ubiquitous cultural phenomenon, adaptation is now understood as a "creative *and* an interpretive act of appropriation/salvaging" (Hutcheon 8); if an adaptation is to a different medium, which is the case with filmic adaptations, remediation can serve as a synonym for adaptation. Thomas Leitch (96–126) has suggested a typology of ten different forms of filmic adaptations of literature which encompasses "celebrations," "adjustment" (which includes compression, expansion, correction and updating), "neoclassic imitation" (the relocation of e. g. a Shakespeare story "to a time and place that are both historically specific and contrary to fact," 103), "revisions" (rewriting of the original), "colonization" (a filmmaker from one country tackles a classic text from another), "(meta)commentary or deconstruction" (film about adaptation and the problems involved in producing adaptations), "analogy" (cf. *Bridget Jones's Diary* in relation to Austen's *Pride and Prejudice*), "parody" or "pastiche," "secondary, tertiary, or quaternary imitations" (adaptations of adaptations), and finally "allusions."

## 5.4.3 | TV

**History and Status.** Television is an electronic medium which has become a central item of everyday life in the Western world since the 1960s, and has subsequently changed our culture radically. Television is a big industry based on a set of technologies which distribute information and frames of interpretation democratically across society as a whole, and is therefore believed to have a homogenizing effect by creating a world of information all people can share. It remediates other media forms (e.g. cinema) and extends "some of its own fiction into multimedia franchises like those cult series such as *Star Trek*" (Jones 585). Despite advances in digitalization by means of the personal computer since the mid-1980s and the subsequent digitalization of other media like photography, film and finally television itself, it remains an important source of knowledge, amusement, boredom, etc. Up until now, not even the Internet has changed this status quo (cf. Adelmann et al. 7). TV is extremely heterogeneous; and due to its status as mixed medium, which combines different "basic" media such as pictures, the spoken and written word as well as music and sound, it is a difficult case for researchers. As TV also combines a wide range of different forms and genres (for instance single drama or television play, mini-series, episodic series and continuing serials and flexi-narratives, cf. Jones 586–87), a precise description of its salient medial features is extremely hard. Among these are the 'flow' (a term coined by Raymond Williams) of the programme, the transmission of live events, commercial breaks, trailers, etc. and the remote control which allows the TV recipient to interrupt the prescribed linear order of the programmes by surfing individually through different channels, and thus to turn from a passive watcher into an active user. Interestingly, on a structural level zapping shows similarities with the clicking technique we rely on when using the Internet and hyperfictions.

**TV and Literature.** If it is true that each new development in the technical history of the media also affects the field of literature, the question arises *how* literary texts react to the new mass media such as TV. The fiction of the famous prize-winning contemporary British writer A. S. Byatt is an ideal test case since her texts can be read as comments on the state of literature in post-modernity. Byatt invites us to view literary texts in a new way, that is, as artistic expressions encoded in one medium, which in turn is situated within a field of other media that influence and complement each other. In her 1978 novel *The Virgin in the Garden*, for instance, Byatt turns to TV and concentrates on the history of this medium in the Western world as

*TV as a heterogeneous medium*

well as on some of its special features. Byatt's novel refers to the first major live transmission in the history of British broadcasting, the coronation of Elizabeth II in 1953:

Before June 2 that year most of the people collected in Mrs Thone's drawing room had never seen a television broadcast. [...] In those days, neither the public nor the private mores that went with the intrusive camera-eye and the obtrusive screen were established. The official BBC report on the coverage of the Coronation enquired of itself, 'Might there not be something unseemly in the chance that a viewer could watch this solemn and significant service with a cup of tea at his elbow?—there were very real doubts ...' Most of the press was democratically statistically ecstatic. 'The coronation brings the tiny screen into its own, turns it into a window on Westminster for 125,000,000 people ... All these millions from Hamburg to Hollywood will see her coach jingle through rejoicing London *this very day* ... 800 microphones are ready for 140 broadcasters to tell the world Elizabeth is crowned. But today is television's day. For it is television, reaching out for the Queen's subjects, which will give a new truth to the Recognition of the Monarch on her Coronation Day ... (ch. 27)

With the help of another medium, namely a printed text, Byatt reflects on the history of television in England and how ordinary people as well as BBC commentators reacted to the new medium. While in Byatt's novel most of the watchers are very critical of it—they fear that it will kill communication within the family and keep people from reading—the commentators are enthusiastic about the fact that TV is a live medium and thus enables millions of people to directly participate in the coronation of Elizabeth II. Byatt's fiction deals with the medium TV by revealing the utopian hopes connected with it. It discusses the fantasies and yearnings as well as the anxieties and fears which are attached to TV. Furthermore, Byatt sometimes also translates **structural specificities** of TV such as channel surfing into new aesthetic strategies in her texts. This is the case in her novella "The Djinn in the Nightingale's Eye" (1994) which demonstrates convincingly that literature's reaction to other media is not just a defensive survival strategy, but rather opens up new possibilities and aesthetic dimensions. In fact, novels such as Bret Easton Ellis's *Less than Zero* (1985), which has been called an "MTV novel," cannot be discussed without taking their intermedial references to TV into account: the short sequences the novel consists of reflect the flow and speed of videos on MTV. While people from media studies have analyzed how TV and other mass media absorb drama ("armchair theatre") and novels (*telenovela*), literary critics are slow in adopting the stepchild of literary studies, namely the reaction of literary texts to the mass media. The resistance of literary scholars to engage in the topic of literature and TV might well have to do with the negative image of TV: Powerful and influential as it may be, TV is infected with the image of entertaining the masses and seen as an instrument of a repressive "culture industry" and a way of exercising social and political control.

## Select Bibliography

**Adelmann, Ralf, et al.** "Perspektiven der Fernsehwissenschaft." *Grundlagentexte zur Fernsehwissenschaft: Theorie – Geschichte – Analyse.* Eds. Ralf Adelmann et al. Konstanz: UVK, 2002. 7–19.

**Arnheim, Rudolf.** *Film as Art.* 1957. Berkeley: University of California Press, 2006.

**Assmann, Aleida.** "Exkarnation. Gedanken zur Grenze zwischen Körper und Schrift." *Raum und Verfahren.* Eds. Jörg Huber and Alois Martin Müller. Zurich: Stroemfeld/Roter Stern, 1993. 133–55.

**Babbitt, Irving.** *The New Laokoon: An Essay on the Confusion of the Arts.* London: Constable, 1910.

**Baer, Ulrich.** *Spectral Evidence: The Photography of Trauma.* Cambridge: MIT Press, 2002.

**Balázs, Béla.** *Schriften zum Film II (1926–1931).* Ed. Wolfgang Gersch. Berlin: Henschel, 1984.

**Balázs, Béla.** *Theory of the Film.* Trans. Edith Bone. London: Dennis Dobson, 1951.

**Barthes, Roland.** *Camera Lucida: Reflections on Photography.* New York: Hill and Wang, 1981.

**Benjamin, Walter.** "A Small History of Photography." 1931. *One-Way Street and Other Writings.* London: Verso, 1985. 225–39.

**Benjamin, Walter.** "The Work of Art in the Age of Mechanical Reproduction." 1936. *Illuminations.* London: Fontana, 1970. 219–53.

**Boehm, Gottfried, and Helmut Pfotenhauer, eds.** *Beschreibungskunst – Kunstbeschreibung: Ekphrasis von der Antike bis zur Gegenwart.* Munich: Fink, 1995.

**Bolter, Jay David.** "Ekphrasis, Virtual Reality, and the Future of Writing." *The Future of the Book.* Ed. Geoffrey Nunberg. Berkeley: University of California Press, 1996. 253–72.

**Bolter, Jay David, and Richard Grusin.** *Remediation: Understanding New Media.* 1999. Cambridge: MIT Press, 2000.

**Bordwell, David.** *The Way Hollywood Tells It: Story and Style in Modern Movies.* Berkeley: University of California Press, 2006.

**Braungart, Georg, Peter Gendolla, and Fotis Jannidis, eds.** *Jahrbuch für Computerphilologie.* Paderborn: Mentis, 1999.

Cartmell, Deborah, and Imelda Whelehan, eds. *The Cambridge Companion to Literature on Screen*. Cambridge: Cambridge University Press, 2007.

Chartier, Roger. "Texts, Printing, Readings." *The New Cultural History*. Ed. Lynn Hunt. Berkeley: University of California Press, 1989. 154–75.

Delany, Paul, and George P. Landow, eds. *Hypermedia and Literary Studies*. Cambridge: MIT Press, 1991.

De Lauretis, Teresa. *Technologies of Gender: Essays on Theory, Film, and Fiction*. Bloomington: Indiana University Press, 1987.

Edel, Leon. "Novel and Camera." *The Theory of the Novel: New Essays*. Ed. John Halperin. Oxford: Oxford University Press, 1974. 177–88.

Edwards, Steve. *Photography: A Very Short History*. Oxford: Oxford University Press, 2006.

Eisenstein, Elizabeth L. *The Printing Press as an Agent of Change: Communications and Cultural Transformation in Early-Modern Europe*. 2 vols. Cambridge: Cambridge University Press, 1979.

Faulstich, Werner. *Mediengeschichte von 1700 bis ins 3. Jahrtausend*. 2 vols. Göttingen: Vandenhoeck & Ruprecht, 2006.

Franck, Georg. *Ökonomie der Aufmerksamkeit*. Munich: Hanser, 1998.

Gaudreault, André, and Philippe Marion. "The Cinema as a Model for the Genealogy of Media." *Convergence* 8.4 (2002): 12–18.

Genette, Gérard. *Palimpsests: Literature in the Second Degree*. Trans. Channa Newman and Claude Doubinsky. Lincoln: University of Nebraska Press, 1997.

Gernsheim, Helmut. *Julia Margaret Cameron: Her Life and Photographic Works*. Millerton: Aperture Found, 1975.

Giesecke, Michael. *Der Buchdruck in der frühen Neuzeit: Eine historische Fallstudie über die Durchsetzung neuer Informations- und Kommunikationstechnologien*. Frankfurt/M.: Suhrkamp, 1991.

Grant, Barry Keith. *Film Genre: From Iconography to Ideology*. London: Wallflower, 2006.

Gumbrecht, Hans Ulrich, and Karl Ludwig Pfeiffer, eds. *Die Materialität der Kommunikation*. Frankfurt/M.: Suhrkamp, 1988.

Hall, Stuart. "Encoding/Decoding." *Media Studies: A Reader*. 2nd ed. Eds. Paul Marris and Sue Thornham. New York: New York University Press, 2000. 51–61.

Hansen-Löve, Aage A. "Intermedialität und Intertextualität: Probleme der Korrelation von Wort- und Bildkunst – am Beispiel der russischen Moderne." *Dialog der Texte*. Eds. Wolf Schmid and Wolf-Dieter Stempel. Vienna: Gesellschaft zur Förderung slawistischer Studien, 1983. 291–360.

Havelock, Eric A. *The Muse Learns to Write: Reflections on Orality and Literacy from Antiquity to the Present*. New Haven: Yale University Press, 1986.

Heffernan, James A. W. "Ekphrasis and Representation." *New Literary History* 22 (1991): 297–316.

Heffernan, James A. W. *Museum of Word: The Poetics of Ekphrasis from Homer to Ashbery*. Chicago: University of Chicago Press, 1993.

Heibach, Christiane. *Literatur im elektronischen Raum*. Frankfurt/M.: Suhrkamp, 2003.

Helbig, Jörg, ed. *Intermedialität: Theorie und Praxis eines interdisziplinären Forschungsgebietes*. Berlin: Erich Schmidt, 1998.

Hiebel, Hans H. "Media: Tabelle zur Geschichte der Medien-Technik." *Medien und Maschinen: Literatur im Technischen Zeitalter*. Eds. Theo Elm and Hans H. Hiebel. Freiburg: Rombach, 1991. 186–224.

Higgins, Dick. "Intermedia." *Something Else Newsletter* 1.1 (1966): 1–6.

Horkheimer, Max, and Theodor W. Adorno. "The Culture Industry: Enlightenment as Mass Deception," *Dialectic of Enlightenment*. Eds. Max Horkheimer and Theodor W. Adorno. London: Verso, 1997. 120-67.

Hutcheon, Linda. *A Theory of Adaptation*. New York: Routledge, 2006.

Innis, Harold A. *The Bias of Communication*. Toronto: University of Toronto Press, 1951.

Jäger, Ludwig. "Die Sprachvergessenheit der Medientheorie: Ein Plädoyer für das Medium Sprache." *Sprache und neue Medien*. Ed. Werner Kallmeyer. Berlin: de Gruyter, 1999. 9–30.

Jäger, Ludwig, Erika Linz, and Irmela Schneider. Preface. *Media, Culture, and Mediality: New Insights into the Current State of Research*. Eds. Ludwig Jäger, Erika Linz, and Irmela Schneider. Bielefeld: transcript, 2010. 9–16.

Jahn, Manfred. "A Guide to Narratological Film Analysis." *Poems, Plays, and Prose: A Guide to the Theory of Literary Genres*. English Department, University of Cologne. 2 Aug. 2003. 17 May 2011 <http://www.uni-koeln.de/~ame02/pppf.htm>.

James, Henry. *The Art of the Novel: Critical Prefaces*. New York: Scribner's, 1962.

Jannidis, Fotis. "Computerphilologie." *Metzler Lexikon Literatur- und Kulturtheorie*. Ed. Ansgar Nünning. 4th ed. Stuttgart: Metzler, 2008. 100–2.

Jenkins, Henry. *Convergence Culture: Where Old and New Media Collide*. New York: New York University Press, 2006.

Jones, Sara Gwenllian. "Television." *Routledge Encyclopedia of Narrative Theory*. Eds. David Herman, Manfred Jahn, and Marie-Laure Ryan. London: Routledge, 2005. 585–89.

Kastan, David Scott. *Shakespeare and the Book*. Cambridge: Cambridge University Press, 2001.

Kittler, Friedrich. *Discourse Networks 1800–1900*. Trans. M. Metteer. Stanford: Stanford University Press, 1990.

Klarer, Mario. *Ekphrasis: Bildbeschreibung als Repräsentationstheorie bei Spenser, Sidney, Lyly und Shakespeare*. Tübingen: Niemeyer, 2001.

Lachmann, Renate. *Gedächtnis und Literatur: Intertextualität in der russischen Moderne*. Frankfurt/M.: Suhrkamp, 1990.

Landow, George, P. *Hypertext: The Convergence of Contemporary Critical Theory and Technology*. Baltimore: Johns Hopkins University Press, 1992.

Leitch, Thomas. *Film Adaptation and Its Discontents*. Baltimore: Johns Hopkins University Press, 2007.

Leschke, Rainer. *Einführung in die Medientheorie*. Munich: Fink, 2003.

Lindsay, Nicholas Vachel. *The Art of the Moving Picture*. 1915. New York: Liveright, 1970.

Luhmann, Niklas. *The Reality of the Mass Media (Cultural Memory in the Present)*. Stanford: Stanford University Press, 1995.

McGann, Jerome. *Radiant Textuality: Literature after the World Wide Web*. New York: Palgrave, 2001.

McLuhan, Marshall. *The Gutenberg Galaxy: The Making of the Typographic Man*. London: Routledge, 1962.

McLuhan, Marshall. *Understanding Media: The Extensions of Man*. New York: McGraw-Hill, 1964.

*Media History Project*. University of Minnesota. 28 August 2007. 19 May 2011 <http://www.mediahistory.umn.edu>.

Metz, Christian. *The Imaginary Signifier: Psychoanalysis and Cinema*. Trans. Celia Brittonet al. Bloomington: Indiana University Press, 1982.

Mirzoeff, Nicholas. "What Is Visual Culture?" *The Visual Culture Reader*. Ed. Nicholas Mirzoeff. London: Routledge, 1998. 3–13.

Mitchell, W. J. T. *Picture Theory*. Chicago: Chicago University Press, 1994.

Mitchell, W. J. T. *The Reconfigured Eye: Visual Truth in the Post-Photographic Era*. Cambridge: MIT Press, 1992.

Mostaf, Franziska. *Metaphorische Intermedialität: Formen und Funktionen der Verarbeitung von Malerei im Roman: Theorie und Praxis in der englischsprachigen Erzählkunst des 19. und 20. Jahrhunderts*. Trier: WVT, 2000.

Ong, Walter J. *Orality and Literacy: The Technologizing of the Word*. London: Methuen, 1982.

Paech, Joachim, ed. *Film, Fernsehen, Video und die Künste: Strategien der Intermedialität*. Stuttgart: Metzler, 1994. 163–78.

Paech, Joachim. "Intermediale Figuration – am Beispiel von Jean-Luc Godards *Histoire(s) du Cinéma*." *Mediale Performanzen: Historische Konzepte und Perspektiven*. Eds. Jutta Eming et al. Freiburg: Rombach Verlag, 2002. 275–95.

Paech, Joachim. "Intermedialität des Films." *Moderne Film Theorie*. Ed. Jürgen Felix. Mainz: Bender, 2002. 287–312.

Paech, Joachim, and Jens Schröter, eds. *Intermedialität analog/digital. Theorien – Methoden – Analysen*. Munich: Fink, 2008.

Peucker, Brigitte. *Incorporating Images: Film and the Rival Arts*. Princeton: Princeton University Press, 1995.

Pross, Harry. *Medienforschung*. Darmstadt: Carl Habel, 1972.

Pross, Harry. *Der Mensch im Mediennetz*. Zurich: Winkler, 1996.

Rajewsky, Irina O. "Intermediality, Intertextuality, and Remediation: A Literary Perspective on Intermediality." *Intermédialités* 6 (2005): 43–64.

Rippl, Gabriele. *Beschreibungskunst: Zur intermedialen Poetik angloamerikanischer Ikontexte (1880–2000)*. Munich: Fink, 2005.

Ryan, Marie-Laure. Introduction. *Narrative across Media: The Languages of Storytelling*. Ed. Marie-Laure Ryan. Lincoln: University of Nebraska Press, 2004. 1–40.

Ryan, Marie-Laure. "Media and Narrative." *Routledge Encyclopedia of Narrative Theory*. Eds. David Herman, Manfred Jahn, and Marie-Laure Ryan. London: Routledge, 2005. 288–92.

Saussure, Ferdinand de. *Course in General Linguistics*. 1916. Trans. Wade Baskin. Eds. Charles Bally and Albert Sechehave. Rev. ed. London: Peter Owen, 1974.

Schmidt, Siegfried J. "Medienkulturwissenschaft." *Metzler Lexikon Literatur- und Kulturtheorie*. 4th ed. Ed. Ansgar Nünning. Stuttgart: Metzler, 2008. 472–74.

Schönert, Jörg. "Germanistik als Medienwissenschaft oder als radikale Philologie?" *Theodor Storm und die Medien*. Eds. Gerd Eversberg and Harro Segeberg. Berlin: Erich Schmidt, 1999. 15–24.

Schröter, Jens. "Intermedialität: Facetten und Probleme eines aktuellen medienwissenschaftlichen Begriffs." *Montage/AV* 7.2 (1998): 129–54.

Segeberg, Harro, and Simone Winko, eds. *Digitalität und Literalität: Zur Zukunft der Literatur*. Munich: Fink, 2005.

Silverman, Kaja. *The Acoustic Mirror: The Female Voice in Psychoanalysis and Cinema*. Bloomington: Indiana University Press, 1988.

Simanowski, Roberto. *Interfictions: Vom Schreiben im Netz*. Frankfurt/M.: Suhrkamp, 2002.

Simonis, Annette. *Intermediales Spiel im Film: Ästhetische Erfahrung zwischen Schrift, Bild und Musik*. Bielefeld: transcript, 2010.

Smith, Murray. *Engaging Characters: Fiction, Emotion, and the Cinema*. Oxford: Clarendon Press, 1995.

Sontag, Susan. *On Photography*. New York: Farrar, Straus and Giroux, 1977.

Spielmann, Yvonne. *Intermedialität: Das System Peter Greenaway*. Munich: Fink, 1998.

Stam, Robert. *Film Theory: An Introduction*. Malden: Blackwell, 2000.

Stam, Robert. "The Theory and Practice of Adaptation." Introduction. Stam and Raengo 1–52.

Stam, Robert, and Alessandra Raengo, eds. *Literature and Film: A Guide to the Theory and Practice of Film Adaptation*. Malden: Blackwell, 2005.

Tan, Ed S. H. *Emotion and the Structure of Narrative Film: Film as an Emotion Machine*. Mahwah: Lawrence Erlbaum, 1996.

Thompson, Kristin, and David Bordwell. *Film History: An Introduction*. New York: McGraw-Hill, 1994.

Todorow, Almut. "Intermedialität." *Historisches Wörterbuch der Rhetorik*. Ed. Gert Ueding. Vol. 10. Tübingen: Max Niemeyer, 2011. 399–410.

Voigts-Virchow, Eckart. *Introduction to Media Studies*. Stuttgart: Ernst Klett, 2005.

Wagner, Peter, ed. *Icons – Texts – Iconotexts: Essays on Ekphrasis and Intermediality*. Berlin: de Gruyter, 1996.

Wenzel, Horst. *Hören und Sehen – Schrift und Bild: Kultur und Gedächtnis im Mittelalter*. Munich: C. H. Beck, 1995.

Williams, Raymond. *Television: Technology and Cultural Form*. London: Fontana, 1974.

Wolf, Werner. "Intermediality." *Routledge Encyclopedia of Narrative Theory*. Eds. David Herman, Manfred Jahn, and Marie-Laure Ryan. London: Routledge, 2005. 252–56.

Wolf, Werner. *The Musicalization of Fiction: A Study in the Theory and History of Intermediality*. Amsterdam: Rodopi, 1999.

*Gabriele Rippl*

# Part IV: Analyzing Literature and Culture

# 1  Analyzing Poetry

**1.1**  William Wordsworth, "Composed upon Westminster Bridge, Sept. 3, 1802"
**1.2**  Robert Hayden, "Night, Death, Mississippi" (1966)

Poetry is often regarded as the most 'difficult' genre, and in some ways it is. A novel or a play tells a story, often in a fairly straightforward way, and even if we do not get a sense of the story at the beginning, things will usually become clearer once we have made our way into the book. Most poems, on the other hand, are too short and too densely written for this mode of reading. If we ignore the details and skip passages we cannot make sense of at first sight, the poem might be over before we even have begun to understand it. In this sense, poetry indeed tends to be more difficult than other genres. However, one of the beliefs that most students of literature come to share is that difficult texts can be more rewarding than easy ones. They force us to read closely, and to wonder why things are expressed the way they are. In other words, when we read poetry, we can hardly help analyzing it at the same time. This makes poetry a paradigmatic genre for literary studies: the techniques of reading we learn here can serve as models for our readings of other genres as well.

This idea was at the core of the formalist approach to literature, which still provides an important foundation for literary studies today (cf. section II.1.2). The formalists developed a method they called '**close reading**.' They studied poems in much detail, with a special focus on stylistic and semantic patterns. Close reading is still an important part of literary analysis, but more recent approaches have raised various larger issues that close reading cannot capture (or that the formalists did not give much thought to): the role of the reader, the implicit cultural assumptions behind our readings, the influence of identity categories such as race or gender, and many others. While these new approaches have sometimes been called '**wide readings**,' they have not escaped the initial problem: most poems are so densely written that even their engagement with larger cultural issues often takes place in complex, implicit, and allusive forms. What we need for analyzing poetry, then, is not a sweeping perspective but a close reading on several levels. To see how such a **multiple close reading** could work in practice, this chapter will discuss two very different poems: first a relatively straightforward one from the early nineteenth century, then a modernist poem from the mid-twentieth century that seems more forbidding at first glance. Its approach to each poem will be guided by three questions:

**1.**  Which topics and issues does the poem raise?
**2.**  How is it written?
**3.**  And why is it written that way?

After discussing these questions, we will try out one of the wider, contextual approaches mentioned earlier.

## 1.1 | Traditional Poetry: William Wordsworth, "Composed upon Westminster Bridge, Sept. 3, 1802"

Earth has not any thing to shew more fair:
Dull would he be of soul who could pass by
A sight so touching in its majesty:
This City now doth like a garment wear
The beauty of the morning; silent, bare,      5
Ships, towers, domes, theatres and temples lie
Open unto the fields, and to the sky;
All bright and glittering in the smokeless air.
Never did sun more beautifully steep
In his first splendor valley, rock, or hill;      10

Ne'er saw I, never felt, a calm so deep!
The river glideth at his own sweet will:
Dear God! the very houses seem asleep;
And all that mighty heart is lying still!

**What is the topic of the poem?** As the title already tells us, the speaker is standing on Westminster Bridge, which means that the "City" he is speaking of is London. Simply put, this is a poem in praise of London.

Analyzing style
and language

**How is the poem written?** Given that London is the central topic of the poem, it is interesting to note that its name is never mentioned. A first formal aspect we can identify, then, is that the poem approaches its topic indirectly. The title does so by means of a metonymic shift: instead of naming the city itself, it names a place we recognize as belonging to it. The poem itself opens with a strong expression of praise and admiration, but information about the object of its praise is delayed: we suspect it is London, but we do not know until the fourth line. Another aspect that stands out from the beginning is the close link the poem establishes between the city and nature. London is described as part of "Earth," in fact as its most beautiful part; it reflects "the beauty of the morning" and belongs "to the fields, and to the sky." The phrasing of lines 9–10 is so vivid that we tend to imagine an actual "valley, rock, or hill" though the speaker is still talking about London, and the "heart" metaphor in the last line depicts the city as part of an organic whole. It also points to a third formal aspect: the frequent use of **personification**. The city is "wearing" the beauty of the morning "like a garment," is described as "fair" and majestic, and has (or is?) a "mighty heart." Lastly, the poem has a conspicuously regular overall structure, with only four different rhymes and pentametric lines throughout. The rhyme scheme divides it into an octave and a sestet, which invokes the tradition of the **Petrarchan sonnet**.

Analyzing perspective

**Why is it written that way?** One can think of a number of reasons why Wordsworth chose an indirect approach to the topic. After all, he wanted to present the largest city in Europe as a calm, beautiful, almost rustic place. Then as now, the sight of London must have been quite overpowering, especially if one stood on a bridge in the middle of the city. The poem solves this potential contradiction by establishing a celebratory, sensual frame for several lines before the city is even mentioned. When it *is* mentioned for the first (and only) time, in line 4, it is immediately cloaked in the "garment" of the beautiful dawn. Another advantage of the indirect approach is that it allows Wordsworth to gloss over the squalid reality of big-city life. It is only in the wide, fuzzy perspective he adopts here that an early-industrial metropolis can become an idyllic landscape; the poem hints at this selective vision when it traces the brightness of the morning to the "smokeless" air. The fact that the absence of smoke is worth mentioning at all indicates that the scenery is very different during the day, when the

chimneys are in use and the steam engines are running. The poem's deceptive atmosphere is evoked not only by the perspective and imagery, however, but also by its **rhythm and meter**. Apart from a few instances where the stress falls on the first word of a line to heighten its rhetorical impact (lines 1, 2, 7, and 9), most of the poem is in iambic pentameter with many run-on lines, which creates an easy flow and a serene mood.

The last two aspects identified above, personification and the sonnet form, allow the speaker to express his close, **emotional relation** to the city. With its beautiful garments and its "mighty heart," London takes the place of the ideal beloved for whom Petrarch and his followers wrote their sonnets. The Petrarchan beloved was admired for her beauty, but also for her virtuous character, of which her beauty was regarded as the outward expression. This formal reference adds depth to Wordsworth's appreciation of London. It suggests that the city is beautiful not just because of the early-morning scene, but that on closer acquaintance it will reveal its deeper, invisible virtues as well. However, the Petrarchan beloved was ideal partly because she was unreachable: she was often either a noblewoman or already married, so that the poet could never hope for fulfillment of his love. Wordsworth's reference to the city's "majesty" (3) might be a hint at this superior status and, by extension, at the ultimate futility of falling in love with either a city or a natural scene. This tension between the speaker's **desire for unity** with his environment and his awareness that such unity cannot be achieved became typical of Romantic poetry (cf. entry I.2.4). If we look at this problem from the environment's side rather than the speaker's, however, the very idea of praising scenery in terms of a human being has something of a falsifying imposition.

**An Ecocritical Reading.** The poem's highly selective view of the city and its questionable use of nature imagery invite a critical examination beyond a 'close reading' of its language. The implications of literary representations of the environment, including their influence on our conception of nature, have been theorized under the label of 'ecocriticism' (cf. entry II.14). In his introduction to ecocriticism, Greg Garrard argues that literature and the environment intersect in widespread metaphorical concepts such as pollution, pastoral, wilderness, dwelling, and apocalypse—concepts that literary critics can analyze. If we look at Wordsworth's poem from this perspective, we can trace the influence of **pastoral ideas** on its description of the cityscape. Pastoral was originally a term for literature that celebrated retreat from city life into an idyllic countryside; it is now defined as "any literature that describes the country with an implicit or explicit contrast to the urban" (Gifford 2). Wordsworth draws on the pastoral, but at the same time turns the concept on its head. He sketches an idyllic scene from which the markers of civilization are noticeably absent (remember the "smokeless air"), but the setting of this scene is the very realm against which the pastoral traditionally defines itself: the city.

In superimposing pastoral images and values on the urban scene, Wordsworth redefines the **nature/culture relation** in two ways. On the one hand, by describing the center of nineteenth-century civilization in natural terms, he subverts the notion that nature is inferior to and must be controlled by culture. In effect, he reverses this hierarchy when he praises London not for its cultural importance but for its resemblance to a natural landscape. The poem can be read as advocating an organic, ecological perspective on human life, in the sense that we should be aware of our embeddedness into a larger ecosystem and of our dependence on our natural (and cultural) environment. On the other hand, however, the pastoral conception of nature relies on a number of problematic assumptions that work against such an ecological perspective. Its tendency to idealize nature, to reduce it to an idyllic leisure park for disaffected urbanites, has not only led to one-sided ecosystemic

models in science but has supported a somewhat touristic view of rural life "that obscures the realities of labour and hardship" (Garrard 33; cf. Garrard 56–58). If such idealization is already problematic in descriptions of the countryside, it is even more so when applied to urban life, as Wordsworth does in the poem. In William Blake's poem "London," published a few years before Wordsworth's, we encounter an alienated, despairing crowd made up of exploited child-workers, disillusioned soldiers, and youthful prostitutes. Wordsworth blanks these problems out; for him, the city is a mere idyll, and with its "ships, towers, domes, theatres and temples" resembles a picturesque ancient landscape rather than an early-industrial metropolis.

These are two very different ecocritical readings of the poem. The first regards it as an ecological text in which the natural environment supplies the terms and values by which the cultural sphere and the speaker himself are measured. The second reading accuses it of anthropocentrism, of putting human civilization and its exigencies at the center while reducing nature to specific cultural purposes such as ornamentation or relaxation. That the text accommodates both readings indicates the complexity not only of its ambiguous language but of its wide-ranging vision of nature/culture interaction. Rather than making a definitive statement about nature, Wordsworth stages a many-faceted encounter of the human and the non-human that raises a variety of fundamental questions about the relationship between the two.

*Complex poems allow for many different readings.*

## 1.2 | Experimental Poetry: Robert Hayden, "Night, Death, Mississippi" (1966)

While Wordsworth's poem was fairly easy to understand on a first reading, our second example is much more elusive:

1

A quavering cry. Screech-owl?
Or one of them?
The old man in his reek
and gauntness laughs—

One of them, I bet—                    5
and turns out the kitchen lamp,

limping to the porch to listen
in the windowless night.

Be there with Boy and the rest
if I was well again.                    10
Time was. Time was.
White robes like moonlight

In the sweetgum dark.
Unbuckled that one then
and him squealing bloody Jesus          15
as we cut it off.

Time was. A cry?
A cry all right.
He hawks and spits,
fevered as by groinfire.                    20

Have us a bottle,

Boy and me—
he's earned him a bottle—
when he gets home.

2

Then we beat them, he said,        25
beat them till our arms was tired
and the big old chains
messy and red.

*O Jesus burning on the lily cross*

Christ, it was better            30
than hunting bear
which don't know why
you want him dead.

*O night, rawhead and bloodybones night*

You kids fetch Paw            35
some water now so's he
can wash that blood
off him, she said.

*O night betrayed by darkness not its own*

**How is the poem written?** This was not the first
question we asked of the Wordsworth poem, but
it is the first question we need to deal with here.
Like many twentieth-century texts, Hayden's
poem, published in 1966, foregrounds style and
language rather than content. We need to get a
sense of the linguistic features before we can understand what the poem is about. The most obvious feature, and the main reason why this poem is
more difficult to understand than Wordsworth's,
is its **elliptical style**: much relevant information is
Approaching    only alluded to or left out altogether. We need to
difficult poems    read carefully: the title is crucial, for example, because it contains information about setting and
theme that will not appear again in the poem. And
we need to add missing pieces while we read: "A
quavering cry (is heard. Is it the cry of a) Screech-
owl? Or (the cry of) one of them?" Here we stum-
ble over an unspecified reference: who is "them"?

The reference reappears three lines further on,
again without explanation, which forces us to
keep the question in mind while we read the rest
of the poem. Another major difficulty we encounter at this point lies in the poem's shifts between
several voices and temporal levels, none of which
is clearly marked. Only a careful reading reveals,
for example, that it is the old man who is speaking
(or thinking) lines 5 and 9–18. The man is listening to something out in the night and reflects that
he would "Be there [...] if I was well again." The
phrase "Time was" introduces his memories of
this earlier period in line 11, and then brings him
back to the present in line 17.

   **What is the poem about?** It is in these **memories**, after we have gone through a shift of voice
and shift of time, that we get the first indications of
what is happening out "there." We are in the
American South at the beginning of the twentieth
century (when the man was young), outside the
town; it is night; there are people in white robes
and one man who is screaming because he is being "unbucked." Whether or not they understood
the slangy sexual reference, which Hayden makes
more explicit two lines later, his readers would immediately have thought of the nightly **lynchings**
of the Ku Klux Klan, which were still happening
in the 1960s. It is one of these lynchings that the
poem is about: the old man is listening to it from
his porch, and a younger man named 'Boy,' most
likely his son, is one of the Klansmen. Once we
are aware of this background, the second part of
the poem becomes easier to understand: the first
two stanzas describe what the Klansmen did to
their victims, and the last stanza is spoken by a
female member of the household. The stanzas
are separated by lines of chant-like prayer that
come from yet another person: from a black
preacher, maybe, or from Hayden himself as an
authorial interjection. Note that the entire second
part could either take place in the old man's
memories—he is out there, and his wife speaks
the last stanza—or in the present after Boy has
returned from the lynching.

   **Why is the poem written that way?** Lynching
poems had been written since the nineteenth century, and most of them were flatly didactic and/or
used brutal, shocking imagery to describe the
burning victim. Hayden approaches the topic indirectly. Of the actual lynching we only hear a
scream, which we cannot identify at this early
point, and we learn at the end that a man will
come back covered in blood. As in a good horror

movie, nothing actually happens before our eyes, on the page—it is all in our imagination. Another difference lies in this poem's general **perspective**: it is the perpetrators that take center stage, not the victim. The main speaker of Hayden's poem is not a sympathetic observer who condemns the lynching but a murderous racist who applauds it and sugarcoats it in nostalgic memories. This dominant perspective is balanced against the prayer in the second part and against the self-revealing brutality of the old man's memories. However, the blending of past and present in the second part suggests that racist ideology persists to the present day and will not simply vanish. Lastly, the **sensual imagery** of the poem is also worth examining: the shifts between light and darkness, the evocation of the colors black, white, and red, and the pervasive device of animalization all contribute to the atmosphere of "rawheaded and bloodybones night" and to the powerful emotional impact of the poem.

Hopefully, these short explications show that analyzing a poem does not necessarily take away from the aesthetic pleasure we experience on a first reading. Ideally, studying the poem in more detail and discovering how it works will add to that pleasure rather than stifle it.

## Further Reading

Bode, Christoph. *Einführung in die Lyrikanalyse*. Trier: WVT, 2001.
Brooks, Cleanth, and Robert Penn Warren. *Understanding Poetry: An Anthology for College Students*. New York: Holt, 1946.

Burdorf, Dieter. *Einführung in die Gedichtanalyse*. 2nd ed. Stuttgart: Metzler, 1997.
Wainwright, Jeffrey. *Poetry: The Basics*. 2nd ed. London: Routledge, 2011.
Williams, Rhian. *The Poetry Toolkit: The Essential Guide to Studying Poetry*. London: Continuum, 2009.

## Works Cited

Garrard, Greg. *Ecocriticism*. London: Routledge, 2004.
Gifford, Terry. *Pastoral*. London: Routledge, 1999.

*Timo Müller*

## 2 Analyzing Prose Fiction

In the university and among a general reading public, the **novel** has become the most popular literary genre. Many readers regard it as more accessible than poetry, more readable than drama, and more captivating than non-fiction. The novel's traditional focus on realistic description and straightforward storytelling, though challenged by experimental writers almost from the beginning, continues to shape reader expectations and has been revived by the strong 'neo-realist' strand in contemporary fiction (cf. entries I.2.6 and I.3.5). Even highly accessible novels (or short stories), however, operate on the level of form as well as the level of content. It is the relation of these two levels that literary studies seek to analyze. As critical readers, we need to keep an eye on a number of **formal aspects** that can support, enhance, or contradict the semantic content of the text. For example, we can ask the following questions of a text:

*The interplay of content and form*

- From which **perspective** is it told? Does that perspective shift? How does it affect our understanding of the story?
- In what **style** is it told? What kinds of linguistic elements are used (word clusters, syntax, dialect, sociolect, degree of formality, etc.)? What does the style tell us about the characters and the narrator?
- Are there recurrent **images** or **symbols**? What are they used for (illustration, characterization, atmosphere, cultural criticism, etc.)?
- What is the significance of the **setting(s)** and the **temporal structure**?

- What is the **cultural background** of the text? Does it raise social and political issues?

This chapter offers a reading of **Nathaniel Hawthorne**'s famous novel ***The Scarlet Letter*** (1850) along the lines of these questions. We will first look at two formal issues that feature prominently both in the introductory sketch and in the main part of the novel: the figure of the narrator and the central image (and symbol) of the letter 'A' that gives the novel its title. Building on this 'close reading,' we will then widen our focus and look at the novel against the historical background of the mid-nineteenth century. This is only one example among many of a 'wide reading'; some other readings inspired by various backgrounds of the novel will be summarized at the end.

**Reader's Toolkit**

> Here are some of the things you should take notes of when you read a text—of any genre—for a literature course at university:
>
> - **characters:** their names, backgrounds, relationships;
> - **setting(s):** their atmosphere and significance;
> - **time:** any dates or indications given; shifts forward or back in time;
> - **motifs:** any objects, topics, or ideas that turn up repeatedly or seem to have special significance;
> - **words and references:** if you don't understand them, look them up!

## 2.1 | The Narrator

Both the Custom House sketch and the main part have a first-person narrator, but the relation of the narrator to the story is very different. The Custom House sketch is a **homodiegetic** narrative: the narrator is telling us about his own experiences during his tenure as surveyor of customs (cf. entry II.9).

As a character in his own story, he cannot claim a perspective superior to that of any other character, or any other person who lives in contemporary Salem. This narrative mode underlines the autobiographical quality of the sketch: any annotated edition of *The Scarlet Letter* will inform us that the descriptions of the Custom House employees and the narrator's background are closely modeled on Hawthorne's own biography. As the sketch progresses, however, it acquires a fictional quality as well, especially in the scene when the narrator holds the scarlet letter against his breast and feels its "burning heat." It is difficult to tell when exactly we move from autobiography to novel, from fact to fiction, and the ambiguous voice of the narrator is crucial in this blurring of boundaries. In the beginning, he is invested with all the authority a narrator can have: as a reliable reporter of fact and as the autobiographical voice of the author. He still has this authority at the point when he finds the manuscript and the letter, so that we cannot be sure whether or not the story of Hester Prynne is really historical. The feeling of uncertainty persists in the opening of the main story, whose narrator seems to be the same person as the narrator of the Custom House sketch. He refers to the same source (Surveyor Pue), situates himself in the same time period (the mid-nineteenth century), and has a similar approach to the story (skeptical but imaginative). In narratological terms, then, Hester's story is an **embedded narrative** told by a second-degree or 'metadiegetic' narrator.

The embedded narrative is set about 200 years earlier and is told from a traditional **authorial perspective**. The second-degree narrator is **heterodiegetic** and knows more than a single person could possibly know. He reports secret meetings, private conversations, the previous and later life of Hester Prynne, and the thoughts and feelings of a number of characters. In keeping with his sovereign authorial position, he does not hesitate to state his own opinions and to judge characters by them. Also, he has a tendency to belittle his characters because they are less progressive and less rational than himself. This authorial perspective is complicated, however, by the narrative frame set up in the Custom House sketch. If the narrator of the main part is the

person who found the manuscript, he cannot really know some of the things he tells. He does warn us in the sketch that he has allowed himself "nearly or altogether as much license as if the facts had been entirely of my own invention," and he stresses that Surveyor Pue collected additional information by talking to witnesses and to friends of Hester's. Nevertheless, it is hardly believable that anyone could know what Hester and Dimmesdale talked about when they met in the forest, or how exactly Dimmesdale felt after the meeting. Moreover, the narrator himself admits his uncertainty at some points, and he often questions the reliability of his sources. When he reports events that contradict his rational view, he usually suggests several possible explanations and avoids choosing between them. In other words, he regularly defers or disclaims the authority his authorial perspective suggests.

Some narratologists have argued that this element of uncertainty and ambiguity establishes a **distance between author and narrator**. It does not necessarily make the narrator unreliable, but as critic Elaine Hansen points out, it allows Hawthorne to make a statement about "the limitations and possibilities of the artist" (148). Since there are always many different perspectives on events and stories, art must be complex and even contradictory, and the narrator is one of the "possibilities" for a fictional text to capture this complexity. Noting the narrator's readiness to report different explanations of crucial events in his story, even at the price of his own consistency, Elaine Hansen suggests that his "ambivalent and self-contradictory attitude" can be seen as "a positive value postulated for artist and reader alike." Hawthorne succeeds in creating an adequately complex rendering of the story, and we as readers are offered several perspectives on the story and thus "have some chance, perhaps, of understanding more of the spirit of the Puritan age and its supernatural personifications of what we know as psychological effects" (155).

*Defining the author-narrator relationship*

## 2.2 | Symbol, Allegory, Image

*The Scarlet Letter* is an unusually poetic novel: much of its atmosphere and characterization relies on **stylistic devices** such as symbol, allegory, and image. As in poetry, the result is a densely written text that conveys several layers of meaning and encourages us to read slowly and carefully. The central stylistic device of the novel is, of course, the

scarlet letter itself. It is an **allegorical** device in that it stands for an abstract idea that Hester is supposed to embody: adultery. By forcing her to wear the letter, the Puritan magistrates hope to turn her into a concrete example of that sin and its consequences, perhaps imitating classics of religious allegory such as Bunyan's *The Pilgrim's Progress* (a favorite of

The **structuralist origins** of the **New Criticism** can be seen, for example, in Hyatt Waggoner's analysis of the novel's general imagery. Waggoner suggests that the cemetery, the prison, and the rose form a **"symbolic pattern"** in which all major concerns of the novel can be placed. He argues that the cemetery stands for the "natural evil" of death, the prison for the "moral evil" of a fundamentalist society, and the rose for "natural good." Another aspect he examines is the **use of color**, which, like Feidelson, he sees as a bridging device between the sensory and the figurative. Blackness, for example, is sometimes a literal, sensory quality (Hester's black eyes), sometimes it may be taken either literally or figuratively (the beadle's statement that in the Puritan colony "iniquity is dragged out into the sunshine"), while at other points the figurative, symbolic quality is dominant (Mr. Wilson's remarks on the "blackness" of Hester's sin).

Hawthorne's), where the characters have names like Christian, Prudence, and Charity. Soon, however, people begin to reinterpret the meaning of the letter and to suggest other interpretations, such as 'able' or 'angel.' This subverts the power of allegory, which relies on a direct, exclusive reference between the idea and the person or thing that embodies it. The letter now becomes **symbolic** rather than allegorical: it is a concrete object that is invested with several, often highly imaginative meanings at the same time. Critics have continued this line of thought and suggested that the 'A' might allude to other, covert issues Hawthorne is concerned with: ambiguity, for example, or America, or the religious dissenters' movement of antinomianism. Aside from the meaning of the letter 'A,' however, the scarlet letter is also important as an **image**. Its colorful vivacity contrasts strongly with the black and grey tones that dominate Puritan society: some Puritans regard the burning red as a sign of the devil, but the novel also relates it to the wild rosebush at the prison door, a sign of hope and of nature's unruliness.

The complexity of the letter, and of the novel's stylistic devices in general, has intrigued readers and critics from the beginning; it made the novel a special favorite with the **New Critics**, who regarded complex, ambiguous use of language as a yardstick for artistic achievement (cf. entry II.1.3). Given this aesthetic creed, it comes as no surprise that the New Critics read the novel as symbolic rather than allegorical. F. O. Matthiessen, the critic who coined the term 'American Renaissance' (cf. entry I.3.2), praised Hawthorne for overcoming "the stiff layers of allegory" in favor a more complex, organic "fusion of idea and image" in the symbol of the scarlet letter (279; 250). Charles Feidelson argued that the novel as a whole is an "exposition of the nature of symbolic perception": inspired in the first place by the narrator's ruminations over the meaning of the letter he finds in the Custom House, it shows how all the characters go through such a process and thus becomes a reflection of "not only the meaning of adultery but also meaning in general: not only *what* the focal symbol means but also *how* it gains significance" (10). Feidelson concludes that symbolism suits Hawthorne's purposes better than allegory, since allegory is a mere "formal correspondence," a mental exercise, whereas the symbol makes the real and the imaginary interact. This interaction has inspired the novel as a whole, according to the Custom House sketch, and it repeats itself in all of the characters in the story: Dimmesdale is seared by the letter both in his mind and on his breast; Hester's entire personality is shaped by the associations of the letter and its real-life consequences; and Pearl, as the narrator repeatedly emphasizes, "*is* the scarlet letter both physically and mentally" (Feidelson 11). This dynamic is expressed most concisely in the narrator's description of these three characters as they are standing on the scaffold after their nightly meeting: "And there stood the minister, with his hand over his heart; and Hester Prynne, with the embroidered letter glimmering on her bosom; and little Pearl, herself a symbol, and the connecting link between those two" (ch. 12). An ambiguous device on several levels, the scarlet letter raises fundamental questions about the relationship of reality and imagination, and it contributes to the uncanny, supernatural atmosphere Hawthorne evokes in the novel.

## 2.3 | Historical Subtexts

The New Critics and their successors were not particularly interested in the historical background of the novel. What little interest there was focused on the seventeenth-century Puritan background against which Hester's story unfolds. From the 1980s, however, scholars influenced by the **New Historicism** pointed out that the historical context of the mid-nineteenth century, the time when

Hawthorne wrote his novel and when the Custom House sketch is set, should also be taken into account. The New Historicists argued that literary texts are sites of contestation where philosophical ideas, political biases, social structures, and other elements of contemporary discourse are consciously discussed or unconsciously reflected (cf. entry II.5; Murfin 412–61). Such reflections, they suggested, often take a covert form: they are a layer underneath the surface of the text and can best be seen when the text is read against historical documents that address these concerns explicitly. One issue that several critics have traced in the subtext of *The Scarlet Letter* is the debate over the abolition of slavery that dominated American public discourse around 1850. There is only one open reference to slavery—the narrator points out that the governor's servant is "a free-born Englishman, but now a seven-year's slave" (ch. 7)—but critics such as Jonathan Arac, Sacvan Bercovitch, and David Reynolds have suggested that Hawthorne's concern with this debate in fact underlies the entire novel. With the possibility of war on the horizon, Arac explains, Hawthorne supported the consensus of the early 1850s that inaction was the best course for the nation as a whole. In a biography of Franklin Pierce he wrote for the latter's 1852 presidential campaign, Hawthorne argued that "preserving our sacred Union" was the most important political goal of the time (ch. 7), and while he opposed slavery, he regarded the abolition movement as dangerous, because it threatened to divide that union. This attitude, Arac suggests, can also be found in the novels Hawthorne wrote in the period. Instead of developing conflictory aspects of the plot, he tries "to erase and undo all action"; his focus is on character rather than action, and more specifically on the "analysis of what prevents a character from acting." Here is a description of Dimmesdale:

The minister [...] had never gone through an experience calculated to lead him beyond the scope of generally received laws; although, in a single instance, he had so fearfully transgressed one of the most sacred of them. But this had been a sin of passion, not of principle, nor even purpose. [...] At the head of a social system, as the clergymen of that day stood, he was only the more trammelled by its regulations, its principles, and even its prejudices. As a priest, the framework of his order inevitably hemmed him in. (ch. 18)

In Arac's reading of this passage, the figure of Dimmesdale comes to embody the political tensions of the time. Like Pierce and other politicians "at the head of [the] social system," he wavers between principle and passion, between regulation and motion, between stability in the present and change in the future, and his societal background demands that it is always the former of the two opposing forces that dominates. Thus, Arac concludes, "the organization of (in)action" in *The Scarlet Letter* "works through a structure of conflicting values related to the political impasse of the 1850s" (259).

Reading novels against their historical background can reveal covert agendas.

## 2.4 | Other Approaches

**Psychoanalysis.** Since *The Scarlet Letter* traces in much detail the characters' inner life and their relationships to each other, critics have often used Freudian and Lacanian concepts to explain the plot dynamic and character behavior (cf. entry II.7; Murfin 297–330; Schwab). James Mellard, for example, suggests that Pearl is going through the 'mirror stage' and the Oedipus complex as she is growing up during the novel; Hester is in a post-Oedipal stage and has to deal with the dynamics of the collective 'gaze' of the town; Dimmesdale shows all the symptoms of a neurosis, including hysteria; and Chillingworth is both an analyst of Dimmesdale's neurosis and a psychotic personality himself. Mellard's chapter on *The Scarlet Letter* explains these analyses in some detail and provides a useful illustration of the psychoanalytical approach.

**Pragmatics/Semiotics.** From a pragmatic perspective (cf. entry II.8), both the historicist and the psychoanalytic approach run into a logical problem at some point: in order to explain the characters' actions, they need to rely on material outside the text—material that is often supplied by or intermingled with their own conjectures and can thus no longer be verified by the text. It is through a study of the characters' responses to signs they encounter in the text, John K. Sheriff claims in his essay on *The Scarlet Letter*, that we can best explain their motivations (cf. Rohr). He distinguishes Hester, Chillingworth, and Dimmesdale by their different 'modes' of responding to the letter and to

The theories introduced in Part II of this book suggest various possible readings of fictional texts.

Pearl. Hester, he suggests, sees signs as indicators of what Peirce called "feeling and possible meaning" (78); she responds to the letter emotionally and aesthetically. Chillingworth sees signs as indicators of empirical truth: just as he perceives his patients' symptoms as signs for a certain illness, he sees the letter on Hester's breast as a mark of adultery, and the letter on Dimmesdale's breast as a proof of his involvement. Dimmesdale, in turn, sees signs "in their relation to theories and laws" (76). Instead of confronting his feelings for Hester and Pearl, he sees them as signs in a religious narrative of guilt and repentance, but also of consecration and holy bonds.

**Reception Theory.** The first characters to appear in *The Scarlet Letter* are not the protagonists, but the Puritans who are waiting in front of the prison. Their responses to Hester and to the letter she is wearing make them the first "readers" of the story. They turn out to be rather inadequate readers, however, and Hawthorne indicates at several points that their responses fall short of the complexity of Hester's situation. They regard her as pure evil at first, and later style her "a Sister of Mercy," while Hester, who shares most of their values in the beginning, becomes more and more estranged from the community. According to reader-response critics (cf. entry II.3), this internal audience is a means of guiding our own interpretation of the novel. Hawthorne encourages us to take a broader perspective and recognize the ambivalences and ambiguities of Hester's case. Stephen

Railton has identified several strategies that contribute to this goal, such as the "strategy of narrative delay," where Hawthorne raises questions without answering them to make the reader aware of the multiplicity of possible interpretations, or his ambiguous style, which upholds or creates uncertainty through such phrases as "it might be," "according to some," "it was reported," etc. (Railton 141–43, 147–48).

**Cultural Ecology.** The inadequacy of the Puritan value system plays an important role not only in guiding the reader's response to the story but also in Hawthorne's general analysis of culture and individuality in seventeenth-century New England. The methods and results of this cultural analysis can be usefully described in ecological terms (cf. entry II.14). The Puritan community has become a prison itself; it is a narrow, stagnant cultural sphere in which every new impulse is stifled or excluded. The novel contrasts this dying 'cultural ecosystem' with the regenerative impulses of individual creativity: Hester's needlework, which transforms the letter of shame into a work of art; Pearl's playful independence from Puritan control and education; Dimmesdale's election sermon, inspired by an illicit meeting outside the community, in the revitalizing natural sphere. Just as the meeting in the forest creates new energy for Hester and Dimmesdale, Hawthorne suggests, it is by bringing together the cultural system and the life-affirming impulses of its excluded or suppressed individuals that society as a whole can be revitalized (cf. Zapf 71–91).

## Further Reading

Bode, Christoph. *Der Roman: Eine Einführung*. Tübingen: Francke, 2011.

Hawthorn, Jeremy. *Studying the Novel*. 5th ed. London: Arnold, 2005.

MacKay, Marina. *The Cambridge Introduction to the Novel*. Cambridge: Cambridge University Press, 2011.

## Works Cited

Arac, Jonathan. "The Politics of *The Scarlet Letter*." *Ideology and Classic American Literature*. Eds. Sacvan Bercovitch and Myra Jehlen. Cambridge: Cambridge University Press, 1986. 247–66.

Bercovitch, Sacvan. *The Office of The Scarlet Letter*. Baltimore: Johns Hopkins University Press, 1991.

Feidelson, Charles, Jr. *Symbolism and American Literature*. Chicago: University of Chicago Press, 1953.

Hansen, Elaine T. "Ambiguity and the Narrator in *The Scarlet Letter*." *Journal of Narrative Technique* 5.3 (1975): 147–63.

Matthiessen, F. O. *American Renaissance: Art and Expression in the Age of Emerson and Whitman*. London: Oxford UP, 1941.

Mellard, James M. "Inscriptions of the Subject." *Using Lacan* 1991, 69–106.

Murfin, Ross C., ed. *Nathaniel Hawthorne: The Scarlet Letter*. Case Studies in Contemporary Criticism. 2nd ed. Boston: Bedford/St. Martin's, 2006.

Railton, Stephen. "The Address of *The Scarlet Letter*." *Readers in History: Nineteenth-Century American Literature and the Contexts of Response*. Ed. James L. Machor. Baltimore: Johns Hopkins University Press, 1993. 138–63.

Reynolds, David S. *Beneath the American Renaissance : The Subversive Imagination in the Age of Emerson and Melville*. New York: Knopf, 1988.

Rohr, Susanne. *Die Wahrheit der Täuschung: Wirklich-keitskonstitution im amerikanischen Roman 1889–1989*. Munich: Fink, 2004.

Schwab, Gabriele. "Seduced by Witches: Nathaniel Haw-thorne's *The Scarlet Letter* in the Context of New En-gland Witchcraft Fiction." *Seduction and Theory: Read-ings of Gender, Representation, and Rhetoric*. Ed. Dianne Hunter. Urbana: University of Illinois Press, 1989. 170–191.

Sheriff, John K. "A Prospectus for a Pragmatic Reading of Hawthorne's *The Scarlet Letter*." *REAL – Yearbook of Research in English and American Literature* 15 (1999): 75–92.

Waggoner, Hyatt. *Hawthorne: A Critical Study*. Cambridge: Belknap Press, 1955.

Zapf, Hubert. *Literatur als kulturelle Ökologie: Zur kulturel-len Funktion imaginativer Texte an Beispielen des ameri-kanischen Romans*. Tübingen: Niemeyer, 2002.

*Timo Müller*

# 3 Analyzing Drama

This chapter aims at introducing exemplary ways of how you can interpret a play. Every drama analysis will have to pay attention to fundamental questions which are outlined in the reader's toolkit below.

In addition, every reading of a play for a term paper will have to use a particular method of analysis and employ a particular literary theory. By focusing on one of the most famous plays of all times, Shakespeare's *The Tragedy of Hamlet, Prince of Denmark* (ca. 1600), we will consider **five approaches** which differ in their methods—and, therefore, in their results as well.

- We will first investigate the text from the point-of-view of **genre**, which always has to do with literary history, too, since a sense of what constitutes a specific genre grows over time—in our case, the notion of 'tragedy' had developed over two thousand years by the time Shakespeare was writing—, but nonetheless experiences important revisions in specific historic epochs, as we shall see with reference to the subgenre of the revenge tragedy.
- In the next step, we will look at *Hamlet* from **a new historicist perspective**, focusing in particular on the portrayal of the ghost. We will explore explanations which an early modern spectator or reader would have had for the spectral apparitions. One of these explanations has to do with the specific political and religious situation in England at the turn of the century, and we will examine the Catholic heritage that resurfaces in *Hamlet* by drawing on the concept of 'cultural memory.'
- In the subsequent section, we will take into account **feminist criticism** of the play by concentrating in particular on its gendering of melancholia.
- We will then reconsider the ghost and melancholia from a theoretic perspective that has been laid out centuries after *Hamlet*'s origin, namely Sigmund Freud's **psychoanalysis**.
- Finally, we will briefly assess the metatheatrical quality of the ghostly apparitions, and thus return to a concept developed within drama theory, **metatheatricality**.

## Reader's Toolkit

Here are some of the things you should take notes of when you read a play for a literature course at university:

- **genre:** is the play a comedy, tragedy, a tragicomedy, a history play? Sometimes, the play's title or subtitle will define its genre; sometimes, you will have to look for cues in the play text itself.
- **epic/absolute drama:** Does the play have a narrator figure or narrative devices such as a chorus, an epilogue or prologue? If it does, we speak of epic drama. If the action ensues as if no such level of fictional mediation were present, we speak of absolute drama.
- **characters:** their names, traits, backgrounds, relationships; the list of characters at the beginning of the play (the *dramatis personae*) might give you relevant information, but also the characters' lines themselves.
- The **constellation of characters** describes the relationships of the characters (antagonists, confidants, relatives, lovers,…), while the **configuration of characters** is a list of which characters are present on stage at the same time; it helps you, for example, to get an overview of their state of information. If one character knows more about the ongoing action than others or if the audience knows more than one or all characters, we speak of **dramatic irony**.
- **setting(s):** despite Aristotle's ideal of a unity of place, many plays include a change of setting; think about the significance of each setting.
- **time:** dates or indications given; linear chronology or shifts forward (flashforward/prolepsis) or back (flashback/analepsis); ellipses of time.
- **motifs:** any objects, topics, or ideas that turn up repeatedly or seem to have special significance.

# 3.1 | Genre and Dramaturgy

As the title signals, *Hamlet* can straightforwardly be categorized as a **tragedy**. Moreover, it belongs to a tragic subgenre that was very popular on the Elizabethan and Jacobean stages, the revenge tragedy (see Prosser 36–73). Like all of Shakespeare's tragedies, *Hamlet* does not fully conform to the classic characteristics of tragedy; for example, it does not quite follow the unities of time and place as laid out in Aristotle's famous *Poetics* that stated that a tragedy's action takes no longer than twenty-four hours and happens at only one place. However, Hamlet is an exemplary tragic protagonist, as he is noble enough to attract the sympathy of the audience, but nonetheless has tragic flaws: He acts, as we will see, too cautiously in some situations, and too impulsively in others.

Dramaturgy. Further, the play realizes in an exemplary manner the tragic dramaturgy represented by Gustav Freytag's pyramid (see illustration). The **complication** and the **rising action** begin when young Hamlet encounters the ghost of his father, learns that his father was killed by his uncle, and is asked to seek revenge. The ensuing conflict between Hamlet and his uncle Claudius carries the rising action further. The **climax** of Hamlet's attempts to determine whether the ghost has spoken the truth happens when Claudius, at least in the eyes of Hamlet, reacts in a guilty manner to a theatrical re-enactment of a regicide, aptly named *The Mousetrap*. The turning point (**peripety**) which initiates the **falling action** is Hamlet's incapacity to kill Claudius while he is at prayer; a few moments later, Hamlet inadvertently kills Polonius, whom he has mistaken for Claudius. These two failures—one committed out of cogitation, the other out of a rash impulse—lead to Hamlet's exile and his loss of control (as much as the loss of his beloved Ophelia, Polonius's daughter). Before the tragic **catastrophe** sets in at the end of the play, a **moment of final suspense** lets audiences hope for a happy ending: Laertes and Hamlet are about to reconcile, which would avert Hamlet's death. Instead, however, the catastrophe leads not only to the demise of the tragic hero, but also to the deaths of his antagonists Laertes and Claudius and of his mother Gertrude. The **denouement** (the resolution) of *Hamlet* can hence be seen as exemplary of Aristotle's demand that the ideal ending of a catastrophe fully dissolve the action.

Genre. *Hamlet* participates in the early modern fashion of **revenge tragedies** that was inspired by successful plays like Thomas Kyd's *The Spanish Tragedy* (1587), which likewise features a ghost crying for vengeance and contains many more characteristics of Shakespeare's later take on the form. Often, the protagonist of a revenge tragedy stands between two mutually exclusive moral principles—this is the case in Shakespeare's play, too. Here, Hamlet has to decide between revenge for the father and the crime of regicide, and for a long time, he is unable to make this decision. Rather than taking action, he ponders his situation in long soliloquies—an aporia which he himself perceives as unmanly and degrading: "That I, the son of the dear murdered, / Prompted to my revenge by heaven and hell, / Must, like a whore, unpack my heart with words" (2.2); "Thus conscience does make cowards of us all" (3.1).

Dramatic Irony. Shakespeare makes extensive use of discrepant awareness to create suspense as well as sympathy for the protagonist. For instance, at the beginning of the third act, in the scene of the play's turning point, audiences are assured that Claudius indeed killed his brother, as he confesses the murder in a soliloquy. Due to Shakespeare's elegant engineering of character configuration, Hamlet arrives a few moments too late on the scene to witness this confession; instead, he mistakes Claudius's pose and words for prayer and refrains from killing him in this situation, as it might mean that Claudius will ascend to heaven. Hamlet also misses Claudius's subsequent admission that he is unable to pray, and the dramatic irony is thus enhanced. For Hamlet himself, the question of whether or not his revenge is justified keeps depending on the nature of the ghost: Are the words of the ghost reliable? Should his demand to "revenge this foul and most unnatural murder" (1.5)

Aspects of genre theory in *Hamlet*: (Revenge) tragedy, tragic dramaturgy, dramatic irony

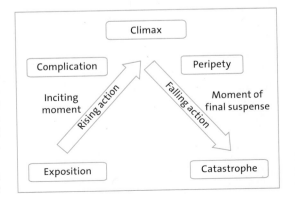

Freytag's Pyramid: Structure of a classical five-act tragedy

be followed? Or is it a figment of young Hamlet's imagination, a symptom of his grief? Might it be a devilish apparition? Critics have found diverging answers to this crucial question and they have employed various theories and methodologies to account for the ghost and Hamlet's task of revenge.

## 3.2 | A New Historicist Reading

Readings of the ghost of Hamlet's father: 1. Early modern medical theory

**Early Modern Melancholia.** Several characters, including Hamlet himself, suggest that Hamlet suffers from melancholia. For example, Claudius declares "There's something in his soul / O'er which his melancholy sits on brood" (3.1). We could hence, from a new historicist perspective (cf. entry II.5), read Hamlet's demeanour, and in particular his visions of the ghost, as melancholic symptoms. In early modern England, melancholia was seen as an affliction that oscillated between a temperament and a severe illness (see Babb; Trevor). Accounts of melancholia were indebted to humour theory, which had given a biological explanation for melancholia as early as the fifth and fourth centuries BC. According to this theory as phrased by Hippocrates, Galen and others, the four elements earth, air, fire, and water are reflected by four humours circulating in the human body, namely, black bile, blood, yellow bile and phlegm. In the healthy person, these four humours are balanced. Therefore, the natural black bile has its place in health, but causes 'melancholia' (the ancient Greek expression for 'black bile') when in excess. Hippocrates names lethargy, coldness, slowness, sleeplessness, irritability, aversion to food, fear, and dejection as symptoms of melancholia, and early modern medical treatises added many more symptoms, most comprehensively in **Robert Burton's The Anatomy of Melancholy** (1621). The ambivalence of melancholia between pathology and a healthy state characterized by increased sorrow and thoughtfulness pervades the history of the concept. An 'ennobled' notion of melancholia as the concomitant of exceptional intellectual or artistic talent had always been typical of the phenomenon, and in Shakespeare's day, the notion of **scholarly melancholia** was well-known—an important background for young Hamlet, too, who arrives at Elsinore from his university at Wittenberg.

Prior to the first performance of *Hamlet*, a number of books on melancholy had commented on ghostly apparitions. For example, Lewes Lavater's *Of Ghostes and Spirites Walking by Night* (translated into English in 1572) explains that melancholics "do falsely persuade themselves that they see or heare ghoasts" (9). Timothie Bright's *A Treatise on Melancholy* (1586) describes how melancholy "counterfetteth terrible objectes to the fantasie" (102) and "forge[s] monstrous fictions" (102) and "disguised shapes" (103). It also comments on another trait of the melancholic that applies to Hamlet: "Their resolution riseth of long deliberation, because of doubt and distrust" (131), but once their resolution is made, they are "not easy to be reconciled" and "out of measure passionate" (124)—as we can see in the quick shift in Hamlet's mood at the play's turning point. Bright also mentions the predisposition of melancholics "to be amorous" (134). In early modern England, an elaborate theory of **love melancholia** existed (see Dawson). It is this form of melancholia that Polonius constantly refers to, as he is convinced that Hamlet's strange behaviour stems from love sickness for his daughter Ophelia, from "the very ecstasy of love" (2.1). Due to the play's use of dramatic irony, the audience knows that Polonius is wrong. He has fallen for Hamlet's strategic use of "an antic disposition" (1.5) to conceal his desire for revenge.

**Cultural Memory.** In addition to melancholia, the play raises another possible explanation for the ghostly visions, which is linked to the concept of cultural memory. Hamlet himself suspects a further reason for the ghostly visions he keeps seeing. He fears that the devil might exploit his melancholic mood:

The spirit that I have seen
May be the devil, and the devil hath power
T'assume a pleasing shape; yea, and perhaps,
Out of my weakness and my melancholy —
As he is very potent with such spirits —
Abuses me to damn me. (2.2)

This remark highlights the context of religion in **Reformation England**, which many critics have found to be a productive new historicist perspective on the ghost in *Hamlet*. In the sixteenth century, England witnessed violent reversals of its state religion, which included the constant rephrasing of central aspects of the Christian fate.

Among them was the Catholic notion of purgatory, which the Reformers criticized and ridiculed and which was officially abandoned in 1563. Nonetheless, as historians and literary critics have come to acknowledge, the old faith might have persisted in people's minds and hearts throughout the century; cultural memory cannot be fully and quickly erased by official degree (cf. entry II.11), especially, as was the case with the idea of purgatory, if people were afraid that they might prolong the suffering of their dead loved ones by not taking care of their souls. In *Hamlet*, several phrases invoke purgatory, an intermediate space between heaven and hell, where souls are tortured for their sins (see Greenblatt, *Hamlet in Purgatory* 225–37). Most prominently, the ghost itself mentions it:

2. Early modern religion

I am thy father's spirit,
Doomed for a certain term to walk the night,
And for the day confined to fast in fires
Till the foul crimes done in my days of nature
Are burnt and purged away. (1.5)

Even though Hamlet does not seem to have Catholic inclinations, and in one speech explicitly defines death as "the undiscovered country from whose bourn / No traveller returns" (3.1), he nonetheless obeys the demands of the paternal figure. Hence, we could argue that the ghost not only represents Hamlet's father and the murdered king, but also refers to the **spectral presence of the old faith**, that is, to the abandoned religion of the fathers which keeps haunting the Protestant sons.

## 3.3 | A Feminist Reading

**The Gendering of Melancholia.** Reading *Hamlet* from a feminist perspective, let us consider the importance of gender for the play's depiction of melancholy and mourning. Hamlet is introduced as a scholar who throughout the action displays his education, intelligence and wit. He conforms to an **ennobled notion of male melancholia**, which had characterised the disease ever since (Pseudo-)Aristotle's notion of melancholia as the concomitant of extraordinary achievements: "Why is it that all men who have become outstanding in philosophy, statesmanship, poetry or the arts are melancholic, and some of them to such an extent that they are infected by the diseases arising from black bile?" (Aristotle 155; 953a). By contrast, female forms of suffering were seen as debilitating affects that diminished rather than enhanced intellectual capacities (see Schiesari). This gendering of melancholia comes to the fore in *Hamlet*, too, when we compare Hamlet's and Ophelia's reactions to the loss of their fathers (cf. entry II.6).

While Hamlet's loss inspires him to long, philosophically profound speeches, Ophelia is presented "as one incapable of her own distress" (4.5). By contrast to Hamlet, the "poison of deep grief" (4.5) does not lead her to deep thought and insightful ponderings on mortality, but divests her of her self-control and reason, as the men who

Aspects of gender

encounter her note. According to Horatio, she "speaks things in doubt / That carry but half sense. Her speech is nothing" (4.5); Claudius declares that "poor Ophelia" is "[d]ivided from herself and her fair judgement / Without the which we are pictures or mere beasts" (4.5); and her brother regrets that "a young maid's wits" are "mortal as an old man's life" (4.5). She is a "document in madness" (4.5) that has to be interpreted by men and that is used as an inspiration for revenge—just as Lavinia, the **inarticulate female victim** in Shakespeare's earlier revenge tragedy *Titus Andronicus*. In her state of madness, Ophelia no longer adheres to the female ideal of her day, which required women to be chaste, silent, and obedient. Quite on the contrary, she speaks shamelessly about sexual matters and seems to imply that she and Hamlet had premarital sexual intercourse (4.5). The gendering of melancholia also concerns the results of the afflictions: while the male mourning of both Laertes and Hamlet is purposeful and has political relevance, as they attempt to take revenge for their fathers, Ophelia retreats into her disturbed psyche and eventually commits suicide in an act of self-aggression. Hamlet himself is buried with all military honours, but only reduced funeral rites are granted to Ophelia.

## 3.4 | A Psychoanalytic Reading

Readings of the ghost:
3. Freud's model
of melancholia

**Mourning and Melancholia.** A more recent theoretical model helps to further illuminate the play and its protagonist (cf. entry II.7). Sigmund Freud in "Trauer und Melancholie" ("Mourning and Melancholia," 1917) developed a new understanding of **melancholia as a response to loss** which shares symptoms of mourning such as painful sadness, loss of the ability to love, and passivity. In both mourning and melancholia, the subject refuses to acknowledge the loss to the point of having hallucinations about the persistent presence of the lost one: "This opposition can be so intense that a turning away from reality takes place and a clinging to the object through the medium of a hallucinatory wishful psychosis. Normally, respect for reality gains the day" (Freud, "Mourning and Melancholia" 244). This theory would explain the ghost as Hamlet's **hallucination**, an interpretation which is plausible for his early remark that he sees his father in his "mind's eye" (1.2) and his second encounter with the ghost, when Gertrude neither sees nor hears the apparition and calls it "the very coinage of your [Hamlet's] brain" (3.4). It raises difficulties, however, for the first apparition, when not only Hamlet, but also Horatio and the guards can see the ghost—this vision would have to be explained as a shared hallucination, as a collective unwillingness to let go of the old ruler.

According to Freud, the loss that results in melancholia is at least partly unconscious; the subject might know whom he has lost, but does not fully grasp the significance of this loss. This seems to be a fruitful perspective on Hamlet, who knows that he has lost his father, but only gradually experiences the further losses caused by the murder: He has lost his throne, but also his belief in justice; what is more, he increasingly loses self-confidence and faith in his own perceptions. Further, he loses trust in his mother, and soon extends his sexual disgust to all women, which leads to a loss of Ophelia as well. The fact that Hamlet is constantly under surveillance makes him—rightly—suspect his friends Rosencrantz and Guildenstern, too.

Freud further argues that mourning ultimately results in the withdrawal of libidinal cathexis from the loved object, which enables the subject to transfer the attachment of the libido to a new object. In melancholia, however, the subject does not eventually regain "respect for reality" (Freud, "Mourning and Melancholia" 244) but, to avoid suffering from loss, he or she introjects the be-loved object and thereby preserves it fantasmatically within the ego. Hamlet's **fixation on his father**, which Claudius criticizes as "obstinate condolement" (1.2) and his compulsive remembrance that includes visions of the deceased can be seen as such an act of incorporation:

Remember thee?
Yea, from the table of my memory
I'll wipe away all trivial fond records,
All saws of books, all forms, all pressures past,
That youth and observation copied there,
And thy commandment all alone shall live
Within the book and volume of my brain (1.5)

As part of this **identification**, Hamlet idealizes the dead father, whom he compares to mythical gods like Hyperion (1.2) and Hercules (1.2), whose martial prowess he cherishes. In his attempt to impersonate the dead father and to take revenge for his murder, Hamlet tries to imitate him and to overcome his own unmanly hesitation:

Rightly to be great
Is not to stir without great argument,
But greatly to find quarrel in a straw
When honour's at the stake. [...]
O, from this time forth
My thoughts be bloody or be nothing worth! (4.4)

Freud argues that once the subject has incorporated the object, it experiences a self-division, since parts of the ego will now judge the incorporated parts and vice versa. Hatred of the object is transformed into hatred of the self, and the critical instance of the super-ego is formed and nourished. This explains the "Kleinheitswahn" (Freud, "Trauer und Melancholie" 431)—the delusion of inferiority—and the **heightened self-criticism** that distinguishes melancholia from mourning and explains why "[i]n mourning it is the world which has become poor and empty; in melancholia it is the ego itself" (Freud, "Mourning and Melancholia" 246). Hamlet's remarks on the futility and **emptiness of the world** and his psyche are famous: "How weary, stale, flat, and unprofitable / Seem to me all the uses of this world!" (1.2); "I have of late—but wherefore I know not—lost all my mirth, forgone all custom of exercise; and indeed it goes so heavily with my disposition that this goodly frame, the earth, seems to me a sterile promontory" (2.2). As we have already seen, he increasingly chastises himself for his incapacity to act, and the conflict within his psyche goes as far as considering suicide in renowned soliloquies like the reflection on "To be or not to be."

Independent of early modern theories of black bile, Hamlet's melancholia can thus be analyzed according to Freud's notion of melancholia—an approach to the play which hardly any critic has chosen so far (for a partial exception see Kirsch; Garber 227–29). Employing Freud's concept of melancholia means that we read the play in the light of a theory which has been developed centuries after Shakespeare wrote *Hamlet*—an approach which some scholars have criticised as a-historical (see for example Greenblatt, "Psychoanalysis"). It is certainly true that we have to pay attention to the historic and cultural specificities of the theory we employ; for example, Freud's notion of the Oedipus complex works only in contexts in which the nuclear family lives together, or Marxist theory can only be applied to industrialized societies ruled by capitalism. However, psychic processes which are instigated by an experience of loss might have been similar at Shakespeare's time and today—and the productivity of Freud's concepts for a reading of Hamlet's state of mind seems to be case in point for reading early modern texts in the light of psychoanalytic theory (see also Mazzio and Trevor).

## 3.5 | Metatheatricality

We can also see the ghost as a potent metatheatrical figure, that is, as a figure that **comments on the theatre's status**. Shakespeare frequently had his actors refer to themselves as 'dreams,' 'illusions,' and 'shadows,' and the ghost can be seen as yet another incorporation of the principle of theatrical embodiment. As Stephen Greenblatt has argued,

[w]hat there is again and again in Shakespeare, far more than in any of his contemporaries, is a sense that ghosts, real or imagined, are good theatre—indeed, that they are good for thinking about theater's capacity to fashion realities, to call realities into question, to tell compelling stories, to puncture the illusions that these stories generate, and to salvage something on the other side of disillusionment. (*Hamlet in Purgatory* 200)

The entrances of the ghost also help Shakespeare to develop a theatrical form which lets audiences participate in the thoughts and fantasies of the protagonist. When the ghost appears for the second time, Gertrude cannot witness it, but audiences share Hamlet's perspective. In this vein, it seems apt that in some performances, the ghost is played by the same actor who later impersonates the murdered king in Hamlet's play-within-the-play—a device whose metatheatrical quality has long been acknowledged. From this perspective, it seems fitting that a brief passage in Lavater's above-mentioned treatise on ghosts presents the melancholic as the quintessential playwright, who in an empty theatre sees a performance in his mind's eye: "A certaine man distraught of his wittes, who going into the Theatre [...] when no man was therein, and there sitting alone, by clapping of his hands, signified that he liked as well every thing there, as if some Comedie or Tragedie had bin notably set forth on a stage" (10).

4. The ghost as metatheatrical comment

### Further Reading

**Asmuth, Bernhard.** *Einführung in die Dramenanalyse.* 7th ed. Stuttgart: Metzler, 2009.

**Buse, Peter.** *Drama and Theory: Critical Approaches to Modern British Drama.* Manchester: Manchester University Press, 2002.

**Dollimore, Jonathan.** *Radical Tragedy: Religion, Ideology and Power in the Drama of Shakespeare and His Contemporaries.* Brighton: Harvester, 1984.

**Jahn, Manfred.** "A Guide to the Theory of Drama." *Poems, Plays, and Prose: A Guide to the Theory of Literary Genres.* 2 Aug. 2003. English Department, University of Cologne. 20 June 2011 <http://www.uni-koeln.de/~ame02/pppd.htm>.

**McEachern, Claire.** *The Cambridge Companion to Shakespearean Tragedy.* Cambridge: Cambridge University Press, 2003.

**Pfister, Manfred.** *Das Drama: Theorie und Analyse.* 11th ed. Stuttgart: UTB, 2001.

**Schößler, Franziska.** *Einführung in die Dramenanalyse.* Stuttgart: Metzler 2012.

## Works Cited

Aristotle. "Book XXX." *Problemata/Problems*. Trans. W. S. Hett. Vol. 2. Cambridge: Harvard University Press, 1965. 154–81.

Babb, Lawrence. *The Elizabethan Malady: A Study of Melancholia in English Literature from 1580 to 1642*. 1951. East Lansing: Michigan State University Press, 1965.

Bright, Timothie. *A Treatise of Melancholie Containing the Causes Thereof, & Reasons of the Strange Effects it Worketh in our Minds and Bodies: With the Physicke Cure, and Spirituall Consolation for such as Haue Thereto Adioyned an Afflicted Conscience. ... by T. Bright Doctor of Physicke*. London: Thomas Vautrollier, 1586.

Dawson, Lesel. *Lovesickness and Gender in Early Modern English Literature*. Oxford: Oxford University Press, 2008.

Freud, Sigmund. "Trauer und Melancholie." 1917. *Gesammelte Werke*. Vol. 10. Frankfurt/M.: Fischer, 1999. 427–46.

Freud, Sigmund. "Mourning and Melancholia." 1917. *The Standard Edition of the Complete Psychological Works of Sigmund Freud*. Ed. James Strachey. Vol. 14. London: Hogarth, 1957. 243–58.

Garber, Marjorie. *Shakespeare's Ghost Writers*. 1987. New York: Routledge, 2010.

Greenblatt, Stephen. *Hamlet in Purgatory*. Princeton: Princeton University Press, 2001.

Greenblatt, Stephen. "Psychoanalysis and Renaissance Culture." *Learning to Curse: Essays in Early Modern Culture*. New York: Routledge, 1990. 131–145.

Kirsch, Arthur. "Hamlet's Grief." *Major Literary Characters: Hamlet*. Ed. Harold Bloom. New York: Chelsea, 1990. 122–38.

Lavater, Lewes [Ludwig]. *Of Ghostes and Spirites Walking by Nyght and of Strange Noyses, Crackes, and Sundry Forewarnynges, Whiche Commonly Happen before the Death of Menne, Great Slaughters, [and] Alterations of Kyngdomes. One Booke, Written by Lewes Lauaterus of Tigurine and Translated into Englyshe by R. H.* London: Henry Benneyman, 1572.

Mazzio, Carla, and Douglas Trevor. "Dreams of History: An Introduction." *Historicism, Psychoanalysis and Early Modern Culture*. Eds. Carla Mazzio and Douglas Trevor. New York: Routledge, 2000. 1–19.

Prosser, Eleanor. *Hamlet and Revenge*. 2nd ed. Stanford: Stanford University Press, 1971.

Schiesari, Juliana. *The Gendering of Melancholia Feminism, Psychoanalysis, and the Symbolics of Loss in Renaissance Literature*. Ithaca: Cornell University Press, 1992.

Trevor, Douglas. *The Poetics of Melancholy in Early Modern England*. Cambridge: Cambridge University Press, 2004.

*Christina Wald*

# 4 Analyzing Film

Just like literature, film has developed a variety of **genres** which help us to understand a film's action and its aesthetics; the Western, the thriller and the romantic comedy belong to the most widespread filmic subgenres. **Casting** is also an important aspect to which you should pay attention; if the film features a well-known actor, his or her star image and the roles he or she previously starred in will contribute to the film's understanding or can signal the film's genre (for example, if an action movie star plays the leading part, you will once again expect an action movie).

When analyzing a film, we have to pay attention to the **visual**, the **acoustic**, as much as the **narrative** level.

Visual Level. The action of a film can be divided into scenes which usually consist of several **shots** that assemble a sequence of **frames**. Every frame is shot in a particular type that is defined by the distance between camera and object shown: Extreme long shots typically show the panorama of a city or landscape and are often used to introduce a setting; they are then also called establishing shot. Other shot types are: long shots, full shots, American shots, medium shots, close ups, and extreme close ups. In addition to the shot type, elements of the **mise en scène** (that is, the visual composition of frames) are the camera's angle and the uses of light and colour.

Shots are spliced into **scenes** by means of **cutting and montage.** The classic form is continuity editing, which tries to assemble shots as seamlessly as possible without drawing the attention of audiences to the techniques of cutting and montage. By contrast, in jump cuts, there is no continuity between the shots and audiences are made aware of the editing. In cross-cutting, two or more simultaneous events are shown alternately; this form of montage is for example used for car chases. In match cuts, there is one common element in the two shots, for example the same object or movement in the same direction. This matching element is often relevant for the film's narrative.

On the acoustic level, not only the characters' dialogue, but also the soundtrack and sound effects are relevant. We differentiate **diegetic sound** (that is, sound that is produced within the narrative shown) from **non-diegetic sound** (coming from the off, e.g. film music). A voice-over is a voice from the off which comments on the action.

While analytic terms developed for drama analysis—such as character constellation and configuration, dramatic irony, flat and round as well as static and dynamic characters etc.—are productive for film analysis, we can also apply a number of concepts and terms from the study of prose fiction, and in particular from narratology.

---

**Focus on Narrative Situations**

Who narrates the film's action?

- **Homo- or autodiegetic narrative situation:** the film's protagonist (or another character) narrates the action, often signalled by the use of voice-over (for example in *American Beauty*)
- **Heterodiegetic narrative situation:** most often, we cannot identify the film's narrator; in these cases, we have a covert, heterodiegetic narrator; this agency has also been called the camera, a "grand image-maker" (Metz), a filmic narrator, an implied filmic author, a shower-narrator (Chatman), and an implied director.
- **Figural narrative situation:** a covert narrative agency relates the action from the perspective of one or more characters, who serve as **focalizers.**

Audiences can be made share the point of view of characters by means of the camera angle and cutting:

- a **gaze shot** shows a character looking.
- a **point-of-view shot** shows an object or person from the character's point-of-view; a series of point-of-view shots are also called **subjective camera**.
- an **eye-line shot** is a gaze shot followed by a point-of-view shot.
- an **over-the-shoulder shot** shows a character's shoulder and what is in front of them.
- a **reaction shot** shows how a character reacts to something he or she has just seen.
- a **mind screen** visualizes thoughts, fantasies, dreams or memories of a character.

---

## 4.1 | Film Narratology: Screening Subjectivity

The definitions above have indicated some forms how films can create a sense of subjectivity, how they can make audiences share the perspective of one or several characters—an issue which has been thoroughly examined in narratology (cf. entries II.9 and IV.2).

Since the 1990s, a number of mainstream films have used rather unusual filmic devices to make audiences participate in the perception of their protagonists. This trend has often involved deceiving audiences regarding the actual plot or character constellation. For example, films like *The Usual Suspects* (1995), *The Sixth Sense* (1999), *Fight Club* (1999), *The Prestige* (2006), and *Shutter Island* (2010) make audiences only belatedly realize to which extent they have shared the protagonist's **unreliable perspective**. This effect is achieved by departing from the usual authorial narrative perspective. In some of these films, the protagonist functions as an autodiegetic narrator; for example, the nameless narrating protagonist of *Fight Club* recounts the events that have led to the film's opening, when he is held at gunpoint in a derelict skyscraper. During his retrospective narration, however, audiences do not share the perspective of the knowledgeable I-as-narrator, but of the deeply disturbed I-as-protagonist. Hence, the protagonist functions as a focalizer whose hallucinations audiences share. In *Fight Club*, the belated realization which will make audiences reconsider the entire plot is that the protagonist's friend Tyler Durden has actually been a projection by the protagonist, that he is an idealized part of himself. In a similar manner, the doppelganger constellation of *The Prestige* is revealed only at the end of the movie, and in *The Sixth Sense* audiences understand only in the finale that the protagonist, who has served as a focalizer throughout the action, is the ghost of a dead man.

The films thus exploit the expectation of audiences that the **camera work** is 'objective,' serving as a reliable narrative authority rather than offering the subjective, potentially deluded view of particular characters. *Fight Club* highlights this clash between the standard work of the camera as an authorial recording device and the unusual appropriation of the camera by the hallucinations of the protagonist when it shows a fight between the protagonist and his alter ego for a second time: Now the colour images of the brutal fight, which audiences have seen before, are interspersed with the objective black-and-white-images shot by a security camera, which show how the protagonist hits himself and throws himself down the stairs. Let us examine in the following one example of screened subjectivity in closer detail.

## 4.2 | The Example of *Memento*: Screening Memory and Oblivion

*Memento* (2000), directed by Christopher Nolan, recounts the quest of a man for revenge; in many ways, it resembles *Hamlet*. Like Shakespeare's protagonist, the revenger figure, called Leonard Shelby, is insecure about his project to avenge the murder of his wife, because he has suffered from anterograde amnesia ever since the traumatic event, which makes it difficult for him to keep in mind and puzzle out the cues he gets regarding his wife's potential murderer. The film's ingenious structure and its use of focalization makes audiences participate in Leonard's condition **by narrating the film backwards**. The opening scene, in which Leonard kills a man and afterwards takes a picture of the corpse, is shown backwards, with the projectile being sucked into the pistol and the Polaroid photo turning from a clear image to a blurred yellow-red surface. All subsequent scenes shown in colour are presented running forwards, but their order is reversed; hence, audiences find themselves, just like the **focalizer** Leonard, in situations without being aware of how and why they entered these circumstances, and causality can only be reconstructed belatedly. One scene in which the resulting difficulties for the focalizer and the audience became acutely apparent is when, at the beginning of a scene shown in crosscuts, Leonard is shown running and audiences can hear his thoughts in a voice-over—Leonard asks himself what he is doing, then decides that he must be chasing a man who is likewise running, and realizes only when this man shoots at him that he must actually be fleeing him (ch. 11).

In addition to the colour scenes in reversed chronological order, the film features a **second strand of narrative** in black-and-white sequences arranged in a linear, forward temporal order. In these scenes, Leonard is shown in his hotel room, repeatedly talking on the phone about his detective work. As part of his phone conversations, he relates the story of a former client of his called Sammy Jankis who had suffered from the same condition as Leonard himself and who inadvertently killed his diabetic wife by giving her insulin shots in quick succession when she tried to test the genuineness of his short-term memory loss. In the final scene of the film, these two narrative strands merge: Elegantly, the filmic image turns from black-and-white to colour together with a developing Polaroid photo which Leonard has taken after killing another man he takes for his wife's murderer (ch. 23). It is only then that audiences can establish their **temporal relation**, namely that the black-and-white sequences have taken place before the sequences shown in colour. Therefore, the film's final scene is, chronologically speaking, its middle part. At the same time, it is the action's **turning point**, but one which audiences only witness at the very end of watching the movie, thus putting them in a position similar to *Fight Club* or *The Sixth Sense*, because they have to reconsider the entire action as well as the protagonist. In this transition scene, audiences learn that Leonard has deliberately written down the license plate number of his acquaintance Teddy as if it were a cue for finding his wife's murder. Leonard thus sets himself the task of tracking down and eventually killing Teddy, and he does so because Teddy has previously confronted him with unbearable truths about his quest: Teddy claims that Leonard already killed two men he took for his wife's murderer, and that the satisfaction and peace of mind which Leonard expects from this act have not lasted due to Leonard's amnesia. Further, he maintains that Leonard has displaced his memories of having accidentally killed his wife with an insulin overdose to the fabricated story about Sammy Jankis. While it is not easy for audiences to decide whether Teddy's account is trustworthy, the film gives a number of **visual cues** that this version can be relied on. For example, when Leonard recounts how Sammy ended up in a hospital after the death of his wife, the film, for a split second, replaces the image of Sammy in his armchair with a shot of Leonard (ch. 22; see illustration), thereby suggesting an identification of the two characters which Teddy's story suggests only later in the film.

By this turn of the action, audiences have to reconsider their view of Leonard, as they realize that he deliberately manipulates himself into killing a man whose guilt he has no proof of at all. *Memento* therefore raises deep-seated questions about **memory, oblivion, guilt, and epistemology**, similar to Nolan's more recent film *Inception* (2010) that likewise deals with the accidental murder of a woman by her husband and the husband's subsequent attempts to come to terms with his guilt. Leonard, like every revenger, is haunted by the past, which determines both his present and his future. While suffering from short-term memory loss, his more distant memories are forceful to the point of being compulsory; he repeatedly has **flashbacks** to the attack on his wife and his prior married life—flashbacks which audiences share with the focalizer—and he tries to re-enact situations from his past to feel at least temporarily at ease. As he admits in a conversation with his dead wife, "I cannot remember to forget you" (ch. 13). Leonard's quest for the murderer of his wife is what gives his life meaning, and Teddy's revelations therefore threaten the very centre of his existence. As Leonard states explicitly, "Just because there are things I don't remember doesn't mean that my actions are meaningless" (ch. 5). And yet, if Teddy is right, the killing of two men has remained meaningless for Leonard himself, as he is unable to remember the fulfilment of his revenge—moreover, his revenge itself is a futile project, as his wife was not killed after all during the attack. Leonard's lack of memory and hence of a sense of time also mean that his acute awareness of the past, of the last things he can remember, does not fade. Similarly to Hamlet, who is confused about the amount of time which has lapsed since his father's death, Leonard does not know for how long his wife has been dead, and his sense of bereavement as well as his desire to take revenge remain acute. He asks himself, "How am I supposed to heal if I can't feel time?" (ch. 8).

Attempting to make sure that Leonard neither forgets his task of taking revenge nor the cues he has already assembled, he has his body tattooed with 'facts' about his wife's murderer, for example his name 'John G__.' Leonard repeatedly points out how much more trustworthy these facts, which he has literally turned into his 'body of evidence,' are in comparison to memories, which can be falsified over time: "Memory can change the shape of a room; it can change the color of a car. And memories can be distorted. They're just an interpretation, they're not a record, and they're irrelevant if you have the facts" (ch. 6).

Filmic experiments with
chronological order

Visual cue to narrative
unreliability

Leonard's 'body
of evidence'

Leonard even has the sentence "memory is treachery" written on his body. And yet, even before the denouement (the resolution) at the film's end, audiences are made to doubt this clear-cut differentiation between reliable facts and potentially **fictitious memories**. For instance, Leonard is confronted with conflicting 'evidence'—when Teddy warns him not to trust Natalie, he finds a handwritten note on his Polaroid photo of Teddy, "Don't believe his lies" (ch. 14). In a similar manner, the tattoo warning him against treacherous memories is contradicted by a highly visible tattoo on his hand, which serves as the backbone of Leonard's sense of self, namely "Remember Sammy Jankis"—it turns out only at the end of the film that these memories are indeed treacherous, too,

and that Leonard betrayed himself (and at the same time, the audience that shares his perspective) about his past and about his project of revenge.

Thus, *Memento*'s **complex narrative structure**, which consists of two strands of narrative that are connected only at the end, one of which is told in reverse chronological order, and its use as a focalizer of a man who suffers from memory loss and who deceives himself about his past, makes the film a good example of how narratological concepts can be productively applied to film analysis. At the same time, *Memento*'s constant intermedial employment of Polaroid photographs that are meant to serve as objective records of the truth, but whose trustworthiness is repeatedly called into question offers audiences a **metacinematic comment** on the unreliability of seemingly objective (moving) images.

## 4.3 | Filmic Adaptations of Literary Texts

The ghost figure
in *Hamlet*, directed by
Laurence Olivier, 1948

The ghost's perspective
in Olivier's *Hamlet*

One important field of film studies within English and American studies is the examination of how literary texts are adapted for the screen. While films have sometimes been judged in view of their 'fidelity' to the original, this attitude has changed in recent years; instead, filmic adaptations are regarded as objects of analysis in their own right, albeit as objects which are intertextually related to original literary text. Nonetheless, for those interested in examining the issue of adaptation, a number of helpful models have been developed that account for the relationship between literary text and its screen version. Among the earliest typologies, Geoffrey Wagner distinguished between

1.   **transpositions**, which come close to the literary text
2.   **commentary**, "where an original is taken and either purposely or inadvertently altered in some respect" (226), for example by changing its setting or its ending
3.   **analogies**, which transplant the whole scenario and have only a loose relationship to the original.

A number of critics have proposed alternative typologies, which usually proceed in three similar stages of closeness to the original (see Cartmell and Whelehan for an overview).

*Screening Hamlet.* To illustrate some of the issues involved in adaptation studies, this section will briefly look at three screenings of *Hamlet*. We will examine their aesthetic choices and their interpretative approach to the play with a particular focus on the **depiction of the ghost** of Hamlet's father that is discussed in the entry on drama analysis as well (cf. entry IV.3). Not only all theatrical stagings, but also every filmic version of *Hamlet* will have to interpret the quality of the ghost, which can range from a haunting spirit returned from purgatory to a figment of young Hamlet's psyche. Moreover, the looks and attitude of the ghost will specify whether Hamlet perceives his father's apparition as frightening, as a nostalgic object, or as comforting.

In the classic black-and-white adaptation directed by Laurence Olivier in 1948, Hamlet's father first appears as a daunting, larger-than-life warrior with a threatening voice; his dark, tall figure is surrounded by fog. In the later closet scene where Hamlet confronts his mother about her betrayal, audiences can only hear the father's voice. Rather than specifying what Hamlet sees, the camera work makes audiences share the ghost's view of

Differing eye-line shots
in *Hamlet*, directed by
Kenneth Branagh, 1996

Hamlet from a **high-angle camera perspective** and thus highlights the awe and the sense of inferiority that the father figure inspires in Hamlet. In the reverse shot, audiences can only make out a blurry fog, and are thus put in a position to understand both Hamlet's discernment of the ghost and Gertrude's conviction that Hamlet must be fantasizing.

In Kenneth Branagh's 1996 version, the ghost is first staged similarly to Olivier's respective scene—here, its menacing quality is even enhanced by the colour scheme and dramatic weather that evokes purgatory or even hell. The differing perceptions of Hamlet and Gertrude in the closet scene are visualized by contrasting **eye-line shots**—while Hamlet's gaze shots are followed by images of the father, Gertrude's point-of-view shots just display her room devoid of any apparitions (see illustrations above); Branagh's film is here more explicit than Olivier's, and audiences will probably trust in Gertrude's view rather than Hamlet's supernatural vision.

The 2000 film version directed by Michael Almereyda transposes the action of *Hamlet* to contemporary New York, where young Hamlet could have been heir to a firm called 'The Denmark Corporation' rather than a kingdom. The film replaces the abundant metatheatrical references of the original by **intermedial and metacinematic** devices. Accordingly, the first apparition of Hamlet's father is registered on a security camera; prior to this scene, young Hamlet has watched videos from his past that featured his father. The spectre of the dead father is thus introduced as akin to a filmic, non-substantial apparition. When Horatio and his friends try to chase the ghost, it accordingly appears translucent, like a filmic projection, and

eventually dissolves. By contrast, in the first conversation between Hamlet and his father, the ghost is presented in a fully realistic manner; father and son interact and touch each other.

Here, the father, who looks and sounds in every respect like the father once alive, is presented as a symptom of the son's grief rather than a religiously inspired ghost; he also lacks the larger-than-life qualities of the menacing warrior which Olivier and Branagh attribute to the ghost. In the closet scene, the father figure is once again presented in a realistic manner and even though Gertrude denies seeing it, audiences never share her view. Because the filmic images only support Hamlet's perception, Gertrude's tearful refutation is called into question, quite in contrast to Olivier's and Branagh's versions.

This brief look at three different screenings of the ghost scenes in *Hamlet*—which we could, drawing on Wagner's typology, perhaps best classify as a **transposition** (Olivier), as a border case between **transposition and commentary** (Branagh), and as a border case between **commentary and analogy** (Almereyda)—suggests how fertile the analysis of filmic adaptations can be to assess the film's own aesthetics and meaning, but also to deepen our understanding of the original literary text.

The ghost in *Hamlet*,
directed by Michael
Almereyda, 2000

## Further Reading

**Andrew, Dudley.** *Concepts in Film Theory*. Oxford: Oxford University Press, 1984.

**Hayward, Susan.** *Cinema Studies: The Key Concepts*. 3rd ed. London: Routledge, 2006.

**Hickethier, Knut.** *Film- und Fernsehanalyse*. 5th ed. Stuttgart: Metzler, 2012.

**McFarlane, Brian.** *Novel to Film: An Introduction to the Theory of Adaptation*. Oxford: Clarendon Press, 1996.

**Monaco, James.** *How to Read a Film*. 4th ed. Oxford: Oxford University Press, 2009.

## Further Reading on Film Narratology

**Chatman, Seymour.** *Coming to Terms: The Rhetoric of Narrative in Fiction and Film*. Ithaca: Cornell UP, 1990.

**Griem, Julika, and Eckard Voigts-Virchow.** "Filmnarratologie: Grundlagen, Tendenzen und Beispielanalysen." *Erzähltheorie transgenerisch, intermedial, interdisziplinär*. Ed. Vera Nünning. Trier: WVT, 2002. 155–83.

**Krützen, Michaela.** *Dramaturgien des Films: Das etwas andere Hollywood*. Frankfurt/M.: Fischer, 2010.

**Laass, Eva.** *Broken Taboos, Subjective Truths: Forms and Functions of Unreliable Narration in Contemporary American Cinema: A Contribution to Film Narratology*. Trier: WVT, 2008.

**Metz, Christian.** *Film Language: A Semiotics of the Cinema*. New York: Oxford UP, 1974.

## Works Cited

**Cartmell, Deborah, and Imelda Whelehan.** "Literature on Screen: A Synoptic View." Introduction. *The Cambridge Companion to Literature on Screen*. Eds. Deborah Cartmell and Imelda Whelehan. Cambridge: Cambridge University Press, 2007. 1–12.

**Wagner, Geoffrey.** *The Novel and the Cinema*. Cranbury: Associated University Press, 1975.

*Christina Wald*

# 5 Analyzing Culture

In comparison to analyses of prose, poetry, drama, and film, examinations of cultural phenomena usually have to take into consideration a much wider **variety of primary sources**. The typical range of materials includes books, newspaper and journal articles, paintings, photographs, TV-shows, movies, advertisement, and internet pages, but fashion, food, music, architecture or other cultural products might be relevant sources, too, depending on your interest.

**Reader's Toolkit**

The scope of **cultural analysis** is so broad that you will have to ask different questions for every field of enquiry. Before starting your analysis, you will always have to ask:
- What are the most relevant **sources** for my enquiry?
- How can I gain **access** to these sources? If newspaper articles are important for your analysis, for example, you should use archives which are available via your home library.
- Among the **databases** which are of particular interest for cultural studies are
  - the Virtual Library of Anglo-American Culture, which offers access to books, journals and digital media,
  - the American Memory Collection, which holds collections of photographs, advertisements, music etc., and
  - the web pages of the British Council, which inform you about British culture, including design, architecture, fashion, music etc. (see entry VII.2 for URLs).

## 5.1 | Football, Nationality, and Multiculturalism

As Christian Huck points out in his entry on British cultural studies, "cultural condensations […] are analysed because they promise access to the social self-interpretation of specific groups" (section III.2.5). This chapter will look at a particular cultural condensation, namely international football matches, in order to examine the self-representation of nations and their perception by others. The importance of football for the perception and celebration of nationality has long been acknowledged in academic research. Attending football matches is a performative, for most spectators iterative, **enactment of belonging**; hence, "[w]hat distinguishes football as a form of popular culture is that it can provide one of the key vehicles for the ritual articulation of identity, be it through the expression of regional pride, local patriotism or national belonging" (Back, Crabbe, and Solomos 83). Eric Hobsbawn has shown in his study of nations and nationalism that

[w]hat has made sport so uniquely effective a medium for inculcating national feelings is the ease with which even the least political or public individuals can identify with the nation […]. The imagined community of millions seems more real as a team of eleven named people. The individual, even the one who only cheers, becomes a symbol of his nation himself. (143)

Hence, both players and fans become metonymies of their nations, and football matches allow for a direct, physical experience of the imagined community of a nation. For the scope of this volume, the encounters between England and the USA and among the national teams of the British Isles are particularly interesting, also because, as Huck emphasizes, "cultures begin to perceive themselves in cultural encounters." While England considers itself the 'home' of football, soccer plays a more marginal role in the USA, where it is also gendered in a different manner, as we will see. In the case of England, football has played an important role for

Football and national identity: England vs. USA

forging a sense of specific '**Englishness**' rather than more inclusive 'Britishness,' which for a long time had provided the chief aim of reference. In this context, Gary Younge, a well-known black British journalist, has argued that "it was not the nation that made the team, but the team that made the nation. Finding evidence of England's material presence beyond the football field is a challenge. I never knew I was English until I went to study in Edinburgh, and even then I had no idea what it meant apart from not being Scottish." The rise of interest in the English national team and the emergence of the St. George's flag during the 1996 European Football Championship might be linked to the decline of Britain's political importance due to decolonization and its marginal role in the European community (Holt and Mason 129; see also Featherstone 1).

By contrast to football clubs, which are nowadays often owned and trained by foreigners and integrate international players, the **national team** is still regarded as representative of its country. In this context, special attention is paid to those players who (or whose parents) once immigrated to the respective country, and who therefore mirror the social developments of that nation. As could be seen during the 2010 World Cup with the rise in popularity of Mesut Özil, a German of Turkish origin, football players can offer positive role models that facilitate the acknowledgement and positive appraisal of **multicultural societies**. This also holds true for the English national team, as Ben Carrington and Ian McDonald point out in their introduction to the collection 'Race', Sport and British Society: "sport is perhaps one of the clearest and most public means in demonstrating how Britain has become a multicultural nation" (3). The inclusion of non-white players in professional football teams also caused tensions, however. Black players, who have become increasingly prominent since the 1970s, were often met with conditional acceptance. Rather than acknowledging and accepting (let alone cherishing) their ethnic difference, it was sometimes symbolically eradicated, thus leaving **racist prejudices** untouched. This was the case, for example, with Tony Witter, of African-Caribbean ethnicity, who in the 1990s played for the English club Millwall FC that had a reputation for racism:

In his blue shirt Tony's racial difference was somehow dissolved, or seen to be irrelevant. The notion of 'wearing the shirt' summons in football vernacular the deepest levels of symbolic identity and commitment. It captures the embodied meanings associated with the football club as an emblem of locality and identity. This is ultimately manifest in the expected style that players perform within the game. (Back, Crabbe, and Solomos 90)

This conditional acceptance in local clubs was mirrored in reactions to the national team, the site of "the most extreme form of racially exclusive nationalism" in football culture (94). One popular song throughout the 1970s and 80s was "There ain't no black in the Union Jack, send the bastards back!" (94; see also Gilroy xi). A similarly racist attitude was enacted against the 'other' on the British Isles, in particular against the team of the Irish Republic, which was often met with songs that demanded "No Surrender to the I.R.A." In 1995 this conflict escalated again, which led to the abandonment of a match between the Republic of Ireland and England in Dublin in February 1995, because of violence in the stands (Back, Crabbe, and Solomos 90). In 2010, however, the attitude of English fans seemed to have changed significantly enough to attract non-white fans, too. As Gary Younge declared in *The New Statesman* prior to the World Cup, he was cheering for the English team, too, whereas he had always identified with the Brazilian team in his youth during the 1970s. He recounts, "[i]n those early and not so early years, this relationship to English football was not merely ambivalent, it was antagonistic. It wasn't just that I did not support the national team, I actively wanted it to lose"—an antagonism that resulted from his experiences outside the football stadium: "It was about flags, anthems, war, migration, race, racism, colonialism, patriotism, nationalism, fascism and family—to name but a few things." Nonetheless, the racist attitude of many football fans on the terraces intensified Younge's unease with his tentative British identity: "if you were looking to try on your English identity, a bit like trying on a suit gifted to you by an elderly relative, a football stadium would not be the fitting room of choice." Today, however, as Younge and others argue, whiteness is no longer the hallmark of Englishness; instead, it depends on a shared culture.

# 5.2 | Football, War, and Colonialism

The competition between national teams usually involves an awareness of cultural difference; despite the internationalization of football, teams are still credited with particular national styles such as Brazilian joyful elegance, German mechanical efficiency, or English masculine toughness (Crolley and Hand 9). As Paul Gilroy and others have shown, this sense of national competition is often aligned with war. In the British context, fans singing "two world wars and one world cup, doo dah, doo dah" make this comparison explicit (Gilroy xi). The **replacement of war by sports** is problematic when it leads to the vilification of the enemy— as with the tabloid newspaper headlines about German 'panzers' and 'Blitzkrieg' that have often accompanied matches between England and Germany. For instance, the front page of *The Sun* placed the match during the Euro 1996 in line with both military and sport history: "We beat them in '45, we beat them in '66, now the battle of '96" (4 July 1996), and *The Daily Mirror* declared 'a state of soccer war' against Germany: "Achtung! Surrender. For you Fritz, ze Euro 96 Championship is over" (24 June 1996, both qtd. in Beck 401). This form of media coverage has a long history, as Peter J. Beck recounts in an assessment of the importance of football for international relations. Thus, before the 1966 World Cup final, *The Daily Mail* commented that "if Germany beats us at Wembley this afternoon at our national sport, we can always point out to them that we have recently beaten them twice at theirs" (qtd. in Beck 403).

Gilroy has suggested understanding Britain's, and in particular England's, nostalgia for the second World War as an attempt at repressing England's less glorious history, namely the brutal aspects of colonialism and the fall of the Empire. In this context, encounters between England and its former colonies, chiefly the USA, are particularly interesting, since the **colonial past** tends to resurface in the discourses accompanying such matches. During the 2010 World Cup, the group match between England and the USA was the most publicized match in the history of American soccer, as USA captain Carlos Bocanegra observed in an interview (Holly). An advertisement of the transmission by the U.S.-American broadcaster ABC activated the colonial subtext. It featured the opening of a pamphlet by Thomas Paine that played a key role in the **American Revolution**. Paine, after having emigrated from England in 1774, became an influential political author during the American Revolution and is hence considered one of the founding figures of the United States of America. During the War of Independence, General George Washington had Paine's 1776 pamphlet "Crisis" read aloud to his soldiers to reinforce their commitment. The abridged opening of this pamphlet is quoted in the TV commercial which aims at recreating a sense of American, revolutionary national unification against the British rule:

> These are the times that try men's souls [...,] but he that stands by it now, deserves the love and thanks of man and woman. Tyranny [...] is not easily conquered; yet we have this consolation with us, that the harder the conflict, the more glorious the triumph. ("2010 FIFA World Cup: Glory (England vs USA)")

The male voice-over reciting these lines in a dramatic fashion is accompanied by images of a military orchestra, celebrating fans with flags, the images of prolific football players of both the American and the English team, a pub signboard advertising the match "England versus USA" and the headlines of *The Sun* that presents England's group as "easy":

> England
> Algeria
> Slovenia
> Yanks (qtd. in "2010 FIFA World Cup: Glory (England vs USA)")

American newspapers after the match likewise compared the game to war when they titled "greatest tie against the British since Bunker Hill" (*New York Post*, 13 June 2010), the site of the first major battle of the American Revolution fought on June 17, 1775. They extended the comparison in their report: "In true revolutionary style, the underdog Americans came from behind and blasted the powerful Brits to a nail-biting 1-1 draw" (qtd. in

England vs. USA: The colonial past resurfaces.

Stills from an advertisement of the 2010 World Cup match England vs. USA

*The Sun*, 14 June 2010). As typical of nationalistic appropriations of football matches, not only military, but also football history was activated when newspapers launched reports about a defeat of the English team by the U.S. in 1950 that amounted to "a moment of national footballing shame" (*The Sun*, 11 May 2010). The fact that, after the 2010 match (which ended 1-1), Scottish newspapers thanked the American team ("Yanks a Million,"

cheered *The Scottish Sun* on 14 June 2010) highlights their **postcolonial identification** with the U.S. against England. From a Scottish perspective, beating the English team, especially at Wembley, for a long time compensated for the lack of political power; one famous chant by football fans was "Give us an assembly, we'll give you back your Wembley" (Holt and Mason 135; see also Dimeo and Finn).

## 5.3 | Football, Gender, and Sexuality

Football/soccer and
sexual normativity

Given the relatively marginal state of football in the U.S. and the fact that it is regarded (and practized) mainly as women's sport there also raised comments about the **gender and sexual implications** of the match. In an episode entitled "World Cup 2010: Into Africa—Two Teams, One Cup," of Jon Stewart's satirical American *Daily Show*, the English football enthusiast John Oliver visits the U.S. training camp, in his eyes the "clown college of football" to talk about their minimal chances to beat the English team that comes, after all, from "the country that lives and breathes the sport. We literally invented the game." Interviewing the U.S. players Jonathan Spector and Jay DeMerit, he implies that becoming an American football player is akin to having to confess one's homosexual inclination to conservative parents: "Of course, being an American soccer player presents its own unique challenges. How did you tell your parents that you wanted to be an American soccer player? [...] I can just imagine the scene. Your dad saying: 'No, please, son. Tell me you're gay.'"

Against the discursive association of football as war and of **masculine, heterosexual toughness**, the 1990s saw the emergence of the football player as fashion icon and of a **new male attitude** towards football as epitomized in football fiction by Nick Hornby (*Fever Pitch*), which arguably "presented the game as a kind of male therapy rather than as an uncomplicated assertion of masculinity" (Featherstone 134; see Williams and Taylor 216–19 for a historical account of the alignment of football and masculinity). One player in particular, **David Beckham**, captain of English national team from 2000 to 2006, aroused media attention for his 'feminine' interests in fashion and cosmetics as much as romance and family matters. Praised by critics as a "powerful and positive image of sensitive masculinity" (Feasy 103) in a field that is usually

characterized by "a specific image of masculinity [...] based on strength, activity, stamina, aggression and competitiveness" (98), Beckham was also championed as the quintessential 'metrosexual'— that is, an affluent, narcissistic, fashion-conscious, young urban man. Mark Simpson, who coined the term 'metrosexuality,' juxtaposed military masculinity and feminine fashionability when he described in his 2002 article "Meet the Metrosexual," how Beckham "recently posed for a glossy gay magazine in the U.K., just before leaving for battle in the Far East." He elaborates: "'Becks' is almost as famous for wearing sarongs and pink nail polish and panties belonging to his wife, Victoria (a.k.a. Posh from the Spice Girls), having a different, tricky haircut every week and posing naked and oiled up on the cover of Esquire, as he is for his impressive ball skills." Despite the broad acceptance of Beckham's unusual gender performance, some tabloids attempted to question his masculinity as much as his patriotism on the ground of his wearing a sarong a few weeks before the onset of the World Cup in 1998; thus, *The Sun* presented an image of Beckham as Eva Peron before England's match against Argentina (30 June 1998; see Miller 8–9).

The **blending of national and gender issues** is also at the heart of one of the many artistic tributes to Beckham. Gurinder Chadha's unusually successful film ***Bend It Like Beckham*** (2004) shows how a young London girl of Indian origin (her Sikh father emigrated to England from Kenya, where he spent his childhood), Jess Bamhra, idolizes Beckham and makes her way against gender and ethnic stereotypes as a promising young football player. The film highlights the neglect of women's football in Britain, where the game is still regarded as a quintessentially male, working-class activity, and contrasts it with the professional state of women's soccer in the U.S. Even as fans watching football matches by male players, women were effectively excluded from English stadiums until the late 1980s, since most venues did not offer ladies' rooms (Williams and Taylor 220). As an Asian female football player, Jess therefore encounters a double exclusion—British-Asian fans, let alone players, have an equally difficult status in football arenas as women, as a 2000 report on the future of multi-ethnic Britain revealed, which stated the exclusion of Asians from both the pitch and the stands (Parekh 173; see also Sedlmayr 179). The film negotiates the sexual stereotypes of women's soccer by having a mother jumping to wrong conclusions about the lesbian inclination of her football-playing daughter; moreover, it depicts one young man who has fallen in love with Beckham, an object of desire for many gay men. *Bend It Like Beckham* also engages with the importance of sports for questions of nationality, by having Jess's father eventually overcome his deep-seated disappointment with having been discriminated against as a cricket player when first arriving in England. By accepting his daughter's activity in a multi-ethnic London team and by supporting her dream to become the "missing piece of the jigsaw" for the English national team, he helps the second-generation immigrant to identify with

her English identity more strongly. Chadha parallels Jess's difficulties with that of her Irish coach Joe, who can share Jess's anger after having been called "Paki" by a player of the other team, thus broadening the postcolonial perspective of the film. As befits the nationalising impulse of international matches, it is during a tournament in Germany that Jess is viewed as an English player and compared to her male precursors. When she has failed to score a penalty, Joe comforts her by saying, "Losing to the Jerries on penalties comes natural to the English. You're part of a tradition now" (cf. Sedlmayr 181).

As the broad spectrum of sources on which this analysis has drawn demonstrates, football has been made the topic of not only journalistic engagements, but also of recent fictional literature, TV satire and commercials, and feature-length films. Due to the popularity of the sport, football has attained a socially metonymic status which has invited cultural negotiations of nationality, gender, and sexuality in both Great Britain and the USA.

The poster of *Bend It Like Beckham* visualizes the protagonist's conflict with her gender and national identity.

## Further Reading

Barker, Chris. *Cultural Studies: Theory and Practice.* London: Sage, 2008.

Nünning, Ansgar and Nünning, Vera, eds. *Einführung in die Kulturwissenschaften: Theoretische Grundlagen, Ansätze, Perspektiven.* Stuttgart: Metzler, 2008.

## Works Cited

"2010 FIFA World Cup: Glory (England vs USA)." Advertisement. ABC. 17 June 2011 <http://www.youtube.com/watch?v=7yc8LljoGDQ>.

Back, Les, Tim Crabbe, and John Solomos. "'Lions and black skins': Race, Nation and Local Patriotism in Football." Carrington and McDonald, *'Race'* 83–102.

Beck, Peter J. "The Relevance of the 'Irrelevant': Football as a Missing Dimension in the Study of British Relations with Germany." *International Affairs* 79.2 (2003): 389–411.

Carrington, Ben, and Ian McDonald, eds. *'Race', Sport and British Society.* London: Routledge, 2001

Carrington, Ben, and Ian McDonald. "'Race', Sport and British Society." Introduction. Carrington and McDonald, *'Race'* 1–26.

Crolley, Liz, and David Hand. *Football, Europe, and the Press.* London: Rank Cass, 2002.

Dimeo, Paul, and Gerry P. T. Finn. "Racism, National Identity and Scottish Football." Carrington and McDonald, *'Race'* 29–48.

Feasy, Rebecca. *Masculinity and Popular Television.* Edinburgh: Edinburgh University Press, 2008.

Featherstone, Simon. *Englishness: Twentieth-Century Popular Culture and the Forming of English Identity.* Edinburgh: Edinburgh University Press, 2009.

Gilroy, Paul. Foreword. Carrington and McDonald, *'Race'* xi–xvii.

Hobsbawn, Eric J. *Nations and Nationalism Since 1780: Programme, Myth, Reality.* Cambridge: Cambridge University Press, 1990.

Holly, Vic. "Yanks Go in Search of History." *The Sun.* 8 June 2010. 10 June 2011 <http://www.thesun.co.uk/sol/homepage/sport/football/worldcup2010/3003705/Yanks-go-in-search-of-history.html#ixzz1PoHL8pCQ>.

Holt, Richard, and Tony Mason. *Sport in Britain: 1945–2000.* Eds. Richard Holt and Tony Mason. Oxford: Blackwell, 2000.

Miller, Toby. *Sportsex.* Philadelphia: Temple University Press, 2001.

Paine, Thomas. "The Crisis." 1776. *The Writings of Thomas Paine.* Ed. Moncure Daniel Conway. 2nd ed. Vol. 1. New York: AMS, 1972. 168–79.

**Parekh, Biku, et al.** *The Future of Multi-Ethnic Britain: Report of the Commission on the Future of Multi-Ethnic Britain*. 2nd ed. London: Profile Books, 2002.

**Sedlmayr, Gerold.** "Negotiating Diasporic Spaces in Contemporary Multi-Ethnic Britain: Gurinder Chadha's *Bend It like Beckham*." *Medialised Britain: Essays on Media, Culture and Society*. Ed. Jürgen Kamm. Passau: Stutz, 2006. 173–84.

**Williams, John, and Rogan Taylor.** "Boys Keep Swinging: Masculinity and Football Culture in England." *Just Boys Doing Business: Men, Masculinities and Crime*. Eds. Tim Newburn and Elizabeth A. Stanko. London: Routledge, 1994. 214–33.

**Younge, Gary.** "Why I'll Be Cheering on England this Year." *New Statesman* 8 June 2010. 1 June 2011 <http://www.newstatesman.com/society/2010/06/british-football-england>.

*Christina Wald*

# Part V: Linguistics

# 1  Introducing Linguistics

Even though the term 'linguistics' is actually a fairly recent coinage (first attested in the second half of the nineteenth century according to the *Oxford English Dictionary*), linguistics as the scientific study of language is of course much older with a respectable tradition of two-and-a-half thousand years. Its roots can be traced back to Pāṇini and other ancient Indian linguists and their the work on the grammar of (the Old Indian language) Sanskrit (fifth or fourth century BC) as well as to early Greek traditions of rhetoric, logic and stylistics in the classical age. Most notably, it was Aristotle who pioneered a number of fundamental ideas of grammar and the form-meaning relationship that have shaped linguistic thinking up to now. However, linguistics as an independent academic discipline concerned with forms and structures, meanings and usages, historical and variational changes of language is much younger. Indeed, it was one of the fundamental tenets shared by students of language in the nineteenth and early twentieth century that linguistics is a field of study in its own right rather than a sub-discipline of stylistics or an auxiliary science assisting literary, philosophical, juridical or theological scholars in their exegetical endeavors.

As an autonomous scientific field, linguistics began to take shape in the nineteenth century with the development of a **historical and comparative approach** to the description of living and extinct languages, their pre-historic roots and their inter-lingual relatedness. Methodologically, historical-comparative linguists advocated a strictly empirical, data based and positivistic stance, which they applied to attested phonetic/phonological, morphological and grammatical forms and structures rather than to meanings, functions and usage. Principal objectives were the search for the common, pre-historic roots of language families such as Indo-European (and, ultimately, the reconstruction of a proto-language), on the one hand, and the establishment of 'laws' to explain how and why languages change over time, on the other.

The historical-comparative paradigm continued to dominate mainstream European linguistics until the advent of **Saussurean structuralism** at the beginning of the twentieth century. The reception of Saussure's ideas marked the turning point from traditional historical (and largely prescriptive) to modern structural (and descriptive) linguistics.

Arguably, this latter conception of linguistics still serves as a fundament for most models of language description, naturally supplemented by more recent theoretical orientations or paradigms. In this volume, we likewise apply an up-to-date approach which amalgamates structuralist as well as poststructural creeds and, accordingly, regard language as a product of cognition and experience, of history, culture and society.

While it is clearly beyond the scope of the five chapters devoted to linguistics in this compendium to provide a comprehensive coverage of the entire field of modern English linguistics, it is nonetheless possible to recount at least its more salient objects and objectives. Setting out to do just that, the following linguistic section presents in-depth treatments of assorted major concepts and topics, developments and variations of present-day English together with a selection of those theories and methods that are pivotal for their description.

The linguistics section is organized in the following way:
1. Theories and Methods
2. History and Change
3. Forms and Structures
4. Text and Context
5. Standard and Varieties

**1. Theories and Methods** paves the way for the scientific treatment of the range of items and issues tackled in the subsequent chapters for which they are deeply relevant. To this end, this opening chapter introduces the most pervasive and commonly used approaches in English linguistics. The emergence of new conceptual and methodological orientations in an individual scientific discipline typically epitomizes paradigmatic shifts within the entirety of the surrounding academic field. Accordingly, fundamental paradigm shifts in the twentieth century have led to the establishment of corresponding theories, 'schools' and methods in linguistics, among them the following turns, which are briefly portrayed because they are of paramount importance for understanding our conception of linguistics as advocated here.

As briefly mentioned above, the **structural turn** (involving the move from causal and historical to structural and system- rather than form-oriented analyses) induced linguists to abandon

Structure of the linguistics chapters

mainstream diachronism and replace it or, rather, complement it with a synchronic stance towards language description. Besides completely changing the way linguistics is understood and practiced up to the present day, structuralism also had a profound impact beyond disciplinary boundaries on literary theory, philosophy and sociology, to name but the most obvious disciplines. Saussure's work bred a number of related (post-)structuralist theories, among them Generative Linguistics.

Another important shift in the study of language is the **pragmatic turn**, which was spawned by the conceptual roots of linguistics in philosophy. Adopting ideas by Wittgenstein, Austin, Grice and other language philosophers, pragmatic linguists shifted their interest from word or sentence meaning to utterance meaning, i.e. to unique historical events created by real speakers to perform linguistic acts aimed at specific goals in actual situational contexts.

The study of linguistics took several 'turns' over the years.

The pragmatic view that meaning emerges in context aligns with the **contextual or interactional turn**'s belief that each unit of language, from individual sounds to composite texts, acquires its function and meaning only in relation to its larger encapsulating linguistic, situational or cultural contexts. Adopting an empirical and inductive approach, interactional linguists rely on authentic language data taken from large corpora for their research findings (rather than on isolated, context-free and constructed sentences) and regard dialogicity as the basic feature of communication.

Finally, linguistic theories inspired by the more recent **cognitive turn** focus on the speaker's knowledge about language as a cognitive ability related to other, more general cognitive abilities. Taking language as a means of reflecting our mental view of the world, cognitive linguists adopt a meaning-, function- and usage-based view of language description.

**2.** History and Change. Many questions concerning the outward appearance and the underlying rules and relations of present-day English can only be answered satisfactorily if linguists resort to a joint synchronic-diachronic perspective. To do so, it is indispensable to consult the **historical development of English**, i.e. to investigate and explain the attested surges of language change that have moulded English as we encounter it today. The driving forces behind the various chronological stages of English and the methods and theories that have been developed for their description are the topic of the next chapter on *History and Change*. On their journey into the language that we are used to refer to as English, the authors forge a bridge from the earliest Old English inscriptions to the rich multimedial and multimodal system of communication we have at our disposal today.

**3.** Forms and Structures, the next chapter, gives an insight into the entire **phonological and grammatical design** of English. To this end, it focuses on those areas of linguistics that are concerned with the description of a specific individual language, *viz.* phonetics and phonology, morphology and word formation, syntax and lexical semantics. The chapter thus discusses the basic features of present-day English: sounds and sound-patterns, words, phrases and clauses together with their structures and meanings. To work out the specific linguistic profile of English, it is intermittently contrasted with German because both languages, while sharing historical roots, have since then developed differently as to their phonology, grammar and lexicon. Furthermore, by resorting to the long and intense history of its contact with other languages, the chapter explains the pronounced tendency of English to prefer analytic to synthetic morphological and syntactic structures.

**4.** Text and Context. This form- and structure-related perspective serves as a springboard for the follow-up chapter on "Text and Context," which investigates how communicators actually use English to perform a plethora of functions and achieve a broad variety of purposes. This is the study of **linguistic pragmatics** (as the outcome of the aforementioned pragmatic turn) and **text analysis**. In their light, linguistics has changed from a science that predominantly concerns itself with forms, lexemes and sentences as units of the abstract language system to a science in which the analysis of textual meanings and functions as construed and negotiated by human interlocutors in their socio-cultural and cognitive environments takes centre stage. In this form, linguistics has entered the field of cultural studies both in conception, theory and application.

**5.** Standard and Varieties, the final chapter, presents theories in variational linguistics and sociolinguistics, which help to take account of the patterns of variation (accents, dialects, registers, etc.) and the parameters that influence them (region, age, sex, culture, social background and position, etc.). The chapter thus amends the fallacious image of English as a static and monolithic block and portrays instead English as an expanding language which constantly gives rise to new regional and social diversity, owed to its multicultural roots and relations. Thus, **dialectology** and **sociolinguistics**, as the disciplines that cover most of these variational issues, set out to describe and explain the impact of society (rather than history) on language in all of its facets.

All articles are written in an intelligible and coherent style and reflect the state of the art as comprehensively as possible, at the same time adopting a critical stance in the light of conflicting evidence and recent findings. The ensuing reliable and authoritative (if unduly concise) overview is designed to serve the needs of students set on analyzing language as a complex socio-cultural, historical and cognitive phenomenon, as well as to promote their appreciation of past and present research in language study.

*Wolfram Bublitz*

# 2 Linguistic Theories, Approaches, and Methods

## 2.1 | Introduction

According to the sociologist Kurt Lewin (169), "there is nothing more practical than a good theory." In stark contrast to the common perception of beginners and even advanced students that linguistic theory is basically a nuisance and no more than an end in itself, this quote is in fact an ideal starting-point for the present chapter of this volume, which is designed to give a sketch of **major theoretical and methodological approaches** in English linguistics. Linguistic theories are no less superfluous than, for example, Newton's theory of gravitation or Einstein's theory of relativity, as both, theories in linguistics and theories in physics, strive essentially for the same goal and serve the same purpose: to identify, formulate and explain a model of the underlying rules and principles of how things work in language or in the world, respectively, by means of observation and generalization. Just as the theory of gravitation allows us to predict that objects which are dropped will fall to the ground rather than begin to float, a good theory of the English language will allow us to predict which sentences and words speakers are likely to produce and understand and which they will not. This means that theories do not merely have enormous explanatory potential, but also massive practical implications. Being familiar with different theoretical models and the methodologies informing and supporting them as well as understanding how they are related to each other is thus an essential aspect of what it means to do linguistics.

From a bird's eye perspective, the aims of linguistic theorizing can be summarized as in the box on the right.

The account of theories and methods given in this chapter essentially follows a chronological pattern, beginning with a glimpse of approaches to the study of language prevalent in the nineteenth century and then concentrating on the major theories proposed in the twentieth and early twenty-first centuries. Throughout the discussion I will make every effort to clarify how different approaches are related to each other and highlight major pathways of how linguistics in general and English linguistics in particular have developed and ramified. A survey summarizing the models discussed will be provided at the end of this contribution. As pragmatic, sociolinguistic and historical approaches are dealt with in separate chapters of this volume, they will not feature prominently here.

---

**Focus on Aims of Linguistic Theorizing**

- Linguistic theories in the fields of **grammar** (including **phonology, morphology, syntax**) and **lexicology** are formulated to understand the nature and structure of language(s).
- Theories in linguistic **semantics** aim at scientific accounts of the rather elusive phenomenon of how linguistic elements and structures can convey meanings.
- **Cognitive-linguistic** theories try to model what speakers know about language and how the structure of languages relates to other cognitive abilities like perception and attention allocation.
- **Psycholinguistic** theories try to model what goes on in the minds of language users during ongoing processing and how languages are acquired by children.
- Theories in linguistic **pragmatics** model how communication works and how understanding comes about (cf. entry V.5).
- Theories in **variational linguistics** and **sociolinguistics** explain patterns of variation (accents, dialects, registers, etc.) and investigate parameters influencing these patterns (age, sex, social and regional background, etc.; cf. entry V.6).
- Theories in **historical linguistics** try to model why and in which ways languages change and are related to each other historically (cf. entry V.3).

## 2.2 | The Turn Towards Modern Linguistics

### 2.2.1 | The Pre-Structuralist Tradition in the Nineteenth Century

Nineteenth-century linguistics is dominated by the comparison of languages, driven to a large extent by the goal of unveiling their historical developments and 'genealogical' relations (cf. Robins 189–221). The period is therefore known as the **comparative-historical tradition**. A key role in the development leading up to this era is usually attributed to Sir William Jones, an eighteenth-century scholar of the ancient Indian language Sanskrit, who discovered that this language shows a similarity to Greek and Latin which could hardly have come about by mere chance. While earlier students of languages had already noticed the similarity of Sanskrit words such as *mātā* 'mother,' *dvāu* 'two' or *trayah* 'three' to the corresponding words in Ancient Greek, Latin and the modern European languages, it was Jones who was the first to propose the correct explanation for these observations: that all three languages were descendants of a common source, known as Proto-Indoeuropean, rather than Sanskrit being the 'mother' of Greek and Latin.

*The influence of German philology*

Dominated by German philologists such as Jakob Grimm, Franz Bopp, August Friedrich Pott, August Schleicher and Hermann Paul, nineteenth-century linguistics is marked by the quest for laws and principles of how languages change and eventually split into mutually unintelligible new languages in long-term developments. Excellent examples of such splits are the modern Romance languages French, Italian, Spanish, Portuguese, Romanian, and others, all of which are essentially descendants of dialects of spoken Latin. Some of the most famous insights gained by nineteenth-century linguists include the so-called Grimm's Law (also known as the First Germanic Sound Shift), the Second or High German Consonant Shift and Verner's Law (for examples see entry V.3.4). The names of these laws indicate the level of language on which research focused at the time, namely sounds. In addition to phonology, nineteenth-century scholars were mainly interested in inflectional morphology and lexical similarities across languages.

Nineteenth-century philologists developed sophisticated data-based methods for the comparison of those languages which are documented by written records, and for the reconstruction of earlier languages. Especially the so-called *Junggrammatiker* or **Neogrammarians** (August Leskien, Karl Brugmann, and others) emphasize that the laws postulated to explain sound changes have to be based on observable facts rather than philosophical speculation in order to have the same quality as laws in physics or other natural sciences—a development which follows the general trend of the time towards a 'positivist' philosophy and theory of science.

### 2.2.2 | Saussure and His Impact

The comparative-historical framework and the *Junggrammatiker* pave the way for the first major turning-point in linguistic theorizing, which is closely associated with the Swiss linguist **Ferdinand de Saussure**. While Saussure is usually given credit for bringing about a sea-change in linguistics at the beginning of the twentieth century, many of the ideas he is famous for were already in the air, so to speak. Saussure himself spent some time studying and researching in Leipzig with Karl Brugmann, but also in Berlin, where—under the influence of Heymann Steinthal, a pupil of Schleiermacher—he became familiar with Wilhelm von Humboldt's ideas of the inner form of language and formed a more critical stance towards the positivist programme envisaged by the *Junggrammatiker* (cf. Prechtl). In hindsight, there can be no doubt that Saussure deserves titles such as 'founder of modern linguistics' and 'founder of structuralism' (cf. section II.1.4), which are often attributed to him. Saussure's seminal ideas are compiled in the famous *Cours de Linguistique Générale*, a collection of his lectures in Geneva; the book was based on Saussure's own and his students' notes and published in 1916 by Charles Bally and Albert Séchehaye after Saussure's death in 1913.

The most consequential 'structuralist' claim made by Saussure—presumably at least partly inspired by his Berlin experience—is that language is a socially shared **system of signs**. This system is considered more important than its parts and defined by the relations between its component parts. The elements in the system have no significance outside it and derive their significance exclusively from the relations to other elements. Saussure's example of hand-written letters provides perhaps the simplest way of illustrating this idea (165):

The significance or value of such letters in the system, Saussure claims, is purely negative and based exclusively on **differences**. The same person can write < t > using any of the substantially different symbols depicted above; what counts for the value or significance of the symbol is only that it does not conflate with the one for < l >, < d > or others. < t > is not < t > by virtue of an inherent quality of the symbol representing it, but it is < t > because it is not < l >, < d > or any other member of the system (Saussure 165). When we talk about *the* letter < t >, this already refers to an abstract construct—a type—generalized over all physically real tokens, which can vary dramatically with regard to their appearance.

The same is true of the **sounds** in spoken language, where the phoneme /t/ may be realized in a large number of ways, in certain environments (e.g. between vowels as in *butter* or *better*) even by a glottal stop (e.g. /bʌʔə/). The essence of /t/ in the system, however, is not the way it is pronounced, but the opposition to /d/, /p/ and so on. Maybe somewhat more surprisingly, the same is even true on the level of meanings and even of whole signs, i.e. combinations of linguistic forms and meanings (see below). A very convincing way of demonstrating the idea that the meanings of words reside in the differences to other word meanings, rather than in their own substance is Saussure's example of the 8:45 pm train from Geneva to Paris. Although, Saussure argues, two 8:45 pm trains on two different days may well have nothing in common regarding their physical substance—there may be different wagons, a different locomotive, conductor and engine driver—we still talk about one and the same train, *the* 8:45 pm from Geneva to Paris, because the differences to other trains in the whole system, for example with regard to time of departure and itinerary, indeed remain the same, irrespective of the day of departure (Saussure 151). Rather than its physical substance or appearance, these indicators of its place in the system give the train its significance.

Another helpful analogy comes from chess: the figures in this game do not assume their significance by virtue of their shape or size, but again by virtue of their place in the system of the game. As argued by Saussure, if, say, a knight goes missing, it can be replaced by any sort of object, such as a cork, which can play the role of knight as long as the two players agree on it. That such an agree-

Figure 1.
Hand-written versions
of the letter <t>
(Saussure 165)

ment is indeed necessary recalls the issue of language being a socially shared system, since it shows that there must be a tacit understanding among the speakers of a speech community regarding the oppositions and differences among the signs in the system.

As an intermediate summary, we can conclude that the essence of a structuralist view of language is that signs are defined by their places in the system, which are defined in turn by the oppositions to other signs, and that therefore the **system** is more important than its component parts. This idea works particularly well for the explanation of the elements of closed systems, i.e. systems with a limited number of elements, such as graphemes or phonemes. With regard to the basically open-ended lexicon, it may well be less convincing at first sight, but can in fact also be applied. Saussure himself points out how this works: within a language, all the words that express neighbouring concepts limit each other; for example, synonyms such as *think, believe, suppose,* or *consider* "n'ont de valeur propre que par leur opposition" ("only have significance by means of their opposition"; 160, my trans.). If one of them did not exist, its content would be divided among its competitors.

To make his thoughts on the nature of the linguistic system convincing, Saussure has to leave behind some of the central ideas of nineteenth-century linguistics:

**1.** Diachronic/synchronic. Saussure makes it clear that there is no point in studying language change and development from a diachronic (lit. 'through time') perspective only, unless the state and structure of a language at a given time, i.e. from a synchronic (lit. 'same time') perspective, is also researched.

**2.** *Langue/parole.* If linguistics is to be a science investigating the system and sub-systems of languages, the study of actual produced texts prevalent in historical-comparative philology falls short of promising to achieve this goal, since, as mentioned above, languages have their own inner structure outside of or over and above actual usage. Saussure, therefore, suggests that the objective of linguistic investigation should not be what

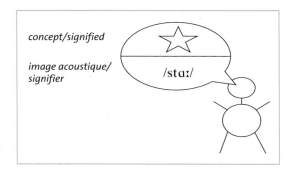

concept/signified

image acoustique/
signifier

/staː/

Figure 2.
Adapted version
of Saussure's model
of the linguistic sign

speakers do with language, i.e. the actual use, to which he refers as *parole*, but the structure of the system itself, i.e. *langue*. Even though Saussure emphasizes that *langue* is not an abstraction but a social fact which is shared by the members of a speech community, in order to describe this system it is necessary to abstract from variants of signs that can occur in actual usage or *parole*. Indeed, the ending *-eme* known from the terms *grapheme, phoneme, morpheme,* and *lexeme* signals that linguistic phenomena at different levels are seen from the *langue* perspective, which does not concern individual tokens, but generalized types. In the system of graphemes, for example, the symbol < t > is an abstraction from actual realizations of the kind illustrated in Figure 1. Likewise the lexeme *drink* as an 'abstract' element in the lexicon on the level of *langue* is a generalization covering actual occurring forms such as *drinks, drinking, drank,* and *drunk* and contextually different meanings such as 'ingest liquids' or 'habitually ingest alcoholic beverages.'

### Focus on Saussure's Main Concepts

Saussure's major contributions to linguistic theorizing can be summarized as follows:
- Language is a socially shared **system of signs**.
- In the study of language, **usage (*parole*)** and **system (*langue*)** have to be kept apart. The target of linguistics should be the generalizations made on the level of *langue* rather than the individual, physically real usage-events taking place in *parole*.
- Linguistic systems should (also) be studied from a purely **synchronic perspective**.
- Signs only have significance or value in the system by virtue of the **differences** (oppositions) to other signs; this gives rise to structure, which is of more fundamental importance than the individual elements of the system.
- The oppositions making up the system are tacitly agreed upon by the members of the speech community by way of **convention**; individual speakers have tacit knowledge about them.

**3.** Signifier/signified. Saussure makes a point of rejecting the anti-mentalist ideas evolving in the positivist climate of his time and stresses the fact that the system has both a social and a psychological dimension. In his well-known binary conception of linguistic signs (cf. Figure 2) in particular, he dwells on the psychological nature of both sides and the associative nature between them. Not only does the concept or signified have to be regarded as a mental entity, but so does the *image acoustique* or signifier, which, as Saussure underlines, is not the physical sound of, say, a word, but its mental image or representation in the mind of a speaker. It is the kind of sound image you can conjure up and 'imagine' when you think of the way a given word sounds, for example *star* in Figure 2.

It is hard to overestimate the impact that Saussure's ideas had on the later development of linguistic theorizing. Addressing various levels of language, this section will discuss a selection of approaches which owe considerably to the insights outlined in the previous section.

The Prague School. As already mentioned above, the closed system of phonemes is, of course, a particularly attractive candidate for applications of the structuralist approach. The earliest and most systematic and consequential efforts were made by a group of Czech linguists known as the Prague School (active in the 1920s and 1930s). Among the leading figures of this linguistic circle are Roman Jakobson and Nikolai Trubetzkoy. Taking up Saussure's distinction between *langue* and *parole*, the Prague School linguists define first of all the difference between phonology and phonetics: while phonetics describes the 'physical' qualities of actual speech, phonology is only interested in those features of sounds which are distinctive in the sense that they differentiate meanings (by virtue of their entering into opposition to other sounds). As a consequence, their main concern is with the distinctive features of phonemes, i.e. the smallest meaning-differentiating units of a language (cf. section V.4.1).

The Theory of Word-Fields. Saussure's ideas on how oppositions between neighbouring words give rise to their meanings inspired a range of structuralist theories in lexical semantics. The first of them is the theory of word-fields or lexical fields introduced by the German linguist Jost Trier, who published an extensive study called *Der deutsche Wortschatz im Sinnbezirk des Verstandes* (1931). By describing historical changes observable in this word-field (including nouns such as *wisheit, list,* and *kunst* which share, with different nuances, the semantic space covered by 'wisdom,' 'knowledge' but also 'capability' and 'science'), Trier is able to confirm what Saussure suggested, showing that in long-term historical developments, one word occupied semantic space left open by a shift of another word. Trier concludes:

Kein ausgesprochenes Wort steht im Bewußtsein des Sprechers und Hörers so vereinzelt da, wie man aus seiner lautlichen Vereinsamung schließen könnte. Jedes ausgesprochene Wort läßt seinen Gegensinn anklingen. Und noch mehr als dies. In der Gesamtheit der beim Aussprechen eines Wortes sich empordrängenden begrifflichen Beziehungen ist die des Gegensinns nur eine und gar nicht die wichtigste. Neben und über ihr taucht eine Fülle anderer Worte auf, die dem ausgesprochenen begrifflich enger oder ferner benachbart sind.

Es sind seine Begriffsverwandten. Sie bilden unter sich und mit dem ausgesprochenen Wort ein gegliedertes Ganzes, ein Gefüge, das man Wortfeld oder sprachliches Zeichenfeld nennen kann. Das Wortfeld ist zeichenhaft zugeordnet einem mehr oder weniger geschlossenen Begriffskomplex, dessen innere Aufteilung sich im gegliederten Gefüge des Zeichenfeldes darstellt, in ihm für die Angehörigen einer Sprachgemeinschaft gegeben ist. (1)

In the consciousness of the speaker and the hearer, no word exists as singularly as one might infer from its phonological isolation. Every uttered word conjures up its opposite meaning (*Gegensinn*). And more than that: Among the totality of the conceptual relations emerging during the utterance of a word, the relation to the opposite meaning is only one and not even the most important one. Above and next to it a multitude of other words appears, words which are closer or more distant conceptual neighbors of the uttered word.

They are its conceptual relatives. Among themselves and with the word uttered they form a structured whole, a pattern one could call lexical field or linguistic-sign field. The lexical field is symbolically assigned to a more or less closed conceptual complex, whose inner partitions are reflected in the organized structure of the sign field, and which presents itself to the members of a speech community in this structure. (my trans.)

**The Theory of Sense Relations.** A second structuralist approach in lexical semantics whose basic assumption can be traced back to Saussure is the theory of sense relations or paradigmatic relations, associated with such linguists as John Lyons, Geoffrey Leech, and Alan Cruse. It was John Lyons (*Structural Semantics*) who presented the first coherent system of sense relations in the 1960s. Lyons argues that the meanings of words—or more precisely in his terminology, their *senses*—are not only describable in terms of their relations to other words but are actually constituted by

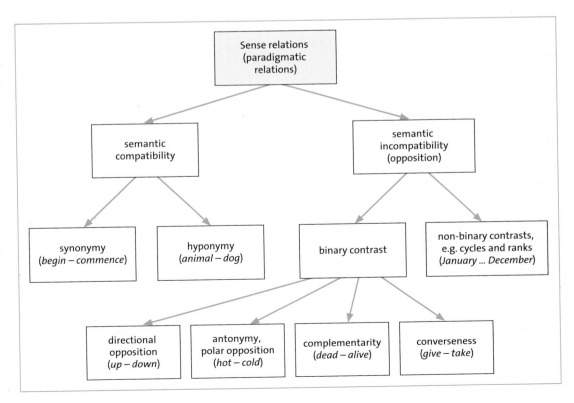

Figure 3.
Survey of sense relations
(based on Lyons, *Semantics*;
Leech; Cruse)

them. Sense relations do not *link* meanings but *give rise* to meaning in the first place as is illustrated by the following examples: the sense of the lexeme *hot* is constituted by its relations to other words, among them the polar opposition (antonymy) to *cold* and the (quasi-)synonymy to words like *burning* or *scorching*. The sense of *give* is constituted by the converse relations to *take* and *receive* and the (quasi-)synonymous relation to *pass, hand over* and many other verbs. The sense of the noun *dog* is constituted by its hyponymic relation to words like *animal* and *mammal*, its hyperonymic relation to *poodle, retriever,* and *German shepherd* and its co-hyponymic relation to *cat, horse, mouse* and other hyponyms of its hyperonym *animal*. It should be stressed that all these relations—semantic incompatability, synonymy, hyponymy and their more specific variants (see Figure 3 for a survey)—are internal to the linguistic system and not a description of things or classes of things in extra-linguistic reality.

A third structuralist approach to semantics inspired by Saussure himself and also indirectly by Prague School phonology and other structuralist approaches is **semantic-feature theory**, which gained momentum in the 1960s and 70s (cf. Lipka 114–36). The basic idea behind this approach is that word meanings are constituted by sets of semantic features very much in the same way that phonemes are constituted by bundles of phonological features. Like distinctive features in phonology, distinctive semantic features can be determined using the main structuralist method, i.e. the comparison of neighbouring elements in the system. For example, just like the comparison of the phonemes /t/ and /d/ yields the phonological feature [±VOICE], a comparison of the meanings of the lexemes *man* and *woman* yields the feature [±MALE], and a comparison of *woman* and *girl* the feature [±ADULT]. It should be emphasized that, at least in theory, these comparisons take place on a purely linguistic level, and are thus indeed comparisons of meanings, rather than on the level of

| Focus on Theories Inspired by Saussure |
|---|
| ▪ Prague School phonology (Jakobson, Trubetzkoy) |
| ▪ Word-field theory (Trier, later also Coseriu, Lipka) |
| ▪ Theory of sense relations (Lyons, Leech, Cruse) |
| ▪ Semantic-feature theory (Leech) |

referents in extra-linguistic reality. We do not compare characteristics of men and women, but of the meanings of the words *man* and *woman*. A well-known illustration of this manner of determining semantic features, rendered in Figure 4, is provided by Leech.

It should be added that this method works quite well for fairly general features such as [±CONCRETE], [±ANIMATE], [±HUMAN] or [±MALE], which are also grammatically relevant, but seems to run into difficulties when applied to finer semantic distinctions relating to semantically more specific words distinguishing, for example, lexemes denoting different kinds of metal such as *iron, steel, copper,* or *lead*. Here Leech resorts to the use of symbols like * or † to simply indicate the fact that meanings differ, emphasizing that even more tangible features like [HUMAN] or [ANIMATE] are essentially just theoretical constructs and descriptive tools. Feature semantic descriptions for the meanings of more abstract words, e.g. *jealousy, boycott,* or *freedom* are even more difficult to come up with.

As in the field of phonology, the aim of an analysis in terms of semantic features is to determine the list of **distinctive features**, i.e. those semantic components which are both individually necessary and collectively sufficient to delimit the class of entities which can be truthfully denoted by the lexeme. A famous example of such an analysis is the decomposition of the meaning of the lexeme *bachelor* into the features [+HUMAN], [+ADULT], [+MALE] and [−MARRIED], all of which are necessary to exclude other animate creatures, children, women as well as married men from the class denoted by the lexeme; that this set of features is indeed sufficient emerges from the fact that there are no entities other than bachelors which meet the conditions defined by this set.

Concerning the methods dominating linguistic investigations in the wake of Saussure we can summarize that the structuralist agenda calls for a new kind of **'comparative' methodology**, one where related or 'neighbouring' elements are compared to each other with the aim of isolating the oppositions relevant for the system. These com-

| | MALE | FEMALE |
|---|---|---|
| ADULT { | *man* | *woman* |
| YOUNG { | *boy* | *girl* |
| | HUMAN | |

Figure 4. Analysis of semantic features (adapted from Leech 89)

parisons are usually carried out in a largely intro-spective manner based on small samples of lin-guistic data representing more or less closed systems such as phonemes or the members of word-fields. Analyses of oppositions are supported by various logical, rather than experimental, tests, e.g. the minimal-pair test in phonology or the en-tailment test in semantic-feature theory. Other lin-guistic methods such as experiments with partici-pants (see section 2.6 below) or the systematic analysis of linguistic corpora (see section 2.7 be-low) are not in line with structuralist thought, as they are only able to tap into the behaviour of speakers (*parole*), thus promising little insight into the structure of the system (*langue*).

## 2.3 | American Structuralism

The period, beginning in the 1920s, commonly re-ferred to as American structuralism and repre-sented by linguists such as Leonard Bloomfield, Charles Fries, H. A. Gleason, and Zellig Harris is united by an interestingly ambivalent stance to-wards Saussure's ideas. On the one hand, the no-tion of language being a structured system is taken up enthusiastically and developed considerably fur-ther; on the other hand, the mentalist approach is fervently rejected. This negative reaction can largely be explained by the general development towards **positivism** in late nineteenth- and early twenti-eth-century philosophy and psychology, which de-manded the total rejection of "psychological pseu-do-explanations," as Bloomfield (17) called them, and a rigorous limitation to the study of objectively observable facts. A well-known catchword is the metaphor of the human mind being a 'black box' not open to introspection or inspection. The **be-haviourist psychology** behind this view, associated with names like J. B. Watson and Frederick Skinner and with the well-known tests on conditioning car-ried out with dogs by Ivan Pavlov, had an enormous effect on the agenda of American structuralists. Their anti-mentalist stance was partly motivated by methodological necessities, as the first decades of the twentieth century were also a time when Amer-ican linguists (among them Franz Boas, Edward Sapir, and Benjamin Whorf) began to investigate indigenous American languages, such as the lan-guage of the Hopi Indians. Since the researchers themselves had no proficiency in these languages, at least not to begin with, there was little tempta-tion to get lost in the study of fine semantic details. Observable facts and patterns on the level of lin-guistic form were much more rewarding start-ing-points for linguistic research.

One of the most well-known and far-reaching consequences of the positivist approach is the ex-plicit reluctance to engage in the study of meaning and to use semantic considerations as arguments in linguistic description and classification. This re-sults in an account of phonological, morphological and syntactic structures that focuses on the distri-bution of forms and their combinatory possibili-ties. Three examples of what linguistic theorizing in American structuralism looks like will be given below: Bloomfield's method of identifying and de-fining phonemes; Fries's analysis and description of word classes; and Gleason's account of syntac-tic structures.

### 2.3.1 | Bloomfield on Phonemes

Definitions of the notion of the phoneme and ap-plications of the minimal-pair test (cf. section V.4.1) typically take recourse to semantic argu-ments: loosely speaking, if phonemes are the smallest meaning-differentiating units of language, and if two sequences of sounds that are identical except for one sound in the same place, e.g. [dʌk] *duck* vs. [dɒk] *dock*, give rise to two different meanings, then these two sounds must have the status of phonemes. Since he rejects arguments based on semantics, Bloomfield faces the problem of how to steer clear of the issue of the differentia-tion of meaning while trying to define the notion of the phoneme. Here is how he goes about deal-ing with this problem:

In order to recognize the distinctive features of forms in our own language, we need only determine which features of sound are 'different' for purposes of communication. Suppose, for instance, that we start with the word *pin*: a few experiments in saying words out loud soon reveal the following resemblances and differences:

(1)  *pin* ends with the same sound as *fin, sin, tin*, but begins differently; this kind of resemblance is familiar to us be-cause of our tradition of using end-rime in verse;

(2) *pin* contains the sound of *in*, but adds something at the beginning;

(3) *pin* ends with the same sound as *man, sun, hen*, but the resemblance is smaller than in (1) and (2);

(4) *pin* begins with the same sound as *pig, pill, pit*, but ends differently;

(5) *pin* begins with the same sound as *pat, push, peg*, but the resemblance is smaller than in (4);

(6) *pin* begins and ends like *pen, pan, pun*, but the middle part is different;

(7) *pin* begins and ends differently from *dig, fish, mill*, but the middle part is the same.

In this way, we can find forms which partially resemble *pin*, by altering any one of the *three* parts of the word. We can alter first one and then a second of the three parts and still have a partial resemblance: if we alter the first part and then the second, we get a series like *pin-tin-tan*; if we alter the first part and then the third, we get a series like *pin-tin-tick*; if we alter the second part and then the third, we get a series like *pin-pan-pack*: and if we alter the three parts, no resemblance is left, as in *pin-tin-tan-tack*.

Further experiment fails to reveal any more replaceable parts in the word *pin*: we conclude that the distinctive features of this word are three indivisible units. Each of these units occurs also in other combinations, but cannot be further analyzed by partial resemblances: each of the three is *a minimum unit of distinctive sound-feature, a phoneme.* (Bloomfield 78-79, emphasis in original)

**Ambivalences of the structuralist approach**

On the one hand, Bloomfield's lucid argumentation illustrates the extent to which it is indeed possible to avoid the use of semantic arguments. On the other hand, his idea that "features of sound are 'different' for purposes of communication," which rests on a behaviourist conception of communication restricted to the observation of visible or audible stimuli and reactions, strikes one as being somewhat elusive as long as the communicative, and hence semantic, impact of utterances is not taken into consideration.

## 2.3.2 | Fries on Word Classes

A similarly ambivalent assessment seems appropriate for the second example to be discussed, Fries's attempt to define the word classes of English without any recourse to traditional meaning-based descriptions such as 'nouns tend to denote things,' 'verbs tend to denote actions' or 'adjectives tend to denote qualities.' It is possible to determine the word class membership of words,

Fries argues, "by the '**positions**' they occupy in the utterances and the **forms** they have, in contrast with other positions and forms" (71–72). To pursue this idea, he proposes three "minimum free utterance test frames" (75) used for an inductive classification of words into word classes, i.e. one that starts out from the observation of linguistic data and does not depend on prior assumptions based on semantic considerations (75).

- Frame A: The concert was good (always)
- Frame B: The clerk remembered the tax (suddenly)
- Frame C: The team went there.

What is interesting is that Fries actually uses authentic data recorded for the purpose of linguistic analysis and description. The application of his methods works as follows: if a given word in his corpus "could be substituted for the word *concert*" in test frame A "with no change of structural meaning" (Fries 75), it is treated as a member of "Class I." Words of Class I typically also occur in the slot occupied by *clerk* in Frame B and *team* in Frame C. Words of Class II are tested using the same procedure of substitution in the frames by checking if they are able to replace *was* in Frame A and/or *remembered* in Frame B and/or *went* in Frame C. Extending this procedure to the other slots in the test frames, Fries is able to define **four major word classes** corresponding roughly to the traditional parts-of-speech of nouns, verbs, adjectives and adverbs on the basis of their potential position in the test frames. This is supplemented by minor classes categorizing various types of function words, among them one class containing the single element *not*. As in the case of Bloomfield, one is struck by the rigour and elegance of the method—relying, as it does, on authentic recordings compiled in a corpus and even on judgments by informants—but also somewhat worried by the fact that the whole procedure depends on a rather ill-defined notion of "structural meaning" mentioned in the quote above.

## 2.3.3 | Gleason on Immediate Constituents

Continuing to pursue this running theme, we can finally look at Gleason's approach to the analysis of syntactic structures, known as immediate constituent analysis or **IC analysis**. The aim of this approach is to exhaustively describe the "interrelationships" between the words in utterances and thereby to accomplish a description of "the syntax of the utterance in its entirety" (129). In such a view, sentences consist of *constructions* which in turn consist of *constituents*; these are *immediate constituents* if the construction is directly formed by them. For example, the word *old* in the sentence *the old man who lives there has gone to his son's house* is an immediate constituent of the larger construction *old man*, which in turn is an immediate constituent of the construction *the old man*, but *old* is not an immediate constituent of the construction *the old man*. In his analysis of immediate constituents, Gleason relies mainly on the following three considerations:

1. the substitutability of potential immediate constituents by other, less complex constituents; for example, *his son's* can be substituted by *John's* without compromising the structure of the sentence, and the whole sequence *the old man who lives there* can be substituted by *he*;

2. the identification of stress and intonation patterns, so-called suprasegmentals; e.g. the pause following *who lives there* is an indicator that *lives* and *there* are more likely to be immediate constituents than *there* and the subsequent *has*.

3. the freedom of potential immediate constituents to occur in other constructions; for instance, if one were in doubt as to whether in the sequence *old light house*, *old* and *light* or *light* and *house* are immediate constituents, one would try to establish which of the two possibilities, *old light* or *light house*, are more likely to occur in other contexts, and presumably arrive at the conclusion that *light house* is more variable than *old light* (cf. *new light*

---

**Focus on American Structuralism**

- Background: influenced by **behaviourist anti-mentalism**; avoids arguments based on semantic considerations;
- Aim: analysis and **description of structure**; reduces observable variability of utterances to distinctive features, components and structures;
- Focus: on **linguistic form** (phonology, morphology, syntax), relegation of meaning;
- Methods: logical argumentation based on selected **datasets**; analysis of authentic materials; application of tests to identify systematic oppositions and interrelations, e.g. substitution tests, testing for freedom of occurrence.

---

*house*, *pretty light house*, *lonely light house*, etc.; Gleason 135–36).

As in the two previous examples, the aim of this procedure is to provide an account of syntactic structures that can do without subjective arguments relating to meanings and functions of constructions and constituents.

The ambitions and achievements of the American structuralists, especially with regard to methodological rigour and objectivity, have had a lasting effect on linguistic theorizing in the area of grammar. The classic test machinery, including the substitution test, the commutation test, the deletion test and others, is still widely applied today in all kinds of syntactic frameworks. However, what caused the next major revolution in linguistics resulting in the pendulum swinging back to a mentalist ideology was the structuralists' self-imposed restriction on the analysis and description of existing linguistic output, which left behind Saussure's idea of investigating the knowledge about the structure of language shared by speakers and stored in their minds.

# 2.4 | Generative Grammar and Case Grammar

## 2.4.1 | Chomsky's Generative Grammar

The revolution referred to in the previous section took place in the late 1950s, and was initiated by the American linguist Noam Chomsky. Basically, Chomsky meets structuralists and behaviourists head on in two arenas:

On the one hand, in his 1957 book *Syntactic Structures*, he argues for an approach to linguistics that does not stop at the description of existing sentences and utterances but aims to come up with an explanation of the knowledge required by speakers for them to be able to potentially generate syntactic representations of all sentences that are considered grammatical in their native language and to decide which sentences are ungrammatical. Partially in parallel to Saussure's distinction between *langue* and *parole*, Chomsky insists that it is the so-called idealized native speaker's **competence** to produce and understand sentences, i.e. his or her tacit mental capacity, which must take centre stage in linguistics rather than speakers' actual **performance**, i.e. their linguistic output. While Saussure conceives of *langue* as a somewhat static socially shared system, Chomsky emphasizes the cognitive nature of *competence* (later termed *I-language*, short for *internal*, and contrasted with *E-language*, short for *external*); he also stresses that *I-language* is not a static system but endows speakers with the creative capacity to produce and understand sentences they have never heard before, hence the term generative grammar. Chomsky is not only interested in the grammars in the mind of the idealized speaker of just one language, but rather also pursues the aim of offering an account of the general grammatical principles on which the structures of all natural languages rest—a notion he refers to as **Universal Grammar**.

The idea of Universal Grammar provides the link to the second blow Chomsky dealt to the behaviourist programme. This is epitomized in a long and devastating review of Skinner's book *Verbal Behavior*, triggering what is now known as the **cognitive turn** in linguistics. With regard to first language acquisition, behaviourists essentially claimed that the use of language is simply a kind of behaviour just like any other and that the use of language itself as well as the process of acquiring language are therefore subject to the same principles as all other kinds of behaviour, namely the positive or negative reinforcement of sequences of stimuli and responses, very much similar to the conditioning taking place in the minds of Pavlov's dogs. In stark contrast to this, Chomsky argues that it is impossible that babies and toddlers acquire language simply by imitation and reinforcement, since the models they get from what they hear around them, i.e. the caregivers' input, are too problematic, marred by all kinds of performance errors such as false starts and incomplete sentences. Known as the 'poverty-of-stimulus argument' or 'Plato's paradox' (Chomsky, *Knowledge*), this and other observations—among them the amazing speed at which toddlers learn to speak—leads Chomsky to argue that the capacity to acquire language must, to a large extent, be innate, i.e. already available in some kind of pre-wired format when children are born. Here we come full circle to the idea of Universal Grammar: since children in different places and speech communities will of course acquire different languages, their innate language acquisition device has to strike the ideal balance between being so specific that it gives a maximum of information on what the local language will be like and being so abstract that it can account for the considerable variability of languages even in the area of syntactic structures. Hence Universal Grammar contains

Chomsky on
Universal Grammar

general principles and parameters that reflect the structural possibilities of all languages and open options to be settled by the child on the basis of the ambient language he or she is confronted with. Parameters of this type are, for example, whether the language has prepositions or postpositions, whether heads tend to follow modifiers or precede them or whether the language can drop pronouns in subject positions (as in Italian, cf. *piove* 'it is raining' or *arrivo* 'I'm coming') or invariably requires subject slots to be filled (as in English).

With regard to the status of language as a type of human behaviour, Chomsky replaces the behaviourist notion with the idea that the linguistic faculty is fundamentally different from other cognitive abilities and indeed the one cognitive ability that distinguishes human beings from all other species. The separation of linguistic from non-linguistic cognition has the extremely far-reaching effect that the linguistic study of language is strictly separated from the psychological study of other human cognitive abilities such as perception, attention-allocation and reasoning. On top of that, Chomsky gives indisputable prominence to the syntactic component within the structure of language and argues that it is also more or less unconnected to other components, notably the lexicon and the semantic, let alone the pragmatic functions of linguistic structures. His explicit aim is to come up with a **context-free grammar**, i.e. a grammar that seeks to explain how speakers know to distinguish grammatical from ungrammatical sentences irrespective of possible contexts of usage.

Chomsky's ideas have undergone a number of substantial **revisions** over the past fifty years. The stages they went through—some named after book titles—are known as the *Standard Theory* (1957), the *Extended Standard Theory* (1965), *Government and Binding* (1981), *Principles and Parameters* (1986) and, most recently, the *Minimalist Program* (1995). What has remained intact throughout this development—in addition to the theoretical background assumptions discussed above—is the idea that sentences are derived from phrase structures by means of certain operations. In the early models, these operations are defined as quite complex transformations such as the passive transformation (turning active sentences in a hypothetical deep structure into passive ones in the surface structure) and the question transformation (turning declarative sentences into interrogative ones). In the *Minimalist Program*, however, the notions of deep structure and surface structure are abandoned, derivations start out from an array of lexical entries in the lexicon and all transformations are essentially traced back to two basic operations called *move α* and *merge*.

For an illustration of how the derivation and the operations work in the Minimalist Program consider the sentence in (1) discussed by Wakabayashi (642).

(1) Which book will the student buy?

This sentence is seen to rest on a simple phrase structure of the kind represented in Figure 5 (adapted from Wakabayashi 642), where *Determiner Phrase* is a notion similar to the traditional *noun phrase*, and V' (pronounced as *V-bar*) stands for a constituent dominating V and DP, reminiscent of the traditional notion of predicate, which also subsumes verb and object.

What is represented by the tree diagram in the figure roughly translates as 'there is a syntactic element of the type VP consisting of the two constituents DP and V'; DP consists of a Determiner and a Noun, lexically represented as *the* and *student* respectively; V' consists of the Verb *buy* and a DP consisting of the Determiner *which* and the noun *book*. To derive sentence (1) from this structure, it

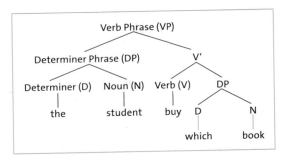

Figure 5.
VP structure of the sentence *Which book will the student buy* (adapted from Wakabayashi 642)

is claimed that the following operations—rendered in a rather simplified way—take place: Tense (T), merges with the structure, creating a Tense Phrase (TP) which introduces the auxiliary *will* and causes the DP *the student* to move to the start of the sentence leaving a trace in the phrase structure (cf. step 1 in Figure 6, adapted from Wakabayahsi 643); then the resulting TP (step 2) merges with a Complementizer (C) indicating essentially that the structure is a sentence (step 3); C brings along the features [+Q] and [+wh], projecting the sentence as a *wh-interrogative* and causing first the auxiliary *will* and then the *wh*-DP *which book* to move to the start of the sentence, thus generating the CP-structure represented in Figure 6 (step 4). Difficult to understand as this brief example may be, it still

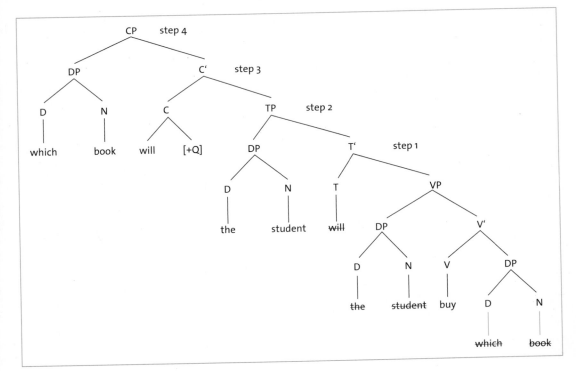

Figure 6.
CP structure of the sentence *Which book will the student buy?*

**Focus on Chomsky's Main Concepts**

**Generativism and productivity**: the target of linguistic theorizing is the description of grammar, largely defined as the generative capacity—i.e. *competence* or *I-language*—of an idealized native speaker to produce and understand an infinite number of sentences and to judge whether sentences are grammatical or ungrammatical.

**Derivation**: sentences are the product of derivations of more complex structures from simpler structures carried out by means of a limited number of clearly defined operations.

**Innateness**: the acquisition of linguistic competence builds on innate knowledge about linguistic structure common to all languages and known as *Universal Grammar*.

**Autonomy**: language is a very special human faculty; *grammar*, in the sense of 'linguistic competence,' does not rely on non-linguistic cognition, and *grammar*, in the sense of 'model of linguistic competence,' *must* not rely on models of non-linguistic cognition.

**Modularity**: within grammar, the generative capacity mainly resides in the syntactic component; the lexicon is, by definition, not rule-governed and therefore of much less interest to linguistic modelling.

**Focus on context-free structure, form, and formalization**: linguistic modelling has to focus on structural and formal aspects of language rather than functional ones and strive for formalized accounts of structures; functional considerations such as 'what is the communicative impact of a sentence?' or 'what are the purposes that syntactic structures serve?' are irrelevant.

provides a glimpse of how the Minimalist Program accounts for syntactic structures and can serve as a backdrop for the description of other approaches to be discussed below.

Chomsky's effect on the development of linguistic theorizing is unrivalled, except maybe by the impact made by Saussure. As in the case of Saussure, Chomsky sparked positive as well as negative reactions, of equally intense quality. On the one hand, his models have been considered the leading linguistic theories by many researchers, especially on the American east coast and in Britain. On the other hand, in view of its fairly strict and strong-minded assumptions regarding the nature of language and the aims of linguistic theorizing, it is not surprising that Chomsky has triggered quite harsh counter-reactions, many of them from former students of his, who cast serious doubts on issues like autonomy, modularity, innateness, and the focus on structure. Notable controversies arising from criticism of Chomsky's positions include the ongoing debate between the formalist and the functionalist camps and the current dispute between two approaches which, ironically, go by the same name of **Cognitive Linguistics**: the Chomskyan autonomous generative

approach, on the one hand, and a set of experientialist, usage-based, functionalist approaches, on the other hand, advocated by linguists like George Lakoff, Ronald Langacker, Leonard Talmy, Paul Hopper, or Joan Bybee, some of which will be discussed in section 5 below. What essentially unites all these reactions to Chomsky is a marked reluctance on the side of his opponents to accept the extent to which he downgrades the significance of functional, use-related, and semantic considerations in his account of the structure of language. An early and particularly influential challenge to Chomsky was mounted by Charles Fillmore, to whose ideas I will now turn.

## 2.4.2 | Case Grammar: Fillmore's 'Semanticization' of Generative Grammar

In a famous paper entitled "The Case for Case" published in 1968, Fillmore introduces a new vision of a generative grammar, known as Case Grammar, which essentially rests on a semantic foundation. He proposes complementing Chomsky's form-focused hierarchical account of syntactic structure with one that regards the verb as some kind of pivot in the sentence, to which the other elements are related by virtue of representing a certain semantic role (originally referred to somewhat confusingly as *deep case*, hence the name *Case Grammar*). It may be noted in passing that the idea that the verb plays a particularly prominent role in determining the structure of a sentence is also key to a range of other syntactic approaches including valency grammar (cf. Herbst and Schüller). These, however, place less emphasis on the semantic foundations of sentence structures and focus instead on descriptions of the number of complements required by a certain verb, their forms and the question of whether these complements are obligatory (i.e. must be expressed) or optional and can thus be left out.

According to Fillmore, prominent **semantic roles** are the AGENT or AGENTIVE, i.e. the person carrying out an action, the INSTRUMENT, i.e. the tool used by the agent to accomplish an action, the PATIENT, i.e. a person affected by an action, and the OBJECTIVE or THEME, an object or entity affected by the action. An account of the sentence in (1) above, inspired by Fillmore's ideas, would argue that the verb *buy* relates to the semantic roles of AGENT (*the student*) and THEME (*the book*). The AGENT will be mapped onto the subject slot in the sentence and the THEME in the object slot, so that a simplified version of the syntactic structure according to Fillmore would look as represented in Figure 7.

As indicated in the figure, the fact that the sentence is a *wh*-interrogative would, just like in Chomsky's framework, have been explained by extra operations subsumed under the labels *tense* and *modality* (which includes a range of clause-related grammatical categories like mood, tense, aspect and negation in Fillmore's terminology).

In later contributions straddling the boundary between syntax and semantics, Fillmore ("Topics") extends his account and argues that basic sentence patterns across languages reflect the conceptual structures of everyday scenes in which events take place and people carry out actions and manipulate objects. The description of a buying scene as expressed in sentence (1) is seen as being based on the activation of a mental structure referred to as a **frame**, which represents general knowledge about commercial events and their recurrent characteristics, participants and props including a BUYER, a SELLER, the GOODS bought and the MONEY transferred from BUYER to SELLER in exchange for the GOODS. Depending on their mental perspec-

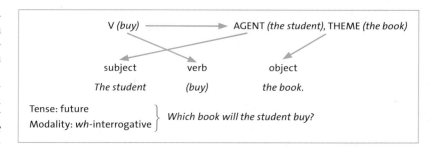

tive on the scene, speakers will choose verbs such as *buy, sell, pay* or *cost* and fill the slots opened up by these verbs according to the prominence of the participants in the scene. The sentence *The student bought the book*, for example, highlights the BUYER and the GOODS while backgrounding the SELLER and the MONEY (which are, however, also implied), whereas the sentence *the book cost ten pounds* directs the hearer's attention to the GOODS and the MONEY while reducing the BUYER and the SELLER in prominence. Ideas of this type, which rely on mental structures and processes related to world knowledge and general cognitive abilities like perception, were very influential for the formation of later cognitive-linguistic theorizing to be discussed in the next section.

Figure 7.
Case grammar account of the sentence *Which book will the student buy?*

## 2.5 | Cognitive Approaches

Approaches to linguistics labelled as 'cognitive' or 'cognitive-linguistic' (in contrast to the Chomskyan kind of cognitivism) share the view of language outlined at the end of the previous section, namely, that linguistic structures reflect our mental representations of the world around us. This implies that the ways they are processed are by no means specific to language but closely related to general cognitive abilities such as categorization, perception, attention-allocation and everyday reasoning on the basis of cognitive models of the world. The cognitive-linguistic position thus rejects Chomsky's autonomy postulate, the modularity postulate and the focus on form, replacing them with a meaning-based and function-oriented perspective regarding language both as a mental mirror of the world and a means of making sense of the world. Three examples will be discussed below to illustrate further implications of such a view.

### 2.5.1 | Prototype Theory

Starting in the field of lexical semantics, it is instructive to compare the feature-semantic approach dominant in the structuralist era and still prevalent in generative grammar to the cognitive-linguistic prototype theory of semantics. As shown above, the aim of feature semantics is to determine those distinctive features that give rise to oppositions between neighbouring word meanings. The meaning of the lexeme *bachelor* was described above by means of the distinctive features [+ HUMAN], [+ ADULT], [+ MALE] and [− MARRIED]. According to feature semantics, entities in the extra-linguistic world which meet these criteria can unequivocally be considered members of the category of BACHELORS and unreservedly be referred to by the word *bachelor*, while entities lacking one or more of the defining conditions are just as unambiguously outside the category. The possibility that there may be more or less typical instances of bachelors to which the word may be more or less appropriately applied—say a thirty-year-old living alone as opposed to a sixty-year-old sharing a house with his long-standing partner—is irrelevant for such a semantic description, since such issues relate to world-knowledge which must not play a part in a model of linguistic meaning.

A prototype-semantic account of the meaning of the lexeme *bachelor* explicitly takes such conceptual and encyclopaedic aspects into account and does not assume that there is a justifiable distinction between meaning proper, defined as a linguistic phenomenon, and conceptual content, considered a psychological one. The central claim of prototype semantics is that the cognitive categories which underlie word meanings are not of the discrete, hard-and-fast type envisaged by feature semantics but rather **conceptually rich, internally graded, and fuzzy** in terms of their boundaries to neighbouring categories. To describe the meaning of *bachelor* according to this approach, it is first necessary to realize that such a concept only makes sense in the framework of a cognitive and cultural model of a society in which people tend to marry, to do so at a certain age and to marry a person belonging to the other sex. For example, although Tarzan and the Pope meet the conditions of being human, adult, male and unmarried, there is not much point in referring to them as *bachelors*, since the general cultural model of marriage does not apply to them. They would be very atypical bachelors at best and the same is true of other potential 'bachelors' as well: What about gay men who do not want to marry a woman anyway? Or an unmarried gay man living in a long-term partnership with another gay man? Could they accurately be referred to by the word *bachelor*? While it may indeed seem that such considerations should not be relevant for a semantic account of the meanings of lexemes *qua* abstract elements in the lexicon of a language, in actual language use speakers are constantly facing the problem of categorizing entities of all sorts once they want to talk about them.

Unlike the categories in scientific classifications, the everyday cognitive categories stored in the minds of the speakers of a language do not seem to be of the either-in-or-out type—'an entity belongs to a category if and only if it meets *all* conditions for membership'—but rather of the more-or-less-good-example type, meaning that an entity can be a good, less good, peripheral or borderline member of a category. That the human mind indeed seems to work with these gradient and fuzzy categories has been shown in various tests. In one type of task, called **goodness-of-example rating**, test subjects are asked to rate test items with regard to how typical they are of a certain category. In the first studies of this kind, which were carried out by the psychologist Eleonor Rosch in the 1970s, students were asked to rate items such as *car, truck,* and *ship* but also *sledge* and *elevator* with regard to their typicality for the category VEHICLE. Not surprisingly, they rated *car* and *truck* as highly prototypical members, *ship* as somewhat less typical and *sledge* and especially *elevator* as fairly peripheral members of the category, but had no problems with seeing all five items as types of vehicles. What is particularly intriguing—and this has also given rise to criticism of this task and the way its results are interpreted—is that even for categories which are basically absolutely clear-cut and non-gradient, e.g. ODD NUMBER and EVEN NUMBER, similar results were obtained. Test participants rated *three* and *seven* as better examples of the category odd number than, say, *877*, in spite of the fact that of course, strictly speaking, all odd numbers are just that, odd numbers, with no difference in typicality. This piece of evidence suggests that we show a strong tendency to anchor cognitive categories in familiar, frequently occurring and salient members, i.e. prototypes, and use our cognitive representations of these prototypes to judge other, especially new entities we are confronted with.

A second method widely used in prototype semantics is a paradigm called **attribute-listing task**. Here participants are instructed to name characteristics they associate with all the things that can be denoted by a given word. For example, confronted with the word *bicycle*, many people associate attributes relating to parts of bicycles such as 'pedals,' 'wheels,' 'handlebar,' 'frame' but also to the way they are used, e.g. 'you ride on them,' 'is used to go from A to B,' 'has no engine' or 'self-propelled.' This is precisely the kind of encyclopaedic knowledge which is strongly associated with word meanings, or indeed constitutes word meanings. If these attributes are highly reminiscent of semantic features, this is of course not by coincidence, as attributes capture semantic components of word meanings—just like semantic features do. Nevertheless, the theoretical and methodological status of attributes differs fundamentally from that of features: attributes are elicited from informants and hence to some extent intersubjectively validated, while features are determined introspectively on the basis of semantic oppositions; attributes represent associations in the minds of speakers and are hence properties of the cognitive system, whereas features are claimed to be a part of meaning and thus a purely linguistic, rather than psychological construct; attributes are conceptually rich, variable, context-dependent, and subjective, while features are by definition generalizations which are stable across different contexts and speakers. While distinctive features clearly demarcate the boundaries of categories in an either-in-or-out fashion, attributes account for the gradient structure and fuzzy boundaries of categories, as different attributes carry different weights. For example, for the category BIRD, attributes like 'lays eggs,' 'can fly,' or 'has feathers' are clearly more important than 'chirps' or 'has thin legs.' In attribute-listing tasks, the weight of attributes shows in the proportion of informants who name a given attribute; conceptually more important attributes are listed by more participants than less central ones. Crucially, even items which share very few of the central attributes of a category, such as penguins or ostriches for the category BIRD, can still be members of the category.

In summary, Table 1 gives a systematic comparison of some of the major differences between feature semantics and prototype semantics.

Unlike semantic features, attributes do not constitute a set of necessary and sufficient criteria for categorisation, as there may in fact not be a single attribute which is shared by all members of a category. This situation is illustrated with the category GAME by the philosopher **Ludwig Wittgenstein**, who argues that it is impossible to suggest a single property which is common to the full range of activities that can be referred to by the word *game*, e.g. chess, bridge, ring-a-ring-a-roses, hide-and-seek, rope-skipping, tennis, and soccer. Wittgenstein notes that the category GAME is still internally coherent even though it is not united by one or several shared attributes, because its members share a pool of common characteristics: some games are of a competitive nature, while others are not; some involve physical activities, others do not; some are of a strategic nature, others are not; one competitive game can also involve physical components (e.g. soccer), while another does not (e.g. chess). This way a network of partially shared attributes is created which holds the members of the category together in what is called a family resemblance fashion. This analogy relies on the idea that the members of a family can resemble each other to a considerable extent without necessarily all having the same colour of eyes, colour of hair, size and shape of mouth and nose, etc.

## 2.5.2 | Conceptual Metaphor Theory

The cognitive models mentioned in the previous section also play a key role in a second highly influential cognitive-linguistic theory called conceptual metaphor theory, proposed by George Lakoff and Mark Johnson in their book *Metaphors We Live By* (first ed. 1980). The central idea of this approach is that metaphors are not just a linguistic phenomenon, i.e. a special way of encoding meanings, but a cognitive one. If a speaker uses an expression like *We had reached a dead-end street*

|  | Semantic-feature theory | Prototype theory |
|---|---|---|
| **word meaning** | clear-cut, discrete, homogeneous | fuzzy boundaries, gradience of typicality |
| **meaning components** | distinctive, i.e. necessary and sufficient features | attributes, possibly distributed in family-resemblance network |
| **nature of components** | linguistic; the sum of features constitutes the meaning | cognitive/associative; 'what comes to people's minds' |
| **locus of meaning** | in language | in the mind |
| **division meaning/knowledge** | (in theory) clear-cut; word meaning ≠ concept | word meaning = concept |
| **methods** | introspective/logical: comparing lexemes, testing for entailments etc. | experimental, asking native speakers: goodness-of-example ratings, attribute-listing tasks |
| **labels** | structuralist, language-immanent | cognitive, encyclopaedic |

Table 1.
Comparison of semantic-feature theory and prototype theory

Table 2.
Conceptual metaphor:
A LOVE RELATIONSHIP
IS A JOURNEY

| Metaphorical expression | Mapped correspondences |
|---|---|
| *we went through a lot together* | • the lovers are travellers<br>• the development of the relationship is the path taken<br>• problems in the relationship are obstacles in the path of the travellers |
| *we found ourselves in a dead-end street* | • stages in the development of the relationship are locations on the journey<br>• problems in the relationship are obstacles in the path of the travellers |
| *we were approaching a crossroads* | • decisions in the relationship are crossroads on the journey |
| *look how far we've come* | • the development of the relationship is progress made in the journey |
| *the relationship isn't going anywhere* | • the development of the relationship is the path taken<br>• purposes of the relationship are destinations of the journey |
| *we've got to leave these arguments behind and look ahead now* | • the development of the relationship is the path taken |

when talking about a difficult situation in a love relationship, then this would be considered to reflect the speaker's way of thinking about the relationship. Many theories of metaphor would consider such conventional expressions to be more or less 'dead' metaphors that have lost their metaphorical quality and are therefore just regular meanings of the words involved. In contrast, conceptual metaphor theory argues that these highly conventionalized ways of talking about one cognitive model or domain (here LOVE) in terms of another (here JOURNEY) are particularly interesting and important because, unnoticed as they presumably go in normal discourse, they represent tacit patterns of thought shared by the members of a speech community.

Conceptual metaphors are defined as mappings from a cognitive **source domain** (JOURNEY) to a **target domain** (LOVE RELATIONSHIP), which transfer or project knowledge about the source onto the target. For this to be useful, the source domains are recruited from fields we know a lot about and are familiar with from everyday experience: our own bodies, location and movement of our bodies and objects in space, the visible physical behaviour of living beings, plants, and objects, and all other kinds of everyday experiences such as moving from one place to another (often labelled JOURNEY in the literature). The target domains, on the other hand, are rather more abstract, less tangible and conceptually structured fields: emotions such as love, anger, or happiness; abstract ideas relating to, for example, structures and processes in society, economics, politics or notions in philosophy and reli-

gion; complex institutions such as companies or organizations. The cognitive advantage of conceptual metaphors lies in their potential to provide these abstract and elusive domains with some sort of tangible conceptual structure by means of the mapping of conceptual correspondences from the source domain to the target domain. Actual metaphorical expressions in language(s) mainly function as evidence for the existence of these mappings, especially if larger numbers of expressions can be traced back to the same metaphorical mappings.

To illustrate these ideas, Table 2 gives examples of metaphorical expressions and correspondences pointing to the existence of the conceptual metaphor A LOVE RELATIONSHIP IS A JOURNEY (cf. Lakoff and Johnson 44–45; Kövecses).

The examples in Table 2 illustrate that metaphorical expressions and conceptual mappings do not occur in isolation, as one-off metaphors so to speak, but form **conceptual systems** projecting crucial elements of the cognitive structure of the source domain onto the target domain: the travellers, the path, progress and stages of the journey as well as obstacles and crossroads are mapped onto the lovers, the development of the relationship, problems and decisions respectively. This way, the rather elusive field of a love relationship acquires an internal structure. Likewise, if we talk about TIME in terms of MONEY—to *spend* time, activities can *cost* a lot of time, people can *give* each other time or *waste* their time—the elusive notion of TIME is supplied with a more tangible conceptual structure (for an application of conceptual metaphor theory to poems see entry II.13).

Conceptual metaphor theory is a **paradigm case** of a cognitive and experientialist theory of language, as it relies heavily on the idea that knowledge distilled from everyday experience about concrete and tangible domains helps us to understand abstract fields of thought. Since its introduction in the early 1980s it has become a mainstay of cognitive-linguistic thinking and has been applied to a huge range of types of discourse, including the discourse of politics, religion, economics, sports, and advertising. In the past years, proponents have been trying to supplement the cognitive aspects with neurological ones and have developed a neural theory of metaphor arguing that the nature and working of conceptual metaphors can be explained on the basis of what we know about the workings of the brain.

## 2.5.3 | Construction Grammar

As we have seen, Chomsky advocates a rather strict separation of the major components of grammar: the most basic division separates the **syntactic module**, which is rule-governed, from the **lexicon**, defined as the repository of all the knowledge about language that resists an account in terms of rules, since it is not generalizable and predictable. Sentences are constructed online by the application of syntactic rules working with lexical items that are stored in and retrieved from the lexicon. Since it is uncontroversial that sentences carry meaning and have a phonetic form, grammar also includes a phonological module and a semantic module; these are somehow linked to the syntactic component, while the lexicon, being the store of information about phonological, semantic and syntactic properties of words, cuts across all the modules in the way represented in Figure 8 (adapted from Croft and Cruse 227). As indicated by the horizontal line in the figure, grammar and usage are strictly separated.

This view of the architecture of grammar has been rejected by cognitive linguists who support competing models subsumed under the label **Construction Grammar**. According to this view, which is represented in Figure 9 (adapted from Croft and Cruse 256), knowledge about language is available in the form of constructions.

Constructions are defined as **form-meaning pairings** and are thus essentially 'signs' in Saussure's sense, except that their sizes vary consider-

ably: words are regarded as constructions in this terminology, and so are smaller units like morphemes, and, notably, larger units such as word-formation patterns (e.g. the prefixation or compounding construction) and even clause-level syntactic patterns like the $SVO_{indir}O_{dir}$ construction or the $SVC_s$ construction. One of the central, and most controversial, claims of Construction Grammar illustrated in Figure 9 is that the stored knowledge about constructions includes information about their phonological, syntactic, semantic, and even pragmatic properties. This idea can be illustrated best with the help of such routine formulae as *good morning* or *pleased to meet you*, which are undoubtedly not put together online by means of rules, but stored and retrieved wholesale, complete with information about the kinds of contextual circumstances of their appropriate use.

The claim that even clause-level patterns have meanings may be much less plausible at first sight. One major justification is the observation that verbs can change their meanings and syntactic properties when they are used in certain constructions. For example, the clause-level construction manifested in SVOA sentences like *The waiter pushed the glass off the table* or *The doctor threw the gloves into the bin* is usually described as having the meaning of caused-motion (cf. Goldberg; Ungerer and Schmid 246–50): an agent causes an object to move to a certain location. Now, speakers can use sentences including verbs that, strictly speaking, do not match this construction from a

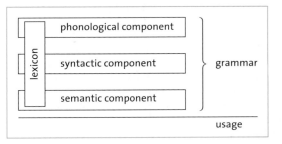

Figure 8.
An idealized version of the architecture of Generative Grammar adapted from Croft and Cruse

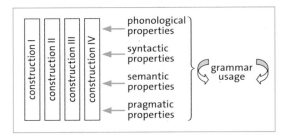

Figure 9.
An idealized version of the architecture of Construction Grammar adapted from Croft and Cruse

syntactic or a semantic point of view. The point is that if they do so, the meaning of the construction seems to override the properties of the verb. The verbs *laugh* and *smile*, for example, are intransitive verbs and thus in principle not eligible to express a caused-motion meaning. In sentences such as *The students laughed the professor out of the room* or *The attractive lawyer smiled the reluctant witness into the witness stand*, however, both verbs seem to acquire the meaning 'cause someone to move to a certain place.' Since the verbs do not bring along this semantic component, the only remaining possibility is that the caused-motion meaning does indeed reside in the construction itself, i.e. in the clause pattern SVOA.

Construction Grammar is a comparatively recent model of grammar, and complete accounts of how fully-fledged sentences are generated have not been proposed as yet. Trying to apply the framework to the sentence *Which book will the student buy?* (cf. example (1) above), one realizes that a considerable number of constructions would have to be activated. Proceeding from more general and schematic constructions to increasingly concrete ones, the following would certainly have to be included:

- some sort of *yes-no* question construction (of the type "aux—NP—main verb—NP"), including information on its interrogative pragmatic function;
- a monotransitive argument-structure construction opening the slots of "AGENT/subject—verb—THEME/object" (filled by *the student, buy,* and *the book* respectively);
- the *will*-future construction;
- the definite NP construction (*the student, the book*);
- lexical constructions representing knowledge about the form and meaning of the lexemes *student, buy,* and *book*.

Somewhat misleading in Figure 9 is the neat arrangement of constructions. If Construction Grammar is to make sense one has to assume that constructions are stored in the form of a huge, densely-knit network where similar constructions are firmly connected and knowledge about constructions can be available on several levels of abstraction.

What has been said about Construction Grammar so far indicates that this model differs substantially from generative approaches in its theoretical background assumptions:

- Construction Grammar is an item-based and network-based model rather than a rule-based one;
- it is not derivational but works on the unique level of constructions;
- it is not modular but holistic in the sense that it unites the phonological, syntactic, semantic and even pragmatic levels of language;
- it is non-autonomous, as it includes information relating to contexts and world-knowledge.

These differences, especially the last one, have extremely far-reaching consequences (indicated by the arrows on the right-hand side in Figure 9): in Construction Grammar and other so-called **usage-based models** (as suggested, for example, by Ronald Langacker, Paul Hopper, and Joan Bybee) the use of language is no longer strictly separated from the linguistic system but seen as constituting the basis and source of a constant renewal of grammar. According to such a view, the structure of grammar is the result of patterns of usage; if certain patterns are sufficiently frequent, they will be stored as chunks and schemata (including open slots and restrictions on how to fill them) in the minds of individual speakers; in addition, the formal, semantic and pragmatic properties will be agreed upon by the members of a speech community—all of which marks and qualifies them as constructions.

## 2.6 | Psycholinguistic Approaches

Psycholinguistics is the study of how language is processed by the human mind. In contrast to cognitive linguists, psycholinguists are only marginally interested in the structure of language, concentrating instead on processes taking place during ongoing language production (writing and speaking) and language comprehension (reading and listening). In addition, a traditional focus of

research in psycholinguistics lies on the study of first language acquisition. A major historical source of what is now known as psycholinguistics was the cognitive turn initiated by Chomsky, who, as outlined above, came up with controversial hypotheses on the nature and structure of sentences which lent themselves to experimental investigations.

Psycholinguists strive to investigate patterns of **language-related behaviour** that are shared by most people, and they do this mainly by means of controlled experiments under laboratory conditions (cf. Sandra). In addition, speech errors such as slips of the tongue as well as linguistic deficits (for instance, of patients suffering from the effects of a stroke) are studied with the aim of investigating how normal language use functions. The central fields of psycholinguistic research include

- the ways in which the forms and meanings of words are stored and retrieved from the **mental lexicon**;
- the processes taking place during written and spoken **language production**;
- the processes taking place during the **comprehension** of written and spoken discourse;
- the patterns and principles underlying **first language acquisition**.

Central controversies in psycholinguistic theorizing revolve around a number of fundamental background assumptions.

**1.** Modularity. Are different aspects of language processing—e.g. the conceptualization of ideas, their lexical, grammatical, and phonological encoding during speech production—taken care of by different, highly specialized modules, and if so, are these modules strictly separated or closely connected? This also touches upon the neurolinguistic question of whether the neurological substrates of these modules can be localized in certain regions of the brain. The fact that there are some stroke patients who have fluent grammar but difficulties finding the right words and some who know all the words they need but cannot assemble them in grammatical sentences is evidence for some sort of neurological specialization in the brain, since these specific deficits can be correlated with the regions in the brain that are damaged.

**2.** Simultaneity vs. Sequentiality. A second, related issue concerns the question of whether these modules do their work in parallel, with, for example, lexical and grammatical encoding taking place simultaneously, or sequentially, which means that the output of one module serves as input for the next one—very much in the way an assembly line in a factory works. For example, in the highly influential model of speech production proposed by Levelt, the conceptualizer provides the input for grammatical encoding, whose output is a syntactic frame filled with material from the mental lexicon.

While Levelt's model is sequential in the sense just explained, it is also incremental, which means that later modules can begin to work before earlier modules have finished.

**3.** Directionality. Especially in sequential models, a further question that comes up is whether information only proceeds in one direction (like in a cascade, cf. Aitchison 222–28) or can flow both forwards and backwards in a much more interactive, network-like fashion. In models of the latter type, so-called interactive network models, it is often assumed that information spreads automatically from the 'point' of access to neighbouring parts of the network. This is demonstrated for example in simple association tasks where a cue like *salt* is more likely to produce responses like *pepper* or *soup* than, say, *pen* or *caterpillar*. Spreading activation is also considered to be a major source of speech errors in which semantically or phonologically similar words, which are supposed to be stored closely together in the network that is the mental lexicon, are inadvertently replaced (e.g. *passion* instead of *fashion*, or the classic case of *right* instead of *left*).

Methods. A large range of methods are applied by psycholinguists, including classic paradigms such as lexical-decision tasks, sentence verification tasks and sentence-completion tasks. For example, in lexical-decision tasks, test participants are presented with a sequence of letters on a computer screen and asked to press one of two keys depending on whether they think the string is a word or not. Typically, participants perform much faster for frequent words than for rare ones (**frequency effect**) and faster for words that have big word families of morphologically similar words than for morphologically isolated ones (**family-size effect**). Another well-known effect is the **recency effect**, which is demonstrated in the fact that words heard or read shortly before the lexical-decision task are identified much faster. As predicted by spreading-activation models, this is also true of words that are semantically and/or phonologically similar to words recently heard or read. The first item, say *doctor*, then acts as a prime for the activation of the second item, for example *patient* or *nurse*. This robust finding can be exploited in so-called priming experiments where two stimuli are presented in a very short time to find out how strongly they are linked up in the mental lexicon.

Psycholinguistic
experiments

## 2.7 | Corpus-Based Approaches

A number of the models and approaches discussed so far are 'corpus-based' in a wider sense of this notion. This means that their theorizing is based on collections of authentic texts (written and spoken), so called **corpora** (from Latin *corpus* 'body,' i.e. a body of texts). For example, being interested in ancient languages, the representatives of the historical-comparative tradition of the nineteenth century basically had no other choice than to proceed from the corpora of texts and documents handed down to us from these earlier periods. Some of the American structuralists, e.g. Charles Fries, also based their descriptions on collections of corpora of spoken language.

The role of computer
technology in corpus
linguistics

The field of linguistics known today as corpus linguistics is not just defined by the use of corpora but to the same extent by the reliance on computers (cf. Mukherjee). Thus, present-day *corpus linguistics* basically means *computer-corpus linguistics*, although notable precursors of systematic corpora in the pre-computer era should be mentioned. As early as the 1950s, Randolph Quirk initiated the Survey of English Usage, which consisted of a huge number of index cards collecting samples of authentic written and spoken language. The 1960s saw a second milestone in the development of corpus linguistics, when Henry Kucera and Francis Nelson compiled the so-called Brown Corpus of American English, consisting of 500 texts containing about 2,000 words each (thus amounting to roughly one million words in total) stored on magnetic tapes. Kucera and Nelson made sure that the texts came from a wide range of sources (e.g. press reportage, fiction, learned texts, texts on 'skills and hobbies'). Following this lead, a group of European scholars based at the universities of Lancaster (Geoffrey Leech and Roger Garside), Oslo (Stig Johansson), and Bergen (Knut Hofland) compiled the analogously structured and equally sized LOB Corpus (short for *Lancaster-Oslo-Bergen Corpus*) as a British-English counterpart to Brown. A little later, in the 1970s, Sidney Greenbaum and Jan Svartvik turned the spoken part of the Survey of English Usage into a 500,000-word corpus of spoken British English known as London-Lund Corpus (for a list of corpora and information on how to access them, see section VII.2.3).

Beginning with the 1980s, corpus sizes started to increase dramatically as a consequence of the development of more powerful computers. Three major projects should be named here: The **Bank of English** was started in the 1980s by John Sinclair in cooperation with Collins publishers. The Bank of English is an open corpus, which means that new material is poured into it continuously; as of April 2011, it contains approximately 450 million words. The **British National Corpus (BNC)** is a closed corpus amounting to 100 million words (roughly 90 million from written text and 10 million originally spoken). The material comes from a huge variety of sources and was collected in the late 1980s and early 1990s with the aim of providing a representative sample of modern English for work in lexicography, grammar and theoretical linguistics. The **International Corpus of English (ICE)** was initiated by Sidney Greenbaum in 1990 and is special in that it consists of several one-million-word corpora collecting material from a wide range of English-speaking areas in Europe (Great Britain, Ireland), Asia (India, Hong Kong, Singapore, the Philippines, etc.), Africa (East Africa, Nigeria, Ghana), the USA and the Caribbean (Jamaica, the Bahamas, Trinidad and Tobago) as well as Australia and New Zealand. Not all ICE corpora are available yet, but work is in progress. Not surprisingly, the main aim of the ICE project is to provide material for systematic comparisons of the world-wide varieties of English (cf. entry V.6).

All modern computer-readable corpora are not just collections of raw text but include various kinds of **annotations** designed to facilitate the retrieval of very specific kinds of information. The annotation usually relates to several linguistic levels. The most common type of annotation is part-of-speech tagging, which marks each individual word in the corpus for its word class. Transcripts of spoken speech contained in the corpora are often annotated with regard to pauses, speaker turns, overlapping speech and other discourse-level phenomena. On the sociolinguistic level, corpus compilers try to make available as much information as possible on the producers of each stretch of language contained in the corpus, for example on speakers' gender, age, education and regional background. The type of situation in which corpus material was recorded, e.g. a council meeting, a business meeting or a parliamentary debate, is also indicated. Most corpora include tailor-made software for the retrieval and further processing of linguistic data. As a result, users of, say, the BNC can run very specific queries such as asking the retrieval software to download all instances of the sequence *why don't you* followed by a verb which were produced by 35- to 44-year-old women and compare the frequency to that of the men in the same age bracket (with the discovery that the women in the corpus use this pattern twice as often as the men do).

More illuminating than mere frequency counts of course is the actual analysis of the output of corpus queries. A basic but very powerful tool used by corpus linguists, lexicographers and grammarians for the analysis of corpus data is the so-called **KWIC-concordance** (key word in context concordance). As illustrated in an exemplary manner in Figure 10, this is a list of all instances found to match the search string in the corpus accompanied by a small number of words surrounding the occurrences in their actual context of usage.

As can be seen, concordances cannot be read like normal text, as each line is basically just a snippet, unconnected to the other lines, which come from different sources. KWIC-concordances provide a handy illustration of how certain words or expressions are used in authentic language. More importantly, they give a first glimpse of lexico-grammatical patterns found in language, which can be investigated more systematically in some corpora, e.g. the BNCweb version, using special tools for the display of **collocations** and the frequency of **word combinations**. As an illustration, Table 3 gives a rank list of the verbs which are most frequently found in questions beginning with *why don't you*. The percentages given in the right-hand column indicate that more than a quarter of these questions include the verbs *go, come,* and *take* and, perhaps more surprisingly, that the first 20 verbs listed here account for a staggering proportion of almost two thirds.

In principle, the field of corpus linguistics is characterized by the aim of systematically investigating authentic linguistic material and by the application of certain methods. In this respect, it is

| | | | | |
|---|---|---|---|---|
| 1 | why don't you | go | 110 | 11.47% |
| 2 | ... | come | 90 | 9.38% |
| 3 | ... | take | 51 | 5.32% |
| 4 | ... | get | 50 | 5.21% |
| 5 | ... | do | 38 | 3.96% |
| 6 | ... | ask | 37 | 3.86% |
| 7 | ... | have | 34 | 3.55% |
| 8 | ... | try | 30 | 3.13% |
| 9 | ... | tell | 24 | 2.5% |
| 10 | ... | put | 20 | 2.09% |
| 11 | ... | use | 19 | 1.98% |
| 12 | ... | give | 18 | 1.88% |
| 13 | ... | make | 16 | 1.67% |
| 14 | ... | sit | 15 | 1.56% |
| 15 | ... | leave | 14 | 1.46% |
| 16 | ... | say | 14 | 1.46% |
| 17 | ... | stay | 12 | 1.25% |
| 18 | ... | let | 11 | 1.15% |
| 19 | ... | like | 11 | 1.15% |
| 20 | ... | start | 10 | 1.04% |
| | | | | 65.07% |

Table 3.
Rank list of most frequent verbs following *why don't you* in the BNC

not comparable to other linguistic disciplines relating to levels of language (such as phonology or syntax) or theoretical approaches like structuralism or generativism. However, as is often the case, the introduction of new methods and methodologies can feed back on theories and scientific ideologies. This also happened in the wake of the introduction of computer-based corpus linguistics.

**1.** The finding that authentic language comes in grammatical and lexical patterns to a surprisingly high degree—as in the case of *why don't you* + Verb—casts doubt on the traditional idea that sentences are constructed by the application of general rules providing syntactic structures and open-

```
  what if it don't work?    Why don't you put    say another pad on top, more pressure, it
    Eleven ten, and eleven.   Why don't you get    them? Thirty quid's just enough. I do
  we'll make a guess alright? Why don't you give   her till half past three? Well that's a
oh its alright oh its lovely  why don't you buy    it then, buy yourself some records its not
        I haven't seen it!    Why don't you take   [unclear]. That one! Oh I did see it
    You must be exhausted?     Why don't you go     to sleep? [unclear] this stuff haven't I ?
Do you have to write it? Oh,  why don't you make   what you've got cos you've got a lot
                 Well         why don't you put    it on the table or on the little table,
Well that's what I'm saying,  why don't you use    the money that Geoffrey and Jean gave you
    ? Cos it's I can. mixed up! Why don't you make  , build houses with that? Yes as long as
Can I take the register. Look! Why don't you sit   down and read a book for five I got minutes
        Oh my god! Hey well    why don't you sell  them at the car boot sale? Well I mean
```

Figure 10.
Sample of a KWIC-concordance for the query *why don't you* from the BNC

ing slots to be filled by words. John Sinclair can be merited with having emphasized that this traditional **open-choice principle**, as he calls it, constantly competes with the **idiom principle**, which suggests that linguistic output relies on more or less prefabricated patterns and chunks. From a cognitive point of view, it is unlikely that speakers assemble these chunks afresh each time they need them; instead, they presumably store them as whole units and retrieve them wholesale in actual language use. The idiom principle not only accounts for genuine idioms like *bite the dust* or *roll out the red carpet* but also for less fixed recurrent lexical bundles (cf. Biber et al. 990–1024) such as *why don't you, the thing is,* or *let me just*. The effects of the idiom principle, for example with regard to the predictability of the parts of lexical bundles, can be demonstrated in psycholinguistic processing experiments.

**2.** As a consequence of these insights, more and more evidence is becoming available that the strict **separation of syntax and lexicon**, with the former being defined as the rule-governed component and latter as the idiosyncratic, item-based component, does not reflect the way languages seem to work.

Important findings
of corpus linguistics

After all, most of these patterns, chunks and schemata are indeed lexico-grammatical in the sense that they combine both types of information.
**3.** Corpus-linguistic work has given further support to the basic assumptions behind the **usage-based models** briefly mentioned in section 2.5.3 above. What the results of corpus-linguistic investigations seem to show is that the way in which linguistic knowledge is stored and represented in the mind depends very much on how frequently speakers use and are confronted with certain patterns and constructions. Frequent patterns are more likely to be stored as chunk-like pieces than are rare sequences of words. On the very mundane level of the formation of past tense forms, this explains why highly frequent irregular forms like *came, took,* or *saw* are much less likely to be replaced by the 'wrong' forms *comed, *taked,* and *seed* than those of rare verbs such as *kneel* or even *beseech*. The reason is that many speakers have not stored the rare irregular forms *knelt* and *besought* and therefore apply the general rule yielding the forms *kneeled* and *beseeched*. As a result, frequent irregular forms remain stable across time, while infrequent ones tend to become regular.

## 2.8 | Summary and Outlook

Omitting the fields of psycholinguistics and corpus linguistics, Figure 11 provides a concluding survey of the major theories and approaches discussed in this chapter. The boxes label the approaches, and indicate their main research areas (e.g. phonology, syntax, etc.) and key proponents. Arrows pointing downwards indicate inspirations provided for later models by earlier ones. Upward-pointing arrows indicate counter-reactions by later approaches to the assumptions of earlier ones. Horizontal double-headed arrows indicate mutual exchanges of ideas. As pointed out at the beginning of this chapter, approaches in historical linguistics, pragmatics and discourse analysis, and sociolinguistics are not included here. The figure shows that the major current approaches in the fields of grammar, semantics and lexicology are the Minimalist Program in the generative framework, a variety of cognitive-linguistic approaches and usage-based models. The general situation, from my personal point of view, is that cognitive, usage-based and other functionalist approaches are increasingly successful in providing

promising alternatives to the generative model. This has had the effect that the study of the core-linguistic components of grammar and the lexicon has increasingly opened up to and been enriched by evidence from the use-related disciplines of pragmatics and sociolinguistics as well as theories of language change.

As far as the methods favoured by the models collected in Figure 11 are concerned, one can basically group them into three classes:

1. **experimental methods** using controlled tests under laboratory conditions,
2. **corpus methods** relying on the analysis of authentic linguistic data collected in computer corpora,
3. methods relying mainly on linguists' **introspection**, often aiming to judge the grammaticality of invented examples.

Of course, the choice of methods tends to be strongly influenced by theoretical and ideological background assumptions. For example, given that Chomsky has always denied the relevance of authentic output data for models of grammar, it is

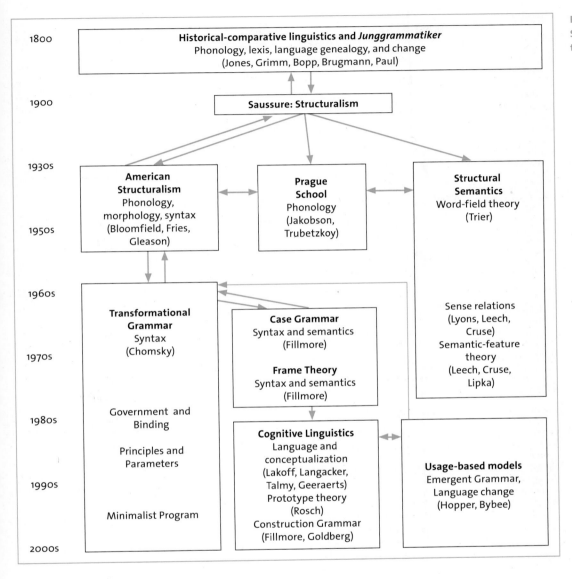

Figure 11.
Survey of major linguistic theories and approaches

hardly surprising that the corpus method has also been used to oppose him. This reliance on introspection is also shared by structuralist semantic approaches. On the other hand, usage-based models, whose proponents subscribe to the view that grammar emerges from actual language use and is continuously adapted to it, are more likely to resort to authentic data. Experimental methods have dominated psycholinguists' research and played a key role in the early development of prototype theory. In the very recent past, more and more linguists, especially those interested in cognitively plausible models of language structure and use, try to produce intersubjectively validated evidence by working with corpus data, carrying out experiments or ideally by searching for converging evidence from introspection, logical argumentation, corpus analysis, and experimental tests.

## Select Bibliography

**Aitchison, Jean.** *Words in the Mind: An Introduction to the Mental Lexicon.* 4th ed. Oxford: Blackwell, 2011.

**Biber, Douglas, et al.** *Longman Grammar of Spoken and Written English.* London: Longman, 1999.

**Bloomfield, Leonhard.** *Language.* New York: Henry Holt, 1933.

**Bybee, Joan.** *Language, Usage and Cognition.* Cambridge: Cambridge University Press, 2010.

**Chomsky, Noam.** *Aspects of the Theory of Syntax.* Cambridge: MIT Press, 1965.

**Chomsky, Noam.** *Knowledge of Language: Its Nature, Origin and Use.* New York: Praeger, 1986.

**Chomsky, Noam.** *Lectures on Government and Binding.* Dordrecht: Foris, 1981.

**Chomsky, Noam.** *The Minimalist Program.* Cambridge: MIT Press, 1995.

**Chomsky, Noam.** "A Review of B. F. Skinner's *Verbal Behavior*." *Language* 35.1 (1959): 26–58.

**Chomsky, Noam.** *Syntactic Structures.* The Hague: Mouton, 1957.

**Croft, William, and D. Allan Cruse.** *Cognitive Linguistics.* Cambridge: Cambridge University Press, 2004.

**Cruse, D. Allan.** *Meaning in Language: An Introduction to Semantics and Pragmatics.* Oxford: Oxford University Press, 2000.

**Fillmore, Charles.** "The Case for Case." *Universals in Linguistic Theory.* Eds. Emmon Bach and Robert T. Harms. New York: Holt, Rinehart and Winston, 1968. 1–88.

**Fillmore, Charles.** "Topics in Lexical Semantics." *Current Issues in Linguistic Theory.* Ed. Roger W. Cole. Bloomington: Indiana University Press, 1977. 76–138.

**Fries, Charles C.** *The Structure of English.* New York: Harcourt Brace, 1952.

**Gleason, H. A.** *An Introduction to Descriptive Linguistics.* New York: Holt, Rinehart and Winston, 1961.

**Goldberg, Adele E.** *A Construction Grammar Approach to Argument Structure.* Chicago: Chicago University Press, 1995.

**Herbst, Thomas, and Susan Schüller.** *Introduction to Syntactic Analysis: A Valency Approach.* Tübingen: Narr, 2008.

**Hopper, Paul.** "Emergent Grammar." *Berkeley Linguistics Society* 13 (1987): 139–57.

**Kövecses, Zoltán.** *Metaphor: A Practical Introduction.* 2nd ed. Oxford: Oxford University Press, 2010.

**Lakoff, George, and Mark Johnson.** *Metaphors We Live By.* Chicago: Chicago University Press, 1980.

**Langacker, Ronald W.** *Cognitive Grammar. A Basic Introduction.* Oxford: Oxford University Press, 2008.

**Leech, Geoffrey.** *Semantics.* 2nd ed. Harmondsworth: Penguin, 1981.

**Levelt, Willem J. M.** *Speaking: From Intention to Articulation.* Cambridge: MIT Press, 1989.

**Lewin, Kurt.** *Field Theory in Social Science: Selected Theoretical Papers by Kurt Lewin.* London: Tavistock, 1952.

**Lipka, Leonhard.** *English Lexicology: Lexical Structure, Word Semantics and Word-Formation.* Tübingen: Narr, 2002.

**Lyons, John.** *Semantics.* 2 vols. Cambridge: Cambridge University Press, 1977.

**Lyons, John.** *Structural Semantics: An Analysis of Part of the Vocabulary of Plato.* Oxford: Blackwell, 1963.

**Mukherjee, Joybrato.** *Anglistische Korpuslinguistik.* Berlin: Erich Schmidt, 2009.

**Prechtl, Peter.** *Saussure zur Einführung.* Hamburg: Junius, 2000.

**Robins, R. H.** *A Short History of Linguistics.* 4th ed. London: Longman, 1997.

**Sandra, Dominiek.** "Experimentation." *Cognition and Pragmatics.* Eds. Dominiek Sandra, Jan-Ola Östman, and Jef Verscheuren. Amsterdam: Benjamins, 2009. 157–200. Vol. 3 of *Handbook of Pragmatics Highlights.* 10 vols. to date. 2009–.

**Saussure, Ferdinand de.** *Cours de Linguistique Générale.* Eds. Charles Bally and Albert Séchehaye. Lausanne: Payot, 1916.

**Trier, Jost.** *Der deutsche Wortschatz im Sinnbezirk des Verstandes.* Heidelberg: Winter, 1931.

**Ungerer, Friedrich, and Hans-Jörg Schmid.** *An Introduction to Cognitive Linguistics.* 2nd. ed. London: Longman, 2006.

**Wakabayashi, Shigenori.** "Generative Grammar." *The Routledge Handbook of Applied Linguistics.* Ed. James Simpson. London: Routledge, 2011. 638–53.

**Wittgenstein, Ludwig.** *Philosophische Untersuchungen.* 2nd ed. Oxford: Macmillan, 1958.

*Hans-Jörg Schmid*

# 3 History and Change

History and change form the two key notions on which **diachronic linguistics**, the scientific study of language through time, rests. Students of linguistics usually first encounter the concept of diachrony in the context of the famous Saussurean dichotomies, but upon entering more deeply into the matter soon realise that, in practice, synchronic and diachronic perspectives are by no means mutually exclusive: the dynamics of language change can only be grasped by a careful diagnosis of the state of the language at different points in time.

This outline thus seeks to combine synchronic observations related to individual stages of English with a process-related diachronic perspective, drawing on insights from three closely related fields: **language history** ('Sprachgeschichte'), **historical linguistics** ('historische Sprachwissenschaft'), and the **history of linguistics** ('Sprachwissenschaftsgeschichte'). Making use of a convenient abstraction, the object of study is 'English,' though linguistic reality, both past and present, attests to a highly diversified range of 'Englishes.'

Employing a subject-oriented rather than a chronological approach, this chapter starts out with a brief discussion of language change, the focal element of historical linguistic study, which during the last decades has increasingly become a matter of theoretical concern (section 3.1). Section 3.2 takes a look at the sources that form the material backbone of English historical linguistics and describes some major tools that have been developed to facilitate access to the available historical evidence and to produce more controlled results. The theoretical problems and practical advantages of dividing the history of the English language into periods and sub-periods are addressed in section 3.3. Section 3.4 charts some changes that have affected English in the core areas of phonology and orthography, grammar, and lexis. Section 3.5, "Variation and Standardisation," adds a historical dimension to the diversified picture of 'real-life English(es)' that is the subject of entry V.6 of this volume. Needless to say, what can be offered here must remain highly selective, with bibliographical references covering only a tiny proportion of relevant literature.

> **Definition**
>
> → **Synchronic linguistics** describes the state of a language, its structure and its features at a specific point in time.
> → **Diachronic linguistics** analyses the development or change of a language over time by comparing different stages of that language.

## 3.1 | Language Change: Forces and Principles

Ye know ek that in forme of speche is chaunge
Withinne a thousand yeer, and wordes tho
That hadden pris, now wonder nyce and straunge
Us thinketh hem, and yet thei spake hem so.
(Geoffrey Chaucer, *Troilus and Criseyde*, lines 22–25)

The famous poetic comment on the instability of human language by England's most prominent medieval writer Geoffrey Chaucer (cf. entry I.2.1) is but one of numerous attestations of a conscious awareness of language change on the part of individual speakers. Historical testimonies of this type at the same time nicely illustrate their subject matter. We can trace manifold instances of "chaunge" affecting several levels of linguistic description when turning the "forme of speche" documented

## Timeline: The History of English

| Date | Major Periods and Historical Events | Languages and Linguistic 'Events' |
|---|---|---|
| **Britain before the Advent of the Anglo-Saxons** | | |
| **from ca. 500 BC** | Celtic settlement | Celtic |
| **ca. 43 BC – 410 AD** | Roman occupation | Celtic, Latin (superstrate) |
| **The Old English Period (ca. 450/700–1100)** | | |
| **ca. 450 AD** | Germanic settlement | Old English, Celtic (substrate) |
| **late 6th/early 7th century** | Christianisation of Britain by Iro-Scottish and Roman missionaries | introduction of the Latin alphabet; Latin ('cultural') borrowings |
| **ca. 700** | first written evidence of Old English | manuscripts in Latin and Old English |
| **late 8th – 11th century** | Viking raids and Scandinavian settlements ('Danelaw') | influx of Scandinavian loans |
| **from ca. 940** | Benedictine Reform: Bishop Æthelwold of Winchester as a major protagonist | 'Standard Old English' and 'Winchester Vocabulary' |
| **The Middle English Period (ca. 1100–1500)** | | |
| **1066** | Norman Conquest and establishment of Anglo-Norman rule by William the Conqueror | sociolinguistic divide between Anglo-Norman and English → superstrate borrowing from French |
| **1204** | loss of Normandy by King John ('Lackland') | decline of French → functional extension of English and adoption of French loans by "interference through shift" |
| **1337–1453** | Hundred Years' War between England and France → growing estrangement and rising nationalism | |
| **1476** | introduction of printing by William Caxton | beginning standardisation of written English |
| **The Early Modern English Period (ca. 1500–1700)** | | |
| **ca. 1500–1650** | Renaissance and Humanism: debate about the status of English: 'inkhorn controversy' | Great Vowel Shift influx of Latin and Greek loans |
| **1604** | beginning of English lexicography | 'hard word' dictionaries |
| **from early 17th century** | expansion of English within the British Isles (Scotland, Ireland) and development of 'extraterritorial Englishes' | growing variation and diversification |
| **The Late Modern English Period (ca. 1700–1900)** | | |
| **18th century** | 'Age of Prescriptivism': attempts to "fix" the language | further standardisation through grammars and dictionaries |
| **1870** | establishment of the English public school system | consolidation of a standard accent (RP) |

## Focus on Studying Historical Linguistics

For a thorough overview of the past states of the English language in the major areas of **historical linguistics** see the six volumes of the *Cambridge History of the English Language* (*CHEL*) and more recent handbooks on the history of English (Bergs and Brinton; Hogg and Denison; van Kemenade and Los; Momma and Matto; Mugglestone, *Oxford History*; Nevalainen and Traugott). A detailed treatment of the theories and methods of historical linguistics with a focus on the study of language change is offered by Joseph and Janda.

in Chaucerian Middle English (ME) manuscripts into Present-Day English (PDE): differences in spelling and pronunciation (e.g. line 22: ME *speche* /spe:tʃ/—PDE *speech* /spi:tʃ/), in inflectional morphology (25: *thinketh—thinks*), grammatical form (22: *ye—you*, 25: *hem—them*), syntactic structure and phraseology (25: *us thinketh hem—we deem them*), vocabulary (22: *ek*—'too, also'; 24: *wonder*—'extraordinarily, exceedingly'), and semantics (24: *nyce*—'strange, extraordinary, remarkable').

While from a linguistic angle it is a truism that all living languages are in a permanent state of change, language users quite often take an evaluative stance—a tendency epitomised in the title of Jean Aitchison's book *Language Change—Progress or Decay?* The history of English language scholarship (cf. Gneuss, *English Language Scholarship*) demonstrates that linguistic thinkers and professional linguists were by no means immune to **value judgements**—mostly of a negative kind, as the long persistence of the 'complaint tradition' in English shows (cf. Milroy and Milroy 24–46). The way from regarding language change as a sign of deterioration to linguistic prescriptivism is a short one, and with some institutional support normative attitudes can themselves act as a quite powerful force of language change or, even more so, its prevention.

**Internal and External Factors.** In categorising language change, the classic distinction is the one between 'internal' and 'external' factors. One of the most powerful language-immanent driving forces is the **principle of analogy**. First used by eighteenth-century scholars in their search for a logical order which, they assumed, was inherent to a 'pure' and rule-governed language, this principle was applied, for instance, in the dismissal of *thereabouts* in favour of *thereabout*—since that word's

basis, *about*, never has final *-s* (cf. Baugh and Cable 281). That regular patterns and more frequent forms tend to exert a regularising influence on irregular, rarer forms was also recognised by the so-called Neogrammarians in the later nineteenth century. As exemplified in section 3.4.2 below, English provides ample evidence for the working of analogy because its morphology was subject to massive reduction and simplification. There is less evidence for another system-immanent force, whose potency has been the subject of intensive linguistic discussion since the later twentieth century: **grammaticalisation**. The term describes a process in which lexical elements acquire a grammatical status as evidenced, for example, by the transformation of *going to* into a futurity marker (and its further reduction to *gonna* in colloquial styles).

External, i.e. extra-linguistic, factors have acted as instigators of language change in English in manifold ways. The most important of these changes resulted from medieval long-term encounters between speakers of different languages on British soil and from the long-lasting influence of Latin. The latter not only served as a sponsor of new words and phrases but also as a metalanguage used in linguistic description and as a standard of comparison, thus influencing English indirectly as well. The socially uneven and often forceful nature of such encounters is reflected in the distinction between '**substrate**' and '**superstrate**' influences. Celtic influences on English, on the one hand, and French on the other can serve as model examples for contact-induced changes 'from below' and 'from above' respectively, while the status of Scandinavian as an '**adstrate**' reflecting a basically non-hierarchical relationship between speakers of Old English and Old Norse is a disputed matter. The potential for change resulting from interdialectal contacts is exemplified by the development of London English into a standard variety in later Middle and early Modern English: the economic and cultural attraction of the metropolis led to an increased immigration from surrounding counties and an influx of east and central midland features that gave the emerging prestige variety its specific shape.

In his monumental three-volume work on *Principles of Linguistic Change*, William Labov adds a third determinant to the traditional dyad of internal and external (social) factors: **cognitive factors**. Their decisive role in language learning and production can substantially add not only to our understanding of how language is acquired, but also

Traditionally, linguists have distinguished various factors of language change.

→ Internal factors are forces operating within the language itself, such as the principle of analogy, by which less common forms are brought into conformity with more frequent, and more regular, ones.

→ External factors are social, political, cultural, or economic forces and events that influence the development of a language 'from the outside,' such as the Scandinavian invasions in Old English times and the Norman Conquest in 1066 (cf. section 3.3 below).

→ Cognitive factors refer to the influence of the speakers' cognitive capacities on language change and vice versa (cf. section V.2.4).

how it is subject to alteration when being transferred from one generation to the next.

Theoretical studies and empirical work have revealed the fundamental role of **variation** in language change. The availability of optional variants, though, "is a necessary but not a sufficient condition for change to occur" (Hogg and Denison 38). To gain a better understanding of the stages involved in successful change, linguists distinguish between the introduction of a variant—variously termed 'innovation,' 'actuation,' or 'implementation'—, and its spread or 'diffusion.' Chaucer's etymologically split usage of the borrowed (Norse-derived) subject form *they* and the inherited object form *hem* demonstrates that innovation within a paradigm may percolate through the system with varying speed and produce different variational patterns depending on region, text type, register, social class, age, etc. The concept of 'lexical diffusion' gives expression to the fact that changes affecting words usually do not affect all potential candidates at the same time, but that some words may "lead the trend" and others lag behind. Likewise, older and newer variants may exist side by side over a long period of time and even become standardised. The conservative nature of English spelling still reveals this. For example, PDE *food*, *foot*, *room*, and *blood* all go back to the same Middle English vowel (/oː/), while the different pronunciations—/fuːd/, /fʊt/, /ruːm/ or /rʊm/, and /blʌd/—show that after undergoing the Great Vowel Shift (/oː/ > /uː/), these lexemes were variously subject to the early Modern English shortening of long vowels in monosyllabic words (/uː/ > /ʊ/) and the successive centralisation of /ʊ/ to /ʌ/.

While in comparing earlier forms with their present-day equivalents historical linguists can, in many cases, come up with convincing explanations, general questions about the directionality and functionality of language change are much more difficult to answer. Textbooks frequently refer to guiding factors such as economy of effort or communicative efficiency and effectiveness. These concepts are, however, by no means easy to define, and the relevant principles may actually work in quite different directions. Thus, from a purely economic point of view, the increasing use of modals and other specific markers in polite English discourse seems a clear case of redundancy (theoretically, a bare imperative phrase would often suffice to get the message across), but successful communication in polite speech evidently follows its own rules. In recent times, a growing awareness of the role of functionally oriented, situation-dependent language use in language change has opened up new directions in linguistic research such as historical pragmatics and register and text type studies (cf. entry V.5), and fostered an increased interest in language materials beyond "literature proper."

## 3.2 | From Manuscript to Corpus Studies: Sources and Tools

In their endeavour to explore the full spectrum of human utterances, historical linguists face a number of specific limitations. The central problem is the restriction to written material for by far the largest part of the time span under inspection. Researchers of English are in a comparatively favourable position, especially as regards the number of early texts that have come down to us. These texts are, however, unevenly distributed across time, region, register, and social class and can thus only convey an incomplete picture of the linguistic reality in former periods. Besides, Old and Middle English manuscripts are often difficult to date and to localise. Many of them were written or copied by anonymous scribes, while autographs, i.e. texts in the author's own hand, are very rare.

Critical Text Editions. From the later nineteenth century onwards, traditional philology facilitated the accessibility of material for linguistic study through the systematic preparation of critical text editions, many of them at the instigation of the Early English Text Society, which has been active since 1864. The publication of facsimile editions, i.e. photographic reproductions of manuscripts and printed texts, is now increasingly supplemented or superseded by digitised versions made available on the internet by libraries and archives. The *Early English Books Online* database offers a wealth of English publications, often in various editions, from the advent of printing to ca. 1700 (cf. entry I.2.2).

Historical Corpora. The most important recent innovation in the field, with important methodological consequences, was the advent of large-sized historical corpora with special facilities for data-driven research. The searchable electronic databases of the two great medieval dictionaries, the *DOE*'s *Dictionary of Old English Web Corpus* and the *MED*'s *Corpus of Middle English Prose and Verse*, have proven to be of immense value to historical linguists. While these welcome by-products of more practical strands of linguistics aim at comprehensiveness and offer their material in 'unfiltered' form, the rapid development of Corpus Linguistics since the 1990s (cf. section V.2.7) has fostered the compilation of language corpora that are specifically tailored to the needs of historical linguists. The pioneer in the field was the diachronic part of the *Helsinki Corpus of English Texts* with approximately 1.6 million words, released in 1991 at the University of Helsinki and covering material from the eighth to the early eighteenth centuries. Its compilers aimed at creating a balanced corpus that offers a representative range of texts (or textual extracts) that were carefully selected according to criteria like time, genre, style, region, and social class. The corpus design thus allows for a systematic study of multiple long-term developments, including sociolinguistic, pragmatic

and text linguistic issues, though the usual caveats apply: major obstacles like the uneven distribution of the evidence, problems of exact categorisation, etc. stand in the way of producing an utterly 'balanced' historical corpus; representative results can only be expected for linguistic phenomena that are sufficiently documented within the scope of a given corpus and can efficiently be retrieved through automatic processing. Another large-scale multi-genre corpus with a historical dimension (1650–1999), incorporating British and American English, is *ARCHER* (*A Representative Corpus of Historical English Registers*). In order to provide a solid material basis for specialised text type studies, the spectrum of electronic research tools has successively been extended by a number of genre-specific collections such as the *Corpus of Early English Correspondence* (*CEEC*), the *Corpus of Early English Medical Writing* (*CEEM*), the *Lampeter Corpus of Early Modern English Tracts*, the *Zurich English Newspaper Corpus* (*ZEN*), and the *Corpus of English Dialogues 1560–1760* (*CED*). A permanently updated list and description of English language corpora is provided on the online *Corpus Resource Database* (*CoRD*) maintained by the Research Unit for Variation, Contacts and Change in English (VARIENG). For detailed information on the most important corpora and on how to access them see section VII.2.3.

Though corpora have by now become standard tools in data-based historical research, it needs to be stressed that text editions—be it in traditional printed or in computerised form—have by no means lost their essential function in linguistic research. The quality of the corpus material, and of the analyses carried out with it, very much depend on the reliability of the texts that enter the compilation, and on the availability of expert information on them.

Resources for historical
corpus studies

## 3.3 | Language History and Linguistic Periodisation

The first general effect of change in a language is that there comes a time when the earliest written documents of the language become obscure, and at last unintelligible, so that we are obliged to admit certain more or less definite periods in the language, such as Old English, Middle English, and Modern English, each of such periods admitting further subdivisions within itself. (Sweet, *History of Language* 76)

Historical linguists have long been aware of how problematic it is to split up a continuous process like language history into separate sections. However, as Henry Sweet indicated in his *History of Language*, the conventional division of English into **three major periods** (and various subperiods) is more than just a convenient reference system; there is some reality behind it, even if this reality is difficult to explicate in detail. It is in fact

Linguistic history
is a process: it eludes
easy categorisation.

not so much the periodisation of English as such but the question where to place the demarcation lines that is controversial among scholars. There are, of course, a number of historical dates, or rather events, whose relevance for the linguistic history of English is undisputed: 449—the year given by Bede in his *Historia ecclesiastica gentis Anglorum* (731) for the Germanic invasion of Britain—marks the beginning of English in many textbook accounts (though we know that the ethnically diverse immigrants came in various stages). 1066, 1476, and 1776—the dates of the Norman Conquest, the introduction of printing in England by William Caxton, and the American Declaration of Independence—serve as boundary markers between volumes 1 to 4 of the *CHEL*. To underpin the process-like rather than the event-driven nature of linguistic history, period divisions are often explicitly marked as rough approximations (see box).

### Definition

> The history of English can roughly be divided into the following periods:
> **Old English:** ca. 450/700–1100
> **Middle English:** ca. 1100–1500
> **Modern English:** ca. 1500 to the present

With manuscript transmission starting around 700, this date indicates a second beginning, that of written documentation in English (and, in much greater proportions, Latin). Some linguists prefer slightly different 'period boundaries' (e.g. ca. 1150/1450/1750) to the ones given above. The long-standing scholarly discussion of the question "When did Middle English begin?" (cf. Kitson, especially 221–22) has demonstrated the relative nature of linguistic dividing lines in an exemplary way: the different speed with which language changes progressed on the various linguistic levels and in different regions of the country does in fact suggest a much earlier 'transition date' from Old to Middle English from a structural rather than from a lexical point of view. Discarding the classic tripartite division into Old, Middle, and Modern English that mainly rests on morphological and morphonological criteria, Lutz ("When did English Begin?" 161–62) posits a two-way periodisation into "Anglo-Saxon" (i.e. Old and Early Middle English) and "English" (i.e. Late Middle English and all subsequent stages) on the basis of the lexicon. Thus, while 'Middle English' features such as the phonetic attrition in inflectional suffixes are found long before the Norman Conquest, the most sweeping changes are lexical ones that become most apparent in the course of the fourteenth century. Taking into account that spoken varieties of English must have been more prone to internal innovation and contact-induced variation than written ones, even more radical views have been proposed, arguably claiming that "outside the East and the South East spoken Middle English, as far as grammar is concerned, began in the sixth and seventh centuries AD" (Tristram 106). In this context it is noteworthy that the periodisation of a language easily falls victim to ideologies, linguistic as well as political ones. If employed with the necessary caveats, period labels and the time frames assigned to them will, however, maintain their usefulness.

## 3.4 | Major Changes on Different Linguistic Levels

### 3.4.1 | Historical Phonology and Orthography

| Though | the | rough | cough | and | hiccough | plough | me | through, |
|---|---|---|---|---|---|---|---|---|
| ðəʊ | ðə | rʌf | kɒf | ən(d) | ˈhɪkʌp | plaʊ | miː | θruː |
| O'er | life's | dark | lough | I | ough | my | way | pursue |
| ɔː(r) | laɪvz | dɑːk | lɒk/lɒx | aɪ | ɔːt | maɪ | weɪ | pəˈsjuː |

This witty couplet ascribed to Horace Mann (1796–1859) still enjoys some popularity as an example for the inconsistency of English spelling— or, for that matter, pronunciation. The two aspects are here treated together, because for most of their material historical linguists can only get down to sounds through letters. This is a difficult enterprise. If *orthography* is taken literally as the art of 'writing correctly,' then English lacked such an art for substantial parts of its recorded history because spelling was not strictly regularised. Nevertheless, writing systems and spellings are invaluable sources—both in their own right and for the **reconstruction of phonological systems and pronunciations**. The great historical dictionaries, the *Oxford English Dictionary* (*OED*), the *MED*, and the *DOE* (see the "Dictionaries" list in section VII.2.3 for details) acknowledge the validity of spelling variants for historical research by offering special attested spelling sections; the additional dating of the spelling forms in the *OED* (by periods and centuries) allows for long-term variational studies.

Other evidence which historical linguists can draw on in reconstructing the history of English sounds is quite unevenly distributed across time: rhymes are available from Middle English onwards, but their reliability (and that of the poet) has to be carefully checked; metalinguistic sources, i.e. works that have language as their subject, become more and more frequent from the sixteenth century onwards. Apart from relevant passages in grammars it is especially the works of spelling reformers and orthoepists—teachers or advocates of 'correct' pronunciation—that yield relevant information, though in the absence of a commonly defined descriptive system or code like the International Phonetic Alphabet (IPA) the evidence is often difficult to interpret.

The changes in the phonemic inventory of English cannot be treated here in any detail, but it seems important to point out that these changes did not only affect individual sounds but the system *per se*. Thus, quite in contrast to the present-day situation, where long and short vowels differ in quality, Old English had a highly **symmetrical vowel system** with /æ/—/æː/, /e/—/eː/, /i/—/iː/, /y/—/yː/, /u/—/uː/, /o/—/oː/ and /a/—/ɑː/ largely corresponding in quantity and quality. Vowel length in Old English was etymologically determined, and the inherited quantities remained quite stable over a long time. On the way to Middle English, however, syllable type became relevant for the actuation of a number of shortening and lengthening processes. Old English also had a length contrast for consonants, with 'long' pronunciation of geminates, i.e. doubled consonants, in words like *æppel* 'apple' or *sittan* 'sit.' A brief outline of two major sound changes—*i*-mutation and the Great Vowel Shift—may serve to demonstrate the effects of such changes on Present-Day English and the explanatory potential of historical linguistics for the shape of the resultant forms.

*I*-mutation, or *i*-umlaut, is a prototypical example for a conditioned sound change, operating only if certain triggers are present in the phonetic neighbourhood. The mechanism described as *umlaut* (a term borrowed from nineteenth-century German philology) is defined by the *OED* as "[a] change in the sound of a vowel produced by partial assimilation to an adjacent sound." The conditioning factors for *i*-mutation, operative around 600, an *i* or *j* in the following syllable, are no longer present in the recorded Old English forms. Yet the palatalising effect of the assimilatory—or, from the angle of speech production—anticipatory process they triggered is still traceable in pairs like *goose/geese* (OE *gōs* [sg]—*gēs* [pl] < Germ *\*gōs-iz*), *doom/deem* (OE *dōm* [n]—*dēman* [v] < Germ *\*dōm-jan*), and in the (semantically specialised) gradation series *old—elder—eldest* (OE *eald—ieldra—ieldest*, with the comparative and superlative originally ending in Germ *\*-izan* and *\*-ista[n]*). Note that unattested, reconstructed forms are marked by an asterisk [*].

The Great Vowel Shift (GVS; sometimes also called 'Tudor Vowel Shift'), by contrast, is an unconditioned sound change: its effects are commonly described as a systematic raising of long vowels, causing diphthongisation for the front/back pair in extreme (high) position. The exact nature of this sound change is, however, still not fully understood; in fact, the ongoing scholarly discussion vividly demonstrates that straightforward explanations of the GVS as put forth by Otto Jespersen (who coined the term in 1909) fall short of linguistic evidence. The traditional view, now often considered too simplistic, describes the GVS as a chain shift, with either /iː/ and /uː/ starting a 'drag chain,' or /eː/ and /oː/ initiating a 'push chain' (cf. the way e.g. *child*, *house*, *green*, and *food* took from Middle English to Modern English: /tʃiːld/ > /tʃaɪld/, /huːs/ > /haʊs/, /greːn/ > /griːn/, /foːd/ > /fuːd/; see illustration on p. 402).

No matter which of the two chain reactions is given precedence, the **controversies around the GVS** make it an excellent candidate for the study of historical phonology. The success by which this theory was met echoes the success of rigid structuralist approaches to linguistic phenomena, here

*Conditioned sound change*

*Unconditioned sound change*

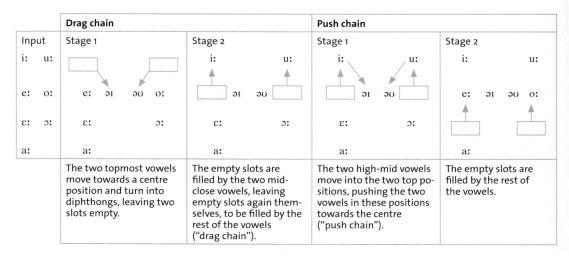

| Drag chain | | | Push chain | |
|---|---|---|---|---|
| Input | Stage 1 | Stage 2 | Stage 1 | Stage 2 |
| i: u:<br><br>e: o:<br><br>ɛ: ɔ:<br><br>a: | e: əɪ əʊ o:<br><br>ɛ: ɔ:<br><br>a: | i: u:<br><br>əɪ əʊ<br><br>ɛ: ɔ:<br><br>a: | i: u:<br><br>əɪ əʊ<br><br>ɛ: ɔ:<br><br>a: | i: u:<br><br>e: əɪ əʊ o:<br><br>ɛ: ɔ:<br><br>a: |
| The two topmost vowels move towards a centre position and turn into diphthongs, leaving two slots empty. | The empty slots are filled by the two mid-close vowels, leaving empty slots again themselves, to be filled by the rest of the vowels ("drag chain"). | | The two high-mid vowels move into the two top positions, pushing the two vowels in these positions towards the centre ("push chain"). | The empty slots are filled by the rest of the vowels. |

in particular the assumption that sound inventories of a given language represent systems with an inherent tendency towards symmetry, economy and distinctiveness. Every gap that may occur due to change will eventually be filled in order to regain symmetrical balance (hence 'chain reaction'). The phonological developments, though, do not match such an ideal picture. The notion of distinctiveness as an essential motor of change is, for instance, called into question by the eventual merger of original /ɛ:/ and /e:/ in /i:/, with low-mid ('open') /ɛ:/ shifting to the former position of its high-mid ('closed') neighbour and continuing to move upwards. The old 'chain debate' has been extended by discussions about the chronology of the individual shifts, their precise temporal extension and, ultimately, the unity of the sound change. Recent accounts stress the 'local' nature of the GVS: it did not affect all English dialects to the same degree and all lexemes that were potentially subject to it at the same time and with the same effect, leaving inconsistencies such as PDE *meat* /i:/ vs. *bread* /e/. Sceptics point out that long-vowel reflexes in modern non-standard varieties suggest a number of processes at work which are not necessarily related; some linguists even go so far as to claim that there was no GVS, at least no shift that could be packaged as *one* in any meaningful way (cf. McMahon 154–77).

Apart from its continuing theoretical interest for linguists, the GVS is of immediate practical relevance for speakers and learners of English as it helps to explain apparently **disparate spelling and pronunciation relationships** in Present-Day En-

glish. The disruptive influence of the GVS on grapheme-phoneme relations is due to the fact that spelling did not follow suit, but by and large continued to reflect late Middle English vowel qualities as conventionalised in early fifteenth-century London English writing practices. The emergence of a regulated orthography, and in particular the (by no means straightforward) role of printing—and printers—in this process, still await close scrutiny. The following table depicts some fairly regular correspondences that attest to the preservation of Middle English pronunciation in Present-Day English orthography:

| ME | PDE | | Examples | |
|---|---|---|---|---|
| phoneme | pronunciation | spelling | PDE | OE |
| /e:/ | /i:/ | ‹ee› | m<u>ee</u>t | < m<u>ē</u>tan |
| /ɛ:/ | /i:/ | ‹ea› | t<u>ea</u>ch, dr<u>ea</u>m | < t<u>æ</u>can, < dr<u>ēa</u>m |
| /o:/ | /u:/ | ‹oo› | t<u>oo</u>th | < t<u>ō</u>þ |
| /ɔ:/ | /əʊ/ | ‹o … e› | b<u>o</u>ne | < b<u>ā</u>n |
| | | ‹oa› | l<u>oa</u>f | < hl<u>ā</u>f |
| /u:/ | /aʊ/ | ‹ou› | h<u>ou</u>se | < h<u>ū</u>s |
| | | ‹ow› | t<u>ow</u>n | < t<u>ū</u>n |

Thus, for example, in words that underwent a regular development, both ‹ee› and ‹ea› represent PDE /i:/; the different spelling, however, still indicates the original quality distinction in the underlying vowels, i.e. ME high-mid /e:/ and low-mid /ɛː/—a difference obscured by their subsequent merger into /iː/. Likewise < oo > and < o ... e/oa > spellings lead us back to ME 'closed' /oː/ and 'open' /ɔː/, respectively.

The history of English consonants is to a considerable extent a history of loss, though the former presence of the corresponding sounds is often still indicated by so-called '**silent letters**,' i.e. graphemes that are not—or no longer—represented in pronunciation. A major case in point is the loss of postvocalic /r/ in non-rhotic varieties of English, which has a long and complex history, taking on a systematic form from the seventeenth century onwards. Speaking (in a more precise manner) about the loss of non-prevocalic /r/ allows us to account for the resurfacing of the silenced consonant that has been preserved in spelling as "linking *r*" as in British Standard English *far away* /faːr əˈweɪ/ vs. *far* /faː/. In variationist studies, rhoticity has turned into an important diagnostic feature which quite often functions as a social marker. The history of word-initial /h/ is an equally complex story, with 'aitch-dropping' reaching much further back than its social stigmatisation, which is linked to the emergence of Received Pronunciation (RP) as an educated and prestigious upper-class accent since the late eighteenth century. In this case, though, spelling has largely followed developments in (standard) pronunciation (with minor, variety-specific exceptions such as *herb*, BrE /hɜːb/, AmE /ɜːrb/).

Spellings like *light*, *right*, *taught* and *bought* attest to the former presence of [ç] and [x]—the voiceless palatal and velar fricatives in allophonic distribution still preserved in German as 'ich-' and 'ach-Laut.' The introduction of < gh > into *delight*—a so-called **inverse spelling** ('umgekehrte Schreibung') that supplanted original ME *delit* (borrowed from Old French) in the sixteenth century (cf. *OED* s.v. *delight* n.)—provides conclusive evidence that at the time of its analogical extension to other lexemes this digraph was no longer pronounced in its original phonetic environment. Another type of conscious interference that produced silent letters is the **orthographic re-Latinisation** of Old French borrowings by humanist scholars, e.g. in *to doubt* ( < ME *d(o)uten* < OF *d(o)uter* < Lat *dubitāre*) and *debt* ( < ME *det(t)e* < OF *det(t)e* < Lat *dēbitum*).

As these examples illustrate, quite a number of modern English spellings that are seemingly irregular "can be explained but not predicted" (Crystal, *Cambridge Encyclopedia* 67). Proposals for "the *Amendment of Orthographie* for English speech"—

as the subtitle of William Bullokar's *Book at Large* (1580) announces—have been brought forward since the mid-sixteenth century. Despite the fact that a reformed orthography found such prominent advocates as Benjamin Franklin and George Bernard Shaw, the history of English spelling reform is on the whole a story of failed attempts. Successful innovations on a minor scale such as Noah Webster's AmE < -or > for BrE < -our > in *color* and AmE < -er > for BrE < -re > in *theater* etc. have been assigned great significance in nineteenth-century America's fight for 'linguistic independence.' These and other small differences in spelling between the major standard varieties do not, however, alter the fact that in times of increasing diversification, a codified orthography—inconsistent as it may be—serves as the major common bond between the many different Englishes and ensures mutual intelligibility between speakers with highly divergent accents.

The long history of orthography reform debate

## 3.4.2 | Changes in Grammar: Inflection and Word Order

If we take Sth E [Southern English] as the standard, we may define OE [Old English] as the period of full endings (*mōna, sunna, sunu, stānas*), ME [Middle English] as the period of levelled endings (*mōne, sunne, sune, stǭnes*)—weak vowels being reduced to a uniform *e* [ə]—, MnE [Modern English] as the period of lost endings (*moon, sun, son*). (Sweet, *History of English Sounds* 154–55)

The lack of the form *stones* in the "lost endings" section makes it immediately clear that Henry Sweet's periodisation of English according to structural criteria is an overgeneralisation. This being conceded, the distinction between "full," "levelled," and "lost" inflections can be taken as a useful illustration of the typological shift of English from a predominantly **synthetic** (inflectional) to a mainly **analytic language** that typically indicates grammatical categories and syntactic functions with invariable elements like prepositions, pronouns, auxiliary verbs, and by means of a fixed word-order (cf. section V.4.3). Germanic stress placement on the root syllable (i.e. the word-initial one if not preceded by a—usually unstressed—prefix) had led to substantial losses of phonetic material in final positions already in pre-Old English times. What remains in terms of inflectional paradigms is still quite impressive from a modern English point of view: a range of declensional

Language change
in Old English

classes with subdistinctions along case, number, and gender lines for the noun, similarly diversified systems for the adjective (with a 'strong,' or definite, and a 'weak,' or indefinite, declension according to information structure and syntactic usage), the demonstrative pronoun (definite article) *se, sēo, þæt* and the personal pronoun, again differentiated according to case, number, and gender, and a host of verb forms with person/number/mood inflection—to mention just the most important elements. But not all these inflectional markings were really distinctive: quite a number of grammatically different forms shared the same marker. Besides, grammatical gender, an inherent property of the noun, was usually not indicated by nominal inflection but can mostly be specified on the basis of an accompanying determiner—if that, in turn, is distinctive enough.

What Roger Lass calls "[t]he **dissolution of Old English**," marked by "the erosion of morphologically important qualitative distinctions," continues an inherited trend, "[b]ut the extent of collapse [...] is much greater, and has a radical systemic effect" (243, 250). The degree of orthographic regulation that characterises the majority of late Old English texts (cf. section 3.5 below) is, however, apt to conceal ongoing language change, especially in the field of inflectional morphology, with vowels merging into indistinct schwa /ə/ and final consonants being increasingly subject to confusion and loss. Scarce though it is, the evidence from the 'progressive' northern dialect areas, as for example the Old English interlinear gloss to the famous *Lindisfarne Gospels*, clearly demonstrates that in the late tenth century the levelling of inflections in unstressed syllables was already well under way—no doubt promoted by interlingual contacts in the areas of Viking settlement. A unique witness to the demise of the Old English grammatical system is the *Peterborough Chronicle*, one of the versions of the *Anglo-Saxon Chronicle*, whose continuations in two scribal hands (up to 1131 and 1154 respectively) gives an impression of what 'transitional English' unimpeded by an established orthographic norm was like.

The **reductive processes** demonstrable in Middle English texts (with partial extensions into the Modern English period) were seldom straightforward ones, but produced a great amount of variation that must have been even greater in spoken discourse. With grammatical gender, a whole category got lost, though the change is a less drastic one if we take into account that natural gender (i.e. sex) was already prevalent in Old English animate, especially personal, nouns. It is still morphologically encoded in the third person singular personal pronouns *he—him, she—her* (as opposed to *it*), as is a distinction between subject and object case and the singular vs. plural opposition that could be upheld thanks to the import of the phonetically distinctive *th*-forms (*they, them, their*) from Old Norse. The word classes most radically affected by inflectional loss and reduction in form are the adjective and the definite article. On a syntactic level, the changes affecting these classes closely interacted with those of the noun (cf. Smith 144–49), which was eventually left with a single homonymic marker {S} for plural and possessive (the latter, strictly speaking, not a case marker but a clitic that attaches to the whole noun phrase; cf. 'group genitives' such as *the king of England's daughter*). With the 'genitive *s*' and the analytic *of*-pattern English has in fact preserved two typologically different forms with varying distinctions in distribution and usage (cf. also synthetic vs. analytic comparison in *big—bigger—biggest* vs. *difficult—more/most difficult*).

The **extension of the *s*-plural** from the Old English masculine *a*-declension (*stān-as* etc.) to the majority of English nouns at the expense of competing patterns (cf. relics like *ox-en, child-r-en, mẹn* and *sheepØ*) serves to demonstrate the effects of analogy, by which speakers make certain forms conform to related ones. The usual path is from less frequent forms (more likely perceived as 'irregular') to more frequent and more familiar ones, resulting in a reduction of complexity and an increase in regularity. The quantitative lead (about a third of the Old English nouns were masculine *a*-stems), combined with a robust phonetic shape (/s/ scores high in terms of consonantal strength), made the *s*-plural a natural candidate for analogical extension, though the *n*-plural also enjoyed some limited success in southern Middle English and is still resonant e.g. in Shakespeare's "Spare none, but such as go in clouted shooen" (*2 Henry VI*, Act 4).

Analogical pressure has also considerably reduced the number of **strong verbs**—those that formed their past by a regular vowel alternation called 'ablaut' (e.g. OE *helpan—healp—hulpon—(ge)holpen*, class III)—in favour of the weak pattern marked by a so-called 'dental element' {D} (e.g. OE *lufian—lufode—(ge)lufod*, class 2) and led to a radical restructuring of the system with a lot of 'hybridisation' or "mixing of forms from more than one class in the conjugation of a given verb" (Lass in *CHEL* 2: 131). Highly irregular as relics such as PDE *cleave—cleft/cleaved/clove—cleft/cleaved/cloven* may seem, the notion of regularity is a relative one or rather a matter of perspective. In Old English, both strong and weak verbs follow regular patterns. However, Old English verbs that kept their ablaut marking (28.6 %; Görlach 74) are always irregular in Present-Day English, while not all verbs that fill the "irregular verbs" section in contemporary grammars and dictionaries were necessarily strong. Thus, in diachronic terms, the development of the two surviving verb forms of OE *cēpan—cēpte—(ge)cēped* (a weak verb, class 1) is completely regular: the infinitive—ME *kēp(en)*— first lost its marker and then went through the Great Vowel Shift (/eː/ > /iː/), while the long vowel in the preterite *cēpte* was subject to shortening in front of a 'consonant cluster' (here the combination /pt/) in early Middle English and thus no candidate for the Great Vowel Shift.

Ernst Leisi's division into **strengthened** ("gestärkte") and **weakened** ("geschwächte") grammatical categories (see Leisi and Mair 112–52) reminds us that the structural development of English is a history of change rather than of mere loss. Among those syntactic phenomena that lost in functionality he lists gender, case, number (to a minor extent), the subjunctive (i.e. one of the moods), and, finally, the distinctions between active, reflexive and passive usages and between main and subordinate clauses, which have become increasingly blurred. On the winning side, with an increase in differentiation and functional load, he sees aspect, tense, the modal verbs, the non-finite verb forms and, last but not least, word-order. The major syntactic changes from Old to Modern English are conveniently listed in Fischer ("History of English Syntax" 60–62). Though the exact nature of causes and effects remains a chicken-and-egg question, there can be no doubt that the growing tendency towards a fixed word order served as a compensation (though not the only one) for morphological loss. The modern SVO (subject-verb-object) order is already represented in Old English, though the older SOV and other types are common as well. The fixation to VO in all types of clauses—including subordinate ones, which were mainly verb-final in Old English (as still in Modern German)—is a Middle English development. Subsequent syntactic changes that have been standardised are frequently associated with the prescriptive grammarians of the eighteenth and nineteenth centuries, though "it may

seem more appropriate to speak of prescriptive tendencies rather than of prescriptive English grammar in the eighteenth century and later" (Gneuss, *English Language Scholarship* 32).

### 3.4.3 | Changes in the Lexicon: Borrowing, Lexical Restructuring, and Semantic Change

I am of this opinion that our own tung shold be written cleane and pure, unmixt and unmangeled with borrowing of other tunges, wherin if we take not heed by tijm, ever borrowing and never payeng, she shall be fain to keep her house as bankrupt. (John Cheke, qtd. in Baugh and Cable 217)

In view of the fact that today English is not only a major donor, but a world language, we can only smile at the fears voiced in 1561 by the Cambridge professor Sir John Cheke that his mother tongue might suffer bankruptcy if it continued to absorb foreign material so liberally. Though in modern contact linguistics the concept of a '**mixed language**' is a disputed one (because there are virtually no 'unmixed'—or, to use Cheke's term, 'pure' languages), there is no denying that the lexis of Modern English is "a unique mixture of Germanic and Romance elements" (Leisi and Mair 41, our trans.). The better part of Modern English vocabulary is of Latin or French origin, while a considerable amount stems from Greek (frequently transmitted through Latin) as well as from Scandinavian and other languages. Judging from a modern standard dictionary and from lexico-statistical evidence (cf. Scheler 9–11 and 70–84), one may arguably call English a Romance language. Indeed, the language used by authors like Shakespeare or even Chaucer has a distinct 'feel of familiarity' when compared with Anglo-Saxon texts such as *Beowulf* or Ælfrician prose: to the untrained modern English eye, these are complete strangers. At first glance, therefore, it is the long-term effects of lexical input that separates the speakers of modern English most obviously from their ancestors, and sets English apart from its Germanic cousins.

For borrowing on such a large scale to occur, direct linguistic contact (through speakers) and indirect contact (through other media) must have persisted over many generations. As Thomason and Kaufman's "borrowing scale" (74–76) demonstrates, the type of material that finds its way into the recipient language by lexical or structural bor-

English:
A Romance language?

rowing correlates significantly with the intensity of contact and with the typological distance between the languages involved. Quite naturally, structural borrowing in the fields of phonology, morphology, and syntax requires much higher levels of bilingual competence on the part of the adoptive speaker community than lexical borrowing. Along with different kinds of community settings, exerting varying degrees of social and cultural pressure, the history of English in contact also provides us with multiple types of linguistic transfer, especially in the prevalent field of lexical borrowing (cf. A. Fischer). Besides 'importation' through the intake of loan words, basically two further techniques were employed involving 'substitution,' i.e. the rendering of foreign concepts with indigenous material, especially by translators and cultural transmitters in Anglo-Saxon times: (a) the coinage of **loan-formations** ('calques') such as OE *þrī-ness* for Lat *trini-tas* 'trinity' (cf. G 'Dreifaltigkeit'), and (b) the creation of **semantic loans** by charging an existing lexeme with a new, borrowed meaning; cf. the extension of OE *hlaford* '(secular) lord' to 'the Lord' (God), on the model of Lat *dominus*. The degree of formal and semantic correspondence with the foreign model allows for further subdivisions into **loan translations** ('Lehnübersetzungen'), **loan renditions** ('Lehnübertragungen'), and **loan creations** ('Lehnschöpfungen') and various types of semantic loans (cf. Gneuss, *Lehnbildungen*).

Celtic Influence. Among the various contact scenarios and their results, which can only be treated in a summary way here, the one with Insular Celtic is particularly difficult to reconstruct (for more detailed accounts cf. Nielsen and the theory-oriented paper by Vennemann). The social inequality between the Anglo-Saxon invaders who entered Britannia around the middle of the fifth century and the conquered Celts suggests a prototypical superstratal contact situation with influence 'from below.' In accordance with theoretical insights that place this type of influence primarily on the structural side, recent research has shifted the focus of attention from the few lexical loans which found their way into Old English—mainly toponyms (*London*, *Kent*) and hydronyms (*Avon*, *Thames*)—to morphosyntactic features such as the progressive form.

Latin Influence. From pre-Old English (Continental) times onwards, Latin has continuously served as a donor to English, first as a living language and, for the larger part of the contact history, as a distinguished functional code used by

the Church, in education, scholarship, science, and as a "language of record." Its role as a cultural superstrate quite typically resulted in lexical borrowing but in fact goes far beyond that: Latin has left its lasting imprint on a considerable number of text types and discourse modes. While loans surviving from the earliest period—Continental ones such as *strǣt*, *chīese* and *wīn* (cf. G *Straße*, *Käse*, *Wein*) and those adopted in the wake of Christianisation from the late sixth century onwards (*mæsse* 'mass,' *prēost* 'priest,' *scōl* 'school')—have become fully integrated into the English lexicon, many of the lexical items borrowed during the Renaissance (ca. 1500–1650) in order to amend the alleged imperfections of the English language are still set apart from the inherited Germanic material by their polysyllabic structure, their accentuation patterns, their specific stylistic value and their technical ring, thus creating a **'hard-word problem'** for less educated speakers (see Leisi and Mair 51–76). A welcome, and commercially successful, side effect of the sixteenth-century dispute over the necessity of 'bookish' imports like *denunciation*, *excrescence*, and *conjectural*, scornfully called 'inkhorn terms,' is the development of monolingual English lexicography, with Robert Cawdrey's *A Table Alphabeticall of Hard Usual English Words* (1604) leading the way. Together with Greek, Latin has also considerably extended the resources of English word-formation with so-called 'neo-classical compounds' such as *audiophile* and *biology*, formed on the basis of 'combining forms' (*audio-*, *-phile*, etc.) and making up large parts of our modern scientific vocabulary.

French Influence. Due to the specific sociolinguistic conditions after the Norman Conquest, French constitutes another prototypical superstrate influence on English. After 1066, Anglo-Norman established itself as the language of power and prestige, and in a different form and under changed contact conditions continued to do so for the entire Middle English period (and beyond). In Thomason and Kaufman's terms (37, 348n1), the politically motivated thirteenth-century switch of the Anglo-Norman elite from French to English and the concomitant transfer of lexical items that surface in large numbers in later fourteenth-century vernacular texts represents a specific type of contact-induced change, namely "interference through shift" (as distinct from 'borrowing'). The rough subdivision into two periods of French influence up to and after ca. 1250 is also borne out by the phonetic nature of the material: cf., for in-

Lexical borrowing is a common type of linguistic transfer.

stance, the preservation of Old French *s* in *feast* (ModF *fête*) and the loan-doublet *catch* with initial /k/ from Old Northern French *cachier* as opposed to *chase* /tʃ/ < CentralF *chacier*. Beside the adoption of more than 10,000 words during the Middle English period, about 75% of which are still in current use (Baugh and Cable 178), French—in tandem with Latin (cf. Lutz, "Types")—also left its traces on word-formation and phraseology, on the sound and writing systems, on accentuation and, by its prestigious status, instigated a specific type of 'pragmatic borrowing': the use of the second person plural pronouns *ye* and *you* (instead of singular *thou* and *thee*) as forms of address.

**Scandinavian Influence.** Chronologically speaking, the Scandinavian, or Old Norse, impact on English clearly precedes the French one, with forced contact by raids starting in the late eighth century. However, the real extent of the influence spreading from the areas of Viking settlement in the north and east of England (the "Danelaw") since the late ninth century becomes apparent only in Middle English times, after the regularising force of the (southern-based) Late Old English *Schriftsprache* had given way to localised, dialectal forms of writing (see the map in section 3.5 below). The exact degree of mutual intelligibility between speakers of Old English and Old Norse, the amount of individual and societal bilingualism and the assumed sociolinguistic status of Old Norse as a non-hierarchical adstrate are still under discussion. But there can be no doubt that the prolonged nature and intensity of the contact and the typological relatedness between the two Germanic languages facilitated borrowing. For the expert, phonetic markers such as /sk/ in *sky*, *skin*, *bask* and imported place name elements such as *-by* in *Whitby*, *Derby*, etc. point to Scandinavian influence; the bulk of the borrowings, however, consists of highly frequent "everyday words" like *fellow*, *take*, and *wrong*. A unique instance of structural borrowing is the gradual adoption of the Norse-derived third person plural pronouns *they*, *them*, and *their* (replacing OE *hīe*, *him*, *hiera*) in later Middle English, which helped to avoid the imminent loss of gender and number distinctions in the personal pronoun paradigm due to phonetic attrition.

Borrowing processes have often been accompanied by **semantic change**: see, for example, instances of semantic differentiation in doublets such as *shirt* (< OE *scyrte*) and *skirt* (ME *skirte* < ON *skyrta*). The causes, paths, and types of such change cannot be dealt with in any detail here (see Görlach 119–36; Moessner 133–51). Suffice it to say that the *OED* and its recently published onomasiological (sense-based) companion tool, the *Historical Thesaurus of the Oxford English Dictionary* (*HTOED*), offer a wealth of insights into the semantic biography of individual words (a printout of the current *OED* entry of *gay*, adj., adv., and n., for instance, yields no less than 28 pages of information), and into the dynamics of meaning relations within whole semantic fields.

Despite substantial losses, the creation of new words (**neologisms**) by borrowing, word-formation or semantic change has not only led to a vast increase in the English lexicon, but also to significant alterations in qualitative terms. While the inherited Germanic word-stock is usually noted for its 'basicness' (cf. *father* and *mother*, *eat* and *drink*, *old* and *young*), for its high frequency, and its structural relevance (most function words belong in this etymological category), borrowing has opened up a wide range of stylistic and register-specific distinctions. Under the (somewhat misleading) heading "Synonyms at Three Levels," Baugh and Cable (186–87) list triplets such as *ask—question—interrogate* or *goodness—virtue—probity*, whose "Saxon," French, and Latin element has respectively been classified as 'popular,' 'literary' and 'learned.' Such schematic categorisations can easily be invalidated. There can, however, be no doubt that the architecture of the English lexicon has substantially been altered through contact-induced change. Proceeding from '**consociated**,' i.e. morphosemantically transparent, word families such as OE *faran* (G *fahren*), *fær* (*Fahrzeug*), *faru* (*Fahrt*), *ofer-faran* (*überfahren*), and contrasting them with etymologically unrelated pairs like *son—filial*, *mouth—oral*, Leisi and Mair (51–52) point to a pervasive tendency of '**dissociation**' (*Dissoziation*), or morphosemantic isolation, in large parts of the modern English vocabulary. A look into a dictionary shows, however, that borrowing and word-formation have created new 'consociative' clusters (*judge*, *judgment*; *judicature*, *judicial*, etc.). The exact nature of their relatedness in the minds of contemporary speakers poses challenging questions for Cognitive Linguistics.

Qualitative changes
through word formation

## 3.5 | Variation and Standardisation

And for ther is so gret diversite
In Englissh and in writing of oure tonge,
So prey I God that non miswrite the,
Ne the mysmetre for defaute of tonge;
And red wherso thow be, or elles songe,
That thow be understonde, God I biseche!

(Chaucer, *Troilus and Criseyde* V.1793–98)

The "gret diversite" which Chaucer refers to at the end of his *Troilus* has been a matter of fact "in Englissh" throughout its history. Conscientious writers thus had good reason to be anxious about the authentic presentation and uncorrupted transmission of their works, especially at times when the amount of regulation and regularisation in written and spoken English was a far cry from modern degrees of standardisation. Chaucer's appeal to scribes and performers not to "miswrite" and "mysmetre" his "litel bok" (line 1786) and to present it in an intelligible way may echo a well-established literary convention, but there is no doubt some linguistic reality behind it: in the absence of a commonly acknowledged norm, "defaute of tonge," i.e. lack of familiarity with the author's dialect, could well lead to alterations and corruptions in spelling and pronunciation (and on other linguistic levels), and the instability of the final -*e* /ə/ added yet another uncontrollable feature, putting the poet's carefully designed metre at risk.

The historiography of English has recently been criticised for marginalizing much of the ever-present variation in support of a '**standard language ideology**,' constructed to bestow legitimacy and exclusiveness on the current prestige variety. As James Milroy (549–50) points out, the "historicization of the language requires that it should possess a continuous unbroken history, a respectable and legitimate ancestry and a long pedigree. It is also highly desirable that it should be as pure and unmixed as possible." In his language history with the programmatic title *The Stories of English*, David Crystal (5) takes a highly critical stance towards such "orthodox histories," written in the "mainstream tradition" with a clear focus on Standard (British) English, and stresses the role of diversity as a primary force in the development of the language. Yet, the "real story," told from a nonstandard perspective with due attention to the broad spectrum of varieties and variation, becomes increasingly difficult to tell the further we move away from modern times (Crystal, *Stories of English* 7).

*Criticizing orthodox language histories*

For the earliest stage of English, these difficulties have been addressed from a theoretically informed perspective in a number of thought-provoking contributions by Richard Hogg. In a paper bearing the provocative title "On the impossibility of Old English dialectology" (1988), Hogg opted for a new theoretical and methodological approach to linguistic variation in Old English, free from presuppositions regarding dialectal discreteness and 'purity': "we must get away from the idea of four more or less homogeneous and discrete speech-communities. What we have to do, rather, is see each individual text, or small group of texts, as separate entities" (Hogg 189). But, as he also pointed out (183, 189–90), it is quite impossible to construct a dialect map on the basis of such micro-studies: fact(or)s such as the scarcity and uneven distribution of the surviving material, problems of dating and localizing manuscripts and texts, and standardizing tendencies in late Anglo-Saxon England prevent the compilation of an Old English dialect atlas parallel to the two Middle English ones (cf. below). That textbook accounts (including the present one) nevertheless usually follow the customary division is partly a matter of convenience and didactic necessity, but also due to the fact that at the present state of research an alternative scenario such as the one outlined above is far from being complete.

It is still a matter of dispute how diversified the speech of the Germanic invaders was prior to their settlement in Britain and how the relation between tribal and speech communities developed over time. The four major Old English dialects distinguished in traditional dialectology are roughly located in the following areas:

- **Northumbrian**, north of the Humber;
- **Mercian**, in the midland area between Humber and Thames;
- **Kentish**, in the southeast, covering Kent and Surrey;
- **West Saxon**, in the southern and south-western parts of England.

As Northumbrian and Mercian share a number of common features, they are classed together as **Anglian**.

There are marked discrepancies in the documentation of these major dialects: while Northumbrian, Mercian, and in particular Kentish are only sparsely attested, West Saxon is amply documented for the tenth and eleventh centuries. It is this variety which in the later tenth century provided the dialectal basis for a written norm that has been variously termed '**Standard Old English**' or the "Late West Saxon *Schriftsprache*." Old English is quite unique among the Germanic languages in developing a literary standard with supraregional extension at so early a stage in its history. Traditional accounts that assign King Alfred the Great (871–899) a decisive role in this process have to be dismissed as unfounded, or, in Milroy's terms, as part of the 'standard ideology.' In a seminal article, Helmut Gneuss ("Origin") linked the origin of standardisation in Old English with the Benedictine reform movement and with the activities of one of its main promoters, Bishop Æthelwold of Winchester (963–984). Among his disciples in the cathedral school of the royal capital was Ælfric, Anglo-Saxon England's most prolific prose writer. Gneuss in fact identified two different types of regulated usage that have often been confounded—the so-called 'Winchester vocabulary,' a set of certain, mainly religious, terms that were given systematic preference in texts with a Winchester affiliation, and 'Standard Old English,' an orthographic norm based on the late West Saxon dialect and adhered to in scriptoria throughout Anglo-Saxon England. Texts transliterated into this prestige variety—albeit with an admixture of Anglian forms that gave rise to assumptions of a "general Old English poetic dialect"—include the four great poetic codices (the *Beowulf* and the Junius manuscripts, the Exeter Book, and the Vercelli Book).

The exact nature of the earliest English 'standard' has recently come under critical scrutiny as scholars have tried to apply general models of language standardisation to the situation in Old English. A taxonomy that is still prominent in the field was proposed by Einar Haugen in 1966. Haugen distinguished four crucial dimensions in the evolution of a standard—(1) selection of norm, (2) codification of form, (3) elaboration of function, and (4) acceptance by the community (933)—, and succinctly defined the "ideal goals of a standard language" as "minimal variation in form" along with "maximal variation in function" (931). It seems hardly surprising that Old English cannot pass this test. To allow for a classification that is less rigid and comes closer to historical reality, scholars have followed Jeremy Smith (66) in distinguishing between a 'standard' or 'fixed' and a 'standardised' or 'focused' language. This distinction not only allows one to classify (modern) Received Pronunciation,

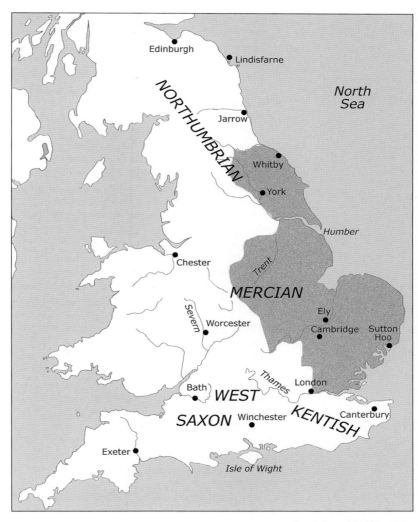

The dialects of Old English and the area of Scandinavian settlement

but also 'Standard Old English' and a number of other medieval literary 'standards' as 'standard*ised*' or 'focused varieties,' i.e. "a centripetal norm towards which speakers [or, as we may add, writers and scribes] tend, rather than a fixed collection of prescribed rules from which any deviation at all is forbidden" (Smith 67–68). Such a modified conceptual approach also appears to do more justice to the role of Ælfric, whose carefully controlled language has all too easily been equated with 'Standard Old English.'

The Norman Conquest brought an end to the productive Old English literary tradition. Texts in the standardised form continued to be copied well into the twelfth century, but French—or, more precisely, Anglo-Norman—now assumed the role of a 'high' language, together with Latin, which continued to serve its elevated functions for literary, official and educational purposes. The vernacular became largely restricted to spoken registers and could thus develop largely uninhibited by conservative regulative forces. As Barbara Strang pointed out, **Middle English** is "par excellence, the dialectal phase of English, in the sense that while dialects have been spoken at all periods, it was in ME that divergent local usage was normally indicated in writing" (224). For the late medieval period from ca. 1350 to 1450 this diversity of written form has been systematically recorded and classified by the *Linguistic Atlas of Late Mediaeval English* (1986). This indispensable research tool broke new ground both in theoretical and methodological respects. The *LALME* takes its material as evidence in its own right, making no assumptions as to how the written forms may have materialised in the spoken language of the time. The compilers also made profitable use of insights gained from dialect atlases of modern languages: by applying the so-called 'fit technique'—a systematic comparison of linguistic profiles consisting in a carefully selected set of features—hitherto unplaced texts and manuscripts were incorporated into a matrix created by localisable 'anchor texts.' The typology of scribal behaviour that emerged from such meticulous research once again confirmed that what we should expect is variation and mixture rather than uniformity and consistency. The *LALME*'s companion piece for the Early Middle English period from 1150 to 1325, the *LAEME*, is currently in the making.

The break 1066 brought about from a 'standard perspective' is not only a diachronic, but also a diatopic one: from the viewpoint of Old English dialectology, the geographical basis for the new prestige norm that started to emerge at the end of the Middle English period was no longer West Saxon, but a sparsely documented subvariety of Anglian: the **East Midland dialect**. It is, however, not only George Puttenham's famous advice to would-be poets in his *Arte of English Poesie* (1589) that leads us to the royal capital as the normative 'trendsetter':

ye shall therefore take the usuall speach of the Court, and that of London and the shires lying about London within lx. myles, and not much above. (qtd. in Baugh and Cable 195)

Baugh and Cable's claim that "[t]he history of Standard English is almost a history of **London English**" (194) holds true if we take into account that 'London English' is an abstraction for a highly diversified linguistic scenario with dialectal input from substantial numbers of immigrants and the necessary infrastructure to provide institutional support for selected forms. In a ground-breaking study of dialect variation in late Middle English manuscripts, M.L. Samuels identified four "types of language that are less obviously dialectal, and can thus cast light on the probable sources of the written standard English that appears in the fifteenth century" (84). Samuels' "Type IV," known as "Chancery English," and represented in the documents issued in the name of the king and the government, has since been propagated as a primary force in the standardisation process (see especially the collected articles of John H. Fisher). Recently though, the notion of a 'Chancery Standard' that served as the immediate ancestor of modern written standard English has come under severe criticism. Michael Benskin's plea is for "a larger study of the beginnings of standard English, in which [...] the Chancery cannot be assigned the leading part" (1).

Fourteenth- and fifteenth-century developments such as the restoration of English "to its dominant place as the language of the country" (Baugh and Cable 149) and its functional extension at the expense of Latin and French were essential preconditions for the **rise of Standard English**. The decisive developments, however, are post-medieval ones. In the wake of the status debate of the sixteenth century, the vernacular turned out to be capable of competing with the major European languages—both classical and modern ones—in a growing number of fields. Increasing elaboration went hand in hand with codification in dictionaries and grammars. Regulation, guided by 'reason,' became a deliberate aim in the eighteenth century, neatly epitomised in Jonathan Swift's "Proposal for Correcting, Improving, and Ascertaining the English Tongue" (1712). Bestsellers like Samuel Johnson's *Dictionary of the English Language* (1755), Robert Lowth's *Short Introduction to English Grammar* (1762), and Lindley Murray's *English Grammar* (1795), with their numerous reprints and revisions, have traditionally been assigned a crucial role in the fixation of certain 'standard' usages and proscriptive rules (such as the notorious "never end a sentence with a preposition"), though again a note of caution seems in order here. Recent research into standardisation has widened its scope from the spelling system as

Instituting a new standard

"the most fully standardised part of standard English" and certain grammatical features to the study of variation and standardisation on all linguistic levels. There, "register variation emerges as one of the key factors setting limits to the codification and generalisation of language standards," with pronunciation—quite unsurprisingly—proving most resistant to regulation (Nevalainen and Tieken-Boon van Ostade 311; see also Mugglestone, *'Talking Proper'*).

## Select Bibliography

Aitchison, Jean. *Language Change: Progress or Decay*. 3rd ed. Cambridge: Cambridge University Press, 2001.

Baugh, Albert C., and Thomas Cable. *A History of the English Language*. 5th ed. London: Routledge, 2002.

Benskin, Michael. "Chancery Standard." *Lexis and Transmission*. Eds. Christian Kay et al. Amsterdam: Benjamins, 2004. 1–40.

Bergs, Alexander, and Laurel Brinton, eds. *English Historical Linguistics: An International Handbook*. 2 vols. Berlin: de Gruyter, 2012.

CHEL: Hogg, Richard M., ed. *The Cambridge History of the English Language*. 6 vols. Cambridge: Cambridge University Press, 1992–2001.

Crystal, David. *The Cambridge Encyclopedia of the English Language*. 2nd ed. Cambridge: Cambridge University Press, 2003.

Crystal, David. *The Stories of English*. London: Allen Lane, 2004.

DOE: Healey, Antonette diPaolo, et al., eds. *Dictionary of Old English in Electronic Form: A to G*. Toronto: University of Toronto Pontifical Institute of Medieval Studies, 2003. 29 Dec. 2011 <www.doe.utoronto.ca/>.

Fischer, Andreas. "Lexical Borrowing and the History of English: A Typology of Typologies." *Language Contact in the History of English*. Eds. Dieter Kastovsky and Arthur Mettinger. 2nd ed. Frankfurt/M.: Lang, 2003. 97–115.

Fischer, Olga. "History of English Syntax." Momma and Matto 57–68.

Fisher, John H. *The Emergence of Standard English*. Lexington: University Press of Kentucky, 1996.

Gneuss, Helmut. *English Language Scholarship: A Survey and Bibliography from the Beginnings to the End of the Nineteenth Century*. Binghamton: Center for Medieval & Early Renaissance Studies, 1996.

Gneuss, Helmut. *Lehnbildungen und Lehnbedeutungen im Altenglischen*. Berlin: Schmidt, 1955.

Gneuss, Helmut. "The Origin of Standard Old English and Æthelwold's School at Winchester." *Anglo-Saxon England* 1 (1972): 63–83.

Görlach, Manfred. *The Linguistic History of English: An Introduction*. Houndmills: Macmillan, 1997.

Haugen, Einar. "Dialect, Language, Nation." *American Anthropologist* 68 (1966): 922–35.

Hogg, Richard M. "On the Impossibility of Old English Dialectology." *Luick Revisited: Papers Read at the Luick-Symposium at Schloss Liechtenstein, 15.-18.9.1985*. Eds. Dieter Kastovsky and Gero Bauer. Tübingen: Narr, 1988. 183–203.

Hogg, Richard, and David Denison, eds. *A History of the English Language*. Cambridge: Cambridge University Press, 2006.

HTOED: Kay, Christian, et al., eds. *Historical Thesaurus of the Oxford English Dictionary, with additional material from A Thesaurus of Old English*. 2 vols. Oxford: Oxford University Press, 2009. 29 Dec. 2011 <http://www.oed.com/thesaurus>.

Joseph, Brian D., and Richard D. Janda, eds. *The Handbook of Historical Linguistics*. Malden: Blackwell, 2003.

Kemenade, Ans van, and Bettelou Los. *The Handbook of the History of English*. Oxford: Blackwell, 2006.

Kitson, Peter R. "When did Middle English begin? Later than you think!" *Studies in Middle English Linguistics*. Ed. Jacek Fisiak. Berlin: de Gruyter, 1997. 221–69.

Labov, William. *Principles of Linguistic Change*. 3 vols. Malden: Wiley-Blackwell, 1994–2010.

LAEME: Laing, Margaret, and Roger Lass. *A Linguistic Atlas of Early Middle English, 1150–1325*. Edinburgh: University of Edinburgh, 2007- . 29 Dec. 2011 <http://www.lel.ed.ac.uk/ihd/laeme1/laeme1.html>.

LALME: McIntosh, Angus, M. L. Samuels, and Michael Benskin. *A Linguistic Atlas of Late Mediaeval English*. 4 vols. Aberdeen: Aberdeen University Press, 1986.

Lass, Roger. *Old English: A Historical Linguistic Companion*. Cambridge: Cambridge University Press, 1994.

Leisi, Ernst, and Christian Mair. *Das heutige Englisch: Wesenszüge und Probleme*. 1955. 9th ed. Heidelberg: Winter, 2008.

Lutz, Angelika. "Types and Degrees of Mixing: A Comparative Assessment of Latin and French Influences on English and German Word Formation." *Interdisciplinary Journal for Germanic Linguistics and Semiotic Analysis* 13 (2008): 131–65.

Lutz, Angelika. "When did English begin?" *Sounds, Words, Texts and Change: Selected Papers from 11 ICEHL, Santiago de Compostela, 7–11 September 2000*. Eds. Teresa Fanego and Elena Seoane. Amsterdam: Benjamins, 2002. 145–71.

McMahon, April. "Restructuring Renaissance English." *The Oxford History of English*. Ed. Lynda Mugglestone. Oxford: Oxford University Press, 2006. 147–77.

MED: Kurath, Hans, et al. *The Middle English Dictionary*. Ann Arbor: University of Michigan Press, 2006. 29 Dec. 2011 <http://quod.lib.umich.edu/m/med/>.

Milroy, James. "Language Ideologies and the Consequences of Standardization." *Journal of Sociolinguistics* 5 (2001): 530–55.

Milroy, James, and Lesley Milroy. *Authority in Language: Investigating Standard English*. 3rd ed. New York: Routledge, 1999.

Moessner, Lilo. *Diachronic English Linguistics: An Introduction*. Tübingen: Narr, 2003.

Momma, Haruko, and Michael Matto, eds. *A Companion to the History of the English Language*. Chichester: Wiley-Blackwell, 2008.

Mugglestone, Lynda, ed. *The Oxford History of English*. Oxford: Oxford University Press, 2006.

Mugglestone, Lynda. *'Talking Proper': The Rise of Accent as a Social Symbol*. 2nd ed. Oxford: Oxford University Press, 2003.

Nevalainen, Terttu, and Ingrid Tieken-Boon van Ostade. "Standardisation." *A History of the English Language*.

Eds. Richard Hogg and David Denison. Cambridge: Cambridge University Press, 2006. 271–311.

**Nevalainen, Terttu, and Elizabeth C. Traugott, eds.** *The Oxford Handbook of the History of English*. Oxford: Oxford University Press, forthcoming.

**Nielsen, Hans Frede.** *A Journey through the History of the English Language in England and America*. 2 vols. Odense: Odense University Press, 1998–2005.

*OED*: **Simpson, John A., ed.** *Oxford English Dictionary Online*. 3rd ed. (in progress). Oxford: Oxford University Press, 2000. 29 Dec. 2011 <http://www.oed.com/>.

**Samuels, M. L.** "Some Applications of Middle English Dialectology." *English Studies* 44 (1963): 81–94.

**Scheler, Manfred.** *Der englische Wortschatz*. Berlin: Erich Schmidt, 1977.

**Smith, Jeremy.** *An Historical Study of English: Function, Form and Change*. London: Routledge, 1996.

**Strang, Barbara.** *A History of English*. London: Methuen, 1970.

**Sweet, Henry.** *A History of English Sounds from the Earliest Period*. Oxford: Clarendon Press, 1888.

**Sweet, Henry.** *The History of Language*. London: Dent, 1900.

**Thomason, Sarah G., and Terrence Kaufman.** *Language Contact, Creolization and Genetic Linguistics*. Berkeley: University of California Press, 1988.

**Tristram, Hildegard.** "Diglossia in Anglo-Saxon England, or What Was Spoken Old English Like?" *Studia Anglica Posnaniensia* 40 (2004): 87–110.

**Vennemann, Theo.** "English as a Contact Language: Typology and Comparison." *Anglia* 129 (2011): 217–57.

*Lucia Kornexl/Dirk Schultze*

# 4 Forms and Structures

As the preceding entry on historical linguistics and language change has shown, the structure of present-day English—its sound system, its grammar and its vocabulary—is the result of almost 1,500 years of historical evolution. Many factors—both internal to the linguistic system and external (historical, social, cultural)—have influenced this process, their influence varying in strength from period to period and depending on the particular structural domains affected. The overall result has been a structural profile of present-day English which is rather different from the historically related languages of Europe with which it has been in continuous contact. This "synchronic" structural profile will be the focus of the present chapter, which will introduce the reader to the sound patterns of English (the subject of the linguistic sub-disciplines of **phonetics** and **phonology**), its words (whose form is studied in **morphology** and **word-formation** and whose meaning is dealt with in **semantics**), and its grammar (largely covered by **syntax**, the study of how words and phrases combine to form clauses and sentences). Given the available space, coverage cannot be complete. Basic design features of present-day English will be discussed in an exemplary fashion, and the author's hope is that readers will take these examples as a starting point for further study and exploration.

Before embarking on a structural sketch of a language, it is necessary to introduce a distinction which has been central to linguistic research since the work of Ferdinand de Saussure, one of the founding figures of modern linguistics (cf. section V.2.2.1). De Saussure distinguished between the levels of

- *langue*, the structural system of a specific individual language;
- *parole*, the concrete manifestation of this system in an individual speaker's utterance or an individual writer's text.

The rationale for this distinction is obvious. We continue to be speakers of a language regardless of whether we are talking or writing in it at a particular moment or not. In other words: there is a sense in which a language exists and can be described independent of the concrete spoken utterance or written text (and even independent of the individual speaker) as the decontextualised underlying system of structural choices collectively available to a community sharing it as a means of communication. Other theoretical approaches, such as Chomskyan generative grammar (cf. section V.2.4.1), suggest a similar distinction between **performance** (comparable to Saussure's *parole*) and **competence**. The latter denotes the human individual's ability to learn and use his or her native language; it is seen as a psycho-cognitive faculty that is part of a human being's genetic endowment. As can be seen from this definition, there is less emphasis on the social nature of language in this tradition than in Saussurean structuralism. Both, however, agree that while *parole* (or performance) provide the immediate observational data for linguistic description the object of linguistic inquiry is to be found on a more abstract level.

Saussure's distinction between *langue* and *parole* is central to modern linguistics.

The Saussurean separation of levels—and the prioritisation of the more abstract one—is absolutely essential to a coherent and efficient description of a language, as the following brief example will illustrate. Imagine a speaker saying:

**Whatcha gonna say about the plans that he is—eh, ehm—so anxious to be put into practice?**

As part of a longer conversation this utterance makes perfect sense. However, it contains at least three features with which we would not want to burden a structural description of English. First, it contains hesitation phenomena (filled pauses, here transcribed as *eh* and *ehm*) which play no role in the grammatical construction but merely point to temporary problems the speaker experiences in recalling the appropriate lexical item from memory. The sequence *whatcha gonna* [wɒtʃə ɡɒnə] is a fast-speech variant of *what are you going to* which is perfectly natural and may be very frequent, but nevertheless it is obvious that a structural sketch of English should refer first to the full underlying forms *what, are, you* etc. and then selectively refer to some of the modifications these forms may undergo on the level of *parole*. Finally, the utterance contains a grammatical construction which is of dubious status. We can see this if we re-phrase the relevant part of the utterance by going back to the main clause which presumably is the basic or underlying form of the relative-clause construction *the plans that he is so anxious to be put into practice*:

**\*He is anxious the plans to be put into practice.**

This does not work, which is why, by convention, the example is marked with an asterisk (\*). (Note that while in synchronically orientated linguistic description, this symbol marks the fact that an example is ungrammatical, in diachronic linguistics it merely indicates that a form is re-constructed but not actually attested.)
The minimum necessary modification required to make the ill-formed example sentence grammatical is to insert *for* before the noun phrase *the plans*: *He is anxious **for** the plans to be put into practice*. Other options are *He is anxious that the plans should be put into practice* or *He is anxious that the plans be put into practice*. What has happened in our case is that these three options have been conflated in illicit ways—presumably because of the relative-clause environment, which blocks the use of the infinitival variant and complicates the deployment of the two finite-clause ones. *\*The plans which he is so anxious for to be carried out* is not grammatical, and the two finite clauses work only if *that* is omitted: *the plans which he is so anxious (\*that) (should) be carried out*. In the trade-off between the pressures on the level of *parole*, where the speaker has to produce a communicatively efficient utterance in real time (and in a very short time at that!) and the requirements for grammatical correctness (in the sense of conformity to the rules formulated at the level of Saussurean *langue*), the latter has lost out here. However, no grammatical description would take the occasional use of such irregular utterances as counter-examples to otherwise well-founded rules for the use of grammatical constructions.

## 4.1 | The Sound Pattern of English

The sounds of a language are described in the linguistic sub-disciplines of phonetics and phonology. The two share their object of study, the sounds of human language, including such phenomena as stress and intonation, but they approach it from two complementary perspectives. This difference is reflected in a different terminology. The central unit for phonetics is the speech sound as a concrete physical object on the level of *parole*, also referred to as the **phone**. The central unit of phonology is the **phoneme**, an abstract unit at the level of *langue*. This fundamental difference in perspective has the following important consequences.

Phonetics approaches speech sounds as natural, physical and physiological phenomena, and a phonetic transcription of an utterance will therefore aim at surface accuracy and rich detail. In a phonetic description of the vowel in the English word *band*, for example, we would point out that it sounds rather different in British and American Standard English (that is in the internationally familiar reference standards of "Received Pronunciation" (RP) and "General American," cf. section

V.6.3). Even greater **variability** may be found in individual British and American regional accents, from Glasgow and Liverpool to Detroit and Alabama. As phoneticians we would try to capture this acoustic impression through phonetic transcription symbols and appropriate technical terminology (on which see below). Suffice it to say here that such phonetic (or "narrow") transcriptions are usually placed between square brackets: [band], [bænd], [bɛnd], [bɪənd]. The number of possible realisations of the vowel sound in this word could be extended by looking at further dialects or merely by refining our techniques of measurement. Indeed it is not possible to give a precise answer to the question of how many distinct realisations of the vowel in *band* there are if we remain on the purely phonetic level.

Deep down, however, we "know" that, the different accents notwithstanding, British and American speakers, or dialect and standard speakers, use the "same" vowel when they pronounce the word *band*. Regardless of the differences, in all the dialects mentioned the contrast between *band* and *bind*, or *band* and *bound*, will be maintained. Such pairs of words, in which the contrast in meaning between two words depends on the contrast of exactly one sound, are called **minimal pairs**, and these minimal pairs are the key to a phonological rather than phonetic perspective on the sounds of human speech. Sounds which are capable of distinguishing meaning in a particular language in such minimal pairs represent phonemes. Phonemic (or "broad") transcriptions appear between slashes: /bænd/ is the only transcription needed for the word *band* at the phonological level for practically all dialects of English, and the many individual realisations of the phoneme /æ/ listed in square brackets above would be regarded as "allophones" of this one abstract sound. To put it in other words: what phonology does is not just look at a concrete sound as a physical object or a product of the human physiological speech apparatus, but at the abstract sound as an element in a language-specific system, which provides the basic mechanism for speakers to distinguish meaning.

Regardless of whether we are "doing" phonetics or phonology, however, we need a system of transcription which helps us visualise on the page what we hear. One of the oldest such systems, and certainly the most widely accepted one, is that first proposed by the International Phonetic Association (IPA) in the late nineteenth century and con-

| **Definition** |
| --- |

→ **Phonetics** deals with the sounds of human speech as physical phenomena, studying how they are produced in the human speech apparatus (articulatory phonetics), how they are transmitted (acoustic phonetics) and how they are perceived (auditory phonetics).
→ **Phonology** studies the organisation of the sound systems of specific languages. The central term in phonology is the phoneme, which is capable of distinguishing meanings in minimal pairs (i.e. pairs of words of different meaning which differ in exactly one sound), such as, for example, *pat-bat, rope-robe, pat-rat, robe-lobe*, etc.

tinually developed ever since. As this **phonetic alphabet** is designed to capture the sounds of all languages of the world, or all the possible speech sounds which human beings can produce, it contains many more symbols than the student of English (or German) has need for. Speech sounds are generally grouped into two major classes: if the air stream coming through the mouth (or nose) in the articulation of a sound is never blocked or obstructed completely, we have a vowel; if there is some kind of blockage or obstruction (for example the lips remaining closed or the tip of the tongue pressing against the upper teeth), we have a consonant.

In the IPA system, vowels are classified as front, central or back, depending on which part of the tongue is active in their production, and as close, mid, or open, depending on how far the active part of the tongue is raised.

In this diagram, [i] figures as a "close and front" vowel because it is articulated in the front of the mouth and with the front part of the tongue close to the palate. The vowel [a], by contrast, is a "front

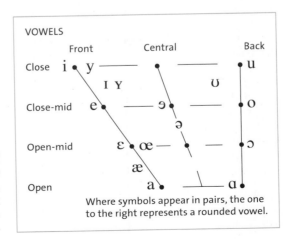

Where symbols appear in pairs, the one to the right represents a rounded vowel.

IPA symbols for vowels

| Vowels and Diphthongs in RP and GA | | | RP | GA |
|---|---|---|---|---|
| **I. Front Vowels** | | | | |
| /iː/ | long closed front vowel | *fleece* | + | + |
| /ɪ/ | short closed front vowel | *kit* | + | + |
| /ɛ/ | short half-open front vowel | *dress* | + | + |
| /æ/ | short open front vowel | *trap* | + | + |
| **II. Central Vowels** | | | | |
| /ɜː/ | long rounded half-open central vowel | *nurse* | + | – |
| /ɝ/ | short rounded half-open central vowel | *nurse* | – | + |
| /ə/ | short half-open central vowel | *letter* | + | + |
| /ʌ/ | short open central vowel | *strut* | + | + |
| **III. Back Vowels** | | | | |
| /uː/ | long rounded closed back vowel | *goose* | + | + |
| /ʊ/ | short rounded closed back vowel | *foot* | + | + |
| /ɔː/ | long rounded half-open back vowel | *force* | + | + |
| /ɑː/ | long open back vowel | *calm* | + | + |
| /ɒ/ | short open back vowel | *cloth* | + | – |
| **IV. Diphthongs** | | | | |
| /aɪ/ | raising diphthong | *price* | + | + |
| /eɪ/ | raising diphthong | *face* | + | + |
| /aʊ/ | raising diphthong | *mouth* | + | + |
| /ɔɪ/ | raising diphthong | *choice* | + | + |
| /əʊ/ | raising diphthong | *goat* | + | – |
| /oʊ/ | raising diphthong | *goat* | – | + |
| /ɪə/ | centring diphthong | *near* | + | – |
| /eə/ | centring diphthong | *square* | + | – |
| /ʊə/ | centring diphthong | *sure* | + | – |

and open" vowel because it is articulated with the tip of the tongue lowered. Diphthongs, i.e. complex vowel sounds, are transcribed by combining their starting and end points. For example, [aɪ] is a diphthong which is produced by a movement of the tongue from the "front and open" to the "front and close" position. For easy reference, the following two charts list the vowel phonemes of the British and American standard accents (R.P. and General American). The two systems are very similar but the British one contains an extra vowel phoneme ([ɒ], as in *shock, hot,* or *stop*) in the back range and a few more diphthongs which are usually rendered as sequences of simple vowels + [r] in American English (e.g. in /bɪə/ vs. /biːr/ for *beer*).

The consonants are defined along three dimensions. The first is **place of articulation**: where in the mouth (or nasal cavity) does the obstruction of the air stream take place? The second is **mode of articulation**: how is the air stream obstructed, by a brief total closure, as in the plosive sounds, or by friction, as in the fricative? The third dimension is **voicing**, with "voiced" sounds showing vibrations of the vocal cords, and "voiceless" sounds showing no such vibration.

The English consonant phoneme /t/ thus presents itself as alveolar on the first dimension (place of articulation): the tongue presses against the "alveolar" ridge just behind the front teeth in its production. On the second dimension (mode of articulation), it is a plosive, as it involves a brief moment of total obstruction or closure of the air stream rather than mere friction. On the third dimension (voicing), it falls into the voiceless class, as the vocal cords are not involved in its production. The sound /s/, by comparison, emerges as a voiceless alveolar fricative, sharing with /t/ its place of articulation but not its mode (friction instead of complete closure).

The following diagram presents the present-day Standard English consonantal phonemes. Strictly speaking, we could do with one column for both British and American English here, as the consonant systems are phonologically identical in the two varieties. However, on the level of phonetic realisation—indicated by square brackets—there are some practically relevant contrasts in the treatment of /t/ and /r/. American /t/s are flapped /ɾ/ when they appear between a stressed and unstressed vowel, as in *water, butter* or *Italy*. If the second vowel is stressed, as in *retire*, the /t/ also remains a plosive ([t]) on the phonetic level.

For students of English, some knowledge of phonetics and phonology is important, not least because it will help them to understand the causes of the foreign or learner accent that they are trying to combat in their practical pronunciation classes. Consider, for example, the contrastive surveys of the phoneme inventories of (Standard) German and British English (RP) on p. 418–19, which show some clear points of mismatch between the two systems.

Not unexpectedly, the points where the two systems do not map onto each other represent well-known **pronunciation problems** for learners—either way. For native speakers of English learning German, for example, the German umlaut vowels will be difficult, as they involve a degree of lip-rounding which is unusual from an English perspective. Conversely, there are different phonemic front vowel distinctions in English than in German, and this leads to learners of English often collapsing the distinction between [e] and [æ] by articulating both in the same way—roughly as German [ɛ]. Minimal pairs such as *bet—bat* or *celery—salary* are then no longer kept distinct in this way. There are similar phenomena among the consonants, English /ð/ and /θ/ being prime examples. Beginners fail to distinguish *think* and *sink*, and even advanced learners keep saying [dɪs] for [ðɪs].

The one feature of a German accent which is probably hardest to erase, however, is due to a different cause. German learners of English consistently fail to produce voiced consonants in sylla-

ble-final position. The contrast between voiced and voiceless consonants is phonemic in German, just as it is in English, as is apparent from minimal pairs such as *heißer—heiser* or *rauben—Raupen*. Thus, native speakers of German can hear the difference between /p/ and /b/, or /s/ and /z/, in principle. Note, however, that while in English the opposition is found syllable-initially, syllable-medially and syllable-finally, in German it is system-

## Focus on English Phonology

English is a language whose inventory of vowel/diphthong and consonant phonemes is slightly more numerous and probably also somewhat **more complex** than some of the more basic ones described for the world's languages. For example, there is no straightforward phonemic contrast between long and short vowels, but a phonological contrast between tense and lax vowels which correlates with phonetic length in complex ways. Also, English allows rather complex consonant clusters in syllable-initial and syllable-final position. An aspect of this greater complexity which is of immediate practical relevance to German learners can be found in the syllable-final position, where the voicing contrast is present in English but not in German. The most unsystematic, intransparent and therefore difficult-to-master aspect of English pronunciation, however, is stress in polysyllabic words (i.e. words consisting of three or more syllables).

Two convenient **introductions** to English phonetics and phonology, with useful accompanying compact discs, are those by Skandera and Burleigh and by Gut. Gimson is an authoritative reference work on Standard British RP, while Jones is the classic British pronunciation dictionary, which has charted the development of standard pronunciations of words since 1917. The pronouncing dictionaries by Wells and by Upton, Kretzschmar and Konopka also provide information on American pronunciations. The *PRAAT: Doing Phonetics by Computer* website offers free software for instrumental phonetic analysis. For weblinks and detailed information see section VII.2.3.

| Consonants in RP and GA | | | RP | GA |
|---|---|---|---|---|
| **I. Plosives** | | | | |
| /p/ | voiceless bilabial plosive | *pan, spill* | + | + |
| /b/ | voiced bilabial plosive | *boat, baby* | + | + |
| /t/ | voiceless alveolar plosive | *tin, still* | + | + |
| [ɾ] | alveolar flap/tap | *city, winter* | − | + |
| [ʔ] | glottal stop | *bottle, but* | + | − |
| /d/ | voiced alveolar plosive | *dark, seed* | + | + |
| /k/ | voiceless velar plosive | *corn, sick* | + | + |
| /g/ | voiced velar plosive | *gold, wig* | + | + |
| **II. Fricatives** | | | | |
| /f/ | voiceless labiodental fricative | *far, off* | + | + |
| /v/ | voiced labiodental fricative | *vet, love* | + | + |
| /θ/ | voiceless dental fricative | *teeth, thief* | + | + |
| /ð/ | voiced dental fricative | *the, (to) teeth* | + | + |
| /s/ | voiceless alveolar fricative | *see, miss* | + | + |
| /z/ | voiced alveolar fricative | *zoo, dogs* | + | + |
| /ʃ/ | voiceless post-alveolar fricative | *shop, flash* | + | + |
| /ʒ/ | voiced post-alveolar fricative | *garage* | + | + |
| /h/ | voiceless glottal fricative | *help* | + | + |
| **III. Affricates** | | | | |
| /ʧ/ | voiceless post-alveolar affricate | *church, match* | + | + |
| /ʤ/ | voiced post-alveolar affricate | *jam, bridge* | + | + |
| **IV. Nasals** | | | | |
| /m/ | bilabial nasal | *meat, woman* | + | + |
| /n/ | alveolar nasal | *nose, winner* | + | + |
| /ŋ/ | velar nasal | *song* | + | + |
| **V. Approximants** | | | | |
| /l/ | alveolar lateral | *live, ball* | + | + |
| /w/ | bilabial glide | *way, wheel* | + | + |
| /j/ | palatal glide | *use, computer* | + | + |
| /r/ | approximant | *rich, sorrow* | + | + |
| [ɹ] | post-alveolar roll | *road, boring* | + | − |
| [ɻ] | retroflex roll | *right, car* | − | + |

| Vowels in RP and German | | | RP | German |
|---|---|---|---|---|
| **I. Front Vowels** | | | | |
| /iː/ | long closed front vowel | *fleece* | + | + |
| /ɪ/ | short closed front vowel | *kit* | + | + |
| /yː/ | long rounded closed front vowel | *Mühle* | – | + |
| /ʏ/ | short rounded closed front vowel | *Müller* | – | + |
| /eː/ | long half-closed front vowel | *Mehl* | – | + |
| /øː/ | long rounded half-closed front vowel | *Höhle* | – | + |
| /ɛː/ | long half-open front vowel | *Bär* | – | + |
| /ɛ/ | short half-open front vowel | *dress* | + | + |
| /œ/ | short rounded half-open front vowel | *Hölle* | – | + |
| /æ/ | short open front vowel | *trap* | + | – |
| **II. Central Vowels** | | | | |
| /ɜː/ | long rounded half-open central vowel | *nurse* | + | – |
| /ə/ | short half-open central vowel | *letter* | + | – |
| /ʌ/ | short open central vowel | *strut* | + | – |
| /aː/ | long open central vowel | *Bad* | – | + |
| /a/ | short open central vowel | *Matte* | – | + |
| **III. Back Vowels** | | | | |
| /uː/ | long rounded closed back vowel | *goose* | + | + |
| /ʊ/ | short rounded closed back vowel | *foot* | + | + |
| /oː/ | long rounded half-closed back vowel | *Kohle* | – | + |
| /ɔː/ | long rounded half-open back vowel | *force* | + | – |
| /ɔ/ | short rounded half-open back vowel | *Sonne* | – | + |
| /ɑː/ | long open back vowel | *bath* | + | – |
| /ɒ/ | short open back vowel | *cloth* | + | – |
| **IV. Diphthongs** | | | | |
| /aɪ/ | raising diphthong | *price* | + | + |
| /eɪ/ | raising diphthong | *face* | + | – |
| /aʊ/ | raising diphthong | *mouth* | + | + |
| /ɔɪ/ | raising diphthong | *choice* | + | + |
| /əʊ/ | raising diphthong | *goat* | + | – |
| /oʊ/ | raising diphthong | *goat* | – | – |
| /ɪə/ | centering diphthong | *near* | + | – |
| /eə/ | centering diphthong | *square* | + | – |
| /ʊə/ | centering diphthong | *sure* | + | – |

atically absent from the final position (and even from the initial position for some sounds in some dialects). The problem of final devoicing (or "Auslautverhärtung") affects all fricatives, affricates and plosives. Any of the following English minimal pairs are thus potential problems for German learners:

tap—tab; leaf—leave; rice—rise; lout—loud; teeth—teethe; lock—log; rich—ridge

Taking a few new expressions from the domain of computing, it is easy to see that *grid* should not be pronounced as *grit*, nor should *cloud computing* come out as *clout computing*, and *are you locked in?* is very different from an intended *are you logged in?*

What examples such as these show is that the linguistic description of a language on the level of *langue*, i.e. of language seen as an abstract, decontextualised system, is not merely an academic end in itself, satisfying the curiosity of the theoretical linguist, but does have **practical relevance** and applications for the work of all sorts of language professionals, from translators and teachers to speech therapists. With regard to the issue of foreign accents, even beginning students of English are likely to profit from some exposure to phonetics and phonology, if they are willing to relate their linguistics teaching to their pronunciation classes.

Phonotactics. So far our discussion has centred on individual speech sounds, which have been approached from the phonetic and phonological perspectives. But even a short introduction should at least briefly mention the supra-segmental domain, with all those many interesting phenomena which extend beyond the single segment in the sound chain. The sounds of a language do not occur in any possible sequence or combination. For example, German contains a lot of words starting in /tsv/ (*zwei, Zwiebel*, etc.), whereas English has none. There are thus clear language-specific constraints that regulate which sounds can occur in which position in the word or syllable. The study of such constraints is the domain of phonotactics. Languages differ considerably with regard to which syllable structures they allow or prefer. If we use the symbol C to refer to any consonant and V to refer to any vowel or diphthong, the structure of the very simple syllable *go* could be represented as CV. Compared to many other languages in the world, English allows very complex clusterings of consonants, be it in syllable-initial or -final position, for example syllables of the abstract pattern CCCVCCC or, if we allow grammatical endings such as the plural *s*, even CCCVCCCC, as in *strengths* [strɛŋkθs]. However, the type of consonant admissible in such clusters and the order in which they are arranged is severely restricted. While the syllable-initial sequence /str-/ is common, /tsr-/ or /rts-/ are not.

Word stress is another important supra-segmental phenomenon. Every English word of more than one syllable has at least one main stress, indicated by ' in the transcription. The word *graphical*, for instance, has a stressed first syllable and two unstressed syllables following it:

['græfɪk(ə)l]

The placement of word stress in present-day English is extremely complicated. Owing to a history of extensive language contact, the language contains elements of three partially incompatible stress systems today: a Germanic one which usually favours stress on the root syllable (in practice often the initial syllable, e.g. '*follow*), a French one which calls for accent on the final syllable (*de'scend*), and one influenced by the movable stress of Latin and Greek (e.g. '*photograph*, *pho'tographer*, *photo'graphical*). Note that over time many borrowed words from French and the classical languages have adopted "Germanic" initial stress (e.g. *nature*, *category*), and some are variable (e.g. *address*, *garage*).

In addition to word-stress, there is, of course, also **sentence stress**. Sentence stress is best treated together with **intonation** as both interact in highlighting important content in an utterance. In spite of its immense importance to the spoken language, linguists have not yet been able to agree on a generally accepted notational system comparable to the IPA symbols used for the individual sound segments. But in principle, the basic intonational unit is structured around a stressed nucleus on which a pitch movement occurs (spelled in capitals in the following examples), a pre-nuclear onset, and a coda. In the most neutral reading of the following sentence, *friend* is the nucleus, showing a falling intonation, *he's your* is the onset and *then* the coda:

| he's your | FRIEND | then |
|-----------|--------|------|
| **onset** | **nucleus** | **coda** |

In an appropriate context, for example if we want to emphasise that the person in question is *your* friend rather than someone else's, the nucleus can, of course, shift back to *your*, and *friend then* together will be the coda.

| he's | YOUR | friend then |
|------|------|-------------|
| onset | nucleus | coda |

**Weak forms.** In yet another context, even the very first word of the tone-group might receive stress:

| Consonants in RP and German | | | RP | German |
|---|---|---|---|---|
| **I. Plosives** | | | | |
| /p/ | voiceless bilabial plosive | *pan, spill* | + | + |
| /b/ | voiced bilabial plosive | *boat, baby* | + | + |
| /t/ | voiceless alveolar plosive | *tin, still* | + | + |
| /d/ | voiced alveolar plosive | *dark, seed* | + | + |
| /k/ | voiceless velar plosive | *corn, sick* | + | + |
| /g/ | voiced velar plosive | *gold, wig* | + | + |
| **II. Fricatives** | | | | |
| /f/ | voiceless labiodental fricative | *far, off* | + | + |
| /v/ | voiced labiodental fricative | *vet, love* | + | + |
| /θ/ | voiceless dental fricative | *teeth, thief* | + | − |
| /ð/ | voiced dental fricative | *the, (to) teeth* | + | − |
| /s/ | voiceless alveolar fricative | *see, miss* | + | + |
| /z/ | voiced alveolar fricative | *zoo, dogs* | + | + |
| /ʃ/ | voiceless post-alveolar fricative | *shop, flash* | + | + |
| /ʒ/ | voiced post-alveolar fricative | *garage* | + | − |
| /x/ | voiceless dorsal fricative | *Licht, Loch* | − | + |
| /h/ | voiceless glottal fricative | *help* | + | + |
| **III. Affricates** | | | | |
| /ʧ/ | voiceless post-alveolar affricate | *church, match* | + | + |
| /ʤ/ | voiced post-alveolar affricate | *jam, bridge* | + | + |
| /pf/ | voiceless bilabial affricate | *Pfau, Topf* | − | + |
| /ts/ | voiceless alveolar affricate | *Zug, Katze* | − | + |
| **IV. Nasals** | | | | |
| /m/ | bilabial nasal | *meat, woman* | + | + |
| /n/ | alveolar nasal | *nose, winner* | + | + |
| /ŋ/ | velar nasal | *song* | + | + |
| **V. Approximants** | | | | |
| /l/ | alveolar lateral | *live, ball* | + | + |
| /w/ | bilabial glide | *way, wheel* | + | − |
| /j/ | palatal glide | *use, computer* | + | + |
| /ɹ/ | post-alveolar roll | *road, boring* | + | − |
| /ʀ/ | uvular roll | *Reise, Haare* | − | + |

*HE's your friend then.* Note in this connection that words such as articles, prepositions, conjunctions and pronouns (i.e. all words which have primarily grammatical function) are usually unstressed in connected speech. Our demonstration tone group contains a relevant example—the auxiliary verb *is*, which would be pronounced [ɪz] in isolation but is reduced to [z] here. Other possible reduced pronunciations of this word that we encounter in connected speech are [s] (after voiceless consonants) or [əz]. The reduced pronunciations of such grammatical words are also known as weak forms.

Many of them contain the vowel [ə], which also happens to be the only English vowel which does not occur in stressed syllables.

## 4.2 | Word Formation

Unlike technical terms such as *phoneme* or *prepositional object*, the concept of *word* is firmly part of our everyday language. However, this does not mean that we can straightforwardly use it in linguistic analysis. While the status of forms such as *table*, *fire*, *greed* (or their German analogues *Tisch*, *Feuer* and *Gier*) as words seems uncontroversial, what about *medical student* and *Medizinstudent*? Have we got two words in English and only one in German, although the two expressions are translation equivalents of each other? How about *critical student*? Is *medical student*, which is superficially parallel, one word because the paraphrase is not just "a student who is medical" (as in "critical student = a student who is critical")? How about contractions such as *isn't* (← *is not*), *zum* (← *zu dem*) or *wanna* (← *want to*)? Many further complications could be added.

*Morpheme, morph, allomorph*

To cut an orderly path into this messy swamp, there is no way around coining another technical term—the **morpheme**. As with the phoneme, the morpheme is an abstract unit, whose concrete realisations are referred to as **morphs**. Thus the morphs which serve as realisations of the same abstract morpheme are called **allomorphs**. By convention, morphemes are represented in curly brackets. For example, the plural morpheme {S} has the following concrete phonetic realisations or allomorphs: [s] as in *cats*, [z] as in *girls*, and [ɪz], as in *buses*. While the phoneme is the smallest linguistic unit capable of distinguishing meaning, the morpheme is the smallest linguistic unit bearing a meaning of its own. Morphemes can be subdivided in several ways. **Free** morphemes can stand alone whereas **bound** morphemes need a free morpheme to which they can be attached. **Lexical** morphemes are an open class, and members have a very specific meaning, for example nouns such as *house*, *pity* or *glory*, verbs such as *to steal*, *to defend* or *to move*, adjectives such as *happy* or *cheap*, and adverbs such as *quickly* or *intelligently*. **Grammatical** morphemes, on the other hand, such as the plural {S}, have a more abstract and general meaning, which is not usually recorded in dictionaries.

While there is a natural correlation between "free" status and "lexical" function of a morpheme (and, by implication, between "bound" status and "grammatical" function), the facts of English are a little more complex, as shown in the cross-tabulation below.

As can be seen, there are elements such as *-cracy*, whose meaning is clearly lexical ("government by") and which nevertheless cannot stand alone. On the other hand the *to* in *give a present to someone* has lost its spatial meaning ("movement toward a goal"), which for example we clearly have in *carry the present to the house*, and just marks the grammatical relation of "receiver." This is why we can say *give someone a present*, but not *\*carry the house the present*.

Words are thus made up of morphemes, the simplest case being a word which consists of just one morpheme, such as—our examples above—*table*, *fire* or *greed*. Other words are more complex. *Overambitiousness* or *motor vehicles*, for example, consist of two free morphemes (*ambitious*, *over*; *motor*, *vehicle*) and one bound one (*-ness*; *-s*) respectively. Note that in spite of the structural parallel, there is an important functional contrast. The

| | free | bound |
|---|---|---|
| lexical | *table, fire, greed, ...* | *electro-* (e.g. *electrocardiography*) <br> *-cracy* (e.g. *aristocracy, meritocracy, democracy*), <br> *-phile* (e.g. *Anglophile, Francophile*) |
| grammatical | *of* (e.g. *cover of the book*) <br> *to* (e.g. *give a present to someone*) <br> *on* (e.g. *depend on*) | plural (*tables, fires, ...*) <br> past (*played, fired, ...*) <br> comparative (*hungrier, cheaper, ...*) |

*Four major types of English morphemes*

function of -*ness* in *overambitiousness* is to derive a new noun from an adjective and thus add a new word to the vocabulary of English. In other words, we are dealing with **word formation**, the creation of new words. The function of the *s* in *motor vehicles*, on the other hand, is a grammatical one—to make an existing word fit for use in a certain grammatical construction (e.g. before a verb not marked for singular) or to modify its reference (to more than one object rather than just one). This latter process is referred to as **inflection** and will be discussed again in section 4.4 below.

Here, we shall conclude with a very brief survey of the most common types of word formation in present-day English.

**Compounding.** A compound is a word which consists of at least two free morphemes. The most common types of compound in English (and German) are noun + noun compounds of the "head + modifier" type: *apple-pie*, *crime statistics*, *bookshop*. An apple pie is a kind of pie made with apples, crime statistics, and a bookshop is a kind of shop selling books. Note that, in contrast to German, spelling rules for English compounds are not very consistent. Thus, I could have written *book-shop* or even *book shop* without a difference. In present-day English, compounds with more than two elements are quite common. While everybody reading newspapers might be able to work out for themselves what the *nuclear energy safety authority director* means, terms such as *variable-region heavy chain 11-mer peptides* are meaningful only to specialists in particular fields. Words such as *blackboard* or *hot dog* illustrate adjective + noun compounds, and *to kick-start* or *to stir-fry* are two of the small number of verb + verb compounds.

Compounds can also be classified according to the semantic relation existing between their elements. The most common type is the **endocentric** compound, in which the first element modifies the second element, or "head." Thus, a *book shop* is a kind of *shop*, like a *jewellery shop*, or a *flower shop*. More fine-grained analysis is possible: thus *corner shop* is also an endocentric compound, but the relation between the modifier and the head is different: a shop on the corner. **Exocentric** compounds have no modifier-head structure. Thus, a *pickpocket* is not a kind of pocket, but refers to a criminal picking other people's pockets. **Copulative** compounds like *to stir-fry* or *writer-director* can be paraphrased by phrases with *and*: "stir and fry"

and someone who is "a writer and a director at the same time," respectively.

Given the analytical grammatical structure of English (see section 4.4 below for an explanation and illustration) and its orthographic conventions, it is very difficult in Modern English to systematically distinguish between grammatical constructions or phrases on the one hand and compounds (i.e. an instance of a complex word), on the other. Compare, for example, the two following noun + noun sequences:

- race problem
- London problem

It is only through applying certain transformation tests that we can establish *race problem* as a lexical unit, and *London problem* as a phrasal one. In *race problem*, we cannot modify *race* or put in material between the modifier and the head, because the noun + noun sequence is an integral complex word; in *London problem*, by contrast, we can modify *London* (e.g. by an adverb: *a largely London problem*) or separate the two nouns: *an almost exclusively London social problem*. Sometimes, stress can be a good clue to the status of a sequence. For example, adjective + noun sequences with stress on the first syllable tend to be compounds (*'blackboard*, *'hothouse*), whereas those with stress on the noun, or level stress, tend to be phrases: *black board*, *hot house*. In these two cases, spelling conforms to pronunciation, but with *short story* (*short-story*, *shortstory*), neither pronunciation nor spelling is a fully reliable clue as to whether we are talking about the literary genre or merely a story which is short.

Another category worth mentioning is the **neo-classical** compounds, which typically consist of morphemes of Latin or Greek origin. Unlike straightforward borrowings from these languages (of which English has many, too), they did not exist as words in the classical languages but were assembled from their constituent parts much later in English or other modern European languages. Examples are particularly common among the technical terms of the various sciences or in learned and academic registers and include words such as *electrocardiography*, *television*, or *Anglophile*. As these cases show, neo-classical compounds frequently feature bound lexical morphemes (e.g. *Anglo-*, *cardio-*, or *-graphy*) or combine Greek and Latin elements (e.g. television, from Greek *tele* "far" and Latin *visio*, "sight"). As contemporary lexical innovations such as *Anglo* ("an English-speaking resident of the U.S. of

Distinguishing compounds from phrasal constructions

British or other European extraction," as opposed to Blacks and Hispanics) or *electro-pop* show, some neo-classical morphemes have entered the more general vocabulary of present-day English as independent words or developed into productive word-formation devices in their own right (see below on "combining forms").

**Derivation** is a process which derives a new word from an existing base by means of adding at least one bound derivational morpheme. Thus, we can add the **prefix** *un-* to the base *happy* to produce another adjective with roughly the opposite meaning, or we can add the suffix *-ness* to create the noun *happiness*. We can also combine the two and derive the noun *unhappiness* from *unhappy*. Note that in English, unlike German, the negative prefix does not combine with simple nouns (as, e.g., in *Unglück* ← *Glück, Unmensch* ← *Mensch*, etc.).

In simple cases such as this one, we get the impression that derivation is largely a process of just sticking morphemes in front or behind their bases. Note, however, that very often, derivation involves a large degree of phonetic irregularity. The verb *act* ends in /t/; the corresponding noun *action* is pronounced very differently. This, incidentally, is a common source for mispronunciation for foreign learners of English, who do not realise that the pronunciation of the noun action [ækʃn] has no [t] in it and produce rather bizarre-sounding approximations such as [ɛktʃn]. Very often, the addition of a **suffix** leads to a shift in word stress: 'photograph, pho'tographer, photo'graphical, photographi'cality*.

The contact history of English is reflected in its present-day word-formation in complex ways. The inherited Germanic affixes (such as *un-* or *-ness*) combine with bases of all etymological origins: *unhappy* (from Anglo-Saxon), *undeliverable* (from French), *unreal* (from Latin); *happiness* (Anglo-Saxon base), *distinctiveness* (Latin). Some affixes which were borrowed from Latin or French have become similarly flexible, for example *-able*: *doable* (Germanic root), *changeable* (French), *deliverable* (Latin). Other borrowed affixes still display a tendency to combine with roots of foreign origin. Thus, *-ity*, similar in function to *-ness* in that it turns adjectives into nouns, does not occur with Germanic roots: *\*happity, \*smallity*, but *density, stupidity, rapidity*, etc.

The foreign component in the derivational apparatus has also produced further complications. Some derivations are transparent but not productive. For example, verbs of the group *to subject, to*

*object, to inject, to reject* have recognisable internal structure although the putative root morpheme *\*ject* is absent from English. The analysability of the forms, however, explains occasional ad-hoc formations such as the trade name *Fast-ject* for a certain type of medical syringe.

Derivational processes differ vastly in their degree of productivity. Morphemes such as *-er*, designating the agent of a verbal action or the inhabitant of a place, or *-ness*, turning adjectives into nouns, are subject to extremely few restrictions and continue to help produce large numbers of new words (e.g. *googler, nangness*). Others have not added new forms to the vocabulary for centuries, for example *-th*, which turns adjectives into nouns in a small number of well-established words such as *warmth, length, width, strength* and *mirth* (from *merry*).

**Conversion** is the process of the creation of new words without changes in the base. Some linguists assume the existence of a phonetically unexpressed "zero" derivational morpheme and therefore regard the core cases of conversion as a special type of derivation by means of a zero-morpheme (hence "zero-derivation").

The most common types of conversion are:

| |
|---|
| ▪ noun → verb: to bottle |
| ▪ verb → noun: a walk |

But other types are found as well:

| |
|---|
| ▪ adjective → noun: a regular |
| ▪ adjective → verb: to ready |
| ▪ preposition/adverb → noun: ups and downs |
| ▪ preposition/adverb → verb: to down a drink, to off (= kill) someone |

In some instances, conversion is partial rather than full (such cases, typically, would not be covered by the more tightly defined concept of "zero derivation"). *Regular*, the example of adjective-noun conversion given above, results in a full noun with all the relevant properties. It has a plural (*the regulars*), and it has a genitive (*the regular's, the regulars'*). Expressions such as *the rich* or *the poor*, on the other hand, are partial conversions only because they have some nominal properties while lacking others. For example, they are plural in meaning but have no plural form.

Note that while compounding and derivation are mainstays of the German word-formation apparatus too, conversion is much more highly developed in present-day English, which is just one consequence of the language's rapid move to the isolating-analytical type after the Old English period.

In all, these three processes account for most of the lexical complexity and current productivity in the vocabulary of English and are thus justifiably referred to as major types of word formation. Any introduction to morphology, however, will list and exemplify numerous additional strategies, minor types, which we will mention and illustrate briefly.

Minor types of word-formation. Several word-formation strategies involve shortening rather than adding to the base. *Prof* (← *professor*) and *dis* (← *to disrespect*) illustrate **clipping**. Merging two bases (*infotainment* ← *information* + *entertainment*) illustrates **blending**, while acronyms and initialisms are constructed using the first letters of groups of words. The difference between the two is that the former are pronounced as a syllable (*AIDS* ← *Acquired Immune Deficiency Syndrome*, pronounced as [eɪdz]), whereas the latter are pronounced as letters (*NGO* ← *Non-Governmental Organisation*, pronounced as [en ʤiː əʊ]).

Another relatively rare but recurrent type of word formation is **back formation**. Here a word is synchronically interpreted as a derived form, although there is no historical evidence that such a derivational process ever took place in the history of the English language. In other words, an assumed but historically spurious base form is constructed after the fact. An example is provided by the word *television*. This was created as a learned neo-classical compound, but was subsequently re-analysed as a derivation from a supposed verbal base *to televise*, in analogy to similar pairs, such as *revise-revision, supervise-supervision*, which were

**Focus on Word Formation**

Summarising the **morphological profile** of present-day English, we observe a small and highly regular inventory of inflectional morphemes, but considerable complexity in its word-formation processes. In direct comparison with German, English reveals a much higher tendency towards conversion, i.e. part-of-speech class change without formal marking, whereas German has the richer range of verbal prefixes (e.g. *kommen* → *ankommen, bekommen, umkommen, verkommen*, etc.).

**Bauer** (*English Word-Formation*) and **Plag** are two classic introductions to the field of English word formation. Stockwell and Minkova is a highly original and competent integrated treatment of the diachronic and synchronic aspects of English word formation, which holds considerable appeal for advanced readers.

already present in the language and served as models. Whereas the *Oxford English Dictionary* (*OED*) documents the priority of the verbal forms in these latter cases (first attestations for *revise* and *supervise* in 1545 and 1596 respectively, for *revision* and *supervision* in 1595 and 1640), *television* is attested from 1907, while the corresponding verb *to televise* is first documented in 1927.

Another process which has become very productive in the recent past is the use of **combining forms**, such as *hyper-, super-, mega-, eco-* or *bio-*. Historically, these usually develop from bound lexical morphemes used in learned words, such as *biology* or *superfluous*. As time goes by, they tend to broaden their meaning and combine with a large number of bases, including common terms of everyday English: *biodynamic, biomass, biodegradable, bio-food, supermarket, supermodel*, etc. Some of them eventually even become free morphemes in their own right: *the party was just mega last night*.

# 4.3 | Grammar

There is a widespread misconception that English grammar is simple and easy, or even that "English has no grammar." This is based on a popular misunderstanding which equates grammar with inflection. Languages such as Latin or Russian, with lots of inflectional endings on their nouns, verbs and adjectives, are thus considered to have a complex grammar, whereas languages without a lot of such endings are considered grammatically simple. The fact of the matter, however, is that inflection is just one dimension of grammatical complexity among several others in human languages, and that the world's 6,000 + languages comprise many which make subtle and complex grammatical distinctions with even less of an inflectional system than English.

### 4.3.1 | Typological Classification of Languages

Probably nowhere is the difference between languages greater than in their grammatical systems. Even languages like English and German, which are closely related historically, can present totally different types of structural organisation.

Early typologies of languages were based on the dominant shape of the word in a given language.

- The **isolating** type tends towards maximally simple words, i.e. a situation in which most words consist of one morpheme only.
- Languages of the **agglutinating** type may have long and complex words, but these are structured transparently and can be assembled and disassembled easily.
- The **inflectional** (or fusional) type has words which are complex and show signs of fusion, i.e. words are much less transparent than in the agglutinating type.
- Languages of the **polysynthetic** (or incorporating) type, finally, have words which are extremely long and complex and very often encompass almost the entire information in a clause.

Some languages correspond rather closely to one or the other of these ideal types. Thus, classical Chinese is said to be a near perfect illustration of the isolating type. Turkish illustrates the agglutinating type, Latin or Russian the inflectional type, and Inuit ( = "Eskimo") the polysynthetic type.

Most languages, however, represent mixed types. English, for example, has many isolating features, which become obvious particularly in comparison with German, for example word-formation by conversion. Depending on the context, *load* corresponds to *laden*, *beladen* or *Ladung*. But on the other hand, English still retains some highly frequent inflectional endings (although, again of course, far fewer than German), for example in the plurals of nouns or the past tenses of verbs.

Another fundamental typological distinction is that between **synthetic** and **analytical** grammars, which is based on clause structure. Languages such as German, Latin or Russian, which strongly rely on inflection to express grammatical functions, are synthetic, whereas those like English or Chinese, which express grammatical function through word-order rules and free grammatical morphemes, are analytical. In a comparison between English and German, the former almost always comes out as more analytical. Thus, the in-

> English has both isolating and inflectional features.

flectional dative of German (e.g. *dem König*) is rendered as an uninflected noun phrase (*the king*—with grammatical function expressed through word order) or as a prepositional phrase (*to the king, for the king*) in English. Comparison of adjectives is by inflection in German. In English, in addition to inflection, there is analytical comparison for some di-syllabic and all polysyllabic adjectives:

polite—politer—politest; polite—more polite—most polite
beautiful—more beautiful—most beautiful

Of course, for someone with a German-language background, learning the English definite article (*the* in writing, and /ðə/ or /ði:/ in speech) is easy, whereas for a native speaker of English to master the definite-article paradigm in German (*der, des, dem, den; die, der, der, die; das, des, dem, das*, to mention the three genders and four cases in the singular) is difficult. However, the inflectional simplicity of English grammar is offset by complex positional rules and the presence of a large number of free morphemes with a grammatical function, as any learner soon realises. Compare

(1a)  Der Lehrer erklärte dem Schüler die Aufgabe.
(1b)  The teacher explained the task to the pupil.

As can be seen, the job of the dative case in German is done by the grammatical function word *to* in English. In this case, it is impossible to turn the order of the two objects around in English. While it is perfectly okay to say *the teacher gave the pupil the task*, it is not possible to say

(1c)  *The teacher explained the pupil the task.

This subtle difference in the constructional potential of the two verbs *give* and *explain* is a grammatical complexity which even very advanced foreign learners of English often fail to master.

The German subject is marked by its nominative case ending. The fact that English does not distinguish nominative, dative and accusative cases on nouns, however, does not mean that it lacks a clear indication of subject status. In English this grammatical function is signalled by the position before the verb. If we swap the position of the two noun phrases *der Lehrer* and *dem Schüler* in the German example, the meaning remains the same (though the emphasis is on a different part of the sentence):

(2a)  Dem Schüler erklärte der Lehrer die Aufgabe.

Doing the same thing in English, by contrast, reverses the meaning; position and word order are all-important in the definition of subject and object:

(2b)  The pupil explained the task to the teacher.

This may be the most obvious instance in which a change in word order serves to signal a change in grammatical structure, but it is by far not the only one. *They had stolen the car* expresses a rather different idea than *They had the car stolen*—certainly another source of complexity in English grammar.

Even without significant inflection, English verb forms can also be taken to great degrees of complexity, as the following variations on our example show:

(3)  The task would have been being explained by the pupil.

This is a combination of the passive (*the task is explained*), the progressive (*the teacher is explaining*), the conditional perfect (*the teacher would have explained*), which we would use for emphasising that the act of explaining should be thought of as being in progress at a hypothetical point of time in the past.

## 4.3.2 | The Formal Description of English Grammar

Playing such grammatical games, however, should not make us forget the basic underlying system. There are many different frameworks for the grammatical description of present-day Standard English, with terminologies that unfortunately sometimes confuse beginners because of their mutual incompatibility and sometimes also because of a degree of internal inconsistency. Practically all of them, though, agree on the basics. There are **formal categories**, which we can identify out of context, and these serve specific **grammatical functions** in the contexts in which they are used. Thus, we can tell that *the happy guests* is a noun phrase (formal category) even before it is used in any particular utterance. However, in order to decide whether this noun phrase serves the grammatical function of a subject or an object, we need to look at the relevant grammatical contexts: *the happy guests left* (subject) or *the hotel owner left the happy guests* (object).

**Formal categories.** With regard to formal categories, it is useful to distinguish between two levels of analysis, words and phrases. **Words** can be categorised into several subclasses, also known as parts-of-speech, with the most important ones being:

- **nouns:** woman, sky, gratification, poetry, …
- **verbs:** be, have, do, turn, expectorate, …
- **adjectives:** happy, expensive, alive, …
- **adverbs:** happily, backwards, yesterday, …
- **articles:** the, a(n)
- **pronouns and determiners other than articles:** I, me, she, her, hers, this, anyone, such, …
- **prepositions:** in, on, at, behind, in front of, …
- **conjunctions:** because, whether, although, …

The number of nouns, verbs, adjectives and—to an extent—also adverbs is extremely large and new members can be added easily. This is why these classes are frequently referred to as "**open**." All the other classes have a more limited membership; new additions are rare, and therefore these are referred to as the **closed** classes. Though small in number, closed-class items are extremely frequent in texts and perform essential grammatical functions.

The next higher level of formal organisation above the single word is the **phrase**. Five types of phrases are commonly distinguished. Nouns function as the heads of noun phrases, verbs head verb phrases, adjectives adjectival phrases, adverbs adverb phrases and prepositions precede prepositional phrases.

This distinction between the part of speech that acts as the head of a phrase (or in the case of prepositional phrase precedes it) and the phrase itself seems trivial at first sight when we look at sentences such as *John felt anxious*. Does it make a difference whether we analyse it as "noun + verb + adjective" or "noun phrase + verb phrase + adjective phrase?" It certainly does, as each of the constituent parts of this very simple sentence can be expanded. Possible replacements of *John*, for example, include substantially sized noun phrases such as *The young man in the corner [felt anxious]* or even *The young man who was slowly approaching through the mist [felt anxious]*. The sentence *John would have been feeling anxious*, on the other hand, illustrates a verb phrase comprising three auxiliary verbs in addition to the one main verb, and *John felt extremely anxious to move on* demonstrates that even adjective phrases can dis-

Five types of phrases

play considerable internal complexity. In a tidy grammatical analysis of the sentence *John is anxious*, there is thus no way around the statement that the adjective *anxious* is the head of an adjectival phrase that consists of only one adjective.

We need the formal category of the phrase in our description of the grammar of a language in order to do justice to the fact that there is order and structure between the level of the individual word (nouns, verbs, adjectives, etc.) and the level of the **clause** or **sentence** (main clause, subordinate clause, ...). However, the fact that most practically relevant grammatical frameworks operate with the category of "phrase" does not mean that they do so in the same way. In fact, there are many differences and complications on the level of descriptive detail.

Defining verb phrases

Probably the most important point of contention is the definition of the **verb phrase**. Grammatical models in which the verb is seen as the structural nucleus of the clause tend to define verb phrases narrowly, as comprising the predicate verb. Subject, object(s) and other complements are seen as independent phrases on the same hierarchical rank. In such a framework, the sentence *Auntie Grace read the children bedtime stories* would be broken up in the following way (VP referring to verb phrases, NP to noun phrases):

[Auntie Grace]$_{NP}$ [read]$_{VP}$ [the children]$_{NP}$ [bedtime stories]$_{NP}$

The verb *read* requires three phrases as complements here. In our examples, all three happen to be noun phrases, *Auntie Grace* functioning as subject and *the children* and *bedtime stories* as indirect and direct objects respectively. In the variant *Auntie Grace read bedtime stories to the children*, the complements would be made up of two noun phrases and one prepositional phrase (*to the children*).

In alternative models, the subject is assumed to have a privileged position, and our example would therefore be divided into a noun phrase, *Auntie Grace*, and a much longer predicate verb phrase, *read the children bedtime stories*. In a second step, this extended verb phrase would be analysed further, as a sequence of a finite verb and two noun phrases.

[Auntie Grace]$_{NP}$ [[read]$_V$ [the children]$_{NP}$ [bedtime stories]$_{NP}$]$_{VP}$

Both ways of parsing our example sentence have specific advantages, disadvantages and conse-

quences, which cannot be discussed further in an introductory sketch, however.

**Grammatical functions.** Having looked at the most important form-categories, let us turn to the functions they serve in the clause. Note that in grammatical analysis, the term *clause* is preferred to *sentence* because of its more specific meaning. While anything from a short exclamation to a 10-line-long stretch taken from a philosophical treatise may qualify as a sentence if it starts with a capital letter and ends with a full stop, the clause is defined as a grammatical construction usually built around a verb as its nucleus. Thus, the following structures would qualify as clauses:

(4)  Tom is making such a good point.
(5)  ... that Tom is making such a good point.
(6)  ... why Tom is making such a good point.
(7)  ... by Tom making such a good point.
(8)  ... to make such a good point.

Only (4) is used alone and is therefore considered a **main clause**. The other four versions illustrate various types of dependent or **subordinate clauses**. They would be used in combination with an appropriate main clause, for example in *I wonder why Tom is making such a good point* or *Tom would be keen to make such a good point*. Note that our main clause is built around a finite verb, i.e. a verb inflected for tense, person and number (present, third singular), whereas two of the four subordinate clauses have a non-finite verb form as their nucleus: a gerund in (7) and an infinitive in (8). These are verb forms not marked for tense, person or number.

The best way to understand the basic clause types in the system of English grammar is to consider various types of verbs and the obligatory extensions they need in order to function in grammatically well-formed clauses.

All English verbs need at least one obligatory complement phrase, typically a noun phrase, which performs the grammatical function of subject. In formal terms, we thus have chains consisting of a noun phrase and a verb phrase (NP-VP); in terms of function, these chains represent subject-predicate (S-P) constructions:

**Basic Two-Element Pattern S-P**
(9)   [The sun] [is shining].
(10)  [The roof] [collapsed].
(11)  [We] [stumbled].

Most verbs, however, require at least one more phrase to make a complete clause. If this phrase introduces a new entity which is affected by the activity or process denoted by the predicate, it is said to serve the grammatical function of object. Typically, objects are made up of noun phrases:

## Basic Three-Element Pattern I: S-P-O

(12) [I] [am shining] [my shoes].
(13) [Are [you] criticising] [your boss]?

To alert the reader to possible complications, (13) shows inversion between the subject and the auxiliary in questions, which is one of the processes which produces discontinuous constituents, i.e. phrases whose components are not positioned adjacent to each other. In other instances, the additional phrase does not introduce a new entity but further defines the subject, thus performing the grammatical function of predicative complement. This constructional pattern is very common, but the number of verbs that occur in it is rather small, typically *to be* or verbs similar in meaning, such as *seem* or *appear*. Such predicative complements of the subject (or subject complements for short) can take a variety of forms. As our examples below show, noun phrases, adjective phrases and even prepositional phrases can all serve as predicative complements.

## Basic Three-Element Pattern II: S-P-predCS

(14) [Your plans] [are] [crazy].
(15) [Your plans] [are] [sheer madness].
(16) [Your plans] [are not] [in your own best interest].

In yet other cases, the additional phrase gives necessary information on temporal duration or the location of the verbal activity or process, its grammatical function being that of an adverbial. Adverbials are typically made up of adverb phrases (*here, right here, not far away from here*), noun phrases (*a whole week, the other day*) or prepositional phrases (*in this town*).

## Basic Three-Element Pattern III: S-P-A

(17) [Very few people] [live] [here].
(18) [Very few people] [live] [in this town].
(19) [The strike] [lasted] [(for) a whole week].

A fair number of verbs, however, require still another phrase to make a complete sentence, thus producing three different types of four-element patterns. The most common among these is a verb with two objects, which are typically realised as noun phrases or as prepositional phrases.

## Basic Four-Element Pattern I: S-P-O-O

(20) [The visitors] [gave] [us] [a splendid present].
(21) [I] [would have congratulated] [you] [on your success].
(22) [I] [will ask] [my sister] [for help].

When the verb is followed by two noun phrases, the first is referred to as the indirect object, while the second one is the direct object. Typically, indirect objects (such as *us* in our example 20) refer to the human or animate referent benefitting from or being otherwise affected by the verbal action. Objects made up of prepositional phrases are often referred to as prepositional objects.

Just like adjective phrases, noun phrases or prepositional phrases can function as predicative complements to the subject, so they can be predicative complements specifying the object:

## Basic Four-Element Pattern II: S-P-O-predCO

(23) [Mary] [considers] [your proposal] [unfair].
(24) [Mary] [considers] [you] [an utter fool].
(25) [Mary] [considers] [your proposal] [out of order].

A small number of verbs, finally, require an extra adverbial:

## Basic Four-Element Pattern III: S-P-O-A

(26) [The student] [put] [the books] [on her desk].
(27) [The salesman] [placed] [the jewels] [in a box].

Note that adverbials in similar clauses are usually optional, which can be represented as S-P-O-(A). For example, if the adverbial is dropped in *I saw the books on her desk*, the rest—*I saw the books*—

---

### Focus on Object and Predicative Complement

Verbs such as *run, taste,* or *make* have several different meanings. Analyse how these meanings correlate with the S-P-O and S-P-predCSs constructional patterns:

Would Peter make a good husband?
Would Peter make a lot of noise?

Who will taste the soup?
This soup tastes delicious.

The country's oil wells are running dry.
Only few people ran the marathon race.

## Focus on English Grammar

In comparison with German and many other languages in the world, the grammar of English represents a clear example of the **analytical** type. Analytical grammars code grammatical relations through word-order rules and free grammatical morphemes (or function words), whereas the opposite type, synthetic languages, largely rely on inflection to do the job. The analytical design features of English include its very rigid S-P-O clause structure, which allows only very few exceptions, the use of prepositions to indicate grammatical function (*of*-genitives such as "the cover of the book," *to*-datives/indirect objects such as "devote oneself to music") and, not least, its very rich inventory of periphrastic verbal forms to indicate notions of tense, mood, aspect, and voice.

The authoritative reference grammars of present-day Standard English are Quirk et al. and Huddleston and Pullum (*Cambridge Grammar*). Beginners are well advised to approach them through their abridged **student versions** (Greenbaum and Quirk; Huddleston and Pullum, *Student's Introduction*). Biber et al. is a rich compendium of information on the stylistic and frequency aspects of grammatical constructions.

is still a grammatically well-formed clause. *The student put the books*, on the other hand, is not. With the verb *place*, we do get grammatically well-formed S-P-O constructions, such as, for example, *Grampa placed a bet*, but the meaning the verb has here is rather different from the literal one illustrated in our example.

It may seem a drastic simplification to reduce the bewildering complexity of actual English sentences to just these seven types. However, even very complex constructions reveal themselves to be instances of the basic types which have had a number of fairly straightforward expansion strategies applied to them:

**Expansions of the pattern.** Any basic clause can be expanded by adding optional further adverbials which give additional information on where, when, how or why an event took place. Take one of our S-P illustrations, *the sun is shining*, for example. By adding further optional adverbials we get S-P-(A)-(A)-(A):

(28)  [The sun] [is shining] [brightly] [on my balcony] [today].

An object may consist of a very simple noun phrase, as in *the scientist demonstrated a new experiment*. In a real academic paper, however, the object may easily be as complex as:

(29)  [In a recent paper (Kemball-Cook et al., 1990)], [we] [demonstrated] [a modified sodium dodecyl sulphate polyacrylamide gel electrophoresis (SDS-PAGE) method for visualization of factor VIII heavy chain (FVIII HC) polypeptides].

Practically limitless complexity is possible once we expand an object into an object clause, a subject into a subject clause, an adverbial into an adverbial clause (and so on), as these processes are recursive, that is, they can be applied again and again in the same sentence. For illustration, consider the following finite object clause, which itself contains a finite subject clause and a further, non-finite, object clause:

(30)  [I] [didn't suspect] [that [what [I] [said]] [would get] [you] [[to react] [in this way]]].

This sentence certainly reads more easily than the complex grammatical analysis would suggest. "Complexifying" a few of its phrases and spicing it up with a few more optional adverbials gets us to a considerable level of complexity with minimal effort:

(31)  [Very few people who were present] [would have [in the least] suspected] [that [what [a low-level official] [said] [in an aside that didn't even make it into the meeting's official minutes]] [could have got] [the visiting representative from the People's Republic] [[to react] [in such an amazingly abrupt way]]].

Example (31) contains two **relative clauses**: *who were present* (in *very few people who were present*) and *that didn't even make it into the meeting's official minutes* (in *in an aside that didn't even make it into the meeting's official minutes*). Unlike the other types of subordinate clauses which we have come across so far, relative clauses do not directly depend on the verbal predicate of a higher clause. Rather, they modify a noun (*people* and *aside*, respectively, in our case). *What she said came as a shock* and *the things she said came as a shock* are two sentences which may not be too different in their message. However, the grammatical status of their subjects is very different. In the first sentence we have a true subject clause (*What she said …*), whereas in the second we have a noun-phrase subject (*the things*) which is post-modified by a relative clause (*she said*).

## 4.4 | The Lexicon

In section 4.3 above, we already had a look at the formal structure of words. In this chapter, we will build on this and study meanings and meaning-based patterns in the English vocabulary. This is the domain of the linguistic sub-discipline of semantics—or to put it precisely, lexical semantics, as there are aspects of meaning, such as negation, which go beyond the scope of the individual word. Currently, two partly incompatible theoretical approaches dominate the field of lexical semantics—a structuralist one and a cognitive one (cf. entry V.2).

**Structuralist Semantics.** As the name suggests, structuralist semantics focuses on meaning in language structure, and not on meanings as they emerge in the minds of speakers and listeners or in the full contexts of actual communication (this latter aspect being the domain of linguistic pragmatics—see entry V.5). Structuralist semantics aims to break down the meanings of words into bundles of semantic features, with the aim of a precise and unambiguous description. In this way, by de-composing their meanings, we can make explicit both the shared and the distinctive aspects of the meanings of the two English words *boy* and *girl*:

boy  [+ human], [– female], [– adult]
girl  [+ human], [+ female], [– adult]

This precision has its merits, but also reaches its limits when we try to extend it too far. How many people would find it natural, for example, to define *woman* and *mother* in the following way?

woman  [+ human], [+ female], [+ adult]
mother  [+ human], [+ female], [+ adult], [+ has given birth]

The superficial precision of this analysis fails us in trying to account for some very common metaphorical expressions containing the word *mother*, for example "Mother Nature" or "mother country," where it is not the notion of giving birth which is crucial but the fact that we think of mothers as caring and nurturing. Of course, we can add this feature and revise our analysis in the following way:

mother  [+ human], [+ female], [+ adult], [+ has given birth],
         [+ caring]

While this solves this particular problem, it introduces another. By making the quality of being caring and nurturing a defining feature of the meaning of *mother*, we will be unable to use the word to describe mothers falling short of this ideal or prototypical standard. The human mind, in handling lexical meaning, seems more tolerant of vagueness and even partial contradiction than structuralist feature analysis gives it credit for.

A classic instance of this is the class of English words denoting containers for liquids (*cup, mug, vase, bowl, jug, pot, …*; see Labov). Typical "features" which we could invoke to distinguish between cups, mugs and bowls might be size, the presence of saucers or handles, etc. In such a feature matrix, cups, mugs and bowls could roughly be represented as follows:

|        | *cup*   | *mug*             | *bowl*        |
|--------|---------|-------------------|---------------|
| **size**   | small   | big               | big or small  |
| **saucer** | present | absent            | absent        |
| **handle** | present | present or absent | absent        |

Clearly, however, this matrix is artificial because it misses out the dimension of shape. Cups are short and round while mugs are taller and more elongated in shape. Unfortunately, this is a dimension which is gradient and allows for any kind of transition, so that it cannot be included in an essentially binary ("either one or the other") matrix of the kind illustrated. Faced with the following two images, we would probably classify the object on the left-hand side as a cup and that on the right as a mug:

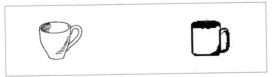

On the other hand, if the object on the right was small and came with a saucer, we would not be bothered if someone called it a cup. By the same token, the object on the left could easily qualify as a mug if it stood five inches tall. It seems that, in categorising objects, the human mind does not check the visual impression against a list of features. Rather, we match what we see against an ideal representative or **prototype**. A category such

Problems of
feature analysis

as "cup," for example, will thus have a clear centre, comprising all those exemplars which match the ideal prototype very closely. Around this centre, but potentially still within the over-all meaning, is a fuzzy periphery which might even partly overlap with neighbouring categories, so that speakers can even use two different terms for one and the same object without this causing misunderstandings.

In general, "binary" constellations of the "boy-girl" type are more difficult to find in natural languages than prototypical or fuzzy ones of the "cup-mug" type. As was pointed out, holistic classification on the basis of prototypes is closer to the way human cognition actually works than analysis into semantic features, which is why the prototype approach is referred to as cognitive semantics.

**Cognitive Semantics** is also in a better position than its structuralist competitor when it comes to explaining a basic truth about the lexicon, namely that hardly any word has only one precise meaning. **Polysemy** (from the Greek words for "many" and "meanings") is a fact of life in natural languages. For example, the current basic meaning of the noun *chip* is "small, flat, hard fragment detached from some larger object." Thus we can think of chips of wood left over after a tree has been felled, or of a chip of porcelain knocked off a cup or mug. Other current meanings have been derived from this basic one through plausible processes of analogical or metaphorical extension. For example, we use the word *chip* to refer to coin-like tokens in various kinds of games or to the small, flat objects bearing the electronic circuits in our computers. A socially and culturally more sensitive case of polysemy is the adjective *gay*, which originally meant "merry" and from this basis was extended to convey the additional meaning of (heterosexual) licentiousness (now obsolete) in the late nineteenth century, before it became the general-purpose term to refer to (male) homosexual orientation in the late twentieth and early twenty-first centuries. The next few decades will show whether these meanings can co-exist or whether a new dominant meaning will oust the original one with which speakers no longer feel it to be compatible.

Unlike grammar, which is governed by largely transparent and highly general rules and conventions, the vocabulary of a language is less regular. However, this does not mean that the lexicon is an unstructured mass (or "mess") of words. A first step towards studying these regularities is to look at relations holding between two words (or more precisely between the specific senses of these words), among which the most prominent ones are synonymy and antonymy.

**Sense relations.** Two words are considered **synonyms** if they mean the same thing or, to give the precise technical description, if they are fully interchangeable in all contexts of use. Such full synonymy is a luxury that natural languages generally don't afford, so that in practice the study of synonyms is concerned with determining the extent of the overlap in meaning between two or more words. Sometimes, one member of a pair of synonyms has a slightly wider or narrower meaning than the other; sometimes, the contrast is a matter of emotional or stylistic connotation. Thus, the meaning of the verb *lay* is more specific than that of *put*; the nouns *yank* and *kraut* are more negatively connoted than their synonyms *American* and *German*; and *expenditure* is more formal in style than *spending*. In more complicated cases, the three dimensions may even intersect. Thus, *solitude* differs from *loneliness* not only because it denotes self-imposed rather than externally imposed deprivation from company, but also because it has a positive emotional connotation and a more elevated stylistic value.

Partial overlap, as in synonymy, is not the only systematic relationship holding between words (or to be precise, between senses of words). Senses can be in various types of opposition to each other. The most common type of such oppositional relationship is **antonymy**. Antonyms mark opposite ends of a scale which allows gradient transitions, as is the case, for example, in the following pairs of adjectives:

tall—short
expensive—cheap
hot—cold
clever—stupid

Each of the two members of the pairs defines points at opposite ends of a scale. Intermediate values can easily be formulated: *less warm, not really very cold*, etc. In addition, one member of each pair is the **unmarked** option, carrying with it no presupposition of any kind, whereas the other is the **marked** option. In the pair *tall—short*, for example, *tall* is the unmarked member. The question *how tall is he?* is a neutral one, leaving open whether the person who is being talked about is tall or short. The question *how short is he?*, which

An example of polysemy

contains the marked choice, on the other hand, comes with a previous assumption that he or she is short.

A somewhat different kind of opposition is illustrated by pairs such as *mortal—immortal* or *dead—alive*. At least on a literal understanding of these words, there are no gradient transitions, and one excludes the other. One cannot be "a little bit immortal" or "very mortal"; if a person is dead, he or she cannot be alive, and vice versa. This is complementary (rather than gradable) antonymy, or—for those who wish to reserve the term *antonym* for gradable contrasts—**complementary opposition**.

Yet another type of semantic opposition is illustrated by verb pairs such as *give—take* or *sell—buy*. Here the first members of the pairs are not so much (gradable or complementary) negations of the second, but rather view the process from opposite perspectives. We can thus speak of **converses**. In pairs such as *forward—backward, up—down* or *come—go* the opposition is **directional**. But in a good many instances, even such a fine-grained taxonomy of semantic opposition reveals itself to be insufficient, for example because the relationship is multi-dimensional. Within the system of English kinship terms, for example, *brother* is opposed to *sister* along one dimension (gender in the same generation), but to *father* or *son* in others. *North* is certainly opposed to *South*, but of course also to *East* and *West* (for a more detailed discussion of such "directional," "antipodal," and "orthogonal" oppositions see Lyons, *Semantics* 2:281–84).

Even the most refined and intricate system of oppositional sense relations will, however, fail in the face of some complications which have evolved in actual language use. The adjectival pair *open—closed*, for instance, appears to be a straightforward case of complementary opposition when we think of shops. If a shop is open, it is not closed, and vice versa. However, it is gradable when talking of doors, which can be wide open or half closed. To complicate matters further, a door can be half closed but apparently not half shut (although *closed* and *shut* are synonyms). In their literal colour-term senses, *black* and *white* are antonyms to the layman, linked in gradable fashion through various shades of grey. Whether this common-sense analysis is acceptable to the expert in optics is an open question. A really messy problem, fraught with a history of centuries of prejudice, however, is presented by their use as designations for racial groups. Here, racist societies such as the slavery-era American South were happy to develop a rich terminology for shades of "black" (*mulatto, quadroon, octoroon*, etc.), treating the concept as gradable, whereas "white" was treated as a non-gradable category, from which anyone with what was referred to as "visible admixture" of "black blood" was excluded. In other words, we have a set of antonyms in which one term is complementary and the other gradable.

**Lexical Fields.** So far, we have focussed on semantic relationships existing between two words—or, to be precise, two senses of words. While these binary relations are very pervasive in language, they are not the only instances of semantic patterning. In many semantic domains, there are lexical fields which comprise more members and thus allow a coherent description of the relevant portions of the lexicon. People are intimidated and fascinated by death, and therefore it is not surprising that lexical creativity flourishes in this domain more than in many others. Consider, as a macabre example, the many synonyms of the English verb *kill*, which can be classified into six sub-groups:

1. **type of victim:** murder, put down, cull, …
2. **method:** shoot, strangle, drown, smother, asphyxiate, starve, slay, poison, hang, electrocute, …
3. **number of victims:** massacre, decimate, butcher, exterminate, …
4. **legal/technical sphere:** murder, lynch, execute, …
5. **euphemisms:** do away with, put to sleep, dispatch, liquidate, put out of one's misery, …
6. **dysphemisms:** rub out, do in, croak, bump off, zap, fix, off, blow to Kingdom Come, …

Sub-group (1) shows that English speakers wish to make distinctions based on the victim of the killing. Whereas the general verb *to kill* can be used for any kind of victim (people, pets and companion animals, other domestic animals or animals in general), *to murder* is reserved for human victims exclusively and additionally conveys that the killing was the result of malicious intention. In tragic circumstances, people can be killed by mistake, but we would not usually say that someone was murdered by mistake. *To put down*, on the other hand, is used for pets; the act is carried out intentionally but not maliciously: *our old dog was so weak and sick he had to be put down*. We would not normally use this verb with objects denoting human beings and wild animals.

**Collocation** is a rather different but extremely important relationship between words. The collo-

## Focus on Collocation Errors

Below you find three extracts from essays written by German students who seem to have a good vocabulary and general command of English grammar. However, the texts do not read naturally because students have not developed the feeling for the **collocational frames** in which the verb *reach* can be used appropriately:

*This is the so-called positive discrimination policy; giving preference to certain 'groups' (e.g. women) in order *to reach a stage of balance between this group and one or more others.*

*[...] whether or not *the gradual change towards a society free from Apartheid can be reached without bloodshed.*

*He or she is faced with a problem, struggles to cope with it, and *reaches a different, more objective view of him- or herself and his or her relation to community.*

(source: *International Corpus of Learner English* (ICLE), German component)

cational relationship is only very partially determined by meaning. Put simply, it refers to the tendency for words to co-occur by convention, and not because their meaning or some grammatical rule would make co-occurrence particularly likely. There is nothing in the meaning of the verb *make*, or in the grammar of English, which should prevent speakers from saying: *\*make one's homework* (a typical foreign learner's error). By convention, however, native speakers of English agree that *do one's homework* is the only possible form in this case. Similarly, *reach* and *achieve* are verbs which have considerable semantic overlap and additionally share the transitive grammatical (S-P-O) pattern. A foreign learner might thus be forgiven for using them interchangeably with the objects *aim*

and *goal*. But in idiomatic native-speaker usage only *reach a goal* and *achieve an aim/a goal* are common, whereas *\*reach an aim* is not (notwithstanding the fact that its German equivalent *ein Ziel erreichen* is perfectly normal).

The pervasiveness of collocations raises interesting theoretical and applied issues. What does it mean to speak a language fluently? Is it enough to have a large vocabulary and to know how to apply the grammatical rules? Or is there a way in which the human mind manages to store the hundreds of thousands of more or less fixed collocations that we find in our language data? For advanced learners of English as a foreign language, collocations remain an irksome learning problem, constantly reminding them of the difference between what is merely correct and what is fully natural and idiomatic.

A relatively trivial problem by comparison is presented by **idioms**, fixed expressions whose meanings are not compositional (that is, cannot be added up from the meanings of the individual words contributing to the fixed expression). Thus, the expression *to spill the beans* means "to tell a secret." We can modify it to some extent, for example by putting it into various tenses, but it is very difficult to make any changes to the object noun phrase. A sentence such as *\*the second edition of the book spilled some more stale old beans* is difficult to understand because the reader will be torn between the intended idiomatic interpretation and the unintended literal one.

## Focus on English Vocabulary

Among the several levels of structural organisation, the vocabulary is probably the one which is least amenable to typological generalisations. One fairly safe generalisation, though, is that the rich history of language contact is reflected in the stylistic stratification of the lexicon even today. Words of Anglo-Saxon or other Germanic origin tend to be general in meaning and colloquial in style, while their French, Latin, or Greek synonyms tend to be more specific and technical in their meaning and more formal stylistically. Two further trends can be noted for English in particular in comparison to German. The first is a tendency toward the creation of **multi-word lexical expressions**. The most prominent example is provided by phrasal and phrasal-prepositional verbs (e. g. *put up, look for, look down, home in on*) and related complex verbal expressions (*take advantage of, get rid of,* etc.). The second is a tendency towards **lexical dissociation**. Unlike German, a noun and its corresponding verb or adjective are frequently derived from different etymological sources in English. While German *Mund* and *mündlich* or *Herz* and *Herzkrankheit* are derived from the same base and thus in a transparent relationship, this is not so for the English equivalents *mouth* and *oral* or *heart* and *coronary disease*.

For introductions to linguistic semantics consult **Lyons**, *Semantics*, a two-volume compendium of still unsurpassed comprehensiveness, and the shorter **Lyons**, *Linguistic Semantics*, or **Cruse**. Issues of English-German contrastive semantics are extensively covered in **Leisi and Mair** (41–111).

# 4.5 | Outlook: English among the European Languages

This brief structural sketch has presented and illustrated the basic design features of present-day English, sometimes highlighting contrasts to German, a language which is closely related to English historically but rather different typologically. As a sketch, it cannot be complete and needs to be fleshed out by consulting more detailed introductions to the various subdomains such as the ones listed in the boxes and in the bibliography. However, the following **structural profile** is probably sufficient to identify English from among the languages of Europe: In comparison to other European languages, English has a moderately rich and complex inventory of phonemes and allows consonantal clusters of considerable complexity. Because of a unique history of language contact, its word stress system is a complex compromise between an inherited "Germanic" tendency to stress the root, a French tendency to stress the final syllable and additional complications introduced by polysyllabic loan words from Latin and Greek. In its word formation, compounding (especially noun + noun compounds) has always been a major strategy of vocabulary extension. Again, however, language contact has led to innovations and complications. In addition to the surviving Germanic derivational morphemes such as -ness and -hood, loans from French and Latin have extended the possibilities of forming new words, but also introduced a large number of phonetic complications. Due to the rapid shift from a synthetic, inflection-based grammar in Old English to an analytical system which depends on word order and free grammatical morphemes, conversion or zero-derivation emerged as an additional major source of new words. This shift has also led to fundamental adjustments in the entire grammatical design of the language. Its most immediate consequence was the fixing of the subject—verb—object order both in main and in subordinate clauses. However, the loss of inflectional case has had numerous additional consequences in the making of the grammar of Modern English—from the development of several prepositions into grammatical function words, the rise of a complex analytical system of tense, aspect and mood in the verb phrase to an enormous flexibility in the mapping of semantic propositional structure on to syntactic form. To give but one example: in a language such as German, in which direct objects are explicitly marked by the accusative case, there is no way of forming passives such as *the kids were read a nice bedtime story*; *that sort of thing has got to be put an end to*; or *my bed must have been slept in by someone else*.

More than in related languages, the structure of Modern English has been shaped by its **history of language contact**, both extensive (English has been in contact with a large number of languages) and intensive (with some of the many contact languages leaving a deep structural imprint through long periods of bilingualism). Contact influence may be least apparent to the eye of the linguistically untrained observer on the phonetic level. It is, however, glaringly obvious in the language's vocabulary, and it may go a long way towards explaining the extreme tendency in English towards analytical grammatical structures. All Indo-European languages display signs of a long-term drift from synthetic to analytical grammars. This drift is working itself out with glacial slowness in Russian and only moderately faster in German. It is strikingly obvious in a comparison between Latin and its daughter languages Italian, French, and Spanish. But it is nowhere more advanced than in English. When the forebears of the Anglo-Saxons started migrating, the drift had been set in motion, but it was certainly speeded up considerably through dialect and language contact from the moment they established themselves in their new island home. Inflectional endings probably wore off when the dialects of the immigrants consolidated into the new language "English," and then even more when English came into contact with Scandinavian.

The development
toward analytical
structures in English

## Select Bibliography

**Aarts, Bas.** *English Syntax and Argumentation*. 2nd ed. Basingstoke: Macmillan, 2001.

**Aarts, Bas, and April McMahon, eds.** *Handbook of English Linguistics*. Oxford: Blackwell, 2006.

**Bauer, Laurie.** *English Word-Formation*. Cambridge: Cambridge University Press, 1983.

**Bauer, Laurie.** *Morphological Productivity*. Cambridge: Cambridge University Press, 2001.

**Biber, Douglas, et al.** *The Longman Grammar of Spoken and Written English*. London: Longman, 1999.

**Brinton, Laurel J., and Donna M. Brinton.** *The Linguistic Structure of Modern English*. 2nd ed. Philadelphia: Benjamins, 2000.

**Cruse, David A.** *Meaning in Language: An Introduction to Semantics and Pragmatics*. 3rd ed. Oxford: Oxford University Press, 2011.

**Cruttenden, Alan.** *Intonation*. 2nd ed. Cambridge: Cambridge University Press, 1997.

**Crystal, David.** *The Cambridge Encyclopedia of the English Language*. 2nd ed. Cambridge: Cambridge University Press, 2003.

**Culpeper, Jonathan, et al., eds.** *English Language: Description, Variation and Context*. Basingstoke: Palgrave Macmillan, 2009.

**Giegerich, Heinz J.** *English Phonology*. Cambridge: Cambridge University Press, 1992.

**Gimson, Alfred C.** *Gimson's Pronunciation of English*. 6th ed. London: Arnold, 2001.

**Greenbaum, Sidney, and Randolph Quirk.** *A Student's Grammar of the English Language*. Harlow: Longman, 1990.

**Gut, Ulrike.** *Introduction to English Phonetics and Phonology*. Frankfurt: Lang, 2009.

**Huddleston, Rodney, and Geoffrey K. Pullum.** *The Cambridge Grammar of the English Language*. Cambridge: Cambridge University Press, 2002.

**Huddleston, Rodney, and Geoffrey K. Pullum.** *A Student's Introduction to English Grammar*. Cambridge: Cambridge University Press, 2004.

**Jones, Daniel.** *English Pronouncing Dictionary*. 17th ed. Cambridge: Cambridge University Press, 2006.

**König, Ekkehard, and Volker Gast.** *Understanding English-German Contrasts*. Berlin: Schmidt, 2007.

**Labov, William.** "The Boundaries of Words and Their Meanings." *New Ways of Analyzing Variation in English*. Eds. Charles-James N. Bailey and Roger W. Shuy. Washington: Georgetown University Press, 1973. 340–73.

**Leisi, Ernst, and Christian Mair.** *Das heutige Englisch*. 8th ed. Heidelberg: Winter, 1999.

**Löbner, Sebastian.** *Understanding Semantics*. London: Arnold, 2002.

**Lyons, John.** *Linguistic Semantics: An Introduction*. Cambridge: Cambridge University Press, 1995.

**Lyons, John.** *Semantics*. 2 vols. Cambridge: Cambridge University Press, 1977.

**Mair, Christian.** *Bachelor-Wissen: English Linguistics*. Tübingen: Narr, 2008.

**Mair, Christian.** *Englisch für Anglisten: Eine Einführung in die englische Sprache*. Tübingen: Stauffenburg, 1995.

**Matthews, Peter H.** *Morphology*. 2nd ed. Cambridge: Cambridge University Press, 1991.

**Plag, Ingo.** *Word-Formation in English*. Cambridge: Cambridge University Press, 2003.

**Quirk, Randolph, et al.** *A Comprehensive Grammar of the English Language*. London: Longman, 1985.

**Radden, Günter, and René Dirven.** *Cognitive English Grammar*. Amsterdam: Benjamins, 2007.

**Saeed, John.** *Semantics*. 3rd ed. Oxford: Blackwell, 2009.

**Schmid, Hans-Jörg.** *English Morphology and Word-Formation: An Introduction*. 2nd ed. Berlin: Schmidt, 2011.

**Skandera, Paul, and Peter Burleigh.** *A Manual of English Phonetics and Phonology*. Tübingen: Narr, 2011.

**Stockwell, Robert P., and Donka Minkova.** *English Words: History and Structure*. Cambridge: Cambridge University Press, 2001.

**Ungerer, Friedrich, and Hans-Jörg Schmid.** *An Introduction to Cognitive Linguistics*. 2nd ed. London: Pearson-Longman, 2006.

**Upton, Clive, William Kretzschmar, and Rafal Konopka.** *The Oxford Dictionary of Pronunciation for Current English*. Oxford: Oxford University Press. 2001.

**Viereck, Wolfgang, Karin Viereck, and Heinrich Ramisch.** *dtv-Atlas Englische Sprache*. Munich: dtv, 2002.

**Wells, John C.** *The Longman Pronunciation Dictionary*. 3rd ed. Harlow: Longman, 2008.

*Christian Mair*

# 5  Text and Context

This chapter will cover the two related areas of pragmatics (as the study of meaning and acting in social contexts) and text analysis (as the study of structures, functions and meanings of texts).

## 5.1 | Pragmatics

### 5.1.1 | Approaching Pragmatics

Pragmatics is both an art and a scientific approach. It is the art of understanding what is meant beyond what is explicitly said. Take, for example, this short extract from a letter written in 1998 by a friend, who lives in Illinois (USA):

(1)  Something happened to me which has never happened to me before this time of year. I was putting Christmas lights up on a tree outside and got buzzed by a mosquito. I was totally stunned!

The non-articulated but nonetheless suggested content (*implicatum*) is much richer than the articulated or stated content (*dictum*); beyond the latter, any reader will infer:

- that *this time of year* refers to the Christmas season,
- that *outside* refers to a place outside the writer's home (which may be a house, a boat, a tent),
- that the *tree* is of a kind that is usually used in those parts of the world as a Christmas tree,
- that it is very atypical for *mosquitos* to *buzz* at that time of the year,
- that the weather was unusually mild (with no snow or heavy rain) for that time of the year (because it still allowed mosquitos to fly),
- that the writer was very much surprised—and other *implicata*.

Additionally, some information can only be inferred by the addressee who is familiar with the writer and the circumstances of the letter, e.g.,

- to whom the personal pronouns refer,
- to what exact location *outside* refers—and other *implicata*.

**Definition**

While → semantics is concerned with the **dictum**, i.e. the commensurable literal and pre-contextual meaning of sentences, → pragmatics is concerned with the **implicatum**, i.e. the incommensurable (and frequently figurative) contextual meaning of utterances that are jointly negotiated and shared *in situ* by the participants involved.

Said meaning or **dictum** and unsaid meaning or **implicatum** are commonly referred to as **semantic** and **pragmatic meaning** respectively. Pragmatic meaning is the outcome of a complex process of interpretive enrichment of semantic meaning. As language users, we are masters in the art of reading between the lines, viz. of ascribing meaning to what is not articulated in so many words. When understanding we cannot help but relate what we hear to our contextual knowledge as well as to the entrenched conceptual schemas and frames of our cognitive knowledge. As linguists, moreover, we employ pragmatics as an approach to describe the principles and mechanisms, the means and procedures that guide both the conveying speaker and the understanding hearer in their endeavour to establish and secure successful communication.

### 5.1.2 | Historical Overview

Even though its roots can be traced back to early classical traditions of rhetorics and stylistics, modern pragmatics is a fairly recent discipline (for a concise overview cf. Koyama). Inaugurated early in the twentieth century as an independent field of study within semiotics (besides syntax and semantics) by Charles Morris, Rudolf Carnap (and ultimately Charles Sanders Peirce), some thirty years elapsed before pragmatics finally made its way into modern linguistics in the late 1960s with linguists' budding interest in so-called performance phenomena (like indexicals, see below). To this end, they adopted ideas developed and advanced by Ludwig Wittgenstein, Gilbert Ryle, Peter Strawson, John L. Austin, and other language philosophers. The ensuing **pragmatic turn** was most notably induced by Austin, John R. Searle and Herbert Paul Grice, who studied how speakers use utterances to perform acts in order to accomplish specific goals. Other scientific movements that nourished pragmatics include anthropology (Bronisław Malinowski, Philipp Wegener, Alan Gardiner), contextualism (John R. Firth) and functionalism (Karl Bühler, Roman Jakobson, Dell Hymes), ethnomethodology (Harold Garfinkel, Erving Goffman, Harvey Sacks) and European sociology (Jürgen Habermas). Since the pragmatic turn, the early Anglo-American framework of pragmatic linguistic study has been immensely expanded and enhanced by research in Continental Europe (and elsewhere).

According to the narrow view, pragmatics is a module of language theory *on a par* with and at the same time in juxtaposition to semantics. Its core issues include deixis, speech acts, presuppositions, implicatures and related types of inferences.

According to the broader view, pragmatics is defined as the scientific study of *all* aspects of linguistic behaviour, encompassing, *inter alia*, language functions, maxims of communication, systems of knowledge, means and strategies of evaluation, principles of text and discourse organization. Unlike syntax or semantics, pragmatics adopts a **functional perspective**. Its focal point is linguistic action and interaction (Greek *prāgma* means *act*). As such, pragmatics takes account of the interactional turn that can be observed in the most recent development of interactive (Web 2.0-based) media formats.

In the following, we will only focus on those key issues that are unanimously regarded as constituting the foundations of pragmatics, to wit: deixis, language functions and speech acts, entailments, presuppositions and implicatures, common ground and context.

### 5.1.3 | Pragmatics Outside and Within Linguistics

When we refer to attitudes and modes of behaviour as pragmatic in non-linguistic discourse, we mean that they have a factual kind of orientation in common. People who act pragmatically or take a pragmatic outlook generally have a preference for a practical, matter of fact and realistic rather than a theoretical, speculative and idealistic way of approaching imminent problems and handling everyday affairs. To assume a pragmatic stance in everyday social encounters as well as in political, historical and related kinds of discourse means to handle the related affairs in a goal- and object-directed, common-sense and down to earth kind of way.

While such everyday understanding of the term has left its traces in linguistics, there is not one generally accepted definition of pragmatics as a unified and homogeneous field of study. In contemporary research, we can identify a narrow and a broad way of delineating pragmatics (of which the former is sometimes allocated to an "Anglo-American" and the latter to a "Continental [European]" tradition of pragmatics, cf. Huang, *Pragmatics* xi).

### 5.1.4 | Deixis

More than any other issue, so-called **indexicals**, like *I*, *you*, *here*, and *now*, puzzled grammarians of whatever shade (and thus spurred the rise of pragmatics), because they do not fall within the scope of grammatical rules. Deixis (compare Greek *deixis* noun and *deiktikós* adjective from the verb *deiknymi*, which means *to show, to point*) concerns the direct relationship between (a small set of) linguistic items (deictics) and those immediate components of the utterance situation to which they refer. Thus, in the following short exchange

(2)  Dave: *I have two scholarship interviews tonight.*
     Kim:  What time? *You're* dressed like *that*?
     Sue:  *You're* not dressed for it.
     Kim:  *Here*?

we need situational knowledge of who is actually talking to whom, where and when, in order to understand the reference of the italicized word forms. The personal pronouns *I* and *you* have no context-independent denotative meaning, but relate a particular participant role (speaker and hearer) to the same referent (Dave). In the same vein, to enrich the restricted denotative meanings of the adverbs *tonight* (*the evening of the day on which 'tonight' is uttered*) and *here* (*the place where 'here' is uttered*), we need to know the speech situation. Metaphorically speaking, deictics are verbal means of pointing, which anchor the ongoing utterance in the speech situation.

The three absolute deictics I, now, here form the **deictic centre** (or, following Bühler 102, the I-now-here-origo) of the speaker's subjective orientation, indicating nearness. They can be juxtaposed with their relative equivalents *you, then, there*, which indicate distance. (A similar distinction can be made for tense: the absolute tenses present, past and future relate temporal events to utterance time, while the relative tenses present perfect, past perfect and future perfect relate temporal events to other, contextually given events that are not identical with the time of utterance.) The deictic centre is constantly shifted in dialogues and also in monologues (e.g. a letter) where time and place do not always coincide. The corresponding problem of deictic projection plays a substantial role in narrative and other forms of fiction (cf. Bühler 80, for different modes of pointing).

While the role-related deictic pronouns *I* and *you* 'point' by themselves (to the current speaker or hearer), other deictics require supporting gestures or gazes (the demonstrative *that* in (2)). Some expressions can be used in a gestural and deictic (*a*-examples), non-gestural and deictic (*b*-examples) and non-deictic (*c*-examples) way:

(3) a. *You, you,* but not *you,* are dismissed
b. What did *you* say?
c. *You* can never tell what sex they are nowadays
(4) a. *This finger* hurts
b. *This* city stinks
c. I met *this* weird guy the other day
(5) a. Push not *now,* but *now*
b. Let's go *now* rather than tomorrow
c. *Now,* that is not what I said
(6) a. Not *that* one, idiot, *that* one
b. *That*'s a beautiful view
c. Oh, I did this and *that*
(7) a. Move it from *there* to *there*
b. Hello, is Harry *there*?
c. *There* we go

(Levinson, *Pragmatics* 66)

Corresponding to the tripartite structure of the I-now-here-origo, there are three central types of deixis: **person deixis**, **time deixis**, and **place deixis**. In view of other parameters of the speech situation, more peripheral types of deixis such as social deixis, text deixis, object deixis can be added (cf. Levinson, "Deixis").

## 5.1.5 | Language Functions

In his seminal work on language theory (1934), the psychologist and linguist **Karl Bühler** examined the idea (originally put forward by Plato) to conceptualize language as a tool in order to explain the functions of language. Tools (hammer, pliers, spoon, computer mouse) are not incidental but serve a particular purpose or function. The broad range of possible functions of language (as a most complex and multifaceted tool) is condensed to only three basic functions by Bühler in his **Organonmodell**. It displays language as a tool (Greek *órganon*) used by one person (the speaker, *I*) to communicate with another person (the hearer, *you*) about something (things, persons, states of affairs, *it*; Bühler 24). These three parameters correspond to three different functions of language; we use language

- to express the speaker's stance and emotions (*Ausdrucksfunktion*),
- to appeal to the hearer (*Appellfunktion*),
- to refer to and represent things and states of affairs in the world (*Darstellungsfunktion*).

Figure 1:
Bühler's *Organonmodell*
(slightly adapted)

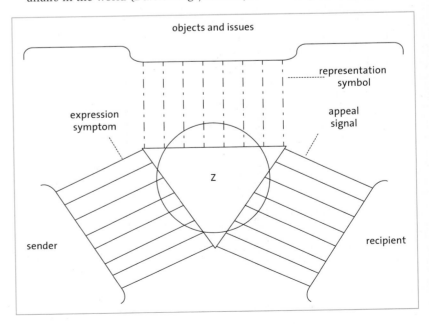

Accordingly, the linguistic sign is *symptom* (or index) of the speaker's frame of mind, *signal* for the hearer to act or behave in a particular way, and *symbol* of the relationship between the sign and what it denotes or refers to (Bühler 28).

Bühler's *Organonmodell* has had a lasting impact on the perception of language as an object of description in modern linguistics. It has also spurred some alternative proposals, of which only **Roman Jakobson**'s deserves a closer look. He prefers a finer grained distinction into six functions, which he relates to the "factors" of addresser, addressee, context, contact, code and message in the following way (Jakobson); we use language

1. to convey our attitudinal and emotional stances with reference to what we say or hear by using modal and prosodic means (**emotive or expressive function**);
2. to affect or influence our interlocutors by using prosody, terms of address, imperatives (**conative function**, Latin *conatio* means *endeavour*);
3. to describe persons, objects, situations (**referential function**);
4. to establish, maintain or terminate the contact with our interlocutors by using summons and routine formulae like *how are you; good to see you* (**phatic function**, Greek *phátis* means *speech*);
5. to ascertain that we (still) draw on the same means of communication by using queries, repairs, paraphrases (**metalingual function**);
6. to direct the hearer's attention to the form and style of the message by using rhyme and rhythm, alliteration and assonance (**poetic function**).

Needless to say, these six functions vary in terms of import and can be found in altering combinations (with one function usually predominating).

| Factor | Function (Jakobson) | Function (Bühler) |
| --- | --- | --- |
| addresser | emotive function | *Ausdrucksfunktion* |
| addressee | conative function | *Appellfunktion* |
| context | referential function | *Darstellungsfunktion* |
| contact | phatic function | |
| code | metalingual function | |
| message | poetic function | |

Functions of language

## 5.1.6 | Speech Acts

Even though the fact that language is multi-functional and well-suited for the accomplishment of a broad range of actions has never been doubted, it was absolutely immaterial in language description over a long period of time. Linguists have always been more interested in exploring grammatical rules than in investigating principles of language usage. The philosophers **John L. Austin** and **John R. Searle** were the first to develop a theory of verbal action in the middle of the last century. Under the name of **speech act theory**, their pioneering work rapidly made inroads into linguistics and instantiated a veritable success story.

**Austin.** Before developing the more complex theory of speech acts, Austin established a new theory of performativity on the grounds that we use language not only (and arguably not even chiefly) to make statements about the world. Denouncing this assumption as "a descriptive fallacy" (3), held too long in the history of (language) philosophy, Austin proposes a fundamental distinction between constative utterances, which we use to describe the world (e.g. *Austin established a theory of performativity*), and a new category of performative utterances, which we use to change the world. For instance, when I say *I promise to be on time next week* I do not describe an act but I *do* act, i.e. *perform* the act denoted by the main clause verb.

Performativity is thus a feature of those utterances where the articulation of the act denoted by the verb coincides with the performance of this act. Austin's (5) examples refer to acts of naming or christening ("'I name this ship the *Queen Elizabeth*'—as uttered when smashing the bottle against the stern"), of betting ("I bet you sixpence it will rain tomorrow") or of agreeing ("I do [sc. take this woman to be my lawful wedded wife]").

**Performative utterances** typically exhibit a verb of saying in first person singular present tense active form that can collocate with *hereby*. Furthermore, performative utterances "are not *true or false*" (Austin 5) for the simple reason that one cannot question (i.e. agree with or disagree with) the performance of an act that has just been performed. The utterance of a promise *is* the promise and its status as a promise can thus not be verified or falsified. **Constative utterances**, on the other hand, can be true or false because any assertion or description of some state of affairs can be matched with what is actually the case in the world. The constative utteranc *Willa Cather won the Pulitzer for her novel 'One of Ours'* is true or false depending on whether or not it is the case that Willa Cather won the Pulitzer for her novel *One of Ours*. Here, truth or falsity are ascribed to the relation between facts outside of the linguistic world to expressions inside the linguistic world (and not to the performance of a linguistic expression itself).

Delving deeper into the constative-performative distinction, Austin finds an increasing amount of restrictions and exceptions. (Arguably, most serious was the insight that constative utterances can easily be turned into performative utterances and *vice versa*. The same act, e.g. CLAIM, can be executed both by the performative *I claim that Joe attended a High School Class reunion over the weekend* and the constative *Joe attended a High School Class reunion over the weekend*.) Eventually this led him to "make a fresh start on the problem" by "reconsider[ing] more generally the senses in which *to say something* may be to do something, or *in saying something* we do something [or] [...] *by saying something* we do something" (Austin 91, our italics). This short quote displays the essence of his speech act theory. Any speech act can be described from three different vantage points corresponding to the three 'sub-acts' of locution, illocution and perlocution in the following way:

Focusing on the act of uttering itself ("the act of *saying something*") renders a **locutionary act** with its component acts of producing
- noises ("a *phonetic* act"),
- lexical, grammatical and intonational constructions ("a *phatic* act"), and
- meanings ("a *rhetic* act") (Austin 92–93).

Focusing on the act of performing a function (e.g. STATEMENT, QUESTION, REQUEST, PROMISE) *in* saying something renders an **illocutionary act** ("*In saying x I was doing y*"). Austin gives the example "In saying I would shoot him I was threatening him" (122). Different illocutions can be performed by using one and the same locution, e.g. REPORT or NARRATION in (8a), QUESTION in (8b), WISH in (8c), PREDICTION or PROMISE or WARNING in (8d), REGRET or CRITICISM in (8e):

(8a) Reggy spent the winter shooting any of God's creatures that were foolish enough to stray past the barrel of his gun.
(8b) Did Reggy spent the winter shooting ...?
(8c) I wish Reggy had spent the winter shooting ...
(8d) Reggy will spend the winter shooting ...
(8e) Regrettably, Reggy spent the winter shooting ...

Focusing on the act of achieving certain effects (e.g. amusement, anger, shame) *by* saying something renders a **perlocutionary act**. Austin gives the example "*By* saying I would shoot him I alarmed him" (122), where *alarm* is the perlocutionary verb which refers to the intended effect. Here are some more perlocutionary verbs (in italics):

(9) By pointing out "I will have an extra bedroom and a study with (I hope) a sofa bed" he *persuaded* us to stay at his house.
(10) By complimenting her on her beautiful purse he *cheered* her *up* and *made* her *happy*.
(11) By arguing that "Latin and Jazz are both dying" she *annoyed* him.

**Searle.** Searle adopts Austin's tripartite structure of the speech act with one very moderate alteration: Within the locutionary act, he distinguishes between an utterance act and a propositional act (performed by the acts of referring and predicating).

| | | Austin | Searle |
|---|---|---|---|
| **locutionary act** | { | phonetic act<br>phatic act | utterance act |
| | | rhetic act | propositional act:<br>• reference act<br>• predicate act |
| **illocutionary act** | | | **illocutionary act** |
| **perlocutionary act** | | | **perlocutionary act** |

Speech act structure according to Austin and Searle

While they generally agree on the structure of the speech act, their theories differ fundamentally as to their ontological quality. Unlike Austin, who simply relates functions to corresponding acts of saying, Searle introduces rule-relatedness as an essential precondition for the metamorphosis of any kind of verbal behaviour into the performance of purposeful speech acts. "Speaking a language," he argues, "is performing acts according to rules" (*Speech Acts* 36–37). In speech act theory, such rules that turn behaving into acting are called **constitutive rules**; they define the conditions under which an utterance X (*I can't reach the salt*) counts as the speech act Y (REQUEST to pass the salt). Constitutive rules, which are essential for the generation of a speech act, are joined by **regulative rules**, which are accidental because they merely regulate the use of already-generated speech acts.

For an utterance to count as the performance of an act, it has to conform to four kinds of **felicity rules**, of which the propositional content rule, the preparatory rule and the sincerity rule are regulative, while the essential rule is constitutive. In the (slightly abridged) table below, Searle (*Speech Acts* 66) defines these rules for the speech acts REQUEST, ASSERT/STATE and QUESTION.

*Searle's five classes of illocutionary acts*

Based on these rules (and a few other conditions), Searle distinguishes between five **classes of illocutionary acts**:

- **representatives** or **assertives** (STATING, SUPPOSING, DISCUSSING), which commit the speaker to the truth of their propositional content,
- **directives** (REQUESTING, PERMITTING, ASKING), which aim at committing the hearer to perform an act or attain a belief,
- **commissives** (PROMISING, OFFERING, REFUSING), which commit the speaker to the performance of the act or belief specified by the propositional content,
- **expressives** (APOLOGIZING, THANKING, CONGRATULATING), which convey the speaker's stance and attitude, and
- **declarations** (CHRISTENING, BLESSING, APPOINTING), which serve to create reality by performing the act denoted by the verb.

### Direct and Indirect Speech Acts

Speech act theory as developed by Austin and Searle promotes a fairly static, autonomous, speaker-oriented and even pre-contextual rather than a dynamic, collaborative, hearer- and context-oriented point of view. It focuses on single utterances rather than on strings of utterances, i.e. texts (even though illocutions and perlocutions are frequently carried by more than one utterance), and on illocutions as matching the speaker's intentions to be inferred by the hearer rather than as the outcome of a mutual process of negotiation. Such speaker-centrism breeds **problems** such as the following two.

Firstly, illocutions are not inherent, invariant and *a priori* given features of utterances that are easily inferred by whoever happens to be the hearer. The inference metaphor falsely conceptualizes utterances as containers and illocutions (or, in fact, intentions) as a material substance within the container to be taken out or 'inferred' by the hearer. The inadequacies and dangers of such metaphorical conceptualization have been convincingly confirmed (by Reddy; cf. Bublitz, *Englische Pragmatik* 40–48). The inference view precludes, for example, that the speaker's illocution can deviate from the hearer's or remain opaque and has to be openly negotiated; a case that is quite common, as can be seen from the following excerpt from Donna Leon's *A Noble Radiance*:

(12) 'Why do they do that to food?' he asked, pointing with his chin to the Count's plate. *'Is that a real question or a criticism of the service?'* the Count asked.

Hence, there is a repertoire of verbal means to handle discrepancies between the meant and the understood illocution, among them *post-factum* corrections by the speaker (*that was a simple question not a statement/threat/promise*) or the hearer (*so that was not a request but just a statement*).

Secondly, it is not at all clear what the process of inference is actually based on. Although there is

*Speech act rules according to Searle*

|  | **Request** | **Assert, state (that)** | **Question** |
|---|---|---|---|
| **Propositional content rule** | Future act *A* of *H[earer]*. | Any proposition *p*. | Any proposition or propositional function |
| **Preparatory rule** | 1. *H* is able to do *A[ct]*. *S[peaker]* believes *H* is able to do *A*.<br>2. It is not obvious to both *S* and *H* that *H* will do *A* in the normal course of events of his own accord. | 1. *S* has evidence (reasons, etc.) for the truth of *p*.<br>2. It is not obvious to both *S* and *H* that *H* knows (does not need to be reminded of, etc.) *p*. | 1. *S* does not know 'the answer,' i.e. does not know if the proposition is true, or, in the case of the propositional function, does not know the information needed to complete the proposition truly.<br>2. It is not obvious to both *S* and *H* that *H* will provide the information at that time without being asked. |
| **Sincerity rule** | *S* wants *H* to do *A*. | *S* believes *p*. | *S* wants this information. |
| **Essential rule** | Counts as an attempt to get *H* to do *A*. | Counts as an undertaking to the effect that *p* represents an actual state of affairs. | Counts as an attempt to elicit this information from *H*. |

a range of verbal and non-verbal means (cf. below), most of them usually function indirectly by indicating possible illocutions. Direct means of indicating a specific illocution are rare and restricted to performative verbs used to explicitly name the illocution:

(13) *I apologize* for not getting this off to you sooner.

Following Searle, the syntactic form of a sentence also counts as a direct means of indicating the illocution:
- declarative sentences are used for representative illocutions like STATEMENTS, ASSERTIONS, ASSUMPTIONS,
- interrogative sentences are used for erotematic (i.e. questioning) illocutions,
- imperative sentences are used for directive illocutions like ORDERS, REQUESTS, INVITATIONS.

Hence, Searle defines **direct speech acts** as those acts that feature such a form-illocution correlation (or else a performative verb). Speech acts lacking such correlation are termed **indirect**. Taking as an example the response *I have to study for an exam*, which is meant and understood not as a STATEMENT but as a REJECTION of the preceding SUGGESTION *Let's go to the movies tonight* ("Indirect Speech Acts" 61), Searle argues for three consecutive interpretive steps: Triggered by the sentence form (or the performative verb), the hearer first infers the "literal" (or direct) illocution (here: STATEMENT), then checks it against the context and, in case of incompatibilty (as is the case here), replaces it by the 'intended' illocution (REJECTION, or to be more precise: the EXPLANATION for the rejection). There are, however, several problems with this "literal force hypothesis" (Levinson, *Pragmatics* 263), among them the following two.

Firstly, the blatant discrepancy between the number of sentence types in English, three (or four if you include exclamatory sentences), and the number of speech acts, several thousand (according to Austin 150), leaves the overwhelming majority of illocutions without a prototypical sentence type of their own. Instead, most other (i.e. non-representative, non-erotematic and non-directive) illocutions are declarative in form (PROMISES, OFFERS, ANNOUNCEMENTS, APOLOGIES, REGRETS, DEFINITIONS, DECLARATIONS, BLESSINGS, etc.), which, however, does not automatically qualify them as direct speech acts. Only the presence of a performative verb can render them direct.

Secondly, even the three sentence types and their corresponding illocutions do not necessarily correlate; we can, *inter alia*, use
- interrogative sentences for STATEMENTS (so-called rhetorical questions): *Don't all Americans love baseball?*,
- interrogative sentences for REQUESTS: *Could you please send us the names and phone numbers of the places you have booked for us to stay?*,
- declarative sentences for QUESTIONS: *Bill: You got confirmed in eighth grade. Sue: Yeah*,
- declarative sentences for REQUESTS: *You always leave the door open.*

Accordingly, there is no fixed one-to-one-correlation but merely a tendency to correlate.

From a less static point of view, it seems more plausible to assume that directness is a gradient phenomenon and that speech acts are simply more or less direct. Even deprived of their contexts, utterances can intuitively be ranked on a **scale of directness** by taking the indicators used into account; the following list of ORDER/REQUEST displays a decreasing degree of directness (cf. Bublitz, *Englische Pragmatik* 146):

(14) I order/ask you to shut the door!
(15) Can I ask you to shut the door.
(16) Shut the door!
(17) Please shut the door!
(18) Can you shut the door?
(19) Would you please shut the door?

A higher degree of directness usually coincides with the use of formal indicators or "inference triggers" (Searle, *Speech Acts* 30) such as performative verbs (14), hedged performatives (15), syntactic forms (the imperative in 16), particles (17), fixed formulae (modal verb + pronoun + main verb in 18 and 19) and, of course, prosody in spoken discourse. Utterances without any of these inference triggers can get increasingly more indirect:

(20) You always leave the door open.
(21) The door seems to be open.
(22) I think people who shut doors when it's cold outside are really considerate.
(23) I hate sitting in a draught.
(24) I love sitting in a draught.

Being highly context-dependent, the illocutions of these utterances are not phenomenologically given but epistemologically constructed according to conventional social rules.

Directness as a gradient phenomenon

## 5.1.7 | Implied and Implicated Meanings

Meanings that language users understand even though they are not explicitly articulated are either intrinsically, i.e. systemically induced meanings or extrinsically, i.e. contextually induced meanings. The former kind includes entailments and semantic presuppositions, which are **implied** by context-independent semantic or structural features; the latter kind comprehends pragmatic presuppositions and implicatures, which are inferred, i.e. supposed and **implicated** by the language user in context.

Entailments and presuppositions are relationships that hold between two sentences or parts thereof, one of which is uttered and made explicit while the other is latent and implicit but understood nonetheless. In

(25)  Joe bought a bicycle that was stolen from him in front of the Law School. He didn't regret the bike, but he regretted losing his two locks that were supposed to hold the bike in place.

both relationships are manifest:

- **Entailment**: The utterances "a bicycle that was stolen" and "he regretted losing his two locks" are related to the non-uttered but implied or *entailed* sentences *the bicycle was gone* and *he had locks / he had one lock*.
- **Presupposition**: The utterances "Joe bought a bicycle" and "he regretted losing his two locks" are related to the non-uttered but inferred or *presupposed* sentences *there is someone called Joe* (or *Joe exists*) and *he lost his two locks*.

Entailments (also called semantic implications) hold in any kind of context because they arise from the intensional semantic features of the lexemes used and/or the grammatical relationships

between them. They are, accordingly, not defeasible or cancellable (unlike implicatures, see below) by negating the entailed sentence: you cannot say *he lost his two locks but he did not have any locks*. We could also say that the truth of the entailed sentence follows necessarily from the truth of the uttered sentence and vice versa:

| Uttered sentence (*Joe had two locks*) | | Entailed sentence (*He had locks*) |
|---|---|---|
| true | → | true |
| false | → | true *or* false |
| true *or* false | ← | true |
| false | ← | false |

Distribution of truth values for entailments

Presuppositions became a key topic in pragmatics subsequent to their investigation in (ordinary) language philosophy (notably by Bertrand Russell, Peter Strawson, and others). There are at least two readings of the term in linguistics.

In a narrower semantic sense, the term refers to the relation between an uttered sentence whose truth is (explicitly or implicitly) asserted and a non-uttered sentence whose truth is taken for granted or presupposed. Such semantic presuppositions are invoked by the semantics of the asserted sentence. There are several types of presuppositions, the most common ones are displayed in the table below (adapted from Yule 30).

As their truth is taken for granted, presuppositions are normally not cancellable (or cannot be questioned) by negating (or interrogating) the asserted (i.e. presupposition-carrying) sentence. In fact, the test of remaining intact under negation or interrogation helps to distinguish between presupposition and entailment:

| Type | | Trigger | Example | Presupposition |
|---|---|---|---|---|
| (a) | *existential p.* | proper noun, pronoun, (in-)definite noun phrase | *Austin, she, the old man* | Austin (etc.) exists |
| (b) | *factive p.* | predicate | *I regret laughing* | I laughed |
| (c) | *counterfactive p.* | predicate | *I imagined flying* | I did not fly |
| (d) | *implicative p.* | predicate | *I managed to pass* | I tried to pass |
| (e) | *change of state p.* | predicate | *I stopped driving* | I had been driving |
| (f) | *iterative p.* | predicate, particle | *I repeat the question* | I asked before |
| (g) | *structural p.* | • question<br>• non-restrictive relative clause | *When did he leave?*<br>*Joe, who loves storks, …* | He left<br>Joe loves storks |
| (h) | *counterfactual p.* | unreal conditional clause | *If I were there, …* | I am not there |

Types of presupposition

- *he lost his two locks* entails *he had locks*
- *he did not lose his two locks* does not entail *he had locks*
- *he regretted losing his two locks* presupposes *he lost his two locks*
- *he did not regret losing his two locks* still presupposes *he lost his two locks*

Hence the different distribution of truth values for semantic presuppositions:

| Assertion (*he regretted losing his two locks*) | | Presupposition (*he lost his two locks*) |
|---|---|---|
| true | → | true |
| false | → | true |
| (neither true nor false | ← | false) |

Distribution of truth values for semantic presuppositions

In actual language use, however, participants can (and frequently do) cancel presuppositions *post festum*, as in the following authentic exchange:

(26)  John: don't you wash your girlfriend's clothes
      Peter: that's a very intimate question about my girlfriend—actually—I don't have a girlfriend

John's utterance carries the existential presupposition that Peter has a girlfriend, which Peter accepts at first (*my girlfriend*) but then cancels (by explicitly negating it).

As they are not always valid but defeasible in context, presuppositions have frequently been defined in a broader pragmatic sense as a relation actually established by the speaker in context. For such pragmatic presuppositions, the structure and lexical meanings of a sentence merely define or delineate the set of possible presuppositions, i.e. the presuppositional potential from which participants choose in actual speech situations. In general, we can say that creating and understanding presuppositions is an essential and indispensable component of any meaning-making communicative process, with shared presuppositions being a prerequisite for the constitution of common ground (cf. below).

**Implicatures** also foster meaning-making in communicative exchanges. The term itself, one of the core concepts of pragmatics, was coined by the philosopher Herbert Paul Grice to refer to a specific way of inferring what is *meant* but not explicitly *said*. This amounts to a clear distinction between two kinds of meanings:

- 'linguistic' or 'said' meaning, which is determined by the pre-contextual lexical and propositional meanings of the utterance, also known as 'literal' or 'natural' meaning, and
- 'speaker's/hearer's' or 'implicated' meaning, which arises in context on the basis of a rational process of reasoning, also known as 'non-literal' or 'non-natural' meaning (Grice, *Studies* 213).

This ingenious distinction between what some call **sentence meaning** and **speaker meaning** for short (readily reflected in German, which has two terms for *to mean*: *bedeuten, was der Satz bedeutet* and *meinen, was der Sprecher meint*) sharply contrasts with traditional approaches to meaning. In Saussurean structural and Chomskyan generative linguistics (cf. sections V.2.2.2 and V.2.4.1), for instance, meaning is reduced to one of two complementary components of the abstract linguistic sign (*signifié* or *concept* interrelating with *signifiant* or *acoustic image*) and of the likewise abstract grammatical phrase or clause (sequences of sounds interrelating with sequences of meanings). Such simplistic coding-decoding models of system-driven *meaning in abstracto* can supplement but never account for use- or context-driven communicative *meaning in situ*. A speaker can say *p* (*I love sitting in a draught*) and mean *q* (*Close the window*) and be confident that the hearer will figure out *q* from *p* by inferring that the speaker *intends* her to implicate *q*. Grice thus sets his intention-recognition model against the traditional semantic coding-decoding model:

'*A* meant something by *x*' is roughly equivalent to '*A* intended the utterance of *x* to produce some effect in an audience by means of the recognition of this intention.' (*Studies* 220)

Following Grice, scholars of semantics as well as pragmatics widely concur that in meaningful verbal exchanges, inferring the interlocutor's **communicative intention** is just as important as decoding the linguistic meaning of the sentence that carries the intention. The hearer, set on recognizing the intention (which the speaker overtly wants her to recognize), resorts to a rational and ordered process of reasoning. Here is Grice's own and often quoted example of such reasoning:

Suppose that A and B are talking about a mutual friend, C, who is now working in a bank. A asks B how C is getting on in his job, and B replies, *Oh quite well, I think; he likes his colleagues, and he hasn't been to prison yet.* At this point, A might well inquire what B was implying, what he was suggesting, or even what he meant by saying that C had not yet been to prison. The answer might be any one of such things as that C is the sort of person likely to yield to the temptation provided by his occupation, that C's col-

Grice's intention-recognition model

leagues are really very unpleasant and treacherous people, and so forth. It might, of course, be quite unnecessary for A to make such an inquiry of B, the answer to it being, in the context, clear in advance. I think it is clear that whatever B implied, suggested, meant, etc., in this example, is distinct from what B said, which was simply that C had not been to prison yet. ("Logic and Conversation" 43–44)

To refer to the rational process geared at deducing the implicated meaning and intended by the speaker for the hearer to understand, Grice invented the term **implicature**. Conversational implicatures rest not only on the hearers' knowledge of the linguistic or said meaning, the context (and further aspects of the necessary common ground shared by the participants), but also on their cognitive skills of drawing conclusions (deductive, inductive or abductive) and making hypotheses on the basis of general principles of rationality and cooperation.

At the heart of any interpretation of implicatures lies the default **principle of cooperation**, which interlocutors actually do and are expected to observe as a matter of course:

Make your conversational contribution such as is required, at the stage at which it occurs, by the accepted purpose or direction of the talk exchange in which you are engaged. ("Logic and Conversation" 45)

Without abiding by such a principle and thus without behaving rationally, interlocutors will fail to converse successfully. Related to this principle are four **maxims of conversation**, which Grice deems to be descriptive rather than normative categories (see box).

---

**Focus on Grice's Four Maxims of Conversation**

**Quantity** "relates to the quantity of information to be provided, and under it fall the following maxims:
1. Make your contribution as informative as is required (for the current purposes of the exchange).
2. Do not make your contribution more informative than is required."
**Quality** includes "a supermaxim—'Try to make your contribution one that is true'—and two more specific maxims:
1. Do not say what you believe to be false.
2. Do not say that for which you lack adequate evidence."
**Relation** is "a single maxim, namely, 'Be relevant.'"
**Manner** relates "not (like the previous categories) to what is said but, rather, to how what is said is to be said, [it includes] [...] the supermaxim—'Be perspicuous'—and various maxims such as: 1. Avoid obscurity of expression. 2. Avoid ambiguity. 3. Be brief (avoid unnecessary prolixity). 4. Be orderly."
("Logic and Conversation" 45–46)

---

Conversational implicatures are evoked by the speaker's violating of one of these maxims while simultaneously and overtly observing the general principle of cooperation. (There are other ways of disregarding these maxims, which, however, do not trigger conversational implicatures; cf. Bublitz, *Englische Pragmatik* 215–18.) This clash gives rise to a process of reasoning on the hearer's side; in Grice's example just quoted, it is the maxim of relevance that triggers the following reasoning process:

in a suitable setting A might reason as follows: '(1) B has apparently violated the maxim 'Be relevant' and so may be regarded as having flouted one of the maxims conjoining perspicuity, yet I have no reason to suppose that he is opting out from the operation of the CP; (2) given the circumstances, I can regard his irrelevance as only apparent if, and only if, I suppose him to think that C is potentially dishonest; (3) B knows that I am capable of working out step (2). So B implicates that C is potentially dishonest.' ("Logic and Conversation" 49–50)

Unlike entailments, conversational implicatures are non-detachable (i.e. not dependent on a particular lexico-grammatical form), usually calculable (i.e. argumentatively reconstructable, cf. above) and thus cancellable. To take up example (25): From "he regretted losing his two locks that were supposed to hold the bike in place," we normally infer (on the basis of the cooperative principle and the maxim of quantity) the conversational implicature that *the writer had not more than two locks*. The implicature can, however, easily be suspended by a following utterance like "… well, three, actually, but the third one was broken."

Grice's theory has since been amended and augmented in various ways by, for example, suggesting other kinds of implicatures (Levinson, *Presumptive Meanings*; Carston), communicative principles and maxims (Leech's principle of politeness; Sperber and Wilson's general principle of relevance) or promoting from a Neo- or Post-Gricean perspective either a more context-oriented or a more semantic-oriented approach; the latter views semantics as pragmatically enriched (cf. Huang, "Types of Inference" and *Pragmatics*) and has consequently effected the semantics-pragmatics interface. Nevertheless, it seems safe to claim that most current scholars of pragmatics adhere to some version of Grice's theory. Its impact on linguistics and adjoining sciences cannot be overrated. It helped to realign the relationship between semantics and pragmatics by shifting explanations of phenomena that had previously burdened semantics into the realm of pragmatics. Pragmatics, therefore, owes its emancipation as a level of linguistic explanation *on a par* with (and *in lieu* of) semantics to Grice more than to any other scholar.

## 5.1.8 | Common Ground and Context

The concept of context is of paramount importance in any kind of pragmatic investigation because it encompasses those textual, social, cultural and other cognitive and knowledge related factors in a speech situation that are responsible for the establishment of common ground, another vital prerequisite for meaning negotiation. Common ground is foremost an epistemological phenomenon. But while it is not 'real' in the sense that it somehow exists 'outside' of communicating participants or observing analysts, it has a cognitive 'reality' and is accordingly best described as a mental representation of knowledge and attitudes assumed to be shared. Being dependent on each participant's own interpretation, it is 'common' to the interlocutors in the sense that they operate on the assumption that their respective grounds are congruent enough to arrive at equally congruent interpretations.

When communicating, we progressively build up common ground not simply by adding but rather by integrating new informational items into existing structures of conceptual and attitudinal knowledge. The accumulation of common ground is an empathetic process of constantly making **hypothetic assumptions** about our interlocutor's state of knowledge and frame of mind. Usually, though, when beginning to listen or read, we do not have to start from scratch, as it were, but can safely predict a certain amount of shared common ground, which chiefly depends on the degree of similarity of, *inter alia*, private, social, professional, cultural and situational background, in short, on 'what we have in common.' However, as people always have 'an awful lot in common,' the question needs to be settled as to what kind of common knowledge etc. we are talking about. Some scholars take a wide view and argue that common ground rests on "a wealth of generic knowledge":

Establishing the common ground is a subtle inference mechanism which capitalizes on many different information sources. [...] [They] include the verbal messages, properties of the speech participants [...], the topic of the interchange, the setting (time, place), the 'channel' (speech, writing, signals), the code (language, dialect), the message form (debate, chat, sermon) and the goals of the participants [as well as] the character roles, the actions [...] of characters (Graesser and Clark 25–26, 14).

According to a narrow view, the notion of common ground is only used to refer to those actually activated fragments of knowledge etc. that are relevant to the ongoing process of understanding and thus currently needed. In fact, only these are induced by the text (i.e. have a textual basis) and through the reactions of the participants.

The establishment of a common ground is often (in ongoing spoken conversation more than in written text) facilitated by the participants, who explicitly add new information (about what they mean and understand) to the text. An obvious example is the way referents are introduced by choosing between the different types of referring expressions available in the language. As readers of the following two fragments, we can easily infer the writers' hypotheses about the assumed readers' familiarity with the persons referred to. On the grounds of their respective hypotheses, the two writers choose referring expressions which they believe to be tailor-made for the assumed state of knowledge of their readers, thus helping them to develop their common grounds.

(27) Then this terrible election. How to explain? Pennsylvania and the whole northeast and Illinois went for Kerry as voters did on the west coast. The south and the middle west went for Bush. The Republicans spent large sums of money in Ohio. Mark Twain said ...

(28) This afternoon I am putting the painting in the Saab for a visit to Alfred and Anne Miller (the couple we had dinner with the night before you left). Alfred is flat in bed.

The use of the proper names (*Pennsylvania, Illinois, Kerry, Bush, Ohio, Mark Twain*) in (27) is a clear indication of the writer's strong assumption

---

**Definition**

→ **Common ground** is an ordered and emergent configuration of shared semantic knowledge, remembered episodes, emotive and evaluative attitudes rather than a random list of bits and pieces of knowledge, memory and stance. Being tightly related to the 'business at hand,' it is not a representation of the entirety of what the participants know, assume and believe. It does not refer to general world knowledge 'commonly' known in speech communities but only to knowledge that is mutually assumed to be shared by the participants involved in that particular situation (cf. Bublitz, "*It Utterly Boggles*").

that the reader knows each referent, and so is the use of the definite noun phrase *The Republicans*. Here, the identification is facilitated (and restricted at the same time) by the previous mention of *this* [...] *election* and the frame it opens. Again, the demonstrative noun phrase points to the writer's assumptions about the reader's familiarity with the referent. In (28), on the other hand, the writer does not assume that the reader can (easily) identify the two referents. The fact that he supplements the proper names with clarifying information (*the couple we had dinner with* [...]) clearly shows his judgment of his reader's state of knowledge and further his concern to secure referent identification. Changing the perspective, from writer to addressed reader, these two examples show how I, as the reader, construct my (view of our) common ground: I infer the writer's hypothesis about my state of knowledge and thus his (view of our) common ground on the basis of the language used. Consulting what is said or written is thus the chief means of making founded assumptions about the interlocutors' hypotheses and thus their shared common ground.

## 5.2 | Text Analysis

### 5.2.1 | The Origins of Text (and Discourse) Analysis

Arguably, the notions of text and discourse suffer from the 'Humpty Dumpty problem' more than other linguistic notions, i.e. they mean different things to different people. While Continental linguists commonly use the term **text** to refer to a stretch of spoken or written language, linguists schooled in the Anglo-American tradition have favored the synonymous concept of **discourse** instead. (An exception is Widdowson, *Discourse Analysis* 5, who defines text as the material substance or medium which underlies the communicative action, while discourse figures as its dynamic interpretation by a specific human individual in a given social and historical context.) In the following, we prefer the term *text* (unless there is an established concept like, for instance, a discourse marker).

Terminology: Text vs. Discourse

Text analysis has in the last three decades emerged as one of the most rapidly growing interdisciplinary fields of linguistic research. Its success springs from the fact that the analysis of texts does not only concern linguists but likewise relates to a wide array of other scientific disciplines, among them psychology, philosophy or literary theory. One result of this interdisciplinary nature is that over the years a plethora of approaches to the study and analysis of any kind of text has been assembled (arguably most prominent among them the socio-philosophical theories attributable to Jürgen Habermas and Michel Foucault, cf. section II.4.2). For linguistics, we can broadly distinguish between **two major approaches** to the analysis of text, which largely correspond to two cumulative stages in the evolution of text analysis. In the **first stage** (approx. 1900–1970), a small number of linguists simply defined text as 'a sequence of sentences' or as 'anything beyond the sentence' (cf. Harris). They mainly extended the rules of syntax, which govern the structure of the sentence, to larger linguistic chunks. Foreseeably, it turned out that these rules could not be transferred to units beyond the sentence because there is no text- or supra-sentential structure akin to sentential and sub-sentential structure. In the shadow of the pragmatic turn, text analysis entered its constitutive **second phase** in the early 1970s. Rather than assuming that text organization is shaped by language-internal rules, it was believed that text organization reflects the socio-cultural context in which it arises. Instead of treating text as a distinct and formally definable unit, linguists regarded text as language in use and as a tool or means to an end. It is this second vantage point which has widely shaped linguists' understanding of text, which is perhaps best captured in Halliday and Hasan's definition:

The word *text* is used in linguistics to refer to any passage, spoken or written, of whatever length, that does form a unified whole. [...] A text may be spoken or written, prose or verse, dialogue or monologue. It may be anything from a single proverb to a whole play, from a momentary cry for help to an all-day discussion on a committee. A text is a unit of language in use. It is not a grammatical unit, like a clause or a sentence; and it is not defined by its size. [...] A text is not something that is like a sentence, only bigger; it is something that differs from a sentence in kind. A text is best regarded as a semantic unit [...]. A text does not consist of sentences; it is realized by, or encoded in, sentences. If we understand it in this way, we shall not expect to find the same kind of structural integration among the parts of a text as we find among the parts of a sentence or clause. The unity of a text is a unity of a different kind. (1–2)

Taking this definition as a springboard, we can now present some central tenets of text:

**1.** Text relates to a linguistic item in use. Text can therefore not be analyzed and interpreted without a given context from which it draws its particular socio-cultural meanings. Going one step further, one can argue that text not only depends on context but creates its own context.

**2.** Text does not comply with any medial or formal limitations. Hence, text can neither be reduced to a specific medium (spoken, written) nor confined to any particular size or length. A single utterance (e.g. a slogan) or even a single word (*Parking*) can be a text in the same vein as a book or a newspaper article. In essence, we define text by its function in context and not by its form.

**3.** Text usually evokes a feeling of unity, which, however, is not structurally induced but the result of language users ascribing unity to the text. In so doing, they enrich texts with socio-cultural information, which they either obtain from the social environment in which the text is embedded or retrieve from their individual background knowledge.

The notion of 'language in use' has a narrow and a broad sense. We have just given a definition of the narrow sense by focusing on a single speech event and its particular use in context. In a broad sense and focusing on the wider social context, text is the umbrella term for a "conglomeration of social practices and ideological assumptions" (Schiffrin, Tannen and Hamilton 1). It then refers to conventional linguistic routines by which social orders and relations are reaffirmed, consolidated, challenged or changed. This broad social reading is adopted by a linguistic group of researchers called **critical discourse analysts** (e.g. Fairclough), who aim to unearth "the way social power abuse, dominance, and inequality are enacted, reproduced, and resisted by text and talk in the social and political context" (van Dijk 352).

In the following, we focus on the most influential concepts and methods devised in text analysis. While the first part explores the structure and organization of spoken and written texts, the second part shows how interlocutors give meaning to texts by relating to contextual phenomena.

## 5.2.2 | Giving Structure to Text: Participation Frameworks and Text Organization

**Participation Frameworks.** The view that communication is dyadic is one of the undisputed principles of communication. As we know from Bühler (cf. V.1.5), communication involves two human participants focussing on each other, i.e. communicating with each other. But research on the duality principle is, of course, much older. Most influential has been Wilhelm von Humboldt's view of **duality** as a universal communicative principle:

It is of particular significance that duality plays a much more important role in language than anywhere else. All speech is based on a dialogic exchange in which the speaker always regards the addressee as a unity even when the latter is not one but several persons. [...] There is an irremediable dualism in the original nature of language, and speaking itself is only possible because it rests on address and response. (138, our trans.)

Duality can surface on multiple linguistic planes. For instance, it comes into play in semantics when we distinguish speaker-induced from hearer-construed meanings, in pragmatics when we juxtapose speaker deixis and hearer deixis (cf. above), or in text analysis when describing adjacency pairs in two-sided conversations (QUESTION-ANSWER, cf. below). In face-to-face conversation as the default kind of communication, the duality principle presupposes two human beings in direct contact acting in a homogeneous social setting. This view can be depicted in the following diagram (cf. Hoffmann, *Cohesive Profiling*):

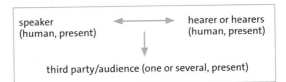

Face-to-face conversation

The advent of artefactual forms of mediation (letter, telephone call, email, chat and other Internet based forms) has, however, spurred various modifications of the participant concept. Both the producing and the receiving agent can be deconstructed in various ways. To account for such diversity, several theoretical models have been developed. The sociologist Erving Goffman (145–46) decomposes textual participation into several social roles according to their deviating personal

| Production Format | Description (cf. Manning 171) |
|---|---|
| *The principal* | The person or party held responsible for the position attested to the meaning of what was spoken |
| *The author* | The "creator" of a textual message |
| *The emitter* | The actual "sounding box," the performing speaker |
| *The animator* | The person engaging in expressive actions accompanying talk |
| *The figure* | The human or non-human characters enacted by the speaker |

*Goffman's production formats*

(propositional and evaluative) commitment to the content and social effect of the textual product.

While in two-party conversations, we may be able to assign all of the above speaker roles to one human individual, other text types such as interviews, newspaper articles, political speeches etc. allocate different roles to different individuals. Each of these persons usually fulfils various necessary tasks in the production and distribution of texts, yet they may distance themselves (in varying degrees) from the intended form, content and purpose of the communicative act. Here is an example: the principal, the author and the emitter of a statement can be

- three different persons, e.g. a government spokesman telling a secretary's account of a cabinet minister's ideas to a journalist,
- two different persons, the secretary telling her own account of a cabinet minister's ideas to a journalist,
- or just one person, the cabinet minister telling the journalist herself her ideas.

Focussing on the reception of communicative messages, Levinson ("Putting Linguistics on a Proper Footing") similarly proposes different roles of readers or hearers, thereby challenging the adequacy of a rigid dual speaker-hearer conception. More precisely, he distinguishes the following recipient types, which differ with respect to three criteria: (a) ratification vs. non-ratification of the recipient, (b) explicit vs. implicit verbal address, (c) intentional vs. unintentional act of reception (e.g. hearing vs. listening).

| Recipient Role | Description |
|---|---|
| Ratified *(Speaker is aware that recipient is listening)* | Addressed recipient |
| | Unaddressed recipient |
| Unratified *(Speaker is unaware that recipient is listening)* | Overhearers (unintentional witness) |
| | Eavesdroppers (intentional witness) |

*Levinson's recipient roles*

An even higher degree of participant deconstruction can be encountered in a few forms of written communication (where the producing and receiving roles amalgamate in varying degrees leading, *inter alia*, to roles such as reader-author) but clearly prevails in the description of some forms of Computer Mediated Communiation. To account for them, Goffman's model has to be adapted, as for example in Hoffmann's (*Cohesive Profiling*) proposal for capturing the specific range of participant activities in weblogs (see box on p. 449).

By inserting hyperlinks into their comments on blog posts, recipients can equally turn into linkers and thus into co-composers of the blog. Thus, the recipient's role may sometimes also adopt features of the producer's role. When combined, the analysis of production and reception formats (by Goffman; Levinson; and Hoffmann) provides a suitable point of departure for sociolinguistic studies which aim to retrace the portrayal and negotiation of cultural and political identity in different communities of practice.

**Text Organisation.** To reduce the complexity of communication in everyday interaction, a broad variety of means and principles serve to give structure to texts. Let us focus on those that structure dialogic communication. The analysis and description of dialogues is a relatively young field of research in linguistics, mostly because the technical equipment which is necessary for a high-quality recording and transcription of spoken language only became available in the late 1960s. Before, most linguists considered spoken language to be too messy to be the object of a viable linguistic description. The task of defining the properties, conventions and regularities by which human beings engage in dialogic interaction fell into the hands of three sociologists, Harvey Sacks, Gail Jefferson, and Emanuel Schegloff. Their combined approach, which maps out a simple methodology to capture the systematic regulations of dialogic text types, is known as (Ethnomethodological or American) **Conversation Analysis**. It centres on the description of **adjacency pairs** in conversation, which each consist of two (usually) verbal contributions: an opening part (first pair part, e.g. QUESTION) by the first speaker and a closing part (second pair part, e.g. ANSWER) by the second speaker. The opening part sets up an expectation for the second speaker to come up with an adequate response. The closing part then fulfils that expectation either by the second speaker responding in the most expectable and unmarked fashion (preferred response) or in a less expectable, marked and usually structurally more complex way (dispreferred response). Adjacency pairs can be linked up as proposed by Levinson (*Pragmatics* 336; see box below):

Sacks, Jefferson and Schegloff call each of these verbal contributions in an ongoing two-sided conversation a **conversational turn**. The speaker is said to hold the floor when she is engaged in such a turn over an extensive period of time without being interrupted or challenged by another interlocutor. Turns can thus become quite extended and complex structures. Due to a lack of planning time, interlocutors are also prone to make a number of performance errors. Sometimes these "communicative disturbances" (Hübler and Bublitz 7) are openly negotiated in ongoing discourse by resorting to metacommunicative utterances. The collaborative patterns which aim to mend a communicative breach are termed **repairs**. They are either triggered by speakers correcting themselves (self-repair), as in (29), or by hearers pointing out the communicative fault to the speaker (other repairs), as in (30):

(29)  I was interested in your advertisement and and but I gather you're after an enormous amount of information and I don't really know that I've got you know whether what I've got is of any help I mean it's really for you to decide really (*LLC*)

(30)  A  I've taken that into account I'm going to have to do a lot of it
      B  you mean domestic work at night
      A  no (laughs) a lot of reading at night (*LLC*)

Once a turn is completed (or is perceived to be completed), interlocutors must renegotiate who may or may not start the next turn. This point of transience between one turn and the next is called a **transition-relevant place**. In an effort to find viable answers to the question of how human beings organize and coordinate their turns at transition-relevant places, Duncan and other linguists have looked at signals which indicate and induce speaker change. Duncan's work represents an extensive body of research on the topic commonly known as **turn-taking**. While turn-taking seems to be a language universal (Duncan, "Some Signals" 285), there are, in

fact, socially distinct ways of doing so. On the grounds that research must focus on (non-)verbal signals generated for the negotiation of speaker rights, we can distinguish speaker signals from hearer signals. Speaker signals demonstrate that speakers wish to continue or yield their turn, hearer signals signpost that hearers are listening and refrain from claiming the role of the speaker.

As illustrated on the next page, interlocutors can select a range of lexical, phonetic, prosodic and other means to regulate their interaction on a macro plane. Additionally, they apply a range of lexical forms to signal how they intend to structure their own contribution with a view to the surrounding ongoing text. In other words, they use these lexical markers to structure individual textual contributions on a micro plane.

Among the most prominent pragmatic devices which serve the aforementioned purpose are **gambits** and **discourse markers**. Gambits are opening moves in chess, which explains why linguistic counterparts occur at the very beginning of a longer stretch of text. Text gambits are fixed expressions which show a low degree of morphological fixity. Their purpose is to reveal how the speaker plans to structure the ensuing topic talk. While gambits commonly serve a **textual function**, they may also fulfil two additional functions:

- an **ideational function** in that they express the speaker's attitude towards the propositional content of the utterance;
- an **interpersonal function** in that they can fine-tune the social relationship between speaker and hearer and thereby act as social lubricants.

| Producer | | Recipient (User(s)) |
|---|---|---|
| Blogger(s) | | 1. ratified<br>• addressed user<br>• unaddressed user |
| (Principal) – Author – Linker – Composer – (Animator) | | 2. unratified<br>• unintentional overseer<br>• intentional overseer |

Hoffmann's decomposition of participant roles in weblogs

| First Pair Parts | request | offer/invite | assessment | question | blame |
|---|---|---|---|---|---|
| **Second Pair Parts:**<br>*preferred* | acceptance | acceptance | agreement | expected answer | denial |
| *dispreferred* | refusal | refusal | disagreement | unexpected answer | admission |

Preference organization of adjacency pairs according to Levinson

Speaker and hearer signals
(adapted from Duncan,
"Structure")

| Purpose | Speaker signals | Hearer signals |
|---------|-----------------|----------------|
| turn-yielding signals | *phonetic and prosodic cues* (e.g. falling vs. rising intonation) *kinesic cues* (e.g. hand gestures, mimics) *discursive cues* (e.g. *but uh, or something*) | *lexical cues* (e.g. interruptions, gambits, discourse markers) *kinesic cues* (e.g. movement of the mouth, inhaling, increase of gestures, widening of eyes, seeking eye contact) |
| attempt-surpressing signals | *kinesic cues* (e.g. one or both hands being engaged in gesticulation | — — |
| speaker/hearer within-turn signals | *kinesic cues* (e.g. turning of the speaker's head toward the auditor) | *lexical cues* (e.g. request for clarification, brief restatements, sentence completion or repairs) |
| speaker/hearer continuation signals | *phonetic and prosodic cues* (e.g. increase in pitch and tempo) *kinesic cues* (e.g. shift away in head direction) | *lexical cues* (e.g. *uhm, uhuh, yes, right*) *kinesic cues* (e.g. nodding, shaking of head) |

Ideational and inter-
personal functions of gambits (adapted from Keller)

| Ideational function | Interpersonal function |
|---------------------|------------------------|
| *proposition-related judgments* (e.g. *I agree with you there ..., I guessed as much ..., no doubt about that ...*) | *mitigating one's own speech act* (e.g. *as far as I know ..., correct me if I'm wrong but ..., normally I wouldn't object at all but ...*) |
| *opinion related judgments* (e.g. *that's for sure ..., I couldn't agree less ..., you must be joking ...*) | *appealing to hearer* (e.g. *let's be fair ..., here's what we'll do ..., keep me posted ..., will you ..., why don't you ...*) |
| *emotive assessment* (e.g. *that must have been just awful ..., what a shame ..., I feel with you ..., serves you right ..., it's your own fault ...*) | *saving one's own face* (a) hedging (e.g. *I know this sounds stupid but ..., what I'm going to do may seem strange but ...*), (b) credentialing (e.g. *I'm not prejudiced but ..., I'm no racist but ...*), (c) sin licenses (e.g. *what I'm going to do is contrary to the letter of the law but not its spirit ...*) (d) appeals for suspension of judgment (e.g. *don't get me wrong ..., hear me out before you ...*) |
| *actions and proposals to act* (e.g. *I'd love to ..., I wouldn't mind ..., why don't we ..., I'd rather not ..., no way ...*) | |

There is an ongoing debate among linguists whether gambits are kinds of **discourse markers** or discourse markers a sub-group of gambits. Sometimes, both are subsumed under the umbrella terms discourse particles or pragmatic particles. Most linguists would agree that the following expressions are discourse markers: *anyway, however, still, incidentally, by the way, actually, what else, I mean, you know, well, now, so*. Typically, these lexical items have both a regular, non-discourse marking meaning (e.g. *now* as temporal adverb) and a discourse marking function (e.g. *now* as signalling the introduction of a new topic). Discourse markers are used to indicate the relevance and the position of the current utterance within the text. To give just one example, some discourse markers help to organize and structure the text by relating current topic talk to the main topic at hand; e.g. *by the way* and *incidentally* mark the beginning of a digression from the topic while *anyway* marks its end (and the return to the previous, i.e. main topic):

(31) B   you see Joe Eccleston wants to do a historical dictionary of Indic pronunciation—but as he says that can't be done until the Indiography comes out—I have *incidentally* persuaded the British Museum to purchase microfilms and or Xerox copies of every single item in my Indiography they don't have
   [...]

A    [...] you mentioned that there was one other thing you
     wanted to say

B    yes the last thing I wanted to say was this [...] (*LLC*)

After the digression, *A* eventually prompts *B* to return to his original main topic.

(32)   C    I went to Barkers the other day and I wanted to get one
        very posh cigar [...] and I went along to the cigarette
        counter—and the bloke said—oh you'll have to go
        round the corner—*it's the same counter* but it sort of
        shifts round you know to where the blue

     B    m

     C    the food counter is—*so anyway I went round there* and
        [...] (*LLC*)

## 5.2.3 | Giving Meaning to Text: Cohesion and Coherence

From the question of how interlocutors organize texts we now turn to the question of how they give meaning to texts, i.e. how they convert sequences of linguistic forms into meaningful wholes. A brief look at the **etymology of the word *text*** might help here. Text can be traced back to the Latin *textus*, which means *texture* in the sense of a woven fabric whose foremost feature is the arrangement and connection of its internal threads. (In medieval times, the expression was generally used to refer to the bible, both the material book and its writing; while *textus* addresses the normative main text of the bible, it excludes the glosses, appendices or additional commentaries added over the years by various clerical authors.) Following up on the original Latin meaning *texture*, we can best define a verbal text as an arrangement of interconnected elements. Such connectivity can arguably be of two sorts. Texts can be either connected 'from within' by utilizing its linguistic means or 'from without' by utilizing the knowledge frames and schemata of the interpreting language users.

**Cohesion.** The first type of connectivity is traditionally called cohesion (Latin *cohaerere* means *to stick together, to hold together*). It can be defined as a "textual prosody" (Bublitz, "*It Utterly Boggles*" 364), which we understand as the supraclausal colouring of linguistic items involving more than one element in a text. (Since J. R. Firth, who perceived prosodic effects as phonological colouring, we use *prosody* to refer to the property of a feature to extend its domain, stretch over and affect not just one but several units.) As cohesion is anchored in its linguistic forms and structures, we can argue that it is an invariant, user- and context-independent property of text. Still, Halliday and Hasan point out that cohesion should not only be regarded as a structural concept (with lexical or structural means linking an item to preceding or following items) but also as a semantic one. Cohesion is semantic because it also refers to inter-clausal semantic relations between propositions such as causality, finality or temporality which typically materialize on the surface level of a text. Temporality, for instance, cannot only be expressed lexically (*today*, *last Sunday*, *later*) or grammatically (as tense), but also as diagrammatic iconicity. The latter relates to the fact that the chronological order of narrated events usually reflects the linear order of the narrated textual elements: *Peter got the cork screw, uncorked the wine and poured two glasses* rather than *He poured two glasses, uncorked the wine and got the cork screw*.

Attempts to classify types of cohesive relations are legion. While de Beaugrande and Dressler, for example, focus only on grammatical cohesive relations, Halliday and Hasan distinguish between grammatical and lexical types of cohesion. In fact, cohesive means can be found on every level of linguistics.

| Phonology | rhythm | metre | rhyme | sound symbolism | intonation | sound rows |
|---|---|---|---|---|---|---|
| Morphology | compounds and derivations whose interpretation is based on and motivated by the text | | | | | |
| Syntax | repetition | parallelism | word order | tense and aspect | theme and rheme | focalization |
| Semantics | determiners | pronouns | conjunctions | anaphoric nouns, verbs, etc. | iconicity | semantic prosody |
| Pragmatics | hedges | gambits | discourse markers | collocation | tags | adjacency pairs |

Exemplary list of cohesive relations

Let us take a closer look at some of these categories to illuminate the concept of cohesion in more detail. As we can see, phonological means of cohesion include metre, rhyme or assonances, as in Lewis Carroll's poem "Jabberwocky":

(33) Twas brillig, and the slithy <u>toves</u>
Did gyre and gimble in the <u>wabe</u>;
All mimsy were the boro<u>goves</u>,
And the mome raths out<u>grabe</u>.
"Beware the Jabberwock, my son!
The jaws that bite, the claws that catch!
Beware the Jubjub bird, and shun
The frumious Bandersnatch!

In contrast, example (34) reveals how similar syntactic structures can likewise induce cohesive effects between two clauses.

(34) I    have    a deep fear    of insects    but
NP + VP    + NP    [ + PP]    =

I    have    a deeper fear    of my editors.
NP + VP    + NP    [ + PP]

("Eating Bugs," *Time*, 16 June 2008)

Analyzing cohesion

Perhaps the most frequent case of cohesion is the use of pronouns to replace preceding lexical expressions. In (35), the speaker Mary introduces the noun phrase *Professor Harrison* in the first clause. The ensuing utterances contain the pronoun *he* which naturally relates to the preceding phrase *Professor Harrison*. Each of these pronouns we may call a cohesive device which, upon reading, induces an **anaphoric** cohesive relation to its antecedent:

(35) Mary I'm supposed to work for *Professor Harrison* grading tests and stuff over Thanksgiving but *he* decided to do them all himself because ... *he* said that ... *he*'s gotten sort of a way of how everybody is doing you know? and *he* wants to make sure *he* knows because they uhm *he* um [...] (*Saarbrücken Corpus of Spoken English*, http://www.uni-saarland.de/fak4/norrick/scose.html)

Apart from anaphoric cohesive relations, we can sometimes spot **cataphoric** cohesive devices, which, rather than substituting a preceding expression, anticipate the occurrence of a following expression. Cataphoric devices are often used at the beginning of short stories. Sometimes, it so happens that authors use this strategy to reveal the identity of protagonists incrementally in the course of their narration. At other times, they seek to draw the readers right into the middle of an ongoing action:

(36) She is like St. Anne. Yes, the concierge is the image of St. Anne, with that black cloth over her head, the whisps of grey hair hanging, and the tiny smoking lamp in her hand. (K. Mansfield, "An Indiscreet Journey")

Recurring nouns, verbs, adjectives or adverbs can likewise build up cohesion, for instance by formal repetition as can be seen in example (37). Note that the noun phrase *hospital* in the second clause triggers a cohesive relation to the preceding noun phrase *hospitals*. In much the same way, lexical items can build semantic cohesive relations between clauses if they induce sense relations such as hyponymy, synonymy, antonymy, etc. (for more comprehensive descriptions consult Halliday and Hasan; and Schubert; see also section V.2.2.2).

(37) At a quarter past seven on Saturday evening in Cairo, a young resident from one of the city's largest *hospitals* called me. I had met him at the *hospital* earlier that day, but the situation, he said, was now much worse [...]. ("Chaos in Cairo," *New Yorker*, 29 Jan 2011)

Another important type of semantic cohesion is **collocation**. Following J. R. Firth's classic work, linguists traditionally define the term as the frequent syntagmatic co-occurrence of at least two linguistic items. Note that linguists commonly take syntagmatic co-occurrence to mean that the collocates (lexical items) must be placed in direct linear adjacency to each other as in *blonde hair* or *a flock of sheep*. In this sense, collocation is entirely intraclausal. Halliday and Hasan, however, redefined the notion of collocation from a textual viewpoint, claiming that collocation is "cohesion that is achieved through the association of lexical items that regularly co-occur" (248). In their view, co-occurrence is not restricted to the clause but refers to the distribution of lexical items across the text which share the same lexico-semantic colouring (educational terms in this example):

(38) [...] and that is the effect of changes in the *curriculum* the ways of *teaching* in *schools*—this is not anything to do necessarily with *comprehensive schools* or the abolition of the *grammar school*—it is notable that in this country it is the *middle classes* who have revolted against the conception of *the eleven plus*—but those of us who thought that you should postpone the age at which irrevocable decisions were taken about a child's *education* [...] (*LLC*)

Connectivity of texts therefore rests on the cohesive relations induced by multiple grammatical, morphological, semantic and pragmatic means. The ubiquity of cohesive relations in spoken and written texts has led linguists to ponder about its general status in texts. After all, in everyday conversation we sometimes encounter stretches of speech which lack cohesive devices and still seem fairly comprehensible to us:

(39) A: That's the telephone. [Get the phone, please!]
B: [I can't because] I'm in the bath. [You get the phone, please!]
A: O. K.
(Widdowson, *Teaching Language* 12, our parentheses)

Our cultural knowledge that person *B* in the bath (possibly showering) cannot answer the telephone allows us to make sense of this conversational exchange even though no cohesive relations hold between the individual contributions. We simply understand that *B*'s response to *A*'s implicit request is an explanation for the implicit rejection. Examples like these may not be the rule in everyday language. But their existence shows that while cohesion is normally a sufficient condition it is not a necessary condition for a meaningful interpretation, or, to put it differently, for the coherence of utterance sequences, i.e. a text.

Coherence. Even though cohesion and coherence refer to meaning resting on relations of connectedness (between individual propositions and sets of propositions), which may or may not be linguistically encoded, they are descriptive categories which differ in kind. Coherence is a cognitive category depending on the language user's interpretation. Unlike cohesion it is not an invariant property of a text, i.e. it is not *given* in a text independently of an interpretation. Consequently, we cannot say "a text has coherence" in the same way as we can say "a text has a beginning or an end," or indeed, "a text has cohesion." We can only say "someone understands a text as coherent."

Coherence is, of course, based on the (cohesive) language of the text but, and this is its defining characteristic, dependent on additional **extra-textual cognitive resources**:

- The interlocutors' knowledge of the general principles and strategies of human communication;
- their immediate, contextual or 'running' knowledge of the situational parameters;
- their episodic or autobiographical knowledge (as described by Tulving);

- their factual or declarative knowledge of social, cultural, historical and related encyclopaedic facts;
- their cognitive skills like drawing conclusions, relating propositional information to mental frames, creating mental spaces, mappings and blendings;
- their empathetic skills of making assumptions about their interlocutor's knowledge and cognitive skills; only shared reciprocal knowledge is coherence-inducing knowledge. It is essentially this empathetic assumption about the writer (with his knowledge and assumptions about me as the reader addressed) that leads to the establishment of a common ground (see above). Ultimately, it is on the basis of the resultant common ground that we arrive at an interpretation of coherence, which we take to match the writer's, if not totally then at least to a sufficiently congruent extent.

Since it is not texts that cohere but rather people who make texts cohere, we can say that for one and the same text there exist a speaker's and a writer's or a hearer's and a reader's (and indeed also an analyst's) coherence, which may or may not match. Normally speakers are set to help create and secure coherence by (more or less subtly) guiding their hearers to a suggested line of understanding. Conversely, hearers use these guiding signals as instructions to align their interpretations with what they take to be the speakers' intentions. Coherence is only approximate and a matter of degree and best described as a scalar notion. Any interpretation of coherence is restricted and, accordingly, partial to different degrees. It is the outcome of the language user's gestalt creating power. People are driven by a strong desire to identify forms, relations, connections which they can maximize in order to turn fragments into whole gestalts, i.e. to 'see' coherence in strings of utterances. As a rule, speakers and hearers alike operate on a standard or default assumption of coherence. This explains why, despite the fact that ascribing coherence frequently involves making difficult and complex acts of inference, cases of disturbed coherence are not abundant, and why people try to understand coherence even though the data to go by may look sadly insufficient.

As a rule of thumb, we can thus draw on the following **central tenets** for cohesion and coherence, which help to delineate these concepts that are essential for textuality.

Central tenets for cohesion
and coherence

| Cohesion | Coherence |
|---|---|
| intratextual connectivity | extratextual connectivity |
| *post festum* | *in actu* |
| invariant and user independent (different participants observe the same range of cohesive means used) | variant (approximant, scalar) and user dependent (different participants may arrive at different interpretations, depending on factors like their individual knowledge) |
| phenomenologically real | epistemologically real |

## 5.3 | Outlook

Pragmatics is becoming
more empirical,
interaction- and
cognition-related.

There is a clear tendency for pragmatics to become more empirical, interaction- and cognition-related. In recent years, Cognitive Pragmatics, Pragmatics of Computer Mediated Communication (CMC) and other novel drifts have been gaining momentum at the expense of traditional mainstream pragmatics. Modern pragmatic research is not only steered by advanced theoretical (cognition-based) or technological (CMC-based) lines of description but also, increasingly so, by new methodological approaches. Thus, established and well-approved methods like intuition, introspection, observation, elicitation or ethnographic field work are supplemented by new modes of analysing data within **corpus-based pragmatics** and **experimental pragmatics**. Furthermore, thanks to advanced technical equipment, data can be dealt with in a much more sophisticated, accurate and thus ultimately enlightening way (as in the case of multi-modal, i.e. audio-visual notations of spoken face-to-face interaction). It is not difficult to envisage that such developments will also further new insights into yet ill-understood, intricate and multifaceted issues of study (as, for example, the concept of *(im-)politeness* in *Interpersonal Pragmatics*). As a field of study with a high degree of topical complexity and heterogeneity, whose openness for new research methods is still continually increasing, pragmatics in linguistics is undoubtedly facing a bright and promising future.

(For up-to-date overviews of *Cognitive Pragmatics*, cf. Schmid; of *Pragmatics of Computer Mediated Communiation*, cf. Herring, Stein and Virtanen; of *Interpersonal Pragmatics*, cf. Locher and Graham; and of the *Foundations*, cf. Bublitz and Norrick.)

In a similar vein, text analysis continues to fine-tune its quantitative, corpus-driven and qualitative, context-based schemes of analysis. It has also started to explore new arenas of study, such as the investigation of writing spaces in new forms of CMC or the complex functional interplay and dissemination of semiotic modes in mass media. Meanwhile, text analysis maintains a strong commitment to its original critical assessment of texts and the evaluation of their social, political and ethical implications for our societies. If nothing else, text analysis has shown in the last three decades that concepts like power, politeness, gender or identity cannot be unmasked without prior recourse to the texts (and contexts) in which they arise. It is this social concern which arguably ties text analysts to a larger interdisciplinary collective of scholars who share an interest in the discursive nature of social affairs. It is in collaborating with scientists, such as social and cognitive psychologists, sociologists, philosophers or literary theorists, that linguistic text analysis will further enhance its perspective and appeal both within linguistics and beyond.

### Select Bibliography

**Austin, John L.** *How to Do Things with Words.* 1962. 2nd ed. London: Oxford University Press, 1975.

**Beaugrande, Robert-Alain de, and Wolfgang U. Dressler.** *Introduction to Text Linguistics.* London: Longman, 1981.

**Bublitz, Wolfram.** *Englische Pragmatik: Eine Einführung.* 2nd ed. Berlin: Erich Schmidt, 2009.

**Bublitz, Wolfram.** "*It Utterly Boggles the Mind*: Knowledge, Common Ground and Coherence." *Language and Memory: Aspects of Knowledge Representations.* Ed. Hanna Pishwa. Berlin: de Gruyter, 2006. 359–86.

**Bublitz, Wolfram, Andreas A. Jucker, and Klaus P. Schneider, eds.** *Handbooks of Pragmatics.* 9 vols. Berlin: de Gruyter Mouton, 2010-.

**Bublitz, Wolfram, and Neal Norrick, eds.** *Foundations of Pragmatics.* Berlin: de Gruyter Mouton, 2011. Vol. 1 of

*Handbooks of Pragmatics.* Bublitz, Jucker, and Schneider, gen. eds.

**Bühler, Karl.** *Sprachtheorie: Die Darstellungsfunktion der Sprache.* 1934. 2nd ed. Stuttgart: Gustav Fischer, 1965.

**Carston, Robyn.** *Thoughts and Utterances: The Pragmatics of Explicit Communication.* Oxford: Blackwell, 2002.

**Dijk, Teun van.** "Critical Discourse Analysis." *Handbook of Discourse Analysis.* Eds. Deborah Tannen, Deborah Schiffrin, and Heidi E. Hamilton. Oxford: Blackwell, 2001. 352–71.

**Duncan, Starkey.** "On the Structure of Speaker-Auditor Interaction During Speaking Turns." *Language in Society* 3 (1974): 161–80.

**Duncan, Starkey.** "Some Signals and Rules for Taking Speaking Turns in Conversations." *Journal of Personality and Social Psychology* 23 (1972): 283–92.

**Fairclough, Norman.** *Discourse and Social Change.* Oxford: Blackwell, 1992.

**Firth, John R.** "Modes of Meaning." *Papers in Linguistics: 1934–1951.* Ed. John R. Firth. London: Oxford University Press, 1951. 190–215.

**Goffman, Erving.** *Forms of Talk.* Oxford: Blackwell, 1981.

**Graesser, Arthur C., and Leslie F. Clark.** *Structures and Procedures of Implicit Knowledge.* Norwood: Ablex, 1985.

**Grice, Herbert Paul.** "Logic and Conversation." *Speech Acts.* Eds. Peter Cole and Jerry L. Morgan. Syntax and Semantics 3. New York: Academic Press, 1975. 41–58.

**Grice, Herbert Paul.** *Studies in the Way of Words.* Cambridge: Harvard University Press, 1989.

**Halliday, Michael A. K., and Ruqaiya Hasan.** *Cohesion in English.* London: Longman, 1976.

**Harris, Zellig S.** "Discourse Analysis: A Sample Text." *Language* 28 (1952): 474–94.

**Herring, Susan, Dieter Stein, and Tuija Virtanen, eds.** *Pragmatics of Computer-Mediated Communication.* Berlin: de Gruyter Mouton, 2013. Vol. 9 of *Handbooks of Pragmatics.* Bublitz, Jucker, and Schneider, gen. eds.

**Hoffmann, Christian.** *Cohesive Profiling: Meaning and Interaction in Personal Weblogs.* Amsterdam: Benjamins, 2013.

**Hoffmann, Christian, ed.** *Narrative Revisited: Telling a Story in the Age of New Media.* Amsterdam: Benjamins, 2010.

**Huang, Yan.** *Pragmatics.* Oxford: Oxford University Press, 2007.

**Huang, Yan.** "Types of Inference: Entailment, Presupposition, and Implicature." Bublitz and Norrick 397–421.

**Hübler, Axel, and Wolfram Bublitz.** "Introducing Metapragmatics in Use." *Metapragmatics in Use.* Eds. Wolfram Bublitz and Axel Hübler. Amsterdam: Benjamins, 2007. 1–26.

**Humboldt, Wilhelm von.** "Ueber den Dualis." 1827. *Schriften zur Sprachphilosophie.* Vol. 3 of *Wilhelm von Humboldt: Werke in 5 Bänden.* Eds. Andreas Flitner and Klaus Giel. 3rd ed. Darmstadt: WBG, 1969. 113–43. 5 vols.

**Jakobson, Roman.** "Linguistics and Poetics." *Style in Language.* Ed. Thomas A. Sebeok. Cambridge: MIT Press, 1960. 350–77.

**Keller, Eric.** "Gambits: Conversational Strategy Signals." *Journal of Pragmatics* 3 (1979): 219–38.

**Koyama, Wataru.** "The Rise of Pragmatics: A Historiographic Overview." Bublitz and Norrick 139–66.

**Leech, Geoffrey.** *Principles of Pragmatics.* London: Longman, 1983.

**Levinson, Stephen.** "Deixis." *The Encyclopedia of Language and Linguistics.* Ed. Ron E. Asher. Oxford: Pergamon Press, 1994. 853–57.

**Levinson, Stephen.** *Pragmatics.* Cambridge: Cambridge University Press, 1983.

**Levinson, Stephen.** *Presumptive Meanings: The Theory of Generalized Conversational Implicature.* Cambridge: MIT Press, 2000.

**Levinson, Stephen.** "Putting Linguistics on a Proper Footing: Explorations in Goffman's Concepts of Participation." *Erving Goffman: Exploring the Interaction Order.* Eds. Paul Drew and Anthony Wootton. Boston: Northeastern University Press, 1988. 161–227.

**Locher, Miriam, and Sage Graham, eds.** *Interpersonal Pragmatics.* Berlin: de Gruyter Mouton, 2010. Vol. 6 of *Handbooks of Pragmatics.* Bublitz, Jucker, and Schneider, gen. eds.

**Manning, Philip.** *Erving Goffman and Modern Sociology.* Stanford: Stanford University Press, 1992.

**Morris, Charles.** "Foundations of the Theory of Signs." *International Encyclopaedia of Unified Science.* Eds. Otto Neurath, Rudolf Carnap, and Charles Morris. Chicago: University of Chicago Press, 1938. 77–138.

**Reddy, Michael J.** "The Conduit Metaphor: A Case of Frame Conflict in Our Language About Language." *Metaphor and Thought.* Ed. Andrew Ortony. Cambridge: Cambridge University Press, 1993. 164–201.

**Sacks, Harvey.** *Lectures on Conversation.* Ed. Gail Jefferson. Oxford: Blackwell, 1992.

**Sacks, Harvey, Emanuel Schegloff, and Gail Jefferson.** "A Simplest Systematics for the Organization of Turn Taking in Conversation." *Language* 50 (1974): 696–735.

**Schiffrin, Deborah, Deborah Tannen, and Heidi E. Hamilton, eds.** *The Handbook of Discourse Analysis.* Oxford: Blackwell, 2001.

**Schmid, Hans-Jörg, ed.** *Cognitive Pragmatics.* Berlin: de Gruyter Mouton, 2012. Vol. 4 of *Handbooks of Pragmatics.* Bublitz, Jucker, and Schneider, gen. eds.

**Schubert, Christoph.** *Englische Textlinguistik: Eine Einführung.* 2nd ed. Berlin: Erich Schmidt, 2012.

**Searle, John R.** "The Classification of Illocutionary Acts." *Language in Society* 5 (1976): 1–24.

**Searle, John R.** "Indirect Speech Acts." *Speech Acts.* Eds. Peter Cole and Jerry L. Morgan. Syntax and Semantics 3. New York: Academic Press, 1975. 59–82.

**Searle, John R.** *Speech Acts.* Cambridge: Cambridge University Press, 1969.

**Sperber, Dan, and Deirdre Wilson.** *Relevance.* Oxford: Blackwell, 1986.

**Tulving, Endel.** *Elements of Episodic Memory.* Oxford: University Press, 1983.

**Widdowson, Henry G.** *Discourse Analysis.* Oxford: Oxford University Press, 2007.

**Widdowson, Henry G.** *Teaching Language as Communication.* Oxford: Oxford University Press, 1978.

**Yule, George.** *Pragmatics.* Oxford: Oxford University Press, 1996.

*Wolfram Bublitz/Christian Hoffmann*

# 6 Standard and Varieties

## 6.1 | Introduction: Notions and Ideologies

An advanced learner of English who travels to any English-speaking country will soon be faced with reality, the observation that many people speak quite differently from the "school English" one was taught. Positing a standard norm of the language for teaching purposes makes sense from a pedagogical perspective, of course, and certainly standard forms of English will also be widely encountered and constitute an important part of linguistic performance. This is only half the story, however. In real-life contexts, English comes in all shapes and sizes, as it were:

- national norms (e.g. American English),
- regional dialects (e.g. Yorkshire dialect, Appalachian English),
- social varieties (e.g. "Valley Girl Talk" in California, working class speech),
- institutionalized second-language forms in postcolonial countries (increasingly important in times of globalization; e.g. Singaporean or Kenyan English),
- strongly contact-induced forms such as creoles (newly-born contact languages, often stemming from colonial plantation cultures; e.g. Jamaican Creole) or pidgins (structurally reduced auxiliary forms used between speakers of different languages),
- and others.

Obviously, the processes which have produced these **varieties** are an important object of investigation and description in linguistic scholarship. The same applies to their structural properties on the levels of pronunciation, lexis, grammar and also pragmatics. A user or learner of English needs to be broadly familiar with certain varieties of the language, at least those in one's environment and some of the more important ones. To some extent this is necessary simply for successful communication. In addition to the ability to understand "real English," however, familiarity with language variation allows us to appreciate the rich sociosemiotic information, the cultural baggage that is encoded in every speech utterance. As soon as anybody opens their mouth, the way one speaks betrays one's regional and social origins but also, possibly, one's social aspirations, one's attitudes towards the situation one is in and the relationship to interlocutors, and so on. Native speakers acquire much of this sociosymbolic competence through regular exposure in the course of time; for non-native speakers it makes sense to acquire at least some strong feel for the social meanings of linguistic forms, in practice or via reading about it.

The relationship between "Standard English" and its varieties is also a topic which is ideologically loaded—it has something to do with power relationships in a society. In many contexts, a command of standard English is acquired in formal, educational settings, but speakers' access to higher education correlates with status, power, and wealth, privileging an upper stratum of a society. In the English-speaking world, language, and one's accent in particular, is an integral part of the deliberate performance of such power and attitudes. An example from England's cultural history in which this is embodied most vividly is George Bernard Shaw's *Pygmalion*: for Eliza Doolittle, the flower girl, the main step towards being accepted as a lady is the acquisition of proper pronunciation, i.e. replacing her Cockney /aɪ/ vowels by standard /eɪ/ realizations in phrases such as the famous *rain in Spain stays mainly in the plain*. Manners count as well, of course, but the symbolic power of accent comes first. This is a highly conservative example, of course. For the last few de-

The uses of studying
language variation

**Definition**

**standard**: a socially accepted norm of a language, associated with formal contexts and high-status speakers, also the target of language education

**RP**: "Received Pronunciation," the pronunciation norm of standard British English

**variety**: any coherent, systematic form of a language associated with specific situational parameters (time, place, typical speakers, also medium of realization), typically associated with characteristic linguistic forms

**dialect**: technically speaking, the same as a *variety* (so that *Standard English*, for instance, is also no more than "just" any dialect, associated with formal contexts and not inherently superior to any other dialect); popularly, a regional or social nonstandard variety

**accent**: the pronunciation (sound level / phonetics and phonology) of any variety

**regional dialect**: a variety associated with a certain place or region

**social dialect**: a variety associated with a specific social group (e.g. male vs. female, young vs. old, white-collar vs. blue-collar speakers)

**sociolect**: a more technical term for *social dialect*

**idiolect**: the speech behavior of any individual

The mistaken notion of "English" equaling "Standard English" only, and of all other forms, including nonstandard varieties, being mere deviations, is widespread. A prescriptive attitude, the insistence on the need to produce "proper English" or "good English," is deeply rooted both in Britain and, perhaps even more so, in North America. It has even been disseminated into postcolonial countries where English is immensely important nowadays. Take Singapore as an example: for a decade or so the government has been running a "Speak Good English Movement" for fear of jeopardizing Singaporeans' international "intelligibility" (another ideologically loaded buzz word) by the widespread use of the popular form known as "Singlish." In contrast, sociolinguists have come to recognize what socially competent speakers have known subconsciously and skillfully manipulated all the time: the ubiquity and importance of variation and the reality of varieties of English. Dialects of English are not just random aberrations, as many people think and conservative gatekeepers of society imply. They provide a stage to subtly perform the management of one's identities, social alignments, and settings in context.

Linguists have come to categorize these varieties of English in several ways, depending upon their social settings and structural properties. Some central terms are explained in the 'Definition' box.

cades, even in Britain, social and linguistic changes such as democratization and colloquialization have, to some extent, resulted in the acceptance of accented forms of English in public and formal domains as well.

## 6.2 | Varieties of English: A Survey

### 6.2.1 | Varieties and Variety Types: Some Illustrative Examples

The previous section introduced the notion that, in reality, "English" is not a monolithic entity, but comes in a myriad of varieties, forms and systems which are tied to specific user groups and usage contexts and have their characteristic properties. Boundaries are fuzzy, and there is no way of delimitating or counting such varieties. On the one hand, there are some supraregional varieties which have become conceptualized as linguistic entities which many people would know something about or have a rough idea of, e.g. "northern English" in England, "Lowland Scots," "Southern" dialect in the U.S., "African American English," or "Philippine English." On the other hand, people commonly tell outsiders that even in the next-door village a "different dialect" is spoken, different words

are used, or some words are pronounced differently. Typically, varieties are associated with characteristic features on the main language levels (sounds, words, grammar).

The following examples (from Schneider, *English Around the World*, where many more examples can be found) offer just a glimpse of the variability we encounter.

(1) Freddie wor sat i' t'chair evvin 'is 'air cut.
(2) Heah, yawl will discovah thet the English language iz spoke like it oughta be spoke.
(3) I know from I small-small say I a' go do somet'ing ina dis worl'. Is my chance dis.
(4) having a knowledge about falling object will create you some ideas how we can change, we can transform energy from one form to another form.

Example (1) is from a website with samples of Yorkshire dialect poetry (www.yorkshire-dialect.org); it illustrates some dialect features such as singular *were* for *was*, article reduction (*t'* 'the'), h-dropping ('*is 'air*') and regional vowel variants (/ʊ/ in *cut*).

Example (2) is from a popularizing booklet on U.S. Southern dialect (Nick and Wilann Powers, *Speakin' Suthern Like It Should Be Spoke!*), with some properties to note, e.g. the distinct second person plural pronoun *yawl* ('you-all'), lack of 'rhoticity,' the phonetic realization of a postvocalic /r/ phoneme (*heah* 'here,' *discovah*), or nonstandard past participle forms (*spoke* 'spoken').

Example (3) is from a Jamaican novel (Michael Thelwell, *The Harder They Come*, 1980), showing typically creole structural forms such as reduplication (*small-small*), deletion of a copula (*I Ø small-small*), the complementizer *say* 'that' after speech act verbs, and the use of a clause-initial copula form as a highlighter (*Is my chance dis.* 'This is …').

And example (4), from a TV speech in Malaysia, displays properties which are characteristic of "New" or Asian Englishes including count uses of uncountable nouns (*a knowledge*), lack of plural marking (*object* 'objects'), innovative verb complementation patterns (*create you some ideas*), monophthongization of diphthongs (/e:/ in *change*), and redundant repetitions (*one form to another form*).

In fact, there is no real boundary of what counts still as English and what doesn't. Görlach once illustrated this fact, somewhat programmatically, in an article entitled "And Is It English?", in which he confronted the reader with texts which are strange and difficult to comprehend but clearly English somehow. Consequently, recent theorizing has come to expand considerably the notion of which types of English there are. Mesthrie and Bhatt (3–6) propose the framework of an "**English Language Complex**," which comprises as many as twelve variety types, including

- "Metropolitan standards" (e.g. British English),
- "Regional dialects" (e.g. East Anglia dialect),
- "Creole Englishes" (e.g. Krio in Sierra Leone),
- "Immigrant Englishes" (e.g. Chicano English in the southwestern US),
- "Language-shift Englishes" (e.g. Irish English),
- "Jargon Englishes" (e.g. unstable speech forms used by sailors), and
- "Hybrid Englishes" (e.g. India's "Hinglish," a constant mix between Hindi and English).

## 6.2.2 | Parameters of Variation

All the varieties of English correlate with specific social settings which determine their conditions of use. Three main parameters of variation can be distinguished: regional, social and stylistic variation.

Regionality operates on different scales, as it were. Differences between the main national varieties, e.g. between British and American English or "World Englishes" (say, South African English, New Zealand English, or Malaysian English) are products of the relationship between space and language variation. Prototypically, however, the notion relates to regional speech differences in the narrow sense, i.e. units like southern vs. northern English (relevant both in Britain and in the U.S., remarkably), Devonshire dialect, or Boston speech forms. And the same principle of one's origin determining one's speech forms operates down to the local level as well, as the existence of speech differences between adjacent villages shows.

Social variation results from the fact that societies are sub-divided into distinct groups of people within which communicative ties are denser than across group boundaries. It is determined by specific speaker parameters, including social class, age, gender, education, or occupation. These will be discussed in greater detail in section 6.5 below.

Style. The concept of style has to be understood in a slightly broader fashion than the non-technical meaning of this notion would imply. In linguistics it denotes the choice of linguistic forms relative to the communicative context of a situation in a broader sense. We typically adjust our linguistic performance to the needs and requirements of a specific context: we speak differently from the way we write; we talk differently in formal, public performances than in leisurely or intimate interactions with friends (saying things like "Will you please support our cause" as compared to "Come on, give me a hand," respectively); and we may signal social distance or proximity to an interlocutor via the choice of alternative speech forms (such as "Mr. Smith" vs. "Jimmy"). In early sociolinguistic theory, following William Labov in the 1960s, the origin of this kind of variability was seen in the fact that speakers self-monitor and adjust their speech behavior according to the needs of the situation. A later approach is Allan Bell's "audience design" concept, suggesting that speakers adjust their talk so that it works most effectively for an intended group of recipients.

'World Englishes'

### 6.2.3 | Contact-Derived Variability

Not infrequently properties of English which characterize certain regional or social varieties have their origin in **contact with other languages**. The historiography of English has been characterized by a tendency to downplay the impact of contact in order to strengthen the "purity" of the language. It is well known that, in the course of time, English has been in contact with many other languages and has been transformed in this process (cf. entry V.3). Contact effects have varied from one group to another, so there is an intrinsic interrelationship between some formal properties of specific varieties and the amount of contact they have experienced. For example, northern English dialects are marked more strongly than others by Scandinavian-derived loans, because this is a core part of the Danelaw, where Danish settlers resided in the Old English period. In contrast, formal and written English are characterized by a higher propensity to use Latinisms, which were borrowed in large numbers during the Renaissance, as so-called "hard words."

Traces of contact are even stronger, however, in younger varieties which have emerged outside of England in the process of the regional and global expansion of the language. This begins with Ireland: **Irish English** is viewed by a number of scholars as shaped by an Irish (Gaelic) substratum (Filppula, Klemola, and Paulasto). Not surprisingly, the effect is even stronger in the cases of **Postcolonial Englishes** (Schneider, *Postcolonial English*). Example (5) illustrates Singapore's *kena*-passive, for instance. A Malay-derived particle has been retained in a regionally distinctive English passive construction with further, innovative constraints (such as a reduced participle morphology and an obligatory adversative reading).

(5) *he also kena play out* 'he was also tricked' (Schneider, *English Around the World* 163)

Similar processes and outcomes, beginning with large-scale lexical borrowing and phonological transfer, can be observed in many of the world's "New Englishes," caused by the vibrant developments of the postcolonial evolution and globalization of English.

Finally, even stronger long-term contact has produced variety types, mentioned and defined earlier, in which contact effects have been even more effective and prominent: English-based **pidgins** and **creoles**. Typically, they originated in very specific sociohistorical settings, marked by unequal distributions of power and restricted access to English, as found mostly in tropical plantation and slave communities. Such varieties are spoken by millions of people, predominantly in the Caribbean, in West Africa, and in the South-West Pacific region.

They have characteristic properties on the levels of words, sounds and grammar:

- Typically, the words of these languages have come from English, even if they are sometimes strongly phonetically modified. For example, in Tok Pisin, spoken in Papua New Guinea, *pinis* derives from *finish*, *paitman* 'warrior' from *fight man*, or *luklukim* 'stare at' from *look-look him*.
- However, their syntax is clearly even more un-English in many ways. For example, preverbal particles express aspect categories such as habituality, and negation is marked simply by placing a negator before the verb: in Barbados, *im does cry* means 'he cries habitually,' and *no cry* means 'don't cry.'

Creolists dispute whether these syntactic patterns have come from transfer effects of indigenous substrate languages or from the impact of universal principles of linguistic evolution or cognition. Traditional creolist scholarship tended to view these varieties, including Jamaican Creole, as distinct, newly-born languages, totally unrelated to English. More modern views regard them as strongly transformed by the impact of language contact but essentially still as varieties of English.

## 6.3 | Standards of English

On the level of writing, the concept of **Standard English** comes close to being supraregionally homogeneous: a formal text, devoid of explicit cultural references, is very difficult to assign to any particular region of origin. (Even this seemingly trivial statement is not fully true, however: when viewed quantitatively, based on larger text corpora, even standard written varieties betray distinct preferences). On the other hand, spoken English is never regionally neutral. There are spoken standard forms of the language, but they always come with a recognizable accent which shows a speaker's origin.

Conventionally, two "reference varieties," or national standard varieties, are recognized, **British English** (BrE) and **American English** (AmE).

## 6.3.1 | Standard British English and RP

The origins of Standard English in Britain date back to the Early Modern English period and can be traced back to social changes and technological advances at the dawn of the modern era:

- Most importantly, the introduction of the **printing press** in England, by Caxton in 1476, resulted in the need for a supraregionally understandable and homogeneous language form.
- An increased demand for **education** produced higher literacy rates and larger reading audiences.
- The **Reformation** called for believers' direct access to the Bible and thus also promoted the diffusion of literacy.

The establishment of Standard English in England can be viewed as an increasing process of conventionalization over a few centuries, culminating in eighteenth-century prescriptive attitudes. Practically, many disputed issues of spelling and vocabulary were settled by the impact of Dr. Johnson's *Dictionary* of 1755. It is important to note, however, that underneath this surface of formal documents which have come down to us the regional dialects continued to be in use. Only dim traces of these forms have been preserved, given that there was hardly any reason to write down "uncouth" speech forms, but even in the absence of written records, the dialects were evolving in unbroken transmission from one generation to the next.

It is also noteworthy that the standard accent of British English, **Received Pronunciation** or **RP**, emerged only in the nineteenth century, as an upper class marker in the exclusive "public schools," which were anything but public in the modern sense. Regionalisms of pronunciation disappeared in that process (and in that variety) and gave way to a supraregionally uniform speech form with a highly effective, socially demarcating role and symbolic value. Essentially, substantial components of this socially exclusive attitude and its associated linguistic form of RP have been preserved to the present day. Public performance in leadership roles still requires RP in Britain, and the ac-

cent has been retained by conservative, class-conscious members of society. Even within RP, however, it is recognized that change is going on: small-scale linguistic differences mark a "conservative" as against a "modern" RP accent.

RP is much less dominant now than it once was, however, and it has been supplemented by changes and attitudes which reflect the social transformations of the latter twentieth century. Recently it has been claimed that **Estuary English**, a south-eastern (Thames Estuary region) near-standard accent with some admixture of London pronunciation features, may be growing into the role of a new prestige variety. Most importantly, however, general attitudes towards the use of regional accents in public have changed dramatically. Just half a century ago it would have been inconceivable to give a public or media speech in anything but immaculate RP. In contrast, nowadays educated regional accents are widely considered acceptable and are performed with some regional pride in such situations.

## 6.3.2 | Standard American English

American English goes back to the accents of the settlers from various parts of the British Isles who brought their speech forms with them. Its structural properties emerged in a process of **koinéization**, defined as a mixture of speech forms from different regions in which communicatively successful forms, those widely understood, are retained and strengthened while the less successful ones, those understood by certain speakers only, gradually fall into disuse, thus generating a "middle-of-the-road" variety in the long run. The conceptualization of American English, i.e. the recognition of the fact that it should be viewed as a distinct linguistic entity in its own right, has its origins in the ideology of the American Revolution, when national leaders called for not only political but also cultural and linguistic independence. The best-known figure in this context is certainly Noah Webster, who gave talks with titles such as (in this case, in Boston in 1786) "Some Differences between the English and the Americans Considered. Corruption of Language in England. Reasons Why the English Should Not Be Standard, Either in Language or Manners." Webster also turned this momentum into a huge business success by producing his bestselling *Ameri-*

Noah Webster and American linguistic independence

can *Spelling Book* and, later, his *American Dictionary of the English Language* (1828). Interestingly enough, from the very beginning language use in the U.S. was associated with political values and motivations like democratization: access to proper (language) education was viewed as a right of every free citizen, and consequently "proper" language use was considered his/her moral obligation at the same time. This explains an exceptionally strongly prescriptive attitude which has prevailed in the U.S. to the present day: striving for and using "proper English" is also a national duty of a good citizen, it is believed.

Unlike in the UK, however, there is no uniform American standard accent, no single norm of pronunciation which is accepted nationwide. In many writings on the subject the term "General American" can be found, but it is highly problematic. It refers to a hypothetically uniform inland-northern-western mode of pronunciation and deliberately excludes at least all of the South and all of New England, regions which have clearly different forms of pronunciation as used even among the educated and in formal contexts. The same applies to the notion of "network English," which is essentially also a myth. Both notions abstract from a complex reality, which is the ubiquity of some degree of regional variation on the levels of pronunciation and word choice. A more realistic and modern notion of "Standard American English" (Kretzschmar, "Pronunciation") regards this variety thus simply as a supraregionally understandable pronunciation form which is devoid of explicit regionalisms. In local contexts, however, localized forms prevail, irrespective of the formality level.

Of course this is not valid for syntax, for which a national standard norm exists. In fact, there is an interesting relationship between regional and social variation on the one hand and the main language levels on the other, somewhat unlike the corresponding pattern in the UK. In America, pronunciation and lexis tend to vary regionally, essentially in all stylistic levels, including formal speech. In contrast, grammar varies socially—there is a set of varying nonstandard grammatical patterns which are diagnostic of one's level of education or status but which can be heard, perhaps with varying frequencies, almost anywhere. A case in point is multiple negation, in clauses like *I don't have no money.*

## 6.3.3 | Differences Between National Standard Varieties

A canonical topic of discussions of the national norms of English are the differences between BrE and AmE. Lists of salient different forms can be widely found in textbooks and are known to many speakers and observers. They include distinctive pairs on the levels of

- **lexis** (*autumn—fall, lorry—truck, pavement—sidewalk,* etc.),
- **pronunciation** (/a:/ vs. /æ/ in words like *staff, dance, can't*; non-rhotic vs. rhotic pronunciation in *car, card,* etc.),
- **grammar** (*got* vs. *gotten*; *Have you got* vs. *Do you have* …), and
- **spelling** (*honour* vs. *honor, centre* vs. *center,* etc.).

Recent research has suggested that that is far from the whole story, however. Differences are much more far-reaching but at the same time subtle and primarily quantitative rather than qualitative: large-scale corpus evidence has shown that on either side of the Atlantic different structural patterns, word choices, phraseological combinations and, in general, different ways of saying the same thing tend to be preferred (see Algeo; Rohdenburg and Schlüter). For example, in pairs of equivalent expressions like *in the circumstances—under the circumstances, right now—at the moment, have a look—take a look* and *ages ago—long time ago* both items occur on both sides of the Atlantic, but British people prefer the former while Americans use the latter much more frequently.

Corpus-linguistic investigations have shown that a similar relationship exists between other and new national varieties of English as well. There are a few stereotypical peculiarities of which speakers are aware (mostly words and some constructions, such as *matatu* 'collective taxi' or *pick someone* rather than *pick someone up* in East Africa) but in addition to that there is a large number of **frequency differences**, word and construction preferences, rather than absolute differences, characterizing certain varieties (e.g. *lady doctor* rather than *female doctor* or *provide somebody something* rather than *provide somebody with something* in India).

## 6.3.4 | The Pluricentricity of English: New Standard Varieties

The final question to be asked when discussing standard(s of) English is whether two are really enough—it has been argued that English by now is a **pluricentric** language, and this notion posits the existence of several standard varieties. There is at least one more national variety which by now can clearly be accepted as a standard norm in its own right, namely **Australian English**. This status does not date back too far—it was roughly in the 1970s when a wave of nationalism contributed to the replacement of the earlier requirement to speak a standard British form in public by the acceptance of Australian ways of speaking in formal domains (such as in the programs of the Australian Broadcasting Corporation). This development was both marked and further promoted by the publication of a first national dictionary, the *Macquarie Dictionary* (Delbridge et al.). Australian English as a distinct accent is not only a local norm, however. Due to the country's location and cultural and business interrelations of all kinds between Australia and Asian countries, it now serves as a refer-ence point in the entire Asia-Pacific region. (Consider the high proportion of Asian immigrants or students in Australia or the foundation of branches of Australian Universities in several Asian states, for example.)

In general, the "Dynamic Model" of the evolution of **Postcolonial Englishes**, proposed by Schneider (*Postcolonial English*) and by now widely accepted, claims that emerging new varieties of English are likely to reach a stage of endo-normative stabilization (i.e. acceptance of their own local usage as correct) after political and cultural independence. New, internally homogeneous forms of regional English grow into the roles of symbols of new national identities in the context of nation building. Debates on whether or not indigenous ways of speaking English might be acceptable as new national norms are going on in many countries where English serves as a second or co-official language (though in the majority of instances so far, authority rests with conservatives who resist such a reorientation). Advanced countries in which regional educated accents enjoy prestige and which may thus be close to this stage include Singapore, India, and Jamaica.

## 6.4 | Regional Variation and Varieties

### 6.4.1 | Dialect Geography: Approaches and Assessments

Regional variation of speech has traditionally been studied by the discipline of **dialect geography**. It emerged as such with late nineteenth and early twentieth century activities first in Germany and then in France and Italy, soon followed by large-scale projects in England and North America. Its main tool has been the production of linguistic (or dialect) atlases, i.e. maps which show the distribution of alternative speech forms in their geographical distributions (see Francis; Davis). These early model projects have jointly produced a set of basic assumptions and methodological procedures observed in the compilation of such an atlas:

- the choice of **localities** spread roughly evenly over the region under investigation;
- the selection of suitable **individuals** (based on criteria such as lifelong residency, lack of speech defects, and typically restricted education) at these localities as representative speakers of the local dialect;
- **data collection** by trained fieldworkers in structured interviews;
- with long lists of **questions** targeting specific items showing (predominantly) certain pronunciation features and regional words; and ultimately
- techniques of **mapping** the results.

The American and British projects of the mid-twentieth-century successfully amassed huge amounts of data representing local dialect forms, and thus they provide valuable baseline documentation of the grassroots variability of British and American speech, even if from a present-day perspective their value is increasingly historical. Some socio-linguists have criticized these projects, arguing that by exclusively focusing upon so-called "NORMs" (non-mobile older rural males) they fail to represent today's social realities marked by regional and social mobility and urbanization. More recent approaches have revitalized these data sets by computerizing them (and thus allowing researchers to mine the data comprehensively along certain parameters) and by applying so-

The making of
a dialect atlas

phisticated statistical techniques in their analysis (see Kretzschmar and Schneider; Shackleton). So, in the long run, these data sets have turned out to produce significant input to new theoretical insights (see Kretzschmar, *Linguistics of Speech*).

### 6.4.2 | Dialectology in Great Britain

In Great Britain, the main dialectological project was the **Survey of English Dialects (SED)**, carried out after 1948 under the directorship of Harold Orton. Its orientation is decidedly diachronic and conservative: the emphasis is on phonology (and Middle English phonemes are used as structural orientation) and lexis, and only rural villages were sampled. The raw data compilation of the results, in list form and narrow transcription, is available as the *Basic Materials* (Orton et al.), subdivided into four main regions each of which is covered in three volumes. Summary maps were then put together in the **Linguistic Atlas of England** (Orton, Sanderson and Widdowson), and in a few spin-off products such as a dictionary (Upton, Parry and Widdowson) and a popularizing book with maps (Upton and Widdowson). Similar projects were later carried out in Wales, Scotland and Ireland (see Raymond Hickey's Irish-English Resource Center at http://www.uni-due.de/IERC and the sources listed there).

Online resources on dialect geography

### 6.4.3 | Dialectology in North America

Dialectology in North America is even older than its British counterpart and at the same time more modern in orientation, as it also investigates urban communities and speakers from higher social classes. In the late 1920s, the Austrian-born linguist Hans Kurath was appointed project director of a "Linguistic Atlas of the United States and Canada"—an intention which has never materialized as such, however. The vastness of the territory to be covered, coupled with limited resources, soon forced Kurath and his colleagues and followers to break the idea down to a series of regional atlas projects (for details, see the **Linguistic Atlas Projects** website at http://us.english.uga.edu/). For most of these, data collection went on during roughly the mid-twentieth century, and the results have either been published or archived. Three

projects have been of special importance and are worth mentioning here. Kurath himself vigorously pushed and systematically organized both the data collection and the publication of the *Linguistic Atlas of New England* (*LANE*; Kurath et al.), which was thus the only project finished and published for a long time to come, and hence a model for many others. Next in line was the *Linguistic Atlas of the Middle and South Atlantic States* (*LAMSAS*), which, together with *LANE*, covered all of the eastern coast, hence the region of earliest settlements and strongest dialectal variation. The *LAMSAS* data have been fully computerized and submitted to sophisticated statistical investigations (Kretzschmar and Schneider; see also later work by Kretzschmar). Finally, the *Linguistic Atlas of the Gulf States* (*LAGS*; Pederson et al.) provided an immensely rich amount of data and an important resource on Southern English, the most conservative of all American dialects. As a consequence of its younger age it built upon modern technology from the outset, with all interviews tape-recorded, the raw data published via microphotography, some sophisticated analytical schemes (such as microfiche "idiolect synopses" and detailed phonetic coding schemes) employed, and data computerized and subjected to electronic analyses.

Another large-scale project, loosely related to the dialectological tradition, has led to a systematic compilation of North America's regional and ethnic vocabulary in an authoritative dictionary modeled upon the *OED*. Work on this *Dictionary of American Regional English* (*DARE*; Cassidy et al.) has been going on for about half a century and is now approaching completion, with the last volumes awaited soon. The project is considered a goldmine of nonstandard lexis, and it has also built upon a comprehensive and modern methodology (including a monumental reading program of dialect writings, computerization of the data base, an atlas-style regional survey of all 50 states, and a computer-generated map display which reflects population density rather than physical geography).

Since the 1960s, traditional dialect geography, focusing as it does on conservative rural dialects, has been complemented by sociolinguistics (see the next section), an approach which many scholars have perceived as more appropriate in times of democratization, urbanization, population mobility, and globalization. The 1990s and after, then, saw a merger of a "**sociolinguistic dialectology**," uniting methods and approaches of both lines of thinking, in work by Guy Bailey and associates in Texas and Oklahoma, J. K. Chambers in Toronto, and, most prominently, William Labov and his colleagues at the University of Pennsylvania. Labov's team, following a model approach by Bailey, used telephone interviews to increase the cost efficiency of sampling, and they were thus able to sample speech data from all of the continent in an unprecedented fashion. They employed cutting-edge sophisticated analytical methods, including acoustic phonology and multivariate statistics. The result of all of this is a monumental publication which will be a benchmark for decades to come, the phonologically orientated *Atlas of North American English* (Labov, Ash, and Boberg). It documents and analyzes pronunciation habits of North Americans from all regions and social spheres, and pays special attention to current sound changes (like the "Northern Cities Shift," an ongoing rotating movement of short vowels).

## 6.4.4 | British and American Dialects: Regional Divisions

So, what have all these investigations taught us about dialects of British and American English? Only a very concise summary is possible here.

Regional **dialects of British English** have been found to have their roots ultimately in the different settlement patterns of the Germanic tribes who, in the pre-Old English period, caused "English" to become a distinct language. Customary divisions tend to distinguish regions such as Southwest, Southeast, East and West Central, Lower North and Northeast, with details varying depending upon the level of granulation and the period focused on (see Trudgill). The main line of division runs between the North and the South, however, distinguished by some well-known pronunciation features such as /ʊ/ vs. /ʌ/ in words like *cut* or *butter*, short vs. long /a/ in *path*, *grass*, etc., and many more. Interestingly enough, considering its low overt prestige, it seems that northern forms have been expanding into the central regions and towards the south over the last few decades. The social changes of the recent past are reflected in Trudgill's fundamental distinction between "Tradi-

tional Dialects," i.e. old-timer rural speech as reflected in the *SED*, and Modern Dialects as spoken by younger people in cities as well. Stereotyped urban varieties, such as London's Cockney, Newcastle's Geordie, Liverpool's Scouse, etc., are undergoing change but essentially still going strong, and in the spirit of the urban sociolinguistic dialectology approach, they have been researched intensely in recent years (e.g. Foulkes and Docherty). Varieties of British English have been subjected to some interesting processes of change, contact and innovation in recent years which have been investigated intensely. Examples include the growth of new contact dialects in "new towns" such as Milton Keynes (Kerswill and Williams), and new contact forms spoken by immigrants from the Caribbean (Sutcliffe), from countries of the former Empire in Asia (e.g. Rasinger), and, most recently, from eastern Europe (Schleef, Meyerhoff, and Clark).

The **dialectal division of the United States** was first established by Kurath (*Word Geography*), based on lexical *LANE* and *LAMSAS* data. He proposed a basically tripartite division into North, Midland and South, each with several sub-regions. This framework was confirmed by later dialectological studies and widely accepted for a long time. It is interesting to note that due to settlement patterns and longer and more intense cultural contact, characteristic features of New England and Southern dialects tend to correspond to those of southern England (such as a non-rhotic pronunciation found with conservative speakers, or the preservation of /j/ in *new*, *tune*, etc.), while the Midlands, the cradle of mainstream inland northern American speech forms, were influenced more strongly by northern, Scottish or Irish speech habits (regarding rhotic pronunciation or some lexical items, for instance). Based on *DARE* lexical data, Carver then suggested that there are only two main dialect areas of AmE, North and South—but with intermediate forms called Lower North and Upper South which are strongly reminiscent of Kurath's subdivision into North and South Midlands. The most recent authoritative division, based on phonological investigations and to be found in Labov, Ash, and Boberg (148), again recognizes a separate Midland and adds the West and Canada as distinct regions of their own.

Identifying dialectal
divisions

## 6.5 | Social Variation and Varieties

With classic studies of ongoing sound changes in Martha's Vineyard and New York City, William Labov redirected the attention of linguists interested in dialect variation to the study of socially motivated speech differences and the relationship between language variation and change, and these studies then became models for many later ones in other locations and communities. **Sociolinguistics** builds upon concepts and methods influenced by sociology, such as representative (and ideally random) sampling of large numbers of informants, focusing upon select linguistic variables (realized by functionally equivalent variant forms), and analyzing data quantitatively. In the early phase, correlations between frequencies of linguistic variants and social groups were sought, and typically presented in tables and graphs.

The frequently reproduced diagram from Labov's 1966 study of New York City (see illustration) may serve to illustrate this approach in a nutshell. The vertical axis shows the percentage of a rhotic realization of postvocalic /r/ in any given context (i.e. how often, out of all possible instances, people pronounce < r > as in [ka:r] and not [ka:]). The lines represent different **social status groups**, roughly between group 0, the lower working class, to group 9, the upper middle class. The positions on the horizontal axis, represented by letters, represent different styles, from casual speech (A) via formal speech (B) to reading style (C), and onward to include the non-natural styles (hence marked by broken lines) of reading word lists (D) and minimal pairs (D'). Notice that style is understood as increasing attention to the form of speech here, a reflex of subconscious prescriptive attitudes. Notice also that we are provided not with speech forms or transcripts here but with figures as represented in a graph—an approach highly typical of the importance of quantification in this discipline.

So, what can the diagram then tell us about New York City's speech, and the pronunciation of /r/ in particular?

- First, rhoticity is rare and thus not typical of the city's speech: in all but one class, realization figures in casual style are close to zero percent.
- Second, it is more often found in the upper classes: with roughly 20 % r's articulated, class 9, the highest, has the highest proportion in natural speech, and in styles A-C, frequencies correlate perfectly well with social class: the higher, the more r's.
- Third, [r] is more frequent in more formal styles throughout (and this effect is strongest in the "artificial" styles when respondents clearly realize that now they should be producing their "best speech" forms).
- These two factors, then, clearly identify it as a prestige form in the community, one that people strive for and value positively (even if most of them hardly ever use it, as we saw).
- Finally, the cross-over of the line of the second-highest status group between styles C and D is interpreted by Labov as an indicator of linguistic insecurity, "hypercorrection of the lower middle class," instability of the system, and hence ongoing change. These speakers aspire to be upwardly mobile and wish to signal this ambition by using the prestige pronunciation, but they lack a feel for how often it is appropriate (to upper class speakers) to use [r]—so involuntarily they exaggerate their usage and outdo the highest status group, as it were.

In such a vein, sociolinguists have identified a number of parameters which determine variation, i.e. which correlate with the more or less frequent use of specific variants.

- **Social class** is a central one, of course—nonstandard forms (such as double negation or the omission of a verbal -s e.g. in *he do*) appear more frequently in working class than in middle class speech.
- Class is a fuzzy, elusive concept, however, so more specific indicators like **occupation**, levels of **education**, income, etc. have frequently been adduced.

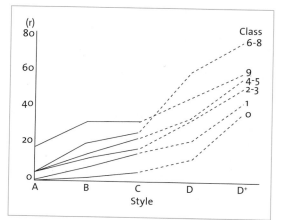

(r)

Class

Style

- **Gender** differences have been a primary topic of interest; women have been shown to prefer prestige variants more than men and to be leaders in linguistic changes.
- **Age** has also been shown to be influential. Young people speak differently from old ones, and the "apparent time" concept of comparing age groups has been developed to track ongoing change.
- In the U.S., **ethnicity** has also been found to be highly influential. African American Vernacular English, the dialect spoken by lower-class black speakers, has been one of the most prominent topics of research for decades.

For five decades, post-Labovian sociolinguistics has been an extremely vibrant discipline, with journals (*Language Variation and Change, Journal of Sociolinguistics*) and a conference series (*NWAV: New Ways of Analyzing Variation*) of its own. Labov's methodology has been adopted at and transferred to many other locations and speech communities, including (to name but a few important ones) Detroit, Washington D.C., Los Angeles, Norwich, Belfast, and so on. The methodological tools developed and the theoretical insights gained have also progressed significantly, however.

- Multivariate **statistical techniques** (most notably the program Varbrul, with its later software versions GoldVarb and Rbrul) have identified factors which contribute to the explanation of observed variability.
- **Acoustic phonetics**, most notably the program Praat, has substantially increased the amount of detail and objectivity in analyzing variation in vowels.
- The view of **sociolinguistic parameters** like class determining one's speech has been sup-

plemented by the idea that one's network relationships or, more recently, participation in "communities of practice," strongly influence speech behavior.
- **Globalization** and the global diffusion of linguistic innovations have been intensely studied. An interesting case in point is the spread of the so-called "new quotatives," above all *be like* to introduce direct speech. Patterns like *I'm like "blabla" and then she's like "blabla"* were recorded for the first time in the western U.S. in the 1980s. By today they can be heard on all continents but are still most strongly characteristic of younger female speech, with speakers having reached roughly the 40s age group.
- Most recent theorizing has viewed speech variability not as passively determined by one's origins but as an active manipulation of one's social alignments, reflecting real or desired group **identities** (Eckert).

It needs to be noted that sociolinguists have never shared the dialectologists' positivistic orientation of viewing data documentation as a valid goal in itself. Labov and his followers have always seen their work as essentially a contribution to an increased understanding of how language variability reflects linguistic change, and hence of the nature of language in a fundamental sense. The essence of these insights has been put together in Labov's theoretical *magnum opus*, his three-volume discussion of internal, social, and, most recently, cognitive factors which determine and reveal *Principles of Linguistic Change*. These books are full of case studies of changing speech forms in American English (and other varieties), most notably from Philadelphia, Labov's research base.

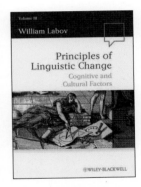

Labov's *Principles of Linguistic Change* is a key work of sociolinguistics.

## 6.6 | World Englishes: New Institutionalized Varieties

For the last three or so decades the topic of the variability of English has been enriched and substantially broadened by another novel facet and perspective, the emergence of new, distinctive, and increasingly stable indigenized varieties around the world. The growth of "World Englishes" has been an extremely vigorous and vibrant process in many countries and on practically all continents, a process which is likely to transform the future shape and status of English more than any other. As in other spheres of life, globalization has also

triggered regionalization, a renewed emphasis on one's local roots, as a reaction, and this applies to English, the main tool of globalization, as well: it is the world's leading international language, but at the same time, distinct local forms of it are mushrooming.

Interestingly enough, after decolonization in the middle of the twentieth century, English has not been abandoned in many former colonies, but it has rather been strengthened locally, resulting in the development of **New Englishes** in many countries of Africa and Asia in particular (Platt, Weber, and Ho). In countries such as Nigeria, Kenya, South Africa, India, Singapore, or the Philippines (and many more), English is a strong second language today, used widely in public domains such as education, the media, business life, etc. Not infrequently, it enjoys an official or co-official status, often promoted by its ethnic neutrality (as in Nigeria or India). In addition to its diffusion in association with its formal status in high domains, however, an enormous grassroots spread is also going on. English is the language which millions of people of whatever walks of life and in many countries strive to acquire, because it promises access to better jobs and a better life. Schneider ("Dynamics"; *Postcolonial English*) proposed that these "Postcolonial Englishes" have been shaped by an essentially similar evolutionary process in which principles of language contact, identity formation and linguistic accommodation between the parties involved in colonization and postcolonial developments have played a decisive role. This "Dynamic Model," accounting for the emergence of these varieties theoretically, has by now been widely discussed and adopted, and largely been accepted.

These new varieties of English typically operate in multilingual and multicultural environments, so in many cases English is a strong second language, often the primary language of speakers' daily interactions. Sometimes it is even more than that: in many countries, native, first-language speakers of such New Englishes can now be found. In African urban contexts, for example, English is chosen not infrequently as a family language by educated couples with different linguistic backgrounds. In Nigeria, millions of speakers grow up speaking Pidgin, locally accepted as a form of English. In Asia, the most strongly anglicized country is Singapore, with roughly a third of all children acquiring English natively, according to recent census data.

All these varieties are characterized by distinctive linguistic features on the levels of lexis, pronunciation, and grammar. Some of these can be accounted for as being contact-induced, resulting from transfer of properties of indigenous languages. Others, however, have evolved internally, restructuring English input in innovative ways. Many of these features as well as the sociolinguistic, functional settings of these new varieties have been described in recent years, for example in articles in the journals *English World-Wide* or *World Englishes*. This is now a thriving scholarly field of investigation, with an *International Association of World Englishes*, annual conferences, the journals mentioned, the book series *Varieties of English Around the World*, and many recent handbooks (Kachru, Kachru, and Nelson; Kirkpatrick) and textbooks (Mesthrie and Bhatt; Schneider, *English Around the World*).

## 6.7 | Outlook

Given space limitations, this chapter has only been able to scratch the surface of a booming field. There is a huge literature on varieties of English, sociolinguistics, World Englishes, and the relationship between language variation and change, and these are regular topics of academic teaching. For readers interested in pursuing the issues further, the "Further Reading" box provides some more, though unavoidably still greatly constrained, guidance to recommended readings.

The principles underlying variation in English and the documentation and investigation of the varieties of the language are highly prominent and important topics in English linguistics nowadays, central to the discipline as a whole. After all, English manifests itself only in the real-life form of its varieties (including standardized forms in formal contexts); the notion of "Standard English" as such is essentially an abstraction. Dialects come from speakers' minds and mouths, and they are close to their hearts, serving as the main modes of expression of solidarity and social relationships.

It has been claimed repeatedly that **dialects** are disappearing in the modern age, due to the impact of modern mass communication. The assumption that the media kill dialects seems mistaken, however. After all, people do not talk to their TV sets, and if this assumption were correct then those who watch TV most should speak perfect standard English as represented in the programs, and this is clearly not true. Actually, the new media have produced new varieties, in a sense. A case in point is the language of **texting**, full of abbreviations which are both creative and opaque to an outsider. It can be viewed as a new sociostylistic dialect, expressed in its own channel.

Educators and conservative gatekeepers still try to brand dialects and social varieties as being somewhere between quaint, uncouth, or broken speech. Nothing could be further from the truth. Local language varieties enjoy an enormous amount of covert prestige, and they are not only successfully resistant but fully alive and kicking, as it were. It is true, of course, that they are constantly changing (as is any language), and that archaic and rural forms, Trudgill's "Traditional Dialects" of England, for instance, have been losing ground and may be disappearing. But the contrary is equally true: new dialectal forms and constellations are constantly emerging, both in traditionally English-speaking regions and, most vividly today, with respect to the expanding New Englishes. **Globalization promotes regionalization**, we found; and in the sociolinguistic literature, it has repeatedly been shown that specific features of disappearing dialects may be recycled and resurface as group identity markers in new environments.

So the varieties of English are sitting on a merry-go-round; they are changing rapidly, and in some cases they are being transformed, down to the loss of some traditional features and dialects. At the same time, however, new varieties are mushrooming, and new feature configurations appear continuously, performing their core social

function of both symbolizing and manipulating social relationships and group alignments. Varieties of English are here to stay.

---

## Focus on Studying Varieties of English

For readers who want to know more about individual varieties of English (both national and regional as well as some social ones, and also pidgins and creoles and the major World Englishes), the source to consult is the authoritative and comprehensive *Handbook of Varieties of English*. On about 2,400 pages and in audio files and maps on an accompanying CD, it describes and documents the linguistic properties of about 70 varieties of English, together with short survey of their historical and sociocultural backgrounds. It is available either as two hardback volumes on phonology and morphosyntax (Schneider et al.; Kortmann et al.) or as four moderately priced paperbacks on major world regions (Kortmann and Upton; Schneider, *Americas*; Burridge and Kortmann; Mesthrie).

There are many **textbooks and handbooks** on English sociolinguistics. Recommended introductions include Chambers, Meyerhoff (with an eye on methodological issues and data analysis procedures), Milroy and Gordon, and Tagliamonte, and the reader by Meyerhoff and Schleef. On global varieties of English, Schneider (*English Around the World*) is a lively introduction with many text samples and commentaries on them, and Mesthrie and Bhatt provide a more technical survey of issues in the field.

There has been a recent surge of handbooks in linguistics, which are usually voluminous, comprehensive and authoritative collections of dozens of articles by renowned scholars. Relevant ones here include Chambers, Trudgill, and Schilling-Estes on variation and change; as well as Kirkpatrick and Kachru, Kachru, and Nelson on World Englishes.

---

## Select Bibliography

**Algeo, John.** *British or American English? A Handbook of Word and Grammar Patterns*. Cambridge: Cambridge University Press, 2006.

**Burridge, Kate, and Bernd Kortmann, eds.** *The Pacific and Australasia*. Vol. 3 of *Varieties of English*. 4 vols. Berlin: Mouton de Gruyter, 2008.

**Carver, Craig M.** *American Regional Dialects: A Word Geography*. Ann Arbor: University of Michigan Press, 1987.

**Cassidy, Frederic G., et al.** *Dictionary of American Regional English*. 4 vols. to date. Cambridge: Belknap Press, 1985-.

**Chambers, J. K.** *Sociolinguistic Theory*. 2nd ed. Malden: Blackwell, 2003.

**Chambers, J. K., Peter Trudgill, and Natalie Schilling-Estes, eds.** *The Handbook of Language Variation and Change*. Malden: Blackwell, 2002.

**Davis, Lawrence M.** *English Dialectology: An Introduction*. Tuscaloosa: University of Alabama Press, 1983.

**Delbridge, Arthur, et al.** *The Macquarie Dictionary*. Sydney: Macquarie Library, 1981.

**Eckert, Penelope.** *Language Variation as Social Practice: The Linguistic Construction of Identity in Belten High*. Malden: Blackwell, 1999.

**Filppula, Markku, Juhani Klemola, and Heli Paulasto.** *English and Celtic in Contact*. London: Routledge, 2008.

**Foulkes, Paul, and Gerard Docherty.** *Urban Voices: Accent Studies in the British Isles*. London: Arnold, 1999.

**Francis, W. Nelson.** *Dialectology: An Introduction*. New York: Longman, 1983.

**Görlach, Manfred.** "And is it English?" *English World-Wide* 17 (1996): 153–74.

**Kachru, Braj, Yamuna Kachru, and Cecil Nelson, eds.** *The Handbook of World Englishes*. Malden: Blackwell, 2006.

**Kerswill, Paul, and Ann Williams.** "New Towns and Koineisation: Linguistic and Social Correlates." *Linguistics* 43 (2005): 1023–48.

**Kirkpatrick, Andy, ed.** *The Routledge Handbook of World Englishes*. London: Routledge, 2010.

**Kortmann, Bernd, Kate Burridge, Rajend Mesthrie, Edgar W. Schneider, and Clive Upton, eds.** *Morphology and Syntax*. Berlin: Mouton de Gruyter, 2004. Vol. 2 of *A Handbook of Varieties of English*. 2 vols.

**Kortmann, Bernd, and Clive Upton, eds.** *The British Isles*. Vol. 1 of *Varieties of English*. 4 vols. Berlin: Mouton de Gruyter, 2008.

**Kretzschmar, William.** *The Linguistics of Speech*. Cambridge: Cambridge University Press, 2009.

**Kretzschmar, William.** "Standard American English Pronunciation." *Phonology*. Eds. Bernd Kortmann et al. Vol. 1 of *A Handbook of Varieties of English*. 2 vols. Berlin: Mouton de Gruyter, 2004. 257–69.

Kretzschmar, William, and Edgar W. Schneider. *Introduction to Quantitative Analysis of Linguistic Survey Data: An Atlas by the Numbers*. Thousand Oaks: Sage, 1996.

Kurath, Hans. *A Word Geography of the Eastern United States*. Ann Arbor: University of Michigan Press, 1949.

Kurath, Hans, et al. *Linguistic Atlas of New England*. 3 vols. Providence: Brown University Press, 1939–43.

Labov, William. *Principles of Linguistic Change*. 3 vols. Malden: Blackwell, 1994–2010.

Labov, William. *The Social Stratification of English in New York City*. 1966. 2nd ed. Cambridge: Cambridge University Press, 2006.

Labov, William. *Sociolinguistic Patterns*. Philadelphia: University of Pennsylvania Press, 1972.

Labov, William, Sharon Ash, and Charles Boberg. *The Atlas of North American English: Phonetics, Phonology, and Sound Change*. Berlin: Mouton de Gruyter, 2006.

Mesthrie, Rajend, and Rakesh Bhatt. *World Englishes*. Cambridge: Cambridge University Press, 2008.

Mesthrie, Rajend, ed. *Africa, South and Southeast Asia*. Vol. 4 of *Varieties of English*. 4 vols. Berlin: Mouton de Gruyter, 2008.

Meyerhoff, Miriam. *Introducing Sociolinguistics*. London: Routledge, 2006.

Meyerhoff, Miriam, and Erik Schleef, eds. *The Routledge Sociolinguistics Reader*. London: Routledge, 2010.

Milroy, Lesley, and Matthew Gordon. *Sociolinguistics: Method and Interpretation*. Malden: Blackwell, 2003.

Orton, Harold, et al. *Survey of English Dialects: Basic Materials*. 4 vols. Leeds: Arnold, 1962–71.

Orton, Harold, Stewart Sanderon, and John D. A. Widdowson. *The Linguistic Atlas of England*. London: Croom Helm, 1978.

Pederson, Lee, et al. *Linguistic Atlas of the Gulf States*. 7 vols. Athens: University of Georgia Press, 1986–91.

Platt, John, Heidi Weber, and Mian Lian Ho. *The New Englishes*. London: Routledge, 1984.

Rasinger, Sebastian. *Bengali-English in East London: A Study in Urban Multilingualism*. Bern: Lang, 2007.

Rohdenburg, Günter, and Julia Schlüter. *One Language, Two Grammars? Differences Between British and American English*. Cambridge: Cambridge University Press, 2009.

Schleef, Erik, Miriam Meyerhoff, and Lynn Clark. "Teenagers' Acquisition of Variation: A Comparison of Locally-Born and Migrant Teens' Realisation of English(ing) in Edinburgh and London." *English World-Wide* 32 (2011): 206–36.

Schneider, Edgar W., ed. *The Americas and the Caribbean*. Vol. 2 of *Varieties of English*. 4 vols. Berlin: Mouton de Gruyter, 2008.

Schneider, Edgar W. "The Dynamics of New Englishes: From Identity Construction to Dialect Birth." *Language* 79 (2003): 233–81.

Schneider, Edgar W. *English Around the World: An Introduction*. Cambridge: Cambridge University Press, 2011.

Schneider, Edgar W. *Postcolonial English: Varieties Around the World*. Cambridge: Cambridge University Press, 2007.

Schneider, Edgar W., Kate Burridge, Bernd Kortmann, Rajend Mesthrie, and Clive Upton, eds. *Phonology*. Berlin: Mouton de Gruyter, 2004. Vol. 1 of *A Handbook of Varieties of English*. 2 vols.

Shackleton, Robert G. *Quantitative Assessment of English-American Speech Relationships*. Groningen: Rijksuniversiteit Groningen, 2010.

Sutcliffe, David. *British Black English*. Oxford: Blackwell, 1984.

Tagliamonte, Sali A. *Analysing Sociolinguistic Variation*. Cambridge: Cambridge University Press, 2006.

Tottie, Gunnel. *An Introduction to American English*. Malden: Blackwell, 2002.

Trudgill, Peter. *The Dialects of England*. Cambridge: Blackwell, 1990.

Upton, Clive, and J. D. A. Widdowson. *An Atlas of English Dialects*. 2nd ed. London: Routledge, 2006.

Upton, Clive, David Parry, and John D. Widdowson. *Survey of English Dialects: The Dictionary and Grammar*. London: Routledge 1994.

*Edgar W. Schneider*

# Part VI: Didactics: The Teaching of English

# 1 The Theory and Politics of English Language Teaching

## 1.1 | The Politics of Global English

"English is now ours, we have colonized it"—this statement by Philippine poet Gémino Abad from 1996 (qtd. in Leitner 7) illustrates recent trends in the global spread of English, especially of English as a foreign language (EFL). First, it hints at how the enormous 'success story' of the English language is continuing to expand. According to recent estimates, up to 1.5 billion people, that is about one in five people in this world, have some kind of competence in English (Leitner 7; Brusch). Further estimates suggest that by the year 2050, about half the world population will have some knowledge of the language. The remarkable **global spread of English** can be attributed to three historical factors (cf. Crystal):

**1.** The Empire. The growth of the British Empire, which peaked in the Age of Imperialism before World War I, at a time when one fifth of the world population was under the British Union Jack.

**2.** The United States. The rise of the English-speaking United States from a dependent colony to the super-power of the twentieth century, and with it the enormous influence of its 'hard power' in the field of economics and geopolitical influence, but also of its 'soft power' in the areas of popular culture, mass entertainment and commercialization.

**3.** Globalization. Partly as a result of U.S. influences, often characterized by mechanisms of push and pull, English has gradually become the language of communication in multifarious settings of international cooperation, in international banking and trade, aviation, tourism, entertainment, film and TV. Recently, this trend has been propelled by the ongoing revolutions in technology (internet, e-mails, easily affordable long-distance calls, etc.) and increased mobility in the age of globalization.

Parallel to the spread of English as the language of the global village, the demand for English language skills has gained tremendous momentum. European as well as German policy makers have reacted by stressing the importance of foreign language acquisition through legislation and political pressure (especially in the wake of the 2001 *Common European Framework of Reference for Languages*' stipulations to propagate and increase foreign language proficiency). Without a doubt, the status of English as 'the fourth r' (i.e., the fourth basic skill with 'reading, writing and 'rithmetic') is here to stay. Learning the foreign language has almost reached the educative significance of mother tongue instruction. This can be evidenced in the fact that English classes, beginning with year three, have become compulsory at the primary/elementary school level in all German *Länder* since the beginning of the twenty-first century (Klippel 443), and there is a growing demand for English at an even earlier stage, beginning with playful exposure to English at the *Kindergarten* level.

Language Imperialism. A second aspect of the spread of English foregrounded in the initial quote appears to be of less relevance in Germany, which has never seriously been exposed to the highly detrimental impact of 'language imperialism.' The darker sides of the success story of English appear of little concern in a country which has occasionally found fault with the deluge of U.S. cultural products and the overabundance of infelicitous *Anglizismen* in German, but has wholeheartedly embraced the idea of English as a key to international communication and professional progress. Elsewhere however, especially in the former British colonies, English still tends to be marred by the reputation of being the language of the former suppressors. It is critically regarded as a tool of dominance and as laden with a history of 'subtractive bilingualism,' i.e. of enforced instruction at the disadvantage of native languages. Moreover, English has been called a 'killer language' whose spread has jeopardized the existence of many indigenous languages, and has always carried with it certain Anglophone or Western cultural, economic and linguistic values and hierarchies (Phillipson).

The significance of English language teaching

**English as *lingua franca*.** However, a pragmatic and proactive approach has gained considerable prevalence recently: that English is no longer the sole possession of the so-called native speakers (whom we tend to associate mostly with the British and the U.S. Americans). They have become a minority (up to 400 million speakers) compared with English speakers from the former colonies (about 150 to 300 million speakers from circa 50 countries and territories worldwide, e.g. from Canada, Australia, South Africa, the West Indies, India, Sri Lanka) and up to 1.5 billion people all over the world speaking English as a foreign language. There is an increasing tendency to prize English away from the native speakers and use it as a versatile tool of international communication. While formerly established models of teaching EFL used to focus on real-life communication with a native speaker, hypothetically in his or her mother country (non-native speaker with native speaker), the new scenario evolving in EFL teaching/learning entails interchanges in what linguists call 'non-native speaker to non-native speaker communication.' This scenario can take place in virtual space via e-mail or chat or in real life situations ranging from a short verbal exchange in one's own country to an extended stay abroad where communicants use EFL but are not necessarily in an English-speak-

New challenges for English
language teaching

ing country. English is increasingly used as a *lingua franca*—and with this development EFL has started to face some drastic changes:

- British or American culture—the culture of the two 'target nations'—is no longer deemed to be the only contextual setting for teaching English language skills. Other cultures—the so-called **new English cultures**, i.e., mainly the former colonies of the British Empire and now chiefly the members of the British Commonwealth—are vying for attention, as are far-away countries such as Japan and China, whose ever-growing global importance asks for inclusion in EFL teaching/learning environments.
- In a similar vein, other Englishes, i.e. other varieties of English (cf. entry V.6), have become the focus of **classroom instruction**, however, with the prestige and privileged status of Standard American or British English (SABE) still continuing. There is a growing trend, though, to accept *lingua franca* forms of English such as 'Denglish,' 'Frenglish' or 'Japlish,' which, from the point of view of linguistic purity, used to be unacceptable.
- With the increase of global communication mostly in its oral form, there is also a trend to accept '**bad English**,' according to the motto 'fluency before accuracy,' where getting a message across is more important than linguistic purity or lexical or grammatical exactness of the utterance. Communicative skills and content are increasingly given preference over correct pronunciation, lexical variation and grammatical perfection. This is a trend, however, which has also been heavily criticized as it, if taken to extremes, would lead to the lowering of instruction standards and disadvantage students who underestimate the significance of correct written language—which is still vital, for example, in letters of application and, generally, in many white-collar professions (see Volkmann 142–56).

## 1.2 | The Politics of EFL in Germany

**Backgrounds.** While Germany has fully accepted the importance of teaching and learning advanced competences in English, as evident in the growing number of bilingual classes at the *Gymnasium* level and the further proliferation of early English instruction from *Kindergarten* on, the German tradition of teaching EFL has always had a unique history with its own theories, concepts, institutions, teaching goals and methodologies. While, at the level of higher education, teachers in most other countries are usually trained in only one foreign language and are often instructed in practical classroom methodology and aspects of language

acquisition and applied linguistics, future German teachers always have a second subject, which can sometimes be a second foreign language, and their exposure to theoretical as well as practical aspects of language teaching at university level can vary extremely. In some *Länder* such as Baden-Württemberg, they may only experience a brief stint of practical training (*Praktikum*), with hardly any teaching experiences of their own, in other *Länder* they will have to attend several seminars on foreign language teaching (FLT) and, in addition, go through a closely linked term of on-the-job training (*Praktikumssemester*). All, however, share a period of teacher's training succeeding the first state exam (*Referendariat*), which is currently between one and a half and two years, a period during which young teachers already teach up to more than thirteen hours per week, get further practical instruction from mentors and are still under supervision. It is only after this second state exam that they have acquired the legal rights to become state teachers (which used to be coupled with the status of a civil servant, but due to fiscal reasons, this is no longer the case in some *Länder*). Alternative, non-state-run schools also accept applications from non-traditionally trained teachers.

*Englischdidaktik.* In analogy to *Didaktik* in other university subjects, the discipline of *Englischdidaktik* is frequently established at Institutes for English and American Studies. It is defined as a link discipline in two regards (cf. section 1.3 below): First, it serves as a connecting, application-oriented 'horizontal link' between various theories and concepts circulating within academic discussions, both in the areas of English Studies and in other academic disciplines. Second, it provides a 'vertical link' between academic agendas and the needs and demands of the EFL classroom. In this context, it must be noted that the term *didactics* carries different connotations in English-speaking countries (implying the idea of overt teacherly instruction); the German discipline could best be translated as English Language Education (Klippel 423). While in other countries terms such as EFL or FLT (foreign language teaching) or applied linguistics or EFL Methodology are preferred, the component of 'education' hints at a typically German (also partly Austrian) tradition of academically informed teaching which goes beyond mere language instruction. It incorporates pedagogical, psychological and, most significantly, educational goals such as intercultural understanding and other more holistic, overarching teaching objectives which are stipulated by the curricula of the *Länder* but also by the *Grundgesetz* (e.g., the demand for tolerance, acceptance of minorities, rights of individuals, preservation of nature).

The subject of English didactics is the theory and practice of teaching and learning English as a foreign language. Studying English didactics, students acquire theoretically grounded knowledge of and skills in planning (conceptualizing), putting into practice and evaluating processes of teaching and learning the target language. Thus, students gain insights into the framework needed for providing their future students with language competences.

---

**Focus on Key Fields of EFL**

- **Fields of influence on English Language Education**: Society, institutions, families, curricula, teacher and students, further external and internal factors (from learning environment to student-teacher ratio).
- **Role of the learner and role of the teacher**: the teacher as instructor and/or mediator; focus on learner-output; questions of learner adequacy and motivation.
- **Teaching goals**: improving language and communicative competences; intercultural learning and overall educative objectives; assessing and evaluating student output.
- **Choice of topics, materials, texts, media**: suitability, comprehensibility, exemplary and representative choices; focus on competences.
- **Choice of methods**: variety of methods; action-, task-, production-, student-oriented; focus on learner autonomy and self-guided learning; developing various competences.
- **Classroom practice**: planning of lesson sequences and individual lessons, methodology, tasks, microstructure of teacher-student interaction.

(cf. Weskamp; Timm)

---

Didactics does not just teach methodological steps or provide a practical 'tool kit' for teaching English, but also has as its important aim to research teaching contents, methods and goals of teaching at schools, from primary schools to advanced learners, and occasionally for lifelong learning.

In its focus, English didactics is both descriptive and normative. That is, it describes and analyses current theories, models and practice *and* it discusses, develops and provides suggestions for implementing improved, more effective theories, models and practices. It is exactly this bridge between theory and practice and the question of how the two perspectives are related respectively that is reflected in the history of English didactics in Germany. Three phases can be discerned here (cf. Klippel 425–44):

Phase 1: before 1970. With the establishment of departments of modern philology in the middle of the nineteenth century, requirements of teacher training came into focus. While the tradition of teaching Latin and Greek and with it the—later much maligned—**Grammar-Translation Method** continued to permeate university instruction in teaching English, already in the last decades of the nineteenth century innovative, more communicatively oriented concepts such as those by Wilhelm Viëtor pointed towards more progressive methods of the future. After *Volkskunde* concepts of teaching English as a key to understanding the target culture's 'spirit and soul' (*das geistige Wesen des*

The Theory and Politics of
English Language Teaching

*Fremden*) evolved in the Weimar Republic and were appropriated in twisted concepts of Aryan superiority in the Nazi years, English language instruction with regard to developing actual language skills became more important in the years after 1945. Teachers trained at universities were still mostly prepared for the *Gymnasium*, which, however, catered only to about ten per cent of the age group. At the *Gymnasien*, classroom English still focused on written English, with oral/aural skills considered of less importance. Didactics began to become increasingly accepted as part of university curricula as the growing need for educating a larger number of the populace demanded substantial **reforms** in the area of teacher education, with the emphasis shifting "towards training students quickly and efficiently for particular professional fields" (Klippel 426).

**Phase 2: 1970–1990.** In these decades, *Englischdidaktik* established itself as an academic discipline, sharpened its profile and—in the wake of the **communicative turn** and influenced by audio-lingual approaches—turned into an academic and theoretical discipline which "derive[d] its leading questions from classroom reality which it needs to analyse and in turn influence" (Klippel 435). Specifically, there was a shift towards more practical orientation as an 'applied discipline.' Major research interests included the history of teaching English, motivational psychology, classroom activities and interaction, classroom games, bilingual methods—and in the late 1980s also intercultural learning and communication skills.

**Phase 3: from 1990 to today.** With the impact of the *Common European Framework of Reference for Languages* (*CEF*), the Language Portfolio project

and a number of recent national surveys and high-profile empirical studies in EFL (for example IGLU and DESI), the demand for competence and **output-oriented teaching** has set in. The new paradigm of **intercultural learning** in connection with a general "pedagogization" of university disciplines, modules and course contents has bolstered up the position of didactics at universities to a considerable degree. Recent introductions to EFL are mushrooming and apparently much coveted by students wishing to be prepared for their future occupation (see for example Bach and Niemeier; Decke-Cornill and Küster; Doff and Klippel; Haß; Müller-Hartmann and Schocker-von Ditfurth; Surkamp; Timm; Volkmann). Given that there are only a few academically prestigious and peer-reviewed journals (*Fremdsprachen Lehren und Lernen* and *Zeitschrift für Fremdsprachenforschung*, edited by *Deutsche Gesellschaft für Fremdsprachenforschung* [DGFF], the academic umbrella-organization of academics involved in foreign language teaching research in Germany), it may be quite telling that most of the publications in the field today have become very practically oriented, including easily applicable, classroom-oriented instructions on how to put theoretical reflections to classroom use. Well-established EFL journals (mainly, *Der Fremdsprachliche Unterricht Englisch*, *Praxis Fremdsprachenunterricht*, *Englisch Betrifft Uns* and the *FMF-Mitteilungen* of various German *Länder* [*Fachverband Moderne Fremdsprachen*]) are forced to compete with a plethora of easily accessible teaching material on the Internet. It is posted there as tailor-made supplementary material by commercial publishing houses and can be accessed partly for free, partly via subscription. There is also material galore posted by teachers themselves, by the international EFL community as well as for specific use in Germany.

It remains to be seen whether the current preference for practical, hands-on, theory-free instruction and its pragmatic-utilitarian dimension will not be to the disadvantage of content-based, knowledge-oriented and theoretically informed course concepts. English didactics, however, which used to be the Cinderella of the English and American Studies departments (cf. Klippel), is increasingly established. However, if it should shift, as many students demand, towards simply offering practical instruction on teaching and learning methods, it may well sink to the status of a low-level, theory-free discipline which had better be part of teacher training courses at the school level.

## Focus on EFL Journals

*Fremdsprachen Lehren und Lernen* (*FLuL*): each issue has its own thematic focus, from teaching literary texts to the history of foreign language teaching

*Zeitschrift für Fremdsprachenforschung* (*ZFF*): focus on research in the field of foreign language teaching/learning in Germany

*Der Fremdsprachliche Unterricht Englisch*: each issue has a thematic focus, offering teaching materials and didactic advice on topics as diverse as "Football" (No. 79), "9/11: Ten Years On" (No. 111) or "Web 2.0" (No. 96)

*Praxis Fremdsprachenunterricht*: six short thematic issues a year that offer teaching ideas based on theoretical discussions—each issue contains teaching material

*Englisch Betrifft Uns*: six thematic issues a year offer teaching material (literature, media, the press, exam suggestions, etc.) for grades 9–13. There are sister magazines for grades 5–9 (*:in Englisch*) and for English at primary school level (*Bausteine Englisch*)

## 1.3 | *Englische Fachdidaktik* as a Bridge or Link Discipline

*Englische Fachdidaktik* as a bridge or link discipline between theory and practice and, in addition, as an interdisciplinary and cross-curricular discipline, taps into several academic disciplines. Its disciplinary hybridity clearly reflects on historical traditions, current trends and on the academic school or position of its respective proponents. While some stress its practical orientation as an applied discipline, one concerned first and foremost with teacher training (Klippel), others stress its groundedness in hermeneutic theories of understanding the other or other cultures (Bredella and Delanoy); still others would grant *Fachdidaktik* the quality of an umbrella discipline, one eclectically selecting from other disciplines what is needed in devising up-to-date and effective curricula (Weskamp).

In the context of English Departments, though, two main traditions have evolved over the decades and have remain highly formative and influential (cf. Hellwig and Keck; Kramer): One—***Literatur- und Kulturdidaktik***—could be defined as the hermeneutical, culture- and literature oriented tradition emphasizing (inter-)cultural teaching (cf. Delanoy and Volkmann). It tends to take as its fields of academic influence the Literature and Culture Departments at university. It also regards as its link disciplines subjects such as philosophy, history, geography, sociology, political science and philosophy. The other tradition—***Sprachdidaktik*** or *sprachwissenschaftliche Didaktik*—is closer to the Linguistic Departments, applied linguistics and the area of teaching methodology, to psychological and pedagogical frameworks of EFL. Here, fields of inquiry cover linguistic topics such as pragmatics, contrastive linguistics, sociolinguistics, lexis and grammar. Classroom-related issues such as language processing, learner adequacy, learning strategies and techniques, motivation, task-based, student-oriented, action and process-oriented and co-operative learning methods are of paramount interest. While the literature and culture position emphasizes the value of *Bildung*, education, reading skills and cultural learning and often regards grammar and vocabulary work as 'below' being treated at the university level, the linguistic or methodological position stresses the importance of teaching 'real English' for real communicative situations, where literature appears of dwindling importance and receives marginal attention. As entrenched as such positions appear at first sight and as clearly visible as they are in the usual categorizations of professorships at university as either *Sprachdidaktik* or *Literatur-/Kulturdidaktik*, the new paradigm of intercultural learning may provide common ground for both areas, because the new teaching/learning goal of '**intercultural competence**' encompasses both linguistic and cultural knowledge, skills and competences.

In addition, the recent shift towards output- and competence-orientation, a result of standardization and internationalization drives, has been instrumental in establishing a new demand for empirical studies—with trends towards empirically grounded Second Language Acquisition and Second Language Learning (*Sprachlehr- und Lernforschung*) experiencing a resounding revival.

There is also an overall trend towards viewing the EFL classroom as the place for teaching intercultural communicative competences such as politeness, sensitivity to and awareness of the 'hidden meaning' of language and behaviour in intercultural settings. The skills learned appear applicable not merely in English-speaking cultures, but on a global scale, and are deemed as transferable to other languages. Furthermore, the following **recent trends** will prevail as important issues of EFL discussions and practice in Germany over the next years:

**1.** The explicit aim of the *CEF* (2001), as postulated by the Council of Europe, that **plurilingualism** is to be promoted in Europe, will continue to have an impact on Germany. The detailed descriptions of six levels of communicative language skills in the form of "can do" statements for a broad range of language competences will further shape and form curriculum planning, teaching and

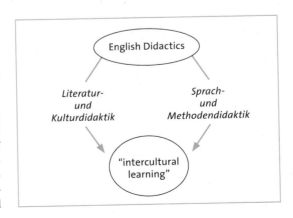

Intercultural learning

The Theory and Politics of
English Language Teaching

criterion-referenced assessment procedures, materials design and the definition of standards for language learning at German schools.

**2.** Traditional goals of the EFL classroom, the imparting of language skills, will further be supplemented not only with communicative skills, but **other competences** such as media competences, genre competences (understanding how a certain text creates meaning) and, apart from traditional literacies, increasingly multiliteracies, i.e., understanding how a combination of different text types (film, pictures, narrative and expository texts) function separately and in unison in a shared act of "textual interplay" (Hallet).

**3.** The trend towards **standardization**, assessment and evaluation on all levels (students, teachers, university instruction) will continue and with it the impact of the empirical turn.

**4.** Moderate forms of constructivism have appeared as the leading paradigm in German EFL publications (students are regarded as active agents, constructing their own meaning and learning contexts) and the idea of **autonomous, lifelong and project-oriented learning** (preferably beyond the spatial confinement of the classroom) will take on a new significance with e-learning and the Internet gaining influence in teaching/learning environments (cf. Rösler).

**5.** The issue of "**Which English(es) do we teach?**" will continue to be hotly discussed—with British and American English slowly losing their privileged positions as the only acceptable varieties in the classroom. With the opening up of global perspectives, the question of whether *lingua franca* forms of English will become widely acceptable remains to be answered. The waning influence of the former 'core countries' (Great Britain and the USA) will cast new cultural issues and topics into relief, such as environmental and political issues of global concern (so-called '**global issues**,' cf. Volkmann 191–205).

**6.** The question of '**differentiation**' will be increasingly important. If learners with different proficiency levels in English are taught in the same class, students must be given tasks in line with their different competence levels (e.g., in ability based groups: teachers organize group work according to the criteria of low, medium and high-level reading competence).

**7.** The trend towards learning English at an **early age** will continue, fervently demanded by parents worried about the future of their children in a globalized world. While, from the point of view of language learning, early instruction can only benefit children linguistically and with regard to intercultural learning (cf. Schmid-Schönbein; Elsner), new inequalities and problems are bound to arise since young pupils achieve very different levels of English before going on to the *Haupt-, Realschule* or *Gymnasium* (*Übergangsproblematik*).

**8.** There will also be an increase of **Content and Language Integrated Learning** (CLIL), that is, subject teaching like History, Geography, Chemistry or Biology in English, with the explicit goal of developing language competence while offering instruction in a non-language subject (cf. Bach and Niemeier; Doff). Influenced by Canadian experiences with immersion teaching, CLIL has been strongly advocated and been widely accepted as a viable option for furthering EFL while keeping up the standard of instruction achieved in the mother tongue.

However, as most researchers in the field would agree, while the future of English Education seems to be promising, the danger inherent in recent trends towards competence orientation and output orientation must be avoided: the threat that English is regarded merely as a linguistic tool, a *lingua franca* instrument without any cultural context and without any needs to consider the cultural implications of learning a language with a long and rich cultural tradition.

Key issues of EFL

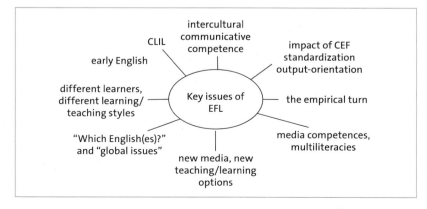

# Select Bibliography

Ahrens, Rüdiger, Wolf-Dieter Bald, and Werner Hüllen, eds. *Handbuch Englisch als Fremdsprache*. Berlin: Erich Schmidt Verlag, 1995.

Bach, Gerhard, and Susanne Niemeier, eds. *Bilingualer Unterricht: Grundlagen, Methoden, Praxis, Perspektiven*. Frankfurt/M.: Lang, 2000.

Bausch, Karl-Richard, Herbert Christ, and Hans-Jürgen Krumm, eds. *Handbuch Fremdsprachenunterricht*. 4th ed. Tübingen: Francke, 2003.

Bredella, Lothar, and Werner Delanoy, eds. *Interkultureller Fremdsprachenunterricht*. Tübingen: Narr, 1999.

Brusch, Wilfried. "Some Thoughts on a Language Policy for Schools and Society." *Praxis des neusprachlichen Unterrichts* 50.2 (2003): 115–124.

*Common European Framework of Reference for Languages (CEF)*. Council of Europe. 20 Dec. 2011 <http://www.coe.int/t/dg4/linguistic/Source/Framework_EN.pdf>. German print version: Europarat et al., eds. *Gemeinsamer europäischer Referenzrahmen für Sprachen: lernen, lehren, beurteilen*. Berlin: Langenscheidt, 2001.

Crystal, David. *English as a Global Language*. 2nd ed. Cambridge: Cambridge University Press, 2003.

Decke-Cornill, Helene, and Lutz Küster. *Fremdsprachendidaktik: Eine Einführung*. Tübingen: Narr, 2010.

Delanoy, Werner, and Laurenz Volkmann, eds. *Cultural Studies in the EFL Classroom*. Heidelberg: Winter, 2006.

Doff, Sabine, ed. *Bilingualer Sachfachunterricht in der Sekundarstufe: Eine Einführung*. Tübingen: Narr, 2010.

Doff, Sabine, and Friederike Klippel. *Englischdidaktik: Praxishandbuch für die Sekundarstufe I und II*. Berlin: Cornelsen Scriptor, 2007.

Elsner, Daniela. *Englisch in der Grundschule unterrichten: Grundlagen, Methoden, Praxisbeispiele*. Munich: Oldenbourg, 2010.

Finkenstaedt, Thomas. *Kleine Geschichte der Anglistik in Deutschland*. Darmstadt: WBG, 1983.

Hallet, Wolfgang. *Fremdsprachenunterricht als Spiel der Texte und Kulturen: Intertextualität als Paradigma einer kulturwissenschaftlichen Didaktik*. Trier: WVT, 2002.

Hallet, Wolfgang, and Ansgar Nünning, eds. *Neue Ansätze und Konzepte der Literatur- und Kulturdidaktik*. Trier: WVT, 2007.

Haß, Frank, ed. *Fachdidaktik Englisch: Tradition, Innovation, Praxis*. Stuttgart: Klett, 2006.

Hellwig, Karlheinz, and Rudolf Keck, eds. *Englisch-Didaktik zwischen Fachwissenschaft und Allgemeiner Didaktik*. Hanover: Fachbereich Erziehungswissenschaften, 1988.

Klippel, Friederike. "The Cinderella of 'Anglistik': Teacher Education." *Anglistik: Research Paradigms and Institutional Politics: 1930–2000*. Ed. Stephan Kohl. Trier: WVT, 2005. 423–44.

Kramer, Jürgen. "Kulturwissenschaft: Anglistik/Amerikanistik." *Kulturwissenschaft Interdisziplinär*. Eds. Klaus Stierstorfer and Laurenz Volkmann. Tübingen: Narr, 2005. 173–92.

Leitner, Gerhard. *Weltsprache Englisch: Vom angelsächsischen Dialekt zur globalen Lingua franca*. Munich: C.H. Beck, 2009.

Müller-Hartmann, Andreas, and Marita Schocker-von Ditfurth. *Introduction to English Language Teaching*. Stuttgart: Klett, 2004.

Nünning, Ansgar, and Andreas H. Jucker. *Orientierung Anglistik/Amerikanistik: Was sie kann, was sie will*. Reinbek: Rowohlt, 1999.

Phillipson, Robert. *Linguistic Imperialism*. Oxford: Oxford University Press, 1992.

Rösler, Dietmar. *E-Learning Fremdsprachen: Eine kritische Einführung*. 2nd ed. Tübingen: Stauffenburg, 2007.

Schmid-Schönbein, Gisela. *Didaktik: Grundschulenglisch*. Berlin: Cornelsen, 2001.

Surkamp, Carola, ed. *Metzler Lexikon Fremdsprachendidaktik*. Stuttgart: Metzler, 2010.

Timm, Johannes-Peter, ed. *Englisch Lernen und Lehren: Didaktik des Englischunterrichts*. 3rd ed. Berlin: Cornelsen, 2005.

Volkmann, Laurenz. *Fachdidaktik Englisch: Kultur und Sprache*. Tübingen: Narr, 2010.

Weskamp, Ralf. *Fachdidaktik: Grundlagen und Konzepte: Anglistik–Amerikanistik*. Berlin: Cornelsen, 2001.

*Laurenz Volkmann*

# 2 Language Learning

## 2.1 | The Limits of Institutionalized Language Teaching/Learning

Unlike teachers of other subjects, teachers of English as a foreign language (EFL) are never quite able to pinpoint how and where their students acquired their skills. Learners can speak a foreign language quite well without formal instruction, and high motivation and language exposure (on holidays or during an extended time abroad) can contribute considerably to EFL proficiency. Some would even state that the level of language proficiency can only be partly attributed to what students are taught in the classroom. Moreover, there is a trend to critically assess the shortcomings of institutionalized language learning at school. A list of drawbacks would include aspects which are all *Problems in the EFL classroom* seen as little conducive to learning a language for everyday use in 'normal' communicative situations:

- Students are forced to learn English in a highly regulated and competitive environment, and their performance in the school subject English, as documented by means of grades, has direct impact on their overall career opportunities. **External circumstances of pressure** can be counter-productive as a constant source of stress and a psychological obstacle fostering discomfort and insecurity.
- They are taught English in a **restricted spatial environment**, in an artificial classroom situation, in a non-communicative seating arrangement and often via methods of teacher-centred frontal teaching.
- Their learning is shaped and formed through official, well-intended political agendas and documents such as the *Common European Framework of Reference for Languages* (*CEF*), the respective region's **curricula** (*Lehrpläne der Länder*), decisions by English members of staff, school routines, the often rigid textbook ('the secret curriculum') and the conventional time-

frame of classroom lessons (on the intermediate level the framework of three times 45 minutes per week begs the question of how students can actually make any progress).
- The **classroom language is artificial**; they are exposed to inauthentic and inaccurate English; they have very little time and opportunity to engage in interchanges.

Some international surveys ('PISA') may cause scepticism about German EFL skills, and the harsh and monotonous German pronunciation, as well as deficiencies in the areas of conversation routines, verbal humour and politeness still need to be addressed in German EFL with plenty of room for improvement. Yet in spite of all these shortcomings, students do acquire sometimes remarkably proficient competences in English, and the need to raise the overall level of skills in English is widely acknowledged. In the age of globalization and its demands for foreign language skills, the need to generally improve English skills is clearly illustrated by the occasional public ridicule caused by those German politicians who embarrass themselves through their atrociously inadequate English.

Increased proficiency in English, specifically in spoken English, and therefore in everyday communication in the foreign language, has been on the agenda of English Language Education since the so-called communicative turn of the 1970s. The focus on '**communication skills**,' informed by theories of applied linguistics, entailed a programmatic turn from former habits of treating English as a written language. The analogy to instruction in the classical languages had shaped foreign language teaching considerably since its beginnings in the middle of the nineteenth century (cf. Doff and Klippel). More recently, the focus on communicative skills was reinforced through the *Common*

*European Framework of Reference for Languages* (2001). This political document, highly influential in the areas of curricula building, course-book design and language output assessment, has basically established two parameters of language teaching/learning: (1) it *defines* and describes general language competences and their sub-competences, and (2) it *categorizes* and describes levels of competency on the general language skills level as well as on various sub-levels ("can-do").

## 2.2 | Defining and Describing Competences

The *Common European Framework of Reference for Languages* defines foreign language competences in a paradigmatic manner:

Language use, embracing language learning, comprises the actions performed by persons who as individuals and as social agents develop a range of **competences**, both **general** and in particular **communicative language competences**. They draw on the competences at their disposal in various contexts under various **conditions** and under various **constraints** to engage in **language activities** involving **language processes** to produce and/or receive **texts** in relation to **themes** in specific **domains**, activating those **strategies** which seem most appropriate for carrying out the **tasks** to be accomplished. The monitoring of these actions by the participants leads to the reinforcement or modification of their competences. (9; emphasis in original)

Communicative competence here is defined in accordance with the seminal theory of linguist Dell Hymes from the 1970s—it is not viewed as an abstract universal language competence innate to all humans no matter what language they speak or acquire (as in Noam Chomsky's concept of a generative grammar). Rather, competence is defined as the performance of an actual speaker in an exchange with other speakers or another speaker in a given, actual space and time and context. According to Canale and Swain, who elaborated on Hymes's theories, communicative competence encompasses four competences (cf. Volkmann 19):

- **Linguistic competence**: the correct use of grammar, lexis, phonology and orthography
- **Sociolinguistic competence**: adequate language use according to a given situation
- **Discursive competence**: cohesion and coherence of utterances or written texts
- **Strategic competence**: using adequate and established communicative strategies (e.g., politeness, turn-taking, feedback)

Communicative language competences accordingly empower a person to take part in communicative interchanges in the target language. Based on these general descriptions of competences, the *CEF*, and with it most curricula at the German *Länder* level, categorize in detail 'sub-competences' which are further described by 'Can Do descriptors' and which can, accordingly, be assessed and evaluated in output-oriented learning/teaching environments. The four basic language skills defined below are given equal importance, which in fact highlights the importance of hitherto rather neglected skills of listening and oral production (cf. Weskamp, *Fremdsprachenunterricht*; Weskamp, *Mehrsprachigkeit*).

In addition to the four traditional skills, the *CEF* foregrounds skills of interaction (such as paralinguistic, non-verbal communication) and mediation, particularly interpreting and translating (here the focus in recent curricula is no longer on word-by-word translation but rather on negotiating between semantically differently-encoded language systems).

While the target language English until recently was associated primarily with 'native speakers' from the USA and Great Britain, there is a growing tendency, as reflected in the *CEF*, to enable learners to use English as a *lingua franca* in international settings, which may entail non-native speaker to non-native speaker communication, e.g., on holiday, or when using social websites. Here, in accordance with influential studies by Michael Byram and Claire Kramsch, the *CEF* stresses the significance of intercultural learning, which is

| Language Activities | |
|---|---|
| **Receptive** | **Productive** |
| **Listening:** this hitherto neglected skill has been given greater significance through obligatory listening comprehension tests in some *Länder* | **Speaking:** this ranges from interactional communication (discussions) to transactional speeches (oral report) |
| **Reading:** this ranges from 'close reading' to 'reading for gist' (scanning: looking for certain aspects; skimming: looking for key words) | **Writing:** tasks can range from comprehension to analysis to opinion to creative responses |

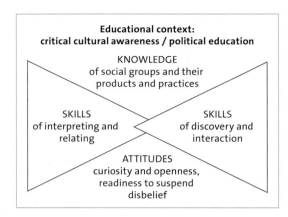

creating tolerance and empathy vis-à-vis other cultures and their individuals.

**2.** This is furthered by **acquiring knowledge** about the other culture. Such knowledge encompasses facts and figures as in earlier concepts of *Landeskunde* (cf. section III.1.2), but also insights into the target culture's areas of small-c culture (popular culture, everyday culture) (cf. Delanoy and Volkmann). This includes knowing about the Do's and Don'ts of another culture.

**3.** This knowledge needs to be converted from declarative, inert knowledge to **procedural know-how**, to skills of dealing with another culture and its members.

**4.** Finally, and most difficult to assess as a competence, intercultural learning enables learners to take on the **perspective of another person**, compare the other person's perspective with one's own perspective and to come to a more complex understanding of another culture, involving affective elements such as empathy, and to overcome stereotyped attitudes. In sum, intercultural competence means "the capacity to fulfil the role of cultural intermediary between one's own culture and the foreign culture and to deal effectively with intercultural misunderstanding and conflict situations" (*CEF* 105).

embodied in the key term 'intercultural communicative competence' or, more recently, reflected in the call for 'transcultural competence' as a social skill and open attitude enabling individuals to communicate effectively and peacefully in a globalized world where national characteristics and boundaries are constantly being blurred or transgressed (cf. Volkmann). The goal of **intercultural competence** is rendered in Michael Byram's definition of its four components (cf. Byram 49–55; Doff and Klippel 120):

**1.** Its overall aims are furthering **intercultural sensitivity**, avoiding ethnocentric attitudes and

## 2.3 | Categorizing Competences

The *CEF* and, under its influence, all recent official documents on foreign language teaching, try to objectify language learning skills and output through a set of taxonomies ('descriptors') with regard to competences in all productive and receptive language areas. The precise formulation of

various sets of common reference points, including the wording of the descriptors, have developed in recent years as the standardized benchmark for all research and teaching sectors of FLT across Europe. Therefore, consulting the *CEF* for lesson and sequence planning as well as student assessment and evaluation is a must for every teacher of EFL. Stating in detail what learners are supposed to be able to do in reading, writing, speaking, listening and other language production fields at each level, the *CEF* divides learners into three broad divisions (basic, independent and proficient user) that are divided into six levels (A1 to C2, see box).

In addition, fields of interest are given where students are supposed to have competences in using language, as in "personal identification; house and home, environment; daily life; free time, entertainment; travel; relations with other people; health and body care; education; shopping; food; drink; services; places; language; weather" (*CEF* 52).

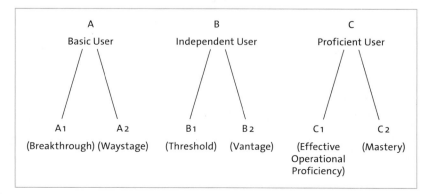

Such description of important contents of communication is reflected in most curricula, which stipulate that early learners start with simple, everyday, pupil-oriented things and matters which they experience in their daily environment (introducing oneself, food, drink, relationships, etc.)

All in all, the *CEF* and the general stress on 'communicative competence' has shifted the focus from product to **process**, from knowledge to **competence**, and from accuracy of language use to **overall fluency**, from the native speaker model to that of the '**intercultural speaker**' (cf. Kramsch;

Kramer 179–80). Importantly, accuracy in both pronunciation and grammar is no longer considered as crucial for effective communication, errors are not avoided at all costs. The most significant shift has been from learning about specific cultural contexts of formerly clearly defined target cultures to everyday communicative skills whose success is tested by means of instruments such as language portfolios or listening comprehension tests which, however, are in danger of testing memorization abilities rather than listening for gist or listening to glean certain, specific items of information.

## 2.4 | Theories and Methods of Language Teaching

Current language teaching/learning is informed by a wide range of theories and methods which could be categorized according to the overall question of whether language skills can be attributed to intelligence, intrinsic motivation and exposure or to explicit instruction ('nature versus nurture'). 'Acquisition' through rich learning environments, comprehensible input and sufficient intake is often pitted against 'learning' through the conscious learning of explicit rules and formal exposure to language (cf. Weskamp, *Fremdsprachenunterricht* 27; Decke-Cornill and Küster 21). Two opposing but not necessarily incompatible theories of language learning inform current EFL teaching/learning: **behaviorism** (a theory based on the findings of psychologist B. F. Skinner) and **nativism** (mainly influenced by the theories of Stephen Krashen), a theory which is often combined with theories of constructivism. By contrast to instructive methods, which would prefer top-down, teacher-centred instruction, the paradigm of **constructivism** stresses individual agency and that the world/ languages are accessible only subjectively; it is a theory influential in the humanities as well as in psychology (cf. Wendt). The following is a survey of these influential theories in key words (cf. Nunan; Brown; Weskamp, *Fremdsprachenunterricht;* Decke-Cornill and Küster):

Behaviorism, also called the 'empiricist' or 'environmentalist' theory: languages are acquired through exposure to an environment; input will create output; learners can be conditioned to produce language (via stimulus-response situations provided by teacher input and/or audio-visual input); learning is enhanced by doing and trial-and-error; reinforcement and habit formation are closely linked to success).

Nativism (usually associated with Noam Chomsky and Stephen Krashen): Based on the 'identity hypothesis': second language (L2) acquisition resembles first language (L1) acquisition; performance is based on universal language competence (Language Acquisition Device). Often linked to the 'natural approach' (Krashen): immersion and acquisition are the key to successful language learning, and the stress is on intuitive, implied knowledge rather than explicit learning of formal knowledge, explicit teaching of rules. Comprehensible input and an anxiety-free environment are most beneficial (Affective Filter Hypothesis): "A learner who is tense, angry, anxious or bored may 'filter out' input, making it unavailable for acquisition. [...] The filter will be 'up' [blocking input] when the learner is stressed, self-conscious, or unmotivated. It will be 'down' when the learner is relaxed and motivated" (Lightbown and Spada 39). Accordingly, teachers should create:

- A positive atmosphere where students are not afraid to make mistakes
- Significant amounts of language production/ experimentation
- Constructivist-based interactional components
- High levels of student comfort, without turning the classroom into a playroom or circus.

You cannot prepare students for the spontaneous conversations they will encounter, but teachers can encourage them to enter into these conversations without fear and with great curiosity and willingness to improve their language and communication skills.

The 'natural approach' to teaching

**Grammar-translation method**: instruction by teacher; explicit teaching of rules; grammar and vocabulary introduced deductively (from abstract definitions and rules to examples); one-to-one translation; focus on reading and writing; often at the expense of communication skills.

**Audio-lingual method**: based on behaviourist theories, focus on aural and visual input (e.g., in the language lab); typical speech acts (typical communicative situations) are rehearsed; 'parrot learning' and 'pattern drill' monotony are to be avoided; modifications are possible through having students practise variations and allowing creativity.

**Total Physical Response**: a holistic approach which combines language use and learning with whole body movements; e.g. with the help of songs, chants, hip hop, etc.

**Suggestopedia**: accelerated learning in the 'alpha brainwave state,' i.e., students relax and enjoy oral input via a technical medium; language is taken in subconsciously; autonomous learning via headphones.

**Natural approach** (also called direct method, immersion, language bath): stress on acquisition of input; instructor provides comprehensible input and creates low anxiety situations (listening to audio-input; silent reading periods); theory of the silent period may be observed: that is, not making pupils speak before they feel ready to do so (speech is delayed until it emerges after a silent period); students will produce language when they are ready to do so.

**Communicative approach**: students are encouraged to use oral English in cooperative settings; the stress is on fluency, not on accuracy.

**Task-based language teaching**: avoidance of teacher-centred learning, focus on self-directed learning; students are offered or choose a task according to their communication or language needs or interests (ranging from a short text-based interpretation to a project covering several lessons); teacher monitors choice of task, provides language and information help, helps students understand tasks and instructions; students do the task in a co-operative manner (pairs, groups); report to class; results are exchanged and compared; instructor monitors and helps with tasks and language processing and presents post-task activities (see Willis 38; Müller-Hartmann and Schocker-von Ditfurth).

**Cognitivist-constructivist theories.** Since humans create their knowledge as active agents, teachers should serve as language facilitators and monitor language acquisition as an individual process furthered by input and interaction. Cognitivist-constructivist theories focus on teaching/learning strategies and techniques (acquisition, retention, use); they prefer holistic approaches to presenting new grammatical and lexical items not as single units but rather as prefabricated 'chunks'; and they aim at enabling learners to reflect on language and acquire language awareness (autonomous learning, task and project based learning). Part of this approach is the creation of an environment that facilitates autonomous learning as through online classes, projects outside of the classroom, etc.

At the very practical level of the classroom, the methods listed above are used eclectically, and are given here in the approximate order of when they gained influence in foreign language teaching.

## 2.5 | Good Language Teachers and Good Language Learners

It is generally agreed that the **teacher-centred classroom** tends to establish and perpetuate fixed communication patterns. Mostly, the teacher tends to open and close the classroom topic and activity, has the power to dominate the topic, controls the turn-taking by selecting a student to respond, initiates most interactions and, finally, evaluates responses. As a result of typical teacher language ('teacherese') and hierarchical and teacher-directed exchanges, students not only internalize artificial and occasionally impractical communication patterns and language skills, they also hardly get time to speak, let alone utter more than just a brief rejoinder to the teacher's question. Typical exchanges consist of three parts: the teacher initiates an exchange, a student responds and the teacher gives feedback. To counterbalance this severe restriction of learning opportunities and to prepare for and enable students to partake of everyday, real-world conversations, the teacher must give students a larger share of the interaction and more opportunities to engage in classroom discourse, also by experimenting with the target language as an 'interlanguage' (cf. Willis 17). The 'good language learner,' much discussed in the literature, is highly dependent on a 'good language teacher.' A good teacher, apart from being equipped with pedagogical, psychological and methodological skills and with cultural and linguistic expertise, knows how to motivate students and monitor as a language facilitator or mediator student activities which are self-directed, cooperative and empower learners to acquire language skills outside of the classroom and after their years at school (e.g., through acquiring dictionary and research skills, language awareness, curiosity and interest in improving English skills). As the 'guide on the side, not the sage on the stage' the good teacher supports the language learner who feels a strong **reason to learn the language** because (cf. Willis 10):

- the learner enjoys seeking opportunities to use English, focuses on communication and meaning rather than on form;
- the learner supplements learning in class and in everyday situations with conscious study, e.g. by keeping a notebook for new words and phrases;
- the learner responds positively to a learning situation which is free of anxiety and inhibitions, offers sufficient comprehensible and relevant input;
- the learner is empowered to analyse, categorise and remember language forms (including grammar) and monitor errors and correct mistakes.
- the learner is prepared to experiment with language ('interlanguage') and not afraid to take risks;
- the learner is flexible and capable of adapting to different learning situations.

## 2.6 | Learning in the Classroom and Learning Beyond the Classroom

In the period of language acquisition, which usually ranges from class 3 (learning at primary/elementary school) to classes 9 or 10, German curricula, language syllabi and with them the 'secret curriculum' of the students' textbook, follow the principle of **sequencing** (*Progression*). According to theories of developmental stages of learners, syntactic and morphological structures of grammar are learned one at a time in a certain sequence (e.g. past tense after present tense): "Research has shown that no matter how language is presented to learners, certain structures are acquired before others" (Lightbown and Spada 166). Sufficient examples of one grammatical structure should be practised before going on to another grammatical phenomenon. However, language learning is not simply linear in its development, and learners incorporate new information about the language according to their own idiosyncratic internal system of rules or habits. The process of readjusting and restructuring the 'mental lexicon' and mental system of language rules is an ongoing and fluctuating process. Thus, many studies in EFL are critical of isolated presentation and practice of one structure at a time as this does not offer learners the chance to develop their own 'interlanguage' and contrasts with normal language use. There is a tendency to advocate the acquisition of pre-fabricated language 'chunks,' i.e. not isolated words or grammatical structures, but complete short utterances, collocations and idiomatic expressions (cf. Taylor; Schmitt).

For the bread and butter job of the foreign language instructor, which is teaching grammar and vocabulary, **inductive** rather than deductive methods have been established. In the case of teaching vocabulary, this implies using word fields which are arranged in a context, possibly in a narrative, and presented in a lively, hands-on manner for beginners, with the aid of pictures, posters, sketches and, whenever feasible, real objects (*Realia*). Verbal explanations (synonyms, defining sentences, etc.) are preferred with advanced learners and if abstract vocabulary is introduced. Correct oral input comes first, with students rehearsing the new words alone and together; exposure to the written form follows; and active use is encouraged only after correct pronunciation and correct use in collocations and typical contexts is ascertained. Vocabulary needs regular revision and correction is needed, if pronunciation mistakes fossilize. However, in general, teachers should not be mis-

*Teaching grammar and vocabulary*

## Focus on Learning: Presentation → Practice → Production

**Presentation**: The teacher presents a sufficient number of typical examples of the new item. This is done in a comprehensible, student-adequate contextual setting, with the support of pictures, stories, etc. For instance, the past tense is introduced by describing with lively illustrations what the students just did in their summer holidays.

**Practice**: While in a first reaction to the teacher's presentation, students merely repeat or respond with simple utterances to the teacher's input, practising the new item gets more complex step by step, includes written forms and moves from simple, rigid tasks (yes/no, 'fill in') to less patterned, free activities.

**Production**: Here the students use the new grammatical item in typical contexts and, through regular revision, incorporate the new structure in their language system. Typical activities in this phase would be role plays and written tasks of free text production.

an open one, with a recent trend back to having students 'discover' basic rules of the new structure themselves after the initial phase(s) of learning. Grammar processing can be divided into the three phases presented on the left.

Already in the period of language acquisition students should become acquainted with learning strategies and techniques, which will lead them towards autonomous and lifelong learning beyond the classroom. The three basic **learning strategies** are the following (Willis 10):

- **Metacognitive**: organizing one's learning, monitoring and evaluating one's language output.
- **Cognitive**: Advance preparation for a class, using a dictionary, listing and categorising new words and phrases, making comparisons with other known languages, learning to understand subtle nuances, the underlying cultural implications and unwritten or unsaid messages behind words.
- **Social**: Including typical conversation routines used in English-speaking countries (politeness, humour, asking for help, asking for correction, interaction with other speakers).

take-seekers, and they should rather not interrupt students' oral production. Instead, they should create awareness of mistakes later (correct 'teacher recasts' comprise an additional option). As to grammar, student- and production-oriented methods are well established (cf. von Ziegésar and von Ziegésar). The question of when and if to include the explicit presentation of grammar rules remains

## Select Bibliography

**Brown, H. Douglas.** *Principles of Language Learning and Teaching.* Englewood Cliffs: Prentice Hall, 1994.

**Bygate, Martin, ed.** *Grammar and the Language Teacher.* New York: Prentice Hall, 1994.

**Byram, Michael.** *Teaching and Assessing Intercultural Communicative Competence.* Clevedon: Multilingual Matters, 1997.

***Common European Framework of Reference for Languages (CEF).*** Council of Europe. 20 Dec. 2011 <http://www.coe.int/t/dg4/linguistic/Source/Framework_EN.pdf>. German print version: Europarat et al., eds. *Gemeinsamer europäischer Referenzrahmen für Sprachen: lernen, lehren, beurteilen.* Berlin: Langenscheidt, 2001.

**Decke-Cornill, Helene, and Lutz Küster.** *Fremdsprachendidaktik: Eine Einführung.* Tübingen: Narr, 2010.

**Delanoy, Werner, and Laurenz Volkmann, eds.** *Cultural Studies in the EFL Classroom.* Heidelberg: Winter, 2006.

**Doff, Sabine, and Friederike Klippel.** *Englischdidaktik. Praxishandbuch für die Sekundarstufe I und II.* Berlin: Cornelsen Scriptor, 2007.

**Edmondson, Willis J.** *Einführung in die Sprachlehrforschung.* 2nd ed. Tübingen: Francke, 2002.

**Haß, Frank, ed.** *Fachdidaktik Englisch: Tradition, Innovation, Praxis.* Stuttgart: Klett, 2006.

**Hymes, D. H.** "On Communicative Competence." 1971. *Sociolinguistics: Selected Readings.* Eds. J. B. Pride and Janet Holmes. Harmondsworth: Penguin, 1972. 269–93.

**Klein, Eberhard.** *Sprachdidaktik Englisch.* Ismaning: Hueber, 2001.

**Klieme, Eckhardt, et al.** *Zur Entwicklung nationaler Bildungsstandards: Eine Expertise.* Berlin: Bundesministerium für Bildung und Forschung, 2003.

**Kramer, Jürgen.** "Kulturwissenschaft: Anglistik/Amerikanistik." *Kulturwissenschaft Interdisziplinär.* Eds. Klaus Stierstorfer and Laurenz Volkmann. Tübingen: Narr, 2005. 173–92.

**Kramsch, Claire.** *Context and Culture in Language Learning.* Oxford: Oxford University Press, 1996.

**Krashen, Stephen D.** *Principles and Practice in Second Language Acquisition.* London: Prentice Hall, 1981.

**Lightbown, Patsy M., and Nina Spada.** *How Languages Are Learned.* Oxford: Oxford University Press, 2004.

**Müller-Hartmann, Andreas, and Marita Schocker-von Ditfurth.** *Introduction to English Language Teaching.* Stuttgart: Klett, 2004.

**Nunan, David.** *Language Teaching Methodology: A Textbook for Teachers.* New York: Prentice Hall, 1991.

**Rösler, Dietmar.** *E-Learning Fremdsprachen: Eine kritische Einführung.* 2nd ed. Tübingen: Stauffenburg, 2007.

**Schmitt, Norbert.** *Vocabulary in Language Teaching.* Cambridge: Cambridge University Press, 2000.

**Taylor, Linda.** *Teaching and Learning Vocabulary.* New York: Prentice Hall, 1990.

**Timm, Johannes-Peter, ed.** *Englisch Lernen und Lehren: Didaktik des Englischunterrichts.* 3rd ed. Berlin: Cornelsen, 2005.

**Volkmann, Laurenz.** *Fachdidaktik Englisch: Kultur und Sprache.* Tübingen: Narr, 2010.

**Wendt, Michael, ed.** *Konstruktion statt Instruktion: Neue Zugänge zu Sprache und Kultur im Fremdsprachenunterricht.* Frankfurt/M.: Lang, 2000.

**Weskamp, Ralf.** *Fremdsprachenunterricht Entwickeln: Grundschule – Sekundarstufe I – Gymnasiale Oberstufe.* Hanover: Diesterweg, 2003.

**Weskamp, Ralf.** *Mehrsprachigkeit: Sprachevolution, Kognitive Sprachverarbeitung und schulischer Fremdsprachenerwerb.* Brunswick: Diesterweg, 2007.

**Willis, Jane.** *A Framework for Task-based Learning.* Harlow: Longman, 2000.

**Ziegésar, Detlef von, and Margarete von Ziegésar.** *Einführung von Grammatik im Englischunterricht.* Munich: Ehrenwirth, 1992.

*Laurenz Volkmann*

# 3 Teaching Literature

## 3.1 | Definition, Field of Tasks, and History of the Discipline

The main goals of a **didactics of literature** in the area of teaching English are to explore why and how literary texts should be employed in foreign language teaching and learning processes, which competences can be developed by dealing with literature and which texts are particularly suitable. The didactics of literature is a relatively young subdiscipline within foreign language didactics. It was not established as a scientifically researched field until the 1970s. Though not always recognized as a field in its own right, the teaching of literature looks back upon a long history. It has been subject to constant changes, resulting from several sources: firstly from the history of literary studies, one of the most important neighbour disciplines of the didactics of literature; secondly from general didactic influences; and thirdly from the varying status literary texts have been assigned in foreign language learning from a didactic and an educational-political perspective at different times.

The use of literature for foreign-language teaching

The use of literary texts in modern language lessons has played an important role ever since the nineteenth century, when English and French were incorporated into the subject canon of humanist grammar schools. At first, the learning objectives and teaching practice were modelled on the ancient languages, i.e. Latin and Greek. This meant that literature lessons consisted primarily of translating significant works of English and French literary history with the goal of conveying the cultural achievements of the countries of the respective target language. These lessons were intended to provide general educational, rather than specifically linguistic, knowledge. This often led to the texts being read in the foreign language, but discussed in German. This orientation towards a humanist educational ideal and the resulting opposition of literature and language learning left its mark on foreign language didactics well into the 1970s (cf. Brusch and Caspari). Up to today, the issue of the integration of language and textual

work has not been finally resolved, even though a first basis has been founded with Wilfried Brusch's concept of 'literary learning as language learning' ("Rolle der Literatur") and the guiding principle of "integrated literary-language learning" outlined by Wolfgang Zydatiß ("Integrierter Literatur-Sprach-Unterricht" 332).

In the twentieth century, two major currents in literary studies particularly influenced how literary texts were approached in foreign language teaching: the New Criticism of the first half of the century and the reader response criticism of the 1970s and 1980s (cf. entry III.3). The continuing impact of literary studies is due to the fact that the university training of future grammar school English teachers was and still is largely grounded in literary studies. The influence that New Criticism (cf. section II.1.3), a text-centred current interested in 'objective literary studies,' had on literature lessons entailed an orientation towards structuralist methods of interpretation, such as close reading, with an emphasis on the formal elements of literary texts. The contemplation of literature was text-immanent and teacher-centred.

In the 1970s and 1980s, dealing with literary texts was largely relegated to the senior classes in grammar schools since 'communicative language learning' was pragmatically modelled on the use of the foreign language in actual speaking situations. The guiding medium for language learning in lower classes was the schoolbook, which hardly contained any literary texts aside from a few songs, poems or cartoons. It was not until well into the 1980s, amid insights gained through research on reading and in reader response criticism as a new concept of text comprehension, that literary texts in English lessons gained momentum again. Following Hans Robert Jauß and Wolfgang Iser, reading was no longer seen as a passive act of extracting information or as the decoding of a particular meaning hidden in a text, but as a creative act of

VI. 3.1

Didactics: The Teaching of English

Definition, Field
of Tasks, and History
of the Discipline

constructing meaning. Against this background, a didactics of literature modelled upon **reader response criticism** developed, which—building on the learners' cognitive and emotional processes of sense-making—conceptualized literature lessons as a place for subjective and individual textual encounters (cf. Bredella and Burwitz-Melzer). This also had methodological consequences for literature classes: the focus was no longer on the text, but on the reception process, i.e. the learners with their individual reactions to the text and their subjective readings. A number of creative methods of dealing with texts were developed in order to mediate between text and learners in terms of a dialogical model of literary understanding. This change brought about by the influence of reader response criticism (also taking into account developments in general didactics) led to a turn towards more learner-orientation, and has an impact on foreign language didactics of literature to this day.

In the 1990s, foreign language didactics was characterized by the new guiding principle of **intercultural learning**. As literature in the foreign language offers learners the opportunity to become acquainted with other models of reality, to take new perspectives and concomitantly to reflect on the inevitable limitedness of their own world view, it gained particular importance within the context of the hermeneutically oriented didactics of what in German is called *Fremdverstehen* (cf. Bredella et al.). The abilities to empathize with others and to change perspectives, both of which are necessary prerequisites for intercultural understanding, are considered an essential component of reading literary texts. Thus, the didactics of literature pursued the idea that reading literary texts in the foreign language classroom was particularly apt to promote intercultural understanding. Supporting this view was the assumption that the protective space provided by the fictionality of literary texts facilitates changing one's attitude by way of trial, a change which can then also take place in the learners' real life (cf. Nünning, "Intermisunderstanding," on the various levels of intercultural understanding when dealing with literary texts). In the 2000s, the emerging discussion about the theoretical concept of transculturality induced the didactics of literature to also turn to the cultural

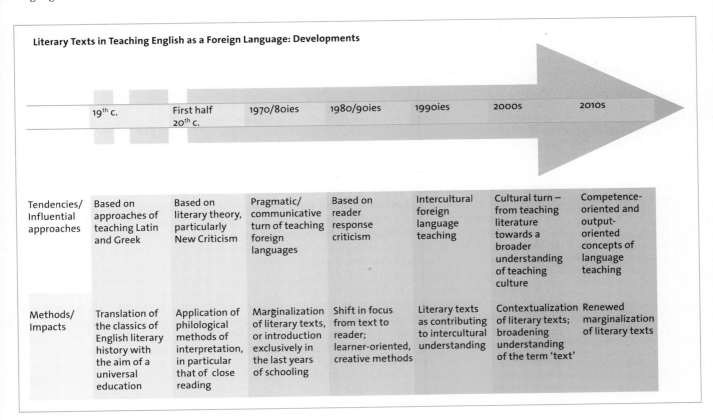

**Literary Texts in Teaching English as a Foreign Language: Developments**

| | 19th c. | First half 20th c. | 1970/80ies | 1980/90ies | 1990ies | 2000s | 2010s |
|---|---|---|---|---|---|---|---|
| Tendencies/ Influential approaches | Based on approaches of teaching Latin and Greek | Based on literary theory, particularly New Criticism | Pragmatic/ communicative turn of teaching foreign languages | Based on reader response criticism | Intercultural foreign language teaching | Cultural turn – from teaching literature towards a broader understanding of teaching culture | Competence-oriented and output-oriented concepts of language teaching |
| Methods/ Impacts | Translation of the classics of English literary history with the aim of a universal education | Application of philological methods of interpretation, in particular that of close reading | Marginalization of literary texts, or introduction exclusively in the last years of schooling | Shift in focus from text to reader; learner-oriented, creative methods | Literary texts as contributing to intercultural understanding | Contextualization of literary texts; broadening understanding of the term 'text' | Renewed marginalization of literary texts |

border crossings and processes of negotiation which go along with the reading of and exchange on literary texts in a foreign language (cf. Eckerth and Wendt; Delanoy).

**At the present time**, the foreign language didactics of literature must be thought of in the plural form. A multitude of **coexistent approaches** have developed under the influence of numerous paradigm shifts within literary and cultural studies, above all the cognitive turn, the cultural turn and the pictorial turn. These shifts make new notions of culture, text and subject fruitful for the teaching of literature in foreign language classes. Furthermore, they have set off a debate on the literary canon and have extended the subject area of the didactics of literature to include visual, auditory and audio-visual texts. The newly developed approaches comprise the broadening of the didactics of literature into a didactics of culture, intertextual and intermedial concepts as well as the inclusion of gender and post-colonial theories into literature classes (cf. the contributions in Hallet and Nünning, *Neue Ansätze*). Wolfgang Hallet, for example, conceptualizes the foreign language classroom as a realm of intercultural and discursive encounters in which texts, utterances and voices of the target language culture(s), but also of the learners and teachers, enter into interplay (*Fremdsprachenunterricht*). He points out that in foreign language lessons, the encounter and communication with other cultures and their representatives generally take place in a textual-discursive or mediated way. Cultural approaches within the didactics of literature emphasize that literary texts are a medium in which culture—understood as the cumulative complex of concepts, mindsets, ways of feeling, values and meanings created by a group of people—materializes. Thus, dealing with a foreign language text in class can allow insights into the cultural knowledge, the world views and lifestyles of the society from which it emerged (Nünning and Surkamp 32–38). Gender-oriented approaches, in turn, deal with the question of how learners can be sensitized to the normativity of a binary thinking of gender as well as to the hybridity and performativity of gender with the help of literary texts (cf. Decke-Cornill, "Identities"; Volkmann). Film-didactic papers discuss the potential movies as multiply coded texts have for foreign language learning—for example with reference to literary adaptations (cf. Surkamp, "Literaturverfilmungen"), but also considering films as works of art in their own right (cf. Blell and Lütge).

**Challenges.** Despite all the differences between the various approaches within literature didactics, important common tasks lie ahead. As Hallet and Nünning note, there is a lack of fundamental theoretical conceptualizations of the newer cultural studies-based orientations, which leads to the fact that the teaching of literature is still largely indebted to structuralist approaches and logocentric concepts ("Neue fachwissenschaftliche Konzepte" 2). Aside from this, ever since the loss of the classical educational mandate of grammar schools, the existence of the *Common European Framework of Reference for Languages* and of the German national educational standards, literary texts have once again run the risk of being marginalized in the foreign language classroom. The competence orientation of today's foreign language teaching is geared to the measurability of learner achievements. However, with regard to teaching literature, this ignores the difference between reading to extract information as it is primarily done with non-fictional texts, and literary reading which includes affective, motivational and attitudinal components which are difficult to measure and evaluate. Moreover, educational standards reduce the concept of communicative competence to the demands of everyday communicative situations, so that there is hardly any space left for literary reading.

**Reactions.** As a consequence, efforts are made in literature didactics which react to this development in two different ways. On the one hand, it is once again discussed in which ways dealing with literary texts can contribute to the learners' general education and personality development (cf. for example Decke-Cornill and Gebhard; Surkamp, "Handlungskompetenz"). On the other hand, efforts aim to show how the use of literary texts can be reconciled with the currently postulated competences and the principle of output orientation. Within the teaching of literature it is contested whether one can define competence levels in the realm of literary comprehension or measure aesthetic competence with test questions. It seems possible to determine individual competences needed when dealing with literary texts in a way that does not measure but rather evaluates them. In line with this, Eva Burwitz-Melzer differentiates sub-competences of literary competence on various levels for grades 10 to 13 ("Lesekompetenzmodell"). These range from reading as merely making sense of the words to determining the particular aesthetic and generic features of a specific

**Cultural approaches to teaching literature**

text to complex linguistic and cultural competences such as intercultural understanding and the capacity for communicating about a literary text. In any case, the new developments entail the insistence on a more strongly empirical didactics of literature in order to prove what literary texts are capable of achieving in teaching and learning a foreign language (cf. also Zydatiß, "Bildungsstandards" 279). So far, however, there is only a small number of initial empirical works on the use of literature in English language teaching (cf. Burwitz-Melzer, *Allmähliche Annäherungen*; Freitag-Hild).

## 3.2 | The Acquisition of Competences

Taking a closer look at current aims of language teaching will show that working with literary texts is well suited to develop the required competences. The primary goal of foreign language classes is the development of **communicative competences**. Dealing with literature can foster this to a high degree: due to their multidimensionality, their openness to different interpretations and their potential for identification processes, literary texts encourage an intensive interaction—both spoken and written—in the foreign language. In the course of discussions on the strengthening of learner autonomy and the encouragement of strategy learning, great importance has been attached to the development of foreign language **reading comprehension**. Learners can be inspired to read extensively with the help of literary texts and appropriate methods (class libraries, book presentations or reading competitions). This in turn helps them to automatize the recognition of words and sentence structures in the foreign language and to expand their vocabulary. In addition to reading competences, learners acquire **aesthetic competences**, for example knowledge of genre-specific features of lyrical, dramatic and narrative texts. This knowledge intensifies the reception process and enables the learners to understand the specific effect a text has on them. In modern literature classes which proceed from a broad understanding of 'text,' learners are also schooled in dealing with different media. They learn to understand texts not simply by reading, but also by listening to them. Beyond this, they are trained in deciphering images. All in all, they learn to decode different cultural signs which belong to various media genres (auditory texts, comics, films, visual arts, hypertexts etc.) and to determine their respective potential effects and functions (**media competence**).

Narrative forms are not only an object of literature classes, but are also and above all a medium of communication. Accordingly, it is of great importance to answer to and to produce stories as competently as possible. Literature classes can contribute to developing **narrative competences** (cf. Nünning and Nünning). As literary texts encourage learners to immerse themselves into a fictional world and empathize with fictional characters, thereby transcending their own horizon of experience, they also call upon **affective and imaginative competences**. They also contribute to the development of **cultural competences** inasmuch as encounters with the culture(s) of the target language in the classroom predominantly take place on the basis of texts. This does not mean that literary texts are to be considered as immediate reflections of the foreign cultural reality. But still the descriptive narration of individual fates can mediate insights into foreign ways of life, values and worldviews. Working with literary texts is of particular importance with regard to the development of empathy and the capacity for changing perspectives. Since **intercultural understanding** is a creative form of understanding by means of which people allow themselves to get involved with something new and unfamiliar, action- and production-oriented forms of textual work can foster the willingness to reconstruct and engage with foreign perspectives.

The acquisition of all these competences in literature classes should always be seen in conjunction with the type of school and age-group level. In general, within the didactics of literature the view is held that literary texts can be used in all stages of language learning—starting with picture books and short poems in elementary school and continuing with children's literature and young adult fiction and (simplified) books in middle school and more complex literary works in the higher grades. The opinions differ when it comes to the question of the advantages and disadvantages of simplified, i.e. shortened and adapted literary texts. Liesel Hermes comes to the conclusion that the advantages of adapted texts outweigh the dis-

*Literary texts can be used in all stages and school types.*

advantages with regard to the first years of language learning. Since the 1990s, the engagement with texts from English children's and young adult literature has increasingly found its way into the foreign language didactics of literature (cf. O'Sullivan and Rösler for an overview).

## 3.3 | Criteria for Text Selection

Choosing appropriate texts is a central responsibility of the didactics of literature. Approaches within literary and cultural studies, with the works of British Cultural Studies leading the way, have criticized the problematic aspects of canon formation since the 1990s, particularly the mechanisms of exclusion and the inherent one-sidedness of some literary histories. Following these approaches, the didactics of literature has also called for canon revisions and for a greater diversity or openness in the choice of texts for foreign language learning (cf. Nünning and Surkamp 39–50). It is by now a consensual principle that literature lessons should include a variety of perspectives. The long-reigning uniformity of texts employed in the English language classroom painted a narrow image of English literature which did not do justice to the diachronic, geographic and cultural diversity of English speaking countries. For this reason, since the 1990s it has been increasingly demanded that subcultural, postcolonial and literature written by ethnic minorities be used in the English language classroom as well. Beyond this, the literature of female authors is to be taken into account to a greater extent. In a diachronic perspective the view is taken that learners should gain insights into as broad a spectrum of foreign language texts from different centuries as possible. Last but not least, a diversity of genres should be employed, and one should proceed from a broad notion of literature. This implies the inclusion of popular literature and of products of mass media.

The aim of including a variety of perspectives in literature classes can also be achieved by engaging with **sequences of texts**, rather than with an individual text. By concentrating on a single text it is not possible to take into account that literature is always embedded in larger textual and cultural contexts. As a consequence, researchers working in foreign language didactics of literature plead for an intertextual engagement with literature, i.e. for a synthesis of both complementary and contrasting, fictional and non-fictional texts on one topic (cf. Decke-Cornill, "Intertextualität"; Hallet, *Fremdsprachenunterricht*). By proceeding like this, learners are able to work out which modes of perception exist in a particular society or culture and in which diverse ways they are expressed in literary works.

There is no patent remedy within the didactics of literature for overcoming canon formation. It is understood that it is necessary to choose the texts with great care, a process in which the following criteria can be helpful. The literary texts selected for English language learning should

- if possible, be authentic English texts,
- conform to the learners' needs and interests and be related to their world,
- encourage the learners to think, talk and write about the represented topic,
- be current and representative,
- do justice to the meaning of different English literatures and, for example, include the realm of New English Literatures,
- also include contemporary literature and texts by female authors,
- offer a well-balanced ratio between texts from different times, genres and media as well as from popular and high culture,
- enable diverse changes of perspective,
- offer numerous options for ensuing narrative production of the students.

*The texts chosen should reflect more than one perspective.*

## 3.4 | Methods of Teaching Literature

The insights gained in reader response criticism into the active role of the reader during the receptive process as well as the general demand for greater learner- and action-orientation in foreign language classes have led to a rethinking of traditional methods of textual analysis during the last twenty years (cf. Nünning and Surkamp 62–70). A multitude of action- and production-oriented pro-

| Action-oriented activities | Production-oriented activities |
|---|---|
| Getting into the text with a fantasy voyage | Documentation of the first reading impressions in a reading diary or reading log |
| Reconstuction of a text divided into many fragments (for example, a poem cut up into individual verses) | Composing letters, diary entries, telegrammes, an "agony aunt" column, a "missing persons" ad, a "Wanted!" poster or an epitaph |
| Approaching a text through reading or acting by testing various ways of speaking through gestures and facial expressions, postures and spatial arrangements, also in the form of freeze frames | Drafting of critical reactions to a text such as a book review or a newspaper article, in the case of positive reactions as an advertising text for a publishing company or as a blurb |
| Presentation of the text through movement and dance | Transformation into dialogues of passages which represent consciousness or formulation of inside views of dialogical texts |
| Visual realization of the text in the form of illustrations, cover illustrations, collages, advertising posters, photos etc. | Rewriting of a text from the perspective of a different character or from a different narrative perspective |
| Selection of suitable background music for specific text passages or the scoring of a text (for example by using Orff-instruments) | Imagining alternatives to the described action (especially in the case of open or ambivalent endings) introduced by "what if" questions |
| Scenic realization of the themes/conflicts of the text as a dialogue, a role-play, an interview or a court hearing | Rewriting of a text by relocating the action to a different place or time, by introducing additional characters or by changing the age or gender of a character |
| Presentation of a text or text excerpt as a puppet or marionette show or as a shadow play | Rewriting of a text as a different text type, for example by turning a short story into a newspaper announcement, a comic into a screenplay |
| Transformation of the text into another type of media, for example into an image, music, a radio play, film, pantomime, a board game | Composition of personal texts by using specified words (for example in the form of a montage poem) or by applying the structure of familiar texts, for example that of poems and fables |
| Gathering of additional information on a text (for example from newspapers, magazines, books, through interviews, letters etc.) and compilation of a documentation | |

cedures have been developed (see table above) which accommodate the readers' individuality and emotionality insofar as they invite them to participate in creative textual work (cf. Caspari). The dual term '**action- and production-oriented**' emphasizes two basic forms of student activity: the active engagement with texts means that the learners become aesthetically and artistically active, for example by acting out the text or by transposing it into a different medium (music, image, film). In production-oriented procedures, the learners generate their own texts. In doing so, they creatively engage with a literary text by expanding, rewriting, updating or alienating it. However, a frequently mentioned point of criticism is that, when employing creative procedures, the literary text itself runs the risk of being lost from sight. But the way in which a text is understood is not merely dependent upon the reader's individuality, but also on textual mechanisms which can be determined with the help of rational analyses. Thus, one task of literature classes is also to offer the learners insights into the effects and functional

principles of textual strategies. Moreover, creative and analytical work should always be combined with each other, for example by referring the results gained through action- and production-oriented procedures back to the original text to assess their plausibility in a concluding consideration of the text.

In order to support the learners' processes of constructing meaning with regard to the language, the content, the manners of representation, and the cultural implications of a text in the foreign language in literature classes, textual work is generally divided into three phases, i.e. before, while and after reading (cf. Nünning and Surkamp 71–82). This tripartite division is accompanied by tasks which prompt the oral and written language production and is intended to promote the learners' interaction with the text. In contrast to the traditional method of simply giving the learners a text without any further preparation (aside from explaining a few unknown words), and subsequently posing comprehension questions, the three-phased-model tries to take into account the

The three phases
of teaching literature

complexity and processual nature of the reading process and to train the learners' textual comprehension step-by-step. This is particularly important in the context of foreign language learning, because literary texts in a foreign language contain obstacles regarding language, content and culture which would not be present to the same extent in comparable texts in the mother tongue. Thus the **pre-reading phase** serves to help the learners adjust to an unknown text, to allow them to draw upon their own experiences with regard to the topic of the text, to activate their prior knowledge, to raise their expectations about the text, to make them familiar with the required vocabulary and possibly to provide them with contextual knowledge. The **while-reading phase** is intended to ensure the learners' textual comprehension and to encourage them to actively read and enter into a dialogue with the text. Active reading can be promoted by prompting the learners to reflect on their impressions and articulate their personal reactions to the text while reading. Furthermore, diverse forms of creatively engaging with a text can support subjectively determined processes of understanding and stimulate processes of making sense (for example by forming hypotheses) while reading. Moreover, specific tasks and activities can record the respective state of comprehension with regard to plot develop-

ment, character representation, and stylistic devices. After reading the text, it is advisable to allow the students to first of all express their personal reactions to the text. The further activities in the **post-reading phase** should then be tied to the tasks worked on in the phases before and while reading in order to support the processual nature of textual comprehension. In the final interpretation of the text, the learners should have the chance to draw on their individual impressions and observations and to meaningfully use the insights gained in the reading process.

*Fostering creativity*

| Pre-reading phase ↓ | lead to the text |
| | raise expectations |
| | activate prior linguistic, cultural and contextual knowledge |
| While-reading phase ↓ | read text |
| | ensure understanding of the text |
| | incite and support a dialogue between reader and text |
| Post-reading phase | talk about the reception (process) |
| | analytical or creative follow-up activities |
| | interpretative classroom discussion |

## Select Bibliography

**Blell, Gabriele, and Christiane Lütge.** "Filmbildung im Fremdsprachenunterricht: Neue Lernziele, Begründungen und Methoden." *Fremdsprachen Lehren und Lernen* 37 (2008): 124–40.

**Bredella, Lothar, and Eva Burwitz-Melzer.** *Rezeptionsästhetische Literaturdidaktik mit Beispielen aus dem Fremdsprachenunterricht Englisch.* Tübingen: Narr, 2004.

**Bredella, Lothar, and Wolfgang Hallet, eds.** *Literaturunterricht, Kompetenzen und Bildung.* Trier: WVT, 2007.

**Bredella, Lothar, et al., eds.** *Wie ist Fremdverstehen lehr- und lernbar?* Tübingen: Narr, 2000.

**Brusch, Wilfried.** "Die Rolle der Literatur beim Spracherwerb." *Neusprachliche Mitteilungen* 42.1 (1989): 11–19.

**Brusch, Wilfried, and Daniela Caspari.** "Verfahren der Textbegegnung: Literarische und andere Texte." *Englisch Lernen und Lehren.* Ed. Johannes-Peter Timm. Berlin: Cornelsen, 1998. 168–77.

**Burwitz-Melzer, Eva.** *Allmähliche Annäherungen: Fiktionale Texte im Interkulturellen Fremdsprachenunterricht der Sekundarstufe I.* Tübingen: Narr, 2003.

**Burwitz-Melzer, Eva.** "Ein Lesekompetenzmodell für den fremdsprachlichen Literaturunterricht." *Literaturunterricht, Kompetenzen und Bildung.* Eds. Lothar Bredella and Wolfgang Hallet. Trier: WVT, 2007. 127–57.

**Burwitz-Melzer, Eva, ed.** *Lehren und Lernen mit literarischen Texten.* Spec. issue of *Fremdsprachen Lehren und Lernen* 37 (2008): 1–315.

**Canale, Michael, and Merrill Swain.** "Theoretical Bases of Communicative Approaches to Second Language Learning and Testing." *Applied Linguistics* 1 (1980): 1–47.

**Caspari, Daniela.** *Kreativität im Umgang mit literarischen Texten im Fremdsprachenunterricht: Theoretische Studien und unterrichtspraktische Erfahrungen.* Frankfurt/M.: Lang, 1994.

**Decke-Cornill, Helene.** "'Identities that cannot exist': Gender Studies und Literaturdidaktik." *Literaturdidaktik im Dialog.* Eds. Lothar Bredella, Werner Delanoy, and Carola Surkamp. Tübingen: Narr, 2004. 181–206.

**Decke-Cornill, Helene.** "Intertextualität als literaturdidaktische Dimension: Zur Frage der Textzusammenstellung bei literarischen Lektürereihen." *Die Neueren Sprachen* 93 (1994): 272–87.

**Decke-Cornill, Helene, and Ulrich Gebhard.** "Ästhetik und Wissenschaft: Zum Verhältnis von literarischer und naturwissenschaftlicher Bildung." *Literaturunterricht, Kompetenzen und Bildung.* Eds. Lothar Bredella and Wolfgang Hallet. Trier: WVT, 2007. 11–29.

**Delanoy, Werner.** "Transculturality and (Inter-) Cultural Learning in the EFL Classroom." *Cultural Studies in the EFL Classroom.* Eds. Werner Delanoy and Laurenz Volkmann. Heidelberg: Winter, 2006. 233–48.

**Eckerth, Johannes, and Michael Wendt, eds.** *Interkulturelles und transkulturelles Lernen im Fremdsprachenunterricht.* Frankfurt/M.: Lang, 2003.

**Freitag-Hild, Britta.** *Theorie, Aufgabentypologie und Unterrichtspraxis inter- und transkultureller Literaturdidaktik: 'British Fictions of Migration' im Fremdsprachenunterricht.* Trier: WVT, 2010.

**Hallet, Wolfgang.** *Fremdsprachenunterricht als Spiel der Texte und Kulturen: Intertextualität als Paradigma einer kulturwissenschaftlichen Didaktik.* Trier: WVT, 2002.

**Hallet, Wolfgang, and Ansgar Nünning, eds.** *Neue Ansätze und Konzepte der Literatur- und Kulturdidaktik.* Trier: WVT, 2007.

**Hallet, Wolfgang, and Ansgar Nünning.** "Neue fachwissenschaftliche Konzepte – neue fachdidaktische Perspektiven: Kontext, Konzeption und Ziele des Bandes." Introduction. Hallet and Nünning 1–10.

**Hermes, Liesel.** "Lektüren." *Metzler Lexikon Fremdsprachendidaktik.* Ed. Carola Surkamp. Stuttgart: Metzler, 2010. 182–84.

**Nünning, Ansgar.** "'Intermisunderstanding': Prolegomena zu einer literaturdidaktischen Theorie des Fremdverstehens: Erzählerische Vermittlung, Perspektivenwechsel und Perspektivenübernahme." Bredella et al. 84–132.

**Nünning, Ansgar, and Carola Surkamp.** *Englische Literatur unterrichten I: Grundlagen und Methoden.* 2nd ed. Seelze-Velber: Kallmeyer-Klett, 2008.

**Nünning, Vera, and Ansgar Nünning.** "Erzählungen verstehen, verständlich erzählen: Dimensionen und Funktionen narrativer Kompetenz." Bredella and Hallet 87–106.

**O'Sullivan, Emer, and Dieter Rösler.** "Fremdsprachenlernen und Kinder- und Jugendliteratur: Eine kritische Bestandsaufnahme." *Zeitschrift für Fremdsprachenforschung* 13.1 (2002): 63–111.

**Surkamp, Carola.** "Handlungskompetenz und Identitätsbildung mit Dramentexten und durch Dramenmethoden." *Sprachen lernen – Menschen bilden.* Eds. Eva Burwitz-Melzer et al. Baltmannsweiler: Schneider-Verlag Hohengehren, 2008. 105–16.

**Surkamp, Carola.** "Literaturverfilmungen im Unterricht: Die Perspektive der Fremdsprachendidaktik." *Film im Fremdsprachenunterricht: Literarische Stoffe, interkulturelle Ziele, mediale Wirkung.* Ed. Eva Leitzke-Ungerer. Stuttgart: Ibidem, 2009. 61–80.

**Volkmann, Laurenz.** "Gender Studies and Literature Didactics: Research and Teaching, Worlds Apart?" *Gender Studies and Foreign Language Teaching.* Eds. Helene Decke-Cornill and Laurenz Volkmann. Tübingen: Narr, 2007. 161–84.

**Zydatiß, Wolfgang.** "Bildungsstandards für den Fremdsprachenunterricht in Deutschland." *Bildungsstandards für den Fremdsprachenunterricht auf dem Prüfstand.* Eds. Richard Bausch et al. Tübingen: Narr, 2005. 272–90.

**Zydatiß, Wolfgang.** "Integrierter Literatur-Sprach-Unterricht in der Oberstufe: Beispiel Englisch." *Kontroversen in der Fremdsprachenforschung.* Eds. Johannes-Peter Timm and Helmut-Johannes Vollmer. Bochum: Brockmeyer, 1993. 326–34.

*Carola Surkamp*

# Part VII: Study Aids

# 1 Methods and Techniques of Research and Academic Writing

An essential part of studying English is writing. Students of English not only find themselves on the *receiving* end of information about English language and literature, but they also need to *produce* various texts as part of course and exam requirements. A scholarly text in English studies has to include several features to be accepted by professors and university teachers: clear statement of topic and thesis, transparent structure, thorough research, argumentative style, precise terminology, clear language, and appropriate form. This chapter will touch upon these **standards** in more detail and give students important **guidelines** for their academic writing projects from start to finish. The following sections will therefore introduce students to (1) preparing and planning a longer essay or term paper in English Studies, (2) conducting efficient research (see also the "Study Aids" entry VII.2), (3) writing a structurally sound and rhetorically effective paper, as well as (4) formatting an academic paper according to common stylistic conventions. If you follow the principles presented here, academic writing will not be the daunting task it might appear to be at first, but a rewarding intellectual activity of communicating knowledge and insight.

## 1.1 | Preparing a Term Paper: Topic and Planning

### 1.1.1 | Finding a Topic

If the topic for your essay/term paper has not been assigned by your teacher, it is important that you find a suitable topic that is neither too broad nor too narrow, neither unspecific nor overly specific for the assignment. For example, "Shakespeare's *A Midsummer Night's Dream*" or "Word Formation in English" are topics that are not specific enough for a term paper that is to be no longer than 10 to 20 pages of text. Instead, you ought to limit your topic to a manageable aspect, e.g. "The Vagaries of Love in *A Midsummer Night's Dream*" or "Back-formation in Selected American Sitcoms of the 2000s."

### 1.1.2 | Planning: Three Phases

Writing a longer paper (between 3,000 and 6,000 words or more) requires organization and good time management. The teacher for who you have to write the paper will give you a deadline by which it has to be submitted. Depending on the length of the assignment, you usually have at least two to four weeks, if not more, between topic assignment and submission of the finished paper. As soon as the clock starts ticking, you need to get organized and plan ahead for the following weeks. Reserve sufficient time for the three phases of a term paper: (1) **project phase**: brainstorming, research, structural planning; (2) **writing phase**: first draft, refinement of thesis, further research into specific points; (3) **revision phase**: formatting, proof-reading and potential rewriting of parts that need improving, double-checking of formal conventions.

You may start your time-planning by allotting half of the available time to the project and revision phases (1 and 3), while reserving the other half for writing (phase 2). However, different topics require different approaches: if the topic calls for lengthy, detailed research (e.g. a linguistic corpus analysis), in which case the writing amounts primarily to a documentation of the results of that research, you might want to plan accordingly and take away, or add, time from the respective phases as you see fit. Yet do not underestimate the revision phase: if you skip revisions because of running out of time, this will most certainly backfire, since submitting an error-strewn, half-baked draft will seriously hurt your chances of getting a good grade.

## 1.2 | Research

### 1.2.1 | The Importance of Research

A scholarly essay/paper requires research into secondary sources concerning your topic. Ideally, you are supposed to reflect the current state of critical discussion among the community of scholars on a given subject. However, first and foremost, a good essay/paper demonstrates proper (and, if possible, original) research into the primary source or object of study! If your subject is a literary text, then your own **original research** should consist of close textual analysis, i.e. your own notes (ideas, observations, annotations, quotations, marked-up passages) concerning the topic after careful reading and re-reading of the text. Correspondingly, for a paper in linguistics, your own research may focus on a careful studying and documenting of a linguistic phenomenon in relevant contexts or media (textual databases etc).

| Definition |
| --- |
| → Secondary sources are "secondary" to a **primary text** or medium (i.e. the immediate target or object of your study) and can range from academic articles, books, compilations etc. specifically written about your primary source to theoretical, methodological or philosophical sources generally relevant to your approach. |

While reading up on prior research in the field of your topic is helpful if you are unsure about what to focus on specifically in your essay, it may also confuse you as there is often an overwhelming number of sources and critical opinions available on a given subject. It is therefore important that you strike a fine balance between drowning in research (to be at the height of critical discussion) and largely ignoring it (to preserve your original stance on a topic).

### 1.2.2 | Research Tools

The first place to look for secondary sources should be the catalogue of your local university library, which records book titles. As virtually every library catalogue comes in the form of an **OPAC** (Online Public Access Catalogue) and can be accessed via the Internet, you may start your research conveniently in front of your own personal computer. To extend the scope of your search for relevant books beyond the holdings of your local library, you may use a *union catalogue* (*Verbundkatalog*), which runs your search terms through many connected OPACs. If you then find a book that is not in your local library, you can order it as an interlibrary loan (*Fernleihe*) to be delivered to your library.

| Writer's Toolkit |
| --- |
| **Library catalogues → books** |
| Library catalogues only list titles of books (monographs, compilations, journals etc.), but not articles! |
| **Bibliographies → articles** |
| To find titles of material published inside of books, you need to look into bibliographies. |

Typically, however, a library catalogue only lists the titles of books and serial volumes, so relevant articles printed *within* a bound volume cannot be found there. This is where **bibliographies** come in as indispensable tools that also record titles of articles published within books, compilations and periodicals. Bibliographies can be either *retrospective* or *current* (updated regularly). The most important current bibliography for literary studies is the **MLA database**, which you should be able to access via your university library (for further information and an overview of research tools see section VII.2). It is the most comprehensive search tool for secondary sources in English (literary) studies, as it registers almost all scholarly output in the United States and the United Kingdom as well as major publications from many other countries, including Germany. More selective in their scope of secondary material are **annotated bibliographies**, which provide helpful summaries of and comment on listed sources. For the different research areas in linguistics, many specialized bibliographies are available on the Internet homepages of scholars and institutions. In order to locate and access these on the web, you need to type relevant keywords into a search engine.

When used intelligently, a search engine like *Google* can be a good point of departure for **Internet-based research**. However, the results yielded by such a search are bound to vary greatly in their degree of quality and usefulness. Just as with *Wikipedia*, the popular grass-roots encyclopaedia on the Web, it is not always immediately apparent whether a webpage has quality content and complies with academic standards. Therefore, *Wikipedia* entries and random Internet pages authored by bloggers, fans or amateurs, are often unreliable sources of scholarly information and, accordingly, are considered unacceptable ("unquotable") by most university teachers.

In order to narrow down Internet search results to reliable academic material, services such as *Google Scholar* can be helpful. Another possibility are specialized **Internet gateways** that provide an abundance of links to scholarly sources on the Web, such as *Voice of the Shuttle* (vos. ucsb.edu), hosted by UC Santa Barbara, and *Literature Guide* (www.anglistikguide.de), hosted by SUB Göttingen.

## 1.2.3 | Compiling a Working Bibliography for a Paper

For your essay or term paper, compile your own working bibliography of relevant secondary sources by using the facilities outlined above: (1) your local OPAC for book titles; (2) additionally a union catalogue; (3) the MLA database and other bibliographies for titles of articles; (4) specific Internet searches for further material.

Often, however, the best place to find helpful sources is the bibliography at the end of a good article or book in the area of your topic. This implies that you may go through different stages of search activity: a first shot at what is all out there,

and a second/third (etc.) more refined search after you have acquired some knowledge of the research area.

For each search, check the availability of sources in your local library. If books or articles cannot be accessed there, use *Google Books* or other online services to look for full-text versions of books (or at least relevant snippets thereof). For journal articles, find out whether your university library has a subscription to scholarly databases, such as *JSTOR*, *Project MUSE*, or *LION* (*Literature Online*). They provide full texts of articles from selected journals (and, in the case of *LION*, even whole books) that can be downloaded as PDF or HTML documents. This way you will often find other means of obtaining texts online even if you cannot have physical access to these sources through your library.

*Checking the availability of sources*

## 1.2.4 | Dealing with Sources Efficiently

You might feel quite overwhelmed by the number of secondary sources available on a topic. In order not to suffer from information overload or loss of orientation in the mass of writing (and loss of valuable time!), three vital strategies are recommended:

**1. Limit the number of sources found to a manageable size** (depending on potential requirements for the number of sources to be used in your paper, set either by your teacher or the department). Include **(a)** sources that appear to be most relevant to your topic, judging from the title of the publication and the keywords in the bibliography or catalogue where you found it; **(b)** sources that are quoted and cross-referenced most often in other publications on your topic; **(c)** sources that your teacher has specifically recommended to you. Now obtain the remaining sources on your list as described in the section before, i.e. access them in your local library and/or download available texts from online databases and Internet services (if necessary, start an interlibrary loan, which will require up to a few weeks for delivery).

**2. Get an overview of the material** you have gathered by skimming through each text: look at the table of contents and the index (in books), read the introduction and conclusion of the text (or parts thereof for long studies), scan other parts of the text (i.e. speed-read headlines and paragraphs for relevant terms and arguments), check foot-/endnotes and the list of works cited at the

**Writer's Toolkit**

**Excerpting** and **note-taking** can be extremely time-consuming if you approach it the wrong way: Do not try to be exhaustive in a misplaced attempt at "doing justice" to the source. Be brief when you quote. Always remind yourself of the fact that you can only mention a fraction of the source's content in your paper due to limited time and space!

end for interesting sources that have escaped your notice so far.

**3. Start a new document for notes and excerpts** on your computer. Now read closely the secondary sources that seem important to you—ignore the other texts (perhaps make a note why you are leaving them out, for a later comment in your paper). While you read, take notes about relevant arguments of a text and copy key passages (or electronically scan them in) so that you can quote them later. Underline important passages in both your primary and secondary texts and make notes

in the margins. This will help you with your current paper and for the future preparation of exams. *Important:* For every idea borrowed and quotation copied you need to document their specific source (e.g. author's name and page number)—if you fail to do so at this stage, you may not be able to distinguish your own ideas from borrowed ones later and thus (involuntarily) plagiarize!

Once you have finished this process, you will have a sizeable document full of ideas, comments, and quotations. This material will form a most valuable basis for outlining the overall structure of your essay/paper. If you combine these research excerpts with your notes and ideas about the primary text/s or study object, you can review all your findings and decide which points you really need to make (and which may be left out). Arrange all remaining points in a logical argumentative order—this will then be the **structural outline** of your paper.

## 1.3 | Writing a Term Paper: Structure and Rhetorical Strategies

### 1.3.1 | General Structure

A term paper represents an extensive *argument* addressed to a scholarly readership. Therefore it should not be written on sudden impulse or from the spontaneous overflow of powerful feelings, but must be well planned and thought through. In other words, it requires you to be clear about the outcome of your paper *before* you start writing! Plan your argument and the evidence and examples required to prove your overall point on the basis of your notes and research excerpts.

In English, an argumentative essay generally consists of (1) the **introduction**, (2) the **main body** of text (middle part), and (3) the **conclusion**.

**Writer's Toolkit**

The rhetorical function of the **three general parts of an essay/paper** corresponds to the following motto:

(1) Tell me what you are going to tell me,
(2) tell me,
(3) and then tell me what you have told me.

### 1.3.2 | Introduction

The introduction should be interesting and inviting for the reader. This is your chance to set the tone for the rest of the paper and make the reader want to keep reading. You may be creative at the beginning and provide a "hook" for the paper with the use of a quote, a definition or even an anecdote to introduce your topic. All this should be brief (the introduction should be no longer than about a tenth of your whole essay/paper).

The introduction needs to give some background information introducing the reader to the field of knowledge in which the concrete topic of your paper is situated. Therefore, introductions often begin in the present perfect tense to report what has been known so far. A typical rhetorical strategy is to move "from the general to the specific" and narrow the provided information down in such a way as to arrive at the precise topic of your paper. You should then proceed to formulate a clear **thesis statement** that informs the reader about what you will show, prove, or find out in your paper. This thesis statement must come in the final sentences of your introduction. If necessary or appropriate, you should make a final remark on the method of analysis that you are using

**Writer's Toolkit**

> Always ensure you state a proper **thesis** in the introduction!
>
> **Wrong (not a thesis):**
>
> "In what follows I will compare the arguments for and against *Oroonoko* being an anti-slavery narrative."
>
> **Right:**
>
> "Despite appearances to the contrary, the following analysis will show that *Oroonoko* is not an anti-slavery narrative because …"

in your paper. You may also give a brief overview of the main points of your paper, if this is not already implied by your thesis statement and/or statement of method.

## 1.3.3 | Main Body

The main part of your paper presents specific analysis based on your thesis stated in the introduction. In a longer paper, the main body should be divided into **sections** (chapters and, if necessary, further subdivisions). Typically, these subdivisions have headings, which should be numbered according to a common and consistent principle (see the sample table of contents on p. 504 for a common principle).

Each section consists of several **paragraphs**. These paragraphs should each focus on a single argumentative aspect and present the reader with **substantial evidence** in a coherent line of reasoning. In literary or linguistic analysis, compelling arguments hinge on clear evidence from primary/secondary sources (quotations, paraphrases). For evidence, do not be exhaustive, but choose the best examples only. Always focus on what you are actually aiming to explain, show or prove—in other words, avoid digressions! Establish **coherence** in your text by connecting the paragraphs with each other through logical link words (e.g. *furthermore, by contrast, consequently, first/second/third/…* etc.) so that the reader understands how the various points relate to, contrast, or support one another.

In English writing, paragraphs require a well-formed **internal structure** themselves. This internal structure mirrors the basic three-part structure of the whole paper (i.e. introduction, main part, conclusion). Each paragraph ideally begins with

- a topic sentence (stating your point, i.e. what is to be shown or proved),
- the evidence or substantiation of that point (examples, quotations, analysis),
- a conclusion sentence, summing up your point/leading over to the next.

Admittedly, there are cases, e.g. if you have many quotations or other evidence for the substantiation of a particular point, where this internal paragraph structure cannot be maintained rigidly. Yet, on the whole, you should stick to it as a basic rhetorical principle.

## 1.3.4 | Conclusion

The conclusion should briefly sum up the results of your paper, i.e. you should highlight the most important points. Typically, the focus of the introduction is reversed by now moving "from the specific to the general" in order to re-contextualize your findings. It is important not to introduce new ideas relevant to your topic in the conclusion (all these must be dealt with in the main body)! Instead, you should make the reader feel that the paper is complete and the arguments are drawn to a proper close. If anything, you may end with a short outlook on possible future research or further interesting aspects that were not part of your approach.

## 1.3.5 | Some Important "Don'ts"

- *Don't* use informal expressions, simple paratactic style, exclamation marks, or flowery language (i.e. do not try to write in a literary style when writing about literature). A term paper is supposed to be a formal piece of scholarly writing. Accordingly, your language should be elaborate but precise, persuasive but matter-of-fact, detailed but succinct.
- *Don't* overuse metacommunicative statements (rhetorical "signposts" or "stage directions") in your text, i.e. announcements of what you are about to present or recapitulations of what you have just shown your readers. Use such statements carefully and sparingly! Otherwise the tone of your paper may become overly didactic and stylistically clumsy. Generally, avoid comments on the progress of your argument unless

you consider them absolutely necessary for following your train of thought.

- *Don't* waste time and space with irrelevant information about your object of study. The plot of a literary text, the biography of an author, or aspects of a linguistic phenomenon etc. must be related argumentatively to the purpose of the paper—otherwise leave them out!
- *Don't* quote indiscriminately (no collage of quotations!) or at excessive length (no hiding behind other people's words!), nor leave longer quotations uncommented (they do not speak for themselves!). Only quote key sentences or passages. Other information you may paraphrase in your own words, but don't forget to

document the source! Create coherence between quotations and your own text by making brief introductory and concluding statements that explain the relevance of a quoted passage to the reader.

- *Don't* plagiarize (i.e. steal ideas or passages from other texts)! Whenever you are aware of your argumentation relying on another source, you must acknowledge it. Thus, for each quotation and paraphrase you present in your paper, you are required to make a bibliographic reference. Otherwise you will fail the assignment and run the risk of being expelled from the course or even the entire study programme!

## 1.4 | Formatting a Term Paper: Stylistic Guidelines

### 1.4.1 | General Format

An acceptable term paper must be submitted as a **computer-printout**. If you are not given specific stylistic guidelines by your teacher, your printout should have (a) page numbers starting on page 2 (i.e. not on the title page); (b) sufficient margins on all sides of a page, preferably 3–4 cm to the left and at least 2 cm to the right; (c) a line-spacing of at least 1.5; (d) a regular font size of 12 pt (more for

headings, less for block quotations and footnotes, if applicable). **Paragraphs** need to have their first line indented (e.g. by 1 cm), with the British exception of *no* first-line indentation for the initial paragraph after a heading or block quotation.

Before the actual text, your paper should have a **title page**, stating the title/subtitle of your term paper (in the middle) and details about you as the author (your name, matriculation/enrolment number, email address, preferably also number of terms studied, study programme and subjects) as well as details about the context of the paper (university, department, academic year or term, course title, professor/teacher).

Following the title page, a **table of contents** lists all headings of sections and further subdivisions of your paper in the same way as they appear in the main text, with their corresponding page numbers (i.e. only the starting page number of a section). The section headings should be kept in nominal style (so avoid verb phrases), and they should be numbered according to a consistent principle (see the box on the left for an example common in German academia). If you use subdivisions, you must have at least two numbered elements in each category (e.g. after 2.1, you must have 2.2, and perhaps 2.3 etc.). But be careful not to overuse subdivisions (not every paragraph needs its own section number!).

After the conclusion of your paper, you need to present a **bibliography** of the sources used in your paper (also called "Works Cited"). List all sources that you have explicitly discussed or referred to by

**Contents:**

– 2 –

quoting or paraphrasing text from them. Do not list sources that make no appearance in your text.

Many university departments nowadays require students to attach to their term papers a signed affidavit (*eidesstattliche Versicherung*) in order to prevent plagiarism. On this page you need to declare that you have written the text yourself and used no other sources than the ones indicated in your paper. Once you sign this you can be held legally responsible for such academic misconduct.

---

### Writer's Toolkit

Titles of **books**, compilations, and periodicals are always set in *italics*.

Titles of **articles** and Internet pages are always put in "quotation marks" (not italicized).

---

## 1.4.2 | Documenting Sources

As indicated above, all sources from which you quote, but also all sources of paraphrased claims, statements, thoughts, and ideas borrowed from other publications or people, have to be clearly documented. There are two places where you need to do this: (a) in the bibliography (or list of works cited) at the end of your paper, and (b) in your main text. In other words, it is not enough to merely list all sources used in the bibliography and forget about referring to them in your main text!

Sources listed in the **bibliography** must have a consistent bibliographic format. There is a bewildering variety of different systems used within both literary/cultural studies and linguistics. Usually your instructor or the department will refer you to their own style sheet, which is often based on an internationally used system. At least for literary studies, the citation system of the Modern Language Association of America (MLA) has become the most widely used. The box on the right gives examples of how to render bibliographic data for the **five most common types of publications**.

In addition, there are also stylistic standards for referencing a CD/DVD and many other types of media. For more detailed information, please consult the latest edition of the *MLA Handbook for Writers of Research Papers*, published by the Modern Language Association of America.

---

**1. Book/monograph (written by one or more authors):**

Tilmouth, Christopher. *Passion's Triumph over Reason: A History of the Moral Imagination from Spenser to Rochester*. Oxford: Oxford UP, 2007. Print.

*Basic format:* Last name, first/middle name(s). *Title: Subtitle.* Place of publication: publisher, year of publication. Medium of publication.

**2. Compilation/anthology of articles (also essays, short stories, poems etc.):**

Middeke, Martin, and Werner Huber, eds. *Biofictions: The Rewriting of Romantic Lives in Contemporary Fiction and Drama*. Rochester, NY: Camden House, 1999. Print.

*Add a comma and* ed. *after the editor's name, or* eds. *when there is more than one. Name sequence for all further persons is reversed (→* Werner Huber*).*

**3. Book article (from a compilation; also applies to essay, story, poem published in a book):**

Shershow, Scott Cutler. "'Punch and Judy' and Cultural Appropriation." *Historical Perspectives on Popular Culture.* Ed. Michael J. Pickering. London: Sage, 2010. 3–22. Print.

*Article's title (in quotation marks) precedes compilation title (in italics), followed by Ed./Eds. plus editor's name(s). Add inclusive page numbers, followed by the medium of publication.*

**4. Journal article (from a scholarly periodical):**

New, Melvyn. "Swift as Ogre, Richardson as Dolt: Rescuing Sterne from the Eighteenth Century." *Shandean* 3 (1991): 49–60. Print.

*Article's title (in quotation marks) precedes journal title (in italics), followed by annual volume number (→ 3). State issue number (if necessary) after the volume number, set off by a dot (e.g.: 3.1). Year of annual volume in brackets. Always leave out publisher and place of publication. Inclusive page numbers are preceded by a colon. Conclude with medium of publication.*

**5. Internet source:**

Nowka, Scott. "Building the Wall: Crusoe and the Other." *Digital Defoe: Studies in Defoe and His Contemporaries* 2.1 (2010): 41–57. Web. 1 June 2011. < http://english.illinoisstate.edu/digitaldefoe/features/nowka.pdf > .

*Example is an article from an online periodical.—Always give date of last access. The URL is optional, but its inclusion is recommended and may indeed be required by your teacher. If you choose to give the URL, put < URL > in angle brackets after the date of last access.*

---

Entries in the actual **bibliography** at the end of your paper are to be arranged in ascending alphabetical order, i.e. with the author's (or editor's, director's etc.) last name as the sorting key—or, whenever the name of the author is not applicable, the source's title.

## 1.4.3 | Referring to Sources: Footnotes versus Short References

There are two basic principles to refer to sources when you quote or paraphrase text: (1) references in notes (i.e. footnotes or endnotes) or (2) short references. Use either one of them consistently, and do not mix them in your paper. (If you use a short-reference system, notes are still allowed for giving additional information.)

The traditional way to acknowledge sources is to cite them in notes attached to quotations or paraphrases, preferably in **footnotes** at the bottom of each page (rather than endnotes appearing after the conclusion). A footnote gives the full citation of a source on its first mention, while subsequent references to the same source may be abbreviated. Footnote references need to follow a consistent standard (see the *MLA Handbook* for a common principle that is very similar to the style for bibliographies/works cited, but differs from it in the use of punctuation).

Short-reference systems have been the norm in linguistics for a long time. Over the past few decades, they have also become increasingly common in literary and cultural studies as an economical alternative to traditional notes. If you are given the choice by your teacher, you might find a short-reference system easier to handle than footnote references.

The most widely used short-reference system in literary/cultural studies is the **MLA style**. Here you simply refer to a source by putting the corresponding page number in brackets behind the quotation or paraphrase. If it is not fully clear from the context to which source you are referring, place the author's last name before the page number. If you refer to more than one source by the same author

or by authors with identical surnames, you will also have to add a shortened form of the source's title before the page number to make the reference clear (see the examples in the box below).

The most common system in linguistics (but also used in literary studies) is the **author-date style**. Here you always state the author's last name plus publication year, and give the page number after a colon (e.g. Barnes 1985:190). Should there be more than one publication with the same author name and year, you need to distinguish between them by putting a, b, c etc. behind the year for each source (e.g. Barnes 1985a: 190 / Barnes 1985b: 12 / …). In this case, the corresponding entries in the bibliography (at the end of your paper) also need to have the same letters.

## 1.4.4 | Formatting Quotations

**Short quotations** can be inserted into your text where you need them, without beginning a new line or paragraph. They must be put in "quotation marks" (American and international standard). If there are quotation marks anywhere within the text you quote, convert those into 'inverted commas.' Never set quotation marks within quotation marks! (If you want to follow the British standard, use inverted commas for regular quotations, and double quotation marks within quotations wherever necessary.)

In turn, quotations extending three lines of text should be formatted as quotation paragraphs (**block quotes**), which are *never* put in enclosing quotation marks. Set a block quote off from your own paragraphs by indenting it as a whole (at least 1 cm). Also desirable are a smaller font size (e.g. 10 pt instead of 12 pt) and narrower line-spacing (e.g. single-spaced instead of double/1.5).

Proofread your quotations thoroughly, they must be accurate! Wording, punctuation and, normally, even font weight and slope (bold print, italics) must not be altered. There are some exceptions. **Permissible modifications** are: (a) italics for emphasis (see box on p. 507); (b) ellipsis, i.e. leaving out unnecessary words or even whole sentences by inserting three dots in square brackets "[…]," unless the omission would distort the meaning of the quotation; (c) short comments within quotes, by using square brackets after individual words (you may add your initials to the comment to make sure your readers notice your

---

**Writer's Toolkit**

Here are some examples of short references in **MLA style**:

In Julian Barnes's novel *Flaubert's Parrot*, the problem of historical truth is represented by "the Case of the Stuffed Parrot" (180).
- Standard form: only page number in brackets if author is clear from the context.

The novel's protagonist Braithwaite remains confident that one of the fifty parrots must be Flaubert's (cf. 189–90).
- Use *cf.* or *see* to refer to a paraphrased passage in a source.

The crucial question is: "How do we seize the past?" (Barnes 90).
- Author's last name added for clarification

Many postmodern authors give the pursuit of history an open end
(e.g. see Barnes, *Parrot* 190). In the work of Julian Barnes, this historical undecidability is a recurring motif (see also "Evermore" 102).
- Use short titles for clear identification of sources with the same author name (omit author's name if context is clear)
- Short title in italics for a book—quotation marks for an article, short story, poem etc.

> **Writer's Toolkit**
>
> Quotations should observe the following conventions:
>
> Pope declares in Epistle I that our experience of a disharmonious world is caused by our limited understanding: "All Nature is but Art, unknown to thee; / […] All Discord, Harmony, not understood" (249).
>
> - Short in-line quotation
> - Ellipsis […] for parts unneeded in the context
> - Slash (/) used to indicate line break in a poem or verse play
>
> In *A Tale of a Tub*, the narrator sneers at the worship of reason in what appears to be just a thinly disguised authorial voice:
>
> > For what man in the natural state or course of thinking, did ever conceive it in his power to reduce the notions of all mankind exactly to the same length, and breadth, and height of his own? Yet this is the first humble and civil design of all innovators in the empire of reason. (Swift 80)
>
> - Block quotation for longer passages—indented as a whole and no enclosing quotation marks
>
> Do not generally italicize quoted text! Use italics in quotations only when words appear so in the original text or if you want to highlight them for the reader (then add "emphasis mine" or "italics mine" to the source reference).

insertion); (d) "[sic]" after a linguistic or typographic mistake in the original (to exonerate yourself from potential blame). In general, such techniques for editing quotations should be used carefully and sparingly.

Avoid quotations from **indirect sources**, i.e. from publications that are quoted in other sources, but to which you did not have direct access. Yet, in cases when this is unavoidable—e.g. you cannot obtain the original book or article—, not only state the source in which you found the quote, but also give the full bibliographic reference to the original source (as stated in the secondary source).

## 1.5 | Conclusion

A final word: practice writing! Academic writing will become easier each time you complete a paper. Putting effort into your essays and term papers in the first semesters of your study helps you improve and get the most out of later ones, especially if it is part of your degree to write a final paper (e.g. a bachelor's or master's thesis). By the time you graduate, you may find academic writing such a pleasure that you decide to enrol in a master's or PhD programme and write an even longer thesis, perhaps in pursuit of an academic career. If not, your academic writing skills will certainly be a benefit to you in your future line of work.

### Select Bibliography

Gibaldi, Joseph. *MLA Handbook for Writers of Research Papers.* 7th ed. New York: Modern Language Association of America, 2009.

McCormack, Joan, and John Slaght. *Extended Writing and Research Skills: Coursebook (English for Academic Study).* Rev. ed. Reading: Garnet, 2009.

Meyer, Michael. *English and American Literatures.* 4th ed. Tübingen: Francke, 2011.

*Virtual Training Suite: English.* 1 Jan. 2012. <http://www.vtstutorials.co.uk>. Path: English.

Wallace, Michael J. *Study Skills in English.* 2nd ed. Cambridge: Cambridge University Press, 2006.

*Christoph Henke*

# 2 Study Aids

This chapter provides general resources for research and background information on Anglophone literature, culture, language, and teaching. Each section opens with a list of introductions to the field ("General Overview"), then proceeds through its main areas, and ends with resources you will need for researching a paper or thesis topic. The sections list both reference books and websites.

## 2.1 | Literature

### General Overview

These works provide a basic overview of the field of literary studies. They outline the general picture. For detailed information about a certain genre or topic of interest, you should consult relevant specialised literature.

- **Böker, Uwe, and Christoph Houswitschka, eds.** *Einführung in das Studium der Anglistik und Amerikanistik.* Munich: Beck, 2007.
- **Klarer, Mario.** *Einführung in die anglistisch-amerikanistische Literaturwissenschaft.* Darmstadt: WBG, 2011. Also available in English as: *An Introduction to Literary Studies.* London: Routledge, 2004.
- **Löffler, Arno.** *Einführung in das Studium der englischen Literatur.* Tübingen: Francke, 2006.
- **Nünning, Ansgar, and Vera Nünning.** *Grundkurs anglistisch-amerikanistische Literaturwissenschaft.* Stuttgart: Klett, 2005. Also available in English as: *An Introduction to the Study of English and American Literature.* Stuttgart: Klett, 2012.

### General Reference Works

Consult these works for concise definitions of terms used in literary studies. These works will provide you with a short overview of the meanings of literary terms and the contexts in which they are used. Your instructors will not accept citations from open-source websites like Wikipedia for definitions of literary terms.

- **Abrams, Meyer H.** *A Glossary of Literary Terms.* Boston: Thomson, 2006.
- **Arnold, Heinz Ludwig, ed.** *Kindlers Literatur Lexikon.* Stuttgart: Metzler, 2009. The standard German-language dictionary of writers and their works. Also available online at < www. kll-online.de > .
- **Baldick, Chris.** *The Oxford Dictionary of Literary Terms.* Oxford: Oxford University Press, 2008.
- **Beck, Rudolf, Hildegard Kuester, and Martin Kuester, eds.** *Basislexikon anglistische Literaturwissenschaft.* Munich: Fink, 2007.
- **Burdorf, Dieter, Christoph Fasbender, and Burkhard Moennighoff, eds.** *Metzler-Lexikon Literatur.* Stuttgart: Metzler, 2007.
- **Cuddon, John A.** *The Penguin Dictionary of Literary Terms and Literary Theory.* London: Penguin, 1999.
- **Engler, Bernd, and Kurt Müller, eds.** *Metzler Lexikon amerikanischer Autoren.* Stuttgart: Metzler, 2000.
- **Kreutzer, Eberhard, and Ansgar Nünning, eds.** *Metzler Lexikon englischsprachiger Autoren.* Stuttgart: Metzler, 2006.
- *The Literary Encyclopedia.* < www.litencyc. com > . A continuously growing online dictionary of works and authors.
- *Oxford Dictionary of National Biography.* < www.oxforddnb.com > . For biographical information on writers.

## Literary Theory

For online resources on literary theory see the last two entries in "Research Databases," below.

- **Barry, Peter.** *Beginning Theory: An Introduction to Literary and Cultural Theory*. Manchester: Manchester University Press, 2009. The most accessible introduction to current theories of literature.
- **Culler, Jonathan.** *Literary Theory: A Very Short Introduction*. Oxford: Oxford University Press, 2011. Very short indeed, but useful as a first overview.
- **Guerin, Wilfred L.** *A Handbook of Critical Approaches to Literature*. Oxford: Oxford University Press, 2011. A detailed guide with practical examples.
- **Harland, Richard.** *Literary Theory from Plato to Barthes: An Introductory History*. Basingstoke: Macmillan, 1999. A survey of literary theory up to the mid-twentieth century.
- **Zapf, Hubert.** *Kurze Geschichte der anglo-amerikanischen Literaturtheorie*. Munich: Fink, 1991. A concise German-language survey of theoretical debate from antiquity to the present day.
- **Nünning, Ansgar, ed.** *Metzler Lexikon Literatur- und Kulturtheorie*. Stuttgart: Metzler, 2008. A handbook with concise entries on a wide range of theories and concepts.
- ***Stanford Encyclopedia of Philosophy.*** < http://plato.stanford.edu/ > . Provides introductions to theories and theorists.
- **"Literary Theory."** *Voice of the Shuttle*. < vos.ucsb.edu > . A list of web resources on literary theory.
- **Lodge, David, and Nigel Wood, eds.** *Modern Criticism and Theory: A Reader*. Harlow: Longman, 2008. A collection of primary texts by influential theorists, from Marx and Saussure to the present.

## Literary History

For online resources on literary history see the last two entries in "Research Databases," below.

- **Seeber, Hans Ulrich, ed.** *Englische Literaturgeschichte*. 5th ed. Stuttgart: Metzler, 2012. The standard German-language history of English literature.
- **Zapf, Hubert.** *Amerikanische Literaturgeschichte*. 3rd ed. Stuttgart: Metzler, 2010. The standard German-language history of American literature.

- **Carter, Ronald, and John McRae.** *The Routledge History of Literature in English: Britain and Ireland*. London: Routledge, 2001.
- **Sanders, Andrew.** *The Short Oxford History of English Literature*. Oxford: Oxford University Press, 2004.
- **Drabble, Margaret, ed.** *The Oxford Companion to English Literature*. Oxford: Oxford University Press, 2006. A dictionary of periods, terms, and writers.
- **Hart, J.D., ed.** *The Oxford Companion to American Literature*. Oxford: Oxford University Press, 1995. A dictionary of periods, terms, and writers.

## Research Databases

When researching a specific topic you should consult both the catalogue of your university library and the most important research databases. The library catalogue usually provides information about entire books and journals. Much relevant literature will have been published in the form of book chapters or journal articles, however, and the research databases will help you find these sources.

Some of the pages listed below contain full-text material you can use directly. Others are online bibliographies that will give you detailed information about relevant material and where to find it. Many databases require a special license. Your university library should hold most of these licenses, but you may need to use the library or university on-campus network in order to access the database.

- ***MLA International Bibliography.*** < www.mla.org > . The most important research tool in literary studies. Always consult this database when researching a topic.
- ***JSTOR.*** < www.jstor.org > . The most important full-text database for secondary literature.
- ***Project Muse.*** < muse.jhu.edu > . Another comprehensive full-text database for secondary literature.
- ***Annual Bibliography of English Language and Literature*** (***ABELL***). < http://collections.chadwyck.com/marketing/home_abell.jsp > . Often yields additional search results not listed in the MLA database.
- ***Annotated Bibliography of English Studies*** (***ABES***). < www.routledgeabes.com > . Lists recent publications according to the field they deal with.

- *Year's Work in English Studies (YWES).* < ywes.oxfordjournals.org >. An annotated bibliography.

More specialized databases, bibliographies, and resources are listed on the following websites:

- *English Language and Literature Research Guide.* Yale University. < http://guides.library.yale.edu/content.php?pid = 8589&sid = 55297 >.
- *Library of Anglo-American Culture & History.* University of Göttingen. < http://aac.sub.uni-goettingen.de/en/literature/guide >.
- *Fachbibliographien und Online-Datenbanken (FabiO) of the BSZ Baden-Württemberg.* < wiki.bsz-bw.de/doku.php?id = linksammlungen:fabio:start >. Select the "Anglistik" category.

For primary literature, especially older texts and full-text versions, consult the following online resources:

- *Literature Online.* < lion.chadwyck.com >. A full-text database for both primary and secondary literature. Provides electronic versions of many literary classics.
- *Perseus Digital Library.* < www.perseus.tufts.edu/hopper/collections >. A primary-literature database for certain periods, e.g. early modern or nineteenth-century American literature.
- *Early English Books Online.* < eebo.chadwyck.com >. A primary-literature database for texts from the medieval and early modern periods.

## 2.2 | Culture

The works and websites listed here provide insights into cultural theory and analysis, as well as historical background information on various English-speaking countries. Use these sources for analyzing cultural texts as explained in Part III and entry IV.5 of this book.

### General Overview

- **Assmann, Aleida.** *Einführung in die Kulturwissenschaft: Grundbegriffe, Themen, Fragestellungen.* Berlin: Schmidt, 2006.
- **Barker, Chris.** *Cultural Studies: Theory and Practice.* 3rd ed. Los Angeles: Sage, 2008.
- **Brown, Keith.** *Oxford Guide to British and American Culture.* Oxford: Oxford University Press, 2007.
- **During, Simon.** *The Cultural Studies Reader.* London: Routledge, 2003.
- **Edgar, Andrew, and Peter Sedgwick.** *Cultural Theory: The Key Concepts.* New York: Routledge, 2005.
- **Jaeger, Friedrich, and Burkard Liebsch, eds.** *Grundlagen und Schlüsselbegriffe.* Stuttgart: Metzler, 2004. Vol. 1 of *Handbuch der Kulturwissenschaften.* 3 Vols.
- **Lewis, Jeff.** *Cultural Studies.* London: Sage, 2008.
- **Longhurst, Brian, et al., eds.** *Introducing Cultural Studies.* London: Pearson, 2008.

- **Nünning, Ansgar, and Vera Nünning, eds.** *Einführung in die Kulturwissenschaften: Theoretische Grundlagen – Ansätze – Perspektiven.* Stuttgart: Metzler, 2008.

### British Cultural Studies

- **Abercrombie, Nicholas, and Alan Warde.** *Contemporary British Society.* Cambridge: Polity, 2007.
- **Beck, Rudolf, and Konrad Schröder, eds.** *Handbuch der britischen Kulturgeschichte.* Stuttgart: UTB, 2006.
- **McCormick, John.** *Contemporary Britain.* Basingstoke: Palgrave, 2007.
- **Nünning, Ansgar, and Vera Nünning, eds.** *Intercultural Studies: Fictions of Empire.* Heidelberg: Winter, 1996.
- **Sommer, Roy.** *Grundkurs Cultural Studies/Kulturwissenschaft Großbritannien.* Stuttgart: Klett, 2003.
- **Storey, John.** *Cultural Studies and the Study of Popular Culture.* Edinburgh: Edinburgh University Press, 2010.
- **Wehling, Hans-Werner.** *Großbritannien: England, Schottland, Wales.* Darmstadt: WBG, 2007.

## American Cultural Studies

- **Burgett, Bruce, and Glenn Hendler, eds.** *Keywords for American Cultural Studies.* New York: New York University Press, 2007.
- **Campbell, Neil, and Alasdair Kean.** *American Cultural Studies: An Introduction to American Culture.* London: Routledge, 2008.
- **Hebel, Udo J.** *Einführung in die Amerikanistik/American Studies.* Stuttgart: Metzler, 2008.
- **Mauk, David, and John Oakland.** *American Civilization: An Introduction.* London: Routledge, 2009.
- **Levander, Caroline Field.** *A Companion to American Literary Studies.* Chichester: Wiley-Blackwell, 2011.
- **Skinner, Jody.** *Anglo-American Cultural Studies.* Tübingen: Francke, 2009.

## Postcolonial Studies

- **Ashcroft, Bill, Gareth Griffiths, and Helen Tiffin.** *Post-Colonial Studies: The Key Concepts.* London: Routledge, 2007.
- **Loomba, Ania, et al., eds.** *Postcolonial Studies and Beyond.* Durham: Duke University Press, 2005.

## Links

- *Library of Anglo-American Culture.* University of Göttingen. < http://aac.sub.uni-goettingen.de >. An online database for cultural studies that provides information on secondary literature and where to find it.
- *British Council.* < www.britishcouncil.org/new/arts >. The "Arts" website provides a list of material for the analysis of various art forms including architecture, film, and music.
- *American Memory Collection.* < memory.loc.gov >. A comprehensive collection of material for cultural analysis, including newspapers, photographs, etc.
- *Allgemeine Informationen über die USA.* University of Mainz. < www.ub.uni-mainz.de/148.php >. A list of resources for American cultural studies.
- *CLCWeb: Comparative Literature and Culture.* < http://docs.lib.purdue.edu/clcweb >. An open-access online journal with a variety of cultural studies articles.

## 2.3 | Language

### General Overview

These publications will introduce you to the various research areas, the methods, and the development of the discipline of linguistics.

- **Herbst, Thomas, Rita Stoll, and Rudolf Westermayr.** *Terminologie der Sprachbeschreibung.* Ismaning: Hueber, 1991. A dictionary-type reference book with concise explanations of key terms.
- **Kortmann, Bernd.** *English Linguistics: Essentials.* Berlin: Cornelsen, 2007.
- **Mair, Christian.** *English Linguistics: An Introduction.* Tübingen: Narr, 2012.

### Historical Linguistics

These are helpful introductions and handbooks on the history of the English language. You may also want to consult the historical corpora listed in the "Corpora" section.

- **Hogg, Richard M., ed.** *The Cambridge History of the English Language (CHEL).* 6 vols. Cambridge: Cambridge University Press, 1992–2001. The most thorough overview of the past states of the English language in the major areas of historical linguistics and of some more recent handbooks on the history of English.
- **Hogg, Richard M., and David Denison, eds.** *A History of the English Language.* Cambridge: Cambridge University Press, 2006.
- **Mugglestone, Lynda, ed.** *The Oxford History of English.* Oxford: Oxford University Press, 2006.
- **Kemenade, Ans van, and Bettelou Los.** *The Handbook of the History of English.* Oxford: Blackwell, 2006.
- **Momma, Haruko, and Michael Matto, eds.** *A Companion to the History of the English Language.* Chichester: Wiley-Blackwell, 2008.

- **Nevalainen, Terttu, and Elizabeth C. Traugott, eds.** *The Oxford Handbook of the History of English.* Oxford: Oxford University Press, 2012.
- **Joseph, Brian D., and Richard D. Janda, eds.** *The Handbook of Historical Linguistics.* Malden: Blackwell, 2003. A detailed treatment of the theories and methods of historical linguistics with a focus on the study of language change.

## Word Formation

These books will give you a thorough overview of the structure, and partly also of the history, of word-formation in English.

- **Bauer, Laurie.** *English Word-Formation.* Cambridge: Cambridge University Press, 1983.
- **Plag, Ingo.** *Word-Formation in English.* Cambridge: Cambridge University Press, 2003.
- **Stockwell, Robert. P., and Donka Minkova.** *English Words: History and Structure.* Cambridge: Cambridge University Press, 2001. An integrated treatment of the diachronic and synchronic aspects of English word formation, which holds considerable appeal for advanced readers.
- **Bauer, Laurie.** *Introducing Linguistic Morphology.* Washington: Georgetown University Press, 2003.
- **Schmid, Hans-Jörg.** *Englische Morphologie und Wortbildung.* Berlin: Schmidt, 2005. The standard German-language introduction.

## Grammar

The authoritative reference grammars of present-day Standard English are:

- **Quirk, Randolph, et al.** *Comprehensive Grammar of the English Language.* London: Longman, 1985.
- **Huddleston, Rodney, and Geoffrey K. Pullum.** *The Cambridge Grammar of the English Language.* Cambridge: Cambridge University Press, 2002.

Beginners might consider using the abridged student versions:

- **Greenbaum, Sidney, and Randolph Quirk.** *A Student's Grammar of the English Language.* Harlow: Longman, 1990.
- **Huddleston, Rodney, and Geoffrey K. Pullum.** *A Student's Introduction to English Grammar.* Cambridge: Cambridge University Press, 2004.

On the stylistic and frequency aspects of grammatical constructions see:

- **Biber, Douglas, et al.** *The Longman Grammar of Spoken and Written English.* London: Longman, 1999.

## Phonology/Phonetics

These two titles are convenient introductions to English phonetics and phonology, with useful accompanying CDs:

- **Skandera, Paul, and Peter Burleigh.** *A Manual of English Phonetics and Phonology.* Tübingen: Narr, 2005.
- **Gut, Ulrike.** *Introduction to English Phonetics and Phonology.* Frankfurt/M.: Lang, 2009.

Other useful resources include:

- **Gimson, Alfred C.** *Gimson's Pronunciation of English.* 6th ed. London: Arnold, 2001. An authoritative reference work on Standard British Received Pronunciation.
- ***PRAAT: Doing Phonetics by Computer.*** < fon. hum.uva.nl/praat > . A website offering free software for instrumental phonetic analysis.

## Pronunciation

Use one of the following standard **dictionaries** to look up the pronunciation of English words:

- **Jones, Daniel.** *English Pronouncing Dictionary.* 17th ed. Cambridge: Cambridge University Press, 2006. The classic British pronunciation dictionary, which has charted the development of standard pronunciations of words since 1917.
- **Wells, John C.** *The Longman Pronunciation Dictionary.* 3rd ed. Harlow: Longman, 2008. A pronunciation dictionary that includes American pronunciations.
- **Upton, Clive, William Kretzschmar, and Rafal Konopka.** *The Oxford Dictionary of Pronunciation for Current English.* Oxford: Oxford University Press, 2001. A pronunciation dictionary that includes American pronunciations.

For **pronunciation samples** go to the following websites:

- ***BBC Voices.*** < bbc.co.uk/voices > .
- ***British Library: Sounds familiar?*** < www. bl.uk/learning/langlit/sounds/index.html > .
- ***How you say.*** < www.howjsay.com > .
- ***IDEA: International Dialects of English Archive.*** < web.ku.edu/ ~ idea > .
- ***The Speech Accent Archive.*** < accent.gmu. edu > .

- *Phonetic Symbols.* < www.phon.ucl.ac.uk/ home/wells/phoneticsymbolsforenglish.htm > . A list of the IPA (International Phonetic Alphabet) symbols you will need to transcribe English words.
- *Type IPA Phonetic Symbols.* < ipa.typeit.org > . A website that enables you to type IPA symbols and copy them into your own document.

## Semantics and Pragmatics

These introductions provide an account of semantics and pragmatics.

- **Lyons, John.** *Semantics*. 2 vols. Cambridge: Cambridge University Press, 1977. Still the most comprehensive introduction to linguistic semantics.
- **Lyons, John.** *Linguistic Semantics: An Introduction*. Cambridge: Cambridge University Press, 1995. A shorter version of the standard introduction.
- **Cruse, David A.** *Meaning in Language: An Introduction to Semantics and Pragmatics*. Oxford: Oxford University Press, 2011.
- **Leisi, Ernst, and Christian Mair.** *Das heutige Englisch: Wesenszüge und Probleme*. 9th ed. Heidelberg: Winter, 2008. Includes an extensive section on English-German contrastive semantics.
- **Bublitz, Wolfram.** *Englische Pragmatik*. Berlin: Schmidt, 2009.

## Varieties

Consult these books for comprehensive accounts of the varieties of the English language.

- **Mesthrie, Rajend, and Rakesh M. Bhatt.** *World Englishes: The Study of New Language Varieties*. Cambridge: Cambridge University Press, 2008.
- **Schneider, Edgar.** *Postcolonial English*. Cambridge: Cambridge University Press, 2007
- **Kortmann, Bernd, et al., eds.** *A Handbook of Varieties of English*. Berlin: de Gruyter, 2004. A comprehensive two-volume resource that includes CDs with audio files and maps. Vol. 1: *Phonology*. Vol. 2: *Morphology and Syntax*.
- **Kortmann, Bernd, and Clive Upton, eds.** *Varieties of English*. Berlin: de Gruyter, 2008. Vol. 1: *The British Isles*. Vol. 2: *The Americas and the Caribbean*. Vol. 3: *The Pacific and Australasia*. Vol. 4: *Africa, South and Southeast Asia*.

For concrete pronunciation samples see the *IDEA* Archive listed under "Pronuncation" above.

## Dictionaries

- *OED: Oxford English Dictionary.* Ed. John A. Simpson. 3rd ed. (in progress). Oxford: Oxford University Press, 2000. < www.oed.com > . The most comprehensive dictionary of English. Not for quick everyday use but indispensable for academic work as it details both the historical usages and the nuances of meaning of a word.

The standard student dictionaries are:

- *Oxford Advanced Learner's Dictionary of Current English.* Oxford: Oxford University Press, 2011.
- *The Concise Oxford Dictionary of Current English.* Oxford: Oxford University Press, 2008.
- *Collins COBUILD English Dictionary for Advanced Learners*. Boston: Heinle Cengage Learning, 2009.
- *Longman Dictionary of Contemporary English.* Harlow: Longman, 2011.

Some academic dictionaries can be consulted online:

- *Oxford Dictionaries Online.* < oxforddictionaries.com > .
- *Longman Dictionary of Contemporary English Online.* < ldoceonline.com > .
- *Online Etymology Dictionary.* < etymonline.com > .

For diachronic linguistics the following historical dictionaries are indispensable (aside from the *OED* of course):

- *DOE: Dictionary of Old English in Electronic Form: A to G*. Eds. Antonette Di Paolo Hearley et al. Toronto: University of Toronto Pontifical Institute of Medieval Studies, 2003. < www.doe.utoronto.ca > .
- *MED: The Middle English Dictionary.* Ed. Hans Kurath et al. Ann Arbor: University of Michigan Press, 2006. < quod.lib.umich.edu/m/med > .

## Corpora

Only corpora maintained by linguists provide reliable samples of language use. Consult the relevant corpora from this list when you need data for your paper or thesis.

- *Survey of English Usage.* < www.ucl.ac.uk/ english-usage > . Index cards collecting samples.

- **Brown Corpus of American English.** < icame. uib.no/brown/bcm.html >. 500 texts containing about 2,000 words each, stored on magnetic tapes.
- **Lancaster-Oslo-Bergen corpus (LOB).** < khnt. hit.uib.no/icame/manuals/lob/index.htm > or < icame.uib.no >. British counterpart to Brown.
- **London-Lund Corpus (LLC).** < khnt.hit.uib. no/icame/manuals/LONDLUND/INDEX. HTM > or < nora.hd.uib.no/corpora.html > or < icame.uib.no/newcd.htm > or < nora.hd. uib.no/whatis.html >. British English spoken part of the Survey of English Usage.
- **The Bank of English.** < www.titania.bham. ac.uk >. Open, computer-based corpus.
- **British National Corpus.** < www.natcorp.ox. ac.uk >. Closed computer corpus, representative sample of modern English for work in lexicography, grammar, and theoretical linguistics.
- **International Corpus of English (ICE).** < ice-corpora.net/ice/index.htm >. Consists of several one-million-word corpora collecting material from a wide range of English-speaking areas in Europe, Asia, Africa, the USA and the Caribbean, Australia, and New Zealand; work is in progress.

For **diachronic linguistics** consult the following historical corpora:

- **Helsinki Corpus of English Texts.** < icame.uib. no/hc >. The diachronic part of this corpus pioneered the field of historical corpus linguistics.

Covers material from the eighth to the early eighteenth centuries.
- **ARCHER: A Representative Corpus of Historical English Registers.** Another large-scale multi-genre corpus with a historical dimension (1650–1999). Incorporates British and American English.
- **The Corpus of Historical American English (COHA).** < corpus.byu.edu/coha >. 400 million words, 1810–2009.

For specialized **text type studies** there is now a number of genre-specific corpora, many of which can be accessed online:

- **Corpus of Early English Correspondence (CEEC).** < www.helsinki.fi/varieng/domains/ CEEC.html >.
- **Corpus of Early English Medical Writing (CEEM).** Available on CD.
- **Lampeter Corpus of Early Modern English Tracts.** < www.tu-chemnitz.de/phil/english/ chairs/linguist/real/independent/lampeter/ lamphome.htm >.
- **Zurich English Newspaper Corpus (ZEN).** < es-zen.unizh.ch >.
- **Corpus of English Dialogues 1560–1760 (CED).**

A permanently updated list and description of historical language corpora is provided by:

- **"Corpus Resource Database."** *Research Unit for Variation, Contacts and Change in English* (VARIENG). < www.helsinki.fi/varieng/CoRD >.

## 2.4 | Teaching

### General Overview

These works provide a basic overview on the field of Didactics and the various subdisciplines as well as definitions for relevant terms within the discourse of Didactics.

- **Bach, Gerhard, and Johannes-Peter Timm, eds.** *Englischunterricht: Grundlagen und Methoden einer handlungsorientierten Unterrichtspraxis.* Tübingen: Francke, 2009.
- **Carter, Ronald, and David Nunan, eds.** *The Cambridge Guide to Teaching English to Speakers of other Languages.* Cambridge: Cambridge University Press, 2001.
- **Decke-Cornill, Helene, and Lutz Küster.** *Fremdsprachendidaktik: Eine Einführung.* Tübingen: Narr, 2010.

- **Haß, Frank, ed.** *Fachdidaktik Englisch: Tradition—Innovation—Praxis.* Stuttgart: Klett, 2006.
- **Johnson, Keith.** *An Introduction to Foreign Language Learning and Teaching.* Harlow: Pearson Education, 2001.
- **Müller-Hartmann, Andreas, and Marita Schocker-von Ditfurth.** *Introduction to English Language Teaching.* Stuttgart: Klett, 2010.
- **Thaler, Engelbert.** *Englisch unterrichten.* Berlin: Cornelsen, 2012.
- **Volkmann, Laurenz.** *Fachdidaktik Englisch: Kultur und Sprache.* Tübingen: Narr, 2010.

## Dictionaries and Reference Books

- **Ahrens, Rüdiger, Wolf-Dietrich Bald, and Werner Hüllen, eds.** *Handbuch Englisch als Fremdsprache.* Berlin: Schmidt, 1994.
- **Bausch, Karl-Richard, Herbert Christ, and Hans-Jürgen Krumm, eds.** *Handbuch Fremdsprachenunterricht.* Tübingen: Francke, 2003.
- **Byram, Michael, ed.** *The Routledge Encyclopedia of Language Teaching and Learning.* London: Taylor & Francis, 2000.
- **Surkamp, Carola, ed.** *Metzler Lexikon Fremdsprachendidaktik: Ansätze—Methoden—Grundbegriffe.* Stuttgart: Metzler, 2010.

## Standards and Guidelines

Consult these websites for the most important institutional standards and guidelines in English language teaching in Germany.
- *Common European Framework of Reference for Languages: Learning, Teaching, Assessment* **(CEFR).** < www.coe.int/T/DG4/Linguistic/CADRE_EN.asp > .
- *Kultusministerkonferenz* **(KMK).** < www.kmk.org/ home.html > .
- **"Entwicklung nationaler Bildungsstandards."** *Bundesministerium für Bildung und Forschung.* < www.bmbf.de/pub/zur_entwicklung_nationaler_bildungsstandards.pdf > .
- *Akademie für Lehrerfortbildung und Personalführung.* < alp.dillingen.de > .

## Journals

These journals provide an overview of new developments in didactic research as well as concrete guidelines and examples for planning lessons.
- *PRAXIS Fremdsprachenunterricht.* < www.oldenbourg-klick.de/zeitschriften/praxis-fremdsprachenunterricht/home > .
- *Modern English Teacher.* < www.onlinemet.com > .
- *Praxis Englisch.* < www.praxisenglisch.de > .

## Online Resources

These websites offer materials for planning lessons or researching a specific topic.
- *BBC: Teaching English.* < www.teachingenglish.org.uk/ > .
- *British Council.* < www.britishcouncil.de/d/english/teachweb.htm > .
- *Yale-New Haven Teacher's Institute.* < www.yale.edu/ynhti/ > .
- *Learning & Teaching Support Centre (LTSC) Karlsruhe.* < http://ltsc.ph-karlsruhe.de > .

# List of Contributors

**Heinz Antor** is Professor of English Literature at the University of Cologne (chapter II.12 "Literary Ethics").

**Klaus Benesch** is Professor of North American Literary History at Ludwig Maximilians University, Munich (chapter I.3.2 "American Renaissance").

**Wolfram Bublitz** is Professor of English Linguistics at the University of Augsburg (chapters V.1 "Introducing Linguistics," V.5 "Text and Context").

**Astrid Erll** is Professor of Anglophone Literatures and Cultures at Goethe University, Frankfurt/Main (chapter II.11 "Cultural Memory").

**Winfried Fluck** is Professor Emeritus of American Studies at the John F. Kennedy Institute for North American Studies, Free University of Berlin (chapter III.3 "American Cultural Studies").

**Monika Fludernik** is Professor of English Literature at the University of Freiburg (chapter II.9 "Narratology").

**Andrea Gutenberg** teaches English Literature at the University of Cologne (chapter I.2.6 "Modernism").

**Ulla Haselstein** is Professor of North American Literature at the John F. Kennedy Institute for North American Studies, Free University of Berlin (chapter II.7 "Psychoanalysis").

**Christoph Henke** teaches English Literature at Augsburg University (chapter VII.1 "Methods and Techniques of Research and Academic Writing").

**Christian Hoffmann** teaches English Linguistics at the University of Augsburg (chapter V.5 "Text and Context").

**Christian Huck** is Professor of Cultural Studies and Media Studies at Christian Albrechts University, Kiel (chapter III.2 "British Cultural Studies").

**Heinz Ickstadt** is Professor Emeritus of North American Literature at the John F. Kennedy Institute for North American Studies, Free University of Berlin (chapter I.3.4 "Modernism").

**Frank Kelleter** is Professor of American Studies at Georg August University, Göttingen (chapter I.3.1 "Early American Literature").

**Annette Kern-Stähler** is Professor of Medieval English Studies at the University of Berne (chapter I.2.1 "The Middle Ages").

**Eveline Kilian** is Professor of English Cultural Studies and Cultural History at Humboldt University, Berlin (chapter II.6 "Gender Studies, Transgender Studies, Queer Studies").

**Stephan Kohl** is Professor Emeritus of English Literature and Culture at Julius Maximilians University, Würzburg (chapter I.2.1 "The Middle Ages").

**Lucia Kornexl** is Professor of English Linguistics at Rostock University (chapter V.3 "History and Change").

**Christian Mair** is Professor of English Linguistics at the University of Freiburg (chapter V.4 "Forms and Structures").

**Martin Middeke** is Professor of English Literature at the University of Augsburg and Visiting Professor of English at the University of Johannesburg, South Africa (chapters I.1 "Introducing Literary Studies," I.2.5 "The Victorian Age," II.3 "Reception Theory," II.4 "Poststructuralism/Deconstruction").

**Timo Müller** teaches American Studies at the University of Augsburg (chapters I.1 "Introducing Literary Studies," II.4 "Poststructuralism/Deconstruction," IV.1 "Analyzing Poetry," IV.2 "Analyzing Prose Fiction").

**Ansgar Nünning** is Professor of English and American Literature and Culture at Justus Liebig University, Gießen (chapter III.1 "Transnational Approaches to the Study of Culture").

**Verena Olejniczak Lobsien** is Professor of English Literature at Humboldt University, Berlin (chapter I.2.2 "The Sixteenth and Seventeenth Centuries").

**Caroline Pirlet** is a Doctoral Candidate at the University of Freiburg (chapter II.9 "Narratology").

**Erik Redling** is currently Deputy Professor of American Studies at the Martin Luther University, Halle-Wittenberg (chapter II.13 "Cognitive Poetics").

**Christoph Reinfandt** is Professor of English Literature at Eberhard Karls University, Tübingen (chapters I.2.4 "Romanticism," II.10 "Systems Theory").

**Gabriele Rippl** is Professor of Literatures in English at the University of Berne (chapter III.5 "Film and Media Studies").

**Susanne Rohr** is Professor of North American Literature and Culture at the University of Hamburg (chapters I.3.3 "Realism and Naturalism," II.8 "Pragmatism and Semiotics").

**Katja Sarkowsky** is Junior Professor of New English Literatures and Cultural Studies at the University of Augsburg (chapters I.4 "The New Literatures in English," III.4 "Postcolonial Studies").

**Oliver Scheiding** is Professor of American Literature at Johannes Gutenberg University, Mainz (chapter II.5 "New Historicism and Discourse Analysis").

**Hans-Jörg Schmid** is Professor of Modern English Linguistics at Ludwig Maximilians University, Munich (chapter V.2 "Linguistic Theories, Approaches, and Methods").

**Edgar W. Schneider** is Professor of English Linguistics at the University of Regensburg (chapter V.6 "Standard and Varieties").

**Ulf Schulenberg** is currently Deputy Professor of American Studies at Catholic University Eichstätt-Ingolstadt (chapters II.1 "Formalism and Structuralism," II.2 "Hermeneutics and Critical Theory").

**Dirk Schultze** teaches English Literature and Linguistics at Rostock University (chapter V.3 "History and Change").

**Frank Schulze-Engler** is Professor of New Anglophone Literatures and Cultures at Johann Wolfgang Goethe University, Frankfurt/Main (chapters I.4 "The New Literatures in English," III.4 "Postcolonial Studies").

**Helga Schwalm** is Professor of English Literature at Humboldt University, Berlin (chapter I.2.3 "The Eighteenth Century").

**Klaus Stierstorfer** is Professor of British Studies at Westfälische Wilhelms University, Münster (chapter I.2.7 "Postmodernism").

**Carola Surkamp** is Professor of English Language Teaching at Georg August University, Göttingen (chapter VI.3 "Teaching Literature").

**Laurenz Volkmann** is Professor of English Language Teaching at Friedrich Schiller University, Jena (chapters VI.1 "The Theory and Politics of English Language Teaching," VI.2 "Language Learning").

**Christina Wald** teaches English Literature at the University of Augsburg (chapters I.1 "Introducing Literary Studies," I.2.2 "The Sixteenth and Seventeenth Centuries," IV.3 "Analyzing Drama," IV.4 "Analyzing Film," IV.5 "Analyzing Culture").

**Hubert Zapf** is Professor of American Literature at the University of Augsburg (chapters I.1 "Introducing Literary Studies," I.3.5 "Postmodern and Contemporary American Literature," II.14 "Ecocriticism and Cultural Ecology").

# Index

# Illustration Credits